T. Ito A. R. Meyer (Eds.)

Theoretical Aspects of Computer Software

International Conference TACS '91
Sendai, Japan, September 24-27, 1991
Proceedings

Springer-Verlag
Berlin Heidelberg New York
London Paris Tokyo
Hong Kong Barcelona
Budapest

Series Editors

Gerhard Goos
GMD Forschungsstelle
Universität Karlsruhe
Vincenz-Priessnitz-Straße 1
W-7500 Karlsruhe, FRG

Juris Hartmanis
Department of Computer Science
Cornell University
Upson Hall
Ithaca, NY 14853, USA

Volume Editors

Takayasu Ito
Department of Information Engineering, Faculty of Engineering
Tohoku University, Sendai, Japan

Albert R. Meyer
MIT Laboratory for Computer Science, NE 43-315
545 Technology Square, Cambridge, MA 02138, USA

CR Subject Classification (1991): D.1-3, F.1, F.3

ISBN 3-540-54415-1 Springer-Verlag Berlin Heidelberg New York
ISBN 0-387-54415-1 Springer-Verlag New York Berlin Heidelberg

Printed in Germany

Typesetting: Camera ready by author
Printing and binding: Druckhaus Beltz, Hemsbach/Bergstr.
2145/3140-543210 - Printed on acid-free paper

Foreword

TACS'91 is the first International Conference on Theoretical Aspects of Computer Software held at Tohoku University, Sendai, Japan, September 24–27, 1991. This volume contains thirty-seven papers and an abstract for talks presented at the conference.

TACS'91 focused on theoretical foundations of programming, and theoretical aspects of the design, analysis and implementation of programming languages and systems. The following topics were mentioned in the call for papers:

- Logic, proof, specification and semantics of programs and languages
- Theories and models of concurrent, parallel and distributed computation
- Constructive logic, category theory, and type theory in computer science
- Theory-based systems for specifying, synthesizing, transforming, testing, and verifying software

The Program Committee members were

Robert Constable (Cornell U.)	Masami Hagiya (Kyoto U.)
Susumu Hayashi (Ryukoku U.)	Takayasu Ito, Co-Chair (Tohoku U.)
J.-L. Lassez (IBM, Yorktown)	Albert R. Meyer, Co-Chair (MIT)
Gordon D. Plotkin (Edinburgh U.)	Amir Pnueli (Weizmann Inst.)
Masahiko Sato (Tohoku U.)	Dana S. Scott (Carnegie-Mellon U.)

The Program Committee received 65 draft papers and accepted 28. The number of worthwhile papers received considerably exceeded the capacity of the conference, and the Program Committee was therefore unable to accept many high-quality submissions. On behalf of the Program Committee, we express our sincere gratitude to all the authors of submitted papers.

Professor Rod Burstall of Edinburgh University accepted our invitation to become the banquet speaker of TACS'91. An evening technical session for demos and informal presentations was included in the program. Other activities included several receptions and a post-conference bus tour to Hiraizumi and Matsushima aimed at promoting discussions and informal contacts among the participants.

Masahiko Sato, Masami Hagiya, Susumu Hayashi and their colleagues helped organize TACS'91 from its beginnings. D. M. Jones (MIT), Y. Kameyama (Tohoku U.), S. Kawamoto (Tohoku U.), M. Ohtomo (Tohoku U.), T. Seino (Tohoku U.), and M. Tatsuta (Tohoku U.) lent their valuable assistance in preparing these Proceedings and in managing the conference. In addition to the Program Committee members, the following people served as reviewers of submitted papers:

Krzysztof R. Apt, Luca Cardelli, Steve German, Carl Gunter, Lalita Jategaonkar, Yukiyoshi Kameyama, A. J. Kfoury, Satoshi Kobayashi, John Mitchell, Hiroshi Nakano, Rishiyur Nikhil, Atsushi Ohori, Phil Pfeiffer, John Reynolds, Jon Riecke, Arie Rudich,

Etsuya Shibayama, Makoto Tatsuta, Boris Trakhtenbrot, Frits Vaandrager, David Wald.

We are very grateful to all those above, as well as the members of the Program Committee and the Invited Speakers for their efforts on behalf of TACS'91.

We gratefully acknowledge the generous sponsorship provided by Tohoku University. We also thank the following organizations for their cooperation:

Information Processing Society of Japan,
Japan Society for Software Science and Technology,
Association for Symbolic Logic,
Association for Computing Machinery–SIGACT,
IEEETC on Mathematical Foundations of Computing.

The papers at TACS'91 offer an outstanding representation of active concerns in the theory of programming by a distinguished international group of researchers. We are happy to have played a role in bringing this group together and in making their work available to the readers of this volume.

June 1991

Takayasu Ito
Albert R. Meyer
Conference Co-Chairs
TACS'91

Contents

Session 6

Session 7

Session 8

Invited Paper

Session 9

Invited Lecture

A Semantics for Type Checking

Gordon Plotkin
Department of Computer Science
University of Edinburgh
Edinburgh, EH9 3JZ, SCOTLAND
gdp@lfcs.edinburgh.ac.uk

Abstract

Curry's system for F-deducibility is the basis for implicit type checking for programming languages such as ML. If a natural "preservation of types by conversion" rule is added it becomes undecidable, but complete relative to a variety of model classes. We show completeness for F-deducibility itself, relative to an extended notion of model which validates reduction but not conversion. Both term model and filter model proofs are given, and the extension to polymorphic typing is also considered.

1 Introduction

Curry's system for F-deducibility is one of the simplest systems for type inference for the untyped λ-calculus [5]. It is a decidable system which can be considered as the basis of type checking algorithms for languages such as ML [9]. It has however a certain defect from a semantical point of view in that it is not complete with respect to any immediately obvious semantics. As Hindley remarks in [5], one would expect that in any decent semantics, interconvertible terms would have the same interpretation. A certain equality rule is then valid. Hindley and others [2, 5, 6] proved that systems equipped with such a rule are indeed complete with respect to various semantical models, which differ only in how types are interpreted (the simple semantics, the F-semantics and the quotient-set semantics). Unfortunately this complete system is not a possible basis for type checking as it is undecidable; we assume here that type checking is to be a terminating process.

Albert Meyer asked whether nonetheless a semantic analysis is possible. We present here one such analysis based on a wider notion of model, called a semi-model, which does not validate conversion, but rather is partially-ordered and validates reduction. The motivation for considering such models is provided by the Subject Reduction theorem which states that for F-deducibility if a term has a type and that term reduces to another then the other has the same type. It can be thought of as stating that once a term has been type checked, then type errors cannot occur in computation (reduction).

For the system of simple functional types we consider a variation on the simple notion of type and give two completeness proofs. One, after the manner of Hindley, uses term models. The other, after the manner of Barendregt, Coppo and Dezani-Ciancaglini, is a filter model. We also obtain a completeness result for the more complex polymorphic type discipline (where decidability is an outstanding open problem) [10].

This work raises interest in models which are sensitive to operational concerns. Various authors have proposed the use of partially ordered categories or 2-categories for such purposes [7, 12, 13]. It would be very interesting to see how the present work would fit into the categorical viewpoint. One has [1] that a model of the λ-calculus is provided by an object in a Cartesian closed category which has the space of its endomorphisms as a retract. It would be pleasing to have an analogous description of the semi-models considered here.

It would also be of interest to extend the analysis to other type disciplines. The intersection type discipline of Coppo *et al* is of immediate interest, and one can also consider, for example, existential and union types and recursive types. Three technical issues are raised below: whether the F-semantics is complete for the simple type discipline, what the proper notion of quotient-set semantics may be, and whether there is a filter model of universal types.

2 The system F

The notation and terminology of Hindley in [5] will be followed, but with a few differences and additions. We write "type expressions" rather than "type schemes." Type assignment statements are written in the form $M\colon \beta$ rather than βM. The letters Γ,Δ are used to vary over finite bases. When writing $\mathcal{B}, x{:}\alpha$ for $\mathcal{B} \cup \{x{:}\alpha\}$ it is assumed that x is a subject of no type assignment statement in $\mathcal{B}$.

There is a convenient sequent-style presentation of F-deducibility for the λ-calculus [10]. This uses sequents of the form $\Gamma \vdash M\colon \alpha$; there are three rules, which we call the system F (of rules).

$$\Gamma \vdash x\colon \alpha \quad (\text{if } x{:}\alpha \text{ is in } \Gamma)$$

$$(\to\mathrm{I}) \qquad \frac{\Gamma, x\colon \alpha \vdash M{:}\beta}{\Gamma \vdash \lambda x.M{:}\alpha\to\beta}$$

$$(\to\mathrm{E}) \qquad \frac{\Gamma \vdash M{:}\alpha\to\beta, \quad \Gamma \vdash N{:}\alpha}{\Gamma \vdash MN{:}\beta}$$

F-deducibility is defined by putting $\Gamma \vdash_F M{:}\alpha$ iff $\Gamma \vdash M{:}\alpha$ is provable using these rules. The equality rule referred to above is parameterized on a notion of conversion. In the case of β-conversion it is:

$$(\mathrm{EQ}\beta) \qquad \frac{\Gamma \vdash M{:}\alpha, \quad M =_\beta N}{\Gamma \vdash N{:}\alpha}$$

Now by the Church-Rosser theorem, we can split this rule up into two parts:

$$(\geq_\beta) \qquad \frac{\Gamma \vdash M{:}\alpha, \quad M \geq_\beta N}{\Gamma \vdash N{:}\alpha}$$

$$(\leq_\beta) \qquad \frac{\Gamma \vdash N{:}\alpha, \quad M \geq_\beta N}{\Gamma \vdash M{:}\alpha}$$

The Subject Reduction theorem says that $(\geq_\beta)$ is an admissible rule of the system F. It is therefore not so surprising that the whole strength of $(\mathrm{EQ}\beta)$ rests with $(\leq_\beta)$:

Proposition 1
$(\mathrm{EQ}\beta)$ is an admissible rule of the system F plus $(\leq_\beta)$.

Proof: We have to show that if $M =_\beta N$ and $\Gamma \vdash M{:}\alpha$ is provable in the system F plus $(\leq_\beta)$ so is $\Gamma \vdash N{:}\alpha$. Under these assumptions $\Gamma \vdash M{:}\alpha$ is provable in the system F plus $(\mathrm{EQ}\beta)$. So by the Equality Postponement theorem [5] there is a term K with $\Gamma \vdash_F K{:}\alpha$ and $K =_\beta M$. So $K =_\beta N$, and by the Church-Rosser theorem there is a term L with $K \geq_\beta L \leq_\beta N$. So by the Subject Reduction theorem we get $\Gamma \vdash_F L{:}\alpha$ and, finally by $(\leq_\beta)$ we get that $\Gamma \vdash N{:}\alpha$ is provable in the extended system.

This proposition gives a computational analysis of $(\mathrm{EQ}\beta)$, showing that it is equivalent to type checking after some computation. For a model-theoretic analysis it seems reasonable to model $(\geq_\beta)$, but not $(\leq_\beta)$. The rule $(\geq_\beta)$ might be read as that if type-theoretic information holds of M and $M \geq_\beta N$ then the information holds of N. So if we follow Scott and model information by a partial order then we would want the denotation of M to be less than that of N, which leads to the notion of semi-model of the next section.

There are two other admissible rules for the system F that will prove useful:

$$(\text{Weakening}) \qquad \frac{\Gamma \vdash M{:}\alpha}{\Gamma, x{:}\alpha \vdash M{:}\alpha}$$

$$(\text{Strengthening}) \qquad \frac{\Gamma, x{:}\alpha \vdash M{:}\alpha}{\Gamma \vdash M{:}\alpha} \quad (\text{provided } x \text{ is not free in } M)$$

The Subject Reduction theorem also holds for $\beta\eta$-reduction, and we can introduce rules $(\mathrm{EQ}\beta\eta)$, $(\geq_{\beta\eta})$ and $(\leq_{\beta\eta})$ like those above. The Equality Postponement theorem holds for $\beta\eta$-conversion, and so we find that $(\mathrm{EQ}\beta\eta)$ is an admissible rule of the system F plus $(\leq_{\beta\eta})$. It would therefore also be reasonable to consider semi-models for $\beta\eta$-conversion.

3 Semi-Models

We work with a variant of the notion of a syntactic λ-model [1, §5]. A *syntactical $\lambda\beta$-semi-model* (*semi-model* for short) is a triple

$$\mathcal{P} = \langle P, \cdot, [\![\cdot]\!]\,(\cdot)\rangle$$

where P is a partial order, and $\cdot$ is a binary monotone operation over P of *application*, and $[\![\cdot]\!]\,(\cdot)$ is a mapping from terms and environments which is monotone in its second argument (environments are given the pointwise ordering where $\rho \leq \rho'$ iff $\rho(x) \leq \rho'(x)$ for all variables x) and such that the following six conditions hold:

(i) $[\![x]\!]\,(\rho) = \rho(x)$

(ii) $[\![MN]\!]\,(\rho) = [\![M]\!]\,(\rho) \cdot [\![N]\!]\,(\rho)$

(iii) if $\rho \restriction \mathrm{FV}(M) = \rho' \restriction \mathrm{FV}(M)$ then $[\![M]\!]\,(\rho) = [\![M]\!]\,(\rho')$

(iv) $[\![[y/x]M]\!]\,(\rho) = [\![M]\!]\,(\rho(x := \rho(y)))$ if $y \notin \mathrm{FV}(M)$

(v) if for all a in P, $[\![M]\!]\,(\rho(x := a)) \leq [\![N]\!]\,(\rho(x := a))$ then $[\![\lambda x.M]\!]\,(\rho) \leq [\![\lambda x.N]\!]\,(\rho)$

(vi) $[\![\lambda x.M]\!]\,(\rho) \cdot a \leq [\![M]\!]\,(\rho(x := a))$

The usual notion of a syntactical λ-model consists of (i), (ii), (iii) and equality versions of (v) and (vi). There (iv) is a consequence and a more general substitution principle holds:

(Sub) $$[\![[N/x]\,M]\!]\,(\rho) = [\![M]\!]\,(\rho\,(x := [\![N]\!]\,(\rho)))$$

The proof in [1] only uses (i), (ii), (iii), the equality version of (v) and a statement equivalent to (iv) in the presence of the equality version of (v). So (Sub) also holds for semi-models.

The following formal system axiomatizes β-reduction:

$$M \leq M$$

$$\frac{M \leq N, \quad N \leq K}{M \leq K}$$

$$\frac{M \leq M', \quad N \leq N'}{MN \leq M'N'}$$

$$\frac{M \leq N}{\lambda x.M \leq \lambda x.N}$$

$$(\lambda x.M)N \leq [N/x]M$$

Now one can see that semi-models model β-reduction in that if $M \geq_\beta N$ then $[\![M]\!] \leq [\![N]\!]$. One proceeds by induction on the proof in the formal system. All cases are evident except for (β) where one calculates that:

$$\begin{aligned} [\![(\lambda x.M)N]\!](\rho) &= [\![\lambda x.M]\!](\rho)\cdot[\![N]\!](\rho) && \text{by (ii)}\\ &\leq [\![M]\!](\rho(x := [\![N]\!](\rho))) && \text{by (vi)}\\ &= [\![[N/x]M]\!](\rho) && \text{by (Sub)} \end{aligned}$$

The class of semi-models is not only consistent for β-reduction, but is also complete for it, as a term model argument shows. This model,

$$\mathcal{T}_\beta = \langle T, \cdot, [\![\cdot]\!](\cdot)\rangle$$

is given by taking equivalence classes of terms. Let

$$[M] = \{N \mid M \geq_\beta N \geq_\beta M\}$$

and then set

$$T = \{[M] \mid M \text{ a } \lambda\text{-term}\}$$

partially ordered by $[M] \leq [N]$ iff $M \geq_\beta N$, and

$$[M]\cdot[N] = [MN]$$

and

$$[\![M]\!](\rho) = [[N_1/x_1, \ldots, N_n/x_n]M],$$

where $\rho(x_1) = [N_1], \ldots, \rho(x_n) = [N_n]$, and $x_1, \ldots, x_n$ are the free variables of M. It is clear that this is a good definition, that application is monotone, that $[\![M]\!](\rho)$ is monotone in ρ, and that conditions (i), (ii), (iii) all hold. Let us verify the others. For (iv) we calculate:

$$[\![M]\!](\rho(x := \rho(y))) = [[K_1/x_1, \ldots, K_n/x_n, K/x]M]$$

(where the x_i are the free variables of M other than x, and K_i is $\rho(x_i)$ and K is $\rho(y)$)

$$= [[K_1/x_1, \ldots, K_n/x_n, K/y][y/x]M]$$

(as $y \notin \mathrm{FV}(M)$)

$$= [\![[y/x]M]\!](\rho)$$

Next (v) is proved by taking a to be $[x]$; we omit the detailed verification. Finally for (vi) we calculate:

$$[\![\lambda x.M]\!](\rho)\cdot[N] = [(\lambda x.[K_1/x_1, \ldots, K_n/x_n]M)N]$$

(where the x_i are the free variables of M other than x and K_i is $\rho(x_i)$)

$$\leq [[K_1/x_1, \ldots, K_n/x_n, N/x]M]$$

(we can assume without loss of generality that x is not a free variable of any K_i)

$$= [\![M]\!]\,(\rho(x := [N]))$$

There is a particularly useful environment ρ_0 defined by $\rho_0(x) = [x]$. It has the property that for any term M, $[\![M]\!]\,(\rho_0) = [M]$.

Completeness Theorem 1
$M \geq_\beta N$ if in all semi-models it is the case that $[\![M]\!] \leq [\![N]\!]$.

Proof: Use the term model and take the denotations of M and N in the environment ρ_0.

Turning to $\beta\eta$-conversion, define a *syntactical $\lambda\beta\eta$-semi-model* to be a semi-model such that

(vii) $\quad [\![\lambda x.Mx]\!]\,(\rho) \leq [\![M]\!]\,(\rho) \quad (\text{if } x \notin \mathrm{FV}(M))$

Now $\beta\eta$-conversion can be axiomatized by adding the scheme

$$\lambda x.Mx \geq M \quad (x \notin \mathrm{FV}(M))$$

to the above rules, and one sees that syntactical $\lambda\beta\eta$-semi-models model $\beta\eta$-conversion. There is a term model $\mathcal{T}_{\beta\eta}$ defined analogously to $\mathcal{T}_\beta$, using $\beta\eta$-reduction rather than β-reduction. This term model can be used to yield the expected completeness result for $\beta\eta$-conversion and syntactical $\lambda\beta\eta$-semi-models.

4 Type Interpretations

Let us begin by considering types as subsets of the domains of semi-models. Fixing a semi-model $\mathcal{P}$ as above, say that a type interpretation is a pair

$$\mathcal{T}y = \langle Ty, \rightarrow\rangle$$

where Ty is a collection of types, which are upper closed subsets of P, and $\rightarrow$ is a binary *arrow* function over Ty such that the following two conditions hold:

(Arrow 1) For any X, Y in Ty, and a in $X{\rightarrow}Y$, $(a \cdot X)$ is a subset of Y.

(Arrow 2) For any X, Y in Ty, if $[\![M]\!]\,(\rho(x := a)) \in Y$ whenever $a \in X$ then $[\![\lambda x.M]\!]\,(\rho) \in X{\rightarrow}Y$.

The above conditions can be rephrased a little. Define operations on upper-closed subsets of P by:

$$(X \rightarrow_S Y) = \{a \mid (a \cdot X) \subset Y\}$$
$$(X \rightarrow_F Y) = \{[\![\lambda x.M]\!](\rho) \mid \forall a \in X.\, [\![M]\!](\rho(x := a)) \in Y\} \uparrow$$

(Here $Z\uparrow$ is $\{b \mid \exists a \in Z.a \leq b\}$, the *upper closure* of Z.) Now the conditions can be rephrased as

$$X \rightarrow_F Y \subset X \rightarrow Y \subset X \rightarrow_S Y$$

We say that an interpretation is *simple* (respectively is an *F-interpretation*) if the arrow operation is $\rightarrow_S$ (respectively $\rightarrow_F$).

In case $\mathcal{P}$ is a model (with the trivial partial order)

$$X \rightarrow_F Y = (X \rightarrow_S Y) \cap F$$

where

$$F = \{[\![\lambda y.xy]\!](\rho) \mid \rho \text{ an environment}\}$$

and the two arrow conditions are a special case of those of Mitchell [10], whose arrow functions operated rather on representations of types. Previously other authors had considered two particular interpretations, the simple semantics and the F-semantics. The simple semantics consists of all subsets of P with $X \rightarrow_S Y$ as the arrow operation; the F-semantics has instead $X \rightarrow_F Y$ as the arrow operation.

Unfortunately these semantics do not seem to be available for semi-models in general. The problem is that it does not seem to be true in general that $X \rightarrow_F Y$ is a subset of $X \rightarrow_S Y$ (and that is needed for the proof of consistency below). So it is possible that taking all upper closed subsets for *Ty* and taking $\rightarrow_S$, say, as the arrow operation will not yield a type interpretation. We will obtain a completeness result for a simple interpretation in which however not all subsets of P are in *Ty*; it is an open problem whether completeness holds for F-interpretations.

It is interesting to contrast this situation with, on the one hand, the case of completeness of (Eq), and, on the other hand, with that of completeness of polymorphic typing with (Eq). In the former case, completeness holds for interpretations where all subsets are allowed as types; in the latter, while there are interpretations with all sets allowed as types, the class of such models fails to be complete (for trivial reasons).

In previous work (see [5, 10] in particular) an extended notion of type was considered, where types were taken as equivalence relations over subsets or, which amounts to the same thing, as partial equivalence relations (the symmetric transitive relations). To formulate such a notion here, one would expect a relation between the order on the semi-models and the partial equivalence relations (just as we ask that, as sets, types be upper closed). For lack of such a condition we do not pursue this notion further here.

Given a type interpretation as above, a *valuation of the type variables*, or *type environment*, is a function, V, assigning elements of *Ty* to type variables. Any such can be extended to all type expressions by putting $V(\alpha \to \beta) = V(\alpha) \to V(\beta)$. Then a statement $M{:}\alpha$ is *satisfied* by ρ, V if $[\![M]\!](\rho) \in V(\alpha)$. We write $\Gamma \models M{:}\alpha$ to mean that whenever any ρ, V satisfy every statement in Γ, then they also satisfy $M{:}\alpha$.

Consistency Theorem 2
If $\Gamma \vdash_F M{:}\alpha$ *then* $\Gamma \models M{:}\alpha$.

Proof: The proof is by induction on the size of the proof that $\Gamma \vdash M{:}\alpha$. Choose ρ, V and assume they satisfy every statement in Γ. The case where x is a variable is trivial, and the case where it is an application is handled by the first arrow condition. If M has the form $\lambda x.N$ then α must have the form $\beta \to \beta'$, and there must be a shorter proof of $\Gamma, x{:}\beta \vdash M{:}\beta'$. Now we can apply the second arrow condition. Choose a in $V(\beta)$. Then $\rho(x := a), V$ satisfy every statement in $\Gamma, x{:}\beta$ and so by the induction hypothesis, they satisfy the statement $M{:}\beta'$, which is to say that $[\![M]\!](\rho(x := a)) \in V(\beta')$. So by the second arrow condition we can conclude that $[\![\lambda x.M]\!](\rho) \in V(\beta) \to V(\beta')$, which is just that ρ, V satisfy the statement $M{:}\alpha$, as required.

The term model We are going to give two proofs of completeness. For the first we begin by describing a type interpretation for the term semi-model $\mathcal{T}_\beta$ given above, and relative to a given finite basis Γ, and term A. Let $\mathcal{B}$ be a basis extending Γ, such that the only type statements in $\mathcal{B}$ with subject a free variable of A are those in Γ, and such that for each type scheme α there are infinitely many statements in $\mathcal{B}$ of the form $x{:}\alpha$. Write $\mathcal{B} \vdash_F M{:}\alpha$ to mean that $\Gamma' \vdash_F M{:}\alpha$, where Γ' is a subset of $\mathcal{B}$. Define:

$$X_\alpha = \{[M] \mid \mathcal{B} \vdash_F M{:}\alpha\}$$

(by the Subject Reduction theorem this is a good definition), and then put

$$Ty = \{X_\alpha \mid \alpha \text{ a type scheme}\}$$

(Note that $X_\alpha = X'_\alpha$ implies that $\alpha = \alpha'$. For, take a variable x with $x{:}\alpha$ in $\mathcal{B}$; then $[x]$ is in X_α; then $[x]$ is in $X_{\alpha'}$ and so $\mathcal{B} \vdash_F x{:}\alpha'$ and so $x{:}\alpha'$ is in $\mathcal{B}$ and so $\alpha = \alpha'$, as required.) Now one can unambiguously define the arrow operation by

$$X_\alpha \to X_\beta = X_{\alpha \to \beta}$$

which concludes our description of the type interpretation.

To see that the first arrow condition holds, suppose that $[M]$ is in $X_{\alpha \to \beta}$ and $[N]$ is in X_α. Then $\mathcal{B} \vdash_F M{:}\alpha \to \beta$ and $\mathcal{B} \vdash_F N{:}\alpha$. It then follows that $\Gamma' \vdash_F M{:}\alpha \to \beta$ and $\Gamma'' \vdash_F N{:}\alpha$, for suitable Γ', Γ''. By the Weakening rule, we have $\Gamma' \cup \Gamma'' \vdash_F M{:}\alpha \to \beta$ and $\Gamma' \cup \Gamma'' \vdash_F N{:}\alpha$. Hence by the $(\to E)$ rule $\Gamma' \cup \Gamma'' \vdash_F MN{:}\beta$, showing that $[MN]$ is in X_β, as required.

To see that the second arrow condition holds, suppose that $[\![M]\!](\rho(x := a)) \in X_\beta$ whenever $a \in X_\alpha$. Suppose that x_i $(i = 1, n)$ are the free variables of M other than x, and K_i is $\rho(x_i)$. Choose $y{:}\alpha$ in $\mathcal{B}$ where y is not free in M or any K_i, and put $a = [y]$. Then we get that

$$\mathcal{B} \vdash_F [K_1/x_1, \ldots, K_n/x_n, y/x]M{:}\beta.$$

So by ($\rightarrow$I)

$$\mathcal{B} \vdash_F \lambda y.[K_1/x_1, \ldots, K_n/x_n, y/x]M{:}\beta$$

and by the choice of y this is

$$\mathcal{B} \vdash_F [K_1/x_1, \ldots, K_n/x_n]\lambda y.[y/x]M{:}\beta$$

and so as y is not free in M we get that $[\![\lambda x.M]\!](\rho) \in X_\alpha \rightarrow X_\beta$ as required.

A particular valuation V_0 of the type variables will be useful. It is defined by:

$$V_0(t) = X_t$$

Clearly, $V_0(\alpha) = X_\alpha$, for any type scheme α.

Completeness Theorem 3
$\Gamma \vdash_F M{:}\alpha$ *if in every semi-model and type interpretation,* $\Gamma \models M{:}\alpha$.

Proof: Suppose that in every semi-model and type interpretation, $\Gamma \models M{:}\alpha$. Choose the semi-model to be the term model and the type interpretation as above, with this Γ and with A taken to be M. Then ρ_0, V_0 satisfies every statement in Γ and so it also satisfies $M{:}\alpha$, and so we have $[M]$ in X_α. Thus we have $\Gamma' \vdash_F M{:}\alpha$ for some $\Gamma' \subset \mathcal{B}$. By applying the Strengthening rule followed, if needed, by weakening we finally obtain that $\Gamma \vdash_F M{:}\alpha$ as required.

The type interpretation used for the completeness proof is simple. To prove this one just has to show that $X_\alpha \rightarrow_S X_\beta$ is a subset of $X_\alpha \rightarrow X_\beta$. To this end, suppose that for all a in X_α that $[M] \cdot a$ is in X_β. Let x be a variable such that the statement $x{:}\alpha$ is in $\mathcal{B}$, and put $a = [x]$. Then we get that $\mathcal{B} \vdash_F Mx{:}\beta$. Now it may easily be proved for the system F that if $\Gamma \vdash_F KL{:}\beta$, then there is an α' such that $\Gamma \vdash_F K{:}\alpha' \rightarrow \beta$ and $\Gamma \vdash_F L{:}\alpha'$. Applying this to the above case we see that $\Gamma \vdash_F x{:}\alpha'$, and so the statement $x{:}\alpha'$ is in Γ, and so as $x{:}\alpha$ is too, $\alpha' = \alpha$, and so $\Gamma \vdash_F M{:}\alpha \rightarrow \beta$, as required.

A filter model It is also possible to try to make a model out of the type expressions themselves. It turns out that this does not work but using a richer collection of types does. This is the idea behind Coppo *et al* [2, 3] and Plotkin [11]. However the collection of type expressions *does* form a semi-model, which can also be used to show the completeness of the system F.

For this model take P to be $\mathcal{P}(\mathit{Type})$ partially ordered by subset, where *Type* is the set of all type expressions. Application is defined by:

$$a \cdot b = \{\beta \mid \text{ for some } \alpha \text{ in } b,\ \alpha \rightarrow \beta \text{ is in } a\}$$

And $[\![\cdot]\!](\cdot)$ is defined by the inductive clauses

$$[\![x]\!](\rho) = \rho(x)$$
$$[\![MN]\!](\rho) = [\![M]\!](\rho) \cdot [\![N]\!](\rho)$$
$$[\![\lambda x.M]\!](\rho) = \{\alpha{\rightarrow}\beta \mid \beta \in [\![M]\!](\rho(x := \alpha))\}$$

Here and below we confuse $\{\alpha\}$ with α. Clearly application is monotone, and $[\![M]\!](\rho)$ is monotone in ρ. Conditions (i), (ii), (iii) and (v) are easily seen to hold, and condition (iv) can be established by a straightforward inductive proof which we omit. For condition (vi), we may calculate that:

$$\begin{aligned}[\![\lambda x.M]\!](\rho) \cdot a &= \{\alpha{\rightarrow}\beta \mid \beta \in [\![M]\!](\rho(x := \alpha))\} \cdot a \\ &= \{\beta \mid \text{ for some } \alpha \text{ in } a,\ \beta \in [\![M]\!](\rho(x := \alpha))\} \\ &\subset [\![M]\!](\rho(x := a)).\end{aligned}$$

For the type interpretation define:

$$X_\alpha = \{a \mid \alpha \in a\}$$

and then put

$$Ty = \{X_\alpha \mid \alpha \text{ a type scheme}\}$$

Noting that X_α determines α since $\{\alpha\}$ is the only singleton in X_α, we can define the arrow operation by

$$X_\alpha{\rightarrow}X_\beta = X_{\alpha\rightarrow\beta}$$

We have to check that the arrow conditions hold. For the first, suppose that a is in $X_{\alpha\rightarrow\beta}$ and b is in X_β. Then $\alpha{\rightarrow}\beta$ is in a, α is in b and so β is in $a \cdot b$. For the second suppose that $[\![M]\!](\rho(x := a)) \in X_\beta$ whenever $a \in X_\alpha$. Then $\beta \in [\![M]\!](\rho(x := \alpha))$ and so $\alpha{\rightarrow}\beta \in [\![\lambda x.M]\!](\rho)$ showing that $[\![\lambda x.M]\!](\rho) \in X_{\alpha\rightarrow\beta}$ as required. One can also see that this semantics is simple. One direction is just the first arrow condition. For the other suppose that for every b in X_α, $a \cdot b \in X_\beta$. Then $\beta \in a \cdot \alpha$, and so $\alpha{\rightarrow}\beta \in a$, showing that $a \in X_{\alpha\rightarrow\beta}$, as required.

To show completeness we will need an appropriate environment and type environment. For the first, for any finite basis Γ define an environment by:

$$\hat{\Gamma}(x) = \{\alpha \mid x{:}\alpha \in \Gamma\}$$

Lemma 1
Let M be a term. Then $[\![M]\!](\hat{\Gamma}) = \{\alpha \mid \Gamma \vdash_F M{:}\alpha\}$.

Proof: The proof is by induction on M. There are three cases. First, if M is a variable x, then:

$$\begin{aligned}[\![M]\!](\hat{\Gamma}) &= \{\alpha \mid x{:}\alpha \in \Gamma\} \\ &= \{\alpha \mid \Gamma \vdash_F x{:}\alpha\}\end{aligned}$$

Second, if M is an application KL, then

$$\begin{aligned}
[\![KL]\!]\,(\hat{\Gamma}) &= [\![K]\!]\,(\hat{\Gamma}) \cdot [\![L]\!]\,(\hat{\Gamma}) \\
&= \{\gamma \mid \Gamma \vdash_F K{:}\gamma\} \cdot \{\alpha \mid \Gamma \vdash_F L{:}\alpha\} \quad \text{(by the induction hypothesis)} \\
&= \{\alpha{\rightarrow}\beta \mid \Gamma \vdash_F K{:}\alpha{\rightarrow}\beta\} \cdot \{\alpha \mid \Gamma \vdash_F L{:}\alpha\} \\
&\qquad\qquad \text{(by the definition of application)} \\
&= \{\beta \mid \Gamma \vdash_F KL{:}\beta\}
\end{aligned}$$

Third, if M is an abstraction $\lambda x.N$, then

$$\begin{aligned}
[\![\lambda x.N]\!]\,(\hat{\Gamma}) &= \{\alpha{\rightarrow}\beta \mid \beta \in [\![N]\!]\,(\hat{\Gamma}(x := a))\} \\
&= \{\alpha{\rightarrow}\beta \mid \Gamma, x{:}\alpha \vdash_F N{:}\beta\} \\
&\qquad \text{(by induction hypothesis, since } \hat{\Gamma}(x := \alpha) \text{ is } (\Gamma, x{:}\alpha)\hat{}\,) \\
&= \{\alpha{\rightarrow}\beta \mid \Gamma \vdash_F \lambda x.N{:}\alpha{\rightarrow}\beta\} \\
&= \{\gamma \mid \Gamma \vdash_F \lambda x.N{:}\gamma\},
\end{aligned}$$

concluding the proof.

Now the type environment is defined by $V_1(t) = X_t$, and one has that $V_1(\alpha) = X_\alpha$. Then one has a second proof of the Completeness theorem. Assume $\Gamma \models M{:}\alpha$ holds. Note that $\hat{\Gamma}, V$ satisfies every type statement $x{:}\alpha$ in Γ as $\{\alpha\} \in X_\alpha$. So $\hat{\Gamma}, V$ satisfies $M{:}\alpha$, which means that $[\![M]\!]\,(\hat{\Gamma})$ is in X_α, and so $\Gamma \vdash_F M{:}\alpha$ by the lemma, concluding the proof.

Since this proof of the Completeness theorem made no use of the Subject Reduction theorem, and since rule $(\geq_\beta)$ is sound for any semi-model and type interpretation, we now have a semantic proof of the Subject Reduction theorem. In fact a direct proof for the system F is very simple, but perhaps the technique would have applications in a more complex setting.

$\beta\eta$-conversion By using $\mathcal{T}_{\beta\eta}$ instead of $\mathcal{T}_\beta$, and working with the analogous simple type interpretation one proves a somewhat stronger completeness theorem:

Completeness Theorem 4
$\Gamma \vdash_F M{:}\alpha$ *if in every syntactical $\lambda\beta\eta$-semi-model and type interpretation,* $\Gamma \models M{:}\alpha$.

The theorem is also an immediate consequence of the fact that the filter model is actually a syntactical $\lambda\beta\eta$-semi-model. This is shown by calculating that for $\lambda x.Mx$ with x not free in M:

$$\begin{aligned}
[\![\lambda x.Mx]\!]\,(\rho) &\leq \{\alpha{\rightarrow}\beta \mid \beta \in [\![Mx]\!]\,(\rho(x := \alpha))\} \\
&= \{\alpha{\rightarrow}\beta \mid \exists \alpha' \in \{\alpha\}.\alpha'{\rightarrow}\beta \in [\![M]\!]\,(\rho(x := \alpha))\} \\
&= \{\alpha{\rightarrow}\beta \mid \alpha{\rightarrow}\beta \in [\![M]\!]\,(\rho(x := \alpha))\} \\
&\subset [\![M]\!]\,(\rho) \quad \text{(as } x \text{ is not free in } M)
\end{aligned}$$

This observation also yields a semantic proof for the Subject Reduction theorem for $\beta\eta$-reduction.

5 Polymorphic Type Inference

A system for polymorphic type inference is obtained by adding universal quantification, $\forall t.\alpha$ to type expressions (see [10, 4, 8, 14, 15] for information on this system and further references). We do not distinguish α-equivalent type expressions—those which differ only in the names of bound variables. There are also evident notions of $\mathrm{FTV}(\alpha)$, the free type variables of α and substitution $[\beta/t]\alpha$. There are two new rules

$$(\forall I) \qquad \frac{\Gamma \vdash M{:}\alpha}{\Gamma \vdash M{:}\forall t.\alpha}$$

(provided that t does not appear free in any type scheme in Γ)

$$(\forall E) \qquad \frac{\Gamma \vdash M{:}\forall t.\alpha}{\Gamma \vdash M{:}[\beta/t]\alpha}$$

The resulting system is called "F∀", and F∀-deducibility, $\Gamma \vdash_{\forall F} M{:}\alpha$, is defined in the evident way. The Subject Reduction theorem for β-reduction, and the Equality Postponement theorem for β-conversion extend to this new setting, and both weakening and strengthening continue to hold. However the Subject Reduction theorem does not hold for $\beta\eta$-reduction [10]; for example, it holds that $y{:}\forall t.\alpha\to\beta \vdash_{\forall F} \lambda x.yx{:}\alpha\to\forall t.\beta$, but not that $y{:}\forall t.\alpha\to\beta \vdash_{\forall F} y{:}\alpha\to\forall t.\beta$.

A *type interpretation* is now a triple

$$\mathcal{T}y = \langle Ty, \to, [\![\cdot]\!]\,(\cdot)\rangle$$

where $\langle Ty, \to\rangle$ is an interpretation as above and $[\![\cdot]\!]\,(\cdot)$ is a mapping from type expressions and valuations of the type variables to types such that:

(i) $\quad [\![t]\!]\,(V) = V(t)$

(ii) $\quad [\![\alpha\to\beta]\!]\,(V) = [\![\alpha]\!]\,(V)\to [\![\beta]\!]\,(V)$

(iii) $\quad [\![\forall t.a]\!]\,(V) = \bigcap\{[\![\alpha]\!]\,(V(t := X)) \mid X \in Ty\}$

Note that we have to take these as conditions rather than as an inductive definition, for in the third case it is needed that the intersection is indeed a type. This definition can be viewed as a special case of the definition in [10] where types represent sets of elements of the model rather than necessarily being such sets. We omit the verification of this claim which would involve embedding $\mathcal{T}y$ in a model of the typed λ-calculus.

Proposition 2
Type interpretations have the following properties:

(iv) $\quad [\![\forall t.\alpha]\!]\,(V) = [\![\forall t'.[t'/t]\alpha]\!]\,(V)$ (if t' is not free in α)

(v) $\quad$ if $V \restriction \mathrm{FTV}(\alpha) = V' \restriction \mathrm{FTV}(\alpha)$ then $[\![\alpha]\!]\,(V) = [\![\alpha]\!]\,(V')$

(vi) if for all X in Ty, $[\![\alpha]\!](V(t := X)) = [\![\beta]\!](V(t := X))$
then $[\![\forall t.\alpha]\!](V) = [\![\forall t.\beta]\!](V)$

(Sub) $[\![[\beta/t]\alpha]\!](V) = [\![\alpha]\!](V(t := [\![\beta]\!](V)))$

Proof: The proof is straightforward, and we omit it.

We now say that a statement $M{:}\alpha$ is *satisfied* by ρ, V if $[\![M]\!](\rho) \in [\![\alpha]\!](V)$, and define what $\Gamma \models M{:}\alpha$ means accordingly.

Consistency Theorem 5
If $\Gamma \vdash_{\forall F} M{:}\alpha$ *then* $\Gamma \models M{:}\alpha$.

Proof: The proof is by induction on the size of the proof that $\Gamma \vdash M{:}\alpha$. Choose ρ, V and assume they satisfy every statement in Γ. The cases other then $(\forall I)$ and $(\forall \mathrm{E})$ are dealt with as before. In the first of these cases, we have that α has the form $\forall t.\beta$, and there is a shorter proof of $\Gamma \vdash M{:}\beta$, where t does not occur free in any type scheme in Γ. Therefore by (v), for any type X it is the case that $\rho, V(t := X)$ satisfy every statement in Γ and so satisfy $M{:}\beta$. That is $[\![M]\!](\rho) \in [\![\alpha]\!](V(t := X))$, and so by (iii), ρ, V satisfy $M{:}\alpha$.

In the second case, we have that for some β, σ the type scheme α has the form $[\sigma/t]\beta$ and there is a shorter proof of $\Gamma \vdash M{:}\forall t.\beta$. So by induction hypothesis, $[\![M]\!](\rho) \in [\![\forall t.\beta]\!](V)$. But

$$\begin{aligned} [\![\forall t.\beta]\!](V) &\subset [\![\beta]\!](V(t := [\![\sigma]\!](V))) && \text{(by (iii))} \\ &= [\![[\sigma/t]\beta]\!](V) && \text{(by (Sub))} \end{aligned}$$

showing that ρ, V satisfy $M{:}[\sigma/t]\beta$, and concluding the proof.

A completeness proof can be based on the term semi-model $\mathcal{T}_\beta$. For a type interpretation, given any finite basis Γ and term A define a basis $\mathcal{B}$ as above, and with the analogous understanding of $\mathcal{B} \vdash_{\forall F} M{:}\alpha$. Define:

$$X_\alpha = \{[M] \mid \mathcal{B} \vdash_{\forall F} M{:}\alpha\}$$

as before, again making use of the Subject Reduction theorem and take

$$Ty = \{X_\alpha \mid \alpha \text{ a type scheme}\}$$

To see that X_α determines α, suppose that $X_\alpha = X_\beta$. Taking a statement of the form $x{:}\alpha$ in $\mathcal{B}$, we get that $\mathcal{B} \vdash_{\forall F} x{:}\beta$, and hence, by strengthening, that $x{:}\alpha \vdash_{\forall F} x{:}\beta$. Then, in the notation of Mitchell, $\alpha \subset \beta$. Similarly $\beta \subset \alpha$, and it follows that α and β are α-equivalent. Now $\rightarrow$ can be defined by:

$$X_\alpha {\rightarrow} X_\beta = X_{\alpha \rightarrow \beta}$$

The arrow conditions hold, with the same proof as before, making use of weakening. It remains to define $[\![\alpha]\!](V)$, and we put:

$$[\![\alpha]\!](V) = X_{[\sigma_1/t_1,\dots,\sigma_n/t_n]\alpha}$$

here $V(t_i) = \sigma_i$, and the t_i are the free type variables of α. We have to verify conditions (i), (ii) and (iii). The first is trivial. For the second, we may calculate that:

$$[\![\alpha\to\beta]\!](V) = X_{[\sigma_1/t_1,\dots,\sigma_n/t_n](\alpha\to\beta)}$$

(where $V(t_i) = \beta_i$ and the t_i are the free type variables of $\alpha\to\beta$)

$$\begin{aligned} &= (X_{[\sigma_1/t_1,\dots,\sigma_n/t_n]\alpha})\to(X_{[\sigma_1/t_1,\dots,\sigma_n/t_n]\beta}) \\ &= [\![\alpha]\!](V)\to[\![\beta]\!](V) \end{aligned}$$

The verification of the third condition is split into two inclusions. In one direction,

$$[\![\forall t.\alpha]\!](V) = X_{[\sigma_1/t_1,\dots,\sigma_n/t_n]\forall t.\alpha}$$

(where $V(t_i) = \sigma_i$, and the t_i are the free type variables of $\forall t.\alpha$, and where we may assume that t differs from all the t_i and does not appear free in any σ_i)

$$\begin{aligned} &= \{[M] \mid \mathcal{B} \vdash_F M{:}\forall t.[\sigma_1/t_1,\dots,\sigma_n/t_n]\alpha\} \\ &\subset \{[M] \mid \mathcal{B} \vdash_F M{:}[\beta/t][\sigma_1/t_1,\dots,\sigma_n/t_n]\alpha\} \quad \text{(by }(\forall\text{E}))\\ &= \{[M] \mid \mathcal{B} \vdash_F M{:}[\beta/t,\sigma_1/t_1,\dots,\sigma_n/t_n]\alpha\} \\ &= [\![\alpha]\!](V(t := [\![\beta]\!](V))) \end{aligned}$$

In the other direction, suppose that $[M]$ is in $[\![\alpha]\!](V(t := X))$ for every type X. Let $t_1,\dots,t_n$ be the free type variables of α other than t, and suppose $V(t_i) = \sigma_i$. Choose t' different from all the t_i, not free in α, or in any σ_i or in any β, where $x{:}\beta$ is a statement in $\mathcal{B}$ whose subject x is free in M. Take X to be $X_{t'}$. Then

$$\Gamma' \vdash_{\forall F} M{:}[t'/t,\sigma_1/t_1,\dots,\sigma_n/t_n]\alpha$$

for some Γ' a subset of $\mathcal{B}$. Applying strengthening as necessary, we can assume that the subject of any statement in Γ' is a free variable of M. Hence by $(\forall\text{I})$

$$\Gamma' \vdash_{\forall F} M{:}\forall t'.[t'/t,\sigma_1/t_1,\dots,\sigma_n/t_n]\alpha.$$

But $\forall t'.[t'/t,\sigma_1/t_1,\dots,\sigma_n/t_n]\alpha$ is α-equivalent to $[\sigma_1/t_1,\dots,\sigma_n/t_n]\forall t.\alpha$, and so M is in $[\![\forall t.\alpha]\!](V)$, as required. Finally, one defines the environments ρ_0 and V_0 as before, and obtains:

Completeness Theorem 6
$\Gamma \vdash_{\forall F} M{:}\alpha$ if in every semi-model and type interpretation, $\Gamma \models M{:}\alpha$.

Proof: The proof is exactly like the term model one for the system F.

We were not able to find a filter semi-model in the polymorphic case.

The simple semantics. Simple type interpretations validate the following rule, introduced by Mitchell:

$$\text{(simple)} \qquad \frac{\Gamma \vdash \lambda x.Mx{:}\alpha \to \beta}{\Gamma \vdash M{:}\alpha \to \beta} \quad (x \notin \mathrm{FV}(M))$$

To see this, suppose we have such an interpretation and $\Gamma \models \lambda x.Mx{:}\alpha \to \beta$, where x is not free in M, and we have environments ρ, V satisfying every statement in Γ. Take a in $V(\alpha)$ to show that $[\![M]\!](\rho) \cdot a \in V(\beta)$. By the assumptions, $[\![\lambda x.Mx]\!](\rho) \cdot a \in V(\beta)$. But $V(\beta)$ is upper closed and $[\![\lambda x.Mx]\!](\rho) \cdot a \leq [\![M]\!](\rho) \cdot a$, yielding the desired conclusion.

The counterexample to Subject Reduction for $\beta\eta$-conversion also shows that (simple) is not a derived rule of the polymorphic typing system. So as simple type interpretations validate (simple) they cannot be complete for the polymorphic typing system. We shall show that, instead, they are complete for that system extended by (simple). Let us call this extended system "$F\forall_s$", and write $\mathcal{B} \vdash_s M{:}\alpha$ to mean $\Gamma \vdash M{:}\alpha$ is provable in it, for some $\Gamma \subset \mathcal{B}$. It is easily seen that both weakening and strengthening hold for this system. The following is implicit in Mitchell's work [10].

Lemma 2
$\Gamma \vdash_s M{:}\alpha$ iff there is a λ-term N such that $N \geq_{\beta\eta} M$ and $\Gamma \vdash_\forall N{:}\alpha$.

Proof: The implication from left to right is a straightforward induction on the size of proof, and is remarked on p228 of *op cit.* Mitchell's lemma 16 shows that the converse holds for his simple containment system, and his theorem 16 shows that system equivalent to the one considered here.

Theorem 7
Subject Reduction holds for the system $F\forall_s$ and $\beta\eta$-conversion.

Proof: Suppose that $\Gamma \vdash_s M{:}\alpha$ and $M \geq_{\beta\eta} N$. By the lemma, there is a λ-term K such that $K \geq_{\beta\eta} M$ and $\Gamma \vdash_\forall K{:}\alpha$. By η-postponement, there is a term L such that $K \geq_\beta L \geq_\eta N$. Then by Subject Reduction for the system $F\forall$ and β-conversion, $\Gamma \vdash_\forall L{:}\alpha$, and it follows from the lemma, that $\Gamma \vdash_s N{:}\alpha$, as desired.

With this result a proof of completeness can be based on the term model $\mathcal{T}_{\beta\eta}$, following the usual lines. For a type interpretation, given any finite basis Γ and term A, define a basis $\mathcal{B}$ as above, and with the analogous understanding of $\mathcal{B} \vdash_s M{:}\alpha$. Define:

$$X_\alpha = \{[M] \mid \mathcal{B} \vdash_s M{:}\alpha\}$$

making use of the above Subject Reduction theorem and take

$$Ty = \{X_\alpha \mid \alpha \text{ a type scheme}\}$$

Here X_α does not quite determine α; we get instead that $X_\alpha = X_\beta$ holds iff $\alpha \subset_s \beta \subset_s \alpha$, where by $\subset_s$ is meant Mitchell's simple containment relation. The implication from left to right is proved as for the system F∀; the other direction follows from an application of rule (cont) of Mitchell's simple containment system. Using his (arrow) rule for simple containment, one then sees that $\rightarrow$ can be defined by:

$$X_\alpha \rightarrow X_\beta = X_{\alpha\rightarrow\beta}$$

as usual. The arrow conditions hold, and are proved as usual. For the interpretation of type expressions, we put:

$$[\![\alpha]\!](V) = X_{[\sigma_1/t_1,\ldots,\sigma_n/t_n]\alpha}$$

and the verification of the three conditions proceeds as before. It remains to see that this semantics is indeed simple. One direction is the first arrow condition. For the other suppose that whenever $[N]$ is in X_α then $[MN]$ is in X_β. Choose $x{:}\alpha$ in $\mathcal{B}$ with $x \notin \mathrm{FV}(M)$. Then $[Mx]$ is in X_β, which is to say that $\mathcal{B} \vdash_s Mx{:}\beta$. So by ($\rightarrow$I), $\mathcal{B} \vdash_s \lambda x.Mx{:}\alpha\rightarrow\beta$, and so by the Subject Reduction theorem $\mathcal{B} \vdash_s M{:}\alpha\rightarrow\beta$ as required. Now one chooses ρ_0, V_0 as before, and obtains:

Completeness Theorem 8
$\Gamma \vdash_s M{:}\alpha$ *if in every syntactical $\lambda\beta\eta$-semi-model and simple type interpretation,* $\Gamma \models M{:}\alpha$.

Acknowledgments

Part of this work was done while the author was visiting the MIT Laboratory for Computer Science, in 1981 and 1982. He would like to thank Albert Meyer for supporting the visit with the aid of an NSF grant.

References

[1] Barendregt, H.P. The lambda calculus: its syntax and semantics. Amsterdam: North-Holland (1984).

[2] Barendregt, H.P., Coppo M., and Dezani-Ciancaglini, M. A filter lambda model and the completeness of type assignment. *J. Symbolic Logic* **48**/4, pp. 931-940 (1984).

[3] Coppo, M., Dezani, M., Honsell F. and Longo, G. Extended type structures and filter lambda models, in *Logic Colloquium '82*, ed. G. Lolli *et al*, pp 241-262. Amsterdam: North Holland (1983)

[4] Giannini, P. and Ronchi Della Rocca, S. Characterisations of typings in polymorphic type discipline. In *Proc. of the Third Annual IEEE Symposium on Logic in Computer Science*, pp. 61-71. Los Alamitos: Computer Society Press of the IEEE (1988).

[5] Hindley, R. The completeness theorem for typing lambda terms. *Theoret. Comput. Sci.* **22**, pp. 1-17 (1983).

[6] Hindley, R. Curry's type rules are complete with respect to the F-semantics too. *Theoret. Comput. Sci.* **22**, pp. 127-133 (1983).

[7] Jay, C. B. Long $\beta\eta$-normal forms in confluent categories. To appear (1991).

[8] Leivant, D. Polymorphic type inference, in *Proceedings, 10th Annual ACM Symposium on Principles of Programming Languages*, pp. 88-89 (1983).

[9] Milner, R. A theory of type polymorphism in programming. *J. Comput. System Sci.* **17**, pp. 348-375 (1985).

[10] Mitchell, J. C. Polymorphic type inference and containment. *Information and Computation* **76**, pp. 211-249 (1988).

[11] Plotkin, G.D. A set-theoretical definition of application. Research Memorandum MIP-R-95, 32 pp. Dept. of Machine Intelligence and Perception, University of Edinburgh (1972).

[12] Rydeheard, D.E. and Stell, J.G. Foundations of equational deduction: a categorical treatment of equational proofs and unification algorithms, in: Pitt *et al*, (eds), Category theory and Computer Science, *Lecture Notes in Computer Science* **283** pp. 114-139. Berlin: Springer Verlag (1987).

[13] Seely, R.A.G. Modelling computations a 2-categorical framework, in: *Proceedings of the Second Annual IEEE Symposium on Logic in Computer Science*, pp. 65-71. Los Alamitos: Computer Society Press of the IEEE (1987).

[14] Tiuryn, J. Type inference problems: a survey, in B. Rovan (ed.) Proceedings, Mathematical Foundations of Computer Science. *Lecture Notes in Computer Science* **452** pp. 105-120. Berlin: Springer Verlag (1990).

[15] Yokouchi, H. Embedding second order type system into intersection type system and its application to type inference. To appear (1991).

Type Inference in Polymorphic Type Discipline

Paola Giannini, Simona Ronchi Della Rocca
Dipartimento di Informatica - Universita' di Torino
Corso Svizzera 185, Torino, (Italy)
giannini,ronchi@di.unito.it

Abstract

A hierarchy of type assignment systems is defined, which is a complete stratification of the polymorphic type assignment system. For each of such systems a type inference algorithm is given.

1. Introduction.

In this paper we study the problem of the automatic inference of types in the polymorphic type discipline for lambda calculus. The polymorphic type discipline is an extension of classical Curry's functionality theory [5] in which types can be universally quantified. We consider the type assignment system for deriving quantified types for terms of untyped lambda calculus introduced in [14]. A typing for an untyped λ-term M is a statement $B\vdash_{\forall}M:\varphi$, provable in such a system, where B is a type assignment (a partial function from λ-variables to types) and φ is a type. In [14] an isomorphism is proved between typings in this system and terms of the second order λ-calculus (see [10] and [18]).

In Curry's type discipline all the typings for a term M are instances of a particular typing of M, the principal one, and there is a decision procedure building the principal typing of M, if it exists [11]. Milner uses this property in designing a type-inference algorithm for the language ML, based on Curry's types [6]. In the polymorphic type discipline, it can be shown that a principal typing in this sense does not exist. In fact consider the term $\lambda x.xx$; both $(\forall t.t)\rightarrow\forall t.t$ and $(\forall t.t\rightarrow t)\rightarrow\forall t.t\rightarrow t$ are types derivable for it, but it can be easily proved that there is no type φ derivable for $\lambda x.xx$ such that both the considered types are instances of φ [4]. Moreover the problem of whether the set of terms having a type in this discipline is recursive is still open; in [9] we proved that this set is a proper subset of the set of strongly normalizing terms which contains all the normal forms.

In this paper we define a countable set of type assignment sytems $\vdash_n$ ($n\in\omega$), which is a complete stratification of the polymorphic type assignment system. I.e., $B\vdash_{\forall}M:\varphi$ if and only if $B\vdash_n M:\varphi$ for some n. Every system $\vdash_n$ is decidable. Then we build a type inference algorithm for every system $\vdash_n$. This algorithm generates, for any untyped term M and integer n, the finite set of the minimal types derivable for M in the system $\vdash_n$, if any. Types are minimal with respect to a partial order relation defined in such a way that, if M has a type in Curry's type discipline, then for any n its principal Curry's type is the minimum of the relation. In fact we are looking for a conservative extension of the ML type inference algorithm.

As pointed out in [13], a type inference problem is always connected to a unification problem. The type inference algorithm for Curry's type discipline is based on the classical first-order unification procedure [19]. It is essentially the solution of a set of equations between Curry's types. For solving the type inference problem in polymorphic type

---

Work partially supported by EEC "Project Stimulation ST2J/0374/C(EDB): Lambda Calcul Type"'.

discipline, we are dealing with particular instances of the semi-unification problem. This problem has been proved to be undecidable in [12].

We give a parameterized solution for a restriction of the semi-unification problem, by defining a unification procedure, which is a conservative extension of Robinson's unification procedure. This procedure works as the classical one, but it never gives a failure as output. A situation that classically is interpreted as a failure here gives a positive information, namely the need of a quantified variable in the place in which the failure occurred. In order to do this, informations about the structure of the terms to be unified must also be supplied to the algorithm. A completely different conservative extension of Robinson's unification algorithm has been defined for solving the problem of type inference in the intersection type discipline. This extension was based not only on substitution but also on other operations on types (see [20] and [3]).

The undecidability of the semi-unification does not imply the undecidability of the type inference. It implies instead that it is undecidable if, in the polymorphic type discipline, a term has a typing satisfying some first order constraints (e.g., having at least a given number of arrows, or a given number of symbols). An undecidability result for the typed case is proved in [16]. Namely it is proved to be undecidable the problem of inferring a type for a partially typed term. There does not seem to be a clear relation between the two results.

Finally we point out that the stratification of the polymorphic type assignment we introduce is not only a technical tool for the type inference, but it seems to be interesting in itself. $\vdash_0$ coincides with the Curry's type assignment system, and in $\vdash_1$ all the normal forms can be typed. Two problems naturally arise:

1) give a characterization of the terms typable in $\vdash_n$, for more n;

2) given a term M, is there a minimum n such that if M cannot be typed in $\vdash_n$ then M cannot be typed in $\vdash_\forall$? This problem is a rephrasation of the problem of asking if the type inference for the polymorphic type discipline is decidable or not.

2. Polymorphic Types and Containment

Let x, y, and z range over *λ-variables*, and M, N, P, and Q range over *λ-terms*. The terms of untyped λ-calculus are defined by the following grammar.

$$M := x \mid MM \mid \lambda x.M$$

Λ is the set of untyped λ-terms, FV(M) denotes the set of the *free variables* of M. Let a, b, and c range over *type variables*, and φ, χ, and ψ range over *type expressions* (*types*). The set of type expressions is defined by the following grammar.

$$\varphi ::= a \mid \varphi\to\varphi \mid \forall a.\varphi$$

We only consider types $\forall a.\varphi$ such that a must be free in φ (λI types). = denotes syntactic equality of types. T is the set of types and $T^- = \{\varphi\in T \mid \text{for no } a \text{ and } \psi\in T,\ \varphi=\forall a.\psi\}$ is the set of *non externally quantified types*. $\varphi_1\to\varphi_2\to\cdots\ \varphi_{n-1}\to\varphi_n$ is an abbreviation for $(\varphi_1\to(\varphi_2\to\cdots(\varphi_{n-1}\to\varphi_n)$ and $\forall a_1a_2\cdots a_n.\varphi$ is an abbreviation for $\forall a_1.\forall a_2.\ldots.\forall a_n.\varphi$. A *type assignment* A is a partial function with finite domain from λ-variables to types.

Notation. (i) Let $\underline{a}$ denote a (possibly empty) string of variables and $\underline{\varphi}$ denote a (possibly empty) sequence of types. $a\in\underline{a}$ denotes that the type variable a occurs in the string $\underline{a}$. Let $\underline{a}$ be the string $a_1a_2\cdots a_n$, where $n\geq 0$, and let φ be a type. $\forall\underline{a}.\varphi$ is an abbreviation for $\forall a_1.\forall a_2.\ldots.\forall a_n.\varphi$ (if n=0 $\forall\underline{a}.\varphi$ is equal to φ).

(ii) Let φ and ψ be types, and a be a type variable. $[\varphi/a]\psi$ denotes the type obtained from ψ by replacing φ for each occurrence of a In the replacement bound variables of φ and ψ can be renamed to avoid collision of free variables. Let $\underline{\varphi}$ be the sequence $\varphi_1\varphi_2\cdots\varphi_n$ and let $\underline{a}$ be $a_1a_2\cdots a_n$: both $[\underline{\varphi}/\underline{a}]\psi$ and $[\varphi_1/a_1, \varphi_2/a_2,\ldots, \varphi_n/a_n]\psi$ denote the type obtained by the simultaneous replacement of the variable a_i by φ_i $(1\leq i\leq n)$. Let A be a type assignment; $[\varphi/a]A$ is the function mapping a to φ, and any x to A(x).

(iii) Let g be a (partial) function from E to F, *domain*(g)=$\{e \in E \mid g(e) \text{ is defined}\}$. If *domain*(g)=$\{e_1, e_2, \ldots, e_n\}$ and $g(e_i)=f_i$, g can be denoted by either

$$[e_1 \Rightarrow f_1, e_2 \Rightarrow f_2, \ldots, e_n \Rightarrow f_n] \text{ or } \Sigma_{1\leq i\leq n} [e_i \Rightarrow f_i].$$

An *extension* of g is a partial function that coincides with g on *domain*(g). Let $e_1, e_2, \ldots, e_n$ be distinct elements of E, and $f_1, f_2, \ldots, f_n$ be elements of F; both

$$g+[e_1 \Rightarrow f_1, e_2 \Rightarrow f_2, \ldots, e_n \Rightarrow f_n] \text{ and } g+\Sigma_{1\leq i\leq n} [e_i \Rightarrow f_i]$$

denote the function that coincides with g on all the elements of $E-\{e_1, e_2, \ldots, e_n\}$ and that for all i, $1\leq i\leq n$, maps e_i into f_i. If g and f are functions and V is a subset of their domains, $f=_V g$ denotes that for all $x\in V$ $f(x)=g(x)$, and fg denotes the composition of f and g, i.e., for all x $fg(x)=f(g(x))$. If C is a subset of E, g-C is a function that coincides with g on all the elements of E that do not belong to C, and it is undefined on the elements of C. The everywhere undefined function is denoted by $\emptyset$. □

Let A be a type assignment, φ be a type, a be a type variable, and M be a λ-term; a is *bindable* in M with respect to A if a is not free in any type A(x) for any free variable x of M. We can derive from A a type φ for M, if $A\vdash_\forall M:\varphi$ is derivable in the following system.

<u>Polymorphic type assignment system</u>

(var) $A\vdash_\forall x: A(x)$

$$(\to I)\ \frac{A+[x\Rightarrow\varphi]\vdash_\forall M:\psi}{A\vdash_\forall \lambda x.M:\varphi\to\psi} \qquad (\to E)\ \frac{A\vdash_\forall M:\varphi\to\psi \quad A\vdash_\forall N:\varphi}{A\vdash_\forall MN:\psi}$$

$$(\forall I)\ \frac{A\vdash_\forall M:\varphi}{A\vdash_\forall M:\forall a.\varphi\ (*)} \qquad (\forall E)\ \frac{A\vdash_\forall M:\forall a.\varphi}{A\vdash_\forall M: [\psi/a]\varphi}$$

(*) a is bindable in M with respect to A.
$\vdash_\forall M:\varphi$ stands for $\emptyset\vdash_\forall M:\varphi$.

A type assignment system is said to be syntax directed if for all term M having a typing in the system, every derivation of a typing for M has a shape depending only on the structure of M. Curry's system is an example of a syntax directed system. For syntax directed systems proofs and reasoning can be easily carried out by structural induction on terms. The type assignment system described above does not have this property, since applications of the rules (∀E) and (∀I) can occur at any point of the derivation. We now present a type assignment system, which is syntax directed and will be proved to be equivalent to the previous one. First let us define a containement relation between types, which is the relation introduced in [6].

<u>Definition 1</u>. $\forall \underline{a}.\varphi\leq[\chi/\underline{a}]\varphi$. □

Clearly the relation ≤ is decidable. Moreover ≤ is reflexive and transitive, and, if $\forall \underline{a}.(\varphi\to\psi)\leq\varphi'\to\psi'$, then $\forall \underline{a}.\varphi\leq\varphi'$ and $\forall \underline{a}.\psi\leq\psi'$.

<u>Containment type assignment system</u>

$$(\text{var}\leq)\ \frac{A(x)\leq\chi}{A\vdash x:\forall \underline{a}.\chi\quad (*)}$$

$$(\to I)\ \frac{A+[x\Rightarrow\varphi]\vdash M:\psi}{A\vdash\lambda x.M:\forall\underline{a}.\varphi\to\psi}\ (*)\qquad\qquad (\to E)\ \frac{A\vdash M:\varphi\to\psi\qquad A\vdash N:\varphi\qquad \psi\leq\chi}{A\vdash MN:\forall\underline{a}.\chi}\ (*)$$

(*) the type variables in $\underline{a}$ are bindable in the subject of the conclusion with respect to A.

<u>Theorem 2</u> [8]. $A\vdash_{\forall}M:\varphi$ if and only if $A\vdash M:\varphi$. □

This containement system is syntax directed. It is immediate to verify that, in the containement type assignment system (as previously defined), we can always assume, without loss of generality, that $\chi\in T^-$ In fact, for any φ and ψ

$$\forall ab.\varphi\leq\forall b.[\psi/a]\varphi \text{ implies } \forall ab.\varphi\leq[\psi/a,\, b/b]\varphi.$$

Therefore if $A\vdash M:\forall b.[\psi/a]\varphi$ then $A\vdash M{:}\ [\psi/a,\, b/b]\varphi$.

<u>Example.</u> Let D_1 be the following derivation of $\vdash_{\forall}\lambda x.xx:\forall b.(\forall a.a)\to b$:

$$(\forall I)\ \cfrac{(\to I)\ \cfrac{(\to E)\ \cfrac{(\forall E)\ \cfrac{(var)\ [x\Rightarrow\forall a.a]\vdash_{\forall}x:\forall a.a}{[x\Rightarrow\forall a.a]\vdash_{\forall}x:a\to b}\qquad (\forall E)\ \cfrac{(var)\ [x\Rightarrow\forall a.a]\vdash_{\forall}x:\forall a.a}{[x\Rightarrow\forall a.a]\vdash_{\forall}x:a}}{[x\Rightarrow\forall a.a]\vdash_{\forall}xx:b}}{\vdash_{\forall}\lambda x.xx:(\forall a.a)\to b}}{\vdash_{\forall}\lambda x.xx:\forall b.(\forall a.a)\to b}$$

and D_2 be the following derivation of $\vdash_{\forall}\lambda x.xx:(\forall a.a\to b)\to b$:

$$(\to I)\ \cfrac{(\to E)\ \cfrac{(\forall E)\ \cfrac{(var)\ [x\Rightarrow\forall a.a\to b]\vdash_{\forall}x:\forall a.a\to b}{[x\Rightarrow\forall a.a\to b]\vdash_{\forall}x:(\forall a.a\to b)\to b}\qquad (var)[x\Rightarrow\forall a.a\to b]\vdash_{\forall}x:\forall a.a\to b}{[x\Rightarrow\forall a.a\to b]\vdash_{\forall}xx:b}}{\vdash_{\forall}\lambda x.xx:(\forall a.a\to b)\to b}$$

The corresponding derivations in the containement system are respectively:
D'_1:

$$(\to I)\ \cfrac{(\to E)\ \cfrac{(var\leq)\ \cfrac{\forall a.a\leq a\to b}{[x\Rightarrow\forall a.a]\vdash x:a\to b}\qquad (var\leq)\ \cfrac{\forall a.a\leq a}{[x\Rightarrow\forall a.a]\vdash x:a}\qquad b\leq b}{[x\Rightarrow\forall a.a]\vdash xx:b}}{\vdash\lambda x.xx:\forall b.(\forall a.a)\to b}$$

D'_2:

$$(\to I)\ \cfrac{(\to E)\ \cfrac{(var\leq)\ \cfrac{\forall a.a\to b\leq(\forall a.a\to b)\to b}{[x\Rightarrow\forall a.a\to b]\vdash x:(\forall a.a\to b)\to b}\qquad (var\leq)\ \cfrac{\forall a.a\to b\leq\forall a.a\to b}{[x\Rightarrow\forall a.a\to b]\vdash x:\forall a.a\to b}\qquad b\leq b}{[x\Rightarrow\forall a.a\to b]\vdash xx:b}}{\vdash_{\forall}\lambda x.xx:\forall b.(\forall a.a\to b)\to b}$$

□

We can represent a derivation in $\vdash$ by a sequence of containements as follows.

<u>Definition 3</u>. Let D be a derivation of $A\vdash M:\varphi$. The *characteristic* of D, C(D), is the sequence

$$\langle\varphi_1\leq\psi_1,\varphi_2\leq\psi_2,\ldots,\varphi_n\leq\psi_n\rangle$$

such that $\varphi_i \leq \psi_i$ occurs in an application of either the rule ($\rightarrow$E) or (var $\leq$) of D and precedes $\varphi_{i+1} \leq \psi_{i+1}$ in the postorder visit of D. □

Example. The characteristics of the previous derivations D'_1 and D'_2 are:

$C(D'_1)=\langle \forall a.a \leq a \rightarrow b, \forall a.a \leq a, b \leq b \rangle$, and

$C(D'_2)=\langle \forall a.a \rightarrow b \leq (\forall a.a \rightarrow b) \rightarrow b, \forall a.a \rightarrow b \leq \forall a.a \rightarrow b, b \leq b \rangle$. □

3. The Principal Typing Scheme of a Term

In this section we breafly rephrase a result already presented in [8], which is an essential tool for the construction of the type inference algorithm. More precisely we define a formal system which, given a term, builds the most general set of constraints that must be satisfied in order to give a typing to the term itself. These constraints are in some sense the analogous of a principal type scheme for the polymorphic type discipline. For representing the constraints, we introduce the schemes, which are representations of type contexts.

Schemes are defined by the following grammar, similar to the one of types, but variables are just names for free places that can be filled by either types or sequences of type variables. Let α, β, γ and δ denote *scheme variables*, r, t ,v and u denote *sequence variables.*

$$\sigma ::= \alpha \mid \forall t.\alpha \mid \sigma \rightarrow \sigma \mid \forall t.\sigma \rightarrow \sigma$$

Let $\equiv$ denote identity between schemes. The set of free variables of a scheme σ, FV(σ), is the set of all scheme and sequence variables occurring in σ, i.e., the symbol $\forall$ does not introduce bound variables. Σ is the set of *schemes.* Schemes are ranged over by ρ, σ, τ and υ. Let Σ^- be $\{\sigma \in \Sigma \mid$ for no t and $\tau \in \Sigma$ $\sigma \equiv \forall t.\tau\}$.

For schemes we introduce two notions of substitutions: ground substitutions, and scheme substitutions. Ground substitutions map schemes into types, whereas scheme substitutions map schemes into schemes.

A *ground substitution,* s, is a function mapping scheme variables in non externally quantified types and sequence variables in (possibly empty) strings of type variables. An empty string will be denoted by ε. So a ground substitution maps a scheme into a type. Then a scheme σ can be viewed as a representation of the set of types that can be obtained from σ by applying a ground substitution to it. For example:

$\forall t.\alpha$ represents the whole set T,

α represents the set T^-,

$(\forall t.\alpha) \rightarrow \forall u.\beta$ represents the set $\{\varphi \rightarrow \psi \mid \varphi, \psi \in T\}$.

A *scheme substitution,* S, is a function mapping scheme variables in elements of Σ^- and sequence variables in sequence variables or the symbol ε. If $S=S'+[t \Rightarrow \varepsilon]$ then $S(\forall t.\sigma)=S'(\sigma)$. Therefore a scheme substitution maps schemes into schemes.

Definition 4.(i) A *scheme system* G is a set of pairs of schemes.

(ii) A set of *variables constraint* F is a function from sequence variables to $\wp_{fin}(\Sigma)$ (finite sets of schemes).

(iii) Let s be a ground substitution, and let G be the scheme system $\{(\sigma_1,\tau_1),(\sigma_2,\tau_2),...,(\sigma_n,\tau_n)\}$. G *is satisfied by* s if for all i, $1 \leq i \leq n$, $s(\sigma_i) \leq s(\tau_i)$ (where $\leq$ is the containement relation between types introduced in definition 1).

(iv) The variables constraint F *is satisfied by* s if for all t such that $F(t)=\Gamma$, if $s(t) = a_1a_2 \cdots a_n$ and $n \geq 1$, then for all i, $1 \leq i \leq n$, a_i does not belong to the free variables of any $s(\sigma)$, where $\sigma \in \Gamma$. □

We now introduce a formal system that proves statements of the shape:

$$\Pi(M)=\langle B,\sigma,G,F \rangle$$

where M is a term of the untyped lambda calculus, B is a scheme assignment (i.e.,partial function with finite domain from λ-variables to schemes), σ is a scheme, G is a scheme system, and F is a set of variables constraints.

Notation. Let B be a scheme assignment, G be a scheme system, and S be a substitution. SB denotes the scheme assignment $\Sigma_{x\in domain(B)}[x\Rightarrow SB(x)]$. SG denotes the scheme system $\{(S(\sigma),S(\tau)) \mid (\sigma,\tau)\in G\}$. □

Definition 5. Let M be a λ-term, B be a scheme assignment, σ be a scheme, G be a scheme system and F be a set of variable constraints. $\Pi(M)=\langle B,\sigma,G,F\rangle$ if and only if the statement is derivable by the following set of rules .

$$\overline{\Pi(x)=\langle[x\Rightarrow\forall t.\alpha],\forall t'.\beta,\{(\forall t.\alpha,\beta)\},[t'\Rightarrow\{\forall t.\alpha\}]\rangle}$$

$$\frac{\Pi(M)=\langle B,\sigma,G,F\rangle,\ B(x)\text{ is undefined},\ \Im=\{B(y)\mid y\in FV(\lambda x.M)\},\text{and } t,\ t',\ \alpha \text{ are fresh}}{\Pi(\lambda x.M)=\langle B,\forall t'.(\forall t.\alpha)\to\sigma,G,F+[t'\Rightarrow\Im]\rangle}$$

$$\frac{\Pi(M)=\langle B,\sigma,G,F\rangle,\ B(x)=\tau,\ \Im=\{B(y)\mid y\in FV(\lambda x.M)\},\text{ and } t \text{ is fresh}}{\Pi(\lambda x.M)=\langle B-\{x\},\forall t.\tau\to\sigma,G,F+[t\Rightarrow\Im]\rangle}$$

$$\frac{\Pi(P)=\langle B,\sigma,G,F\rangle\quad \Pi(Q)=\langle B',\sigma',G',F'\rangle\quad S=UNIFY(B,B',\sigma,\sigma'\to\forall t.\alpha)\quad \Im=\{SB(y)\mid y\in FV(P)\}\cup\{SB'(y)\mid y\in FV(Q)\},\text{ and } t,\ t',\ \alpha,\ \beta \text{ are fresh}}{\Pi(PQ)=\langle SB+SB',\forall t'.\beta,SG\cup SG'\cup\{(S(\forall t.\alpha),\beta)\},SF+SF'+[t'\Rightarrow\Im]\rangle}$$

Given a term M, let $\Pi(M)=\langle B,\sigma,G,F\rangle$ be derivable in the previous system. We will call $\langle B,\sigma,G,F\rangle$ the *principal typing scheme* of M. □

The UNIFY previously used is defined using the formal system $\twoheadrightarrow_U$. $\twoheadrightarrow_U$ is a simple generalization to the syntax of schemes of the classical Robinson's unification. UNIFY is defined by: $UNIFY(B,B',\sigma,\sigma')=S_m\ldots S_1S'$ if and only if: $\sigma,\sigma'\twoheadrightarrow_U S'$, $S'\tau_1,S'\tau'_1\twoheadrightarrow_U S_1$, and for all i, $2\le i\le m$, $S_{i-1}(\tau_i),S_{i-1}(\tau'_i)\twoheadrightarrow_U S_i$, where $\{x_1,\ldots,x_m\}= dom(B)\cap dom(B')$, and $B(x_j)=\tau_j$, $B'(x_j)=\tau'_j$ $(1\le j\le m)$.

Definition 6. The formal system $\twoheadrightarrow_U$, defined as follows, proves judgements of the shape $\sigma,\tau\twoheadrightarrow_U S$ where σ and τ are schemes and S is a scheme substitution.

$$\frac{\alpha\text{ does not occur in }\sigma}{\alpha,\sigma\twoheadrightarrow_U[\alpha\Rightarrow\sigma]}\qquad\qquad \frac{\sigma',\sigma\twoheadrightarrow_U S}{\sigma,\sigma'\twoheadrightarrow_U S}$$

$$\frac{\sigma\in\Sigma^-,\ \alpha\text{ does not occur in }\sigma}{\forall t.\alpha,\sigma\twoheadrightarrow_U[\alpha\Rightarrow\sigma,t\Rightarrow\varepsilon]}\qquad\qquad \frac{\alpha\text{ does not occur in }\sigma}{\forall t.\alpha,\forall t'.\sigma\twoheadrightarrow_U[\alpha\Rightarrow\sigma,t\Rightarrow t']}$$

$$\frac{\sigma_1,\tau_1\twoheadrightarrow_U S_1\quad S_1\sigma_2,S_1\tau_2\twoheadrightarrow_U S_2}{\sigma_1\to\sigma_2,\tau_1\to\tau_2\twoheadrightarrow_U S_2S_1}\qquad\qquad \frac{\sigma_1,\tau_1\twoheadrightarrow_U S_1\quad S_1\sigma_2,S_1\tau_2\twoheadrightarrow_U S_2}{\forall t.\sigma_1\to\sigma_2,\forall t'.\tau_1\to\tau_2\twoheadrightarrow_U S_2S_1+[t\Rightarrow t']}$$

$$\frac{\sigma_1,\tau_1 \twoheadrightarrow_U S_1 \quad S_1\sigma_2, S_1\tau_2 \twoheadrightarrow_U S_2}{\forall t.\sigma_1\to\sigma_2, \tau_1\to\tau_2 \twoheadrightarrow_U S_2S_1+[t\Rightarrow\varepsilon]} \qquad \square$$

It is immediate to verify that if $\sigma,\tau \twoheadrightarrow_U S$ then S is the most general unifier for σ and τ.

The following theorem asserts that $\Pi(M)$ is the *minimum* set of constraints that must be satisfied by any typing for M.

Theorem 7. Let M be a λ-term and let $\Pi(M)=\langle B,\sigma,G,F\rangle$. $A\vdash M:\varphi$ if and only if for some ground substitution s, for all $x\in FV(M)$, $A(x)=sB(x)$, $s(\sigma)=\varphi$ and s satisfies G and F. $\square$

The proof of the previous theorem relays on the following properties of the schemes generated by Π and of the UNIFY used in it.

Let a scheme τ be *simple* if it does not contain repeated variables.

Property 8. If $\Pi(M)=\langle B,\sigma,G,F\rangle$ then:
(i) σ is simple, and for all x in FV(M), B(x) is simple,
(ii) for x and y distinct, FV(B(x)) and FV(B(y)) are disjoint, and they are disjoint from $FV(\sigma)$. $\square$

From the previous property it is easy to prove that: for all M in the derivation of $\Pi(M)$ every application of UNIFY is defined. Moreover it can be proved that: if $\Pi(M)=\langle B,\sigma,G,F\rangle$ then the scheme system G has a particular structure.

Definition 9. (i) A scheme system G is *simple* if and only if it is of the shape $\{(\forall t.\sigma,\tau_1), (\forall t.\sigma,\tau_2),\ldots,(\forall t.\sigma,\tau_n)\}$, where for all i, $1\leq i\leq n$, σ and τ_i are simple, $\tau_i\in\Sigma^-$, and $FV(\sigma)$ and $FV(\tau_i)$ are disjoint. t is the *index* of G.
(ii) A scheme system is *canonical* if and only if it is the union of simple scheme systems with different indexes. $\square$

Corollary 10. If $\Pi(M)=\langle B,\sigma,G,F\rangle$ then G is canonical. $\square$

4. The Type Inference and the Scheme Checking Problem.

The type inference problem is the problem of determining, for any term M, whether there is a typing for M in $\vdash$; i.e., if there is A and φ such that $A\vdash M:\varphi$. From the results of the previous section, it follows that this problem for the polymorphic type discipline can be equivalently stated as:

Type Inference Problem. Given a term M, let $\Pi(M)=\langle B,\sigma,G,F\rangle$. Determine if there exists a ground substitution satisfying G and F.

So the type inference problem is equivalent to the problem of solving type scheme systems which are generated by the algorithm Π, i.e., canonical type scheme systems.

The general problem of solving scheme systems is undecidable, as a consequence of the undecidability of the semi-unification problem, proved in [12]. Let us recall the semi-unification problem.

Semi-unification problem. Let *S* be a signature containing at least one binary function symbol and X be a set of variables. Let T be a set of terms over *S* and X. An instance Ω of the semi-unification problem is a finite set of pairs

$$\{(f_1, g_1),\ldots,(f_n, g_n)\}$$

where f_i, and g_i are in $\mathcal{T}$. A substitution is a function from X to the set $\mathcal{T}$. A substitution S is a *solution* for Ω if and only if there are substitutions $S_1,\ldots,S_n$ such that

$$S_1(S(f_1))=S(g_1),\ldots,S_n(S(f_n))=S(g_n)$$

The *semi-unification problem* is the problem of deciding for any instance Ω, whether Ω has a solution or not.

From the undecidability of semi-unification we derive the undecidability of the following problem.

Scheme checking problem. For any term M and scheme substitution S, if $\Pi(M)$ is $\langle B,\sigma,G,F\rangle$ determine if there is a ground substitution s such that $sSB\vdash M:sS(\sigma)$.

This problem corresponds to ask if a term has a type satisfying some minimal structural constraints. For example: let I be $\lambda x.x$. $\Pi(I)$ is $\langle\varnothing,\forall u.(\forall t.\alpha)\rightarrow\forall t'.\beta,G,F\rangle$, where G is $\{(\forall t.\alpha,\beta)\}$ and F is $[t'\Rightarrow\{\forall t.\alpha\}]$. Let S be $[\alpha\Rightarrow\alpha,t\Rightarrow t,,u\Rightarrow u,\beta\Rightarrow(\forall t.\alpha)\rightarrow\beta,t'\Rightarrow\varepsilon]$. Then to ask if there is s such that $\vdash I:sS(\forall u.(\forall t.\alpha)\rightarrow\forall t'.\beta)=s(\forall u.(\forall t.\alpha)\rightarrow(\forall t.\alpha)\rightarrow\beta)$ corresponds to ask if I has a type with at least two arrows, with the first component equal to the second one and the third component belonging to T^-. In this case the answer is positive. For example a type of this shape derivable for the identity is $(\forall a.a)\rightarrow(\forall a.a)\rightarrow b$ (this is the minimum with respect to the number of symbols, between all types satisfying the given constraints).

The following result was first announced in [9].

Proposition 11. The scheme checking problem is undecidable.
Proof (hint). Let *S* be $\{\rightarrow\}$ and X be the set of schemes variables, i.e., schemes without any occurrence of $\forall$ are our term language. Let Ω be

$$\{(\tau_1,\sigma_1),(\tau_2,\sigma_2),\ldots,(\tau_n,\sigma_n)\}$$

Consider the term $\lambda x.xII\ldots I$, where the number of occurrences of I is n. $\Pi(\lambda x.xII\ldots I)$ is $\langle\varnothing,\forall u.(\forall t.\alpha)\rightarrow\forall t'.\gamma,G,F\rangle$, where G is $\{(\forall t.\alpha,(\forall w_1.(\forall t_1.\alpha_1\rightarrow\forall t'_1.\beta_1))\rightarrow\forall v_1.\gamma_1)\}\cup$ $\{(\forall v_i.\gamma_i,(\forall w_{i+1}.(\forall t_{i+1}.\alpha_{i+1}\rightarrow\forall t'_{i+1}.\beta_{i+1}))\rightarrow\forall v_{i+1}.\gamma_{i+1})\mid 1\leq i\leq n-1\}\cup\{(\forall t_i.\alpha_i,\beta_i)\mid 1\leq i\leq n\}\cup\{(\forall v_n.\gamma_n,\gamma)\}$ and F is $[v_i\Rightarrow\{\forall t.\alpha\},t'_i\Rightarrow\{\forall t_i.\alpha_i\}\mid 1\leq i\leq n]$. Let S be the following substitution

$$[\alpha_1\Rightarrow\tau_1,\ldots,\alpha_n\Rightarrow\tau_n,\beta_1\Rightarrow\sigma_1,\ldots,\beta_n\Rightarrow\sigma_n,t'\Rightarrow\varepsilon,t\Rightarrow\varepsilon,u\Rightarrow\varepsilon].$$

Claim 1. Let G' be $\{(\forall t_i.\tau_i,\sigma_i)\mid 1\leq i\leq n\}$. SG is satisfiable if and only G' is satisfiable.
Claim 2. Ω has a solution if and only if G' is satisfiable.
The two claims imply the result. □

Notice that this result does not imply the undecidability of the type inference problem. In fact the undecidability of the semiunification problem does not imply the undecidability of the solution of canonical scheme systems.

5. A complete stratification of $\vdash$.

It is well known that in the polymorphic type discipline, there is no *principal typing* for terms in the classical sense. So a question naturally arises: "if a term M can be assigned a type in the type assignment system $\vdash$, are there some typings for M which can be considered *the most interesting typings*?" In trying to give an answer to such a question, let us consider two examples. First consider the term representing the identity function: $\lambda x.x$. All the typings for $\lambda x.x$ are of the following shape:

$$A\vdash\lambda x.x:\forall\underline{b}.(\forall\underline{a}.\varphi)\rightarrow[\underline{\psi}/\underline{a}]\varphi$$

for each sequence of types $\underline{\psi}$ and basis A. We claim that *the most interesting typing* for $\lambda x.x$ is the instance: $\vdash\lambda x.x:\forall b.b\rightarrow b$, since it gives more information about the applicative behaviour of the term. In fact, if $\lambda x.x$ has type $\forall b.b\rightarrow b$, it can be applied to any typed term, by substituting the type of the term itself to the variable b, while in the other cases it can be applied only to terms of a particular shape. Note that $b \to b$ is the principal type of $\lambda x.x$ in the Curry's type discipline. By extending the reasoning, we claim that, if a term has a type in the Curry's type discipline, then its (quantified) principal type is the most interesting type for it also in the polymorphic type discipline.

Now consider the term $\Delta \equiv \lambda x.xx$. $\Pi(\Delta)$ is $\langle \emptyset, \forall u.(\forall t.\alpha) \to \forall t'.\beta, G_\Delta, F_\Delta \rangle$ where G_Δ is $\{(\forall t.\alpha, (\forall u.\gamma) \to \forall v.\delta), (\forall t.\alpha, \gamma), (\forall v.\delta, \beta)\}$ and F_Δ is $[u \Rightarrow \{\forall t.\alpha\}, t' \Rightarrow \{\forall t.\alpha\}]$. This means that every typing for Δ is of the shape:

$$A \vdash \Delta : \forall \underline{b}.(\forall \underline{a}.\varphi) \to \forall \underline{c}.\psi$$

for all A, and the following properties hold: $\psi = [\underline{a}''/\chi]\psi'$ for some χ, $[\underline{a}/\chi']\varphi = \varphi' \to \forall \underline{a}''.\psi'$ for some χ', $[\underline{a}/\chi'']\varphi = \varphi'$ for some χ''. In order to define more precisely these constraints, let us introduce a definition.

Definition 12. i) A *path* is a sequence of elements of the set $\{0,1\}$. ε denotes the empty path. If c and c' are paths, cc' denotes their *concatenation*. If c'=cc" for some c" then c is a *subpath* of c' and c' is a *superpath* of c. Moreover c *is near to* c' if either c is a subpath or a superpath of c'.
ii) A path can be used to identify an occurrence of a subtype in a type (of a subscheme in a scheme), according to the following definition.

$$\varphi/\varepsilon = \varphi$$

$$\varphi/0c = \begin{cases} \varphi_1/c & \text{if } \varphi = \forall \underline{a}.\varphi_1 \to \varphi_2 \\ \text{undefined} & \text{otherwise} \end{cases}$$

$$\varphi/1c = \begin{cases} \varphi_2/c & \text{if } \varphi = \forall \underline{a}.\varphi_1 \to \varphi_2 \\ \text{undefined} & \text{otherwise} \end{cases}$$

iii) The path c is *maximal* in φ if $\varphi/c = \forall a.a$ or $\varphi/c = a$ where a is a type variable. If $\varphi/c = \forall a_1 \ldots a_m.\psi$ we will say also that ψ $(\forall a_1 \ldots a_m.\psi)$ occurs at path c in φ. □

It will be proved in the following that if $A \vdash \lambda x.xx : \forall \underline{b}.(\forall \underline{a}.\varphi) \to \forall \underline{c}.\psi$ then the type $\forall \underline{a}.\varphi$ has an occurence of a type variable $a \in \underline{a}$ at the path 00000...For example,

1. $\vdash \lambda x.xx : \forall b.(\forall a.a) \to b$ (see example in section 2)
2. $\vdash \lambda x.xx : \forall \underline{b}.(\forall a.a) \to \varphi$ (*)
3. $\vdash \lambda x.xx : \forall b.(\forall a.a \to b) \to b$ (see example in section 2)
4. $\vdash \lambda x.xx : \forall \underline{b}.(\forall a.a \to \varphi) \to \varphi$ (*)
5. $\vdash \lambda x.xx : \forall \underline{b}.(\forall a.a \to a) \to \varphi \to \psi$ (*)
6. $\vdash \lambda x.xx : \forall bcd.(\forall a.a \to d \to b \to c) \to d \to b \to c$

(*) for all φ and ψ containing the variables in $\underline{b}$.
Certainly, typing 1 seems more general than typing 2, since $\forall b.(\forall a.a) \to b \leq \forall \underline{b}.(\forall a.a) \to \varphi$. Moreover both typings 3 and 4 seem more general than typing 5, since if $\lambda x.xx$ has typing 3 or 4 then it can be applied to any term having an arrow type whereas if it has typing 5 then it can be applied only to terms with the behaviour of the identity. Moreover since $\forall b.(\forall a.a \to b) \to b \leq \forall b.(\forall a.a \to \varphi) \to \varphi$, typing 3 seems more general than typing 4. Finally note that it seems meaningless to compare the typings in the sets: $\{1,2\}$, $\{4,5\}$, and $\{6\}$, since any of these sets contains types which can be used for application to terms of different functionality. Therefore we introduce a countable set of type derivation systems, $\vdash_n$. Each system $\vdash_n$ is decidable. We claim that , if a term M has a typing in $\vdash_n$, then the most interesting types for it are of the shape $\forall \underline{a}.\varphi$, where the number of occurrences of bound variables in φ is as minimum as possible.

Definition 13. (i) Let $\varphi/c=a$. This occurence of a in φ is at level n if and only if the length of the path c is n+1, where the length of ε is 0. (Note that a occurs at level 0 in φ if and only if a does not occur in φ.)
(ii) $\forall a_1...a_m.\varphi\leq_n\psi$ if and only if $\forall a_1...a_m.\varphi\leq\psi$ and every occurrence of a_i is at level less than or equal to n in φ $(1\leq i\leq m)$.
(iii) Let $n\leq m$; $\forall a_1...a_p.\varphi$ is a *n-m-proper type* if and only if for all i, $1\leq i\leq p$, a_i occurs in φ at level j $(n\leq j\leq m)$, i.e., a_i occurs at a level included between n and m in φ.
(iv) Let $\vdash_n$ be the type assignment system obtained from $\vdash$ by replacing every occurrence of $\leq$ by $\leq_n$. Let D: $B\vdash_n M:\varphi$, and let $C(D)=\langle\forall\underline{a}_1.\varphi_1\leq_n\psi_1,...,\forall\underline{a}_q.\varphi_q\leq_n\psi_q\rangle$. D is *n-m-proper* if and only if $a\in\underline{a}_i$ occurs at level j in φ_i $(n\leq j\leq m)$ $(1\leq i\leq q)$. □

Note that $\varphi\leq_0\varphi$, and $\varphi\leq_n\psi$ implies $\varphi\leq_m\psi$ for every $m\geq n$.

The set of systems $\vdash_n$ is a complete stratification of $\vdash$. In fact the following theorem holds.

Theorem 14. $A\vdash M:\varphi$ if and only if for some n $A\vdash_n M:\varphi$. □

We now introduce a partial order relation between types, <<, that compares types with respect to the number of (significant) quantified variables that they contain and moreover with respect to the standard notion of instance by substitution. Derivations in $\vdash_n$ can then be ordered by this relation.

Definition 15. (i) $\forall\underline{a}.\varphi<<\forall\underline{b}.\psi$ if and only if for all paths c
if $\forall\underline{a}.\varphi/c=a\in\underline{a}$ then there is a subpath c' of c such that $\forall\underline{b}.\psi/c'=b\in\underline{b}$, and
if $\forall\underline{a}.\varphi/c=d$ where d is free in $\forall\underline{a}.\varphi$ then: either there is a φ' such that $\forall\underline{b}.\psi/c=\varphi'$, or there is a c' subpath of c such that $\forall\underline{b}.\psi/c'=d'$ and d' is bound in $\forall\underline{b}.\psi$.
(ii) The partial order relation << between types can be extended to a partial order relation between derivations in the following way. Let D: $A\vdash_n M:\varphi$ and D': $A\vdash_n M:\psi$, and let $C(D)=\langle\forall\underline{a}_1.\varphi_1\leq_n\varphi'_1,...,\forall\underline{a}_m.\varphi_m\leq_n\varphi'_m\rangle$ and $C(D')=\langle\forall\underline{b}_1.\psi_1\leq_n\psi'_1,...,\forall\underline{b}_m.\psi_m\leq_n\psi'_m\rangle$. D<<D' if and only if for all i, $\forall\underline{a}_i.\varphi_i<<\forall\underline{b}_i.\psi_i$ and $\varphi'_i<<\psi'_i$ and $\varphi<<\psi$ $(1\leq i\leq m)$.
(iii) Let s and s' be substitutions satisfying a scheme system G. $s<<_G s'$ if for all $(\sigma,\tau)\in G$, $s(\sigma)<<s'(\sigma)$ and $s(\tau)<<s'(\tau)$. □

Note that a type variable a is such that $a<<\varphi$ for all φ, $\forall b.\varphi<<\forall a.a$ for all φ, and $a\rightarrow b\rightarrow c<<a\rightarrow\forall b.b$.

The relation << seems a good candidate for formalizing the notion of *the most interesting typings for a term.* In the following sections we will show an algorithm which, given in input $\Pi(M)$ and an integer n, builds the set of minimal (with respect to <<) derivations of a type for M in the $\vdash_n$ type assignment system.

Note that, given a term M, if there exists a derivation D such that D: $B\vdash M:\varphi$ and D is a Curry's derivation (i.e., every type in D is a Curry's type), then for all n, D: $B\vdash_n M:\varphi$. The principal of such derivations is the minimum between all the derivations D': $B\vdash_n M:\varphi'$. Therefore, if M has a type in Curry's type assignment system, the algorithm builds its principal typing.

6. The Pre-Unification System

For solving canonical systems we need to define a unification algorithm. In fact, let consider the following canonical system $G=\{(\forall t.\alpha,\beta\rightarrow\gamma),(\forall t.\alpha,\delta)\}$ which, for simplicity, is composed by only one simple system. Clearly G is satisfied by the substitution

$$s=[\alpha\Rightarrow b\rightarrow c,\beta\Rightarrow b,\gamma\Rightarrow c,\delta\Rightarrow b\rightarrow c,t\Rightarrow\varepsilon]$$

which is a substitution unifying the set of schemes $\{\alpha,\beta\rightarrow\gamma,\delta\}$. (So in this case a solution can be found by classical unification.) But now consider a slight modification of G, say

$G'=\{(\forall t.\alpha,\beta\to\gamma),(\forall t.\alpha,\beta)\}$. In this case there is no substitution unifying $\{\alpha,\beta\to\gamma,\beta\}$. However G' has infinite solutions. For example, the substitution $s=[\alpha\Rightarrow a,\beta\Rightarrow b,\gamma\Rightarrow c,t\Rightarrow a]$ satisfies G'. In fact sG' is the set of inequalities of types: $\{(\forall a.a\leq b\to c, \forall a.a\leq b)\}$.

Since we want to find the minimal solutions of G (with respect to <<) we define a pre-unification system that never gives a failure as output. A situation that classically is interpreted as a failure here gives a positive information, namely the necessity of having a quantified variable in the place in which the failure occurred. In order to do this, information about the structure of terms and the name of the sequence variables needed to solve the failure must be supplied to the system.

To identify the occurrence of a bound variable in a type scheme we extend the syntax of schemes adding clauses that allow to relate type variables to the corresponding sequence variables. The syntax of type schemes is modified adding the clauses:

$$a_t \mid \forall r.a_t$$

where a_t, b_t, c_t, and d_t denote *seq-scheme* variables (where t is any sequence variable). The *kind of a seq-scheme* variable a_t is t. Ground substitutions are extended to map any seq-scheme variable a_t in a type variable a such that $a\in s(t)$. Scheme substitutions are extended to map seq-scheme variables in seq-scheme variables and are such that $S(t)=t'$ implies $S(a_t)=a_{t'}$ and viceversa. The intended meaning of seq-scheme variables is explained by the following examples: $\forall t.a_t\to b_t$ represents the set of types $\{\forall ab.a\to b, \forall a.a\to a\}$ and $\forall t.a_t\to\alpha$ represents the types $\{\forall \underline{a}.a_i\to\varphi \mid a_i\in\underline{a} \text{ and } \varphi\in T^-\}$.

The pre-unification system $\twoheadrightarrow_{UU}$ manipulates *unification triples* $\langle\wp,E,D\rangle$: where $\wp$, called *unification set*, is a set of sets of schemes that have to be unified, E is a relation on the set of sequence variables plus $\{\varepsilon\}$, which is a partial equivalence relation when restricted to the set of sequence variables, and D is a symmetric relation on sequence variables. The meaning of the triple $\langle\wp,E,D\rangle$ is the following: the schemes in $\wp$ have to be unified with the constraint that the sequence variables in E may be equal and the one in D different. Sets in $\wp$ are indexed by pairs: paths, sequence variables, i.e., they are of the shape:

$$P=\{\sigma_1,\ldots,\sigma_n\}^{\{(c_1,t_1),\ldots,(c_k,t_k)\}}$$

Moreover E and D in a unification triple have to satisfy the following constraint: if $(t,t')\in D$ then for all $u\in[t]_E$ and $u'\in[t']_E$ $(u,u')\in D$ ($[t]_E$ is the equivalence class of t in E).

Definition 16. The system $\twoheadrightarrow_{UU}$ proving statements of the shape $\langle\wp,E,D\rangle\twoheadrightarrow_{UU}\langle\wp',E',D'\rangle$ is the transistive closure of the following rules.

$$1)\ \frac{P=\{\forall t_1.\sigma_1,\ldots,\forall t_n.\sigma_n\}^C,\ P'=\{\sigma_1,\ldots,\sigma_n\}^C,\ P'\notin\wp\cup\{P\},\quad E'=E\cup\{(t_i,t_j)\mid 1\leq i,j\leq n\},\text{ and }\langle E',D\rangle\twoheadrightarrow_{EQ}D'}{\langle\wp\cup\{P\},E,D\rangle\twoheadrightarrow_{UU}\langle\wp\cup\{P'\},E',D'\rangle}$$

$$1')\ \frac{P_1=\{\forall t_1.\sigma_1,\ldots,\forall t_n.\sigma_n\},P_2=\{\tau_1,\ldots,\tau_m\mid\tau_i\in\Sigma^-,1\leq i\leq m\},\ P'=\{\sigma_1,\ldots,\sigma_n,\tau_1,\ldots,\tau_m\}^C,\quad P'\notin\wp\cup\{(P_1\cup P_2)^C\},\ E'=E\cup\{(t_i,\varepsilon)\mid 1\leq i\leq n\},\text{ and }\langle E',D\rangle\twoheadrightarrow_{EQ}D'}{\langle\wp\cup\{(P_1\cup P_2)^C\},E,D\rangle\twoheadrightarrow_{UU}\langle\wp\cup\{P'\},E',D'\rangle}$$

$$2)\ \frac{P'=\{\sigma_1,\ldots,\sigma_n\}^{\{(c0,t)\mid(c,t)\in C\}},\ P''=\{\tau_1,\ldots,\tau_n\}^{\{(c1,t)\mid(c,t)\in C\}}\quad P=\{\sigma_1\to\tau_1,\ldots,\sigma_n\to\tau_n\}^C\text{ and }(P'\notin\wp\cup\{P\}\text{ or }P''\notin\wp\cup\{P\})}{\langle\wp\cup\{P\},E,D\rangle\twoheadrightarrow_{UU}\langle\wp\cup\{P',P''\},E,D\rangle}$$

$$3)\ \frac{P=\{\alpha,\sigma_1,\ldots,\sigma_n\}^C,\ P'=\{\alpha,\tau_1,\ldots,\tau_m\}^{C'} \quad P''=\{\sigma_1,\ldots,\sigma_n,\tau_1,\ldots,\tau_m\}^{C\cup C'} \text{ and } P''\notin \wp\cup\{P,P'\}}{\langle \wp\cup\{P,P'\},E,D\rangle \twoheadrightarrow_{UU} \langle \wp\cup\{P,P',P''\},E,D\rangle}$$

$$3')\ \frac{P=\{a_t,\sigma_1,\ldots,\sigma_n\}^C,\ P'=\{a_t,\tau_1,\ldots,\tau_m\}^{C'} \quad P''=\{\sigma_1,\ldots,\sigma_n,\tau_1,\ldots,\tau_m\}^{C\cup C'} \text{ and } P''\notin \wp\cup\{P,P'\}}{\langle \wp\cup\{P,P'\},E,D\rangle \twoheadrightarrow_{UU} \langle \wp\cup\{P,P',P''\},E,D\rangle}$$

$$4)\ \frac{P=\{\alpha,\sigma_1,\ldots,\sigma_n\}^C,\ P'=\{\sigma_1,\ldots,\sigma_n\}^C\ n>1 \text{ and } P'\notin \wp\cup\{P\}}{\langle \wp\cup\{P\},E,D\rangle \twoheadrightarrow_{UU} \langle \wp\cup\{P,P'\},E,D\rangle}$$

$$4')\ \frac{P=\{a_t,\sigma_1,\ldots,\sigma_n\}^C,\ P'=\{\sigma_1,\ldots,\sigma_n\}^C\ n>1 \text{ and } P'\notin \wp\cup\{P\}}{\langle \wp\cup\{P\},E,D\rangle \twoheadrightarrow_{UU} \langle \wp\cup\{P,P'\},E,D\rangle}$$

where the rules for the system $\twoheadrightarrow_{EQ}$ mantaining the consistency of the relations E and D are:

$$\frac{\langle E,D\rangle \twoheadrightarrow_{EQ} D',\ (t,t')\notin D,\ (t,\varepsilon)\notin E, \text{ and } (t',\varepsilon)\notin E}{\langle E\cup\{(t,t')\},D\rangle \twoheadrightarrow_{EQ} D'\cup\{(t'',t'),\ (t',t'') \mid (t'',t)\in D\}}$$

$$\frac{\langle E,D\rangle \twoheadrightarrow_{EQ} D',\ (t,t')\notin D, \text{ and either } (t,\varepsilon)\notin E, \text{ or } (t',\varepsilon)\notin E}{\langle E\cup\{(t,t')\},D\rangle \twoheadrightarrow_{EQ} D}$$

$$\frac{}{\langle \varnothing,D\rangle \twoheadrightarrow_{EQ} D} \qquad \square$$

We can read $\twoheadrightarrow_{UU}$ as a conditional term rewriting system, acting on unification triples. The system is terminating and confluent. Let $UU(\langle \wp,E,D\rangle)$ denote the normal form of $\langle \wp,E,D\rangle$ with repect to $\twoheadrightarrow_{UU}$. Note that each element of $UU(\langle \wp,E,D\rangle)$ is a set of the shape either $\{\alpha, \sigma_1,\ldots,\sigma_n\}^C$ or $\{a_t, \sigma_1,\ldots,\sigma_n\}^C$ $(n\geq 1)$.

Notation. Let $\sigma[]$ denote a context for schemes, i.e., a scheme with one hole. Let $\sigma[\tau]$ be the context σ in which the hole is filled by τ. The hole can be only in positions where the scheme variables (or schemes) may occur. $\square$

Definition 17. (i) Let $\wp$ be a unification set. The sequence of sets $\langle P_1,\ldots,P_n\rangle$ is a *cyclic sequence* of $\wp$ if for all i, $1\leq i\leq n$:

a) $P_i=\{\beta_i,\sigma_i[\beta_{i+1}]\}^{C_i}$ and there is $Q_i^{C_i}\in \wp$ such that $Q_i\supseteq\{\beta_i,\sigma_i[\beta_{i+1}]\}$,

b) $\beta_1=\beta_{n+1}$ and for all j, $i\neq j$ implies $\beta_i\neq\beta_j$.

Moreover

c) there is j, $1\leq j\leq n$, such that $\sigma_j[]\neq[]$.

Cyclic sequences are considered modulo the equivalence $\cong$ defined by:

$$\langle P_1,\ldots,P_n\rangle\cong\langle P_j,P_{j+1},\ldots,P_n,P_1,\ldots,P_{j-1}\rangle$$

for all j, $1\leq j\leq n$.

(ii) Let $\langle\{\beta_1,\sigma_1[\beta_2]\}^{C_1},\ldots,\{\beta_n,\sigma_n[\beta_1]\}^{C_n}\rangle$ be a cyclic sequence; the *cyclic occurrence of* β_i is the infinite path

$$(c''_i\ldots c''_n c''_1\ldots c''_{i-1})^*$$

where c''_j is the path of the occurrence of the hole in σ_j and c^* denotes the infinite path cccccccc......($1 \le j \le n$).
(iii) Let $\langle\{\beta_1,\sigma_1[\beta_2]\}^{C_1},...,\{\beta_n,\sigma_n[\beta_1]\}^{C_n}\rangle$ be a cyclic sequence; its set of *cyclic paths* is the set:

$\{(cc',t) \mid \exists i, 1 \le i \le n$ such that $(c,t) \in C_i$, and c' is the cyclic occurrence of $\beta_i\}$. □

A cyclic path is always an infinite path identified by a prefix followed by a repeated part.

Definition 18. Let $\langle \wp,E,D\rangle$ be a unification triple. The sets $\{a_t,\sigma_1 \to \sigma_2,....\}^C \in \wp$ (or $\{a_t, \forall t.\sigma_1 \to \sigma_2,....\}^C$), and $\{a_t,b_{t'},...\}^C \in \wp$ such that $(t,t') \in D$, are called *critical sets*. □

Example. Let $\sigma_1[]=[] \to \alpha$ and $\sigma_2[]=\alpha \to []$. The unification set $\{\{\alpha, \alpha \to \alpha,\}^{\{(c,t),(c',t')\}}\}$ has two cyclic sequences:

(1) $\langle\{(\alpha,\sigma_1[\alpha]\}^{\{(c,t),(c',t')\}}\rangle$ and
(2) $\langle\{\alpha,\sigma_2[\alpha]\}^{\{(c,t),(c',t')\}}\rangle$.

The set of cyclic paths associated with (1) is $\{(c(0)^*,t), (c'(0)^*,t')\}$. For (2) the set of cyclic paths is $\{(c(1)^*,t), (c'(1)^*,t')\}$. □

Let s be a ground substitution, s *is a unifier of* $\langle \wp,E,D\rangle$ if s is such that for all $P^C \in \wp$: for all $\sigma,\tau \in P$, $s(\sigma)=s(\tau)$, and if $(t,t') \in D$ then s(t) and s(t') do not have variables in common (in case one of them gets mapped to the empty sequence this property is satisfied). Observe that: if $\langle \wp,E,D\rangle \twoheadrightarrow_{UU} \langle \wp',E',D'\rangle$, s is a unifier of $\langle \wp,E,D\rangle$ if and only if s is a unifier of $\langle \wp',E',D'\rangle$.

The system above can be easily extended to a unification algorithm that subsumes the classical Robinson's unification, as shown by the following lemma.

Lemma 19. Let $\langle \wp,E,D\rangle$ be a unification triple. $UU(\langle \wp,E,D\rangle)$ does not contain neither a cyclic sequence nor a critical set if and only if there exists a unifier of $\langle \wp,E,D\rangle$. Moreover there exists a most general unifier of $\langle \wp,E,D\rangle$.
Proof (hint). Extend the formal system $\twoheadrightarrow_U$ of definition 6 with the following rules:

$$\frac{}{a_t, \alpha \twoheadrightarrow_U [\alpha \Rightarrow a_t]} \qquad \frac{}{a_t, b_{t'} \twoheadrightarrow_U [a_t \Rightarrow b_{t'}]}$$

It is immediate to verify that this system finds the most general unifier of two schemes where seq-scheme variables may occur. Extend, in the classical way, the system $\twoheadrightarrow_U$ to a system $\twoheadrightarrow_{U^*}$ that unifies sets of schemes. Let $\wp$ be $\{P_1,...,P_r\}$. For all j, $1 \le j \le r$, let S_j be $\{S_{j-1}\sigma \mid \sigma \in P_j\} \twoheadrightarrow_{U^*} S_j$ where S_0 is the identity. Define the *associated scheme substitution* of $\langle \wp,E,D\rangle$ as

$$S=S_rS_{r-1}...S_1+[t \Rightarrow t \mid t \text{ is a seq-scheme variable occurring in } \wp]+$$
$$[t \Rightarrow t' \mid \text{there is } a_t, b_{t'}\ S(a_t)=S(b_{t'})]$$

The fact that there is neither a cyclic sequence nor a critical set insures that S always exists. Then the desired substitution is the composition of S with a ground substitution s which is a one-to-one mapping between schemes and type variables and which maps every sequence variable in ε. □

7. Normalization of Scheme Systems

Normalization is one of the essential steps of the algorithm. The idea is that if there is a substitution s such that $s(\sigma) \le s(\tau)$, then every path defined in $s(\sigma)$ is also defined in $s(\tau)$. Some components of the substitution s are just meant to adjust the shape of τ in such a way that this condition is satisfied. Normalization generates such components of the substitution which can be expressed with a scheme substitution.

Definition 20. (i) A system G is *normalized* if for all $(\sigma,\tau)\in G$, for every path c, c defined in σ implies c defined in τ. G is *normalizable* if there is a scheme substitution S such that SG is normalized.
(ii) $\alpha \ll_G \beta$, if and only if there is a pair $(\sigma,\tau)\in G$ such that $\alpha\in FV(\sigma)$ and $\beta\in FV(\tau)$. □

It is clear that if G is not normalizable then G cannot be satisfiable. We now give a sufficient condition for the normalizability of a system. Let a scheme substitution S be *monotone for a set of schemes* $\{\sigma_1,...,\sigma_n\}$ if and only if: for all α, $S(\alpha)$ is simple and does not contain variables in $FV(\{\sigma_1,...,\sigma_n\})$. Moreover for all α and β, $FV(S(\alpha))$ and $FV(S(\beta))$ are disjoint.

Theorem 21. Let G be a system such that all the schemes in G are simple and the relation $\ll_G$ is acyclic. Then there is (always) a scheme substitution S_G such that:
(i) $S_G G$ is normalized,
(ii) s satisfies G if and only if for some s', $s =_{FV(G)} s'S_G$ and s' satisfies $S_G G$,
(iii) S_G is monotone for the set of schemes in G. □

If G is a scheme system, let $(G)^N$ be $S_G G$. S_G is the *normalizing substitution* of G. When G is obtained by the algorithm Π the conditions of the theorem are satisfied. Therefore there is always a normalizing substitution for G. Normalization is extended to work with occurrences of seq-scheme variables in an obvious way. Observe that there are canonical systems with some occurrences of seq-scheme variables which cannot be normalized.

8. A Parameterized Solution of Canonical Scheme Systems

A normalized simple scheme system $\{(\forall t.\sigma,\tau_1),(\forall t.\sigma,\tau_2),...,(\forall t.\sigma,\tau_n)\}$ has always a trivial solution. Just consider a bijection, f, between scheme variables and type variables. Let $\underline{a}$ be a sequence of variables containing all the variables in $f(\alpha)$ for all α in σ (the order of the variables in the sequence is inessential). The substitution $s=f+\Sigma_{t'\in Q}[t'\Rightarrow\varepsilon]+[t\Rightarrow\underline{a}]$, where Q is the set of sequence variables occurring in σ, τ_1, ..., τ_n, satisfies G.

A canonical system may have no solution even though its simple components do. Consider, for example, $G=G_1\cup G_2$, where $G_1=\{(\forall t.\alpha\rightarrow\forall v.\beta,\gamma\rightarrow\delta),(\forall t.\alpha\rightarrow\forall v.\beta,\gamma)\}$, and $G_2=\{(\forall v.\alpha\rightarrow\varepsilon,\mu\rightarrow\nu),(\forall v.\alpha\rightarrow\varepsilon,\mu)\}$. As it will be clear in the following , every solution of G_1 must be such that, if c=0...0 (with n 0's) is maximal in $s_1(\alpha)$, then $s_1(\alpha)/c\in s_1(t)$. Similarly in every solution s_2 of G_2, if c=0...0 (with n 0's) is maximal in $s_2(\alpha)$, then $s_2(\alpha)/c\in s_2(v)$. But there is no substitution, s, satisfying both these conditions, since variables in s(t) and s(v) are bounded in different subtypes of the same type, and therefore cannot be identified.

Moreover, even in the case a normalized canonical system is satisfiable, a sum of the trivial solutions of its simple components it is not always a solution for the whole system. For example, let $G=G_1\cup G_2$, where $G_1=\{(\forall t.\alpha\rightarrow\forall v.\beta,\gamma\rightarrow\delta),(\forall t.\alpha\rightarrow\forall v.\beta,\gamma\rightarrow\delta')\}$, and $G_2=\{(\forall v.\alpha,\theta),(\forall v.\alpha,\theta')\}$ where γ, δ, θ, θ' are scheme variables. Let f be a one-to-one mapping between scheme variables and type variables. A trivial solution for G_1 is: $s_1=f+[v\Rightarrow\varepsilon]+[t\Rightarrow f(\alpha)f(\beta)]$. A trivial solution for G_2 is: $f+[v\Rightarrow f(\alpha)]$. For the same reason of the example before, s_1+s_2 is not a solution of G. Moreover, even though the sum of the trivial solutions of the components is a solution of the whole system, this is not the kind of solution we have in mind. We are indeed interested in exploring the properties that all the solutions have in common and choosing the minimal solutions with respect to the relation $\ll$ defined in definition 14.

In the following, we define an algorithm that, given a normalized canonical system G, a relation on sequence variables D', and two integers n, and m, finds the minimal set of substitutions satisfying G according to the order relation between substitutions defined in definition 15 (iii). Such substitutions are such that variables related in D' are not identified.

The algorithm, which will be described as a formal system, consists of iterating the pre-unification defined in the previous section. The unification triple input of the pre-unification, $\langle \wp,E,D\rangle$, collects the following information about the scheme system:

- $P\in\wp$ contains a set of schemes that must be identified in order to find a substitution replacing them with types without bound variables. Initially all the schemes of G occur in $\wp$, then at every iteration some sets of $\wp$ are erased, if not unifiable.
- E contains pairs of sequence variables which may be identified by a substitution satisfying G.
- D is a superset of D' that contains pairs of sequence variables which cannot be identified by a substitution satisfying G. For example sequence variables occurring in the scope of each other in the same scheme of G.

The formal definition of the initial unification triple follows. In the rest of the section we deal only with normalized canonical systems.

Definition 22. Let $G=\cup_{1\le i\le q} G_i$ where $G_i=\{(\forall t_i.\sigma_i,\tau_{i,1}), (\forall t_i.\sigma_i,\tau_{i,2}), ..., (\forall t_i.\sigma_i,\tau_{i,k(i)})\}$. Let $E=\{(t_i,t_i) \mid 1\le i\le q\}$ and $D=\{(t,t'), (t',t) \mid$ t and t' occur in the same scheme of G and t is in the scope of t'$\}$.
Let $\langle\{\{\sigma_i,\tau_{i,1},..., \tau_{i,k(i)}\}^{\{(\varepsilon,t_i)\}} \mid 1\le i\le q\}, E,D\rangle \twoheadrightarrow_{UU}\langle \wp,E_G,D_G\rangle$ using rules 1, 1', and 2 of $\twoheadrightarrow_{UU}$. Let $\wp_G$ be $\{P^C \mid P^C\in \wp$ and P^C does not contain an a_t where a_t is of kind t_i and a_t is a subscheme of a σ_i $(1\le i\le q)\}$. The *unification triple associated with* G is $\langle \wp_G,E_G,D_G\rangle$. □

In the following we will use UU(G) for $UU(\langle \wp_G,E_G,D_G\rangle)$.

Example. 1) Remember that $\Pi(\Delta)=\langle\varnothing,\forall u.(\forall t.\alpha)\to\forall t'.\beta,G_\Delta,[u\Rightarrow\{\forall t.\alpha\},t'\Rightarrow\{\forall t.\alpha\}]\rangle$ where G_Δ is $\{(\forall t.\alpha,(\forall u.\gamma)\to\forall v.\delta),(\forall t.\alpha,\gamma),(\forall v.\delta,\beta)\}$. $UU(G_\Delta)$ is the normal form of

$$\langle\{\{\alpha,(\forall u.\gamma)\to\forall v.\delta\}^{\{(\varepsilon,t)\}},\{\alpha,\gamma\}^{\{(\varepsilon,t)\}},\{\delta,\beta\}^{\{(\varepsilon,v)\}}\},$$
$$\{(t,t),(v,v)\},\{(u,t),(u,t'),(t,u),(t',u)\}\rangle,$$

i.e., $\langle \wp'_\Delta,E'_\Delta,D'_\Delta\rangle=$

$$\langle\{\{\alpha,(\forall u.\gamma)\to\forall v.\delta\}^{\{(\varepsilon,t)\}},\{\alpha,\gamma\}^{\{(\varepsilon,t)\}},\{\gamma,(\forall u.\gamma)\to\forall v.\delta\}^{\{(\varepsilon,t)\}},\{\delta,\beta\}^{\{(\varepsilon,v\}}\},$$
$$\{(t,t),(v,v)\},\{(u,t),(u,t'),(t,u),(t',u)\}\rangle.$$

Note that $\wp'_\Delta$ has one critical sequence: $\{\gamma,(\forall u.\gamma)\to\forall v.\delta\}^{\{(\varepsilon,t)\}}$ whose critical path is $(0)^*$.

2) Consider the scheme system $G=\{(\forall t.a_t\to\forall t'.\alpha,(\forall t'.\beta\to\forall u.\gamma)\to\forall v.\delta)$, $(\forall t.a_t\to\forall t'.\alpha,\forall t'.\beta\to\forall u.\gamma),(\forall u.\gamma,\rho)\}$, $\langle \wp_G,E_G,D_G\rangle$ is

$$\langle\{\{\alpha,\delta\}^{\{(1,t)\}},\{\alpha,\gamma\}^{\{(1,t)\}},\{\rho,\gamma\}^{\{(\varepsilon,u)\}}\},E,D\rangle$$

where $[t']_E=\{t',v,u\}$ and $[t]_E=\{t\}$ and D is the symmetric closure of $\{(t,t'),(v,t),(u,t)\}$. In fact since a_t must be replaced by a bound variable, the system will be satisfied by a substitution s independently from the value of $s(\beta)$. □

Remark. Let $\langle \wp,E,D\rangle$ be $UU(\langle \wp_G,E_G,D_G\rangle)$.
(i) If $\{\rho_1,...,\rho_n\}^C\in\wp$ then for all h, ρ_h is a subscheme of either one of the σ_i's or one of the $\tau_{i,j}$. Moreover for some $(c,t_i)\in C$, ρ_h occurs at the path c of either σ_i or one of the $\tau_{i,j}$ $(1\le i\le q,\ 1\le j\le k(i))$.
(ii) The equivalence E is such that $(t,t')\in E$ if and only if: either $t=t'$, or for some $\langle \wp',E',D'\rangle$ used in the derivation of $\twoheadrightarrow_{UU}$ there is a $P^C\in\wp'$ such that $\forall t.\rho,\forall t'.\rho'\in P$ for some ρ and ρ'. □

In the following lemma we prove that, given G, in case in UU(G) there are some cyclic sequences or critical sets any substitution satifying the system G must transform the left-hand-side of G in types containing some bound variables. Moreover these bound variables must occur: for a cyclic sequence along some cyclic paths of the sequence and for critical sets along some subpaths of the sets of paths indexing the critical set.

Lemma 23. Let G be $\cup_{1\leq i\leq q} G_i$ where $G_i=\{(\forall t_i.\sigma_i,\tau_{i,1}), (\forall t_i.\sigma_i,\tau_{i,2}), ..., (\forall t_i.\sigma_i,\tau_{i,k(i)})\}$, let $\langle \wp,E,D\rangle$ be UU(G), and let s be a substitution satisfying G.
(a) Let $Q=\langle\{\beta_1,\rho_1[\beta_2]\}^{C_1},...,\{\beta_n,\rho_n[\beta_1]\}^{C_n}\rangle$ be a cyclic sequence of $\wp$. Then there is a cyclic path of Q, say (c',t_i), such that, if c is the subpath of c' maximal in $s(\sigma_i)$, then $s(\sigma_i)/c\in s(t_i)$ $(1\leq i\leq q)$.
(b) Let $P^C\in\wp$ be a critical set. Then there is $(c,t_i)\in C$ such that if c' is the subpath of c maximal in $s(\sigma_i)$, then $s(\sigma_i)/c'\in s(t_i)$ $(1\leq i\leq q)$.
Proof. Let s be such that s satisfies G and let $\langle \wp'',E'',D''\rangle$ be UU(G).
Claim. Let $\{\rho'_1, ..., \rho'_m\}^C\in\wp''$. For all c maximal in $s(\sigma_i)$ such that c is near to c' and $(c',t_i)\in C$: if $s(\sigma_i)/c\notin s(t_i)$, and there is ρ'_j, $1\leq j\leq m$, such that either $\rho'_j=\sigma_i/c'$ or $\rho'_j=\tau_{i,h}/c'$ for some h, $1\leq h\leq k(i)$, then c=c'c" (for some c") and
 (i) either $s(\sigma_i)/c=s(\rho'_1)/c''=...=s(\rho'_m)/c''$ or
 (ii) there is $(c_1,t_j)\in C$ and c_2 maximal in $s(\sigma_j)$ and subpath of c_1c'' such that $s(\sigma_j)/c_2\in s(t_j)$.
Proof of the claim. We will prove a stronger result, i.e., the claim holds at every step of the derivation of UU(G). The result is proved by induction on the number of steps of the derivation of UU(G). For the initial sets $\{\{\sigma_i,\tau_{i,1},..., \tau_{i,k(i)}\}^{\{(\varepsilon,t_i)\}} \mid 1\leq i\leq q\}$ the claim derives by the fact that s satisfies G and hence $s(\forall t_i.\sigma_i)\leq s(\tau_{i,j})$ for all i,j. It is immediate then to prove that the claim holds for all the elements of $\langle\wp_G,E_G,D_G\rangle$. Now, assuming the claim for all the elements of $\langle\wp,E,D\rangle$, we have to prove it for all the elements of $\langle\wp',E',D'\rangle$ such that $\langle\wp,E,D\rangle\twoheadrightarrow_{UU}\langle\wp',E',D'\rangle$. The only rule for which the proof is interesting is rule 3 (and rule 3' that is similar). Assume the claim for $P=\{\alpha,\rho'_1,...,\rho'_n\}^C\in\wp$ and $P'=\{\alpha,\upsilon_1,...,\upsilon_m\}^{C'}\in\wp$. We will prove it for $P''=\{\rho'_1,...,\rho'_n,\upsilon_1,...,\upsilon_m\}^{C\cup C'}$. Let $s(\sigma_i)/c\notin s(t_i)$, and for some c' in $C\cup C'$ let c be near to c'. Assume without loss of generality that c' is in C and either ρ'_j (for some j) or α are defined at c' in either σ_i or one of the $\tau_{i,h}$. If $s(\sigma_i)/c\notin s(t_i)$ then c=c'c" (for some c"). By inductive hypothesis either (i) or (ii) holds for P. If (ii) holds for P then (ii) holds also for P". If (i) holds for P with c then $s(\sigma_i)/c=s(\alpha)/c''=s(\rho'_1)/c''=...=s(\rho'_n)/c''$. Hence $s(\alpha)/c''$ is maximal. Therefore there is $(c_1,t_j)\in C'$ and c_2 maximal in $s(\sigma_j)$ such that c_2 is a subpath of c_1c'' and α is defined at c_1. By inductive hypothesis for P' with respect to c_2, if (ii) holds for c_2 in P', i.e., $s(\sigma_j)/c_2\in s(t_j)$, then (ii) holds also for P" and c_2. Now let $s(\sigma_j)/c_2\notin s(t_j)$ and therefore $c_2=c_1c_3$ where c_3 is a subpath of c". If (ii) holds for P' with c_2 then (ii) holds for P" with c. Instead if (i) holds for P' $s(\sigma_j)/c_2=s(\alpha)/c_3=s(\upsilon_1)/c_3=...=s(\upsilon_n)/c_3$ where c_3 is a subpath of c". But since $s(\alpha)/c''$ is maximal $c_3=c''$ and $s(\alpha)/c''= s(\rho'_1)/c''=...=s(\rho'_n)/c''$. Hence (i) holds for P" with c. End Proof of the Claim.
(a) Let s be such that for every path that is a prefix of a cyclic sequence and is maximal in $s(\sigma_j)$, $s(\sigma_j)$ at this path is a variable not in $s(t_j)$ $(1\leq j\leq q)$. Let us consider any $\{\beta_i,\rho_i[\beta_{i+1}]\}^{C_i}$. Let c be the maximal subpath of the cyclic occurrence of β_i that is defined in $s(\beta_i)$ and let c' be such that there is k, $(c',t_k)\in C_i$ and c' is a path at which β_i occurs (in either σ_k or $\tau_{k,r}$ for some r); c'c is a subpath of a cyclic path. Then there is a c" maximal in $s(\sigma_k)$ such that c" is a subpath of c'c. Let $c''=c'c_i$. Clearly c" is a subpath of the cyclic path $(c'c^*,t_k)$ where c^* is the cyclic occurrence of β_i. Hence by hypothesis it cannot be that $s(\sigma_k)/c''\in s(t_k)$. By the claim: either
 (a) $s(\sigma_k)/c''=s(\beta_i)/c_i=s(\rho_i[\beta_{i+1}])/c_i$ or
 (b) there is a $(c^+,t_r)\in C_i$ and a c^{++} maximal in $s(\sigma_r)$ and subpath of c^+c_i such that $s(\sigma_r)/c^{++}\in s(t_r)$ $(1\leq r\leq q)$.
But (b) cannot hold since such a c^{++} would be a subpath of the cyclic path (c^+c^*,t_r). Therefore $s(\sigma_k)/c''= s(\beta_i)/c_i=s(\rho_i[\beta_{i+1}])/c_i$. This means that $c_i=c''_ic'_i$, where c''_i is the path of the occurrence of the hole in ρ_i and c'_i is a subpath of the cyclic occurrence of β_{i+1}. Moreover c_i is a maximal path in $s(\beta_i)$ (since c" is maximal in $s(\sigma_k)$) and a subpath of the cyclic occurrence of β_i and c'_i is a maximal path in $s(\beta_{i+1})$ subpath of the cyclic occurrence of β_{i+1}. Repeating the same reasoning for $\{\beta_{i+1},\rho_{i+1}[\beta_{i+2}]\}^{C_{i+1}}$ defining c_{i+1} such that $c_i=c''_ic_{i+1}$ and c''_i is the occurrence of the hole in ρ_{i+1}, we obtain that both c_{i+1} and c'_i are

maximal paths in $s(\beta_{i+1})$; therefore $c_{i+1}=c'_i$. Since this holds for all i, $1\leq i\leq n$, and by definition $c'_n=c_1$, $c_1=c''_1c''_2...c''_nc_1$ where by definition of cyclic path at least one of the c''_i is not empty. This is a contraddiction, so it must be that there is a path c such that c is a prefix of c' where there is k such that (c',t_k) is a cyclic paths in the cyclic sequence and $s(\sigma_k)/c\in s(t_k)$.
(b) Let us consider a critical set $\{a_t,\rho_1\to\rho_2,....\}^C$. Assume that for all c' such that $s(\sigma_i)/c'$ is maximal and c' is a subpath of c such that $(c,t_i)\in C$, $s(\sigma_i)/c'\notin s(t_i)$. Let c' and k be such that $(c',t_k)\in C$ is a path at which a_t occurs (in either σ_k or $\tau_{k,q}$). Since $s(a_t)$ must be a type variable, $s(\sigma_k)$ must be defined at a subpath of c', say c. If $s(\sigma_k)/c\notin s(t_k)$ by the claim c=c'c" and by hypothesis (ii) cannot holds. Hence $s(a_t)/c''=s(\rho_1\to\rho_2)/c''$. But this is absurd. A similar proof holds for the other case of the definition of critical set. □

Before defining the algorithm we need another technical definition. Since sometimes we need to insert bound variables in suitable positions we may have to lengthen some paths of a scheme in the most general way.

Definition 24. Let c be a path, and t be a sequence variable, *scheme*(c,t) is the type scheme defined as follows.

$$scheme(c,t)=\begin{cases} a_t & \text{if } c=\varepsilon \\ \forall t'.\forall u.\beta\to scheme(c',t) & \text{if } c=1c' \\ \forall t'.scheme(c',t)\to\forall u.\beta & \text{if } c=0c' \end{cases}$$

where all the variables (a_t, t', u, and β) are fresh. □

Informally *scheme*(c,t) is the most general type scheme in which the path c is maximal and identifies a seq-scheme variable, and any other variable occurs once in it, and it is fresh.

Definition 25. (i) Let G be $\cup_{1\leq i\leq q}$ G_i where $G_i=\{(\forall t_i.\sigma_i,\tau_{i,1}), (\forall t_i.\sigma_i,\tau_{i,2}), ..., (\forall t_i.\sigma_i,\tau_{i,k(i)})\}$. A solution s of G is n-m-proper if $s(\forall t_i.\sigma_i)$ is a n-m-proper type for all i, $1\leq i\leq q$. A solution s of G is of *degree n* if $s(\sigma)\leq_n s(\tau)$ for all $(\sigma,\tau)\in G$.
(ii) Let a substitution s *satisfy a symmetric relation* D on sequence variables if and only if for all $(t,u)\in D$, either s(t) or s(u) are ε or s(t) is different from s(u). □

With the previous results we can define the desired algorithm, through the formal system $\twoheadrightarrow_{T,n,m}$. Judgements of the system are of the form $G,D\twoheadrightarrow_{T,n,m}\{s_1,...,s_r\}$ where G is a canonical system and D is a symmetric relation on sequence variables. A judgement $G,D\twoheadrightarrow_{T,n,m}\{s_1,...,s_r\}$ means that $\{s_1,..., s_r\}$ is the set of minimal (with respect to <<) n-m-proper solutions of G satisfying D. If the set is empty G does not have any n-m-proper solution satisfying the previous condition. The system has five rules. The first one corresponds to the case in which the unification triple associated with the system has a unifier. Hence the algorithm returns the most general unifier. The second rule deals with cyclic sequences. For each cyclic path the algorithm tries to find the maximum path of length less than m and bigger than n at which we can place a bound variable to get a substitution satisfying the system. The third rule is similar and deals with critical sets. The fourth and fifth rules deal with cases in which there is not a substitution satisfying G and D.

Definition 26. Let G be $\cup_{1\leq i\leq q}$ G_i where $G_i=\{(\forall t_i.\sigma_i,\tau_{i,1}), (\forall t_i.\sigma_i,\tau_{i,2}), ..., (\forall t_i.\sigma_i,\tau_{i,k(i)})\}$. Let D be a symmetric relation on sequence variables. Let $\langle\wp,E,D\rangle$ be $UU(\langle\wp_G,E_G,D_G\cup D'\rangle)$. The formal system $\twoheadrightarrow_{T,n,m}$ is defined by the following five rules.

$\langle \wp, E, D\rangle$ has neither cyclic sequences nor critical sets,
S is the associated scheme substitution for $\langle \wp, E, D\rangle$,
f is an injective mapping from scheme variables to type variables,
$s=f+[t_i \Rightarrow a_{i,1}...a_{i,r(i)} \mid \{a_{i,1},...,a_{i,r(i)}\}$ is the set of seq-scheme variables of kind t_i in $S(G)$, $1 \leq i \leq q]+[t_i \Rightarrow \varepsilon \mid$ there are no seq-scheme variables of kind t_i in $S(G)$, $1 \leq i \leq q]$,
sS satisfies G.

$$G, D' \twoheadrightarrow_{T,n,m} \{sS\}$$

$C=\{(c_1,t'_1),...,(c_r,t'_r)\}$ $(t'_i \in \{t_1,...,t_q\})$ is the set of cyclic paths of $\wp$ such that: $(c,t_i) \in C$ implies that σ_i is not defined at a subpath of c of length bigger than m $(1 \leq i \leq q)$.
For all k, $1 \leq k \leq r$,
let j be the maximum integer, $n \leq j \leq m$ such that:
if $c_k = c_k' c^*$ where c'_k is of length j,
S_k is the scheme substitution:

$$S_k(\beta)=\begin{cases} \mathit{scheme}(c'', t_{k'}) & \text{if } t_{k'}=t_k,\ \forall t.\beta=\sigma_{k'}/c', \text{ and } c_k'=c'c'' \\ \beta & \text{otherwise} \end{cases}$$

the normalizing substitution of S_kG exists and is S_k',
$S_k' S_k G, D' \twoheadrightarrow_{T,j,m} \{s_{k,1},...,s_{k,p(k)}\}$ with $p(k)>0$.

$$G, D' \twoheadrightarrow_{T,n,m} \cup_{1 \leq i \leq r} \{s_{i,1} S_i' S_i, ..., s_{i,p(i)} S_i' S_i\}$$

$\wp$ is the set of critical sets of UU(G).
For all $P^C \in \wp$, for all $(c,t_k) \in C$, if r=length(c) is between n and m and σ_k is not defined at a superpath of c,
let j be the maximum integer $n \leq j \leq r$ such that:
$c=c'c''$ where c' is of length j,
S is the scheme substitution:

$$S(\beta)=\begin{cases} \mathit{scheme}(c'', t_k) & \text{if } \forall t.\beta=\sigma_k/c', \\ \beta & \text{otherwise} \end{cases}$$

the normalizing substitution of SG exists and is S',
let $\mathit{Solution}(P^C, (c,t_k))$ be such that $S'SG, D' \twoheadrightarrow_{T,j,m} \mathit{Solution}(P^C, (c,t_k))$

$$G, D' \twoheadrightarrow_{T,n,m} \cup_{P^C \in \wp', (c,t_k) \in C} \mathit{Solution}(P^C, (c,t_k))$$

C is the set of critical paths.
For all $(c,t_i) \in C$ $(1 \leq i \leq q)$, σ_i is defined at a subpath of c of length bigger than m

---

$$G, D' \twoheadrightarrow \varnothing$$

$\wp$ is the set of critical sets of UU(G).
For all $P^C \in \wp$, for all $(c,t_i) \in C$ $(1 \leq i \leq q)$, σ_i is defined at a path near to c of length bigger than m or less than n.

$$G, D' \twoheadrightarrow_{T,n,m} \varnothing$$

□

The system finds solutions in which bound variables are at level between n and m.

Remark. The system $\twoheadrightarrow_{T,n,m}$ can be thought as doing an exaustive search only on paths that need to have bound variables. As presented the system yields a quite inefficient algorithm. However various kinds of optimizations can be made. For instance the unification sets associated to the system do not need to be recomputed every time. This would lead to a system with judgements of the shape $G,D,\langle \wp,E,D\rangle \twoheadrightarrow_{T,n,m}\{s_1,...,s_r\}$.

The following theorem asserts that the system $\twoheadrightarrow_{T,n,m}$ finds the set of minimal n-m-proper solutions of the canonical system G. I.e., if $G,D \twoheadrightarrow_{T,n,m}\{s_1,...,s_p\}$, s_i is a solution for G satisfying D ($1\leq i\leq p$), , and if s is an n-m-proper solution of G satisfying D then there is j, $s_j <<_G s$ ($1\leq j\leq p$).

Theorem 27. Let G be a canonical system.
i) If $G,D \twoheadrightarrow_{T,n,m}\{s_1,...,s_p\}$, then $\{s_1,...,s_p\}$ is the set of the minimal n-m-proper solutions of G satisfying D.
ii) If $G,D \twoheadrightarrow_{T,0,m}\{s_1,...,s_p\}$, then $\{s_1,...,s_p\}$ is the set of minimal solutions of G satisfying D of degree m.
Sketch of the proof. (i) The proof is by induction on the derivation of $G,D\twoheadrightarrow_{T,n,m}\{s_1,...,s_q\}$, and is based on Lemma 23.
(ii) From (i) observing that a 0-m-solution is a solution of degree m. □

From this theorem we can derive the main result of the paper. Namely that the system $\twoheadrightarrow_{T,0,n}$ finds the set of minimal derivations in the system $\vdash_n$.

Main Theorem. Let $\Pi(M)=\langle B,\sigma,G,F\rangle$. Let $D=\{(t,t') \mid t$ is in the scope of t' in σ or viceversa$\}$, and $G,D\twoheadrightarrow_{T,0,n}\{s_1,...,s_p\}$ ($p\geq 0$). Let $\{s'_1,...,s'_h\}$ be the subset of $\{s_1,...,s_p\}$ ($p\geq 0$) such that s'_i satisfies F for all i, $1\leq i\leq h$.
(i) $s'_iB\vdash_n M:s'_i\sigma$. (This is the soundness of the algorithm.)
(ii) If $A \vdash_n M:\varphi$, let s be such that $sB(x)=A(x)$ for all $x\in FV(M)$, $s(\sigma)=\varphi$, and s satisfies G and F. There is j, ($1\leq j\leq p$), such that $s'_j<<_G s$. (This is the completeness of $\twoheadrightarrow_{T,0,n}$.) □

Note that, if G and D are as in the theorem, either $G,D\twoheadrightarrow_{T,0,n}\emptyset$ or $G,D\twoheadrightarrow_{T,0,n}\{s_1,...,s_p\}$ ($p>0$), and if for no s in $\{s_1,...,s_p\}$ s satisfies F, then M has no typing in $\vdash_n$.

Example. Consider the term Δ. Let $\Pi(\Delta)=\langle\emptyset,\sigma_\Delta,G_\Delta,F_\Delta\rangle$ as defined in the previous example, D_Δ is $\{(u,t),(u,t'),(t,u),(t',u)\}$.
1) Let us first analize the system $\twoheadrightarrow_{T,0,0}$. It is immediate to verify that, since $UU(G_\Delta)$ has a cyclic path, namely $(0)^*$ (see the previous example), $G_\Delta\twoheadrightarrow_{T,0,0}\emptyset$. This means that Δ has no type in Curry's type discipline.
2) Now consider the system $\twoheadrightarrow_{T,0,1}$. $G_\Delta\twoheadrightarrow_{T,0,1}\{s\}$ where s is

$$[t\Rightarrow a,a_t\Rightarrow a,\delta\Rightarrow b,\beta\Rightarrow b,\gamma\Rightarrow c,u\Rightarrow\varepsilon,v\Rightarrow\varepsilon],$$

since ε is the only subpath of the cyclic path $(0)^*$ of length 1, $S=[\alpha\Rightarrow a_t]$, SG_Δ is normalized, and $SG_\Delta\twoheadrightarrow_{T,0,1}\{s\}$. This is because $UU(SG_\Delta)=\langle\{\delta,\beta\}^{\{(\varepsilon,v)\}},\{(t,t),(v,v)\},D_\Delta\rangle$ and $\{\{\delta,\beta\}^{\{(\varepsilon,v)\}}\}$ has no cyclic paths. So the first rule is applied, and its associated scheme substitution is $[\delta\Rightarrow\beta]$. This means that: $\vdash_1\Delta$: $\forall b.(\forall a.a)\to b$.
3) Similarly, it can be verified that $G_\Delta\twoheadrightarrow_{T,0,2}\{s\}$, where s is such that

$$s(\sigma_\Delta)=\forall b.(\forall a.a\to b)\to b$$

i.e., $\vdash_2\Delta$: $\forall b.(\forall a.a\to b)\to b$, and this is the minimum typing for Δ in $\vdash_2$. □

Acknowledgements: We would like to thank Mariangiola Dezani-Ciancaglini for several comments and suggestions on earlier versions of this paper.

References

[1] Barendregt, H.P., *The Lambda Calculus: its Syntax and Semantics*. North Holland, 1984 (revised version).
[2] Ben-Yelles, C., *Type Assignment in the Lambda-Calculus: Syntax and Semantics*.

Ph. D. Thesis, University College of Swansea, 1979.

[3] Bosio, E., Ronchi Della Rocca, S., Type Synthesis for Intersection Type Discipline. Prooceedings of *Third Italian Conference on Theoretical Computer Science*. Word Scientific, 1989, pp.109-122.

[4] Coppo, M., *Tipi e polimorfismo nei linguaggi di programmazione,* Atti degli Incontri di Logica Matematica, Siena, 1985.

[5] Curry, H.B., Modified Basic Functionality in Combinatory Logic. *Dialectica*, 1969.

[6] Damas, L. and Milner, R., The Principal Type Schemes for Functional Programs. In *Symposium on Principles of Programming Languages*, ACM, 1982, pp.207-212.

[7] Giannini,P.,Honsell , F., Ronchi Della Rocca, S., *A strongly normalizing term having no type in the system F (second order λ-calculus)*, Rapporto Interno, Dipartimento di Informatica, Torino, 1987.

[8] Giannini, P., Ronchi Della Rocca, S., Characterization of typings in polymorphic type discipline. In *Logic in Computer Science*, IEEE, 1988, pp. 61-70.

[9] Giannini, P., Ronchi Della Rocca, S., Message on the Type-Net, November 1989.

[10] Girard, J.Y., *Interpretation Fonctionelle et Elimination des Coupures de l'Arithmetique dOrdre Superieur*. These D'Etat, Universite Paris VII, 1972.

[11] Hindley, R.,The Principal Type Scheme of an Object in Combinatory Logic. *Transactions of American Mathematical Society*, 1969, pp. 1-17.

[12] Kfoury, A.J., Tiuryn J., Urzyczyn P., The Undecidability of Semiunification Problem. *Tec. Report, Computer Science Dept., Boston University*, 1989.

[13] Le Chenadec P., On the Logic of Unification. *Journal of Symbolic Computation*, 8, 1/2, 1989, pp. 141-199.

[14] Leivant, D., Polymorphic Type Inference. In *Symposium on Principles of Programming Languages*, ACM, 1983, pp.88-98.

[15] Mitchell, J.C., Polymorphic Type Inference and Containment. *Information and Computation* 76, 2/3, 1988, pp.211-249.

[16] Pfenning, F., Partial Polymorphic Type Inference and Higher-Order Unification. In *Conference on LISP and Functional Programming*, ACM, 1988.

[17] Prawitz, D., *Natural Deduction, a Proof Theoretic Study*. Almquist and Wiksell, Amsterdam, 1965.

[18] Reynolds, J.C., Towards a Theory of Type Structures. In *Paris Colloquium on Programming*, Springer Verlag, 1974, pp.408-425.

[19] Robinson, J.A., A Machine Oriented Logic Based on the Resolution Principle. *Journal of the ACM*, 1965, pp.24-41.

[20] Ronchi Della Rocca, S., Principal Type Scheme and Unification for Intersection Type Discipline. *Theoretical Computer Science* 59, 1988, pp.181-209.

Monotone Recursive Definition of Predicates and Its Realizability Interpretation

Makoto Tatsuta
Research Institute of Electrical Communication
Tohoku University
Sendai 980, JAPAN
tatsuta@riec.tohoku.ac.jp

Abstract

The main aim of the paper is to construct a logic by which we can formalize properties of programs. Inductive definition or recursive definition plays a very important role for this purpose. Inductive definition has been studied for untyped theories, predicative typed theories and impredicative typed theories. Monotone recursive definition in an untyped theory is studied in this paper. The main point is realizability interpretation of monotone recursive definition.

Untyped predicative theory $\mathbf{TID_0}$ and $\mathbf{TID_1}$ are presented, which have monotone recursive definition of predicates. $\mathbf{TID_1}$ has full monotone recursive definition and $\mathbf{TID_0}$ has only restricted monotone recursive definition. q-realizability interpretation of $\mathbf{TID_0}$ and $\mathbf{TID_1}$ is defined. It is proved that the realizability interpretation of $\mathbf{TID_0}$ is sound and that the realizability interpretation of $\mathbf{TID_1}$ is not sound, though $\mathbf{TID_1}$ and its interpretation seem very natural.

1 Introduction

Our main aim is to construct a logic by which we can formalize properties of programs for verification, synthesis and transformation of programs. We present a theory $\mathbf{TID_0}$ for this aim.

Inductive definition or recursive definition plays a very important role for this purpose. Many important data structures programs use such as natural numbers, lists and trees are recursively defined by nature. The essence of control structures of programs is a loop structure, which is realized by recursive calls. Specifications and properties of programs can be formally represented in a natural way by recursive definition if the logic has the facility of recursive definition.

Inductive definition in formal theories was studies in the area of mathematical logic. The main purpose of these research was placed on proof theoretic strength of formal theories.

Many formal systems have been studied to formalize programs in the area of computer science. They are almost divided into two groups. One is typed theories and the other is untyped theories. Typed theories are also divided into two groups, which are predicative typed theories and impredicative typed theories.

Inductive definition was studied for theories of each group. For predicative typed theories, extensions of Martin-Löf's type theory by adding inductive definition were studied [7, 2]. For impredicative typed theories, inductive definition attached to CC was studied [3, 9, 8]. For untyped theories, inductive generation of $\mathbf{T_0}$ [4], CIG of **PX**[5], μ of $\mathbf{EON} + \mu$ [10, 6] were studied.

We study monotone recursive definition in an untyped theory $\mathbf{TID_0}$. Only positive inductive definition has been studied [6] for constructive untyped theories before this time. Inductive generation of $\mathbf{T_0}$ and CIG of **PX** treat only a positive rank 0 case. $\mathbf{EON} + \mu$ [10] can use only an almost strictly positive case and $\mathbf{EON} + \mu$ [6] can treat only a positive case.

The semantics of inductive definition is given by the least fixed point. From the point of view of this semantics, an extension of a monotone case is natural. We try to extend inductive definition to a monotone case and point out some difficulty in this study.

Program extraction is one of the benefits we get when we use a constructive formal theory to treat properties of programs. Program extraction is to get a program from a constructive proof of its specification formula. One method of program extraction is to use realizability interpretation. In **PX**, for example, a LISP program is extracted from a proof of its specification by realizability. We want to use this facility of program extraction by realizability for $\mathbf{TID_0}$.

The main point of this paper is realizability interpretation of monotone recursive definition.

We present untyped predicative theory $\mathbf{TID_0}$ and $\mathbf{TID_1}$, which have monotone recursive definition of predicates. $\mathbf{TID_1}$ has full monotone recursive definition, which is one of our aims and $\mathbf{TID_0}$ has only restricted monotone recursive definition. We define **q**-realizability interpretation of $\mathbf{TID_0}$ and $\mathbf{TID_1}$. This **q**-realizability interpretation is essentially the same as the realizability of $\mathbf{EON} + \mu$ [10, 6]. We show that the realizability interpretation of $\mathbf{TID_0}$ in $\mathbf{TID_1}$ is sound and that the realizability interpretation of $\mathbf{TID_1}$ in $\mathbf{TID_1}$ is not sound, though $\mathbf{TID_1}$ and its interpretation seem very natural. The soundness proof for $\mathbf{TID_0}$ includes the soundness proof for a positive case of $\mathbf{EON} + \mu$ [6] as a special case, though the proof for $\mathbf{EON} + \mu$ seems much more complicated than the one for $\mathbf{TID_0}$. The simplicity of our proof is brought by simplifying the condition to monotonicity.

In Section 2, we give definition of theory $\mathbf{TID_0}$ and $\mathbf{TID_1}$. In Section 3, we briefly explain how useful the facility of recursive definition of predicates is and discuss related works. In Section 4, we discuss a model of $\mathbf{TID_1}$ and prove its consistency. In Section

5, we present **q**-realizability interpretation of $\mathbf{TID_0}$ and $\mathbf{TID_1}$. We explain that this realizability interpretation of recursively defined predicates is natural. We prove the soundness theorem for $\mathbf{TID_0}$. We show that the interpretation of $\mathbf{TID_1}$ is not sound.

2 Theory $\mathbf{TID_0}$ and $\mathbf{TID_1}$

We present theory $\mathbf{TID_0}$ and $\mathbf{TID_1}$ in this section. Both are the same as Beeson's **EON**[1] except for the rules of recursive definition of predicates. $\mathbf{TID_0}$ and $\mathbf{TID_1}$ are different only in the rules of recursive definition of predicates.

Definition 2.1. (Language of $\mathbf{TID_0}$ and $\mathbf{TID_1}$)

The language of $\mathbf{TID_0}$ and the one of $\mathbf{TID_1}$ are the same. This is based on a first order language but extended for recursive definition of predicates.

The constants are:

$\mathbf{K},\quad \mathbf{S},\quad \mathbf{p},\quad \mathbf{p}_0,\quad \mathbf{p}_1,\quad 0,\quad \mathbf{s_N},\quad \mathbf{p_N},\quad \mathbf{E}.$

We choose combinators as a target programming language for simplicity. **K** and **S** mean the usual basic combinators. We have natural numbers as primitives, which are given by 0, a successor function $\mathbf{s_N}$ and a predecessor function $\mathbf{p_N}$. We also have paring functions $\mathbf{p}$, $\mathbf{p}_0$ and $\mathbf{p}_1$ as built-in, which correspond to `cons`, `car` and `cdr` in LISP respectively. **E** is a combinator judging equality of terms and corresponds to an if-then-else statement in a usual programming language.

We have only one function symbol:

App

whose arity is 2. This means a functional application of combinators.

Terms are defined in the same way as for a usual first order logic. For terms s, t, we abbreviate $\mathbf{App}(s,t)$ as st. For terms s, t, we also use an abbreviation $\langle s,t\rangle \equiv \mathbf{p}st$, $t_0 \equiv \mathbf{p}_0 t$ and $t_1 \equiv \mathbf{p}_1 t$.

The predicate symbols are:

$\bot,\quad \downarrow,\quad \mathbf{N},\quad =.$

We have predicate variables, which a first order language does not have. The predicate variables are:

$X, Y, Z, \ldots, X^*, Y^*, Z^*, \ldots.$

Each predicate variable has a fixed arity. We assume that the arity of X^* is $n+1$ if the arity of X is n.

Definition 2.2. (Formula)

1. If a, b are terms,

   $\bot,\quad a\downarrow,\quad \mathbf{N}(a),\quad a=b$

   are formulas.

2. If X is a predicate variable whose arity is n, $X(x_1, \ldots, x_n)$ is a formula.
3. A formula is constructed from logical connectives &, $\vee$, $\rightarrow$, $\forall$, $\exists$ in the same way as a first order language.
4. $(\mu X.\lambda x_1 \ldots x_n.A)(t_1, \ldots, t_n)$ is a formula where X is a predicate variable whose arity is n, A is a formula and $t_1, \ldots, t_n$ are terms.

$\bot$ means contradiction. $\mathbf{N}(a)$ means that a is a natural number. $a = b$ means that a equals to b.

We adopt a logic of partial terms, where some terms may fail to have any values [1]. $a\downarrow$ means that a has a value.

The last case corresponds to recursively defined predicates. Remark that X and $x_1, \ldots, x_n$ may occur freely in A. The intuitive meaning of a formula

$$(\mu X.\lambda x_1 \ldots x_n.A(X, x_1, \ldots, x_n))(t_1, \ldots, t_n)$$

is as follows: Let P be a predicate of arity n such that P is the least solution of an equation

$$P(x_1, \ldots, x_n) \leftrightarrow A(P, x_1, \ldots, x_n).$$

Then $(\mu X.\lambda x_1 \ldots x_n.A(X, x_1, \ldots, x_n))(t_1, \ldots, t_n)$ means $P(t_1, \ldots, t_n)$ intuitively.

We abbreviate a sequence as a bold type symbol, for example, $x_1, \ldots, x_n$ as $\mathbf{x}$.

Example 2.3.

We give an example of a formula. We assume the arity of a predicate variable P is 1. Then

$$(\mu P.\lambda x.x = 0 \vee \exists y(P(y) \mathbin{\&} x = \mathrm{s_N} y))(x)$$

is a formula.

Among many axioms and inference rules of $\mathbf{TID_0}$ and $\mathbf{TID_1}$, we discuss only inference rules of recursive definition of predicates here. The rest of axioms and inference rules are almost the same as **EON** [1] and we only list them in the appendix.

Let $\mu \equiv \mu P.\lambda \mathbf{x}.A(P)$ where $\mathbf{x}$ is a sequence of variables whose length is the same as the arity of a predicate variable P and $A(P)$ is a formula displaying all the occurrences of P in a formula A. Suppose that

$$(\mu 1) \equiv A(\mu) \rightarrow \mu(\mathbf{x}),$$
$$(\mu 2) \equiv \forall \mathbf{x}(A(C) \rightarrow C(\mathbf{x})) \rightarrow \forall \mathbf{x}(\mu(\mathbf{x}) \rightarrow C(\mathbf{x})),$$

$$(\mathrm{MONO}) \equiv \forall \mathbf{x}(X(\mathbf{x}) \rightarrow Y(\mathbf{x})) \rightarrow \forall \mathbf{x}(A(X) \rightarrow A(Y)),$$
$$(\mathrm{MONO\text{-}Q}) \equiv \forall \mathbf{x}r(X^*(r, \mathbf{x}) \rightarrow Y^*(r, \mathbf{x})) \rightarrow$$
$$\forall \mathbf{x}r((r \;\; \mathbf{q}_X[X, X^*] \;\; A(X)) \rightarrow (r \;\; \mathbf{q}_X[X, Y^*] \;\; A(X)))$$

where X, Y, X^*, Y^* are predicate variables, $A(X)$ is a formula displaying all the occurrences of a predicate variable X in a formula A, $C(\mathbf{x})$ is a formula displaying all the occurrences of variables $\mathbf{x}$ in a formula C and $\mathbf{x}$ covers all the free variables of $A(X)$. The notation $\mathbf{q}_X[X, X^*]$ is defined in a later section.

We have 2 inference rules for $\mathbf{TID_0}$ and $\mathbf{TID_1}$ respectively. For $\mathbf{TID_0}$ the inference rules are as follows:

$$\frac{\text{(MONO)} \quad \text{(MONO-Q)}}{(\mu 1)} \; (\mu R1')$$

$$\frac{\text{(MONO)} \quad \text{(MONO-Q)}}{(\mu 2)} \; (\mu R2')$$

where X, Y, X^*, Y^* do not occur freely in open assumptions of deductions of the premises.

For $\mathbf{TID_1}$ the inference rules are as follows:

$$\frac{\text{(MONO)}}{(\mu 1)} \; (\mu R1)$$

$$\frac{\text{(MONO)}}{(\mu 2)} \; (\mu R2)$$

where X, Y do not occur freely in open assumptions of deductions of the premises.

The condition (MONO) states that a formula $A(X)$ is monotone with respect to X.

The additional condition (MONO-Q) states that a formula $e \;\; \mathbf{q}_X[X, X^*] \;\; A(X)$ is monotone with respect to X^*.

We define $\mathbf{TID}^-$ as a theory $\mathbf{TID_1}$ except for the 2 inference rules of recursive definition of predicates.

3 Monotone Recursive Definition of Predicates

We will explain how useful the recursive definition of predicates is and discuss related works.

Let $\mu \equiv \mu P.\lambda \mathbf{x}.A(P)$ where $\mathbf{x}$ is a sequence of variables whose length is the same as the arity of a predicate variable P and $A(P)$ is a formula displaying all the occurrences of P in a formula A. Suppose that (MONO) and (MONO-Q) hold for this A. So we can use $(\mu 1)$ and $(\mu 2)$ for A in each theory $\mathbf{TID_0}$ and $\mathbf{TID_1}$. We will discuss $(\mu 1)$ and $(\mu 2)$.

By $(\mu 1)$ and $(\mu 2)$,

$$\mu(\mathbf{x}) \leftrightarrow A(\mu). \qquad (\mu 1')$$

holds. This μ is the least solution of an equation for a predicate variable X:

$$X(\mathbf{x}) \leftrightarrow A(X).$$

Because

$$\forall \mathbf{x}(A(C) \leftrightarrow C(\mathbf{x})) \rightarrow \forall \mathbf{x}(\mu(\mathbf{x}) \rightarrow C(\mathbf{x}))$$

holds by $(\mu 2)$ for any formula $C(\mathbf{x})$.

We often want to define a predicate recursively. For example, we will define the predicate *Nat* which judges whether the argument is a natural number or not. One way to define it is as follows:

$$Nat(x) \equiv x = 0 \vee \exists y(Nat(y) \,\&\, x = \mathbf{s}_{\mathrm{N}}y).$$

But it is not a definition in a usual sense since *Nat* appears also in the right hand side which is the body of the definition of the predicate. What we want to present by this equation is the least solution of a recursion equation for a predicate variable X:

$$X(x) \leftrightarrow x = 0 \vee \exists y(X(y) \,\&\, x = \mathbf{s}_{\mathrm{N}}y).$$

In $\mathbf{TID_0}$ and $\mathbf{TID_1}$ this solution can be represented by a formula

$$(\mu P.\lambda x.x = 0 \vee \exists y(P(y) \,\&\, x = \mathbf{s}_{\mathrm{N}}y))(x)$$

and (μ1) and (μ2) state this formula is actually the least solution of the equation. By this facility we can define *Nat* in $\mathbf{TID_0}$ and $\mathbf{TID_1}$ as follows:

$$Nat(x) \equiv (\mu P.\lambda x.x = 0 \vee \exists y(P(y) \,\&\, x = \mathbf{s}_{\mathrm{N}}y))(x)$$

For this example, (μ2) represents the mathematical induction for natural numbers classified by *Nat*. (μ2) represents the generalized induction principle in general.

By the facility of recursive definition of predicates, many useful recursive data structures such as natural numbers, lists and trees can be defined inside the theory [10]. The induction principle corresponding to each data structure is derived from (μ2) for each case. The list induction is derived from (μ2) for a definition of lists and the tree induction is derived from (μ2) for a definition of trees.

We want to write specification formulas of programs in the theory. Recursive calls are one of the most important control structures of programs. In this case recursively defined predicates are also useful since recursive calls can be represented naturally by recursively defined predicates. Especially predicates defined recursively by Horn clauses in Prolog can be represented directly in the theory [10].

Recursive definition or inductive definition has been studied in untyped predicative theories. The restricting condition for $A(P)$ varies for the theories. In **PX**[5], we can use $(\mu P.\lambda x.A(P))(t)$ only when every occurrence of P in $A(P)$ is positive and $A(P)$ is a Harrop formula. In $\mathbf{EON} + \mu$ [10], we can use it only when every occurrence of P in $A(P)$ is positive and for each occurrence P one of the following 2 conditions holds:

1. the occurrence appears in some Harrop subformula of $A(P)$.
2. the occurrence is strictly positive in $A(P)$.

In $\mathbf{EON} + \mu$ [6], we can use it only when every occurrence of P in $A(P)$ is positive. In $\mathbf{TID_0}$ we have presented, we can use it only when both of the following 2 conditions hold:

1. (MONO) $A(P)$ is monotone with respect to P,
2. (MONO-Q) r **q** $A(P)$ is monotone with respect to P^*.

$\mathbf{TID_0}$ has the weakest restrictions on $A(P)$ among the above theories.

We want to relax the restricting conditions since recursively defined predicates can be used more widely and more flexibly in the case of weaker restrictions. But the theory is inconsistent if there are no restrictions because we can use $\mu P.\neg P$ and $(\mu P.\neg P) \leftrightarrow \neg(\mu P.\neg P)$ holds by $(\mu 1)$ and $(\mu 2)$. From the point of view of an intended model, recursively defined predicates means the least fixed point. In this model construction we use only monotonicity. Therefore we have a question: Can we use recursively defined predicates on only the condition that a formula $A(P)$ is monotone with respect to a predicate variable P ? From the point of view of consistency of the theory, the answer is yes. This is stated by the fact $\mathbf{TID_1}$ is consistent. But the restriction of **PX** and **EON** $+\ \mu$ were made also for soundness of realizability interpretation. So we have another question: Is realizability interpretation of monotone recursive definition sound ? The answer is no for our realizability interpretation defined in a later section, though it seems very natural. This is stated by the fact realizability interpretation of $\mathbf{TID_1}$ is not sound. We can relax the restriction more than positivity, but still we need some restrictions besides monotonicity for our realizability interpretation. This corresponds to $\mathbf{TID_0}$ and actually realizability interpretation of $\mathbf{TID_0}$ is sound.

4 Model of $\mathbf{TID_1}$

We will briefly explain semantics of $\mathbf{TID_1}$ by giving its intended model. Since $\mathbf{TID_1}$ includes $\mathbf{TID_0}$, this model also explains semantics of $\mathbf{TID_0}$.

We will use the well-known least fixed point theorem for model construction.

Theorem 4.1. (Least Fixed Point)

Suppose S be a set, $p(S)$ be a power set of S. If $f : p(S) \to p(S)$ is a monotone function, there exists a such that $a \in p(S)$ and

1. $f(a) = a$,
2. For any $b \in p(S)$, if $f(b) \subset b$, then $a \subset b$.

a is abbreviated as $\mathrm{lfp}(f)$.

We will construct a model M' of $\mathbf{TID_1}$ extending an arbitrary model M of $\mathbf{TID^-}$. Our intended model of $\mathbf{TID^-}$ is the closed normal term model whose universe is the set of closed normal terms and in which equality of elements is decidable [1]. We denote the universe by U.

We will define $\rho \models A$ in almost the same way as for a first order logic where A is a formula and ρ is an environment which assigns a first order variable to an element of U and a predicate variable of arity n to a subset of U^n and which covers all the free first order variables and all the free predicate variables of A. We present only the definition for the case $(\mu P.\lambda \mathbf{x}.A(P))(\mathbf{t})$.

Define F as follows:

$$|\mathbf{x}| = n,$$

$$F : p(U^n) \to p(U^n),$$

$$F(X) = \{\mathbf{x} \in U^n \mid \rho[P := X] \models A(P)\},$$

where $\rho[P := X]$ is defined as follows:

$$\rho[P := X](P) = X,$$

$$\rho[P := X](x) = \rho(x) \qquad \text{if } x \text{ is not } P.$$

Then $\rho \models (\mu P.\lambda\mathbf{x}.A(P))(\mathbf{t})$ is defined as $\mathbf{t} \in \mathrm{lfp}(F)$ if F is monotone. $\rho \models (\mu P.\lambda\mathbf{x}.A(P))(\mathbf{t})$ is defined as true if F is not monotone.

Theorem 4.2.

If $\mathbf{TID_1} \vdash A$, then $\rho \models A$ for any environment ρ which covers all the free variables of A.

Theorem 4.3.

$\mathbf{TID_0}$ and $\mathbf{TID_1}$ are consistent.

5 q-realizability Interpretation of $\mathbf{TID_0}$ and $\mathbf{TID_1}$

We will explain motivation of our realizability. We start with a usual **q**-realizability and try to interpret $(\mu P.\lambda x.A(P,x))(x)$. Let μ be $\mu P.\lambda x.A(P,x)$ and suppose that $(\mu 1)$ and $(\mu 2)$ hold for this μ. Then $\mu(x) \leftrightarrow A(\mu, x)$ holds. We want to treat $\mu(x)$ and $A(\mu, x)$ in the same manner. So we require $(e \ \mathbf{q} \ \mu(x)) \leftrightarrow (e \ \mathbf{q} \ A(\mu, x))$. Therefore it is very natural to define $e \ \mathbf{q} \ \mu(x)$ as $\mu^*(e,x)$ where $\mu^*(e,x)$ is the least solution of a recursive equation for a predicate variable X^*:

$$X^*(e,x) \leftrightarrow (e \ \mathbf{q} \ A(\mu,x))[(r \ \mathbf{q} \ \mu(y)) := X^*(r,y)].$$

where $[(r \ \mathbf{q} \ \mu(y)) := X^*(r,y)]$ of the right hand side means replacing each subformula $r \ \mathbf{q} \ \mu(y)$ by a subformula $X^*(r,y)$ in a formula $e \ \mathbf{q} \ A(\mu,x)$. We get the following definition of our realizability by describing syntactically this idea. This interpretation is an immediate extension of [10, 6].

Our **q**-realizability interpretation of $\mathbf{TID_0}$ and the one of $\mathbf{TID_1}$ are the same, for the language of $\mathbf{TID_0}$ and the one of $\mathbf{TID_1}$ are also the same.

Definition 5.1. (Harrop formula)

1. Atomic formulas $\bot$, $a\downarrow$, $\mathbf{N}(a)$ and $a = b$ are Harrop.
2. If A and B are Harrop, then $A \,\&\, B$, $C \to B$, $\forall x A$ and $(\mu P.\lambda\mathbf{x}.A)(\mathbf{x})$ are also Harrop.

Since a Harrop formula does not have computational meanings, we can simplify the **q**-realizability interpretation of them.

Definition 5.2. (Abstract)

1. A predicate constant of arity n is an abstract of arity n.
2. A predicate variable of arity n is an abstract of arity n.
3. If A is a formula, $\lambda x_1 \ldots x_n.A$ is an abstract of arity n.

We identify $(\lambda x_1 \ldots x_n.A)(t_1, \ldots, t_n)$ with $A[x_1 := t_1, \ldots, x_n := t_n]$ where $[x_1 := t_1, \ldots, x_n := t_n]$ denotes a substitution.

Definition 5.3. (q-realizability Interpretation)

Suppose A is a formula, $P_1, \ldots, P_n$ is a sequence of predicate variables whose arities are $m_1, \ldots, m_n$ respectively and $F_1, G_1, \ldots, F_n, G_n$ is a sequence of abstracts whose arities are $m_1, m_1 + 1, \ldots, m_n, m_n + 1$ respectively.
$(e \;\; \mathbf{q}_{P_1,\ldots,P_n}[F_1, G_1, \ldots, F_n, G_n] \;\; A)$
is defined by induction on the construction of A as follows.

We abbreviate $\mathbf{q}_{P_1,\ldots,P_n}[F_1, G_1, \ldots, F_n, G_n]$ as $\mathbf{q}'$, $\mathbf{q}_{P_1,\ldots,P_n,P}[F_1, G_1, \ldots, F_n, G_n, F, G]$ as $\mathbf{q}'_P[F, G]$, $F_1, \ldots, F_n$ as $\mathbf{F}$ and $P_1, \ldots, P_n$ as $\mathbf{P}$.

1. $(e \;\; \mathbf{q}' \;\; A) \equiv e = 0 \,\&\, A_{\mathbf{P}}[\mathbf{F}]$ where A is Harrop.
2. $(e \;\; \mathbf{q}' \;\; P_i(\mathbf{t})) \equiv G_i(e, \mathbf{t}) \,\&\, e{\downarrow}$.
3. $(e \;\; \mathbf{q}' \;\; Q(\mathbf{t})) \equiv Q^*(e, \mathbf{t}) \,\&\, e{\downarrow}$ where $Q \not\equiv P_i \quad (1 \leq i \leq n)$.
4. $(e \;\; \mathbf{q}' \;\; A \,\&\, B) \equiv (e_0 \;\; \mathbf{q}' \;\; A) \,\&\, (e_1 \;\; \mathbf{q}' \;\; B)$.
5. $(e \;\; \mathbf{q}' \;\; A \vee B) \equiv \mathbf{N}(e_0) \,\&$
   $(e_0 = 0 \rightarrow (e_1 \;\; \mathbf{q}' \;\; A) \,\&\, A_{\mathbf{P}}[\mathbf{F}]) \,\&$
   $(e_0 \neq 0 \rightarrow (e_1 \;\; \mathbf{q}' \;\; B) \,\&\, B_{\mathbf{P}}[\mathbf{F}])$.
6. $(e \;\; \mathbf{q}' \;\; A \rightarrow B) \equiv \forall q((q \;\; \mathbf{q}' \;\; A) \,\&\, A_{\mathbf{P}}[\mathbf{F}] \rightarrow (eq \;\; \mathbf{q}' \;\; B)) \,\&\, e{\downarrow}$.
7. $(e \;\; \mathbf{q}' \;\; \forall x A(x)) \equiv \forall x(ex \;\; \mathbf{q}' \;\; A(x))$.
8. $(e \;\; \mathbf{q}' \;\; \exists x A(x)) \equiv (e_1 \;\; \mathbf{q}' \;\; A(e_0)) \,\&\, A(e_0)_{\mathbf{P}}[\mathbf{F}]$.
9. $(e \;\; \mathbf{q}' \;\; (\mu X.\lambda \mathbf{x}.A(X))(\mathbf{t})) \equiv (\mu X^*.\lambda e\mathbf{x}.(e \;\; \mathbf{q}'_X[\mu_{\mathbf{P}}[\mathbf{F}], X^*] \;\; A(X)))(e, \mathbf{t})$ where $\mu \equiv \mu X.\lambda \mathbf{x}.A(X)$.

In the above definition, ${}_{P_1,\ldots,P_n}[F_1, G_1, \ldots, F_n, G_n]$ means a substitution. Our realizability interpretation is something like a realizability interpretation with a substitution.

This interpretation works well for $\mathbf{TID_0}$ but goes wrong for $\mathbf{TID_1}$. The interpretation of $\mathbf{TID_0}$ is sound but the interpretation of $\mathbf{TID_1}$ is not sound. The difference is brought by the additional condition (MONO-Q). In general, we cannot conclude that $e \;\; \mathbf{q}_X[X, X^*] \;\; A$ is monotone with respect to X^* even if A is monotone with respect to X. For such A, we in general cannot use $(\mu 1)$ and $(\mu 2)$ for $e \;\; \mathbf{q} \;\; (\mu X.\lambda x.A)(t)$ in $\mathbf{TID_1}$. On the other hand, we can always use $(\mu 1)$ and $(\mu 2)$ for $e \;\; \mathbf{q} \;\; (\mu X.\lambda x.A)(t)$ in $\mathbf{TID_1}$ if the additional (MONO-Q) guarantees that $e \;\; \mathbf{q}_X[X, X^*] \;\; A$ is monotone with respect to X^*.

Theorem 5.4.

The **q**-realizability interpretation is not sound for $\mathbf{TID_1}$. That is, there is a formula A such that $\mathbf{TID_1} \vdash A$ holds but $\mathbf{TID_1} \vdash e\ \mathbf{q}\ A$ does not hold for any e.

Proof 5.5.

Let X,Y be predicate variables of arity 0 and

$\mu \equiv \mu X.(X \to X) \,\&\, Y,$

$\mu^*(r) \equiv (r\ \mathbf{q}\ \mu),$

$A \equiv \mu \to Y.$

Then clearly $\mathbf{TID_1} \vdash A$ holds. But $\mathbf{TID_1} \vdash e\ \mathbf{q}\ A$ does not hold for any e. We will show it by a model given in Section 4. We have

$(e\ \mathbf{q}\ A) \leftrightarrow \forall r(\mu^*(r) \,\&\, \mu \to Y^*(er) \,\&\, er\downarrow) \,\&\, e\downarrow,$

$$\begin{aligned} \mu^*(r) &\equiv (\mu X^*.\lambda r.(r\ \mathbf{q}[\mu, X^*]\ (X \to X) \,\&\, Y))(r) \\ &\leftrightarrow (\mu X^*.\lambda r.\forall q(X^*(q) \,\&\, \mu \to X^*(r_0 q) \,\&\, r_0 q\downarrow) \,\&\, r\downarrow \,\&\, Y^*(r_1))(r). \end{aligned}$$

Choose ρ such that $\rho \models Y$ and $\rho[Y^*] = \phi$. Define F as follows:

$F : p(U) \to p(U),$

$F(V) = \{r \in U \mid \rho[X^* := V] \models \forall q(X^*(q) \,\&\, \mu \to X^*(r_0 q) \,\&\, r_0 q\downarrow) \,\&\, r\downarrow \,\&\, Y^*(r_1)\}.$

Since F is not monotone, $\rho' \models \mu^*(r)$ holds for any $u \in U$ and $\rho' = \rho[r := u]$. Put $u = 0$ and $\rho' = \rho[r := 0]$. Then we have

$\rho' \models \mu^*(r),$

$\rho' \models \mu,$

$\rho' \not\models Y^*(er).$

Therefore we have

$\rho' \not\models \mu^*(r) \,\&\, \mu \to Y^*(er) \,\&\, er\downarrow.$

Hence

$\rho \not\models \forall r(\mu^*(r) \,\&\, \mu \to Y(er) \,\&\, er\downarrow).$

Therefore $\mathbf{TID_1} \not\vdash e\ \mathbf{q}\ A$. □

We will discuss the realizability interpretation of $\mathbf{TID_0}$ in $\mathbf{TID_1}$.

Proposition 5.6.

Suppose that (MONO-Q) holds for every $B(X)$ such that A has a subformula $(\mu X.\lambda \mathbf{x}.B(X))(\mathbf{t})$. Then

$\mathbf{TID_1} \vdash (e\ \mathbf{q}\ A) \to e\downarrow.$

Proof 5.7.

By induction on A. □

Proposition 5.8.

Let $\mu \equiv \mu P.\lambda \mathbf{x}.A(P)$ and suppose that (MONO-Q) holds for $A(P)$. Then

$$\mathbf{TID_1} \vdash (e \ \ \mathbf{q} \ \ \mu(\mathbf{x})) \leftrightarrow (e \ \ \mathbf{q} \ \ A(\mu))$$

holds.

Proof 5.9.

From (μ1) and (μ2). □

This proposition shows that the definition of realizability satisfies our first motivation.

Proposition 5.10.

If $\mathbf{TID_0} \vdash$ (MONO) and $\mathbf{TID_0} \vdash$ (MONO-Q) hold,

$$\mathbf{TID_1} \vdash \lambda x.x \ \ \mathbf{q} \ \ (\mu 1)$$

holds.

Proof 5.11.

Immediate from proposition 5.8. □

Proposition 5.12.

$$\mathbf{TID_1} \vdash \lambda q.\mu f.\lambda \mathbf{x}r.q\mathbf{x}(mf\mathbf{x}(m(\lambda \mathbf{x}r.r)\mathbf{x}r)) \ \ \mathbf{q} \ \ (\mu 2),$$

where

$$\mathbf{TID_1} \vdash m \ \ \mathbf{q} \ \ (\text{MONO}).$$

We prove it in the appendix.

Theorem 5.13. (Soundness Theorem)

If $\mathbf{TID_0} \vdash A$, we can get a term e from a proof and $\mathbf{TID_1} \vdash (e \ \ \mathbf{q} \ \ A)$ holds where all the free variables of e are included in all the free variables of A.

Proof 5.14.

By induction on the proof of $\mathbf{TID_0} \vdash A$. Use proposition 5.10 and proposition 5.12. □

By the soundness of realizability, we get the term existence property, the disjunction property, the program extraction theorem and consistency with some choice axioms in a usual way.

Theorem 5.15. (Term Existence Property)

If $\mathbf{TID_0} \vdash \exists x A(x)$, we can get a term t from a proof and $\mathbf{TID_1} \vdash A(t)$ holds.

Theorem 5.16. (Program Extraction)
If there exists a term j such that $\mathbf{TID_1} \vdash \forall x(A(x) \to (j(x) \;\; \mathbf{q} \;\; A(x)))$ and $\mathbf{TID_0} \vdash \forall x(A(x) \to \exists y B(x,y))$, we can get a program f from a proof and $\mathbf{TID_1} \vdash \forall x(A(x) \to f(x)\downarrow \,\&\, B(x, f(x)))$ holds.

We show the discussion of realizability of [10, 6] is a special case of the above discussion.

Proposition 5.17.
If P occurs only positively in $A(P)$, (MONO) and (MONO-Q) hold.

Corollary 5.18.
$\mathbf{TID_0}$ is an extension of $\mathbf{EON} + \mu$ where $\mathbf{EON} + \mu$ is presented in [6].

If we choose an appropriate monotone realizer m for $A(P)$ where P is positive in $A(P)$, we get almost the same soundness proof for $\mathbf{EON} + \mu$ as in [10, 6]. But the soundness proof of this paper is simpler than soundness proofs for $\mathbf{EON} + \mu$ in [10, 6] because of the monotonicity condition.

Acknowledgements

I'm deeply grateful to Prof. Masahiko Sato for invaluable discussions and comments.

References

[1] M. Beeson. *Foundations of Constructive Mathematics.* Springer, 1985.

[2] R.L. Constable et al. *Implementing Mathematics with the Nuprl Proof Development System.* Prentice-Hall, 1986.

[3] T. Coquand and C. Paulin. *Inductively Defined Types.* Manuscript, 1989.

[4] S. Feferman. Constructive theories of functions and classes, In: M. Boffa, D. van Dalen and K. McAloon, editors. *Logic Colloquium '78, Proceedings of the Logic Colloquium at Mons,* pages 159–224. North-Holland, 1979.

[5] S. Hayashi and H. Nakano. **PX***: A Computational Logic.* MIT Press, 1988.

[6] S. Kobayashi and M. Tatsuta. *Realizability Interpretation of Generalized Inductive Definitions.* Submitted, 1989.

[7] P. Martin-Löf. *Intuitionistic Type Theory.* Bibliopolis, 1984.

[8] C. Paulin-Mohring. Extracting F_ω's programs from proofs in the Calculus of Constructions. In 16th *Symp. Principles of Programming Languages,* pages 89–104. ACM, 1989.

[9] F. Pfenning and C. Paulin-Mohring. *Inductively Defined Types in the Calculus of Constructions.* Technical Report CMU-CS-89-209, School of Computer Science, Carnegie Melon University, 1989.

[10] M. Tatsuta. Program Synthesis Using Realizability. *Theoretical Computer Science,* to appear.

A Axioms and Inference Rules of TID_0 and TID_1

Axioms for Partial Terms:

$$x\downarrow \quad (x \text{ is a variable}) \tag{T1}$$

$$c\downarrow \quad (c \text{ is a constant}) \tag{T2}$$

$$\mathbf{N}(t) \to t\downarrow \quad (t \text{ is a term}) \tag{T3}$$

$$s = t \to s\downarrow \mathbin{\&} t\downarrow \quad (s,\, t \text{ are terms}) \tag{T4}$$

$$st\downarrow \to s\downarrow \mathbin{\&} t\downarrow \quad (s,\, t \text{ are terms}) \tag{T5}$$

$(s\downarrow \to s = t) \mathbin{\&} (t\downarrow \to s = t)$ is abbreviated as $s \simeq t$.

The logical axioms and inference rules are the same as the ones of a usual intuitionistic logic except for the following quantifier rules.

$$\frac{A(a)}{\forall x A(x)}\ (\forall I) \qquad \frac{\forall x A(x) \quad t\downarrow}{A(t)}\ (\forall E)$$

$$\frac{A(t) \quad t\downarrow}{\exists x A(x)}\ (\exists I) \qquad \frac{\exists x A(x) \quad \begin{matrix}[A(a)] \\ \vdots \\ C\end{matrix}}{C}\ (\exists E)$$

Axioms for Equality:

$$\forall x(x = x) \tag{E1}$$

$$\forall x, y(x = y \mathbin{\&} A(x) \to A(y)) \tag{E2}$$

Axioms for Combinators:

$$\forall x, y(\mathbf{K}xy = x) \tag{C1}$$

$$\forall x, y(\mathbf{S}xy\downarrow) \tag{C2}$$

$$\forall x, y, z(\mathbf{S}xyz \simeq xz(yz)) \tag{C3}$$

Axioms for Pairing:

$$\forall x, y(\mathbf{p}_0(\mathbf{p}xy) = x) \tag{P1}$$

$$\forall x, y(\mathbf{p}_1(\mathbf{p}xy) = y) \tag{P2}$$

$$\forall x(\mathbf{p}_0 x\downarrow) \tag{P3}$$

$$\forall x(\mathbf{p}_1 x\downarrow) \tag{P4}$$

Axioms for Natural Numbers:

$$\mathbf{N}(0) \tag{N1}$$

$$\forall x(\mathbf{N}(x) \to \mathbf{N}(\mathbf{s}_{\mathrm{N}}x)) \tag{N2}$$

$$\forall x(\mathbf{N}(x) \to \mathbf{p}_{\mathrm{N}}(\mathbf{s}_{\mathrm{N}}x) = x) \tag{N3}$$

$$\forall x(\mathbf{N}(x) \to \mathbf{s}_{\mathrm{N}}x \neq 0) \tag{N4}$$

$$A(0) \mathbin{\&} \forall x(\mathbf{N}(x) \mathbin{\&} A(x) \to A(\mathbf{s}_{\mathrm{N}}x)) \to \forall x(\mathbf{N}(x) \to A(x)) \tag{N5}$$

Decidable Equality:

$$\forall x, y(x = y \lor x \neq y) \tag{D1}$$

$$\forall x, y, a, b(x = y \to \mathbf{E}xyab = a) \tag{D2}$$

$$\forall x, y, a, b(x \neq y \rightarrow \mathbf{E}xyab = b) \qquad \text{(D3)}$$
$$s \neq t \qquad (s \text{ and } t \text{ are closed normal terms and } s \not\equiv t) \qquad \text{(D4)}$$

B Proof of proposition 5.12

Suppose that
$$m \ \mathbf{q} \ \forall \mathbf{x}(X(\mathbf{x}) \rightarrow Y(\mathbf{x})) \rightarrow \forall \mathbf{x}(A(X) \rightarrow A(Y)).$$
By expanding it, we get
$$\forall f(\forall \mathbf{x}r(X^*(r, \mathbf{x}) \,\&\, X(\mathbf{x}) \rightarrow Y^*(f\mathbf{x}r, \mathbf{x})) \,\&\, \forall \mathbf{x}(X(\mathbf{x}) \rightarrow Y(\mathbf{x})) \rightarrow$$
$$\forall \mathbf{x}r((r \ \ \mathbf{q}_X[X, X^*] \ \ A(X)) \,\&\, A(X) \rightarrow (mf\mathbf{x}r \ \ \mathbf{q}_X[Y, Y^*] \ \ A(X)))). \text{ (1)}$$

Lemma B.1.

Suppose that
$$m \ \mathbf{q} \ \forall \mathbf{x}(X(\mathbf{x}) \rightarrow Y(\mathbf{x})) \rightarrow \forall \mathbf{x}(A(X) \rightarrow A(Y)).$$
Then
$$(r \ \ \mathbf{q}_X[F, G] \ \ A(X)) \,\&\, A(F) \rightarrow (m(\lambda \mathbf{x}r.r)\mathbf{x}r \ \ \mathbf{q}_X[F, \lambda r\mathbf{x}.(F(\mathbf{x}) \,\&\, G(r, \mathbf{x}))] \ \ A(X))$$
holds.

Proof B.2.

Put
$$X := F,$$
$$Y := F,$$
$$X^* := G,$$
$$Y^* := \lambda r\mathbf{x}.(F(\mathbf{x}) \,\&\, G(r, \mathbf{x})),$$
$$f := \lambda \mathbf{x}r.r$$
in (1). Then we get the conclusion of the lemma. □

Proof B.3. (of proposition 5.12)

We assume that
$$q \ \ \mathbf{q} \ \ \forall \mathbf{x}(A(C) \rightarrow C(\mathbf{x})), \qquad (2)$$
$$A(C) \rightarrow C(x). \qquad (3)$$
Let
$$f \equiv \mu f.\lambda \mathbf{x}r.q\mathbf{x}(mf\mathbf{x}(m(\lambda \mathbf{x}r.r)\mathbf{x}r)).$$
We will show
$$f \ \ \mathbf{q} \ \ \forall \mathbf{x}(\mu(\mathbf{x}) \rightarrow C(\mathbf{x}))$$
under these conditions. This is equivalent to
$$\forall \mathbf{x}r((\mu P^*.\lambda r\mathbf{x}.(r \ \ \mathbf{q}_P[\mu, P^*] \ \ A(P)))(r, \mathbf{x}) \,\&\, \mu(\mathbf{x}) \rightarrow (f\mathbf{x}r \ \ \mathbf{q} \ \ C(\mathbf{x}))).$$
Therefore by (μ2) it is sufficient to show
$$\forall \mathbf{x}r((r \ \ \mathbf{q}_P[\mu, \lambda r\mathbf{x}.(\mu(\mathbf{x}) \rightarrow (f\mathbf{x}r \ \ \mathbf{q} \ \ C(\mathbf{x})))] \ \ A(P)) \rightarrow \mu(\mathbf{x}) \rightarrow (f\mathbf{x}r \ \ \mathbf{q} \ \ C(\mathbf{x}))).$$
From lemma B.1 and (MONO-Q) it is sufficient to show

$$\forall \mathbf{x} r((m(\lambda \mathbf{x} r.r)\mathbf{x} r \ \ \mathbf{q}_P[\mu, \lambda r\mathbf{x}.(f\mathbf{x} r \ \ \mathbf{q} \ \ C(\mathbf{x}))] \ \ A(P))\&A(\mu)\rightarrow(f\mathbf{x} r \ \ \mathbf{q} \ \ C(\mathbf{x}))).(4)$$

Put

$X := \mu,$
$Y := C,$
$X^* := \lambda r\mathbf{x}.(f\mathbf{x} r \ \ \mathbf{q} \ \ C(\mathbf{x})),$
$Y^* := \lambda r\mathbf{x}.(r \ \ \mathbf{q} \ \ C(\mathbf{x})),$
$f := f$

in (1), then we get

$$\forall \mathbf{x} r((r \ \ \mathbf{q}_X[\mu, \lambda r\mathbf{x}.(f\mathbf{x} r \ \ \mathbf{q} \ \ C(\mathbf{x}))] \ \ A(X)) \,\&\, A(\mu) \rightarrow (mf\mathbf{x} r \ \ \mathbf{q} \ \ A(C))). \quad (5)$$

We will show (4). Fix $\mathbf{x}$ and r and suppose that

$m(\lambda \mathbf{x} r.r)\mathbf{x} r \ \ \mathbf{q}_P[\mu, \lambda r\mathbf{x}.(f\mathbf{x} r \ \ \mathbf{q} \ \ C(\mathbf{x}))] \ \ A(P),$ (6)

$A(\mu).$ (7)

We will show $f\mathbf{x} r \ \ \mathbf{q} \ \ C(\mathbf{x})$ under these conditions. By (5), (6) and (7), we have

$mf\mathbf{x}(m(\lambda \mathbf{x} r.r)\mathbf{x} r) \ \ \mathbf{q} \ \ A(C).$

By (2),

$q\mathbf{x}(mf\mathbf{x}(m(\lambda \mathbf{x} r.r)\mathbf{x} r)) \ \ \mathbf{q} \ \ C(\mathbf{x}).$

By the definition of f, we have

$f\mathbf{x} r \ \ \mathbf{q} \ \ C(\mathbf{x}).\square$

Adding Proof Objects and Inductive Definition Mechanisms to Frege Structures

Masahiko Sato
Research Institute of Electrical Communication
Tohoku University, Sendai 980, Japan
masahiko@sato.riec.tohoku.ac.jp

Abstract

A constructive theory RPT (Reflective Proof Theory) of proofs which has the following three features is introduced. (1) Proofs as objects. (2) Hierarchies of propositions and truths. (3) The mechanisms of inductive definitions of predicates. Three kinds of structures called Frege structures with inductively defined predicates, Frege structures with proof objects and proof structures are also introduced. These structures are obtained by generalizing certain aspects of RPT and they are all closely related to Frege structures.

1 Introduction

Aczel [1] introduced the notion of Frege structure as a lambda structure equipped with the collections of objects called *propositions* and *truths* satisfying specific *logical schemata.* In a Frege structure, truth of a proposition is determined by reflecting the metalogic. For instance, the proposition $a \vee b$ is true if and only if a is true *or* b is true. The truths of a Frege structure is just the collection of true propositions. In a Frege structure, *sets* may be defined simply as propositional functions. A propositional function is determined by an object a such that $\mathrm{APP}(a, b)$ is a proposition for any object b. Then b is in the set a iff the proposition $\mathrm{APP}(a, b)$ is true.

In this paper, we extend Frege structures in two directions by (i) adding proof objects and (ii) adding the mechanisms of inductive definitions to Frege structures.

The motivation for adding proofs to Frege structures comes from the intuitionistic principle: "To assert is to prove." This principle requires that each true proposition be equipped with its *proof*, so we simply throw in proofs to Frege structures as their objects.

The motivation for adding the mechanisms of inductive definitions to Frege structures is simply because we cannot even define the set of natural numbers without them. In a Frege structure, if it cannot internally define a certain set like the set of natural numbers, we must extend it by adding a unary logical constant, say N, and add an appropriate logical schema for it.

In our case we can internally define such sets by inductively defining predicates which characterize these sets. With each such inductively defined predicate, we can associate an induction principle which can be used to prove properties of the set defined by the predicate. We add such mechanisms uniformly to Frege structures.

The organization of the paper is as follows. The paper is divided into two parts where sections 2-6 constitute the first part and sections 7-9 constitute the second part.

In the first part, we introduce a constructive theory of proofs which we call reflective proof theory (RPT, for short). The theory will be developed on a specific domain $\Lambda_=$. The domain $\Lambda_=$ is constructed from a fairly simple type free functional programming language called Λ. Λ contains λ-calculus with $\beta\eta$ equality. We give the semantics of Λ by means of the reduction relation $\rhd$. The Church-Rosser theorem for $\rhd$ enables us to define an equality relation $=$ on Λ in such a way that two Λ-terms a and b are equal iff there exists a Λ-term c such that $a \rhd c$ and $b \rhd c$. We define $\Lambda_=$ as the structure on the set of terms equipped with this equality relation.

RPT is then defined on $\Lambda_=$ as an indexed family of theories RPT_α $(\alpha < \Omega)$, where Ω may be any ordinal as long as each $\alpha < \Omega$ has a distinct name for it in $\Lambda_=$. So, from a nonconstructive point of view, we can take as Ω any countable ordinal. However, since we would like to develop RPT constructively, and since we do not need a very large ordinal for our purpose, in this paper we take as Ω the ordinal $\omega + 1$.

Each RPT_α has the notions of proposition, inductively defined predicate and a binary provability relation of level α. If $\alpha < \beta$ then RPT_β is a conservative extension of RPT_α in the following sense. First, if a is a proposition of level α then it is also a proposition of level β, and there is a proposition b of level β which is not a proposition of level α. The same is true for predicates. Finally if c proves a at level α then c proves a also at level β, and the provability relations are conservative in the sense that if, for a proposition a of level α, b proves a at level β, then b already proves a at level α. RPT_β becomes a metatheory of RPT_α in the following way. For any objects c and a, there is a proposition $c \vdash_\alpha a$ of level β such that it is true iff c proves a at level α. Therefore, if we can prove the proposition $c \vdash_\alpha a$ in a metatheory RPT_β of RPT_α we can reflect this result back to the object theory RPT_α and may conclude that c proves a at level α. This is the reason why we call our theory reflective proof theory.

In the second part of this paper, we introduce three kinds of structures, namely, Frege structures with inductively defined predicates, Frege structures with proof objects and proof structures.

A Frege structure with inductively defined predicates is defined as a Frege structure satisfying some further conditions which endow the structure with an ability to internally define predicates inductively. We will show that any lambda structure can be enlarged to a Frege structure with inductively defined predicates. This result extends a theorem in [1] which says that any lambda structure can be enlarged to an N-standard Frege structure.

A Frege structure with proof objects is defined as a Frege structure equipped with a provability relation which satisfies the principle of 'to assert is to prove'. From this principle, however, it will turn out that such a structure is incompatible with the classical metalogic. Existence of these structures is shown assuming an appropriate constructive metalogic. In fact, assuming a constructive metalogic, RPT_α becomes a Frege structure with proof objects for each $\alpha < \Omega$.

Finally, a proof structure is defined as a lambda structure equipped with a unary relation *Prop* and a binary relation *Proves*. Such a structure does not have the notion of truth, and we can construct proof structures when our metalogic is classical as well as when it is intuitionistic.

2 Syntax and Semantics of Λ

In this section we define a programming language called Λ. Λ contains λ-calculus. It is theoretically possible to formulate our theory in λ-calculus, but we prefer our extended language because we can encode syntactic objects more directly and naturally.

We will first define the syntax of Λ and then define its semantics by the reduction rules for them. The Church-Rosser property for the language enables us to define (undecidable) equality relation between Λ-terms.

The syntax of our programming language Λ is defined as follows. Below we define *terms*. Terms are also called *programs*. In the following definition, t stands for terms and x stands for variables where we assume that there are countably many variables. We will identify two α-congruent terms, and consider them as syntactically the same.

$$
\begin{array}{rcl}
t & ::= & x \\
& | & \texttt{nil} \mid \texttt{null?}(t) \\
& | & \texttt{false} \mid \texttt{false?}(t) \\
& | & \texttt{true} \mid \texttt{true?}(t) \\
& | & [t \mathbin{\texttt{.}} t] \mid \texttt{pair?}(t) \mid \texttt{car}(t) \mid \texttt{cdr}(t) \\
& | & \lambda x.t \mid \texttt{fun?}(t) \mid t(t) \\
& | & \mu(t) \\
& | & \texttt{if}\ t\ \texttt{then}\ t\ \texttt{else}\ t\ \texttt{fi}
\end{array}
$$

In the following, a, b, c etc. will stand for terms and x, y, z will stand for variables. We classify terms into the following categories:

- Variables: x.

- Constructor terms: $\texttt{nil}$, $\texttt{false}$, $\texttt{true}$, $\texttt{[}a \texttt{ . } b\texttt{]}$ and $\lambda x.a$. They are called constructor terms of the first, second, third, fourth and fifth kind, respectively.
- Recognizer terms: $\texttt{null?}(a)$, $\texttt{false?}(a)$, $\texttt{true?}(a)$, $\texttt{pair?}(a)$ and $\texttt{fun?}(a)$. They are called recognizer terms of the first, second, third, fourth and fifth kind, respectively.
- Selector terms: $\texttt{car}(a)$, $\texttt{cdr}(a)$ and $a(b)$.
- Recursive terms: $\mu(a)$.
- Conditional terms: $\texttt{if } a \texttt{ then } b \texttt{ else } c \texttt{ fi}$.

We define semantics of Λ by giving reduction rules for terms. For this purpose we use parallel reduction ($\rightarrow$) which is defined as follows.

1. If a is a variable, $\texttt{nil}$, $\texttt{false}$ or $\texttt{true}$, then $a \rightarrow a$.
2. If $a \rightarrow d$ and $\#$ is $\texttt{null?}$, $\texttt{false?}$, $\texttt{true?}$, $\texttt{pair?}$, $\texttt{fun?}$, $\texttt{car}$, $\texttt{cdr}$ or μ then $\#(a) \rightarrow \#(d)$.
3. If $a \rightarrow d$ then $\lambda x.a \rightarrow \lambda x.d$.
4. If $a \rightarrow d$ and $b \rightarrow e$ then $\texttt{[}a \texttt{ . } b\texttt{]} \rightarrow \texttt{[}d \texttt{ . } e\texttt{]}$.
5. If $a \rightarrow d$ and $b \rightarrow e$ then $a(b) \rightarrow d(e)$.
6. If $a \rightarrow d$, $b \rightarrow e$ and $c \rightarrow f$ then $\texttt{if } a \texttt{ then } b \texttt{ else } c \texttt{ fi} \rightarrow \texttt{if } d \texttt{ then } e \texttt{ else } f \texttt{ fi}$.
7. If $\#(a)$ is a recognizer term of some kind and a is a constructor term of the same kind, then $\#(a) \rightarrow \texttt{true}$.
8. If $\#(a)$ is a recognizer term of some kind and a is a constructor term of different kind, then $\#(a) \rightarrow \texttt{false}$.
9. If $a \rightarrow d$ then $\texttt{car}(\texttt{[}a \texttt{ . } b\texttt{]}) \rightarrow d$.
10. If $b \rightarrow e$ then $\texttt{cdr}(\texttt{[}a \texttt{ . } b\texttt{]}) \rightarrow e$.
11. If $\lambda y.a \rightarrow d$ then $\lambda x.(\lambda y.a)(x) \rightarrow d$ where x is not free in $\lambda y.a$.
12. If $a \rightarrow d$ and $b \rightarrow e$ then $(\lambda x.a)(b) \rightarrow d_x[e]$.
13. If $a \rightarrow d$ then $\mu(a) \rightarrow d(\mu(d))$.
14. If $b \rightarrow e$ then $\texttt{if true then } b \texttt{ else } c \texttt{ fi} \rightarrow e$.
15. If $c \rightarrow f$ then $\texttt{if false then } b \texttt{ else } c \texttt{ fi} \rightarrow f$.

We may characterize the basic one step reduction by the following theorem.

Theorem 2.1

1. *If* $\#(a)$ *is a recognizer term of some kind and* a *is a constructor term of the same kind, then* $\#(a) \rightarrow$ `true`.

2. *If* $\#(a)$ *is a recognizer term of some kind and* a *is a constructor term of different kind, then* $\#(a) \rightarrow$ `false`.

3. `car`$([a\ .\ b]) \rightarrow a$.

4. `cdr`$([a\ .\ b]) \rightarrow b$.

5. $\lambda x.(\lambda y.a)(x) \rightarrow \lambda y.a$ *where* x *is not free in* $\lambda y.a$.

6. $(\lambda x.a)(b) \rightarrow a_x[b]$.

7. $\mu(a) \rightarrow a(\mu(a))$.

8. `if true then` b `else` c `fi` $\rightarrow b$.

9. `if false then` b `else` c `fi` $\rightarrow c$.

For each term a we associate a term a^* inductively as follows. If several of the following rules are applicable to a particular term, we understand that only the first one applies.

1. If a is a variable, `nil`, `false` or `true`, then $a^* \triangleq a$.

2. $[a\ .\ b]^* \triangleq [a^*\ .\ b^*]$.

3. If $\#(a)$ is a recognizer term of some kind and a is a constructor term of the same kind, then $\#(a)^* \triangleq$ `true`.

4. If $\#(a)$ is a recognizer term of some kind and a is a constructor term of different kind, then $\#(a)^* \triangleq$ `false`.

5. If $\#(a)$ is a recognizer term and a is not a constructor term, then $\#(a)^* \triangleq \#(a^*)$.

6. `car`$([a\ .\ b])^* \triangleq a^*$.

7. `car`$(a)^* \triangleq$ `car`(a^*).

8. `cdr`$([a\ .\ b])^* \triangleq b^*$.

9. `cdr`$(a)^* \triangleq$ `cdr`(a^*).

10. $(\lambda x.(\lambda y.a)(x))^* \triangleq (\lambda y.a)^*$ where x is not free in $\lambda y.a$.

11. $(\lambda x.a)^* \triangleq \lambda x.a^*$.

12. $(\lambda x.a)(b)^* \triangleq a^*_x[b^*]$.

13. $a(b)^* \triangleq a^*(b^*)$.

14. $\mu(a)^* \triangleq a^*(\mu(a^*))$.

15. $\texttt{if true then } b \texttt{ else } c \texttt{ fi}^* \triangleq b^*$.

16. $\texttt{if false then } b \texttt{ else } c \texttt{ fi}^* \triangleq c^*$.

17. $\texttt{if } a \texttt{ then } b \texttt{ else } c \texttt{ fi}^* \triangleq \texttt{if } a^* \texttt{ then } b^* \texttt{ else } c^* \texttt{ fi}$.

We have the following:

Theorem 2.2

(1) $a \to a$.

(2) If $a \to d$ *and* $b \to e$ *then* $a_x[b] \to d_x[e]$.

(3) If $a \to d$ *then* $d \to a^*$.

This theorem can be easily proved by induction. We define $\triangleright$ as the transitive closure of $\to$. The Church-Rosser property for $\triangleright$ easily follows from the above theorem. We have thus used Takahashi's method (see Takahashi [7]) to prove the Church-Rosser Theorem for Λ.

Theorem 2.3 *If* $a \triangleright b$ *and* $a \triangleright c$ *then* $b \triangleright d$ *and* $c \triangleright d$ *hold for some* d.

We can define an equality relation on terms, by stipulating that $a = b$ if and only if $a \triangleright c$ and $b \triangleright c$ for some c. The equality relation just defined has the following property:

Theorem 2.4

(1) $=$ *is an equivalence relation on terms.*

(2) If $a = b$ *and* $c = d$ *then* $a_x[c] = b_x[d]$.

(3) If $\texttt{fun?}(a) = \texttt{fun?}(b) = \texttt{true}$ *and* $a(c) = b(c)$ *for any* c *then* $a = b$.

3 The logical structure of $\Lambda_=$

We are interested in studying the mathematical structure of the collection of the Λ-terms equipped with the equality relation defined in the previous section. Let us call the structure $\Lambda_=$. Each element of $\Lambda_=$ will be called an *object* rather than a term. Two syntactically distinct but equal terms denote one and and the same object and they are indistiguishable as objects.

We would like to define the notions of *proposition* and *proof* within $\Lambda_=$. Before we present the precise definitions of these two notions, we will explain them very briefly in an informal way. It will later turn out that with each proposition and proof a level is associated which measures the complexity of the proposition and proof, but in this brief explanation we will completely ignore this as we have already explained it to some extent in the introduction.

A *proposition* will be introduced as a certain object for which we can talk about its *proof*, where a proof is also a certain object. More precisely, we will define a unary relation $\mathit{Prop}(a)$ and a binary relation $\mathit{Proves}(p, a)$ on our domain $\Lambda_=$. Then an object a will be called a proposition if the relation $\mathit{Prop}(a)$ holds, and an object p will be called a proof if the relation $\mathit{Proves}(p, a)$ holds for some object a. In fact, we will define $\mathit{Proves}(p, a)$ so that $\mathit{Proves}(p, a)$ implies $\mathit{Prop}(a)$. An object a will be called a *truth* if $\mathit{Proves}(p, a)$ holds for some p. A truth is always a proposition and it is also called a *true proposition.* Proofs are polymorphic. For instance, for any object a, $\mathit{Prop}(a)$ implies $\mathit{Proves}(\lambda x.x, a \supset a)$.

That $\mathit{Prop}(a)$ is a unary relation on $\Lambda_=$ means that if $\mathit{Prop}(a)$ and $a = b$, then $\mathit{Prop}(b)$ also holds. Since the equality relation on $\Lambda_=$ is undecidable, we can easily see that the relation $\mathit{Prop}(a)$ is also undecidable. The same remark applies to the provability relation $\mathit{Proves}(p, a)$. As we will see, there are other reasons that make these relations undecidable. Because of this fact our theory of proofs and propositions necessarily becomes a semantical theory.

Except for some important cases, these notions are defined by means of usual inductive clauses. For example, we have the following clause in our definition of propositions (precise definition will be given later): If $\mathit{Prop}(a)$ and $\mathit{Prop}(b)$ then $\mathit{Prop}(a \vee b)$. Similarly, we have the following clause in our definition of proofs: If $\mathit{Proves}(p, a)$ and $\mathit{Proves}(q, b)$ then $\mathit{Proves}([p\ .\ q], a \wedge b)$.

For any objects a and b we have informal mathematical proposition $a = b$ which means that a and b are equal objects. We will encode this informal proposition as the following formal proposition: $a \mathtt{=} b$, where it is written using a notation to be defined soon. Thus for any objects a and b, $\mathit{Prop}(a \mathtt{=} b)$ holds and they constitute the atomic propositions.

As in Martin-Löf [5] and Aczel [1], the following clause, among others, makes the definition of *Prop* and *Proves* depend on each other:

> If $\mathit{Prop}(a)$ and $\mathit{Prop}(b)$ holds under the assumption that a is a true proposition, then $\mathit{Prop}(a \supset b)$.

Also, in the above definition, the clause 'a is a true proposition' appears negatively in the assumption part of the inductive clause. Because of this, the definition is not monotonic with respect to the predicates being defined. Technically this difficulty can be taken care of by the method of Aczel [1] or Feferman [3]. It is also possible to accept this definition as one accepts Martin-Löf's explanation of sets and their elements in [5]. Here we follow the last alternative and ask the reader to accept the Definition 3.1 as given as a legitimate definition. In section 9, we will explain how we can define these notions within the framework of classical set theory. If we define these notions by the method of section 9, then Definition 3.1 will become a theorem which characterizes these notions.

Note that, in our approach, provability relation is more basic than truth, since we can define the latter by the former but not vice versa. This is one point where we differ from Aczel's approach, and because we define the provability relation by reflecting the constructive interpretation of the logical connectives, the internal logic of $\Lambda_=$ becomes constructive.

Next, we explain how we will introduce inductively defined predicates. We define these predicates simultaneously with the definitions of propositions and provability relations. Let us write, for the moment, $Pred(p)$ to indicate that p is an inductively defined predicate. Then, if $Pred(p)$ and a is an object then we would like to have $Prop(p[a])$, where $p[a]$ is an object (to be defined below) such that it is possible to recover both p and a from $p[a]$. To define an inductively defined predicate, we will simulate the syntactic definitions of the μ-predicates as in Sato [6] or Tatsuta [8]. A μ-predicate is defined from a formula schema where the schematic predicate variable occurs only in the strictly positive part of the schema. This restriction ensures the existence of the least predicate satisfying the schema, and we can associate induction schema for the predicate. However, we cannot follow this approach directly here, because what we are dealing with are propositions and are not formulas. For instance, consider the object $A = \lambda p.\texttt{if}\ a\ \texttt{then}\ p\ \texttt{else}\ \neg p\ \texttt{fi}$ where a is a certain object. Then we will say that A is strictly positive if and only if $a = \texttt{true}$. We cannot mechanically decide if A is strictly positive or not, sinc the equality $a = \texttt{true}$ is undecidable. Thus we cannot determine if a given object is strictly positive or not by a simple syntactic analysis of the object. Our definition here is again semantical.

We now give precise definitions of the propositions and provability relations. In the following, a, b, c, d, e and u, v, w etc. will denote objects. i, j, k will denote nonnegative integers.

We will also use the following abbreviations.

- $\texttt{0} \triangleq \texttt{nil}$, $\texttt{1} \triangleq \texttt{[0 . 0]}$, $\texttt{2} \triangleq \texttt{[0 . 1]}$, $\texttt{3} \triangleq \texttt{[0 . 2]}$, $\cdots$
- $\texttt{[]} \triangleq \texttt{nil}$, $\texttt{[}a\texttt{]} \triangleq \texttt{[}a\ \texttt{. nil]}$, $\texttt{[}a, b\texttt{]} \triangleq \texttt{[}a\ \texttt{. [}b\ \texttt{. nil]]}$, $\cdots$
- $a\texttt{\^{}} \triangleq (\lambda x.\lambda y.x)(a)$
- $\top \triangleq \texttt{true\^{}\^{}}$

- $a = b \triangleq$ `[1, a, b]`
- $a[b] \triangleq$ `[2, a, b]`
- $\models_i b \triangleq$ `[3, i, b]`
- $\not\models_i b \triangleq$ `[4, i, b]`
- $a \vdash_i b \triangleq$ `[5, i, a, b]`
- $a \vdash_{i,c} b \triangleq$ `[6, i, c, a, b]`
- $a \wedge b \triangleq$ `[7, a, b]`
- $a \mathbin{\&} b \triangleq$ `[8, a, b]`
- $a \vee b \triangleq$ `[9, a, b]`
- $a \supset b \triangleq$ `[10, a, b]`
- $\neg a \triangleq a \supset$ `false`
- $\forall a \triangleq$ `[11, a]`
- $\forall x.A \triangleq$ `[11, λx.A]`
- $\exists a \triangleq$ `[12, a]`
- $\exists x.A \triangleq$ `[12, λx.A]`

In the above, we have introduced the notation $a\hat{}$ as an abbreviation for $(\lambda x.\lambda y.x)(a)$ where x and y are any two distinct variables. What will happen, if, instead of this, we define $a\hat{}$ as an abbreviation for $\lambda y.a$? We would get the same result if the equality:

$$(\lambda x.\lambda y.x)(a) = \lambda y.a$$

holds. To make the argument precise, let us assume that the variables x and y above are the first and the second variable in our list of Λ-variables. Furthermore, let z be the third variable, and consider the case where $a = y$. (Note that this case is possible since a can be any object in $\Lambda_=$.) Then the left hand side of the above equality is equal to $\lambda z.y$ (because in the β reduction we must change the bound variable y to z to avoid clash) and the right hand side is equal to $\lambda y.y$. So, the expected equality does not hold in general. In spite of this fact, in the following, we will use $\lambda y.a$ as an incorrect but convenient abbreviation for $(\lambda x.\lambda y.x)(a)$. We will use similar notations too. For instance, for any object a, we will understand that $\lambda x.\lambda y.x(a)(y)$ stands for $(\lambda z.\lambda x.\lambda y.x(z)(y))(a)$.

For each i, we will define two unary relations $\models_i$ and $\models_i^+$ and two binary relations $\vdash_i$ and $\vdash_{i,A}$ on $\Lambda_=$. The intended meaning of $a \vdash_i b$ is that a is a proof of the i-th level proposition b, and that of $\models_i b$ is that b is an i-th level proposition. $\models_i^+ b$ will mean that b is a schematic proposition such that the proposition schema occurs only in the strictly positive part of the schematic proposition.

The level of a proposition refers to the degree of the complexity of that proposition. For instance, if a is an i-th level proposition, then the proposition 'a is an i-th level proposition' becomes an $i+1$-st level proposition.

We define these four relations in essentially the same way as Martin-Löf does in [5]. Namely, we define these relations for all non-negative integers by means of the following inductive clauses. In the following definition, we will say that A is a level i *predicate* if $\models_i^+ \lambda g.A(g)(a)$ holds for all objects a. Also, the variables u, v, w, i will be implicitly existentially quantified.

Definition 3.1 *Let a, b and A be objects and i be a nonnegative integer.*

(i) $\models_i^+ a$ *holds if and only if one of the following conditions hold:*

1. $a = \lambda g.g[v]$.
2. $a = u[v]\hat{}$ *and u is a level i predicate.*
3. $a = \texttt{false}\hat{}$.
4. $a = \texttt{true}\hat{}$.
5. $a = (u = v)\hat{}$.
6. $a = (\Vdash_j v)\hat{}$ *where* $j < i$.
7. $a = (\Vdash_j^+ v)\hat{}$ *where* $j < i$.
8. $a = (u \vdash_j v)\hat{}$ *where* $j < i$.
9. $a = (u \vdash_{j,w} v)\hat{}$ *where* $j < i$.
10. $a = \lambda g.u(g) \wedge v(g)$, $\models_i^+ u$ *and* $\models_i^+ v$.
11. $a = \lambda g.u \,\&\, v(g)$, $\models_i^+ u\hat{}$ *and for any c,* $c \vdash_{i,\top} u\hat{}$ *implies* $\models_i^+ v$.
12. $a = \lambda g.u(g) \vee v(g)$, $\models_i^+ u$ *and* $\models_i^+ v$.
13. $a = \lambda g.u \supset v(g)$, $\models_i^+ u\hat{}$ *and for any c,* $c \vdash_{i,\top} u\hat{}$ *implies* $\models_i^+ v$.
14. $a = \lambda g.\forall u(g)$ *and for any v,* $\models_i^+ \lambda g.u(g)(v)$.
15. $a = \lambda g.\exists u(g)$ *and for any v,* $\models_i^+ \lambda g.u(g)(v)$.

(ii) $b \vdash_{i,A} a$ *if and only if* A *is a level* i *predicate,* $\models_i^+ a$ *and one of the following conditions hold:*

1. $a = \lambda g.g[v]$ *and* $b \vdash_{i,A} \lambda g.A(g)(v)$.
2. $a = u[v]\hat{}$ *and* $b \vdash_{i,u} \lambda g.u(g)(v)$.
3. $a = \texttt{false}\hat{}$ *and* $0 = 1$. *(This is a void case.)*
4. $a = \texttt{true}\hat{}$ *and* $b = 0$.
5. $a = (u = v)\hat{}$, $u = v$ *and* $b = 0$.
6. $a = (\Vdash_j v)\hat{}$ *where* $j < i$, $\models_j^+ v\hat{}$ *and* $b = 0$.
7. $a = (\Vdash_j^+ v)\hat{}$ *where* $j < i$, $\models_j^+ v$ *and* $b = 0$.
8. $a = (u \vdash_j v)\hat{}$ *where* $j < i$, $u \vdash_{j,\top} v\hat{}$ *and* $b = 0$.
9. $a = (u \vdash_{j,w} v)\hat{}$ *where* $j < i$, $u \vdash_{j,w} v$ *and* $b = 0$.
10. $a = \lambda g.u(g) \wedge v(g)$, $\texttt{car}(b) \vdash_{i,A} u$ *and* $\texttt{cdr}(b) \vdash_{i,A} v$.
11. $a = \lambda g.u \,\&\, v(g)$, $\texttt{car}(b) \vdash_{i,A} u\hat{}$ *and* $\texttt{cdr}(b) \vdash_{i,A} v$.
12. $a = \lambda g.u(g) \vee v(g)$ *and either (i)* $\texttt{car}(b) = \texttt{true}$ *and* $\texttt{cdr}(b) \vdash_{i,A} u$ *or (ii)* $\texttt{car}(b) = \texttt{false}$ *and* $\texttt{cdr}(b) \vdash_{i,A} v$.
13. $a = \lambda g.u \supset v(g)$ *and for any* c, $c \vdash_{i,\top} u\hat{}$ *implies* $b(c) \vdash_{i,A} v$.
14. $a = \lambda g.\forall u(g)$ *and for any* v, $b(v) \vdash_{i,A} \lambda g.u(g)(v)$.
15. $a = \lambda g.\exists u(g)$ *and* $\texttt{cdr}(b) \vdash_{i,A} \lambda g.u(g)(\texttt{car}(b))$.

(iii) $\models_i a$ *holds if and only if* $\models_i^+ a\hat{}$ *holds.*

(iv) $b \vdash_i a$ *holds if and only if* $b \vdash_{i,\top} a\hat{}$ *holds.*

We can easily prove by induction on the above definition that for any objects a, b and predicates A, B, $b \vdash_{i,A} a\hat{}$ holds iff $b \vdash_{i,B} a\hat{}$ holds. Namely, the provability of $a\hat{}$ under $\vdash_{i,A}$ does not depend on the predicate A.

We have the following theorem which characterizes $\models$ and $\vdash$.

Theorem 3.1 (i) $\models_i a$ *holds if and only if one of the following conditions hold:*

1. $a = u[v]$ *and* u *is a level* i *predicate.*
2. $a = \texttt{false}$.

3. $a = \texttt{true}$.

4. $a = u = v$.

5. $a = \models_j v$ *where* $j < i$.

6. $a = \models_j^+ v$ *where* $j < i$.

7. $a = u \vdash_j v$ *where* $j < i$.

8. $a = u \vdash_{j,w} v$ *where* $j < i$.

9. $a = u \wedge v$, $\models_i u$ *and* $\models_i v$.

10. $a = u \,\&\, v$, $\models_i u$ *and for any* c, $c \vdash_i u$ *implies* $\models_i v$.

11. $a = u \vee v$, $\models_i u$ *and* $\models_i v$.

12. $a = u \supset v$, $\models_i u$ *and for any* c, $c \vdash_i u$ *implies* $\models_i v$.

13. $a = \forall u$ *and for any* v, $\models_i u(v)$.

14. $a = \exists u$ *and for any* v, $\models_i u(v)$.

(ii) $b \vdash_i a$ *if and only if* $\models_i a$ *and one of the following conditions hold:*

1. $a = u[v]$ *and* $b \vdash_{i,u} \lambda g.u(g)(v)$.

2. $a = \texttt{false}$ *and* $0 = 1$.

3. $a = \texttt{true}$ *and* $b = 0$.

4. $a = u = v$, $u = v$ *and* $b = 0$.

5. $a = \models_j v$ *where* $j < i$ *and* $\models_j v$.

6. $a = \models_j^+ v$ *where* $j < i$ *and* $\models_j^+ v$.

7. $a = u \vdash_j v$ *where* $j < i$ *and* $u \vdash_j v$.

8. $a = u \vdash_{j,w} v$ *where* $j < i$ *and* $u \vdash_{j,w} v$.

9. $a = u \wedge v$, $\texttt{car}(b) \vdash_i u$ *and* $\texttt{cdr}(b) \vdash_i v$.

10. $a = u \,\&\, v$, $\texttt{car}(b) \vdash_i u$ *and* $\texttt{cdr}(b) \vdash_i v$.

11. $a = u \vee v$ *and either (i)* $\texttt{car}(b) = \texttt{true}$ *and* $\texttt{cdr}(b) \vdash_i u$ *or (ii)* $\texttt{car}(b) = \texttt{false}$ *and* $\texttt{cdr}(b) \vdash_i v$.

12. $a = u \supset v$ *and for any* c, $c \vdash_i u$ *implies* $b(c) \vdash_i v$.

13. $a = \forall u$ *and for any* v, $b(v) \vdash_i u(v)$.

14. $a = \exists u$ *and* $\mathtt{cdr}(b) \vdash_i u(\mathtt{car}(b))$.

An object a is said to be a level i *truth* (or, a level i *theorem*) if $b \vdash_i a$ holds for some b. The notation $\vdash_i a$ will mean that a is a level i truth.

An object a is said to be a level i *propositional function* if $\models_i a(b)$ holds for any object b.

4 Inductively defined predicates

In this section we take an arbitrary level i and fix it. Therefore, we will often omit the subscript i in the following.

Recall that an object A is a (level i) *predicate* if $\models_i^+ \lambda g.A(g)(v)$ holds for any term v. Such an object is also called an *inductively defined predicate.* It is easy to see that A is a predicate if and only if $A[v]$ is a proposition for any object v.
We have the following basic lemma:

Lemma 4.1 *Let A be a predicate and p, a objects. Then $p \vdash_A a$ if and only if $p \vdash a(A)$.*

Proof. By induction on the definition of $\models^+ a$. We prove only the first case here. In this case, there exists an object v such that $a(g) = g[v]$ holds for any g and $p \vdash_A a$ iff $p \vdash_A \lambda g.A(g)(v)$. Since $a(A) = A[v]$, we have $p \vdash a(A)$ iff $p \vdash_\top a(A)\hat{}$ iff $p \vdash_A a(A)\hat{}$ iff $p \vdash_A A[v]\hat{}$ iff $p \vdash_A \lambda g.A(g)(v)$. □

If we put $a \triangleq \lambda g.A(g)(v)$ in the above lemma, we have:

$$\begin{aligned} p \vdash A[v] &\iff p \vdash_\top A[v]\hat{} \\ &\iff p \vdash_A \lambda g.A(g)(v) \\ &\iff p \vdash A(A)(v) \end{aligned}$$

Namely, we have:

Theorem 4.1 *Let A be a predicate and v, p objects. Then $p \vdash A[v]$ if and only if $p \vdash A(A)(v)$.*

For example, if we put:

$$\mathtt{nat} \triangleq \lambda g.\lambda x.(x = 0 \lor \exists y.(x = \mathtt{[0\ .\ }y\mathtt{]} \land g[y]))$$

then, we see that nat is a predicate, and by the above lemma we have:

$$\mathtt{nat}[v] \supset\subset v = 0 \lor \exists y.(v = \mathtt{[0\ .\ }y\mathtt{]} \land \mathtt{nat}[y])$$

for any v.

With each predicate A, we can associate the following induction principle:

$$\forall x.(A(\Phi)(x) \supset \Phi[x]) \supset \forall x.(A[x] \supset \Phi[x])$$

where Φ is any predicate.

Since $\forall x.(A(A)(x) \supset A[x])$ holds by the above theorem, the induction principle says that A is the least predicate among the predicates Φ satisfying the condition $\forall x.(A(\Phi)(x) \supset \Phi[x])$.

A predicate A is said to be *simple* if $A = a\hat{}$ for some a. A simple predicate is not really inductively defined. In fact, if A is simple, the induction principle becomes trivial since for any v, $A(\Phi)(v) = A(A)(v) \supset\subset A[v]$.

Now, let us verify the induction principle. We assume that the predicates A and Φ are given and fixed. First, for each a such that $\models^+ a$, we assign an object a^* inductively as follows. In the following definition, each item defines a^* for a defined by the corresponding item in the definition of $\models^+ a$. It is easy to rewrite this definition into a Λ-program S with the property that for any object a, $S(a) = a^*$ if $\models^+ a$. But we leave this as an exercise for the reader.

1. $\lambda f.\lambda q.f(v)(q)$.
2. $\lambda f.\lambda q.q$.
3. $\lambda f.\lambda q.q$.
4. $\lambda f.\lambda q.q$.
5. $\lambda f.\lambda q.q$.
6. $\lambda f.\lambda q.q$.
7. $\lambda f.\lambda q.q$.
8. $\lambda f.\lambda q.q$.
9. $\lambda f.\lambda q.q$.
10. $\lambda f.\lambda q.\texttt{[}u^*(f)(\texttt{car}(q))\ \texttt{.}\ v^*(f)(\texttt{cdr}(q))\texttt{]}$.
11. $\lambda f.\lambda q.\texttt{[}u^*(f)(\texttt{car}(q))\ \texttt{.}\ v^*(f)(\texttt{cdr}(q))\texttt{]}$.
12. $\lambda f.\lambda q.\texttt{if car}(q)\ \texttt{then}\ u^*(f)(\texttt{cdr}(q))\ \texttt{else}\ v^*(f)(\texttt{cdr}(q))\ \texttt{fi}$.
13. $\lambda f.\lambda q.\lambda x.v^*(f)(q(x))$.
14. $\lambda f.\lambda q.\lambda x.(\lambda g.u(g)(x))^*(f)(q(x))$.
15. $\lambda f.\lambda q.\texttt{[car}(q)\ \texttt{.}\ (\lambda g.u(g)(\texttt{car}(q)))^*(f)(\texttt{cdr}(q))\texttt{]}$.

Now suppose that $\forall x.(A(\Phi)(x) \supset \Phi[x])$ holds, and let p be such that $p \vdash \forall x.(A(\Phi)(x) \supset \Phi[x])$. We put:

$$F \triangleq \mu(\lambda f.\lambda x.\lambda q.p(x)((\lambda g.A(g)(x))^*(f)(q)))$$

Then, under these assumptions, we have the following lemma:

Lemma 4.2 *For any q and a, $q \vdash_A a$ implies $a^*(F)(q) \vdash a(\Phi)$.*

Proof. Proof by induction on the definition of $q \vdash_A a$. Here, we consider only case 1, 13 and 15.

Case 1) In this case we have $q \vdash_A \lambda g.A(g)(v)$. Then, by induction hypothesis, we have:

$$(\lambda g.A(g)(v))^*(F)(q) \vdash A(\Phi)(v)$$

Since $p \vdash \forall x.(A(\Phi)(x) \supset \Phi[x])$, we have:

$$p(v)((\lambda g.A(g)(v))^*(F)(q)) \vdash \Phi(v)$$

On the other hand,

$$a^*(F)(q) = F(v)(q) = p(v)((\lambda g.A(g)(v))^*(F)(q))$$

and $a(\Phi) = \Phi[v]$. Hence, we have $a^*(F)(q) \vdash a(\Phi)$ in this case.

Case 13) In this case we have $a(\Phi) = u \supset v(\Phi)$ and for any c, $c \vdash_T u\hat{}$ implies $q(c) \vdash_A v$. Hence, by induction hypothesis, we have, for any c

$$c \vdash u \Longrightarrow v^*(F)(q(c)) \vdash v(\Phi)$$

Namely, we have

$$\lambda x.v^*(F)(q(x)) \vdash a(\Phi)$$

Since $a^* = \lambda f.\lambda q.\lambda x.v^*(f)(q(x))$, we have the desired result.

Case 15) In this case we have:

$$\mathtt{cdr}(q) \vdash_A \lambda g.u(g)(\mathtt{car}(q))$$

Then, by induction hypothesis, we have:

$$(\lambda g.u(g)(\mathtt{car}(q)))^*(F)(\mathtt{cdr}(q)) \vdash u(\Phi)(\mathtt{car}(q))$$

Hence,

$$[\mathtt{car}(q)\ .\ (\lambda g.u(g)(\mathtt{car}(q))^*(F)(\mathtt{cdr}(q)))] \vdash \exists u(\Phi)$$

This means that $a^*(F)(q) \vdash a(\Phi)$ holds in this case. □

Now we can prove the induction principle as follows:

Theorem 4.2

$$\lambda p.\lambda x.\lambda q.F(x)(q) \vdash \forall x.(A(\Phi)(x) \supset \Phi[x]) \supset \forall x.(A[x] \supset \Phi[x])$$

Proof. Let $p \vdash \forall x.(A(\Phi)(x) \supset \Phi[x])$ and $q \vdash A[x]$. Then we have $q \vdash_A \lambda g.A(g)(x)$. By the above lemma, we have:

$$(\lambda g.A(g)(x))^*(F)(q) \vdash A(\Phi)(x)$$

Hence we have:

$$p(x)(\lambda g.A(g)(x))^*(F)(q) \vdash \Phi[x]$$

On the other hand, we have

$$F(x)(q) = p(x)(\lambda g.A(g)(x))^*(F)(q)$$

Thus we have:

$$\lambda p.\lambda x.\lambda q.F(x)(q) \vdash \forall x.(A(\Phi)(x) \supset \Phi[x]) \supset \forall x.(A[x] \supset \Phi[x])$$

□

Let us consider a very simple case where $A = \mathtt{nat}$ and $\Phi = \lambda g.(\lambda x.x = 0 \vee \neg(x = 0))$. We would like to prove $\forall x.A[x] \supset \Phi[x]$ using the induction principle. So, our goal is:

$$\forall x.(A(\Phi)(x) \supset \Phi[x])$$

To prove this, let us take any v and suppose $p \vdash A(\Phi)(v)$, i.e.,

$$p \vdash v = 0 \vee \exists y.(v = [0 \;.\; y] \wedge \Phi[y])$$

If $\mathtt{car}(p) = \mathtt{true}$ we have $v = 0$ and if $\mathtt{car}(p) = \mathtt{false}$ we have $v \neq 0$. Hence, in any case, we have $\Phi[v]$. From this we can easily prove our goal, and using the induction principle, we have the theorem which says that for any natural number v, we can decide if it is 0 or not.

5 Internalization

For each nonnegative integer i, we have defined level i propositions and level i proofs, by induction on i. After the induction is completed, we are, so to speak, at ω level, and we can make the following observations at this level.

Let u_0 be a 0-level proposition so that $\models_0 u_0$, and suppose that it has a proof v_0 so that $v_0 \vdash_0 u_0$. Since the metaproposition $v_0 \vdash_0 u_0$ is true, we can formalize and prove it at level 1, i.e., letting $u_1 \triangleq v_0 \vdash_0 u_0$ and $v_1 \triangleq 0$, we have $v_1 \vdash_1 u_1$.

We can continue this by putting $v_i \triangleq 0$ and $u_{i+1} \triangleq v_i \vdash_i u_i$ for $i > 1$. Then, we have $\models_i u_i$ and $v_i \vdash_i u_i$ for $i > 1$. Thus, for example, we have

$$0 \vdash_4 0 \vdash_3 0 \vdash_2 0 \vdash_1 v_0 \vdash_0 u_0$$

We can also see that for any i and j, u_i is a level j proposition if and only if $j \geq i$, and u_i is a level j truth if and only if $j \geq i$. It is also true that any level i proposition (truth) is also a level j proposition (truth, respectively) for any $j > i$. We now have the following theorem:

Theorem 5.1 *If $j > i$ then the j-level propositions (truths) properly contain the i-level propositions (truths, respectively).*

Can we formalize this theorem? For any particular j and i such that $j > i$, we can formalize and prove the instance of this theorem at level $j + 1$.

However, the theorem itself cannot be stated at any particular level k since at level k, we can only talk about propositions and truths whose levels are below k. We can see this as follows. The argument below is similar to Aczel's in [1].

Let S be a collection of objects and s be a level i propositional function. Then, we say that s *internally defines* S (at level i) if for any v, v is in S if and only if $\vdash_i s(v)$. We say that S is *internally definable* (at level i) if there exists some s such that s internally defines S (at level i).

Now let T be the collection of level i truths and suppose that t internally defines T at level i. Then we see that for any v, $\vdash_i v$ iff $\vdash_i t(v)$. Let us put $r \triangleq \lambda x.t(\neg x(x))$ and $R \triangleq r(r)$. Then we have

$$R = r(r) = t(\neg r(r)) = t(\neg R) \tag{1}$$

and this is a level i proposition since t is a level i propositional function. Assume that

$$\vdash_i R \tag{2}$$

Then we have

$$\vdash_i t(\neg R) \tag{3}$$

Hence, we have

$$\vdash_i \neg R \tag{4}$$

From (2) and (4), we have

$$\vdash_i \bot \tag{5}$$

Since, this is impossible, we know that our assumption (2) was wrong. Namely, we have, $\not\vdash_i R$. From this we see that $a \vdash_i \neg R$ for any object a, according to the defintion of what constitutes a (level i) proof of $\neg R$. That $\vdash_i \neg R$ holds implies that $\vdash_i t(\neg R)$, and this implies $\vdash_i R$. But, this is contrary to the fact that $\not\vdash_i R$. We thus see that the collection of level i truths is not internally definable at level i.

This T, however, is internally definable at level i+1 simply by putting $t \triangleq \lambda x.(\models_i x) \mathbin{\&} x$. From this, we also see that, $\lambda x.\models_i x$ is a level $i+1$ propositional function but is not a level i propositional function (for, if it were so, t internally defines T at level i).

Now, we remark that, although we have defined two fundamental relations $\models_i$ and $\vdash_i$ for each $i < \omega$ by transfinite induction up to ω, the choice of ω was, arbitrary in a sense, because the definition itself could be carried out in the same way for any other ordinal Ω such that each $\alpha < \Omega$ can be encoded as a distinct object. In this section we take $\omega + 1$ as such an ordinal by encoding ω as [1 . 0].

We can then define $\models_\alpha$ and $\vdash_\alpha$ for each $\alpha < \omega + 1$. We define the theory RPT_α ($\alpha < \omega+1$) as the structure on $\Lambda_=$ equipped with the three relations $\models_\alpha$, $\vdash_\alpha$ and $\models^+_\alpha$. We note that, by Lemma 4.1, $\vdash_{\alpha,A}$ is definable by $\vdash_\alpha$. In the following, $\models_\omega$ and $\vdash_\omega$ will simply be written as $\models$ and $\vdash$ respectively.

We can formalize and prove Theorem 3.1 as follows:

Theorem 5.2 *Let*

$$
\begin{aligned}
A \triangleq\ & \forall a.\forall i.(\mathtt{nat}[i] \supset \\
& \quad \models_i a \supset\subset \\
& \qquad \exists u.\exists v.(a = u[v] \wedge \forall w. \models^+_i \lambda g.u(g)(w)) \\
& \quad \vee\ a = \mathtt{false} \\
& \quad \vee\ a = \mathtt{true} \\
& \quad \vee\ \exists u.\exists v.(a = (u = v)) \\
& \quad \vee\ \exists j.\exists v.(j < i \wedge a = \models_j v) \\
& \quad \vee\ \exists j.\exists v.(j < i \wedge a = \models^+_j v) \\
& \quad \vee\ \exists j.\exists u.\exists v.(j < i \wedge a = u \vdash_j v) \\
& \quad \vee\ \exists j.\exists u.\exists v.\exists w.(j < i \wedge a = u \vdash_{j,w} v) \\
& \quad \vee\ \exists u.\exists v.(a = (u \wedge v) \wedge \models_i u \wedge \models_i v) \\
& \quad \vee\ \exists u.\exists v.(a = (u \,\&\, v) \wedge \models_i u \wedge \forall c.(c \vdash_i u \supset \models_i v)) \\
& \quad \vee\ \exists u.\exists v.(a = (u \vee v) \wedge \models_i u \wedge \models_i v) \\
& \quad \vee\ \exists u.\exists v.(a = (u \supset v) \wedge \models_i u \wedge \forall c.(c \vdash_i u \supset \models_i v)) \\
& \quad \vee\ \exists u.(a = \forall u \wedge \forall v. \models_i u(v)) \\
& \quad \vee\ \exists u.(a = \exists u \wedge \forall v. \models_i u(v))
\end{aligned}
$$

and

$$
\begin{aligned}
B \triangleq\ & \forall a.\forall b.\forall i.(\mathtt{nat}[i] \supset \\
& \quad b \vdash_i a \supset\subset \models_i a \wedge (\\
& \qquad \exists u.\exists v.(a = u[v] \wedge b \vdash_{i,u} \lambda g.u(g)(v)) \\
& \quad \vee\ a = \mathtt{false} \wedge 0 = 1 \\
& \quad \vee\ a = \mathtt{true} \wedge b = 0 \\
& \quad \vee\ \exists u.\exists v.(a = (u = v)) \wedge u = v \wedge b = 0 \\
& \quad \vee\ \exists j.\exists v.(j < i \wedge a = \models_j v \wedge \models_j v \wedge b = 0) \\
& \quad \vee\ \exists j.\exists v.(j < i \wedge a = \models^+_j v \wedge \models^+_j v \wedge b = 0) \\
& \quad \vee\ \exists j.\exists u.\exists v.(j < i \wedge a = u \vdash_j v \wedge u \vdash_j v \wedge b = 0) \\
& \quad \vee\ \exists j.\exists u.\exists v \exists w.(j < i \wedge a = u \vdash_{j,w} v \wedge u \vdash_{j,w} v \wedge b = 0) \\
& \quad \vee\ \exists u.\exists v.(a = (u \wedge v) \wedge \mathtt{car}(b) \vdash_i u \wedge \mathtt{cdr}(b) \vdash_i v)
\end{aligned}
$$

$$
\begin{aligned}
&\vee\ \exists u.\exists v.(a = (u \mathbin{\&} v) \wedge \models_i u \wedge \texttt{car}(b) \vdash_i u \wedge \texttt{cdr}(b) \vdash_i v)\\
&\vee\ \exists u.\exists v.(a = (u \vee v) \wedge\\
&\qquad ((\texttt{car}(b) = \texttt{true} \wedge \texttt{cdr}(b) \vdash_i u) \vee (\texttt{car}(b) = \texttt{false} \wedge \texttt{cdr}(b) \vdash_i v)))\\
&\vee\ \exists u.\exists v.(a = (u \supset v) \wedge \models_i u \wedge \forall c.(c \vdash_i u \supset b(c) \vdash_i v))\\
&\vee\ \exists u.(a = \forall u \wedge \forall v.(b(v) \vdash_i u(v)))\\
&\vee\ \exists u.(a = \exists u \wedge \texttt{cdr}(b) \vdash_i u(\texttt{car}(b))))
\end{aligned}
$$

Then we have $\vdash A$ *and* $\vdash B$.

In the above theorem, $i < j$ stands for the proposition $L[[i, j]]$ where L is the predicate defined as follows:

$$
\begin{aligned}
L \triangleq\ & \lambda g.\lambda x.\exists i.(\texttt{nat}[i] \wedge \exists j.(\texttt{nat}[j] \wedge x = [i, j] \wedge (\\
&\quad (i = 0 \wedge \exists l.j = [0 \mathbin{.} l])\\
&\quad \vee\ \exists k.\exists l.(i = [0 \mathbin{.} k] \wedge j = [0 \mathbin{.} l] \wedge L[[k, l]]))))
\end{aligned}
$$

We define (formal) *truths* (of level i) as follows. Namely, we are defining truths as propositions having proofs, i.e., as *provable* propositions.

- $\vdash_i a \triangleq \exists x.(x \vdash_i a)$

The following theorem says that any object is provable at level i if and only if it is a true proposition of level i.

Theorem 5.3 $\vdash \forall i.(\texttt{nat}[i] \supset \forall a.((\vdash_i a) \supset\subset (\models_i a) \mathbin{\&} a))$

Proof. Let A be the object to be proved. Then for the following P, we have $P \vdash A$.

$$P \triangleq \lambda i.\lambda p.\lambda a.[\lambda q.[0 \mathbin{.} \texttt{cdr}(q)] \mathbin{.} \lambda q.[\texttt{cdr}(q) \mathbin{.} 0]]$$

□

This theorem can also be written in the following form:

$$\vdash \forall i.(\texttt{nat}[i] \supset \forall a.(\models_i a \supset (a \supset\subset \vdash_i a))$$

In this form, the theorem says that the principle of 'to assert is to prove' is valid for any natural number i. We can use this theorem to get the following true proposition:

$$\vdash \forall i.(\texttt{nat}[i] \supset \forall a.(\models_i a \supset (\neg \vdash_i a) \supset \vdash_i \neg a))$$

This proposition says that if we can show that a certain proposition a (of level i) is not provable (at level i), then we may conclude that $\neg a$ is provable (at level i).

We can formalize and prove Theorem 5.1 in RPT_ω as follows:

Theorem 5.4

$$\vdash \forall i. \forall j.\ i < j \supset \forall a.(\models_i a \supset \models_j a) \land \exists b.(\models_j b \land \neg \models_i b)$$

$$\vdash \forall i. \forall j.\ i < j \supset \forall a.(\ \vdash_i a \supset\ \vdash_j a) \land \exists b.(\ \vdash_j b \land \neg\ \vdash_i b)$$

We define *predicates* of level i internally as follows.

- $\pi_i(A) \triangleq \forall x.(\overset{+}{\models}_i \lambda g.A(g)(x))$

Then we can internally prove our induction principle as follows:

Theorem 5.5

$$\vdash \forall i.\mathtt{nat}[i] \supset \forall A.\pi_i(A) \supset \forall \Phi.\pi_i(\Phi) \supset \forall x.(A(\Phi)(x) \supset \Phi[x]) \supset \forall x.(A[x] \supset \Phi[x]))$$

6 Sets and Russell paradox

As in Aczel [1], we introduce the notion of *set* as the extension of a propositional function. Namely, we introduce a level i set a by the following abbreviation:

$$\sigma_i(a) \triangleq \forall x. \models_i a(x)$$

We also introduce the following notations.

- $\{x \mid A\} \triangleq \lambda x.A$
- $b \in_i a \triangleq \sigma_i(a)\ \&\ a(b)$

$b \in_i a$ means that b is a member of the level i set a. (Note that & is used in the definition of $\in_i$, since $a(b)$ becomes a proposition only under the condition that a is a level i set.)

Level i sets have the following expected properties:

$$\begin{array}{rl} \text{Predication:} & \vdash_{i+1} \forall a.(\sigma_i(a) \supset \forall b.(\models_i b \in_i a)) \\ \text{Comprehension:} & \vdash_{i+1} \forall a.(\sigma_i(a) \supset \forall x.(x \in_i a \supset\subset a(x))) \end{array}$$

In order that $b \in_i a$ becomes true, it is necessary that a is a level i set. This requirement is the key to avoid Russell paradox, as we are going to see now. We put:

$$R_i \triangleq \{x \mid x \notin_i x\}$$

Then, we have:

$$R_i \in_i R_i \ \equiv\ \sigma_i(R_i)\ \&\ R_i(R_i) \tag{6}$$

Assume now that R_i is a level i set, namely, that $\sigma_i(R_i)$ is true. Then $R_i \in_i R_i$ becomes equivalent to $R_i(R_i)$, which then becomes equal to $R_i \not\in_i R_i$. This is a contradiction. So we have (instead of Russell paradox) that R_i is not a level i set, and hence also, not $R_i \in_i R_i$ (see (6)). We can formalize this argument at level $i+1$, and we get the following negative assertions:

$$\vdash_{i+1} \neg\sigma_i(R_i)$$

and

$$\vdash_{i+1} R_i \not\in_i R_i$$

We have thus seen that $R_i \in_i R_i$ is not the case, because R_i is not a level i set. On the other hand, it is easy to see that R_i is a level $i+1$ set. We can now see that, as a level $i+1$ set, R_i contains itself as its member as follows. We have:

$$R_i \in_{i+1} R_i \quad \equiv \quad \sigma_{i+1}(R_i) \mathbin{\&} R_i(R_i) \tag{7}$$

This time, since $\sigma_{i+1}(R_i)$ is true, $R_i \in_{i+1} R_i$ becomes equivalent to $R_i(R_i)$, which then becomes equal to $R_i \not\in_i R_i$ which is true as we saw above. Hence $R_i \in_{i+1} R_i$ is true. This argument can be formalized at level $i+2$, and we get the following positive assertions.

$$\vdash_{i+2} \sigma_{i+1}(R_i)$$

and

$$\vdash_{i+2} R_i \in_{i+1} R_i$$

We have thus seen that at each level $i+1$, we can introduce a new set R_i which is not definable at any lower level. Although the set R_i itself is not definable at level i, there still remains the possibility of defining at level i a set S which is not intensionally the same as R_i but extensionally the same as R_i. Namely, there may be a level i set S for which $\forall x.(x \in_{i+1} R_i \supset\subset x \in_i S)$ is true. We can refute this possibility as follows. Assume that S is a level i set with this property. Then $S \in_i S$ becomes equivalent to $S \in_{i+1} R_i$, which is equivalent to $S \not\in_i S$. This is a contradiction.

Let us now see what kind of sets we can construct in the theory. First of all the smallest set (*empty set*), largest set (*universe*) and the set of natural numbers are already available at level 0: $\emptyset \triangleq \{x \mid \mathtt{false}\}$, $\mathbf{V} \triangleq \{x \mid \mathtt{true}\}$, $\mathbf{Nat} \triangleq \{x \mid \mathtt{nat}[x]\}$.

Suppose that A and B are level i sets, then we can define the followings sets as level i sets: $A \cup B$, $A \cap B$, $A + B$, $A \times B$ and $A \to B$. For example, we can define $A \to B$ by $A \to B \triangleq \{f \mid \forall x.(A(x) \supset B(f(x))\}$, and see that the identity function has the following polymorphic type:

$$\vdash_{i+1} \forall A.(\sigma_i(A) \supset \lambda x.x \in_i A \to A)$$

Next, suppose that A is a level i set and $B(x)$ is a level i set whenever $x \in_i A$. Then we can define the *sum* and the *product* of $B(x)$ over $x \in_i A$ as level i sets as follows:

$$\sum_{x \in A} B(x) \quad \triangleq \quad \{z \mid A(\mathtt{car}(z)) \mathbin{\&} B(\mathtt{car}(z))(\mathtt{cdr}(z))\}$$

$$\prod_{x \in A} B(x) \quad \triangleq \quad \{f \mid \forall x.(A(x) \supset B(x)(f(x))\}$$

7 Frege structures with inductively defined predicates

In this section we will introduce Frege structures with inductively defined predicates. These structures are defined as Frege structures satisfying some extra conditions. These extra conditions make it possible to internally define various recursive predicates in a uniform way in such structures.

We refer the reader to [1] for the definitions of basic notions necessary to define Frege structures. We will, however, use slightly different notations from Aczel's. In particular, we will write $a \wedge b$ instead of $a \ \& \ b$, and our $a \ \& \ b$ stands for Aczel's $a \ \&\!\supset b$. Our $a = b$ corresponds to $a \doteq b$ in [1], etc. Also, we will write $a(b)$ and $a(b)(c)$ for $\mathrm{APP}(a, b)$ and $\mathrm{APP}(\mathrm{APP}(a, b), c)$.

We define a *Frege structure with inductively defined predicates* (**FSID**, for short) as a Frege structure which has the notion of inductively defined predicate in addition to those of proposition and truth. Now, suppose that a Frege structure relative to an explicitly closed family $\mathcal{F} = \mathcal{F}_0, \mathcal{F}_1, \ldots$ is given. Then it is said to be a Frege structure with inductively defined predicates if it has an additional logical constant:

$$[] : \mathcal{F}_0 \times \mathcal{F}_0 \to \mathcal{F}_0$$

(we write $a[b]$ for $[](a, b)$) and it also has the notion of *monotone proposition generator* (MPG, for short) and a binary relation $\mathit{hold}(a, X)$ (between objects a in MPG and collections X of objects) satisfying the following four conditions (ID-1)-(ID-4). We will write a *holds for* X, instead of $\mathit{hold}(a, X)$ for readability.

(ID-1) *(monotonicity) Any MPG a is monotonic in the sense that for any collections X, Y of objects such that X is a subcollection of Y, if a holds for X then a also holds for Y.*

We call this condition the *monotonicity condition for a*. We say that an object p is an *inductively defined predicate* if $\lambda g p(g)(a)$ is an MPG for all objects a, where, as in [1], $\lambda g p(g)(a)$ is an abbreviation for $\lambda(<p(g)(a) \mid g>)$ which is a function in $\mathcal{F}_1$ sending each object b in $\mathcal{F}_0$ to another object $p(b)(a)$ in $\mathcal{F}_0$. For any collection X of objects, we define another collection of objects $\hat{p}(X)$ as the collection of objects a such that $\lambda g p(g)(a)$ holds for X. Then, p is monotonic in the sense that for any two collections X, Y of objects such that X is a subcollection of Y, $\hat{p}(X)$ is a subcollection of $\hat{p}(Y)$.

Because of the monotonicity of p, for any inductively defined predicate p, there exists the smallest collection X of objects such that $\hat{p}(X)$ is a subcollection of X. We call this X the *extension* of p and write $[\![p]\!]$ for it. We note that $[\![p]\!]$ satisfies the equality $[\![p]\!] = \hat{p}([\![p]\!])$.

(ID-2) *If p is an inductively defined predicate then for all objects a, $p[a]$ is a proposition and it is true iff a is in $[\![p]\!]$.*

(ID-3) *The following schemata for monotone proposition generators are all valid.*

1. *For any object a, $\lambda gg[a]$ is an MPG such that for any X, it holds for X iff a is in X.*

2. *If p is an inductively defined predicate and a is an object then $\lambda gp[a]$ is an MPG such that for any X, it holds for X iff a is in the extension $[\![p]\!]$ of p.*

3. *If a is a proposition then λga is an MPG such that for any X, it holds for X iff a is true.*

4. *If p and q are MPGs then $\lambda gp(g) \wedge q(g)$ is an MPG such that for any X, it holds for X iff p holds for X and q holds for X.*

5. *If p and q are MPGs then $\lambda gp(g) \vee q(g)$ is an MPG such that for any X, it holds for X iff p holds for X or q holds for X.*

6. *If a is a proposition and q is an MPG provided that a is true then $\lambda ga \supset q(g)$ is an MPG such that for any X, it holds for X iff q holds for X provided that a is true.*

7. *If f is a function in $\mathcal{F}_1$ such that $\lambda gf(a)(g)$ is an MPG for all objects a, then $\lambda g\forall(<(f(z))(g) \mid z>)$ is an MPG such that for any X, it holds for X iff $\lambda gf(a)(g)$ holds for X for all objects a.*

8. *If f is a function in $\mathcal{F}_1$ such that $\lambda gf(a)(g)$ is an MPG for all objects a, then $\lambda g\exists(<(f(z))(g) \mid z>)$ is an MPG such that for any X, it holds for X iff $\lambda gf(a)(g)$ holds for X for some object a.*

(ID-4) *If a is an MPG and p is an inductively defined predicate, then $a(p)$ is a proposition and it is true iff a holds for $[\![p]\!]$.*

Now, we can prove the following theorems for any **FSID**.

Theorem 7.1 *If p is an inductively defined predicate, then for all objects a, $p[a]$ is true iff $p(p)(a)$ is true.*

Proof.

$$\begin{aligned} & p[a] \text{ is true} \\ \Longleftrightarrow\ & a \text{ is in } [\![p]\!] \text{ (by (ID-2))} \\ \Longleftrightarrow\ & \lambda gp(g)(a) \text{ holds for } [\![p]\!] \text{ (by the definition of } [\![p]\!]) \\ \Longleftrightarrow\ & (\lambda gp(g)(a))(p) \text{ is true (by (ID-4))} \\ \Longleftrightarrow\ & p(p)(a) \text{ is true (by the property of APP)} \end{aligned}$$

□

Theorem 7.2 *If p and q are inductively defined predicates then the following induction proposition for p is true:*

$$\forall x(p(q)(x) \supset q[x]) \supset \forall x(p[x] \supset q[x])$$

Proof. Assume that $\forall x(p(q)(x) \supset q[x])$ is true, and let a be any object. Then:

$$\begin{aligned} & p(q)(a) \text{ is true} \\ \iff & (\lambda g p(g)(a))(q) \text{ is true (by the property of APPLY)} \\ \iff & \lambda g p(g)(a) \text{ holds for } [\![q]\!] \text{ (by (ID-4))} \\ \iff & a \text{ is in } \hat{p}([\![q]\!]) \text{ (by the definition of } \hat{p}) \end{aligned}$$

So, our assumption implies that $\hat{p}([\![q]\!])$ is a subcollection of $[\![q]\!]$. Since $[\![p]\!]$ is the smallest collection X of objects such that $\hat{p}(X)$ is a subcollection of X, we see that $[\![p]\!]$ is a subcollection of $[\![q]\!]$. This implies the truth of the desired conclusion: $\forall x(p[x] \supset q[x])$. □

In an **FSID**, we can define, for example, the natural number predicate and define the set of natural numbers internally. The method is similar to the one we had in section 4. More precisely, since any **FSID** is a Frege structure, we can introduce an object 0 and $\mathcal{F}$-functions $s, \mathrm{PRED}, \mathrm{DEC} : \mathcal{F}_0 \rightarrow \mathcal{F}_0$ such that for all objects a:

$$\begin{aligned} \mathrm{PRED}(s(a)) &= a, \\ \mathrm{DEC}(s(a)) &= \Delta_2, \\ \mathrm{DEC}(0) &= \Delta_1 \end{aligned}$$

hold. (Δ_1 and Δ_2 are distinct objects. See [1], for details.) Then we define an object $\mathtt{nat}$ by:

$$\mathtt{nat} \triangleq \lambda g \lambda x(x = 0 \vee \exists y(x = s(y) \wedge g[y]))$$

It is easy to see that $\mathtt{nat}$ is a predicate, and the induction proposition for $\mathtt{nat}$ is equivalent to the following form of mathematical induction:

$$q[0] \wedge \forall x(q[x] \supset q[s(x)]) \supset \forall x(\mathtt{nat}[x] \supset q[x])$$

We note the following in passing. As in [1], a *propositional function* is a function whose values are all propositions. Let f be a propositional function in $\mathcal{F}_1$. Then $p = \lambda g f$ is a predicate such that the proposition $\forall x(p[x] \supset\subset f(x))$ is true. Conversely, let p be any predicate. Then $f = <p[x] \mid x>$ is a propositional function in $\mathcal{F}_1$ such that the proposition $\forall x(p[x] \supset\subset f(x))$ is true. So, the above mathematical induction can be equivalently formulated as follows:

> *Let f be any propositional function in $\mathcal{F}_1$. Then the following proposition is true:*
>
> $$f(0) \wedge \forall x(f(x) \supset f(s(x))) \supset \forall x(\mathtt{nat}[x] \supset f(x))$$

Aczel [1] defined the collection of *natural numbers* as the smallest collection of objects containing 0 and closed under the successor function s. We can also prove the following

Lemma 7.1 *For any object a, a is a natural number iff* $\mathtt{nat}[a]$ *is true.*

Proof. ($\Rightarrow$) By Theorem 7.1 we have the following true proposition:

$$\forall x(\mathtt{nat}[x] \supset\subset x = 0 \vee \exists y(x = s(y) \wedge \mathtt{nat}[y]))$$

From this, we see that the propositions $\mathtt{nat}[0]$ and $\forall x(\mathtt{nat}[x] \supset \mathtt{nat}[s(x)])$ are both true. Therefore, by induction on the construction of natural numbers, we see that $\mathtt{nat}[a]$ is true for all natural numbers a.

($\Leftarrow$) Let **N** denote the collection of natural numbers. Clearly, we will be done if we could show that $[\![\mathtt{nat}]\!]$ is a subcollection of **N**. We first show that $\hat{\mathtt{nat}}(\mathbf{N})$ is a subcollection of **N**. Let a be any object. Then:

$$\begin{array}{ll} & a \text{ is in } \hat{\mathtt{nat}}(\mathbf{N}) \\ \Longleftrightarrow & \lambda g \mathtt{nat}(g)(a) \text{ holds for } \mathbf{N} \\ \Longleftrightarrow & \lambda g(a = 0 \vee \exists y(a = s(y) \wedge g[y])) \text{ holds for } \mathbf{N} \\ \Longleftrightarrow & \lambda g(a = 0) \text{ holds for } \mathbf{N} \text{ or } \lambda g \exists y(a = s(y) \wedge g[y]) \text{ holds for } \mathbf{N} \\ \Longleftrightarrow & a = 0 \text{ or there exists an object } b \text{ such that } \lambda g(a = s(b) \wedge g[b]) \text{ holds for } \mathbf{N} \\ \Longleftrightarrow & a = 0 \text{ or there exists an object } b \text{ such that } a = s(b) \text{ and } b \text{ is in } \mathbf{N} \\ \Longleftrightarrow & a = 0 \text{ or there exists a natural number } b \text{ such that } a = s(b) \end{array}$$

Since the collection of natural numbers contains 0 and is closed under the function s, we see that a is in $\hat{\mathtt{nat}}(\mathbf{N})$ implies that a is in **N**. Namely $\hat{\mathtt{nat}}(\mathbf{N})$ becomes a subcollection of **N**. Then, by the definition of $[\![\mathtt{nat}]\!]$, we see that $[\![\mathtt{nat}]\!]$ is a subcollection of **N**.

We can immediately get the following theorem from this lemma.

Theorem 7.3 *In any* **FSID**, *the collection* **N** *of all the natural numbers are internally definable.*

In Aczel's terminology, this theorem says that any **FSID** is an *N-standard* Frege structure.

8 Frege structures with proof objects and proof structures

In this section we define two kinds of structures. One is Frege structures with proof objects (**FSP** for short). An **FSP** is obtained as a special Frege structure which has a provability relation satisfying suitable conditions. One such condition is the principle of 'to assert is to prove'. So, in an **FSP**, truth of a proposition is equivalent to its provability. This has the following consequence. On one hand, since an **FSP** is a Frege structure, truth is defined by reflecting the metalogic (for instance the meaning of the logical constant $\supset$ is determined by using the metalogical connective 'implies'), and on the other hand, provability will be defined by reflecting the constructive reading of logical constants (for instance, a proof c of the proposition $a \supset b$ is defined to be an object which transforms each proof e of a to a proof $c(e)$ of b). Therefore our definition of **FSP** will be meaningful only if we assume that our metalogic is constructive. In fact, we will show that **FSP** cannot exist if our metalogic is classical.

The other structures we introduce in this section are called proof structures. Proof structures are very similar to **FSP**. The difference is that they are not based on Frege structures. We define proof structures directly without assuming Frege structures. Proof structures are determined by the two notions of *proposition* and *provability relation.*

In any Frege structure we can construct the functions:

$$\begin{aligned} \text{PAIR} &: \mathcal{F}_0 \times \mathcal{F}_0 \to \mathcal{F}_0 \\ P, Q &: \mathcal{F}_0 \to \mathcal{F}_0 \end{aligned}$$

such that for all objects a and b in $\mathcal{F}_0$:

$$P(\text{PAIR}(a, b)) = a \text{ and } Q(\text{PAIR}(a, b)) = b.$$

(See [1] for details.)

We now turn to the definition of Frege structures with proof objects.

A *Frege structure with proofs* is a Frege structure with a binary relation $Proves(a, b)$ between objects a and b satisfying the following two conditions (PR-1) and (PR-2). We will write a *proves* b instead of $Proves(a, b)$ for readability.

(PR-1) *(To assert is to prove) For all objects a, a is true iff a is provable (i.e., there exists an object b such that b proves a).*

(PR-2) *The following provability schemata are all valid.*

1. *(Negation) For all objects c and a, c proves $\neg a$ iff a is a proposition and there does not exists an object b such that b proves a.*

2. *(Conjunction) For all objects c, a and b, c proves $a \wedge b$ iff $P(c)$ proves a and $Q(c)$ proves b.*

3. *(Disjunction) For all objects c, a and b, c proves $a \vee b$ iff (i) $a \vee b$ is a proposition and (ii) $P(c) = \Delta_1$ and $Q(c)$ proves a or $P(c) = \Delta_2$ and $Q(c)$ proves b.*

4. *(Implication) For all objects c, a and b, c proves $a \supset b$ iff a is a proposition and for any object e, e proves a implies $c(e)$ proves b.*

5. *(Universal quantification) If f is a propositional function in $\mathcal{F}_1$ then for all objects c, c proves $\forall(f)$ iff for all objects a, $c(a)$ proves $f(a)$.*

6. *(Existential quantification) If f is a propositional function in $\mathcal{F}_1$ then for all objects c, c proves $\exists(f)$ iff $Q(c)$ proves $f(P(c))$.*

7. *(Equality)* For all objects c, a and b, c proves $a = b$ iff $a = b$ and $c = 0$.

In [6], we have called the style of programming in which programs are developed within a constructive mathematical system (which is preferably implemented on a computer) *constructive programming*. In an **FSP**, constructive programming is possible in the following way. Let S be a function in $\mathcal{F}_0 \to \mathcal{F}_0 \to \mathcal{F}_0$ such that $S(a)(b)$ becomes a proposition for any objects a and b, and consider the *specification* proposition: $\forall x \exists y S(x)(y)$. Suppose that the specification is true. Then by the principle of 'to assert is to prove', it has a proof p. Since p proves $\forall x \exists y S(x)(y)$, we have that for all objects a, $p(a)$ proves $\exists y S(a)(y)$. This means that $Q(p(a))$ proves $S(a)(P(p(a)))$. So, if we put $g = <P(p(x)) \mid x>$ and $h = <Q(p(x)) \mid x>$, we see that for any *input* object a, the *output* object $g(a)$ satisfies the *input-output relation* $S(a)(g(a))$ required by the specification. $h(a)$ gives a proof that the relation $S(a)(g(a))$ indeed holds.

We now show that we cannot construct an instance of an **FSP** if our metalogic is classical. To see this, we first show that the proposition $\forall x (x = \Delta_1 \vee \neg(x = \Delta_1))$ is not provable. So, suppose that we have a proof p of the proposition and consider the function $f = <|P(p(x))|_2(\Delta_2, \Delta_1) \mid x>$ in $\mathcal{F}_1$. By the fixed-point theorem (Theorem 5.5) in [1], we can construct an object a such that $f(a) = a$. Now, $p(a)$ proves the proposition $a = \Delta_1 \vee \neg(a = \Delta_1)$. Since, $p(a)$ proves a disjunction, we have one of the following two cases:

1. $P(p(a)) = \Delta_1$ and $Q(p(a))$ proves $a = \Delta_1$: In this case, we have, $a = f(a) = |P(p(a))|_2(\Delta_2, \Delta_1) = \Delta_2$. On the other hand, since $a = \Delta_1$ is provable, we have, $a = \Delta_1$. So, we have $\Delta_1 = \Delta_2$, but this is impossible.

2. $P(p(a)) = \Delta_2$ and $Q(p(a))$ proves $\neg(a = \Delta_1)$: In this case, we have, $a = f(a) = |P(p(a))|_2(\Delta_2, \Delta_1) = \Delta_1$. On the other hand, since $\neg(a = \Delta_1)$ is provable, there are no proofs for $a = \Delta_1$. So we have $a \neq \Delta_1$ (because, if $a = \Delta_1$ then 0 proves $a = \Delta_1$). We have a contradiction in this case too.

Now, if we look at this proposition classically, we see that this is a true proposition. Then the principle of 'to assert is to prove' says that it is also provable. But this is impossible as we have just seen. In the next section, we will show the existence of **FSP**s, but to accept the argument used there we need to accept a constructive metalogic.

Next, we define proof structures. Assume that we have an explicitly closed family $\mathcal{F}$ and the following list of distinct $\mathcal{F}$-functionals called *logical constants*:

$$\neg \;:\; \mathcal{F}_0 \to \mathcal{F}_0$$
$$\wedge, \vee, \supset, = \;:\; \mathcal{F}_0 \times \mathcal{F}_0 \to \mathcal{F}_0$$
$$\forall, \exists \;:\; \mathcal{F}_1 \to \mathcal{F}_0$$

and *operator constants*:

$$0, \Delta_1, \Delta_2 \;:\; \to \mathcal{F}_0$$

$$\text{PAIR} \ : \ \mathcal{F}_0 \times \mathcal{F}_0 \to \mathcal{F}_0$$
$$P, Q \ : \ \mathcal{F}_0 \to \mathcal{F}_0$$
$$\lambda \ : \ \mathcal{F}_1 \to \mathcal{F}_0$$
$$\text{APP} \ : \ \mathcal{F}_0 \times \mathcal{F}_0$$

such that for all objects a and b in $\mathcal{F}_0$ and for all f in $\mathcal{F}_1$,

$$P(\text{PAIR}(a, b)) = a, Q(\text{PAIR}(a, b)) = b \text{ and } \text{APP}(\lambda(f), a) = f(a)$$

hold. Then a *proof structure* consists of two relations *Prop*, which is unary, and *Proves*, which is binary, such that the following two conditions (PS-1) and (PS-2) are satisfied. In the following we will write a *is a proposition* for *Prop(a)* and c *proves* a for *Proves(c, a)*. Also, we will say that a *is provable* if c proves a for some object c.

(PS-1) *If a is provable then a is a proposition.*

(PS-2) *The following provability schemata are all valid.*

1. *(Negation) For all objects a, if a is a proposition then $\neg a$ is a proposition such that for all objects c, c proves $\neg a$ iff there does not exists an object b such that b proves a.*

2. *(Conjunction) For all objects a and b, if both a and b are propositions then $a \wedge b$ is a proposition such that for all objects c, c proves $a \wedge b$ iff $P(c)$ proves a and $Q(c)$ proves b.*

3. *(Disjunction) For all objects a and b, if both a and b are propositions then $a \vee b$ is a proposition such that for all objects c, c proves $a \vee b$ iff $P(c) = \Delta_1$ and $Q(c)$ proves a or $P(c) = \Delta_2$ and $Q(c)$ proves b.*

4. *(Implication) For all objects a and b, if a is a proposition and b is a proposition provided that a is provable then $a \supset b$ is a proposition such that for all objects c, c proves $a \supset b$ iff a is a proposition and for any object e, e proves a implies $c(e)$ proves b.*

5. *(Universal quantification) If f is a propositional function in $\mathcal{F}_1$ then $\forall(f)$ is a proposition such that for all objects c, c proves $\forall(f)$ iff for any object a, $c(a)$ proves $f(a)$.*

6. *(Existential quantification) If f is a propositional function in $\mathcal{F}_1$ then $\exists(f)$ is a proposition such that for all objects c, c proves $\exists(f)$ iff $Q(c)$ proves $f(P(c))$.*

7. *(Equality) For all objects a and b, $a = b$ is a proposition such that for all objects c, c proves $a = b$ iff $a = b$ and $c = 0$.*

Proof structures do not have the notion of truth. If we wish to add the notion of truth to proof structures, how should we do this? We will probably want that any provable proposition to be true. And if we want this, we arrive at the conclusion that we must define truths as provable propositions here again. For, otherwise, there exist a true but unprovable proposition a. Then by the schema for the provability of $\neg a$, we see that $\neg a$ is provable and hence true.

Based on this argument, in any proof structure, we will say that a proposition is *true* iff it is provable. Thus the principle of 'to assert is to prove' holds for any proof structure and its internal logic is constructive. However, since truth is defined internally via provability without directly reflecting the metalogic, proof structures are compatible with classical metalogic as well as with intuitionistic metalogic.

9 The construction of the structures

In this section we construct concrete examples of the three structures we introduced in the previous two sections.

We will use $\Lambda_=$ as the basic domain for our construction. We now define a family $\mathcal{L}$ as follows. We put $\mathcal{L}_0 = \Lambda_=$ and for $n > 0$, we put $\mathcal{L}_n$ as the collection of those functions $f : \mathcal{L}_0^n \rightarrow \mathcal{L}_0$ such that there exists a Λ-term b and distinct variables $x_1, \ldots, x_n$ with the property that for all objects $a_1, \ldots, a_n$, $f(a_1, \ldots, a_n) = b_{x_1,\ldots,x_n}[a_1, \ldots, a_n]$. Here, $b_{x_1,\ldots,x_n}[a_1, \ldots, a_n]$ denotes the result of simultaneously substituting $a_1, \ldots, a_n$ for $x_1, \ldots, x_n$ in b. It is easy to see that the family $\mathcal{L}$ is explicitly closed. It becomes a lambda structure if we define

$$\begin{aligned} \lambda &: \mathcal{L}_1 \rightarrow \mathcal{L}_0 \\ \mathrm{APP} &: \mathcal{L}_0 \times \mathcal{L}_0 \rightarrow \mathcal{L}_0 \end{aligned}$$

by putting $\lambda(f) = \lambda x.b$, where b is a Λ-term and x is a variable such that for all objects a, $f(a) = b_x[a]$ and $\mathrm{APP}(a, b) = a(b)$.

Based on this lambda structure, we first construct a proof structure. The logical constants other than $\neg$ are defined using the notations introduced in section 3. For instance $\wedge : \mathcal{L}_0 \times \mathcal{L}_0 \rightarrow \mathcal{L}_0$ is defined by putting $\wedge = <\![\mathtt{7}, x, y] \mid x, y\!>$. We define $\neg$ by putting $\neg = <\!x \supset \mathtt{false} \mid x\!>$. The operator constants are defined as follows. $0 = \mathtt{0}$, $\Delta_1 = \mathtt{true}$, $\Delta_2 = \mathtt{false}$, $\mathrm{PAIR} = <\![x\ .\ y] \mid x, y\!>$, $P = <\!\mathtt{car}(x) \mid x\!>$, $Q = <\!\mathtt{cdr}(x) \mid x\!>$. Finally, we define the relation *Prop* by the condition that a is a proposition iff $\models_0 a$ holds, and define the relation *Proves* by the condition that c *proves* a iff $c \vdash_0 a$ holds. Then by Theorem 3.1, we see that we have a proof structure here. In fact we could use any pair of $\models_\alpha$ and $\vdash_\alpha$ such that $\alpha < \Omega$ instead of $\models_0$ and $\vdash_0$.

Next, we consider the construction of Frege structures with proof objects. We use the proof structure we just constructed for this purpose. So, let the proof structure be as above. We define an object to be *true* iff it is provable in it. In other words, an object a is true iff there exists an object c such that c proves a. Then, according to the definition of **FSP**, this proof structure with the notion of truth defined as above will become an **FSP** if we can verify the logical schemata which must hold for any Frege structure.

But, as we have shown in the previous section, if we interpret these schemata by using classical metalogic, we arrive at a contradiction. So, we must interpret these schemata constructively. And if we do so properly, we see that these logical schemata have the same meaning as the provability schemata for Frege structures with proof objects. Thus, the principle of 'to assert is to prove' forces us a very specific interpretation of logical schemata. This is in contrast with Frege structures in general where metalogic can be either classical or constructive.

The last structures to be constructed are Frege structures with inductively defined predicates. We will use the lambda structure $\mathcal{L}$ for the construction.

First we add a logical constant $[] : \mathcal{L}_0 \times \mathcal{L}_0 \to \mathcal{L}_0$ by putting $[] = <x[y] \mid x, y>$, where $a[b]$ is an abbreviation of `[2, a, b]`, if we recall the notation introduced in section 3.

We will give explicit definitions of the notions of proposition, truth, MPG and a binary relation *hold* by transfinite induction on the ordinals.

For each ordinal α, we do the following $(\mathrm{A})_\alpha$-$(\mathrm{H})_\alpha$ by transfinite induction.

$(\mathrm{A})_\alpha$ State and prove a certain statement P_α.

$(\mathrm{B})_\alpha$ State and prove a certain statement Q_α.

$(\mathrm{C})_\alpha$ Define a notion of MPG_α.

$(\mathrm{D})_\alpha$ Define a binary relation $hold_\alpha$ between any objects and any collections of objects.

$(\mathrm{E})_\alpha$ Define a notion of truth_α.

$(\mathrm{F})_\alpha$ State and prove a certain statement R_α.

$(\mathrm{G})_\alpha$ Define a notion of $\mathrm{predicate}_\alpha$.

$(\mathrm{H})_\alpha$ For any $\mathrm{predicate}_\alpha$ p, define its extension $[\![p]\!]_\alpha$.

Let α be any ordinal. We may assume that we have done $(\mathrm{A})_\beta$-$(\mathrm{H})_\beta$ for all $\beta < \alpha$. We will refer to this assumption as *the induction hypothesis* in the following construction.

(A)$_\alpha$ The statement P_α is:

> *Let a be an object and suppose that there exist ordinals β and γ such that $\beta < \alpha$, $\gamma < \alpha$, a is an* MPG_β *and a is an* MPG_γ*. Then the two ordinals β and γ are equal.*

We prove this as follows. Suppose the assumption of the statement, and suppose further that β and γ are different, so that $\beta < \gamma$ or $\gamma < \beta$. If $\beta < \gamma$ ($\gamma < \beta$), we get a contradiction from the definition of MPG_γ (MPG_β) which was given by $(\mathrm{C})_\gamma$ ($(\mathrm{C})_\beta$, resp.) Therefore, β and γ must be equal. This β will be referred to as the *birthday* of a and we will write $|a|$ for it.

(B)$_\alpha$ The statement Q_α is:

Let a be an object and suppose that there exist ordinals β and γ such that $\beta < \alpha$, $\gamma < \alpha$, a is a predicate$_\beta$ *and a is a* predicate$_\gamma$. *Then the two ordinals β and γ are equal.*

The proof is very similar to the proof of P_α. The ordinal determined by this fact is called the *birthday of the predicate a*.

(C)$_\alpha$ Let a be any object. Then a is an MPG$_\alpha$ iff (i) for all $\beta < \alpha$, a is *not* an MPG$_\beta$ and (ii) one of the following conditions hold:

1. There exists an object v such that $a = \lambda g.g[v]$.
2. There exist objects u, v and $\beta < \alpha$ such that $a = u[v]\hat{}$ and u is a predicate$_\beta$.
3. There exist an object u and $\beta < \alpha$ such that $a = (\neg u)\hat{}$ and $u\hat{}$ is an MPG$_\beta$.
4. There exist objects u, v, $\beta < \alpha$ and $\gamma < \alpha$ such that $a = \lambda g.u(g) \wedge v(g)$, u is an MPG$_\beta$ and v is an MPG$_\gamma$.
5. There exist objects u, v, $\beta < \alpha$ and $\gamma < \alpha$ such that $a = \lambda g.u(g) \vee v(g)$, u is an MPG$_\beta$ and v is an MPG$_\gamma$.
6. There exist objects u, v and $\beta < \alpha$ such that $a = \lambda g.u \supset v(g)$, $u\hat{}$ is an MPG$_\beta$ and u is true$_\beta$ implies that v is an MPG$_\gamma$ for some $\gamma < \alpha$.
7. There exists an object u such that $a = \lambda g.\forall u(g)$ and for any v, there exists a $\beta < \alpha$ such that $\lambda g.u(g)(v)$ is an MPG$_\beta$.
8. There exists an object u such that $a = \lambda g.\exists u(g)$ and for any v, there exists a $\beta < \alpha$ such that $\lambda g.u(g)(v)$ is an MPG$_\beta$.
9. There exist objects u and v such that $a = (u = v)\hat{}$.

(D)$_\alpha$ Let a be any object and let X be any collection of objects. Then a holds$_\alpha$ for X iff a is an MPG$_\alpha$ and one of the following conditions hold:

1. There exists an object v such that $a = \lambda g.g[v]$ and v is in X.
2. There exist objects u and v such that $a = u[v]\hat{}$ and u is a predicate$_\beta$ and v is in $[\![u]\!]_\beta$ where β is the birthday of the predicate u.
3. There exists an object u such that $a = \neg u\hat{}$ and u is not true$_{|u|}$.
4. There exist objects u and v such that $a = \lambda g.u(g) \wedge v(g)$, u holds$_{|u|}$ for X and v holds$_{|v|}$ for X.
5. There exist objects u and v such that $a = \lambda g.u(g) \vee v(g)$ and u holds$_{|u|}$ for X or v holds$_{|u|}$ for X.

6. There exist objects u and v such that $a = \lambda g.u \supset v(g)$ and u is $\text{true}_{|u|}$ implies v $\text{holds}_{|v|}$ for X.

7. There exists an object u such that $a = \lambda g.\forall u(g)$ and for any v, $\lambda g.u(g)(v)$ $\text{holds}_{|\lambda g.u(g)(v)|}$ for X.

8. There exists an object u such that $a = \lambda g.\exists u(g)$ and for some v, $\lambda g.u(g)(v)$ $\text{holds}_{|\lambda g.u(g)(v)|}$ for X.

9. There exist objects u and v such that $a = (u = v)^\frown$ and $u = v$.

(E)$_\alpha$ Let a be any object. Then a is true_α iff $a^\frown$ holds_α for the empty collection $\emptyset$ of objects.

(F)$_\alpha$ The statement R_α is:

> *Let a be any* MPG_α*, let X and Y be any collections of objects such that X is a subcollection of Y. Then if a* holds_α *for X then a also* holds_α *for Y.*

This can be proved by a simple inductive argument.

(G)$_\alpha$ Let a be any object. Then a is a predicate_α iff for all $\beta < \alpha$, a is *not* a predicate_β and (ii) for any object e there exists a $\beta < \alpha$ such that $\lambda g.a(g)(e)$ is an MPG_β.

(H)$_\alpha$ Let p be a predicate_α. For any collection X of objects, we define $\hat{p}(X)$ as the collection of objects a such that $\lambda g.p(g)(a)$ $\text{holds}_{|\lambda g.p(g)(a)|}$ for X. Then $(\text{G})_\alpha$ and the induction hypothesis guarantees that $\hat{p}(X)$ is well-defined for any X. By $(\text{F})_\alpha$, we see that $\hat{p}(X)$ is monononic in X. So, we can define $[\![p]\!]_\alpha$ as the smallest collection X of objects such that $\hat{p}(X)$ is a subcollection of X.

We have now carried out $(\text{A})_\alpha$-$(\text{H})_\alpha$ for each ordinal α. We will complete the construction of an **FSID**, by defining the notions of proposition, truth, MPG and a binary relation *hold*, and showing that they enjoy the expected properties. Let a be an object and X be a collection of objects. Then a is an *MPG* iff a is an MPG_α for some α and a *holds* for X iff a is an MPG and a $\text{holds}_{|a|}$ for X. Furthermore, a is a *proposition* iff $a^\frown$ is an MPG and a is *true* iff $a^\frown$ holds for $\emptyset$.

In order to see that we have actually obtained an **FSID**, we have to verify the logical schemata for the Frege structures and the conditions (ID-1)-(ID-4) for **FSID**. Since most of the verification is straightforward, we only verify a part of (ID-4) here. Let a be an MPG and p be a predicate. We show that $a(p)$ is a proposition and it is true iff a holds for $[\![p]\!]$ by induction on the birthday $|a|$ of a. By $(\text{C})_{|a|}$, there are 9 cases to be considered, but we prove only the three cases below.

- There exists an object v such that $a = \lambda g.g[v]$: $a(p) = p[v]$ becomes a proposition by (ID-2). Now, $a(p)$ is true iff $a(p)^\frown$ holds for $\emptyset$ iff $\lambda g.p[v]$ holds for $\emptyset$ iff v is in $[\![p]\!]$ iff a holds for $[\![p]\!]$.

- There exist objects u and v such that $a = u[v]^\frown$ and u is a predicate$_\beta$ and v is in $[\![u]\!]_\beta$ where β is the birthday of the predicate u: $a(p) = u[v]$ is a proposition, since u is a predicate. Now, $a(p)$ is true iff $u[v]^\frown$ holds for $\emptyset$ iff a holds for $[\![p]\!]$.
- There exist a proposition u and an object v such that $a = \lambda g.u \supset v(g)$ and u is true$_{|u|}$ implies v holds$_{|v|}$ for X: $a(p) = u \supset v(p)$ is a proposition since u is a proposition and $|v| < |a|$. Now, $a(p)$ is true iff u is true implies $v(p)$ is true, and by the induction hypothesis, this is equivalent to, u is true implies v holds for $[\![p]\!]$, which is equivalent to, a holds for $[\![p]\!]$.

We have thus constructed an **FSID** on the lambda structure $\mathcal{L}$. However the construction did not depend much on the particular structure of $\mathcal{L}$. We have used $\mathcal{L}$ only for the convenience of the explanation. In fact a complete parallel construction as above is possible for any lambda structure $\mathcal{F}$. So, suppose that a lambda structure $\mathcal{F}$ is given. As the initial setting for the construction, we take an independent family of primitive $\mathcal{F}$-functionals which include a logical constant $[] : \mathcal{F}_0 \times \mathcal{F}_0 \to \mathcal{F}_0$ as well as a list of other logical constants: $\neg, \wedge, \vee, \supset, =, \forall, \exists$. This is possible by Theorem 5.15 in [1]. Then a completely parallel construction as above gives us an **FSID** on $\mathcal{F}$. Thus we have the following theorem.

Theorem 9.1 *Any lambda structure can be enlarged to an* **FSID**.

Since any **FSID** is an N-standard Frege structure (Theorem 7.3), this theorem is a generalization of Theorem 6.10 in [1] which says that any lambda structure can be enlarged to an N-standard Frege structure,

Essentially the same method as above can be used to define RPT_ω within classical set theory.

10 Concluding remarks

We have introduced a constructive theory of proofs RPT_ω. For each $i < \omega$, RPT_ω contains RPT_i as its subtheory. Namely, for any objects a and b, $b \vdash_i a$ is a proposition of RPT_ω such that it is true if and only if b proves a at level i, and, similarly, $\models_i a$ is a proposition of RPT_ω such that it is true if and only if a is a proposition of level i. In this way, the concept of proposition (of level i) and the binary provability relation (of level i) are faithfully reflected in RPT_ω.

For any natural numbers i, j such that $i < j < \omega$, RPT_j becomes a metatheory of RPT_i. Because of this, for instance, we can prove in RPT_j, the fact that there are no propositional functions t of level i such that for all objects a, a is true at level i iff $t(a)$ is true at level i. In this way, we can state and prove most of the results in [1] concerning the properties of Frege structures, as internal theorems of RPT_1 (by considering the Frege structure determined by RPT_0).

We have not discussed about the formalization of the theory RPT_ω as a formal system in this paper. It is possible to formalize RPT_ω in a rather straightforward way. In fact Yukiyoshi Kameyama of our institute is now implementing such a system on a computer. The system is unique in that it is developed on top of (a slight extension of) Λ. The results of this development will be reported elsewhere.

Of course, once formalized as a formal system, we can capture only part of the whole truths due to the incompleteness of the formalized system. RPT_ω itself is given semantically and is free from such incompleteness. Assuming that the system has correctly formalized RPT_ω, and moreover it has been correctly implemented on a computer, the advantage of having such a computerized system is that we can use it as an error-free guide to arrive at true propositions of RPT_ω. Another advantage is that we can automatically get an executable programs from the proofs of these theorems and then, if we wish, we can execute them on the computer. We can then have a computer environment for constructive programming.

We have introduced the notion of Frege structures with inductively defined predicates, and showed that any lambda structure can be enlarged to a Frege structure with inductively defined predicates. So, for instance, starting from any lambda structure we can internally define the set of natural numbers and use mathematical induction as an admissible proof schema.

The idea of adding proof objects to Frege structures comes from Beeson [2]. Beeson, however, did not introduce these structures semantically. Instead, he proposed a formal system called RPS which has the predicate for provability relation in addition to the predicates for proposition and truth. He did not prove the consistency of RPT and left it as a conjecture. The conjecture was positively solved by Kobayashi [4]. We have introduced Frege structures with proof objects and proof structures semantically by generalizing some aspects of RPT.

References

[1] Aczel, P., Frege structures and the notions of proposition, truth and set, pp. 31-59 in *The Kleene Symposium*, Barwise, J., Keisler, H.J., Kunen, K. (eds.), North-Holland, 1980.

[2] Beeson, M.J., *Foundations of Constructive Mathematics*, Springer-Verlag, 1985.

[3] Feferman, S., A language and axioms for explicit mathematics, pp. 87-139 in *Algebra and Logic*, Lect. Notes in Math. 450, Crossley, J.N. (ed.), Springer-Verlag, 1975.

[4] Kobayashi, S., Consistency of Beeson's formal system RPS and some related results, pp. 120-140 in *Mathematical Logic and Applications*, Lect. Notes in Math. 1388, Shinoda, J., Slaman, T.A. and Tugué, T. (eds.), Springer-Verlag, 1987.

[5] Martin-Löf, P., *Intuitionistic Type Theory*, Bibliopolis, 1984.

[6] Sato, M. and Kameyama, Y., Constructive Programming in SST, pp. 23-30 in *Proceedings of the Japanese-Czechoslovak Seminar on Theoretical Foundations of Knowledge Information Processing* (ed. Arikawa, S. and Vlach, M.), Inorga, 1990.

[7] Takahashi, M., Parallel Reductions in λ-Calculus, *J. Symbolic Computation*, **7**, pp. 113-123, 1989.

[8] Tatsuta, M., Program Synthesis Using Realizability, *Theoret. Computer Sci.*, to appear.

From Term Models to Domains

Wesley Phoa
Department of Pure Mathematics and Mathematical Statistics
16 Mill Lane, Cambridge CB2 1SB, United Kingdom
wksp1@phx.cam.ac.uk

Abstract

Let B be the closed term model of the λ-calculus [illegible] ame Böhm tree are identified. We investigate which [illegible] ons (PERs) on B can be regarded as predomains or [illegible] the realizability topos on B, such PERs can be regard [illegible] ular model of constructive set theory.

No well-behaved partial order has been identi [illegible] out it is still possible to isolate those PERs which have [illegible] rtain sense, and all maps between such PERs in the [illegible] ma of chains. One can also define what it means for [illegible] ttom'; partial function spaces provide an example. [illegible] nts of arbitrary endofunctions exist and are compute [illegible] binator y. There is also a notion of meet-closure for which all maps are [illegible]

The categories of predomains are closed under the formation of total and partial function spaces, polymorphic types and convex powerdomains. (Subtyping and bounded quantification can also be modelled.) They in fact form reflective subcategories of the realizability topos; and in this set-theoretic context, these constructions are very simple to describe.

1 Introduction

This paper is an example of a new approach to domain theory: one in which a category of domains is built up directly from a particular model of computation, in a natural and intuitive framework, and using the tools of category theory and topos theory.

Domains are traditionally thought of as complete partial orders, of one kind or another. This makes it possible to interpret recursion, and to solve recursive domain equations; and indeed, classical domain theory has been quite successful. But it has its shortcomings: the mathematics can get very complicated; some programming language features (such as polymorphism and nondeterminism) are difficult to model, especially in combination; the treatment of effectivity is not very convincing; it's difficult to establish a relationship with operational semantics; and so on. The problem seems to be that domain theory throws away the idea of computability and replaces it with a mathematical analogy, namely continuity.

For a few years now, a different approach towards domain theory has been emerging, one incorporating computability in a direct and concrete way. Not everyone agrees on what it is, but it seems to combine at least two ideas:

- *A domains is a particular kind of set* in some appropriate model of constructive set theory. That is, we don't need to impose a complete partial order or any such additional structure; this is automatic, all set-theoretic functions between domains respect this automatic structure, and we can reason about domains—and perform constructions on domains—in a purely set-theoretic way. For example, exponentials are the full set-theoretic function spaces.

- *A domains is a particular kind of partial equivalence relation* on some model of the λ-calculus; or more generally, on some partial combinatory algebra. That is, we look for classes of domains sitting inside PER models for polymorphism.

(Both are due, in one way or another, to Dana Scott: see [21].) Note that one can regard *computability* as being built into both approaches; rather than singling out 'effective domains' and 'computable functions', *all* maps are computable: from the second point of view by definition, from the first by virtue of the particular model we pick.

The best way to combine the two approaches is to work inside a realizability topos. Roughly speaking, a *topos* is a category-theoretic model of constructive set theory; a *realizability topos* is a topos constructed using a partial combinatory algebra—for example, the partial recursive functions, or a model of the untyped λ-calculus. Such a topos contains a counterpart of the category of PERs, namely the (internal) category of *modest sets*: see [6] and [10].

A lot of effort has been concentrated on looking for domains in the effective topos (the realizability topos based on the partial recursive functions): first came the work of Rosolini [20], and later Phoa [12] and Freyd et al. [5], among others. More recently, people have been looking at continuous models of the λ-calculus: see, for example, Abadi and Plotkin [1] (these results have not yet been fitted into the topos-theoretic framework).

Before we start talking about a particular model, it will be useful to review the theory of realizability toposes and modest sets, and this is done in section 2. In view of the popularity of PER models for polymorphism, it's surprising that so few people are familiar with this point of view—for it is in this context that PER models seem most natural, since then they reduce to ordinary set theory.

In particular, results proved using the internal logic of a topos yield—when viewed externally—apparently stronger 'indexed' or 'uniform' results, which are often exactly what we need to model theories of dependent types or the calculus of constructions.

So in this case, the use of topos theory is not just conceptually attractive; it's saving us work as well.

Even more is true. Completeness in an appropriate sense ensures reflectivity; and this has good consequences (see [15] for an account). For example, the categories we will define admit a *convex powerdomain* construction, which exists for quite a trivial reason. This is not something we can deduce immediately if we insist on taking an external point of view, speaking only of closure under intersection, and so on....

The reader uncomfortable with topos theory should not be put off. The definitions and proofs in this paper make sense, word for word, as statements about PERs in the usual ('external') sense—though, read in this way, they are of course weaker. The fact that we're actually talking about PERs in an odd constructive universe is somehow transparent. So perhaps, on a first reading, it's safe just to ignore the words 'topos' and 'internal logic' and imagine that the statements and proofs are about PERs in the ordinary sense; we then obtain results similar in flavour to those presented in [1], though of course the underlying model is different and so the same techniques cannot be applied.

The actual results These are contained in section 3. The goal is to unify domain theory and the λ-calculus: not by using domains to model the λ-calculus, but by showing that the λ-calculus gives rise to categories of 'domains'. The whole approach relies on the basic fact that application is continuous with respect to the tree topology; the aim is to lift this result to a suitable class of PERs.

We work inside a certain realizability topos based on a particular (total) combinatory algebra: the closed term model B of the λ-calculus in which terms having the same Böhm tree are identified. This turns out to be just the right identification to make to get the continuity properties we need. Our reference for facts about this model, and the λ-calculus in general, is the book [2].

In contrast to, say, [12] or [8], this paper has quite a concrete flavour: we are interested in PERs themselves, and in the relationship between the type structure and the untyped computations. The idea is that computation really goes on at an untyped level—the type structure is just semantic scaffolding that falls away at run-time—and the theory should reflect this.

First we isolate a suitable notion of 'computable partial map' applicable to any object in the topos. (We need to do this so that we can model non-terminating programs.) The idea is to find an appropriate *dominance* (see [20]). The computable partial map classifier of an object will turn out to be the correct lifted domain construction.

The next step is to define a category of predomains. We say what it means for a PER (a modest set) to be **complete**—that is, to have 'sups of chains'—and show that *all* maps between complete PERs automatically preserve these sups. This is *not* achieved by defining a partial order on the PER, but more directly: the method is based on the idea of continuity in the sense of Böhm trees. Anyway, these PERs will be our predomains.

We say that a PER is **canonically focal**—has a 'bottom element'—if the unsolvable term is in its domain. It turns out that a complete, canonically focal PER has fixed points of endofunctions—and these may be calculated using the fixed point combinator y, as we might hope. Such a PER can thus be regarded as a domain.

The categories of predomains is, in an appropriate sense (see [10], [19]), *small* and *complete.* As mentioned before, this means that it's possible to construct polymorphic types; they provide models for the theory of constructions ([4], [9]). It's also possible to solve covariant domain equations (and hence to model recursively defined algebraic data types); and to construct convex powerdomains as free semilattices, in the way that was sketched in [12].

One can also say when a PER is 'meet-closed': the definition is again related to meets (intersections) of Böhm trees. And it can then be shown that all maps between meet-closed PERs must automatically be stable. The meet-relation also behaves properly with respect to the formation of products, exponentials and polymorphic types. However, this notion of stability is not yet well understood.

Note. The theorems we'll be proving are nearly all statements in the internal language. However, not all the proofs can be carried out entirely in the internal language; we'll need to use particular properties of the model, together with the characterization of validity in the internal language of a realizability topos as explained in [6]. So someone unfamiliar with these matters will find many of the arguments a bit mysterious. Hopefully a more satisfactory presentation will be available one day.

2 Realizability toposes and modest sets

2.1 Realizability toposes

I have to assume some familiarity with topos theory. But for those who know nothing about it: a topos $\mathcal{E}$ is a category with some additional structure that lets us regard it, very roughly speaking, as a model of constructive set theory. If we are working inside a fixed topos $\mathcal{E}$, we often abuse language by calling its objects 'sets'.

Any topos $\mathcal{E}$ has an *internal logic*: (almost) any set-theoretic or mathematical statement ϕ can be interpreted in $\mathcal{E}$, and it makes sense to say that ϕ is or is not 'true'—i.e. valid—in $\mathcal{E}$. And in general, any statement that is constructively provable is valid in any topos; for example,

$$\forall n \in \mathbb{N}.\, \exists p \in \mathbb{N}.\, p \text{ is prime} \wedge p > n.$$

However, a classically provable statement need not be valid in an arbitrary topos; for example, $\neg\neg\phi \rightarrow \phi$ and $\phi \vee \neg\phi$ will not in general be valid.

Recall that a **partial combinatory algebra** A is a set equipped with a partial binary operation $\mathsf{A} \times \mathsf{A} \rightharpoonup \mathsf{A}$, 'application', and with designated elements $\mathsf{s}, \mathsf{k} \in \mathsf{A}$ satisfying the usual axioms. For example, any model of the λ-calculus is a partial (in fact, a total) combinatory algebra; another example would be the partial recursive functions.

The particular toposes we are concerned with will be constructed using partial combinatory algebras. A statement of set theory is 'true' in such a topos exactly when there is an element of the algebra (an operation) that computes evidence for its truth. The logic we must use is constructive just because we have this computational interpretation of truth.

Thought of as models of constructive set theory, these toposes extend the realizability interpretation of constructive logic. For example, to say that

$$\forall n \in \mathbb{N}.\, \exists p \in \mathbb{N}.\, p \text{ is prime} \wedge p > n$$

is valid amounts to saying that there exists an element $a \in \mathsf{A}$ such that for any Church numeral c_n, $a\mathsf{c}_n$ is a Church numeral c_p where p is a prime $> n$.

The construction of the realizability topos $\mathcal{E}$ associated to a partial combinatory algebra A is due to Hyland: see [6] (Powell had the same idea a little earlier, but his work has never appeared in print; in any case, Hyland's categorical framework will be more useful for the purposes of this paper).

Assemblies Rather than describe the construction of these categories—which is rather complicated—I just want to describe a subcategory of $\mathcal{E}$ that is more familiar and easier to think about.

Let A be a combinatory algebra. An **A-valued assembly** (or just an **assembly** if A is understood) consists of a set X together with, for each $x \in X$, a nonempty subset $|x \in X| \subseteq \mathsf{A}$. We think of this as a set of 'codes for x'; as x varies, these subsets need not necessarily be disjoint. (In the case $\mathsf{A} = \mathbb{N}$, the indices for partial recursive functions, A-valued assemblies are usually called **ω-sets**; they have been widely used in the semantics of various typed λ-calculi.)

If X and Y are two assemblies, a map $X \to Y$ is defined to be a function $f\colon X \to Y$ between the underlying sets, for which there exists an element $a \in \mathsf{A}$ such that for all $x \in X$,

$$p \in |x \in X| \longrightarrow ap \in |f(x) \in Y|$$

(we say that a **tracks** f).

Let *Sep* be the category of (A-valued) assemblies; it has finite limits and is cartesian closed. It also contains the ordinary category of sets: there is a full embedding *Sets* $\hookrightarrow$ *Sep*. This even has a left adjoint. On the other hand, there are plenty of objects which are not in the image of this embedding. For example, A itself gives rise to an assembly $\mathbb{A}$, with underlying set A and

$$|a| = \{a\}$$

for all $a \in \mathsf{A}$.

Sep is not a topos. The authors of [5] show how to construct a topos $\mathcal{E}$ out of *Sep* in a fairly simple way; this is called the **realizability topos** on A, basically because it provides a realizability interpretation of (a certain kind of) constructive set theory. *Sep* turns out to be a reflective subcategory of $\mathcal{E}$; in fact, a lot more can be said, though for this it's better to look at Hyland's original construction. See [6] for details, and in particular an explanation of why *Sep* is called '*Sep*'.

Some remarks on the logic Any topos contains an object Ω of truth-values, endowed with an entailment relation $\leq$. For example, in *Sets* (the ordinary category of sets), $\Omega = \{\top, \bot\}$ where $\bot \leq \top$.

In the realizability topos $\mathcal{E}$ arising from a partial combinatory algebra A, Ω looks roughly as follows: the truth-values are subsets of A, and if $p, q \subseteq \mathsf{A}$ then $p \leq q$ exactly when there is an element $a \in \mathsf{A}$ such that $ab \in q$ for all $b \in p$. (This is not a precise description of Ω; in fact, as Ω is not an assembly, we aren't in a position to describe it precisely. So be warned that the preceding remarks are an oversimplification.)

If X is an object of $\mathcal{E}$, we can regard a mono $X' \rightarrowtail X$ as giving us a 'subset' of X. To each such subset there corresponds a map $\phi\colon X \to \Omega$, its characteristic function. Such a map ϕ can be identified with a predicate on X, whose extension is X'. In other words, we can think of X' as being

$$\{x \mid \phi(x)\} \rightarrowtail X$$

(and in fact, we often define subsets of X by specifying predicates on X). ϕ is 'true' or valid if X' is the whole of X.

Because the logic of $\mathcal{E}$ is constructive, if ϕ is a predicate on X then ϕ and $\neg\neg\phi$ are not in general the same: if they do happen to coincide, ϕ is called **$\neg\neg$-closed**. If X is an A-valued assembly, thought of as an object of $\mathcal{E}$, the $\neg\neg$-closed predicates on X correspond exactly to the (ordinary) subsets of the underlying set of X. More general predicates on X correspond to subsets whose elements are endowed with extra intensional information.

The following example may help, though it's not needed in what follows. Let A be $\mathbb{N}$, the set of indices for partial recursive functions; the corresponding realizability topos is called *Eff*, the effective topos. As before, $\mathbb{N}$ is the underlying set of an assembly, where we simply put

$$|n| = \{n\}$$

as above; we will also call this assembly $\mathbb{N}$.

If $C \subseteq \mathbb{N}$ is a subset of natural numbers (in the ordinary sense) then it is the underlying set of an assembly: just put

$$|n| = \{n\}$$

again. The identity function tracks a mono $\bar{C} \rightarrowtail \mathbb{N}$ in *Sep* (and so in *Eff*, since *Sep* is a full subcategory of *Eff*) and this mono corresponds to a $\neg\neg$-closed predicate ϕ on $\mathbb{N}$.

However, $\phi \vee \neg\phi$ is not a $\neg\neg$-closed predicate on $\mathbb{N}$. It corresponds to a mono $\bar{C} \vee \neg\bar{C} \rightarrowtail \mathbb{N}$, where $\bar{C} \vee \neg\bar{C}$ denotes the assembly with underlying set $\mathbb{N}$ where we put

$$|n| = \begin{cases} \{\langle n, 0\rangle\} & n \notin C \\ \{\langle n, 1\rangle\} & n \in C \end{cases}$$

There is one particular example of a $\neg\neg$-closed predicate that is worth mentioning. The diagonal inclusion $\mathsf{A} \rightarrowtail \mathsf{A} \times \mathsf{A}$ gives us a mono $\mathbb{A} \rightarrowtail \mathbb{A} \times \mathbb{A}$ that corresponds to the equality predicate $\mathbb{A} \times \mathbb{A} \to \Omega$ taking $\langle a, b \rangle \mapsto |a = b|$. So the equality predicate is $\neg\neg$-closed:

$$\neg\neg|a = b| \;\to\; |a = b|.$$

More information may be found in [6]; for example, it is proved there that $\mathcal{S}ep$ is simply the category of $\neg\neg$-separated objects in $\mathcal{E}$ (from which it follows immediately that $\mathcal{S}ep$ is reflective in $\mathcal{E}$, locally cartesian closed and so on). $\mathcal{S}ets$ is also a full reflective subcategory of $\mathcal{E}$, via the embedding $\mathcal{S}ets \hookrightarrow \mathcal{S}ep$; it can be identified with the category of $\neg\neg$-sheaves.

2.2 Modest sets and completeness

Call an assembly a **modest set** if two different elements never share a common code; that is, if for all $x, x' \in X$,

$$x \neq x' \longrightarrow |x \in X| \cap |x' \in X| = \varnothing.$$

Let $\mathcal{M}od$ be the full subcategory of $\mathcal{S}ep$ whose objects are the modest sets; it contains, for example, the object $\mathbb{A}$. Indeed, the modest sets are exactly the quotients of $\mathbb{A}$ in $\mathcal{E}$ under $\neg\neg$-closed partial equivalence relations: that is, symmetric, transitive relations R on $\mathbb{A}$ satisfying

$$\neg\neg(aRa') \to aRa'.$$

(Remember that the logic is constructive, so this is a nontrivial condition; it says, somehow, that the statement aRa' contains no intensional information.)

This category is essentially the same as the category Per of ordinary PERs on A: for these are certain subsets of $\mathsf{A} \times \mathsf{A}$, which correspond to $\neg\neg$-closed predicates on $\mathbb{A} \times \mathbb{A}$.

Another way to see this is as follows: notice that any PER R gives rise to an assembly, where we have

- underlying set $\mathsf{A}/R = \{R\text{-equivalence classes}\}$;
- if $u \in \mathsf{A}/R$, $|u \in \mathsf{A}/R| = u \subseteq \mathsf{A}$.

(That is, the codes for an equivalence class are the elements of the equivalence class.) Then we get another full embedding $\mathsf{Per} \hookrightarrow \mathcal{S}ep$ that preserves finite limits and the cartesian closed structure; and the image of I is equivalent to $\mathcal{M}od$.

So far this is rather external. The point is that there is an internal category $\mathbb{M}\mathbf{od}$ in $\mathcal{E}$—the category of $\neg\neg$-closed partial equivalence relations on $\mathbb{A}$ and maps between them—whose 'externalization' (in a certain sense) is $\mathcal{M}od$. The fact that any map between modest sets is tracked by an element of A can also be expressed by a valid formula in the internal language, which for $\mathcal{E}\!f\!f$ is called *generalized Church's thesis*: see [6].

The reason why the PER model of polymorphism works is that **Mod** is, in a suitable sense (see [10] and [20]), *complete.* Hence, for example, polymorphic types $\Pi X.T(X)$ can be taken to be $\mathbf{Mod}_0$-indexed products $\Pi_{X \in \mathbf{Mod}} T(X)$, where $\mathbf{Mod}_0$ is the object-of-objects of the internal category **Mod**. This is the so-called Moggi-Hyland 'set-theoretic' interpretation of polymorphism. (Other interpretations based on modest sets do exist, some of them better behaved.)

Note. Actually, we need the language of indexed categories or fibrations to formulate all this properly; everything ought to be regarded as a fibration: see [10]. The theory of fibrations won't be discussed here; what this approach amounts to, though, is considering families $\{X_i\}_{i \in I}$ of modest sets 'indexed' by arbitrary objects $I \in \mathcal{E}$ (not just by ordinary sets); by 'completeness' we mean, for example, closure under 'products' indexed by objects $I \in \mathcal{E}$. See also [19].

In fact, it is only those families indexed by assemblies $I \in \mathcal{S}ep$ that are well-behaved, and $\mathcal{M}od$ is really only complete (in the sense appropriate to fibrations) indexed over $\mathcal{S}ep$; however, this is enough to deduce all the results we need. For example, **Mod** is an internal category in $\mathcal{S}ep$, not just in $\mathcal{E}f\!f$, and in particular $\mathbf{Mod}_0 \in \mathcal{S}ep$; so the Moggi-Hyland interpretation does carry through.

2.3 Partial maps and dominances

If we restrict ourselves to the ordinary category of modest sets, then all maps are computable; that is, all *total* functions. But (as usual in computer science) we will also be interested in partial functions; and because the notion of subobject in a realizability topos is very flexible, there are many partial maps which cannot be regarded as computable. We want to be able to isolate a smaller class of computable partial maps.

Building on ideas due to Mulry and Scott, Rosolini developed a general category-theoretic framework for discussing partial maps. The idea is to single out an appropriate subset $\Sigma \rightarrowtail \Omega$ of truth-values—which may be regarded as the 'computable' truth-values. A subobject $X' \rightarrowtail X$ whose characteristic function takes values in Σ will be called a **Σ-subset** (we then write $X' \subset_\Sigma X$); it will turn out that—if we choose the right Σ—the partial maps whose domains are Σ-subsets are exactly the ones which can be regarded as computable.

Let $\Sigma \rightarrowtail \Omega$ be a subset of the object of truth-values. Then Σ is a **dominance** if

$$\top \in \Sigma;$$
$$p \in \Sigma \wedge (p = \top \rightarrow q \in \Sigma) \rightarrow (p \wedge q) \in \Sigma.$$

(That is, if these statements are valid in the internal logic.) These conditions ensure that partial maps whose domains are Σ-subsets form a category: they contain identity maps and are closed under composition.

It may be more enlightening to cast these conditions in an 'external' form. Stated this way, they say that

- $X \subset_\Sigma X$ for any object X; and
- if $X \subset_\Sigma Y$ and $Y \subset_\Sigma Z$ then $X \subset_\Sigma Z$.

These conditions have to be interpreted in a suitable 'indexed' or fibred sense, however; that is, we have to talk about (internal) families of objects, and families of Σ-subsets. I won't spell this out.

The most well-known example of a dominance is the *r.e. subobject classifier* (see [20]) in the effective topos $\mathcal{E}\!f\!f$. Σ-subsets in this case are a generalization of r.e. subsets—we can talk about a Σ-subset of any object of $\mathcal{E}\!f\!f$, not just of $\mathbb{N}$)—and partial maps whose domains are Σ-subsets are generalized partial recursive functions.

Once we've fixed a dominance Σ, we have a notion of partial map classifier. Given an object $X \in \mathcal{E}$, we say that another object $X_\perp$ is a **Σ-partial map classifier** for X if, for any object Y, there is a natural bijection between partial maps $Y \rightharpoonup X$ with domain a Σ-subset and (total) maps $Y \to X_\perp$. (The object $X_\perp$ is necessarily unique; it is also called the **lift** of X.)

Note that we then have partial function spaces: the partial function space $[Y \rightharpoonup X]$ is just the ordinary exponential ${X_\perp}^Y$.

The preceding remarks apply when we want to talk about computable partial maps between any two objects of the topos. However, it's sometimes the case that we're only interested in a particular subcategory $\mathcal{C}$ of a topos: for example, $\mathcal{S}ep$ or $\mathcal{M}od$. In this case we would only require that Σ satisfy the (external) conditions for being a dominance in the case where all the objects lie in $\mathcal{C}$; and similarly, we would require that for $X \in \mathcal{C}$ there was an object $X_\perp \in \mathcal{C}$ satisfying an appropriate universal property for Σ-partial maps $Y \rightharpoonup X$ with $Y \in \mathcal{C}$. (Again, these statements have to be read in an appropriate 'indexed' sense.) We could say that we had a dominance, and partial map classifiers, *relative to* $\mathcal{C}$.

There are several general methods for constructing the Σ-partial map classifier $X_\perp$; rather than give a categorical construction here, we will give an explicit description later on once we've defined the particular dominance Σ we need.

2.4 A criterion for reflectivity

In [12], the category of complete Σ-spaces was shown to be complete; one could deduce from this that it was reflective—see [14],[15] for more of the technical details. In this paper we will be working the other way: we'll show that certain categories of PERs (i.e. subcategories of $\mathbb{M}\mathbf{od}$) are reflective, and deduce that they are complete.

The following result will be a useful tool. Note that all the statements are meant to be interpreted in the internal language.

Proposition 2.4.1 *Let $\mathbb{C}_0$ be an (internal) collection of PERs such that*

- *if $(R_i)_{i\in I}$ is any internal family of PERs in $\mathbb{C}_0$, then their intersection $\bigcap_{i\in I} R_i$ is also in $\mathbb{C}_0$;*

- *if $a \in \mathbb{A}$ and $R \in \mathbb{C}_0$ then $a^{-1}R \in \mathbb{C}_0$, where*

$$p(a^{-1}R)q \quad\longleftrightarrow\quad (ap)R(aq);$$

- *the full subcategory $\mathbb{C}$ of $\mathbf{Mod}$ with object-of-objects $\mathbb{C}_0$ is closed under the formation of equalizers in $\mathbf{Mod}$; that is, if $R, S \in \mathbb{C}_0$ and $a, b \in \mathbb{A}$ track maps $\mathbb{A}/R \rightrightarrows \mathbb{A}/S$ then the PER E is in $\mathbb{C}_0$, where*

$$pEq \quad\longleftrightarrow\quad (pRq \wedge (ap)S(bq)).$$

Then there is a reflection functor $\mathbf{Mod} \to \mathbb{C}$.

Proof. (Sketch.) Let R be any PER in $\mathbf{Mod}_0$; we'll construct a PER $\tilde{R}$ that's its reflection into $\mathbb{C}$. In fact, let

$$\tilde{R} = \bigcap_{S\in\mathbb{C}_0, R\subseteq S} S$$

and note that the identity $\mathsf{i} \in \mathbb{A}$ tracks a map $r\colon \mathbb{A}/R \to \mathbb{A}/\tilde{R}$.

To see that this gives us the reflection, let $a \in \mathbb{A}$ track a map $f\colon \mathbb{A}/R \to \mathbb{A}/T$ where $T \in \mathbb{C}_0$. Then since $\tilde{R} \subseteq a^{-1}T$, this map f factors through $\mathbb{A}/\tilde{R}$ (a tracks a map $\mathbb{A}/a^{-1}T \to \mathbb{A}/T$, hence $\mathbb{A}/\tilde{R} \to \mathbb{A}/T$).

To see that this factorization is unique, let a, a' track maps $\mathbb{A}/\tilde{R} \rightrightarrows \mathbb{A}/T$, and let $E \subseteq \tilde{R}$ be a PER representing their equalizer, as above. Then $E \in \mathbb{C}_0$ and $R \subseteq E$ (because a and a' both track factorizations of f); so $\tilde{R} \subseteq E$, i.e. $E = \tilde{R}$. ■

2.5 Calculating indexed products

The following result lets us avoid a few calculations when we're trying to show that some class of modest sets is closed under arbitrary products (indexed by objects of $\mathcal{E}$). Closure under exponentiation by arbitrary objects of $\mathcal{E}$ will follow, since the exponential X^Y is just a Y-indexed product.

Proposition 2.5.1 *Let $\mathbb{C}_0$ be a $\neg\neg$-closed subobject of $\mathbf{Mod}_0$; think of it as defining a full subfibration $\mathcal{C}$ of $\mathcal{M}od$ (over $\mathcal{S}ep$). Then to show that $\mathcal{C}$ is closed under indexed products along all arrows in $\mathcal{S}ep$, it suffices to show that*

- *$\mathcal{C}$ is an exponential ideal (that is, if $X \in \mathcal{C}$ then $X^Y \in \mathcal{C}$ for any object Y); and*

- *if $(R_i)_{i\in I}$ is a family of PERs in $\mathbb{C}_0$ indexed by an object I in the image of $\mathcal{S}ets \hookrightarrow \mathcal{E}$ then their intersection $\bigcap_{i\in I} R_i \in \mathbb{C}_0$.*

Note. We use the same argument that was used in [7], and the proof assumes that the reader is familiar with [7]. Actually, the result is really about completeness over $\mathcal{S}ep$; but the result implies closure under indexed products (in a weak sense, cf. [10]) along arbitrary maps of the topos.

Proof. (Sketch; section numbers in this proof refer to [7].) We can conclude from the second condition that $\mathcal{C}$ is closed under indexed products along all maps of $\neg\neg$-sheaves (that is, thought of as fibred over $\mathcal{S}ets$, it's closed under indexed products).

Since $\mathbb{C}_0$ is a $\neg\neg$-closed subobject of a $\neg\neg$-sheaf, and hence itself a $\neg\neg$-sheaf, any map $X \to \mathbb{C}_0$ determines (as in 2.5) a diagram

$$\begin{array}{ccccc} R & \longrightarrow & R' & \longrightarrow & R'' \\ \downarrow & & \downarrow & & \downarrow \\ X & \longrightarrow & sX & \longrightarrow & aX \end{array}$$

(where sX is the reflection of X into $\mathcal{S}ep$, and aX is its $\neg\neg$-sheafification), in which both squares are pullbacks.

Now apply the argument of 2.7. ∎

Of course, checking the hypotheses still involves *some* stuffing around with PERs.

3 Categories of predomains (and domains)

3.1 Partial maps and lifting

As I mentioned, in this section we'll be dealing with the closed term model B of the λ-calculus in which terms having the same Böhm tree are identified. $\mathcal{E}$ will denote the corresponding realizability topos, and $\mathbb{B}$ the assembly constructed from B in the standard way, as described earlier; we can regard $\mathbb{B}$ as an object of $\mathcal{E}$. By they way, the results in this section also hold for the Böhm tree model (see [2]), and can probably be extended to some other models.

We'll sometimes talk about a combinator like k or s as if it were an element of the model; what we really mean is the corresponding λ-expression. For example, we'll write i instead of $\lambda x.x$. Also, if M is a term, we will write $\mathrm{BT}(M)$ for the Böhm tree of M. Finally, the symbol Ω will stand for the term $\Omega = (\lambda x.xx)(\lambda x.xx)$ (or any other unsolvable term; all are identified in the model).

[This is an unfortunate clash of notation, since we previously used Ω to denote the subobject classifier of $\mathcal{E}$. But both usages are standard; and anyway, one can always tell from the context whether Ω is a term or an object.]

Let Σ be the B-valued assembly with underlying set $\{\top, \bot\}$ and

$$|\bot| = \Omega, \quad |\top| = \mathsf{i}.$$

The idea is that Ω represents divergence and i flags convergence. We think of Σ as being an object of $\mathcal{E}$. In fact it can be defined using the internal logic: it is simply the subset $\{M|\phi(M)\}$ of $\mathbb{B}$, where $\phi(M)$ is the predicate

$$\neg(M = \Omega) \to (M = \mathsf{i}).$$

ϕ is clearly $\neg\neg$-closed, so Σ is in fact a modest set. The important fact is that Σ is actually a subset of Ω, the object of truth-values. More precisely,

Proposition 3.1.1 *Σ is isomorphic to the subset*

$$\Sigma_1 = \{p|\,\exists! M \in \mathbb{B}.\,(\neg p \leftrightarrow (M = \Omega)) \wedge (p \leftrightarrow (M = \mathsf{i}))\}$$

of Ω.

Proof. There is a map $\Sigma_1 \to \Sigma$ taking $p \mapsto M$. We can also define a map $\Sigma \to \Omega$ taking $M \mapsto |M = \mathsf{i}|$; this actually maps into Σ_1 (we must check that $\neg(M = \mathsf{i}) \leftrightarrow (M = \Omega)$ and $(M = \mathsf{i}) \leftrightarrow (M = \mathsf{i})$, which is easy). These two maps are mutually inverse. ■

It seems likely that Σ is a dominance, but the proof would be rather messy. In any case we only need the following, weaker, result.

Proposition 3.1.2 *Σ is a dominance relative to $\mathcal{S}ep$.*

Proof. We need to prove that $X \subset_\Sigma X$ for any object X, and that a Σ-subset of a Σ-subset is a Σ-subset. The first statement is easily seen to be true; so we simply need to show that if $X \subset_\Sigma Y$ and $Y \subset_\Sigma Z$ then $X \subset_\Sigma Z$.

Suppose M tracks the classifying map of $X \subset_\Sigma Y$, and N tracks the classifying map of $Y \subset_\Sigma Z$; then the classifier of $X \subset_\Sigma Z$ is tracked by

$$\lambda x.Nx(Mx)$$

(and observe that for any term P, if NP is unsolvable then so is $NP(MP)$, no matter what MP is).
[Note that this proof is very 'uniform' in character; it can easily be modified to prove the indexed versions of the conditions, which are what we really have to verify.] ■

Now to describe the lift of a modest set. Intuitively, if R is a PER then the 'lifted PER' $R_\perp$ is defined by: $\Omega R_\perp \Omega$, and if MRM then $M_\bullet R_\perp M_\bullet$ where $M_\bullet = \lambda z.z\mathsf{i}M$. (The motivation is that i is a 'flag' indicating convergence of a computation; note that a computation might converge and yield the answer Ω, and this is different from diverging.) But we need to be able to formalize this definition in the internal logic; and we want the PER $R_\perp$ to be $\neg\neg$-closed. We need to be a bit more careful.

So if R is a PER, define a PER $R_\perp$ by

$$MR_\perp N \quad \longleftrightarrow \quad \neg(M = N = \Omega) \rightarrow (((M\mathsf{f})R(N\mathsf{f}) \wedge M\mathsf{k} = N\mathsf{k} = \mathsf{i}))$$

(where $\mathsf{f} = \lambda xy.y$). Some fiddling with intuitionistic logic verifies that this gives us a $\neg\neg$-closed relation (using the fact that R is $\neg\neg$-closed), as we'd like. Note that if we'd tried to define $R_\perp$ by cases—that is, by a formula containing a disjunction—it would not have been $\neg\neg$-closed.

Proposition 3.1.3 *If $Y \cong \mathbb{B}/R$, then $Y_\perp \cong \mathbb{B}/R_\perp$ (where $Y_\perp$ denotes the Σ-partial map classifier relative to Sep).*

Proof. First observe that $Y \subset_\Sigma \mathbb{B}/R_\perp$; its classifier $\mathbb{B}/R_\perp \rightarrow \Sigma$ is tracked by

$$\lambda x.x\mathsf{i}.$$

Suppose $X' \subset_\Sigma X$, M tracks a map $X' \rightarrow Y$ and N tracks the classifier $X \rightarrow \Sigma$ of X'. Then the corresponding map $X \rightarrow \mathbb{B}/R_\perp$ is tracked by

$$\lambda x.(Nx)(\lambda z.z(Mx))$$

(and note again that if NP is unsolvable then applying NP to $\lambda z.z(MP)$ will give us something unsolvable).

The converse is easy. ■

Call a PER R **canonically focal** if $\Omega R\Omega$; call a modest set a **canonically focal set** if it's the quotient of $\mathbb{B}$ by a canonically focal PER. It follows from the above discussion that lifts of modest sets may be taken to be canonically focal. And 2.5.1 can be used to prove:

Proposition 3.1.4 *The fibration of canonically focal sets is closed under indexed products (over Sep).*

A reminder: Since the class of canonically focal PERs isn't closed under isomorphism, a statement like this has to be interpreted with care.

3.2 A kind of chain completeness

In contrast to the situation in $\mathcal{E}\!f\!f$, described in [12], there's no obvious way to define an intrinsic preorder on objects of the topos, or even just on modest sets (see the remark in the next section). We have to define 'chain completeness' in a more concrete way, looking at the PERs themselves.

We will constantly be using the fact that 'application is continuous with respect to the Böhm tree topology': that is, if M is any term and N_n, N are terms with

$$\mathrm{BT}(N_1) \subseteq \mathrm{BT}(N_2) \subseteq \mathrm{BT}(N_3) \ldots$$

and

$$\mathrm{BT}(N) = \bigcup_n \mathrm{BT}(N_n)$$

then

$$\mathrm{BT}(MN) = \bigcup_n \mathrm{BT}(MN_n).$$

(This is actually a special case of a more general theorem; see [2, chapter 19]). We will abuse notation and write

$$M(\bigcup_n N_n) = \bigcup_n MN_n.$$

Now, let c_n denote the nth Church numeral and define

$$\ulcorner n \urcorner = \lambda f.\mathsf{c}_n f \Omega;$$

that is,

$$\ulcorner 0 \urcorner = \lambda f.\Omega,\ \ulcorner 1 \urcorner = \lambda f.f\Omega,\ \ulcorner 2 \urcorner = \lambda f.f(f\Omega), \ldots$$

Observe that, in a sense, the terms $\ulcorner n \urcorner$ form a sequence of approximations to the fixed point combinator

$$\mathsf{y} = \lambda f.(\lambda x.f(xx))(\lambda x.f(xx))\ ;$$

we say this because

$$\mathrm{BT}(\mathsf{y}) = \bigcup_n \mathrm{BT}(\ulcorner n \urcorner).$$

Call a PER R **complete** if it satisfies the following condition: for all terms M and N,

$$(\forall n.\,(M\ulcorner n \urcorner)R(N\ulcorner n \urcorner)) \longrightarrow (M\mathsf{y})R(N\mathsf{y}).$$

And call a modest set **complete** if it's the quotient of $\mathbb{B}$ by a complete PER.

Proposition 3.2.1 *The category of complete modest sets is reflective.*

Proof. Closure under intersection is obvious; and it's straightforward to show, using the fact that application is continuous, that the other hypotheses of 2.4.1 also hold. ■

There is one particularly interesting example of a complete PER. Let ω be the B-valued assembly with underlying set $\{0, 1, 2, \ldots\}$ and put

$$|n| = \{\ulcorner n \urcorner\};$$

and let $\bar{\omega}$ be the B-valued assembly with underlying set $\{0, 1, 2, \ldots, \infty\}$ and put

$$|n| = \{\ulcorner n \urcorner\},\ |\infty| = \{\mathsf{y}\};$$

there is an obvious mono $\omega \rightarrowtail \bar{\omega}$.

Note that any map from ω into a complete modest set extends uniquely to $\bar{\omega}$; in fact, the defining condition for complete PERs tells us that if M tracks a map $\omega \to X$ then it also tracks the extension $\bar{\omega} \to X$.

We have a continuity result which is easy but important: Any map between complete modest sets 'preserves sups of chains'; more precisely,

Proposition 3.2.2 *Let X and Y be complete modest sets, and let $f: X \to Y$. If $g: \omega \to X$ extends (uniquely) to $h: \bar{\omega} \to X$, then the unique extension of $fg: \omega \to Y$ to a map $\bar{\omega} \to Y$ is just fh.*

Proof. By the uniqueness of extensions, it suffices to show that fh extends fg; that is, that they agree on ω. But they do, because h extends g. ■

And we do have sups of enough chains to be able to calculate fixed points (which, after all, was the main reason why we wanted 'chain completeness').

Proposition 3.2.3 *Suppose X is complete and canonically focal; then any map $X \to X$ has a fixed point. In fact, there is a fixed point operator $X^X \to X$.*

Remark. In other words, X has the so-called *fixed point property.* This property was first studied by Lawvere, and many years later Scott suggested that it could prove useful in an axiomatic treatment of domain theory.

Proof. Suppose we have a map $X \to X$ tracked by a term P. Define $\omega \to X$ to be the map tracked by the term

$$M = \lambda x.xP;$$

this extends to a map $\bar{\omega} \to X$.

By the definition of complete PER, M tracks the extended map $\bar{\omega} \to X$. But $M\mathsf{y} = \mathsf{y}P$ is a code for a fixed point of the map $X \to X$ (indeed, a fixed point 'on the nose' for codes).

The internal version—that there exists a fixed point operator $X^X \to X$, tracked by y—follows from this argument by adding some λ's. ■

Note the oddly intensional nature of this proof (y actually computes a fixed point 'on the nose' for codes); it has a rather different flavour from the usual fixed-point theorem for domains. I have not tried to formulate an appropriate notion of fixed-point induction yet.

3.3 All maps are stable?

One interesting feature of the approach we've taken is that we can easily incorporate stability; this is because of the theorems of Berry about stability in the λ-calculus (again, see [2]). The actual results in this section are extremely simple. The main thing to notice is that we have to be careful in the way we talk about meets.

In the λ-calculus this is how things go: Given terms M and N, say that $M \uparrow N$ if there exists a term P such that

$$\mathrm{BT}(M), \mathrm{BT}(N) \subseteq \mathrm{BT}(P)$$

(we call M and N a 'bounded pair of terms'). If $M \uparrow N$ then we define $M \sqcap N$ to be the term with Böhm tree

$$\mathrm{BT}(M) \cap \mathrm{BT}(N).$$

(Note that this defines $M \sqcap N$ uniquely as an element of B.) But this doesn't internalize; there is no 'meet' map $\sqcap\colon \mathbb{B} \times \mathbb{B} \rightharpoonup \mathbb{B}$ in $\mathcal{E}$ that takes a bounded pair of terms to their meet:

Proposition 3.3.1 *There does not exist a term Q such that*

$$M \uparrow N \longrightarrow QMN \simeq M \sqcap N$$

where $\simeq$ denotes equality of Böhm trees (equality in B).

Proof. This is an easy consequence of [2, theorem 14.4.12]: Observe that for any terms M and N, $\Omega \uparrow N$ and $M \uparrow \Omega$; so if Q exists,

$$Q\Omega N \simeq QM\Omega \simeq \Omega\,;$$

it follows that $QMN \simeq \Omega$ for all M, N. ∎

However, we do have a $\neg\neg$-closed relation

$$\mathbf{Meet} \stackrel{\mathrm{def}}{=} \{\langle M, N, P\rangle \,|\, (M \uparrow N) \wedge (P = M \sqcap N)\} \rightarrowtail \mathbb{B} \times \mathbb{B} \times \mathbb{B}$$

This is just the subobject of $\mathbb{B} \times \mathbb{B} \times \mathbb{B}$ corresponding to the ordinary subset

$$\{\langle M, N, P\rangle \,|\, (M \uparrow N) \wedge (P = M \sqcap N)\} \subset \mathsf{B} \times \mathsf{B} \times \mathsf{B};$$

in the absence of a 'meet' map we have to state everything in terms of this relation. But we will generally abuse notation and write

$$P = M \sqcap N$$

as an abbreviation for $\langle M, N, P\rangle \in \mathbf{Meet}$.

Call a PER R **meet-closed** if

$$\forall P = M \sqcap N,\ P' = M' \sqcap N'.\ (MRM' \wedge NRN') \rightarrow (PRP');$$

and call a modest set $X \cong \mathbb{B}/R$ **meet-closed** if R is meet-closed. Note that we can then define a certain $\neg\neg$-closed relation

$$\mathbf{Meet}_X \rightarrowtail X \times X \times X,$$

namely the quotient of **Meet** by R (in the obvious sense). And given $x_1, x_2, x \in X$, we will write

$$x = x_1 \sqcap x_2$$

as an abbreviation for $\langle x_1, x_2, x\rangle \in \mathbf{Meet}_X$.

The following results say that all maps between meet-closed PERs are stable, and that the category of meet-closed PERs is well-behaved.

Proposition 3.3.2 *If X and Y are meet-closed modest sets and $f: X \rightarrow Y$, then for all $x_1, x_2, x \in X$,*

$$x = x_1 \sqcap x_2 \longrightarrow f(x) = f(x_1) \sqcap f(x_2).$$

Proof. Immediate from the fact that application of λ-terms is stable: [2, corollary 14.4.11]. (Spelled out, this result says that if $P = M \sqcap N$ then $QP = QM \sqcap QN$.) ■

Proposition 3.3.3 *The category of meet-closed modest sets is reflective.*

Proof. We'll use 2.4.1 again. It's clear that the meet-closed PERs are closed under arbitrary intersection.

Suppose $Q \in \mathbb{B}$ and R is meet-closed; we must show that $Q^{-1}R$ is meet-closed. But if

$$M(Q^{-1}R)M', N(Q^{-1}R)N'$$

then by definition,

$$(QM)R(QM'), (QN)R(QN');$$

but if

$$P = M \sqcap N, P' = M' \sqcap N'$$

then

$$QP = QM \sqcap QN, QP' = QM' \sqcap QN'$$

and so $(QP)R(QP')$, i.e. $P(Q^{-1}R)P'$.

As for equalizers: Suppose we have meet-closed PERs R, S, and Q_1, Q_2 track maps $\mathbb{B}/R \rightrightarrows \mathbb{B}/S$; define the PER E as in proposition 2.4.1. Given

$$MEM', NEN'$$

and

$$P = M \sqcap N, P' = M' \sqcap N',$$

a similar calculation shows that PEP'. ■

Unfortunately, I don't know much about the behaviour of the meet relation under various constructions on objects. If we restrict ourselves to canonically focal meet-closed PERs, then binary products, function spaces and products indexed by objects like $\mathbf{Mod}_0$) (technically, indexed by $\neg\neg$-sheaves)—which can be calculated simply by taking the intersection of the relevant family of PERs—all have the right meet relations on them. But I can't prove any more general results; so at the moment, the usefulness of this concept is rather limited.

3.4 Closure under lifting

We would like to use the category of complete PERs (identified with the complete modest sets) as our category of predomains, and the complete, canonically focal PERs as our category of domains. Alternatively, if we want to talk about stability, we could use the complete, meet-closed PERs as our predomains and the complete, meet-closed, canonically focal PERs as our domains.

For these categories to be useful as categories of predomains, they'd better be closed under the lift construction so that they contain Σ-partial function spaces as well as total ones. So this is the last thing we need to check.

First we need a lemma that says we are allowed to prove these facts 'externally', and another that states the—external—continuity of application 'the other way round' (there's an internal counterpart, of course, but we won't need it).

Lemma 3.4.1 *Let C be a class of PERs, corresponding to a $\neg\neg$-closed predicate ϕ on $\mathbf{Mod}_0$ (the internal object of $\neg\neg$-closed PERs, which is a $\neg\neg$-sheaf). That is, C comes from an ordinary subset of the set of PERs on B. In order to prove that*

$$\forall R \in \mathbf{Mod}_0.\, \phi(R)$$

is valid, it suffices to prove the external fact that $R \in C$ for all PERs R.

Proof. This proof requires some familiarity with the internal logic of realizability toposes, as described in [6].

Since $\mathbf{Mod}_0$ is a $\neg\neg$-sheaf, the formula will be valid if and only if

$$\bigcap_R |\phi(R)| \neq \varnothing$$

(this follows from the description of the internal logic in terms of the tripos, and a little unwinding of the definitions). But since ϕ is the $\neg\neg$-closed predicate corresponding to $\mathcal{C}$,

$$\phi(R) = \begin{cases} \mathsf{B} & \text{if } R \in \mathcal{C}; \\ \varnothing & \text{otherwise.} \end{cases}$$

So the intersection is nonempty precisely when $R \in \mathcal{C}$ for all R. ■

Lemma 3.4.2 *If* $M = \bigcup_n M_n$ *then* $MN = \bigcup_n M_n N$.

Proof. Define $\mathsf{a} = \lambda xf.fx$. Then

$$MN = \mathsf{a}NM = \mathsf{a}N(\bigcup_n M_n) = \bigcup_n \mathsf{a}NM_n = \bigcup_n M_n N$$

by continuity of application. ■

Proposition 3.4.3 *The category of complete PERs is closed under lifting.*

Proof. Let $\mathcal{C}$ be the collection of PERs R on B such that

$$\text{if } R \text{ is complete, so is } R_\perp$$

(where $R_\perp$ is the PER defined in section 3.1; we are taking the external analogues of all the internal definitions). It corresponds to a certain predicate ϕ on $\mathbf{Mod}_0$ of the form

$$R \text{ complete} \longrightarrow R_\perp \text{ complete}$$

which is $\neg\neg$-closed since the formulas on either side of the implication symbol are $\neg\neg$-closed.

The proposition is equivalent to the validity of

$$\forall R \in \mathbf{Mod}_0.\, \phi(R)$$

and so, by the first lemma, it suffices to prove the external fact that all PERs R on B belong to $\mathcal{C}$; that is: whenever R is a complete PER, then so is $R_\perp$.

First some preliminary definitions. For each $i \in \mathbb{N}$ let

$$\mathsf{s}_i = \lambda f.f^i(\ulcorner n \urcorner f);$$

then $\mathsf{s}_i \ulcorner n \urcorner = \ulcorner n+i \urcorner$ for all n. Now if M is any term let

$$M^{(i)} = \lambda x.M(\mathsf{s}_i x);$$

then $M^{(i)}\ulcorner n \urcorner = M \ulcorner n+i \urcorner$ for all n. Observe that

$$M\mathsf{y} = \bigcup_n M\ulcorner n\urcorner = \bigcup_n M\ulcorner n+i\urcorner = \bigcup_n M^{(i)}\ulcorner n\urcorner = M^{(i)}\mathsf{y}.$$

Now: Let R be a complete PER and suppose we have terms M, N such that for all n, $(M\ulcorner n\urcorner)R_\perp(N\ulcorner n\urcorner)$; we want to show that $(M\mathsf{y})R_\perp(N\mathsf{y})$. By the definition of $R_\perp$, for all n we have that if $\neg(M\ulcorner n\urcorner = N\ulcorner n\urcorner = \Omega)$ then

$$(M\ulcorner n\urcorner\mathsf{f})R(N\ulcorner n\urcorner\mathsf{f}) \wedge M\ulcorner n\urcorner\mathsf{k} = N\ulcorner n\urcorner\mathsf{k} = \mathsf{i}.$$

Suppose that $\neg(M\mathsf{y} = N\mathsf{y} = \Omega)$. Since $M\mathsf{y} = \bigcup_n M\ulcorner n\urcorner$ and $N\mathsf{y} = \bigcup_n N\ulcorner n\urcorner$, we must have

$$\neg(M\ulcorner i\urcorner = N\ulcorner i\urcorner = \Omega)$$

for some i sufficiently large. Then for all n, we have

$$\neg(M^{(i)}\ulcorner n\urcorner = N^{(i)}\ulcorner n\urcorner = \Omega)$$

and hence

$$(M^{(i)}\ulcorner n\urcorner\mathsf{f})R(N^{(i)}\ulcorner n\urcorner\mathsf{f});$$

this shows that $(M^{(i)}\mathsf{y}\mathsf{f})R(N^{(i)}\mathsf{y}\mathsf{f})$ and hence $(M\mathsf{y})R(N\mathsf{y})$. Also,

$$M^{(i)}\ulcorner n\urcorner\mathsf{k} = N^{(i)}\ulcorner n\urcorner\mathsf{k} = \mathsf{i},$$

and hence

$$M\mathsf{yk} = M(\bigcup_n \ulcorner n\urcorner)\mathsf{k} = (\bigcup_n M\ulcorner n\urcorner)\mathsf{k} = \bigcup_n M\ulcorner n\urcorner\mathsf{k} = \bigcup_n M^{(i)}\ulcorner n\urcorner\mathsf{k} = \bigcup_n \mathsf{i} = \mathsf{i};$$

and so $M\mathsf{yk} = \mathsf{i}$. Similarly for N. So we are done. ■

It would be nice to have a proof entirely in the internal language (as in [12]); but I haven't been able to find one.

Proposition 3.4.4 *The category of meet-closed PERs is closed under lifting.*

Proof. Similar, but easier; instead of continuity of application, we use stability of application. The details are left to the reader. ■

We can combine the proofs of these two propositions to show that the category of complete, meet-closed PERs is closed under lifting—which is what we wanted.

4 Final remarks

Perhaps the first thing to say is that the results described above are only a beginning. We are far from understanding any of the categories of domains that live in various realizability toposes, and when we do, it seems likely that they will be understood in quite a different way from the way we see them now. The categories described in this paper are particularly mysterious, because they do not seem to fit in well with the 'synthetic' point of view underlying the programme of Hyland (see [8], for example, though this is still work in progress).

That said, there are a couple of more concrete matters worth raising.

On the interpretation of polymorphic types The predicates that carve the objects-of-objects of these two categories out of $\mathbf{Mod}_0$ are both $\neg\neg$-stable, so

- The object of complete PERs and the object of meet-closed PERs are both in the image of the inclusion $\mathcal{S}ets \hookrightarrow \mathcal{E}$.

(In fact, so is the object of canonically focal PERs.)

That is, because of the 'canonical' nature of the sups of chains, meets and bottoms that are required to exist, the underlying objects of these categories can be thought of as ordinary sets in the usual sense. Some other authors would call them 'uniformizable' objects. In particular, we can calculate products indexed by these objects simply by taking the intersection of the given collection of PERs.

This is, of course, just the usual interpretation of polymorphic types in PER models. The point is that for some categories of domains—such as the complete Σ-spaces of [12]—the object-of-objects is not an ordinary set and so polymorphic types, while they exist, cannot be calculated simply as intersections. This has something to do with the fact that while the definition of complete Σ-space implicitly includes some intensional information (the existence of a realizer that computes suprema of chains) the definition of complete PER does not. Complete PERs could be compared with the complete extensional PERs of [5] in this respect; in both cases, we gain this nice property, but pay a price: the categories are not closed under isomorphism, and the definitions are not so clean.

(For another approach to this problem, applicable to arbitrary reflective subcategories of modest sets, see the remarks on the 'uniformized interpretation' in [16].)

Applications of completeness We have not mentioned the practical consequences of the fact that our predomains form small complete categories (cf. [12], [13]). For example, we can interpret

- polymorphic types, in various ways;

- 'covariant' recursive types;
- subtypes and bounded quantification (this is work in progress);
- nondeterminism, via convex powerdomains (i.e. free semilattices).

These constructions have not been analysed in detail. There are problems: for example, we might like a convex powerdomain construction that preserved the property of being canonically focal, but there is no obvious candidate.

What happened to the order relation? In contrast to the situation in [12] and [14], there's no partial order floating around. We don't need one for the to find fixed points, but it would be handy to be able to use the inverse limit construction to solve domain equations, and to be able to make sense of upper and lower powerdomains (which have an order-theoretic characterization as free meet- and join-semilattices; see [14] or [15]).

Since there is a partial order on the underlying model—the specialization order arising from the tree topology—it should be possible to define a sensible partial order on certain PERs. But I don't know how to proceed. For example, you wouldn't expect the partial order on a function space to be the pointwise order; it should be something like the stable order. But you might expect the order on a product indexed by a $\neg\neg$-sheaf to be pointwise. And how do we tie this up with the notion of meet-closure?

Are we looking at the right model? The particular model B we chose to look at is not the only possibility. In view of some of the arguments we've used, it seems as if it might be more natural to use Nakajima trees ('infinite η-expansions' of Böhm trees) rather than Böhm trees (see [2, exercise 19.4.4]); this means we would have the η-rule available. That is, η-equivalence would be incorporated into our notion of equality on terms. But then one would have to reprove the continuity theorems, and so on; this should be possible, but might be tedious.

Alternatively, one could say that since many modern functional languages are lazy, the notion of Böhm tree is not the right one; it would be better to look for a theory based on the lazy λ-calculus. But I'm not sure if this is possible.

The model studied in [13] (the r.e. graph model) can be regarded as a term model for Scott's language LAMBDA—albeit one in which we have no syntactic characterization of equality. It may be interesting to look at other term models of combinatory logic; after all, functional languages are often implemented using combinators.

A more general problem is that we have no good techniques for relating categories of domains in different toposes. In fact, the whole question of how different realizability toposes can be related is still largely open.

Acknowledgements

The work described here formed part of a Ph.D. dissertation written under the supervision of Martin Hyland; I must thank him for being so patient and helpful. I also benefited from discussions and correspondence with many other people—too many to list here.

The final version of this paper was prepared with the support of the Australian Research Council.

References

[1] M. Abadi, G. Plotkin: A PER model of polymorphism and recursive types, in: Proc. of 5th Annual Symposium on Logic in Computer Science, 1990.

[2] H. P. Barendregt: *The Lambda-Calculus: Its Syntax and Semantics (revised edition)*, North-Holland, 1984.

[3] M. Beeson: *Foundations of Constructive Mathematics*, Springer, 1985.

[4] T. Coquand, G. Huet: Constructions: a higher-order proof system for mechanizing mathematics, in: *EUROCAL '85: European Conference on Computer Algebra*, Springer, 1985.

[5] P. Freyd, P. Mulry, G. Rosolini, D.S. Scott: Extensional PERs, in: Proc. of 5th Annual Symposium on Logic in Computer Science, 1990.

[6] J.M.E. Hyland: The effective topos, in: *The L.E.J. Brouwer Centenary Symposium* (ed. A. S. Troelstra, D. van Dalen), North-Holland, 1982.

[7] J.M.E. Hyland: A small complete category, *Annals of Pure and Applied Logic* 40 (1988) 135-165.

[8] J.M.E. Hyland: Synthetic domains—the story so far, *Abstracts EACTS*, 1990.

[9] J.M.E Hyland, A.M. Pitts: The theory of constructions, categorical semantics and topos-theoretic models, in *Categories in Computer Science and Logic (Proc. Boulder 1987)*, *Contemp. Math.* **92** (1989) 137–199.

[10] J.M.E. Hyland, E.P. Robinson, G. Rosolini: The discrete objects in the effective topos, *Proc. Lond. Math. Soc.* (3) 60 (1990) 1–36.

[11] P. T. Johnstone: *Topos Theory*, Academic Press, 1977.

[12] W. K.-S. Phoa: Effective domains and intrinsic structure, in: Proc. of 5th Annual Symposium on Logic in Computer Science, 1990.

[13] W. K.-S. Phoa: Building domains from models of computation, submitted.

[14] W. K.-S. Phoa: *Domain Theory in Realizability Toposes*, Ph.D. dissertation, University of Cambridge, November 1990.

[15] W. K.-S. Phoa: Reflectivity for categories of synthetic domains, submitted, 1990.

[16] W. K.-S. Phoa: Two results on set-theoretic polymorphism, submitted, 1991.

[17] W. K.-S. Phoa, P. Taylor: The synthetic Plotkin powerdomain, preprint.

[18] G. D. Plotkin, M. B. Smyth: The category-theoretic solution of recursive domain equations, *Siam Journal of Computing* vol. 11 no. 4, 1982.

[19] E. Robinson: How complete is PER? in: Proc. of 4th Annual Symposium on Logic in Computer Science, 1989.

[20] G. Rosolini: Categories and [illegible] computations, in: Lecture Notes in Computer Science 283, Springer [illegible]

[21] D.S. Scott: Data types as [illegible] *t.* 5 (3) (1976) 522-587.

An Abstract Interpretation for ML Equality Kinds

Carl A. Gunter
Dept. of Computer and Information Science
University of Pennsylvania
200 S. 33rd St.
Philadelphia, PA 19104
gunter@cis.upenn.edu

Elsa L. Gunter
AT&T Bell Laboratories, Room 2C-454
600 Mountain Ave.
Murray Hill, NJ 07974-2070
elsa@research.att.com

David B. MacQueen
AT&T Bell Laboratories, Room 2C-322
600 Mountain Ave.
Murray Hill, NJ 07974-2070
macqueen@research.att.com

Abstract

The definition of Standard ML provides a form of generic equality which is inferred for certain types, called *equality types,* on which it is possible to define a computable equality relation. However, the standard definition is incomplete in the sense that there are interesting and useful types which are *not* inferred to be equality types but which nevertheless have a computable equality relation. In this paper, a refinement of the Standard ML system of equality types is introduced and is proven sound and *complete* with respect to the existence of a computable equality. The technique used here is based on an abstract interpretation of ML operators as monotone functions over a three point lattice. It is shown how the equality relation can be defined (as an ML program) from the definition of a type with our equality property. Finally, a sound, efficient algorithm for inferring the equality property which corrects the limitations of the standard definition in all cases of practical interest is demonstrated.

1 Equality Types in Standard ML

The ML language provides an extensible algebra of type constructions. The Standard ML dialect divides types into two classes, those which *admit equality* (also called *equality types*) and those which do not. This distinction is based on the structure of types. Primitive types like `int` and `string` have a predefined equality operation, while equality can be defined over compound types built up from primitive types using "concrete" constructions like product and disjoint union in the usual componentwise manner. Function types on the other hand do not posses an equality operation, nor, by convention, do user–defined abstract types. As a first approximation, therefore, the types admitting equality can be identified with the "hereditarily concrete" types built from primitive types using concrete type constructions. Some recursively defined datatype constructors such as `list` also qualify as concrete, producing equality types when applied to equality types.

Having identified a class of types possessing canonical equality operations, the next step is to introduce a restricted form of polymorphism by abstracting over polymorphic type variables which are constrained to range only over such types. Using this restricted form of polymorphism one can define functions like the generic list membership function:

```
fun member x nil = false
  | member x (y::r) = if x = y then true else member x r
```

which searches a list for an appearance of a value. The type inferred for `member` is

```
member : ''a * ''a list -> bool
```

where `''a` is a polymorphic type variable ranging over equality types. (In Standard ML, an ordinary polymorphic type variable ranging over arbitrary types begins with a single quote, e.g. `'a`.)

The goal of this research is to investigate some problems that arise from oversimplifications in the treatment of equality types in the Definition of Standard ML [MTH90, MT91]. We propose a refined treatment of equality types using equality *kinds* defined in terms of an abstract interpretation of type expressions that we prove to be sound and complete with respect to the denotational semantics of Standard ML types.

In the Definition of Standard ML, a unary type constructor `'a F` is said to *admit equality* if `t F` is an equality type whenever the parameter type `t` is. A constructed type `t F` admits equality only if both `t` and `F` admit equality. This extends to n-ary type constructors in the obvious way. Unfortunately, this definition is incomplete for the inference of equality properties because of the presence of certain special type constructors that have stronger equality properties. For example, the type `t ref` admits equality regardless of whether `t` does. Therefore a type constructor defined as

```
datatype ('a,'b) F = mkF of 'a * 'b ref
```

has a more complex equality preservation behavior than the standard definition is capable of expressing. For example, `(int, unit->int) F` should admit equality even though one of its arguments, `(unit->int)`, does not. However this will not be inferred based on the definition.

To correct this problem requires a more precise notion of equality properties of type constructors. A simple binary property distinguishing between type constructors which admit equality and those which do not must be replaced by an *equality kind* that specifies how the equality property of the result depends on the equality properties of the arguments of the constructor.

We start in Section 2 by developing a standard denotational interpretation of types and an abstract interpretation mapping types into a three point lattice $\mathcal{E} = \{\mathsf{void}, \mathsf{eq}, \mathsf{type}\}$, where the top element type represents arbitrary types, the middle element eq represents types admitting equality and the bottom element void represents empty types (*i.e.* types containing no defined elements).

This abstract interpretation of types is also extended to type constructors, whose interpretations will be mappings from appropriate products of $\mathcal{E}$ to $\mathcal{E}$. To interpret recursively defined constructors we simply calculate a least fixed point of the abstract interpretations. For example, if we define

```
datatype ('a,'b) F = A of 'a | B of (unit -> 'b, 'b) G
     and ('c,'d) G = C of ('c ref, 'd) F | D of 'd
```

then neither `F` nor `G` are considered to admit equality according to the Standard ML definition. However, both `F` and `G` admit equality under the abstract interpretation, and their interpretations f, g satisfy $f(\mathsf{eq}, \mathsf{eq}) = \mathsf{eq}$ and $g(\mathsf{type}, \mathsf{eq}) = \mathsf{eq}$ respectively.

In Section 3 we relate the denotational and abstract interpretations by showing that the denotation of a type is a flat domain if and only if the abstract interpretation of that type is eq.

In Section 4 we show that if a type has eq as its abstract interpretation we can generate a computable equality operation for that type. This involves defining equality functionals corresponding to the type constructors used to build the type. It is also shown that only the flat domains may have a computable equality operation, so that the equality types are exactly the types having a computable equality.

The structure of the recursive definition of a type constructor is used as a format for creating a recursive definition of the corresponding equality function. In the case of `F` and `G`, this recursive function is parameterized by equality tests for `'a`, `'b`, `'d` and a "dummy parameter" for `'c`. In fact, the equality test for `'c` will be never be invoked in an equality test for a type built with `F` or `G` because it is not used to compute equality on `'c ref`.

In Section 5 we show that by avoiding void the abstract interpretation can be simplified, and *equality kinds* are introduced as succinct characterizations of the interpretation of type constructors. In practice, normal type constructor definitions are indeed "void-avoiding".

We conclude by discussing future research directions, particularly the interaction of equality types and ML modules, and the impact of equality types on implementations of ML.

2 Interpretations of Types

For the purposes of this paper, we shall assume that the expressions of the type algebra in ML are given by the following grammar:

$$t = \textbf{void} \mid \textbf{unit} \mid t * t \mid t + t \mid t \to t \mid \textbf{ref}\ t \mid F_i(t_1, \ldots, t_{n_i}) \qquad (i = 1, \ldots m)$$

where the type constructors $F_1, \ldots F_m$ are all the user-defined datatypes. Associated with the user-defined type constructors there is a system of equations

$$\begin{aligned} F_1(\alpha_1, \ldots, \alpha_{n_1}) &= \mathcal{F}_1(F_1, \ldots, F_m)(\alpha_1, \ldots, \alpha_{n_1}) \\ &\vdots \\ F_m(\alpha_1, \ldots, \alpha_{n_m}) &= \mathcal{F}_m(F_1, \ldots, F_m)(\alpha_1, \ldots, \alpha_{n_m}). \end{aligned}$$

which any interpretation should treat as one large mutual recursion. For example, the recursive definition from the previous section would be use the following operators:

$$\begin{aligned} \mathcal{F} &= \lambda(F, G)\lambda(\alpha, \beta).\alpha + G(\textbf{unit} \to \beta, \beta) \\ \mathcal{G} &= \lambda(F, G)\lambda(\gamma, \delta).F(\textbf{ref}\ \gamma, \delta) + \delta \end{aligned}$$

We shall refer to the non-recursive type constructors, namely **void**, **unit**, $*$, $+$, $\to$, and **ref**, as *basic* constructors. In the above recursive equations, the functions $\mathcal{F}_i$ are second-order λ-expressions over our type algebra, containing no free occurrences of the symbols F_1, ..., F_m. That is, the bodies of the functions $\mathcal{F}_i$ are composed only of first-order and second-order bound variables and basic constructors.

In this section we wish to define two interpretations of these type expressions, one domain-theoretic and the other an abstract interpretation. In order to do so, it will be beneficial in both cases to have associated with each of our recursive constructors, F_1, ..., F_m, a sequence of functions which are first-order λ-expressions over our basic type algebra whose bodies are composed only of first-order variables and basic constructors. Under each of the interpretations these functions will provide finite approximates to the recursive constructors. These functions are given by the following recursive definition:

$$\begin{aligned} F_i^0(\alpha_1, \ldots, \alpha_{n_i}) &= \textbf{void} \\ F_i^{j+1}(\alpha_1, \ldots, \alpha_{n_i}) &= \mathcal{F}_i(F_1^j, \ldots, F_m^j)(\alpha_1, \ldots, \alpha_{n_1}). \end{aligned}$$

With these we are now in a position to describe our two interpretations.

2.1 A Domain-theoretic Interpretation

We now sketch the standard fixed-point semantics of ML's types. To do this we must briefly introduce some domain-theoretic terminology. A somewhat fuller discussion of domain theory can be found in [GS90]. A subset $M \subseteq D$ of a poset D is *directed* if, for every finite set $u \subseteq M$, there is an upper bound $x \in M$ for u. D is a *complete* partial order (cpo) if every directed subset $M \subseteq D$ has a least upper bound $\bigvee M$ and there is a least element $\bot_D$ in D. To interpret ML's types, we need a collection of operators on cpo's.

Given cpo's D and E, we define the *coalesced sum* $D \oplus E$ to be the set

$$\Big((D - \{\bot_D\}) \times \{0\}\Big) \cup \Big((E - \{\bot_E\}) \times \{1\}\Big) \cup \{\bot_{D \oplus E}\}$$

where $D - \{\bot_D\}$ and $E - \{\bot_E\}$ are the sets D and E with their respective bottom elements removed and $\bot_{D\oplus E}$ is a new element which is not a pair. It is ordered by taking $\bot_{D\oplus E} \leq z$ for all $z \in D \oplus E$ and taking $(x, m) \leq (y, n)$ if and only if $m = n$ and $x \leq y$.

Given a cpo D, we define the *lift* of D to be the poset obtained by adding a new bottom to D. More precisely, the set $D_\bot = (D \times \{0\}) \cup \{\bot\}$, where $\bot$ is a new element which is not a pair, together with a partial ordering $\leq$ which is given by stipulating that $(x, 0) \leq (y, 0)$ whenever $x \leq y$ and $\bot \leq z$ for every $z \in D_\bot$.

For cpo's D and E, the *smash product* $D \otimes E$ is the set

$$\{(x, y) \in D \times E \mid x \neq \bot \text{ and } y \neq \bot\} \cup \{\bot_{D\otimes E}\}$$

where $\bot_{D\otimes E}$ is some new element which is not a pair. The ordering on pairs is coordinatewise and we stipulate that $\bot_{D\otimes E} \leq z$ for every $z \in D \otimes E$.

The two point lattice $\mathbf{1}$ is a unit for the smash product: $D \otimes \mathbf{1} \cong \mathbf{1} \otimes D \cong D$. The one point lattice $\mathbf{0}$ is a unit for the coalesced sum, $D \oplus \mathbf{0} \cong \mathbf{0} \oplus D \cong D$, and an eliminator for the smash product, $D \otimes \mathbf{0} \cong \mathbf{0} \otimes D \cong \mathbf{0}$. A cpo is said to be *void* if it is isomorphic to $\mathbf{0}$. A cpo D is said to be *flat* if it is not void and any two distinct elements of D are comparable only when one of them is $\bot$. Up to isomorphism, there is a unique countably infinite flat cpo which we denote $N_\bot$. The domain $\mathbf{B}$ of *booleans* is the flat domain with three distinct elements true, false, $\bot$. The *equality function* $=_D$ on a flat domain D is a mapping from $D \otimes D$ into D such that

- $=_D (x, y)$ is true when $x = y \neq \bot$
- $=_D (x, y)$ is false when $x, y \neq \bot$ and $x \neq y$
- $=_D (x, y)$ is $\bot$ when x or y is $\bot$.

A monotone function between two cpo's is *continuous* if it preserves least upper bounds of directed collections. A function between cpo's is *strict* if it takes $\bot$ to $\bot$. Given two cpo's D and E, the space of all strict continuous functions between D and E, denoted by $D \multimap E$, is again a cpo under the point-wise ordering.

For an ML type expression t, let $\check{t}$ be the standard domain-theoretic interpretation of t. This definition can be given inductively as follows. First of all, we define $\check{\mathbf{void}} = \mathbf{0}$ and $\check{\mathbf{unit}} = \mathbf{1}$. The interpretations of the basic constructors are defined on domains D and E as follows:

- $D \check{*} E = D \otimes E$
- $D \check{+} E = D \oplus E$
- $D \check{\rightarrow} E = (D \multimap E)_\perp$
- $\check{\mathbf{ref}}\ \mathbf{0} = \mathbf{0}$
- $\check{\mathbf{ref}}\ D = N_\perp \quad \text{if } D \neq \mathbf{0}$

The interpretation of recursive types can be given as described in [SP82] using colimits. These methods also apply to provide a semantics for the recursively defined type constructors provided by ML. For example, an ML definition of lists such as

```
datatype 'a list = Cons of 'a * 'a list | Nil
```

is a recursive definition of a constructor `list`. At the domain-theoretic level, this is a recursive definition of a *functor.* The solution is obtained as a colimit of a sequence of functors, where the colimit is obtained in a category of functors and natural transformations. To prove that the equality functions we define later as ML programs are indeed the ones we expect, it is essential for us to know something about the exact mathematical operator which we obtain as the solution of this equation.

Fortunately, it is not necessary to work in a functor category in order to do this. Instead, we can employ a technique of Scott which uses a *universal domain.* The first use of the idea appears in [Sco76] using what one might call a "closure-universal" domain, but we will employ a related technique introduced in [Sco82b, Sco82a] using a "projection-universal" domain. Both techniques are described and illustrated in [GS90]. For the purposes of the remainder of this paper, a *domain* is a bounded complete algebraic cpo (these are sometimes called "Scott domains"). It will not be necessary for us to define these structures here since we will simply rely on properties of their universal domain. The universal domain technique can be summarized as follows. Given a domain D, let us say that a subset E is a subdomain of D and write $E \lhd D$ if E forms a domain under the ordering inherited from D and there is a projection from D onto E, *i.e.* there is is a mapping $p : D \to E$ such that $p \circ p = p$ and $p(x) \leq x$ for each $x \in D$. Roughly speaking, a *universal domain* is a domain U which has a copy of every other domain D as a subdomain, *i.e.* $D \lhd U$ up to isomorphism. Moreover, the set of all subdomains of U again forms a domain, and hence there is a special subdomain $T \lhd U$, called the *type of types*, which is isomorphic to the domain of

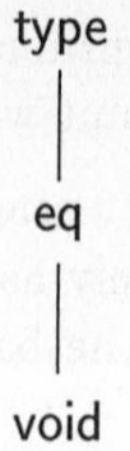

Figure 1: The Equality Properties Lattice $\mathcal{E}$.

subdomains of U. More specifically, there is a bijection τ between T and the domain of subdomains of U such that $D \lhd E$ iff $\tau(D) \leq \tau(E)$ for any pair of subdomains $D, E \lhd U$. In the remainder of the paper we will make no distinction between a domain D (which is to be viewed as a subdomain of U) and its image in T under τ.

The existence of a universal domain allows us to interpret operators on *types* as continuous functions on the *domain* T. For example, the function space operator $\rightarrow$ can be viewed as a continuous function from $T \times T$ into T. Hence, a fixed point specification such as the one given for `list` above can be solved as a fixed point equation over a cpo without the need to introduce functor categories, *etc.* explicitly (see Theorem 7.10 of [GS90]). Therefore, if $D_1, \ldots, D_{n_i}$ are domains, then we can define

$$\check{F}_i(D_1, \ldots, D_{n_i}) = \bigvee(\check{F}_i^j(D_1, \ldots, D_{n_i}))$$

where the least upper bound is being taken in T and the isomorphism between domains and elements of T is being taken for granted.

Another useful perspective that we are able to obtain by working in a universal domains is a simple way to compare functions between domains. If we are given a continuous function $f : D \rightarrow E$ between subdomains D and E, then we may view this as a continuous function $f' : U \rightarrow U$ where $f'(x) = f(p(x))$ where p is the projection onto D. In particular, if $D \lhd D'$ are flat subdomains, then their equality functions are related $=_D \leq =_{D'}$ (where we are suppressing the distinction between the equality functions on the domains and their extensions to all of U). One further note which will be important to our discussion later is that when we have a tower of flat domains $D_0 \lhd D_1 \lhd \cdots$, then their limit in T corresponds to their *union* $\bigcup_i D_i$ as subdomains of U. In particular, the limit of their equality functions is the equality function on their limit (the union of the D_i's).

2.2 An Abstract Interpretation

Next we wish to describe an abstract interpretation function mapping closed ML type expressions into the three point lattice $\mathcal{E}$ pictured in Figure 1. To do so, we will define the interpretation on the constructors and extend by structural induction to closed type expressions. For any $v_1, v_2 \in \mathcal{E}$, we have:

- $\hat{\textbf{void}} = \mathsf{void}$
- $\hat{\textbf{unit}} = \mathsf{eq}$
- $v_1 \mathbin{\hat{+}} v_2 = \max\{v_1, v_2\}$
- If either $v_1 = \mathsf{void}$ or $v_2 = \mathsf{void}$ then $v_1 \mathbin{\hat{*}} v_2 = \mathsf{void}$, if $v_1 = v_2 = \mathsf{eq}$ then $v_1 \mathbin{\hat{*}} v_2 = \mathsf{eq}$ and otherwise $v_1 \mathbin{\hat{*}} v_2 = \mathsf{type}$
- If $v_1 = \mathsf{void}$ or $v_2 = \mathsf{void}$, then $v_1 \mathbin{\hat{\to}} v_2 = \mathsf{eq}$, and otherwise $v_1 \mathbin{\hat{\to}} v_2 = \mathsf{type}$
- $\hat{\textbf{ref}}\ \mathsf{void} = \mathsf{void}$ and if $v \neq \mathsf{void}$ then $\hat{\textbf{ref}}\ v = \mathsf{eq}$.

Notice that each of the the basic constructors is interpreted as a monotone function over the n-ary product $(n = 0, 1, 2)$ of $\mathcal{E}$ with itself.

Having defined our interpretation for the basic constructors, by structural induction we have the interpretations $\hat{F}_i^j$ for the functions F_i^j, since they are composed only of basic constructors. Using these, we define the interpretations of the recursive constructors by

$$\hat{F}_i(v_1, \ldots, v_{n_i}) = \max_j\{\hat{F}_i^j(v_1, \ldots, v_{n_i})\}.$$

By structural induction, we can in fact extend our interpretation function to the second-order functions $\mathcal{F}_i$. Since these are also composed only of basic constructors (and first- and second-order bound variables), and since all the basic constructors are interpreted as monotone functions, the interpretation of $\mathcal{F}_i$ will itself be a function which is monotone in both its first-order and second-order arguments.

Lemma 1 *For all i, j, we have $\hat{F}_i^j \leq \hat{F}_i^{j+1}$. Moreover, there exists a k such that for all i, $\hat{F}_i^k = \hat{F}_i^{k+1}$, and hence for all i, $\hat{F}_i = \hat{F}_i^k$.*

Proof. For the first part, the proof is by induction on j. Suppose $v_1, \ldots, v_{n_i} \in \mathcal{E}$. For the base step, $\hat{F}_i^0(v_1, \ldots, v_{n_i}) = \mathsf{void} \leq \hat{F}_i^1(v_1, \ldots, v_{n_i})$. For the inductive step suppose that for all i

$$\hat{F}_i^{j-1}(v_1, \ldots, v_{n_i}) \leq \hat{F}_i^j(v_1, \ldots, v_{n_i})$$

Then, by applying $\hat{\mathcal{F}}_i$, for each i, since $\hat{\mathcal{F}}_i$ is monotonic, we have

$$\hat{\mathcal{F}}_i(\hat{F}_1^j, \ldots, \hat{F}_m^j)(v_1, \ldots, v_{n_i}) \leq \hat{\mathcal{F}}_i(\hat{F}_1^{j+1}, \ldots, \hat{F}_m^{j+1})(v_1, \ldots, v_{n_i})$$

and hence

$$\hat{F}_i^j(v_1, \ldots, v_{n_i}) \leq \hat{F}_i^{j+1}(v_1, \ldots, v_{n_i}).$$

For the second part, since the set of functions mapping $\mathcal{E}^{n_i}$ into $\mathcal{E}$ is finite and the $\hat{F}_i^j$'s form an increasing sequence, it is immediate that there exists a k such that for all i we have $\hat{F}_i^k = \hat{F}_i^{k+1}$. By the definition of the F_i^j's, for all $j > k$ we therefore have $\hat{F}_i^j = \hat{F}_i^k$. Again since the $\hat{F}_i^j$'s form an increasing sequence, we have that $\hat{F}_i = max_j\{\hat{F}_i^j\} = \hat{F}_i^k$. ∎

Notice that the previous lemma tells us that the computation of the $\hat{F}_i$'s is a finite process.

3 Relating Interpretations

The purpose of this section is to demonstrate that, for any type expression t, the standard interpretation $\check{t}$ is flat if and only if $\hat{t} = \mathsf{eq}$. This describes the soundness and completeness property of our interpretation. Because of the presence of recursive definitions and the constant type **void** itself, it is necessary to deal with the possibility that there are type expressions t such that every program of type t is divergent. For example, the following types

```
datatype empty = Mknothing of empty

datatype product = Infiniteprod of product * product
```

have only divergent programs. The following definition and lemma show how such types are abstractly interpreted as void.

Definition 2 A closed type expression t *has property* $\mathcal{V}$ provided that $\hat{t} = \mathsf{void}$ iff $\check{t} = \mathbf{0}$. ∎

Lemma 3 *1. The types* **void** *and* **unit** *both have property* $\mathcal{V}$.

2. If the types t_1 and t_2 both have property $\mathcal{V}$, then so do $t_1 + t_2$ and $t_1 * t_2$.

3. For all types t_1 and t_2, the type $t_1 \to t_2$ has property $\mathcal{V}$.

4. If a type t has property $\mathcal{V}$ then so does **ref** *t.*

5. If types $t_1, \ldots, t_{n_i}$ have property $\mathcal{V}$, then so does $F_i(t_1, \ldots, t_{n_i})$.

Proof. 1) The type **void** has property $\mathcal{V}$ since $\widehat{\mathbf{void}} = \mathsf{void}$ and $\check{\mathbf{void}} = \mathbf{0}$. The type **unit** has property $\mathcal{V}$ since $\widehat{\mathbf{unit}} = \mathsf{eq} \neq \mathsf{void}$ and $\check{\mathbf{unit}} = \mathbf{1} \neq \mathbf{0}$.

2) Suppose t_1 and t_2 both have property $\mathcal{V}$. Then

$$\begin{aligned} \hat{t_1} \mathbin{\hat{+}} \hat{t_2} = \mathsf{void} &\Leftrightarrow \text{ both } \hat{t_1} = \mathsf{void} \text{ and } \hat{t_2} = \mathsf{void} \\ &\Leftrightarrow \text{ both } \check{t_1} = \mathbf{0} \text{ and } \check{t_2} = \mathbf{0} \\ &\Leftrightarrow \check{t_1} \mathbin{\check{+}} \check{t_2} = \mathbf{0}. \end{aligned}$$

Therefore, $t_1 + t_2$ has property $\mathcal{V}$. Also,

$$\begin{aligned}\hat{t_1} \mathbin{\hat{*}} \hat{t_2} = \mathsf{void} &\Leftrightarrow \text{ either } \hat{t_1} = \mathsf{void} \text{ or } \hat{t_2} = \mathsf{void} \\ &\Leftrightarrow \text{ either } \check{t_1} = \mathbf{0} \text{ or } \check{t_2} = \mathbf{0} \\ &\Leftrightarrow \check{t_1} \mathbin{\check{*}} \check{t_2} = \mathbf{0}.\end{aligned}$$

Therefore, $t_1 * t_2$ has property $\mathcal{V}$.

3) For all types t_1 and t_2, the domain $\check{t_1} \mathbin{\check{\rightarrow}} \check{t_2} = (\check{t_1} \circ\!\!\rightarrow \check{t_2})_\perp$ always has at least two elements, namely $\perp$ and $\lambda x.\perp$, and hence is not $\mathbf{0}$. Moreover, by the definition of $\hat{\rightarrow}$, $\hat{t_1} \mathbin{\hat{\rightarrow}} \hat{t_2}$ is never equal to void. Therefore, $t_1 \rightarrow t_2$ always has property $\mathcal{V}$.

4) Suppose that the type t has property $\mathcal{V}$. Then

$$\begin{aligned}\hat{\mathbf{ref}}\ \hat{t} = \mathsf{void} &\Leftrightarrow \hat{t} = \mathsf{void} \\ &\Leftrightarrow \check{t} = \mathbf{0} \\ &\Leftrightarrow \check{\mathbf{ref}}\ \check{t} = \mathbf{0}\end{aligned}$$

Therefore, **ref** t has property $\mathcal{V}$.

As a result of parts 1 through 4 of the lemma, we have by structural induction that any type operator that is composed solely of basic constructors preserves property $\mathcal{V}$.

5) Let $t_1, \ldots, t_{n_i}$ be a collection of types having property $\mathcal{V}$. By the previous remark, for each j, the type $F_i^j(t_1, \ldots, t_{n_i})$ has property $\mathcal{V}$. Therefore

$$\begin{aligned}\hat{F_i}(\hat{t_1}, \ldots, \hat{t_{n_i}}) = \mathsf{void} &\Leftrightarrow \hat{F_i^j}(\hat{t_1}, \ldots, \hat{t_{n_i}}) = \mathsf{void}, \text{ for all } j \\ &\Leftrightarrow \check{F_i^j}(\check{t_1}, \ldots, \check{t_{n_i}}) = \mathbf{0}, \text{ for all } j \\ &\Leftrightarrow \check{F_i}(\check{t_1}, \ldots, \check{t_{n_i}}) = \bigvee_j \check{F_i^j}(\check{t_1}, \ldots, \check{t_{n_i}}) = \mathbf{0}.\end{aligned}$$

where the least upper bound is taken in T, the type of types. Therefore, $F_i(t_1, \ldots, t_{n_i})$ has property $\mathcal{V}$. ∎

Corollary 4 *For all closed ML type expressions t, we have that $\hat{t} = \mathsf{void}$ iff $\check{t} = \mathbf{0}$.*

Proof. By structural induction and the previous lemma, all closed type expressions in ML have property $\mathcal{V}$. ∎

Our primary interest is not in types which are void, but in those which are equality types. We may now characterize the types having eq as their abstract interpretation as exactly those with a flat standard interpretation.

Definition 5 A closed type expression t *has property $\mathcal{SC}$* (for "sound and complete") provided that $\hat{t} = \mathsf{eq}$ iff $\check{t}$ is flat. ∎

Lemma 6 *1. The types* **void** *and* **unit** *both have property* $\mathcal{SC}$.

2. If the types t_1 *and* t_2 *both have property* $\mathcal{SC}$, *then so do* $t_1 + t_2$ *and* $t_1 * t_2$.

3. For all types t_1 *and* t_2, *the type* $t_1 \rightarrow t_2$ *has property* $\mathcal{SC}$.

4. For all types t, *the type* **ref** t *has property* $\mathcal{SC}$.

5. If types $t_1, \ldots, t_{n_i}$ *have property* $\mathcal{SC}$, *then so does* $F_i(t_1, \ldots, t_{n_i})$.

Proof. 1) Since $\widehat{\textbf{void}} \neq \mathsf{eq}$ and $\check{\textbf{void}}$ is not flat, **void** has property $\mathcal{SC}$. Since $\widehat{\textbf{unit}} = \mathsf{eq}$ and $\check{\textbf{unit}}$ is flat, **unit** also has property $\mathcal{SC}$.

2) Suppose that both types t_1 and t_2 have property $\mathcal{SC}$. Then

$\hat{t_1} \mathbin{\hat{+}} \hat{t_2} = \mathsf{eq}$

$\Leftrightarrow$ each of $\hat{t_1}$ and $\hat{t_2}$ is either void or eq, and at least one of them is eq

$\Leftrightarrow$ each of $\check{t_1}$ and $\check{t_2}$ is either void or flat (by Corollary 3 and property SC), and at least one is not void

$\Leftrightarrow$ $\check{t_1} \mathbin{\check{+}} \check{t_2}$ is flat.

Therefore, $t_1 + t_2$ has property $\mathcal{SC}$. Also,

$\hat{t_1} \mathbin{\hat{*}} \hat{t_2} = \mathsf{eq}$

$\Leftrightarrow$ both $\hat{t_1}$ and $\hat{t_2}$ are eq

$\Leftrightarrow$ both $\check{t_1}$ and $\check{t_2}$ are flat

$\Leftrightarrow$ $\check{t_1} \mathbin{\check{*}} \check{t_2}$ is flat,

and hence, $t_1 * t_2$ has property $\mathcal{SC}$.

3) For any types t_1 and t_2, we have that

$$\begin{aligned} \hat{t_1} \mathbin{\hat{\rightarrow}} \hat{t_2} = \mathsf{eq} &\Leftrightarrow \hat{t_1} = \mathsf{void} \text{ or } \hat{t_1} = \mathsf{void} \\ &\Leftrightarrow \check{t_1} = \mathbf{0} \text{ or } \check{t_1} = \mathbf{0} \text{ (by Corollary 3)} \\ &\Leftrightarrow \check{t_1} \mathbin{\check{\rightarrow}} \check{t_2} = \mathbf{1}, \text{ which is flat.} \end{aligned}$$

Therefore, $t_1 \rightarrow t_2$ has property $\mathcal{SC}$.

4) Given any type t, we have

$$\begin{aligned} \widehat{\textbf{ref}}\ \hat{t} \neq \mathsf{eq} &\Leftrightarrow \hat{t} = \mathsf{void} \\ &\Leftrightarrow \check{t} = \mathbf{0} \text{ (by Corollary 3)} \\ &\Leftrightarrow \check{\textbf{ref}}\ \check{t} = \mathbf{0} \\ &\Leftrightarrow \check{\textbf{ref}}\ \check{t} \text{ is not flat.} \end{aligned}$$

Therefore, **ref** t has property $\mathcal{SC}$.

As before, by 1 through 4 of this lemma, we know by structural induction that any type operator that is composed solely of basic constructors preserves property $\mathcal{SC}$.

5)Let $t_1, \ldots, t_{n_i}$ be a collection of types having property $\mathcal{SC}$. By the previous remark we have that $F_i^j(t_1, \ldots, t_{n_i})$ has property $\mathcal{SC}$, for each j. Thus

$\hat{F}_i(\hat{t_1},\ldots,\hat{t_{n_i}}) = \mathsf{eq}$
$\Leftrightarrow$ there exists a k such that $\hat{F}_i^j(\hat{t_1},\ldots,\hat{t_{n_i}}) = \mathsf{void}$ for all $j < k$, and $\hat{F}_i^j(\hat{t_1},\ldots,\hat{t_{n_i}}) = \mathsf{eq}$ for all $j \geq k$ (by Lemma 1).
$\Leftrightarrow$ there exists a k such that $\check{F}_i^j(\check{t_1},\ldots,\check{t_{n_i}}) = \mathbf{0}$ for all $j < k$, and $\check{F}_i^j(\check{t_1},\ldots,\check{t_{n_i}})$ is (non-void) flat for all $j \geq k$
$\Leftrightarrow$ $\check{F}_i(\check{t_1},\ldots,\check{t_{n_i}})$ is flat, being the least upper bound of a chain of flat domains.

Therefore, $F_i(t_1,\ldots,t_{n_i})$ has property $\mathcal{SC}$. ∎

Corollary 7 *(Soundness and Completeness) For all closed ML type expressions t, we have that $\check{t}$ is flat iff $\hat{t} = \mathsf{eq}$.*

Proof. By structural induction and the previous lemma, all closed type expressions in ML have property $\mathcal{SC}$. ∎

4 Equality Functions

Having derived an abstract interpretation for equality types, we now have a theory that tells us when we should expect to find an equality function on a type. However, there is no *a priori* reason to believe that this function is definable in ML or that we can provide a way to uniformly produce a program for computing the function from the structure of the type. However, it is not at all difficult to see that we can do this for the basic operators. For example, to get the equality function on a *product* `s * t`, given equality functions `f` and `g` on `s` and `t` respectively, one just uses the given equality functions to compute the equality on the respective coordinates of the product:

```
fun eqtimes (f,g) ((x,y), (x',y'))
    = f(x,x') andalso g(y,y')
```

The *sum* is similar; the given equality functions should be used in their respective components:

```
fun eqsum (f,g) (inl x, inl y) = f(x,y)
  | eqsum (f,g) (inr x, inr y) = g(x,y)
  | eqsum (f,g) _ = false
```

where the sum type is represented by the following concrete type operator:

```
datatype ('a,'b) sum = inl of 'a | inr of 'b;
```

What should be done for the *arrow* types? These are never equality types except when the domain or codomain of the type is void. In this case, the interpretation of the type has two elements; one of these represents the undefined program at the type and the other represents "delayed divergence". Hence, if two arguments to an equality test for such a type both converge, then they are equal. Noting the call-by-value evaluation of ML programs, we may therefore take the following definition:

```
fun eqarrow (f,g) = fn (x,y) => true
```

Note that the equality function parameters `f` and `g` are not used. That this is the "correct" equality function on arrow types presupposes that it will only be used in the case where the arrow type is flat.

Equality on *reference* types must be computed by a primitive function which determines identity of memory locations.

How is the equality function on *recursive* types computed? Recursively, of course! For example, consider the definition of the operator `list`:

```
datatype 'a list = Cons of 'a * 'a list | Nil
```

given earlier. To calculate equality on `''a list`, given an equality function aeq for `''a`, the constructors which build the list must be recursively unwound:

```
fun eqlist aeq (Cons (x,l), Cons (y, m))
     = (aeq (x,y)) andalso (eqlist aeq (l, m))
  | eqlist aeq (Nil, Nil) = true
  | eqlist _ _ = false
```

Now we give the formal definitions of the equality interpretation of types. Given a type t, we define the equality function $\overline{\overline{t}}$ by induction on the structure of t. First, the equality function on products is given by

$$(f \mathbin{\overline{\overline{*}}} g)(x,y) = \begin{cases} \mathsf{true} & \text{if } x = (x_1, x_2) \text{ and } y = (y_1, y_2) \\ & \quad \text{and } f(x_1, y_1) = g(x_2, y_2) = \mathsf{true} \\ \mathsf{false} & \text{if } x = (x_1, x_2) \text{ and } y = (y_1, y_2) \\ & \quad \text{and } f(x_1, y_1) = \mathsf{false} \text{ or } g = (x_2, y_2)\mathsf{false} \\ \bot & \text{otherwise} \end{cases}$$

and on sums by

$$(f \mathbin{\overline{\overline{+}}} g)(x,y) = \begin{cases} f(x', y') & \text{if } x = (x', 0) \text{ and } y = (y', 0) \\ g(x', y') & \text{if } x = (x', 1) \text{ and } y = (y', 1) \\ \mathsf{false} & \text{if } x = (x', i) \text{ and } y = (y', j) \text{ and } i \neq j \\ \bot & \text{if } x = \bot \text{ or } y = \bot \end{cases}$$

A we saw with the definition of eqarrow the interpretation for the function spaces is essentially trivial

$$(f \overline{\overline{\rightarrow}}\, g)(x,y) = \begin{cases} \mathsf{true} & \text{if } x \neq \bot \text{ and } y \neq \bot \\ \bot & \text{otherwise.} \end{cases}$$

The interpretation for unit is similar:

$$(\overline{\overline{\textbf{unit}}})(x,y) = \begin{cases} \mathsf{true} & \text{if } x \neq \bot \text{ and } y \neq \bot \\ \bot & \text{otherwise.} \end{cases}$$

$\overline{\overline{\textbf{void}}}$ is the constant function to $\bot$. $\overline{\overline{\textbf{ref}}}\ (f)$ is the equality function on $N_\bot$.

The equality function for the recursive type operators is the limit of the equality functions associated with their finite approximates:

$$\overline{\overline{F_i}} = \bigvee_i \overline{\overline{F_i^j}}.$$

Theorem 8 *For any type expression t, if $\hat{t} = \mathsf{eq}$, then $\overline{\overline{t}}$ is the equality function on $\check{t}$.*

Proof. The proof is by an induction on the structure of t. The cases involving the primitive operators are straightforward. For the recursive type constructors F_i, note first that $\check{F}_i^j(\check{t}_1, \ldots, \check{t}_{n_i})$ is flat if $\hat{F}_i^j(\hat{t}_1, \ldots, \hat{t}_{n_i}) = \mathsf{eq}$ by Corollary 7. If $\overline{\overline{F_i^j}}$ is the equality function on

$$D_j = \check{F}_i^j(\check{t}_1, \ldots, \check{t}_{n_i})$$

for each j then $\overline{\overline{F_i}}$ is a limit of equality functions on domains D_j. Since these domains are all flat their limit is simply their union $\bigcup_j D_j$ and the limit of the equality functions on the parts is the equality function on the whole. Hence $\overline{\overline{F_i}}$ is the equality function on $\check{F}_i(\check{t}_1, \ldots, \check{t}_{n_i})$. ∎

The reader may now be curious why we have restricted ourselves to types with flat interpretations for those having an equality property. Could there be other types on which equality could be defined? Our domain-theoretic semantics offers some guidance on this point. Let us try to generalize our earlier definition of an equality function $=_D$ by relaxing the requirement that D is flat. It is clear that such a function can be defined on void and makes sense on any domain, but let us consider the simplest non-flat, non-trivial domain. This domain has three elements; indeed it is isomorphic to $\mathcal{E}$, but to avoid confusing matters, let us name its elements by $\bot < x < y$. This is the interpretation of the type **unit** $\rightarrow$ **unit** (which has precisely three distinct programs). Following the standard denotational interpretation of ML terms, the equality function on this type cannot be defined in ML because the equality function on this three point domain is not *monotone.* Indeed, no domain with a three element chain could have a definable equality function for this reason.

We may conclude that our abstract interpretation describes all and exactly the ML types on which a definable equality exists.

Figure 2: The Equality Kinds Lattice $\mathcal{O}$.

5 Calculating Equality Kinds

There is a problem with the abstract interpretation of types given in the previous sections. We cannot say of a type constructor that the type it yields will admit equality if and only if certain of its arguments admit equality. The difficulty is with the combination of the function space type constructor and void types. The type **unit** $\to$ **void** admits equality and the type **void** $\to$ **unit** admits equality, but **unit** $\to$ **unit** does not admit equality. There is a lack of independence between the two arguments to $\to$ when determining whether their resultant type admits equality. This example also shows why it was necessary for us to introduce void as a separate element of the equality properties lattice, $\mathcal{E}$. If we were to interpret $\widehat{\mathbf{void}}$ as eq, then what would be the correct value of eq $\hat{\to}$ eq? If we choose it to be eq, then we lose soundness, and if we choose it to be type, then we lose completeness. It is too naive to try to solve these problems by saying that "there are no elements of type void, so there is no reason to have it." Firstly, **void** may be a subexpression of a nonvoid type, such as **void** $\to$ **unit**. More importantly, we can only understand the recursive types by successive approximations, starting with the void type. Still, there is a useful, sensible theory that we can cull out based on the idea of banning void.

To begin with let us focus attention on the sublattice $\mathcal{O}$ of $\mathcal{E}$ consisting of the points $\{\mathsf{eq}, \mathsf{type}\}$ as picture in Figure 2. In this section, we will develop another abstract interpretation of ML types, using $\mathcal{O}$ instead of $\mathcal{E}$. This new interpretation has a succinct representation, which is readily computed from the types and type constructors. Moreover, if our recursive type constructors satisfy a reasonable void-avoiding property, when we restrict to the subalgebra of types not involving **void**, the two abstract interpretations turn out to be the same. Therefore, on this subalgebra, this new abstract interpretation will also turn out to be sound and complete.

As before, the definition of the abstract interpretation over $\mathcal{O}$ is given by first defining it on the constructors, and then extending it to closed type expressions by structural induction. The definition for the constructors is as follows:

- $\widetilde{\mathbf{void}} = \mathsf{eq}$;
- $\widetilde{\mathbf{unit}} = \mathsf{eq}$;
- $v_1 \tilde{+} v_2 = \max\{v_1, v_2\}$;

- $v_1 \tilde{*} v_2 = \max\{v_1, v_2\}$;
- for all $v_1, v_2 \in \mathcal{O}$ we have $v_1 \tilde{\rightarrow} v_2 = \mathsf{type}$;
- for all $v \in \mathcal{O}$ we have $\tilde{\mathbf{ref}}\ v = \mathsf{eq}$; and
- $\tilde{F}_i(v_1, \ldots, v_{n_i}) = \max_j\{\tilde{F}_i^j(v_1, \ldots, v_n)\}$.

Lemma 9 *For all i, j, we have $\tilde{F}_i^j \leq \tilde{F}_i^{j+1}$. Moreover, there exists a k such that for all i, $\tilde{F}_i^k = \tilde{F}_i^{k+1}$, and hence, $\tilde{F}_i = \tilde{F}_i^k$.*

Proof. The proof is the same as for Lemma 1. ∎

Lemma 10 *Given any n-ary type operator G over our type algebra, either for all $(v_1, \ldots, v_n) \in \mathcal{O}^n$ we have $\tilde{G}(v_1, \ldots, v_n) = \mathsf{type}$, or there exists a point $(z_1, \ldots, z_n)$ such that $\tilde{G}(v_1, \ldots, v_n) = \mathsf{eq}$ iff $v_i \leq z_i$, $i = 1, \ldots, n$.*

Proof. The proof is by structural induction on the body of G. The result follows immediately for the basic constructors. Therefore, by structural induction, we have the result for type operators composed solely of the basic operators. In particular, we have the result for the operators F_i^j. But then, the result for the recursive constructors follows immediately from the previous lemma, since for some k, $\tilde{F}_i = \tilde{F}_i^k$. ∎

Definition 11 Given any n-ary type operator G over our type algebra, if for all $(v_1, \ldots, v_n) \in \mathcal{O}^n$ we have $\tilde{G}(v_1, \ldots, v_n) = \mathsf{type}$, then the *equality kind* of G is $\not\ominus$, and we say that G does *not* admit equality. Otherwise, the *equality kind* of G is the point $(z_1, \ldots, z_n)$ such that $\tilde{G}(v_1, \ldots, v_n) = \mathsf{eq}$ iff $v_i \leq z_i$ for all $i = 1, \ldots, n$. ∎

In particular, if t is a closed (nullary) type expression, then either it does not admit equality, and therefore has equality kind $\not\ominus$, or it does admit equality and has equality kind $()$.

The equality kinds for the basic constructors is as follows:

- The equality kind of **void** is $()$.
- The equality kind of **unit** is $()$.
- The equality kind of both $+$ and $*$ is $(\mathsf{eq}, \mathsf{eq})$.
- The equality kind of $\rightarrow$ is $\not\ominus$.
- The equality kind of **ref** is type.

Notice that for n-ary type operators F and G that admit equality, we have that $\tilde{F} \leq \tilde{G}$ iff $(w_1, \ldots, w_n) \geq (z_1, \ldots, z_n)$ where $(w_1, \ldots, w_n)$ is the equality kind of F and $(z_1, \ldots, z_n)$ is the equality kind of G.

With these definitions it is possible to describe how to calculate the equality kind of a recursive type constructor. One simply carries out the iterations of the fixed point. By Lemma 9, this will terminate. The number of iterations required is bounded by the number of parameters in the type recursion, so the algorithm is quite efficient. This calculation will miss some types for which equality is computable, but only in cases that are uninteresting in practice. To state a crisp theorem, we must formulate a notion of "void avoidance". To do this, we now restrict our attention to that subalgebra of type expressions over basic constructors **unit**, $+$, $*$, $\rightarrow$, and **ref**, and the recursive operators, provided that the associated recursive equations are over just these basic constructors.

Definition 12 A set of recursive type constructor $F_1, \ldots, F_m$ is *void avoiding* provided that the second-order recursive operators $\mathcal{F}_i$ giving the recursive equations associated with them involve only the basic constructors **unit**, $+$, $*$, $\rightarrow$, and **ref**, and whenever the constructor F_i is applied to argument types $t_1 \ldots, t_{n_i}$, each of which has a non-void domain-theoretic interpretation, the resulting type has a domain-theoretic interpretation which is non-void, *i.e.* $\check{F}_i(\check{t_1}, \ldots, \check{t_{n_i}}) \neq \mathbf{0}$. ∎

Lemma 13 *Suppose that the set of recursive type operators $F_1, \ldots, F_m$ are void-avoiding. Then, for every closed type expression t not containing* **void** *as a subexpression, we have that $\hat{t} = \tilde{t}$.*

Proof. First notice that any closed type expression in this subalgebra will have an interpretation under $\frown$ of either eq or type. Therefore, we may view the abstract interpretation under $\frown$ of any n-ary type operator as a function from $\mathcal{O}^n$ into $\mathcal{O}$. To prove the lemma, it suffices to show that given any n-ary type operator G, the function $\hat{G}$, when restricted to $\mathcal{O}^n$ is the same as the function $\tilde{G}$. By structural induction, in fact it suffices to show this for the basic constructors (excluding **void**) and for the recursive constructors. The result follows immediately from the definitions of $\frown$ and $\sim$ for the basic constructors **unit**, $+$, $*$, $\rightarrow$, and **ref**.

Since the second-order operators $\mathcal{F}_i$ are composed solely of basic constructors, by structural induction we have that $\hat{\mathcal{F}}_i = \tilde{\mathcal{F}}_i$. Also, since $\hat{G} \leq \tilde{G}$ for every basic constructor G, we have that for each of the finite approximates $\hat{F}_i^j \leq \tilde{F}_i^j$. By Lemma 1, there exists a k such that

$$\hat{F}_i^k = \hat{\mathcal{F}}_i(\hat{F}_1^k, \ldots, \hat{F}_m^k) = \tilde{\mathcal{F}}_i(\hat{F}_1^k, \ldots, \hat{F}_m^k)$$

and $\hat{F}_i = \hat{F}_i^k$. Therefore, the operators $\hat{F}_i^k$ form a fixed point of the system $\tilde{\mathcal{F}}_1, \ldots, \tilde{\mathcal{F}}_m$. However, by their construction the functions $\tilde{F}_i$, $i = 1, \ldots, m$ form the least fix point of the operators $\tilde{\mathcal{F}}_i$. Since $\hat{F}_i = \hat{F}_i^k \leq \tilde{F}_i^k \leq \tilde{F}_i$, we must have that $\hat{F}_i = \tilde{F}_i$. ∎

Corollary 14 *(Soundness and Completeness) Suppose that the set of recursive type operators $F_1, \ldots, F_m$ are void-avoiding. Let G be a type operator defined in terms of the basic constructors* **unit**, $+$, $*$, $\rightarrow$ *and* **ref** *and the recursive constructors. Then G admits equality iff the equality kind of G is not $\not\oplus$. Moreover, if G admits equality with equality kind $(z_1, \ldots, z_n)$, then for any types $t_1, \ldots t_n$ which do not contain* **void** *as a subexpression, $\check{G}(\check{t}_1, \ldots, \check{t}_n)$ is flat iff $\tilde{t}_i \leq z_i$ for all $i = 1, \ldots, n$.*

6 Conclusions and Future Work

We have provided a sound and complete semantic analysis of the equality property for ML types and demonstrated an efficient algorithm for carrying out the inference of equality properties for void-avoiding systems of user-defined types. Our results are based on theorems that relate the standard denotational semantics of type constructors to an abstract interpretation that describes the equality kind of the operator.

The motivation for this work was to provide a more accurate version of the notion of equality types in Standard ML. Introducing the refined notion of equality kinds into Standard ML itself raises the question of how they would be integrated with the module system.

The easiest problem is specifying the equality kinds of type constructors in signatures. The current language definition provides a simple type specification

```
type ('a,'b) F
```

that does not constrain the equality kind of `F` at all, and the equality type specification

```
eqtype ('a,'b) F
```

that specifies that `F` has equality kind with succinct representation (eq, eq). To specify that `F` has the equality kind (eq, type) we might use the following notation:

```
type F: (eq,ty) => eq
```

A more complex interaction with modules involves the effect of sharing constraints in signatures. If two type constructor specifications are identified as a consequence of sharing constraints, it seems clear that they should have the same equality kind. This brings up the issue of compatibility of equality kind specifications and the problem of determining the resultant kind when two specifications share.

A third problem is how equality kinds are affected by functor applications. The definition of a type constructor in the body of a functor may depend on type constructors in the functor parameter with unspecified equality kinds, making it impossible to completely infer the equality kind of the defined constructor. When the functor is applied, the actual parameter supplies additional information that should be taken into account to recalculate the equality kind of the defined type constructor. This suggests partial and incremental calculation of equality kind information may be required.

These problems of integrating equality kinds with the module system are the subject of continuing research, with the experience with the current Standard ML treatment of equality kinds providing a starting point.

It is our belief that there are broader issues relating to equality types that involve other properties and operators which are defined uniformly from the structure of types. One might refer to this as *structural polymorphism.* It has come up in other contexts such as the study of subtyping and coercions between recursive types [BGS89]. Whether there is any general theory that connects these apparently similar phenomenon remains to be seen.

References

[BGS89] V. Breazu-Tannen, … *tational Semantics for Subtyping between R…* … MS-CIS-89-63/Logic & Computation 12, D… … nation Science, University of Pennsylvania…

[GS90] C. A. Gunter and D. S. … J. van Leeuwen, editor, *Handbook of Theoretical …*, pages 633–674, North Holland, 1990.

[MT91] R. Milner and M. Tofte. *Commentary on Standard ML.* MIT Press, 1991.

[MTH90] R. Milner, M. Tofte, and R. Harper. *The Definition of Standard ML.* MIT Press, 1990.

[Sco76] D. S. Scott. Data types as lattices. *SIAM Journal of Computing*, 5:522–587, 1976.

[Sco82a] D. S. Scott. Domains for denotational semantics. In M. Nielsen and E. M. Schmidt, editors, *International Colloquium on Automata, Languages and Programs*, pages 577–613, *Lecture Notes in Computer Science vol. 140*, Springer, 1982.

[Sco82b] D. S. Scott. Lectures on a mathematical theory of computation. In M. Broy and G. Schmidt, editors, *Theoretical Foundations of Programming Methodology*, pages 145–292, *NATO Advanced Study Institutes Series*, D. Reidel, 1982.

[SP82] M. Smyth and G. D. Plotkin. The category-theoretic solution of recursive domain equations. *SIAM Journal of Computing*, 11:761–783, 1982.

Full Abstraction and the Context Lemma (Preliminary Report)

Trevor Jim* and Albert R. Meyer†
MIT Laboratory for Computer Science

Abstract

A general notion of rewriting system of the kind used for evaluating simply typed λ-terms in Scott's PCF is defined. Any simply typed λ-calculus with PCF-like rewriting semantics is shown necessarily to satisfy Milner's Context Lemma. A simple argument demonstrates that any denotational semantics which is adequate for PCF and in which certain simple Boolean functionals exist, cannot be fully abstract for *any* extension of PCF satisfying the Context Lemma. An immediate corollary is that Berry's stable domains cannot be fully abstract for any extension of PCF definable by PCF-like rules. Thus, the idea of adding a combinator to PCF analogous to the "parallel-or" combinator which establishes full abstraction for the familiar cpo model cannot be generalized for models such as stable domains.

1 Introduction

Modern programming languages typically offer a variety of phrase types which are designated as "functional". One of the great successes of the Scott-Strachey approach to denotational semantics is the characterization of spaces of functions which rigorously capture and explain *prima facie* paradoxical properties of functional phrases involving self-application and recursion [32, 29]. Of course, the computational behavior of phrase types designated as functional must have some special character in order for functional meanings to capture the behavior directly with accuracy. The Context Lemma of Milner [21] provides one natural, purely operational criterion for assessing how "functional" the computational behavior of a programming language phrase may be.

Informally, the Context Lemma requires that if two phrases M, N of the same syntactic functional type yield visibly distinct computational outcomes when used in *some*

---

*E-mail: trevor@theory.lcs.mit.edu. Supported in part by ARO grant DAAL03-89-G-0071.

†E-mail: meyer@theory.lcs.mit.edu. Supported in part by ONR grant N00014-89-J-1988 and NSF grant 8819761-CCR.

language context, then there are actual parameters of appropriate argument type, such that M and N each simply *applied* to these arguments, yield visibly distinct computational outcomes. This property, more perspicuously dubbed *operational extensionality* by Bloom [9], has been identified by many authors as technically significant in program semantics [33, 23, 18, 1, 14, 2, 30]

The paradigmatic example of a functional programming language is PCF, Scott's simply typed λ-calculus for recursive functions on the integers [26]. The main technical contribution of this paper is a simple, modest restriction on the format of rewrite rules which is sufficient to guarantee the Context Lemma for PCF extensions defined by such rules. That is, we formulate a simple syntactic characterization of "PCF-like" rewrite rules. Any extension of PCF with simply typed combinators whose operational behavior is specified by such rules will satisfy the Context Lemma when, as usual, numerals are taken to be the visible outputs of programs. Key to the proof of the Context Lemma is a new Standard Reduction Theorem 14 for PCF-like rewrite systems; the Standard Reduction proof is only sketched in this preliminary version.

The most familiar model for PCF is the cpo model, which assigns "continuous" functions as meanings of phrases of functional type. The cpo model is *adequate* to explain the computational behavior of PCF in a precise technical sense: a PCF term evaluates to the numeral $\underline{n}$ iff its meaning in the cpo model is the integer n. But there are pairs of terms with distinct meanings in the cpo model which nevertheless are computationally indistinguishable in PCF. Only when PCF is extended with a "parallel-or" combinator can the language express enough computations to be *fully abstract* with the cpo semantics, *i.e.*, semantical distinctions and computational distinctions between terms coincide [25, 24].

The problem of characterizing the fully abstract model of unextended PCF remains open after nearly two decades, *cf.* [21, 7, 22, 31]. Efforts to construct spaces of "sequential" functions corresponding to those definable in the original PCF without parallelism have led to the discovery of a number of new domains suitable for denotational semantics. Although none are fully abstract for PCF, one motivation for the development of spaces such as the *stable* functions, *bistable* functions, *sequential algorithms* [4, 3, 7, 6, 12], and most recently the *strongly stable* functions [11] was that they captured various aspects of sequentiality and so seemed "closer" to full abstraction for unextended PCF than the cpo model .

The stable function model in particular has a simple definition and attractive category-theoretic properties. Its only apparent technical peculiarity is that stable domains of functions are not partially ordered pointwise; in general, the stable ordering strictly refines the pointwise ordering. Nevertheless, just as for the cpo model, the elements of stable domains of type $\sigma \to \tau$ are actually total functions from elements of type σ to elements of type τ. Likewise, there is a natural notion of finite and effective elements of stable domains, and these domains yield an adequate least fixed-point model for PCF. Further, they form a Cartesian Closed Category with solutions for domain equations [4]. This category was also independently discovered and used in constructing a model of polymorphic λ-calculus [13]. So the stable domains seem to offer a setting for a theory for higher-order recursive computation with many of the attractions of the popular cpo category.

However, one important result about cpo's is not known for stable domains, namely, full abstraction with respect to some extension of PCF analogous to the parallel-or extension which Plotkin-Sazonov provided for the cpo model. What might a symbolic-evaluator for an extended PCF look like if it was well matched—fully abstract—with the stable domain? We conclude as the main corollary of our analysis of the Context Lemma that such an evaluator will have to be unusual looking: it cannot be specified by the kind of term-rewriting based evaluation rules known for PCF and its extensions.

The significance of this negative result hinges heavily on how drastic we judge it to go beyond the scope of PCF-like rules. It is of course possible that some operational behavior that we declare to be non-PCF-like in our technical sense, will nevertheless offer a useful extension of PCF for which stable domains are fully abstract. For example, Bloom [9] provides such an extension for complete lattice models, though he goes on to criticize the rather complex algorithmic specification of the combinators in his extension. The general benefits of structured approaches to operational semantics and connections to full abstraction are discussed in [20, 10]

To illustrate the generality of our notion of PCF-like rules, we note that the standard extensions to PCF by parallel-or and existential combinators are easily seen to be PCF-like. For example, we can define an evaluator for Plotkin's $\exists$ constant [24] while remaining within a term rewriting discipline. Namely, let $p : \iota \rightarrow o$ be an "integer predicate" variable, and use the rules:

$$\begin{aligned} \exists p &\rightarrow \mathtt{cond}\,(p\underline{n})\,\mathtt{tt}\,\Omega, \\ \exists p &\rightarrow \mathtt{cond}\,(p\Omega)\,\Omega\,\mathtt{ff}. \end{aligned}$$

The resulting PCF-like language no longer has a confluent rewriting system, though it remains single-valued, *viz.*, every term rewrites to at most one numeral. In general, our PCF-like rules need not even be single valued.

Our work borrows much from Bloom [8, 9]. Scott [27, 28] originally proposed complete lattices as denotational models for PCF and for untyped lambda calculus as well. However, it was eventually agreed that the "extra" top elements in the lattices were technically distracting and, for example, caused a failure of full abstraction even in the presence of parallel-or. The second author raised the question of whether there was a "reasonable" extension of PCF that would yield an accurate evaluator for lattice models. Bloom recognized that the Context Lemma and full abstraction were incompatible with *single-valued* evaluators for the lattice model. He also characterized a general class of rewrite rules that ensured the soundness of the Context Lemma. However, Bloom's kind of rules were necessarily consistent, confluent, and single-valued, and in order to capture the computational behavior of the $\exists$ combinator, he needed to develop an auxiliary notion of "observation calculi".

Our PCF-like rules are, in an appropriate sense, as powerful as Bloom's observational calculi, and thus strictly subsume Bloom's class of rules. Indeed, as Bloom remarks [8], it is easy to sidestep his negative results with some very simple *multi-valued* PCF-like rules, namely, using multi-valued rules yields a PCF-extension both fully abstract for the lattice model and also satisfying the Context Lemma. No such maneuver sidesteps our results: not even multi-valued systems can achieve full abstraction for stable domains. Our wish to simplify Bloom's criteria while dealing with nonconfluent rewriting systems forced us, however, to a rather elaborate theory of standard reductions.

As an aside, we also point out that it is questionable whether the (bi)stable and similar domains are closer to full abstraction for PCF. In particular, although some operationally valid equations that fail in the cpo model do hold, for example, in the stable model, we note in Corollary 9 that the converse also happens: some equations that hold in the cpo model fail in the stable model. The cpo, stable and likewise the bistable models thus offer information about the operational behavior of PCF terms that is not apparently comparable, and it is hard to see how to judge which is a more accurate model.

The outline of our argument is as follows: We begin in Section 2, Theorem 8, with an easy proof that any denotational semantics that is adequate for PCF, and in which a certain simple Boolean functional exists, cannot be fully abstract for *any* extension of PCF satisfying the Context Lemma. The Boolean functional is obviously not continuous in Scott's sense, but it is stably continuous, and so does appear in the stable model. We then formulate in Section 3 our general notion of term rewriting systems of the kind used for symbolic evaluation of PCF terms. In Section 4, we show that any such system defines an observational congruence relation that must satisfy the Context Lemma [21]. An immediate corollary is Theorem 16 that there is no extension of PCF defined by PCF-like rewriting rules for which the stable domain semantics is fully abstract.

2 Full abstraction

We work with a language, $\mathcal{L}$, that is a simply typed λ-calculus with some typed constants. The behavior of terms will be defined through predicates on terms called *observations*. If an observation holds of a term we say that the term *yields* the observation, and we will base theories of program behavior on the observations yielded by terms.

We call any set $\mathcal{O}$ of observations a *notion of observation*. For example, $\mathcal{O}_{\text{eval}}$ captures the familiar notion of observing the final numerical outcome of an evaluation:

$$\mathcal{O}_{\text{eval}} = \{\text{ “evaluates to numeral } \underline{n}\text{” } \mid n \geq 0\,\}.$$

Another common notion of observation is $\mathcal{O}_{\text{int}}$, defined for a model $[\![\cdot]\!]$ of $\mathcal{L}$ in which the “integer” type ι actually contains the nonnegative integers:

$$\mathcal{O}_{\text{int}} = \{\text{ “has meaning approximated by } n\text{” } \mid n \geq 0\,\}.$$

Any notion of observation induces a preordering on terms as follows.

Definition 1

- Let $\mathcal{L}$ be a language with a notion of observation $\mathcal{O}$. We say a term M *observationally approximates* a term N, written $M \sqsubseteq_{obs} N$, if for all contexts $C[\cdot]$, whenever $C[M]$ yields an observation from $\mathcal{O}$, $C[N]$ yields it as well.

- We say that M and N are *observationally equivalent*, written $M \equiv_{obs} N$, if $M \sqsubseteq_{obs} N$ and $N \sqsubseteq_{obs} M$.

Proofs of observational equivalence can often be simplified by appealing to the *Context Lemma*.

Definition 2

- Let $\mathcal{L}$ be a language with a notion of observation $\mathcal{O}$. We say a closed term M *applicatively approximates* a closed term N, written $M \sqsubseteq_{app} N$, if for all vectors of terms, $\vec{P}$, whenever $M\vec{P}$ yields an observation from $\mathcal{O}$, $N\vec{P}$ yields it as well.

- A language $\mathcal{L}$ with notion of observation $\mathcal{O}$ is said to *satisfy the Context Lemma* if for all closed terms M and N,

$$M \sqsubseteq_{app} N \quad \text{iff} \quad M \sqsubseteq_{obs} N.$$

Lemma 3 (Milner) *PCF under $\mathcal{O}_{\text{eval}}$ satisfies the Context Lemma.*

We will see later that the Context Lemma holds for all languages defined in a "PCF-like" operational discipline, including, of course, PCF itself.

In the setting of the simply typed λ-calculus with a ground type ι corresponding to the integers, the fundamental notion of computational observation is $\mathcal{O}_{\text{eval}}$. Models in which the ordering $\sqsubseteq_{obs}$ induced by $\mathcal{O}_{\text{eval}}$ coincides with that induced by $\mathcal{O}_{\text{int}}$ are called *adequate*:

Definition 4 Let $[\![\cdot]\!]$ be a model for a language $\mathcal{L}$ with numerals $\underline{n} : \iota$ for $n \geq 0$ such that $[\![\underline{n}]\!] = n$. Then the model is *computationally adequate at integer type* if for all closed terms $M : \iota$ and $n \geq 0$,

$$n \sqsubseteq [\![M]\!] \quad \text{iff} \quad M \text{ evaluates to } \underline{n}.$$

We will only work with such adequate models throughout the rest of the paper, and henceforth assume that $\sqsubseteq_{obs}$ and $\sqsubseteq_{app}$ are the observational relations determined by $\mathcal{O}_{\text{eval}}$, or equivalently, by $\mathcal{O}_{\text{int}}$, as convenient.

The definition of model (*cf.* Appendix B) implies that for such adequate models, the relation $\sqsubseteq$ on the meanings of terms refines observational approximation with respect to $\mathcal{O}_{\text{int}}$:

Lemma 5 *Let $[\![\cdot]\!]$ be a model for a language $\mathcal{L}$ with numerals $\underline{n} : \iota$ for $n \geq 0$ such that $[\![\underline{n}]\!] = n$. If the model is computationally adequate at integer type, then for all closed terms M, N of the same type, $[\![M]\!] \sqsubseteq [\![N]\!]$ implies $M \sqsubseteq_{obs} N$.*

Note that in general the relation $\sqsubseteq$ in a model may be *strictly* finer on the meanings of terms than the relation $\sqsubseteq_{obs}$. When they coincide, the model is said to be (inequationally) fully abstract:

Definition 6 Let $[\![\cdot]\!]$ be a model for a language $\mathcal{L}$. We say $[\![\cdot]\!]$ is *inequationally fully abstract* with a notion of observation $\mathcal{O}$, if for all terms M and N,

$$[\![M]\!] \sqsubseteq [\![N]\!] \quad \text{iff} \quad M \sqsubseteq_{obs} N.$$

It is *equationally fully abstract* if for all M and N,

$$[\![M]\!] = [\![N]\!] \quad \text{iff} \quad M \equiv_{obs} N.$$

Henceforth, we consider full abstraction only with respect to $\mathcal{O}_{\text{int}}$—or equivalently $\mathcal{O}_{eval}$, since models will be computationally adequate.

The rest of this section is concerned specifically with the language PCF and its extensions. We defer precise definitions to Appendices A and B, giving only a few relevant facts here.

PCF is a simply typed λ-calculus with Boolean and natural number base types, and simple arithmetic, recursion, and conditional operators. Two models will be highlighted: the cpo model $\mathcal{C}[\![\cdot]\!]$ and the stable model $\mathcal{S}[\![\cdot]\!]$. Both models are adequate but not fully abstract for PCF.

Our theorems apply to adequate models of PCF in which the ground domain $[\![o]\!]$, corresponding to the Booleans, is the flat cpo $\{tt, ff, \bot\}$, and in which $[\![\mathtt{tt}]\!] = tt$. (Adequacy then implies that also $[\![\mathtt{ff}]\!] = ff$.) The first theorem is predicated on the existence of certain simple functionals over the flat Booleans.

Definition 7 Let *True* be the constant *tt* function on the flat Booleans, and *True!* be the strict constant *tt* function. A *true-separator* is a function f satisfying

$$\begin{aligned} f(\mathit{True}) &= tt, \\ f(\mathit{True!}) &= ff. \end{aligned}$$

Theorem 8 *Let $[\![\cdot]\!]$ be a model that is adequate for some extension of PCF satisfying the Context Lemma. If $[\![\cdot]\!]$ contains a true-separator, it is not equationally fully abstract.*

Proof: First consider the terms `True` and `True!`:

$$\begin{aligned} \mathtt{True} &\stackrel{\text{def}}{\equiv} \lambda x.\mathtt{tt}, \\ \mathtt{True!} &\stackrel{\text{def}}{\equiv} \lambda x.\mathtt{cond}\ x\ \mathtt{tt}\ \mathtt{tt}. \end{aligned}$$

With $[\![o]\!]$ equal to the flat Booleans, we have by the definition of adequate model that $[\![\mathtt{True}]\!] = \mathit{True}$, $[\![\mathtt{True!}]\!] = \mathit{True!}$, and $\mathtt{True!} \sqsubseteq_{app} \mathtt{True}$. So by the Context Lemma, $\mathtt{True!} \sqsubseteq_{obs} \mathtt{True}$.

We conclude that there is no term P defining a true-separator; otherwise `True!` and `True` yield distinct observations in the context $(\mathtt{cond}\,(P[\cdot])\,\underline{0}\,\underline{1})$, contradicting the fact that $\mathtt{True!} \sqsubseteq_{obs} \mathtt{True}$.

However, we can define a true-separator *detector*, D, as follows:

$$D \stackrel{\text{def}}{\equiv} \lambda x.\mathtt{cond}\,(x\,\mathtt{True})\,(\mathtt{cond}\,(x\,\mathtt{True!})\,\Omega^o\,\underline{\mathtt{tt}})\,\Omega^o,$$

where Ω^o is a divergent term, say, $(\mathtt{Y}_o\lambda z^o.z)$. By the definition of adequate model, $[\![\Omega^o]\!] = \bot$, and

$$[\![D]\!](x) = \begin{cases} tt & \text{if } x \text{ is a true-separator,} \\ \bot & \text{otherwise.} \end{cases}$$

Now from the definition of model, it follows that the term $\lambda x.\Omega^o$ must denote the constant $\bot$ function. So $[\![D]\!] \neq [\![\lambda x.\Omega^o]\!]$, since they differ exactly on arguments which are true-separators. But since true-separators are not definable by terms, D and $\lambda x.\Omega^o$ are applicatively congruent. Then by the Context Lemma, they are observationally congruent, contradicting equational full abstraction. ■

Corollary 9 *If a stable function model is adequate for an extension of PCF that satisfies the Context Lemma, then the model is not equationally fully abstract.*

Proof: Every stable model in which $[\![o]\!]$ is the flat Boolean cpo contains a true-separator *truesep*, defined as follows:

$$truesep(x) = \begin{cases} tt & \text{if } x = True, \\ ff & \text{if } x = True!, \\ \bot & \text{otherwise.} \end{cases}$$

■

Corollary 10 *The PCF equations valid in the stable model do not include those valid in the cpo model.*

Proof: Just note that $\mathcal{C}[\![D]\!] = \mathcal{C}[\![\lambda x.\Omega^o]\!]$ but $\mathcal{S}[\![D]\!] \neq \mathcal{S}[\![\lambda x.\Omega^o]\!]$. ■

Our proof of Corollary 9 of course takes advantage of the notable fact that the stable ordering of functions differs from the pointwise ordering, *e.g.*, the pair of functions *True* and *True!* are ordered pointwise but are stable-incomparable. In fact, the first few lines of the proof of Theorem 8 already show that *in*equational full abstraction is incompatible with the Context Lemma for any model in which *True* and *True!* are incomparable; the rest of the proof justifies the stronger conclusion that *equational* full abstraction fails as well.

Berry realized that altering the pointwise ordering of functions caused difficulties, and he proposed from the start an additional *bistable* model which combines stability with pointwise ordering. The counterexample of Corollary 10 does not apply to the bistable model, but a similar argument nevertheless shows that bistable domains are not an obvious improvement on cpo's as models of PCF. This will be discussed in the full version of this paper, *cf.* [16].

3 PCF-like rewrite systems

Symbolic evaluators for PCF terms are often presented as term rewriting systems. In this section, we give the basic definitions for such systems, and give our criteria for calling such a system "PCF-like". Our evaluator for PCF is given in Appendix A.

A *rewrite rule* is a pair $l \to r$ of terms of the same type, such that the free variables of the right-hand side r are included in those of the left-hand side l. We write $M \xrightarrow{\Delta}_\pi N$ if for some subterm Δ of M, $\Delta \to \Delta'$ is an instance of the rule π, and N is obtained from M by replacing Δ with Δ'. We will omit Δ or π as convenient.

Since all of our languages are simply typed λ-calculi, we will always include β-reduction in the rewrite rules of the language. Additionally, we may specify some set Θ of *δ-rules* defining the behavior of the constants. Together, Θ and β define the *rewriting relation* $\to_{\Theta,\beta}$ on the language $\mathcal{L}$. We omit Θ and β when they can be recovered from context.

The δ-rules of PCF have a particularly simple form:

Definition 11

(i) A *linear ground δ-rule* is a rewrite rule of the form

$$\delta\vec{m} \to P,$$

where each m_i is either a ground constant c_i or a variable x_i. The variables x_i must be distinct.

(ii) A *PCF-like rewrite system* is a language $\mathcal{L}$ together with a set Θ of linear ground δ-rules on the constants of $\mathcal{L}$.

Note that this definition of "PCF-like" is meant to be generous. In particular, although the system for pure, unextended PCF is both single-valued—every term reduces to at most one constant—and confluent, PCF-like systems in general may be multiple-valued and nonconfluent.

An interesting example of a multiple-valued PCF-like system arises in [8]. There, Bloom defines an extension of PCF that is both fully abstract and denotationally universal for the lattice model of PCF. The key to the construction is the addition of a top constant, $\top^\sigma$, for each ground type σ; and it is the top constants that make the language multiple-valued. Each $\top^\sigma$ rewrites to all other ground constants of type σ; for example, the Boolean top constant $\top^o$ rewrites to both $\mathtt{tt}$ and $\mathtt{ff}$.

Nonconfluent but single-valued systems are also of interest. For example, [24] extends parallel PCF by an existential operator, $\exists : (\iota \to o) \to o$, to achieve a language that is fully abstract and denotationally universal for the cpo model. There, $\exists$ is defined by the deductive rules

$$\frac{p\underline{n} \twoheadrightarrow \mathtt{tt}}{\exists p \to \mathtt{tt}}, \qquad \frac{p\Omega \twoheadrightarrow \mathtt{ff}}{\exists p \to \mathtt{ff}},$$

where $\twoheadrightarrow$ is the reflexive transitive closure of $\rightarrow$. The resulting language is indeed confluent, but goes beyond mere term rewriting. To capture the deductive style for specifying constants like $\exists$, Bloom [9] introduces *observation calculi* as a definition of "PCF-like" deductive rules. By giving up confluence, we can define an $\exists$ constant while remaining within a term rewriting discipline, as indicated in the Introduction. This kind of rewriting is more straightforward, but actually as powerful as the deductive discipline.

Since PCF-like systems are not confluent in general, we will not be able to use confluence in our proof of the Context Lemma. Instead we will rely on a *standardization theorem*, which states that if a term M rewrites to a term N, then there is a "standard" reduction from M to N. Thus we only need consider these standard reductions in our proof.

The technical machinery required just for the precise definition of standard reductions, excluding the proofs, is extensive, and we defer it to the full version of this paper. Instead, we now provide an informal description of standardization sufficient for the proof of the Context Lemma in the next section.

First, we introduce some useful notation. Consider the set of indices i such that m_i is a constant in rule $\theta : \delta\vec{m} \rightarrow P$. These indices identify what we call the *critical* arguments of θ, since the rule θ applies to a term $\delta\vec{Q}$ iff $Q_i \equiv c_i$ for i in the set. For expository purposes it will be convenient to separate the critical and non-critical arguments of a constant δ (relative to some linear ground δ-rule θ).

Notation 12 Let $\theta : \delta\vec{m} \rightarrow P$ be a linear ground δ-rule with j critical arguments and k non-critical arguments. Then for vectors $\vec{A} \equiv A_1 \cdots A_j$ and $\vec{B} \equiv B_1 \cdots B_k$, we let

$$\delta_\theta\langle\vec{A}, \vec{B}\rangle \stackrel{\text{def}}{\equiv} \delta\vec{Q},$$

where $\vec{Q}$ is the interleaving of $\vec{A}$ and $\vec{B}$ such that the A_i's appear at the critical indices of $\vec{Q}$. We drop the subscript θ when it can be recovered from context.

Note that we do not require that $\delta\vec{Q}$ be an instance of $\delta\vec{m}$; we will want to use the $\delta\langle\cdot,\cdot\rangle$ notation on terms that we anticipate becoming θ-redexes over the course of a reduction.

In this notation, we write linear ground δ-rules as

$$\theta : \delta\langle\vec{c}, \vec{x}\rangle \rightarrow P$$

or even

$$\theta : \delta\langle\vec{c}, \vec{x}\rangle \rightarrow P(\vec{x})$$

when we wish to make the dependence of P on $\vec{x}$ explicit.

Typically, the standard reductions are a class of reductions with a particularly nice structure and description. For instance, in the pure, typed λ-calculus, a standard reduction is one in which redexes are contracted from left to right.

The definition of standard reductions in PCF-like rewrite systems is more complicated because they admit the upwards creation of redexes, *cf.* [15]. For instance the term

$$\delta_\theta\langle c_1 \cdots c_{n-1} C, \vec{D}\rangle$$

is not a θ-redex, but the contraction of the subterm $C \to c_n$ creates the redex $\delta_\theta\langle \vec{c}, \vec{D}\rangle$. The new redex is to the left of C, but clearly cannot be contracted before it.

Definition 13 (informal) A *standard reduction* in a PCF-like rewrite system is a reduction in which redexes are contracted from left to right, except that redexes in the critical arguments of a δ-term contract before the δ-redex and before redexes in non-critical arguments. We will write $M \twoheadrightarrow_s N$ for a standard reduction from M to N.

Thus a standard reduction involving a δ-contraction might look like:

$$\begin{aligned} \delta\langle \vec{C}, \vec{D}\rangle \vec{E} &\twoheadrightarrow_s \delta\langle c_1 C_2 \cdots C_n, \vec{D}\rangle \vec{E} \\ &\twoheadrightarrow_s \cdots \\ &\twoheadrightarrow_s \delta\langle \vec{c}, \vec{D}\rangle \vec{E} \\ &\to_\theta P(\vec{D})\vec{E} \\ &\twoheadrightarrow_s \cdots \end{aligned}$$

where each $C_i \twoheadrightarrow_s c_i$.

Theorem 14 (Standardization) *For any PCF-like rewrite system with δ-rules Θ, if $M \twoheadrightarrow_{\Theta,\beta} N$, then there is a standard reduction $M \twoheadrightarrow_s N$.*

Note that if we require our rules to be *consistent* and *non-overlapping*, as did [9], then they are a special case of *orthogonal* rewrite systems, for which standardization has been known for some time [15]. However then we would lose the ability to define constants like $\exists$.

4 The Context Lemma

Given standardization, we prove the Context Lemma by a straightforward adaptation of Bloom's proof for his observation calculi [9].

Lemma 15 (Context Lemma) *In any PCF-like rewrite system,*

$$M \sqsubseteq_{obs} N \quad \text{iff} \quad M \sqsubseteq_{app} N$$

for all closed terms M and N.

Proof:

($\Longrightarrow$) Trivial.

($\Longleftarrow$) Suppose $M \sqsubseteq_{app} N$, and $C[\cdot]$ is a program context for M such that $C[M] \twoheadrightarrow_s c$. We show $C[N] \twoheadrightarrow c$ by induction on the length of the reduction $C[M] \twoheadrightarrow_s c$.

1. The only reductions $C[M] \twoheadrightarrow_s c$ of length zero are $c \twoheadrightarrow c$. Then one of the following holds:

   (a) $C[\cdot] \equiv c$. Then clearly $C[N] \equiv c \twoheadrightarrow c$.

   (b) $C[\cdot] \equiv [\cdot]$ and $M \equiv c$. Here $C[N] \twoheadrightarrow c$ because $M \sqsubseteq_{app} N$.

For the induction, we consider subcases on the form of $C[\cdot]$.

2. $C[\cdot] \equiv (\lambda x C_1[\cdot])C_2[\cdot] \cdots C_n[\cdot]$. Then the reduction $C[M] \twoheadrightarrow_s c$ is of the form

$$\begin{array}{rcl} C[M] & \equiv & (\lambda x C_1[M])C_2[M] \cdots C_n[M] \\ & \rightarrow_\beta & (C_1[M])[x := C_2[M]]C_3[M] \cdots C_n[M] \\ & \twoheadrightarrow_s & c. \end{array}$$

Define the context $C'[\cdot]$ as follows:

$$C'[\cdot] \stackrel{\text{def}}{\equiv} C_0[\cdot]C_3[\cdot] \cdots C_n[\cdot],$$

where $C_0[\cdot]$ is the context obtained from $C_1[\cdot]$ by replacing free occurrences of x by $C_2[\cdot]$.

Because M and N are closed, we have

$$\begin{array}{rrcl} & C'[M] & \equiv & (C_1[M])[x := C_2[M]]C_3[M] \cdots C_n[M] \\ \text{and} & C'[N] & \equiv & (C_1[N])[x := C_2[N]]C_3[N] \cdots C_n[N]. \end{array}$$

Then since $C'[M] \twoheadrightarrow_s c$, by induction $C'[N] \twoheadrightarrow c$. And since $C[N] \rightarrow_\beta C'[N]$, we have $C[N] \twoheadrightarrow c$ as desired.

3. $C[\cdot] \equiv \delta C_1[\cdot] \cdots C_n[\cdot]$. Then the reduction $C[M] \twoheadrightarrow_s c$ must contract the head δ by some rule $\theta : \delta_\theta\langle \vec{c}, \vec{x}\rangle \rightarrow P(\vec{x})$. Accordingly, we rewrite $C[\cdot]$ as

$$C[\cdot] \equiv \delta_\theta\langle \vec{D}[\cdot], \vec{E}[\cdot]\rangle \vec{F}[\cdot].$$

Then the reduction $C[M] \twoheadrightarrow_s c$ is of the form

$$\begin{array}{rcl} C[M] & \equiv & \delta_\theta\langle \vec{D}[M], \vec{E}[M]\rangle \vec{F}[M] \\ & \twoheadrightarrow_s & \delta_\theta\langle \vec{c}, \vec{E}[M]\rangle \vec{F}[M] \\ & \rightarrow_\theta & P(\vec{E}[M])\vec{F}[M] \\ & \twoheadrightarrow_s & c. \end{array}$$

By induction, we have $D_i[N] \twoheadrightarrow c_i$. And as in case 2, by defining $C'[\cdot]$ to be the context obtained from $P(\vec{x})\vec{F}[\cdot]$ by replacing each free x_j in P by $E_j[\cdot]$, we have

$$\begin{array}{rrcl} & C'[M] & \equiv & P(\vec{E}[M])\vec{F}[M] \\ \text{and} & C'[N] & \equiv & P(\vec{E}[N])\vec{F}[N]. \end{array}$$

And since $C'[M] \twoheadrightarrow_s c$, by induction we know $C'[N] \twoheadrightarrow c$. Thus we have found a reduction

$$\begin{array}{rcl} C[N] & \equiv & \delta_\theta\langle \vec{D}[N], \vec{E}[N]\rangle \vec{F}[N] \\ & \twoheadrightarrow & \delta_\theta\langle \vec{c}, \vec{E}[N]\rangle \vec{F}[N] \\ & \rightarrow_\theta & P(\vec{E}[N])\vec{F}[N] \\ & \twoheadrightarrow & c. \end{array}$$

4. $C[\cdot] \equiv [\cdot]C_1[\cdot]\cdots C_n[\cdot]$. Then consider the context

$$C'[\cdot] \stackrel{\text{def}}{\equiv} MC_1[\cdot]\cdots C_n[\cdot].$$

Note that $C[M] \equiv C'[M]$, so $C'[M] \twoheadrightarrow_s c$. Moreover $C'[\cdot]$ must be of a form considered in the two previous cases, and so by the previous argument we conclude $C'[N] \twoheadrightarrow c$. Now consider the applicative context

$$C''[\cdot] \stackrel{\text{def}}{\equiv} [\cdot]C_1[N]\cdots C_n[N].$$

Since $C''[M] \equiv C'[N]$, we have $C''[M] \twoheadrightarrow c$. Finally, $M \sqsubseteq_{app} N$ implies $C''[N] \twoheadrightarrow c$; and

$$\begin{array}{rcl} C''[N] & \equiv & [N]C_1[N]\cdots C_n[N] \\ & \equiv & C[N], \end{array}$$

so $C[N] \twoheadrightarrow c$.

■

We have immediately from Corollary 9:

Theorem 16 *Every stable function model that is adequate for an extension of PCF defined by PCF-like rewrite rules is not equationally fully abstract.*

5 Conclusions and Future Work

We have extended the metatheory of term rewriting operational semantics for simply typed λ-calculi and shown that certain denotational models, in particular the stable domains, cannot be fully abstract for such operational semantics. We believe that our results should apply straightforwardly to the strongly stable model, but we have not had time to verify this.

The category of sequential algorithms [5] is technically not a model in our sense, but is like the stable model in that it is a Cartesian Closed Category with partially ordered function objects which are not pointwise ordered. We believe that with some minor modifications our results will apply to it as well. (This claim stands in apparent contradiction to the results of [5], which shows that the language CDS, based on concrete data structures [17], is fully abstract for the sequential algorithm model. However, it seems questionable to us to call a language such as CDS "PCF-like", since it does not have λ-abstraction or even variables.)

An important open question is whether our methods can be refined to cover the bistable and bisequential models, which are pointwise ordered. We show in the full version of this paper that full abstraction for these order-extensional models is inconsistent with a version of the Context Lemma involving "comparability" in place of approximation, where M and N are *observationally comparable* iff for each context $C[\cdot]$, the observations yielded by $C[M]$ are setwise comparable to those yielded by $C[N]$. However, fully general PCF-like rewrite rules do not guarantee a Comparability Context Lemma, so we must require more restrictions on the definition of "PCF-like" in order to obtain a version of Theorem 16 for order-extensional models.

Finally, it might be interesting to extend our results to lazy, call-by-value, and untyped languages.

Acknowledgments

We are grateful to B. Bloom, G. Berry, P.-L. Curien, J.-J. Lévy, G.D. Plotkin, and Scott Smith for helpful discussions.

References

[1] S. Abramsky. The lazy lambda calculus. In D. L. Turner, editor, *Research Topics in Functional Programming.* Addison-Wesley Publishing Co., 1989.

[2] S. Abramsky. Domain theory in logical form. *Ann. Pure Appl. Logic*, 51:1–77, 1991.

[3] G. Berry. Séquentialité de l'evaluation formelle des lambda-expressions. In B. Robinet, editor, *Program Transformations, 3eme Colloque International sur la programmation*, pages 67–80, 1978.

[4] G. Berry. Stable models of typed lambda-calculi. In G. Ausiello and C. Böhm, editors, *Automata, Languages and Programming: Fifth Colloquium*, volume 62 of *Lecture Notes in Computer Science*, pages 72–89. Springer-Verlag, July 1978.

[5] G. Berry and P.-L. Curien. Sequential algorithms on concrete data structures. *Theor. Comput. Sci.*, 20(3):265–321, July 1982.

[6] G. Berry and P.-L. Curien. Theory and practice of sequential algorithms: the kernel of the programming language CDS. In M. Nivat and J. C. Reynolds, editors,

Algebraic Methods in Semantics, chapter 2, pages 35–87. Cambridge Univ. Press, 1985.

[7] G. Berry, P.-L. Curien, and J.-J. Lévy. Full abstraction for sequential languages: the state of the art. In M. Nivat and J. C. Reynolds, editors, *Algebraic Methods in Semantics*, chapter 3, pages 89–132. Cambridge Univ. Press, 1985.

[8] B. Bloom. Can LCF be topped? Flat lattice models of typed lambda calculus (preliminary report). In *Third Annual Symposium on Logic in Computer Science*, pages 282–295. IEEE, 1988.

[9] B. Bloom. Can LCF be topped? Flat lattice models of typed λ-calculus. *Information and Computation*, 87(1/2):263–300, July/Aug. 1990.

[10] B. Bloom, S. Istrail, and A. R. Meyer. Bisimulation can't be traced (preliminary report). In *Conference Record of the Fifteenth Annual ACM Symposium on Principles of Programming Languages*, pages 229–239, 1988. Also appears as MIT Technical Memo MIT/LCS/TM-345; submitted for journal publication.

[11] A. Bucciarelli and T. Ehrard. Sequentiality and strong stability. In *Proceedings, Sixth Annual IEEE Symposium on Logic in Computer Science*, 1991. to appear.

[12] P.-L. Curien. *Categorical Combinators, Sequential Algorithms and Functional Programming.* John Wiley and Sons, 1986.

[13] J.-Y. Girard. The system F of variable types, fifteen years later. *Theor. Comput. Sci.*, 45:152–192, 1986.

[14] D. J. Howe. Equality in lazy computation systems. In *Proceedings, Fourth Annual Symposium on Logic in Computer Science*, pages 198–203. IEEE, 1989.

[15] G. Huet and J.-J. Lévy. Computations in nonambiguous term rewriting systems. Technical Report 359, INRIA, Rocquencourt, France, 1979.

[16] T. Jim and A. R. Meyer. Communication in the TYPES electronic forum (types@theory.lcs.mit.edu). June 17th, 1989.

[17] G. Kahn and D. B. MacQueen. Coroutines and networks of parallel processes. In B. Gilchrist, editor, *Information Processing '77*, pages 993–998. North-Holland Publishing Co., 1977.

[18] I. Mason and C. Talcott. Programming, transforming, and proving with function abstractions and memories. In G. Ausiello, M. Dezani-Ciancaglini, and S. R. D. Rocca, editors, *Automata, Languages and Programming: 16th International Colloquium*, volume 372 of *Lecture Notes in Computer Science*. Springer-Verlag, 1989.

[19] A. R. Meyer. What is a model of the lambda calculus? *Information and Control*, 52(1):87–122, Jan. 1982.

[20] A. R. Meyer. Semantical paradigms: Notes for an invited lecture, with two appendices by Stavros Cosmadakis. In *Third Annual Symposium on Logic in Computer Science*, pages 236–253. IEEE, 1988.

[21] R. Milner. Fully abstract models of the typed lambda calculus. *Theor. Comput. Sci.*, 4:1–22, 1977.

[22] K. Mulmuley. *Full Abstraction and Semantic Equivalence.* ACM Doctoral Dissertation Award 1986. MIT Press, 1987.

[23] C.-H. L. Ong. *The Lazy Lambda Calculus: An Investigation into the Foundations of Functional Programming.* PhD thesis, Imperial College, University of London, 1988.

[24] G. D. Plotkin. LCF considered as a programming language. *Theor. Comput. Sci.*, 5(3):223–256, Dec. 1977.

[25] V. Sazonov. Expressibility of functions in D. Scott's LCF language. *Algebra i Logika*, 15:308–330, 1976. (Russian).

[26] D. S. Scott. A type theoretical alternative to CUCH, ISWIM, OWHY. Manuscript, Oxford Univ., 1969.

[27] D. S. Scott. Continuous lattices. In F. W. Lawvere, editor, *Toposes, Algebraic Geometry and Logic*, volume 274 of *Lecture Notes in Mathematics*, pages 97–136. Springer-Verlag, 1972.

[28] D. S. Scott. Data types as lattices. *SIAM J. Comput.*, 5:522–587, 1976.

[29] D. S. Scott. Logic and programming languages. *Commun. ACM*, 20:634–645, 1977.

[30] S. Smith. From operational to denotational semantics. In *Mathematical Foundations of Programming Semantics*, 1991. To appear.

[31] A. Stoughton. *Fully Abstract Models of Progamming Languages.* Research Notes in Theoretical Computer Science. Pitman/Wiley, 1988. Revision of Ph.D thesis, Dept. of Computer Science, Univ. Edinburgh, Report No. CST-40-86, 1986.

[32] C. Strachey. Fundamental concepts in programming languages. Lecture Notes, Int'l. Summer School in Computer Programming, Copenhagen., 1967.

[33] C. Talcott. Programming and proving with function and control abstractions. Technical Report STAN-CS-89-1288, Stanford Univ., 1988.

$$\begin{array}{rcll} \texttt{tt},\texttt{ff} & : & o & \\ \underline{n} & : & \iota & \text{for each integer } n \geq 0 \\ \texttt{succ},\texttt{pred} & : & \iota \to \iota & \\ \texttt{zero?} & : & \iota \to o & \\ \texttt{cond}_o & : & o \to o \to o \to o & \\ \texttt{cond}_\iota & : & o \to \iota \to \iota \to \iota & \\ \texttt{Y}_\sigma & : & (\sigma \to \sigma) \to \sigma & \text{for each type } \sigma \end{array}$$

Figure 1: Constants of PCF

A PCF

Because we will work with both PCF and its extensions, we give the general definitions for simply typed λ-calculi. A language is parameterized by its ground types and typed constants; for instance, PCF's ground types are the Booleans o and the numerals ι, and its constants are listed in Figure 1.

The set of *types* of the language is the least set containing the ground types and $(\sigma \to \tau)$ for types σ and τ. The typed *terms* of the language are defined inductively:

- A constant δ^σ is a term of type σ.
- A variable x^σ is a term of type σ.
- If M is a term of type $(\sigma \to \tau)$ and N is a term of type σ, then (MN) is a term of type τ.
- If M is a term of type τ, then $(\lambda x^\sigma M)$ is a term of type $(\sigma \to \tau)$.

We omit types and parentheses whenever possible, adopting the standard conventions of association: application associates to the left, and types associate to the right. We will use $M, N, P, \ldots$ to denote arbitrary terms; $x, y, z, \ldots$ to denote arbitrary variables; and $\sigma, \tau, \gamma, \ldots$ to denote arbitrary types. δ will always denote a constant, and c will always be a ground constant. The binary relation symbol $\equiv$ denotes syntactic equality.

Free and bound variables are defined as usual, and we consider terms that are identical modulo a change of bound variables to be syntactically identical. A term is *closed* if it has no free variables; otherwise it is *open*. A *program* is a closed term of ground type.

A *substitution* is a well-typed mapping of variables to terms. Substitutions are extended to terms as usual (taking care to avoid capture of free variables), and are written postfix, so that $M\rho$ is the application of the substitution ρ to the term M. We call $M\rho$ an *instance* of M. If $\vec{x} \equiv x_1, \ldots, x_n$ and $\vec{N} \equiv N_1, \ldots, N_n$, then $[\vec{x} := \vec{N}]$ is the substitution that maps each x_i to N_i (simultaneously), and is the identity otherwise. A special case is $[x := N]$, so that $M[x := N]$ is the result of substituting N for x in M. Sometimes we write $M \equiv M(\vec{x})$, with the intent that $M(\vec{N}) \equiv M[\vec{x} := \vec{N}]$.

$$\begin{aligned}
\texttt{cond}\,\texttt{tt}\,x\,y &\rightarrow x \\
\texttt{cond}\,\texttt{ff}\,x\,y &\rightarrow y \\[1em]
\texttt{zero?}\,\underline{0} &\rightarrow \texttt{tt} \\
\texttt{zero?}\,\underline{n+1} &\rightarrow \texttt{ff} \\[1em]
\texttt{succ}\,\underline{n} &\rightarrow \underline{n+1} \\[1em]
\texttt{pred}\,\underline{0} &\rightarrow \underline{0} \\
\texttt{pred}\,\underline{n+1} &\rightarrow \underline{n} \\[1em]
\texttt{Y}\,f &\rightarrow f(\texttt{Y}\,f)
\end{aligned}$$

Figure 2: Rewrite rules for PCF

A *context* $C[\cdot]$ is a term with some holes. $C[M]$ denotes the result of putting M into the holes of $C[\cdot]$, which may cause free variables of M to become bound. We say $C[\cdot]$ is a *program context* for M if $C[M]$ is a closed term of ground type.

The interpreter of the language is defined via a rewrite system; any set of δ-rules, together with the classical rule (β), induces the one-step reduction relation $\rightarrow$. The relation $\twoheadrightarrow$ is the reflexive transitive closure of $\rightarrow$. Figure 2 gives the δ-rules for PCF.

Definition 17 An *extension of PCF* is a language and set of linear ground δ-rules satisfying the following conditions.

- The ground types are o and ι.
- The constants must include those of PCF.
- The δ-rules whose left-hand sides involve no new (non-PCF) constants are exactly the rules of PCF.

B Simply Typed Models

Here we develop the general framework for function-based models of simply typed λ-calculi.

A *type frame* $\{[\![\sigma]\!]\}$ is collection of sets indexed by type such that $[\![\sigma \rightarrow \tau]\!]$ is a set of functions from $[\![\sigma]\!]$ to $[\![\tau]\!]$. The sets $[\![\sigma]\!]$ are called *domains*, and the elements of each $[\![\sigma]\!]$ are called *meanings* or *values* of type σ.

Since our discussion focuses on issues of adequacy and full abstraction, we also require the following:

- there is a binary relation $\sqsubseteq_\sigma$ associated with each domain;
- the functions of $[\![\sigma \to \tau]\!]$ are monotone with respect to the orderings $\sqsubseteq_\sigma$ and $\sqsubseteq_\tau$;
- and the relation $\sqsubseteq_{\sigma\to\tau}$ refines the pointwise relation on functions $f, g \in [\![\sigma \to \tau]\!]$, namely

$$f \sqsubseteq_{\sigma\to\tau} g \text{ implies } f(d) \sqsubseteq_\tau g(d) \text{ for all } d \in [\![\sigma]\!].$$

An *environment* is a type-respecting mapping from variables to values. If ρ is an environment, then the environment $\rho[x := d]$ is ρ with the value of x updated to d:

$$\rho[x := d](y) = \begin{cases} d & \text{if } y \equiv x, \\ \rho(y) & \text{otherwise.} \end{cases}$$

An *interpretation* is a type-respecting mapping from constants to values. For a given type frame $\{[\![\sigma]\!]\}$ and interpretation $\mathcal{I}$ we can try to define a *model* $[\![\cdot]\!]$ that maps each term to a meaning with respect to an environment:

$$\begin{aligned} [\![\delta]\!]\rho &= \mathcal{I}(\delta) & (1)\\ [\![x]\!]\rho &= \rho(x) & (2)\\ [\![(MN)]\!]\rho &= ([\![M]\!]\rho)([\![N]\!]\rho) & (3)\\ ([\![\lambda x M]\!]\rho)(d) &= [\![M]\!]\rho[x := d] & (4) \end{aligned}$$

Implicit in condition (4) is the requirement that the function defined to be $([\![\lambda x M]\!]\rho)$ must be an element of the type frame. In other words, a model is a type frame which is closed under lambda-definability. Such closure certainly does not hold for all type frames (*cf.* [19]).

The meaning of a closed term is the same in any environment:

$$[\![M]\!]\rho = [\![M]\!]\rho'$$

for all closed M and arbitrary ρ, ρ'. Therefore we sometimes write $[\![M]\!]$ for the meaning of a closed term M, omitting the environment.

Continuity

We give the standard definitions for cpo's and continuous functions, then define the cpo model of PCF.

A *partial order* or *poset* is a set D together with a binary relation $\sqsubseteq$ that is reflexive, transitive, and anti-symmetric. We will refer to the partial order $\langle D, \sqsubseteq\rangle$ as just D. A subset $X \subseteq D$ is *directed* if every finite subset of X has an upper bound in X. A partial order D is a *complete partial order* or *cpo* if it has a least element $\bot_D$ and every directed subset $X \subseteq D$ has a least upper bound $\sqcup X$. We omit the subscript D

in $\perp_D$ when it can be recovered from context. For any set X we define the cpo $X_\perp$, with elements $X \cup \{\perp_X\}$, ordered $x \sqsubseteq y$ iff $x = y$ or $x = \perp_X$.

A function $f : D \to E$ between posets is *monotone* if $f(x) \sqsubseteq_E f(y)$ whenever $x \sqsubseteq_D y$. We say f is *continuous* if it is monotone and $f(\sqcup X) = \sqcup f(X)$ for every directed $X \subseteq D$.

The set $D \to_c E$ of continuous functions from cpo D to cpo E is a cpo under the pointwise order $\sqsubseteq_p$, defined as follows:

$$f \sqsubseteq_p g \quad \text{iff} \quad f(x) \sqsubseteq_E g(x) \text{ for all } x \in D$$

If D is a cpo and $f : D \to D$ is continuous, then f has a least fixed point $\mathit{fix}(f)$. The function fix itself is continuous, which will allow us to interpret the recursion operator Y.

Now we define the cpo model $\mathcal{C}[\![\cdot]\!]$ of PCF, based on continuous functions and cpos. First we construct a type frame with ground domains $\mathcal{C}[\![o]\!] = \{\mathit{tt}, \mathit{ff}\}_\perp$ and $\mathcal{C}[\![\iota]\!] = \{0, 1, 2, \ldots\}_\perp$, and higher-order domains $\mathcal{C}[\![\sigma \to \tau]\!] = \mathcal{C}[\![\sigma]\!] \to_c \mathcal{C}[\![\tau]\!]$. The cpo model of PCF is then the model $\mathcal{C}[\![\cdot]\!]$ associated with $\{\mathcal{C}[\![\sigma]\!]\}$ and the *standard interpretation*: the ground constants are interpreted in the obvious way; the constants Y_σ are interpreted as *least* fixed-point operators; and the interpretation of the remaining function constants is determined by the condition that the rewrite rules of Figure 2 be valid as equations.

Theorem 18 (Plotkin[24], Sazonov[25]) *The cpo model $\mathcal{C}[\![\cdot]\!]$ is adequate but not fully abstract for PCF.*

Stability

If D is a partial order and $X \subseteq D$, then X is *bounded* or *consistent* if there is an element $y \in D$ such that $x \sqsubseteq y$ for all $x \in X$. If elements x and y are consistent we will write $x \uparrow y$. We say D is *bounded complete* if every bounded subset $X \subseteq D$ has a least upper bound $\sqcup X$.

An element $a \in D$ is *compact* if, for every directed $X \subseteq D$ with $a \sqsubseteq \sqcup X$, there is some $x \in X$ such that $a \sqsubseteq x$. We define $\mathbf{K}D$, the *kernel* of D, to be the set of compact elements of D. The cpo D is *algebraic* if, for every $x \in D$, the set $\downarrow x = \{ a \in \mathbf{K}D \mid a \sqsubseteq x \}$ is directed and $\sqcup \downarrow x = x$.

A cpo is *distributive* if $x \sqcap (y \sqcup z) = (x \sqcap y) \sqcup (x \sqcap z)$ whenever y and z are consistent. An algebraic cpo D *has property I* if $\downarrow a$ is finite for each $a \in \mathbf{K}D$. A *dI-domain* is a distributive, bounded complete cpo which has property I.

A continuous function f between dI-domains is *stable* if whenever $x \uparrow y$, we have that $f(x \sqcap y) = f(x) \sqcap f(y)$. We let $D \to_s E$ be the set of stable functions between dI-domains D and E. As noted in [4], $D \to_s E$ ordered pointwise is *not* a dI-domain; accordingly we define the stable ordering $\sqsubseteq_s$:

$$f \sqsubseteq_s g \qquad \text{iff} \qquad f(x) = f(y) \sqcap g(x) \text{ whenever } x \sqsubseteq y$$

Function	tt	ff	$\bot$
True	tt	tt	tt
False	ff	ff	ff
True!	tt	tt	$\bot$
False!	ff	ff	$\bot$
Id	tt	ff	$\bot$
Not	ff	tt	$\bot$
$(tt \Rightarrow tt)$	tt	$\bot$	$\bot$
$(tt \Rightarrow ff)$	ff	$\bot$	$\bot$
$(ff \Rightarrow tt)$	$\bot$	tt	$\bot$
$(ff \Rightarrow ff)$	$\bot$	ff	$\bot$
Bot	$\bot$	$\bot$	$\bot$

Figure 3: Boolean functions

If D and E are dI-domains, then $D \to_s E$ is a dI-domain under the stable order.

It must be noted that the stable order is quite different from the pointwise order. For instance, consider the monotone Boolean functions, listed in Figure 3. These functions are both continuous and stable, and so they are elements of both the continuous and stable type frames. However the stable ordering of $o \to o$ (Figure 5) is different from its pointwise ordering (Figure 4). In particular, consider *True*, the constant tt function, and *True!*, the strict constant tt function. Although $True! \sqsubseteq_p True$, we have $True! \not\sqsubseteq_s True$ since $\bot \sqsubseteq_s tt$ but

$$True!(\bot) = \bot \quad \neq \quad tt = (True!(tt) \sqcap True(\bot))$$

(It is this that permits the existence of the function *truesep* that was needed in Corollary 9.)

Nevertheless, a stable model $\mathcal{S}[\![\cdot]\!]$ of PCF, based on dI-domains and stable functions, can be defined in much the same way as the cpo model. The ground domains $\mathcal{S}[\![o]\!]$ and $\mathcal{S}[\![\iota]\!]$ of the stable type frame are identical to the ground domains of the cpo model. At higher types, however, we use stable functions: $\mathcal{S}[\![\sigma \to \tau]\!] = \mathcal{S}[\![\sigma]\!] \to_s \mathcal{S}[\![\tau]\!]$. Then we let $\mathcal{S}[\![\cdot]\!]$ be the model associated with the stable type frame and the (stable) standard interpretation (*cf.* the interpretation of the cpo model).

Theorem 19 (Berry[4]) *The stable model $\mathcal{S}[\![\cdot]\!]$ is adequate but not fully abstract for PCF.*

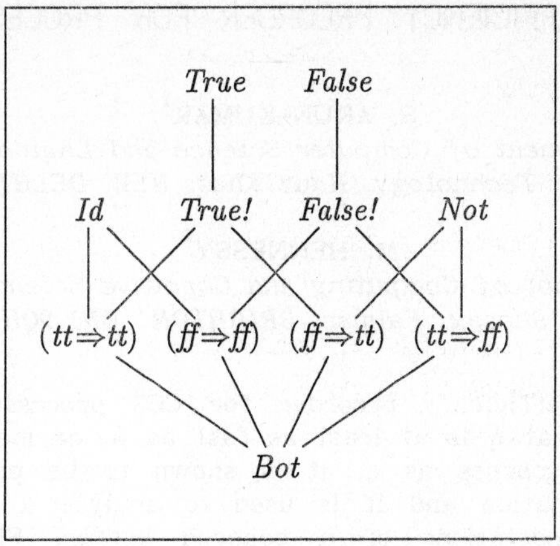

Figure 4: Pointwise ordering of $o \rightarrow o$

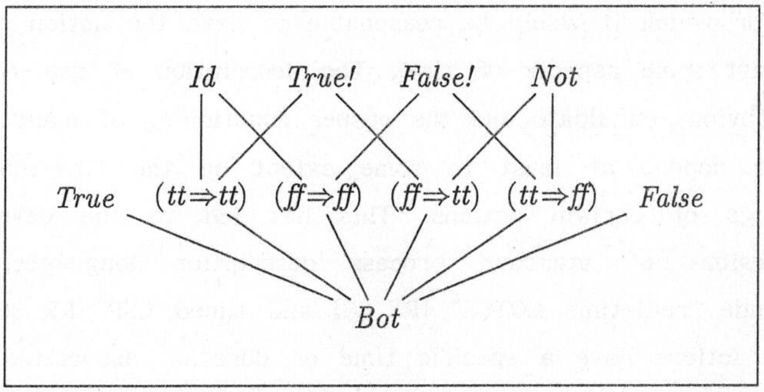

Figure 5: Stable ordering of $o \rightarrow o$

AN EFFICIENCY PREORDER FOR PROCESSES

S. ARUN-KUMAR[1]
Department of Computer Science and Engineering
Indian Institute of Technology, Hauz Khas, NEW DELHI 110 016 INDIA.

M. HENNESSY[2]
School of Computing and Cognitive Sciences
University of Sussex, Falmer, BRIGHTON BN1 9QH, ENGLAND.

Abstract. A simple efficiency preorder for CCS processes is introduced in which $p \lesssim q$ means that q is at least as fast as p, or more generally, p uses at least as much resources as q. It is shown to be preserved by all CCS contexts except summation and it is used to analyse a non-trivial example: two different implementations of a bounded buffer. Finally a sound and complete proof system for finite processes is given.

1. Introduction

A large number of behavioural equivalences for process description languages have been studied in recent years ([Mil 89], [Hoa 85], [Hen 88]). If $\approx$ is such an equivalence then $p \approx q$ means intuitively that p and q offer essentially the same behaviour to the environment. When comparing the behaviour of processes, many of these equivalences, often called asynchronous equivalences, do not take timing considerations into account; internal actions are considered to be instantaneous. On the other hand there are many applications for which it would be reasonable to have the notion of behaviour include at least some aspects of time. The description of real-time systems is the most obvious candidate and the proper functioning of many communication protocols depend at least to some extent on the fine-tuning of the relative timings of certain actions. This has led to the development of real-time versions of standard process description languages. Typical examples include "real-time LOTOS" [RS 88] and timed CSP [RR 86]. In these languages all actions have a specific time or duration associated with them and, roughly speaking, two processes are deemed to be equivalent if they offer the same potential actions of the same duration at more or less the same time during a computation. Let us call this intuitive idea "real-time equivalence".

---

[1] Most of this work was done while the first author was at the University of Sussex and supported by SERC grant GR/D 97368 of the Science and Engineering Research Council of Great Britain.

[2] The second author would like to acknowledge the support of the ESPRIT II

For many applications this treatment of time is much too detailed. One ends up being forced to carry out long and precise timing calculations, the details of which are often superfluous. Indeed, many descriptions which one feels should be equivalent are not so because the comparison is too fine-grained. We would like to develop methods of comparing processes which are finer than the asynchronous equivalences in that they take time into consideration but are not as restrictive as real-time equivalences.

In this paper we develop one such method. The idea is very simple and although it will not be universally applicable, we feel that it will be useful in many applications. We develop a preorder on process descriptions which has approximately the following meaning: $p \lesssim q$ if p and q are bisimulation equivalent and q is at least as fast as p.

So in this approach there is no assignment of absolute values to the actions or constructs of a process. Instead it is purely comparative; the comparison is made by assuming all external actions take the same time and that internal actions take some indefinite but non-zero time. Hence if α and β are actions and 1 represents an internal move then it turns out that $\alpha.1.\beta.\mathbb{0} \lesssim \alpha.\beta.\mathbb{0}$ but $\alpha.\beta.\mathbb{0} \not\lesssim \alpha.1.\beta.\mathbb{0}$.

One obvious advantage of such a treatment as opposed to the usual real-time equivalences such as [RR 86] and [GB 86] is that "1" may be used not just as a unit or measure of time but to denote some more general quantities such as "energy consumed in a computation" or the "complexity of communication and synchronization" as well.

We will show in this paper that a mathematically tractable behavioural theory of processes based on these ideas can be developed. It is applied to the standard version of CCS although in principle there is no reason why it should not be equally applicable to more general languages with real-time features.

In section 2 we define the syntax and operational semantics of CCS. This is completely standard and may be omitted by readers familiar with CCS. In section 3 we show how to modify the usual recursive definition of bisimulation equivalence [Mil 89], so as to obtain $\lesssim$. Roughly speaking for $p \lesssim q$ to hold, every "weak arrow", $\stackrel{\alpha}{\Longrightarrow}$, from p must be matched by a corresponding "weak arrow" from q which performs at most the same number of internal moves and conversely, every "weak arrow" from q must be matched by a "weak arrow" from p which uses at least as many internal moves. Alternative and more useful formulations of $\lesssim$ are also given. We develop most of these concepts by confining ourselves to "pure CCS", where no values are passed between processes. The extension to value-passing may be done in the usual fashion. We then investigate the algebraic properties of $\lesssim$. For the same reasons as for observational equivalence (see [Mil 89]) it is not preserved by the "+" operation of CCS, but we can apply the usual method to overcome this problem. We show that the resulting relation is preserved by all the operators of CCS including recursion. We also justify fixpoint induction. In section 4, we consider an example which examines different methods of implementing a FIFO buffer. In section 5 we show how a complete proof system may be obtained for finite processes. This involves modifying the equations in [HM 86] but it appears that an extra proof rule is also necessary. The paper ends with a brief comparison with other related work in the literature.

2. CCS and Labelled Transition Systems

2.1 Syntax and operational semantics of CCS.

Let Λ and $\bar{\Lambda}$ (the complement of Λ) be disjoint sets in bijection under the complementation operation "$\bar{\ }$". Then $V = \Lambda \cup \bar{\Lambda}$ is the set of **ports** and complementation is extended to the whole of V so that $\bar{\bar{\alpha}} = \alpha$ for all $\alpha \in V$. If D is any domain of values, $V \times D$ denotes the set of **visible actions** with "$\bar{\ }$" extended to $V \times D$ in the usual way. That is, for $\alpha \in V$ and $d \in D$, $\alpha(d)$ will denote an element of $V \times D$ and $\bar{\alpha}(d)$ its complement. Let "1" be a special action called the **internal (silent** or **invisible)** action, such that $\bar{1} = 1$. Then $A = (V \times D) \cup \{ 1 \}$ is the set of all **actions**. In particular, when D is a single-valued domain we shall identify V with $V \times D$.

Unless otherwise mentioned, we use the following notational conventions. Typically α, β, γ, ... (suitably decorated) denote elements of V and a, b, c, ... (suitably decorated) stand for (visible or invisible) actions. Let X be a set of process variable symbols and U a set of value variable symbols. Then x, y, z, ... (possibly decorated) represent process variable names and u, v, w, ... (possibly decorated) stand for value variable symbols. The language of CCS expressions is then given by the following BNF.

$$e ::= x \mid \mathbb{0} \mid \alpha(u).e \mid \bar{\alpha}(d).e \mid 1.e \mid e+e \mid e|e \mid e\backslash L \mid e[h] \mid \mu_i \underline{x}{:}\underline{e}$$

where $\mathbb{0}$ is a constant (or 0-ary operator), $u \in U$, $d \in D$ and $L \subseteq V$. $\underline{x}$ and $\underline{e}$ denote vectors of process variables and process expressions respectively, and $\mu\underline{x}{:}\underline{e}$ denotes the solution of a system of recursive process equations, whose i-th component is $\mu_i\underline{x}{:}\underline{e}$. In e[h], $h : A \longrightarrow A$ is the relabelling function satisfying the conditions $\overline{h(\alpha)} = h(\bar{\alpha})$, $h(1) = 1$ and $h(\alpha) \neq 1$ for all $\alpha \in V$.

Any term generated by the above BNF is called a **process expression** and E, ranged over by e, f, g, ... (possibly decorated), denotes the set of process expressions. For any process expression e, FPV(e) is the set of free process variables in e. **Processes** are closed process expressions (i.e. expressions with no free process variables). p, q, r (possibly decorated) range over the set P of all processes.

We have defined a subset of CCS with value-passing that is sufficient for our purposes. A more complete language would have a conditional statement and a "sublanguage" for value expressions. Since these extra features are not used in our examples we have excluded them for the sake of simplicity.

The operational semantics of the language is defined in terms of labelled transition systems in the usual fashion. Let $\langle E, A, \{ \xrightarrow{a} \mid a \in A \}\rangle$ be a labelled transition system (LTS) where the transition relation $\longrightarrow \subseteq E \times A \times E$ is the smallest relation satisfying the following axioms and rules of inference.

1. Prefix	1.1	$\alpha(u).e \xrightarrow{\alpha(d)} e\{d/u\}$, for all $d \in D$
	1.2	$\bar{\alpha}(d).e \xrightarrow{\bar{\alpha}(d)} e$
	1.3	$1.e \xrightarrow{1} e$
2. Summation	2.1	$e_1 \xrightarrow{a} e'_1 \;\Rightarrow\; e_1 + e_2 \xrightarrow{a} e'_1$
	2.2	$e_2 \xrightarrow{a} e'_2 \;\Rightarrow\; e_1 + e_2 \xrightarrow{a} e'_2$
3. Composition	3.1	$e_1 \xrightarrow{a} e'_1 \;\Rightarrow\; e_1 \mid e_2 \xrightarrow{a} e'_1 \mid e_2$
	3.2	$e_2 \xrightarrow{a} e'_2 \;\Rightarrow\; e_1 \mid e_2 \xrightarrow{a} e_1 \mid e'_2$
	3.3	$e_1 \xrightarrow{\alpha} e'_1,\ e_2 \xrightarrow{\bar{\alpha}} e'_2 \;\Rightarrow\; e_1 \mid e_2 \xrightarrow{1} e'_1 \mid e'_2$
4. Hiding		$e \xrightarrow{a} e',\ a, \bar{a} \notin L \;\Rightarrow\; e\backslash L \xrightarrow{a} e'\backslash L$
5. Relabelling		$e \xrightarrow{a} e' \;\Rightarrow\; e[h] \xrightarrow{h(a)} e'[h]$
6. Recursion		$e_i\{\mu\underline{x}{:}\underline{e}/\underline{x}\} \xrightarrow{a} e' \;\Rightarrow\; \mu_i\underline{x}{:}\underline{e} \xrightarrow{a} e'$

where "$f\{\underline{r}/\underline{x}\}$" denotes the syntactic substitution of all free occurrences of the variable x_j ($x_j \in \underline{x}$) in the expression f by r_j ($r_j \in \underline{r}$) for each j in the indexing set of the vectors $\underline{x}$ and $\underline{r}$.

2.2 Derived Labelled Transition Systems

We may readily extend the notion of labelled transition systems to derived LTS (DLTS) and weak LTS (WLTS) such that a transition is over a sequence of actions.

Definition 2.1. A derived LTS is a structure $\langle E, A^*, \{ \xrightarrow{s} \mid s \in A^* \}\rangle$, where $\longrightarrow \subseteq E \times A^* \times E$ is the least relation satisfying the following conditions:

(i) $e \xrightarrow{\varepsilon} e$, for all $e \in E$, where ε is the empty sequence,

(ii) $e \xrightarrow{as} e'$ if for some $e \in E$, $e \xrightarrow{a} e$ and $e \xrightarrow{s} e'$.

Definition 2.2. A weak LTS is a structure $\langle E, V^*, \{ \overset{s}{\Longrightarrow} \mid s \in V^* \}\rangle$, where for $s = \alpha_1 \ldots \alpha_n \in V^*$, $e \overset{s}{\Longrightarrow} e'$ iff there exists $t = 1^{m_0}\alpha_1 1^{m_1} \ldots 1^{m_{n-1}}\alpha_n 1^{m_n}$ in A^*, for $m_0, m_1, \ldots, m_n \geq 0$ such that $e \overset{t}{\longrightarrow} e'$.

For any $t \in A^*$, let $\hat{t}$ denote the sequence (of visible actions) obtained by deleting all occurrences of the internal action 1 from t. In the above definition $\hat{t} = s$. Following Milner we use the notation $p \Longrightarrow p'$ to denote $p \overset{1\,*}{\longrightarrow} p'$ and $p \overset{1}{\Longrightarrow} p'$ to denote $p \overset{1\,+}{\longrightarrow} p'$.

Definition 2.3. Let $\leq$ be the binary relation on A^* generated by the inequation $1s \leq s$, i.e. $\leq$ is closed under reflexivity, transitivity, and substitution under catenation contexts. An **extended action** is an element of A^* containing at most one visible action. The set EA of all extended actions is partially ordered by $\leq$.

Note that the empty sequence and any finite sequence of internal actions belong to EA. In fact, $A \subseteq EA \subseteq A^*$. It is also clear that $\leq$ is antisymmetric and hence a partial order on A^* and EA.

In the next section we proceed with our analysis of the effect of this partial order on process behaviours. However to enable the reader to look at our definitions and theorems in the proper perspective, we also intersperse in our theory some results (stated without proof) due to Milner. The reader may consult [Mil 89] for the relevant proofs.

3. Weak Bisimulations and Efficiency Prebisimulations

Definition 3.1. If $FPV(e) \cup FPV(f) \subseteq \underline{x}$ and $\blacktriangleleft$ is a binary relation on processes, then $e \blacktriangleleft f$ iff for every vector of processes $\underline{p}$, $e\{\underline{p}/\underline{x}\} \blacktriangleleft f\{\underline{p}/\underline{x}\}$.

The above definition enables us to extend every behavioural relation on processes to process expressions. In the sequel we will assume that every behavioural relation that we define is thus extended. We now define the notion of weak bisimulations [Mil 83] and state some of its properties.

Definition 3.2. A binary relation $R \subseteq P \times P$ is a **weak bisimulation** (abbreviated to **wb**) if for every $\langle p, q\rangle \in R$ and $t \in V^*$ the following conditions are satisfied.

WB1. $p \overset{t}{\Longrightarrow} p' \;\Rightarrow\; \exists q'\colon q \overset{t}{\Longrightarrow} q' \wedge p'Rq'$

WB2. $q \overset{t}{\Longrightarrow} q' \;\Rightarrow\; \exists p'\colon p \overset{t}{\Longrightarrow} p' \wedge p'Rq'$.

Proposition 3.3.

1. If R_1 and R_2 are wbs then so is $R_1 \circ R_2$.
2. The union of a family of wbs is a wb.
3. $\approx\; = \bigcup\{ R \mid R \text{ is a wb} \}$ is the largest wb.
4. $p \approx q$ iff for some wb R, pRq.

5. $\approx$ is an equivalence relation on P. □

The relation $\approx$ is called **observational equivalence.**

Definition 3.4. A binary relation $R \subseteq P \times P$ is an **efficiency prebisimulation** (**ep** for short) if for every $\langle p, q \rangle \in R$ and $s \in EA$ the following conditions are satisfied.

EP1. $p \xrightarrow{s} p' \Rightarrow \exists s': s \le s': \exists q': q \xrightarrow{s'} q' \wedge p'Rq'$

EP2. $q \xrightarrow{s'} q' \Rightarrow \exists s: s \le s': \exists p': p \xrightarrow{s} p' \wedge p'Rq'$

It is easy to show that every efficiency prebisimulation is, in fact, a weak bisimulation. In addition, results analogous to those of weak bisimulation in proposition 3.3 may be proved as stated in the following proposition.

Proposition 3.5.

1. Every efficiency prebisimulation is a weak bisimulation.
2. If R_1 and R_2 are eps then so is their relational composition $R_1 \circ R_2$.
3. The union of a family of eps is an ep.
4. $\precsim \; = \bigcup \{ R \mid R \text{ is an ep} \}$ is the largest ep.
5. $p \precsim q$ iff for some ep R, pRq.
6. $\precsim$ is a preorder on P. □

We give below a formulation of efficiency prebisimulations that is both simpler and more convenient to use than definition 3.4.

Proposition 3.6. A binary relation $R \subseteq P \times P$ is an ep iff for every $\langle p, q \rangle \in R$, $\alpha \in V$, $a \in A$, the following conditions are satisfied.

EP'1. $p \xrightarrow{\alpha} p' \Rightarrow \exists q': q \xrightarrow{\alpha} q' \wedge p'Rq'$

EP'2. $p \xrightarrow{1} p' \Rightarrow p'Rq \vee (\exists q': q \xrightarrow{1} q' \wedge p'Rq')$

EP'3. $q \xrightarrow{a} q' \Rightarrow \exists p': p \stackrel{a}{\Longrightarrow} p' \wedge p'Rq'$

<u>Proof.</u> ($\Longrightarrow$) EP1 implies EP'1 because for $s = \alpha$, $s \le s'$ implies $s' = \alpha$. EP1 also implies EP'2 since for $s = 1$, $s \le s'$ implies either $s' = \varepsilon$ or $s' = 1$. Also it is obvious that EP2 implies EP'3 for $s' = \alpha \in V$. For $s' = 1$, from EP2 we have $p \xrightarrow{s} p'$ for some $s \le s'$, that is, $p \stackrel{1}{\Longrightarrow} p'$. Hence EP implies EP'.

($\Longleftarrow$) Suppose R is a relation satisfying the conditions EP'. Let $\langle p, q \rangle \in R$ and for some $s \in EA$, let $p \xrightarrow{s} p'$. We proceed by induction on the length of s. If $s = \varepsilon$ there is nothing to prove. Otherwise $s = as_1$ for some $a \in A$ and $s_1 \in EA$. There exists p_1 such that $p \xrightarrow{a} p_1 \xrightarrow{s_1} p'$. Now we have two cases to consider.

Case (i) $a = \alpha \in V$. By EP'1 there is a q_1 such that $q \xrightarrow{\alpha} q_1$ and p_1Rq_1. By the induction hypothesis there exists $s_1' \in EA$ and q' such that $s_1 \le s_1'$, $q_1 \xrightarrow{s_1'} q'$ and $p'Rq'$. Letting $s' = \alpha s_1'$ it is easy to see that EP1 holds.

Case (ii) $a = 1$. Then either $\langle p_1, q \rangle \in R$ or there is a q_1 such that $q \xrightarrow{1} q_1$

and p_1Rq_1. In the latter case the proof proceeds as in case (i). In the former instance, again by the induction hypothesis there must exist s'_1, $s_1 \leq s'_1$ and q' such that $q \xrightarrow{s_1} q'$ and p'Rq'. Letting $s' = s'_1$ we have $s = 1s_1 \leq s'_1 = s'$ and EP1 follows. □

As in the case of $\approx$ [Mil 89] we may show that $\lesssim$ is preserved by all operators except summation. As the following example shows, it is due to the preemptive power of the silent action that $\lesssim$ and $\approx$ are not preserved under summation.

Example 3.7. $1.\alpha.0 \lesssim \alpha.0$ whereas $1.\alpha.0 + \beta.0 \not\lesssim \alpha.0 + \beta.0$ because $1.\alpha.0 + \beta.0 \xrightarrow{1} \alpha.0$ while $\alpha.0 + \beta.0 \xrightarrow{\varepsilon} \alpha.0 + \beta.0$. For the same reasons $1.\alpha.0 \approx \alpha.0$ holds but $1.\alpha.0 + \beta.0 \approx \alpha.0 + \beta.0$ does not.

In order to obtain a precongruence we therefore follow the usual method of defining the largest precongruence contained in $\lesssim$. In the following lemma we state without proof the result that all the operators, except summation and recursion, preserve the preorder.

Lemma 3.8. Let $\lhd \in \{\lesssim, \approx\}$. Then for all p, q $\in$ P, $p \lhd q$ implies

(a) $a.p \lhd a.q$ for all $a \in A$,

(b) $p|r \lhd q|r$ and $r|p \lhd r|q$ for all $r \in P$,

(c) $p\backslash L \lhd q\backslash L$ for $L \subseteq V$,

(d) $p[h] \lhd q[h]$ for any relabelling function h. □

It is also easy to verify that the 1-laws (called "τ-laws" in [Mil 89]) no longer hold symmetrically for the preorder $\lesssim$. We state these laws in the next lemma. In the sequel we always use $\lhd$ to denote either $\lesssim$ or $\approx$.

Lemma 3.9.

1. $1.p \lhd p$
2. $1.p \lhd p + 1.p \lhd p$
3. $a.1.p \lhd a.p$
4. $a.(p + 1.q) \lhd a.(p + 1.q) + a.q$ □

This lemma may be proved for both $\lesssim$ and $\approx$ by constructing appropriate eps (note that it is not enough to construct wbs for the purpose of $\lesssim$, though every ep is a wb by proposition 3.5.1).

Definition 3.10. For $\lhd \in \{\lesssim, \approx\}$, $p \lhd^+ q$ iff for some visible action α not occurring in p or q, $p + \alpha.0 \lhd q + \alpha.0$.

For reasons that will become clear in theorem 3.15, the relations $\lesssim^+$ and $\approx^+$ defined above (definition 3.10) are called **efficiency precongruence** and **observational congruence** respectively. In the next proposition we give a useful behavioural characterization of $\lesssim^+$.

Proposition 3.11.

1. $p \lesssim^+ q$ implies $p \lesssim q$.
2. $p \lesssim^+ q$ and $p \xrightarrow{1} p'$ implies $\exists q'$: $q \xrightarrow{1} q' \wedge p' \lesssim q'$
3. $p \lesssim^+ q$ iff for every $a \in A$, the following conditions hold.

   EP$^+$1. $p \xrightarrow{a} p' \;\Rightarrow\; \exists q'$: $q \xrightarrow{a} q' \wedge p' \lesssim q'$

   EP$^+$2. $q \xrightarrow{a} q' \;\Rightarrow\; \exists p'$: $p \overset{a}{\Longrightarrow} p' \wedge p' \lesssim q'$

Proof. 1. Obvious.

2. Let $p \lesssim^+ q$. Then by definition 3.10 $p + \alpha.\mathbb{0} \lesssim q + \alpha.\mathbb{0}$, for some visible action α that does not occur in p or q. If $p \xrightarrow{1} p'$ then $p + \alpha.\mathbb{0} \xrightarrow{1} p'$. From condition EP'2 (proposition 3.6) $p' \lesssim q + \alpha.\mathbb{0}$ or for some q', $q + \alpha.\mathbb{0} \xrightarrow{1} q'$ and $p' \lesssim q'$. But $p' \not\lesssim q + \alpha.\mathbb{0}$ since $q + \alpha.\mathbb{0} \xrightarrow{\alpha} \mathbb{0}$, whereas p' can never perform an α action. Hence there must be a q' such that $q \xrightarrow{1} q'$ and $p' \lesssim q'$.

3.($\Rightarrow$) Follows from parts 1 and 2.

($\Leftarrow$) It suffices to show from EP$^+$ that $p + \alpha.\mathbb{0} \lesssim q + \alpha.\mathbb{0}$. It is easy to show from EP$^+$ that EP'1 and EP'3 are satisfied by the pair $\langle p + \alpha.\mathbb{0}, q + \alpha.\mathbb{0}\rangle$. Let $p + \alpha.\mathbb{0} \xrightarrow{1} p'$, then since $\alpha \in V$ we have $p \xrightarrow{1} p'$ and from EP$^+$1 it follows that for some q', $q \xrightarrow{1} q'$ and $p' \lesssim q'$. Hence $q + \alpha.\mathbb{0} \xrightarrow{1} q'$ and $p' \lesssim q'$ which proves EP'2. □

A similar behavioural characterization exists for $\approx^+$ which we merely reproduce without proof [Mil 89].

Proposition 3.12. $p \approx^+ q$ iff for every $a \in A$, the following conditions hold.

WB$^+$1. $p \xrightarrow{a} p' \;\Rightarrow\; \exists q'$: $q \overset{a}{\Longrightarrow} q' \wedge p' \approx q'$

WB$^+$2. $q \xrightarrow{a} q' \;\Rightarrow\; \exists p'$: $p \overset{a}{\Longrightarrow} p' \wedge p' \approx q'$. □

It is then a simple matter to prove the following proposition for $\lhd^+ \in \{ \lesssim^+, \approx^+ \}$. We leave the proof to the reader.

Proposition 3.13. $\lhd^+$ is preserved under prefix, summation, composition, hiding and relabelling. □

To show that $\lhd^+$ is a precongruence it is now only necessary to prove that it is preserved under recursion.

Lemma 3.14. Let $\underline{e}$ and $\underline{f}$ be process expressions such that $\underline{e} \lhd^+ \underline{f}$ and $FPV(\underline{e}) \cup FPV(\underline{f}) \subseteq \underline{x}$. Then $\mu\underline{x}{:}\underline{e} \lhd^+ \mu\underline{x}{:}\underline{f}$.

Proof outline. This was originally proved in [Mil 89] for $\approx^+$ and the same proof may be easily adapted for $\lhd^+$. We give an outline for the case of e and f having at most one free variable, say x. That is, we prove that $e \lhd^+ f$ implies $p \lhd^+ q$ where $p \equiv \mu x{:}e$ and $q \equiv \mu x{:}f$. Now consider the relation

$$R = \{\langle g\{p/x\}, g\{q/x\}\rangle \mid g \in E, FPV(g) \subseteq \{x\} \}.$$

By induction on the depth of the inferences $g\{p/x\} \xrightarrow{a} p'$ and $g\{q/x\} \xrightarrow{a} q'$

respectively, one may show that the following conditions hold for all $a \in A$.

(i) $g\{p/x\} \xrightarrow{a} p' \;\Rightarrow\; \exists q' : g\{q/x\} \xrightarrow{a} q' \wedge p' R \circ \lhd q'$

(ii) $g\{q/x\} \xrightarrow{a} q' \;\Rightarrow\; \exists p' : g\{p/x\} \xrightarrow{a} p' \wedge p' \lhd \circ R q'$

From (i) and (ii) we may show that $\lhd \circ R \circ \lhd$ is an ep if $\lhd = \lesssim$ and a wb if $\lhd = \approx$, and since $R \subseteq \lhd \circ R \circ \lhd$ it follows that $R \subseteq \lhd$. Letting $g \equiv x$ it is clear that $\langle p, q \rangle \in R$ and hence $p \lhd q$. But from (i) and (ii) above and the conditions EP^+ in proposition 3.11.3, we obtain the stronger result $p \lhd^+ q$. □

Theorem 3.15. $\lhd^+$ is a precongruence on CCS process expressions.

<u>Proof.</u> Follows from proposition 3.13 and lemma 3.14. □

Definition 3.16. The kernel of $\lesssim^+$, defined by $\simeq^+ = \lesssim^+ \cap \gtrsim^+$, where $\gtrsim^+$ denotes the converse of $\lesssim^+$, is called **efficiency congruence.**

We will also have occasion to refer to another relation which we briefly describe here. If definition 3.2 were strengthened by letting $t \in A^*$ and replacing " $\overset{t}{\Longrightarrow}$ " everywhere by " $\xrightarrow{t}$ " in the conditions WB, then the relation obtained is a **strong bisimulation** and $\sim$, called **strong bisimulation congruence,** denotes the largest strong bisimulation (for details see [Mil 89]). It turns out that efficiency congruence strictly contains strong congruence, and is, in turn, strictly contained in observational congruence i.e., $\sim \subset \simeq^+ \subset \approx^+$. The following example makes clear the difference between the three relations.

Example 3.17.

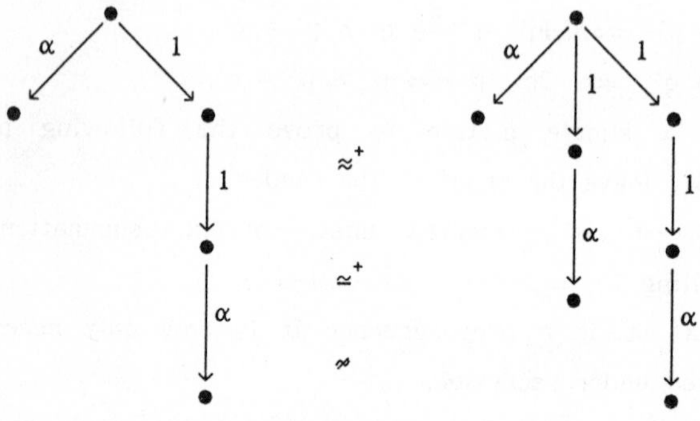

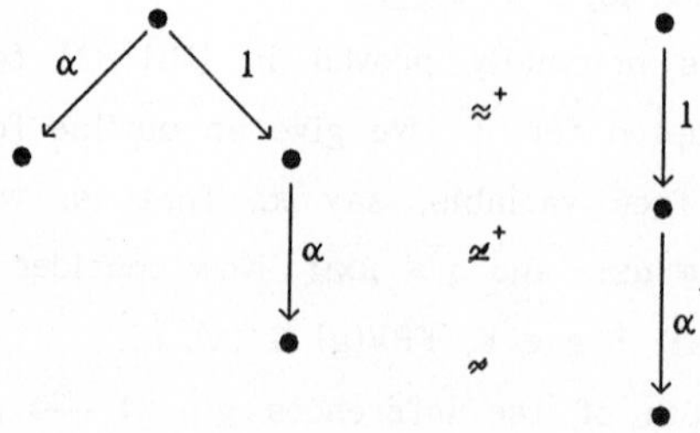

4. An Example: The (N+2)-Buffer

In this example we use the value-passing version to specify a bounded buffer of capacity N+2, $N > 0$, and compare two different implementations of the specification. The problem may be stated informally as follows. Values are to be accepted from a process SOURCE and delivered *in order* to another process DEST independent of the speeds of execution of SOURCE and DEST. We give three different processes which carry out this task and which are strictly ordered with respect to $\lesssim$.

Let D be a value domain and for $n \geq 0$, let D^n denote the set of strings of length n and $D_n = \bigcup \{ D^k \mid 0 \leq k \leq n \}$ the set of strings of length at most n. The state of the buffer at any instant of its execution is determined by the string it contains. The state space of the buffer is given by D_{N+2}. We may then formally specify the behaviour of the buffer by the CCS process FIFO(t), where $t \in D_{N+2}$, $a, d \in D$, α is the input port and $\bar{\delta}$ is the output port as shown in figure 1.

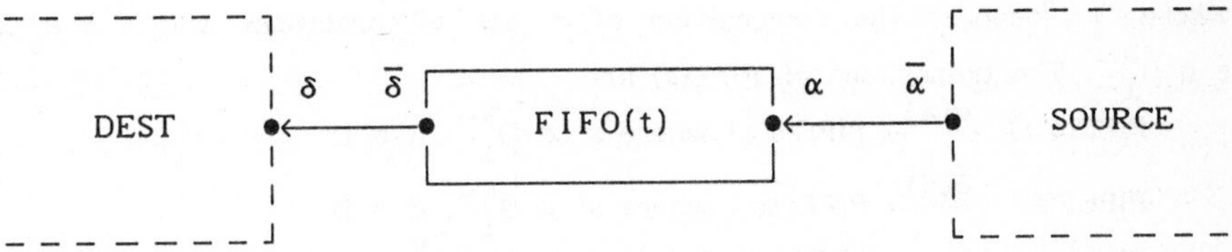

Fig. 1. *Specification of Buffer*

$$\mathrm{FIFO}(t) \equiv \begin{cases} \alpha(a).\mathrm{FIFO}(a) \text{ if } t = \varepsilon \text{ (or } |t| = 0) \\ \bar{\delta}(d).\mathrm{FIFO}(t_1) + \alpha(a).\mathrm{FIFO}(ta) \quad \text{if } t = dt_1 \text{ and } 0 < |t| \leq N+1 \\ \bar{\delta}(d).\mathrm{FIFO}(t_1) \text{ if } t = dt_1 \text{ and } |t| = N+2 \end{cases}$$

Hence for any string t, FIFO(t) has the following transitions.

$$\mathrm{FIFO}(t) \xrightarrow{\alpha(a)} \mathrm{FIFO}(ta) \quad \text{if } 0 \leq |t| < N+2$$

$$\mathrm{FIFO}(t) \xrightarrow{\bar{\delta}(d)} \mathrm{FIFO}(t_1) \quad \text{if } 0 < |t| \leq N+2 \text{ and } t = dt_1$$

Throughout this section we shall use the word "implementation" to refer to any CCS process that is observationally congruent to FIFO(ε). We shall also override some of the notational conventions specified in section 2.1 as regards variables and values.

The process PIPE. A simple implementation of this buffer is in terms of cells, where a cell is an elementary i-o device that may be defined as $C \equiv \iota(x).C'(x)$ and $C'(x) \equiv \bar{o}(x).C$. For the sake of uniformity we denote the state C as $C(\bot)$ and $C'(d)$ as $C(d)$. A buffer of capacity N+2 may be created simply by connecting cells end to end and relabelling the ports appropriately (see figure 2).

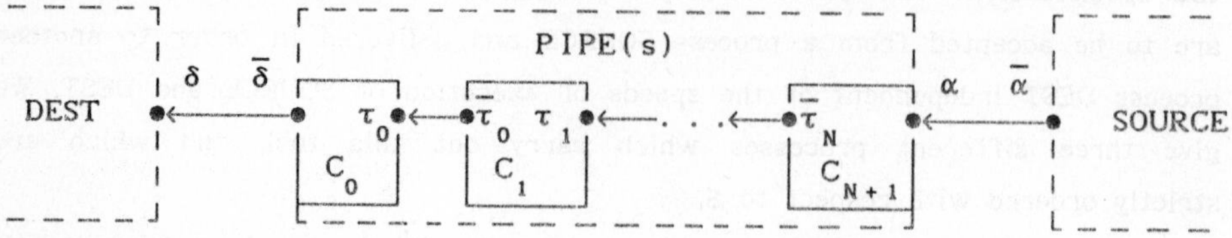

Fig. 2. *First Implementation of Buffer*

We have for $D_\bot = D \cup \{ \bot \}$ and all $x \in D_\bot$,

$$C_0(x) \equiv C(x)[\tau_0/\iota,\ \delta/o]$$
$$C_j(x) \equiv C(x)[\tau_j/\iota,\ \tau_{j-1}/o] \quad \text{for } 0 < j \le N$$
$$C_{N+1}(x) \equiv C(x)[\alpha/\iota,\ \tau_N/o]$$
$$PIPE(s) \equiv (\Gamma \{ C_j(x_j) \mid 0 \le j \le N{+}1 \}) \backslash \{ \tau_k \mid 1 \le k \le N{+}1 \}$$

where "Γ" denotes the composition of a set of processes and $s = x_0 \ldots x_{N+1}$, $s \in D_\bot^{N+2}$. The transitions of PIPE(s) are

$$PIPE(s'\bot) \xrightarrow{\alpha(a)} PIPE(s'a) \text{ where } s' \in D_\bot^{N+1},\ a \in D$$
$$PIPE(ds') \xrightarrow{\bar{\delta}(d)} PIPE(\bot s') \text{ where } s' \in D_\bot^{N+1},\ d \in D$$
$$PIPE(s'\bot v s'') \xrightarrow{1} PIPE(s'v\bot s'') \text{ where } s's'' \in D_\bot^{N},\ v \in D$$

To prove that PIPE is an implementation of FIFO, it is sufficient to display a weak bisimulation between their state spaces. However it is possible to prove the stronger result given in the following lemma, whose detailed proof we leave to the interested reader.

Proposition 4.1. Let $f : D_\bot^{N+2} \longrightarrow D^{N+2}$ be the function which strips off all occurrences of "$\bot$" from any string in $D_\bot^{N+2}$. Then

1. $R = \{ \langle PIPE(s), FIFO(f(s)) \rangle \mid s \in D_\bot^{N+2} \}$ is an ep.
2. $PIPE(\bot^{N+2}) \lesssim^+ FIFO(\varepsilon)$.

<u>Proof Outline.</u> 1. Clearly f is surjective, so every possible state of PIPE and FIFO is present in R. Then it is a simple matter to show from the transitions of PIPE and FIFO that R is indeed an ep.

2. For $t = \varepsilon$ and $s = \bot^{N+2}$, it is clear that $f(s) = \varepsilon$ and also $PIPE(\bot^{N+2})$ has no silent transitions. Then PIPE(s) and FIFO(t) satisfy the conditions EP^+ of proposition 3.11.3. Hence $PIPE(\bot^{N+2}) \lesssim^+ FIFO(\varepsilon)$. □

The process BUFF. Now consider a different implementation of the buffer, in which N cells are used (numbered from 0 to N-1) simply as storage and each cell interacts only with a centralized buffer controller which may store an additional two values. We define the store as follows.

$B_j(x) \equiv C(x)[\omega_j/\iota,\ \rho_j/o]$, for $0 \le j < N$

$MEM(s) \equiv \Gamma\ \{B_j(x_j)\ |\ 0 \le j < N\}$

where $s = x_0 \ldots x_{N-1}$ and $x_j \in D_\perp$, is the state of cell B_j for $0 \le j < N$.

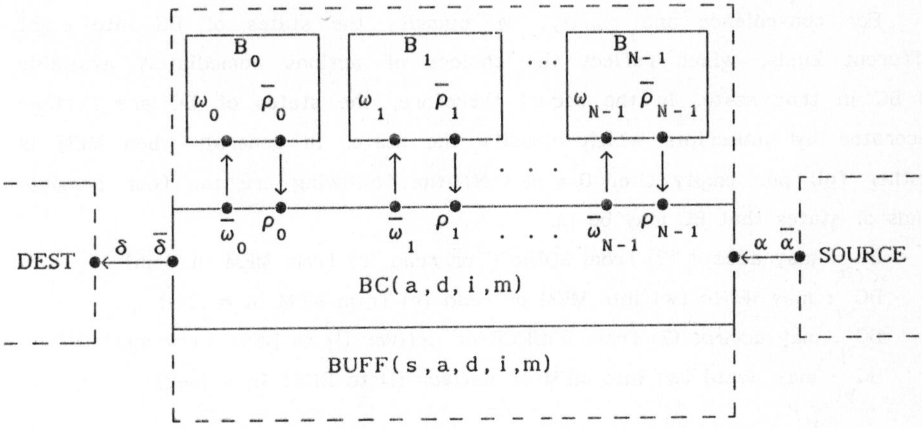

Fig. 3. *Second Implementation of Buffer*

The buffer controller, BC, whose schematic design is shown in fig. 3, may store at most 2 values at any instant. It performs the following functions.

(a) it *accepts* a value from SOURCE through the port α, and does not accept another till the first one is stored in one of the N cells.

(b) it *writes* the most recently accepted value in the first available empty cell, say B_j, through the port $\bar{\omega}_j$.

(c) it retains the oldest undelivered value, (after *reading* from, say B_i through port ρ_i) and keeps it ready for delivery.

(d) it *delivers* whatever value it has retained, whenever possible, to DEST, through the port $\bar{\delta}$. The next value is not delivered till it has been retrieved from the appropriate cell.

(e) The N cells are treated as a *circular queue* of length N (with the indices of the cells ordered as follows: $0 < 1 < \ldots < N-1 < 0$). It is clear that the controller requires to maintain the following information: i, the index of the cell containing the oldest undelivered message and j, the index of the first available empty cell. Equivalently, since the values are stored *in order* in contiguous cells of the circular queue, instead of j, it may retain m the number of cells in MEM containing undelivered messages.

The state of BC is therefore determined by four arguments — the value

$a \in D$ at the port α, which it may *accept* from SOURCE, the value $d \in D$ at the port $\bar{\delta}$, which it may *deliver* to DEST, the index i and the number m. As before $a = \perp$ if there is no value at α and similarly $d = \perp$ if there is no value at δ. Further, if n denotes the total number of messages in the memory-buffer controller system, then $m \le n \le m+2$ always holds.

For convenience and clarity, we classify the states of BC into eight different kinds, which reflect the choices of actions immediately available to BC in that state. In the sequel therefore, the states of BC are further decorated by subscripts which classify the state. In general, when MEM is neither full nor empty (i.e. $0 < m < N$) the following are the four possible kinds of states that BC may be in.

$BC_{?r}$: may *accept* (?) from SOURCE or *read* (r) from MEM ($n = m$)

BC_{wr}: may *write* (w) into MEM or *read* (r) from MEM ($n = m+1$)

$BC_{?!}$: may *accept* (?) from SOURCE or *deliver* (!) to DEST ($n = m+1$)

$BC_{w!}$: may *write* (w) into MEM or *deliver* (!) to DEST ($n = m+2$)

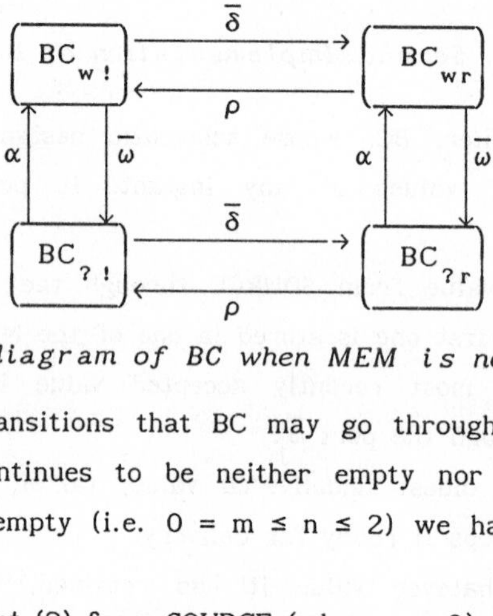

Fig. 4a. *Transition diagram of BC when MEM is neither full nor empty*

Figure 4a shows the transitions that BC may go through between these four states provided MEM continues to be neither empty nor full. Otherwise, for instance, when MEM is empty (i.e. $0 = m \le n \le 2$) we have the two kinds of states

$BC_{?}$: may only *accept* (?) from SOURCE (when $n = 0$) and

BC_{w}: may only *write* (w) into MEM (when $n = 1$).

When $m = 0$ and $n = 2$, clearly the only kind of state possible is $BC_{w!}$. Similarly, when MEM is full (i.e. $N = m < n \le N+2$), we get two more, viz.

BC_{r}: may only *read* (r) from MEM (when $n = N+1$) and

$BC_{!}$: may only *deliver* (!) to DEST (when $n = N+2$).

When $N = m = n$, we have $BC_{?r}$ as the only possible kind of state. The state transition diagrams for these "boundary" conditions are shown in figures 4b and 4c repectively. We may then define BC(a,d,i,m) as follows, using "$\oplus$" and "$\ominus$" to denote addition and subtraction modulo N respectively.

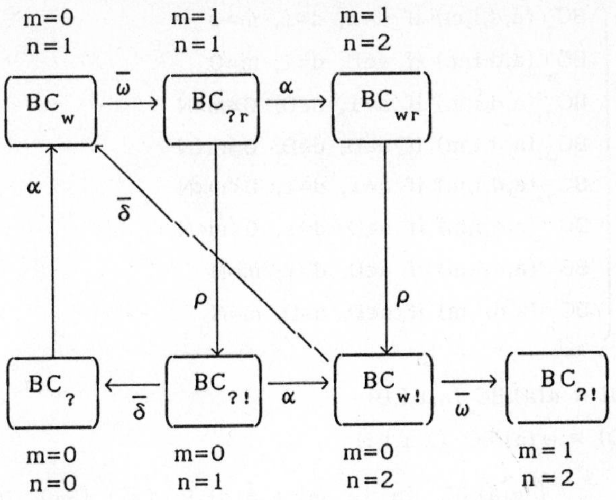

Fig. 4b. *Transition diagram of BC when MEM is empty*

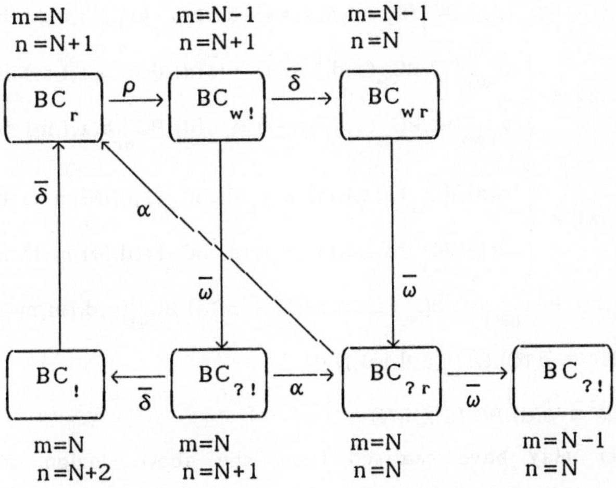

Fig. 4c. *Transition diagram of BC when MEM is full*

$$BC(a,d,i,m) \equiv \begin{cases} BC_{?}\ (a,d,i,m) \text{ if } a=\perp,\ d=\perp,\ m=0 \\ BC_{w}\ (a,d,i,m) \text{ if } a\in D,\ d=\perp,\ m=0 \\ BC_{?!}(a,d,i,m) \text{ if } a=\perp,\ d\in D,\ 0\le m\le N \\ BC_{w!}(a,d,i,m) \text{ if } a\in D,\ d\in D,\ 0\le m<N \\ BC_{?r}(a,d,i,m) \text{ if } a=\perp,\ d=\perp,\ 0<m\le N \\ BC_{wr}(a,d,i,m) \text{ if } a\in D,\ d=\perp,\ 0<m<N \\ BC_{r}\ (a,d,i,m) \text{ if } a\in D,\ d=\perp,\ m=N \\ BC_{!}\ (a,d,i,m) \text{ if } a\in D,\ d\in D,\ m=N \end{cases}$$

where

$$BC_{?}(\perp,\perp,i,0) \equiv \alpha(a).BC_{w}(a,\perp,i,0)$$

$$BC_{w}(a,\perp,i,0) \equiv \overline{\omega}_{i}(a).BC_{?r}(\perp,\perp,i,1)$$

$$BC_{?!}(\perp,d,i,m) \equiv \begin{cases} \alpha(a).BC_{w!}(a,d,i,m) + \overline{\delta}(d).BC_{?}(\perp,\perp,i,m) & \text{if } m=0 \\ \alpha(a).BC_{w!}(a,d,i,m) + \overline{\delta}(d).BC_{?r}(\perp,\perp,i,m) & \text{if } 0<m<N \\ \alpha(a).BC_{!}(a,d,i,m) + \overline{\delta}(d).BC_{?r}(\perp,\perp,i,m) & \text{if } m=N \end{cases}$$

$$BC_{w!}(a,d,i,m) \equiv \begin{cases} \overline{\omega}_{i\oplus m}(a).BC_{?!}(\perp,d,i,m+1) + \overline{\delta}(d).BC_{w}(a,\perp,i,m) & \text{if } m=0 \\ \overline{\omega}_{i\oplus m}(a).BC_{?!}(\perp,d,i,m+1) + \overline{\delta}(d).BC_{wr}(a,\perp,i,m) & \text{if } 0<m<N \end{cases}$$

$$BC_{?r}(\perp,\perp,i,m) \equiv \begin{cases} \alpha(a).BC_{wr}(a,\perp,i,m) + \rho_{i}(d).BC_{?!}(\perp,d,i\oplus 1,m-1) & \text{if } 0<m<N \\ \alpha(a).BC_{r}(a,\perp,i,m) + \rho_{i}(d).BC_{?!}(\perp,d,i\oplus 1,m-1) & \text{if } m=N \end{cases}$$

$$BC_{wr}(a,\perp,i,m) \equiv \overline{\omega}_{i\oplus m}(a).BC_{?r}(\perp,\perp,i,m+1) + \rho_{i}(d).BC_{w!}(a,d,i\oplus 1,m-1)$$

$$BC_{r}(a,\perp,i,N) \equiv \rho_{i}(d).BC_{w!}(a,d,i\oplus 1,N-1)$$

$$BC_{!}(a,d,i,N) \equiv \overline{\delta}(d).BC_{r}(a,\perp,i,N)$$

The reader may have realised from the above design of BC that the subscripts on the states of BC are unnecessary since its state (given by the values of the four arguments) completely determines its immediate choices. However we shall continue to use these subscripts wherever convenient, as they help in understanding the functioning of both the controller and the system as a whole. Before composing BC with MEM to obtain the complete system, we define a function

$$g : D_{\perp}^{N} \times \{0,\dots,N-1\} \times \{0,\dots,N\} \longrightarrow D_{N}$$

such that

$$g(s,i,m) = \begin{cases} \varepsilon & \text{if } m = 0 \\ x_{i} & \text{if } m = 1 \\ x_{i}x_{i\oplus 1}\dots x_{i\oplus m\ominus 1} & \text{otherwise.} \end{cases}$$

where x_j is the value stored in cell B_j, for all $i \le j < i\oplus m$. The function g abstracts away the details of *where* in MEM messages are located and yields merely the sequence, in the order of their arrivals, of undelivered messages stored in MEM. That is, for any given $r \in D_N$ and $m = |r|$, $g(s,i,m) = r$ may hold for several different values of s, and i. Let

$$BUFF_*(s,a,d,i,m) \equiv (MEM(s) \mid BC_*(a,d,i,m)) \backslash \{\rho_k, \omega_k \mid 0 \le k < N\}$$

where $* \in \{ ?, !, w, r, ?!, w!, ?r, wr \}$ as appropriate to the states of MEM and BC. It is easy to show that for all s, a, d, i, m and appropriately chosen values of s', a', i', m' (which may be determined from the definition), BUFF may undergo the following transitions.

$$BUFF(s,\bot,d,i,m) \xrightarrow{\alpha(a)} BUFF(s,a,d,i,m) \quad \text{if } a \in D,\ d \in D_\bot$$

$$BUFF(s,a,d,i,m) \xrightarrow{\bar{\delta}(d)} BUFF(s,a,\bot,i,m) \quad \text{if } a \in D_\bot,\ d \in D$$

$$BUFF(s,a,d,i,m) \xrightarrow{1} BUFF(s',a',d',i',m') \quad \text{otherwise.}$$

The last transition given above holds because the ports $\rho_k, \bar{\rho}_k, \omega_k, \bar{\omega}_k$, for all k, $0 \le k < N$, are hidden. The hiding operation (by internalising the various *read* and *write* operations between MEM and BC) too has the effect of abstracting away the details of storage of the undelivered messages in MEM. We now have the following lemma.

Lemma 4.2.

1. Let $s = x_0 \ldots x_{N-1}$ and $t = y_0 \ldots y_{N-1}$, then $g(s,i,m) = g(t,j,m)$ iff for all k, $0 \le k < m$, $x_{i \oplus k} = y_{j \oplus k}$.
2. For $s, s' \in D_\bot^N$, $i, i' \in \{0, \ldots, N-1\}$ and $m \in \{0, \ldots, N\}$ if $g(s,i,m) = g(s',i',m)$ then $BUFF_*(s,a,d,i,m) \simeq^+ BUFF_*(s',a,d,i',m)$. In fact they are strong congruent.

<u>Proof outline.</u> 1. Follows from the fact that $g(s,i,m) = x_i \ldots x_{i \oplus m \ominus 1}$ and $g(t,j,m) = y_j \ldots y_{j \oplus m \ominus 1}$.

2. Since the hiding operation $\backslash \{\rho_k, \omega_k \mid 0 \le k < N\}$ plays essentially the same role in the overall system as the function g (in abstracting away the details of storage), it is easy to show, using the transitions of BUFF and the result in part 1 above, that the relation R,

$$R = \{ \langle BUFF_*(s,a,d,i,m), BUFF_*(s',a,d,i',m) \rangle \mid g(s,i,m) = g(s',i',m) \}$$

is a strong bisimulation. □

As a consequence of lemma 4.2 we may abbreviate the state of BUFF to

$$BUFF_*(dra) \equiv BUFF_*(s,a,d,i,m),$$

where $r = g(s,i,m) \in D_N$. Further, since the value of "*" determines whether the ports α and/or $\bar{\delta}$ are empty or not, we may extend the function f to $\hat{f} : (D_\bot)_{N+2} \longrightarrow D_{N+2}$, which removes all occurrences of "$\bot$" from any string of length at most N+2. This means for $r \in D_N$ and $a, d \in D_\bot$ we have

$$\hat{f}(dra) = \begin{cases} r & \text{if } d = a = \bot \\ dr & \text{if } d \in D,\ a = \bot \\ ra & \text{if } d = \bot,\ a \in D \\ dra & \text{if } d,\ a \in D \end{cases}$$

Letting $t = \hat{f}(dra)$ it is easy to see that the values of $*$ and t together completely specify the state of BUFF upto strong congruence. Hence we may further simplify our definition of BUFF to

$BUFF_*(t) \equiv BUFF_*(dra)$

where $\hat{f}(dra) = t \in D_{N+2}$.

Proposition 4.3. Let $S = \{ \langle BUFF_*(t), FIFO(t)\rangle \mid t \in D_{N+2} \}$.

1. S is an efficiency prebisimulation.
2. $BUFF_*(\varepsilon) \lesssim^+ FIFO(\varepsilon)$.

Proof Outline. 1. Follows from the transitions of FIFO and BUFF.

2. When $t = \varepsilon$, $* = ?$ and $BUFF_*(t)$ has no internal transitions. In fact, both $BUFF(\varepsilon)$ and $FIFO(\varepsilon)$ have only an α-transition, satisfying the conditions EP^+ of proposition 3.11.3. □

Proposition 4.4. Let $T = \{ \langle PIPE(dsa), BUFF(dra)\rangle \mid \hat{f}(s) = r,\ \ a, d \in D_\bot \}$

1. T is an efficiency prebisimulation for all $N \geq 1$.
2. For $N = 1$ and $s, r \in D_\bot$ such that $\hat{f}(s) = r$, $PIPE(dsa) \simeq^+ BUFF(dra)$ for all $a, d \in D_\bot$.
3. For $N > 1$ and $s, r \in (D_\bot)_N$ such that $\hat{f}(s) = r$, $PIPE(dsa) \lesssim^+ BUFF(dra)$ for all $a, d \in D_\bot$. In particular, $PIPE(\bot^{N+2}) \lesssim^+ BUFF_?(\varepsilon)$.

Proof Outline. 1. Similar to the proof of proposition 4.3.1. The condition $N \geq 1$ is absolutely necessary because if $N = 0$ then BUFF is not an implementation at all (there is no MEM)!

2. It may be seen that when $N = 1$, the relation T defined in part 1 is a strong bisimulation.

3. It suffices to consider only the internal transitions of the the two implementations. Intuitively speaking, for every message that is accepted, PIPE has to perform N+1 internal actions (i.e. passing the message from cell C_{N+1} to C_N and so on till it reaches C_0) before it can deliver it to DEST. On the other hand, BUFF needs to perform exactly two internal actions (one to store the message in MEM and the other to retrieve it) before delivering it to DEST. Consider any ordered pair ⟨PIPE(dsa), BUFF(dra)⟩ in the ep T given in part 1 and let $N > 1$. The following claims may then be proved easily.

Claim 1. Let p be an integer such that $0 \leq p \leq N+1$, and $q = \min(2, p)$. Then for every ⟨PIPE(dsa), BUFF(dra)⟩ in T, $PIPE(dsa) \xrightarrow{1^p} PIPE(d's'a')$ implies there exists $r' \in D_N$ such that $BUFF(dra) \xrightarrow{1^q} BUFF(d'r'a')$ and

$\langle PIPE(d's'a'), BUFF(d'r'a')\rangle \in T$.

Claim 2. If $BUFF(dra) \xrightarrow{1} BUFF(d'r'a')$ then there exists $p \geq 1$ and s' such that $PIPE(dsa) \xrightarrow{1^p} PIPE(d's'a')$ and $\langle PIPE(d's'a'), BUFF(d'r'a')\rangle \in T$.

$PIPE(\bot^{N+2}) \lesssim^{+} BUFF(\varepsilon)$ follows from the fact that both processes have no internal transitions and both may only perform α-transitions. □

5. Proof System for Finite Processes.

In this section, we give a sound and complete (in)equational proof system for finite processes, that is, processes in which there is no occurrence of recursion.

In any proof system for finite processes in CCS, it turns out that for a precongruence which is coarser than strong bisimulation congruence (~) it is enough to restrict attention to what are referred to by Milner as "finite serial processes", i.e. processes which are built up only from prefix and summation operations. This is because, any finite process containing one or more of the so called "static operators", viz. composition, hiding and relabelling, may be transformed into a finite serial process using equations which are sound for strong bisimulation congruence. The reader may verify from the following proposition (stated without proof) that this is indeed true. It is easy to show that "|" is both commutative and associative, hence we use the unary operation "Γ" over a set of processes to denote their composition. For similar reasons "Σ" is used for summation.

Proposition 5.1. [Mil 89].

1. *The Expansion Law.* Let $p \equiv \Gamma P'$, where $P' \equiv \{ p_i \mid 1 \leq i \leq n \}$. Then

$$p \sim \Sigma \{ a_i.p' \mid p_i \xrightarrow{a_i} p'_i,\ p' \equiv \Gamma((P' - \{p_i\}) \cup \{p'_i\}) \} +$$

$$\Sigma \{ 1.p'' \mid p_i \xrightarrow{\alpha_i} p'_i,\ p_j \xrightarrow{\bar{\alpha}_i} p'_j,\ i<j,\ p'' \equiv \Gamma((P'-\{p_i,p_j\}) \cup \{p'_i,p'_j\}) \}$$

2. $(a.p)\backslash L \sim \begin{cases} \mathbb{O} \text{ if } a \in L \cup \bar{L} \\ a.(p\backslash L) \text{ otherwise} \end{cases}$
3. $(a.p)[h] \sim h(a).p[h]$
4. $(p + q)\backslash L \sim (p\backslash L) + (q\backslash L)$
5. $(p + q)[h] \sim p[h] + q[h]$ □

The five parts of the above proposition may be combined and generalized into a single monolithic expansion law. However, we have given it in the above form for the sake of clarity.

A proof system for efficiency precongruence, strictly speaking, should also incorporate proposition 5.1 as an infinitary equation (since A is an infinite set). However, it is enough for our purposes to know that such an equation exists. Our main concern therefore, will be to obtain a proof system for finite serial processes that characterizes efficiency precongruence. Our proof system, denoted $\mathcal{A}$, is shown below.

A1. $x + y = y + x$

A2. $x + (y + z) = (x + y) + z$

A3. $x + x = x$

A4. $x + \mathbb{0} = x$

A5. $a.(x + 1.x) \sqsubseteq a.x$

A6. $1.x \sqsubseteq x + 1.x$

A7. $a.(x + 1.y) \sqsubseteq a.(x + 1.y) + a.y$

R0. $$\frac{x \sqsubseteq x + y + z}{x \sqsubseteq x + z}$$

As with any inequational axiom system (see [Hen 88]) provability is assumed to be closed under the following rules -- reflexivity (R1), equality (R2), transitivity (R3), substitutivity (R4) and instantiation (R5). Further, each of the equations A1-4 given above, actually denotes a pair of inequations which may be obtained by applying rule R2.

The proof system $\mathcal{A}$ consists of the axioms A1-7 and rules R0-6. The axioms A1-4 and rules R1-5 are the usual ones and require no explanation. A5-7 are asymmetric because of the differing numbers of silent actions on the two sides of the respective inequations, i.e. their converses do not hold. Note that using A6 a slightly weaker version of A5 may be derived, $a.1.x \sqsubseteq a.x$. However, rule R0 may require some detailed intuitive explanation to justify its introduction. Let $\mathcal{A}^-$ denote the proof system $\mathcal{A}$ without the rule R0.

To explain the need for R0, it is necessary to be able to compare the proof system $\mathcal{A}^-$ with the system $\mathcal{A}'$ for observational congruence. $\mathcal{A}'$ consists of the equations A1-4, and the following equations (A5'-7') in lieu of A5-7.

A5'. $a.1.x = a.x$

A6'. $1.x = x + 1.x$

A7'. $a.(x + 1.y) = a.(x + 1.y) + a.y$

In place of A5' we could have used $a.(x + 1.x) = a.x$, but in view of A6' our choice seems more straightforward. Moreover these are precisely the axioms used in [HM 86]. Further we also have the rules R1'-5', which are obtained by replacing all occurrences of "$\sqsubseteq$" in R1-5 by "=" respectively. $\mathcal{A}'$ has been shown to be complete for finite processes (see [HM 86] or [Mil 89]). Now consider the following equation.

T1'. $z + 1.(x + y) = z + 1.(x + y) + y$

It may be easily shown that T1' is provable in $\mathcal{A}'$ using the equation

A8'. $1.(x + y) = 1.(x + y) + y$.

A8' in turn may be derived from A6' in the following manner.

$$\begin{aligned} & 1.(x + y) \\ &= 1.(x + y) + (x + y) && \text{by A6'} \\ &= (1.(x + y) + (x + y)) + y && \text{by A3 and A2} \\ &= 1.(x + y) + y && \text{by A6'} \end{aligned}$$

However, to prove the analogue of T1', viz.

T1. $z + 1.(x + y) \sqsubseteq z + 1.(x + y) + y$

in $\mathcal{A}^-$, it would be necessary to introduce

A8. $1.(x + y) \sqsubseteq 1.(x + y) + y$

as an extra axiom, since A8 cannot be derived from A6 in a similar fashion. Even if A8 were added to the system $\mathcal{A}$, it is not possible to prove

T2. $1.(x_1 + 1.(x_2 + y)) \sqsubseteq 1.(x_1 + 1.(x_2 + y)) + y$,

whereas, the analogue of T2, viz. T2' is provable in $\mathcal{A}'$, without the addition of any more axioms or inference rules.

Let X denote the sequence $\langle x_i \mid 1 \le i \le m \rangle$ and for any y, let $a \succ X\Box y$ denote $a.(x_1 + a.(x_2 + a.(\dots + a.(x_m + y)\dots)))$. In general, in the system $\mathcal{A}^-$, it does not seem possible to derive valid inequalities of the form,

T3. $1 \succ X\Box y \sqsubseteq (1 \succ X\Box y) + y$

without adding an infinite number of axioms starting with A8. On the other hand, by using R0 in conjunction with A6, we would be able to prove inequations like T3. For instance, T2 may be derived in $\mathcal{A}$ as follows:

$$\begin{aligned} & 1.(x_1 + 1.(x_2 + y)) \\ &\sqsubseteq 1.(x_1 + 1.(x_2 + y)) + x_1 + 1.(x_2 + y) && \text{by A6} \\ &\sqsubseteq 1.(x_1 + 1.(x_2 + y)) + x_1 + (1.(x_2 + y) + x_2 + y) && \text{by A6} \\ &\sqsubseteq 1.(x_1 + 1.(x_2 + y)) + (x_1 + 1.(x_2 + y) + x_2) + y && \text{by A2} \\ &\sqsubseteq 1.(x_1 + 1.(x_2 + y)) + y && \text{by R0} \end{aligned}$$

A6 therefore enables us to extract y from an expression of the form given in T3, in which y may be nested at an arbitrary depth. However R0 enables us to discard certain other superfluous terms which also come up by the application of A6. A similar phenomenon occurs with A7. For example,

T4. $a.(x_1 + 1.(x_2 + 1.y)) \sqsubseteq a.(x_1 + 1.(x_2 + 1.y)) + a.y$

cannot be derived in $\mathcal{A}$ although its analogue T4' is a theorem in $\mathcal{A}'$.

We give below the proof of soundness of R0 and leave the other proofs of soundness to the reader. We then proceed to show that the proof system $\mathcal{A}$ is complete for finite processes.

Proposition 5.2. Rule R0 is sound.

Proof. Suppose $p \lesssim^{+} p + q + r$. Let $pqr \equiv p + q + r$ and $pr \equiv p + r$. By proposition 3.11.3 we have

$$p \xrightarrow{a} p' \Rightarrow \exists pqr': pqr \xrightarrow{a} pqr' \wedge p' \lesssim pqr' \quad (1)$$

$$pqr \xrightarrow{a} pqr' \Rightarrow \exists p': p \overset{a}{\Longrightarrow} p' \wedge p' \lesssim pqr' \quad (2)$$

Letting $pr' \equiv p'$ we have

$$p \xrightarrow{a} p' \Rightarrow \exists pr': pr \xrightarrow{a} pr' \wedge p' \lesssim pr' \quad (3)$$

From (2) it follows that

$$pr \xrightarrow{a} pr' \Rightarrow \exists p': p \overset{a}{\Longrightarrow} p' \wedge p' \lesssim pr' \quad (4)$$

By (3), (4) and proposition 3.11.3 we get $p \lesssim^{+} p + r$. □

Lemma 5.3. For all processes p, q, $p \lesssim q$ implies $p \lesssim^{+} q$ or $p \lesssim^{+} q + 1.q$.

Proof. Assume $p \lesssim q$ and $p \not\lesssim^{+} q$. We have to show $p \lesssim^{+} q + 1.q$. By proposition 3.11 it is sufficient to show

$$p \xrightarrow{a} p' \Rightarrow \exists q': q + 1.q \xrightarrow{a} q' \wedge p' \lesssim q' \quad (1)$$

$$q + 1.q \xrightarrow{a} q' \Rightarrow \exists p': p \overset{a}{\Longrightarrow} p' \wedge p' \lesssim q' \quad (2)$$

(1) follows from the fact that $p \lesssim q$ using the characterization of $\lesssim$ given in proposition 3.6. The same characterization ensures (2) whenever $q \xrightarrow{a} q'$. Hence it remains to prove $\exists p': p \overset{1}{\Longrightarrow} p' \wedge p' \lesssim q$ when $q + 1.q \xrightarrow{1} q$. Since $p \lesssim q$ and $p \not\lesssim^{+} q$, EP'2 and the negation of $EP^{+}2$ for a = 1 yield

$$p \xrightarrow{1} p' \wedge p' \lesssim q \wedge (\forall q': q \xrightarrow{1} q': p' \not\lesssim q').$$

Hence

$$q + 1.q \xrightarrow{1} q \Rightarrow \exists p': p \overset{1}{\Longrightarrow} p' \wedge p' \lesssim q$$

which was required. □

Lemma 5.4. $p \xrightarrow{a} p'$ implies $\mathcal{A} \vdash p = p + a.p'$.

Proof. By induction on the depth of inference of $p \xrightarrow{a} p'$. □

Lemma 5.5. $p \overset{a}{\Longrightarrow} p'$ implies $\mathcal{A} \vdash p \sqsubseteq p + a.p'$.

Proof. By induction on the number of silent actions involved in the transition $p \overset{a}{\Longrightarrow} p'$. If $p \xrightarrow{a} p'$ then the result follows from lemma 5.4. Otherwise we have two cases to consider. Either $p \xrightarrow{1} q \overset{a}{\Longrightarrow} p'$ or $p \overset{a}{\Longrightarrow} q \xrightarrow{1} p'$. In the former case by lemma 5.4 we have

$\mathcal{A} \vdash p = p + 1.q$		(1)
$\mathcal{A} \vdash q \sqsubseteq q + a.p'$	by induction hypothesis	
$\mathcal{A} \vdash 1.q \sqsubseteq 1.(q + a.p')$	by R4	
$\mathcal{A} \vdash 1.q \sqsubseteq 1.(q + a.p') + q + a.p'$	A6	(2)
$\mathcal{A} \vdash p \sqsubseteq p + (1.(q + a.p') + q) + a.p'$	by (1), (2), R3 and A2	(3)

Applying rule R0 to (3) we obtain

$$\mathcal{A} \vdash p \sqsubseteq p + a.p'.$$

In the latter case by the induction hypothesis

$\mathcal{A} \vdash p \sqsubseteq p + a.q$ (4)

$\mathcal{A} \vdash q = q + 1.p'$ by lemma 5.4

$\mathcal{A} \vdash a.q = a.(q + 1.p')$ by R4

$\mathcal{A} \vdash a.q \sqsubseteq a.(q + 1.p') + a.q$ by A7 (5)

$\mathcal{A} \vdash p \sqsubseteq p + a.(q + 1.p') + a.q$ from (4), (5) and R3 (6)

Again applying R0 to (6) we get

$\mathcal{A} \vdash p \sqsubseteq p + a.p'$ □

Theorem 5.6 (Completeness). $p \lesssim^{+} q$ implies $\mathcal{A} \vdash p \sqsubseteq q$.

Proof. We prove this by induction on the sum of the *depths* of p and q, where the *depth* of p is the maximum number of nested prefixes in p. We may assume p and q have the standard forms $\Sigma \{ a_i.p_i \mid 1 \le i \le m \}$ and $\Sigma \{ b_j.q_j \mid 1 \le j \le n \}$ respectively (and for all i, j, $1 \le i \le m$, $1 \le j \le n$, p_i, q_j are in standard form). If the sum of the depths is 0 (i.e. m = n = 0), there is nothing to prove since $p \equiv \mathbb{0} \equiv q$. Otherwise, by repeated applications of A4, all summands that are $\mathbb{0}$ may be eliminated leaving p and q in standard form (m, n > 0). We prove the following claim.

Claim. (i) $\mathcal{A} \vdash a_i.p_i + q \sqsubseteq q$ for every i, $1 \le i \le m$.

(ii) $\mathcal{A} \vdash p \sqsubseteq p + b_j.q_j$ for every j, $1 \le j \le n$.

(i) If $p \lesssim^{+} q$ then since $p \xrightarrow{a_i} p_i$ there exists $b_j = a_i$ with $q \xrightarrow{b_j} q_j$ and $p_i \lesssim q_j$. By lemma 5.3 $p_i \lesssim^{+} q_j$ or $p_i \lesssim^{+} q_j + 1.q_j$. By the induction hypothesis we have $\mathcal{A} \vdash p_i \sqsubseteq q_j$ or $\mathcal{A} \vdash p_i \sqsubseteq q + 1.q_j$. In the former case $\mathcal{A} \vdash a_i.p_i \sqsubseteq b_j.q_j$ by R4, and in the latter we get the same by applying R4 followed by A5. The result then follows.

(ii) If $q \xrightarrow{b_j} q_j$ then by proposition 3.11.3 there exists p' and some $a_i = b_j$ such that $p \stackrel{a_i}{\Longrightarrow} p'$ and $p' \lesssim q_j$. By lemma 5.3 and the induction hypothesis we get $\mathcal{A} \vdash p' \sqsubseteq q_j$ or $\mathcal{A} \vdash p' \sqsubseteq q_j + 1.q_j$. It then follows (by applying A5 in the latter case) that $\mathcal{A} \vdash b_j.p' \sqsubseteq b_j.q_j$ and by lemma 5.5 $\mathcal{A} \vdash p \sqsubseteq p + b_j.p'$ from which we obtain $\mathcal{A} \vdash p \sqsubseteq p + b_j.q_j$.

Having proved the claim, we proceed as follows. By R4, we may sum up (i) for all i, reorder the terms (by A1 and A2) and repeatedly apply A3, to obtain $\mathcal{A} \vdash p + q \sqsubseteq q$. By performing similar operations with (ii) for all j, we get $\mathcal{A} \vdash p \sqsubseteq p + q$. The result then follows by R3. □

6. Conclusion

The efficiency preorder we have introduced, $\lesssim$, is based on the simple idea of, essentially, counting the number of internal moves made by a process. We have shown that this idea may be successfully incorporated within the general framework of bisimulations, [Mil 89], to obtain a mathematically tractable preorder, which, in common with the standard notions of bisimulation equivalence, is sensitive to the branching structure of processes yet supports abstraction. It is mathematically tractable in that it is preserved by all CCS contexts and we have given a complete proof system for finite terms, based on a modification of the standard τ-laws for CCS. Moreover the usual algorithms for checking bisimulations or finding bisimulations, [CPS 89], may easily be adapted to $\lesssim$. It supports abstraction in that it is insensitive to many of the internal details of processes. For example, the usual laws associated with port restrictions are true as are variations on the τ-laws. It differs from the abstraction supported by weak bisimulation only in that processes may be differentiated if their response times to external stimuli are different. This is also the basis of comparing and ordering processes: $p \lesssim q$ if the response time of q to external stimuli is uniformly faster than that of p.

Although the basis of the preorder is very simple, we have demonstrated its usefulness by applying it to an example of the implementation of a FIFO queue. In future work we hope to apply it to more significant examples. We also intend to investigate the possibility of characterising $\lesssim$ completely using a finite set of inequations. Recall that the proof rule R0 is essential to our proof system.

There has been much recent work on introducing notions of time into process algebras. [BB 89] and [RR 86] are typical examples of one approach, where real-time durations are associated with actions. [NRSV 89] and [HR 89] are examples of another approach where actions are still instantaneous but a special action is introduced to represent the passage of time. Neither of these approaches is directly comparable with the one presented here, which we believe to be the first "improvement" preorder based on time.

REFERENCES

("LNCS" denotes "Lecture Notes in Computer Science")

[BB 89] J. Baeton, J. Bergstra: *Real Time Process Algebra*, Technical Report CWI Amsterdam, 1989.

[CPS 89] R. Cleaveland, J. Parrow, B. Steffen: *The Concurrency Workbench: A Semantics-Based Verification Tool for Finite-State Systems*, Technical Report ECS-LFCS-89-83, University of Edinburgh, 1989.

[DS 89] J. Davies, S. Schneider: *An Introduction to Timed CSP*, Technical Report, PRG, Oxford, 1989.

[GB 86] R. Gerth, A. Boucher: *A Timed Failures Model for Extended Communicating Sequential Processes*, LNCS 267, Springer-Verlag, 1986.

[Hoa 85] C.A.R. Hoare: **Communicating Sequential Processes**, Prentice Hall, 1985.

[Hen 88]M. Hennessy: **Algebraic Theory of Processes**, MIT Press, 1988.

[HM 86] M. Hennessy, R. Milner: *Algebraic Laws for Nondeterminism and Concurrency*, Journal of the ACM, 32, 1, 137-161, 1985.

[HR 90] M. Hennessy, T. Regan: *A Temporal Process Algebra*, Technical Report 2/90, University of Sussex, 1990.

[Mil 83] R. Milner: *Calculi for Synchrony and Asynchrony*, Theoretical Computer Science, 25, 267-310, 1983.

[Mil 89]R. Milner: **Communication and Concurrency**, Prentice Hall, 1989.

[NRSV 89] X. Nicollin, J.L. Richier, J. Sifakis, J. Voiron: *ATP: An Algebra for Timed Processes*, Technical Report, Grenoble 1989.

[Pa 80] D. Park: *Concurrency and Automata on Infinite Sequences*, LNCS 104, Springer-Verlag 1980.

[RR 86] G.M. Reed, A. Roscoe: *A Timed Model for Communicating Sequential Processes*, LNCS 226, Springer-Verlag, 1986.

[RS 88] S. Rudkin, C.R. Smith: *A Temporal Enhancement for LOTOS*, British Telecom, 1988.

On Nets, Algebras and Modularity

Alexander Rabinovich
IBM Research Division
T.J. Watson Research Center
P.O. Box 218, Yorktown Heights, NY 10598, USA
alik@watson.ibm.com

Boris A. Trakhtenbrot*
MIT Lab. for Computer Science
boris@theory.lcs.mit.edu
and
Dep. of Computer Science
Raymond and Beverly Sackler Faculty of Exact Sciences
Tel Aviv University, Tel Aviv, Israel 69978
trakhte@taurus.bitnet

Abstract

We aim at a unified and coherent presentation of net models for concurrency like Petri nets and dataflow networks from the perspective of modularity and substitutivity. The major goal is to achieve a better understanding of the links between modularity issues for nets and laws (or anomalies) in algebras of processes and algebras of relations. To this end we develop Mazurkiewicz's compositional approach which requires a careful analysis of homomorphisms from algebras of nets into algebras of processes and relations.

0 Introduction

0.1 Modularity, Substitutivity, Compositionality

Modularity reflects the Frege Principle: any two expressions $expr_1$ and $expr_2$ which have the same meaning (semantics) can be replaced by each other in every appropriate context $C[\,]$ without changing the meaning of the overall expression

*Supported by NSF Grant No. 9002826–CCR.

$$sem(expr_1) = sem(expr_2) \text{ implies } sem(C[expr_1]) = sem(C[expr_2])$$

$R - substitutivity$, where R is a given a binary relation R in the semantical domain of meanings, is a broader notion. It means that

$$sem(expr_1) R sem(expr_2) \text{ implies } sem(C[expr_1]) R sem(C[expr_2])$$

In particular, R may happen to be an equivalence relation in the semantical domain. For example, a dataflow net may specify a process Pr but what one is mainly interested in is the input-output behavior $rel(Pr)$ of this process i.e., the relation between the input histories and output histories of Pr. Hence of fundamental importance is $\equiv_{rel}$-substitutivity i.e., substitutivity of the equivalence $rel(Pr_1) = rel(Pr_2)$. However, in general R is not necessarily an equivalence relation. As a matter of fact for dataflow nets we consider also substitutivity of $\leq_{rel}$ i.e. of $rel(Pr_1) \subseteq rel(Pr_2)$.

A conventional syntax (call it TEXTUAL as opposed to NET-syntax) is based on a signature Σ. Morever, a complex piece of syntax $expr$ may be *uniquely* decomposed into simpler subpieces: $expr = op(expr_1, \cdots expr_k)$, where op is in Σ. If *compositional* semantics is used, then there is a corresponding semantical clause with the format: $sem(expr) =_{def} OP(sem(expr_1), ..., sem(expr_k))$. Here OP is the semantical constructor which corresponds to op. In this situation there is a natural and clear notion of context; it is also quite evident that compositional semantics guarantees modularity. Compositional semantics may be characterized as a homomorphism from the Σ-algebra of the syntactical domain into the Σ-algebra of the semantical domain.

Typically, denotational semantics is formulated in compositional style and hence supports modularity. However, often one starts with an operational semantics which lacks compositional structure. Then a standard way to prove modularity is to discover a compositional semantics which is equivalent to the given operational one.

In net models of concurrency syntax is provided by some specific class NN of labelled graphs called *nets*. On the other hand, semantics is usually defined in an operational style through appropriate firing (enabling) rules. Though NN is not necessarily equipped with a signature Σ of operations (i.e. no algebra of nets must be assumed) the notions of *context, subnet* and *substitution* may make sense and therefore $R - substitutivity$ (in particular modularity) may be defined and investigated.

0.2 Historical Background

Petri nets and dataflow nets are fundamental paradigms in concurrency. Historically, modularity topics appeared wrt them as follows:

1. *Dataflow.* Substitutivity issues for dataflow nets were identified early and in a sharp way. The Kahn Principle [7] implies that dataflow nets over functional agents are $\equiv_{rel}$-substitutive . On the other hand, as Brock and Ackerman observed, $\equiv_{rel}$-substitutivity in general fails if nonfunctional agents (like MERGE) are also allowed. The celebrated counterexample from [3] illustrates this so called Brock-Ackerman anomaly.

2. *Petri Nets.* For elementary Petri nets modularity was established by Mazurkiewicz [8] following the pattern mentioned above wrt TEXTUAL syntax. Namely, he discovered a compositional semantics for elementary Petri nets which is equivalent to the original 'token game' semantics. Yet, the novelty is that (unlike the case of textual syntax) there may be *different* decompositions of a net into subnets. In other words, for textual syntax compositional semantics is an homomorphism from an Σ-algebra over a system of *free generators* whereas in the case of nets the generators obey some nontrivial relations. Clearly in order to support homomorphism, these relations must hold also in the semantical domain as well. Mazurkiewicz made the fundamental observation that for elementary Petri nets the signature Σ consists of one binary operation to be interpreted as *combination* of nets (at the syntactical leval) and *synchronization* of processes (at the semantical level); the nontrivial relations amount to commutativity and associativity of the operation. In the sequel [9] he formulated compositional semantics of this kind also for the more general classes of P/T-nets but without to compare it with the already existing token game semantics.

These seminal works in dataflow nets and in Petri nets inspired and strongly influenced the research of modularity for net models. [2, 4, 5, 6, 11, 12, 13, 15, 16, 17, 18]. Note that in these works 'modularity' and 'compositionality' are not clearly distinguished.

Modularity issues for models based on the net concept constitute also one of the major goals in our previous papers [5, 15, 16, 17]. In [5] we used the Mazurkiewicz algebraical approach to formulate an alternative compositional semantics for the token game semantics of P/T-nets. In this way we established modularity for this, more general class of nets. On the other hand, in [15, 16] where our main concern was about the phenomena around the Brock-Ackerman-anomaly, we did not rely on any specific algebraical arguments. An important conceptual and technical novelty we started in [16] and developed in [17] is the idea to consider semantics of nets of relations in addition to semantics of nets of processes. As a result of a careful comparison of these two kinds of nets we came very close to answering the following question: what nonfunctional agents may be used in dataflow nets without to produce anomalies?

As shown in [16], if such nontrivial agents exist they may implement only so called unambiguous relations. This seems to be too a strong restriction which cannot offer much to practice. However, the full answer to the question is an exciting challenge and we have more to say about that in the sequel.

0.3 Goals of the Paper

They are better explained after some preliminary comments about the conceptual and notational framework we are going to use.

A possible formalization of the models we consider is through triples:

$MM =_{def} < NN, DD, SEM >$, where
NN is the syntactical domain, a class of 'nets',

DD is the semantical domain, usually a class of 'processes',
SEM is a function from $NN \times ENV$ into DD. Here ENV is an appropriately defined class of 'environments'.

Syntax. A great diversity of nets is actually used in the literature. Roughly speaking the nets we consider are *bipartite* graphs as in the theory of Petri nets with the additional requirement that the set of all transitions (we call them *ports*) is divided into the set of visible ports and the set of hidden ports. It may happen that for the whole class of nets (we denote it as NN_1) modularity cannot be guaranteed. In order to regain modularity one has to consider subclasses of NN_1, which reflect reasonable restrictions on the topology of the net or on the status of visible/hidden nodes. We find the following restrictions enough representative: NN_2-nets without hiding, NN_4-nets without loops, NN_3-nets with exactly the internal ports hidden. In most of dataflow papers (including our [16]) one prefers to deal with simpler (nonbipartite) graphs in which edges do not necessarily have nodes, or may have nodes of different kinds. It is easy to see that these kinds of nets are shorthands of our bipartite nets and in particular of nets in NN_3. Summarizing we believe that our approach to nets is quite general.

Semantical domains. Here our choice is very specific and debatable. We consider only processes which are prefix closed sets of finite runs. This may be too a strong restriction. Yet it still allows to explain many phenomena concerning modularity and anomalies. But note that in addition to processes we consider also the semantical domain of (connected) relations, which are the behaviors of processes. These objects are interesting in their own (see [10, 16, 17]) but we use them here also for the explanation of $\equiv_{rel}$-substitutivity and anomalies.

Semantics. Our starting point is an operational semantics we call SEM_{proc} which provides meanings for nets of processes in the style of firing (enabling) rules. A semantics SEM_{rel} for nets of relations is derived from SEM_{proc}. In [16, 17] we analyzed different possible approaches and they provide evidence to the naturalness of the semantics SEM_{rel}.

In this paper we pursue two major interrelated goals.

The first is to develop our previous results to a level which presents in an unified and coherent way the status of different models from the perspective of modularity. To be more concrete one can imagine a table with 4 rows (corresponding to our four kinds of nets) and with 3 columns (corresponding to modularity for processes, modularity for relations and $\equiv_{rel}$-substitutivity). At each of the 12 intersections we would expect the characterization of those classes of processes or relations (if any!) which support the required version of modularity/substitutivity wrt the class of nets under consideration.

Our second goal is to achieve a better understanding of the links between modularity/substitutivity issues for nets and laws (or 'anomalies') in algebras of processes and relations. To this end, following Mazurkiewicz, we aim at a careful analysis of homomorphisms from algebras of nets into algebras of processes or relations. This may be illustrated by the following comparison with [8]. There, for nets without hiding, modularity is argued by the fact that process synchronization obeys the laws of commutativity and associativity. For other models we expect to discover in a similar way appropriate laws which support modularity (in particular - their violation spoils modularity).

0.4 Survey of Contributions

Let us now proceed with the survey of the paper and its main contributions.

Section 1 presents nets as syntax and also the concept of modular net semantics. This material is mainly folklore, but note the accurate definition of substitution (for nets some of whose nodes may be hidden!) and of substitutional classes of nets.

Sections 2-4 contain the definitions of input processes, input relations and of the semantical functions SEM_{proc}, SEM_{rel}. In general, processes are dealt with in a more or less routine way. However our treatment of relations is not routine and heavily relies on the notion of *kernel* which transfers on relations the idea of least fixed points. This notion appears in [17, 10] and comes close to Misra's 'smooth solution' [11].

The conceptual framework covered in sections 1-4 suffices for the formulation of the modularity (relational substitutivity) problems we investigate in this paper. It suffices also to formulate most of the facts (though not their proofs) according to the 4×3 - table we mentioned above. Not surprisingly (though we never met this fact in the literature) modularity for processes holds for all nets and all processes (Claim 2.1). The real problems arise with modularity for relations and for $\equiv_{rel}$-substitutivity; both fail if all nets are allowed. Moreover, they fail even for trivial subdomains of processes or relations. Here is where restrictions on the class of nets have to be considered. If hiding is not allowed (the case of class NN_2) or if the nets under consideration don't contain loops (the case of class NN_4) no anomalies appear for relations. This analysis shows that the real challenge is with nets which allow both hiding and loops but are still tractable. In our classification the appropriate candidate is just the class NN_3 which requires exactly the hiding of the internal ports of the net (additional fanin and fanout restrictions are imposed only to make the exposition readable). Note, that in most of works on dataflow such nets (or more precisely - their shorthands) are considered. Earlier in [16] we also investigated these nets; it appears that for them the two following tasks are reducible to each other:
Task 1. Find a class of processes which is relational substitutive.
Task 2. Find a class of relations which is modular.

Sections 5-8 contain the algebraical part of the paper.

In Section 5 the classes NN_1, NN_2, NN_3, NN_4 of nets are characterized as algebras with appropriate signatures. Moreover the corresponding nontrivial relations for their generators are explicitly formulated. Among them the most prominent are: the existential quantifier law - 5.2(4) and the looping law - 5.2(5).

Section 6 deals with algebra of processes to an extent which exceeds the direct necessities of our modularity issues (in particular we consider the union operation which is not in the signature of the net algebras). Nevertheless, we included claim 6.1 which shows that well known logical laws hold in the algebra of processes. Beyond of being a generally stimulating observation, this fact may be also useful for other related applications (e.g., for the proof of the generalized Kahn Principle as in [17]).

Section 7 deals briefly with the algebra of relations. Again we notice similarities of the operations in this algebra with logical operations, but unlike for processes these similarities are much more limited and exhibit anomalies.

Section 8 contains the main technical result (claim 8.3) which establishes the links between the algebras investigated in the previous sections and their relationship to the original semantical functions SEM_{proc} and SEM_{rel}. It extends the Mazurkiewicz compositional approach to a broad class of net models and paves the way to the discovery of modular models or to the prediction that they are impossible under given circumstances. Actually, that is how most of the claims in sections 1-4 may be proved. In particular a model $< NN_3,\ RR,\ SEM_{rel} >$ is modular iff the looping law holds in the class RR of relations. Recalling the connection between modularity for nets of relations and $\equiv_{rel}$-substitutivity (see Task 1 and Task 2 on the previous page) we can see that this fact opens the way to the full characterization of nonfunctional agents which avoid the Brock-Ackerman anomaly. However, the *explicit* description of *all* classes of relations which obey the looping rule appears to be a subtle task and will be the subject of a separate paper [14].

1 Nets

1.1 General Definitions

A *net* is an appropriately labeled bipartite directed graph with nodes of two kinds, pictured as circles and boxes and called respectively **places** and **ports**. The edges of the net are called **channels**. If there is a channel between port p and place pl they are said to be adjacent. If there is a channel from port p to place pl then p is called an input port of pl. If there is a channel to port p from place pl then p is called an output port of pl. Channels connecting place pl to its input ports and output ports are numbered. This allows to refer to the first input channel of pl, to its second input channel, $\cdots$, first output channel etc. The difference between ports and places is relevant for the notion of subnet.

Definition 1 *A subgraph N_1 of N is considered to be a subnet of N if the set of its nodes consists of some places and all ports and channels adjacent to these places.*

Ports of a net are partitioned into input, output and internal ports as follows:

Input ports - ports with no entering channel.

Output ports - ports with no exiting channel.

Internal ports - all the other ports.

Output and internal ports are called **local** ports.

In the sequel we consider marked nets i.e. nets in which some ports are declared as visible ports; all the other ports are said to be hidden.

Labeling. Ports are labeled by port names. Different ports of a net are labeled by different names. Places are labeled by identifiers together with pair of natural numbers (rank). An identifier assigned to a place *pl* with n input ports and m output ports should have the rank $(n; m)$

The type of place *pl* is the set of names of port adjacent to it. We use the notation *Port(pl)* for the type of *pl*. A net with only one place and any number of ports is called **atomic**. $At(a_1, \cdots a_n; b_1, \cdots b_m)$ is a typical notation for an atomic net with place labeled by $At(n; m)$, with input ports labeled by $a_1, \cdots a_n$ and output ports labeled by $b_1, \cdots b_m$. Different ports of a net have different labels. Hence we may identify ports with their labels. We always assume in the sequel that no parallel channels are allowed in the net: given an arbitrary place and an arbitrary port in the net there may be no more than one channel which connects them. Therefore, in any atomic subnet $At_1(a_1, \cdots a_n; b_1, \cdots b_m)$ all the port labels $a_1, \cdots a_n, b_1, \cdots b_m$ are different.

Fig. 1 suggest itself. For example in N_2 place pl_1 has two adjacent ports. Port a is adjacent to places pl_1, pl_2, pl_3. As usual nets are to be considered up to isomorphism. Two nets are isomorphic if there is a bijection between them which preserves adjacency, visibility status of ports and also the labeling.

Here are some possible restrictions concerning hiding and the topology of directed nets:

1. *No hiding at all*
2. *No Confluence* - For every port there is at most one channel entering it.
3. *No Forks* - For every port there is at most one channel exiting it.
4. All internal ports are hidden.
5. *No Loops* - No directed cycles in the net.

1.2 Substitution

Let *pl* be a place of a net N. We say that a net N_1 is substitutable for a place *pl* in N if:

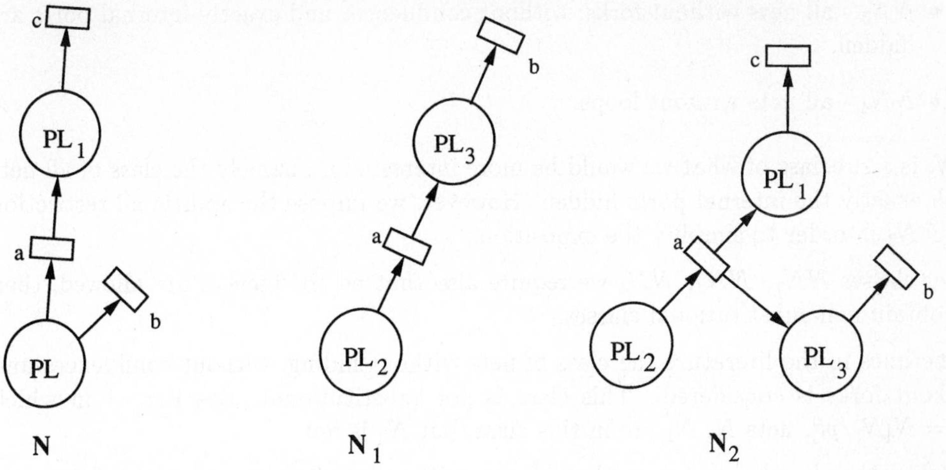

Figure 1: $N_2 = N[N_1/pl]$

1. The sets of input and local visible ports of N_1 are the same as the sets of input and output ports of pl.

2. No hidden port of N_1 is a port of N.

3. N_1 and N do not have common places.

The result of substitution $N[N_1/pl]$ is the net N_2 defined as follows:

1. $Places(N_2) = Places(N) - \{pl\} \cup Places(N_1)$

2. $Ports(N_2) = Ports(N) \cup Ports(N_1)$

3. A port and a place are connected in N_2 if they are connected in N or in N_1 and the edges preserves their direction.

4. A port is visible in N_2 if it is visible in N.

5. All nodes inherit their labelling.

For example in Fig. 1 $N_2 = N[N_1/pl]$.

A class of nets is called **substitutional** if it is closed under substitutions.

Notations. In the sequel we will refer to some specific substitutional classes of nets and denote them as follows:

- NN_1 - all nets

- NN_2 - all nets with only visible ports

- NN_3 - all nets without forks, without confluences and exactly internal ports are hidden.
- NN_4 - all nets without loops.

NN_3 is a subclass of what we would be more interested in, namely the class of all nets with exactly the internal ports hidden. However, we impose the additional restriction for NN_3 in order to simplify the exposition.

If for classes NN_1, NN_2, NN_4 we require also that no confluences are allowed, then we obtain non substitutional classes.

Sometimes in the literature the class of nets without hiding, without confluences and without forks is considered. This class is not substitutional. See Fig. 1 in which $N_2 = N[N_1/pl]$, nets N, N_1 are in this class, but N_2 is not.

On the other hand the class without forks, without confluence and with all internal ports hidden is substitutional.

1.3 Modular Net Semantics

A model of net semantics is a triple $< NN, D, SEM >$ where: NN is a substitutional class of nets, D is an 'appropriate' semantical domain we do not specify here (In the sequel classes of relations or classes of processes are intended mainly). SEM is a function from $NN \times ENV$ into D. Here ENV is the set of environments; each environment is a mapping from (all) atomic nets into D which respects types and renaming (see definition 3 below). An *interpreted net* is a net together with an environment. Notations $< N, env >$ and $SEM(N, env)$ are used for an interpreted net and its semantics. Since the places of a net are uniquely identified with its atomic subnets we refer (by abuse of notation) to env in $< N, env >$ also as to a function from the places of N into D. As always a *net context* is a net with partial environment (an environment which assigns value not to all places of N). $N[pl]$ is a typical notation for the net with one hole pl.

Definition 2 (Modularity) *We say that model $< NN, D, SEM >$ is modular (or briefly - that semantics SEM is modular) iff $SEM(N_1, env) = SEM(N_2, env)$ implies that for arbitrary context $N[pl]$*

$$SEM(N[N_1/pl], env) = SEM(N[N_2/pl], env)$$

From the particular case when N_2 is atomic it follows that a modular semantics SEM has the following

Property: Assume that pl is a place in N and $SEM(N_1, env) = env(pl)$; then $SEM(N, env) = SEM(N[N_1/pl], env)$.

It is easy to see that if NN contains all atomic nets then this property is equivalent to modularity.

2 Processes

2.1 Basic Definitions

Let P be a set of ports and Δ be a fixed data set. A communication event over P is a pair $< port,\ d >$ with $port \in P$ and $d \in \Delta$. A linear run over P is a finite string of communications over P. A linear process of type P is a pair $(T,\ P)$, where T is a prefix closed set of runs over P. Note, that processes of different types might contain the same set of string; such processes are different. The type of a process is its important attribute; we use notations $ports(Pr)$ for the type of process Pr. On processes of a given type one considers the subset preorder: $Pr_1 \leq Pr_2$ iff every run of Pr_1 is a run of Pr_2.

Example 1 Buffer. Usually under 'buffer' one has in mind an automaton with one input port one output port; it reads values and outputs them according to the FIFO discipline. As a linear process a buffer with input port p and output port q (notation - $buf(p \rightarrow q)$) consists of all strings s which obey the condition: in every prefix of s the sequence of data communicated through q is a prefix of the sequence of data communicated through p.

Example 2 Labeled transition systems and linear processes A Labeled Transition System (LTS) of type P is an automaton whose alphabet (set of actions) is the set of communications over P and the special invisible action τ. It consists of:

- Set of states Q.
- Initial state $q_0 \in Q$.
- Transition Relation: a subset of $Q \times Alphabet \times Q$.

We use $q \xrightarrow{<p,d>} q'$ as a notation for a transition from state q via communication $< p, d >$ to state q'; we say that $< p, d >$ is enabled at state q if there is a transition $q \xrightarrow{<p,d>} q'$ for some q'.

An alternating sequense $q_0,\ a_0,\ q_1,\ a_1, \cdots a_{n-1},\ q_n$ of states of LTS T and actions of T is an *execution sequence* of T if q_0 is the initial state of T and $q_i \xrightarrow{a_i} q_{i+1}$ are transitions of T for $i = 0 \cdots n-1$. A run of T is the sequence of communications which is obtained from an execution sequence by deleting the states of T and τ actions. For every LTS T the process of the same type as T is assigned. This process consists of the runs of T. It is clear that the set of runs of T is a prefix closed set of strings. It is also clear that for every process Pr there corresponds a LTS whose set of runs consists of the strings of Pr.

2.2 Operational Semantics Sem_{proc} for nets of processes

Let us consider first operational semantics for a net of LTS.

Let N be a net with n places and let ρ be a function which assigns to every place pl_i of N a LTS of the same type as pl. N and ρ define the LTS T as follows:

- States of T are the tuples $(q_1, \cdots q_n)$, where q_i is a state of $\rho(pl_i)$.
- The initial state of T is the tuple of the initial states of $\rho(pl_i)$.
- The transitions of T are defined as follows:
  1. If $q_i \xrightarrow{\tau} q_i'$ is a transitions of $\rho(pl_i)$ then $(q_1, \cdots q_{i-1}q_i, q_{i+1}, \cdots q_n) \xrightarrow{\tau} (q_1, \cdots q_{i-1}q_i', q_{i+1}, \cdots q_n)$ is a transitions of T.
  2. If in each of the places $pl_{i_1}, \cdots pl_{i_k}$ which are adjacent to the port p the communication $< p, d >$ is enabled at state $(q_1, \cdots q_{i-1}q_i, q_{i+1}, \cdots q_n)$, and $q_{i_1} \xrightarrow{<p,d>} q_{i_1}' \cdots q_{i_k} \xrightarrow{<p,d>} q_{i_k}'$ are transitions of $\rho(pl_{i_1}) \cdots \rho(pl_{i_k})$ then $(q_1, \cdots q_{i-1}q_i, q_{i+1}, \cdots q_n) \xrightarrow{\tau} (q_1, \cdots q_{i_1}', \cdots q_{i_k}' \cdots q_n)$ is a transitions of T if p is a hidden port of N and $(q_1, \cdots q_{i-1}q_i, q_{i+1}, \cdots q_n) \xrightarrow{<p,d>} (q_1, \cdots q_{i_1}', \cdots q_{i_k}' \cdots q_n)$ is a transitions of T if p is a visible port of N.

Definition 3 *A process* **environment** *pp is a mapping from atomic nets into processes which*

- *Respects types: $pp(At(a_1, \cdots a_n; b_1, \cdots b_m))$ has the same type as $At(a_1, \cdots a_n; b_1, \cdots b_m)$.*
- *Respects renaming: the processes $pp(At(a_1, \cdots a_n; b_1, \cdots b_m))$ and $pp(At(a_1', \cdots a_n'; b_1', \cdots b_m'))$ are the same up to appropriate renaming of their ports.*

Semantics of a net of processes Let $< N, pp >$ be an interpreted net of processes and let ρ be a function which maps the places of N into labeled transition systems such that the sets of runs of $\rho(pl_i)$ is the same as the process $pp(pl_i)$. The process semantics Sem_{proc} of $< N, pp >$ is the process assigned to the LTS for $< N, \rho >$.

It is easy to see that $Sem_{proc}(N, pp)$ does not depend on the choice of ρ. Therefore process semantics is well defined.

2.3 Input Processes

Definition 4 *Pr is an* **input process** *if its ports are divided into input ports and local ports with the only demand that if p is declared as an input port it should be 'input buffered' in the following sense: Assume s in Pr; then Pr contains also all strings one can construct via the following operations:*

- *Input extension. Extend s appending to the right arbitrary many communications through p.*
- *Input anticipation. If a communication $< p, d >$ follows immediately after a communication through a port different from p, permute them.*

The following remarks explain the intuition behind these conditions. Let Pr' be a process of type $p' \cup P$. Consider the process Pr specified by the net N with hidden port p' and two places: one for Pr' and another for $buf(p \longrightarrow p')$ (here p is not a port of Pr). Then port p in Pr satisfies input extension and input anticipation conditions.

If a process is obtained by the construction above, we say that its port p contains a buffer. It is easy to check that a process is input buffered at ports $p_1, \cdots p_k$ iff it contains buffers at these ports. Additional remarks about input bufferness will be given in section 6.2 when we consider operations on processes.

Example 3 *$buf(p \rightarrow q)$ is a linear process with input port p and local port q.*

Example 4 *(Rudimentary Processes [15]). Start with an arbitrary run s over ports $P \cup Q$. Let $Prefix(s)$ be the closure of s under prefixes. Finally, close $Prefix(s)$ under input extension and input anticipation wrt ports in P. The resulting process Rudim(s, P, Q) is called the rudimentary process generated by s, P, Q. It is an input process with input ports P and local ports Q.*

From now on when we refer to an interpreted net of processes we will have in mind that its environment assigns to the atoms input processes and to an atom At with input ports $p_1, \cdots, p_k$ and output ports $q_1, \cdots, q_m$ the environment assigns a process with input ports $p_1, \cdots, p_k$ and local ports $q_1, \cdots, q_m$. It is easy to check that the process Pr specified by such an interpreted net is an input process wrt to the set of visible inputs in N. Hence, the general notion of semantics for a net of processes consistently restricts to semantics for nets of input processes.

Claim 2.1 *(Modularity of SEM_{proc}). Let PP_1 be the the class of all input processes. Then $< NN_1, PP_1, SEM_{proc} >$ is a modular model.*

For the proof see later section 8.3. As a straightforward consequence we mention:

Corollary 2.2 *Let $< NN, PP, SEM_{proc} >$ be a model with arbitrary substitutional set NN and arbitrary set PP of input processes; then this model is modular.*

3 Implementing Relations

3.1 Basic Definitions

Let D be a domain and P be a set of (port) names. A **port** relation R of type P over D is a subset of D^P. We will designate the type P of R as $ports(R)$. Below we will consider port relations over stream domains.

Definition 5 *Let Δ be an arbitrary set. The stream domain $D = STREAM(\Delta)$ over Δ consists of all finite and infinite strings over Δ, including the empty string and is partially ordered by the relation 'x is a prefix of y'.*

Obviously the set of streams ordered as above is a CPO.

Let D be a CPO. Recall that an element x of D is called **finite** if it satisfies the following condition: assume that $x \leq a$, where a is the least upper bound (lub) of a sequence $a_1 \leq a_2 \leq \ldots$; then $x \leq a_n$ for some n.

For a finite set of ports P, the finite elements of $STREAM(\Delta)^P$ are functions which map ports into finite streams. Let s be a run of process Pr. The behavior of run s at port p is the stream of data communicated through p in s. Therefore, to each run there corresponds a function from ports to $STREAM(\Delta)$. And to a process Pr of type P there corresponds a port relation of type P which we denote by $rel(Pr)$. We say that process Pr **implements** this relation. We say that processes Pr_1, Pr_2 are relationally equivalent (notation $Pr_1 \equiv_{rel} Pr_2$) if $rel(Pr_1) = rel(Pr_2)$. Among the processes which implement a relation R there is a maximal process (i.e. each other process implementing R is its subset). This maximal process is said to be **fat** and is denoted by $fat(R)$. We also introduce a preorder $\leq_{rel}$ on processes: $Pr_1 \leq_{rel} Pr_2$ if $rel(Pr_1)$ is a subset of $rel(Pr_2)$.

3.2 About $\equiv_{rel}$-substitutivity issues for SEM_{proc}

Consider a model $< NN, PP, SEM_{proc} >$ where NN is a substitutional set of nets and PP is a set of processes. We know already what it means that such a model is modular. Say that it respects $\equiv_{rel}$ (or that it is $\equiv_{rel}$ substitutive) if the following holds: Assume that two interpreted nets $< N_1, pp_1 >$ and $< N_2, pp_2 >$ in this model specify processes Pr_1, Pr_2 which implement the same relation (i.e. $rel(Pr_1) = rel(Pr_2)$) and that they are both substitutable in some context. Then they are replaceable by each other without changing the relation of the overall net. Similarly one defines 'respecting $\leq_{rel}$' (or $\leq_{rel}$ substitutivity): require that if ($Pr_1 \leq_{rel} Pr_2$ then replacing $< N_1, pp_1 >$ by $< N_2, pp_2 >$ may only increase the relation of the overall net. Clearly $\leq_{rel}$ substitutivity implies $\equiv_{rel}$ substitutivity. The Brock-Ackerman example (Brock-Ackerman anomaly) is a warning that substitutive reasoning of this kind is generally impossible; nevertheless, it still does not exclude specific cases when this is possible.

Given a substitutional set of nets NN and a set of processes PP the closure of PP under NN consists of all processes which can be specified by nets from NN over processes from PP. Say that PP is modular wrt NN if $< NN, closure(PP), SEM_{proc} >$ is a modular model. In a similar way we refer to PP as being $\leq_{rel}$-substitutive wrt NN.

Looking for $\leq_{rel}$ substitutive sets of processes we prefer to deal with sets PP of processes which have enough computational power [15]. The formalization is in terms of powerful sets. PP is said to be a powerful set if it contains at least all the rudimentary processes (see example 4 in 2.3).

Here is a slightly rephrased version of our result in [16], adapted to the notations of this paper:
Assume that PP is a powerful set of processes which is closed under NN_3. Then the model $< NN_3, PP, SEM_{proc} >$ is $\leq_{rel}$ substitutive iff all the processes in PP are fat.

One direction of this claim is easy. Note (1) SEM_{proc} is monotonic wrt inclusion of processes. (2) for fat processes, $Pr_1 \subseteq Pr_2$ iff $rel(Pr_1) \subseteq rel(Pr_2)$. Hence, if all processes in PP are fat then the model $< NN_3, PP, SEM_{proc} >$ is $\leq_{rel}$ substitutive. The second direction that a modular powerful set of processes contains only fat processes is more subtle and its proof is based on full abstractness.

What powerful sets of processes are $\leq_{rel}$-substitutive wrt NN_1, NN_2, NN_3, NN_4?

Claim 3.1 *1. NN_1. No powerful set is $\leq_{rel}$-substitutive wrt NN_1.*

2. NN_2. A powerful set is $\leq_{rel}$-substitutive wrt NN_2 iff it consists of only fat processes.

3. NN_3. A powerful set is $\leq_{rel}$-substitutive wrt NN_3 iff its closure under NN_3 consists of only fat processes.

4. NN_4. Each set of processes is $\leq_{rel}$-substitutive wrt NN_4.

Comment. (Comparing classes NN_2 and NN_3.) If a set PP consists of only fat processes then its closure under NN_2 will also consist of only fat processes. That is not the case for NN_3. Hence, it is easy to give examples of $\leq_{rel}$-subsitutive (and powerful) sets for NN_2; just take all fat input buffered processes. On the other hand, it is not even simple to check that the closure of the rudimentary processes under NN_3 consists only of fat processes. Therefore, the construction of all powerful $\leq_{rel}$-substitutive sets is a difficult problem. This issue is better handled in connection with modularity for relations (see 4.3).

4 Connected Relations

4.1 Basic Definitions

Since processes are prefix closed their relations may not be arbitrary.

We are going to characterize briefly this particular kind of relations, we call *connected relations* (see [17, 10]).

Definition 6 *We will write $x_1 \ll x_2$ (x_1 immediately precedes x_2, or x_2 covers x_1) if $x_1 < x_2$ and there is no element between x_1 and x_2. A finite chain $s = \{x_i : i = 1...n\}$ is called* strict *if it begins with $\bot$ and $x_i \ll x_{i+1}$ for all $i < n$.*

Let R be a subset of D. $chain(R)$ denotes the set of all strict chains contained in R. The kernel of R (denoted $Kern(R)$) is the subset of R such that x is in $Kern(R)$ if it belongs to a chain in $chain(R)$.

Definition 7 *A relation R is called* **connected** *if $R = Kern(R)$.*

Obviously, $Kern(R)$ is the maximal connected subset of R. Every connected relation over a stream domain consists only of finite elements.

Example 5 *(kernel vs least fixed point) Consider the relations: $S =_{def} \{y = f(x, y)\}$ and $S' =_{def} \{y < f(x, y)\}$. Assume that f is the constant function which returns the stream 00. Then S consists of all pairs $< x, 00 >$ and its kernel is obviously empty. On the other hand for arbitrary continuous f: $Kern(S')$ consists of all finite x, y such that $y < h(x)$, where $h(x) =_{def} lfp.\lambda y.f(x, y)$.*

Definition 8 *Given a relation R of type P (i.e., $R \subset STREAM(\Delta)^P$) we say that R increases at port p if the following holds: Assume that x, y are finite elements in $STREAM(\Delta)^P$) which differ only on p and moreover $x(p) \leq y(p)$. Then $x \in R$ implies that $y \in R$.*

Similarly one defines 'R decreases in p'. We will refer to a relation R as to an input relation if its ports are divided (someway!) into input ports and local ports with the only requirement that R increases on each of its input ports. Notations like $R(\vec{x}; \vec{y})$ are used to point on the vector $\vec{x}$ of input ports and on the vector $\vec{y}$ of local ports.

Example 6 *$buf(p \to q)$ implements the relation R we designate as $p \geq q$. It contains only finite elements and $x \in R \Leftrightarrow x(p) \geq x(q)$. Note that this relation increases in p and decreases in q.*

It is easily seen that if p is an input port of Pr then $rel(Pr)$ increases on this port. Hence $rel(Pr)$ may be considered as an input relation with the same inputs as Pr.

Fact 4.1 *1. R is a connected relation iff it is implemented by a linear process.*

2. R is an input relation with input ports P and local ports Q iff it is implemented by input process with input ports P and local ports Q.

4.2 Nets of Relations and their Semantics

Relational environments are defined similarly to process environments. Let rr be a relational environment. Given the interpreted net $< N, rr >$ choose a process environment pp such that for each place pl in N the process $pp(pl)$ implements the relation $rr(pl)$. Now consider the relation S implemented by the process $SEM_{proc}(N, pp)$. Since a relation may be implemented by different processes neither pp nor S are uniquely determined by $< N, rr >$

Fact 4.2 *[16, 17] There is an extreme environment pp which returns the maximal among all possible S; namely, this is the environment which assigns to each pl the fat implementation of rr(pl).*

Definition 9 *The maximal relation S achievable in this way is called the relational semantics of the net and is denoted by* $SEM_{rel}(N, rr)$.

Hence, $SEM_{rel}(N,\ rr) = rel(SEM_{proc}(N,\ fat(rr)))$.

4.3 Modularity of Sem_{rel} and $\leq_{rel}$ substitutivity of Sem_{proc}

Given a substitutional class of nets NN and a set of connected relations RR. We define 'RR is modular wrt NN' in the same way as for processes in 3.2. A set RR of relations is said to be powerful if it contains all the rudimentary relations, i.e. those relations which are implemented by rudimentary processes (see example 4 in section 2.3).

There is a simple relationship between modularity for relations and $\equiv_{rel}$-substitutivity for processes.

Claim 4.3 *Let RR and PP be corresponding sets of relations and fat processes, i.e.* $Pr \in PP$ *iff* $Pr = fat(R)$ *for R in RR. Then PP is* $\equiv_{rel}$*-substitutive wrt* NN_3 *iff RR is modular wrt* NN_3.

This claim is the starting point for improvements which show that problems about rel-substitutivity may be reduced to problems about modularity for relations.

What sets RR of relations are modular wrt NN_1, NN_2, NN_3, NN_4?

Claim 4.4

1. *NN_1. No powerful set RR is modular wrt NN_1.*
2. *NN_2. Every set RR is modular wrt NN_2.*
3. *NN_3. A powerful set RR is modular wrt NN_3 iff the corresponding set of processes $fat(RR)$ is $\leq_{rel}$-substitutive wrt NN_3.*

4. NN_4. Every set RR is modular wrt NN_4.

Comment. Claims 3.1.3 and 4.4.3 provide the reductions between the following tasks:

1. Find powerful sets of processes which are $\leq_{rel}$-substitutive wrt NN_3.
2. Find powerful sets of relations which are modular wrt NN_3.(Such sets will be directly characterized later through claim 8.4)

Indeed, if RR is a modular and powerful set of relations, then according to claim 4.4.3, the set $fat(RR)$ of processes is powerful and $\leq_{rel}$-substitutive. On the other hand, if PP is a powerful and $\leq_{rel}$-substitutive set of processes then by claim 3.1.3 it consists only of fat processes. Therefore, PP coincides with $fat(rel(PP))$ and is $\leq_{rel}$-substitutive. Hence, by claim 4.4.3, $rel(PP)$ is modular.

5 Algebra of Nets

5.1 Net Constructors

Below we consider a set Σ of operations on nets which allow to construct complex nets from more elementary ones. For all these operations labelling of nodes is unchanged.

Combination. N_1 and N_2 may be combined if they do not have a hidden port with the same name. The set of nodes in the resulting net is union of the set of nodes of N_1 and N_2. A port and a place are connected in N if they are connected in N_1 or in N_2. Ports inherit their visibility status; edges inherit their directions and numbering.

Aggregation: is combination of nets which do not have common port names. (neither hidden, nor visible).

Sequential composition (notation *seq*) is combination of two nets N_1, N_2 such that every common port name is the name of a visible local port in N_1 and the name of a visible input port in N_2.

Hiding. If p is a visible port in N it becomes hidden in $\exists p.N$.

Note that for all operations above the set of atomic subnets of resulting net is the union of the sets of atomic subnets of components. The following operations do not possess this property.

LOOPing of a local port y and an input port x which are visible in a net N.

The operation $LOOP(y \rightarrow x)$ **in** N is defined as following:

1. Delete x from N.
2. Connect y to all places which were connected to x.

3. The visibility status of all ports is unchanged.

looping (note the low case spelling). $loop(y \to x)$ in N is defined as $LOOP(y \to x)$ in N, but the status of y changes from visible to hidden.

Simultaneous $LOOP(\vec{y} \to \vec{x})$ in N and $loop(\vec{y} \to \vec{x})$ in N are defined in a similar way.

Note that all looping constructors are only partially defined in order to avoid the creation of nets with parallel channels. Note also that all constructors preserve the number of ports adjacent to a given place. (If parallel channels have been allowed, the looping constructors would be totally defined, but the above invariant would be violated).

Relying on the signature Σ and on some appropriate notations for atomic nets one can formulate a language NET (in the spirit of [4]) for the description of nets. For example, both terms $(At(;a,b) comb At_1(a;c))$ and $(LOOP(a \to a')$ in $(At(;a,b) aggr At_1(a';c)))$ describe the net N in Fig. 1. If two terms t_1, t_2 of NET describe the same net, we say that they are graph equivalent and write $t_1 \equiv_{graph} t_2$.

5.2 Equivalences in NET

Below are equivalences which allow to prove that terms in NET describe the same net:

1. combination is commutative and associative.
2. aggregation is commutative and associative.
3. $\exists p \exists q.N = \exists q \exists p.N$
4. $\exists p.\ (N_1 comb N_2) = (\exists p.\ N_1) comb N_2$, provided p is not visible in N_2.
5. $loop(\vec{y}_1 \to \vec{x}_1)$ in $(loop(\vec{y}_2 \to \vec{x}_2)$ in $N) = loop(\vec{y}_1,\ \vec{y}_2 \to \vec{x}_1,\ \vec{x}_2)$ in N
6. $loop(y \to x)$ in $(N_1 aggr N_2) = (loop(y \to x)$ in $N_1) aggr N_2$, provided y and x are not visible ports of N_2.

5.3 Constructor sets for specific classes of nets

Say that the class NN of nets is generated by the subsignature $\Sigma' \subset \Sigma$ if it contains exactly the nets generated from atomic nets by the operations in Σ' (in other words - the nets expressible in the language NET with the use of only Σ')

Claim 5.1 *1. The classes NN_i below are generated as follows:*

(a) (All nets.) NN_1 is generated by comb and hide.

(b) *(All nets with only visible ports.)* NN_2 *is generated by comb.*

(c) *(All nets without forks, without confluences and exactly internal ports hidden.)* NN_3 *is generated by aggr and loop.*

(d) *(All nets without loops.)* NN_4 *is generated by aggr, seq and hide.*

2. *(Standard systems of equivalences.) For each of the classes* NN_i *above and their corresponding constructor set* Σ_i *there is a standard system of equivalences from which all other equivalences are provable by equational reasoning.*

   (a) *For* NN_1*: equivalences 1,3,4;*

   (b) *For* NN_2*: equivalences 1;*

   (c) *For* NN_3*: equivalences 2,5,6;*

   (d) *For* NN_4*: omitted;*

6 Algebra of Processes

6.1 Preliminary Remarks

We consider below the special interpretation of Σ (the signature of net constructors) wrt processes (see 6.2). Σ_{proc} will designate the set of these operations on processes.

We preserve the terminology and notations used wrt nets except for combination, to which there corresponds synchronization ($\|$) of processes. All the definitions implicitly include an appropriate classification of the ports (in the result of the operation) into input and local ports exactly as for the corresponding constructors. It is easy to check that the ports declared as input ports indeed obey the input buffering condition. We consider also union of processes.

As an immediate consequence of the interpretation Σ_{proc} one can use the syntax of NET for specification of processes.

6.2 Operations on Processes

First we consider operations on processes which correspond to the signature Σ of the net constructs.

Synchronization (notations: $\|$)

$$\begin{gathered} ports(Pr_1\|Pr_2) = ports(Pr_1) \cup ports(Pr_2) \\ s \in Pr_1\|Pr_2 \text{ iff for } i = 1,2 \\ s|ports(Pr_i) \in Pr_i \end{gathered}$$

where $ports(Pr)$ is the type of process Pr and $s|A$ is the notation for the string one gets from s by deleting all events which are not on ports A.

Aggregation. In the case when Pr_1 and Pr_2 do not have common ports, their synchronization is called aggregation.

Hiding. $\exists\, p.\ Pr$ results in the process of type $ports(Pr) - p$; its strings are obtained from the strings of Pr by deleting all occurrences of communications on p.

Next we consider two versions of the looping operation. Note that we use for them upper cases notations (when the local port is not hidden) and lower case notation (when the local port is hidden).

LOOPing of a local port y and an input port x of process Pr.

$LOOP(y \to x)$ in $Pr =_{def} \exists x.(Pr \| buf(y \to x))$

looping. $loop(y \to x)$ in $Pr =_{def} \exists y.(LOOP(y \to x)$ in $Pr)$.

Another useful operation on processes is
Union. For processes Pr_1, Pr_2 of the same type, $Pr_1 \cup Pr_2$ inherits this alphabet and contains all strings in Pr_1 and in Pr_2.

Remark about the relevance of input bufferness. Let Pr be a process and p be its port. One can show that Pr is input buffered at p (see definition 4) iff for any port r not in Pr the process $\exists p.Pr \| buf(r \to p)$ is the same as the process obtained from Pr by renaming p by r. Therefore, in input processes a buffer is attached to every input port.

In our definition of the looping operations we explicitly rely on buffers. The input buferness is needed later only to show that the semantics based on aggregation and LOOPing coincides with the semantics based on synchronization. For example, net N_1 in Fig 1 can be described as $At_1(;a) comb At_2(a;b)$ and as $LOOP\ (a \to a')\ in\ At_1(;a) aggr At_2(a';b)$. If an environment pp assigns to At_1 and At_2 input buffered processes, then these two terms will specify the same process in pp; otherwise these terms might specify different processes.

In the sequel under a process we have in mind an input process.

6.3 Some Laws

In order to characterize the algebras of processes we notice similarities between the logical operations conjunction, disjunction and existential quantifier on one hand and the operations synchronization, union and hiding for processes on the other hand. Let t be a first order term which uses only conjunction, disjunction and existential quantifiers. In addition to the usual logical interpretations of such terms one can consider also their process interpretations following a way similar to that we used in section 6.1 for terms in NET. For example, $(At_1(b', c) \wedge At_2(a, b))$ is interpreted in logic as the conjunction of the relations assigned by a logical environment to symbols

At_1, At_2. In the process algebra this term is interpreted as the synchronization of the processes assigned by a process environment to symbols $At_1(b', c)$, $At_2(a, b)$.

Given two terms t_1, t_2 of the same type $\{a_1 \cdots a_n\}$; say that t_1 implies t_2 in logic if the formula $\forall a_1 \cdots a_n(t_1 \rightarrow t_2)$ is first order valid formula. The following claims are valid for arbitrary not just input processes.

Claim 6.1 *(Relationship of process algebra to logic).*
If t_1 implies t_2 in logic then the process specified by (t_1, pp) is a subset of the process specified by (t_2, pp) in arbitrary process environment pp.

Corollary 6.2 *All basic equivalences for net constructors (see 5.3) hold in the algebra of processes, i.e., for every constructor set Σ_i considered above and terms t_1 and t_2 over Σ_i the equivalence $t_1 \equiv_{graph} t_2$ implies that for each process environment pp the interpreted terms (t_1, pp) and (t_2, pp) define the same process.*

Proof: The equivalences 1, 3, 4 from section 5.2 hold in logic and hence by claim 6.1 we obtain immediately the equivalences for combination and hiding. For other operations it may be inferred from their definition based on synchronization and hiding. □

7 Algebra of Connected relations

7.1 Preliminary Remarks

As for processes we consider below the special interpretation of Σ (the signature of net constructors) wrt relations. Σ_{rel} will designates the set of these operations on relations.

We preserve the terminology and notations used wrt nets except for combination, to which there corresponds strong conjunction ($\underline{\&}$) of relations. In addition to Σ_{rel} we consider also union (disjunction) of relations.

As an immediate consequence of the interpretation Σ_{rel}, one can use the syntax of NET for specification of relations. Let rr be a relational environment and let t be an arbitrary term in NET; then the pair $< t, rr >$ is an interpreted term whose meaning, denoted (t, rr), is a port relation which is fully determined by the environment rr and the interpretation Σ_{rel} of the net constructor symbols.

7.2 Operations on Relations

Given $x \in D^P$ and $x_1 \in D^{P_1}$, assume that $P_1 \subseteq P$ and for every port p in P_1 the equality $x_1(p) = x(p)$ holds; in this case we say that x_1 is the **projection** of x onto P_1.

First we consider the operations join and disjunction.

Join. Let R_1 be a relation of type P_1 and let R_2 be a relation of type P_2. The join of R_1 and R_2 is the relations of type $P_1 \cup P_2$ defined as follows: $x \in R_1 \& R_2$ if the projection of x on P_1 is in R_1 and the projection of x on P_2 is in R_2.

Disjunction. Let R_1 and R_2 be relations of the same type P. $R_1 \cup R_2$ is the relation of the type P which denotes the union of R_1 and R_2.

Disjunction of connected relations is a connected relation. But the result of the join of connected relations is not always a connected relation.

Now we list the operations in Σ_{rel}.

Strong Conjunction - (notation $\underline{\&}$). Let R_1 be a relation of type P_1 and R_2 be a relation of type P_2. The strong conjunction of R_1 and R_2 is the kernel of their join.

Example 7 *Consider the system of equation S_1 and the corresponding system of inequalities S_2.*

$$S_1 = \begin{cases} y = & f(x,z) \\ x = & y \end{cases} \quad S_2 = \begin{cases} y \leq & f(x,z) \\ x \leq & y \end{cases}$$

The solutions of S_1 is $R_1 = \{(x,y,z) : \ x = y = lfp\lambda x.f(x,z)\}$.
The strong conjunction of the two inequalities in S_2 is $R_2 = \{finite\ (x,y,z) : \ x \leq y \leq lfp\ \lambda x.f(x,z)\}$

Aggregation. In the case when R_1 and R_2 do not have common ports their strong conjunction is called aggregation.

It is easy to see that aggregation of connected relations coincides with their join.

Hiding. $\exists p.R$ is the relation of type $ports(R) - \{p\}$ which consists of projections of elements of R on these ports.

Again as for processes we consider two versions of looping: without and with hiding of local ports.

LOOPing of a local port y and an input port x of relation R.

$LOOP(y \to x)$ in $R =_{def} \exists x.Kern(R \underline{\&} (x \leq y))$.

$loop(y \to x)$ in $R =_{def} \exists y.LOOP(y \to x)$ in R.

7.3 Some Laws and Anomalies

As for processes we notice similarities between the logical operations conjunction, disjunction and existential quantifier on one hand and the operations strong conjunction, disjunction and hiding for relations. However, the algebra of connected relations is not rich as the algebra of processes. Some laws are valid; in particular strong conjunction is commutative and associative, hiding is commutative. But note equivalence 4 (from section 5.2); we refer to it in the sequel as $\exists$-rule:

$\exists p.\ (N_1 comb N_2) = (\exists p\ in N_1) comb N_2$, provided p is not visible port of N_2.

The rule is not valid for the set of all connected relations; in other words, for this set there holds $\exists$-anomaly. Also equivalences 5 and 6 (from section 5.2) fail. Hence, for connected relations there is no analog of corollary 6.2 we established for processes in section 6.3

8 Modularity and Robustness

8.1 Term Semantics

Sometimes (see [4, 18]) when referring to net semantics $SEM(N, env)$ what one really has in mind is term semantics $(t,\ env)$, where t belongs to some chosen set TN of descriptions of the net N. In such a case one has to make sure that for all t_i in TN the meaning of (t_i, env) is the same. Otherwise the net-semantics is not well defined.

In particular, given an interpreted net $< N, pp >$, consider the set TN of N's descriptions which perform first the combination of all atomic subnets and after that all the hidings. Due to the commutativity and associativity of process synchronization and of process hiding one can use interpreted terms $< t, pp >$ with t in TN for a well defined semantics $< N, pp >$. The same remark holds for strong conjunction and hiding wrt relations and hence for a well defined semantics of nets of relations.

Fact 8.1 *Semantics defined this way coincides with SEM_{proc} for processes and with SEM_{rel} for relations*

But what about other descriptions for (N, env). Do they provide also the same meaning as (t, pp) and (t, rr) for t in TN?

8.2 Compositional Semantics

Consider one of the sets NN_i of nets (see 5.3) equipped with its constructor set Σ_i. Below $t_1,\ t_2, \cdots$ are terms in NET which use only constructors from Σ_i; PP and RR denote some sets of input processes and relations respectively which are supposed to be closed under Σ_{proc} and Σ_{rel} respectively.

Definition 10 *The semantical model $< NN_i, PP, SEM >$ is compositional (SEM is a compositional semantics from NN_i into PP) iff for each environment (types respected!) SEM induces a Σ_i homomorphism from NN_i into PP.*

Corollary 8.2 *Every compositional model is modular.*

Claim 8.3 *1. A compositional semantics from NN_i into PP is possible (and if possible is unique) if there holds the following* **robustness condition:** *Given arbitrary terms t_1, t_2 over Σ_i the equivalence $t_i \equiv_{graph} t_2$ implies that for every environment env in PP the processes specified by $(t_1,\ env)$, $(t_2,\ env)$ are equal.*

2. Under the conditions above SEM coincides with SEM_{proc}.

3. If $< NN_i, PP, SEM_{proc} >$ is a modular model then SEM_{proc} is a compositional semantics from NN_i into PP.

Similarly for semantics from NN_i into RR.

8.3 Modular Models

Relying on corollary 8.2 and on claim 8.3 we are going to characterize some modular models $< NN_i, PP, SEM_{proc} >$ and $< NN_i, RR, SEM_{rel} >$. To this end we survey situations when the robustness condition holds.

a) Robustness holds for all models $< NN_i, PP, SEM_{proc} >$.

That is due to corollary 6.2, and it proves modularity of SEM_{proc} (see claim 2.1 from section 2.3).

For relations the situation is quite different. This can be shown directly by counterexamples, but is also evident from the $\exists$-anomaly (see section 7.3), which violates a basic equivalence for $\{comb, hide\}$. Therefore, it makes sense to look for more specific situations in which robustness and hence modularity hold. The following cases are easy and prove claim 4.4 (see section 4.3) for NN_1, NN_2 and NN_4.

b) NN_2 (No hiding). Robustness holds for arbitrary RR. That is because the only relevant equivalences are commutativity and associativity for both comb and &.

c) NN_4 (No loops). Robustness holds for all relations. We omit the details.

d) NN_1 (arbitrary nets). Robustness fails for every powerful set RR. Actually, the $\exists$-rule (see 7.3) is violated in such set.

Hence, if we want to allow both loops and hiding and at the same time to have robustness we must restrict the set NN_1. An instructive case is the set NN_3 with the constructors $\{aggr,\ loop\}$. The basic equivalences 2 and 6 (see 5.2) wrt $\{aggr,\ loop\}$ hold in general for all relations. There is still one kind of basic equivalences which should be explicitly postulated:

The looping law: For each relation R in the class RR there holds

$$loop(\vec{x}_1 \to \vec{y}_1)\ in\ (loop(\vec{x}_2 \to \vec{y}_2)\ in\ R) =$$
$$= loop(\vec{x}_2 \to \vec{y}_2)\ in\ (loop(\vec{x}_1 \to \vec{y}_1)\ in\ R) =$$
$$= loop(\vec{x}_1, \vec{x}_2 \to \vec{y}_1, \vec{y}_2)\ in\ R$$

Therefore we conclude:

Claim 8.4 *A model* $< NN_3, RR, SEM_{rel} >$ *is modular iff for all* R *in* RR *there holds the looping law.*

A powerful model of this kind is provided by the class of all functional relations. Recall [16] that a relation $R(\vec{x};\ \vec{y})$ is functional if for some continuous function f

$$R(\vec{x};\ \vec{y}) \text{ iff } \vec{x} \text{ and } \vec{y} \text{ are finite elements and } \vec{y} \leq f(\vec{x}).$$

Note that such a relation is not only input increasing but it is also decreasing wrt all local ports. (In our previous papers [16, 17] we used the terminology 'observable relations' for relations with this property). The looping law for functional relations is a consequence of the well known fact that for functions the least fixed point operators commute. Note that usually the proof of modularity for functional relations is based on the Kahn Principle for dataflow nets. Here we inferred it directly from the robustness condition. Are there other nontrivial classes RR which obey the looping equivalence and hence are modular? We know that there are such classes. According to claim 4.4.3 in section 4.3 these classes correspond exactly to powerful classes of processes which are $\leq_{rel}$-substitutive, i.e. avoid Brock-Ackerman anomaly.

9 Concluding Remarks

9.1 Comments to 8.2

It is not difficult to understand that processes and relations are not exceptions and that claim 8.3.1 (and the definitions it is based on) can be generalized to a broad class of domains. For such a domain D and for an appropriate interpretation of the signature of net constructors one can consider the robustness condition and its relationship to modularity. First, observe that under the robustness condition a net semantics is induced in a natural way. For example, in the cases of processes we would define $semrobust(N, pp)$ as the value (t, pp), where t is an arbitrary description of N over NN_i, the point being that this definition does not depend on the particular choice of the description t for N. This definition of semantics may be adapted to 'arbitrary' domain D and, what is more, one can show that the semantics will be modular. In the case of processes and relations the use of Σ_{proc} and Σ_{rel} implies also 8.3.2 and 8.3.3 i.e., the robust semantics coincides with SEM_{proc} and SEM_{rel} respectively. In the general case at this stage we do not have any a priory net semantics to compare with. But assume that we started with a modular model $< NN_i, D, SEM >$; is it the case that the signature Σ_i may be interpreted in D in such a way that robustness holds? It appears that in the general case some additional assumptions about SEM are needed. In the particular case of processes or relations these assumptions are implicit in the requirements about input buffering and input increasing.

9.2 The impact of hiding

It seems clear that nets without loops are too poor to support an interesting theory of dataflow networks. On the other hand, it makes sense to look to what extent the theory may (or should) be developed without hiding. In particular: do there exist interesting models without hiding for which the Kahn Principle and its generalization [2] hold?

It seems that in [2] Abramsky had in mind just such model. Here is a quotation from [1]: 'I didn't forget about hiding in my paper. I left it out because I didn't consider it germane for the Kahn Principle. It is no need for me to build hiding into my definition of network composition ... It is well known that this (hiding) spoils the nice properties of of composition-this is why it isn't done e.g. in CCS and CSP'.

Unfortunately, there is some slight inconsistency in [2] which can be easily repaired without affecting the results of the paper. This can be done in two ways. One of them would preserve the definition of 'process P computes function f' chosen in [2], but would require hiding internal ports of the net. The other one seems to correspond to Abramsky's idea of justifying Kahn Principle without building on hiding. It amounts to weaken the definition of 'process P computes function f'.

However, now there may be different processes which implement different relations, but compute the same functions. Therefore, unlike the case of relational substitutivity it would not make sense to distinguish between different relations to which there corresponds the same function (an idea advocated by those who insist on considering complete computations). Hence, instead of $\equiv_{rel}$-substitutivity one should consider a weaker equivalence between processes. But then anomalies would appear without hiding exactly as they appeared wrt $\equiv_{rel}$ substitutivity in the presence of hiding. As a matter of fact, the original Brock-Ackerman example illustrates this kind of anomaly without hiding.

The moral: though one can justify the Kahn Principle in models without hiding, this approach does not rescue from anomalies.

9.3 Further Research

1. We considered processes and relations over stream domains. The generalization to F-domains [17] is straightforward.

2. Technically more involved seems to be the accurate extension of the the theory to other sets and algebras of nets. But we do not see any serious difficulties on this way.

3. Deepening the knowledge about the algebras of processes and relations. We conjecture that 'logical laws' for processes (see section 6.3) may be essentially improved. On the other hand, despite the stigma of anomalies, the algebra of relations is worth to be explored carefully. Though anomalies cannot be avoided, facing them may still be possible in many situations.

4. This paper as well as our previous works [15, 16, 17] is based on a simple model of processes which does not take into account such discriminating features as branching, terminating, etc.. It seems that ignoring these features is not harmful and may be even useful as long as one can develop the theory without them. But finally we have to face the challenge of analyzing more sophisticated models which take into account, for example, complete runs [2, 3, 6, 11, 18].

Acknowledgements

We are indebted to Antoni Mazurkiewicz whose compositional approach to Petri nets provided the initial stimulus to this work. We would also like to thank Samson Abramsky and Albert R. Meyer for stimulating discussions.

References

[1] S. Abramsky. e-mail correspondence.

[2] S. Abramsky. A generalized Kahn principle for abstract asynchronous networks. In M. Main, A. Melton, M. Mislove, and D. Scmidt, editors, *Mathematical Foundations of Programming Languages Semantics*, volume 442 of *Lect. Notes in Computer Science*. Springer Verlag, 1990.

[3] J. D. Brock and W. B. Ackerman. Scenarios: A model of non-determinate computation. In *Formalization of Programming Concepts*, volume 107 of *Lect. Notes in Computer Science*, pages 252–259. Springer Verlag, 1981.

[4] M. Broy. Semantics of finite and infinite networks of concurrent communicating agents. *Distributed Computing*, 2, 1987.

[5] J. Hirshfeld, A. Rabinovich, and B. A. Trakhtenbrot. Discerning causality in interleaving behavior. In A. R. Meyer and M. A. Taitsin, editors, *Proceedings of Logic at Botik 89*, volume 363 of *Lect. Notes in Computer Science*. Springer Verlag, 1989.

[6] B. Jonsson. A fully abstract trace model for dataflow networks. In *Proceedings of the 16-th ACM Symposium on Principles of Programming Languages*, 1989.

[7] G. Kahn. The semantics of a simple language for parallel programming. In J. L. Rosenfeld, editor, *Information Processing 74*. North Holland Publ. Co., 1974.

[8] A. Mazurkiewicz. Semantics of concurrent systems: A modular fixed point trace approach. In *Advanced in Petri Nets*, volume 188 of *Lect. Notes in Computer Science*. Springer Verlag, 1984.

[9] A. Mazurkiewicz. Concurrency, modularity and synchronization. In *Mathematical Foundation of Computer Science*, volume 379 of *Lect. Notes in Computer Science*. Springer Verlag, 1989.

[10] A. Mazurkiewicz, A. Rabinovich, and B. A. Trakhtenbrot. Connectedness and synchronization. In D. Bjorner and V. Kotov, editors, *Images of Programming (dedicated to the memory of A. Ershov)*. North Holland Publ. Co., 1991.

[11] J. Misra. Equational reasoning about nondeterministic processes. In *Proceedings of 8th ACM Symposium on Principles of Distributed Computing*, 1989.

[12] D. Park. The fairness problem and nondeterministic computing networks. In J. W. de Bakker and J. van Leeuwen, editors, *Proceedings, 4th Advanced Cource on Theoretical Computer Science*. Mathematisch Centrum, 1982.

[13] V. R. Pratt. On composition of processes. In *Proceedings of the Ninth Annual ACM Symposium on Principle of Programming Languages*, 1982.

[14] A. Rabinovich. in preparation.

[15] A. Rabinovich and B. A. Trakhtenbrot. Nets of processes and data flow. In *Proceedings of Rex Workshop on Linear Time, Branching Time and Partial Order in Logics and Models for Concurrency*, volume 354 of *Lect. Notes in Computer Science*. Springer Verlag, 1988.

[16] A. Rabinovich and B. A. Trakhtenbrot. Nets and data flow interpreters. In *the Proceedings of the Fourth Symposium on Logic in Computer Science*, 1989.

[17] A. Rabinovich and B. A. Trakhtenbrot. Communication among relations. In *International Conference on Automata, Languages and Programming*, volume 443 of *Lect. Notes in Computer Science*. Springer Verlag, 1990.

[18] E. W. Stark. A simple generalization of Kahn's principle to indeterminate dataflow networks. In M. Z. Kwiatkowska, M. W. Shields, and R. M. Thomas, editors, *Semantics for concurrency*, Workshops in Computing. Springer Verlag, 1990.

Towards a Complete Hierarchy of Compositional Dataflow Models

Bengt Jonsson*
Swedish Institute of Computer Science and Uppsala University
Box 1263
164 28 Kista, Sweden
bengt@sics.se

Joost N. Kok
Dept. of Computer Science
Utrecht University
P.O. Box 80.089
3508 TB Utrecht, the Netherlands
joost@cs.ruu.nl

Abstract

A dataflow network consists of nodes that communicate by passing data over unbounded FIFO channels. For dataflow networks containing only deterministic nodes, Kahn has presented a simple and elegant semantic model. However, the generalization of this model is not compositional for nondeterministic networks. Past work has shown that compositionality can be attained by models based on traces. In the paper, we investigate trace models of dataflow networks, with the aim of characterizing compositional and non-compositional models. We study several compositional trace models, which differ in whether they model liveness, termination or divergence. We relate the models into a hierarchy, according to their capability to distinguish networks. A hierarchy is called *complete* if any gap between two models in the hierarchy contains no compositional models. Our main contribution is to prove that most of the gaps in our hierarchy do not contain compositional models. Several full abstraction results in the literature follow directly from the gaps in our hierarchy. We also show that by restricting the networks to contain less powerful nondeterministic processes, additional models become compositional. This means that additional models are added to the hierarchy.

*Supported in part by the Swedish Board for Technical Development (STU) under contract No. 89–01220P as part of Esprit BRA project SPEC, No. 3096.

1 Introduction

Semantical models of communicating systems has been a topic of intensive study in the last years (e.g. [4, 8, 21, 7, 24]). A purpose of that study is a better understanding of how to describe and reason about the behavior of communicating systems. A semantic model should abstract from the internal activity of a system, describing only its externally observable behavior. It should also be *compositional*, meaning that the denotation of a composed network can be obtained using only the denotations of its components. A compositional model can serve as a basis for modular spefication and verification methods, (e.g. [1, 9, 22, 23, 37]).

This paper is concerned with semantic models of dataflow networks. Dataflow networks are an important model for asynchronous parallel computation, in which streams of data items are exchanged along FIFO channels between executing processes. The interest in semantics of dataflow networks is to a large extent due to the work by Kahn [14], who proposed an elegant semantic model for dataflow networks with only deterministic processes. However, the straight-forward generlaization of Kahn's model is not compositional if networks may contain nondeterministic processes [3]. Since the work by Kahn, many compositional models for nondeterministic networks have been proposed [1, 2, 3, 5, 6, 11, 17, 18, 19, 15, 16, 28, 29, 30, 35]. Recently, a number of models have appeared that are in addition fully abstract, i.e., they have to Kahn's model added precisely the information that is necessary for attaining compositionality [11, 18, 31, 34]. Of these models, the ones presented in [11, 18, 34] are isomorphic to each other [13]. However, the model in [31] is different from these in that it does not represent infinite behaviors or liveness properties.

In the literature, there are thus at least two essentially different compositional models of dataflow networks which are also fully abstract. In this paper, we consider the question of investigating which are the compositional models of dataflow networks and which models cannot be compositional. Since the fully abstract models in [11, 31] are both trace models, we start our investigation by a hierarchy of trace-based models. We define several compositional trace models, which differ in whether or not they model safety properties, liveness properties, termination, and divergence. For instance, safety properties can be represented by prefix-closed sets of finite traces (as in [31]), whereas liveness and fairness properties are represented by (possibly infinite) traces of completed executions of a network (as in [11, 18, 34]).

In order to investigate compositional models, we relate the models according to how fine distinctions they make between the modeled networks. If any two networks that are distinguished by model 1 are also distinguished by model 2, then model 2 makes more distinctions than model 1. Our compositional models can thus be organized into a hierarchy. Our main contribution is that using this hierarchy, we prove the nonexistence of certain compositional models: instead of just saying that a model 2 is makes more distinctions than a model 1, we also prove that in some cases there is no compositional model which is strictly more distinguishing than model 1 and strictly less distinguishing than model 2. Thus there is a "gap" between model 1 and 2, in which no other compositional model exists. Assume for example that model 1 represents safety properties, and that model 2 represents safety and liveness properties. Then the nonexistence of a model between model 1 and 2 means that liveness properties cannot be represented in less detail than they are in model 2, without sacrificing compositionality (assuming that safety properties are represented). Several full abstraction results, e.g. those by Jonsson [11] and Rabinovich and Trakhtenbrot [31] follow immediately from our hierarchy with associated gaps. Allthough all the models in the hierarchy are trace based models, the results about the gaps also show that there are no other compositional (possibly non trace based) models in the gaps.

In some of our models (the models which represents liveness properties), the denotation of a network contains infinite traces, which correspond to infinite observations. It may be argued that the status of such infinite observations is debatable. Our results show that it is necessary to make distinctions based on infinite traces necessary because of compositionality even if only some finite completed traces can be observed. Of course, we then assume the existence of contexts which are sufficiently powerful to make infinite observations and transform these into finite observations. For the case that such contexts are not at hand, we extend our results to less general classes of nondeterministic networks which do not include fair merge processes and without interrupt capabilities. Panangaden et al [25, 26, 27] have found that there are several inequivalent forms of indeterminacy and fairness in dataflow. For the class of networks without interrupt capabilities, we prove that there exist additional, inequivalent, compositional models, which are not compositional if fair merge primitives are allowed. In this way, we show that under certain circumstances one can use less powerful observation criteria in a semantic model.

The idea of proving gaps between compositional models in a hierarchy has appeared earlier, for I/O-automata ([20]), in the thesis of the first author [10], and in [12]. For synchronously communicating systems, hierarchies of models have been studied by Reed and Roscoe [32, 33], by Olderog and Hoare [24], and by van Glabbeek and Vaandrager [36].

In the next section, we present dataflow networks. In Section 3 we present the general framework for relating models according to information content and for establishing gaps. In Section 4 we define our models of dataflow networks and prove that they are compositional. In Section 5 we relate the models and establish the gaps. Section 6 contains an example of an additional compositional model between the models that represent safety and liveness for the restricted class of dataflow networks. Section 7 contains conclusions.

2 Dataflow Networks

In this section, we give an informal presentation of dataflow networks. A more careful treatment of the subject would require a more thorough definition, e.g. by means of transition systems. Such a definition is given in e.g. [11, 18, 13].

A *dataflow network* consists of a set of *nodes* connected by directed *channels.* Each channel is distinctly named. The nodes communicate with each other and with the environment by passing *data items* over the channels. The channels are of three different types:

input channels are used to transmit data items from the environment to a node.

output channels are used to transmit data items from a node to the environment.

internal channels are used to transmit data items from a node to another node of the network.

Larger networks can be built by *composition* of smaller networks as follows. The networks $N_1, \ldots, N_k$ are *compatible* if each channel name occurs at most once as an input channel and at most once as an output channel. Given compatible networks $N_1, \ldots, N_k$, a composite network is obtained by connecting input channels to output channels with the same name. The resulting network can also, if we disregard its input and output channels, be viewed as a node which can be connected to other nodes. As an example, Figure 1 shows how two networks, N_1 and N_2, are composed to yield a network with input channel a and output channels b and d. The composition of the nodes N_1 and N_2 and channel c can also be viewed as a node which receives data items from channel a and transmits data items over channels b and d.

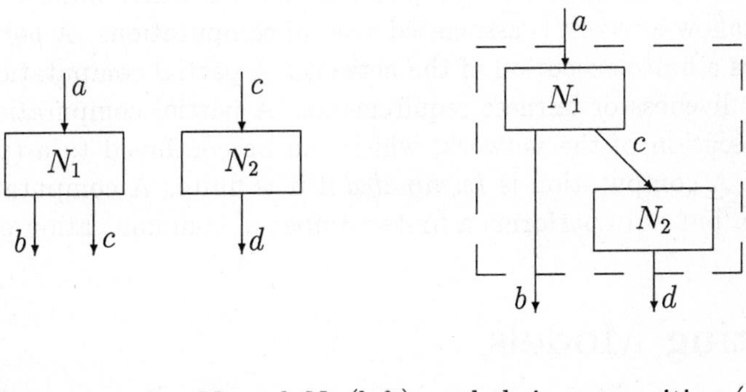

Figure 1: Two networks, N_1 and N_2 (left), and their composition (right).

The channels of a network behave like perfect, unbounded FIFO queues. That is, data items sent over a channel are delivered in unchanged order, after a finite unspecified delay. Note that this also applies to the input and output channels of the network.

The nodes have in general an internal state, they can consume data items from incoming channels, produce data items on outgoing channels, and perform internal computations. Some of the states are designated as initial states. With each node of a network is, in addition, associated a set of liveness and fairness requirements. These requirements are specific to each node. Examples of such requirements are: a node may be required eventually to consume a data item from a certain incoming channel if that channel is not empty, a certain operation may not be enabled indefinitely without being executed, etc. For instance, with a fair merge node is associated the requirements that data items on an incoming channel must eventually be consumed and thereafter produced on the outgoing channel.

With each output channel is associated the following liveness requirement: Each data item in the queue of the output channel must eventually be delivered to the environment.

A *communication event* of a dataflow network N is a pair $c(d)$, where c is an input or output channel of N, and d is a data item. A communication event $c(d)$ represents the transmission of data item d from the environment into channel c, or from channel c to the environment, depending on whether c is an input or output channel.

An *execution step* of a network is either

- an operation by a node of the network which is internal and possibly produces, or consumes a data item from some channel or
- the exchange of a data item between a channel and the environment.

An *execution* of a network is a sequence of execution steps that starts in a state where each node is in its initial state and all channels are empty. A *computation* is an execution of the network that satisfies the liveness and fairness requirements associated with the network. A computation can be either finite or infinite. Thus, with each dataflow network is associated a set of computations. A *partial computation* of a network is a finite execution of the network. A partial computation does not have to satisfy any liveness or fairness requirements. A partial computation represents an unfinished execution of the network, which can be continued to a (possibly infinite) computation. A computation is *terminated* if it is finite. A computation is *divergent* if it is infinite, but only performs a finite number of communication events.

3 Relating Models

Before presenting our models of dataflow networks, we shall present the general framework for the relationships between the models that will be established subsequently.

A *model* $[\![\cdot]\!]$ (of dataflow networks) is a mapping that maps dataflow networks to some domain. A model $[\![\cdot]\!]$ is *compositional* iff there is a partial operation $\|_{\mathcal{M}}$ on the domain of $[\![\cdot]\!]$ such that $[\![\|(N_1,\cdots,N_k)]\!] = \|_{\mathcal{M}}([\![N_1]\!],\cdots,[\![N_k]\!])$ whenever the dataflow networks $N_1,\ldots,N_k$ can be composed.

Examples of rather uninteresting compositional models is the (uninformative) model that maps all dataflow networks to the same single denotation, and the model which maps any dataflow network to itself.

We next define how two models are compared according to their ability to distinguish between dataflow networks.

Definition 3.1 A model $[\![\cdot]\!]_1$ is *more abstract* than another model $[\![\cdot]\!]_2$, denoted $[\![\cdot]\!]_1 \sqsubseteq [\![\cdot]\!]_2$ if $[\![N_1]\!]_2 = [\![N_2]\!]_2$ implies $[\![N_1]\!]_1 = [\![N_2]\!]_1$ for all dataflow networks N_1, N_2. We use $[\![\cdot]\!]_1 \cong [\![\cdot]\!]_2$ to denote that $[\![\cdot]\!]_1 \sqsubseteq [\![\cdot]\!]_2 \sqsubseteq [\![\cdot]\!]_1$, and use $[\![\cdot]\!]_1 \sqsubset [\![\cdot]\!]_2$ to denote that $[\![\cdot]\!]_1 \sqsubseteq [\![\cdot]\!]_2 \not\sqsubseteq [\![\cdot]\!]_1$. □

Intuitively, if $[\![\cdot]\!]_1 \sqsubseteq [\![\cdot]\!]_2$, then the model $[\![\cdot]\!]_2$ distinguishes between all pairs of networks that are distinguished by $[\![\cdot]\!]_1$.

When establishing results about models, we shall instead of Definition 3.1, use the following alternative characterization, which follows immediately from Definition 3.1

Lemma 3.2 Let $[\![\cdot]\!]_1$ and $[\![\cdot]\!]_2$ be models. Then $[\![\cdot]\!]_1 \sqsubset [\![\cdot]\!]_2$ if and only if

1. For all dataflow networks N_1, N_2 we have that $[\![N_1]\!]_2 = [\![N_2]\!]_2$ implies $[\![N_1]\!]_1 = [\![N_2]\!]_1$.
2. There are dataflow networks N_3, N_4 that $[\![N_3]\!]_2 \neq [\![N_4]\!]_2$ and $[\![N_3]\!]_1 = [\![N_4]\!]_1$.

□

The most important concept to be studied in the remainder of the paper is the following, which excludes the existence of compositional models that lie between other models.

Definition 3.3 If $[\![\cdot]\!]_1$ and $[\![\cdot]\!]_2$ are models such that $[\![\cdot]\!]_1 \sqsubset [\![\cdot]\!]_2$, then the relation $[\![\cdot]\!]_1 \sqsubset [\![\cdot]\!]_2$, is a *minimal proper inclusion* (or a *proper gap*) if there is no compositional model $[\![\cdot]\!]_3$ such that $[\![\cdot]\!]_1 \sqsubset [\![\cdot]\!]_3 \sqsubset [\![\cdot]\!]_2$. □

4 Models of Dataflow Networks

In this section, we define the denotational models of dataflow networks that will be studied in this paper.

Let N be a dataflow network.

- A *trace* of N is the sequence of communication events in a computation of N. A trace can be both finite and infinite.
- A *partial trace* of N is the sequence of communication events in a partial computation of N.
- A *terminated trace* of N is the sequence of communication events in a finite computation of N. Note that in the last state of a finite computation, all output channels of the network must be empty, due to the liveness requirement that each data item in an output channel must eventually be delivered to the environment.
- A *divergent trace* of N is a finite sequence of communication events which occurs in an infinite computation of N.

Intuitively, a partial trace records the sequence of communication events that has occured until some moment in an execution. Such a recording can be made within finite time. In contrast, a trace records the sequence of communication events that has occured during a completed computation. A trace can be recorded only after the whole computation, i.e., an infinite stretch of time has passed, because at any point in time during the computation one cannot be sure whether the computation has indeed produced all its communication events. In order to record terminated or divergent traces, one must also assume that one can observe when no more internal execution steps, i.e. execution steps which do not produce communication events, will occur. This cannot be observed from the communication events alone, but one could imagine a lamp which indicates when the system will not perform any more execution steps unless more input is supplied.

As an example, consider a network with only a *copy* node, which copies data items from its single input channel to its single output channel. A partial trace of the network is a finite sequence t of communication events such that for any prefix t' of t, the sequence of data output in t' is a prefix of the sequence of data input in t'. A trace of the network is a (finite or infinite) sequence t of communication events such that all prefixes of t are partial traces of the network, and such that the sequence of data output in t is the same as the sequence of data input in t. A terminated trace of the network is simply a trace of the network which is finite. There are no divergent traces of the network. However, suppose that the network in addition to the copy node contains an internal clock, which performs an infinite sequence of internal execution steps that are unobservable using the communication events performed. In this case, no computation stops after a finite number of steps, all finite traces are divergent, and there are no terminated traces.

Let N be a dataflow network. Define

$I(N)$ as the set of input channels of N

$O(N)$ as the set of output channels of N

$E(N) = I(N) \cup O(N)$, the set of channels of N

$P(N)$ as the set of partial traces of N

$Q(N)$ as the set of terminated traces of N

$D(N)$ as the set of divergent traces of N

$T(N)$ as the set of traces of N

We can now define models of dataflow networks by letting the denotation of a network be a tuple with some of the above defined sets of traces and channels. We shall only consider models that include the sets $I(N)$ and $O(N)$, since these are necessary for determining when networks can be composed. We define the model $[\![\cdot]\!]_{Ev}$ by letting the denotation $[\![N]\!]_{Ev}$ of N be the tuple $\langle I(N), O(N)\rangle$. For the other models, we use the letters P, T, Q, and D as subscripts to indicate which sets of traces are included in addition to the input and output channels. For instance, the model $[\![\cdot]\!]_P$ is defined by letting the denotation $[\![N]\!]_P$ of N be the tuple $\langle I(N), O(N), P(N)\rangle$. The model $[\![N]\!]_{TQ}$ is defined by letting the denotation $[\![N]\!]_{TQ}$ of N be the tuple $\langle I(N), O(N), T(N), Q(N)\rangle$.

By noting that the set $P(N)$ can be obtained from the set $T(N)$, we find that there are twelve inequivalent models that can be obtained in the above way. Of these only 8 are compositional, as we shall see.

Let E be a set of channels and q a sequence of communication events.

$q\lceil_E$ denotes the restriction of q to the channels in E, i.e., the subsequence of q containing only events on channels in E.

$q \setminus E$ denotes the subsequence of q that are not on the channels in E, i.e., the result of deleting the events on channels in E from q.

E^* denotes the set of finite sequences of events on channels in E.

E^ω denotes the set of infinite sequences of events on channels in E.

$E^\dagger$ denotes the set of finite and infinite sequences of events on channels in E.

Theorem 4.1 *All models defined through combinations of P, T, Q, and D are compositional, except for the models $[\![\cdot]\!]_D$, $[\![\cdot]\!]_{PD}$, $[\![\cdot]\!]_{QD}$, and $[\![\cdot]\!]_{PQD}$.* □

Proof: The theorem follows from the following rules for composing the individual sets in the tuples. If $N_1, \ldots, N_k$ can be composed, and N is their composition $N_1 \| \ldots \| N_k$, we have the following facts:

$$I(N) = \bigcup_{i=1}^{k} I(N_i) - \bigcup_{i=1}^{k} O(N_i)$$

$$O(N) = \bigcup_{i=1}^{k} O(N_i) - \bigcup_{i=1}^{k} I(N_i)$$

$$P(N) = \{p\lceil_{(E(N))} : p \in (\bigcup_{i=1}^{k} E(N_i))^* \wedge (\forall i) \ p\lceil_{E(N_i)} \in P(N_i)\}$$

$$T(N) = \{t\lceil_{(E(N))} : t \in (\bigcup_{i=1}^{k} E(N_i))^\dagger \wedge (\forall i) \ t\lceil_{E(N_i)} \in T(N_i)\}$$

$$Q(N) = \{q\lceil_{(E(N))} : q \in (\bigcup_{i=1}^{k} E(N_i))^* \wedge (\forall i) \ q\lceil_{E(N_i)} \in Q(N_i)\}$$

$$D(N) = \{d\lceil_{(E(N))} : d \in (\bigcup_{i=1}^{k} E(N_i))^* \wedge (\exists i) \ [d\lceil_{E(N_i)} \in D(N_i) \wedge (\forall j) \ d\lceil_{E(N_j)} \in T(N_j)]\}$$

The proof of these rules is analogous to other proofs of similar results. See e.g. [11]. □

5 Comparison between models of dataflow networks

We can now state the main result of the paper, which relates the compositional models of dataflow networks that have been defined in Section 4.

$$\begin{array}{ccc}
[\![\cdot]\!]_{TD} & \sqsubset & [\![\cdot]\!]_{TQD} \\
\sqcup & & \sqcup \\
[\![\cdot]\!]_{T} & \sqsubset & [\![\cdot]\!]_{TQ} \\
\sqcup & & \sqcup \\
[\![\cdot]\!]_{P} & \sqsubset & [\![\cdot]\!]_{PQ} \\
\sqcup & & \sqcup \\
[\![\cdot]\!]_{Ev} & \sqsubset & [\![\cdot]\!]_{Q}
\end{array}$$

Figure 2: Relation between the models

Theorem 5.1 *The models defined in Section 4 have relationships as shown in Figure 2. Moreover, all the relations in Figure 2, except for the ones involving divergence and* $[\![\cdot]\!]_Q \sqsubset [\![\cdot]\!]_{PQ}$ *and* $[\![\cdot]\!]_{PQ} \sqsubset [\![\cdot]\!]_{TQ}$, *are minimal proper inclusions.* □

Proof: The first part of the proof, that of showing that the relationships exist, is straightforward, using the obvious mappings between the models. To show that the relations are minimal proper inclusions requires a separate proof using a separate construction for each relation. In the following, we shall devote one section to each relation.

5.1 Proof that $[\![\cdot]\!]_{Ev} \sqsubset [\![\cdot]\!]_P$ is a minimal proper inclusion

The central ingredient in the proof that $[\![\cdot]\!]_{Ev} \sqsubset [\![\cdot]\!]_P$ is a minimal proper inclusion is a construction of a context, which is given in the following lemma. For a channel c, let the network $0token_c$ be the network with one output channel c and no input channels, which never produces any data items, i.e., $0token_c$ has only one trace, the empty one. Let $01token_c$ be the network with one output channel c and no input channels, which either behaves as $0token_c$ or produces one data item, called *token*, and thereafter does nothing.

Lemma 5.2 Let N_1 and N_2 be dataflow networks for which $[\![N_1]\!]_{Ev} = [\![N_2]\!]_{Ev}$ such that there is a finite sequence t of communication events with $t \notin P(N_1)$ and $t \in P(N_2)$. Let c be a channel which is not a channel of N_1. Then there is a context $C[\cdot]$, built from deterministic dataflow networks, such that

$$\begin{array}{rcl} [\![C[N_1]]\!]_P & = & [\![0token_c]\!]_P \\ [\![C[N_2]]\!]_P & = & [\![01token_c]\!]_P \end{array}$$

□

Proof: The structure of the context $C[\cdot]$ is shown in Figure 3.

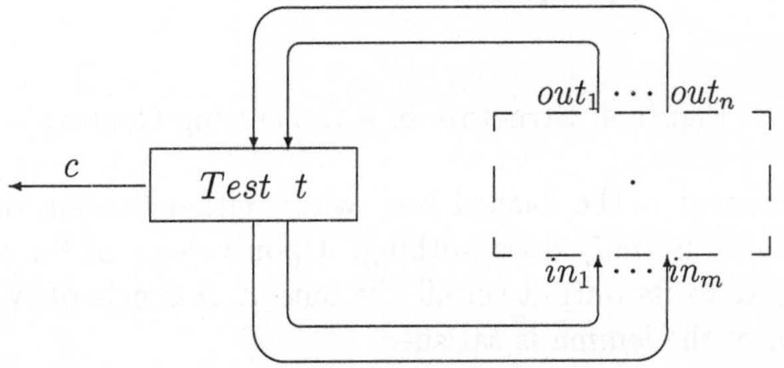

Figure 3: Structure of a Tester Context

The hole of the context is the dashed box, where either N_1 or N_2 will be put. We have assumed that $in_1, \ldots, in_m$ and $out_1, \ldots, out_n$ are the input and output channels of N_1 and N_2. The node $Test\ \ t$ can perform the sequence of events in t and thereafter sends the data item *token* on channel c. If the sequence of data items that arrives to $Test\ \ t$ on the channels $out_1, \ldots, out_n$ does not correspond to the sequence t then $Test\ \ t$ stops and does nothing more. It is easy to see that the context satisfies the conclusion of the lemma. □

For a pair $\langle I, O\rangle$ of disjoint sets of channels, let the network $NIL(I, O)$ be the network which has the denotation $\langle I, O, I^*\rangle$ in the partial trace model. That is, $NIL(I, O)$ has input channels I, output channels O and as traces all finite sequences of events on channels in I, i.e. no output is produced.

Lemma 5.3 Let N be a dataflow network which does not have the channel c. Then there is a context $\mathcal{C}[\cdot]$ such that

$$\begin{aligned} [\![\mathcal{C}[0token_c]]\!]_P &= [\![NIL(I,O)]\!]_P \\ [\![\mathcal{C}[01token_c]]\!]_P &= [\![N]\!]_P \end{aligned}$$

□

Proof: In the proof, we construct a context $\mathcal{C}[\cdot]$, whose structure is given in Figure 4.

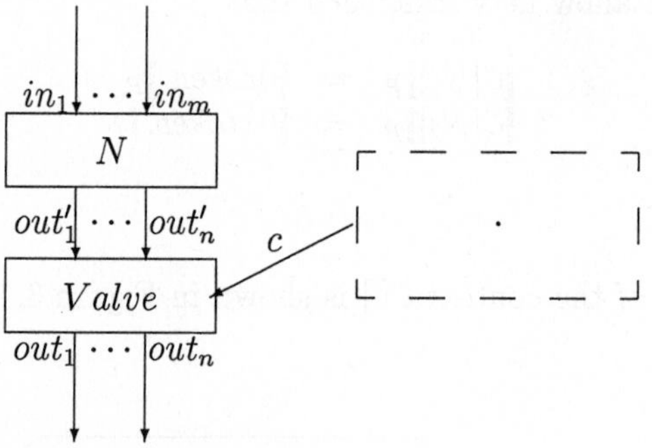

Figure 4: Structure of a Generating Context

The hole of the context is the dashed box, where either $0token_c$ or $01token_c$ will be put. The node $Valve$ initially does nothing. Upon receipt of the data item *token* it starts copying input to its output on all the output channels of N. It is easy to see the the conclusion of the lemma is satisfied. □

Theorem 5.4 *The gap* $[\![\cdot]\!]_{Ev} \sqsubset [\![\cdot]\!]_P$ *is a minimal proper inclusion for the classes of dataflow networks which includes the deterministic ones.* □

Proof: Assume that there exists a model $[\![\cdot]\!]$ such that $[\![\cdot]\!]_{Ev} \sqsubset [\![\cdot]\!] \sqsubset [\![\cdot]\!]_P$. We shall derive a contradiction. By $[\![\cdot]\!] \sqsubset [\![\cdot]\!]_P$ and Lemma 3.2, there are dataflow networks N_1, N_2 such that

$$[\![N_1]\!] = [\![N_2]\!] \quad \text{and} \quad [\![N_1]\!]_P \neq [\![N_2]\!]_P \tag{1}$$

By $[\![\cdot]\!]_{Ev} \sqsubset [\![\cdot]\!]$ and Lemma 3.2, there are dataflow networks N_3, N_4 such that

$$[\![N_3]\!]_{Ev} = [\![N_4]\!]_{Ev} \quad \text{and} \quad [\![N_3]\!] \neq [\![N_4]\!] \tag{2}$$

By (1) there is a finite sequence t of communication events such that $t \in P(N_2)$ but $t \notin P(N_1)$. By Lemma 5.2 we conclude that there is a context $\mathcal{C}[\cdot]$, such that $[\![\mathcal{C}[N_1]]\!]_P = [\![0token_c]\!]_P$ and $[\![\mathcal{C}[N_2]]\!]_P = [\![01token_c]\!]_P$. By (1) and the fact that $[\![\cdot]\!]$ is compositional we then conclude that $[\![0token_c]\!] = [\![01token_c]\!]$. By lemma 5.3 we then conclude that $[\![NIL(I(N_3), O(N_3))]\!] = [\![N_3]\!]$ and $[\![NIL(I(N_4), O(N_4))]\!] = [\![N_4]\!]$. It follows (because $[\![N_3]\!]_{Ev} = [\![N_4]\!]_{Ev}$ implies $[\![NIL(I(N_3), O(N_3))]\!]_P = [\![NIL(I(N_4), O(N_4))]\!]_P$) that $[\![N_3]\!] = [\![N_4]\!]$ contradicting (2). □

5.2 Proof that $[\![\cdot]\!]_P \sqsubset [\![\cdot]\!]_T$ is a minimal proper inclusion

In this section, we shall first establish a set of constructions of contexts. From these constructions, we can infer that $[\![\cdot]\!]_P \sqsubset [\![\cdot]\!]_T$ is a minimal proper inclusion for the class of nondeterministic dataflow networks. In contrast to the preceding section, it is not enough to use only deterministic process in these contexts, one must also use merge nodes. After the sequence of lemmas, we supply theorems which show that the gap $[\![\cdot]\!]_P \sqsubset [\![\cdot]\!]_T$ is a minimal proper inclusion for the class of all nondeterministic dataflow networks, which includes fair merge nodes. The essential reason for needing fair merge nodes is that we need to use interrupts and timeouts in the contexts.

For a channel c, let $1token_c$ be the network with one output channel c and no input channels, which produces one data item, called *token* and thereafter does nothing.

Lemma 5.5 Let N_1 and N_2 be dataflow networks for which $[\![N_1]\!]_P = [\![N_2]\!]_P$ such that there is a finite or infinite sequence t of communication events with $t \notin T(N_1)$ and $t \in T(N_2)$. Let c be a channel which is not a channel of N_1. Then there is a context $\mathcal{C}[\cdot]$, such that

$$\begin{aligned} [\![\mathcal{C}[N_1]]\!]_T &= [\![1token_c]\!]_T \\ [\![\mathcal{C}[N_2]]\!]_T &= [\![01token_c]\!]_T \end{aligned}$$

□

Proof: The structure of the context $\mathcal{C}[\cdot]$ is shown in Figure 5.

The hole of the context is the dashed box, where either N_1 or N_2 will be put. We have assumed that $in_1, \ldots, in_m$ and $out_1, \ldots, out_n$ are the input and output channels of N_1 and N_2.

The intuition behind the node $Test\ \neg t$ is that it will try to perform the sequence of events in t and outputs a token if something is wrong (either timeout and there are communication events to be received or wrong communication events arrive). At the arrival of a timeout token at a channel all the communication events at that channel should have occurred.

If t is infinite then $Test\ \neg t$ tries to perform an infinite sequence of events corresponding to t. If this goes well, then there will be no token on the channel c. If a wrong communication event arrives, then a token is put on the channel c. If timeout arrives on a channel, then it is checked if there are still communication events expected (in

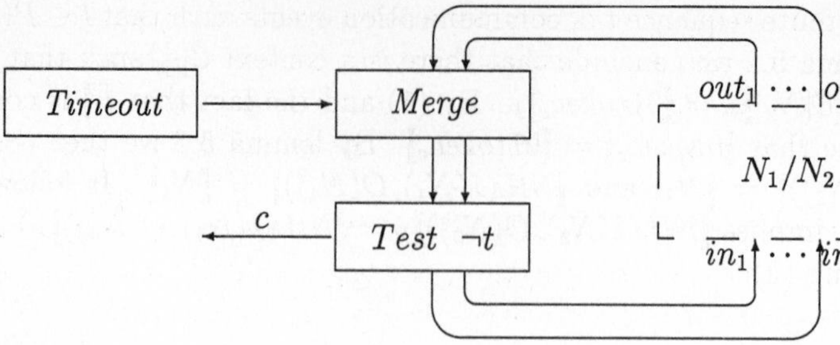

Figure 5: Structure of an Timeout-Tester Context

the rest of the trace t) at that channel. If this is the case, a token is put on the channel c.

If t is finite, then *Test* $\neg t$ will output no token on c if it can perform the sequence t followed by reception of an *timeout* token on each input channel. However, if before the sequence t is completed a token caused by a network in the hole arrives which does not correspond with the sequence t then *Test* $\neg t$ sends the data item *token* on channel c and thereafter does nothing. Again, if timeout arrives on a channel, then it is checked if there are still communication events expected at that channel. If this is the case, a token is put on the channel c. The item *token* will also be sent if t is finite, but more input, which is not the item *timeout*, arrives after t has been performed. The node *Test* $\neg t$ always stops execution after sending *token*.

The node *Timeout* sends a single distinguished data item *timeout* on its output channel. The node *Merge* forwards all incoming data items on channels $out_1, \ldots, out_n$ to the corresponding outgoing channels. It can also receive the data item *timeout* from *Timeout* and forward *timeout* on all its outgoing channels. The node *Merge* is fair in the sense that it must continue forwarding some input as long as some input arrives, but it does not need to be fair to any particular input channel. Thus *Merge* must forward the *timeout* token if no more input arrives on the other incoming channels, but it is also possible for *Merge* to neglect the input from *Timeout* if infinitely many data items arrive on the other incoming channels.

To see that the context satisfies the conclusion of the lemma, note that *Test* $\neg t$ will never perform the sequence t if the hole is filled with N_1 and that if N_1 performs a sequence which is a proper prefix of t then the item *timeout* will arrive to *Test* $\neg t$ and generate the item *token*. Further note that if the hole is filled with N_2 then there is a computation in which *Test* $\neg t$ sees the sequence t, and in which if t has infinite number of output events, the *timeout* is never input by *Merge* and if t is finite, *timeout* arrives to *Test* $\neg t$ after all other data items. □

For a network N let $\lceil T(N) \rceil$ be all finite and infinite sequences of comunication events of $E(N)$ that can be obtained by appending a finite or infinite sequence of input events to some sequence in $P(N)$. Intuitively, $\lceil T(N) \rceil$ contains the sequences that can be obtained by performing first a part of a computation of N with a sequence of communication events in $P(N)$ and thereafter blocking all further output so that the remaining communication events in the computation are input events. Let $FinOut(N)$ be the network which has the denotation $\langle I(N), O(N), \lceil T(N) \rceil \rangle$. Intuitively, $FinOut(N)$ can be thought of as the network N where output is blocked after some finite time of each computation so that each computation has only finitely many output events. Let $FinInfOut(N)$ be the network which has the denotation $\langle I(N), O(N), \lceil T(N) \rceil \cup T(N) \rangle$. Intuitively, $FinInfOut(N)$ is a network which behaves either like $FinOut(N)$ or like N.

Lemma 5.6 Let N be a dataflow network which does not have the channel c. Then there is a context $\mathcal{C}[\cdot]$ such that

$$\begin{aligned} [\![\mathcal{C}[1\,token_c]]\!]_T &= [\![FinOut(N)]\!]_T \\ [\![\mathcal{C}[01\,token_c]]\!]_T &= [\![FinInfOut(N)]\!]_T \end{aligned}$$

□

Proof: In the proof, we use a context $\mathcal{C}[\cdot]$ with the same structure as that in Figure 4. The hole of the context is the dashed box, where either $1\,token_c$ or $01\,token_c$ will be put. The node $Valve$ is initially copying input to its output on all the output channels of N. Upon receipt of the datum *token* it stops copying data items and does nothing further. This implies that if *token* is received, then only a finite portion of the output of the network is produced. The conclusion of the lemma follows. □

Lemma 5.7 Let N be a dataflow network which does not have the channel c. Then there is a context $\mathcal{C}[\cdot]$ such that

$$\begin{aligned} [\![\mathcal{C}[1\,token_c]]\!]_T &= [\![N]\!]_T \\ [\![\mathcal{C}[01\,token_c]]\!]_T &= [\![FinInfOut(N)]\!]_T \end{aligned}$$

□

Proof: In the proof, we use a context $\mathcal{C}[\cdot]$ with the same structure as that in Figure 4. The hole of the context is the dashed box, where either $1\,token_c$ or $01\,token_c$ will be put. The difference is that this time the node $Valve$ is initially copying input to its output on all the output channels of N. At some randomly chosen finite time, it stops copying data items and blocks further output and only waits for the datum *token* from the network in the hole of the context. Upon recept of *token* it again starts copying input to its output on all the output channels of N. This implies that if *token* is received, then a normal computation of the network is observed. If *token* is never received, then only a finite portion of the output of the network is produced. The conclusion of the lemma follows. □

Theorem 5.8 *The gap* $[\![\cdot]\!]_P \sqsubset [\![\cdot]\!]_T$ *is a minimal proper inclusion for the class of all dataflow networks.* □

Proof: Assume that there exists a model $[\![\cdot]\!]$ such that $[\![\cdot]\!]_P \sqsubset [\![\cdot]\!] \sqsubset [\![\cdot]\!]_T$. We shall derive a contradiction. By $[\![\cdot]\!] \sqsubset [\![\cdot]\!]_T$ and Lemma 3.2, there are dataflow networks N_1, N_2 such that

$$[\![N_1]\!] = [\![N_2]\!] \qquad \text{and} \qquad [\![N_1]\!]_T \neq [\![N_2]\!]_T \qquad (1)$$

By $[\![\cdot]\!]_P \sqsubset [\![\cdot]\!]$ and Lemma 3.2, there are dataflow networks N_3, N_4 such that

$$[\![N_3]\!]_P = [\![N_4]\!]_P \qquad \text{and} \qquad [\![N_3]\!] \neq [\![N_4]\!] \qquad (2)$$

By (1) there is a finite or infinite sequence t of communication events such that $t \in [\![N_2]\!]_T$ but $t \notin [\![N_1]\!]_T$. By Lemma 5.5 we conclude that there is a context $\mathcal{C}[\cdot]$, such that $[\![\mathcal{C}[N_1]]\!]_T = [\![1token_c]\!]_T$ and $[\![\mathcal{C}[N_2]]\!]_T = [\![01token_c]\!]_T$. By (1), the assumption $[\![\cdot]\!] \sqsubset [\![\cdot]\!]_T$, and the fact that $[\![\cdot]\!]$ is compositional we then conclude that $[\![1token_c]\!] = [\![01token_c]\!]$. By Lemma 5.7 we then conclude that $[\![N_3]\!] = [\![FinInfOut(N_3)]\!]$. By lemma 5.6 we conclude that $[\![FinOut(N_3)]\!] = [\![FinInfOut(N_3)]\!]$, which implies that $[\![N_3]\!] = [\![FinOut(N_3)]\!]$. We similarly conclude that $[\![N_4]\!] = [\![FinOut(N_4)]\!]$. By the fact that for all networks N_1 and N_2 we have that $[\![N_1]\!]_P = [\![N_2]\!]_P$ implies $[\![FinOut(N_1)]\!]_T = [\![FinOut(N_2)]\!]_T$ we infer $[\![N_3]\!] = [\![N_4]\!]$ contradicting (2). □

5.3 Proof that $[\![\cdot]\!]_P \sqsubset [\![\cdot]\!]_{PQ}$ is a minimal proper inclusion

Let *DIV* be the network with only the empty partial trace, which always diverges, i.e., it has no terminated trace. let *HALFDIV* the the network with the same partial trace, which sometimes diverges and sometimes terminates, i.e., the empty trace is both terminated and divergent.

Lemma 5.9 Let N_1 and N_2 be dataflow networks for which $[\![N_1]\!]_P = [\![N_2]\!]_P$. Assume that there is a finite sequence of events t such that $t \notin Q(N_1)$ but $t \in Q(N_2)$. Then there is a context $\mathcal{C}[\cdot]$, such that

$$\begin{aligned} [\![\mathcal{C}[N_1]]\!]_{PQ} &= [\![DIV]\!]_{PQ} \\ [\![\mathcal{C}[N_2]]\!]_{PQ} &= [\![HALFDIV]\!]_{PQ} \end{aligned}$$

□

Proof: The proof uses the context in Figure 6. The nodes perform the following functions:

Test t can perform the sequence t of communication events, and thereafter sends the datum *stop* to *Clock*. If any more input appears from the hole in the context, then the datum *start* is sent to *Clock*.

Clock Initially performs internal activity without stopping. Upon receiving the datum *stop* it stops its activity. When receiving the datum *start* it again starts its activity.

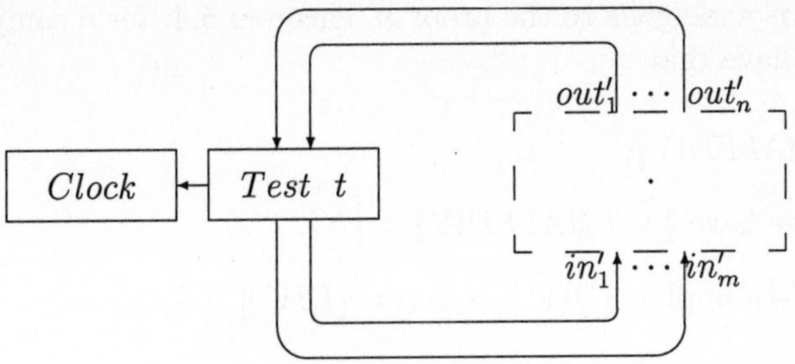

Figure 6: Context in the proof of Lemma 5.9

The consequence of this context is that if in a computation, the sequence of communication events on $E(N_1)$ is not t, the clock is switched on, whereas if the sequence actually is t, then the clock is switched off. It follows that the whole network wil always diverge unless the hole performs t (and nothing more). □

Lemma 5.10 Let N be a dataflow network. Then there is a context such that

$$\begin{aligned} [\![\mathcal{C}[HALFDIV]]\!]_{PQ} &= [\![N]\!]_{PQ} \\ [\![\mathcal{C}[DIV]]\!]_{PQ} &= [\![DIV \parallel N]\!]_{PQ} \end{aligned}$$

□

Proof: The proof uses the context in Figure 7. The conclusion of the theorem obviously

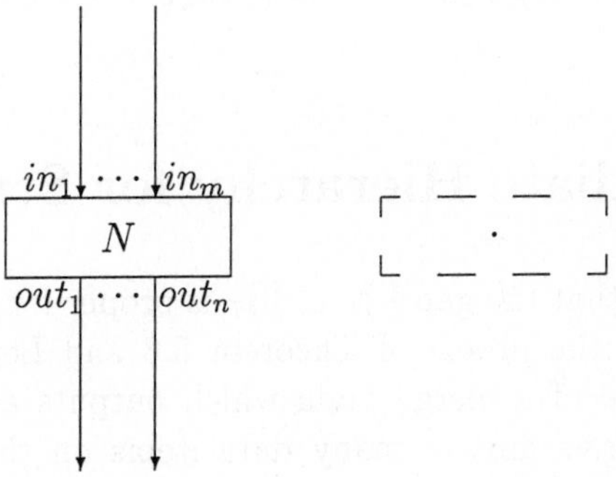

Figure 7: Context in the proof of Lemma 5.10

follows from this context. □

Theorem 5.11 *The gap* $[\![\cdot]\!]_P \sqsubset [\![\cdot]\!]_{PQ}$ *is a minimal proper inclusion for the class of all dataflow networks.* □

Proof: The proof is analogous to the proof of Theorem 5.4: for a compositional model $[\![\cdot]\!]$ in the gap we have that

1. $[\![DIV]\!] = [\![HALFDIV]\!]$,
2. for any N we have $[\![N \parallel HALFDIV]\!] = [\![N]\!]$,
3. $[\![N_3]\!]_P = [\![N_4]\!]_P$ implies $[\![DIV \parallel N_3]\!]_{PQ} = [\![DIV \parallel N_4]\!]_{PQ}$.

□

5.4 Proofs that $[\![\cdot]\!]_{Ev} \sqsubset [\![\cdot]\!]_Q$ and $[\![\cdot]\!]_T \sqsubset [\![\cdot]\!]_{TQ}$ are minimal proper inclusions

Follow the same patterns as the proofs in subsection 5.3.

5.5 Other gaps

We conjecture that the gaps $[\![\cdot]\!]_Q \sqsubset [\![\cdot]\!]_{PQ}$ and $[\![\cdot]\!]_{PQ} \sqsubset [\![\cdot]\!]_{TQ}$ contain both one compositional model. Consider networks that only have divergent traces. This class is closed under parallel composition with any other network. In both gaps we can find a model in between by taking for this subclass as denotation the left-model of the gap and for other networks as the denotation the right-model.
Alexander Rabinovich has showed us in a personal communication that the model $[\![\cdot]\!]_{TD}$ is fully abstract with respect to $[\![\cdot]\!]_D$ and that $[\![\cdot]\!]_{TQD}$ is fully abstract with respect to the $[\![\cdot]\!]_{QD}$.

6 An Intermediate Hierarchy for Strict Networks

In Section 5.2, we proved that the gap $[\![\cdot]\!]_P \sqsubset [\![\cdot]\!]_T$ is proper for the class of all dataflow networks. By examining the proofs of Theorem 5.8 and Lemma 5.5, we find that they rely on the existence of a merge node which outputs all data items from one input channel if there arrive finitely many data items on the other input channel. Such a merge is sometimes called an angelic merge node. In this section, we shall look at a less powerful class of networks which does not contain the angelic merge node. This class is characterized by the property that a node may only read from one input channel at a time, and that a read operation does not time out if no input arrives. This implies that if a read operation is performed when there is no data item in the channel, then the node is blocked forever unless data arrives in the channel. Nodes may exhibit nondeterminism, but only if it is the result of internal choices of a node and independent of whether or not data items arrive on input channels. This class of networks does not include the angelic merge node. If we allow unbounded nondeterministic internal choices, then the class includes the so-called infinity-fair merge. We shall call this the class of *strict networks* because of its unability to produce output if no input appears during a read operation. As a distinguishing property of this class of networks, we shall take the *prefix property* which is defined by Panangaden and Shanbhogue [25] to prove that the infinity-fair merge is strictly less expressive than the angelic merge.

For sequences h_1 and h_2, we use $h_1 \leq h_2$ to denote that h_1 is a prefix of h_2. The prefix relation is extended to tuples of sequences in the natural way. If t_1 and t_2 are sequences of communication events and E is a set of channels, let $t_1 \preceq_E t_2$ denote that

1. for each channel c in E $t_1\lceil_c \leq t_2\lceil_c$,
2. for each channel c not in E $t_1\lceil_c = t_2\lceil_c$, and
3. for all channels c, c' and integers i, j, such that the ith event on c and the jth event on c' are both in t_1, we have that the ith event on c precedes the jth event on c' in t_1 iff it does so in t_2.

We shall use vector notation to denote tuples of channels. If $\overline{c}$ is a tuple of channels, then $t\lceil_{\overline{c}}$ denotes the tuple of histories on the channels in $\overline{c}$.

Definition 6.1 Let N be a network with a tuple $\overline{in}$ of input channels and a tuple $\overline{out}$ of output channels. N is said to have the *prefix property* if whenever $\overline{h}'$ is a tuple and t is a trace of N with $\overline{h}' \leq t\lceil_{\overline{in}}$ then there is a trace t' of N such that $t'\lceil_{\overline{in}} = \overline{h}'$ and $t' \preceq_{E(N)} t$. □

Intuitively, if a certain input produces a certain output, then any prefix of the input produces some prefix of the same output as one possibility. The following theorem, which is a variant of a theorem proven in [25], shows that the prefix property is preserved by composition of networks.

Theorem 6.2 *If N_1 and N_2 are compatible networks that both have the prefix property, then $N_1 \| N_2$ also has the prefix property.* □

Proof: Assume that t is a trace of $N = N_1 \| N_2$. Then there exists a sequence $\hat{t}$ of communication events on the channels $E(N_1) \cup E(N_2)$ such that $\hat{t}\lceil_{E(N)} = t$ and $t_i = \hat{t}\lceil_{E(N_i)}$ is a trace of N_i for $i = 1, 2$. We shall use the following notation for the channels of N_1 and N_2. Let $\overline{in}_1$ be the tuple of input channels of N_1 which are in $I(N)$, let $\overline{out}_1$ be the tuple of output channels of N_1 which are in $O(N)$, and let $\overline{c}_{12}$ be the tuple of channels that are both output channels of N_1 and input channels of N_2. Define $\overline{in}_2$, $\overline{out}_2$, and $\overline{c}_{21}$ analogously. Now let $\overline{h}_1' \leq t\lceil_{\overline{in}_1}$ and $\overline{h}_2' \leq t\lceil_{\overline{in}_2}$. We must show that there is a trace t' of N such that $t'\lceil_{\overline{in}_i} = \overline{h}_i'$ for $i = 1, 2$, and $t' \preceq_{E(N)} t$. Since N_1 has the prefix property, there is a trace t_1^1 of N_1 such that $t_1^1\lceil_{\overline{in}_1} = \overline{h}_1'$, and $t_1^1\lceil_{\overline{c}_{12},\overline{out}_1} \leq t_1\lceil_{\overline{c}_{12},\overline{out}_1}$, and $t_1^1 \preceq_{E(N_1)} t_1$. Analogously, there is a trace t_2^1 with analogous properties. If now

t_1^1 and t_2^1 match, i.e. $t_1^1\lceil_{\overline{c}_{12},\overline{c}_{21}} = t_2^1\lceil_{\overline{c}_{12},\overline{c}_{21}}$, then we are done. If not, we must have an inequality in either $t_1^1\lceil_{\overline{c}_{12}} \leq t_2^1\lceil_{\overline{c}_{12}}$ or in $t_2^1\lceil_{\overline{c}_{21}} \leq t_1^1\lceil_{\overline{c}_{21}}$. Since N_1 again has the prefix property, there is a trace t_1^2 of N_1 such that $t_1^2\lceil_{\overline{c}_{21}} = t_2^1\lceil_{\overline{c}_{21}}$, and $t_1^2\lceil_{\overline{c}_{12},\overline{out}_1} \leq t_1^1\lceil_{\overline{c}_{12},\overline{out}_1}$, and $t_1^2 \preceq_{E(N_1)} t_1^1$. Analogously, there is a trace t_2^2 with analogous properties. If now t_1^2 and t_2^2 match, then we are done. Otherwise we continue the process until we find a matching pair t_1^m and t_2^m of traces. The process must terminate wich such a pair, since $\leq$ is a well-founded ordering, and when we hit the empty sequences on $\overline{c}_{12}$ and $\overline{c}_{21}$ they certainly match. The pair t_1^m and t_2^m satisfies $t_1^m\lceil_{\overline{in}_1} = \overline{h}'_1$ and $t_2^m\lceil_{\overline{in}_2} = \overline{h}'_2$, and also $t_1^m\lceil_{\overline{out}_1} \leq t_1\lceil_{\overline{out}_1}$ and $t_2^m\lceil_{\overline{out}_2} \leq t_2\lceil_{\overline{out}_2}$. Together with the fact that t_1^m and t_2^m match, this proves the theorem. □

We shall now define a new compositional model for strict networks. For a network N, define a *shortest trace* of N to be a trace t such that there is no trace t' with $t' \preceq_{O(N)} t$. Intuitively, a shortest trace is a minimal result of a computation where the input of the trace is supplied in the particular way described by the trace. Given any trace t of N, there is always a shortest trace of N which can obtained by removing communication events on some output channels. For a network N let $S(N)$ denote the set of shortest traces of N. As an example, consider a node *copy*123 with one input channel *in* and one output channel *out*, which upon receiving a data item decides internally to produce either one, two, or three copies of the data item onto channel *out*. The shortest traces of *copy*123 are those in which only one copy of each data item is produced, i.e., *copy*123 has the same shortest traces as the simple node *copy* described in Section 4, which just copies without duplication.

Using the set $S(N)$, new models of dataflow networks can defined, analogously to the preceding ones. The following theorem shows that the model $[\![\cdot]\!]_S$ is indeed compositional for the class of strict networks.

Theorem 6.3 *Let N_1 and N_2 be two compatible strict dataflow networks and let N be their composition. Let $C(N) = E(N_1) \cup E(N_2)$. Assume that $t \in S(N)$. Then there is a sequence $t' \in C(N)^\dagger$ such that $t'\lceil_{E(N_i)} \in S(N_i)$ for $i = 1, 2$ and $t'\lceil_{E(N)} = t$.* □

Proof: By Theorem 4.1 there is a sequence $\hat{t} \in C(N)^\dagger$ such that $t_i = \hat{t}\lceil_{E(N_i)} \in T(N_i)$ for $i = 1, 2$ and $\hat{t}\lceil_{E(N)} = t$. If $t_i \in S(N_i)$ for $i = 1, 2$ then we are done. Otherwise, define $\overline{in}_1$, $\overline{out}_1$, $\overline{c}_{12}$, $\overline{in}_2$, $\overline{out}_2$, and $\overline{c}_{21}$ as in the proof of Theorem 6.2. Then there exist shortest traces $t_1^1 \in S(N_1)$ and $t_2^1 \in S(N_2)$ with $t_1^1 \preceq_{O(N_1)} t_1$ and $t_2^1 \preceq_{O(N_2)} t_2$. If now t_1^1 and t_2^1 match, i.e., $t_1^1\lceil_{\overline{c}_{12},\overline{c}_{21}} = t_2^1\lceil_{\overline{c}_{12},\overline{c}_{21}}$, then we are done. If not, we must have an inequality in either $t_1^1\lceil_{\overline{c}_{12}} \leq t_2^1\lceil_{\overline{c}_{12}}$ or in $t_2^1\lceil_{\overline{c}_{21}} \leq t_1^1\lceil_{\overline{c}_{21}}$. Since N_1 again has the prefix property, there is a shortest trace $t_1^2 \in S(N_1)$ with $t_1^2\lceil_{\overline{c}_{21}} = t_2^1\lceil_{\overline{c}_{21}}$, and $t_1^2\lceil_{\overline{c}_{12},\overline{out}_1} \leq t_1^1\lceil_{\overline{c}_{12},\overline{out}_1}$, and $t_1^2 \preceq_{E(N_1)} t_1^1$. Analogously, there is a shortest trace t_2^2 with analogous properties. If now t_1^2 and t_2^2 match, then we are done. Otherwise we continue the process until we find a matching pair t_1^m and t_2^m of shortest traces. The process must terminate wich such a pair, since $\leq$ is a well-founded ordering, and when we hit the empty sequences on $\overline{c}_{12}$ and $\overline{c}_{21}$ they certainly match. The pair t_1^m and t_2^m satisfies $t_1^m\lceil_{\overline{in}_1} = t_1\lceil_{\overline{in}_1}$ and $t_2^m\lceil_{\overline{in}_2} = t_2\lceil_{\overline{in}_2}$, and also $t_1^m\lceil_{\overline{out}_1} = t_1\lceil_{\overline{out}_1}$ and $t_2^m\lceil_{\overline{out}_2} = t_2\lceil_{\overline{out}_2}$ since because t is a shortest trace of $N_1 \| N_2$ we cannot further shorten the output histories in the composition of t_1^m and t_2^m. The fact that t_1^m and t_2^m match proves the theorem by taking t' such that $t_i^m = t' \lceil_{E(N_i)} \in T(N_i)$ for $i = 1, 2$. □

Using Theorem 6.3 it is easy to see that the shortest-trace model is compositional for strict networks. In the composition, simply compose the shortest traces of the components to yield the shortest traces of the composition. One may in the result have to delete some traces, which have shorter output sequences, but the last theorem shows that we only need the shortest traces of the components to find the shortest traces of the composition. As a remark, the model $[\![\cdot]\!]_{PS}$ is also compositional.

7 Conclusions and Further Work

We have presented a hierarchy of compositional trace models for dataflow networks, and investigated their relationship. The models have been related according to their ability to distinguish networks, and as a major contribution, results about proper gaps have been established.

A conclusion of the work is that in compositional models, the concepts of fairness as represented by infinite traces, and termination represent "indivisible units of description", in the sense that there is no model which can describe a part of the information provided by e.g. the termination component in a compositional way.

We showed that when we restrict the class of dataflow networks, we can add models to the hierarchy. We would like to explore further the hierarchy of compositional models for these networks. It would be interesting to see whether similar ideas can be applied to models of synchronously communicating systems, e.g. CSP, thus extending the work of e.g. [24] and Reed and Roscoe [32, 33].

References

[1] R. Back and H. Mannila. On the suitability of trace semantics for modular proofs of communicating processes. *Theoretical Computer Science*, 39(1):47–68, 1985.

[2] F. Boussinot. Proposition de semantique denotationelle pur des processus avec operateur de melange equitable. *Theoretical Computer Science*, 18(2):173–206, 1982.

[3] J. Brock and W. Ackerman. Scenarios: a model of non-determinate computation. In *Formalization of Programming Concepts, LNCS 107*, pages 252–259. 1981.

[4] S. Brookes, C. Hoare, and A. Roscoe. A theory of communicating sequential processes. *J. ACM*, 31(3):560–599, 1984.

[5] M. Broy. Fixed point theory for communication and concurrency. In Bjoerner, editor, *Formal Description of Programming Concepts II*, pages 125–146, 1983. North-Holland.

[6] M. Broy. Nondeterministic data flow programs: How to avoid the merge anomaly. *Science of Computer Programming*, 10:65–85, 1988.

[7] R. de Nicola and M. Hennessy. Testing equivalences for processes. *Theoretical Computer Science*, 34:83–133, 1984.

[8] C. Hoare. *Communicating Sequential Processes.* Prentice-Hall, 1985.

[9] B. Jonsson. A model and proof system for asynchronous networks. In *Proc. 4th ACM PoDC*, pages 49–58, 1985.

[10] B. Jonsson. *Compositional Verification of Distributed Systems.* PhD thesis, Uppsala University, Sweden, 1987.

[11] B. Jonsson. A fully abstract trace model for dataflow networks. In *Proc. 16th ACM PoPL*, pages 155–165, 1989.

[12] B. Jonsson. A hiearchy of compositional models of I/O-automata. In *Proc. MFCS, LNCS 452*, pages 347–354. 1990.

[13] B. Jonsson and J. Kok. Comparing two fully absttract dataflow models. In *Proc. PARLE 89, LNCS 365*, pages 217–234. 1989.

[14] G. Kahn. The semantics of a simple language for parallel programming. In *IFIP 74*, pages 471–475. North-Holland, 1974.

[15] R. Keller and P. Panangaden. Semantics of networks containing indeterminate operators. In *Seminar on Concurrency 1984, LNCS 197*, pages 479–496, 1985.

[16] R. Keller and P. Panangaden. Semantics of networks containing indeterminate operators. *Distributed Computing*, 1:235–245, 1986.

[17] J. Kok. Denotational semantics of nets with nondeterminism. In *European Symposium on Programming, Saarbrücken, LNCS 206*, pages 237–249. 1986.

[18] J. Kok. A fully abstract semantics for data flow nets. In *Proc. PARLE, LNCS 259*, pages 351–368. 1987.

[19] P. Kosinski. A straight-forward denotational semantics for nondeterminate data flow programs. In *Proc. 5th ACM PoPL*, pages 214–219, 1978.

[20] N. Lynch and M. Tuttle. Hierarchical correctness proofs for distributed algorithms. In *Proc. 6th ACM PoDC*, pages 137–151, 1987.

[21] R. Milner. *Communication and Concurrency.* Prentice-Hall, 1989.

[22] J. Misra and K. M. Chandy. Proofs of networks of processes. *IEEE Trans. on Software Engineering*, SE-7(4):417–426, July 1981.

[23] V. Nguyen, A. Demers, D. Gries, and S. Owicki. A model and temporal proof system for networks of processes. *Distributed Computing*, 1(1):7–25, 1986.

[24] E. Olderog and C. Hoare. Specification-oriented semantics for communicating processes. *Acta Informatica*, 23(1):9–66, 1986.

[25] P. Panangaden and V. Shanbhogue. The expressive power of indeterminate dataflow primitives, May 1989. Manuscript.

[26] P. Panangaden, V. Shanbhogue, and E. Stark. Stability and sequentiality in dataflow networks. TR 89-1055, Cornell University, Nov. 1989.

[27] P. Panangaden and E. Stark. Computations, residuals, and the power of indeterminiacy. In *Proc. ICALP '88, LNCS 317*, volume 317 of *Lecture Notes in Computer Science*, pages 439–454. Springer Verlag, 1988.

[28] D. Park. The 'fairness' problem and nondeterministic computing networks. In, *Foundations of Computer Science IV, Part 2*, pages 133–161, Amsterdam, 1983. Mathematical Centre Tracts 159.

[29] V. Pratt. On the composition of processes. In *Proc. 9th ACM PoPL*, pages 213–223, 1982.

[30] V. Pratt. The pomset model of parallel processes: Unifying the temporal and the spatial. In *Proc. Seminar on Concurrency, LNCS 197*, pages 180–196. 1984.

[31] A. Rabinovich and B. Trakhtenbrot. Nets of processes and data flow. In *Linear Time, Branching Time and Partial Order in Logics and Models for Concurrency, LNCS 354*, pages 574–602. 1989.

[32] G. Reed and A. Roscoe. A timed model for communicating sequential processes. In *Proc. ICALP '86, LNCS 226*, pages 314–323. 1986.

[33] G. Reed and A. Roscoe. Metric spaces as models for real-time concurrency. In *Proc. 3rd Workshop on Math. Found. of Progr. Lang. Semantics, LNCS 298.* Springer Verlag, 1988.

[34] J. Russell. Full abstraction for nondeterministic dataflow networks. In *Proc. 30th IEEE FoCS*, 1989.

[35] J. Staples and V. Nguyen. A fixpoint semantics for nondeterministic data flow. *J. ACM*, 32(2):411–444, April 1985.

[36] R. J. van Glabbeek and F. W. Vaandrager. Petri net models for algebraic theories of concurency. In *Proc. PARLE, LNCS 259*, pages 224–242. 1987.

[37] J. Zwiers. *Compositionality, Concurrency and Partial Correctness, LNCS 321.* 1989.

Type Theory as a Foundation for Computer Science

Robert L. Constable*
Department of Computer Science
Cornell University
Ithaca, NY 14853
rc@cs.cornell.edu

Abstract

We discuss some of the boons as well as shortcomings of constructive type theory as a foundation for computer science. Certain new concepts are offered for tailoring these theories to this task including an idea for collecting objects into subtypes and a proposal for using logic variables and treating them as part of the definition of the logic.

1 Introduction

It would be good if there were a formal logical theory that expressed the basic concepts of computer science well. It has been a goal of logicians to find such a foundational theory for mathematics, and many people are happy with Set Theory in that role. But for computer science the formal theory should offer a programming notation as well since computing involves programming in a central way; and a formal notation is needed for that. If the programming notation were independent of the foundational theory, then we could not directly use the theoretical insights in programming and vise versa. Once we are committed to a formalized theory for computing, we need one that can express arguments about algorithms and systems actually built, that is, it should be a programming logic as well as a foundational theory.

These two requirements place a large burden on such a theory. Simply adding a programming notation to Set Theory for example results in a costly and cumbersome solution. Constructive type theories have arisen as a more elegant and lean approach. In this article we examine some of their advantages and deficiencies.

*This research supported by NSF grant CCR86-16552 and ONR grant N00014-88K-0490.

2 Advantages of type theory

I do not intend to survey all of the candidate type theories, but there are at least three main species: Martin-Löf's predicative type theories and their extensions [22, 23, 10, 29, 18, 25, 26, 9], Girard's impredicative theories and their extensions [13, 14, 11, 21] [3], and Fefeman's theories of functions and classes [12, 17, 7]. In some ways these are converging in that they are treating the same class of concepts, and none is clearly right at the expense of the others. Indeed all are not right, but they represent the best we can do at present. They all offer the following advantages over taking the union of Set Theory and Programming Logic (say over ones favorite programming language).

1. Simple connections between programs and specifications

These type theories all use a functional programming notation and assign types essentially as for the typed lambda calculus. The connection to logic in the case of the ML and Girard theories is via the propositions-as-types principle. These two mechanisms combine elegantly, and the connection is robust, supporting many extensions to both type and programs. It offers also a richer type system than any in existing functional programming language, so in principle the result is a richer programming notation.

A Simple Type Theory

Here is a simple type theory that illustrates the basic concepts needed in the rest of the paper. The basic syntactic concept is a *term*. The terms are divided into two groups, the *canonical* ones and the *noncanonical* ones. Here are all of the canonical terms: $prod(A; x.B)$, $fun(A; x.B)$, $union(A; B)$, $void$, $Type$, $pair(a; b)$, $\lambda(x.b)$, $inl(a)$, $inr(b)$, $any(b)$.

Here are the noncanonical ones: $spread(p; u, v.t)$, $ap(f; a)$, $decide(d; u.t1; v.t2)$.

There are *computation rules* telling how to *reduce* the noncanonical terms; the canonical ones reduce to themselves. In these rules the notation $exp[a/x]$ denotes the term obtained from exp by substituting a for each occurrence of x in exp.

To reduce $spread(p; u, v.t)$, first reduce p. If the result is $pair(a; b)$, then continue by reducing $t[a/u, b/v]$.

To reduce $ap(f; a)$, first reduce f; if the result is $\lambda(x.b)$, then continue by reducing $b[a/x]$.

To reduce $decide(d; u.t1; v.t2)$, first reduce d; if the result is $inl(a)$, then continue by reducing $t1[a/u]$; if the result is $inr(b)$, then continue by reducing $t2[b/v]$.

Typing Rules These terms are the basis of a simple type theory. A type will be defined when we say which canonical terms are elements of it and what canonical name is. One type is determined by the term *void*. It is a type with no members. We generally speak of the term which is the canonical name of a type as a type, so we say *void* is a type.

Another type is determined by the name *Type*. To define its canonical members we proceed inductively, and we introduce the auxiliary concept of a family of types over a type A. If B is a term and A is a type, and if for every element a of A the term $B[a/x]$ is a type, then B is a family of types indexed by A (using index variable x).

If A and C are types and if B is a type indexed by A (with index variable x) then $prod(A; x.B)$, $fun(A; x.B)$ and $union(A; C)$ are types. If x does not occur in B, then we omitt the $x.$ binding operator. To specify what types these are, we must define their canonical elements.

The canonical elements of the types $union(A; C)$ are those terms $inl(a)$ and $inr(c)$ where a is a term of type A and c is one of type C; neither a nor c need be canonical, so we must also to define what it means generally for a term to be of some type T. We do this below.

The canonical elements of $prod(A, x.B)$ are the terms $pair(a; b)$ where a is of type A and b is of type $B[a/x]$. We know that these $B[a/x]$ are types since $prod(A; x.B)$ is.

The canonical element of $fun(A; x.B)$ are the terms $\lambda(x.b)$ such that for each a of type A, $b[a/x]$ is of type A.

A term with no free variable (i.e. a *closed term*) is of type A if it reduces to a canonical term of type A. Thus if $t[a/x, b/y]$ reduces to a canonical term type T, then $spread(pair(a; b); x, y.t)$ is of type T.

A term with free variables can be contingently of type A depending on assumption about the types of the free variables. To define this, let $x_1, \ldots, x_n$ be the free variables of t assume A_1, is a type, and say that A_2 is a type, possibly depending on A_1, if for each a_1 of type A_1, $A_2[a/x]$ is a type. Likewise for A_n depending on $A_1, \ldots, A_{n-1}$, and T depending on $x_1, \ldots, x_n$. Now t is of type T if for each a_1 of type A_1, A_2 of type $A_2[a_1/x], \ldots, a_n$ of type $A_n[a_1/x_1, \ldots, a_{nil}/x_{nil}]$, $t[a_1/x_1, \ldots, a_n/x_n]$ is of type $T[a_1/x_1, \ldots, a_n/x_n]$. For example, $inr(x)$ is of type $union(A; B)$ if x is assumed to be of type A.

Encoding constructive logic The *propositions-as-types principle* establishes a correspondence between types and propositions based on the idea that a proposition is true if and only if the corresponding type is inhabited. For decidable atomic propositions it is easy to begin the correspondence, namely a proposition P is taken to be an empty type if it is false and a type with at least one element if it is true; so $false$ corresponds to the type *void*. One can use the proposition itself as a type. The correspondence is extended to compound propositions by the following definitions.

$A\&B$ corresponds to $prod(A; B)$
$A \vee B$ corresponds to $union(A; B)$
$A \Rightarrow B$ corresponds to $fun(A; B)$.

This correspondence is justified on semantic grounds and can be seen as a *realizability* semantics for constructive logic as is by now well-known.

2. Rich specification languages

These type theories can express a great deal of mathematics. One reason for this is that they allow quantification over propositions. This is possible in Martin-Löf style theories because the notion *Type* presented above is refined into a hierarchy of types called *universes.* A universe is a type closed under all the type forming operations, so it looks like the collection of all types. But it is itself a type and is not contained in itself. The first of these is called $U1$. There is a larger universe $U2$ which contains all of the types from $U1$ plus $U1$ itself. Indeed there is a sequence of universes, Ui with Ui contained in $Ui+1$.

These universes allow the user to define recursive types, and with recursive types one can encode some versions of infinitary logic. It is also possible to represent dynamic logic and other programming logics. In the case of the type theories with partial objects [33, 9] [3] this can be done directly taking programs as partial functions on state.

Of course Set Theory allows all of these concepts as well and can represent higher-order logic by taking propositions to be boolean valued functions. It is simple to define sets inductively and to provide a denotational semantics for dynamic logic and programming logics. However, the encoding of these ideas in Set Theory does not help us keep track of what can be computed and what can't be. So typically although we can for example define a model of a programming language, the partial functions used in it will not be computable, so we cannot actually execute the semantic definition. Also the definition of a mathematical concept in Set Theory is often not the one we want to compute with. Let us examine two examples of this phenomenon, first consider the definition of *multi-sets*, say as in [Manna&Waldinger/89book].

A multi-set is defined axiomatically as a set with the operations of adding an element, say $add(a, S)$. There is an empty mulit-set, say []. There is an axiom about equality, saying that $add(x, add(y, S)) = add(y, add(x, S))$, and there is a principle of induction for proving things about such sets. It has the form that if we can prove P on [] and if for every multi-set S and any element a we can prove that P holding on S implies that it holds on $add(a, S)$, then we know P on any multi-set. From this basis Manna&Waldinger show that we can define a choice function, *choose*, from any nonempty multi-set S to an element, $choose(S)$. They also show how to define the function $count(a, S)$ which denotes the number of times that the element a appears in S. Now a constructive account of multi-sets requires a more delicate approach. A complete account occurs in [4]. First these sets must be defined over some underlying type, say A. Then some concrete representation must be defined, say the sets of Lists over A. An equality relation is imposed on these representations, the same as above, and an induction combinator must be defined. It is like the induction principle stated above except that one must explicitly say that the method of proving P on $add(x, S)$

from P on S must respect the defined equality. It turns out that this restriction prevents us from defining the choice function, *choose*(x, S), which is a good thing since it is not in general computable for multi-sets over any base A.

As a second example, consider the definition of the real numbers in Set Theory. There one can choose from among many equivalent definitions, say Dedekind cuts versus Cauchy sequences versus nested intervals and so forth. But one cannot compute with any of these definitions, and some of them are difficult to modify to make them computable. Dedekind cuts do not lead to a notion of computable reals in a natural way whereas the Cauchy definition does. Namely, following Bishop, [6], we say that a constructive real number is a sequence of rational numbers, $x_1, x_2, \ldots$ such that $|x_i - x_j| < 1/i + 1/j$. Two of them , $x_1, x_2, \ldots.$ and $y_1, y_2, \ldots.$ are equal iff for all i, $|x_i - y_i| < 2/i$. These are examples of two very basic mathematical concepts which arise frequently in computer science and for which the set theoretic definitions do not necessarily lead to good data structures for practical computation. So new computational definitions must be introduced and related to the other definitions. In most cases this process requires an elaborate definition of computability prior to the definitions. In type theory we can start with the computationally sensible definition right at the start because the right computing concepts are part of the basic theory.

3. A range of programming styles

functional programming The terms of constructive type theories include those that constitute a functional programming language, so they support directly the functional programming style. In fact in a system like Nuprl we expect to be able to achieve the performance of a language like Standard ML on the subset of programs common to both languages, which is essentially the functional subset of Standard ML. This is sufficient performance for a wide range of algorithms and systems, including by the way the implementation of Nuprl itself [27].

object oriented programming The richness of these type theories allows them to express directly concepts such as modules and algebraic data types, ADT's. So it is possible to program in the style of the so-called object oriented languages to some extent. For instance in [4] there are many examples including lists, multi-sets, formulas and proofs all formulated as ADT's using the constructors fun and $prod$. However, no one has explored in detail the adequacy with which type theory can represent the various operations on algebraic structures that make this kind of programming so attractive. I would conjecture that many of these operations will have a pleasant formulation.

logic programming In a system like Nuprl it is possible to use the metalanguage to enable a logic programming style. Lipton [20] has actually built a Prolog engine in Nuprl in just this way. But we can see the main idea by looking at an example of a Prolog style computation done using just the basic types of a Martin-Löf theory plus the Nuprl-style tactics. This will be done in section 3 where we also discuss logic variables.

imperative programming There is good evidence to believe that the mechanisms being used in functional programming to attain the performance levels of imperative programming languages will be available in these type theories, either in the implementation or in some cases in the logic as well. For example the work of Griffin and Murthy [16, 27] shows how to type the control operator call/cc (the "go to's" of functional programming). Moreover this work reveals a deep connection between these evaluation strategies in functional programming and certain transformations important in proof theory.

4. Expressing basic ideas from computer science

The constructive type theories are able to explain and generalize some of the concepts basic to computer science. In the first place they provide a rigorous and general notion of data type which generalizes many of the earlier notions. For example, variant records become dependent products, function spaces can be seen as special cases of dependent function spaces, set types can be defined over any type, modules are instances of parameterized dependent products (as are abstract types) and recursive types can be generalized to include the constructive ordinals. In addition new relationships are revealed by the definitions as in the case of lazy data types being the co-inductive types [24].

The underlying deductive mechanism of a system such as Nuprl can be used to unify many important basic concepts. For instance there is one uniform notion of binding and scope which applies to the entire system. Also the notion of a transformation tactic gives as well the concept of a program transformation. The use of tactics to define the idea of a high-level proof applies as well to defining high-level programs.

One of the most important unifications provided by constructive type theories occurs at the interface between mathematics and computer science. Here we see that many of the concepts from constructive mathematics are exactly what is needed in computing, e.g. the real numbers, and conversely many of the algorithms needed in constructive mathematics can be developed by techniques from computer science. An illustration of this later point occurs in Howe's library of basic real analysis, [Howe&Chirimar89], the proof of the Intermediate Value Theorem is based on a simple binary search algorithm whose structure is directly apparent from the proof. In contrast the same proof in Bishop&Bridges hides the algorithm. In another field, the constructive proof of Higman's lemma provided by Murthy and Russell [28] gives an algorithm based on regular expressions which is much simpler to understand than the one which can be obtained from the classical proofs, [27].

5. Naturally automated

One of the most successful and interesting approaches to automating reasoning is the method of tactics pioneered by the LCF system [15]. This approach fits very well with type theory because it involves using a richly typed programming language as a metalanguage for proof construction. These type theories can use themselves as programming notations for automating reasoning in them. So for example it is possible to write and prove correct a theorem proving procedure for Intuitionistic propositional calculus in any of the programming styles suggested above and then use this for facilitating formal reasoning in the type theory. One of the most interesting examples of this is [35].

3 Improvements to the type theories

The use of constructive type theory in framing basic computing concepts is relatively new, and the community is learning how to adjust and improve the exact definitions of the basic concepts. The same process went on in set theory for many years before the elegant and polished accounts that we now see were developed. Indeed work along these lines is still being done. In the case of type theory we can see for example that the treatment of inductively defined types has improved over the past five years. The first accounts, [8, 24] led to an implementation in Nuprl. Experience with these types showed that the full notion of parameterized mutually inductive types was awkward. Subsequent work by Coquand, Paulin, and Dybjer has led to a more elegant and polished set of rules for the general case [Paulin&Coquand] [30] [Dybjer], and extensive experience with the simple unparameterized case has shown just how vital the concept is in defining basic concepts [18]. Likewise new type constructors have been studied such as intersection types [Backhouse] [1] and partial types [33, 9, 32]. In this section I want to suggest some other possible improvements to these type theories. In two cases we look at new type constructors and in the other we consider logic variables.

3.1 new set types

Both Nuprl and the Göteborg proof development systems are based on type theories that use some version of a *set type*. We will refer to the Nuprl version, but the observations apply as well to the other notion. The key idea is that for any type A and predicate P on A, there is a type $\{x : A|P(x)\}$ of those elements of A that satisfy the predicate P. For example the positive natural numbers N^+ can be defined as $\{z : integer|\ 0 < z\}$. But since when computing with this type we do not want to provide as data to functions defined on it the proofs of the proposition $P(x)$, we need to "hide that information." To see this point think of defining a function on N^+, we do not want it to need two arguments, one for the number n and one for the proof that $0 < n$. So we require that when defining a function f from $\{x : A|P(x)\}$ on input a, say f(a), the value of f cannot use the proof that P(a) holds. The value of this construct is illustrated and discussed in the two books on these type theories, [10, 29].

There are cases when the set type lets us down. For example if we define the positive real numbers as $\{r : Real \mid 0 < r\}$ then we cannot define the function $1/r$ on them. The reason is that to compute $1/r$ we need to know how far r is from 0; that information is given in the proof of $0 < r$, but this proof is not available in defining $1/r$ because of the design of the set type.

Let us consider now another version of the set type to be used as a companion to the one described above. The idea will be to allow access to the proof component as long as that does not introduce a dependence on the exact form of the proof. So as long as the concept being defined over the set is *independent of the proof* of the predicate, then we can have access to the information in that predicate. This is a way of encorporating the independence-of-proofs idea from Automath [deBruijn68] into the theory. The way we will capture this idea is to require that any object b built from a member a of $\{x : A||P(x)\}$, the notation for the new set type, and a proof p of $P(a)$ will have the property that it is equal to any object built in the same way from a and any other proof of q of $P(a)$. That is, if $p = q$, then $b(p) = b(q)$. We give the exact form of the rule for this below and then show that with this type we can define the positive reals in a useful way.

The new set type, $\{x : A||P\}$ is well formed when A is a type and $P[a/x]$ is a type for a in A. The rule for introducing a member of the type $\{x : A||P\}$ is written in the Nuprl format. This format is discussed further in section 3 below on logic variables.

$H \quad >> \{x : A||P\}$ by intro a extract $st(a;p)$
  1. $H >> a$ in A
  2. $H >> P[a/x]$ extract p.

This is the same rule as for the introduction of elements in an ordinary set type which is in turn the same as the rule for the dependent product. The elimination rule distinguishes the type. It is this.

$H, \quad u : \{x : A||P\} >> G$ by elim u extract $g[u/x, pf(u)/p]$
  1. $H, x : A, p : P >> G$ extract g
  2. $H, x : A, p1 : P, p2 : P >> g[p1/p] = g[p2/p] in G.$

The term $pf(u)$ denotes the proof component of u, and the computation rule for it is $pf(st(a;p))$ reduces to p. The interesting new computation rule concerns the pairing constructor $st(a;p)$ which is meant to be read "a such that p". We want that $f(st(a;p))$ reduces to $f(a)$ for any operator f except pf. The actual form of the rule needs to be a bit more general and refer to any argument position of any operator other than pf, but we need not go into such detail here.

Now the definition of the positive reals can be taken as $\{x : Real||\exists n : N.x(n) > 1/n\}$. When we are computing with positive reals $st(u;p)$, $st(v;q)$ we can write expressions like $u+v$ where $+$ is defined on the reals, and this will be equivalent to $st(u;p)+st(v;q)$. This simple mechanism offers an easy way to extend all operations on the reals to the positive reals. So it is providing one kind of inheritance mechanism between types and the sets built over them.

We can also define $1/u$ which is the sequence $y_1, y_2, \ldots$ where y_1 to y_n are n^3, for n the witness part of the proof $pf(u)$, and for all $k > n$, $y(k) = 1/u(k) \times n^3$. It can be shown that regardless of which proof is used to show $u > 0$, the real numbers $1/st(x;p)$ and $1/st(x;q)$ will be equal over the reals. The operation $1/x$ on positive reals cannot be extended to the reals because it requires the proof component.

3.2 represented types

The disjoint union type in Martin-Lof type theory, say of types A and B, can be thought of as the set $\{inl(x), inr(y)|x \text{ in } A \text{ and } y \text{ in } B\}$ where *inr* and *inl* are operator names used just to build this type. This is one way of incorporating the categorical idea that $union(A;B)$ is the type such that for any maps $g : A \Rightarrow C$ and $h : B \Rightarrow C$ there is a unique map $f : union(A;B) \Rightarrow C$ such that on A it equals g and on B it equals C. This categorical construction is not directly represented in type theory. If we generalize the above way of defining unions, then we get a version of the categorical notion. This way of forming types can be thought of as building new elements by using previously constructed ones to represent them and "tagging the new elements" to give them names.

Consider first a simple version of this type. Given a type A and a new operator name op, let $\{op(x)|x : A\}$ be a type *represented by A*. The interesting feature is the elimination rule which lets us get at the representative. If u belongs to $\{op(x)|x : A\}$, say it is $op(a)$, and if given any x in A we can build g in G, then we can build g from $op(x)$ and we denote that object as $case_1(u; x.g)$, a member of G. The rule for computing with $case_1(u; x.g)$ is that $case_1(op(a); x.g)$ reduces to $g[a/x]$.

We can generalize this type constructor to allow several operators, say op_1 to op_n. The type would be $\{op_1(x1), op_2(x_2), \ldots, op_n(x_n)|x_1 : A_1, \ldots, x_n : A_n\}$. The elimination form for this type would be $case_n(z; x_1.g_1; \ldots; x_n.g_n)$ with the computation rule that $case_n(op_i(a_i); x_1.g_1; \ldots; x_n.g_n)$ reduces to $g_i[a_i/x_i]$. With this type constructor we could define not only $union(A;B)$ but an n-ary union, $union(A_1; \ldots; A_n)$ whose operator names might be $in_1, \ldots, in_n$.

One especially natural definition that this constructor makes possible is the natural numbers using a recursive type. We could define 0 and *succ* as new operator names and define Nat as $rec(N.\{0, succ(n)|n : N\})$. The elements of this type are exactly 0, $succ(0)$, $succ(succ(0))$, ... This is somewhat clearer than encoding the natural numbers as $rec(N.union(\{0\}; N))$.

3.3 Logic variables in refinement logic

refinement logics When proving a theorem we often work backwards from the goal to axioms or assumptions. This is sometimes called *top-down development.* For instance we argue that $((A \Rightarrow B)\ \&\ (B \Rightarrow C)) \Rightarrow (A \Rightarrow C)$ by saying we need a proof of $(A \Rightarrow C)$ from a proof of $(A \Rightarrow B)\ \&\ (B \Rightarrow C)$. To prove $A \Rightarrow C$, we need a proof of C from A and the other assumptions. We can prove C if we can prove B because we are assuming $B \Rightarrow C$. But we can prove B if we can prove A because we assume $A \Rightarrow B$. But we assume A, so there is a proof.

The *tableau* proof style [34] is top-down, and Nuprl's logic is top-down. This kind of logic was also called a *refinement logic* by Bates [5]. The convenient way to present the rules of a refinement logic is to state the goal first, then the rule name and any information needed to determine the subgoals, and finally the subgoals. So for example the rule for proving $A\&B$ from assumption H is written in Nuprl as

$$\begin{array}{ll} H >> & A\ \&\ B \text{ by and intro} \\ & 1.\ H >> A \\ & 2.\ H >> B. \end{array}$$

The sign ">>" is used as a replacement for "$\vdash$" to indicate that the proofs are being generated top-down. A rule which requires information beyond the rule name to generate the subgoals is

$$\begin{array}{l} H,\ \forall x\colon A.B >> G \text{ by all elimination on } a \\ \quad H >> a \epsilon A \\ \quad H, \forall x\colon A.B\ ,\ B[a/x] >> G \end{array}$$

We need the name of the element of A to generate the subgoals.

In Nuprl the existential introduction rule also requires extra information. It is

$$\begin{array}{ll} H >> & \exists x\colon A.B \text{ by intro } a \\ & H >> a \epsilon A \\ & H >> B[a/x]. \end{array}$$

This rule is inconvenient because it interrupts the top-down development, forcing the user to choose a early in the proof.

One of the powerful features of logic programming languages, which are also top-down, is that they employ the concept of a *logic variable* to delay existential choices. If Nurpl had logic variables, for now let's write them a s capitals, $X, Y, Z, \ldots$, then the existential introduction rule could be written as

$$\begin{array}{ll} H >> & \exists x : A.B \text{ by intro } X \\ & 1.\ H >> X \epsilon A \\ & 2.\ H >> B[X/x]. \end{array}$$

The key assumption underlying the use of logic variables is that they are instantiated simultaneously at all occurrences. So if in the subproof of $B[X/x]$ we learn that X must be a particular value a, and we set X to a, then the first subgoal becomes $H >> a \epsilon A$.

We will discuss below one way to treat logic variables in refinement logics, and we apply it in a logic programming setting. But first we consider the Prolog computation mechanism as it can be explained in a refinement logic like Nuprl without logic variable.

Prolog proof procedure A "program" in Prolog is a set of inductive definitions of relations. For instance here is a Prolog form of the primitive recursive function definition

$$f(0, y) = y$$
$$f(s(n), y) = h(n, f(n, y)).$$

It is a pair of relations

$$\forall y R(0, y, y)$$
$$\forall u, z, y(R(z, y, v) \Rightarrow R(s(z), y, h(z, v)).$$

In general a program can consists of several relations or program *clauses*, say $C_1, \ldots, C_n$. Each of them defines a relation in the form $\forall \bar{x}.(A_1 \&, \ldots, \& A_n \Rightarrow B)$ where the A_i, B are atomic formulas, be maybe 0. We say B is the "head" of its clause.

A goal clause has the form $\forall \bar{x}.(A \Rightarrow \exists \bar{y}.B)$. A constructive proof of this will find functions which compute a witness for this existential quantifier. The form of the function is simply an expression for the vector $\bar{y}$ of values in terms of the primitives. The expression is presented as a substitution for $\bar{y}$. The proof procedure can find many expressions, so it is finding more than one function.

The Prolog proof procedure can be expressed without logic variables. It is just a specific search which uses unification and backchaining. The unification can be done "under the existential quantifiers." Let Prog be the primitive recurssive program above. Consider this Prolog goal

$$Prog >> \exists u.R(s(s(0)), b, u)$$

The first step is to unify $R(s(s(0)), b, u)$ against the head's of the program clauses. There are only two choices, one succeeds.

$$R(s(s(0)), b, u) \quad \text{unifies with}$$

$$R(s(z), y, h(z, v)).$$

The resulting substitution is $z := s(0), y := b\ ,\ u := h(s(0), v)$. We need to know whether there is a value for v. This generates a subgoal of the form

$$\exists v_2.R(s(0), b, v_2)$$

by backchaining on the second program clause. We can express the proof obligation by sequencing in this subgoal. The proof starts as

$$Prog >> \exists v.R(s(s(0)), b, v) \text{ by seq } \exists v_2.R(s(0), b, v_2$$

$$\begin{array}{ll} 1. & Prog, \exists v_2.R(s(0), b, v_2) >> \exists u.R(s(s(0)), b, u) \\ 2. & \qquad Prog \quad >> \exists v_2.R(s(0), b, v_2). \end{array}$$

Now the interesting point is that the entire first subgoal can be proved simply by elimination on $\exists V_2$ and backchaining. The first step results in the subgoal

$$Prog, \quad v_2 : N, \quad R(s(0), b, v_2) >> \exists u.R(s(s(0)), b, u).$$

Then we substitute properly in the second program clause (the rule is $\forall$-elimination) to obtain

$$Prog,\ v_2 : N,\ R(s(0), b, v_2),\ R(s(0), b, v_2) \Rightarrow R(s(s(0)), b, h(s(0), v_2) >> \exists u.\ R(s(s(0)), b, u).$$

Now we know that is we take u to be $h(s(0), v_2)$ the proof is finished by simple backchaining.

Notice that the definition of u as $h(s(0), v_2)$ is not complete until we know v_2, but finding it has been relegated to the second subgoal, and substituting it into $h(s(0), v_2)$ is part of the definition of the sequent rule. So the entire problem has h reduced to proving the second subgoal, and it *is of the exact same form* as the original goal. This means we can apply the same method. We call this method the *Prolog search procedure.*

In Nuprl this method can be coded as a *proof tactic*, so we can see Prolog evaluation as the result of trying a fixed tactic on goals of the form $Prog >> \exists v.B$. The tactic is guaranteed to generate only subgoals of this form; the other subgoals are automatically proved.

proof expressions in refinement logics Before we can discuss the role of logic variable in refinement logics we need to consider how the justification for the goal of a sequent can be written as an algebraic expression. First consider the simple case of a step taken by *and introduction.*

$$\begin{array}{ll} H >> & A\&B \text{ by intro} \\ & 1.\ H >> A \\ & 2.\ H >> B. \end{array}$$

Let us write after each proved sequent an expression that codes why it is true, that is how it was proved; call these *proof expressions.* If we are looking at a complete proof of $H >> A\&B$, then $H >> A$ is proved and so is $H >> B$. Suppose the proof expression for the first is a and for the second b. Then we can propagate up the proof tree an expression for $H >> A\&B$; we synthesize it out of expression for the subproofs. In this case we can take $pair(a; b)$ as the expression required; and we show these expressions as in this example

$$H >> A\&B \ : \ pair(a;b)$$
$$1.\ H >> A : a$$
$$2.\ H >> B : b.$$

We read the synthesis of proof expressions *bottom-up* and the subgoals top-down. Here are the rules for the Intuitionistic Predicate Calculus written with proof expressions indicated.

$H, x : A >> A : hyp(x)$

$H >> A\&B \ : \ pair(a;b)$
  $H >> A : a$
  $H >> B : b$

$H, s : A\&B >> G \ : \ spread(z; x, y, g)$
  $H, x : A, y : B >> G = g$

$H >> A \vee B : inl(a)$
  $H >> A : a$

---

or $H >> A \vee B \ : \ inr(b)$
  $H >> B : b$

$H, z : A \vee B >> G \ : \ decide(z; x.g_1; y.g_2)$
  $H,\ x : A >> G : g_1$
  $H, y : B >> G : g_2$

$H >> A \Rightarrow B \ : \ \lambda(x.b)$
  $H, x : A >> B : B$

$H, f : A \Rightarrow B >> G \ : op(f; a; y.g)$
  $H, f : A \Rightarrow B >> A : a$
  $H, y.B >> G : g$

$H, x : false >> G \ : \ any(x)$

$H >> G \quad seq(a; x.g)$
  $H >> A : a$
  $H,\ x : A >> g$

$H >> \exists x : A.B \ : \ pair(a;p)$
  $H >> A : a$
  $H >> B[a/x] : p$

$H, z : \exists x : A.B >> G \ : \ spread(z; x, y.g)$
  $H, xA, y : P >> G : g$

$H >> \forall x : A.B \ : \ \lambda(x.b)$
  $H, x : A >> B$

$H, f : \forall x : A.B >> G \ : \ op(f; a; y.g)$
  $H, f.\forall x : A.B >> A : a$
  $H, y.B >> G : g$

logic variables One approach to introducing logic variables into a refinement logic is suggested by looking at the existential introduction rule. If we want to introduce a variable as a witness for the quantifier, then it needs to be typed and "declared." There does not seem to be a natural way to do it in the pure logic, but in the presence of proof expression we can try this idea. We allow variables to range over these proof expressions. So a possible existential introduction rule is

$$\begin{aligned} H >> \ & \exists x : A.B \text{ by intro } X \\ & 1.\ H >> A : X \\ & 2.\ H >> P[X/x] \end{aligned}$$

The advantage of this approach is that X of this approach is that x is available in the entire proof tree, just as we want, without having to add it to the hypothesis lists. Also we need just two rules for using these variables. First we need a definition rule saying that X satisfies these conditions, and it is of type A and satisfies P. We also need a rule to refine it or specify its value further.

In order for this notion to be flexible enough, we nee to be able to indicate the dependence if X on variables declared in H. Then we could see X as a name for the function from H into A. So the complete account of logic variables must treat them as *second-order* variables. We write $X[z_i, \ldots, z_b]$ where z_i are declared in H. Now $X[\bar{z}]$ can be used in those contexts that provide the values needed for $\bar{z}$.

4 Shortcomings of type theories

1. Universe hierarchy

The hierarchy of universes arises because we cannot see a consistent way to enable the notion that Type is itself a type, say Type in Type. It appears to be an *ad hoc* mechanism. In the case of the original type theory of Russell, it was this feature of levels that made it so unappealing to mathematicians. In Principia Mathematica the notion of a real number was stratified among the levels so that there was no one type which captured that concept. In constructive type theories there are definitions of the reals which stay in the first universe, but there are others which get stratified. When this happens to a concept we feel that it is not being formalized properly, but that is a subjective judgement. So for example we can define the notion of a group as a type, G, with a unit,0, a binary operation, +, and a unary operation, −. If we take the carrier type, G, to be in U1, then we get only the notion of a "small group". This seems awkward although in Set Theory if we tried to take the class of all sets as the carrier of a group we would become aware that what we defined inside the set theory was only the notion of a relatively small group. So the question is one of convenience, how often do we need groups bigger than those in U1?

There are ways known to ameliorate this difficulty. In Lego [21, 31] there is a scheme to automatically keep track of the universe levels without the user having to write the index. Stuart Allen of Cornell has a theory of universes that is completely polymorphic, one does not ever write a specific universe. Recently we noticed at Cornell a way to use the reflection mechanism of Nuprl to provide a way to lift arguments from one universe to another when that is legal. So there are ways to improve handling of universes, but none has settled out as the correct answer.

2. Equalities abound

In Martin-Löf style type theories each type comes equipped with an equality. One might think that this gave enough of them to keep the most democratic type theorist happy, but alas, one of the most basic and useful ones is not expressible. We often want to express the idea that two programs are equal in all contexts regardless of type. For example, spread(pair(a;b);x,y.x) is equal to a regardless of whether or not this expression is well-typed because this spread term computes down to a. But if a is a nonsensical term, such as U1(2), then there is no way to write this computational equality.

Douglas Howe [19] has analyzed this computational equality and shown that it is a congruence relation on the type theory. So it is mathematically sensible. But as yet none of the type theories can express this idea inside. Nuprl comes the closest by allowing direct computation rules that permit the evaluation of a term in any context.

3. Model theory of Girard theories is daunting

The Martin-Löf type theories can all be explained in terms of a simple and elegant semantic model due to Stuart Allen [2]. This semantics is a powerful tool for assessing the consistency of proposed extensions and for proving relative consistency of the theories, as with constructive and classical set theories, and for explaining the theory from a mathematical perspective. The corresponding models for the Girard theories are much more difficult [references??], and one can question the foundational value of a theory whose semantics is not easily understood or whose consistency rests on a deep normalization theorem.

4. Theory size is still large

When we look at the type theories that are being used, they are large. In the case of Nuprl with reflection, there will be over a hundred rules. Is that too big? Who can say what is too big, but the interesting point is that much of Nuprl is generated by a few principles, say Martin-Löf's basic notion of type, Allen's semantic framework, the direct computation idea, the universe hierarchy, the use of a refinement logic, and the desire for a tactic-tree concept of proof. Extending the logic is a matter of generating the right syntax and rules based on these principles. The interesting question is whether or not we can isolate and formalize these deeper principles lying behind the type theories and then generate a specific "complete" theory from them. In a way this is the eternal struggle of logic, and it explains why it is good to see the variety of type theories now, from this variety will emerge a deeper set of principles.

Acknowledgements

I would like to thank Randy Pollack for many hours of stimulating discussions of type theory and especially for his help with formulating the concept of a logic variable. We may produce joint results on this topic in the near future showing how the concept defined here can be used to describe higher-order unification in a refinement logic.

References

[1] S. F. Allen. *A non-type-theoretic semantics for type-theoretic language.* PhD thesis, Cornell University, 1987.

[2] S. F. Allen. A non-type-theoretic definition of martin-löf's types. *Proc. of Second Symp. on Logics in Computer Science, IEEE*, pages 215–224., June 1987.

[3] P. Audebaud. Partial objects in the calculus of constructions. In *Sixth Symp. on Logic in Computer Science, IEEE*, Vrije University, Amsterdam, The Netherlands, 1991.

[4] D. Basin and R. Constable. Meta-logical frameworks. In *Proc. of the Second Workshop on Logical Frameworks*, Edinburgh, UK, June 1991.

[5] J. L. Bates. *A logic for correct program development.* PhD thesis, Cornell University, 1979.

[6] E. Bishop and D. Bridges. *Constructive Analysis.* NY:Springer-Verlag, 1985.

[7] W. Buchholtz et al. Iterated inductive definitions and subsystems of analysis. *Recent Proof-Theoretical Studies, Lecture Notes in Mathematics*, 897, 1981.

[8] R. Constable and N. Mendler. Recursive Definitions in Type Theory. In *Proc. of Logics of Prog. Conf.*, pages 61–78, January 1985. Cornell TR 85-659.

[9] R. Constable and S. F. Smith. Computational foundations of basic function theory. In *Third Symp. on Logic in Somp. Sci.* IEEE, 1988. (Cornell TR 88-904).

[10] R. L. Constable et al. *Implementing Mathematics with the Nuprl Development System.* NJ:Prentice-Hall, 1986.

[11] T. Coquand and G. Huet. The calculus of construction. *Information and Computation*, 76:95–120., 1988.

[12] S. Feferman. Formal theories for transfinite iterations of generalized inductive definitions and some subsystems of analysis. In *Proc. Conf. Intuitionism and Proof Theory*, pages 303–326, Buffalo, NY, 1970. North-Holland.

[13] J.-Y. Girard. Une extension de l'interpretation de godel a l'analyse, et son application a l'elimination des coupures dans l'analyse et la theorie des types. In *2nd Scandinavian Logic Symp.*, pages 63–69. NY:Springer-Verlag, 1971.

[14] J.-Y. Girard, Y. Lafont, and P. Taylor. *Proofs and Types.* Cambridge University Press, 1988.

[15] M. Gordon, R. Milner, and C. Wadsworth. Edinburgh LCF: a mechanized logic of computation. *Lecture Notes in Computer Science*, 78, 1979.

[16] T. Griffin. A formulas-as-types notion of control. In *POPL*, 1990.

[17] S. Hayashi and H. Nakano. *PX: A Computational Logic.* Foundations of Computing. MIT Press, Cambridge, MA, 1988.

[18] D. J. Howe. *Automating Reasoning in an Implementation of Constructive Type Theory.* PhD thesis, Cornell University, 1988.

[19] D. J. Howe. Equality in lazy computation systems. *Proc. Fourth Symp. Logic in Computer Science, IEEE*, 1989.

[20] J. Lipton. Logic programming in the nuprl type theory environment. Technical report, Cornell University, Ithaca, NY, 1991. To appear as a technical report, summer 1991.

[21] Z. Luo. Ecc, an extended calculus of construction. In *Proc. Fourth Symp. on Logics in Computer Science, IEEE*, Washington, DC, June 1989.

[22] P. Martin-Lof. An intuitionistic theory of types: predicative part. In *Logic Colloquium '73.*, pages 73–118. Amsterdam:North-Holland, 1973.

[23] P. Martin-Lof. Constructive mathematics and computer programming. In *Sixth International Congress for Logic, Methodology, and Philosophy of Science*, pages 153–75. Amsterdam:North Holland, 1982.

[24] P. Mendler. Recursive Types and Type Constraints in Second-Order Lambda Calculus. *Proc. in Second Symp. on Logic in Comp. Sci., IEEE*, pages 30–36, June 1987.

[25] P. Mendler. *Inductive Definition in Type Theory.* PhD thesis, Cornell University, Ithaca, NY, 1988.

[26] C. Murthy. *Extracting Constructive Content for Classical Proofs.* PhD thesis, Cornell University, Dept. of Computer Science, 1990. TR 89-1151.

[27] C. Murthy. An evaluation semantics for classical proofs. In *LICS, '91*, Amsterdam, The Netherlands, July 1991.

[28] C. Murthy and J. Russell. A constructive proof of higman's lemma. Technical Report TR 89-1049, Cornell University, Ithaca, NY 14853, January 1989.

[29] B. Nordstrom, K. Peterson, and J. Smith. *Programming in Martin-Lof's Type Theory.* Oxford Sciences Publication, Oxford, 1990.

[30] C. Paulin-Mohring. *Extraction in the calculus of constructions.* PhD thesis, University of Paris VII, 1989.

[31] R. Pollack. Lego user's guide. Technical report, University of Edinburgh, 1990.

[32] S. Smith. *Partial Objects in Type Theory.* PhD thesis, Cornell University, Ithaca, NY, 1989.

[33] S. F. Smith and R. L. Constable. Partial objects in constructive type theory. In *Symposium on Logic in Computer Science.*, pages 183–93. Washington, D.C.:IEEE., 1987.

[34] R. M. Smullyan. *First–Order Logic.* Springer–Verlag, New York, 1968.

[35] J. Underwood. A constructive completeness proof for the intuitionistic propositional calculus. Technical report, Cornell University, 1990.

What is in a Step: On the Semantics of Statecharts *

A. Pnueli † M. Shalev ‡
Department of Applied Mathematics and Computer Science
The Weizmann Institute of Science
Rehovot 76100, Israel
amir@wisdom.weizmann.ac.il

Abstract

This paper presents a proposal for the definition of a step in the execution of a statechart. The proposed semantics maintains the *synchrony hypothesis*, by which the system is infinitely faster than its environment, and can always finish computing its response before the next stimulus arrives. However, it corrects some inconsistencies present in previous definitions, by requiring global consistency of the step.

1 Introduction

The language of Statecharts has been proposed by D. Harel [3] as a visual language for the specification and modeling of *reactive systems.* While the (graphical) syntax of the language has been firmed up quite early, the definition of its formal semantics proved to be more difficult than originally expected. These difficulties may be explained as resulting from several requirements that seem to be desirable in a specification language for reactive systems, but yet may conflict with one another in some interpretations. Below, we list and shortly discuss each of these basic requirements.

To illustrate the discussed points we will use a restricted subset of the statechart syntax. The basic reaction of the system to external stimuli (events) is performed by *transitions.* Transitions in the system are graphically represented by arrows connecting

---

*A preliminary version of this paper appeared in [10]

†Research supported in part by the European Community ESPRIT project 937 (DESCARTES) and Basic Research Action Project 3096 (SPEC). This paper has been written while the author was visiting INRIA-IRISA, Rennes, France, whose hospitality is most gratefully acknowledged.

‡Research done as part of a M.Sc. thesis at the Weizmann Institute.

one state to another, and are labeled by a *label* which typically has the form e/a. In such a label, the *event* e *triggers* (enables) the transition, i.e., allows it to be taken. The optional *action* a is performed when the transition is actually taken. Typically, the action has the form $g_1, \ldots, g_m$, which means that events $g_1, \ldots, g_m$ are *generated* by the transition when it is taken. Two transitions may be *parallel* to one another (also referred to as *orthogonal*), which means that they can be performed in the same step. Alternately, two transitions may be *conflicting*, e.g., if they depart from the same state, and then, at most one of them can be taken at any given step.

Synchrony Hypothesis

One of the main requirements one may wish to associate with a specification language for reactive systems is the *synchrony hypothesis*, formulated by Berry [1]. This hypothesis assumes that the system is infinitely faster than the environment and, hence, the response to an external stimulus is always generated in the same step that the stimulus is introduced. We may view this hypothesis as stating that the response is always simultaneous with the stimulus. We remind the reader that a long sequence of internal communications may be required to generate the outgoing response.

For example, we may have a set of parallel transitions with the following labels:

$$t_0\colon a/e_1 \quad t_1\colon e_1/e_2 \;\ldots\; t_n\colon e_n/b$$

An external incoming stimulus represented by event a causes transition t_0 to be activated and generate event e_1. In turn, transition t_1 responds to e_1 by generating e_2. This chain reaction continues until transition t_n responds to e_n by generating b, which may be the final response of the system. According to the synchrony hypothesis, b (and $e_1, \ldots, e_n$) are all generated in the same step in which the event a is presented to the system.

The synchrony hypothesis is an abstraction that limits the interference that may occur in the time period separating the stimulus from the response and, hence, provides a guaranteed response as a primitive construct. In later stages of the development of the system, a more realistic modeling of the actual implementation can be done by introducing explicit delay elements if necessary.

Yet, Retaining Causality

In spite of the simultaneity abstraction, we should retain the distinction between cause and effect.

Consider for example the case that no external stimulus is given, and the system has two ready parallel transitions, with labels

$$t_1\colon a/b \qquad t_2\colon b/a$$

In principle, one may consider a semantics in which both transitions are taken while generating the events a and b. The justification for taking transition t_1 with trigger a is that a is generated by transition t_2 at the same step. Similarly, the generation of b by t_1 justifies taking t_2.

This is a situation we like to exclude. The principle of causality requires that there is a clear causal ordering among the transitions taken in a step, such that no transition t relies for its activation on events generated by transitions appearing later than t in the causal ordering.

Expressing Priorities

An important feature of specification formalisms for real-time and reactive systems is the ability to assign *priorities* to responses.

Assume, for example, a system with two conflicting transitions with labels

$$t_1 \colon a \qquad t_2 \colon b$$

Note that when a transition does not generate any events, we omit the separator '/' from its label.

We may consider t_1 to be a response to the event a while t_2 is a response to the event b. In the (probably infrequent) case that both a and b occur in the same step, the response is chosen non-deterministically. In many cases we may want to stipulate that, in the case both a and b occur, the response to b should have the higher priority. In Statecharts, this is expressed by using the *negation* of events. The general syntax of labels allows a *triggering expression* which is a boolean expression over events. In the simplified syntax we consider here, a triggering expression has the form $\ell_1 \cdots \ell_k$, where each ℓ_i is a *literal* that can be an event or a negation of an event. Negation of event a is denoted by $\overline{a}$. This expression is interpreted as a conjunction of the literals, requiring all of them to hold.

The labels

$$t_1 \colon a \cdot \overline{b} \qquad t_2 \colon b$$

ensure that if a or b occur exclusively then, as before, t_1 or t_2 is taken, respectively. However, if a and b occur together in the same step, then only t_2 can be taken.

The three requirements listed above, i.e., *synchrony, causality,* and *priorities*, led to the semantics defined in [5].

The basic approach presented in [5] is that the behavior of a statechart is described as a sequence of *steps*, each step leading from one stable configuration to the next. The environment may introduce new external events at the beginning of each step. The response of the system to these input events is built up of a sequence of *micro-steps.* The first micro-step consists of all the transitions that are triggered by the input events. Subsequent micro-steps consist of all the transitions triggered by the set of events containing the input events, as well as all the events generated by previous micro-steps. Since there are only finitely many transitions that can be taken in a step, the sequence of micro-steps always terminates when there are no additional enabled transitions. This concludes a single step, and the set of events generated in any of the micro-steps is defined as the events generated during this step. It is not difficult to see that all the three requirements of *synchrony, causality* and expressing *priorities* via negations of events, are satisfied by the [5] semantics. It also has the distinct advantage of being computationally feasible, which implies existence of an efficient implementation.

Unfortunately, the approach presented in [5] has several deficiencies. The main ones are that it is highly operational, strongly depends on the ordering between micro-steps, and does not possess the property of *global consistency.* To illustrate the last point, consider two parallel transitions with the labels

$$t_1 : \overline{a}/b \qquad t_2 : b/a$$

The semantics of [5] constructs for this case the step $\{t_1, t_2\}$, even when there are no external input events. This step generates the events $\{a, b\}$. To see how this step is generated, consider an initially empty set of present events $E = \phi$. Since $a \notin E$, t_1 is enabled, and the first micro-step takes t_1, generating b which is added to E. In the next micro-step, $b \in E$ and t_2 is taken, generating a.

One may complain that this step is not globally consistent, because it includes both the event a and the transition t_1, whose triggering condition requires that a is not generated during the current step. We refer to this phenomenon as *global* inconsistency, since the sequence of micro-steps, consisting of $\{t_1\}$ followed by $\{t_2\}$, is *locally* consistent. It is justified to take t_1 in the first micro-step and t_2 in the second micro-step, since they are both enabled at these points. It is only when we sum the effect of the complete sequence, that the inconsistency is discovered.

Well defined programming and specification languages usually possess two types of semantics. An *operational* semantics defines the behavior of a program or a specification in terms of a sequence of simple and atomic *operations.* It usually provides important guidelines for the implementor of the execution engine of such programs or specifications (compiler or interpreter). The other type of semantics is a *declarative* one, which bases the definition of the meaning of a program on some kind of equational theory (using fixpoints for iteration and recursion), and attempts to ignore operational details such as order of execution, etc. We have intentionally avoided using the term *denotational* semantics which implies *compositionality* in addition to declarativity.

The declarative semantics, being based on simpler mathematical principles, is the one that underlies formal reasoning about programs and specifications, such as comparing two programs for equivalence or inclusion.

A proven sign of healthy and robust understanding of the meaning of a programming or a specification language is the possession of both an operational and declarative semantics, which are consistent with one another. Based on this criterion, our first attempt was to define a declarative semantics consistent with the operational semantics of [5]. We soon found out that one of the main requisites for a declarative semantics is global consistency which is absent from [5].

The present paper attempts to achieve the goal of assigning mutually consistent operational and declarative semantics to the specification language of Statecharts. The resulting operational semantics differs from that of [5] in some situations.

As seen below, the declarative semantics is based on fixpoints as is often the case. However, in the case considered here, the situation is more complex because, due to the presence of negations, the right hand side of the fixpoint equation is, in general, non-monotonic.

Anticipating the formal development below, the basic fixpoint equation associated with a step is

$$T = En(T)$$

In this equation, T is a set of transitions which are candidates for being taken together in a step. The function $En(T)$ yields the transitions which are consistent with the transitions in T and are triggered by the events generated by the transitions T. We can translate each of the requirements listed above into a condition on the solution T^* which is an acceptable set of transitions that can be jointly taken in a step.

- **Synchrony Hypothesis.** This requirement can be represented by the condition

  $$En(T^*) \subseteq T^*,$$

  which states that all the transitions triggered by the events generated by T^* and consistent with T^* are already in T^*. This implies that T^* is *maximal* in the sense that no additional transitions can be taken in this step.

- **Causality.** This is represented by the requirement of *inseparability* expressed by the requirement that there exists no $T \subset T^*$, such that

  $$En(T) \cap (T - T^*) = \phi$$

  This means that if we try to stop at any subset T which is strictly contained in T^*, there is always an additional enabled transition in $T - T^*$ that can be added to T. In the usual case of monotonic operators this corresponds to *minimality.*

- **Expressing Priorities.** This is provided by allowing negations of events in the triggering expressions.

- **Global Consistency.** This is represented by the condition

  $$T^* \subseteq En(T^*),$$

  which states that each transition in T^* is enabled on the *complete* set of transitions T^*.

The main concerns considered in this paper are not unique to Statecharts, and have to be faced by any language intended for the specification of reactive systems, such as *Esterel* [1] and *Lustre* [2]. These two languages have also adopted the principles of *synchrony, causality* and *global consistency.* However, they avoid the complex interplay between non-determinism and priorities, present in Statecharts, by ruling out as illegal any program giving rise to these problems.

We should realize that this paper considers only the *micro-semantics* of statecharts, by defining the fine structure of a single step. Single steps can be combined into an operational semantics, following the treatment of [5]. We refer the reader to [8], where a denotational semantics for some versions of the operational semantics is considered, and to [7], [6] for a comparative discussion of the different factors determining the semantics of a reactive language.

An interesting recent development is presented by the language *Argos* [9]. This visual language is a simpler dialect of Statecharts which is distinguished by a more modular structure. The paper [9] presents a *compositional* semantics for *Argos*, which can also be adopted for Statecharts. The main difference between the simple semantics presented in [9] and the semantics presented here is in the treatment of causality issues. A typical distinguishing example is the pair of parallel transitions

$$t_1\colon\ a/b \qquad t_2\colon\ b/a.$$

In the absence of external stimuli and the assumption that events a and b are internal, the semantics of [9] will take $\{t_1, t_2\}$ as a step, while the semantics presented here identifies ϕ as the only possible step.

A preliminary version of this paper appeared in [10].

2 An Informal Introduction to Statecharts

It is beyond the scope of this paper to present a full description of the visual language of statecharts and examples of its use. We refer the reader to [3] and [4] for such a presentation.

However, we will illustrate the basic concepts of the language on the single example of a Binary Stopwatch, presented in Fig. 1.

The specification of the watch consists of a single all encompassing state, called *Binary_Stopwatch.* The activity of the watch is partitioned into the two modes *ShowTime* and *Stopwatch.* The system switches between these two states at the occurrence of the event a which may represent a user pressing some button on the watch.

When entering the *Stopwatch* mode, the systems moves to the initial state *Off*, intended to represent the state in which the stopwatch is not running and counting time yet. When the user presses button b, the system moves to state *On*, which represents

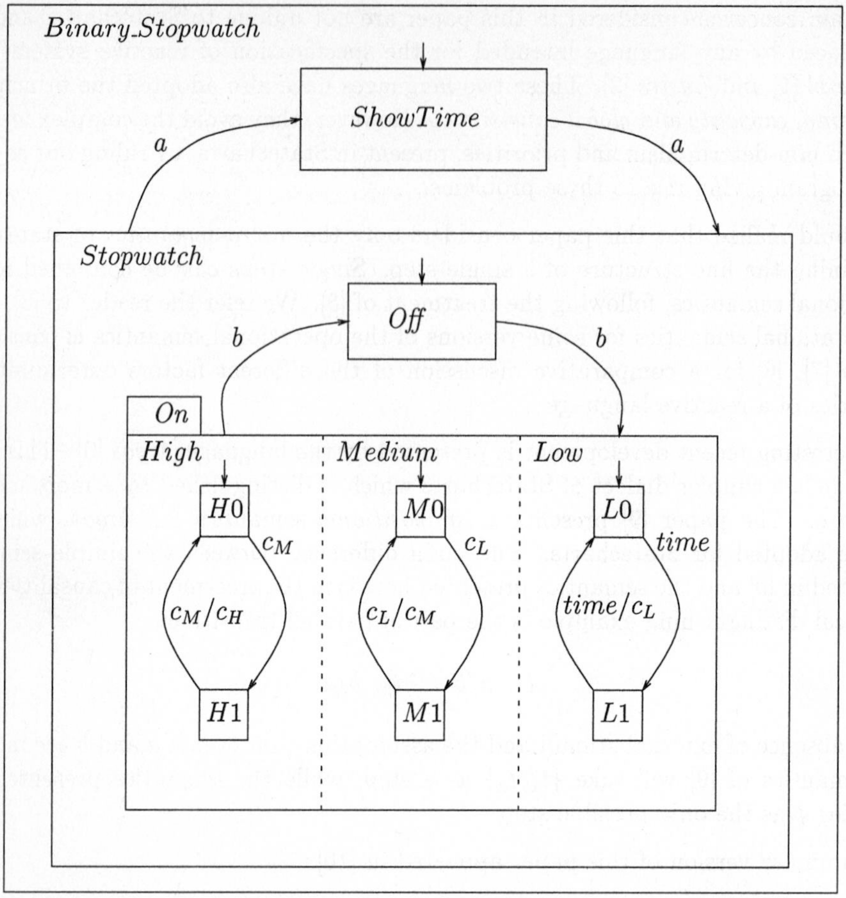

Figure 1: A Binary Stopwatch.

the time counting activity. State *On* is an *and*-state, consisting of the three parallel substates: *Low*, *Medium*, and *High*, intended to represent three bits of a binary counter. Each of these single bit counters can be in a 0 or in a 1 mode. Initially, they are all set to the 0 mode.

Counting is triggered by the external input *time*. Whenever the event *time* occur, state *Low* responds by switching between its two internal modes. If it moves from $L1$ to $L0$, it emits at the same time the output signal c_L, signifying a carry from the low position to the medium position. On receiving the c_L signal, state *Medium* responds by switching between its own modes. On moving from $M1$ to $M0$, the signal c_M is emitted. All these internal reactions are taking place at the same step that the external event *time* occurs.

If, at any point of this activity, the user presses either the *b* or the *a* button, the system immediately stops what it is currently doing (preemption) and moves to state *Off* or *ShowTime*, respectively.

3 Syntax

In this section we present a precise syntax for statecharts and introduce some notations that are used in the following sections. The syntax presented here is based on the syntax that was introduced in [5] with necessary modifications due to the special approach we adopted here to the semantics of statecharts. To simplify the presentation, we consider first a restricted version of the syntax. Some of the restrictions will be later removed.

A Statechart is a structure consisting of the components

$$\langle \Pi, S, \mathcal{T}, r, V \rangle$$

where

- Π is a set of *primitive events.*
- S is a set of *states.*
- $\mathcal{T}$ is a set of *transitions.*
- $r \in S$ is the *root* state.
- V is a set of *variables.* For the restricted syntax considered first, $V = \phi$.

States and Their Structure

The set of states S represents both basic states and composite states which contain other states as substates. There are three functions which describe structural relations between states.

The function *children* : $S \rightarrow 2^S$ defines for each state the set of its children (immediate substates). A state s is called *basic* if $children(s) = \phi$. Otherwise it is called *composite.* We denote by *Basic* the set of basic states. For $s_2 \in children(s_1)$, we say that s_1 is a *parent* of s_2 and that s_2 is a *child* of s_1. There exists a unique state $r \in S$ which has no parent, i.e., such that $\forall s \in S$, $r \notin children(s)$. This state r is called the *root* of the statechart.

We define *children** and *children*$^+$, the reflexive-transitive and transitive closures of *children*, by

$$children^* = \bigcup_{i \geq 0} children^i(s) \quad \text{and} \quad children^+ = \bigcup_{i \geq 1} children^i(s),$$

where $children^0(s) = \{s\}$, $children^1(s) = children(s)$ and, for each $i \geq 1$,

$$children^{i+1}(s) = \bigcup_{s' \in children(s)} children^i(s').$$

The function *children** can be extended to *sets of states* by defining, for a set $X \subseteq S$,

$$children^*(X) = \bigcup_{s \in X} children^*(s).$$

For $s_2 \in children^*(s_1)$, we say that s_1 is an *ancestor* of s_2 and that s_2 is a *descendant* of s_1. Note that s is both an ancestor and a descendant of itself. If s_1 is either an ancestor or a descendant of s_2, we say that s_1 and s_2 are *ancestrally related.* For $s_2 \in children^+(s_2)$ we say that s_1 is a *strict ancestor* of s_2 and that s_2 is a *strict descendant* of s_1.

It is required that the root r is an ancestor of every state $s \in S$ and that any state, except the root, has a single parent. This leads to the fact that the childhood relation arranges the states of a statechart in a tree with root r, whose leaves are the basic states and whose intermediate nodes are the composite states.

The function $type : S \rightarrow \{and, or\}$ is a partial function that assigns to each composite state its type, and identifies it as either an *or*-state or an *and*-state. If $children(s) \neq \phi$ and $type(s) = or$ then $children(s)$ is an (exclusive) *or*-decomposition of s, i.e., when the system is in the state s it is in one and only one of its immediate substates (descendants). If $children(s) \neq \phi$ and $type(s) = and$ then $children(s)$ is an *and*-decomposition of s, i.e., when the system is in the state s it is simultaneously in all of its immediate substates. The function *type* is undefined on basic states. It is required that the root r be an *or*-state.

The function $default : S \rightarrow S$ identifies for each *or*-state s one of its immediate descendants $default(s) \in children(s)$ as the *default state.* The intended meaning of the default state $default(s)$, is that any transition that enters state s, also causes $default(s)$ to be entered.

In the table of Fig. 2, we present the states of the Binary Stopwatch statechart with their *children*, *type*, and *default* parameters.

Orthogonal States and Sets of States

The following definitions are taken from [5].

- For a set of states $X \subseteq S$, the *Least Common Ancestor* of X, denoted by $lca(X)$ is defined to be the state x such that
  - $X \subseteq children^*(x)$.
  - For every other $s \in S$, such that $X \subseteq children^*(s)$, it follows that $x \in children^*(s)$.

  It is not difficult to see that, for any statechart, there exists a unique least common ancestor for every set of states $X \subseteq S$.

  For example, the least common ancestor of states *M*1 and *Off* of Fig. 1 is the state *Stopwatch*.

State	children	type	default
Binary_Stopwatch	$\{ShowTime, Stopwatch\}$	*or*	*ShowTime*
ShowTime	ϕ	Basic	
Stopwatch	$\{Off, On\}$	*or*	*Off*
Off	ϕ	Basic	
On	$\{High, Medium, Low\}$	*and*	
High	$\{H0, H1\}$	*or*	*H0*
Medium	$\{M0, M1\}$	*or*	*M0*
Low	$\{L0, L1\}$	*or*	*L0*
H0	ϕ	Basic	
H1	ϕ	Basic	
M0	ϕ	Basic	
M1	ϕ	Basic	
L0	ϕ	Basic	
L1	ϕ	Basic	

Figure 2: Table of States and Their Parameters.

- Two states x, y are *orthogonal*, denoted by $x \perp y$, if x and y are not ancestrally related and their *lca* is an *and*-state.

  For example, states $M1$ and $L0$ of Fig. 1 are orthogonal, but states $M0$ and *Off* are not, and neither are $M0$ and *On* even though their least common ancestor is the *and*-state *On*.

- A set of states X, is called an *orthogonal set* if, for every $x, y \in X$, either $x = y$ or $x \perp y$. Note that the singleton set $\{x\}$ is always an *orthogonal* set.

  For example, $\{H0, M1, L0\}$ is an orthogonal set.

- A set of states $X \subseteq S$ is called *consistent* if, for every two states $s_1, s_2 \in X$, either s_1 and s_2 are ancestrally related, or $s_1 \perp s_2$. A consistent set X is called *maximally consistent* if, for every state $s \in S - X$, $X \cup \{s\}$ is not consistent. We refer to a maximally consistent subset of S as a *configuration* of the statechart. Configurations are intended to represent the global state of a statechart.

  For example, the set $\{H1, Low, Stopwatch\}$ is a consistent set, and the set $\{Binary\_Stopwatch, Stopwatch, On, High, Medium, Low, H1, M0, L0\}$ is a configuration.

- Let X be a consistent set. The *default completion* of X, denoted by *completion*(X), is the configuration Y containing X such that, for every *or*-state $s \in Y$, if $X \cap$ *children*$(s) = \phi$ then *default*$(s) \in Y$. It can be shown that the above requirement identifies a unique configuration Y.

  For example, the default completion of the consistent set $\{H1, Low, Stopwatch\}$ is the configuration

  $$\{Binary\_Stopwatch, Stopwatch, On, High, Medium, Low, H1, M0, L0\}.$$

- The *initial configuration* X_0, is the default completion of the root r.

  For example, {*Binary_Stopwatch*, *ShowTime*} is the initial configuration of the Binary Stopwatch statechart of Fig. 1.

Transitions

There are several functions which identify the parameters of transitions.

For each transition $t \in \mathcal{T}$, $source(t)$ identifies a non-empty set of *source states*, from which the transition departs. In a graphical representation, the transition is drawn as a composite arrow that may have several heads and several tails that must eventually share a common stem. The set of states from which the various tails depart is $source(t)$.

Consider, for example, the statechart presented in Fig. 3. Transition t_1 is represented by a composite arrow, whose tails are C_2 and D_2, and whose heads are G_1, H_1, and I_1. Consequently $source(t_1) = \{C_2, D_2\}$.

Symmetrically, $target(t)$ identifies the set of *target states*, which are represented graphically as the states to which the heads connect. It is required that both $source(t)$ and $target(t)$ be orthogonal sets.

For example, $target(t_1) = \{G_1, H_1, I_1\}$.

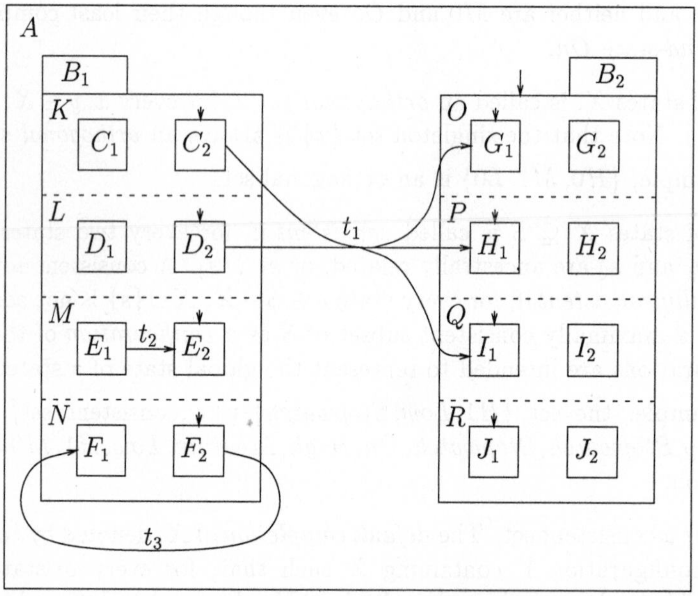

Figure 3: Transitions and Their Arenas.

The *arena* of a transition t, denoted by $arena(t)$, identifies an *or*-state which contains both $source(t)$ and $target(t)$. Graphically, the arena is represented as the smallest *or*-state which contains all parts of the transition. The intention is that this is the minimal context that contains all the changes caused by the transition. Usually the arena is the smallest *or*-state containing $source(t) \cup target(t)$, but there are exceptional cases.

Thus the arenas of transitions t_1, t_2, and t_3, of Fig. 3 are A, M, and A, respectively, even though the smallest common *or*-ancestor containing $source(t_3) \cup target(t_3) = \{F_1, F_2\}$ is N.

The *trigger* of a transition t, denoted by $trigger(t)$, consists (in the restricted syntax considered at this stage) of a set of literals $\ell_1 \cdots \ell_k$, $k \geq 0$, each of which is either a primitive event $e \in \Pi$, or the negation $\overline{e}$ of such an event. Given a set of events $E \subseteq \Pi$, we say that transition t is *triggered* by E if $e \in E$, for each $e \in trigger(t)$, and $e \notin E$ for each $\overline{e} \in trigger(t)$. Denote by $triggered(E)$ the set of transitions that are triggered by E.

Considering transitions in Fig. 1, the triggers of transitions $Stopwatch \rightarrow ShowTime$, $L0 \rightarrow L1$, and $H1 \rightarrow H0$, are the single events a, $time$, and c_M, respectively.

The *action set* of a transition, denoted by $actions(t)$, is a set of events $g_1, \ldots, g_m$, where $g_i \in \Pi$, for $i = 1, \ldots, m$. The intended meaning of this set is that, when transition t is taken, it generates the events $g_1, \ldots, g_m$. For a set of transitions T, we denote by $generated(T)$ the set

$$generated(T) = \bigcup_{t \in T} actions(t).$$

Graphically, the trigger and action sets of a transition t are represented by labeling the transition by the label

$$t: \ \ell_1 \cdots \ell_k / g_1, \ldots, g_m$$

where the transition name t is often omitted.

For example, the action sets of transitions $L1 \rightarrow L0$ and $H1 \rightarrow H0$ of Fig. 1 are $\{c_L\}$ and $\{c_M\}$, respectively, while $M0 \rightarrow M1$ has an empty action set.

Relations Between Transitions

Transitions t_1 and t_2 are said to be *consistent* if either $t_1 = t_2$ or

$$arena(t_1) \perp arena(t_2).$$

Otherwise, t_1 and t_2 are said to be *in conflict.* Note that every transition is consistent with itself.

A set of transitions T is said to be a *consistent set* if t_1 and t_2 are consistent, for every $t_1, t_2 \in T$. Denote by $consistent(T)$ the set of all transitions that are consistent with every $t \in T$.

For example, transitions $L0 \rightarrow L1$ and $H1 \rightarrow H0$ in Fig. 1 are consistent, but $L0 \rightarrow L1$ and $Stopwatch \rightarrow ShowTime$ are not.

4 The Enabling Function *En*

Consider a fixed configuration C and a set of primitive events $I \subseteq \Pi$. Our main purpose is to define the set of transitions T that is taken in a single step in response to the external inputs I. As is implied by the concept of *micro-steps*, this step is built incrementally, by taking first transitions that are enabled by I which, when taken, generate additional events, enabling additional transitions, and so on.

Consequently, a key concept in the process of step construction is the enabling function $En(T)$, which assumes that we have already decided to take the set of transitions T, and identifies all transitions that are enabled as a result of that decision.

The function En is defined by

$$En(T) \;=\; relevant(C) \,\cap\, consistent(T) \,\cap\, triggered(I \cup generated(T))$$

As we see, this function is composed of the intersection of three sets of transitions. The set $relevant(C)$ is the set of all transitions, whose source sets are contained in the configuration C which is assumed to be fixed for the state and is independent of T. The set $consistent(T)$ selects out of this set only those transitions that are consistent with each $t \in T$. The last set is computed by taking the union of $generated(T)$ the set of all events generated by T and the initial inputs I, and checking which transitions are triggered by this set of events.

Consider, for example the configuration

$$C: \quad \{Binary\_Stopwatch, Stopwatch, On, H0, M1, L1\}$$

of Fig. 1. Note that, to provide a non-redundant identification of C, it is sufficient to specify that it contains $H0, M1$, and $L1$. The transitions relevant to C are

$$Stopwatch \rightarrow ShowTime,\;\; On \rightarrow Off,\;\; H0 \rightarrow H1,\;\; M1 \rightarrow M0,\;\; L1 \rightarrow L0.$$

Consider the set of input events $I = \{a, time\}$, and assume that we have already decided to take $T = \{L1 \rightarrow L0\}$. Then, the set $consistent(T)$ is given by

$$\{L1 \rightarrow L0,\;\; M0 \rightarrow M1,\;\; M1 \rightarrow M0,\;\; H0 \rightarrow H1,\;\; H1 \rightarrow H0\}.$$

Note that $L0 \rightarrow L1$ is in conflict with $L1 \rightarrow L0$. The set of events $I \cup generated(T)$ is $\{a, time, c_L\}$. The set $triggered(I \cup generated(T))$ is given by

$$\begin{array}{ll} \{ & L0 \rightarrow L1,\;\; L1 \rightarrow L0,\;\; M0 \rightarrow M1,\;\; M1 \rightarrow M0, \\ & Stopwatch \rightarrow ShowTime,\;\; ShowTime \rightarrow Stopwatch \quad \}. \end{array}$$

The intersection of the three sets yield

$$\{L1 \rightarrow L0,\;\; M1 \rightarrow M0\}$$

as the set $En(\{L1 \rightarrow L0\})$.

The Concavity Property

An important property of the enabling function *En* is that it is *concave*. We study here some of the properties of concave functions.

Let X and Y be two domains. A function $f : 2^X \mapsto 2^Y$ is called concave if, for every X_1, X_2, and X_3, such that $X_1 \subseteq X_2 \subseteq X_3 \subseteq X$, it follows that

$$f(X_1) \cap f(X_3) \quad \subseteq \quad f(X_2)$$

We observe first that if f and g are concave functions, then so is their intersection $f \cap g$. This is based on

$$(f(X_1) \cap g(X_1)) \cap (f(X_3) \cap g(X_3)) = (f(X_1) \cap f(X_3)) \cap (g(X_1) \cap g(X_3)) \subseteq f(X_2) \cap g(X_2).$$

A function $f : 2^X \mapsto 2^Y$ is called *monotonically decreasing* if, for every $X_1 \subseteq X_2$, it follows that $f(X_1) \supseteq f(X_2)$. It is not difficult to show that a monotonically decreasing function is concave. Assuming that f is a monotonically decreasing function, we observe that, for $X_1 \subseteq X_2 \subseteq X_3$, it follows that

$$f(X_1) \cap f(X_3) = f(X_3) \subseteq f(X_2).$$

Obviously, *relevant*(C), being independent of T, is concave. The function *consistent*(T) is clearly monotonically decreasing, and hence is concave. Since concavity is closed under intersection, it only remains to show that *triggered*$(I \cup$ *generated*$(T))$ is a concave function of T. As $I \cup$ *generated*(T) is monotonically increasing in T, it is sufficient to show that *triggered*(E) is a concave function from 2^{Π} to $2^{\mathcal{T}}$. For that, it is enough to show that if $E_1 \subseteq E_2 \subseteq E_3$ are three sets of events, and a transition t is triggered by both E_1 and E_3, then it is also triggered by E_2. Consider any event $e \in$ *trigger*(t). Since $t \in$ *triggered*(E_1), it follows that $e \in E_1$ and therefore belongs also to $E_2 \supseteq E_1$. On the other hand, if $\overline{e} \in$ *trigger*(t) and t is triggered by E_3, then $e \notin E_3$. It follows that $e \notin E_2 \subseteq E_3$.

This shows that *En*(T) is a concave function of T.

5 Two Definitions of a Step

In this section we introduce two definitions of the sets of transitions that are considered to be admissible steps from a given configuration C in response to a set of external events I.

The first definition is operational and suggests a non-deterministic algorithm for computing all the possible steps. This approach resembles very much the micro-step approach presented in [5]. The second definition is declarative and is based on solving a fixpoint equation. We then show that, due to the property of concavity, the two definitions coincide.

An operational Definition

The operational definition is based on a non-deterministic procedure that constructs a step T, adding one transition at a time.

Procedure: STEP-CONSTRUCTION

1. *Initially* $T = \phi$.

2. *Compare* $En(T)$ *to* T.

   2.1 *If* $T = En(T)$ *terminate and report success.*

   2.2 *If* $T \subset En(T)$, *pick a transition* $t \in En(T) - T$ *and add it to* T. *Repeat step 2.*

   2.3 *Otherwise, i.e.,* $T \not\subseteq En(T)$, *report failure.*

A set T which can be obtained by a sequence of choices of transitions $t \in En(T) - T$ is called *constructible.*

A Declarative Definition

A set of transitions T is defined to be *separable* if there exists a subset $T' \subset T$, such that

$$En(T') \cap (T - T') = \phi.$$

A set T is called *inseparable* if it is not separable.

A set of transitions T which is inseparable and satisfies the equation

$$T = En(T)$$

is called an *admissible step* of the system.

We refer to such a set also as an *inseparable solution.*

Proposition :
A set of transitions T *is an inseparable solution to the equation* $T = En(T)$ *iff it is constructible.*

Proof : Assume that T_0 is an inseparable solution to the equation $T_0 = En(T_0)$. We will show that T_0 is constructible.

Apply procedure STEP-CONSTRUCTION, where only transitions from $(En(T) - T) \cap T_0$ are added to T in step *2.2*. We show:

The procedure cannot fail.

Initially $T = \phi$ which implies $T \subseteq En(T)$. Assume that the procedure fails after adding a transition t to some $T \subset T_0$. This implies that $T \subseteq En(T)$, but there exists some $t' \in T \cup \{t\}$ such that $t' \notin En(T \cup \{t\})$.

If $t' = t$ then, since $t \in (En(T) - T) \cap T_0$, it follows that $t' \in En(T)$. Otherwise, $t' \in T \subset En(T)$, which also leads to $t' \in En(T)$. Also, since $t' \in T \cup \{t\} \subseteq T_0$ and $T_0 = En(T_0)$, it follows that $t' \in En(T_0)$.

Thus, we have identified three sets of transitions, $T \subseteq T \cup \{t\} \subseteq T_0$, such that t' belongs to $En(T)$ and to $En(T_0)$, but does not belong to $En(T \cup \{t\})$. This contradicts the concavity property of the function En.

It follows that the procedure cannot fail.

The procedure cannot stop at $T \subset T_0$.

The procedure can stop at $T \subset T_0$, only if $(En(T) - T) \cap T_0 = En(T) \cap (T_0 - T) = \phi$, contradicting the fact that T_0 is inseparable.

To show the other direction, let T be a set obtained by procedure STEP-CONSTRUCTION. We show that T is an inseparable solution. Let the transitions in T be ordered in a sequence $t_1, t_2, \ldots, t_n$, according to the order of their addition to T. Clearly, since the construction stopped at T, we have that T satisfies

$$T = En(T).$$

It only remains to show that T is inseparable.

Consider any $T' \subset T$. Let t_k be the first transition, in the above ordering, which belongs to $T - T'$. We claim that $t_k \in En(T')$ which leads to the fact that $En(T') \cap (T - T') \neq \phi$. Assume to the contrary, that $t_k \notin En(T')$. Then we have three sets

$$T_1 = \{t_1, \ldots, t_{k-1}\}, \qquad T_2 = T', \qquad T_3 = T,$$

such that $T_1 \subseteq T_2 \subseteq T_3$, and yet

1. $t_k \in En(\{t_1, \ldots, t_{k-1}\})$
2. $t_k \notin En(T')$
3. $t_k \in En(T)$.

Claim 1 follows from the fact that procedure STEP-CONSTRUCTION picks transitions to be added only if they are enabled under the current approximation. Claim 2 is our contrary assumption. Claim 3 follows from the fact that $t_k \in T = En(T)$.

This contradicts again the property of concavity.

We must conclude that $En(T') \cap (T - T') \neq \phi$ for any $T' \subset T$, and hence T is inseparable. ∎

The Yield and Next Configuration of a Step

Let C be a configuration and T an admissible step from C. What are the effects of taking the step T? Obviously, taking T generates some output events of the system, which are its reaction to the inputs I. These events are given by

$$\mathit{Yield}(T) = \mathit{generated}(T).$$

The other effect of taking T is that it leads to a new global state (configuration) C'. This next configuration can be defined by

$$\mathit{NextConfig}(C,T) = \mathit{completion}((C - \bigcup_{t\in T} \mathit{children}^*(\mathit{arena}(t))) \cup \bigcup_{t\in T} \mathit{target}(t)).$$

Thus, the effect of each transition $t \in T$ on the configuration C is to remove from C all states that are among the descendants of $\mathit{arena}(t)$ and to add to C all the states that are in $\mathit{target}(t)$. This yields a partial configuration, whose default completion is the new configuration resulting from taking the step T.

For example, assume that C is the (unique) default completion of the consistent set of states $\{H0, M1, L1\}$. Let I consist of the single input event *time*. Then, the only possible step T contains the three transitions

$$\{L1 \rightarrow L0,\ M1 \rightarrow M0,\ H0 \rightarrow H1\},$$

which generate the additional events $\{c_L, c_M\}$. To compute the new configuration, we first subtract from C the arenas of the three transitions belonging to T and all of their children. The arenas are the states $High, Medium$, and Low, and altogether, this removes from C the states

$$\{High,\ H0,\ Medium,\ M1,\ Low,\ L1\}.$$

We then add to C the targets of the three transitions, which are $H1$, $M0$, and $L1$. Taking the default completion of this set, adds back the states $High$, $Medium$, and Low.

6 Extending the Syntax

The restricted syntax we have so far considered, in which the trigger of transition is a conjunction of literals, was specially designed to guarantee the property of concavity. Let us show that allowing more general event expressions as triggers, such as disjunctions of events, leads to the loss of concavity and of the equivalence between the operational and declarative definitions of a step.

Example : Consider the two consistent transitions

$$t_1 :\ (\overline{a} \vee b)/a \qquad \text{and} \qquad t_2 :\ a/b$$

under the external input set $I = \phi$.

This situation admits no constructible step. At the first micro-step, $T = E = \phi$. The only transition triggered at this stage is t_1, due to the fact that $a \notin E$. In the second micro-step, $En(\{t_1\}) = \{t_2\} \not\subseteq \{t_1\}$ and procedure STEP-CONSTRUCTION stops, reporting failure. Obviously, t_2 is triggered by $generated(t_1) = \{a\}$ but t_1 is not.

On the other hand, the set $T = \{t_1, t_2\}$ is an inseparable solution of the equation $T = En(T)$. Obviously, $generated(T) = \{a, b\}$, which triggers both t_1 and t_2. Also, T is inseparable, as can be seen by trying to separate it by any of ϕ, $\{t_1\}$, or $\{t_2\}$.

Extensions by Transition Splitting

It is still possible to accommodate more general event expressions, provided we give them a different interpretation.

Consider the example presented above, in which the trigger of t_1 is the disjunction $\overline{a} \vee b$. We interpret this set of candidate transitions as consisting of the *three* transitions

$$t'_1 : \overline{a}/a \qquad t''_1 : b/a \qquad t_2 : a/b$$

obtained by splitting transition t_1 into the two transitions t'_1 and t''_1. Now, all triggers obey our restricted syntax, and the declarative and operational definitions of a step will coincide. In the case of no external input events, both will fail to identify any possible step.

It is clear how to apply this idea to the general case in which we allow arbitrary boolean expressions over Π as triggers of transitions. A boolean expression *exp* which is the trigger for transition t can be expanded into a disjunctive normal form $exp = e_1 \vee \cdots \vee e_m$, where each e_i is a conjunction of literals. Transition t can then be split into the m transitions

$$t_1 : e_1/a, \quad \ldots, \quad t_m : e_m/a,$$

where a is the action set $actions(t)$.

Implicitly Generated Events

All the events we considered so far are primitive events belonging to Π. There are some events that are implicitly generated by entering and exiting states without having to list them explicitly in the action set of a transition. The syntax of two such *implicit events* is

$$entered(s) \qquad \text{and} \qquad exited(s),$$

for some state $s \in S$.

Being in a configuration C, transition t generates event $exited(s)$, for every $s \in C \cap children^+(arena(t))$. That is, each strict descendant of $arena(t)$ which is active in C is considered to be *exited* when t is taken.

Transition t generates event $entered(s)$, for every s such that $s \in completion(target(t)) \cap children^+(arena(t))$. That is, each strict descendant of $arena(t)$ which is in the default completion of $target(s)$ is considered to be *entered* when t is taken.

We extend the syntax by allowing the events $entered(s)$ and $exited(s)$ to appear in the trigger expression of transitions.

Conditions

An important extension of the syntax admits triggering expressions of the form $e[c]$, where e is an event expression consisting of a conjunction of event literals, and c is a *boolean expression*. As a first step, boolean expressions are built out of the basic predicate $in(s)$ for an arbitrary state $s \in S$. For a given configuration C, we say that $in(s)$ *holds over* C, denoted by $C \models in(s)$, iff $s \in C$. It is clear how an arbitrary boolean condition over in predicates can be evaluated over a configuration C.

Given a configuration C, a set of events E, and a transition t with trigger $e[c]$, we add to the definition of t being triggered by E at C, the requirement $C \models c$.

Such conditions can be used, for example, to reduce multiple-source transitions, such as t_1 in Fig. 3, to a single-source transition. We can, for example, draw t_1 as having only D_2 as a single source, but add to its trigger (which is not given in that figure) the condition $[in(C_2)]$. This has the effect that the transition can be taken only if both C_2 and D_2 are active in the configuration.

Variables and Assignments

The most significant and enriching extension of the syntax is to allow variables of arbitrary types and assignments to them.

We sketch below the extensions that are necessary to accommodate these extensions. We illustrate these concepts on variables ranging over the domain of natural numbers $\mathcal{N}$. The extensions to additional data domains is straightforward.

Syntax of Operations on Data

The following are added to the syntax:

- The action set of transitions may contain *assignments* having the form $y := exp$, where $y \in V$ is a variable, and exp is an arithmetical expression over the natural numbers.

- The condition part of a triggering expression may contain predicates over natural numbers.

- The event part of a triggering expression may contain the special event *assigned*(y) for any variable $y \in V$.

For example, the transition

$$t: \ (\neg \mathit{assigned}(y))[y > 0]/(y := y - 1),$$

is intended as a representation of a semaphore. It is enabled in a step only if $y$is positive and no previous transition in the same step has assigned any value to variable y. When taken, transition t subtracts 1 from y, and implicitly generates the event *assigned*(y).

We strengthen the definition of consistent transitions by defining as inconsistent any two transitions that have in their actions sets assignments to the same variable .

Semantic Extensions

The notion of the global state of a system is extended to consist of a pair $\langle C, St\rangle$, where C is a configuration and St is a *store*, which is a mapping from V to $\mathcal{N}$.

Given a global state and a set of events E, we extend the definition of a transition with label $e[c]/a$ being triggered by E by requiring, in addition to the standard requirements concerning triggering of e, also:

- $\langle C, St\rangle \models c$. When evaluating condition c that may contain references to variables, we use $St[y]$ as the current value of the variable $y \in V$.
- If the action part a contains an assignment to variable y, then it is required that $\mathit{assigned}(y) \notin E$.
- If the action part a contains an assignment to y, then *assigned*(y) is considered as part of *generated*(t).

On taking a complete step T, we update the global state by changing the configuration C to $\mathit{NextConfig}(C, T)$, as defined above. In addition, for each y such that $\mathit{assigned}(y) \in \mathit{generated}(T)$, which means that precisely one transition with action part containing an assignment $y := \mathit{exp}$ is included in T, we update $St[y]$ to the value of *exp* as evaluated over the current store St.

Additional details and additions are described in [10].

Acknowledgements

We wish to thank Rivi Sherman for many constructive comments and identification of bugs in previous versions of the manuscript. We gratefully acknowledge many enjoyable discussions with W.P. de Roever, F. Maraninchi, R. Gerth, C. Huizing,

J. Hooman, R. Koymans and R. Kuiper, which significantly contributed to our understanding of the tradeoffs between the various requirements expected from a good semantics. We thank Carol Weintraub and Sarah Fliegelmann for typing the numerous versions of the manuscript.

References

[1] G. Berry and G. Gonthier. *The Synchronous Programming Language Esterel, Design, Semantics, Implementation.* Technical Report, Technical Report 327, INRIA, 1988. to Appear in *Science of Computer Programming.*

[2] P. Caspi, N. Halbwachs, D. Pilaud, and J. Plaice. Lustre, a declarative language for programming synchronous systems. In *Proc. 14th ACM Symp. Princ. of Prog. Lang.*, pages 178–188, 1987.

[3] D. Harel. Statecharts: A visual formalism for complex systems. *Sci. Comp. Prog.*, 8:231–274, 1987.

[4] D. Harel, H. Lachover, A. Naamad, A. Pnueli, M. Politi, R. Sherman, A. Shtull-Trauring, and M. Trakhtenbrot. Statemate: a working environment for the development of complex reactive systems. *IEEE Trans. Software Engin.*, 16:403–414, 1990.

[5] D. Harel, A. Pnueli, J. Schmidt, and R. Sherman. On the formal semantics of statecharts. In *Proc. First IEEE Symp. Logic in Comp. Sci.*, pages 54–64, 1986.

[6] C. Huizing. *Semantics of reactive systems: comparison and full abstraction.* PhD thesis, Technical University Eindhoven, 1991.

[7] C. Huizing and R. Gerth. *On the Semantics of Reactive Systems.* Technical Report, Eindhoven University of Technology, 1988.

[8] C. Huizing, R. Gerth, and W. de Roever. Modeling statecharts behavior in a fully abstract way. In *Proc. 13th CAAP*, pages 271–294, Lecture Notes in Comp. Sci. 299, Springer-Verlag, 1988.

[9] F. Maraninchi. Argonaute: graphical description, semantics and verification of reactive systems by using a process algebra. In J. Sifakis, editor, *Automatic Verification Methods for Finite State Systems*, Lecture Notes in Comp. Sci. 407, Springer-Verlag, 1989.

[10] A. Pnueli and M. Shalev. What is in a step? In J. Klop, J. Meijer, and J. Rutten, editors, *J.W. De Bakker, Liber Amicorum*, pages 373–400, CWI, Amsterdam, 1989.

Proving Termination of General Prolog Programs

Krzysztof R. Apt
Centre for Mathematics and Computer Science
Kruislaan 413, 1098 SJ Amsterdam, The Netherlands

Dino Pedreschi
Dipartimento di Informatica, Università di Pisa
Corso Italia 40, 56125 Pisa, Italy

Abstract

We study here termination of general logic programs with the Prolog selection rule. To this end we extend the approach of Apt and Pedreschi [AP90] and consider the class of *left terminating* general programs. These are general logic programs that terminate with the Prolog selection rule for all ground goals. We introduce the notion of an *acceptable program* and prove that acceptable programs are left terminating. This provides us with a practical method of proving termination.

The converse implication does not hold but we show that under the assumption of non-floundering from ground goals every left terminating program is acceptable. Finally, we prove that various ways of defining semantics coincide for acceptable programs. The method is illustrated by giving simple proofs of termination of a "game" program and the transitive closure program for the desired class of goals.

Note. First author's work was partly supported by ESPRIT Basic Research Action 3020 (Integration). Second author's work was partly supported by ESPRIT Basic Research Action 3012 (Compulog).

1 Introduction

Motivation

Prolog is a programming language based on logic programming. However, the use of a fixed selection rule combined with the depth first search in the resulting search trees makes Prolog and logic programming different. As a consequence various completeness results linking the procedural and declarative interpretation of logic programs cannot be directly applied to Prolog programs. This mismatch makes it difficult to study Prolog programs using only the logic programming theory. Clearly the main problem is the issue of termination: a Prolog interpreter will miss a solution if all success nodes lie to the right of an infinite path in the search tree.

In our previous paper we proposed to study pure Prolog programs that terminate for all ground goals. We called such programs left terminating and claimed that most pure Prolog programs are left terminating. Then we offered a characterization of left terminating programs which allowed us to provide simple termination proofs of various "troublesome" pure Prolog programs.

The aim of this paper is to extend this approach to termination to general Prolog programs, i.e. programs allowing negative literals. More precisely, we consider here general logic programs executed with the leftmost selection rule used in Prolog. Our approach uses the concept of a level mapping (a function assigning natural numbers to ground atoms) in combination with a limited declarative knowledge about the program embodied in some interpretation I. I should be a model of the considered program P *and* a model of Clark's completion of the "negative" fragment of P.

These two concepts are combined in the notion of an acceptable program. Intuitively, a general program P is acceptable w.r.t. a level mapping and a model I if for all ground instances of the clauses of P the level of the head is greater than the level of the atoms in a certain prefix of the body. Which prefix is considered is determined by the model I. We prove that acceptable general programs are left terminating. Consequently, to prove left termination it suffices to prove acceptability.

The converse implication does not hold due to the possibility of floundering. On the other hand, we show that for programs that do not flounder from ground goals the concepts of left termination and acceptability do coincide. Also, we prove that various ways of defining semantics coincide for acceptable programs.

Once the left termination of a general Prolog program is established, non-ground terminating goals can be identified by using the concept of a bounded goal. We illustrate the use of this method by providing simple proofs of termination of a "game" program and the transitive closure program for the desired class of goals.

The problem of termination of Prolog programs attracted a lot of attention in the literature. A short overview can be found in Apt and Pedreschi [AP90]. In particular, it is interesting to contrast our approach with that of Ullman and Van Gelder [UvG88], later improved by Plümer [Plü90b, Plü90a], aimed at the automatic verification of termination of a pure Prolog program and a goal. In their approach, some sufficient conditions for termination are identified, which can be statically checked. Obviously, such an approach cannot be complete due to the undecidability of the halting problem.

We propose instead a complete method, which characterizes precisely the left terminating, non floundering programs. Additionally, in the present paper and in [AP90] we provide simple proofs of termination for programs and goals which cannot be handled using the cited approach. On the other hand, we do not determine here any conditions under which our method could be automated. This should form part of a future research.

We are aware of only one paper in which a method of proving termination of general Prolog programs is proposed — Baudinet [Bau88]. In her proposal negation is treated indirectly by dealing with termination in presence of the *cut* operator using which negation can be simulated. The present paper seems to be the first one in which negation is treated in a direct way. By virtue of our approach the termination proofs can be built in a modular way and the limited declarative knowledge ensuring termination of the program can be identified. This results in our opinion in simple arguments which formalize the reasoning used informally.

Preliminaries

Throughout this paper we use the standard notation and terminology of Lloyd [Llo87] or Apt [Apt90]. Recall that a *general clause* is a construct of the form

$$A \leftarrow L_1, \ldots, L_n$$

($n \geq 0$) where A is an atom and $L_1, \ldots, L_n$ are literals. In turn, a *general goal* is a construct of the form

$$\leftarrow L_1, \ldots, L_n$$

($n \geq 0$) where $L_1, \ldots, L_n$ are literals. A *general program* is a finite set of general clauses.

From now on we simply say *clause, goal* and *program* instead of *general clause, general goal* and *general program*. When each L_i is positive, we call a clause a *positive clause* and a goal a *positive goal*. A program whose all clauses are positive is called a *positive program*.

We use the following abbreviations for a program P:
B_P for the Herbrand Base of P,
T_P for the immediate consequence operator of P,
$ground(P)$ for the set of all ground instances of clauses from P,
$comp(P)$ for Clark's completion of P.

Also, we use Prolog's convention identifying in the context of a program each string starting with a capital letter with a variable, reserving other strings for the names of constants, terms or relations.

In the programs we use the usual list notation. The constant $[\,]$ denotes the empty list and $[\,.\mid.\,]$ is a binary function which given a term x and a list xs produces a new list $[\,x \mid xs\,]$ with head x and tail xs. The standard notation $[\,x_1, \ldots, x_n\,]$, for $n \geq 0$, is used as an abbreviation of $[x_1 \mid [\ldots [x_n \mid [\,]] \ldots]]$. Given a list $[\,x_1, \ldots, x_n\,]$, each x_i is called an *element* of $[\,x_1, \ldots, x_n\,]$. In general, the Herbrand Universe will also contain "impure" elements that contain $[\,]$ or $[\,.\mid.\,]$ but are not lists - for example $s([\,])$ or $[s(0) \mid 0]$ where 0 is a constant and s a unary function symbol. They will not cause any complications.

Left Termination

In this paper we consider *SLDNF*-resolution with one selection rule only – namely that of Prolog, usually called the leftmost selection rule. As S in *SLDNF* stands for "selection rule", we denote this form of resolution by *LDNF* (*L*inear resolution for *D*efinite clauses with *N*egation as *F*ailure).

When studying termination of general Prolog programs, i.e. programs executed using the *LDNF*-resolution it is necessary to revise the standard definitions of Lloyd [Llo87]. Indeed, according to his definitions there is no *LDNF*-derivation for $\{p \leftarrow \neg p\} \cup \{\leftarrow p\}$ whereas the corresponding Prolog execution diverges.

The appropriate revision is achieved by viewing the *LDNF*-resolution as a top down interpreter which given a program P and a goal G attempts to build a search tree for $P \cup \{G\}$ by constructing its branches in parallel. The branches in this tree are called *LDNF*-derivations for $P \cup \{G\}$ and the tree itself is called the *LDNF*-tree for $P \cup \{G\}$.

Negative literals are resolved using the negation as failure rule which calls for the construction of a subsidiary search tree. If during this subsidiary construction the interpreter diverges, the main *LDNF*-derivation *is considered* to be infinite. Adopting this view the *LDNF*-derivation for $\{p \leftarrow \neg p\} \cup \{\leftarrow p\}$ diverges because the goal $\leftarrow p$ is resolved to $\leftarrow \neg p$ and the subsequent construction of the subsidiary *LDNF*-tree for $\{p \leftarrow \neg p\} \cup \{\leftarrow p\}$ diverges.

Summarizing, by termination of a general Prolog program we actually mean termination of the underlying interpreter. By choosing variables of the input clauses and the used mgu's in a fixed way we can assume that for every program P and goal G there exists exactly one *LDNF*-tree for $P \cup \{G\}$. The subsidiary *LDNF*-trees formed during the construction of this tree are called *subsidiary LDNF-trees for* $P \cup \{G\}$.

The following notion plays an important role in our considerations.

Definition 1.1 A program P is called *left terminating* if all *LDNF*-derivations of P starting in a ground goal are finite. □

In other words, a program is left terminating if all *LDNF*-trees for P with a ground root are finite. When studying Prolog programs, one is actually interested in proving termination of a given program not only for all ground goals but also for a class of non-ground goals constituting the intended queries. Our method of proving left termination will allow us to identify for each program such a class of non-ground goals.

The following lemma will be of use later.

Lemma 1.2 *Suppose that all LDNF-derivations of P starting in a ground positive goal are finite. Then P is left terminating.*

Proof. It suffices to show that for all ground literals L all *LDNF*-derivations of $P \cup \{\leftarrow L\}$ are finite. When L is positive it is a part of the assumptions and when L is negative, say $L = \neg A$, it follows from the fact that by assumption the subsidiary *LDNF*-tree for $P \cup \{\leftarrow A\}$ is finite.

□

2 Acceptable Programs

Definitions

The subject of termination of Prolog programs has been studied in several articles (see Apt and Pedreschi [AP90] for a short overview). Our approach to termination of general Prolog programs is based on a generalization of the approach of Apt and Pedreschi [AP90]. We begin by recalling the relevant notions.

A *level mapping* for a positive program P (see Bezem [Bez89] and Cavedon [Cav89]) is a function $|\ | : B_P \rightarrow N$ from ground atoms to natural numbers. For $A \in B_P$, $|A|$ is the level of A.

Definition 2.1 Let P be a positive program, $|\ |$ a level mapping for P and I a (not necessarily Herbrand) model of P. P is called *acceptable with respect to* $|\ |$ *and* I if for every clause $A \leftarrow B_1, \ldots, B_n$ in *ground*(P)

$$|A| > |B_i| \text{ for } i \in [1, \bar{n}],$$

where

$$\bar{n} = \min(\{n\} \cup \{i \in [1,n] \mid I \not\models B_i\}).$$

Alternatively, we may define $\bar{n}$ by

$$\bar{n} = \begin{cases} n & \text{if } I \models B_1 \wedge \ldots \wedge B_n, \\ i & \text{if } I \models B_1 \wedge \ldots \wedge B_{i-1} \text{ and } I \not\models B_1 \wedge \cdots \wedge B_i. \end{cases}$$

P is called *acceptable* if it is acceptable with respect to some level mapping and a model of P. □

Our aim is to generalize the above concept of acceptability to general Prolog programs. First , we extend in a natural way a level mapping to a mapping from ground literals to natural numbers by putting $|\neg A| = |A|$. Next, given a program P, we define its subset P^-. In P^- we collect the definitions of the negated relations and relations on which these relations depend. More precisely, we define P^- as follows.

Definition 2.2 Let P be a program and p, q relations.

(i) We say that p *refers to* q iff there is a clause in P that uses p in its head and q in its body.

(ii) We say that p *depends on* q iff (p, q) is in the reflexive, transitive closure of the relation *refers to*.

□

Of course, not every relation needs to refer to itself, but by reflexivity every relation depends on itself.

Definition 2.3 Let P be a program. Denote by Neg_P the set of relations in P which occur in a negative literal in a body of a clause from P and by Neg_P^* the set of relations in P on which the relations in Neg_P depend on. We define P^- to be the set of clauses in P in whose head a relation from Neg_P^* occurs. □

We can now introduce the desired generalization of the notion of acceptability.

Definition 2.4 Let P be a program, $|\,|$ a level mapping for P and I a model of P whose restriction to the relations from Neg_P^* is a model of $comp(P^-)$. P is called *acceptable with respect to* $|\,|$ *and* I if for every clause $A \leftarrow L_1, \ldots, L_n$ in $ground(P)$

$$|A| > |L_i| \text{ for } i \in [1, \bar{n}],$$

where

$$\bar{n} = \min(\{n\} \cup \{i \in [1,n] \mid I \not\models L_i\}).$$

P is called *acceptable* if it is acceptable with respect to some level mapping and a model of P whose restriction to the relations from Neg_P^* is a model of $comp(P^-)$. □

Note that for a positive program P we have $Neg_P^* = \emptyset$, so P^- is empty and the above definition coincides with the definition of acceptability for positive programs.

The concept of an acceptable program also generalizes that of an acyclic program studied in Cavedon [Cav89] and Apt and Bezem [AB90].

Definition 2.5 Let P be a program, $|\,|$ a level mapping for P. P is called *acyclic with respect to* $|\,|$ if for every clause $A \leftarrow L_1, \ldots, L_n$ in $ground(P)$

$$|A| > |L_i| \text{ for } i \in [1, n].$$

P is called *acyclic* if it is acyclic with respect to some level mapping. □

Lemma 2.6 *Every acyclic program is acceptable.*

Proof. Let P be acyclic w.r.t. some level mapping $|\,|$. By Theorem 4.1 of Apt and Bezem [AB90] $comp(P)$ has a unique Herbrand model, M_P. Then P is acceptable w.r.t. $|\,|$ and M_P. □

Apt and Bezem [AB90] proved among others that all $SLDNF$-derivations of an acyclic program starting in a ground goal are finite. This implies that all acyclic programs are left terminating, so the concept of acyclicity is of obvious importance when studying termination of Prolog programs. Indeed, in Apt and Bezem [AB90] the usefulness of this concept was demonstrated by proving termination of a program which formalizes the Yale Shooting problem of Hanks and McDermott [HM87]. However, as we shall see in the final section of this paper, there exist natural left terminating programs which are not acyclic. Thus the concept of acyclicity is of limited applicability when considering Prolog programs.

Multiset ordering

In our considerations below we use the multiset ordering. A *multiset*, sometimes called *bag*, is an unordered sequence. Given a (non-reflexive) ordering $<$ on a set W, the *multiset ordering over* $(W, <)$ is an ordering on finite multisets of the set W. It is defined as the transitive closure of the relation in which X is smaller than Y if X can be obtained from Y by replacing an element a of Y by a finite (possibly empty) multiset each of whose elements is smaller than a in the ordering $<$.

In symbols, first we define the relation $\prec$ by

$$X \prec Y \text{ iff } X = Y - \{a\} \cup Z \text{ for some } Z \text{ such that } b < a \text{ for } b \in Z,$$

where X, Y, Z are finite multisets of elements of W, and then define the multiset ordering over $(W, <)$ as the transitive closure of the relation $\prec$.

It is well-known (see e.g. Dershowitz [Der87]) that multiset ordering over a well-founded ordering is again well-founded. Thus it can be iterated while maintaining well-foundedness. What we need here is, as in Apt and Pedreschi [AP90], two fold iteration. We start with the set of natural numbers N ordered by $<$ and apply the multiset ordering twice. We call the first iteration multiset ordering and the second *double multiset ordering.* Both are well-founded. The double multiset ordering is defined on the finite *multisets* of finite multisets of natural numbers, but we shall use it only on the finite *sets* of finite multisets of natural numbers. The following simple lemma (see Apt and Pedreschi [AP90]) will be of help when using the double multiset ordering.

Lemma 2.7 *Let X and Y be two finite sets of finite multisets of natural numbers. Suppose that*

$$\forall x \in X \, \exists y \in Y \; (y \textit{ majorizes } x),$$

where y majorizes x means that x is smaller than y in the multiset ordering.

Then X is smaller than Y in the double multiset ordering.

Proof. We call an element $y \in Y$ *majorizing* if it majorizes some $x \in X$. X can be obtained from Y by first replacing each majorizing $y \in Y$ by the multiset M_y of elements of X it majorizes and then removing from Y the non-majorizing elements. This proves the claim. □

Below we use the notation bag $(a_1, \ldots, a_n)$ to denote the multiset consisting of the unordered sequence $a_1, \ldots, a_n$.

Boundedness

Another important concept is that of boundedness, originally introduced in Bezem [Bez89]. It allows us to identify goals from which no divergence can arise. Recall that an atom A is called *bounded* w.r.t. a level mapping $|\,|$ if $|\,|$ is bounded on the set $[A]$ of ground instances of A. If A is bounded, then $|[A]|$ denotes the maximum that $|\,|$ takes on $[A]$. Note that every ground atom is bounded.

Our concept of a bounded general goal directly generalizes that of a bounded goal given in Apt and Pedreschi [AP90].

Definition 2.8 Let P be a program, $|\,|$ a level mapping for P, I model of P whose restriction to the relations from Neg_P^* is a model of *comp*(P^-) and $k \geq 0$.

(i) With each ground general goal $G = \leftarrow L_1, \ldots, L_n$ we associate a finite multiset $|G|_I$ of natural numbers defined by

$$|G|_I \;=\; \text{bag}\,(|L_1|, \ldots, |L_{\bar{n}}|),$$

where

$$\bar{n} = \min(\{n\} \cup \{i \in [1, n] \mid I \not\models L_i\}).$$

(ii) With each general goal G we associate a set of multisets $|[G]|_I$ defined by

$$|[G]|_I = \{|G'|_I \mid G' \text{ is a ground instance of } G\}.$$

(iii) A general goal G is called *bounded by* k w.r.t. $|\,|$ and I if $k \geq \ell$ for $\ell \in \bigcup|[G]|_I$, where $\bigcup|[G]|_I$ stands for the set-theoretic union of the elements of $|[G]|_I$.

(iv) A general goal is called *bounded* w.r.t. $|\,|$ and I if it is bounded by some $k \geq 0$ w.r.t. $|\,|$ and I.

□

It is useful to note the following.

Lemma 2.9 *Let P be a program, $|\,|$ a level mapping for P and I a model of P whose restriction to the relations from Neg_P^* is a model of $comp(P^-)$. A general goal G is bounded w.r.t. $|\,|$ and I iff the set $|[G]|_I$ is finite.*

Proof. Consider a general goal G that is bounded by some k. Suppose that G has n atoms. Then each element of $|[G]|_I$ is a multiset of at most n numbers selected from $[0, k]$. The number of such multisets is finite.

The other implication is obvious. □

The following lemma is an analogue of Lemma 3.7 of Apt and Pedreschi [AP90]. Recall that a goal is called *positive* if it contains only positive literals.

Lemma 2.10 *Let P be a program that is acceptable w.r.t. a level mapping $|\,|$ and an interpretation I. Let G be a goal which is a descendant of a positive goal and which is bounded (w.r.t. $|\,|$ and I) and let H be an LDNF-resolvent of G from P. Then*

(i) H is bounded,

(ii) $|[H]|_I$ is smaller than $|[G]|_I$ in the double multiset ordering.

Proof. The proof is analogous to the proof of Lemma 3.7 of Apt and Pedreschi [AP90]. Due to the presence of negative literals we only have to consider one additional case.

Let $G = \leftarrow L_1, \ldots, L_n\ (n \geq 1)$. For some literals $M_1, \ldots, M_k\ (k \geq 0)$ and a substitution θ we have $H = \leftarrow (M_1, \ldots, M_k, L_2, \ldots, L_n)\theta$.

First we show that for every ground instance H_0 of H there exists a ground instance G' of G such that $|H_0|_I$ is smaller that $|G'|_I$ in the multiset ordering.

Case 1 H is obtained from G by the negation as failure rule.
Then L_1 is a ground negative literal, say $L_1 = \neg A$, and $H = \leftarrow L_2, \ldots, L_n$, i.e. $k = 0$ and $\theta = \epsilon$ (ϵ stands for the empty substitution).

Denote by T the finitely failed *LDNF*-tree for $P \cup \{\leftarrow A\}$. By the definition of Neg_P and the fact that G is a descendant of a positive goal, the relation occurring in A is in Neg_P. Thus all relations which occur in the goals of the tree T are elements of Neg_P^*. So T is in fact a finitely failed *LDNF*-tree for $P^- \cup \{\leftarrow A\}$. By the soundness of the *SLDNF*-resolution, $comp(P^-) \models \neg A$, so $I \models L_1$.

Let H_0 be a ground instance of H. For some substitution δ

$$H_0 = \leftarrow L'_2, \ldots, L'_n,$$

where L'_i denotes $L_i\delta$. Thus

$$G' = \leftarrow L_1, L'_2, \ldots, L'_n,$$

is a ground instance of G. Then

$$|H_0|_I = \text{bag}\,(|L'_2|, \ldots, |L'_n|)$$

where

$$\bar{n} = \min(\{n\} \cup \{i \in [2,n] \,|\, I \not\models L'_i\}).$$

and, since $I \models L_1$,

$$|G'|_I = \text{bag}\,(|L_1|,\ |L'_2|, \ldots, |L'_{\bar{n}}|).$$

This shows that $|H_0|_I$ is smaller than $|G'|_I$ in the multiset ordering. □

Case 2 H is obtained from G by the proper resolution step.
Then L_1 is a positive literal, so for some atom A, $C = A \leftarrow M_1, \ldots, M_k$ is an input clause of P and θ is an mgu of A and L_1. Let H_0 be a ground instance of H. For some substitution δ

$$H_0 = \leftarrow M'_1, \ldots, M'_k, L'_2, \ldots, L'_n,$$

where for brevity for any atom, clause or goal M, M' denotes $M\theta\delta$. Note that

$$C' = L'_1 \leftarrow M'_1, \ldots, M'_k$$

and

$$G' = \leftarrow L'_1, \ldots, L'_n,$$

since $A' = L'_1$ as $A\theta = L_1\theta$.

Subcase 1 For $i \in [1,k]$ $I \models M'_i$.
Then

$$|H_0|_I = \text{bag}\,(|M'_1|, \ldots, |M'_k|,\ |L'_2|, \ldots, |L'_{\bar{n}}|)$$

where

$$\bar{n} = \min(\{n\} \cup \{i \in [2,n] \,|\, I \not\models L'_i\}).$$

Additionally $I \models L'_1$ because I is a model of P and a fortiori a model of the clause C'. Thus

$$|G'|_I = \text{bag}\,(|L'_1|,\ |L'_2|, \ldots, |L'_{\bar{n}}|).$$

This means that $|H_0|_I$ is obtained from $|G'|_I$ by replacing $|L'_1|$ by $|M'_1|, \ldots, |M'_k|$. But by the definition of acceptability

$$|M'_i| < |L'_1|$$

for $i \in [1,k]$, so $|H_0|_I$ is smaller than $|G'|_I$ in the multiset ordering. □

Subcase 2 For some $i \in [1,k]$ $I \not\models M'_i$.
Then

$$|H_0|_I = \text{bag}(|M'_1|, \ldots, |M'_{\bar{k}}|)$$

where

$$\bar{k} = \min(\{i \in [1,k] \,|\, I \not\models M'_i\}).$$

Also, by the definition of acceptability

$$|M'_i| < |L'_1|$$

for $i \in [1, \bar{k}]$, so $|H_0|_I$ is smaller than $|G'|_I$ in the multiset ordering. □
□

The statement we just proved implies claim (i) since G is bounded. By Lemma 2.9 $|[H]|_I$ is finite and claim (ii) now follows by Lemma 2.7. □

Corollary 2.11 *Let P be an acceptable program and G a bounded positive goal. Then all LDNF-derivations of $P \cup \{G\}$ are finite.*

Proof. The double multiset ordering is well-founded. □

Corollary 2.12 *Every acceptable program is left terminating.*

Proof. By the fact that every ground goal is bounded, Corollary 2.11 and Lemma 1.2. □

Thus to prove that a program is left terminating it suffices to show that it is acceptable.

To apply Corollaries 2.11 and 2.12 we need a method for verifying that an interpretation is a model of $comp(P^-)$. In the case of Herbrand interpretations this task becomes much simpler thanks to the following theorem due to Apt, Blair and Walker [ABW88]. Here an interpretation is *supported* if for all ground atoms A, $I \models A$ implies that for some clause $A \leftarrow L_1, \ldots, L_n$ in $ground(P)$ we have $I \models L_1 \wedge \ldots \wedge L_n$.

Theorem 2.13 *A Herbrand interpretation I is a model of $comp(P)$ iff it is a supported model of P.* □

3 Acceptability versus Left Termination

The converse of Corollary 2.12 does not hold. This is in contrast to the case of positive programs. Below we say that an $LDNF$-derivation *flounders* if there occurs in it or in any of its subsidiary $LDNF$-trees a goal with the first literal being non-ground and negative. An $LDNF$-tree is called *non-floundering* if none of its branches flounders.

Example 3.1 Consider the program P which consists of only one clause: $p(0) \leftarrow \neg p(X)$. Then the only $LDNF$-derivation of $P \cup \{\leftarrow p(0)\}$ flounders, so it is finite. By the definition of $SLDNF$-resolution the only $LDNF$-derivation of $P \cup \{\leftarrow \neg p(0)\}$ flounders, as well. Thus P is left terminating, since the only ground goals are of the form $G = \leftarrow L_1, \ldots, L_n$ $(n \geq 1)$ where each L_i is either $p(0)$ or $\neg p(0)$. On the other hand P is not acceptable since $p(0) \leftarrow \neg p(0)$ is in $ground(P)$ and by definition for any level mapping $|p(0)| = |\neg p(0)|$. □

The above example exploits the fact that $SLDNF$-derivations may terminate by floundering. We now show that in the absence of floundering Corollary 2.12 can be reversed. We proceed analogously to the case of positive programs and study the size of finite $LDNF$-trees. We need the following lemma, where $nodes_P(G)$ for a program P and a goal G denotes the total number of nodes in the $LDNF$-tree for $P \cup \{G\}$ and in all the subsidiary $LDNF$-trees for $P \cup \{G\}$.

Lemma 3.2 *Let P be a program and G a goal such that the $LDNF$-tree for $P \cup \{G\}$ is finite and non-floundering. Then*

(i) for all substitutions θ, the $LDNF$-tree for $P \cup \{G\theta\}$ is finite and non-floundering and $nodes_P(G\theta) \leq nodes_P(G)$,

(ii) for all prefixes H of G, the $LDNF$-tree for $P \cup \{H\}$ is finite and non-floundering and $nodes_P(H) \leq nodes_P(G)$,

(iii) for all non-root nodes H in the $LDNF$-tree for $P \cup \{G\}$, $nodes_P(H) < nodes_P(G)$.

Proof.
(i) The proof proceeds by structural induction on the $LDNF$-tree T for $P \cup \{G\}$.

The Base Case. Then T is formed by the only node G. The following three subcases arise.

Subcase 1 $G = \square$. Then $G = G\theta$, and the claim trivially holds.
Subcase 2 $G = \leftarrow A, L_2, \ldots, L_k$. Then A does not unify with the head of any clause in P and neither $A\theta$ does. As a consequence, the goal $G\theta$ also immediately fails, and the $LDNF$-tree T for $P \cup \{G\theta\}$ is formed by the only node $G\theta$.
Subcase 3 $G = \leftarrow \neg A, L_2, \ldots, L_k$. By the fact that T has no floundering derivation, A is ground. The goal G immediately fails, so by the definition of the $LDNF$-resolution there is an $LDNF$-refutation of $P \cup \{\leftarrow A\}$. Then $G\theta$ also immediately fails as $A = A\theta$. Hence the $LDNF$-tree T for $P \cup \{G\theta\}$ is formed by the only node $G\theta$. By definition

$$nodes_P(G\theta) = 1 + nodes_P(\leftarrow A\theta) = 1 + nodes_P(\leftarrow A) = nodes_P(G).$$

The Induction Case. Two subcases arise here.

Subcase 1 $G = \leftarrow A, L_2, \ldots, L_k$. Assume that $H_1, \ldots, H_m$ are the resolvents of G from P. Consider $G\theta = \leftarrow (A, L_2, \ldots, L_k)\theta$, and let $H'_1, \ldots, H'_l$ be the resolvents of $G\theta$ from P. Clearly, for all i in $[1, l]$ there exist j in $[1, m]$ and a substitution δ such that $H'_i = H_j\delta$. By the induction hypothesis, $nodes_P(H'_i) \leq nodes_P(H_j)$. Hence:

$$nodes_P(G\theta) = 1 + nodes_P(H'_1) + \ldots + nodes_P(H'_l) \leq$$
$$1 + nodes_P(H_1) + \ldots + nodes_P(H_m) = nodes_P(G).$$

Moreover, the $LDNF$-tree for $P \cup \{G\theta\}$ is finite and non-floundering and by the induction hypothesis the $LDNF$-trees for the resolvents of $G\theta$ are finite and non-floundering.
Subcase 2 $G = \leftarrow \neg A, L_2, \ldots, L_k$. By the fact that T has no floundering derivation, A is ground. The fact that G is not a terminal node in T implies that there exists an $LDNF$-refutation of $P \cup \{\leftarrow \neg A\}$, i.e. the $LDNF$-tree for $P \cup \{\leftarrow A\}$ is finitely failed. Then G

has only one resolvent, namely $\leftarrow L_2, \ldots, L_k$. Moreover, $G\theta = \leftarrow \neg A, (L_2, \ldots, L_k)\theta$, since A is ground, so $\leftarrow (L_2, \ldots, L_k)\theta$ is the only resolvent of $G\theta$. By the induction hypothesis, $nodes_P(\leftarrow (L_2, \ldots, L_k)\theta) \leq nodes_P(\leftarrow L_2, \ldots, L_k)$. Hence:

$$nodes_P(G\theta) = 1 + nodes_P(\leftarrow A) + nodes_P(\leftarrow (L_2, \ldots, L_k)\theta) \leq$$
$$1 + nodes_P(\leftarrow A) + nodes_P(\leftarrow L_2, \ldots, L_k) = nodes_P(G).$$

Moreover, the *LDNF*-tree for $P \cup \{G\theta\}$ is finite and non-floundering, since by the induction hypothesis the *LDNF*-tree for the resolvent of $G\theta$ is finite and non-floundering.

(ii) Consider a prefix $H = \leftarrow L_1, \ldots, L_k$ of $G = \leftarrow L_1, \ldots, L_n$ $(n \geq k)$. By an appropriate renaming of variables (formally justified by a straightforward extension to the *LDNF*-resolution of the Variant Lemma 2.8 in Apt [Apt90]) we can assume that all input clauses used in the *LDNF*-tree for $P \cup \{H\}$ have no variables in common with G. We can now transform the *LDNF*-tree for $P \cup \{H\}$ into an initial subtree of the *LDNF*-tree for $P \cup \{G\}$ by replacing in it a node $\leftarrow M_1, \ldots, M_l$ by $\leftarrow M_1, \ldots, M_l, L_{k+1}\theta, \ldots, L_n\theta$, where θ is the composition of the mgu's used on the path from the root H to the node $\leftarrow M_1, \ldots, M_l$. This implies the claim, since every subsidiary *LDNF*-tree for $P \cup \{H\}$ is also a subsidiary *LDNF*-tree for $P \cup \{G\}$.

(iii) Immediate by the definition. □

The following definition will now be useful.

Definition 3.3 We call a program P *non-floundering* if all its *LDNF*-derivations starting in a ground goal are non-floundering.

Theorem 3.4 *Let P be a left terminating, non-floundering program. Then for some level mapping $|\;|$ and a model I of comp(P)*

(i) P is acceptable w.r.t. $|\;|$ and I,

(ii) for every goal G, G is bounded w.r.t. $|\;|$ and I iff all LDNF-derivations of $P \cup \{G\}$ are finite.

Proof. Define the level mapping by putting for $A \in B_P$

$$|A| = nodes_P\,(\leftarrow A).$$

Since P is left terminating, this level mapping is well defined. Note that by definition, for $A \in B_P$

$$nodes_P(\leftarrow \neg A) > nodes_P(\leftarrow A) = |A| = |\neg A|,$$

so

$$nodes_P(\leftarrow \neg A) \geq |\neg A|.$$

Next, choose

$$I = \{A \in B_P \mid \text{there is an } LDNF\text{-refutation of } P \cup \{\leftarrow A\}\}.$$

Let us show that I is a model of $comp(P)$. To this end, we use Theorem 2.13 and show that I is a supported model of P.

To establish that I is a model of P, assume by contradiction that some ground instance $A \leftarrow L'_1, \ldots, L'_n$ of a clause C from P is false in I. Then $I \models L'_1 \wedge \ldots \wedge L'_n$ and $I \not\models A$. Since P is left terminating and non-floundering, $I \not\models A$ implies that the $LDNF$-tree for $P \cup \{\leftarrow A\}$ is finitely failed and non-floundering.

For some ground substitution γ, $A = B\gamma$ where B is the head of the clause C. Thus $A\gamma = B\gamma\gamma = B\gamma$, so A and B unify.

Let $\leftarrow L_1, \ldots, L_n$ be the resolvent of $\leftarrow A$ from the clause C. The $LDNF$-tree for $P \cup \{\leftarrow L_1, \ldots, L_n\}$ is also finitely failed and non-floundering. As $L'_1, \ldots, L'_n = (L_1, \ldots, L_n)\theta$ for some substitution θ, we have by Lemma 3.2(i) that the $LDNF$-tree for $P \cup \{\leftarrow L'_1, \ldots, L'_n\}$ is non-floundering. Moreover, it is finitely failed, since a direct consequence of the proof of Lemma 3.2(i) is that the goals present in the $LDNF$-tree for $P \cup \{\leftarrow L'_1, \ldots, L'_n\}$ are all instances of the goals present in the $LDNF$-tree for $P \cup \{\leftarrow L_1, \ldots, L_n\}$. But the fact that the $LDNF$-tree for $P \cup \{\leftarrow L'_1, \ldots, L'_n\}$ is finitely failed and non-floundering contradicts the hypothesis that $I \models L'_1 \wedge \ldots \wedge L'_n$.

To establish that I is a supported interpretation of P, consider $A \in B_P$ such that $I \models A$, and let C be the first input clause used in the leftmost $LDNF$-refutation of $P \cup \{\leftarrow A\}$. Let $\leftarrow L_1, \ldots, L_n$ be the resolvent of $\leftarrow A$ from the clause C. Clearly, an $LDNF$-refutation for $P \cup \{\leftarrow L_1, \ldots, L_n\}$, with a computed answer substitution θ, can be extracted from the $LDNF$-refutation of $P \cup \{\leftarrow A\}$. Let $L'_1, \ldots, L'_n$ be a ground instance of $(L_1, \ldots, L_n)\theta$. By a straightforward generalization of Lemma 3.20 in [Apt90] to the $LDNF$-resolution there exists an $LDNF$-refutation for $P \cup \{\leftarrow L'_1, \ldots, L'_n\}$. We conclude that $I \models L'_1 \wedge \ldots \wedge L'_n$. This establishes that I is a supported interpretation of P.

We are now in the position to prove (i) and (ii). First we prove one implication of (ii).

(ii1) Consider a goal G such that all $LDNF$-derivations of $P \cup \{G\}$ are finite. We prove that G is bounded by $nodes_P(G)$ w.r.t. $|\ |$ and I.

To this end take $\ell \in \cup|[G]|_I$. For some ground instance $\leftarrow L_1, \ldots, L_n$ of G and $i \in [1, \bar{n}]$, where

$$\bar{n} = \min(\{n\} \cup \{i \in [1, n] \mid I \not\models L_i\}),$$

we have $\ell = |L_i|$. We now calculate

$$
\begin{array}{ll}
 & nodes_P(G) \\
\geq & \quad \{\text{Lemma 3.2 (i)}\} \\
 & nodes_P(\leftarrow L_1, \ldots, L_n) \\
\geq & \quad \{\text{Lemma 3.2 (ii)}\} \\
 & nodes_P(\leftarrow L_1, \ldots, L_{\bar{n}}) \\
\geq & \quad \{\text{Lemma 3.2 (iii), noting that for } j \in [1, \bar{n} - 1] \\
 & \quad \text{there is an } LDNF\text{-refutation of } P \cup \{\leftarrow L_1, \ldots, L_j\}\} \\
 & nodes_P(\leftarrow L_i, \ldots, L_{\bar{n}})
\end{array}
$$

$$
\begin{array}{ll}
\geq & \{\text{Lemma 3.2 (ii)}\} \\
 & nodes_P\,(\leftarrow L_i) \\
\geq & \{\text{definition of } |\;|,\ L_i \text{ is ground}\} \\
 & |L_i| \\
= & \ell.
\end{array}
$$

(i) We now prove that P is acceptable w.r.t. $|\;|$ and I. We showed that I is a model of *comp*(P), so the restriction of I to the relations in Neg^*_P is trivially a model of *comp*(P^-). To complete the proof, take a clause $A \leftarrow L_1, \ldots, L_n$ in P and its ground instance $A\theta \leftarrow L_1\theta, \ldots, L_n\theta$. We need to show that

$$|A\theta| > |L_i\theta| \text{ for } i \in [1, \bar{n}],$$

where

$$\bar{n} = \min(\{n\} \cup \{i \in [1,n] \mid I \not\models L_i\theta\}).$$

We have $A\theta\theta \equiv A\theta$, so $A\theta$ and A unify. Let $\mu = \text{mgu}(A\theta, A)$. Then $\theta = \mu\delta$ for some δ. By the definition of *LDNF*-resolution, $\leftarrow L_1\mu, \ldots, L_n\mu$ is an *LDNF*-resolvent of $\leftarrow A\theta$. Then for $i \in [1, \bar{n}]$

$$
\begin{array}{ll}
 & |A\theta| \\
= & \{\text{definition of } |\;|\} \\
 & nodes_P\,(\leftarrow A\theta) \\
> & \{\text{Lemma 3.2(iii)}, \leftarrow L_1\mu, \ldots, L_n\mu \text{ is a resolvent of } \leftarrow A\theta\} \\
 & nodes_P\,(\leftarrow L_1\mu, \ldots, L_n\mu) \\
\geq & \{\text{part (ii1), noting that } L_i\theta \in \cup|[\leftarrow L_1\mu, \ldots, L_n\mu]|_I\} \\
 & |L_i\theta|.
\end{array}
$$

(ii2) Consider a goal G which is bounded w.r.t. $|\;|$ and I. Then by (i) and Corollary 2.10 all *LDNF*-derivations of $P \cup \{G\}$ are finite. □

Corollary 3.5 *A non-floundering program is left terminating iff it is acceptable.*

Proof. By Corollary 2.12 and Theorem 3.4. □

4 Semantic Considerations

In this section we study semantics of acceptable programs. We show here that various ways of defining their semantics coincide.

We recall first the relevant definitions and results. We use below Fitting's approach to the semantics of general programs. Fitting [Fit85] uses a 3-valued logic based on a logic due to Kleene [Kle52]. In Kleene's logic there are three truth values: **t** for true, **f** for false and **u** for undefined.

A Herbrand interpretation for this logic (called a 3-*valued* Herbrand interpretation) is defined as a pair (T, F) of disjoint sets of ground atoms. Given such an interpretation $I = (T, F)$ a ground atom A is true in I if $A \in T$, false in I if $A \in F$ and undefined otherwise; $\neg A$ is true in I if A is false in I and $\neg A$ is false in I if A is true in I.

Every binary connective takes the value **t** or **f** if it takes that value in 2-valued logic for all possible substitutions of **u**'s by **t** or **f**; otherwise it takes value **u**.

Given a formula ϕ and a 3-valued Herbrand interpretation I, we write ϕ is $true_3$ in I (respectively ϕ is $false_3$ in I) to denote the fact that ϕ is true in I (respectively that ϕ is false in I) in the above defined sense.

Given $I = (T, F)$ we denote T by I^+ and F by I^-. Thus $I = (I^+, I^-)$. If $I^+ \cup I^- = B_P$, we call I a *total* 3-valued Herbrand interpretation for the program P.

Every (2-valued) Herbrand interpretation I for a program P determines a total 3-valued Herbrand interpretation $(I, B_P - I)$ for P. This allows us to identify every 2-valued Herbrand interpretation I for a program P with its 3-valued counterpart $(I, B_P - I)$. For uniformity, given a (2-valued) Herbrand interpretation I we write ϕ is $true_2$ in I instead of $I \models \phi$ and ϕ is $false_2$ in I instead of $I \not\models \phi$. The following proposition relates truth in 3- and 2-valued intepretations and will be useful later.

Proposition 4.1 *Let I be a 3-valued interpretation and L a literal. Then*

(i) L is $true_3$ in I implies L is $true_2$ in I^+,

(ii) L is $true_2$ in I^+ implies L is not $false_3$ in I, i.e. L is either $true_3$ or undefined in I.

Proof.
(i) If $L = A$, L is $true_3$ in I implies $A \in I^+$, hence A is $true_2$ in I^+. If $L = \neg A$, $\neg A$ is $true_3$ in I implies $A \in I^-$, which implies $A \notin I^+$. Hence $\neg A$ is $true_2$ in I^+.
(ii) If $L = A$, L is $true_2$ in I^+ implies $A \in I^+$, hence A is $true_3$ in I. If $L = \neg A$, $\neg A$ is $true_2$ in I^+ implies $A \notin I^+$. Hence $\neg A$ is either $true_3$ or undefined in I. □

Given a program P, the 3-valued Herbrand interpretations for P form a complete partial ordering with the ordering $\subseteq$ defined by

$$I \subseteq J \text{ iff } I^+ \subseteq J^+ \wedge I^- \subseteq J^-$$

and with the least element $(\emptyset, \emptyset)$. Note that in this ordering every total 3-valued Herbrand interpretation is $\subseteq$-maximal. Intuitively, $I \subseteq J$ if J decides both truth and falsity for more atoms than I does.

Following Fitting [Fit85], given a program P we define an operator Φ_P on the complete partial ordering of 3-valued Herbrand interpretations for P as follows:

$$\Phi_P(I) = (T, F),$$

where

$$T = \{A \mid \text{for some } A \leftarrow L_1, \ldots, L_k \text{ in } ground(P),\ L_1 \wedge \ldots \wedge L_k \text{ is } true_3 \text{ in } I\},$$
$$F = \{A \mid \text{for all } A \leftarrow L_1, \ldots, L_k \text{ in } ground(P),\ L_1 \wedge \ldots \wedge L_k \text{ is } false_3 \text{ in } I\}.$$

It is easy to see that T and F are disjoint, so $\Phi_P(I)$ is indeed a 3-valued Herbrand interpretation. Φ_P is a natural generalization of the usual immediate consequence operator T_P to the case of 3-valued logic. Φ_P is easily seen to be monotonic.

The *upward ordinal powers* of Φ_P, denoted by $\Phi_P \uparrow \alpha$, are defined in the usual way starting the iteration at the $\subseteq$-least 3-valued Herbrand interpretation, $(\emptyset, \emptyset)$. In particular

$$\Phi_P \uparrow \omega = \bigcup_{n<\omega} \Phi_P \uparrow n.$$

Before studying semantics of acceptable programs we prove a number of auxiliary results about the operators T_P and Φ_P. The following lemma relates these two operators.

Lemma 4.2 *Let I be a 3-valued interpretation and P a program. Then*

$$\Phi_P(I)^+ \subseteq T_P(I^+) \subseteq B_P - \Phi_P(I)^-.$$

Moreover, if I is total then $\Phi_P(I)^+ = T_P(I^+) = B_P - \Phi_P(I)^-$.

Proof. By definition of T_P and Φ_P we obtain:

$A \in \Phi_P(I)^+$	iff for some $A \leftarrow L_1, \ldots, L_k$ in $ground(P)$ $L_1 \wedge \ldots \wedge L_k$ is $true_3$ in I,
$A \in T_P(I^+)$	iff for some $A \leftarrow L_1, \ldots, L_k$ in $ground(P)$ $L_1 \wedge \ldots \wedge L_k$ is $true_2$ in I^+,
$A \in B_P - \Phi_P(I)^-$	iff for some $A \leftarrow L_1, \ldots, L_k$ in $ground(P)$ $L_1 \wedge \ldots \wedge L_k$ is not $false_3$ in I.

Hence, the implication $A \in \Phi_P(I)^+ \Rightarrow A \in T_P(I^+)$ (respectively $A \in T_P(I^+) \Rightarrow A \in B_P - \Phi_P(I)^-$) directly follows from Proposition 4.1(i) (respectively Proposition 4.1(ii)).

If I is total, then $L_1 \wedge \ldots \wedge L_k$ is $true_3$ in I iff $L_1 \wedge \ldots \wedge L_k$ is $true_2$ in I^+ iff $L_1 \wedge \ldots \wedge L_k$ is not $false_3$ in I. □

The following corollaries relate the fixpoints of the operators T_P and Φ_P.

Corollary 4.3 *Let $I = (I^+, B_P - I^+)$ be a total 3-valued interpretation and P a program. Then I^+ is a fixpoint of T_P if and only if I is a fixpoint of Φ_P.*

Proof.
($\Rightarrow$) Assume $I^+ = T_P(I^+)$. By Lemma 4.2 we have $\Phi_P(I)^+ = T_P(I^+) = B_P - \Phi_P(I)^-$. Hence $I^+ = \Phi_P(I)^+$ and $I^- = B_P - I^+ = \Phi_P(I)^-$, i.e. $I = \Phi_P(I)$.
($\Leftarrow$) Assume $I = \Phi_P(I)$. Then by Lemma 4.2 we have

$$I^+ = \Phi_P(I)^+ \subseteq T_P(I^+) \subseteq B_P - \Phi_P(I)^- = B_P - I^- = I^+.$$

Hence I^+ is a fixpoint of T_P. □

Corollary 4.4 *If Φ_P has exactly one fixpoint I and I is total, then I^+ is the unique fixpoint of T_P.*

Proof. By Corollary 4.3. □

The fixpoints of the operator T_P are of interest for us because of the following result of Apt, Blair and Walker [ABW88].

Theorem 4.5 *A Herbrand interpretation I is a model of comp(P) iff it is a fixpoint of T_P.* □

Corollary 4.6 *If I is a Herbrand model of comp(P) then $\Phi_P \uparrow \omega \subseteq (I, B_P - I)$.*

Proof. Suppose I is a Herbrand model of *comp(P)*. Then by Theorem 4.5 I is a fixpoint of T_P, so by Corollary 4.3 $(I, B_P - I)$ is fixpoint of Φ_P. By the monotonicity of Φ_P the least fixpoint of Φ_P, $lfp(\Phi_P)$, exists and $\Phi_P \uparrow \omega \subseteq lfp(\Phi_P)$. But $lfp(\Phi_P) \subseteq (I, B_P - I)$, so $\Phi_P \uparrow \omega \subseteq (I, B_P - I)$. □

We are now ready to analyze the semantics of acceptable programs.

Theorem 4.7 *Let P be an acceptable program w.r.t. $||$ and I. Then $\Phi_P \uparrow \omega$ is total.*

Proof. To establish that $\Phi_P \uparrow \omega$ is total we prove that, for $n \in \omega$ and $A \in B_P$, $|A| = n$ implies that A is not undefined in $\Phi_P \uparrow (n+1)$, i.e. A is either $true_3$ or $false_3$ in $\Phi_P \uparrow (n+1)$. The proof proceeds by induction on n. Fix $A \in B_P$.

In the base case we have $|A| = 0$ and since P is acceptable, two possibilities arise: (i) there is a unit clause $A \leftarrow$ in *ground(P)* and (ii) there is no clause in *ground(P)* with A as conclusion. In case (i) A is $true_3$ in $\Phi_P \uparrow 1$, and in case (ii) A is $false_3$ in $\Phi_P \uparrow 1$.

In the induction case we have $|A| = n > 0$. Consider the set C_A of the clauses in *ground(P)* with A as conclusion. If C_A is empty then A is $false_3$ in $\Phi_P \uparrow 1$ and, by the monotonicity of Φ_P, it is $false_3$ in $\Phi_P \uparrow (n+1)$. If C_A is non-empty, take a clause $A \leftarrow L_1, \ldots, L_k$ from C_A, and let $\bar{k} = \min(\{k\} \cup \{i \in [1,k] \mid L_i \text{ is } false_2 \text{ in } I\}$. We now prove that $L_1 \wedge \ldots \wedge L_k$ is not undefined in $\Phi_P \uparrow n$. To this end we consider two subcases.

Subcase 1. $\bar{k} = k$ and L_k is $true_2$ in I. Then, by the acceptability of P, $n = |A| > |L_k|$ for $i \in [1,k]$. By the induction hypothesis L_i is either $true_3$ or $false_3$ in $\Phi_P \uparrow n$, for $i \in [1,k]$.

Subcase 2. $\bar{k} \leq k$ and $L_{\bar{k}}$ is $false_2$ in I. Then $n = |A| > |L_k|$ for $i \in [1,\bar{k}]$. By the induction hypothesis, L_i is either $true_3$ or $false_3$ in $\Phi_P \uparrow n$, for $i \in [1,\bar{k}]$. Moreover, we claim that $L_{\bar{k}}$ is $false_3$ in $\Phi_P \uparrow n$. To establish this point, the following two possibilities have to be taken into account.

Suppose the relation occurring in $L_{\bar{k}}$ is in Neg_P^*. A simple proof by induction on n shows that $\Phi_P \uparrow n$ and $\Phi_{P^-} \uparrow n$ coincide on the relations in Neg_P^*. Thus $L_{\bar{k}}$ is $true_3$ in $\Phi_P \uparrow n$ implies $L_{\bar{k}}$ is $true_3$ in $\Phi_{P^-} \uparrow n$. Hence, by Corollary 4.6 and Proposition 4.1(i), $L_{\bar{k}}$ is $true_2$ in the restriction of I to the relations in Neg_P^* which is a model of $comp(P^-)$. This contradicts the fact that $L_{\bar{k}}$ is $false_2$ in I.

If the relation occurring in $L_{\bar{k}}$ is not in Neg_P^*, then $L_{\bar{k}}$ is a positive literal. We show that in this case $L_{\bar{k}}$ is $true_3$ in $\Phi_P \uparrow n$ implies $L_{\bar{k}}$ is $true_2$ in I by induction on the stage i at which $L_{\bar{k}}$ becomes $true_3$ in $\Phi_P \uparrow i$. For $i = 0$ there is nothing to prove. If $L_{\bar{k}}$ becomes $true_3$ in $\Phi_P \uparrow i$, then there is a clause $L_{\bar{k}} \leftarrow M_1, \ldots, M_m$ in $ground(P)$ with $M_1 \wedge \ldots \wedge M_m$ being $true_3$ in $\Phi_P \uparrow (i-1)$. For $j \in [1, m]$, if the relation occurring in M_j is in Neg_P^*, then M_j is $true_3$ in $\Phi_P \uparrow (i-1)$ implies M_j is $true_2$ in I by Corollary 4.6 and Proposition 4.1(i). If the relation occurring in M_j is not in Neg_P^*, then M_j is $true_3$ in $\Phi_P \uparrow (i-1)$ implies M_j is $true_2$ in I by the induction hypothesis. Hence $M_1 \wedge \ldots \wedge M_m$ is $true_2$ in I, which implies $L_{\bar{k}}$ is $true_2$ in I, since I is a model of $L_{\bar{k}} \leftarrow M_1, \ldots, M_m$. This contradicts the fact that $L_{\bar{k}}$ is $false_2$ in I.

In both Subcase 1 and 2, we have that $L_1 \wedge \ldots \wedge L_k$ is not undefined in $\Phi_P \uparrow n$, as it is either $true_3$ or $false_3$ in Subcase 1, and $false_3$ in Subcase 2. As a consequence, A is either $true_3$ or $false_3$ in $\Phi_P \uparrow (n+1)$, which establishes the claim. □

Corollary 4.8 *Let P be an acceptable program. Then $\Phi_P \uparrow \omega$ is the unique fixpoint of Φ_P.*

Proof. We have $\Phi_P \uparrow \omega \subseteq \Phi_P \uparrow (\omega + 1)$, i.e. $\Phi_P \uparrow \omega \subseteq \Phi_P(\Phi_P \uparrow \omega)$. By Theorem 4.7 $\Phi_P \uparrow \omega$ is total, so in fact $\Phi_P \uparrow \omega = \Phi_P(\Phi_P \uparrow \omega)$, i.e. $\Phi_P \uparrow \omega$ is a fixpoint of Φ_P. Moreover, by the monotonicity of Φ_P, every fixpoint of Φ_P of the form $\Phi_P \uparrow \alpha$ is contained in any other fixpoint, so in fact $\Phi_P \uparrow \omega$ is the unique fixpoint of Φ_P. □

The following corollary summarizes the relevant properties of $M_P = \Phi_P \uparrow \omega$.

Corollary 4.9 *Let P be an acceptable program. Then*

(i) M_P is total,

(ii) M_P is the unique fixpoint of Φ_P,

(iii) M_P is the unique 3-valued Herbrand model of comp(P),

(iv) M_P^+ is the unique fixpoint of T_P,

(v) M_P^+ is the unique Herbrand model of comp(P),

(vi) for all ground atoms A such that no LDNF-derivation of $P \cup \{\leftarrow A\}$ flounders,

$$A \in M_P^+ \text{ iff there exists an LDNF-refutation of } P \cup \{\leftarrow A\}.$$

In particular, this equivalence holds for all ground atoms A when P is non-floundering.

Proof.
(i) By Theorem 4.7.
(ii) By Corollary 4.8.
(iii) By (ii) and the result of Fitting [Fit85] stating that a 3-valued Herbrand interpretation is a model of *comp*(P) iff it is a fixpoint of Φ_P.

(iv) By Theorem 4.7 and Corollaries 4.8 and 4.4.
(v) By Theorem 4.5.
(vi) Consider a ground atom A such that no $LDNF$-derivation of $P \cup \{\leftarrow A\}$ flounders. By the soundness of the $SLDNF$-resolution and (v) if there exists an $LDNF$-refutation of $P \cup \{\leftarrow A\}$ then $A \in M_P^+$. To prove the converse implication assume $A \in M_P^+$. By Corollary 2.11 all $LDNF$-derivations of $P \cup \{\leftarrow A\}$ are finite. Suppose by contradiction that none of them is successful. Then the $LDNF$-tree for $P \cup \{\leftarrow A\}$ is non-floundering and finitely failed. By the soundness of the $SLDNF$-resolution and (v), $M_P^+ \models \neg A$, i.e. $A \notin M_P^+$ which is a contradiction.

□

Clause (vi) of the above Corollary can be seen as a completeness result for acceptable programs relating the $LDNF$-resolution to the model M_P^+.

5 Applications

Theorem 3.4 shows that our method of proving termination based on the concepts of acceptability and boundedness is complete for left terminating, non-floundering general Prolog programs. In this section we illustrate its use by proving termination of two simple, well-known programs. None of them can be handled within the framework of Apt and Bezem [AB90].

A GAME Program

Suppose that $\mathcal{G}$ is an acyclic finite graph. Consider the following program GAME:

```
win(X) ← move(X,Y), ¬ win(Y).
move(a,b) ←        for (a,b) ∈ 𝒢.
```

Lemma 5.1 GAME *is not acyclic.*

Proof. For any ground instance $win(a) \leftarrow move(a,a), \neg win(a)$ of the first clause and a level mapping $|\;|$ we have $|win(a)| = |\neg win(a)|$. □

We now proceed to show that GAME is acceptable. Since $\mathcal{G}$ is acyclic and finite, there exists a function f from the elements of its domain to natural numbers such that for $a \in dom(\mathcal{G})$

$$f(a) = \begin{cases} 0 & \text{if for no } b,\ (a,b) \in \mathcal{G} \\ 1 + max\ \{f(b) \mid (a,b) \in \mathcal{G}\} & \text{otherwise.} \end{cases}$$

We define appropriate level mapping by putting for all $(a,b) \in dom(\mathcal{G})$

$$|move(a,b)| = f(a)$$

and for $a \in dom(\mathcal{G})$

$$|win(a)| = f(a) + 1.$$

Next, since $\mathcal{G}$ is acyclic and finite, there exists a function g from the elements of its domain to $\{0, 1\}$ such that for $a \in dom(\mathcal{G})$

$$g(a) = \begin{cases} 0 & \text{if for no } b, (a,b) \in \mathcal{G} \\ 1 - min\ \{g(b) \mid (a,b) \in \mathcal{G}\} & \text{otherwise.} \end{cases}$$

Let

$$\begin{aligned} I \ = \quad & \{move(a,b) \mid \ (a,b) \in \mathcal{G}\} \\ \cup \ & \{win(a) \mid \ g(a) = 1\}. \end{aligned}$$

Lemma 5.2 *I is a model of comp(*`GAME`*).*

Proof. The following two statements hold.
(a) I is a model of `GAME`.

Indeed, consider a ground instance

$$win(a) \leftarrow move(a,b), \neg win(b)$$

of the first clause of `GAME` and suppose that

$$I \models move(a,b) \wedge \neg win(b).$$

Then $(a,b) \in \mathcal{G}$ and $g(b) = 0$, so $g(a) = 1$ and consequently

$$I \models win(a).$$

Additionally, I is a model for all `move` clauses.

(b) I is a supported interpretation of `GAME`.

Indeed, consider an atom $win(a) \in I$. Then $g(a) = 1$, so for some $b \in \mathcal{G}$ we have $(a,b) \in \mathcal{G}$ and $g(b) = 0$. We conclude that

$$I \models move(a,b) \wedge \neg win(b).$$

By Theorem 2.13 we conclude that I is a model of *comp*(`GAME`). □

We can now prove the desired result.

Theorem 5.3 `GAME` *is acceptable w.r.t.* $|\ |$ *and* I.

Proof. For a program P every model of $comp(P)$ is also a model of P, thus I is a model of `GAME`. Moreover, $\texttt{GAME}^- = \texttt{GAME}$.

Consider a ground instance

$$win(a) \leftarrow move(a,b), \neg win(b)$$

of the first clause of GAME. Then by definition

$$|win(a)| = f(a) + 1 > f(a) = |move(a, b)|.$$

Suppose now that $I \models move(a, b)$. Then $move(a, b) \in I$, so $(a, b) \in \mathcal{G}$ and consequently $f(a) > f(b)$. Thus

$$|win(a)| = f(a) + 1 > f(b) + 1 = |\neg win(b)|.$$

□

Corollary 5.4 GAME *is left terminating.*

Proof. By Corollary 2.12. □

Corollary 5.5 *For all terms t, the goal* $\leftarrow win(t)$ *is bounded w.r.t.* $|\ |$ *and* I.

Proof. The goal $\leftarrow win(t)$ is bounded by $max\ \{f(a) + 1 \mid a \in dom(\mathcal{G})\}$. Note that because of the syntax of GAME, t is either a variable or a constant. In the latter case we can improve the bound to $f(t) + 1$. □

Corollary 5.6 *For all terms t, all LDNF-derivations of* GAME $\cup \{\leftarrow win(t)\}$ *are finite.*

Proof. By Corollary 2.11. □

Transitive Closure

Consider the following program computing the transitive closure of a graph.

```
(r1)  r(X,Y,E,V) ←
         member([X,Y],E).
(r2)  r(X,Z,E,V) ←
         member([X,Y],E),
         ¬ member(Y,V),
         r(Y,Z,E,[Y|V]).

(m1)  member(X,[X|T]) ←.
(m2)  member(X,[Y|T]) ←
         member(X,T).
```

In a typical use of this program one evaluates a goal $\leftarrow r(x, y, e, [\,])$ where x, y are nodes and e is a graph specified by a list of its edges. The nodes of e belong to a finite set $\mathcal{A}$. This goal is supposed to succeed when $[x, y]$ is in the transitive closure of e. The last argument of $r(x, y, e, v)$ acts as an accumulator in which one maintains the list of nodes which should not be reused when looking for a path connecting x with y in e (to keep the path acyclic).

To ensure that the elements of $\mathcal{A}$ are in the Herbrand Universe of the program we add to the program the clauses

(e) `element(a) ←` *for* a $\in \mathcal{A}$,

and call the resulting program TRANS.

Lemma 5.7 TRANS *is not acyclic.*

Proof. By Lemma 4.1 of Apt and Bezem [AB90] all *SLDNF*-derivations of an acyclic program P starting with a ground goal are finite. Thus it suffices to exhibit an infinite *SLDNF*-derivation of TRANS starting in a ground goal. Such a derivation is obtained by using the rightmost selection rule and starting with the ground goal $\leftarrow r(x, z, e, v)$ repeatedly using clause (r_2). □

We now prove that TRANS is acceptable. Below we call a list consisting of two elements a *pair.*

First, we define by structural induction two functions on ground terms. We denote the first function by $|\ |$:

$$|[x|xs]| = |xs| + 1,$$
$$|f(x_1, \ldots, x_n)| = 0 \text{ if } f \neq [\,.\,|\,.\,].$$

Then for a list xs, $|xs|$ equals its length. We denote the second function by *set*:

$$set([x|xs]) = \{x\} \cup set(xs),$$
$$set(f(x_1, \ldots, x_n)) = \emptyset \text{ if } f \neq [\,.\,|\,.\,].$$

Then for a list xs, $set(xs)$ is the set of its elements.

Define now a Herbrand interpretation I by

$$I = [r(X, Y, E, V)] \cup I_1 \cup \{element(x) \mid x \in \mathcal{A}\}$$

where

$$I_1 = \{member(x, xs) \mid x \in set(xs)\}.$$

Recall that for an atom A, $[A]$ stands for the set of all ground instances of A.

We now prove two lemmata about I and I_1.

Lemma 5.8 I *is a model of* TRANS.

Proof. I is clearly a model of (r_1), (r_2) and of the clauses (e). I is also a model of the clauses (m_1) and (m_2) because by definition $x \in set([x|t])$ holds and $x \in set(t)$ implies $x \in set([y|t])$. □

Lemma 5.9 I_1 *is a model of comp*(TRANS$^-$).

Proof. Note that $\texttt{TRANS}^- = \{(m_1), (m_2)\}$. We prove that I_1 is a supported interpretation of $\{(m_1), (m_2)\}$. Consider an atom $member(x, xs) \in I_1$. We prove that there exists a ground instance $member(x, xs) \leftarrow L_1, \ldots, L_n$ of (m_1) or (m_2) such that $I \models L_1 \wedge \ldots \wedge L_n$.

By definition $x \in set(xs)$, so for some y and t we have $xs = [y|t]$ and $x \in \{y\} \cup set(t)$. If $x = y$, then $xs = [x|t]$, and the desired clause is an instance of (m_1). Otherwise $x \in set(t)$, so $member(x, t) \in I$, i.e. $I \models member(x, t)$. In this case the desired clause is an instance of (m_2).

By Lemma 5.8 I_1 is a model of $\{(m_1), (m_2)\}$, so by Theorem 2.13 we now conclude that I_1 is a model of $comp(\{(m_1), (m_2)\})$. □

We now define an appropriate level mapping. It is clear that by putting

$$|member(x, y)| = |y|$$

we obtain the desired decrease for clause (m_2). Having made this choice in order to obtain the desired decrease for clause (r_1) we need to have

$$|r(x, z, e, v)| > |e|. \tag{1}$$

Additionally, to obtain the desired decrease for clause (r_2) we need to have (assuming that $I \models member([x, y], e)$)

$$|r(x, z, e, v)| > |v| \tag{2}$$

and, assuming

$$I \models member([x, y], e) \wedge \neg member(y, v), \tag{3}$$

we need to prove

$$|r(x, z, e, v)| > |r(y, z, e, [y|v])|. \tag{4}$$

To define $|r(x, z, e, v)|$ we first define two auxiliary functions. Let

$$nodes(e) = \{x \mid \text{for some pair } b,\ x \in set(b) \text{ and } b \in set(e)\}.$$

If e is a list of pairs that specifies the edges of a graph $\mathcal{G}$, then $nodes(e)$ is the set of nodes of $\mathcal{G}$.

Let

$$out(e, v) = \{x \mid x \in nodes(e) \text{ and } x \notin set(v)\}.$$

If e is a list of pairs that specify the edges of a graph $\mathcal{G}$ and v is a list, then $out(e, v)$ is the set of nodes of $\mathcal{G}$ that are not elements of v.

We now put

$$|r(x, z, e, v)| = |e| + |v| + 2 \cdot card\ out(e, v) + 1,$$

where $card\ X$ stands for the cardinality of the set X.

Then (1) and (2) hold. Assume now (3). Then $[x, y] \in set(e)$ and $y \notin set(v)$. Thus $y \in nodes(e)$ and consequently $y \in out(e, v)$.

On the other hand $set([y|v]) = \{y\} \cup set(v)$. Thus $y \notin out(e, [y|v])$ and $out(e, v) = \{y\} \cup out(e, [y|v])$ so $card\ out(e, v) = card\ out(e, [y|v]) + 1$.

We now have

$$\begin{aligned} |r(x, z, e, v)| &= |e| + |v| + 2 \cdot card\ out(e, v) + 1 \\ &= |e| + |v| + 2 \cdot card\ out(e, [y|v]) + 3 \\ &> |e| + |[y|v]| + 2 \cdot card\ out(e, [y|v]) + 1 \\ &= |r(y, z, e, [y|v])| \end{aligned}$$

which proves (4).

Summarizing, we proved the following result.

Theorem 5.10 TRANS *is acceptable w.r.t.* $|\ |$ *and* I. □

Corollary 5.11 TRANS *is left terminating.*

Proof. By Corollary 2.12. □

Corollary 5.12 *For all terms* x, y *and lists* e, v, *the goal* $\leftarrow r(x, y, e, v)$ *is bounded w.r.t.* $|\ |$ *and* I.

Proof. The goal $\leftarrow r(x, y, e, v)$ is bounded by $|e| + |v| + 2 \cdot card\ out(e, v) + 1$. □

Corollary 5.13 *For all terms* x, y *and lists* e, v, *all LDNF-derivations of* TRANS $\cup \{\leftarrow r(x, y, e, v)\}$ *are finite.*

Proof. By Corollary 2.11. □

Acknowledgement

Marc Bezem made us aware of the importance of including subsidiary *LDNF*-trees in the definition of $nodes_P(G)$.

References

[AB90] K. R. Apt and M. Bezem. Acyclic programs. In D. H. D. Warren and P. Szeredi, editors, *Proceedings of the Seventh International Conference on Logic Programming*, pages 617–633. The MIT Press, 1990.

[ABW88] K. R. Apt, H. A. Blair, and A. Walker. Towards a theory of declarative knowledge. In J. Minker, editor, *Foundations of Deductive Databases and Logic Programming*, pages 89–148. Morgan Kaufmann, 1988.

[AP90] K. R. Apt and D. Pedreschi. Studies in pure Prolog: termination. In J.W. Lloyd, editor, *Symposium on Computional Logic*, pages 150–176, Berlin, 1990. Springer-Verlag.

[Apt90] K. R. Apt. Logic programming. In J. van Leeuwen, editor, *Handbook of Theoretical Computer Science*, pages 493–574. Elsevier, 1990. Vol. B.

[Bau88] M. Baudinet. Proving termination properties of PROLOG programs. In *Proceedings of the 3rd Annual Symposium on Logic in Computer Science (LICS)*, pages 336–347, Edinburgh, Scotland, 1988.

[Bez89] M. Bezem. Characterizing termination of logic programs with level mappings. In E. L. Lusk and R. A. Overbeek, editors, *Proceedings of the North American Conference on Logic Programming*, pages 69–80. The MIT Press, 1989.

[Cav89] L. Cavedon. Continuity, consistency, and completeness properties for logic programs. In G. Levi and M. Martelli, editors, *Proceedings of the Sixth International Conference on Logic Programming*, pages 571–584. The MIT Press, 1989.

[Der87] N. Dershowitz. Termination of rewriting. *Journal of Symbolic Computation*, 8:69–116, 1987.

[Fit85] M. Fitting. A Kripke-Kleene semantics for general logic programs. *Journal of Logic Programming*, 2:295–312, 1985.

[HM87] S. Hanks and D. McDermott. Nonmonotonic logic and temporal projection. *Artificial Intelligence*, 33:379–412, 1987.

[Kle52] S. C. Kleene. *Introduction to Metamathematics.* van Nostrand, New York, 1952.

[Llo87] J. W. Lloyd. *Foundations of Logic Programming.* Springer-Verlag, Berlin, second edition, 1987.

[Plü90a] L. Plümer. *Termination Proofs for Logic Programs.* Lecture Notes in Artificial Intelligence 446, Springer-Verlag, Berlin, 1990.

[Plü90b] L. Plümer. Termination proofs for logic programs based on predicate inequalities. In D. H. D. Warren and P. Szeredi, editors, *Proceedings of the Seventh International Conference on Logic Programming*, pages 634–648. The MIT Press, 1990.

[UvG88] J. D. Ullman and A. van Gelder. Efficient tests for top-down termination of logical rules. *J. ACM*, 35(2):345–373, 1988.

On Abstraction and the Expressive Power of Programming Languages

John C. Mitchell*
Department of Computer Science
Stanford University
Stanford, CA 94305
jcm@cs.stanford.edu

Abstract

We present a tentative theory of programming language expressiveness based on reductions (language translations) that preserve observational equivalence. These are called "abstraction-preserving" because of a connection with a definition of "abstraction" or "information-hiding" mechanism. If there is an abstraction-preserving reduction from one language to another, then essentially every function on natural numbers that is definable in the first is also definable in the second. Moreover, regardless of the set of first-order functions definable in either language, no programming language with an abstraction mechanism can be reduced to a language without. Since Lisp with user-defined special forms does not have an abstraction mechanism, it is therefore not "universal" in this theory, in spite of the ability to define every partial recursive function on the natural numbers. Several examples and counter-examples to abstraction-preserving reductions are given. We do not know whether there is a natural universal language with respect to abstraction-preserving reduction.

1 Introduction

This paper presents a tentative theory of programming language expressiveness, originally described in unpublished notes that were circulated in 1986. The original motivation was to compare languages according to the ability to make sections of a program "abstract" by hiding some details of the internal workings of the code. This led

*Supported in part by an NSF PYI Award, matching funds from Digital Equipment Corporation, the Powell Foundation, and Xerox Corporation; NSF grant CCR-8814921 and the Wallace F. and Lucille M. Davis Faculty Scholarship.

to the definition of abstraction-preserving reductions, which are syntax-directed (homomorphic) language translations that preserve observational equivalence. Common translations such as replacing a block by a function declaration and call are abstraction-preserving, as is the addition of recursive types to a functional language that already allows recursive definition of functions. A motivating example was the comparison of weak sums (existential types) with strong sums, which were debated as the basis for data abstraction and module facilities in programming languages. In addition to showing that the replacement of weak sums by strong sums is not abstraction-preserving, we point out that many languages are not reducible to Lisp (with FEXPR), in spite of the fact that any partial recursive function on the natural numbers may be written in Lisp.

Since the first version of this paper was circulated, abstraction-preserving reductions have been used by Riecke, with some insightful refinements, to compare call-by-name, call-by-value and lazy lambda calculus [16]. In addition, Felleisen has proposed an alternative theory of expressiveness that has different motivations and consequences [2]. Both of these papers are discussed in Section 8.

We will give some motivation for abstraction-preserving reductions in the next section, and give precise definitions in Section 3. Some examples of reductions and non-reductions appear in Sections 4 through 6. In Section 7, we observe that since no language with an abstraction mechanism can be reduced to a language without, languages like Lisp (with FEXPR) that can distinguish program phrases by their syntactic form are not universal with respect to our reductions. We do not know whether there is a reasonable language that is capable of simulating every other programming languages in an abstraction-preserving way. Some concluding remarks appear in Section 9.

The original title of this paper was "Lisp is not universal." This was catchy, but gave the mistaken implication that the main topic is Lisp. The discussion of Lisp in this paper is not intended to be a criticism of the language. In particular, it is recognized that most Lisp programmers use FEXPR's sparingly. The main point of the Lisp example is to demonstrate the kind of programming construct that can prevent abstraction-preserving reduction.

2 What properties should a "reduction" preserve?

Intuitively, a programming language $\mathcal{L}_1$ is no more expressive than a language $\mathcal{L}_2$ if there is a function θ "reducing" each construct of $\mathcal{L}_1$ to an essentially equivalent construct in $\mathcal{L}_2$. To gain some perspective, we review some forms of reduction from the literature.

We may view recursion equations, Turing machine descriptions and untyped lambda terms as languages for programming functions on the integers. Each formalism has a way of representing integers and a way of coding functions between integers. We may compare the ability to express numeric functions using recursion-theoretic reductions:

a language $\mathcal{L}_1$ is reducible to another language $\mathcal{L}_2$ if there is a mapping θ from $\mathcal{L}_1$ to $\mathcal{L}_2$ which sends every coding f of a numeric function in $\mathcal{L}_1$ to a coding θf of the same numeric function in $\mathcal{L}_2$. Since all of the languages for partial recursive functions define the same class of numeric functions, each is reducible to any other.

A more useful definition of reduction is the one adopted in "program schematology" [3, 13]. In this theory, simple imperative programs are "run" on arbitrary data types, or first-order structures. To simplify our discussion, let us consider deterministic programs only. A program S may mention some set $x_1 \ldots x_i$ of variables, some set $f_1 \ldots f_j$ of function symbols in its expressions and some set $P_1 \ldots P_k$ of predicate symbols in its boolean tests. For any set A, functions $f_1^A \ldots f_j^A$ on A and predicates $P_1 \ldots P_k$ on A, a deterministic imperative program computes a partial function from sequences of initial values for $x_1 \ldots x_i$ from A to final values of $x_1 \ldots x_i$. Thus, for any first-order structure $\mathcal{A} = \langle A, f_1^A \ldots f_j^A, P_1^A \ldots P_k^A \rangle$ interpreting the function and predicate symbols in P, a program P computes an input-output function on sequences of values from A. In program schematology, language $\mathcal{L}_1$ is reducible to $\mathcal{L}_2$ if, for every program P in $\mathcal{L}_1$ there is a program $Q = \theta P$ in $\mathcal{L}_2$ computing the same input-output function for every $\mathcal{A}$. (Often a simulating program is allowed to use extra "scratch" variables.) Using this definition of reduction, we can distinguish between recursion and iteration, for example [13]. Thus program schematology does a better job of explaining the intuitive "expressive power" of programming languages than recursion theory. We can actually view program schematology as a theory of "higher-order expressiveness," as follows. For most classes of imperative programs, we could fix the carrier A to be some suitably large set without loss of generality, and think of a program text S as defining the higher-order function

$$\lambda f_1. \ldots \lambda f_j. \lambda P_1. \ldots \lambda P_k. \lambda x_1. \ldots \lambda x_i. \langle S_1, \ldots, S_i \rangle$$

where S_n is the final value of x_n after running S on the indicated input. Then a reduction from $\mathcal{L}_1$ to $\mathcal{L}_2$ becomes a mapping which preserves the set of higher-order functions definable in the language.

A more general approach to higher-order expressiveness would be to use denotational semantics. We discuss this possibility as an intermediate step towards a definition that is essentially based on operational semantics, but has a close connection to a traditional topic in denotational semantics. If languages $\mathcal{L}_1$ and $\mathcal{L}_2$ come equipped with denotational semantics, then for every class of phrases in each language, the denotational semantics gives us some way of determining whether phrases of this class are equivalent. For example, the usual denotational semantics of languages with higher-order procedures determines an equivalence of higher-order procedures. A useful notation is to write $P \stackrel{\text{den}}{=} Q$ if expressions P and Q of $\mathcal{L}_1$ have the same meaning according to the denotational semantics of $\mathcal{L}_1$. A natural definition of reduction is a mapping θ from $\mathcal{L}_1$ to $\mathcal{L}_2$ with

$$P \stackrel{\text{den}}{=} Q \text{ iff } \theta P \stackrel{\text{den}}{=} \theta Q.$$

If we think of the denotation of a set of recursion equations as a numeric function, or the denotation of a program scheme as a mapping from predicate and function symbols in the first-order signature to functions, then the reductions we have discussed so far may be put in this form.

An important property of denotational semantics is substitutivity: if $P \stackrel{\text{den}}{=} Q$, then P may be substituted for Q in any program without changing the meaning of a program. As a consequence of substitutivity, whenever one language is reducible to another by a mapping that preserves denotational equivalence, we know that every expression in the first language may be translated to an expression in the second which serves the same purpose in every program context. This gives a good justification for using mappings that preserve denotational equivalence. The problem, however, is that many programming languages have many semantic interpretations, and it is not clear whether we want reductions to respect equivalence for all semantics, or for some "standard" one.

A natural equivalence relation on program phrases is observational equivalence. This is defined using operational semantics, but coincides with denotational equivalence in the fully-abstract model of the language [7, 14, 18], if it exists. We describe observational equivalence in this paragraph, and give the full, standard definition in the next section. Independent of any denotation semantics, observational equivalence is substitutive. We assume that full programs of a language $\mathcal{L}$ either run forever, or produce some kind of basic value as output. To simplify matters, we may assume that the inputs to a program are built into the program, and there is only one output. There is no harm in doing this because we will be able to compare programs with inputs and outputs by comparing their behaviors inside all possible "full programs" that supply inputs and select a single output. We say that two program phrases P and Q are *observationally equivalent* if, for any full program $\mathcal{C}[P]$ which produces a basic output value, the program $\mathcal{C}[Q]$ with Q replacing P produces the same value, and vice versa. Generally speaking, observational equivalence does not depend much on what we choose as the "basic values." Observational equivalence is more robust than arbitrary denotational equivalence, and seems to lead to a plausible study of expressiveness and abstraction mechanisms. One technical difficulty, however, is that since fully abstract models are difficult to construct, there is a shortage of techniques for reasoning about observational equivalence.

3 Programming languages and abstraction-preserving reductions

Before defining reductions, we describe the assumptions we need to make about programming languages. In addition to a set of expressions, we need program contexts. Intuitively, a program context $\mathcal{C}[\ ]$ is a program with a hole in it (represented by the empty brackets [ ]). When a language is presented by, say, a BNF grammar, it is easy to see what the contexts are. However, we can develop at least part of the theory by taking the more abstract view that we are given some set of expressions and some set of contexts. We also need a set of observables, intuitively corresponding to the printable values of the language, and an operational semantics.

For the purposes of this paper, a *programming language* $\mathcal{L} = \langle \mathcal{E}, \mathcal{C}t, \mathcal{O}, \stackrel{\text{eval}}{\rightarrow} \rangle$ consists of a set $\mathcal{E}$ of expressions, a set $\mathcal{C}t$ of contexts, a subset $\mathcal{O} \subseteq \mathcal{L}$ of expressions which we will call the *observables* of the language, and an evaluation relation $\stackrel{\text{eval}}{\rightarrow}$ on $\mathcal{L}$. We assume that every observable evaluates only to itself, *i.e.*,

$$\text{If } M \in \mathcal{O}, \text{ then } M \stackrel{\text{eval}}{\rightarrow} N \text{ iff } M \equiv N,$$

where $\equiv$ is syntactic equivalence, and that every expression evaluates to at most one observable. A context $\mathcal{C}[\,] \in \mathcal{C}t$ may be any mapping from expressions to expressions[1]. We will assume that every context is *syntactically nontrivial* in the sense that for any $\mathcal{C}[\,]$, the expression M must occur as a subexpression of $\mathcal{C}[M]$. We also assume, since we have not specified how contexts are derived from expressions, that the identity context $\mathcal{C}_I[\,]$ is included in $\mathcal{C}t$. This is the context that maps each expression of $\mathcal{L}$ to itself.

As the name suggests, two expressions M and N are observationally equivalent if we cannot observe any difference between them. Since the only way we can "observe" the behavior of an expression is by inserting it in a context which then yields an observable value, observational equivalence is defined as follows. Expressions M and N of a language $\mathcal{L}$ are observationally equivalent, written $M \stackrel{\text{obs}}{=} N$, if for every context $\mathcal{C}[\,]$,

$$\text{For all } P \in \mathcal{O},\ \mathcal{C}[M] \stackrel{\text{eval}}{\rightarrow} P \text{ iff } \mathcal{C}[N] \stackrel{\text{eval}}{\rightarrow} P.$$

In other words, whenever $\mathcal{C}[M]$ or $\mathcal{C}[N]$ evaluates to an observable, both evaluate to the same observable. A simple property of observational equivalence is that it is syntactic equality for observables.

Lemma 3.1 *If $M, N \in \mathcal{O}$ are observables, then $M \stackrel{\text{obs}}{=} N$ iff $M \equiv N$.*

This follows from our assumption that there is an identity context $\mathcal{C}_I[\,]$.

It is important to realize that the observational equivalence of two expressions M and N depends on the entire language, not just the way that M and N are evaluated. For example, if we could form pairs of basic values, but could not examine the components of a pair, then any two pairs might be observationally equivalent. However, if we add projection functions to the language, then pairs become observationally equivalent only if their components are equivalent. Thus adding new features to a language may make observationally equivalent expression inequivalent. For this reason, we must say which language we have in mind when we use the symbol $\stackrel{\text{obs}}{=}$.

Intuitively, an abstraction mechanism is a way of hiding some of the differences between program phrases. For example, in Algol-like languages, procedures with local

[1] Ordinarily, a context might be considered a partial function, since $\mathcal{C}[M]$ might not be well-formed. However, since evaluation is partial and we will only be concerned with programs that evaluate to observables, we can account for the partiality of contexts by taking evaluation to be undefined on expressions that are not well-formed.

variable declarations provide abstraction because we can take algorithms which work in different ways and hide their differences by placing them inside procedure declarations. To be more concrete, we may take two sorting algorithms which have different effects on temporary variables and enclose the two algorithms inside procedure bodies with local declarations of temporaries. If the two algorithms have the same effect on arrays, the two procedures will be equivalent. Thus, we can explain how procedures provide abstraction by observing that the context

procedure sort (a : int array)
    begin temp : int; [ ] **end**

allows us to transform inequivalent expressions (sorting algorithms with different side effects on temporary variables) into equivalent ones. For the purpose of this paper, it seems reasonable to define abstraction by this property.

A context $\mathcal{C}[\ ]$ is an *abstraction context for* $\mathcal{L}$ if $\mathcal{C}[M] \stackrel{\text{obs}}{=} \mathcal{C}[N]$ for some expressions $M \stackrel{\text{obs}}{\neq} N$ which are not observationally equivalent. The reason why such a context is called an "abstraction context" is that it obscures the difference between two otherwise distinguishable phrases. If we allowed syntactically trivial contexts $\mathcal{C}[\ ]$ with M not occurring in $\mathcal{C}[M]$, then every language would have an abstraction context. However, we do not consider syntactically trivial contexts. Even among the syntactically nontrivial contexts, there may be contexts $\mathcal{C}[\ ]$ with $\mathcal{C}[M] \stackrel{\text{obs}}{=} \mathcal{C}[N]$ for all M, N. Any of these *semantically trivial* contexts fits our definition since it maps inequivalent arguments to equivalent results. This is not very satisfactory, but it is not clear how far to go in patching the definition to avoid this.

An *abstraction-preserving reduction* from $\mathcal{L}_1$ to $\mathcal{L}_2$ is a mapping θ of expressions to expressions and contexts to contexts satisfying the following two conditions.

$$\begin{array}{ll} \text{(R1)} & \theta(\mathcal{C}[M]) \stackrel{\text{obs}}{=} (\theta\mathcal{C})[\theta M], \\ \text{(R2)} & M \stackrel{\text{obs}}{=} N \text{ iff } \theta M \stackrel{\text{obs}}{=} \theta N. \end{array}$$

Intuitively, the first condition says that θ respects the compositional meaning of programs, while the second condition is that θ must preserve observational equivalence (and inequivalence).

The name "abstraction-preserving reduction" is now explained by the following lemma.

Lemma 3.2 *Suppose language $\mathcal{L}_1$ has an abstraction context $\mathcal{C}$ and θ is an abstraction-preserving reduction from $\mathcal{L}_1$ to $\mathcal{L}_2$. Then $\theta\mathcal{C}$ is an abstraction context for $\mathcal{L}_2$. Moreover, if $\mathcal{C}$ hides the difference between inequivalent $M \stackrel{\text{obs}}{\neq} N$ in $\mathcal{L}_1$, by $\mathcal{C}[M] \stackrel{\text{obs}}{=} \mathcal{C}[N]$, then $\theta\mathcal{C}$ similarly hides the difference between inequivalent $\theta M \stackrel{\text{obs}}{\neq} \theta N$ in $\mathcal{L}_2$.*

An immediate consequence of the lemma is that if $\mathcal{L}_1$ has an abstraction context and $\mathcal{L}_2$ does not, then there is no abstraction-preserving reduction from $\mathcal{L}_1$ to $\mathcal{L}_2$. This will lead us to conclude, in Section 7, that no language with an abstraction context is reducible to Lisp with FEXPR.

Proof of Lemma 3.2: We assume that $\mathcal{C}[\,]$ is an abstraction context for $\mathcal{L}_1$ and θ is an abstraction-preserving reduction from $\mathcal{L}_1$ to $\mathcal{L}_2$. Since $\mathcal{C}[\,]$ is an abstraction context, $\mathcal{C}[M] \overset{\text{obs}}{=} \mathcal{C}[N]$ for some $M \overset{\text{obs}}{\neq} N$ in $\mathcal{L}_1$.

From the definition of abstraction-preserving reduction, we know that

$$\theta(\mathcal{C}[M]) = (\theta\mathcal{C})[\theta M]$$

and similarly for N. Since $\mathcal{C}[M] \overset{\text{obs}}{=} \mathcal{C}[N]$, it follows that

$$(\theta\mathcal{C})[\theta M] \overset{\text{obs}}{=} (\theta\mathcal{C})[\theta N].$$

If we can show that $\theta M \overset{\text{obs}}{\neq} \theta N$, then it will follow that $\theta\mathcal{C}$ is an abstraction context for $\mathcal{L}_2$. But $\theta M \overset{\text{obs}}{\neq} \theta N$ follows directly from the assumption that $M \overset{\text{obs}}{\neq} N$ and the fact that θ preserves observational equivalence (and inequivalence). ∎

Before considering the implications for parts of programs, we show that given a correspondence between observables, the existence of an abstraction-preserving reduction from $\mathcal{L}_1$ to $\mathcal{L}_2$ implies that every function on observables definable in $\mathcal{L}_1$ is also definable in $\mathcal{L}_2$. To explain this concretely, let us assume that the observables for each language are the natural numbers, and that we have an abstraction-preserving reduction $\theta : \mathcal{L}_1 \to \mathcal{L}_2$ which maps each natural number $n \in \mathcal{N}$ to itself. A partial function f on natural numbers is definable in $\mathcal{L}_i$ if there is a context $\mathcal{C}_f[\,]$ with the property that for all $n, m \in \mathcal{N}$, $\mathcal{C}_f[n] \overset{\text{eval}}{\to} m$ iff $f(n)$ is defined and equal to m. It is easy to see that if f is definable in $\mathcal{L}_1$, and $\theta : \mathcal{L}_1 \to \mathcal{L}_2$ preserves natural numbers, then f is definable in $\mathcal{L}_2$, as follows. If f is defined by by $\mathcal{C}_f[\,]$, then since θ maps contexts to contexts, there is a context $\theta\mathcal{C}_f[\,]$ in $\mathcal{L}_2$ with the property

$$\theta\mathcal{C}_f[n] \overset{\text{eval}}{\to} m \text{ iff } \theta\mathcal{C}_f[\theta n] \overset{\text{eval}}{\to} \theta m \text{ iff } \mathcal{C}_f[n] \overset{\text{eval}}{\to} m \text{ iff } f(n) \text{ is defined and equal to } m.$$

Therefore, $\theta\mathcal{C}_f[\,]$ defines f in $\mathcal{L}_2$. A more general statement, with essentially the same proof, follows.

Proposition 3.3 *Suppose $\theta : \mathcal{L}_1 \to \mathcal{L}_2$ is an abstraction-preserving reduction giving a bijective correspondence between some subset $\mathcal{N}_1 \subseteq \mathcal{O}_1$ of the $\mathcal{L}_1$ observables and some subset $\mathcal{N}_2 \subseteq \mathcal{O}_2$ of the $\mathcal{L}_2$ observables. If partial function $f : \mathcal{N}_1 \to \mathcal{N}_1$ is definable in $\mathcal{L}_1$ by context $\mathcal{C}_f[\,]$, then $\theta\mathcal{C}_f[\,]$ defines the partial function $\theta \circ f \circ \theta^{-1} : \mathcal{N}_2 \to \mathcal{N}_2$ in $\mathcal{L}_2$.*

Therefore, an abstraction-preserving reduction not only preserves abstraction contexts, but also the set of definable functions on observable values. It is easy to show that the composition of two abstraction-preserving reductions is abstraction preserving.

Proposition 3.4 *The composition of two abstraction-preserving reductions is an abstractio preserving reduction.*

4 A Simple Abstraction-Preserving Reduction

Many commonly-used equivalences between program constructs, such as the equivalence between a block with an initialized local variable, and a procedure declaration followed by a call may be described as abstraction-preserving reductions. Instead of proving this for a language with assignment, we will consider a similar translation in a functional setting. Specifically, we can reduce lambda calculus with `let` declarations

$$\texttt{let } x = M \texttt{ in } N$$

to pure lambda calculus by mapping a `let` declaration (as above) the the lambda term

$$(\lambda x.N)M.$$

To demonstrate what is involved in proving that a very simple translation is abstraction-preserving, we will go through this in some detail.

Let $\mathcal{L}_1$ be the ordinary untyped lambda calculus, with expressions defined by

$$M ::= x \mid M_1 M_2 \mid \lambda x.M$$

and evaluation the least congruence relation containing α-conversion (renaming of bound variables) and β-reduction

$$(\lambda x.M)N \xrightarrow{\beta} [N/x]M,$$

where $[N/x]M$ is the result of substituting N for free occurrences of x in M. (We assume bound variables are renamed during substitution to avoid capture, as usual). Let $\mathcal{L}_2$ be the lambda calculus extended with the additional construct

$$\texttt{let } x = M \texttt{ in } N$$

and associated evaluation rule

$$\texttt{let } x = M \texttt{ in } N \rightarrow [N/x]M.$$

The contexts of each language are obtained by deleting one subexpression from any expression of the language. We take the normal forms, expressions which cannot be reduced, as the observables of both languages.

We will give an abstraction-preserving reduction of $\mathcal{L}_2$ to $\mathcal{L}_1$. The reduction θ is defined inductively as follows.

$$\begin{array}{ll}
\theta x = & x \\
\theta(M_1 M_2) = & (\theta M_1)\,(\theta M_2) \\
\theta(\lambda x.M) = & \lambda x.\theta M \\
\theta(\texttt{let } x = M \texttt{ in } N) = & (\lambda x.\theta N)(\theta M)
\end{array}$$

Since contexts are derived from expressions, this is also a translation of $\mathcal{L}_2$ contexts to $\mathcal{L}_1$ contexts. Furthermore, since θ is defined by induction on the structure of expressions, it is easy to verify $(R1)$. It remains to verify condition $(R2)$ of the definition of abstraction-preserving reduction.

We will show that $M \stackrel{\text{obs}}{=} N$ iff $\theta M \stackrel{\text{obs}}{=} \theta N$ using properties of lambda calculus reduction. It is helpful to first realize that for any M in $\mathcal{L}_2$, the terms M and θM have a common reduct P. We reduce M to P by reducing all the `let` redexes (from the bottom of the parse tree of the term up, so as to eliminate all `let`'s from M), and reduce θM to P by "mimicking" this reduction in θM. Another helpful observation is that every $\mathcal{L}_1$ context is an $\mathcal{L}_2$ context and, similarly, every $\mathcal{L}_2$ context may be converted to an equivalent $\mathcal{L}_1$ context.

Suppose that $M \stackrel{\text{obs}}{=} N$. Let $\mathcal{C}[\,]$ be any $\mathcal{L}_1$ context with $\mathcal{C}[\theta M]$ reducing to a normal form P. Let Q be any common reduct of M and θM. Then $\mathcal{C}[M]$ reduces to $\mathcal{C}[Q]$ and so $\mathcal{C}[M]$ reduces to P. Since $M \stackrel{\text{obs}}{=} N$, we know that $\mathcal{C}[N]$ also reduces to P. By similar reasoning we can show that $\mathcal{C}[\theta N]$ reduces to P. This demonstrates that $\theta M \stackrel{\text{obs}}{=} \theta N$. The converse implication is proved using the same ideas.

5 Abstraction-Preserving Extensions

If the expressions and contexts of one language are subsets of the expressions and contexts of another (respectively), we might ask whether the identity map on expressions and contexts is abstraction-preserving. In general, if we have two languages, $\mathcal{L}_1 =< \mathfrak{E}_1, Ct_1, \mathcal{O}_1, \stackrel{\text{eval}}{\rightarrow}_1>$ and $\mathcal{L}_2 =< \mathfrak{E}_2, Ct_2, \mathcal{O}_2, \stackrel{\text{eval}}{\rightarrow}_2>$ with $\mathfrak{E}_1 \subseteq \mathfrak{E}_2$ and $Ct_1 \subseteq Ct_2$, then the identity map from $\mathcal{L}_1$ expressions and contexts to $\mathcal{L}_2$ expressions and contexts is abstraction-preserving iff we have

$$M \stackrel{\text{obs}}{=}_1 N \text{ iff } M \stackrel{\text{obs}}{=}_2 N$$

for all expressions M and N of $\mathcal{L}_1$, where $\stackrel{\text{obs}}{=}_i$ is observational equivalence in language $\mathcal{L}_i$. This amounts to saying that the observational equivalence theory of $\mathcal{L}_2$ is a *conservative extension* of the observational equivalence theory of $\mathcal{L}_1$. It does not follow that the observables of $\mathcal{L}_1$ are a subset of those of $\mathcal{L}_2$, or that $\stackrel{\text{eval}}{\rightarrow}_2$ restricted to $\mathfrak{E}_1$ coincides with $\stackrel{\text{eval}}{\rightarrow}_1$. Since all of the examples we wish to consider have these additional properties, we will incorporate them into the definition of "abstraction-preserving extension" below.

We say language $\mathcal{L}_1$ is a *sublanguage* of $\mathcal{L}_2$, written $\mathcal{L}_1 \subseteq \mathcal{L}_2$ or $\mathcal{L}_2 \supseteq \mathcal{L}_1$, if the $\mathfrak{E}_1 \subseteq \mathfrak{E}_2$, $Ct_1 \subseteq Ct_2$, $\mathcal{O}_1 \subseteq \mathcal{O}_2$, and the restriction of $\stackrel{\text{eval}}{\rightarrow}_2$ to $\mathfrak{E}_1$ expressions is $\stackrel{\text{eval}}{\rightarrow}_1$. It is easy to show that if $\mathcal{L}_1$ is a sublanguage of $\mathcal{L}_2$, then whenever $M, N \in \mathcal{L}_1$ are distinguishable in $\mathcal{L}_1$, they are also distinguishable in $\mathcal{L}_2$. (This would not follow from only $\mathfrak{E}_1 \subseteq \mathfrak{E}_2$ and $Ct_1 \subseteq Ct_2$.) However, two expressions $M, N \in \mathcal{L}_1$ may be observationally equivalent in $\mathcal{L}_1$ and observationally distinct in $\mathcal{L}_2$. This is because the richer language $\mathcal{L}_2$ may provide more contexts for observing M and N. We will say that $\mathcal{L}_2 \supseteq \mathcal{L}_1$ is an *abstraction-preserving extension of* $\mathcal{L}_1$ if $M \stackrel{\text{obs}}{=} N \in \mathcal{L}_1$ iff $M \stackrel{\text{obs}}{=} N \in \mathcal{L}_2$ for all $M, N \in \mathcal{L}_1$.

There are many trivial examples of abstraction-preserving extensions, and some non-trivial ones. A relatively trivial example is the extension of untyped lambda calculus (language $\mathcal{L}_1$ of the last section) to lambda calculus with `let` (language $\mathcal{L}_2$ of the last section). In general, an abstraction-preserving extension $\mathcal{L}_2 \supseteq \mathcal{L}_1$ may contain many more constructs than $\mathcal{L}_1$, or only a few. The definition does not require any particular relationship between $\mathcal{L}_1$ and $\mathcal{L}_2$ other than when we compare $\mathcal{L}_1$ expressions using $\mathcal{L}_2$ contexts, we make precisely the same distinctions as if we only consider $\mathcal{L}_1$ contexts.

A non-example that may be intuitively familiar is the relationship between a simple concurrent extension of an Algol-like language and its sequential sublanguage. We explain this using the construct

$$\texttt{cobegin } S_1 \texttt{ and } S_2 \texttt{ end}$$

which executes statements S_1 and S_2 concurrently. The same phenomenon occurs in a variety of concurrent programming languages. The single assignment $x{:}= 2$ is observationally equivalent to the sequence of assignments $x{:}= 1;\ x{:}= x + 1$ in many common sequential languages. However, assuming we compare programs by printed output, these may be distinguished by the concurrent context

$$\mathcal{C}[\ ] ::= \texttt{cobegin } [\ ] \texttt{ and } x{:}= 2 \texttt{ end; print } x$$

which executes the inserted statement in parallel with another assignment to the variable x. If we assume that assignments to x are atomic, but sequences of assignments are not, then $\mathcal{C}[x{:}= 1;\ x{:}= x + 1]$ may produce more possible final values of x than $\mathcal{C}[x{:}= 2]$. An interesting variation on this example is that if we have an atomicity primitive in our concurrent language, then it appears that we could embed the sequential sublanguage into the full language in an abstraction-preserving way. The main idea is to reduce a sequential statement S to the statement $atomic(S)$ which would be guaranteed atomic. We conjecture that with suitable treatment of procedure declarations and other constructs, a language embedding along these lines could be proved abstraction-preserving.

An interesting abstraction-preserving language extension involves the addition of recursive types to typed functional languages. Let $\mathcal{L}_1$ be a typed lambda calculus with an arbitrary selection of base types like the integers and booleans, and functional types like int → int, int → bool, and so on. We assume that $\mathcal{L}_1$ allows recursive function declarations, and may add sum or product types if we wish. Let $\mathcal{L}_2$ be obtained from $\mathcal{L}_1$ by adding recursively-defined types. The richer language $\mathcal{L}_2$ lets us write type declarations like

$$\text{tree} = \text{atom} + \text{tree} \times \text{tree}$$

which we could not write in $\mathcal{L}_1$. It follows immediately from the construction in [12, Chapter 4] that $\mathcal{L}_2$ is an abstraction-preserving extension of $\mathcal{L}_1$. This follows from the fact, summarized in [12, Section 4.6], that the fully-abstract (sub)model for typed lambda calculus with recursive types is an extension of the fully-abstract (sub)model for typed lambda calculus without recursive types.

6 A Translation Which is Not Abstraction Preserving

At the time the first version of this paper was written, there was some debate about the application of so-called strong and weak sums from type theory to programming languages. In particular, MacQueen argued against existential types, or weak sums, as a basis for the ML module facility [5]. Instead, he used strong sums. In retrospect, the argument seems to be one of apples vs. oranges: weaks sums provide data abstraction, while strong sums allow programs to be modularized with minimum restriction. Clarifying the difference between strong and weak sums and, in particular, showing that weak sums have an advantage for providing abstraction, was one of the original motivations for formulating the theory presented here. In this section, we show that the obvious map from weak to strong sums is not abstraction-preserving. The proof is essentially straightforward, drawing on [15, 8], but requires some definitions.

We extend the typed lambda calculus with two forms of sums. To keep the notation as simple as possible, the syntax of the two extensions will overlap. We will refer to the language with weak sums as $\lambda^{\rightarrow,\ \mathrm{weak}\ \Sigma}$ and the language with strong sums as $\lambda^{\rightarrow,\ \mathrm{strong}\ \Sigma}$. In both languages, there are two universes of type expressions (*c.f.* [6, 10]). The types of the first universe, U_1, have the form

$$\tau \ ::= \ t \,|\, b \,|\, \tau_1 \rightarrow \tau_2$$

where t is any type variable, b a type constant, $\tau_1 \rightarrow \tau_2$ the type of functions from τ_1 to τ_2. The additional types of the second universe are sums

$$\sigma \ ::= \ \tau \,|\, \Sigma t.\sigma,$$

where $\Sigma t.\sigma$ is the the sum type whose elements are a form of pair consisting of a type and an element of a type, and first projections applied to strong sums (described below). The terms common to both languages have the form

$$M \ ::= \ x \,|\, c \,|\, \lambda x:\tau.M \,|\, M_1 M_2 \,|\, \langle t=\tau, M:\sigma \rangle$$

where $\langle t=\tau, M:\sigma\rangle$ has type $\Sigma t.\sigma$ if M has type $[\tau/t]\sigma$. Precise typing rules for the whole language are given in the Appendix. For weak sums, we add the form

$$\texttt{abstype}\ t\ \texttt{with}\ x:\sigma\ \texttt{is}\ M\ \texttt{in}\ N$$

which binds type variable t and term variable x to the first and second components of $M:\Sigma t.\sigma$ with scope N. The additional typing constraints associated with `abstype` are that t cannot be free in the type of any free variable of N other than x, and t cannot occur free in the type of N. The evaluation rule for abstype is

$$\texttt{abstype}\ t\ \texttt{with}\ x:\sigma\ \texttt{is}\ \langle t=\tau, M:\sigma\rangle\ \texttt{in}\ N \rightarrow [M/x][\tau/t]N.$$

Further description of the correspondence between this construct and abstract types in programming languages may be found in [11], and also [1].

Strong sums are similar to weak sums, but with fewer typing restrictions. Instead of abstype, we add projection functions *Fst* and *Snd*. If M has type $\Sigma t.\sigma$, then

$$\textit{Fst}\, M \text{ is a type expression, and}$$

$$\textit{Snd}\, M \text{ is a term with type } [\textit{Fst}\, M/t]\sigma.$$

The evaluation rules for *Fst* and *Snd* are

$$\begin{aligned} \textit{Fst}\,\langle t=\tau, M:\sigma\rangle &\rightarrow \tau \\ \textit{Snd}\,\langle t=\tau, M:\sigma\rangle &\rightarrow M \end{aligned}$$

There are several translations from weak to strong sums which leave all the common type and term expressions fixed. For example, we may map abstype expressions to a combination of *Fst* and *Snd* according to the scheme

$$\begin{aligned} &\texttt{abstype}\ t\ \texttt{with}\ x:\sigma\ \texttt{is}\ \langle t=\tau, M:\sigma\rangle\ \texttt{in}\ N \\ &\quad\mapsto (\lambda y:(\Sigma t.\sigma).[\textit{Snd}\ y/x][\textit{Fst}\ y/t]N)\langle t=\tau, M:\sigma\rangle. \end{aligned}$$

We show that no translation which leaves expressions of sum type fixed is abstraction-preserving.

Proposition 6.1 *No translation from $\lambda^{\rightarrow,\ \text{weak}\ \Sigma}$ to $\lambda^{\rightarrow,\ \text{strong}\ \Sigma}$ which maps each expression $M:\Sigma t.\sigma$ not containing Fst or Snd to itself is abstraction preserving.*

Proof. We will give two expressions, $\langle t=\tau, M_1:\sigma\rangle$ and $\langle t=\tau, M_2:\sigma\rangle$ of type $\Sigma t.\sigma$, not containing *Fst* or *Snd*, which are observationally equivalent in $\lambda^{\rightarrow,\ \text{weak}\ \Sigma}$, but distinguishable using strong sums. From the results of [15, 8], it follows that if there is a binary relation on the set of elements of type τ such that M_1 and M_2 map related arguments to related results, then if we take elements of some basic type (named by a type constant) as observables, $\langle t=\tau, M_1:\sigma\rangle$ and $\langle t=\tau, M_2:\sigma\rangle$ will be indistinguishable. In particular, if M_1 and M_2 both define elements of τ or first-order functions from τ to τ, and the pairs $\langle t=\tau, M_1:\sigma\rangle$ and $\langle t=\tau, M_2:\sigma\rangle$ define isomorphic algebras (with carriers given by τ and operations given by M_1 or M_2), then they will be indistinguishable. A simple example, therefore, is just to let

$$\begin{aligned} \tau &::= b\rightarrow b\rightarrow b \\ M_1 &::= \lambda x:b.\lambda y:b.\,x \\ M_2 &::= \lambda x:b.\lambda y:b.\,y \\ \sigma &::= t \end{aligned}$$

so that $\langle t = \tau, M_1{:}\sigma\rangle, \langle t = \tau, M_2{:}\sigma\rangle{:}\Sigma t.t$ are trivially indistinguishable using only weak sums, but easily distinguished using *Snd* and application to a pair of distinguishable elements of type b. ■

An analogous situation exists in the programming language Ada. Ada packages may have public and private types. It may seem that we can eliminate private types, since any program with private types may be written using public types without changing the output of the program. However, merely changing private types to public types does not preserve abstraction.

7 Lisp is Not Universal

Recall that an abstraction context is a context $\mathcal{C}[\;]$ with $\mathcal{C}[M] \overset{\text{obs}}{=} \mathcal{C}[N]$ for some expressions $M \overset{\text{obs}}{\neq} N$ which are not observationally equivalent. In languages where expressions can examine the text of their subexpressions, there are no abstraction contexts. An example is Lisp, when we have the ability to define special forms that do not evaluate their arguments.

Claim 7.1 *Lisp (with* FEXPR*) has no abstraction contexts.*

The justification of this claim rests on the fact that if two Lisp expressions M and N are syntactically different, then there is some context $\mathcal{C}[\;]$ using FEXPR which distinguishes M from N. Recall that a FEXPR is a function which does not evaluate its arguments [19]. Instead, the unevaluated arguments are put together in a list and passed to the FEXPR. For example, if we apply the function f defined by

(DEFUN f FEXPR (x) (CAR x)).

to the arguments A, B, C, as in

$(f\;\; A\;\; B\;\; C)$,

the result is the unevaluated first argument A. Thus, given any syntactically distinct M and N, a context $\mathcal{C}[\;]$ which applies a FEXPR to its argument may distinguish between M and N. The context may return an observable value like 0 or 1 depending on what the n-th character is. For n chosen properly, we will have $\mathcal{C}[M] \overset{\text{eval}}{\to} 0$ and $\mathcal{C}[N] \overset{\text{eval}}{\to} 1$, so $M \overset{\text{obs}}{\neq} N$. Thus syntactically different Lisp expressions are not observationally equivalent.

Now suppose $\mathcal{C}[\;]$ is an abstraction context for Lisp. We will see that this leads to a contradiction. We have $\mathcal{C}[M] \overset{\text{obs}}{=} \mathcal{C}[N]$ for some $M \overset{\text{obs}}{\neq} N$. But $\mathcal{C}[M] \overset{\text{obs}}{=} \mathcal{C}[N]$ implies that $\mathcal{C}[M]$ and $\mathcal{C}[N]$ are syntactically identical. Therefore, since M and N appear in $\mathcal{C}[M]$ and $\mathcal{C}[N]$ (respectively), it follows that M and N are syntactically identical. This contradicts the assumption that $\mathcal{C}[\ ]$ is an abstraction context and justifies the claim.

We have the following consequence of Lemma 3.2 and Claim 7.1.

Proposition 7.2 *If $\mathcal{L}$ is a language with an abstraction context, then there is no abstraction-preserving reduction from $\mathcal{L}$ to Lisp with* FEXPR.

It is worth recalling from Lemma 3.2 that if $\mathcal{C}[\ ]$ is an abstraction context and θ an abstraction-preserving reduction, then the behavior of $\mathcal{C}[\ ]$ on equivalence classes of expressions determines the behavior of $\theta\mathcal{C}[\ ]$ on equivalence classes in the range of θ. Consequently, if $\mathcal{C}[\ ]$ is semantically nontrivial, $\theta\mathcal{C}[\ ]$ must be as well. Thus no language with a semantically nontrivial abstraction context can be reduced to a language with only semantically trivial abstraction contexts. In future research, it would be worthwhile to explore this form of argument more carefully. It would be interesting to use the way that the translation $\theta\mathcal{C}$ of an abstraction context $\mathcal{C}$ must hide differences between translations of inequivalent expressions to derive more significant negative results.

8 Comparison with related work

Two related papers are Riecke's comparative study of three standard evaluation strategies [16] and Felleisen's general theory of programming language expressiveness [2]. Since Riecke's paper uses abstraction-preserving reductions, we discuss this first.

Riecke compares call-by-value, call-by-name and lazy versions of the language PCF, which is a typed lambda calculus with natural numbers, parallel and sequential conditional and recursion operators. In rough terms, the main results are that call-by-value and lazy PCF are equally expressive, and both are more expressive than call-by-name PCF. In symbols,

$$\textit{call-by-name} \ \overset{<}{\not\sim}\ \textit{call-by-value} \cong \textit{lazy PCF}$$

The three reductions, from call-by-name to call-by-value, and between call-by-value and lazy PCF are first given as abstraction preserving reductions, as defined in this paper. However, to show that neither call-by-value nor lazy PCF may be reduced to call-by-name PCF, Riecke requires additional assumptions in the form of a stronger notion of reduction. The stronger definition, called *functional translation,* is roughly similar to an abstraction-preserving reduction induced by a logical relation between the two languages [17, 9]. This relies on the type structures of the two languages, which apparently must be identical. Along with the negative results based on functional translations, Riecke observes that his reductions from call-by-name to call-by-value, and between call-by-value and lazy PCF are all functional translations. An apparently minor point is that the paper leaves open whether the composition of two functional translations is a functional translation.

The difference between the three versions of PCF is essentially evaluation order, except for an additional construct in lazy PCF. For all of the languages, the observables are the numerals. Call-by-value evaluation of an application MN first evaluates the function and argument to "values," which are either lambda abstractions or atomic symbols, and then evaluates the function application. In call-by-name evaluation of MN, only M must be evaluated. If M ignores its argument, and the evaluation of N does not terminate, the application MN will terminate in call-by-name but not in call-by-value. In lazy PCF we use call-by-name evaluation order, but also observe termination of function expressions. Termination in lazy PCF is observed using convergence testing primitive $conv^{\sigma,\tau} : \sigma \rightarrow \tau \rightarrow \tau$. We may observe convergence at type σ using the context $\mathcal{C}_\sigma[\,] \equiv conv^{\sigma,nat}[\,]\,0$ which has the property that if M has type σ, then $\mathcal{C}_\sigma[M]$ either diverges or evaluates to the numeral 0.

A technically important construct of all three language is parallel conditional. With this operator, we have standard domain-theoretic constructions of fully abstract models [14, 18]. These are used in an essential way to prove that the reductions from call-by-name to call-by-value, and between call-by-value and lazy PCF preserve observational equivalence. Without fully-abstract models, it seems difficult to show that such reductions are abstraction-preserving.

In motivating functional translations, Riecke makes some important observations about the weaker possibility of effective (computable) translations that preserve observational equivalence. By a simple Gödel-numbering trick, we may construct such a reduction from any language, $\mathcal{L}_1$, to any other, $\mathcal{L}_2$, provided only that we are able to write an interpreter $interp_{1,2}$ for $\mathcal{L}_1$ in $\mathcal{L}_2$. Given such an interpreter, we reduce $\mathcal{L}_1$ to $\mathcal{L}_2$ by mapping a term M to the application $(interp_{1,2}\lceil M \rceil)$, where $\lceil M \rceil$ is the Gödel number of M. This translation is *almost* compositional (and therefore *almost* abstraction-preserving, by the definition of this paper), since $\lceil M \rceil$ may be defined compositionally from M. However, the way $interp_{1,2}$ is used keeps this translation from being compositional, strictly speaking. An interesting open problem is whether there is an abstraction-preserving reduction from either call-by-value or lazy PCF to call-by-name PCF. To show that no abstraction-preserving reductions exist would strengthen Riecke's negative results. Another interesting direction would be to develop the theory of functional translations in greater depth, including the generalization to languages with other type structures.

Felleisen proposes a general theory for determining whether a set of constructs within a language are "eliminable," or expressible by the remaining constructs [2]. The apparent connection with language reductions is that when $\mathcal{L}_1 \subseteq \mathcal{L}_2$, we might expect there to be a reduction from $\mathcal{L}_2$ to $\mathcal{L}_1$ exactly if the additional constructs of $\mathcal{L}_2$ are eliminable, relative to $\mathcal{L}_1$. Felleisen's theory is described as an adaptation of Kleene's notion of definitional extension from logic [4] to programming languages. The paper discusses two forms of expressiveness, called *eliminability* and *macro-eliminability*. Since the first is much closer to the concepts discussed here, we will not consider the more restrictive notion of macro-eliminability. If the constructs of $\mathcal{L}_2 \supseteq \mathcal{L}_1$ are eliminable, we say $\mathcal{L}_2$ is a *definitional extension* of $\mathcal{L}_1$.

In Felleisen's theory, a programming language is modeled as a set of *phrases,* freely generated by a set of *constructors* $\mathbf{F}_1, \mathbf{F}_2, \ldots$, each with a specificed arity. The set of well-formed *programs* must be some recursive subset of the phrases. Programs are compared using a predicate *halts*? which is true if the program halts under the implicit operational semantics. (Felleisen calls this predicate *eval,* but we will write *halts*? to avoid confusion with the notation of the present paper.) A significant difference between Felleisen's theory and the one suggested here is the difference between the termination theory of a language and the observational equivalence theory. Termination is determined directly by evaluation, while observational equivalence involves consideration of all program contexts, and therefore depends on the surrounding language. A recursion-theoretic distinction is that the termination theory of a language is typically re-complete, while the observational equivalence theory is typically Π_2-complete. This makes Felleisen's definitional extensions easier to reason about, but perhaps less informative than abstraction-preserving reductions.

An important subsidiary definition in Felleisen's theory is that $\mathcal{L}_2$ is a *conservative extension* of $\mathcal{L}_1$ if the phrases of $\mathcal{L}_2$ contain those of $\mathcal{L}_1$, program-hood is conservative, and the termination theory of $\mathcal{L}_2$ is conservative over the termination theory of $\mathcal{L}_1$. This is very similar to our definition of language extension, given in Section 5, except for the difference between the two models of programming languages. The main definition is that when $\mathcal{L}_2$ is a conservative extension of $\mathcal{L}_1$, the additional constructs of $\mathcal{L}_2$ are *eliminable* if there is a recursive mapping Φ of $\mathcal{L}_2$ phrases to $\mathcal{L}_1$ phrases which is compositional with respect to $\mathcal{L}_1$ *constructors only,* maps programs to programs, and which preserves the termination theory. The main positive example is that `let` is eliminable from a λ-calculus extended with `let`, which is analogous to the abstraction-preserving reduction given in Section 4 of this paper. The only negative example claimed in [2] is that call-by-name lambda abstraction is not eliminable from a lambda calculus containing both call-by-value and call-by-name lambda abstraction. This is similar to Riecke's theorem showing that there is no functional translation from call-by-name to call-by-value.

As mentioned above, we might compare Felleisen's theory of eliminability with our definition of reduction by seeing whether, given $\mathcal{L}_2$ conservative over $\mathcal{L}_1$, there is an abstraction-preserving reduction from $\mathcal{L}_2$ to $\mathcal{L}_1$ iff $\mathcal{L}_2$ is a definitional extension of $\mathcal{L}_1$. A special case of conservative extension makes it easy to see that these two conditions are *not* equivalent, on very general grounds. Given any two languages, $\mathcal{L}_1$ and $\mathcal{L}_2$, modeled either as in Felleisen's paper or this one, there is an obvious definition of their disjoint union, which we will write symbolically as $\mathcal{L}_1 \uplus \mathcal{L}_2$. By Felleisen's definition of conservative extension, $\mathcal{L}_2 \uplus \mathcal{L}_1$ is always a conservative extension of $\mathcal{L}_1$. Thus, we might conjecture, *a priori,* that there is an abstraction-preserving reductions from $\mathcal{L}_2$ to $\mathcal{L}_1$ iff $\mathcal{L}_2 \uplus \mathcal{L}_1$ is a definitional extension of $\mathcal{L}_1$. However, in this situation, definitional extension is a largely degenerate concept. All that is required for $\mathcal{L}_2 \uplus \mathcal{L}_1$ to be a definitional extension of $\mathcal{L}_1$ is a recursive map Φ from $\mathcal{L}_2$ phrases to $\mathcal{L}_1$ phrases such that for every $\mathcal{L}_2$ program e, we have $halts?_{L2}(e)$ iff $halts?_{L1}(\Phi e)$. Riecke's Gödel numbering argument, summarized above, shows that there exists such a recursive, and in fact almost compositional, map from $\mathcal{L}_2$ to $\mathcal{L}_1$ whenever an $\mathcal{L}_2$ interpreter is definable in $\mathcal{L}_1$. More specifically, we can see that $\mathcal{L}_2 \uplus \mathcal{L}_1$ is a definitional extension of $\mathcal{L}_1$ whenever the halting predicate for $\mathcal{L}_2$ is derived from an effective (computable) operational semantics, there is a Gödel numbering of $\mathcal{L}_2$ phrases as $\mathcal{L}_1$ expressions, and all partial recursive functions are definable in $\mathcal{L}_1$.

For the reader familiar with [2], we give a few additional comparisons. Theorems 3.6 and 3.8 of [2] relate definitional extension to the existence of compositional (homomorphic) mappings that send each $\mathcal{L}_2$ expression to an $\mathcal{L}_2$-observationally equivalent $\mathcal{L}_1$ expression. Theorem 3.6 gives a sufficient condition, in these terms, for $\mathcal{L}_2$ being a definitional extension of $\mathcal{L}_1$, and Theorem 3.8 relates non-existence of homomorphic mappings to $\mathcal{L}_2$ *not* being a definitional extension of $\mathcal{L}_1$. Together, these two theorems provide an intuitive point of comparison between Felleisen's theory of expressiveness and the existence of abstraction-preserving reductions. However, both of these theorems are uninformative if we wish to compare $\mathcal{L}_2 \uplus \mathcal{L}_1$ with $\mathcal{L}_1$. This problematic special case makes it difficult to prove any precise connections between the theories. In more detail, Theorem 3.6 does not apply to $\mathcal{L}_2 \uplus \mathcal{L}_1$ and $\mathcal{L}_1$, due to a detail in Felleisen's definition of observational equivalence that allows e and e' to be equivalent only if there is a context $C[\,]$ such that both $C[e]$ and $C[e']$ are programs. This makes e from $\mathcal{L}_2$ and e' from $\mathcal{L}_1$ observationally *inequivalent* in the disjoint union $\mathcal{L}_2 \uplus \mathcal{L}_1$, and therefore no translation Φ satisfying the hypotheses of the theorem could possibly exist. For similar reasons, Theorem 3.8 does not give any sufficient condition implying that $\mathcal{L}_2 \uplus \mathcal{L}_1$ is not a definitional extension of $\mathcal{L}_1$. In addition, these theorems only require the maps from $\mathcal{L}_2$ to $\mathcal{L}_1$ to be compositional on $\mathcal{L}_1$ only, not on all of $\mathcal{L}_2$. Therefore, by Riecke's argument, these allow Gödel numbering translations. However, with some modification to eliminate this degenerate form of translation, the criteria given in Theorems 3.6 and 3.8 of [2] might provide a basis for an interesting general theory.

9 Conclusions and Directions for Further Investigation

This paper defines *abstraction-preserving reductions,* which are syntax-directed (homomorphic) reductions that preserve observational equivalence. Some simple translations and language embeddings are easily seen to be abstraction preserving. One example is the translation of blocks to function declarations and calls. A nontrivial example is the extension of a functional language with finite types to a language with recursively-defined types. The proof that this extension is abstraction-preserving involves detailed reasoning about the inclusive predicates which link the operational and denotational semantics of each language. One kind of reduction that is not abstraction preserving is the kind of reduction which replaces abstract "private" types with concrete "public" types (to use Ada terminology). In addition, we show that many languages are not reducible to Lisp with user-defined special forms.

The general theory sketched here is tentative, and it would be interesting to extend the preliminary definitions in several ways. One refinement would be to adopt a more specific language model, in which a context-free or context-sensitive grammar determines both the expressions and the contexts. Some related comments and suggestions may be found in [16]. Another direction is to examine the two clauses of our definition more closely. The constraint (R2) that a reduction must preserve observational equivalence seems quite natural, although we could consider weakening the "iff" to an implication. The intent of clause (R1), which forces reductions to preserve contexts, or be "homomorphic," is intended to rule out language reductions such as Gödel numberings. An open question is whether (R1) actually eliminates all reductions that we would intuitively recognize as Gödel-numberings. Therefore, it may be desirable to strengthen or alter this condition on the basis of further investigation, as discussed in [16]. An open question is whether abstract data type declarations can be reduced to polymorphic function declarations and calls. Two translations have been proposed [15, 11], and one is easily shown not to preserve abstraction. It would be interesting to determine whether the other one is abstraction preserving.

It is easy to argue that Lisp with FEXPR is not a "universal" language, since no language with an abstraction mechanism can be reduced to Lisp in an abstraction-preserving manner. We do not know whether there is a natural universal language for the theory outlined here, restricting our attention to languages with a finite presentation and computable evaluation relation. An additional condition which might impose some useful structure on the problem of finding a universal language is to require that if $M \stackrel{\text{eval}}{\to} N$, then $M \stackrel{\text{obs}}{=} N$. This is relevant to Lisp with user-defined special forms since our proof that Lisp has no abstraction contexts involves showing that this general principle is violated.

Acknowledgements

Thanks to Jon Riecke, Kim Bruce and an anonymous referee for helpful suggestions.

References

[1] L. Cardelli and P. Wegner. On understanding types, data abstraction, and polymorphism. *Computing Surveys*, 17(4):471–522, 1985.

[2] M. Felleisen. On the expressive power of programming languages. In *Proc. European Symp. on Programming*, pages 134–151. Springer-Verlag LNCS 432, 1990.

[3] S. Greibach. *Theory of Program Structures: Schemes, Semantics, Verification*, volume 36 of *Lecture Notes in Computer Science*. Springer-Verlag, 1975.

[4] S. Kleene. *Introduction to Metamathematics*. Van Nostrand, New York, 1952.

[5] D. MacQueen. Using dependent types to express modular structure. In *Proc. 13-th ACM Symp. on Principles of Programming Languages*, pages 277–286, 1986.

[6] P. Martin-Löf. *Intuitionistic Type Theory.* Bibliopolis, Napoli, 1984.

[7] R. Milner. Fully abstract models of typed lambda calculi. *Theoretical Computer Science*, 4(1), 1977.

[8] J. Mitchell. Representation independence and data abstraction. In *Proc. 13-th ACM Symp. on Principles of Programming Languages*, pages 263–276, January 1986.

[9] J. Mitchell. Type systems for programming languages. In J. van Leeuwen, editor, *Handbook of Theoretical Computer Science, Volume B*, pages 365–458. North-Holland, 1990.

[10] J. Mitchell and R. Harper. The essence of ML. In *Proc. 15-th ACM Symp. on Principles of Programming Languages*, pages 28–46, January 1988.

[11] J. Mitchell and G. Plotkin. Abstract types have existential types. *ACM Trans. on Programming Languages and Systems*, 10(3):470–502, 1988. Preliminary version appeared in *Proc. 12-th ACM Symp. on Principles of Programming Languages*, 1985.

[12] K. Mulmuley. *Full abstraction and semantic equivalence.* The MIT Press, 1987.

[13] M. Paterson and C. Hewitt. Comparative schematology. In *Proj. MAC Conf. on Concurrent Systems and Parallel Computation.* MIT, 1970.

[14] G. Plotkin. LCF considered as a programming language. *Theoretical Computer Science*, 5:223–255, 1977.

[15] J. Reynolds. Types, abstraction, and parametric polymorphism. In *Information Processing '83*, pages 513–523, Amsterdam, 1983. North-Holland.

[16] J. Riecke. Fully abstract translations between functional languages. In *Proc. 17-th ACM Symp. on Principles of Programming Languages*, pages 245–254, January 1990.

[17] R. Statman. Logical relations and the typed lambda calculus. *Information and Control*, 65:85–97, 1985.

[18] A. Stoughton. *Fully Abstract Models of Programming Languages.* Pitman/John Wiley and Sons, 1988.

[19] P. Winston and B. Horn. *Lisp.* Addison-Wesley, 1981.

Appendix. Typing rules for weak and strong sums

$$\frac{}{\langle\rangle \text{ environment}} \qquad \frac{\Gamma \rhd \tau : U_1}{\Gamma, x : \tau \text{ environment}} \qquad \frac{\Gamma \rhd \sigma : U_2}{\Gamma, x : \sigma \text{ environment}}$$

$$(x \notin \mathrm{Dom}(\Gamma))$$

$$\frac{\Gamma \text{ environment} \quad \Gamma(x) = \tau}{\Gamma \rhd x : \tau} \qquad \frac{\Gamma \text{ environment} \quad \Gamma(x) = \sigma}{\Gamma \rhd x : \sigma}$$

$$\frac{\Gamma \rhd \alpha \quad \Gamma \rhd \tau : U_1}{\Gamma, x : \tau \rhd \alpha} \qquad \frac{\Gamma \rhd \alpha \quad \Gamma \rhd \sigma : U_2}{\Gamma, x : \sigma \rhd \alpha}$$

$$(x \notin \mathrm{Dom}(\Gamma),\ \alpha \textit{ is } M : \tau \textit{ or } M : \sigma)$$

$$\frac{\Gamma \rhd M : \tau \quad \Gamma \rhd \tau = \tau' : U_1}{\Gamma \rhd M : \tau'} \qquad \frac{\Gamma \rhd M : \sigma \quad \Gamma \rhd \sigma = \sigma' : U_2}{\Gamma \rhd M : \sigma'}$$

Table 1: Environment and structural rules

$$\frac{\Gamma \text{ environment}}{\Gamma \rhd U_1 : U_2} \qquad \frac{\Gamma \rhd \tau : U_1}{\Gamma \rhd \tau : U_2}$$

Table 2: Universes

$$\frac{\Gamma \rhd \tau : U_1 \quad \Gamma \rhd \tau' : U_1}{\Gamma \rhd \tau \rightarrow \tau' : U_1}$$

$$\frac{\Gamma \rhd \tau : U_1 \quad \Gamma \rhd \tau' : U_1 \quad \Gamma, x : \tau \rhd M : \tau'}{\Gamma \rhd \lambda x : \tau . M : \tau \rightarrow \tau'} \qquad (x \notin \mathrm{Dom}(\Gamma))$$

$$\frac{\Gamma \rhd M : \tau \rightarrow \tau' \quad \Gamma \rhd N : \tau}{\Gamma \rhd MN : \tau'}$$

Table 3: Types and terms in U_1

$$\frac{\Gamma, t : U_1 \rhd \sigma : U_2}{\Gamma \rhd \Sigma t.\sigma : U_2} \quad (t \notin \mathrm{Dom}(\Gamma))$$

$$\frac{\Gamma \rhd \tau : U_1 \quad \Gamma \rhd [\tau/t]M : [\tau/t]\sigma \quad \Gamma, t : U_1 \rhd \sigma : U_2}{\Gamma \rhd \langle t{=}\tau, M : \sigma\rangle : \Sigma t.\sigma} \quad (x \notin \mathrm{Dom}(\Gamma))$$

$$\frac{\Gamma \rhd M : \Sigma t.\sigma}{\Gamma \rhd \mathit{Fst}(M) : U_1} \qquad \frac{\Gamma \rhd M : \Sigma t.\sigma}{\Gamma \rhd \mathit{Snd}(M) : [\mathit{Fst}(M)/t]\sigma}$$

$$\frac{\Gamma \rhd M : \Sigma t.\sigma \quad \Gamma, t : U_1, x : \sigma \rhd N : \tau}{\Gamma \rhd \texttt{abstype}\ t\ \texttt{with}\ x : \sigma\ \texttt{is}\ M\ \texttt{in}\ N : \tau} \quad t\ \textit{not free in}\ \Gamma\ \textit{or}\ \tau$$

Table 4: Types and terms in U_2

Role of Logic Programming in the FGCS Project

Kazuhiro Fuchi, Koichi Furukawa
fuchi@icot.or.jp, furukawa@icot.or.jp
ICOT Research Center
Institute for New Generation Computer technology
1-4-28, Mita, Minato-ku,
Tokyo 108, JAPAN

Abstract

The research of the Fifth Generation Computer Project was conducted based on a single principle: Logic Programming. Logic programming unifies the ideas of retrieval and computation. Both of these can be regarded as forms of deduction. Research shows that logic programming plays a central role in the project. This role is as the foundation of a very high level programming language based on constraint logic programming, and as a formalization of a very powerful concurrent programming language, which also gives specifications for multi-processor architecture.

1 Introduction

The Fifth Generation Computer Systems (FGCS) project started in 1982. The goal of the project was to establish knowledge information processing technology that was compatible with parallel computers. The combination of knowledge information processing and parallel processing was commonly believed to be very difficult to achieve.

Three years before the FGCS project started, a committee was organized to investigate how to achieve this goal. The committee studied two different aspects of the problem: the software aspect, including programming languages, and the hardware aspect, including architecture. The study of programming languages was devoted to investigating future programming languages for knowledge information processing and parallel processing. There were apparently two candidates: Lisp and Prolog. Although Lisp was much more advanced and used predominantly in the area of artificial intelligence, we selected Prolog as our first language candidate.

There were several reasons for this selection. One was the ubiquity of logic and logic programming in the field of knowledge information processing. As a programming language, Prolog provides list-processing and exhaustive searching capabilities, which provide bases for knowledge information processing technology. As a representation scheme, logic is a universal language for knowledge representation and is supported by strong mathematical theory. Logic plays very important roles in software engineering, as a means of specification and verification; in databases, as a query language and as integrity constraints; and in natural language processing, for parsing.

Another reason was its possibility of providing a specification for architectural design of parallel processors due to its simple computation mechanism and its inherent parallelism.

Logic programming is based on the well established mathematical theory of logic and inherits many good features such as soundness, completeness, and semantic characterization based on fix point theory and least model.

As a result, we concluded that logic programming would become the latest unified principle in computer science.

Based on this conclusion, we proposed the FGCS project with logic programming as its key concept. The combination of knowledge information processing and parallel processing was commonly believed very difficult to achieve and was criticized a lot during our first FGCS Conference. To solve this difficult problem, we promoted logic programming, as a working hypothesis, between the two components, expecting it to assume the role of a bridge connecting them [Fuchi 87].

2 Unification as Computation

In logic programming, there are two important computation aspects: proof strategy for control and unification. Here we concentrate on unification. Unification is an operation to unify two terms (or two literals) by appropriately instantiating variables. For example, two terms, $f(X, g(Y), a)$ and $f(g(Z), g(Z), U)$, can be unified by instantiating variables, X to g(Z), Y to Z, and U to a, where we adopt the Prolog convention of representing variables by words starting with capital letters. Note that variables can appear in both terms of unification. This differs from matching where one of the terms should be a ground term. Also, we compute only the most general unification. In the above example, the value of Z could be arbitrarily chosen to unify them. But we keep it uninstantiated to make it more general.

It is easily shown that list processing can be done by unification. We define a list constructor, *cons*, and a special constant, *nil*, to represent an empty list. Assume we are given a list element, X, whose value is a, and a list, Y, whose value is $cons(b, nil)$. Then, the list construction operation of making a new list Z by adding element X to list Y, is realized by the unification of two terms, Z and $cons(X, Y)$. Let us use "=" to represent unification. Then, the list construction can be expressed as:

$$\{X = a, Y = cons(b, nil), Z = cons(X, Y)\}.$$

By solving this simultaneous equation, we obtain

$$Z = cons(a, cons(b, nil)).$$

This is actually a result of adding element a to list $cons(b, nil)$. The reverse operation of *cons*, represented by *car* and *cdr* in Lisp, can be done also by the following unification:

$$\{Z = cons(a, cons(b, nil)), Z = cons(X, Y)\}.$$

By solving this simultaneous equation, we obtain

$$\{X = a, Y = cons(b, nil)\}.$$

Note that Z has been instantiated but X and Y are not instantiated before the the last unification, $Z = cons(X, Y)\}$. Also, note that this unification is the same as the last one for the list construction.

For more complicated list operations, we need to write a program. Since a list is a recursive data structure, most natural programs for list manipulation are recursive programs. The following example is a list append program:

```
append(nil,X,X).
append(cons(A,X),Y,cons(A,Z)) :- append(X,Y,Z).
```

where `append(A,B,C)` means that the result of appending list `B` to list `A`, is list `C`, and "`:-`" means logical implication. Therefore the second clause of the append program is read as: "if the result of appending `Y`, to `X` is `Z`, then the result of appending `Y` to `cons(A,X)` is `cons(A,Z)`. The first clause of append describes a terminating condition: the result of appending arbitrary list `X` to an empty list is `X`. Note that this definition is readable and understandable. It is said that the invention of this append program took three months from the completion of Prolog. It can be said that Prolog became the true list processing language only after the invention of the append program.

3 Search and Unify as Retrieval

The retrieval process depends on proof strategy, another important aspect of logic programming, as well as unification. The proof strategies adopted by logic programming are variations of resolution strategies [Robinson 65]. The main issues of resolution strategies are how to select the next pair of clauses and the pair of literals to be resolved. In Prolog, one of the clauses to be resolved is always a goal clause representing a problem to be solved, and one of the literals to be resolved is the left most literal of the goal clause. The other clause to be resolved is searched through, linearly from the top to the bottom of the clause database, looking for a head literal (a literal appearing on the left hand side of the implication, which represents a consequent of the implication) which is unifiable to the selected goal literal. The resolvent is obtained by replacing the resolved goal with a list of literals on the right hand side (the antecedent of the implication) from the other resolved clause. Since the implication can be interpreted as a goal-subgoal relation by corresponding a consequent to a goal and an antecedent to a subgoal, the resolution step can be regarded as a goal-subgoal problem reduction.

It is straight forward enough to represent a database with a set of ground unit clauses (clauses whose antecedents are empty, representing true). A database query is then a goal to be solved. We need no mechanisms other than a Prolog interpreter to evaluate any queries represented by Prolog goals. Database retrieval is realized by a clause-search- and-unify mechanism embedded in the Prolog interpreter.

It is interesting to observe the similarity of computation and retrieval. In Prolog, they are both realized by the same mechanism, *clause-search-and-unify*. This is not surprising because computation can be realized by retrieval once functions tables are made. Actually, a tabular method has been used in computing logarithmic functions. It involves trade-off between space and time for computation. If we want to represent everything in a tabular form, then we need vast amounts of memories for the table. However, since table retrieval is often more efficient than computation for complex problems, there are cases where it is preferable to represent some part of the functions using a table. In Prolog, since the representations of tables and programs are the same, it is rather easy to represent the mix strategy in a single framework. This argument is also related to a well known optimization technique called *partial evaluation* [Futamura 71]. Much work has been done in developing partial evaluation techniques in the field of logic programming [Komorowski 82], [Takeuchi 86], [Fujita 88]. This work produced many fruitful results, like a straight forward realization of a self-applicable partial evaluator for Prolog programs in Prolog [Fujita 88].

4 Bidirectionality in Logic Programming

One of the advantages of logic programming is the bidirectionality of its arguments. You can use a single append program to either append the second argument to the first one to obtain the result at the third argument, or to partition a list in the third argument into two lists appearing at the first and the second argument position.

Note that this nature derives the equivalence of two different permutation algorithms, insertion permutation and deletion permutation. Both of these compute every possible permutation of a given list each time it is retried by failure.

Insertion permutation computes a permutation of a given list, `[X|Xs]`[1]. First it permutes list `Xs`, a list starting from the second element of the given list, to obtain an intermediate result, `Zs`, and then it inserts the first element, `X`, to an arbitrary position in `Zs`. The Prolog program is as follows:

```
iperm([X|Xs],Ys) :- iperm(Xs,Zs), insert(X,Zs,Ys).
iperm([],[]).
```

[1] `[A|B]` represents a list whose first element is `A` while the rest of the list is `B`.

Next, we define an *insert* program. There are two possible ways of inserting a given element to an *arbitrary* position in a list: one is to put the given element at the front of the list and the other is to insert recursively the given element to a list starting form the second element of the given list. These two alternatives can be coded into two different clauses chosen alternatively when failure propagates, as follows:

```
insert(X,Us,[X|Us]).
insert(X,[U|Us],[U|Vs]) :- insert(X,Us,Vs).
```

Similarly, we can define a permutation algorithm based on *deletion*. In deletion permutation, we first delete an arbitrary element from the given list to be permuted, then permute the rest and put the deleted element in front of the permutation result. The Prolog program for this algorithm is as follows:

```
dperm(Ys,[X|Xs]) :- delete(X,Ys,Zs),dperm(Xs,Zs).
dperm([],[]).

delete(X,[X|Us],Us).
delete(X,[U|Vs],[U|Us]) :- delete(X,Vs,Us).
```

By carefully comparing these two programs one can easily find that

(1) `insert(A,B,C)` = `delete(A,C,B)`, and

(2) `iperm(A,B)` = `dperm(B,A)`.

Furthermore, we can derive two well-known sorting algorithms, *insertion sort* (`isort`) and *selection sort* (`ssort`), from `iperm` and `dperm`. `isort` is a specialization of `iperm` by adding an ordering constraint to `insert`. We define a restricted insertion algorithm called *op_insert* which means order-preserving insertion as follows:

```
op_insert(X,[],[X]).
op_insert(X,[U|Us],[X,U|Us]) :- X=<U.
op_insert(X,[U|Us],[U|Vs]) :-
    X>U, op_insert(X,Us,Vs).
```

If we replace `insert` with `op_insert` in `iperm`, the resulting permutation program will actually sort a given list in ascending order. Therefore, it will become an *insertion sort* program as follows.

```
isort([X|Xs],Ys) :- isort(Xs,Zs), op_insert(X,Zs,Ys).
isort([],[]).
```

It was shown by Seki and Furukawa [Seki 87] that the *insertion sort* program is deduced from a naive exhaustive search program, nsort, defined by:

```
nsort(Xs,Ys) :- iperm(Xs,Ys),ordered(Ys).
```

using the following equivalence formula:

```
insert(X,Zs,Ys) & ordered(Ys)
    = ordered(Zs) & op_insert(X,Zs,Ys)
```

Similarly, we can derive a *selection sort* program by replacing delete with the delete_min program in dperm:

```
ssort(Ys,[X|Xs]) :- delete_min(X,Ys,Zs),ssort(Xs,Zs).
ssort([],[]).

delete_min(X,[X],[]).
delete_min(X,[U,V|Us],[V|Vs]) :-
     U=<V, delete_min(X,[U|Us],Vs).
delete_min(X,[U,V|Us],[U|Vs]) :-
     U>V, delete_min(X,[V|Us],Vs).
```

The *ssort* program can also be derived form the *nsort* program using the following equivalence relation:

```
delete(X,Ys,Zs) & perm(Zs,Xs) & ordered([X|Xs])
    = delete_min(X,Ys,Zs) & perm(Zs,Xs) & ordered(Xs)
```

As a result, it is shown that *isort* and *ssort* are equivalent.

5 Constraint LP by Unification Extension

Constraint logic programming is one of the most promising approaches in the field of logic programming. It enables the domain of the language to be extended to cover most AI problems.The idea is to combine constraint satisfaction and logic programming. The reasons why it is so successful are 1) it is a straight forward extension of Prolog by extending the notion of unification to deal with constraint satisfaction, and 2) it extends the primitive domain of the system allowing declarative programming in a wider class of problems such as linear equations and inequations in a uniform way as unifications between terms. From the viewpoint of constraint satisfaction, it allows descriptions of problem solving based on constraint satisfaction to be programmed. Jaffar and Lassez [Jaffar 86] gave a criterion for a proposed constraint logic

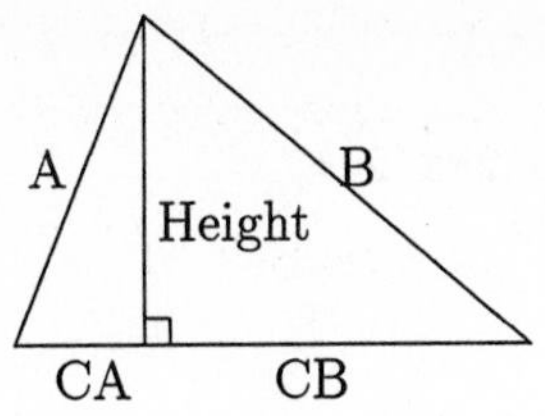

Figure 1: An arbitrary triangle divided into two right triangles

programming system to inherit good logic programming characteristics like soundness, completeness and fixpoint semantics. It is worth noting that constraint logic programming is derived by extending unification. We will discuss later the fact that concurrent logic programming is derived by restricting unification.

We have our own constraint logic programming language, CAL [Sakai 89]. CAL is a CLP language for dealing with nonlinear equations, i.e. polynomial ring. Execution is based on an algorithm for computing Groebner basis for a set of nonlinear equations. It is a kind of term rewriting system and a version of Knuth-Bendix completion. Let us show a simple example of using CAL in geometry. Here, we try to deduce Heron's formula from a set of geometric definitions of surfaces, right triangles and general triangles.

[An Example Program in CAL]

```
surface(Base,Height,Surface) :-
    2*Surface = Base*Height.

right_tri(X,Y,Z) :- X^2 + Y^2 = Z^2.

tri(A,B,C,Surface) :-
    C = CA + CB,
    right_tri(CA,Height,A),
    right_tri(CB,Height,B),
    surface(C,Height,Surface).
```

The meaning of the last clause, defining a general triangle, is shown in Fig. 1.

The Heron's formula is obtained by executing the following query.

[Query and Answer]

```
?- tri(a,b,c,s).

s^2 = (-c^4+ -1*a^4+2*(2*b^2*a^2)+
      -1*b-4+2*(2*c^2*a^2)+
      2*(2*c^2*b^2))/16
```

The execution of the goal, "?- tri(a,b,c,s)." proceeds as follows: first, a set of constraints are collected during the execution of goals. Then, the solver tries to solve the simultaneous equation by eliminating intermediate variables, *CA, CB* and *Heights*. Internal variables are eliminated during the computation of the Groebner Basis of the equations.

We worked on the field of the robot arm control to compute a desired amount of rotation and arm extension given the target position of the arm [Sato 91]. We succeeded in modeling many different types of robots in a very similar way without any difficulty in programming.

6 Concurrent LP as Specifications of Parallel Architecture

One of the most important achievements of the FGCS project is the development of a concurrent logic programming language, Guarded Horn Clauses (GHC) [Ueda 86], and its realistic extension, KL1 [Chikayama 88],[Ueda 90]. GHC follows Relational Language [Clark 81], Concurrent Prolog [Shapiro 83] and PARLOG [Clark 84]. They share the common feature of committed choice nondeterminism and are often called as committed choice nondeterministic languages. In contrast with constraint logic programming languages, they restrict head unifications into one-way unifications. The restriction causes the information to flow from a caller (an active goal) to a callee (a candidate program for the goal) only. Each goal represents a process which runs in parallel. Shared variables between them represent communication channels connecting them. Messages are sent by variable instantiation. The process which performs the instantiation is the sender of the message. The other processes sharing the same variable are the receivers of the message. Variable instantiations are by (one-way) unification. The restriction of head unification gives the rule of synchronization: whenever one-way head unification is impossible due to lack of information (lack of instantiation in the caller variables), the unification will be suspended. More precisely, the suspension condition goes beyond the head unification: you can add additional conditions for synchronization. To identify part of the conditions for each clause, a commitment operator (represented by a vertical bar, "|") is introduced to separate an entire clause into two parts; a guard part which is the left of the commitment operator and the body part which is the rest of the goals. A more precise suspension condition is: "If not enough data has arrived to judge the guard part (a lack of instantiations in the caller variables), then guard computation will be suspended."

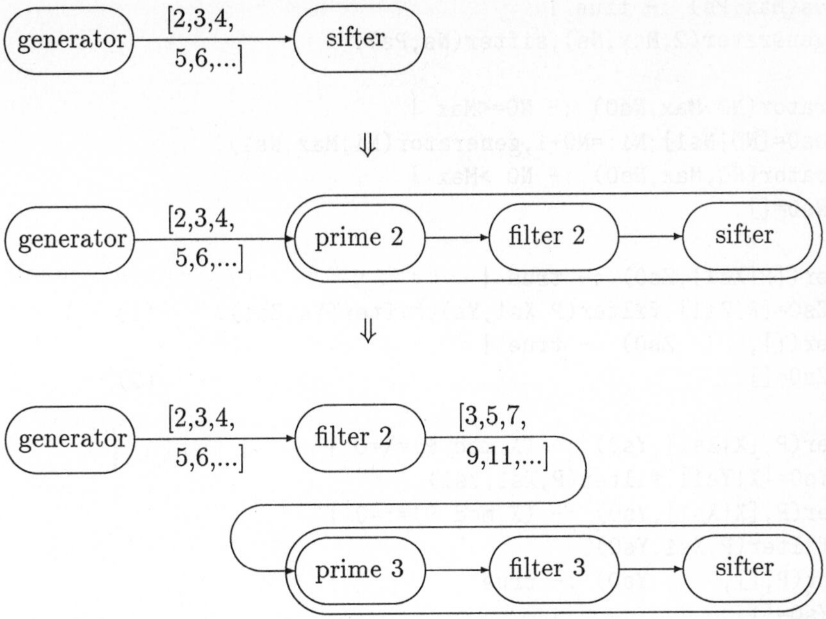

Figure 2: Dynamic behavior of Eratosthenese's sieve

Let us explain in more detail with an example.

[An Example of GHC Program]

Consider a well known algorithm of computing prime numbers. The behavior of the algorithm is described in Fig. 2. It is best explained as a dynamically changing assembly-line factory. In its initial stage, there are only two workers: one, called *generator*, is to produce integer sequences starting at two until a given maximum number is reached. The other, called *sifter*, is to produce prime number sequences from an integer sequence. The job of the later worker is divided into three sub tasks. The first is to add the first element of its input to the prime number list. The second is to create a *filter* to eliminate all subsequent numbers which can be divided by the newly added prime number in the first step and output the rest of the elements. Lastly, the *sifter* replaces himself with a new *sifter* who is responsible for producing subsequent prime numbers from a new input sequence coming from the *filter*. Note that every time a new *sifter* is created, the first element it receives is always a prime number.

The GHC program of the algorithm is given in Fig. 3. Note that each worker is represented by a goal in the body of a clause. Long life workers such as sifters and filters are represented by recursive programs which call the same workers repeatedly. The behavior of the sifter is shown in the sifter clauses. The first sifter clause, (1), shows the creation of two new workers, the new prime reporter and a filter, and the

```
primes(Max,Ps) :- true |
    generator(2,Max,Ns),sifter(Ns,Ps).

generator(N0,Max,Ns0) :- N0=<Max |
    Ns0=[N0|Ns1],N1:=N0+1,generator(N1,Max,Ns1).
generator(N0,Max,Ns0) :- N0 >Max |
    Ns0=[].

sifter([P|Xs1],Zs0) :- true |
    Zs0=[P|Zs1],filter(P,Xs1,Ys),sifter(Ys,Zs1).      (1)
sifter([],     Zs0) :- true |
    Zs0=[].                                            (2)

filter(P,[X|Xs1],Ys0) :- (X mod P)=\=0 |
    Ys0=[X|Ys1],filter(P,Xs1,Ys1).
filter(P,[X|Xs1],Ys0) :- (X mod P)=:=0 |
    filter(P,Xs1,Ys0).
filter(P,[],     Ys0) :- true          |
    Ys0=[].
```

Figure 3: A GHC program of the Eratosthenese's Sieve

clause's replacement by a new sifter (see the three goals appearing in the body of the clause). The second clause, (2), expresses that if an empty sequence is received, then it terminates its job and deletes itself.

Let us see how the synchronization scheme works in this example. We concentrate on the behavior of the **filter** and **sifter** processes appearing in clause (1). Note that they are connected by a shared variable, Ys, representing a sequence of integers for the further production of prime numbers. The instantiation of the variable, Ys, is done be the filter process. Now the synchronization problem is that the sifter process cannot run before the filter finishes its instantiation to the variable, Ys. This problem is solved by the suspension conditions in the sifter clauses. When the sifter goal tries to call the first sifter clause, then Ys must be unified to [P|Xs1] by one way unification from the caller to the callee. If the filter process has not instantiated variable Ys, then it remains an unbound variable and one way unification is not successful. A similar situation happens when the sifter process tries to call the second sifter clause. Note that instantiation by the filter process need not be ground. As soon as it computes a part of the values of Ys, the sifter process can start to run and one of the candidate clauses is properly selected depending upon the content of Ys.

As a final remark of concurrent logic programming, let us introduce our language KL1

(Kernel Language version 1). This is a realistic extension to FGHC, the flat version of GHC.[2] KL1 consists of two sublanguages, KL1c (KL1 core), and KL1p (KL1 pragma). KL1c is an extension of FGHC to enable the language to realize the meta hierarchical structure needed to develop our operating system for Multi-PSI and PIM. KL1p is a sublanguage for annotating run time information on process allocation to processors and for priority scheduling.

6.1 Parallel hardware and operating system

We have been developing two kinds of parallel processors dedicated to KL1. One is the Multi-PSI [Taki 88], consisting of 8 to 64 PSI machines connected by a mesh network. Here, PSI is our workstation for Prolog and KL1 developed at an early stage in this project. Multi-PSI was completed in 1988 and has been used for developing software technology in KL1.

The other parallel processor is PIM [Taki 89], our final target machine. We are now developing five different models of PIM: three large and two small.

Let us introduce the largest one in more detail. It is called PIM/p and has 512 processing elements [Goto 90]. They are divided into 64 clusters each consisting of 8 PEs. Each cluster has a shared memory architecture with two 64K bytes sets of coherent cache memory, one for instructions and one for data. These 64 clusters are then connected by two hyper-cube networks. Every processing element has a connection to one of the networks. Each communication path has a throughput of 20M bytes/second in both directions.

The PIM/p processing element is designed for the efficient execution of KL1-B, which is an abstract instruction set for the KL1 used commonly in our different PIM models. The role of KL1-B is similar to that of WAM [Warren 83]. The major differences from WAM are the synchronization feature and the functions for incremental garbage collection, called MRB [Chikayama 87]. Performance is expected to be 200K to 500K LIPS for one PE and around 100M LIPS for the entire PIM/p.

PIMOS [Chikayama 88] is an operating system for both Multi-PSI and PIM. It has been developed totally in KL1. The core part of PIMOS is a program of around 20,000 lines. The primary functions of PIMOS are I/O resource management, execution control of user tasks, and management of program codes. It is a single operating system which runs in parallel. Since the implementation language, KL1, supports synchronization, it is not surprising that we succeeded in developing the operating system entirely in KL1, our concurrent logic programming language. Every I/O device connected to the PIM has a *logical* interface, so it looks like a perpetual process (a recursive program) connected to user programs by a shared variable working as a message channel. Indeed, it is the largest program written in KL1, which shows the potential of the language for developing realistic applications.

[2]FGHC is a restricted GHC which does not allow the writing of any user defined predicates in its guard part. This prevents the guard environment from becoming nested during execution.

7 Theorem Prover in KL1

Since unification is limited to one way in GHC/KL1, it is generally hard to realize a first order theorem prover since these usually need to make heavy use of full unification. There are two ways to solve this problem. One is to write the full unification program in GHC/KL1 (regarding it as a very low level language like C). The result is not very attractive because efficiency is decreased 10 to 100 times compared with direct use of unification (in case of one way unification). The other way is to limit the usage of unification to only one way. Manthey and Bry invented a new bottom up theorem prover, called SATCHMO, based on model generation [Manthey 88].

SATCHMO tries to generate all possible models incrementally by bottom up evaluation of clauses. It tries to prove the antecedent conjunction of literals by searching their instances in each model. If it succeeds in finding a model in which the proof succeeds, then it extends the model by adding the consequent disjunctive ground literals. If there is more than one literal in its disjunct, then SATCHMO splits the model into the number of literals in the disjunct, and adds each literal to each of the split model. Since every element in every model is ground, we need one way unification only to search models when proving antecedent conjuncts. This enables us to realize an efficient theorem prover in GHC/KL1. One big problem was how to realize multiple binding to find all possible proofs by different instantiations of variables. In the case of Prolog, this function is achieved by utilizing backtracking. However, there is no backtracking mechanism in GHC/KL1. Fuchi [Fuchi 90] invented an elegant coding technique for implementing SATCHMO in GHC by utilizing GHC variables as object variables appearing in theories to be proved. This technique was improved by Fujita and Hasegawa [Fujita 91]. In their coding technique, this problem is avoided by reversing the role of the caller and the callee: instead of trying to find a model element having a pattern appearing in a theorem, their method tries to find a theorem having a given model element as an instantiation of a literal of the theorem. Since every model element is a ground literal, there is no variable in the caller. The variable instantiations occur when a theorem database is searched and an appropriate clause representing a literal of some theorem is found to match a given model element.

Actually, the same trick can be applied in database searching. The KL1 program in Fig. 4 is a realization of the **select** operation of Relational Database.

Note that we need to compile a query each time it is to be retrieved. Also, we need an extra **query** clause to match to every data item no match can be made to the real **query** clause. To make the selection of the exceptional clause last, we need a control primitive, **otherwise** in KL1.

8 Conclusion

The research activities of the FGCS project can be regarded as a continuous effort to prove the correctness of our conjecture that logic programming will be the bridge

```
select([],Ans) :- true | Ans=[].
select([Q|DB], Ans) :- true |
        query(Q,R),
        cont_select(Q,DB,R,Ans).

cont_select(Q,DB,fail,Ans) :- true |
        select(DB,Ans).
cont_select(Q,DB,true,Ans) :- true |
        Ans=[Q|Ans1],
        select(DB,Ans1).

query(address(Employee,tokyo),T) :- true | T=true.
otherwise.
query(_,T) :- true | T=fail.
```

Figure 4: A KL1 program of the **select** operation

that connects knowledge information processing and parallel processing. Our research results strongly suggest that out proof is valid.

We succeeded in developing a family of logic programming languages for knowledge information processing applications and for parallel processing. These include the constraint logic programming language CAL, and the concurrent logic programming language KL1. Although more effort is needed to completely integrate these two languages into a single framework, we have shown much evidence that integration will be possible in the future.

The new computational environment being provided through our project will certainly invoke new application areas in large scale knowledge information processing. One of the most challenging topics of such new areas is machine learning based on a new logic programming paradigm: abduction / induction. This new paradigm, together with efficient theorem proving techniques, will create a new era in knowledge information processing.

References

[Chikayama 87] T. Chikayama and Y. Kimura, *Multiple Reference Management in Flat GHC.* In Proc. of the Fourth International Conference on Logic Programming, MIT Press, 1987.

[Chikayama 88] T. CHikayama, H. Sato and T. Miyazaki, *Overview of the Parallel Inference Machine Operating System(PIMOS).* In Proc. of the International Conf. on Fifth Generation Computing Systems 1988, Tokyo, 1988.

[Clark 81] K. L. Clark and S. Gregory, *A Relational Language for Parallel Programming.* In Proc. ACM Conf. on Functional Programming Languages and Computer Architecture, ACM, 1981.

[Clark 84] K. L. Clark and S. Gregory, *PARLOG: Parallel Programming in Logic.* Research Report DOC 84/4, Dept. of Computing, Imperial College of Science and Technology, London. Also in *ACM. Trans. Prog. Lang. Syst.*, Vol. 8, No. 1, 1986.

[Fuchi 87] Fuchi, K. and Furukawa, K. "The Role of Logic Programming in the Fifth Generation Computer Project," New Generation Computing, Vol. 5, No. 1, Ohmsha-springer, 1987.

[Fuchi 90] K. Fuchi, *Impression of KL1 Programming - from my experience with writing parallel provers -.* In Proc. of KL1 Programming Workshop '90, Institute for New Generation Computer Technology, Tokyo, 1990 (in Japanese).

[Fujita 88] H. Fujita and K. Furukawa, *A Self-Applicable Partial Evaluator and Its Use in Incremental Compilation.* New Generation Computing, Vol. 6, Nos.2,3, Ohmsha/Springer-Verlag, 1988.

[Fujita 91] H. Fujita and R. Hasegawa, *A Model Generation Theorem Prover in KL1 Using a Ramified-Stack Algorithm.* In Proc. of the Eighth International Conference on Logic Programming, Paris, 1991.

[Futamura 71] Futamura, Y. (1971) Partial Evaluation of Computation Process: An Approach to a Compiler-Compiler. *Systems, Computers, Controls 2.*

[Goto 90] A. Goto, *Research and Development of the Parallel Inference Machine in the FGCS Project.* Technical Report TR-437, Institute for New Generation Computer Technology, Tokyo, 1989.

[Jaffar 86] J. Jaffar and J-L. Lassez, *Constraint Logic Programming.* Technical Report, Department of Computer Science, Monash University, 1986.

[Komorowski 82] H. J. Komorowski, *Partial Evaluation as a Means for Inferencing Data Structure in an Applicative Language: A Theory and Implementation in the Case of Prolog.* Ninth ACM Symposium on Principles of Programming Languages, Albuquerque, New Mexico, 1982.

[Manthey 88] R. Manthey and F. Bry, *SATCHMO: A Theorem Prover Implemented in Prolog.* In Proc. of CADE-88, Argonne, Illinois, 1988.

[Robinson 65] J. A. Robinson, *A Machine-Oriented Logic Based on Resolution Principle.* J. ACM 12, 1965.

[Sakai 89] Sakai, K. and Aiba, A. "CAL: A Theoretical Background of Constraint Logic Programming and its Applications," J. Symbolic Computation, Vol.8, No.6, pp.589-603, 1989.

[Sato 91] S. Sato and A. Aiba, *An Application of CAL to Robotics.* Tech. Memo TM 1032, Institute for New Generation Computer Technology, Tokyo, 1991.

[Seki 87] H. Seki and K. Furukawa, *Notes on Transformation techniques for Generate and Test Logic Programs.* In Proc. 1987 Symposium on Logic Programming, IEEE Computer Society Press, 1987.

[Shapiro 83] E. Y. Shapiro, *A Subset of Concurrent Prolog and Its Interpreter.* Tech. Report TR-003, Institute for New Generation Computer Technology, Tokyo, 1983.

[Takeuchi 86] A. Takeuchi and K. Furukawa, *Partial Evaluation of Prolog Programs and Its Application to Meta Programming.* In Proc. IFIP'86, North-Holland, 1986.

[Taki 88] K. Taki, *The Parallel Software Research and Development Tool: Multi-PSI system.* In Programming of Future Generation Computers, K. Fuchi and M. Nivat, eds, North-Holland, 1988.

[Taki 89] K. Taki, *The FGCS Computing Archtecture.* In Proc. IFIP'89, North-Holland, 1989.

[Ueda 86] K. Ueda, *Guarded Horn Clauses.* In Logic Programming '85, E. Wada, ed, Lecture Notes in Computer Science, 221, Springer-Verlag, 1986.

[Ueda 90] Ueda, K. and Chikayama, T. "Design of the Kernel Language for the Parallel Inference Machine," The Computer Journal, Vol. 33, No. 6 (Dec., 1990), pp. 494–500.

[Warren 83] D. H. D. Warren, *An Abstract Prolog Instruction Set.* Technical Note 304, Artificial Intelligence Center, SRI, 1983.

Authentication and Delegation with Smart-cards

M. Abadi* M. Burrows* C. Kaufman† B. Lampson*

Abstract

The authentication of users in distributed systems poses special problems because users lack the ability to encrypt and decrypt. The same problems arise when users wish to delegate some of their authority to nodes, after mutual authentication.

In most systems today, the user is forced to trust the node he wants to use. In a more satisfactory design, the user carries a smart-card with sufficient computing power to assist him; the card provides encryption and decryption capabilities for authentication and delegation.

Authentication is relatively straightforward with a powerful enough smart-card. However, for practical reasons, protocols that place few demands on smart-cards should be considered. These protocols are subtle, as they rely on fairly complex trust relations between the principals in the system (users, hosts, services). In this paper, we discuss a range of public-key smart-card protocols, and analyze their assumptions and the guarantees they offer.

1 Introduction

In a secure distributed environment, there is a need for users to prove their identities to nodes, from mainframes to automatic teller machines. There is also a need, though less recognized, for nodes to prove their identities to users, as each user may trust different nodes to different extents. Furthermore, users must be able to delegate some of their authority to the nodes that they trust.

Authentication protocols serve for these purposes, typically relying on secrets and encryption (e.g., [3, 11, 12]). The authentication of users poses special problems, because users lack the ability to encrypt and decrypt.

*Digital Equipment Corporation, Systems Research Center, 130 Lytton Avenue, Palo Alto, California 94301, USA.

†Digital Equipment Corporation, Telecommunications and Networks, 550 King Street, Littleton, Massachusetts 01460, USA.

In the simplest approach to user authentication, the user owns a secret (his password) that he gives to a node that he wishes to use. It is likely that the password will be short and memorable, or that the user will need to write it down. In either case, it may be easy for an attacker to discover the user's password and hence obtain all his rights.

This weakness can be eliminated by introducing a simple card with a small amount of read-only memory. Each user carries a card, and each card contains a different secret, which the node verifies before granting access to the user. The secret can be quite long, and hence hard to guess, but theft of the card is a significant danger.

A further improvement consists in introducing a Personal Identification Number (PIN), which the user types when he presents his card. Thus, theft of the card alone no longer suffices for a security breach. This scheme is essentially that used by most Automated Teller Machines (ATMs).

All of these approaches suffer from a serious flaw: the node must be completely trusted, as it obtains all of the user's secrets. It is impossible for a user to delegate only part of his authority, or to delegate his authority for only a limited time. Moreover, a malicious node could remember the user's secrets for future mischief. This threat seems important—consider, for example, the users of public terminals in hotels.

A smart-card with sufficient computing power solves these problems. The smart-card we envision has its own keyboard, display, clock, logic for performing public-key encryption [6, 13], and can be electrically coupled to the node.

Authentication would be relatively straightforward with this powerful smart-card. The smart-card might operate only when fed a PIN, so an attacker would need to steal the smart-card and to discover the user's PIN in order to impersonate the user. The keyboard and display allow the user to communicate directly with the smart-card, so that the node never sees the password. Since the smart-card performs public-key encryption, no secrets ever need be revealed to the node.

After authentication, the smart-card can sign timestamped certificates to delegate part of the user's authority for a limited time. For example, the smart-card could issue a certificate that allows the node to manipulate the user's remote files for the next hour. The timestamp provides protection against replay attacks, and careful use of lifetimes can prevent mischief by the node at a later time.

Unfortunately, no one is currently selling a smart-card of the type we have described, though one may be available at some time in the future. More realistic protocols that place weaker demands on smart-cards should therefore be considered. Various compatible solutions can be implemented with reduced degrees of security and user convenience. The protocols are subtler, as they rely on more complex trust relations between the principals (users, hosts, services) in the system.

Consider, for example, a smart-card with no clock. Such a smart-card is attractive because it avoids the need for a battery. Unfortunately, the smart-card can no longer generate timestamps for its certificates, and it cannot check that other certificates have not expired. A variety of replay attacks becomes possible, unless the card can obtain the time somehow. To counter replay attacks effectively, the card may obtain the time from a network time service, which must then be secure and trusted.

In this paper, we describe a range of public-key smart-card authentication protocols, with different compromises between cost and security. The protocols were developed in the context of the Digital Distributed System Security Architecture [7]. Most previous work focuses on user authentication using shared-key cryptography, with little discussion of delegation (see, for example, [4]). We believe that public-key cryptography is more suitable than shared-key cryptography for authentication and delegation, and that it is not prohibitively expensive when used wisely. The protocols considered can be based on RSA encryption [13], but other algorithms (e.g., [8]) could also be used.

We analyze the protocols with a logic of authentication. This is essentially the logic of Burrows, Abadi, and Needham [2], with a simple extension to handle secure and timely channels. It should be noted that our logical account is not the only one possible. However, the formalism enables us to describe the assumptions and the guarantees of each protocol, clarifying the trust relations between principals. Moreover, a logical account helps in avoiding certain security flaws commonly present in authentication protocols [2].

In the next section, we summarize the notation of the logic; the logic is discussed further in an Appendix. In later sections, we describe smart-card authentication protocols, starting with those that require the more ambitious smart-card designs and the weaker trust relations. We analyze three cases in some detail; the reader can interpolate between these. The informal descriptions (without the logic) are self-contained, and the formal passages may be skipped in a first reading.

2 Notation

In the analysis of smart-card protocols, we apply a logic for describing the beliefs of the principals in the course of authentication. Several sorts of objects appear in the logic: principals, encryption keys, formulas, and communication links. (The original logic does not discuss links.) In what follows, the symbols P, Q, and R range over principals; X and Y range over formulas; K ranges over encryption keys; L ranges over communication links. The constructs that we use are listed below.

P **believes** X

P **controls** X: P has *jurisdiction* over X. The principal P is an authority on X and should be trusted on this matter. For example, a certification authority may be trusted to provide the public keys of principals.

P **said** X: P *once said* X. The principal P sent a message including X, either long ago or during the current run of the protocol. In any case, P believed X when he sent the message.

P **said**$_L$ X: P *once said* X on the communication link L.

P **sees** X: P *sees* X. A message containing X has been sent to P, who can read and repeat X (possibly after doing some decryption).

P **sees**$_L$ X: P *sees* X on the communication link L.

fresh(X): X is *fresh*, that is, X has not been sent in a message at any time before the current run of the protocol. This usually holds for timestamps and for *nonces*—expressions invented for the purpose of being fresh.

timely(L): The link L is a *timely channel*: all messages on link L are known to have been sent recently.

$\overset{K}{\mapsto} P$: P has K as a *public key*. The matching *secret key* (the inverse of K, denoted K^{-1}) will never be discovered by any principal except P, or a principal trusted by P.

$\overset{L}{\prec} P$: The link L is a *secure channel* from P: all messages on link L are known to have been sent by P, or a principal trusted by P.

$P \overset{X}{\rightleftharpoons} Q$: X is a *secret* that will never be known to anyone but P and Q, and possibly to principals trusted by them. Only P and Q may use X to prove their identities to one another. An example of a shared secret is a password or a PIN.

$\{X\}_K$: This represents the formula X encrypted under the key K.

$\langle X\rangle_Y$: This represents X combined with the formula Y; it is intended that Y be a secret, and that its presence prove the identity of whoever utters $\langle X\rangle_Y$. In implementations, X may simply be concatenated with Y; our notation highlights that Y plays a special rôle, as proof of origin for X.

3 A protocol for ideal smart-cards

We start with a description of how user authentication would work given the ultimate smart-card, with its own keyboard, display, clock, and logic for performing public-key encryption. Other schemes are best thought of in terms of their differences from this scheme.

We assume that a distributed name service is available. The name service contains *certificates* with information about which nodes each user should trust and which public keys belong to which agents. A certificate is a statement that has been signed by a principal. Often, certificates are signed by a widely trusted service, known as a *certification authority*. A certificate typically includes a timestamp, with its time of issue, and sometimes an explicit lifetime, which limits its validity. The certification authority need not be on-line; the name service need not be trusted.

We also assume that principals know the time accurately enough to check the validity of certificates and to detect the replay of timestamped messages. A trusted time service is one way of achieving this.

We first describe the protocol informally, and then more formally.

3.1 Discussion

For the sake of concreteness, let us imagine that a user wants to prove his identity to a workstation. Moreover, the user wishes to allow the workstation to access files on his behalf.

1. The user sits down at the workstation and presents his smart-card. The smart-card is willing to give certain information, including the name of the user, to anyone.

2. The workstation now authenticates itself to the smart-card. Given the name of the user, the workstation can retrieve all the certificates the smart-card needs to determine that it is allowed to delegate authority to the workstation; it forwards these to the smart-card. The workstation also generates a new public key and a matching secret key; we refer to these keys as *delegation keys.* It sends the public key and a timestamp to the smart-card, signed with its own secret key.

3. The smart-card examines the information presented by the workstation, verifying the signatures and lifetimes on all of the certificates. At this point, the smart-card knows the public key of the workstation and that the workstation can be trusted to act on behalf of the user. The smart-card shows that it is satisfied on its display and requests the user's PIN. In addition, it might give the identity of the workstation, or at least an indication, such as a group nickname. It might also provide some means to identify the workstation's display, such as a name or location.

4. Now the user has some evidence of the workstation's identity. The user responds by entering a PIN into the keyboard of the smart-card, thus authorizing the use of this workstation.

5. The entry of the correct PIN indicates that the genuine user is present, rather than some smart-card thief. Hence, the card constructs and signs a *delegation certificate.* This delegation certificate authorizes anyone who can demonstrate knowledge of the secret delegation key to act on behalf of the user for a limited period of time. It sends that certificate to the workstation.

6. The workstation verifies that the delegation certificate is signed with the card's secret key and contains the public delegation key. At this point, the workstation

has authenticated the user, in the sense that it knows that whoever is at the keyboard has a particular public key. The workstation has enough information to consult an access control list and to determine whether it should provide its services to this user. Moreover, the delegation certificate enables the workstation to convince another node, such as a file server, that the workstation acts on behalf of the user.

This completes the authentication process. The workstation now knows the user's identity. It can prove that it acts on the user's behalf by presenting the delegation certificate and proving that it knows the secret delegation key. The user also knows something about the workstation—perhaps its name, but at least that the workstation can be trusted, according to the certification authority.

For authentication, it does not suffice for the user and the workstation to know each other's names. They must also know that they are communicating via a particular keyboard and a particular display, and for example that no malicious principal is interposed between the user and the workstation. An implementation of this protocol should provide this guarantee.

An important variation on this scheme has to do with rôles. A user may need and want different privileges when he acts as member of a research group and as manager, for example. A user may also want different privileges depending on his trust of the systems that act on his behalf. Software and hardware trusted in one rôle should be prevented from gaining privileges reserved for another rôle. One way of providing this capability is to issue multiple smart-cards to the user, one for each rôle. A more satisfactory solution is to have a single smart-card support multiple rôles. By typing at the card's keyboard, the user could select a rôle, to be mentioned in the delegation certificate. In addition, the smart-card could restrict the rôles available, to save the user from misplaced trust in unsafe environments.

For the purposes of a logical analysis, it would be adequate to conceive of the user in each of his rôles as a different user. For simplicity, we do not discuss rôles further in this paper.

3.2 Notation and assumptions

The notation used in the remainder of this section is as follows:

- S is the certification authority, W the workstation, C the smart-card, U the user, and F a file server (or any other node) that the workstation contacts on behalf of the user;
- K_s, K_w, and K_c are the public keys of S, W, and C, respectively;
- K_d is the public delegation key, generated by W;
- *PIN* is U's personal identification number;

- T_w, T_c, T_s, T'_s, and T''_s are timestamps;
- I_c is the smart-card's keyboard (input to the card);
- O_c is the smart-card's display (output from the card);
- I_w is the workstation's keyboard (input to the workstation); and
- O_w is the workstation's display (output from the workstation).

The name C is useful only in connecting U with K_c, and need not be present in an implementation. Similarly, the names for I_w and O_w will quite likely be related to one another, and to W. For example, if I_w and O_w are referred to by location, then the names could be identical.

In order to analyze the protocol with the logic, we have to state its assumptions and describe it more formally. We leave the description of the protocol to the next subsection, and now proceed to discuss its assumptions. The assumptions naturally fall into several classes:

Assumptions about timestamps: the smart-card, the workstation, and the file server believe that certain timestamps were generated recently:

1. C **believes fresh**(T_s), C **believes fresh**(T'_s), C **believes fresh**(T_w);
2. W **believes fresh**(T_c), W **believes fresh**(T''_s);
3. F **believes fresh**(T_c), F **believes fresh**(T''_s).

Assumptions about keys and secrets:

1. S **believes** $\overset{K_c}{\mapsto} C$, S **believes** $\overset{K_w}{\mapsto} W$: the certification authority believes the smart-card's public key is K_c, and the workstation's public key is K_w;
2. C **believes** $\overset{K_s}{\mapsto} S$: the smart-card believes the certification authority's public key is K_s;
3. C **believes** $C \overset{PIN}{\rightleftharpoons} U$: the smart-card believes that PIN is a secret shared with the user;
4. W **believes** $\overset{K_s}{\mapsto} S$: the workstation believes the certification authority's public key is K_s;
5. W **believes** $\overset{K_d}{\mapsto} U$: the workstation believes that K_d is a good key for U (probably because W has constructed the key);
6. F **believes** $\overset{K_s}{\mapsto} S$: the file server believes the certification authority's public key is K_s.

Assumptions about channels:

1. W **believes** $\overset{O_w}{\prec} W$: the workstation believes that the display is a secure channel from it;
2. U **believes** $\overset{O_c}{\prec} C$, U **believes timely**(O_c): the user believes that the smart-card's display is a secure and timely channel from the smart-card;
3. U **believes** $\overset{I_w}{\prec} U$: the user believes that the workstation's keyboard is a secure channel from him;
4. C **believes timely**(I_c): the smart-card believes that its keypad is a timely channel.

Assumptions about trust:

1. U **believes** $\forall K.(W$ **controls** $\overset{K}{\mapsto} U)$: the user believes that the workstation can choose an appropriate public key; intuitively, the user is willing to delegate to this workstation;
2. S **believes** U **controls** $\forall K.(W$ **controls** $\overset{K}{\mapsto} U)$: W is believed to be a safe workstation for the user to delegate to; more precisely, the certification authority trusts the user to decide whether to trust this workstation in the choice of a key;
3. S **believes** $\forall X.(C$ **controls** U **believes** $X)$: the certification authority trusts the smart-card to relay the user's beliefs;
4. S **believes** $\forall K.(C$ **controls** $\overset{K}{\mapsto} U)$: the certification authority trusts the smart-card to set a key for the user;
5. U **believes** W **controls** $\overset{O_w}{\prec} W$: the user trusts the workstation when it says that the display O_w is a channel from it;
6. U **believes** $\forall W.(C$ **controls** W **believes** $\overset{O_w}{\prec} W)$: the user trusts his card to pass on beliefs of the workstation;
7. W **believes** U **controls** $\overset{I_w}{\prec} U$: the workstation trusts the user when he claims to be at the keyboard.

In addition, there are a few assumptions about trust in the server; for the sake of brevity, we assume that every principal trusts the server completely.

Some of the assumptions are rather strong, and could be weakened. In particular, the assumption

$$W \textbf{ believes } U \textbf{ controls } \overset{I_w}{\prec} U$$

is a simplification of the more accurate "the workstation trusts whoever claims to be at its keyboard to identify himself properly *through the smart-card*." Our simple logic is unable to express this satisfactorily in a single formula.

3.3 The protocol analyzed

Now we discuss the protocol in detail, and show that it establishes channels (the keyboard and the display) between the user and the workstation, and that it provides a delegation key that the workstation can use on behalf of the user in dealing with other nodes:

$$U \textbf{ believes } \overset{O_w}{\prec} W, \qquad W \textbf{ believes } \overset{I_w}{\prec} U, \qquad F \textbf{ believes } \overset{K_d}{\mapsto} U$$

Step by step, we can follow the evolution of the beliefs of the participants, from the initial assumptions to these conclusions. We summarize the major deductions, and at the same time we explain the messages in the protocol.

The reasoning deals with an idealized version of the protocol, in which messages are replaced by formulas of the logic. These formulas should be believed by the principals that send them. An implementation of the protocol need not transmit these formulas literally; any unambiguous bit representation will do, and one is typically obvious from the context.

The transmission of certificates is represented explicitly. We do not show the exact routes these follow, however, as the routes do not affect the properties of the protocol—they are merely an implementation choice. In practice, one would expect certificates to be cached, so that they do not need to be transmitted or checked repeatedly.

1. $W \to C$: $\{\overset{K_d}{\mapsto} U,\ \overset{O_w}{\prec} W,\ T_w\}_{K_w^{-1}}$
   The workstation asserts that it has a public key K_d for the user and that the display O_w is a secure channel from W.

2. $S \to C$: $\{\overset{K_w}{\mapsto} W,\ T_s\}_{K_s^{-1}},\ \{U \textbf{ controls } \forall K.(W \textbf{ controls } \overset{K}{\mapsto} U),\ T_s'\}_{K_s^{-1}}$
   The certification authority provides the public key of the workstation to the smart-card. At this point, the smart-card can decrypt and attribute the previous message, as well as check the freshness of the timestamp T_w. The certification authority also states that the user can let this workstation choose a delegation key. The smart-card trusts the certification authority; in the logic, we obtain:

   $$C \textbf{ believes } \overset{K_w}{\mapsto} W, \quad C \textbf{ believes } U \textbf{ controls } \forall K.(W \textbf{ controls } \overset{K}{\mapsto} U)$$

   and then also

   $$C \textbf{ believes } W \textbf{ believes } \overset{O_w}{\prec} W$$

3. $C \to U$: $W \textbf{ believes } \overset{O_w}{\prec} W$ *on* O_c
   On its display, the card provides the name of the workstation to the user; the card also gives enough information for the user to check whether the display in front of him is W's. More precisely, the smart-card states that W believes that O_w is its display (formally, that O_w is a secure channel from W). Since the user

trusts the smart-card on this matter and it knows that the smart-card's display is both secure and timely, it believes the card's assertion. We can now derive:

$$U \textbf{ believes } \stackrel{O_w}{\prec} W$$

because the user trusts W on $\stackrel{O_w}{\prec} W$. Thus, the workstation has authenticated itself to the user.

4. $U \rightarrow C$: $\langle \forall K.(W \textbf{ controls } \stackrel{K}{\mapsto} U), \stackrel{I_w}{\prec} U \rangle_{PIN}$ *on* I_c
If the user wishes to proceed, he enters his PIN on the card's keypad. Thus, the user indicates that he trusts the workstation to choose a key and that he is at the keyboard I_w. He uses his personal identification number to convince the smart-card of his identity. We can prove:

$$C \textbf{ believes } \forall K.(W \textbf{ controls } \stackrel{K}{\mapsto} U), \quad C \textbf{ believes } U \textbf{ believes } \stackrel{I_w}{\prec} U$$

Using S's certificates and W's claims, we can also obtain:

$$C \textbf{ believes } \stackrel{K_d}{\mapsto} U$$

5. $C \rightarrow W$: $\{U \textbf{ believes } \stackrel{I_w}{\prec} U, T_c\}_{K_c^{-1}}$
The smart-card communicates to the workstation that the user believes he is at the keyboard. In an implementation where U and I_w are clear from context, it suffices for C to send a signed message to W, such as the delegation certificate below.

6. $S \rightarrow W$: $\{\stackrel{K_c}{\mapsto} C, \forall X.(C \textbf{ controls } U \textbf{ believes } X), T_s''\}_{K_s^{-1}}$
The certification authority gives the smart-card's public key to the workstation, and connects this key to U. At this point, the workstation can decrypt the previous message and check its timestamp. With a few applications of the logical postulates, we prove:

$$W \textbf{ believes } \stackrel{I_w}{\prec} U$$

This statement means that the workstation believes that the user is at its keyboard, and hence that the user has authenticated himself to the workstation.

7. $C \rightarrow F$: $\{\stackrel{K_d}{\mapsto} U, T_c\}_{K_c^{-1}}$
The smart-card certifies that K_d is a delegation key for the user.

8. $S \rightarrow F$: $\{\stackrel{K_c}{\mapsto} C, \forall K.(C \textbf{ controls } \stackrel{K}{\mapsto} U), T_s''\}_{K_s^{-1}}$
The certification authority gives the smart-card's key to the file server. At this point, the file server can decrypt the certificate from the smart-card and check the timestamp in it. Furthermore, the certification authority asserts that the card can set a key for the user, and the file server trusts the certification authority in this matter as well. Hence, we obtain:

$$F \textbf{ believes } \stackrel{K_d}{\mapsto} U$$

Informally, the file server has accepted the delegation key generated by the workstation, and thus the workstation can act on the user's behalf.

After this message sequence, the file server F has not heard about W. All the responsibility for checking the suitability of W rests on the user and the smart-card. This is not entirely unreasonable, as we are assuming a powerful smart-card. In the next section, we describe protocols where F participates in this checking.

4 A more realistic smart-card protocol

The smart-card design required for the protocol of the previous section is rather ambitious with today's technology. In this section, we consider a protocol that requires much less from the smart-card. Another one appears in the next section.

4.1 Concessions in smart-card design

The first feature to eliminate is the clock on the card. Having a clock on the card is particularly difficult because it requires a battery. The clock could be eliminated by having the user enter the time; it is equivalent, but much more practical, to have the workstation supply the time to the card and the user verify it on the display. This solution is not as convenient or as secure (the user will probably not check very carefully), but it works. There are two threats if the smart-card has an incorrect notion of time. First, the card could be tricked into signing a delegation certificate for some time far in the future and the workstation could then impersonate the user without the smart-card being physically present. Second, a workstation whose certificate has expired at some time in the past could convince the smart-card the certificate is still valid.

Another feature we could eliminate is the keyboard on the card. It may be quite difficult to make a small, mechanically strong keyboard that can be reached even when the card has been connected to a reader. The user could instead enter his PIN on the workstation's keyboard, which could forward the PIN in a message to the card. The danger here, though not a particularly worrisome one, is that a misbehaving workstation could capture the PIN. The workstation could give the PIN to someone who subsequently steals the card, or the workstation could use the PIN more than once on a single insertion of the card to obtain the delegation of more rôles than the user intended. These threats can be avoided entirely by having the card display a nonce secret and having the user "modify" it into the PIN with a series of '+' and 'nextdigit' operations sent via the workstation keyboard. We can view this nonce secret as an encryption key (or a one-time pad) that the card supplies to the user to establish a secure channel that the workstation cannot read or write. In this way, PIN entry goes through the keyboard but is not subject to replay.

A similar concession is to remove the display from the card, instead of the keyboard. In this case, it is straightforward for the user to enter the PIN, but it is much harder for the smart-card to identify the workstation to the user. A single LED is a partial substitute for a display.

A final compromise consists in limiting the smart-card's ability to encrypt and decrypt. We consider the extreme case where the smart-card signs one message but is not able to decrypt. In this case, it is desirable to provide a secure channel from the workstation (such as a secure card reader).

In the remainder of this section, we study a protocol where the smart-card has a display, but has neither a clock nor a keyboard, and has reduced encryption capabilities. (We leave to the reader the derivation and analysis of variants.)

These concessions in smart-card design may leave the user at the mercy of the workstation. It is therefore desirable to transfer some trust from the workstation to other principals in the distributed environment.

The simplest choice is to give a more prominent rôle to the principals that check delegation certificates, such as the file server F. Thus, F takes into account W's identity before accepting a delegation key for U. Moreover, F may grant some requests from W on behalf of U, and not others (as in the general approach to delegation of [9]). The user obtains no real guarantee of the identity of the workstation, since the card cannot decrypt. However, the user can be sure that his authority is not delegated inappropriately, because of the check performed by F. This is the approach we adopt in the following protocol.

In the next section, we discuss a more elaborate design, where dedicated *trusted agents* assist the smart-card in the process of delegation.

4.2 Notation and assumptions

Some additional notation is needed:

- K_{cu} is a short secret nonce generated by the card, to protect the entry of the user's PIN—as the notation suggests, we view the secret as an encryption key for the PIN;
- L_r is the smart-card reader; and
- $\{T_b\}_{K_b^{-1}}$ is a timestamp signed by B, a trusted time service; B is trusted never to sign a timestamp for a time in the future; W obtains the certified timestamp by whatever means, and may check T_b.

The following are the main novelties in the initial assumptions; we omit a full list. In these, it is convenient to use the name W' for the workstation that controls the channel L_r. (With any luck, of course, W' is the intended W.) We need this notation because the user must reason about the workstation connected to L_r before believing it is W.

1. C **believes** $\overset{L_r}{\prec} W'$, C **believes timely**(L_r): the smart-card believes that the smart-card reader provides a timely, secure channel to the workstation W';

2. C **believes** $C \overset{K_{cu}}{\leftrightarrow} U$, C **believes fresh**$(C \overset{K_{cu}}{\leftrightarrow} U)$: the smart-card has a secret, to be used to hide the PIN from the workstation; this secret is a nonce, and hence its mention in a message proves the freshness of this message.

3. U **believes** W' **controls** $\overset{O_w}{\prec} W$: the user trusts the workstation connected to the smart-card reader to give its name correctly, asserting that the display is a secure channel from W—the user may reject outrageous names, though; this assumption is strong, since the user gets no real guarantee of the workstation's identity;

4. F **believes fresh**$(\{T_b\}_{K_b^{-1}})$: the file server believes in the timeliness of the certified timestamp; B's signature convinces F of the validity of T_b, even though C does not have a clock, because B is trusted not to sign future timestamps.

4.3 The protocol analyzed

The protocol presented here achieves the same properties as the one for ultimate smart-cards, namely,

$$U \textbf{ believes } \overset{O_w}{\prec} W, \qquad W \textbf{ believes } \overset{I_w}{\prec} U, \qquad F \textbf{ believes } \overset{K_d}{\mapsto} U$$

This amounts to mutual authentication and delegation. However, stronger assumptions are required here, particularly for the first conclusion.

The messages and the deductions can be explained thus:

1. $W \to C$: $\overset{O_w}{\prec} W$ *on* L_r
   The workstation names itself and its display.

2. $C \to U$: W' **believes** $\overset{O_w}{\prec} W, C \overset{K_{cu}}{\leftrightarrow} U$ *on* O_c
   The card passes the workstation's message on to the user. It also provides a one-time pad K_{cu}. Notice that the user has no assurance that the named workstation is actually the workstation in front of him. However, he can be sure that he is delegating authority only to the machine named. The user simply trusts the workstation to give its name correctly. Thus, we have:

$$U \textbf{ believes } \overset{O_w}{\prec} W$$

3. $U \to C$: $\{\overset{I_w}{\prec} U, \forall K.(W \textbf{ controls } \overset{K}{\mapsto} U), C \overset{K_{cu}}{\leftrightarrow} U\}_{Kcu}$
   The user enters his PIN. The PIN is not entered directly; instead, the user types a sequence of keys which modify the displayed value K_{cu} until the PIN is displayed.

Thus, the user asserts that he is at the keyboard, and gives jurisdiction to the workstation over the choice of a key. The key K_{cu} appears inside the message as proof of timeliness. (In an implementation, the use of K_{cu} as a one-time pad suffices as proof of timeliness.)

4. $C \rightarrow W$: $\{U$ **believes** $\overset{I_w}{\prec} U, \{T_b\}_{K_b^{-1}}\}_{K_c^{-1}}$
   As in the previous protocol, the smart-card communicates to the workstation that the user believes he is at the keyboard. The certified timestamp, which may have been obtained via W, is included as proof of timeliness.

5. $S \rightarrow W$: $\{\overset{K_c}{\mapsto} C, \forall X.(C$ **controls** U **believes** $X), T_s''\}_{K_s^{-1}}$
   The certification authority provides the smart-card's public key to the workstation and certifies that the smart-card is allowed to transmit the user's beliefs. At this point the workstation can interpret the previous message. As in the previous protocol, the user has authenticated to the workstation:

$$W \textbf{ believes } \overset{I_w}{\prec} U$$

6. $C \rightarrow F$: $\{U$ **believes** W **controls** $\overset{K_d}{\mapsto} U, \{T_b\}_{K_b^{-1}}\}_{K_c^{-1}}$
   In this delegation certificate, the smart-card asserts that the user has delegated to the workstation: it says that the user believes that the workstation has jurisdiction over setting K_d as his delegation key. The certificate includes $\{T_b\}_{K_b^{-1}}$ as proof of timeliness.

7. $W \rightarrow F$: $\{\overset{K_d}{\mapsto} U, \{T_b\}_{K_b^{-1}}\}_{K_w^{-1}}$
   The workstation asserts that K_d is a delegation key for U.

8. $S \rightarrow F$: $\{\overset{K_w}{\mapsto} W, T_s\}_{K_s^{-1}}$, $\{\forall K.(U$ **controls** W **controls** $\overset{K}{\mapsto} U), T_s'\}_{K_s^{-1}}$,
   $\{\overset{K_c}{\mapsto} C, \forall X.(C$ **controls** U **believes** $X), T_s''\}_{K_s^{-1}}$
   The certification authority provides the public keys of the smart-card and the workstation. It certifies that the user can delegate to this workstation, and that the smart-card is allowed to transmit the user's beliefs. Using the previous messages, we obtain the desired delegation result:

$$F \textbf{ believes } \overset{K_d}{\mapsto} U$$

It is not strictly necessary to include the key K_d in the delegation certificate, as we have. However, the mention of the key makes it simple for the workstation to renounce delegated powers when they are no longer needed, by forgetting the matching secret key K_d^{-1}. Thus, the user is protected against future compromise of the workstation, even if the delegation certificate has a long lifetime.

As usual, the number of messages can be reduced by caching commonly used certificates. Furthermore, the smart-card need perform only one signing operation, and this can be done while the user enters his PIN. Hence the card need not be particularly fast. The total complexity of the protocol has increased slightly, but the demands on the smart-card have decreased. This protocol, or similar ones, may well be practical.

5 A protocol with trusted agents

An alternative approach to reducing the demands on the smart-card is based on the use of trusted agents. We discuss this solution here.

5.1 Trusted agents

An on-line trusted agent can relieve the smart-card from the elaborate rituals of generating timestamps and verifying certificates. As this trusted agent can check that W is a suitable workstation for U, this burden is removed from principals such as F. Moreover, a trusted agent simplifies the process of revocation for a compromised workstation—a trusted agent may be a convenient place for a workstation black list. The workstation and the trusted agents can check on one another.

As we envision them, these trusted agents are dedicated, physically protected machines. There would be a large number of trusted agents widely dispersed. Each trusted agent assists a community of users under a single domain or management. Any such arrangement reduces availability (when all replicas are down or inaccessible, the user cannot work) and lessens security (the agents are an attractive target).

If the smart-card can execute only the DES algorithm [5], then the trusted agent will get access to the user's private key during the login process. It can still be arranged that compromise of a trusted agent will not permit the impersonation of all users who trust it—only of those who use it while it is compromised.

If the smart-card can perform the RSA signing operation, a protocol can be obtained whereby the trusted agent cannot impersonate the user. The compromise of a trusted agent does not destroy security per se. In the solution explored in the rest of this section, the smart-card will sign anything the workstation gives it, but no one will believe anything signed by the smart-card without a certificate from a suitable trusted agent. As in the previous protocol, the user obtains no real guarantee of the identity of the workstation, since the card cannot decrypt. However, the user can be sure that his authority is not delegated inappropriately, because of the check performed by the trusted agent.

5.2 Notation and assumptions

Let A be a trusted agent, K_a his public key, and T_a a timestamp he generates.

The most important new assumptions are:

1. S **believes** $\forall K \forall W.(A$ **controls** W **believes** $\stackrel{K}{\mapsto} U)$,
   S **believes** $\forall K \forall W.(A$ **controls** U **controls** W **controls** $\stackrel{K}{\mapsto} U)$: the certification authority believes that the user is in the domain of the trusted agent A; the formulas represent consequences of this belief.

2. **A believes** $\forall K.(U$ **controls** W **controls** $\overset{K}{\mapsto} U)$: the trusted agent A believes that U can delegate to W.

We treat A as different from B, the trusted time provider, although A and B could obviously be implemented by a single node.

5.3 The protocol analyzed

Many of the messages are identical to those of the previous protocol. We discuss only the changes.

1. $W \rightarrow A$: $\{\overset{K_d}{\mapsto} U, T_w\}_{K_w^{-1}}$
   The workstation asserts that K_d is a delegation key for U.

2. $S \rightarrow A$: $\{\overset{K_w}{\mapsto} W, T_s\}_{K_s^{-1}}$
   The trusted agent consults a certificate that contains W's key.

3. $W \rightarrow C$: $\overset{O_w}{\prec} W \quad on\ L_r$

4. $C \rightarrow U$: W' **believes** $\overset{O_w}{\prec} W$, $C \overset{K_{cu}}{\leftrightarrow} U \quad on\ O_c$

5. $U \rightarrow C$: $\{\overset{I_w}{\prec} U$, $\forall K.(W$ **controls** $\overset{K}{\mapsto} U)$, $C \overset{K_{cu}}{\leftrightarrow} U\}_{K_{cu}}$

6. $C \rightarrow W$: $\{U$ **believes** $\overset{I_w}{\prec} U$, $\{T_b\}_{K_b^{-1}}\}_{K_c^{-1}}$

7. $A \rightarrow F$: $\{W$ **believes** $\overset{K_d}{\mapsto} U$, U **controls** W **controls** $\overset{K_d}{\mapsto} U$, $T_a\}_{K_a^{-1}}$
   The trusted agent checks that the workstation is a reasonable machine for the user to trust. It signs a certificate to that effect, including the delegation key for the subsequent session. The trusted agent states that W has chosen K_d, and that U can let W use K_d as a delegation key.

8. $C \rightarrow F$: $\{U$ **believes** W **controls** $\overset{K_d}{\mapsto} U$, $\{T_b\}_{K_b^{-1}}\}_{K_c^{-1}}$
   The file server checks that values of U and W match those in the previous message. This check ensures that both the user and the trusted agent refer to the same workstation.

9. $S \rightarrow F$: $\{\overset{K_a}{\mapsto} A, T_s'\}_{K_s^{-1}}$
   $\{\forall K \forall W.(A$ **controls** W **believes** $\overset{K}{\mapsto} U)$,
   $\forall K \forall W.(A$ **controls** U **controls** W **controls** $\overset{K}{\mapsto} U)$, $T_s''\}_{K_s^{-1}}$
   $\{\overset{K_c}{\mapsto} C$, $\forall X.(C$ **controls** U **believes** $X)$, $T_s'''\}_{K_s^{-1}}$
   The file server obtains certificates for A and C.

The result is the usual one: mutual authentication and delegation.

6 Conclusions

Authentication protocols that use smart-cards are a significant improvement over those that use simple passwords. We have described a few smart-card protocols and the guarantees they offer. We feel that the use of a formalism has helped us elucidate and compare some of the subtle trust relations that underlie these protocols.

A trade-off is inevitable, between the trust that the user needs to place in the environment, and the power, cost, and size of his smart-card. Each of the protocols—and there are others—has its own problems and addresses specific threats, with specific technological requirements.

Acknowledgements

Jim Saxe invented the method for entering a PIN by modifying a nonce with a series of '+' and 'nextdigit' operations. Dorothy Denning and Roger Needham read drafts of this paper. Cynthia Hibbard provided comments on the presentation.

References

[1] M. Abadi and M. Tuttle. A Semantics for a Logic of Authentication, to appear in *Proceedings of the Tenth Annual ACM Symposium on Principles of Distributed Computing*, Montreal, August 1991.

[2] M. Burrows, M. Abadi, and R.M. Needham. A Logic of Authentication, *Proceedings of the Royal Society of London A* Vol. 426, 1989, pp. 233–271. A preliminary version appeared as Digital Equipment Corporation Systems Research Center report No. 39, February 1989.

[3] CCITT. CCITT Blue Book, Recommendation X.509 and ISO 9594-8: The Directory-Authentication Framework. Geneva, March 1988.

[4] D. Chaum and I. Schaumüller-Bichl, editors. *Smart Card 2000: The Future of IC Cards*, Proceedings of the IFIP WG 11.6 International Conference on Smart Card 2000: The Future of IC Cards, Laxenburg, Austria, October, 1987. North-Holland, Amsterdam, 1989.

[5] National Bureau of Standards. Data Encryption Standard. Fed. Inform. Processing Standards Pub. 46. Washington DC, January 1977.

[6] W. Diffie and M. Hellman. New Directions in Cryptography. *IEEE Transactions on Information Theory* IT-22, No. 6, November 1976, pp. 644–654.

[7] M. Gasser, A. Goldstein, C. Kaufman, B. Lampson. The Digital Distributed System Security Architecture. *Proceedings of the 1989 National Computer Security Conference*, Baltimore, October 1989, pp. 305-319.

[8] U. Feige, A. Fiat, A. Shamir. Zero Knowledge Proofs of Identity. *Proceedings of the Nineteenth Annual ACM Symposium on Theory of Computing*, New York, May 1987, pp. 210–217.

[9] M. Gasser, E. McDermott. An Architecture for Practical Delegation in a Distributed System. *Proceedings of the 1990 IEEE Symposium on Security and Privacy*, Oakland, May 1990, pp. 20–30.

[10] C.A.R. Hoare. An Axiomatic Basis for Computer Programming, *CACM* Vol. 12, No. 10, October 1969, pp. 576–580.

[11] S.P. Miller, C. Neuman, J.I. Schiller, and J.H. Saltzer. Kerberos Authentication and Authorization System. *Project Athena Technical Plan* Section E.2.1, MIT, July 1987.

[12] R.M. Needham and M.D. Schroeder. Using Encryption for Authentication in Large Networks of Computers. *CACM* Vol. 21, No. 12, December 1978, pp. 993–999.

[13] R.L. Rivest, A. Shamir, and L. Adleman. A Method for Obtaining Digital Signatures and Public-key Cryptosystems, *CACM* Vol. 21, No. 2, February 1978, pp. 120-126.

Appendix: The logic

In the analysis of smart-card protocols, we apply a logic of authentication. The notation is as given in Section 2; here we give a few of the main rules of inference and briefly explain how to use them. The logic is presented in [2], and discussed further in [1], which includes a Kripke semantics.

Rules of inference

We manipulate formulas of the logic with rules of inference, such as the following.

- The jurisdiction rule reflects that if P believes that Q is an authority on X then P trusts Q on the truth of X:

$$\frac{P \textbf{ believes } Q \textbf{ controls } X, \quad P \textbf{ believes } Q \textbf{ believes } X}{P \textbf{ believes } X}$$

- The public-key message-meaning rule concerns the interpretation of encrypted messages:

$$\frac{P \textbf{ believes } \stackrel{K}{\mapsto} Q, \quad P \textbf{ sees } \{X\}_{K^{-1}}}{P \textbf{ believes } Q \textbf{ said } X}$$

  That is, if P believes that the key K is Q's public key and P sees X encrypted under K's inverse, then P believes that Q once said X.

- A similar message-meaning rule applies to links:

$$\frac{P \textbf{ believes } \overset{L}{\prec} Q, \quad P \textbf{ sees}_L\ X}{P \textbf{ believes } Q \textbf{ said}_L\ X}$$

- A nonce-verification rule expresses the check that a part of a message is recent, and hence that the sender still believes in the message:

$$\frac{P \textbf{ believes fresh}(X), \quad P \textbf{ believes } Q \textbf{ said } X}{P \textbf{ believes } Q \textbf{ believes } X}$$

That is, if P believes that X could have been uttered only recently and that Q once said X, then P believes that Q has said X recently, and hence that Q believes X. A variant of this rule is sometimes useful:

$$\frac{P \textbf{ believes fresh}(Y), \quad P \textbf{ believes } Q \textbf{ said } (X, Y)}{P \textbf{ believes } Q \textbf{ believes } X}$$

For the sake of simplicity, we use this rule only when X is cleartext, that is, it has no subformulas of the form $\{Y\}_K$. A similar remark applies to all other rules that introduce the **believes** operator.

- Another way to guarantee timeliness is by using timely communication links:

$$\frac{P \textbf{ believes timely}(L), \quad P \textbf{ believes } Q \textbf{ said}_L\ X}{P \textbf{ believes } Q \textbf{ believes } X}$$

On quantifiers in delegations

Delegation statements usually mention one or more variables. For example, the user U may let the workstation W generate an arbitrary delegation key. We can express this as

$$U \textbf{ believes } W \textbf{ controls } \overset{K}{\mapsto} U$$

Here the key K is universally quantified, and we can make explicit this quantification by writing

$$U \textbf{ believes } \forall K.(W \textbf{ controls } \overset{K}{\mapsto} U)$$

For complex delegation statements, it is generally necessary to write quantifiers explicitly in order to avoid ambiguities. In some previous works on the logic, this need was not recognized, as in fact it did not arise. (There were no nested jurisdiction statements.) This need does arise in the proofs above.

Our formal manipulation of quantifiers is quite straightforward. All we use is the ability to instantiate variables in jurisdiction statements, as reflected by the rule

$$\frac{P \textbf{ believes } \forall V_1 \ldots V_n.(Q \textbf{ controls } X)}{P \textbf{ believes } Q' \textbf{ controls } X'}$$

where Q' **controls** X' is the result of simultaneously instantiating all of the variables $V_1, \ldots, V_n$ in Q **controls** X.

Protocol analysis

Authentication protocols are typically described by listing their messages in the form

$$P \rightarrow Q : message$$

This denotes that P sends the message to Q. Occasionally, it is stated that the message follows a particular route, such as a secure channel.

The message is presented in an informal notation designed to suggest the bit-string that a particular concrete implementation would use. In the interest of formal analysis, we rewrite each message as a logical formula. For instance, the protocol step

$$A \rightarrow F : K_a \textit{ on link } L_1$$

may tell F, who knows that L_1 is a secure channel from A, that K_a is A's public key. This step should then be idealized as

$$A \rightarrow F : \stackrel{K_a}{\mapsto} A \quad \textit{on } L_1$$

We annotate idealized protocols with logical formulas, much as in a proof in Hoare logic [10]. We write formulas before the first message and after each message. The main rules for deriving legal annotations are:

- if X holds before the message $P \rightarrow Q : Y$ then both X and Q **sees** Y hold afterwards;
- if X holds before the message $P \rightarrow Q : Y$ *on* L then both X and Q **sees**$_L$ Y hold afterwards;
- if Y can be derived from X by the logical postulates then Y holds whenever X holds.

An annotation of a protocol is like a sequence of comments about the beliefs of principals and what they see in the course of authentication, from initial assumptions to conclusions.

Data Flow Analysis as Model Checking

Bernhard Steffen
Lehrstuhl für Informatik II
RWTH – Aachen
D-5100 Aachen

Abstract

The paper develops a framework that is based on the idea that modal logic provides an appropriate framework for the specification of data flow analysis (DFA) algorithms as soon as programs are represented as models of the logic. This can be exploited to construct a DFA-*generator* that generates efficient implementations of DFA-algorithms from modal specifications by partially evaluating a specific model checker with respect to the specifying modal formula. Moreover, the use of a modal logic as specification language for DFA-algorithms supports the compositional development of specifications and structured proofs of properties of DFA-algorithms. – The framework is illustrated by means of a real life example: the problem of determining optimal computation points within flow graphs.

1 Introduction

Data flow analysis (DFA) is concerned with the automatic identification of program points enjoying specific properties, like for example, lifeness of variables or equivalence of program terms. Typically, data flow analysis algorithms are constructed for a given program property of interest and therefore have the following functionality:

DFA-algorithm for a property: programs $\rightarrow$ program points enjoying the property

Model checking is concerned with the automatic identification of those states of a finite system satisfying a specific modal (or temporal) formula that expresses, for example, properties like deadlock, divergence or liveness. Typically, model checkers are parameterized on the formula of interest and therefore have the following functionality:

model checker: modal formulas $\times$ model $\rightarrow$ states satisfying the argument formula

Identifying programs with models, program points with states and program properties with modal formulas, model checkers can be seen as DFA algorithms that have the program property of interest as a parameter.

In this paper, we exploit this observation in order to develop an algorithm that automatically generates efficient implementations of DFA-algorithms from specifications written in a modal logic. In essence, this DFA-*generator* works by *partially evaluating* an appropriate model checker with respect to its modal formula parameter; the result is a standard iterative DFA-algorithm (cf. [Kil]), which directly runs on the machine the model checker is implemented on. For simplicity, we will refer to these implementations just as DFA-algorithms.

Our framework covers the standard bit-vector DFA algorithms [1] in an efficient manner: it allows concise high level specifications, and the generated algorithms are guaranteed to be linear in the size of the program being analysed. Moreover it supports the specification of and reasoning about DFA-algorithms. Both can be done modularly by reasoning within the modal logic serving as specification language.

The framework is illustrated by means of an example of practical relevance: an improved version of Morel/Renvoise's algorithm for eliminating partial redundancies [MR]. The algorithm generated here from a one line specification[2] is linear in the size of the argument program and its results are optimal. This improves on the complexity estimation $O(n \log(n))$ given in [Dha][3]. Moreover, to our knowledge, the only comparable optimality results that have been proved before are the ones in [SKR1, SKR2], which concern more complex placement algorithms.

Summary of Technical Results

Section 2 presents the program representation, which consists of transition systems, where nodes and states are labeled. This representation is very close to the standard models for modal logics [Sti1], and it allows a simple adaptation of the program representations used in DFA. For example, nondeterministic flow graphs, a standard program representation in DFA, can be easily transformed into this format.

Section 3 develops two specification languages: a low level specification language with a general fixpoint operator, and a high level specification language, where the general fixpoint operator is replaced by intuitively easy to understand derived operators. The section closes with logical characterizations of structural constraints of certain program models.

Section 4 deals with a "real life" example. A bidirectional DFA-algorithm determining the optimal placement of computations within programs is specified and its correctness and optimality is established. All the reasoning is done purely within the high level specification language.

---

[1]Typically, such algorithms determine things like life variables, (very) busy expressions or use-definition chains[He].

[2]Usually, this type of algorithm is given by means of a complex equation system.

[3]Here n stands for the number of edges in the flow graph. — Dhamdhere also mentions that his algorithm is $O(n)$ for specific graph structures. In contrast, the estimation here does not depend on any structural requirements.

Section 5 provides a correct and complete model checker, which is linear in the size of the program model being investigated[4]. Our DFA-generator works by partially evaluating this model checker with respect to to the modal formula used to specify the DFA-property of interest. This partial evaluation process is illustrated by generating a DFA-algorithm from the specification developed in Section 4.

Finally, Section 6 contains conclusions and directions for future work.

Related Work

Already in the seventies a DFA-generator has been developed, which essentially works on syntax trees and generates DFA-algorithms from specifications given as computation functions for attribute values [Wil1, Wil2]. Thus its specifications explicitly describe the way in which the program properties of interest are determined. To our knowledge, this principle has been maintained in all later developments (cf. [Gie, Nie2, LPRS, SFRW, Ven]). In contrast, we specify DFA-algorithms just by means of the program property under consideration. All the details about the corresponding analysis algorithm are hidden in the model checker our approach is based upon. This yields concise high level specifications, simplifies the specification development and supports the reasoning about features, such as correctness and optimality, of the corresponding DFA-algorithms.

2 Models for Programs

We model programs as transition systems, whose states and transitions are labeled with sets of atomic propositions and actions, respectively. Intuitively, atomic propositions describe properties of states, while actions describe (properties of) statements. As usual, the control flow is modelled by the graph structure of the transition system.

Definition 2.1 *A* program model $\mathcal{P}$ *is a quintuple* $(\mathcal{S}, \mathcal{A}, \rightarrow, \mathcal{B}, \lambda)$ *where*

1. $\mathcal{S}$ *is a finite set of* nodes *or* program states.

2. $\mathcal{A}$ *is a set of* atoms. *The subsets of* $\mathcal{A}$ *play the role of what is usually called* actions. *We will denote this set of actions by Act.*

3. $\rightarrow \subseteq \mathcal{S} \times Act \times \mathcal{S}$ *is a set of* labeled transitions, *which define the control flow of* $\mathcal{P}$.

4. $\mathcal{B}$ *is a set of* atomic propositions.

5. λ *is a function* $\lambda : \mathcal{S} \rightarrow 2^{\mathcal{B}}$ *that labels states with subsets of* $\mathcal{B}$.

[4]This algorithm is a variant of the algorithm presented in [CES], modified to simplify partial evaluation.

We will write $p \xrightarrow{A} q$ *instead of* $(p, A, q) \in \rightarrow$*, and given* $\alpha \subseteq Act$*, we will call* p *an* α-predecessor *of* q *and* q *an* α-successor *of* p *if* $A \in \alpha$*. The set of all* α*-predecessors and* α*-successors will be abbreviated by* $Pred_\alpha$ *and* $Succ_\alpha$*, respectively*[5]*.*

Essentially, a program model is a combination of a standard labeled transition system and a Kripke structure, which allows us to speak about state and statement properties explicitly and separately without using any complicated encodings. New is only the set structure of the actions. This is necessary, because we want to deal with *abstract interpretations*, which treat concrete statements as sets of properties (cf. [CC]). However, one should abstract from the internal structure of actions, where it is unimportant, like e.g. in Section 3.1 and most of Section 3.2.

Definition 2.2 *A* DFA-model *is a program model with two distinct states* **s** *(the* start *state) and* **e** *(the* end *start) satisfying:*

1. **s** *and* **e** *do not possess any predecessor and successor, respectively.*
2. *Every program state is reachable from* **s***.*
3. **e** *is reachable from every program state.*

The additional requirements for DFA-models are standard in data flow analysis. In fact, they do not impose any restrictions there, because one can always reach this format by eliminating unreachable parts and adding nodes **s** and **e** appropriately.

Modelling Nondeterministic Flow Graphs

We will consider *nondeterministic flow graphs* as DFA-models. Nondeterministic flow graphs are directed graphs whose nodes represent statements (as usual, we will concentrate on assignments here) and whose edges represent the flow of control. As mentioned above, we can additionally assume that they possess unique start and end nodes. There are two straightforward ways to transform flow graphs into DFA-models. First, by pushing the statements from the nodes into the outgoing edges. In this case, we arrive at a *precondition model*, because here the nodes will characterize preconditions to the statements that have been originally associated with the nodes. Second, and dually, by pushing the statements upwards into the ingoing edges. Here one arrives at a *postcondition model*[6]. In the discussion of our example we will deal with precondition models. In general, the appropriate choice of model depends on the particular application.

[5]Note that the *Act*-predecessors and *Act*-successors are just the predecessors and successors in the usual sense.

[6]In order to make these transformations work in general, we assume that start and end nodes of flow graphs represent skip statements.

In order to establish the setup for our "real life" example (see Section 4), let $\mathbf{V}$ and $\mathbf{T}$ be sets of program variables and program terms, respectively, and A_c be the set of all assignments of the form $v := t$, where $v \in \mathbf{V}$ and $t \in \mathbf{T}$. Furthermore, let $\mathcal{B} =_{df} \{\texttt{start, end}\}$ be a set of atomic propositions, and λ_c the labeling function, which associated the empty set of properties with each node of the model except for $\lambda_c(\mathtt{s}) = \{\texttt{start}\}$ and $\lambda_c(\mathtt{e}) = \{\texttt{end}\}$. Then the precondition model (or equivalently the postcondition model) of a flow graph forms a DFA-model $(\mathcal{S}, A_c, \rightarrow, \mathcal{B}, \lambda_c)$, where the state labeling just identifies the start and the end state, and the transition labeling the statement corresponding to a state transition.

We will refer to such DFA-models as *concrete* DFA-models. However, the DFA-models we want to deal with, and which allow an automatic analysis, arise as abstractions from concrete DFA-models. A typical abstraction is given by choosing $A_a = \{\texttt{mod}(t) \mid t \in \mathbf{T}\} \cup \{\texttt{use}(t) \mid t \in \mathbf{T}\}$ as the set of transition labels together with the abstraction function $abstr : A_c \rightarrow A_a$ which is defined by:

$$abstr(\{v := t\}) =_{df} \{\texttt{mod}\,(t') \mid v \text{ is subterm of } t'\} \cup \{use\,(t') \mid t' \text{ is a subterm of } t\}$$

and the (additivity) property:

$$abstr(A) = \bigcup \{\, abstr(v := t) \mid v := t \in A\}$$

Transitions labeled with $\texttt{mod}(t)$ or $\texttt{use}(t)$ represent statements that *modify* or *use* the term t. Our illustrating example will work with this abstraction, which is tailored to address problems dealing with *invariance* and *usage* of program terms, and in particular, program variables. In fact, many DFA-problems can be dealt with by means of this abstraction or slight extensions. However, in general, the appropriate abstract interpretation of the statements must be chosen problem dependently.

3 The Specification Languages

We present two specification languages, a *low level* language, which is primary, and a derived *high level* language. Whereas the low level language is used to formally define the semantics of formulas, the high level language is easier to understand and should be used for specification.

3.1 Low Level Specifications

Our low-level specification language is essentially a sublanguage of the modal mu-calculus [Koz], which is characterized by a restricted use of fixpoint constructions. The syntax of our low level specification language is parameterized by denumerable sets *Var*, $\mathcal{B}$ and *Act* of propositional variables, atomic propositions and actions, respectively, where X ranges over *Var*, β over $\mathcal{B}$ and α over subsets of *Act*:

$$\Phi ::= X \mid tt \mid \Phi \wedge \Phi \mid \neg\Phi \mid \beta \mid [\alpha]\Phi \mid \overline{[\alpha]}\,\Phi \mid \nu X.\Phi$$

$$
\begin{aligned}
[\![tt]\!] &= \mathcal{S} \\
[\![\Phi_1 \wedge \Phi_2]\!] &= [\![\Phi_1]\!] \cap [\![\Phi_2]\!] \\
[\![\neg\Phi]\!] &= \mathcal{S} \setminus [\![\Phi]\!] \\
[\![\beta]\!] &= \{ p \in \mathcal{S} \mid \beta \in \lambda(p) \} \\
[\![[\,\alpha\,]\,\Phi]\!] &= \{ p \in \mathcal{S} \mid \forall q \in \mathit{Succ}_\alpha(p).\ q \in [\![\Phi]\!] \} \\
[\![\overline{[\,\alpha\,]}\,\Phi]\!] &= \{ q \in \mathcal{S} \mid \forall p \in \mathit{Pred}_\alpha(q).\ p \in [\![\Phi]\!] \} \\
[\![\nu X.\Phi]\!] &= \bigcup \{ S' \subseteq \mathcal{S} \mid S' \subseteq [\![\Phi_{S'}]\!], \text{ where } \Phi_{S'} \text{ is } \Phi \text{ with } X \text{ interpreted as } S' \}
\end{aligned}
$$

Figure 1: The semantics of formulas.

The semantics of *closed* formulas, where all occurrences of variables are bound by some fixpoint operator ν, is defined with respect to a program model $\mathcal{P}$ according to the following intuition: Every program state satisfies the formula *tt*, while program state p satisfies $\Phi_1 \wedge \Phi_2$ if it satisfies both Φ_1 and Φ_2. Moreover, a program state satisfies $\neg\Phi$ if it does not satisfy Φ, it satisfies β if it is labeled by a set containing β and it satisfies $[\,\alpha\,]\,\Phi$ if every of its α-successors satisfies Φ. Note that this implies that a program state p satisfies $[\,\alpha\,]\mathit{ff}$ exactly when p has no α-successors. Analogously, a program state p satisfies $\overline{[\,\alpha\,]}\,\Phi$ if every α-predecessor satisfies Φ. Thus in analogy, a program state p satisfies $\overline{[\,\alpha\,]}\mathit{ff}$ exactly when p has no α-predecessors. The formula $\nu X.\Phi$ is a recursive formula and should be thought of as the "largest" solution to the "equation" $X = \Phi$. Since $\mathcal{P}$ is finite-state, this formula is equivalent to the infinite conjunction $\bigwedge_{i=0}^{\infty} \Phi_i$, where

$$
\begin{aligned}
\Phi_0 &= tt \\
\Phi_{i+1} &= \Phi[\Phi_i/X]
\end{aligned}
$$

and the substitution $\Phi[\Gamma/X]$ is defined in the standard way

As usual, there is a syntactic restriction on expressions of the form $\nu X.\Phi$, which is necessary to ensure the continuity of the fixpoint operator: X is required to appear within the range of an even number of negations in Φ. — All this is completely standard, except for the meaning of modalities, which is defined for sets of actions here, rather than just for single actions. This is a convenient generalization, which simplifies the representation of certain properties enormously (cf. [BS]).

The formal semantic definition of the logic is given in Figure 1. It maps closed formulas to sets of program states—intuitively, the program states for which the formula is "true". Note that the semantics of $\nu X.\Phi$ is based on Tarski's fixpoint theorem [Tar]: its meaning is defined as the greatest fixpoint of a continuous function over the powerset of the set of states. The continuity of this function follows from the syntactic restriction mentioned above and the continuity of the semantic interpretations of the other propositional constructors.

In the following we will write $[\,.\,]$ or $\overline{[\,.\,]}$ instead of $[\,Act\,]$ or $\overline{[\,Act\,]}$. Moreover, we will use $\mathcal{P} \models \Phi$ (or just $\models \Phi$ if $\mathcal{P}$ is understood) to indicate that every state of the program model $\mathcal{P}$ satisfies Φ. As usual, we can define the following duals to the operators of our language and the implication operator $\Rightarrow$ by:

$$\begin{aligned} \mathit{ff} &= \neg tt \\ \Phi_1 \vee \Phi_2 &= \neg(\neg\Phi_1 \wedge \neg\Phi_2) \\ \langle\, \alpha \,\rangle\, \Phi &= \neg[\,\alpha\,]\,(\neg\Phi) \\ \overline{\langle\, \alpha \,\rangle}\, \Phi &= \neg\overline{[\,\alpha\,]}\,(\neg\Phi) \\ \mu X.\Phi &= \neg\,\nu X.\neg(\Phi[\neg X/X]) \\ \Phi \Rightarrow \Psi &= \neg\Phi \vee \Psi \end{aligned}$$

Our low level specification language consists of all *closed* and *guarded* formulas, where no variables occur free inside the scope of a fixpoint expression[7]. Closed means that all variables are bound by a fixpoint operator, and guarded that they all occur inside the range of a modality.

In future, we will also use the derived operators except for the minimal fixpoint operator, which we avoid here in order to keep the presentation of the model checker (Section 5.1) as simple as possible.

3.2 High Level Specifications

The recursive proposition constructors add a tremendous amount of expressive power to the logic (cf. [EL, Ste1]). For example, they allow the description of invariance (or *safety*) and eventuality (or *liveness*) properties. However, general fixpoint formulas are in general unintuitive and difficult to understand. We will therefore define a collection of intuitively easy to understand derived operators that are based on the following "Henceforth"-operator of the temporal logic CTL [CES]:

$$\mathbf{AG}\,\Phi \;=\; \nu X.(\Phi \wedge [\,.\,]\,X)$$

and its past-time counterpart:

$$\overline{\mathbf{AG}}\,\Phi \;=\; \nu X.(\Phi \wedge \overline{[\,.\,]}\,X)$$

AG Φ holds of p if Φ holds for every state of every path that starts in p, while $\overline{\mathbf{AG}}\,\Phi$ holds of p, if Φ holds for every state of every path that ends in p.

DFA is concerned with a specific kind of *eventuality* properties: certain program

[7]The point of this condition is to avoid the possibility of *alternated nesting* [EL]. Of course, there are weaker conditions to guarantee this, but they are unnecessarily complicated for our purpose.

transformations are only admissible (or safe[8]) if a specific value must be computed before the program terminates, i.e. before the end state is reached (cf. Section 4). This cannot be expressed with the standard CTL operators. However, the following parameterized version of the Henceforth-operator suites this purpose:

$$\begin{aligned} \mathbf{AG}_\alpha\,\Phi &= \nu X.(\Phi \wedge [\,\alpha\,]X) \\ \overline{\mathbf{AG}_\alpha}\,\Phi &= \nu X.(\Phi \wedge \overline{[\,\alpha\,]}X) \end{aligned}$$

Intuitively, the parameter reduces the set of relevant paths to those being labeled with elements of α. Thus in order to express that a computation must happen before the end state is reached, one may equivalently express that one never reaches the end state on a path, whose transitions do not perform this computation. Formally, this is expressed by setting $\Phi = \neg\texttt{end}$ and $\alpha = 2^{\mathcal{A}\setminus\{\texttt{comp}\}}$, where $\texttt{comp}$ represents the computation of interest. This pattern is typical for specifications in our framework.

Our high level specification language arises from the low level specification language by replacing the general fixpoint operator with the operators established above. This language is quite expressive and it allows concise specifications of the standard bit-vector algorithms. In addition to this, our specification language is expressive enough to cover structural properties of program models as well. This allows us to prove properties of DFA-algorithms within our logical framework, even if these properties depend on structural restrictions of the program models under consideration. For example, the three structural restrictions for DFA-models given in Definition 2.2 are characterized by:

Proposition 3.1 (DFA-Models)
A DFA-model is characterized by the following three properties:

1. $\models (\texttt{start} \Rightarrow \overline{[\,.\,]}\,f\!f) \wedge (\texttt{end} \Rightarrow [\,.\,]\,f\!f)$
2. $\models \neg(\,\overline{\mathbf{AG}}\ \neg\texttt{start}\,)$
3. $\models \neg(\,\mathbf{AG}\ \neg\texttt{end}\,)$

Whereas part (1) is obvious, parts (2) and (3) express the corresponding properties of a DFA-model in the indirect sense explained above. Intuitively, part (2) says: "for every state of the model it is not the case that all the path never reach the end state", which is equivalent to: "from every state there exists a path reaching the end state". Part (3) is analogous.

Also a property of precondition models, which is important for the proof of the Correctness Theorem 4.2 and the Optimality Theorem 4.6, can be stated within our specification language:

---

[8]This notion of safety is different from the logical notion of safety we referred to above: a program transformation is safe, if it does not affect the program semantics. Moreover, there is a notion of safety for DFA's: a DFA is safe, if the properties claimed by its results definitely hold of the analysed program. The latter two notions of safety relate in the following way: usually, a safe DFA is the central ingredient of a safe program transformation.

Proposition 3.2 (Precondition Models)
In a precondition model we have for ever $A \in Act$: $\models \langle \{A\} \rangle tt \;\Rightarrow\; [\{A\}^c]ff$, *where "^{c}" denotes the set complement operator.*

Intuitively, this property means that all the transitions of a state (program point) in a precondition model are labelled identically. This property is valid in precondition models, because there, the labels of all the transitions leaving a specific state are derived from the same statement.

4 Example: Optimal Placement of Computations

In this section, we will develop a specification for a bi-directional DFA-algorithm that determines optimal computation points for a given term t within a DFA-model (flow graph). During this development we will fix t, in order to be able to drop it from the argument list of the predicates and therefore simplify the notation.

4.1 Specifying the DFA-Algorithm

It is well-known that in completely arbitrary graph structures the placement process may deliver unsatisfactory results, because specific patterns may cause that the code motion process gets blocked. This problem can be solved by means of the following transformation: insert an artificial state into each transition that starts at a state with more than one successor and ends at a state with more than one predecessor (cf. [Dha, SKR1, SKR2][9]). For DFA-models, the essence of this transformation can be characterized logically as follows:

Characterization of Placement Models

1. $\models (\Phi \Rightarrow \overline{[\,.\,]}[\,.\,]\Phi) \vee (\overline{\langle\,.\,\rangle}\Phi \Rightarrow \overline{[\,.\,]}\Phi)$ and
2. $\models (\Phi \Rightarrow [\,.\,]\overline{[\,.\,]}\Phi) \vee (\langle\,.\,\rangle\Phi \Rightarrow [\,.\,]\Phi)$

Intuitively the first property means that there are two classes of states in a placement model:

- the ones that are "similar" to (have exactly the same properties as) all their brothers, and
- the ones whose predecessors are all "similar".

[9] In [Dha] this is done implicitly by placing the computations in the edges of the flow graph under consideration.

The second property is the "forward" analogon of the first property.

In fact, it is possible to obtain an optimal placement algorithm, as soon as we restrict ourselves to precondition models with this property, which we call *precondition placement models* (cf. Optimality Theorem 4.6).

In our framework, DFA-algorithms are specified by means of the program property they are checking for. Thus the DFA-algorithm to determine the optimal placement of computations is specified by means of the specification of the optimal computation points. These can be characterized in two steps.

First, the placement of a computation at a computation point must be *safe*, i.e. it must not introduce the computation of a new value on a path. This requirement is necessary in order to guarantee that no run time errors (e.g. "division by 0" or "overflow") are introduced: a safe placement does not change the potential for run time errors. This property is satisfied, if all the inserted computations are *necessary*, i.e. if their values will be computed on every continuation of a program execution that terminates in **e**. Logically, this property of a program point can be characterized by:

Guaranteeing Safety $\texttt{NEC} =_{df} \mathbf{AG}_{U^c}(\neg\texttt{end} \wedge [M \cap U^c]\mathit{ff})$

where $M =_{df} \{A \mid \texttt{mod} \in A\}$ and $U =_{df} \{A \mid \texttt{use} \in A\}$. Note that in a transition (i.e. in an assignment statement), which uses and and modifies the value of a term t, the usage always comes first. Thus the subformula $[M \cap U^c]\mathit{ff}$ characterizes the states, which do not have any transition that modifies the value of t without using it beforehand.

Second, in order to achieve optimality, we require that computations should be placed as "early" as possible. This can be logically characterized by $\overline{[M^c]}(\overline{\mathbf{AG}}_{M^c}\neg\texttt{NEC})$, meaning that a placement at an "earlier" position would either be unnecessary for t or an evaluation of t there would not always yield the required value.

The combination of these two properties yields the desired specification:

The Computation Points $\texttt{OCP} =_{df} \texttt{NEC} \;\wedge\; \overline{[M^c]}(\overline{\mathbf{AG}}_{M^c}\neg\texttt{NEC})$

As will be established in the next subsection, `OCP` is already the complete specification of the DFA-algorithm that determines the optimal computation points (for t). Thus, a subsequent program transformation, which

- initializes an auxiliary variable at these program points and
- replaces all the original computations (of t) by this auxiliary variable

places the computations of t optimally within a precondition placement model.

4.2 Correctness and Optimality of the Placement

In this section we are going to show that the placement of computations specified by OCP is *better* than every other placement that is *correct* and *safe* (see Theorems 4.2, 4.4 and 4.6). In order to establish this result within our logical framework, we need to formalize in the logic, what it means to be "correct", "safe" and "better". This requires the introduction of some further notation. Let $S \subseteq \mathcal{S}$ be an arbitrary set of states. Then we:

- assume that their exists an atom $\mathtt{from_S} \in Act$.
- define $Acts_S =_{df} \{ A \mid \mathtt{from_S} \in A \}$.
- require that transitions ending in S are characterized by having $\mathtt{from_S}$ in their label set.

These conventions reflect the idea of inserting computations at the computation points in a precondition model. Note however, that the initialization statement is inserted before the original statement of the considered transition. Thus $\langle U \cap Acts_S \rangle tt$ is a property, stating that the transitions leaving the state under consideration first initialize an auxiliary variable with t and subsequently use the value of t in their second (their original) statement[10]. This is important for the understanding of Definition 4.1.

Correctness of a placement of computations means that all computations of the original flow graph are covered by the corresponding computation points, i.e. the initialization of an auxiliary variable at the computation points allows to replace all original computations of the flow graph by the auxiliary variable without changing the program semantics. The following notion of placement correctness formalizes this intention:

Definition 4.1 *A subset set $S \subseteq \mathcal{S}$ (here regarded as a set of computation points) is* placement correct *if every state of the program model satisfies:*

$$\mathtt{P\text{-}Cor}\,(S) =_{df} \langle U \cap Acts_S{}^c \rangle tt \Rightarrow \overline{\mathbf{AG}}_{Acts_S{}^c}(\neg\mathtt{start} \wedge \overline{[M]}\,ff)$$

Intuitively, $\langle U \cap Acts_S{}^c \rangle tt$ characterizes the states, whose transitions use t without initializing the corresponding auxiliary variable. Thus it must be guaranteed that the auxiliary variable is initialized beforehand. This is expressed in the conclusion, in the indirect way, which is characteristic for specifications in our framework.

From now on, let $S_I =_{df} \{ s \mid s \models \mathtt{OCP} \}$. Then the following theorem yields that OCP specifies a placement correct set of program points (or states):

Theorem 4.2 (Correctness) $\models \mathtt{P\text{-}Cor}\,(S_I)$

[10]In fact, this interpretation already exploits the fact that we are dealing with precondition models. In general, this property only guarantees the existence of such a transition.

The proof of this theorem strongly depends on the specific properties of placement models. It can be found in the long version of this paper [Ste2].

A placement of computations is safe, if it does not introduce any computations of new values on any path. This is expressed by requiring that the computations must either occur before or after each computation point:

Definition 4.3 *A subset set $S \subseteq \mathcal{S}$ (again viewed as a set of computation points) is* placement safe *if the following predicate* P-Safe (S) *holds of all states:*

$$\langle\, Acts_S \,\rangle tt \;\Rightarrow\; (\overline{\mathbf{AG}}_{U^c}\,(\neg\mathtt{start} \wedge \overline{[\,M\,]}\,ff) \;\vee\; \mathbf{AG}_{U^c}\,(\neg\mathtt{end} \wedge [\,M \cap U^c\,]\,ff))$$

In fact, OCP also specifies a placement safe set of program points (or states):

Theorem 4.4 (Safety) $\models$ P-Safe (S_I)

The correctness of this theorem is immediate from the fact that $\langle\, Acts_S \,\rangle tt$ is logically equivalent to OCP and that the second disjunct in the conclusion is the defining expression for NEC.

Given two arbitrary subsets S and S' of $\mathcal{S}$, we consider S' as being better than S if on every path through the program model the number of occurrences of states of S is as least as large as the number of occurrences of states of S'. This reflects the intuition that a set of computation points is better than another if it causes less computations during the program execution. Additionally, our logical formulation requires that a better set of computation points leads to "earlier" computations:

Definition 4.5 *Let $S, S' \subseteq \mathcal{S}$ be arbitrary sets of states. Then S' is* better *than S if every precondition placement model satisfies:*

$$\models\; [\, Acts_{S'} \cap Acts_S{}^c\,]\; (\,\mathbf{AG}_{Acts_S{}^c}\,(\neg\mathtt{end} \wedge [\, Acts_{S'}\,]\,ff\,))$$

Our DFA-algorithm is optimal in the strong sense of this definition:

Theorem 4.6 (Optimality)
The placement of computations specified by OCP *is* better *than every other placement which is* correct *and* safe.

The proof of this theorem, which is actually new for Morel/Renvoise-like placement algorithms, can be found in [Ste2]. Here we only want to stress the fact that properties (of implementations) of DFA-algorithms can be proved on the specification level, i.e. logically, without reference to implementation details[11].

[11] Further information about placement algorithms can be found in [Dha, MR, RWZ, SKR1, SKR2].

5 DFA-Generation

5.1 The Principle

The principle of the DFA-generator proposed here is *partial evaluation* of an appropriate model checker with respect to the modal formula that serves as the specification of the DFA-algorithm. The model checker we are going to use is a variant of the algorithm presented in [CES], modified to support partial evaluation with respect to to the specifying formula. It iteratively determines the set of all states of the program model under consideration that satisfy the argument formula. This is done by computing a maximal fixpoint over a node labeling consisting of bit-vectors that represent approximate truth values of certain (low level) modal formulas. Our model checker works in four steps:

The Model Checker

1. Translate the high level specification into the corresponding low level specification. This can be done in a straightforward manner. However, one can also add "optimizations" here that yield an equivalent, but more compact representation, as for example the *shared representation* used in Section 5.2.

2. Construct a (higher order) function from the low level formula that associates every program state of every potential program model with its corresponding *predicate transformer*, i.e. with a function that computes the next approximate bit-vector labeling for a given program state from the current approximate solutions (bit-vector values) of its predecessors and successors. The resulting predicate transformers operate on bit-vectors that have one component corresponding to each subformula containing a variable that appears as an operand of a modality. We will refer to these subformulas as *critical* subformulas. Given a program point p and a critical subformula Φ the predicate transformers update the corresponding bit-vector component with the truth value of the formula that arises from Φ by replacing all subformulas having a modality as the top most operator by their truth value under the current approximation.

   All this is rather straightforward, except for the following fact: approximations for critical subformulas that are separated by negation operations must be computed in a hierarchical manner, in order to guarantee the monotonicity of the iteration process. Therefore, the low level formula is also partitioned into *monotonicity levels*, the iteration mechanism of the third step depends upon. Note however that all this can be done *independently* of the particular program model under consideration.

3. Compute the greatest fixpoint over the bit-vector labeling of the program model under consideration with respect to the predicate transformers that have been generated by the algorithm of the second step. This can be done by means of a

standard *work list algorithm*[12] modified to determine the fixpoints monotonicity-level-wise: a level gets executed, if all its sub-levels are already dealt with.

The computation of the greatest fixpoint for a given monotonicity level proceeds in two steps:

(a) Initialize the bit-vectors of all program states to *tt*. Note that the usual frame conditions are implicit in the atomic propositions the states are labeled with, e.g. `start` and end (see Section 4).

(b) Process the elements of the work list by applying their corresponding predicate transformer, until the maximal fixpoint is reached.

4. Finally, for each state the value of the complete specifying formula Φ_s is determined using the fixpoint values computed in the third step. We will write $p \vdash \Phi_s$ if this yields *tt* for p.

This model checker is quite general: it can easily be extended to larger high level languages just by extending the first step. In particular, an extension covering CTL can be obtained straightforwardly. – In analogy to [CES] we have:

Theorem 5.1 (Correctness, Completeness and Efficiency)
Let $\mathcal{P}$ be a program model and p be a state of $\mathcal{P}$. Then we have: $p \vdash \Phi$ iff $p \in [\![\Phi]\!]$. Moreover, the effort to determine the set of all states satisfying Φ is proportional to the size of $\mathcal{P}$.

Partial evaluation of this model checker with respect to a high level specification consists of executing the first two (program independent) steps. This can be automated, yielding a generator that produces nested bit-vector algorithms from modal specifications, whose worst case run time complexity is proportional to the size of $\mathcal{P}$.

Instead of going into formal detail here, we will rather continue our real life example for illustration:

5.2 Continuation of the Example: Generating the DFA-Algorithm

The evaluation of the first step transforms the specifying formula

$$\mathtt{OCP} \;=\; \mathtt{NEC} \wedge \overline{[M^c]}(\overline{\mathbf{AG}}_{M^c}\, \neg\mathtt{NEC})$$

by means of macro substitution into the following diagram:

[12] A work list is a mean to obtain a fair and therefore terminating computation.

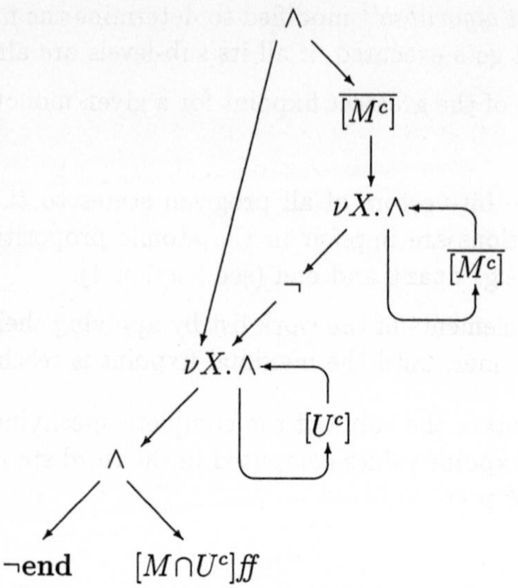

Figure 5.2

Such shared representations take care of common subexpressions and therefore improve the efficiency of the DFA-algorithm generated.

The second step constructs a higher order function that associates every state of a program model with a predicate transformer, which realizes the evaluation of the formula above in the current approximation. In our example, the predicates are represented by means of bit-vectors of length two, whose first and second components hold the current approximations of the value of

$$\mathtt{NEC} \;=\; \mathbf{AG}_{U^c}(\neg\mathbf{end} \wedge [\,M \cap U^c\,]\,ff) \quad \text{and} \quad \overline{\mathbf{AG}}_{M^c}\,\neg\mathtt{NEC}$$

respectively[13]. The following figure shows how the bit-vector labeling is updated in step 3(b):

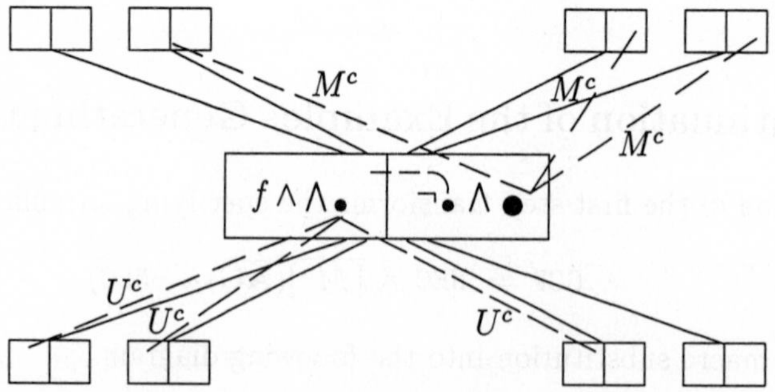

Figure 5.3

[13]These are exactly the subformulas that contain a variable and appear as an operand of a modality.

Here, the next approximation for the first bit of the bit-vector in the center of the picture is computed as the conjunction of $f =_{df} \neg\mathrm{end} \wedge [\,M \cap U^c\,]\, ff$ and the approximate values of the first bits of the bit-vectors of its U^c-successors. Analogously, the value of the second component of this bit-vector is updated as the conjunction of the negation of its own first bit and the approximate values of the second components of its M^c-predecessors. Note that the fixpoints for these two bits must be computed hierarchically, because they belong to different monotonicity levels.

The two (automatic) evaluation steps described above generate an iterative DFA-algorithm for the placement problem, which directly runs on the machine the model checker is implemented on.

It is worth noting that we only need to iterate according to two Boolean values here; one for each fixpoint expression, or, one for the forward flow and one for the backward flow. This flow structure is much cleaner and simpler than in previous algorithms, where backward and forward flow are interwoven (cf. [Dha, MR]). Besides yielding clarity, this simplicity also improves the run time behaviour of the algorithm, because it allows to statically determine a "good" evaluation ordering for the iteration process.

6 Conclusion and Future Work

A framework has been developed, using a modal logic for the specification of DFA-algorithms. Main achievements of this development are the DFA-generator, which works by partial evaluation of a specific model checker, and the modularity of both the development of DFA-specifications and the structure of proofs of properties of the DFA-algorithms generated. All these features have been illustrated by means of the problem of optimally placing computations within a program. This example is particularly suitable for illustration, because it is complex enough to require a non-trivial specification and verification phase, and the hierarchical evaluation of fixpoint expressions. Other DFA-problems like the detection of very busy expressions and life variables are much simpler to deal with, and therefore would not have allowed to demonstrate all the features of our framework.

Currently, we focus on imperative languages and plan, as a first step, to implement a generator for intraprocedural DFA-algorithms as an extension of the Edinburgh Concurrency Workbench [CPS1, CPS2]. Subsequently, this generator will be extended to automatically generate interprocedural algorithms as well. This can be done along the lines indicated in [SP].

Ultimately, it is planned to achieve language independency by using Mosses' *action notation* (cf. [Mos, MW]) as a common intermediate language. The program models for our DFA-generator will then be given by abstractly interpreted transitions systems, which arise from the corresponding structured operational semantics (cf. [Plo]).

This will allow us to uniformly deal with imperative and functional languages and distributed systems.

Current research (cf. [CS1, CS2]) has shown that one can analyze formulas containing mutually recursive equation systems in linear time, as long as there is no alternated nesting [EL]. This suggests to use such formulas for low level specification, with the advantage of allowing to express the shared representation used in Section 5.2 directly on this level. We plan to investigate this change in detail, in particular with respect to its impact on the partial evaluation process.

Acknowledgements

I am very grateful to Rance Cleaveland, Marion Dreimüller, Hardi Hungar, Jens Knoop, Jens Palsberg and Oliver Rüthing for their careful proof reading and their helpful comments.

References

[BS] J. Bradfield, C.Stirling. *Local Model Checking for Finite State Spaces.* LFCS Report Series ECS-LFCS-90-115, June 1990

[CC] P. Cousot, R. Cousot. *Abstract interpretation: A unified Lattice Model for static Analysis of Programs by Construction or Approximation of Fixpoints.* In Proceedings 4th POPL, Los Angeles, California, January, 1977

[CES] E. Clarke, E.A. Emerson, A.P. Sistla. *Automatic Verification of Finite State Concurrent Systems using Temporal Logic Specifications: A Practical Approach.* In Proceedings 10th POPL'83, 1983

[CPS1] R. Cleaveland, J.G. Parrow, B. Steffen. *A Semantic-Based Verification Tool for Finite-State-Systems.* Protocol Specification, Testing and Verification, IX, Elsevier Science Publications B.V. (North Holland), 287-302, 1990

[CPS2] R. Cleaveland, J.G. Parrow, B. Steffen. *The Concurrency Workbench.* Workshop on Automatic Verification Methods for Finite State Systems, LNCS 407, 1989

[CS1] R. Cleaveland, B. Steffen. *Computing Behavioural Relations, Logically.* In Proceedings ICALP'91, LNCS, 1991

[CS2] R. Cleaveland, B. Steffen. *A Linear-Time Model-Checking Alogorithm for the Alternation-Free Modal Mu-Calculus.* In Proceedings CAV'91

[Dha] D. Dhamdhere. *A Fast Algorithm for Code Movement Optimization.* SIGPLAN Notices, Vol. 23, 1988

[EL] E. Emerson, J. Lei, *Efficient model checking in fragments of the propositional mu-calculus.* In Proceedings LICS'86, 267-278, 1986

[Gie] R. Giegerich. *Automatic Generation of Machine Specific Code Generation.* In Proceedings 9th POPL, Albuquerque, New Mexico, January, 1982

[He] S.M. Hecht *Flow Analysis of Computer Programs.* Elsevier, North Holland, 1977

[Kil] G.A. Kildall. *A Unified Approach to Global Program Optimization.* In Proceedings 1st POPL, Boston, Massachusetts, 194-206, 1973

[Koz] D. Kozen. *Results on the Propositional mu-Calculus.* TCS 27, 333-354, 1983

[La] K. Larsen. *Proof Systems for Hennessy–Milner Logic with Recursion*, in Proceedings CAAP 1988.

[Mos] P.D. Mosses. *Action Semantics.* To appear 1991

[MR] E. Morel, C. Renvoise. *Global Optimization by Suppression of Partial Redundancies.* CACM 22, 96-103, 1979

[MW] P.D. Mosses, A.A. Watt. *The Use of Action Semantics.* In Formal Description of Programming Concepts - III, 1986

[Nie1] F. Nielson. *A Bibliography on Abstract Interpretations.* ACM SIGPLAN Notices 21, 31-38, 1986

[Nie2] F. Nielson. *A Denotational Framework for Data Flow Analysis.* Acta Informatica 18, 265-287, 1982

[Plo] G. Plotkin. *A Structural Approach to Operational Semantics.* University of Aarhus, DAIMI FN-19, 1981

[LPRS] Peter Lee, Frank Pfenning, Gene Rollins, and William Scherlis. *The Ergo Support System: An Integrated Set of Tools for Prototyping Integrated Environments.* SIGPLAN Notices, Vol. 24, No. 2, 25-34, February 1989

[RWZ] B. K. Rosen, M. N. Wegman and F. K. Zadeck. *"Global Value Numbers and Redundant Computations".* 15th POPL, San Diego, California, 12 - 27, 1988

[SFRW] S. Sagiv, N. Francez, M. Rodeh, R. Wilhelm. *A Logic-Based Approach to Data Flow Analysis Problems.* To appear 1990

[SKR1] B. Steffen, J. Knoop, O. Rüthing. *The Value Flow Graph: A Program Representation for Optimal Program Transformations.* In Proceedings ESOP'90, LNCS 432, 1990

[SKR2] B. Steffen, J. Knoop, O. Rüthing. *Optimal Placement of Computations within Flow Graphs: A Practical Approach.* In Proceedings TAPSOFT'91, LNCS, 1991

[SP] M. Sharir, A. Pnueli. *Two Approaches to Interprocedural Data Flow Analysis. In: S.S. Muchnick, N.D. Jones. Program Flow Analysis: Theory and Applications.* Prentice-Hall, Englewood Cliffs , N.J., 1981

[Ste1] B. Steffen. *Characteristic Formulae.* In Proceedings ICALP'89, LNCS 372, 1989

[Ste2] B. Steffen. *Generating Data Flow Analysis Algorithms from Modal Specifications.* Technical Report of the RWTH–Aachen, to appear 1991

[Sti1] C. Stirling. *Modal and Temporal Logics.* In *Handbook of Logics in Computer Science*, Vol. 1, Oxford University Press, to appear 1990.

[Tar] Tarski, A. "A Lattice-Theoretical Fixpoint Theorem and its Applications." *Pacific Journal of Mathematics*, v. 5, 1955.

[Ven] G.A. Venkatesh. *A framework for construction and evaluation of high-level specifications for program analysis techniques.* In Proceedings SIGPLAN'89, 1989

[Wil1] R. Wilhelm. *Global Flow Analysis and Optimization in the MUG2 Compiler Generating System. In: S.S. Muchnick, N.D. Jones. Program Flow Analysis: Theory and Applications.* Prentice-Hall, Englewood Cliffs, N.J., 1981

[Wil2] R. Wilhelm. *Codeoptimierung mittels attributierter Transformationsgrammatiken.* LNCS 26, 257-266, 1974

On the Adequacy of Dependence-Based Representations for Programs with Heaps

Phil Pfeiffer
University of Wisconsin–Madison
pfeiffer@cs.wisc.edu

Rebecca Parsons Selke
Rice University
selke@rice.edu

Abstract

Program dependence graphs (*pdgs*) are popular tools for reasoning about a program's semantics. This report proves two fundamental theorems about the representational soundness of *pdgs* for languages with heap-allocated storage and reference variables. The first, the *Pointer-Language Equivalence Theorem*, asserts that *pdgs* adequately represent a program's meaning. The second, the *Pointer-Language Slicing Theorem*, asserts that *pdgs* adequately represent a program's threads of computation. These theorems are demonstrated with two new lemmas about the semantics of *pdgs* for languages that lack pointer variables. These lemmas, the *Dynamic Equivalence* and *Dynamic Slicing Theorems*, state that an edge can safely be removed from a program's *pdg* if this edge represents a static dependence that does not arise at run-time.

1. Introduction

Program dependence graphs (*pdgs*) are popular tools for manipulating imperative programs. A *pdg* is a directed labeled graph that depicts a program's *dependences*—possible constraints on that program's evaluation. *Pdgs* have been used in optimizing and parallelizing compilers to restructure programs [1, 7, 15, 16], and in debuggers, program-integration tools, and semantic-differencing utilities to identify a program's threads of computation [6, 11, 12, 18]. *Pdgs* are useful because they simplify program analysis; dependences abstract away from a program's statement-list operator, and expose its underlying threads of computation.

This work was supported in part by a David and Lucile Packard Fellowship for Science and Engineering, by the National Science Foundation under grants DCR-8552602 and CCR-8958530, by the Defense Advanced Research Projects Agency, monitored by the Office of Naval Research under contract N00014-88-K-0590, as well as by grants from IBM, DEC, and Xerox.

Early research on *pdgs* was limited to languages like FORTRAN that support scalar variables and arrays, but lack heap-allocated storage. Recently, *pdgs* have been used to represent programs in *pointer languages*—languages like Pascal that support heap-allocated storage, reference variables, and a destructive assignment statement. Several authors have proposed techniques for computing dependences in the presence of heaps [4, 8, 10, 16]. One of these authors [16] also shows how dependences can be used to parallelize Lisp-like programs.

An important limitation of the work on pointer-language *pdgs* is the lack of theoretical justification for using *pdgs* to reason about programs with pointers. This report takes a first step towards providing such justification by proving two fundamental theorems about pointer-language *pdgs*. The first, the *Pointer-Language Equivalence Theorem*, states that two pointer-language programs that have isomorphic *pdgs* represent equivalent programs. The second, the *Pointer-Language Slicing Theorem*, states that a program's *pdg* adequately characterizes its threads of computation.

The Pointer-Language Equivalence and Slicing Theorems are proved by reducing assertions about the semantics of pointer-language *pdgs* to assertions about the semantics of *pdgs* for pointer-free languages. Example pointer-language programs are first reduced to programs in a simpler language (called $\mathcal{S}$) that supports neither references nor allocation. The reduction ensures that a reduced computation simulates the evaluation of an unreduced computation, up to the exhaustion of the simulated freelist. The reduction also ensures that programs with isomorphic *pdgs* are reduced to pointer-free programs with isomorphic *pdgs*. The problem of proving the Pointer-Language Equivalence and Slicing Theorems is therefore reduced to the task of proving two lemmas about the semantics of *pdgs* for $\mathcal{S}$-like languages:

* The first lemma, the *Dynamic Equivalence Theorem*, states that two programs in $\mathcal{S}$ that have isomorphic *dynamic pdgs* represent equivalent programs.
* The second lemma, the *Dynamic Slicing Theorem*, states that a *dynamic pdg* adequately represents a program's threads of computation.

These lemmas generalize existing adequacy theorems for $\mathcal{S}$-like languages by relaxing the requirements on a *pdg*'s set of edges. Earlier versions of the Equivalence and Slicing Theorems (*e.g.*, [21]) assume that program *P*'s *pdg* contains an edge $p \longrightarrow q$ if paths between *p* and *q* in *P*'s control-flow graph satisfy certain criteria—even if these paths are never evaluated. The Dynamic Equivalence and Slicing Theorems, on the other hand, allow $p \longrightarrow q$ to be removed from *P*'s *pdg* if none of *P*'s possible evaluations exhibits $p \longrightarrow q$.

The proof of the Equivalence Theorem exposes an interesting shortcoming of using dependences to reason about programs with pointers. The proof assumes that a terminating computation can always allocate as much memory as it needs to complete. This assumption implies that any dependence-based reordering of a computation's prescribed evaluation strategy is safe, regardless of whether that reordering increases a computation's peak memory requirements. The assumption that an evaluation strategy's memory requirements can safely be ignored may of course prove false for applications that use most of a machine's available memory. The assumption is needed, however, since standard notions of (data) dependence do not account for how operations consume storage.

The rest of the report contains four sections. Section 2 defines an example language whose features typify those exhibited by pointer languages. Section 3 defines a *pdg* for this language. Section 4 proves that this *pdg* provides an adequate representation of a program's semantics. Section 5 describes related research, and discusses the limitations of the theorems presented in this paper.

2. A Language with Heap-Allocated Storage

This report argues that a dependence-graph representation of a program that uses pointers adequately characterizes that program's meaning and threads of computation. These claims are proved for the language $\mathcal{H}$, an example imperative language that exhibits the following features:

- Memory is represented as a map from locations to *structures*—cons cells and environments.
- Environments are maps from identifiers to *values* (*i.e.*, locations and atoms). Every store contains exactly one environment.
- Cons cells are maps from *selectors*—elements of { hd, tl }—to values.
- Programs are finite syntactic objects that map *finite* stores to stores. A store is finite if it contains finitely many structures that are accessible from (*i.e.*, can be reached from) that store's environment.
- Cons cells are allocated by expressions of the form *exp* :: *exp*.
- Storage is accessed by expressions like *x*.hd and *x*.tl.
- Assignment statements alter the fields of environments and cons cells. For example, the statement *x*.hd := 0 overwrites the current contents of *x*.hd with the value 0.

The following grammar defines $\mathcal{H}$'s concrete syntax:

Program → *Stmts*
Stmts → *Stmt* {; *Stmt*}*
Stmt → **while** *Cond* **do** *Stmts* **od** | **if** *Cond* **then** *Stmts* {**else** *Stmts*} **fi** | *IdExp* := *Exp*
Cond → **isAtom** *SimplExp* | **isNil** *SimplExp* | **not** *Cond*
Exp → *SimpleExp* | *Exp* :: *Exp*
SimplExp → ATOM | *IdExp*
IdExp → IDENT{.*Sel*}*
Sel → hd | tl

ATOM is a set of primitive objects—*e.g*, integers. IDENT is a set of lower-case alphanumeric identifier names. Members of IDENT are called *identifiers*. Members of

IdExp are called *identifier expressions.*

Figure 1 gives an operational semantics for $\mathcal{H}$. This semantics makes the simplifying assumption that a program's freelist is unbounded; *i.e.*, that programs never fail for want of storage. How the difference between this idealized freelist and actual implementations of *alloc* affects the validity of these results is discussed in the final section of this paper.

The expression $P:\sigma$ denotes the sequence of states that results from evaluating the program P with respect to the store σ. The expression $P(\sigma)$ is a synonym for $\mathbf{M}_{\mathcal{H}}(P, \sigma)$, the *meaning* of the computation $P:\sigma$. $P(\sigma)$ is the error state $\perp$ if either $P:\sigma$ is not finite or $P:\sigma$ *terminates abnormally*—*i.e.*, if a statement either reads an undefined identifier, or applies a selector expression to an atom.

3. Program Dependence Graphs

A *program dependence graph* (*pdg*) is a graph that depicts interactions between a program's component statements. *Pdgs* consist of nodes that represent a program's syntactic points of control, linked by edges $p \longrightarrow q$ that represent how one statement p might exchange information with, or control the evaluation of, a second statement q. The exact definition of a *pdg*—how its nodes and edges are labeled, and the notion of dependence it portrays—depends on the graph's intended use.

This report is concerned with two kinds of *pdgs*. The first, the *dynamic heap pdg* (*hpdg*), represents programs in $\mathcal{H}$. The second, the *dynamic scalar pdg* (*spdg*), is used to prove assertions about *hpdgs*. Both *spdgs* and *hpdgs* are related to a third *pdg*, referred to here as a *static pdg*. Static *pdgs* were developed for imperative languages with conditionals, loops, and scalar variables. A static *pdg* for program P, G_P, contains one entry vertex, which represents P's initial point of control; one initial-definition and one final-use vertex for every variable in P; and one *if*, *while*, and *assignment* vertex for every *if* predicate, *while* predicate, and assignment in P, respectively. G_P also contains one edge for each of P's static *control*, *loop-carried flow*, *loop-independent flow*, *loop-carried def-order*, and *loop-independent def-order* dependences. The definitions of these dependences and the labeling requirements for the edges that represent them are summarized in Figure 2. Figure 3 depicts an example of a static *pdg*.

The only difference between a static *pdg* and an *spdg* is that an *spdg* portrays a *dynamic* notion of data dependence (*cf.* Figure 4). A static *pdg* for program P *must* contain the edge $p \longrightarrow q$ when P's control-flow graph contains paths from p to q that satisfy certain criteria—even if these paths are never evaluated. An *spdg* for P, on the other hand, may omit $p \longrightarrow q$ if none of P's *evaluations* exhibit $p \longrightarrow q$. An *spdg* for the program "[1] **if** *pred* **then** [2] $x := 1$ **fi**; [3] $y := x$", for example, may omit a flow edge from [2] to [3] when *pred* is uniformly false. Similarly, an *spdg* for a program P may omit $p \longrightarrow_{do\,(r)} q$ when none of P's evaluations exhibit both $p \longrightarrow_f r$ and $q \longrightarrow_f r$.

$State = Point \times Store \qquad Store = Loc \rightarrow Env + Cons \qquad Env = Ident \rightarrow Val_{\perp}$

$Cons = Sel \rightarrow Val \qquad Val = Loc + Atom$

$\mathbf{M}_{\mathcal{H}}: Prog \times Store \rightarrow Store_{\perp}$

$\mathbf{M}_{\mathcal{H}}(prog, \sigma) =$ **let** *freelist* be an unbounded list of locations that are not in $Domain(\sigma)$ **in**

  let *firstPoint* be *prog*'s initial program point **in**

  let $evalPgm = fix\ \lambda f.\ (\lambda((p, \sigma')) .\ p \stackrel{?}{=} \mathbf{final} \rightarrow \sigma' \ [\!]\ f(next(prog, (p, \sigma'))))$

  in $evalPgm((firstPoint, \sigma))$

end*

$next : Prog \times State \rightarrow State_{\perp}$

$next(prog, (p, \sigma)) =$ **case** p **in**

  $If(cexp), While(cexp)$: $(nextPoint(prog, p, cond(\sigma, cexp)), \sigma)$

  $Assign(lexp, rexp)$: $(nextPoint(prog, p), assign(\sigma, lexp, rexp))$

esac

$cond : Store \times Cond \rightarrow Bool_{\perp}$

$cond(\sigma, cexp) =$

case *cexp* **in**

  isNil(*exp*): $(idexp(\sigma, exp) \stackrel{?}{=} \mathbf{nil})$

  isAtom(*exp*): $(idexp(\sigma, exp) \in Atom)$

  not(*exp*): $\neg\ cond(\sigma, exp)$

esac

$rvalue : Store \times Exp \rightarrow (Store \times Val)_{\perp}$

$rvalue(\sigma, rvexp) =$

case *rvexp* **in**

  Atom: $(\sigma, rvexp)$

  Idexp: $(\sigma, idexp(\sigma, rvexp))$

  $lexp :: rexp$: $cons(\sigma, lexp, rexp)$

esac

$assign : Store \times Exp \times Exp \rightarrow Store_{\perp}$

$assign(\sigma, lexp, rexp) =$

let $lv = idexp(\sigma, front(lexp))$ **in**

  $lv \in Atom \rightarrow \perp\ [\!]$

  let $(\sigma', rv) = rvalue(\sigma, rexp)$ **in**

   $\sigma'[\ (\sigma(lv))\ [rv\ /\ last(lexp)]\ \ /\ lv]$

end*

$cons : Store \times Exp \times Exp \rightarrow (Store \times Val)_{\perp}$

$cons(\sigma, lexp, rexp) =$

let $(\sigma', headv) = rvalue(\sigma, lexp)$ **in**

  let $(\sigma'', tailv) = rvalue(\sigma', rexp)$ **in**

   let $loc = alloc()$ **in**

   $(\sigma''[\,[\mathrm{hd} \mapsto headv, \mathrm{tl} \mapsto tailv]\ /\ loc], loc)$

end*

$idexp : Store \rightarrow (Idexp \cup \{\varepsilon\}) \rightarrow Val_{\perp}$

$idexp(\sigma, idexpr) =$ **let** *env* be the location of σ's environment **in** $selexp(\sigma, env, idexpr)$ **end**

$selexp : Store \times Val \times (Ident + Sel)^{*} \rightarrow Val_{\perp}$

$selexp(\sigma, val, selexpr) =$

  $selexpr \stackrel{?}{=} \varepsilon \rightarrow val\ [\!]\ (val \in Atom \rightarrow \perp\ [\!]\ selexp(\sigma, (\sigma(val))(first(selexpr)), tail(selexpr)))$

$alloc : () \rightarrow Loc = \lambda().\ loc := first(freelist);\ freelist := tail(freelist);$ **return**(loc)

fix is the least fixpoint functional. $nextPoint(prog, p, cond)$ and $nextPoint(prog, p)$ denote point p's control-flow successors. ε is the empty sequence. $first(seq)$ and $last(seq)$ denote the first and last elements of sequence *seq*. $tail(seq)$ denotes all but the first, and $front(seq)$ all but the last, element of *seq*.

Figure 1. Language $\mathcal{H}$'s meaning function, $\mathbf{M}_{\mathcal{H}}$. Every function is strict in each argument.

Let $l(p)$, the *level* of p, be the number of *while* and *if* statements enclosing p. Program P has a ***control dependence*** $p \longrightarrow_c q$ iff either

1. p is the entry vertex, q is not the entry vertex, and $l(q) = 0$;
2. p is a *while* predicate, the *while* statement at p encloses q, and $l(q) = l(p) + 1$;
3. p is an *if* predicate, the **true** branch of the *if* statement at p encloses q, and $l(q) = l(p) + 1$; or
4. p is an *if* predicate, the **false** branch of the *if* statement at p encloses q, and $l(q) = l(p) + 1$.

P's static *pdg* contains one edge for each of P's control dependences. Edges that correspond to cases 1-3 are labeled **true**; edges that correspond to case 4 are labeled **false**.

P has a ***flow (output) dependence*** $p \longrightarrow_f q$ ($p \longrightarrow_o q$) iff there exists a path in P's control-flow graph from p to q such that p defines a variable x; x is not redefined between p and q; and q accesses (redefines) x. Dependence $p \longrightarrow q$ is ***carried*** by loop L iff L contains p and q, a path π gives rise to $p \longrightarrow q$, and π contains L's entry point. Dependence $p \longrightarrow q$ is ***loop-independent*** iff there exists a path π such that π gives rise to $p \longrightarrow q$ and, for all L that contain both p and q, π does not contain L's entry point. (*N.B.*: a loop L contains its own entry point).

P's *pdg* contains one edge $p \longrightarrow_{f(L)} q$ for every loop L that carries $p \longrightarrow_f q$. P's *pdg* also contains one edge $p \longrightarrow_{f(li)} q$ if $p \longrightarrow_f q$ is loop-independent.

P has a ***transitive*** output dependence $p_0 \overset{+}{\longrightarrow}_o p_n$ iff there exist $p_2 \cdots p_{n-1}$ such that $p_0 \longrightarrow_o p_1 \cdots \longrightarrow_o p_n$. $p_0 \overset{+}{\longrightarrow}_o p_n$ is carried by L if any of the $p_i \longrightarrow_o p_{i+1}$ are carried by L.

P has a ***def-order dependence*** $p \longrightarrow_{do(r)} q$ iff P has two dependences $p \longrightarrow_f r$ and $q \longrightarrow_f r$ through a variable x, and p precedes q in P's abstract syntax tree. P's *pdg* contains one edge $p \longrightarrow_{do(r,L)} q$ for every loop L that carries $p \overset{+}{\longrightarrow}_o q$. P's *pdg* also contains one edge $p \longrightarrow_{do(r,li)} q$ if $p \longrightarrow_o q$ is loop-independent.

Figure 2. Edges that make up a static *pdg*.

Hpdgs differ from *spdgs* in two ways. *Hpdgs* contain *one* initial definition vertex and *one* final use vertex, corresponding to every accessible structure in a program's initial and final stores, respectively. *Hpdgs* also portray a slightly different notion of data dependence—one that describes accesses of structures and fields (*cf.* Figure 5). To simplify the presentation—more specifically, the reduction described in Section 4—edges that arise from accesses of structures are omitted from *hpdgs*. Such edges can be omitted because they are accompanied by corresponding, transitive edges that arise from accesses of fields. This point may be illustrated by examining the dependences exhibited by an example program; for instance, "[1] $a :=$ **nil** :: **nil**; [2] $b := a$; [3] **if** *isAtom*(b) $\cdots$". This program exhibits [1] $\longrightarrow_f$ [3], since statement [3] checks the type of a cons cell that statement [1] creates. The program, however, also exhibits a transitive dependence [1] $\longrightarrow_f$ [2] $\longrightarrow_f$ [3] that arises from the accesses of a and b.

The definition of an *spdg* implies that programs can have multiple *spdgs*. Let P be a program that can be represented by a *pdg*. Let $static(P)$ and $dynamic(P)$ be program P's static and dynamic dependences, respectively. Let $S \subseteq static(P)$ be any *def-order-consistent* superset of $dynamic(P)$; *i.e.*, any superset of $dynamic(P)$ such that, for all p, q, r, and L, $p \rightarrow_{do(r)} q \in S$ iff $p \rightarrow_f r \in S \wedge q \rightarrow_f r \in S$. Then the *spdg* that depicts only those data dependences in S is a valid *spdg* for program P. Similarly, let P_h be a program that manipulates pointers. Let $static(P_h)$ be the set of dependences that P_h exhibits with respect to worst-case aliasing assumptions about P_h. Let $S_h \subseteq static(P_h)$ be any def-order-consistent superset of $dynamic(P_h)$. Then the *hpdg* that depicts only those data dependences in S_h is valid for program P_h.

The most accurate representation of a program P's dependences is given by that dynamic *pdg* that depicts only those data dependences in $dynamic(P)$. A program's dynamic dependences, unfortunately, are not always computable. This assertion follows from the observation that it is not always possible to determine which of a program's statements will evaluate [17]. (*N.B.*: Dependence-computation algorithms for pointer languages typically compute a consistent superset of $dynamic(P)$; see, for example, [10].)

4. The Adequacy of Hpdgs

This section proves two theorems about *hpdgs*. The first, the *Pointer-Language Equivalence Theorem*, shows that an *hpdg* provides an adequate characterization of a

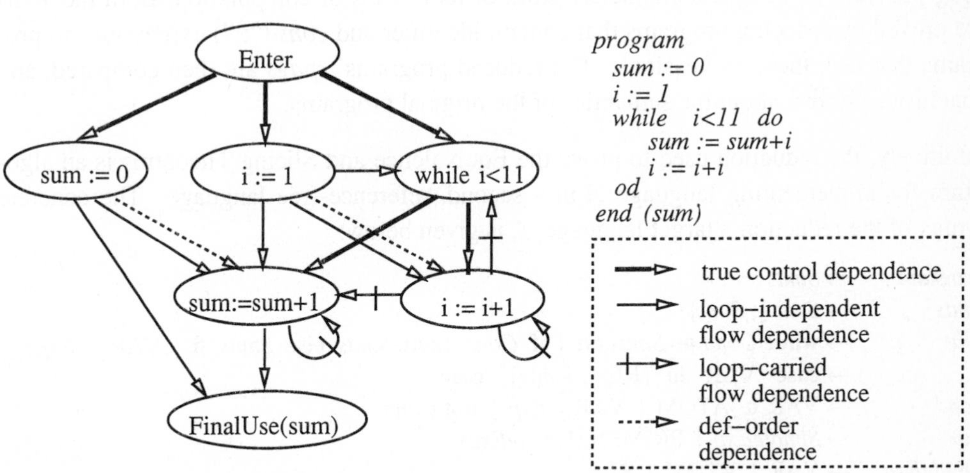

Figure 3. A static *pdg* for an example program that sums the integers from 1 to 10.

P exhibits a ***flow (output) dependence*** $p \longrightarrow_f q$ ($p \longrightarrow_o q$) iff there exists a store σ such that $P{:}\sigma$ generates a sequence of states $(p, \sigma_1) \cdots (q, \sigma_n)$; p defines a variable x in σ_1; x is not redefined between (p, σ_1) and (q, σ_n); and q accesses (redefines) x in σ_n. Dependence $p \longrightarrow q$ is ***carried*** by loop L iff L contains p and q, and there exists a store σ and a sequence of states $\pi = (p, \sigma_1) \cdots (q, \sigma_n)$ such that $P{:}\sigma$ generates π; π gives rise to $p \longrightarrow q$; and π contains a state at L's entry point. Dependence $p \longrightarrow q$ is ***loop-independent*** if there exists a store σ and a sequence of states $\pi = (p, \sigma_1) \cdots (q, \sigma_n)$ such that π gives rise to $p \longrightarrow q$ and, for all L that contain both p and q, π does not contain a state at L's entry point.
(*N.B.:* π contains a state at point p iff $\pi = (p_1, \sigma_1) \cdots (p_n, \sigma_n)$, and $p = p_i$ for some i between 1 and n inclusive.)

P's *pdg* contains one edge $p \longrightarrow_{f(L)} q$ for every loop L that carries $p \longrightarrow_f q$. P's *pdg* also contains one edge $p \longrightarrow_{f(li)} q$ if $p \longrightarrow_f q$ is loop-independent.

P exhibits a ***def-order dependence*** $p \longrightarrow_{do\,(r)} q$ iff P exhibits two dependences $p \longrightarrow_f r$ and $q \longrightarrow_f r$ through a variable x, and p precedes q in P's abstract syntax tree. P's *pdg* contains one edge $p \longrightarrow_{do(r,L)} q$ for every loop L that carries $p \stackrel{+}{\longrightarrow}_o q$. P's *pdg* also contains one edge $p \longrightarrow_{do\,(r,li)} q$ if $p \stackrel{+}{\longrightarrow}_o q$ is loop-independent.
(*N.B.:* The definition of transitive output dependence is similar to the one given in Figure 1.)

Figure 4. Data-dependence edges that must be included in an *spdg*.

program's meaning. The second, the *Pointer-Language Slicing Theorem*, shows that an *hpdg* provides an adequate characterization of its threads of computation. Both theorems are proved by reducing programs that contain identifier and *cons* ("::") expressions to programs that lack these expressions. The reduced programs' *spdgs* are then compared, and conclusions drawn about the semantics of the original programs.

Intuitively, the reduction used to prove the Equivalence and Slicing Theorems is an algorithm for implementing language $\mathcal{H}$ in a second, reference-free language. The concrete syntax of the reduction's target language, $\mathcal{S}$, is given below:

Program	→ *Stmts*
Stmts	→ *Stmt* {; *Stmt*}*
Stmt	→ **while** *Cond* **do** *Stmts* **od** | **if** *Cond* **then** *Stmts* **else** *Stmts* **fi** | VAR := *Exp*
	→ **case** VAR **in** {REF : *Stmts*}* **esac**
Cond	→ VAR ∈ ATOM | VAR $\stackrel{?}{=}$ *Exp* | **not** *Cond*
Exp	→ *SimpleExp* | PRIMFN (*SimpleExp*)
SimpleExp	→ VAR | ATOM | REF
REF	→ **&1** | **&2** | ···

VAR is a set of alphanumeric variable names. Variables that are special to the reduction are given upper-case names; note that such names are not members of IDENT. PRIMFN

P exhibits a ***flow (output) dependence*** $p \rightarrow_f q$ ($p \rightarrow_o q$) iff there exists a store σ such that $P{:}\sigma$ generates a sequence of states $(p, \sigma_1) \cdots (q, \sigma_n)$; p defines a structure or field x in σ_1; x is not redefined between (p, σ_1) and (q, σ_n); and q accesses (redefines) x in σ_n.

P's *pdg* contains one edge $p \rightarrow_{f(L)} q$ for every loop L that carries $p \rightarrow_f q$. P's *pdg* also contains one edge $p \rightarrow_{f(li)} q$ if $p \rightarrow_f q$ is loop-independent.

P exhibits a ***def-order dependence*** $p \rightarrow_{do(r)} q$ iff P exhibits two dependences $p \rightarrow_f r$ and $q \rightarrow_f r$ through a field x, and p precedes q in P's abstract syntax tree. P's *pdg* contains one edge $p \rightarrow_{do(r,L)} q$ for every loop L that carries a $p \overset{+}{\rightarrow}_o q$ that arises through x. P's *pdg* also contains one edge $p \rightarrow_{do(r,li)} q$ if a $p \overset{+}{\rightarrow}_o q$ that arises through x is loop-independent.
(*N.B.*: The definitions of loop-carried, loop-independent, and transitive dependence are similar to those given in Figures 1 and 2.)

Figure 5. Data-dependence edges that must be included in an *hpdg*.

is a collection of value-returning, side-effect-free, non-nested functions. The subscripts $\mathcal{H}$ and $\mathcal{S}$ are used when needed to distinguish between semantic objects in $\mathcal{H}$ and $\mathcal{S}$.

An operational semantics is assumed for $\mathcal{S}$, similar to one given in [23]. Conditional expressions, *while* loops, assignment statements, and statement lists have their usual meaning. The *case* statement is equivalent to a nested if-then-else statement that causes a program to fail if none of its guards are matched. Language $\mathcal{S}$ has one unusual feature: its meaning function maps a computation $P_*{:}\sigma_*$ to $\perp$ when P_* and σ_* fail to satisfy certain consistency constraints. These constraints, which ensure that every computation in $\mathcal{S}$ corresponds to some computation in $\mathcal{H}$, are described below.

Two functions are used to reduce computations in $\mathcal{H}$ to computations in $\mathcal{S}$. The one, *reduceStore*$_k$, reduces a $\sigma \in Store_{\mathcal{H}}$ to a comparable $\sigma_* \in Store_{\mathcal{S}}$. Store σ_* consists of three sets of variables. The first contains one variable x for every identifier x in σ's environment. The second contains $2n$ variables that correspond to the n accessible cons cells in σ's heap: every accessible cell is reduced to a unique pair of variables (L_jHD, L_jTL), where j is an arbitrary value between 1 and n. The third set, which contains $2k$ variables named $L_{n+1}HD \cdots L_{n+k}TL$, simulates σ's infinitely-long freelist.

Function *reduceStore* reduces atoms to atoms. If σ's environment, for example, maps the identifier x to the value "3", then variable x in σ_* contains "3". References to the jth cons cell in σ are reduced to the value **&j** $\in$ REF. If σ's environment, for example, maps x to the jth cons cell in σ, then variable x in σ_* contains **&j**.

Function *reduceStore*, in effect, maps a $\sigma \in Store_{\mathcal{H}}$ to a *congruent* $\sigma_* \in Store_{\mathcal{S}}$. Two stores σ and σ_* are congruent, written $\sigma \approx_{\mathcal{HS}} \sigma_*$ ($\sigma_* \approx_{\mathcal{SH}} \sigma$), if for all *idexp* and *idexp'* in *IDEXP*:

- *idexp* denotes the atom *at* in σ iff *idexp* corresponds to a variable v in σ_* that contains *at*.[1]
- *idexp* denotes a cons cell in σ iff *idexp* corresponds to a variable in σ_* that contains an element of REF.
- *idexp* and *idexp'* denote the same structure in σ iff *idexp* and *idexp'* correspond to variables in σ_* that contain the same element of REF.

Two other relations given in this report are similar to $\approx_{\mathcal{HS}}$. The one, $\approx_{\mathcal{H}}$, identifies isomorphic members of $Store_{\mathcal{H}}$. The other, $\approx_{\mathcal{S}}$, identifies members of $Store_{\mathcal{S}}$ that have comparable interpretations. The definitions of $\approx_{\mathcal{H}}$, $\approx_{\mathcal{HS}}$, and $\approx_{\mathcal{S}}$ ensure that $\sigma \approx_{\mathcal{H}} \sigma'$ when there exist σ_* and σ'_* such that $\sigma \approx_{\mathcal{HS}} \sigma_* \approx_{\mathcal{S}} \sigma'_* \approx_{\mathcal{SH}} \sigma'$.

Function *reducePgm*, the other reduction function, maps a $P \in Program_{\mathcal{H}}$ to a comparable $P_* \in Program_{\mathcal{S}}$. The expression $reducePgm_{n,k,ident}(P)$ denotes a P_* that comprises a prologue and a body. P_*'s prologue is a sequence of assignment statements that initialize a special variable, *NFREE*, to *n*, and every $x \in ident$ to the special atom *undefined*. P_*'s body is obtained by recursively reducing *P* according to the rules given below:

A statement list "$stmt_1$; $\cdots$; $stmt_s$" is reduced by reducing each $stmt_i$ individually, according to the following rules for reducing statements.

An assignment such as "*x* := *at*", where *at* is an atom, is reduced to itself.

An assignment such as "*x.hd* := *y.tl*" is reduced to a nested **case** statement that first determines which variable corresponds to *y.tl*, then assigns the contents of this variable to the variable corresponding to *x.hd*:

case *y* **in**
 &1: **case** *x* **in** **&1**: $L_1HD := L_1TL$; $\cdots$ **&n+k**: $L_{n+k}HD := L_1TL$; **esac**
 $\cdots$
 &n+k: **case** *x* **in** **&1**: $L_1HD := L_{n+k}TL$; $\cdots$ **&n+k**: $L_{n+k}HD := L_{n+k}TL$; **esac**
esac

Note that the reduction proscribes the use of an infinite simulated address space, since *n* and *k* must be finite to ensure that reduced programs contain finitely many points.

An assignment such as "*x* := *lexp* ::*rexp*" is reduced to the four-statement sequence "*NFREE* := *NFREE* +1; *x* := *makeRef* (*NFREE*); *x.hd* := *lexp*; *x.tl* := *rexp*". Variable *NFREE* simulates *P*'s internal pointer to the head of a store's freelist. Function

[1] *idexp* corresponds to v in σ_* if $v = idexp$, or if $v = L_jSEL$, *idexp* is of the form $x.sel_1 \cdots sel_{n-1}SEL$, and $x.sel_1 \cdots sel_{n-1}$ denotes a variable containing the value **&j**.

makeRef (*NFREE*) returns **&j** when *NFREE* = *j* and $j \le n+k$, and *undefined* otherwise. The assignments "*x.hd* := *lexp*" and "*x.tl* := *rexp*" must then be reduced by applying the reductions given above.

A conditional statement such as "**if** *isAtom* (*lexp*) **then** *SL* **fi**" is first reduced to the pair of statements "*TMP* := *lexp*; **if** *TMP* ∉ REF **then** *SL* **fi**". Statement list *SL* and the assignment to *TMP* must then be reduced by applying the reductions given in this section.

The proofs of the Pointer-Language Equivalence and Slicing Theorems impose two constraints on the reduction from $\mathcal{H}$ to $\mathcal{S}$. Constraint (1) is that reduced computations must mimic unreduced computations up to heap overflow:

(1a) A computation $P_*{:}\sigma_*$ must denote $\perp$ when either P_* names an identifier that is not present in σ_*, or the initial configuration of $P_*{:}\sigma_*$'s address space or freelist is invalid; for example, when any of the simulated cons cells in σ_*'s simulated initial freelist can be accessed by an identifier expression. Requirement (1a) ensures that every reduced computation in $\mathcal{S}$ corresponds to a valid computation in $\mathcal{H}$.

(1b) If σ is a store and $\sigma_* = reduceStore_k(\sigma)$ for a suitable k, then $P{:}\sigma$ and $P_*{:}\sigma_*$ must generate comparable sequences of states and congruent final stores—unless $P_*{:}\sigma_*$ fails by overflowing its simulated heap.

Requirement (1a) can be satisfied by defining $\mathcal{S}$'s meaning function so that it maps invalid combinations of stores and programs to $\perp$. Requirement (1b) can be satisfied by using *reducePgm* and *reduceStore* to define a reduction from $\mathcal{H}$ to $\mathcal{S}$, as follows:

DEFINITION. Let $P \in Program_{\mathcal{H}}$ and $\sigma \in Store_{\mathcal{H}}$. Let n be the number of accessible cons cells in σ. Let *idset* be the set of all identifiers not defined in σ, but referenced in P. Let k be an integer, $\sigma_* = reduceStore_k(\sigma)$, and $P_* = reducePgm_{n,k,idset}(P)$. The expression $reduce_k(P{:}\sigma)$ denotes $P_*{:}\sigma_*$. The expression $reduce_k(P(\sigma))$ denotes $P_*(\sigma_*)$. □

LEMMA 1. Let $P \in Program_{\mathcal{H}}$, $\sigma \in Store_{\mathcal{H}}$, and k be a non-negative integer. Then $reduce_k(P{:}\sigma)$ fails if $P{:}\sigma$ allocates more than k cons cells; otherwise, $P{:}\sigma$ and $reduce_k(P{:}\sigma)$ generate corresponding sequences of states, with $P(\sigma) \approx_{\mathcal{HS}} reduce_k(P(\sigma))$.

PROOF. Lemma 1 is proved by induction on the number of steps in $P{:}\sigma$. This induction shows that P and P_* generate comparable sequences of states, so long as $P_*{:}\sigma_*$ does not exhaust its simulated freelist. □

The proofs of the Pointer-Language Equivalence and Slicing Theorems also require that (2) P and P_* exhibit *comparable* dependences. More formally, let $R(s)$ be the set of program points in P_* that correspond under this reduction to a point s in P. Let p and q be distinct points in P_* such that $p \not\rightarrow_c q$. Then, for all $p_* \in R(p)$ and all $q_* \in R(q)$, the reduction must ensure that $p_* \not\rightarrow_c q_*$. Similar constraints hold for flow and def-order dependences. Intuitively, constraint (2) allows programs with isomorphic *hpdgs* to be reduced to programs with isomorphic *spdgs*.

The reduction defined in Lemma 1, unfortunately, fails to satisfy constraint (2). The reduction's use of a global freelist to parcel out storage, which provides a reasonable model of how programs allocate cells, can introduce unwanted dependences into reduced programs. Figure 6 illustrates an example reduced program, P_*, that exhibits a flow dependence ([1.1] $\longrightarrow_f$ [2.1]) that corresponds to none of the dependences in the original. This new dependence, which arises from [2.1]'s read of *NFREE*, represents a needless constraint on the order in which P_* removes cells from its (simulated) freelist.

A second reduction depicted in Figure 7 (*cf.* program P'_*) eliminates freelist-related dependences by partitioning the original program's freelist into a set of local freelists—one per program point. Lemma 2 shows that the alternative reduction yields (1) an equivalent computation to the one obtained from the standard reduction of *cons*, and (2) a program whose dependences are comparable to those of the original program.

DEFINITION. Let program P contain p points. Let $free_1 \cdots free_p$ be functions from *Nat*, the natural numbers, to $\{ n+1, \cdots, n+k, undefined \}$. The expression

Program $\overline{P}$		Program $\overline{P'}$	
[0]	$NFREE := 0$	[0]	$NFREE_1 := 0; NFREE_2 := 0$
[1.1]	$NFREE := NFREE + 1;$	[1.1]	$NFREE_1 := NFREE_1 + 1$
[1.2]	$a := makeRef\,(NFREE);$	[1.2]	$a := free_1\,(NFREE_1)$
[1.3]	**case** a **in**	[1.3]	**case** a **in**
	&1: $L_1HD := 7;\ L_1TL := 7$		**&1**: $L_1HD := 7;\ L_1TL := 7$
	...		...
	&n+k: $L_{n+k}HD := 7;\ L_{n+k}TL := 7$		**&n+k**: $L_{n+k}HD := 7;\ L_{n+k}TL := 7$
	esac		**esac**
[2.1]	$NFREE := NFREE + 1;$	[2.1]	$NFREE_2 := NFREE_2 + 1$
[2.2]	$b := makeRef\,(NFREE);$	[2.2]	$b := free_2\,(NFREE_2)$
[2.3]	**case** b **in**	[2.3]	**case** b **in**
	&1: $L_1HD := 8;\ L_1TL := 8$		**&1**: $L_1HD := 8;\ L_1TL := 8$
	...		...
	&n+k: $L_{n+k}HD := 8;\ L_{n+k}TL := 8$		**&n+k**: $L_{n+k}HD := 8;\ L_{n+k}TL := 8$
	esac		**esac**
			$free_1 = \lambda x\,.\,x \stackrel{?}{=} 1 \rightarrow$ **&1** [] *undefined*
			$free_2 = \lambda x\,.\,x \stackrel{?}{=} 1 \rightarrow$ **&2** [] *undefined*

Figure 6. Two reductions of "[1] $a := 7 :: 7$; [2] $b := 8 :: 8$" that produce different dependences. Program $\overline{P}$ exhibits [1.1] $\longrightarrow_f$ [2.1] through *NFREE*. Program $\overline{P'}$, which has two different freelist variables, does not exhibit [1.1] $\longrightarrow_f$ [2.1].

$reducePgm'_{n,k,ident}(P,\ free_1, \cdots, free_p)$ denotes a program that differs from $reducePgm_{n,k,ident}(P)$ in the following two ways:

- The statement "*NFREE* := 0" in P's prologue is replaced by p statements that set the variables $NFREE_1 \cdots NFREE_p$ to 0.
- An assignment such as "[q] x := *lexp* ::*rexp*" is reduced to "$NFREE_q := NFREE_q + 1$; $x := free_q(NFREE_q)$; *x.hd* := *lexp*; *x.tl* := *rexp*". □

DEFINITION. Let $free_1 \cdots free_p$ be functions from *Nat* to *Nat* ∪ { *undefined* }. The $free_j$ are *mutually independent* iff $free_d(f) = free_e(g)$ implies that either $free_d(f) = undefined$ or $d = e$ and $f = g$. □

LEMMA 2. Let $P \in Program_{\mathcal{H}}$, $\sigma \in Store_{\mathcal{H}}$, and k be a non-negative integer. Let $\sigma_* = reduceStore_k(\sigma)$. Let $free_1 \cdots free_p$ be mutually independent functions from *Nat* to $\{n+1, \cdots, n+k, undefined\}$. Let $P_* = reducePgm_{n,k,ident}(P)$ and $P'_* = reducePgm'_{n,k,ident}(P,\ free_1, \cdots, free_p)$. Then $P_*{:}\sigma_*$ and $P'_*{:}\sigma_*$ generate equivalent sequences of stores, unless $P'_*{:}\sigma_*$ fails because of the evaluation of a variable containing the value *undefined* (*i.e.*, because of a call to a $free_j$). Furthermore, P and P'_* have comparable dependences.

PROOF. The assertion that $P_*{:}\sigma_*$ and $P'_*{:}\sigma_*$ generate equivalent sequences of stores (up to the possible failure of $P'_*{:}\sigma_*$) follows from the independence of the $free_i$ and the referential transparency of $\mathcal{H}$.

The assertion that P and P'_* have comparable dependences is proved by reasoning about the reduction. The claim that P and P'_* have comparable sets of control dependences follows directly from the definition of *reducePgm*. The claim that P and P'_* also have comparable data dependences is proved by using P's *hpdg* to reason about the dynamic dependences exhibited by P'_*. Figure 7 illustrates how a program P'_* may have static data dependences that fail to correspond to any of P's dependences, due to the use of *case* statements to simulate the interpretation of identifier expressions. Static dependences in P'_* of the form $[1.i] \longrightarrow_f [3.i]$ fail to correspond to dependences in P (*i.e.*, to $[1] \longrightarrow_f [3]$) when a and b are always aliased. Static dependences in P'_* of the form $[2.i] \longrightarrow_f [3.i]$ fail to correspond to dependences in P (*i.e.*, to $[2] \longrightarrow_f [3]$) when a and b are never aliased. Finally, static dependences in P'_* of the form $[1.i] \longrightarrow_{do([3.i])} [2.i]$ fail to correspond to dependences in P (*i.e.*, to $[1] \longrightarrow_{do([3])} [2]$) unless P exhibits both $[1] \longrightarrow_f [3]$ and $[2] \longrightarrow_f [3]$.

It can be shown, however, that P'_* and P exhibit comparable sets of dynamic data dependences. Let H_P be an arbitrary *hpdg* for P. Let $depend(H_P)$ be the set of data dependences depicted in H_P. Let $static(P'_*)$ be the set of static data dependences exhibited by P'_*. Construct $induced(P'_*, H_P)$ from $static(P'_*)$ by removing $p_* \longrightarrow q_*$ from $static(P'_*)$ when there exist p and q in P such that $p \neq q$, $p_* \in R(p)$, $q_* \in R(q)$, and

Program P	[1] $a.hd := 7$; [2] $b.hd := 8$; [3] $a := a.hd$		
Program $\overline{P}$	**case** a **in** [1.1] **&1**: $L_1 HD := 7$	$\cdots$ [1.n+k] **&n+k**: $L_{n+k} HD := 7$	**esac**
	case b **in** [2.1] **&1**: $L_1 HD := 8$	$\cdots$ [2.n+k] **&n+k**: $L_{n+k} HD := 8$	**esac**
	case a **in** [3.1] **&1**: $a := L_1 HD$	$\cdots$ [3.n+k] **&n+k**: $a := L_{n+k} HD$	**esac**

Figure 7. Illustration of how the reduction adds static dependences to a program. A static dependence of the form $[1.i] \longrightarrow_f [3.i]$ will fail to correspond to a dependence in P (*i.e.*, to $[1] \longrightarrow_f [3]$) when a and b are always aliased. Similar observations hold for the $[2.i] \longrightarrow_f [3.i]$ and the $[1.i] \longrightarrow_{do([3.i])} [2.i]$.

$p \longrightarrow q \notin depend(H_P)$. Lemma 2 may now proved by arguing that:

i. $induced(P'_*, P)$ contains all P'_*'s dynamic dependences, and
ii. $depend(H_P)$ and $induced(P'_*, H_P)$ are comparable sets of dependences.

Proof of (i). Let $dynamic(P'_*)$ denote P'_*'s set of dynamic dependences. Let $removed(P'_*, H_P)$ denote $static(P'_*) - induced(P'_*, H_P)$. Since $dynamic(P'_*) \subseteq static(P'_*)$, claim (i) can be proved by showing that (*) $dynamic(P'_*) \cap removed(P'_*, H_P) = \emptyset$. To see the correctness of claim (*), assume to the contrary that some $p_* \longrightarrow q_*$ in $dynamic(P'_*)$ was removed from $static(P'_*)$. By the definition of a dynamic data dependence, there exists some σ'_* such that $P'_*:\sigma'_*$ exhibits $p_* \longrightarrow q_*$. However, the definition of $\mathcal{S}$'s meaning function (*cf.* constraint (1a)) and Lemma 1 then ensure the existence of a σ such that $P{:}\sigma$ exhibits $p \longrightarrow q$. Then $p \longrightarrow q \in depend(P)$, and $p_* \longrightarrow q_*$ could not have been removed from $static(P'_*)$—a contradiction.

Proof of (ii). Claim (ii) is proved by showing that $p \longrightarrow q \notin depend(H_P)$ iff $p_* \longrightarrow q_* \notin induced(P'_*, H_P)$ for all $p_* \in R(p)$ and $q_* \in R(q)$. The *only if* direction—$p \longrightarrow q \notin depend(P)$ implies $p_* \longrightarrow q_* \notin induced(P'_*, H_P)$—is immediate from the definition of $induced(P'_*, H_P)$. To show the *if* direction, assume that $p \longrightarrow q \in depend(H_P)$. By the definition of data dependence, P's control-flow graph must contain a path from p to q. By the definition of the reduction, P'_*'s control-flow graph must also contain paths from the points in $R(p)$ to the points in $R(q)$. By the definition of the reduction, there must be a $p_* \in R(p)$ and a $q_* \in R(q)$ such that P'_* exhibits a static dependence from p_* to q_*. Then, by the definition of *induced*, $p_* \longrightarrow q_* \in induced(P'_*, H_P)$. □

The proof of Lemma 2 concludes the characterization of the reduction proper. The proofs of the Pointer-Language Equivalence and Slicing Theorems use two additional lemmas, the Dynamic Equivalence and Slicing Theorems, to obtain a characterization of a reduced program's semantics. These lemmas are used to show that a reduced program's *spdg* provides an adequate characterization of its meaning and threads of computation, respectively.

The Dynamic Equivalence and Slicing Theorems are proved by using the graph-rewriting semantics for static *pdgs* given in [22] to show that a data-dependence edge that does not correspond to a dynamic dependence can safely be removed from a program's *pdg*. This semantics is a *pdg*-rewriting system that identifies *redexes*—nodes with no remaining incoming dependences—and updates the *pdg* to reflect the impact of the node. For example, the rewriting of an assignment node causes the propagation of the value of its expression to all other nodes with incoming flow edges from the redex. In this semantics, nodes are removed from the *pdg* when they are rewritten, and nodes that do not execute due to the outcome of a predicate node are removed without being rewritten. A *rewriting sequence* shows the order in which the redexes are rewritten. The result of a rewriting is the set of final use nodes containing identifiers and their final values.

LEMMA (*Dynamic Equivalence Theorem*). Suppose that P and Q are members of $Program_S$ that have isomorphic *spdgs*. Let σ and σ' agree on the values of all variables named by P's initial-definition vertices. If P halts on σ then (1) Q halts on σ', (2) P and Q compute identical sequences of values at corresponding program points, and (3) P and Q compute stores that agree on the values of all store-access expressions named by P's final-use vertices.

PROOF. Since the *spdgs* for P and Q are isomorphic, their meanings under the rewriting semantics from [22] are the same. If the rewriting semantics holds for *spdgs* as well as *pdgs*, the lemma is shown. The proof for the following claim appears below.

CLAIM. Let P be a program in $Program_S$, let G be its static *pdg* and let G' be an *spdg* for P. Then G rewrites to the set $\{ (x_1, v_1) \cdots (x_n, v_n) \}$ for all x_i appearing in the final-use vertices iff G' rewrites to the same set.

PROOF OF CLAIM. By the definition of *spdgs*, G and G' have the same node set and control edge set. The proof proceeds by induction on the length of the rewriting sequence. The induction hypothesis includes the following three claims:

1. The same values are computed for corresponding redexes in G and G'.
2. The same values flow over corresponding edges in G and G'.
3. The nodes removed in G and G' by the rewriting are the same.

The base step is trivial. Since G and G' only differ in the flow and def-order edge sets, there are three cases to consider for the induction step: the same redex is available for rewriting in both G and G', the node in G corresponding to the redex in G' has an incoming flow edge, and the node in G corresponding to the redex in G' has an incoming def-order edge.

The first case of the induction step is trivial.

For the second case, let n and n' be the nodes in G and G' respectively, and let (p,n) be the edge in G. Since this edge is not in G' and by the induction hypothesis, this edge must *not* be exhibited by any rewriting of P. Since n' is a redex, all control edges for n must have been resolved so n will execute. Thus, either (i) p does not send a value to n, or (ii) the value that p sends to n will be overwritten by some other node p'. If (i) holds, then n becomes a redex that is, by part 2 of the induction hypothesis, not different from n'. Otherwise, if (ii) holds, the def-order consistency condition for *pdgs* (*cf.* Section 3) and part 3 of the induction hypothesis ensure the presence of a def-order edge (p,p') in G. The value sent to n' by p' must therefore overwrite any value sent by p. By part 2 of the induction hypothesis, when n does become a redex, its expression will evaluate to the same value as n'.

The arguments for the third case are similar to those of the second case, but there are more possibilities to consider in the differences in the graphs. These differences arise because there are more situations where a def-order edge can be removed from the *spdg* than there are situations for flow edges.

This concludes the proof of the claim. With this claim, the main lemma follows directly from the *pdg* Equivalence Theorem given in [22]. □

DEFINITION. A (backward) *slice* of a *pdg* G with respect to vertex set S, written G / S, is the subgraph of G induced by $V(G / S)$, the set of vertices v such that there exists a path from v to a vertex in S—less all edges $u \longrightarrow_{do\ (w)} v$ such that $w \notin V(G / S)$. □

Intuitively, G / S is safe approximation to the set of all points in G that could contribute to the sequence of values computed at points in S. A slice of an example program's (static) *pdg* is illustrated in Figure 8.

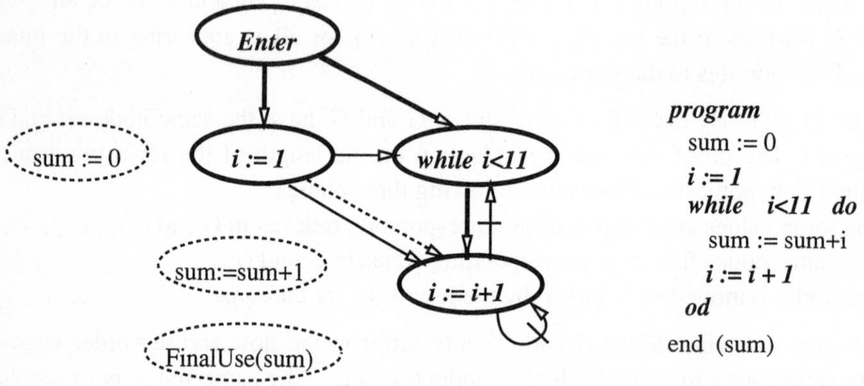

Figure 8. The slice of the example program depicted in Figure 3, computed w.r.t. the statement "$i := i + 1$. This slice shows the set of points that could affect the values of i computed at this statement in the example program's evaluation.

LEMMA (*Dynamic Slicing Theorem*). Let Q be a slice of a $P \in Program_S$ with respect to a set of vertices. Let σ and σ' agree on the values of all variables named by Q's initial-definition vertices. If P halts on σ, then (1) Q halts on σ', (2) P and Q compute identical sequences of values at each program point of Q, and (3) P and Q agree on the values of all variables named in Q's final-definition vertices.

PROOF. Let G and H be the *spdg*s for the program and the slice respectively. Since P halts, the rewriting sequence for G is finite. A finite rewriting sequence for H can be constructed from this sequence by simply selecting the steps for nodes that exist in H. From the definition of a slice, this sequence results in a final value for Q and is a valid rewriting sequence. Thus, Q halts. Since the steps are identical for all nodes in H, and since the rewriting semantics shows that the effects of rewriting a node are confined to nodes with edges from the rewritten node, the rest of the theorem follows directly. □

This concludes the presentation of the auxiliary lemmas used in the Pointer-Language Equivalence and Slicing Theorems. Proofs of these theorems now follow.

THEOREM (*Pointer-Language Equivalence Theorem*). Let P and Q be programs that have isomorphic hpdgs, H_P and H_Q. If P terminates successfully on σ, then (1) Q terminates successfully on σ, (2) P and Q compute equivalent sequences of values at corresponding program points, and (3) $P(\sigma) \approx_{\mathcal{H}} Q(\sigma)$.

PROOF. Let *ident* be the set of identifiers named in P but not defined in σ. Let n be the number of accessible cells in σ. Let k be an upper bound on the number of cells that $P{:}\sigma$ allocates; such a bound must exist because P terminates. Let $\sigma_* = reduceStore_k(\sigma)$ and $P_* = reducePgm_{n,k,ident}(P)$. By Lemma 1, $P_*(\sigma_*)$ succeeds, with $P(\sigma) \approx_{\mathcal{H}S} P_*(\sigma_*)$. Since $P_*(\sigma_*)$ terminates, there exist mutually independent $free_1 \cdots free_p$ and a $P'_* = reducePgm'_{n,k,ident}(P, free_1, \cdots, free_p)$ such that $P_*(\sigma_*) \approx_S P'_*(\sigma_*)$.

Let $Q'_* = reducePgm'_{n,k,ident}(Q, free_{\pi^{-1}(1)}, \cdots, free_{\pi^{-1}(p)})$, where $\pi(j)$ denotes that program point in H_Q that corresponds under the isomorphism to point j in H_P. If programs P'_* and Q'_* have isomorphic *spdgs*, then it follows from the Dynamic Equivalence Theorem that P'_* and Q'_* are equivalent programs.

Let $spdg(P'_*)$ denote that *spdg* for program P'_* that depicts only those data dependences in $induced(P'_*, H_P)$ (*cf.* the proof of Lemma 2). Similarly, let $spdg(Q'_*)$ denote that *spdg* for Q'_* that depicts only those dependences in $induced(Q'_*, H_Q)$. A two-part argument can now be used to show that $spdg(Q'_*)$ and $spdg(P'_*)$ are isomorphic. It must first be shown that (1) P_* and Q_* have isomorphic sets of program points. This claim, however, follows immediately from the choice of the $free_{\pi(j)}$. It must then be shown that (2) $spdg(P'_*)$ and $spdg(Q'_*)$ have isomorphic edge sets. The proof of assertion (2) can be divided into two cases. If p_* and q_* are two points in $spdg(P'_*)$ that correspond to a single point in P, then the reduction ensures that edges between p_* and q_* in $spdg(P'_*)$ are isomorphic to edges between $\pi(p_*)$ and $\pi(q_*)$ in $spdg(Q'_*)$. Otherwise, p_* and q_* correspond to distinct points in P. Then Lemma 2 and the reduction ensure that edges between p_* and q_* are isomorphic to edges between $\pi(p_*)$ and $\pi(q_*)$. Graph $spdg(Q'_*)$ is therefore isomorphic to $spdg(P'_*)$.

Since P'_* and Q'_* have isomorphic *spdgs*, the Dynamic Equivalence Theorem now implies that $Q'_*(\sigma_*)$ terminates successfully, with $P'_*(\sigma_*) = Q'_*(\sigma_*)$. In particular, computation $Q'_*:\sigma_*$ does not overflow, since $P'_*(\sigma_*)$ and $Q'_*(\sigma_*)$ compute the same $NFREE_i$.

Let $Q_* = reducePgm_{n,k,ident}(Q)$. By Lemma 2, the mutual independence of the $free_i$, and the observation that $Q'_*(\sigma_*)$ terminates successfully, $Q_*(\sigma_*)$ must also succeed, with $Q'_*(\sigma_*) \approx_S Q_*(\sigma_*)$. Since $Q_*(\sigma_*)$ succeeds, Lemma 1 now implies that $Q_*(\sigma_*) \approx_{S\mathcal{H}} Q(\sigma)$.

To summarize the preceding argument, $P(\sigma) \approx_{\mathcal{H}S} P_*(\sigma_*) \approx_S P'_*(\sigma_*) = Q'_*(\sigma_*) \approx_S Q_*(\sigma_*) \approx_{S\mathcal{H}} Q(\sigma)$. The definitions of these relations now imply that $P(\sigma) \approx_{\mathcal{H}} Q(\sigma)$. An extension of this argument shows that P and Q generate equivalent values at corresponding program points. □

COROLLARY. If $\sigma \approx_{\mathcal{H}} \sigma'$, then (1) Q halts on σ', (2) P and Q compute corresponding sequences of values at corresponding program points, and (3) $P(\sigma) \approx_{\mathcal{H}} Q(\sigma')$.

PROOF. Since language $\mathcal{H}$ is referentially transparent, $P(\sigma) \approx_{\mathcal{H}} P(\sigma')$. The corollary now follows from the main theorem and the transitivity of $\approx_{\mathcal{H}}$. □

THEOREM (*Pointer-Language Slicing Theorem*). Let Q be a slice of a program P with respect to a set of vertices. Let σ and σ' be stores that agree on the values of all store-access expressions named by Q's initial-definition vertices. If P halts on σ, then (1) Q halts on σ', (2) P and Q compute equivalent values on each program point of Q, and (3) P and Q agree on the values of all store-access expressions named in Q's final-definition vertices.

PROOF. This claim follows from the Dynamic Slicing Theorem and the assertion that the reduction based on *reducePgm′* maps dependences in a program to comparable dependences in a reduced program. □

5. Discussion

This report presents what we believe are the first proofs of the Equivalence and Slicing Theorems, relative to a language with heap allocation and pointer variables. These proofs can be extended to an expanded language that supports other structures and referentially-transparent operators and predicates. The limitations imposed by the lack of multiple initial-definition and final-use vertices can be overcome by adding input and output statements to $\mathcal{H}$, using the techniques outlined in [22].

The idea that a program's semantics can be represented by its data dependences was proposed by Kuck *et. al.* in [14]. The various kinds of dependence graphs that have been proposed since [14]—such as *pdgs* [7, 11, 18, 22], *system dependence graphs* (*sdgs*) [13], *program representation graphs* (*prgs*) [12], *program dependence webs* [2], and *dependence flow graphs* [19]—represent different extensions of [14]. None of the these representations were intended for languages with heaps.

Horwitz, Reps, and Prins were the first to investigate whether dependence graphs provide an adequate representation of a program's semantics [9]. Horwitz *et. al.* proved that programs with isomorphic *pdgs* computed identical final stores, relative to a structured language with scalar variables. Reps and Yang strengthed this result by showing that terminating programs with isomorphic *pdgs* computed identical sequences of values at corresponding program points [21]. A second proof of the Equivalence Theorem that develops a graph-rewriting semantics for *pdgs* was given by Selke [22].

Reps and Yang were the first to investigate the semantics of program slicing. In [21], Reps and Yang showed that *pdgs* provide an adequate characterization of a program's slices, relative to a structured language with scalar variables. A second proof of the Slicing Theorem has been given by Selke [23].

Other reports on the semantics of dependence-graph representations include [24], which gives a calculus for *pdgs*; [20], which gives a semantics for *prgs*; [19], which gives a semantics for *dependence-flow graphs*; and [3], which proves an equivalence theorem for *sdgs*—a *pdg*-like representation for languages with procedures. Binkley *et. al.*'s proof of the *sdg* Equivalence Theorem, which reduces two programs with isomorphic *sdgs* to two programs with isomorphic scalar *pdgs*, inspired the approach used here.

The Dynamic Equivalence and Slicing Theorems are believed to be the first soundness theorems for dependence-based program representations that use a dynamic notion of data dependence.

Horwitz *et. al.* were the first to give, and prove the correctness of, an algorithm for computing a program's dependences for an $\mathcal{H}$-like language [10]. Larus was the first to describe how dependences can be used to find parallelism in Lisp-like programs [16]. Bodin and Guarna have also given dependence-computation algorithms for programs with heaps and pointers [4, 8]. None of these reports, however, show that dependence-based representations for programs are sound.

The theorems demonstrated in this report do not guarantee the soundness of many common dependence-based program transformations, such as loop unrolling and parallel evaluation (*cf.* [16]). Such concerns, though important, are beyond the scope of this paper. The report also fails to consider whether the classic kinds of dependences that are represented in *pdgs* adequately portray how "real" programs manipulate storage. The theorems presented in Section 4 make claims about how programs evaluate when their freelists contain arbitrarily many cons cells. It can be argued that this assumption is not a crucial limitation, so long as a program's heap is large enough to support any of its feasible evaluation orders: the freelist may be viewed as a list of virtual cons cells, and a garbage-collector as an oracle that maps virtual cells onto free locations. This use of an oracle, however, begs the question of whether a statement that allocates cells should be regarded as being dependent on statements that deallocate cells. A more serious problem with the failure to account for storage limitations is that a naive, but apparently safe, rearrangement of a program's execution order may cause that program to overflow its heap.

Acknowledgements

Thanks are extended to Tom Reps, Tom Ball, David Binkley, and G. Ramalingam for providing valuable critiques of this report. Thanks are also extended to David Chase, whose observations about how transformations affect storage consumption inspired the observations about heap overflow [5].

References

1. Allen, J.R., "Dependence Analysis for Subscripted Variables and its Application to Program Transformations," Ph.D. dissertation, Dept. of Math. Sciences, Rice Univ., Houston, TX (April 1983).

2. Ballance, R.A., Maccabe, A.B., and Ottenstein, K.J., "The Program Dependence Web: A Representation Supporting Control-, Data-, and Demand-Driven Interpretation of Imperative Languages," *Proceedings of the ACM SIGPLAN 90 Conference on Programming Language Design and Implementation,* (White Plains, NY, June 20-22, 1990), *ACM SIGPLAN Notices* **25**(6) pp. 257-271 (June 1990).

3. Binkley, D., Horwitz, S., and Reps, T., "The Multi-Procedure Equivalence Theorem," TR-890, Computer Sciences Department, University of Wisconsin, Madison, WI (November 1989).

4. Bodin, F., "Preliminary Report: Data Structure Analysis in C Programs," *Proceedings of the Workshop on Parallelism in the Presence of Pointers and Dynamically-allocated Objects* (Leesburg, Virginia, March 1990), *Technical Note SRC-TN-90-292,* pp. 4.3.1-4.3.34 Supercomputing Research Center/Institute for Defense Analysis, (1990).

5. Chase, D.R., "Safety Considerations for Storage Allocation Optimization," *Proceedings of the ACM SIGPLAN 88 Conference on Programming Language Design and Implementation,* (Atlanta, GA, June 22-24, 1988), *ACM SIGPLAN Notices* **23**(7) pp. 1-10 (July 1988).

6. Choi, J., "Parallel Program Debugging with Flowback Analysis," Ph.D. dissertation and TR-871, Computer Sciences Department, University of Wisconsin, Madison, WI (August 1989).

7. Ferrante, J., Ottenstein, K., and Warren, J., "The Program Dependence Graph and Its Use in Optimization," *ACM Transactions on Programming Languages and Systems* **9**(3) pp. 319-349 (July 1987).

8. Guarna Jr., V.A., "Dependence Analysis for C Programs Containing Pointers and Dynamic Data Structures," *Proceedings of the Workshop on Parallelism in the Presence of Pointers and Dynamically-allocated Objects* (Leesburg, Virginia, March 1990), *Technical Note SRC-TN-90-292*, pp. 5.15.1-5.15.25 Supercomputing Research Center/Institute for Defense Analysis, (1990).

9. Horwitz, S., Prins, J., and Reps, T., "On the Adequacy of Program Dependence Graphs for Representing Programs," pp. 146-157 in *Conference Record of the Fifteenth ACM Symposium on Principles of Programming Languages,* (San Diego, CA, January 13-15, 1988), ACM, New York, NY (1988).

10. Horwitz, S., Pfeiffer, P., and Reps, T., "Dependence Analysis for Pointer Variables," *Proceedings of the ACM SIGPLAN 89 Conference on Programming Language Design and Implementation,* (Portland, OR, June 21-23, 1989), *ACM SIGPLAN Notices* **24**(7) pp. 28-40 (July 1989).

11. Horwitz, S., Prins, J., and Reps, T., "Integrating Non-interfering Versions of Programs," *ACM Transactions on Programming Languages and Systems* **11**(3) pp. 345-387 (July 1989).

12. Horwitz, S., "Identifying the Semantic and Textual Differences Between Two Versions of a Program," *Proceedings of the ACM SIGPLAN 90 Conference on Programming Language Design and Implementation,* (White Plains, NY, June 20-22, 1990), *ACM SIGPLAN Notices* **25**(6)(July 1990).

13. Horwitz, S., Reps, T., and Binkley, D., "Interprocedural Slicing Using Dependence Graphs," *ACM Transactions on Programming Languages and Systems* **12**(1) pp. 26-60 (January 1990).

14. Kuck, D.J., Muraoka, Y., and Chen, S.C., "On the number of operations simultaneously executable in FORTRAN-like programs and their resulting speed-up," *IEEE Trans. on Computers* **C-21**(12) pp. 1293-1310 (December 1972).

15. Kuck, D.J., Kuhn, R.H., Leasure, B., Padua, D.A., and Wolfe, M., "Dependence Graphs and Compiler Optimizations," pp. 207-218 in *Conference Record of the Eighth ACM Symposium on Principles of Programming Languages,* (Williamsburg, VA, January 26-28, 1981), ACM, New York, NY (1981).

16. Larus, J.R., "Restructuring Symbolic Programs for Concurrent Execution on Multiprocessors," Ph.D. dissertation and Tech. Rep. UCB/CSD 89/502, Computer Science Division, Dept. of Elec. Eng. and Comp. Sci., Univ. of California – Berkeley, Berkeley, CA (May 1989).

17. Manna, Z., *Mathematical Theory of Computation,* McGraw-Hill, New York, NY (1974).

18. Ottenstein, K.J. and Ottenstein, L.M., "The Program Dependence Graph in a Software Development Environment," *Proceedings of the ACM SIGSOFT/SIGPLAN Software Engineering Symposium on Practical Software Development Environments,* (Pittsburgh, PA, Apr. 23-25, 1984), *ACM SIGPLAN Notices* **19**(5) pp. 177-184 (May 1984).

19. Pingali, K., Beck, M., Johnson, R., Moudgill, M., and Stodghill, P., "Dependence Flow Graphs: An Algebraic Approach to Program Dependencies," pp. 67-78 in *Conference Record of the Eighteenth ACM Symposium on Principles of Programming Languages,* (Orlando, FL, January 21-23, 1991), ACM, New York, NY (1991).

20. Ramalingam, G. and Reps, T., "Semantics of program representation graphs," TR-900, Computer Sciences Department, University of Wisconsin, Madison, WI (December 1989).

21. Reps, T. and Yang, W., "The Semantics of Program Slicing and Program Integration," *Proceedings of the International Joint Conference on Theory and Practice of Software Development (Colloquium on Current Issues in Programming Languages),* (Barcelona, Spain, March 13-17, 1989), *Lecture Notes in Computer Science* **352** pp. 360-374 Springer-Verlag, (1989).

22. Selke, R.P., "A Rewriting Semantics for Program Dependence Graphs," pp. 12-24 in *Conference Record of the Sixteenth ACM Symposium on Principles of Programming Languages,* (Austin, TX, Jan. 11-13, 1989), ACM, New York, NY (1989).

23. Selke, R.P., "Program Dependence Graphs: A Formal Treatment," Technical Report TR90-130, Dept. of Computer Science, Rice Univ., Houston, TX (1990).

24. Selke, R.P., "Transforming Program Dependence Graphs," Technical Report TR90-131, Dept. of Computer Science, Rice Univ., Houston, TX (August 1990).

From Programming-by-Example to Proving-by-Example

Masami Hagiya
RIMS, Kyoto University
Kyoto 606-01, JAPAN
hagiya@kurims.kyoto-u.ac.jp

Abstract

In the machine learning community, it is widely recognized that there are two fundamentally different approaches to learning: *inductive learning* and *deductive learning.* This paper formalizes both of the approaches to learning under a uniform framework of type theory and investigates the use of higher-order unification to solve learning problems in both.

I first introduce the simply typed λ-calculus with inductive definitions and give a unification procedure for the calculus. I then formalize a problem of *programming-by-example* (i.e., inductive learning) as a system of equations in the calculus and reformulate existing methods for programming-by-example as restricted versions of the unification procedure.

It is a new attempt to formalize a problem of *proving-by-example* (i.e., deductive learning) as an equation in a typed λ-calculus. For that purpose, I extend **LF** with inductive definitions and consider a unification procedure for it.

1 Introduction

1.1 Inductive Learning and Deductive Learning

In the machine learning community, it is widely recognized that there are two fundamentally different approaches to learning: *inductive learning* and *deductive learning* [6]. For understanding the difference between the two approaches, consider a situation in which a mother is trying to teach her child the concept of *a cup* (more precisely, *a coffee cup*). The approach of inductive learning is easy to understand in this situation. In inductive learning, in order to teach what is a cup to her child, the mother simply shows examples and counter-examples of cups to the child (Figure 1). He then inductively learns what is a cup by finding the similarities among the examples that are not

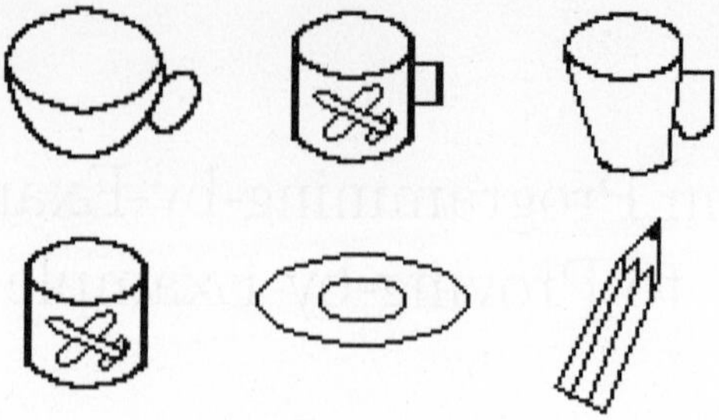

Figure 1: Examples and counter-examples of cups

Figure 2: An example of a cup

seen in the counter-examples. In this sense, inductive learning is also called *similarity-based learning.* Since examples and counter-examples are both given, examples are called *positive examples* and counter-examples *negative examples.*

The approach of deductive learning is rather hard to understand. This approach usually involves a single positive example. To teach what is a cup, the mother first prepares an example of a cup and shows it to her child (Figure 2). She then actually pours coffee into the cup and sips coffee to show the functionality of a cup. This is considered as the *original* definition of a cup:

A cup is something with which one can drink coffee.

She then explains why it is really a cup; she says that it is a cup because it has a round open top so that one can pour coffee into it and because it has a small rectangular handle so that one can pick it up to sip coffee from it. She also says that it is white, it has a picture of an airplane on it, it is made of plastic, etc. This explanation is only about the very cup shown to the child, but he can generalize the explanation and obtain the general concept of a cup. In this process, he must extract from the explanation the sufficient condition for the shown cup to be a cup. For example, he must ignore the shape of the handle, the color of the cup, the picture of an airplane, etc. He finally obtains the following *alternative* definition of a cup:

If something has an open top and a handle, then it is a cup.

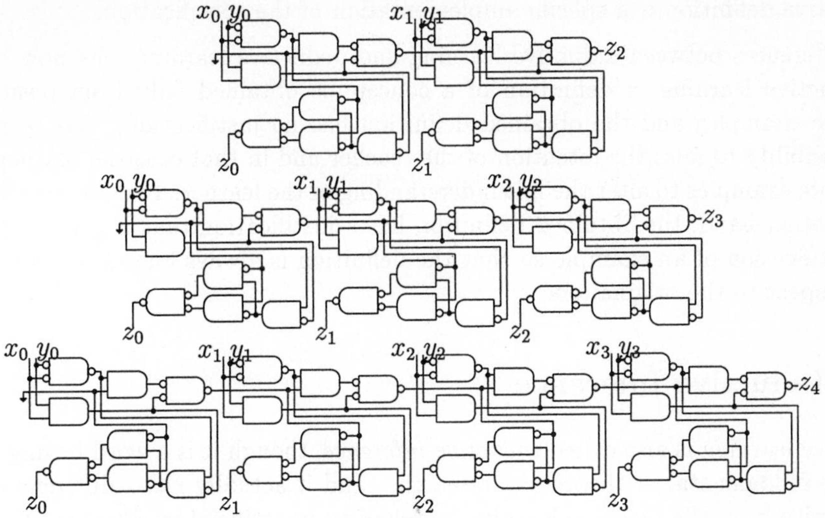

Figure 3: Adders

Because of the use of explanations, deductive learning is also called *explanation-based learning.*

In the machine learning community, there has been a long controversy on what is learned in deductive learning. It is now recognized that deductive learning is a method to learn through an example and an explanation an alternative definition of a concept that is more *efficient* than the original definition of the concept and that can be *deduced* from the original one under a certain deductive system. A definition is considered efficient if its condition is easy to check or justify. For example, the obtained alternative definition of a cup is only about physical properties of a cup and is therefore easier to check than the original one. In this sense, deductive learning is also called *performance learning.*

As another situation for understanding the difference between inductive learning and deductive learning, consider an intelligent CAD system trying to learn the concept of an adder circuit. Adders of two, three and four digits are listed in Figure 3. In inductive learning, the system generalizes these circuits to an n-digit adder for arbitrary n. This is similar to obtaining a definition of Fibonacci numbers from their initial segment: $0, 1, 1, 2, 3, 5, 8$.

In deductive learning, on the other hand, the CAD system is given a single adder, say a 3-digit adder, and a justification of why the circuit is really a 3-digit adder, i.e., $x_2x_1x_0 + y_2y_1y_0 = z_3z_2z_1z_0$. In computer science terminology, the justification is called a correctness proof of the circuit with respect to a specification of an adder. The system then generalizes the given circuit and its correctness proof at the same time, and obtains an n-digit adder with a correctness proof. In this situation, the original definition of the concept of an adder is a specification of an adder, and the obtained alternative definition is a specific implementation of the specification.

The differences between inductive learning and deductive learning may now be clear. In inductive learning, a definition of a concept is obtained only from positive and negative examples and the obtained definition has no justification. The learner has the possibility to miss the intention of the teacher and in that case the teacher should give more examples to alter the misunderstanding of the learner. In deductive learning, on the other hand, the obtained definition has a justification that is generalized from the justification of an example so that the definition is always guaranteed to be valid with respect to the original one.

1.2 Inductive Inference

Inductive learning is also called *inductive inference,* though it is a word having a flavor of more fundamental or theoretical researches and it actually has a different research community from the machine learning community in artificial intelligence [1].

Methods for inductive inference can be divided into two classes according to what to infer: inductive inference of predicates and inductive inference of functions. The former is also called *model inference* because a set of predicates determines a model in the usual sense.

In this paper, I only consider inductive inference of functions. Since predicates are regarded as functions with return values `true` and `false`, methods for inferring functions can also be used for inferring predicates. However, inductive inference of predicates differs in many respects from inductive inference of functions and therefore has been studied using different frameworks.

In function inference, a function is inferred from examples of inputs and corresponding outputs. Since what is actually inferred is not a function itself but is a function definition written in some programming language, function inference is also called *programming-by-example.* Methods for function inference, of course, vary according to what kind of programming language to use. Below are some of the methods to define functions:

- a procedural language like Pascal or C,
- a functional language like the functional subset of Lisp or Scheme,
- a term rewriting system, and
- a typed or untyped λ-calculus.

In the very early stage of programming-by-example, some works were done that tried to infer function definitions written in procedural languages. However, since procedural languages are not suitable for theoretical investigations, most works in programming-by-example have been done using functional languages, particularly, the functional subset of Lisp.

Early works of programming-by-example in Lisp were done by Summers, Kodratoff, Biremann, etc. For example, using the method of Summers [17], from the input-output pairs

```
      ()  →  ()
    (A B)  →  (A)
(A B C D)  →  (A C),
```

one can obtain the following Lisp program.

```
(defun f (x)
  (if (null x)
      nil
      (cons (car x) (f (cdr (cdr x))))))
```

Using the method extended by Kodratoff [13], from the input-output pairs

```
     ()  →  ()
    (A)  →  (A)
  (A B)  →  (B A)
(A B C)  →  (C B A),
```

one can obtain the following Lisp program.

```
(defun app nd (x y)
  (if (nul  x)
      y
      (cons (car x) (append (cdr x) y))))
(defun reverse (x)
  (if (null x)
      nil
      (append (reverse (cdr x)) (cons (car x) nil))))
```

In this paper, I take the most natural and fundamental approach to programming-by-example. Given n pairs of inputs x_i and corresponding outputs y_i, i.e,

$$\langle x_1, y_1 \rangle,\ \langle x_2, y_2 \rangle,\ \cdots,\ \langle x_n, y_n \rangle,$$

a problem of programming-by-example is to find function f such that

$$\begin{cases} f(x_1) &= y_1 \\ f(x_2) &= y_2 \\ \quad\vdots & \\ f(x_n) &= y_n. \end{cases}$$

This is nothing but a system of simultaneous equations with unknown f. Since f denotes a function, it is a system of *functional equations.* Therefore, if there exsits a method to solve functional equations as above, the problem of function inference is also solved.

Among the methods for defining functions, λ-calculi are the most fundamental and theoretical. In λ-calculi, one can also introduce data types, define higher-order functions, etc. In this paper, I use the simply typed λ-calculus with inductive definitions as a language for defining functions. It is a natural extension of Gödel's **T**, the calculus of primitive recursive functionals.

Unification, in its broadest sense, is nothing but a method to solve equations. For example, first-order unification used in resolution theorem proving or logic programming is a method to solve equations consisting of first-order unknowns and constructors. (In logic programming, unknowns are also called *free variables, substitutible variables,* etc. In this paper, I consistently use the word *unknown* to avoid confusion.) Recently, in *constraint logic programming,* solvers for various kinds of equation, including a solver for linear equations, have been built into the unifier of Prolog. This is one of the indications that the difference between unification and equation solving is becoming more and more vague.

Higher-order unification is a method to solve equations that contain unknowns denoting functions in typed λ-calculi [11, 16]. Therefore, it is very natural to use higher-order unification to solve problems of programming-by-example. One of the purposes of this paper is to investigate the possibility of using higher-order unification to infer functions from examples.

1.3 Explanation-Based Generalization

Explanation-based generalization (*EBG* for short) is a formalization of deductive learning [6]. It formalizes deductive learning as a process consisting of the following steps:

- A set of facts and a set of inference rules are first given. The set of inference rules is usually called the *domain knowledge.* It contains the original definition of the concept whose alternative definition is to be learned.
- An instance of the concept is given as a goal. This is the example used in deductive learning.
- The goal is proved under the set of facts and the set of inference rules by a human or a prover. The constructed proof is called the *explanation* of the goal.
- The goal and the explanation are generalized. This leads to an alternative definition of the concept.

One of the most widely used examples for explaining the process of EBG is that of *John's suicide.* In this example, the set of facts and the set of inference rules are given as Prolog clauses. Facts:

```
depressed(john).
buy(john,gun1).
gun(gun1).
```

Inference rules:

```
hate(X,X) :- depressed(X).
kill(X,Y) :- hate(X,Y), possess(X,Z), weapon(Z).
possess(X,Z) :- buy(X,Z).
weapon(Z) :- gun(Z).
```

Notice that the set of inference rules defines the concept `kill`, whose alternative definition is to be learned.

As an instance of the concept, the goal

```
?- kill(john,john).
```

is given. One can then construct the following explanation of `kill(john,john)` by simply proving it under Prolog.

```
 depressed(john)        buy(john,gun1)        gun(gun1)
-----------------     ------------------     -----------
 hate(john,john)      possess(john,gun1)     weapon(gun1)
------------------------------------------------------------
                     kill(john,john)
```

The explanation is then generalized by replacing constants with variables.

```
 depressed(X)        buy(X,Z)       gun(Z)
--------------     ------------    ---------
  hate(X,X)        possess(X,Z)    weapon(Z)
-------------------------------------------
                kill(X,X)
```

By collecting the leaves of this generalized explanation, one can obtain the following clause for `kill`.

```
kill(X,X) :- depressed(X), buy(X,Z), gun(Z).
```

This is the result of EBG. Notice that the clause is a deductive consequence of the domain knowledge and gives one of the sufficient conditions for `kill` to hold.

As is pointed out in [18], a process of EBG is nothing but a process of *partial evaluation.* The above clause can also be obtained by partially evaluating the general goal `kill(X,Y)` using the well established method for partial evaluation in logic programming. Efficiency is the objective of both partial evaluation and performance learning. Proving `kill(john,john)` with the new clause is obviously faster than proving it under the original definition of `kill`.

However, the most important difference between deductive learning and partial evaluation is that in deductive learning, the process of partial evaluation is guided by an example. In general, there are a number of possibilities to partially evaluate the given general goal. Giving an instance of the goal can reduce the number of possibilities and guide the process of partial evaluation.

1.4 Generalizing Number

In deductive learning of the concept of an adder circuit, the 3-digit adder given as an example has a recurrent structure that is iterated for each digit, and accordingly its correctness proof also has a recurrent structure. In order to generalize the 3-digit adder and its correctness proof to obtain an n-digit adder with a correctness proof, one must discover a recurrent structure in both of the circuit and its correctness proof. Moreover, the n-digit adder must be defined recursively and its correctness proof must be a proof by mathematical induction.

In general, replacing constants with variables is not enough for generalizing a proof. It is often necessary to discover a recurrent structure of a proof and construct an inductive proof from the discovered structure. In the machine learning community, this problem was first studied by Shavlik [15] and is called the problem of *generalizing number* or *generalization to n,* because a concrete number, say 3, is generalized to a variable, say n, while an inductive proof is being constructed.

Generalizing a given proof to obtain an inductive proof has close relationship with inferring a recursive function from examples in that a recurrent structure in examples must be correctly analyzed. Using the notion of *Curry-Howard isomorphism,* deductive learning can also be formalized as a problem of solving a function equation. Let $P(n)$ be a predicate on natural number n and let p_3 be a proof of $P(3)$. The objective of deductive learning is to obtain a proof f of the universal formula $\forall n P(n)$. In Curry-Howard isomophism, a proof of $\forall n P(n)$ is regarded as a function that returns a proof of $P(n)$ given a natural number n as an input. The type of such a function is denoted by a Π-type $\Pi n{:}\mathbf{N}.P(n)$, which mathematically means the indexed product

$$\prod_{n \in \mathbf{N}} P(n),$$

where $\mathbf{N}$ denotes the type of natural numbers. Since a function of type $\Pi n{:}\mathbf{N}.P(n)$ produces a proof of $P(n)$, when applied to n, the application of the unknown function f to the argument 3 must be equal to the proof p_3, i.e.,

$$f(3) \; = \; p_3.$$

This is the only equation that f must satisfy. Therefore, if there exsits a method to solve an equation as above, the problem of deductive learning is also solved.

In this paper, a problem of obtaining a proof of a universal formula from a proof of an example (by solving an equation as above) is called *proving-by-example.*

For the problem of generalizing an adder and a correctness proof, $P(n)$ is defined as the existential formula $\exists a Q(n,a)$, where $Q(n,a)$ means that a is an n-digit adder. In Curry-Howard isomorphism, a proof of $\exists a Q(n,a)$ is considered as a pair of a and a proof of $Q(n,a)$. Therefore, if a_3 is a 3-digit adder and q_3 is a proof of $Q(3,a_3)$, the following equation must be solved.

$$f(3) = \langle a_3, q_3 \rangle$$

Since f is a proof of $\forall n \exists a Q(n,a)$, it is a function that returns a pair of an n-digit adder and a correctness proof given a natural number n as an input.

Outline of the Rest of the Paper

In Section 2, I first introduce the simply typed λ-calculus with inductive definitions and give a unification procedure for the calculus. I then formalize a problem of programming-by-example as a system of equations in the calculus and reformulate existing methods for programming-by-example as restricted versions of the unification procedure. In order to synthesize programs with a general recursion schema, I introduce the notion of a generator of unknowns.

Section 3 is devoted to proving-by-example. It is a new attempt to formalize a problem of proving-by-example as an equation in a typed λ-calculus. For that purpose, I extend **LF** with inductive definitions and consider a unification procedure for it. In order to represent various kinds of induction schema, generators of unknowns are also used in proving-by-example.

In Section 4, I list remaining issues in programming-by-example and proving-by-example, and suggest some research directions in the future.

I assume that the reader has fundamental knowledge on typed λ-calculi, though I try to give basic definitions and enough explanations on key concepts to make the paper self-contained. In particular, a brief introduction on higher-order unification is given. On the other hand, I assume no knowledge on machine learning or inductive inference.

2 Programming-by-Example

2.1 Simply Typed λ-calculus with Inductive Definitions

I use, in this paper, the simply typed λ-calculus with inductive definitions as a framework for defining functions. Refer to [9] for more detailed treatments of the calculus. It is a subsystem of many existing calculi, such as that in [3].

A type in this calculus is either an atomic type or a function type of the form $A \to B$, where A and B are arbitrary types. The operator $\to$ associates to the right as usual. An atomic type is either *inductive* or *non-inductive.* An inductive atomic type is defined by an *inductive definition,* which is a finite set of *production rules* of the form

$$\frac{A_1 \quad \cdots \quad A_n \quad B_1 \quad \cdots \quad B_r}{\alpha}\, c,$$

where α is the inductive type being defined and c is the *constructor* of this production rule. A_j and B_k are the types of the arguments of c. A_j must be a type consisting of only non-inductive types and already defined inductive types. B_k contains α besides those types. As a consequence, mutually inductive types are not permitted here. The first n arguments of c are called *non-recursive* while the last r arguments *recursive.* An inductive type is called *recursive* if its inductive definition has a constructor with at least one recursive argument, and *non-recursive* otherwise. I use letters α, β, etc. for atomic types and letters A, B, etc. for types.

Inductive definitions are usually classified according to how α occurs in B_k; e.g, strictly positive, positive, monotone, etc. For simplicity in this paper, I assume that B_k is of the form $C_{k1} \to \cdots \to C_{kq_k} \to \alpha$ and α does not occur in $C_{k1}, \cdots, C_{kq_k}$; i.e., inductive definitions are supposed to be strictly positive. (In fact, $q_k = 0$ in all the examples in this paper.)

Examples of inductive definitions:

$$\left\{\frac{}{\texttt{Bool}}\,\texttt{true},\quad \frac{}{\texttt{Bool}}\,\texttt{false}\right\}$$

$$\left\{\frac{}{\mathbf{N}}\,0,\quad \frac{\mathbf{N}}{\mathbf{N}}\,\mathbf{S}\right\}$$

$$\left\{\frac{}{\mathbf{L}}\,\texttt{nil},\quad \frac{\mathbf{N} \quad \mathbf{L}}{\mathbf{L}}\,\texttt{cons}\right\}$$

`Bool` is a non-recursive type and has two constructors `true` and `false`, both of which take no arguments. $\mathbf{N}$ is the type of natural numbers. It is a recursive type and has two constructors 0 and $\mathbf{S}$, from which numerals of the form $\mathbf{S}(\cdots(\mathbf{S}0)\cdots)$ are constructed. $\mathbf{L}$ is the type of lists of natural numbers and has two constructors `nil` and `cons`. `cons` takes one non-recursive argument of type $\mathbf{N}$ and one recursive argument of type $\mathbf{L}$.

A term in this calculus is one of

- a variable x,
- an abstraction $\lambda x{:}A.M$,
- an application MN,
- a *constructor term* of the form $cM_1 \cdots M_{n+r}$, or
- an elimination term, which I will explain below.

The application associates to the left as usual. Terms are denoted by letters M, N, etc. and variables by letters x, y, etc.

If M is a term of type $\mathbf{N}$, an *elimination term* beginning with M is of the form

$$e(M;\ 0..N_1,\ \mathbf{S}y.z.N_2),$$

where $0..N_1$ and $\mathbf{S}y.z.N_2$ are called the *branches* of this elimination term. The first branch $0..N_1$ is also written $0.N_1$. Variables y and z in the second branch $\mathbf{S}y.z.N_2$ are considered to be bound in N_2. The elimination term means an application of the following primitive recursive function f to the argument M.

$$\begin{cases} f0 & = & N_1 \\ f(\mathbf{S}y) & = & N_2[fy/z] \end{cases}$$

$N_2[fy/z]$ denotes the result of substituting fy for z in N_2. According to this meaning of the elimination term, the calculus has the following reduction rules.

$$\begin{array}{rcl} e(0;\ 0.N_1,\ \mathbf{S}y.z.N_2) & \triangleright & N_1 \\ e(\mathbf{S}M;\ 0.N_1,\ \mathbf{S}y.z.N_2) & \triangleright & N_2[M/y,\ e(M;\ 0.N_1,\ \mathbf{S}y.z.N_2)/z] \end{array}$$

$N_2[M/y,\ e(M;\ 0.N_1,\ \mathbf{S}y.z.N_2)/z]$ denotes the result of substituting M for y and $e(M;\ 0.N_1,\ \mathbf{S}y.z.N_2)$ for z in N_2. In Gödel's $\mathbf{T}$, $e(M;\ 0.N_1,\ \mathbf{S}y.z.N_2)$ is written $\mathbf{R}N_1(\lambda y.\lambda z.N_2)M$ using the recursion operator $\mathbf{R}$ of $\mathbf{T}$.

In general, if M is of inductive type α and the inductive definition of α consists of m production rules, an elimination term $e(M;\ \cdots)$ also has m branches, and its i-th branch is of the form

$$cx_1 \cdots x_n y_1 \cdots y_r.z_1 \cdots z_r.N,$$

where the i-th constructor of α has n non-recursive arguments and r recursive arguments. x_j and y_k denote arguments of c and z_k denotes the result of a recursive call on y_k. The formal definition of reduction rules for elimination terms is given in Appendix B.

A *typing context* is a sequence of expressions, each of which is of the form $x{:}A$, and is used as an environment of variables and their types. Typing contexts are denoted by letters Γ, Δ, etc. $\Gamma \vdash M \in A$ means that the type of the term M is A under the typing context Γ. The typing rules of the calculus are given in Appendix A. Notice that the unicity of the type of a term holds if each inductive type has at least one constructor.

Besides the reduction rules for elimination terms, the calculus has the usual β and η rules. (The α rule is implicit.) The β rule is of the form

$$(\lambda x{:}A.M)N \ \triangleright\ M[N/x].$$

The η rule is used in the opposite direction and is of the form

$$M \ \triangleright\ \lambda x{:}A.Mx,$$

where M is of type $A \to B$ and x is a new variable. This rule is usually called η *expansion.* In order to avoid an infinite reduction sequence

$$M \rhd \lambda x{:}A.Mx \rhd \lambda x{:}A.(\lambda x{:}A.Mx)x \rhd \lambda x{:}A.(\lambda x{:}A.(\lambda x{:}A.Mx)x)x \rhd \cdots,$$

the left hand side of $M \rhd \lambda x{:}A.Mx$ should not be applied to an argument and should not begin with λ.

It is assumed that if $M \rhd M'$ holds then $N[M] \rhd N[M']$ also holds, provided that $N[\,]$ is a context satisfying the condition for the η expansion rule. The reflexive and transitive closure of $\rhd$ is denoted by $\rhd^*$. The reflexive, transitive and symmetric closure of $\rhd$ is denoted by $=$. Syntactical identity between terms is denoted by $\equiv$.

The calculus has the usual properties of typed λ-calculi: Church-Rosser property, strong normalizability, subject reducibility, etc.

2.2 Higher-Order Unification

Methods for solving equations are classified into two kinds: those by *propagation* and those by *generating and testing.* Propagation is a process in which values of unknowns are successively obtained from known values and values of already solved unknowns. Solving homogeneous linear equations by elimination is a typical example of propagation. A method by generating and testing consists of a procedure for generating candidates of a solution and a procedure for testing if a generated candidate is really a solution. Naïve ways for solving puzzles such as eight queens' puzzle are usually of this kind.

In general, propagation is more efficient than generating and testing because known information is directly used to construct a solution. In this sense, propagation is called *constructive.* On the other hand, it is easy to guarantee the completeness of a method by generating and testing, because it is enough to check if the procedure for generating a candidate eventually *enumerates* all the possible candidates.

The procedure for higher-order unification has both of the features; it has a constructive operation as well as an enumerative one. The former is called *imitation* and the latter *projection* [11, 16].

Projection (in the broader sense) is the most fundamental operation in higher-order unification because it is this operation that enumerates all the terms of a given type and guarantees the completeness of the higher-order unification procedure. The other operation, i.e., imitation, can be considered as a variant of projection that works more efficiently in some cases by directly using known information. (In this paper, I use the word projection in two ways. Projection in the narrower sense means projection in Huet's original definition. Projection in the broader sense means both projection in the narrower sense and imitation.)

Projection is based on the so-called long normal forms. A *long normal form* in the simply typed λ-calculus *without* inductive definitions is a term of the form

$$\lambda x_1{:}A_1.\cdots.\lambda x_m{:}A_m.aM_1\cdots M_n,$$

where a is a variable of type $B_1 \to \cdots \to B_n \to \alpha$ and M_j is a long normal form of type B_j. Every term of type $A_1 \to \cdots \to A_m \to \alpha$ can be reduced into this form. Recall that η expansion is used instead of η reduction. Given an unknown of type $A_1 \to \cdots \to A_m \to \alpha$, it is only necessary to generate a term of the above form as a value of the unknown because terms that are equal under reduction rules are considered to represent the same solution.

Let f be an unknown of type $A_1 \to \cdots \to A_m \to \alpha$, and let Γ be a typing context. Consider a problem of substituting for f a term whose type is the same as that of f and whose free variables are all from Γ. Since only long normal forms are taken into account, a term of the following form is substituted for f.

$$\lambda x_1{:}A_1.\cdots.\lambda x_m{:}A_m.af_1\cdots f_n$$

a is a variable arbitrarily chosen from Γ or from among x_i. f_j is a newly created unknown of type B_j. Free variables of a term that is substituted for f_j should be from the context $\Gamma, x_1{:}A_1, \cdots, x_m{:}A_m$.

Instead of recording a different typing context for each unknown, one can explicitly add parameters to newly created unknowns. In this formulation, the typing context Γ is fixed, and a term of the following form is substituted for f.

$$\lambda x_1{:}A_1.\cdots.\lambda x_m{:}A_m.a(f_1\bar{x})\cdots(f_n\bar{x})$$

a is an arbitrarily chosen variable as before. $\bar{x}$ denotes the sequence of variables $x_1\cdots x_m$. f_j is a newly created unknown of type $A_1 \to \cdots \to A_m \to B_j$. Free variables of a term substituted for f_j should also be from Γ. In this paper, I call this operation *projection* (in the broader sense). (The above term is called a *partial binding* in [16].)

Pre-unification, formulated by Huet, is a practical procedure for higher-order unification in the simply-typed λ-calculus [11]. It consists of the following operations on a system of equations:

- imitation
- projection (in the narrower sense)
- decomposition (*or* simplification).

In pre-unification, long normal forms are classified into two kinds: flexible terms and rigid terms. A long normal form

$$\lambda x_1{:}A_1.\cdots.\lambda x_m{:}A_m.aM_1\cdots M_n,$$

is called *flexible* if a is an unknown, and is called *rigid* if a is a constant or a bound variable, where variables in Γ are regarded as *constants*.

Pre-unification first selects an equation from the given system of equations, and reduces both sides into long normal forms.

$$\lambda w_1{:}C_1.\cdots.\lambda w_q{:}C_q.bM_1\cdots M_m \;=\; \lambda w_1{:}C_1.\cdots.\lambda w_q{:}C_q.cN_1\cdots N_n$$

Notice that bound variables are renamed so that both sides have the same bound variables $w_1,\cdots,w_q$.

If both sides of the equation are rigid and $b \equiv c$ (and $n = m$), *decomposition* is applied and the equation is decomposed into the following equations.

$$\begin{aligned}\lambda w_1{:}C_1.\cdots.\lambda w_q{:}C_q.M_1 &= \lambda w_1{:}C_1.\cdots.\lambda w_q{:}C_q.N_1\\ &\vdots\\ \lambda w_1{:}C_1.\cdots.\lambda w_q{:}C_q.M_m &= \lambda w_1{:}C_1.\cdots.\lambda w_q{:}C_q.N_m\end{aligned}$$

If the left hand side of the equation is flexible and the right hand side is rigid, i.e., $b \equiv f$ and f is an unknown of type $A_1 \to \cdots \to A_m \to \alpha$, then the following term is substituted for f.

$$\lambda x_1{:}A_1.\cdots.\lambda x_m{:}A_m.a(f_1\bar{x})\cdots(f_n\bar{x})$$

This operation is called *projection* (in the narrower sense) if a is chosen from among x_i, i.e., a is a bound variable, and is called *imitation* if a is chosen from Γ, i.e., a is a constant. Imitation, however, is allowed only when c is a constant and $a \equiv c$. This restriction makes imitation a constructive operation because a solution is directly constructed using information in the equation.

If both sides are flexible, the equation is not processed further. In pre-unification, equations between flexible terms are not solved but are left as constraints because they generally have an infinite number of solutions. This is one of the reasons that make pre-unification practical.

This ends the explanation of pre-unification. It may now be clear that projection (in the broader sense) plays the central role in the unification procedure.

If there are inductive definitions, the notion of a long normal form should also be extended. If c is a constructor of inductive type α with $n+r$ arguments, then a term of the form

$$\lambda x_1{:}A_1.\cdots.\lambda x_m{:}A_m.cM_1\cdots M_{n+r}$$

is also a long normal form of type $A_1 \to \cdots \to A_m \to \alpha$, where M_j is a long normal form of an appropriate type. Projection corresponding to this long normal form is a substitution of the following term.

$$\lambda x_1{:}A_1.\cdots.\lambda x_m{:}A_m.c(f_1\bar{x})\cdots(f_{n+r}\bar{x})$$

I call this operation *c-projection* here. In the pre-unification procedure for the calculus with inductive definitions, the use of c-projection is restricted to those equations whose left hand side is flexible and whose right hand side is of the form

$$\lambda x_1{:}A_1.\cdots.\lambda x_m{:}A_m.cM_1\cdots M_{n+r}.$$

Under this restriction, c-projection is called *c-imitation.*

Moreover, since the calculus has elimination terms, if $\lambda x_1{:}A_1.\cdots.\lambda x_m{:}A_m.M$ is a long normal form, then a term of the form

$$\lambda x_1{:}A_1.\cdots.\lambda x_m{:}A_m.e(M;\ \cdots)N_1\cdots N_n$$

is also a long normal form. In general,

$$\lambda x_1{:}A_1.\cdots.\lambda x_m{:}A_m.\mathcal{C}[aM_1\cdots M_n]$$

is a long normal form, where a is a variable and $\mathcal{C}[\,]$ is a context defined as follows.

$$\mathcal{C}[\,]\ ::=\ [\,]\ \mid\ \mathcal{C}[\,]M\ \mid\ e(\mathcal{C}[\,];\ \cdots,\ c\bar{x}'\bar{y}'.\bar{z}'.N,\ \cdots)$$

Projection corresponding to this long normal form is a substitution of the following term.

$$\lambda x_1{:}A_1.\cdots.\lambda x_m{:}A_m.\mathcal{F}_{\bar{x}}[a(f_1\bar{x})\cdots(f_n\bar{x})]$$

$\mathcal{F}_{\bar{x}}[\,]$ is a context defined as follows.

$$\mathcal{F}_{\bar{x}}[\,]\ ::=\ [\,]\ \mid\ \mathcal{F}_{\bar{x}}[\,](f\bar{x})\ \mid\ e(\mathcal{F}_{\bar{x}}[\,];\ \cdots,\ c\bar{x}'\bar{y}'.\bar{z}'.(f'\bar{x}\bar{x}'\bar{y}'\bar{z}'),\ \cdots)$$

I call this operation *e-projection* if $\mathcal{F}_{\bar{x}}[\,]$ is not the identity context $[\,]$. In case $\mathcal{F}_{\bar{x}}[\,]$ is $[\,]$, it is called *simple projection* (in the broader sense). Since $\mathcal{F}_{\bar{x}}[\,]$ should be chosen from among an infinite number of possibilities, e-projection is hopelessly nondeterministic and it is almost impossible to naïvely implement the unification procedure.

2.3 Synthesis of Primitive Recursive Functions

As is explained in Introduction, a problem of inferring a function from examples of inputs and corresponding outputs is a problem of solving a system of equations with an unknown denoting a function. Under the calculus of this paper, a problem of inferring an m-ary function from examples is formalized as a system of equations of the form

$$\begin{cases} fM_{11}\cdots M_{1m} & = & N_1 \\ \vdots & & \\ fM_{n1}\cdots M_{nm} & = & N_n, \end{cases}$$

where f is an unknown of type $A_1 \to \cdots \to A_m \to B$, and M_{ij} is an input of type A_j and N_i is an output of type B.

In general, a problem of inferring a recursive function from examples consists of the following two subproblems:

- the subproblem of selecting an appropriate recursion schema, and
- the subproblem of appropriately instantiating the selected schema.

Within the framework of this paper, the former corresponds to the e-projection operation while the latter corresponds to other kinds of projection operation, i.e., c-projection and simple projection.

As a sample problem of programming-by-example, consider that of inferring a binary function f of type $\mathbf{L} \to \mathbf{L} \to \mathbf{L}$ by simultaneously solving the following equations.

$$\begin{cases} f\,\texttt{[]}\,\texttt{[4,5]} &= \texttt{[4,5]} \\ f\,\texttt{[3]}\,\texttt{[4,5]} &= \texttt{[3,4,5]} \\ f\,\texttt{[2,3]}\,\texttt{[4,5]} &= \texttt{[2,3,4,5]} \\ f\,\texttt{[1,2,3]}\,\texttt{[4,5]} &= \texttt{[1,2,3,4,5]} \end{cases}$$

The type of the unknown f is $\mathbf{L} \to \mathbf{L} \to \mathbf{L}$. The ML-like notation is used to write a list of natural numbers; e.g., [1, 2, 3] is an abbreviation of cons 1 (cons 2 (cons 3 nil)). I also use the notation x::y for cons x y.

Since the inputs for the first argument of f are given in the increasing order of the number of elements in a list, it is natural to use, as a recursion schema, the usual list recursion with respect to the first argument of f. This is exactly the simplest form of e-projection on f, in which the following term is substituted for f.

$$\lambda x_1{:}\mathbf{L}.\lambda x_2{:}\mathbf{L}.e(x_1;\ \texttt{[]}.f_1 x_1 x_2,\ x_1'{::}y_1'.z_1'.f_2 x_1 x_2 x_1' y_1' z_1')$$

f_1 and f_2 are newly created unknowns. The type of f_1 is $\mathbf{L} \to \mathbf{L} \to \mathbf{L}$ and the type of f_2 is $\mathbf{L} \to \mathbf{L} \to \mathbf{N} \to \mathbf{L} \to \mathbf{L} \to \mathbf{L}$.

If the further use of e-projection is disallowed, the problem of finding the values of f_1 and f_2 becomes decidable. In fact, one can obtain the following solution.

$$\begin{aligned} f_1 &= \lambda x_1{:}\mathbf{L}.\lambda x_2{:}\mathbf{L}.\texttt{[]} \\ f_2 &= \lambda x_1{:}\mathbf{L}.\lambda x_2{:}\mathbf{L}.\lambda x_1'{:}\mathbf{N}.\lambda y_1'{:}\mathbf{L}.\lambda z_1'{:}\mathbf{L}.x_1'{::}z_1' \end{aligned}$$

This is due to the fact corresponding to the well known theorem that second-order matching problems in the simply typed λ-calculus are decidable because their search space by pre-unification is finite [12].

In the following, I will extend the theorem to the calculus of this paper and discuss its application in programming-by-example. I first make the following definition.

Definition 1 A system of equations is called a *matching problem* if unknowns occur only in one side of each equation.

The order ord(A) of type A is defined as follows.

$$\begin{aligned} \mathrm{ord}(\alpha) &= 1 \\ \mathrm{ord}(A \to B) &= \max(\mathrm{ord}(A)+1,\ \mathrm{ord}(B)) \end{aligned}$$

The order of a variable (or a constant) is defined as the order of its type. The order of a constructor, introduced by a production rule

$$\frac{A_1 \quad \cdots \quad A_n \quad B_1 \quad \cdots \quad B_r}{\alpha}\, c,$$

is defined as

$$\max(\mathrm{ord}(A_1),\ \cdots,\ \mathrm{ord}(A_n),\ \mathrm{ord}(B_1),\ \cdots,\ \mathrm{ord}(B_r)) + 1.$$

This corresponds to regarding the constructor as a function of type $A_1 \to \cdots \to A_n \to B_1 \to \cdots \to B_r \to \alpha$. For example, the order of 0 and `nil` is one. The order of **S** and `cons` is two. The order of f, f_1 and f_2 in the above problem of programming-by-example is also two. Below is the definition for a system of equations to be second-order.

Definition 2 A system of equations is called *second-order* if constants, constructors and unknowns appearing in its equations are all of order at most two.

(One may allow constants and constructors to be of order at most three.)

I finally define the notion of stability.

Definition 3 An elimination term $e(M;\ \cdots)$ is called *unstable* if M begins with an unknown, i.e., M is of the form $fM_1 \cdots M_n$ for some unknown f. A system of equations is called *stable* if both sides of each equation do not contain unstable elimination terms after they are reduced into long normal forms.

For example, the original system of equations in the above problem is stable. The system of equations after the substitution for f is also stable.

The *pre-unification procedure without e-projection* consists of the following operations:

- imitation
- c-imitation
- simple projection (in the narrower sense)
- decomposition.

Imitation, c-imitation and simple projection are allowed only on an equation between flexible and rigid terms. Decomposition is allowed on an equation between rigid terms. A rigid term is defined as a long normal form of the form

$$\lambda x_1{:}A_1.\cdots.\lambda x_m{:}A_m.\mathcal{C}[aM_1 \cdots M_n],$$

where a is a constant or a bound variable, or a term of the form

$$\lambda x_1{:}A_1.\cdots.\lambda x_m{:}A_m.cM_1 \cdots M_{n+r},$$

where c is a constructor. Imitation and decomposition are extended to cope with this definition of rigid terms. Flexible terms are defined as before.

I can now state the following theorem.

Theorem 1 *If a second-order matching problem is stable, its search space by pre-unification without e-projection is finite.*

The proof is similar to that for the calculus without inductive definitions. It is obvious that beginning with a matching problem, the pre-unification procedure does not encounter an equation between flexible terms. Therefore, for a stable second-order matching problem, the procedure without e-projection either terminates with a finite set of solutions or finitely fails.

Ignoring the efficiency of higher-order unification, the above theorem solves the second subproblem of programming-by-example, i.e., that of appropriately instantiating a recursion schema by examples. The remaining problem is how to find an appropriate recursion schema that preserves the order and stability.

Let f be an unknown of type $\alpha_1 \to \cdots \to \alpha_m \to \alpha$. Consider the substitution of the following term for f.

$$\lambda x_1{:}\alpha_1.\cdots.\lambda x_m{:}\alpha_m.e(x_i;\ \cdots,\ c\bar{x}'\bar{y}'.\bar{z}'.f'\bar{x}\bar{x}'\bar{y}'\bar{z}',\ \cdots)(f_1\bar{x})\cdots(f_n\bar{x})$$

In this term, constructors and newly created unknowns are supposed to be of order at most two. (One may allow constructors to be of order at most three.)

Assume that in a system of equations between long normal forms, the arguments of f contain no unknowns. Then the system of equations obtained by the above substitution is stable and second-order if the original one is stable and second-order. Moreover, the arguments of the newly created unknowns also contain no unknowns.

Most of the schemata used in programming-by-example fall into the above form. For example, the simplest schema for list recursion is a substitution of the following term for an unknown.

$$\lambda x_1{:}\alpha_1.\cdots.\lambda x_m{:}\alpha_m.e(x_i;\ \texttt{[]}.f_1\bar{x},\ x_1'{::}y_1'.z_1'.f_2\bar{x}x_1'y_1'z_1')$$

x_i is supposed to be of type $\mathbf{L}$. Functions such as `append`, `length`, etc. can be synthesized with this schema.

The `reverse` function, which uses an auxiliary function with an additional accumulator parameter, can be synthesized using the following schema.

$$\lambda x_1{:}\mathbf{L}.e(x_1;\ \texttt{[]}.f_1x_1,\ x_1'{::}y_1'.z_1'.f_2x_1x_1'y_1'z_1')(f_3x_1)$$

In fact, for the equations

$$\begin{cases} f\,\texttt{[]} &= \texttt{[]} \\ f\,\texttt{[1]} &= \texttt{[1]} \\ f\,\texttt{[1,2]} &= \texttt{[2,1]} \\ f\,\texttt{[1,2,3]} &= \texttt{[3,2,1]}, \end{cases}$$

one can obtain the following solution.

$$\begin{aligned} f_1 &= \lambda x_1{:}\mathbf{L}.\lambda w{:}\mathbf{L}.w \\ f_2 &= \lambda x_1{:}\mathbf{L}.\lambda x_1'{:}\mathbf{N}.\lambda y_1'{:}\mathbf{L}.\lambda z_1'{:}\mathbf{L} \to \mathbf{L}.\lambda w{:}\mathbf{L}.z_1'(x_1'{::}w) \\ f_3 &= \lambda x_1{:}\mathbf{L}.\texttt{[]} \end{aligned}$$

In this schema, the elimination term denotes a function of type $\mathbf{L} \to \mathbf{L}$, which corresponds to the auxiliary function with an additional parameter. In [17], this function is synthesized by the method called *generalization.* In general, introduction of auxiliary functions by generalization corresponds to using recursion schemata of the above form.

The naïve `reverse` function can be synthesized by first using the schema

$$\lambda x_1{:}\mathbf{L}.e(x_1;\ \texttt{[]}.f_1 x_1,\ x_1'{::}y_1'.z_1'.f_2 x_1 x_1' y_1' z_1')$$

and then using the same kind of schema on f_2 to synthesize the `append` function. In [13], Kodratoff proposes to use higher-order derivatives for synthesizing auxiliary functions. This corresponds to successively applying recursion schemata of the above form. In [14], Ling discusses the *constructive* use of the schemata to synthesize auxiliary functions. In general, auxiliary functions synthesized during inductive inference are called *theoretical terms.*

2.4 Synthesis with Library Functions

Synthesizing a function using existing library functions can also be formalized as a variant of the projection operation; i.e., a substitution of a term

$$\lambda x_1{:}\alpha_1.\cdots.\lambda x_m{:}\alpha_m.g(f_1\bar{x})\cdots(f_n\bar{x})$$

for an unknown can introduce a library function denoted by g (see [8]). However, this substitution does not preserve stability in general.

Another approach to use library functions is to rewrite before unification each output in terms of the corresponding input and library functions (and constructors). Consider, for example, the equations

$$\begin{cases} f\,\texttt{[]} &= \texttt{[]} \\ f\,\texttt{[1,2]} &= \texttt{[1]} \\ f\,\texttt{[1,2,3,4]} &= \texttt{[1,3]} \end{cases}$$

and assume that `hd` (head) and `tl` (tail) are in the library. One can then rewrite the equations as follows.

$$\begin{cases} f x_1 &= \texttt{[]} \\ f x_2 &= \texttt{[hd } x_2\texttt{]} \\ f x_3 &= \texttt{[hd } x_3\texttt{, hd (tl (tl } x_3\texttt{))]} \end{cases}$$

x_1, x_2 and x_3 denote the inputs. Selectors are typical library functions in programming-by-example [17, 13], and the result of rewriting is usually called a *computational trace.*

After rewriting outputs, one can solve the equations by unification, regarding library functions as constants. In general, however, there are an infinite number of possibilities to rewrite outputs using library functions, and one must enumerate those possibilities in some manner.

In proving-by-example, the type structure of a proof can be used for appropriately rewriting the outputs. See Section 3.5.

The above example is continued to the next section.

2.5 General Recursion and Generators of Unknowns

General recursion schemata such as

$$fx = \textbf{if } px \textbf{ then } bx \textbf{ else } ax(f(dx))$$

cannot be directly formulated within the framework of this paper. One approach to synthesize the function f defined by the above schema is to assume the existence of the function that returns the number of recursion steps of f for the input x. In order to formalize the idea, I first introduce the recursion operator $\mathbf{R}$, which is defined by an elimination term as follows.

$$\mathbf{R}nxdab \equiv e(n;\ 0.\lambda x{:}D.bx,\ \mathbf{S}y.z.\lambda x{:}D.ax(z(dx)))x$$

The arguments of $\mathbf{R}$ have the following types.

$$\begin{aligned} n &\in \mathbf{N} \\ x &\in D \\ d &\in D \to D \\ a &\in D \to R \to R \\ b &\in D \to R \end{aligned}$$

D denotes the domain and R denotes the range of f. $\mathbf{R}$ satisfies the following reduction rules.

$$\begin{aligned} \mathbf{R}0xdab &\rhd^* bx \\ \mathbf{R}(\mathbf{S}n)xdab &\rhd^* ax(\mathbf{R}n(dx)dab) \end{aligned}$$

Let s be a function of type $D \to \mathbf{N}$. If sx denotes the number of recursion steps of f for x, f can be defined as follows.

$$f = \lambda x{:}D.\mathbf{R}(sx)xdab$$

The functions d, a and b are unknowns whose values must be obtained by unification from examples. The function s is also an unknown, but instead of trying to obtain the value of s by unification, I treat it as a generator of unknowns.

A *generator of unknowns* is a function variable that generates a new unknown for each sequence of arguments. When a generator g of unknowns appears in a long normal form

$$\lambda x_1{:}A_m.\cdots.\lambda x_m{:}A_m.C[gM_1\cdots M_n],$$

the term $gM_1\cdots M_n$ is replaced with the term $f'\bar{x}$, where f' is a newly created unknown corresponding to the arguments $M_1,\cdots,M_n$. In an actual implementation, the arguments $M_1,\cdots,M_n$ are required to contain no unknowns.

Generators of unknowns are objects outside the calculus of this paper. In some cases, however, by tracing the values of the unknowns that replaced an application of a generator, one can reconstruct the value of the generator as a term of the calculus.

After the substitution of $\lambda x{:}D.\mathbf{R}(sx)xdab$ for f, an equation of the form $fM = N$ becomes

$$\mathbf{R}nMdab = N,$$

where n is a new unknown of type $\mathbf{N}$ corresponding to the argument M of the generator s. For example, the equations in the previous section become

$$\left\{\begin{array}{rcl} \mathbf{R}n_1x_1dab & = & \texttt{[]} \\ \mathbf{R}n_2x_2dab & = & \texttt{[hd } x_2\texttt{]} \\ \mathbf{R}n_3x_3dab & = & \texttt{[hd } x_3\texttt{, hd (tl (tl } x_3\texttt{))]}, \end{array}\right.$$

where n_1, n_2 and n_3 are unknowns corresponding to sx_1, sx_2 and sx_3.

By solving equations of the form $\mathbf{R}nMdab = N$, one can obtain the values of d, a and b. Notice that equations of this form are not stable because n is an unknown. Therefore, one must extend the pre-unification procedure by allowing c-projection on n. This means that the following terms are successively substituted for n.

$$0,\ \mathbf{S}n',\ \mathbf{S}0,\ \mathbf{S}(\mathbf{S}n''),\ \cdots$$

$n', n'', \cdots$ are new unknowns of type $\mathbf{N}$. The search space of pre-unification is therefore infinite in general. But for equations of the above form, it is possible to set an upper bound on the value of n.

For the above equations, one can obtain the following solution.

$$\begin{array}{rcl} d & = & \lambda x{:}\mathbf{L}.\texttt{tl (tl } x\texttt{)} \\ a & = & \lambda x{:}\mathbf{L}.\lambda y{:}\mathbf{L}.x{::}y \\ b & = & \lambda x{:}\mathbf{L}.\texttt{[]} \end{array}$$

Moreover, one also obtains

$$\begin{array}{rcl} sx_1 & = & 0 \\ sx_2 & = & \mathbf{S}0 \\ sx_3 & = & \mathbf{S}(\mathbf{S}0) \end{array}$$

as the values of the generator s.

The value of p in the schema cannot be obtained by unification. In some cases, it can be inferred from the values of s. For the above equations, one can infer

$$p = \lambda x{:}\mathbf{L}.\texttt{null } x.$$

3 Proving-by-Example

3.1 LF

A typed λ-calculus that has the so-called dependent types can be used as a framework for defining formal systems of logic by Curry-Howard isomorphism. Recently,

Barendregt introduced the notion of a λ-*cube,* in which typed λ-calculi are classified according to three dimensions [2]. The simplest calculus in the λ-cube that has dependent types is the calculus called λ**P** or **LF**, which stands for *Logical Framework*. **LF** was originally formulated by Harper et al. and was actually used to represent various kinds of logic, including first-order predicate calculus, Peano arithmetic, modal logic, etc. [10].

The difference between the simply typed λ-calculus and **LF** is that in **LF**, a type may contain terms of already defined types. For example, having defined the type **N** of natural numbers, one can introduce the type `Narray` n of an array of n natural numbers. `Narray` n is called a *dependent type* because it depends on the term n. Since `Narray` is considered as a function that returns a type given a natural number as an input, the type of `Narray` itself can be represented by the expression $\mathbf{N} \rightarrow \mathrm{Type}$, where Type denotes the type of all the types. I write `Narray` $\in \mathbf{N} \rightarrow \mathrm{Type}$ just as I write $n \in \mathbf{N}$ when n is of type **N**. Expressions such as Type and $\mathbf{N} \rightarrow \mathrm{Type}$ are called *kinds.*

If there are dependent types, one can consider a function whose output type depends on its inputs. For example, consider the function `zeroarray`, which is given a natural number n as an input and returns an array whose elements are all zero and whose length is n. The type of this function cannot be represented by a simple function type of the form $A \rightarrow B$ because its output type `Narray` n depends on its input n. Mathematically, the function belongs to the indexed product

$$\prod_{n \in \mathbf{N}} \mathtt{Narray}\ n,$$

and in **LF**, this type is written $\Pi n{:}\mathbf{N}.$`Narray` n and is called a Π-*type.* In general, a Π-type is of the form $\Pi x{:}A.B$, where B is a type that may depend on x. A simple function type $A \rightarrow B$ is considered as an abbreviation of $\Pi x{:}A.B$ if B does not depend on x.

In summary, a type of **LF** is either an atomic type of the form $cM_1 \cdots M_n$ or a Π-type of the form $\Pi x{:}A.B$. A term of **LF** is a term in the simply typed λ-calculus. A kind of **LF** is an expression of the form

$$\Pi x_1{:}A_1. \cdots .\Pi x_n{:}A_n.\mathrm{Type},$$

where A_i is a type possibly containing variables $x_1, \cdots x_{i-1}$. If K is a kind that does not depend on x, the kind $\Pi x{:}A.K$ can be abbreviated to $A \rightarrow K$. If c is a type function whose kind is $\Pi x_1{:}A_1. \cdots .\Pi x_n{:}A_n.\mathrm{Type}$, then $cM_1 \cdots M_n$ is an atomic type provided that M_i is a term of type $A_i[M_1/x_1,\ \cdots,\ M_{i-1}/x_{i-1}]$.

Curry-Howard isomorphism is a notion that was independently and almost simultaneously formulated by many people, including Howard, de Bruijn, etc. It is also called *formulae-as-types notion* or *proof-as-program paradigm.* In Curry-Howard isomorphism, a proposition is represented by a type, and a proof of the proposition by a term of the corresponding type. An implication $A \supset B$ is represented by a function type $A \to B$ and a universal quantification $\forall x B$ by a Π-type $\Pi x{:}A.B$, where A is the type of the variable x. Representation of a proof by a term is based on the constructive reading of propositions. $A \to B$ is considered to be true if one can construct a witness of B from a witness of A. A proof of $A \to B$ is therefore a function that returns a proof of B given a proof of A. $\Pi x{:}A.B$ is considered to be true if one can construct a witness of B for each element x of A. A proof of $\Pi x{:}A.B$ is therefore a function that returns a proof of B given an element x of type A.

I formalize in **LF** the proof of John's suicide given in Introduction. First, the following types and constants are introduced.

$$\begin{array}{rcl} \iota & \in & \text{Type} \\ \texttt{depressed, weapon, gun} & \in & \iota \to \text{Type} \\ \texttt{hate, possess, buy} & \in & \iota \to \iota \to \text{Type} \\ \texttt{John, gun}_1 & \in & \iota \end{array}$$

ι is the type of persons, weapons, etc. The unary predicates `depressed`, `weapon` and `gun` are introduced as type functions whose kind is $\iota \to$ Type. The kind of binary predicates is $\iota \to \iota \to$ Type. Facts and inference rules are introduced as constants; i.e., for each fact or inference rule A, a constant of type A is introduced, which is used as a name of the fact or inference rule. The example has the following facts and inference rules.

$$\begin{array}{lcl} \texttt{Fact}_1 & \in & \texttt{depressed John} \\ \texttt{Fact}_2 & \in & \texttt{buy John gun}_1 \\ \texttt{Fact}_3 & \in & \texttt{gun gun}_1 \\ \texttt{Rule}_1 & \in & \Pi x{:}\iota.(\texttt{depressed } x) \to (\texttt{hate } x\ x) \\ \texttt{Rule}_2 & \in & \Pi x{:}\iota.\Pi y{:}\iota.\Pi z{:}\iota. \\ & & (\texttt{hate } x\ y) \to (\texttt{possess } x\ z) \to (\texttt{weapon } z) \to (\texttt{kill } x\ y) \\ \texttt{Rule}_3 & \in & \Pi x{:}\iota.\Pi z{:}\iota.(\texttt{buy } x\ z) \to (\texttt{possess } x\ z) \\ \texttt{Rule}_4 & \in & \Pi z{:}\iota.(\texttt{gun } z) \to (\texttt{weapon } z) \end{array}$$

The proof of the proposition `kill John John` is then represented by the term

$$\begin{array}{l} \texttt{Rule}_2\ \texttt{John John gun}_1\ (\texttt{Rule}_1\ \texttt{John Fact}_1) \\ (\texttt{Rule}_3\ \texttt{John gun}_1\ \texttt{Fact}_2)\ (\texttt{Rule}_4\ \texttt{gun}_1\ \texttt{Fact}_3), \end{array}$$

whose type is `kill John John`. Let M denote the above proof.

In Introduction, the proof was generalized into a proof of the following general proposition.

$$(\texttt{depressed } x) \to (\texttt{buy } x\ z) \to (\texttt{gun } z) \to (\texttt{kill } x\ x)$$

In EBG, this proposition was also obtained during the process of EBG. In this paper, however, for a problem of proving-by-example, I assume that a generalized proposition is fixed and given in advance. Therefore, I consider the problem of obtaining a proof of the universal formula

$$\forall x \forall z\ (\texttt{depressed}\ x) \rightarrow (\texttt{buy}\ x\ z) \rightarrow (\texttt{gun}\ z) \rightarrow (\texttt{kill}\ x\ x)$$

from the given proof M of `kill John John`.

Since the universal formula is represented by the Π-type

$$\Pi x{:}\iota.\Pi z{:}\iota.(\texttt{depressed}\ x) \rightarrow (\texttt{buy}\ x\ z) \rightarrow (\texttt{gun}\ z) \rightarrow (\texttt{kill}\ x\ x),$$

I introduce an unknown f of the above Π-type and the following unknowns of the specified types.

$$\begin{aligned} X &\in \iota \\ Z &\in \iota \\ V_1 &\in \texttt{depressed}\ X \\ V_2 &\in \texttt{buy}\ X\ Z \\ V_3 &\in \texttt{gun}\ Z \end{aligned}$$

The problem of generalizing the proof M is then formalized as that of solving the following equation between proofs.

$$fXYV_1V_2V_3 = M$$

By the unification procedure between proofs, one can obtain the following solution of this equation:

$$\begin{aligned} X &= \texttt{John} \\ Z &= \texttt{gun}_1 \\ V_1 &= \texttt{Fact}_1 \\ V_2 &= \texttt{Fact}_2 \\ V_3 &= \texttt{Fact}_3 \end{aligned}$$

and

$$\begin{aligned} f = {} & \lambda x{:}\iota.\lambda z{:}\iota.\lambda v_1{:}(\texttt{depressed}\ x).\lambda v_2{:}(\texttt{buy}\ x\ z).\lambda v_3{:}(\texttt{gun}\ z). \\ & \texttt{Rule}_2\ x\ x\ z\ (\texttt{Rule}_1\ x\ v_1)\ (\texttt{Rule}_3\ x\ z\ v_2)\ (\texttt{Rule}_4\ z\ v_3). \end{aligned}$$

3.2 Higher-Order Unification between Proofs

A unification procedure for **LF**, which is an extension of Huet's pre-unification procedure, was first formulated by Elliott [4]. The essential idea of the extension is very natural and is also based on long normal forms.

A long normal form of **LF** is also a term of the form

$$\lambda x_1{:}A_1.\cdots.\lambda x_m{:}A_m.aM_1\cdots M_n.$$

Therefore, the projection operation (in the broader sense) for an unknown f is a substitution of the following term for f.

$$\lambda x_1{:}A_1.\cdots.x_m{:}A_m.a(f_1\bar{x})\cdots(f_n\bar{x})$$

a is a variable as before. In **LF**, however, the type of f and that of a may contain terms including unknowns. This makes it necessary to add a new equation for the above substitution to be well typed in **LF**.

To be more precise, let f be an unknown of type $\Pi x_1{:}A_1.\cdots.\Pi x_m{:}A_m.\alpha$ and a be a variable of type $\Pi y_1{:}B_1.\cdots.\Pi y_n{:}B_n.\beta$. Then the type of the term $\lambda x_1{:}A_1.\cdots.x_m{:}A_m.a(f_1\bar{x})\cdots(f_n\bar{x})$ is

$$\Pi x_1{:}A_1.\cdots.\Pi x_m{:}A_m.\beta[f_1\bar{x}/y_1,\ \cdots,\ f_n\bar{x}/y_n].$$

Therefore, the equation

$$\lambda x_1{:}A_1.\cdots.\lambda x_m{:}A_m.\alpha \;=\; \lambda x_1{:}A_1.\cdots.\lambda x_m{:}A_m.\beta[f_1\bar{x}/y_1,\ \cdots,\ f_n\bar{x}/y_n]$$

should be added to the system of equations. This equation contains the newly created unknowns as well as those that were originally in α and β.

The most serious consequence of the above extension is that even if the original system of equations is a matching problem, the added equation may contain unknowns in both sides. This means that while solving a matching problem in **LF**, one may have to solve a system of equations that is not a matching problem. Since it is well known that second-order unification in the simply typed λ-calculus is undecidable, a second-order matching problem in **LF** is also undecidable in general. This makes proving-by-example inherently more difficult than programming-by-example.

3.3 Induction

In order to represent inductive proofs, I extend **LF** by adding the inductive definitions of the same form as those added to the simply typed λ-calculus. The typing rule for elimination terms in this extension of **LF** is such that if M is of inductive type α, the type of an elimination term $e(M;\ \cdots)$ is in general of the form $A[M]$, where $A[w]$ denotes a type that may depend on w of type α. For example, the type of the elimination term

$$e(M;\ 0.N_1,\ \mathbf{S}y.z.N_2)$$

is $A[M]$ if M is of type $\mathbf{N}$, N_1 is of type $A[0]$ and N_2 is of type $A[\mathbf{S}y]$ provided that y is of type $\mathbf{N}$ and z is of type $A[y]$.

In **LF**, in order to gain the unicity of the type of an elimination term, one must explicitly add the type information $\Pi w{:}\alpha.A[w]$ as a suffix. For example, after $\Pi w{:}\mathbf{N}.A[w]$ is added as a suffix, the above elimination term becomes

$$e(M;\ 0.N_1,\ \mathbf{S}y.z.N_2)_{\Pi w:\mathbf{N}.A[w]}.$$

The e-projection operation can be defined as in the simply typed λ-calculus except that the type information of an elimination term must also be inferred. Let f be an unknown of type $\Pi x_1{:}A_1.\cdots\Pi x_m{:}A_m.cM_1\cdots M_n$. If x_i is of type $\mathbf{N}$ (i.e., $A_i \equiv \mathbf{N}$), the substitution of the term

$$\lambda x_1{:}A_1.\cdots.\lambda x_m{:}A_m.e(x_i;\ 0.f_1\bar{x},\ \mathbf{S}y.z.f_2\bar{x}yz)_{\Pi w:\mathbf{N}.A[w]}$$

for f is an application of e-projection, where $A[w]$ is defined as follows.

$$A[w]\ \equiv\ c(f_1'\bar{x}w)\cdots(f_n'\bar{x}w)$$

$f_1', \cdots, f_n'$ are newly created unknowns whose values must also be inferred.

As a sample problem of proving-by-example, consider that of obtaining a proof of the formula

$$\Pi x{:}\mathbf{N}.\mathsf{add}\ 0\ x\ x$$

from a proof of an example, where $\mathsf{add}\ x\ y\ z$ means $x+y=z$. The predicate add and the axioms for add are declared as follows.

$$\begin{aligned}\mathsf{add} &\in \mathbf{N}\to\mathbf{N}\to\mathbf{N}\to\mathrm{Type}\\ \mathsf{add_0} &\in \Pi x{:}\mathbf{N}.\mathsf{add}\ x\ 0\ x\\ \mathsf{add_S} &\in \Pi x{:}\mathbf{N}.\Pi y{:}\mathbf{N}.\Pi z{:}\mathbf{N}.(\mathsf{add}\ x\ y\ z)\to(\mathsf{add}\ x\ (\mathbf{S}y)\ (\mathbf{S}z))\end{aligned}$$

Then

$$\mathsf{add_S}\ 0\ 2\ 2\ (\mathsf{add_S}\ 0\ 1\ 1\ (\mathsf{add_S}\ 0\ 0\ 0\ (\mathsf{add_0}\ 0)))$$

is a proof of the formula add 0 3 3. Numerals $1, 2, 3, \cdots$ are considered as abbreviations of terms made of 0 and **S**. Let M denote the above proof, and let f be an unknown of type $\Pi x{:}\mathbf{N}.\mathsf{add}\ 0\ x\ x$. The problem is then represented by the equation

$$f3\ =\ M.$$

The substitution of the term

$$\lambda x{:}\mathbf{N}.e(x;\ 0.f_1x,\ \mathbf{S}y.z.f_2xyz)_{\Pi w:\mathbf{N}.A[w]}$$

for f is an application of e-projection, where $A[w]$ is defined as follows.

$$A[w]\ \equiv\ \mathsf{add}\ (f_3xw)\ (f_4xw)\ (f_5xw)$$

The equation

$$\lambda x{:}\mathbf{N}.\mathsf{add}\ 0\ x\ x\ =\ \lambda x{:}\mathbf{N}.\mathsf{add}\ (f_3xx)\ (f_4xx)\ (f_5xx)$$

should be added in order for the substitution to be well typed in **LF**. After solving these equations, one can obtain the following solution.

$$\begin{aligned} f_1 &= \lambda x{:}\mathbf{N}.\mathsf{add}_0\ 0 \\ f_2 &= \lambda x{:}\mathbf{N}.\lambda y{:}\mathbf{N}.\lambda z{:}(\mathsf{add}\ 0\ y\ y).\mathsf{add}_\mathsf{S}\ 0\ y\ y\ z \\ f_3 &= \lambda x{:}\mathbf{N}.\lambda w{:}\mathbf{N}.0 \\ f_4 &= \lambda x{:}\mathbf{N}.\lambda w{:}\mathbf{N}.w \\ f_5 &= \lambda x{:}\mathbf{N}.\lambda w{:}\mathbf{N}.w \end{aligned}$$

As a consequence, the following inductive proof of $\Pi x{:}\mathbf{N}.\mathsf{add}\ 0\ x\ x$ is constructed.

$$\lambda x{:}\mathbf{N}.(x;\ 0.\mathsf{add}_0,\ \mathbf{S}y.z.\mathsf{add}_\mathsf{S}\ 0\ y\ y\ z)$$

For representing various kinds of induction schema, generators of unknowns can also be used. For example, consider the following induction schema.

$$\frac{\begin{array}{c}[P_2[x]] \\ \vdots \\ A[x]\end{array} \qquad \begin{array}{c}[P_1[x]] \quad [A[dx]] \\ \vdots \\ A[x]\end{array}}{\forall x A[x]}$$

$P_2[x]$ denotes the base case; $A[x]$ must be proved from $P_2[x]$. $P_1[x]$ denotes the induction step; $A[x]$ must be proved from $P_1[x]$ and the induction hypothesis $A[dx]$. It is assumed that for each x, either $P_1[x]$ or $P_2[x]$ is true, and $P_2[d^i x]$ becomes true for some i. A proof using the above schema is represented by a term of the form

$$\lambda x{:}D.\mathbf{R}^+(sx)xp_1p_2dab,$$

where the induction operator $\mathbf{R}^+$ is defined as follows.

$$\mathbf{R}^+nxp_1p_2dab \equiv e(n;\ 0.\lambda x{:}D.b(p_2x),\ \mathbf{S}y.z.\lambda x{:}D.ax(p_1x)(z(dx)))x$$

The arguments of $\mathbf{R}$ have the following types.

$$\begin{aligned} n &\in \mathbf{N} \\ x &\in D \\ d &\in D \to D \\ p_1 &\in \Pi x{:}D.P_1[x] \\ p_2 &\in \Pi x{:}D.P_2[x] \\ a &\in \Pi x{:}D.P_1[x] \to A[dx] \to A[x] \\ b &\in \Pi x{:}D.P_2[x] \to A[x]. \end{aligned}$$

$\mathbf{R}^+$ satisfies the following reduction rules.

$$\begin{aligned} \mathbf{R}^+0xp_1p_2dab &\rhd^* bx(p_2x) \\ \mathbf{R}^+(\mathbf{S}n)xp_1p_2dab &\rhd^* ax(p_1x)(\mathbf{R}^+nxp_1p_2dab) \end{aligned}$$

In proving-by-example, the functions d, a and b in $\lambda x{:}D.\mathbf{R}^+(sx)xp_1p_2dab$ are treated as unknowns and the functions s, p_1 and p_2 are treated as generators of unknowns. Therefore, p_1x and p_2x in the above reduction rules will be replaced with new unknowns. A sample problem of proving-by-example using this schema is give in Section 3.5.

3.4 Σ-type

In order to represent an existential formula $\exists xB$ as a type, one must introduce a Σ-type

$$\Sigma x{:}A.B,$$

which is the type of the following pair.

$$\langle M, N\rangle_{\Sigma x:A.B}$$

The suffix $\Sigma x{:}A.B$ is added for the unicity of the type of the pair. In $\langle M, N\rangle$, M is of type A and N is of type $B[M/x]$; i.e., a proof of $\Sigma x{:}A.B$ is a pair of M and a proof of $B[M/x]$. π_1 and π_2 denote projections on a pair, satisfying the following reduction rules.

$$\begin{array}{rcl} \pi_1\langle M, N\rangle_{\Sigma x:A.B} & \triangleright & M \\ \pi_2\langle M, N\rangle_{\Sigma x:A.B} & \triangleright & N \end{array}$$

Besides these rules, I assume the rule of *surjective pairing*

$$M \;\triangleright\; \langle \pi_1 M, \pi_2 M\rangle_{\Sigma x:A.B},$$

provided that M itself is not a pair and neither π_1 nor π_2 is applied to M in the left hand side. This rule corresponds to the η expansion rule.

If B does not depend on x, $\Sigma x{:}A.B$ is abbreviated to $A \times B$.

The extension of **LF** by Σ-types is almost straight-forward, and the unification procedure is also easy to formulate if the extension has surjective pairing [5]. A sample problem of proving-by-example using Σ-types is given in the next section.

3.5 Relation with Type Checking

As a sample problem of proving-by-example using the induction operator $\mathbf{R}^+$ and Σ-types, consider that of obtaining an indictive proof of the GCD theorem from a proof of an example.

Let `mod` denote a function of type $\mathbf{N} \to \mathbf{N} \to \mathbf{N}$ that computes the remainder of the first argument divided by the second. `mod` can be defined as a primitive recursive function. Let `iszero` and `isnonzero` denote functions of type $\mathbf{N} \to$ `Bool` that check if their argument is zero or nonzero. They are also defined as primitive recursive functions. The following constants are also declared.

$$\begin{array}{rcl}
|\cdot| & \in & \texttt{Bool} \to \text{Type} \\
\texttt{True} & \in & |\texttt{true}| \\
\texttt{gcd} & \in & \mathbf{N} \to \mathbf{N} \to \mathbf{N} \to \text{Type} \\
\texttt{Lemma}_1 & \in & \Pi x{:}\mathbf{N}.\Pi y{:}\mathbf{N}.|\texttt{iszero}\ x| \to (\texttt{gcd}\ x\ y\ y) \\
\texttt{Lemma}_2 & \in & \Pi x{:}\mathbf{N}.\Pi y{:}\mathbf{N}.\Pi z{:}\mathbf{N}. \\
& & |\texttt{isnonzero}\ x| \to (\texttt{gcd}\ (\texttt{mod}\ y\ x)\ x\ z) \to (\texttt{gcd}\ x\ y\ z)
\end{array}$$

If M is of type $\texttt{Bool}$, $|M|$ denotes the proposition that M is true. $\texttt{gcd}\ x\ y\ z$ means that z is the GCD of x and y.

Let $\texttt{hasgcd}\ x$ be an abbreviation of the type $\Sigma y{:}\mathbf{N}.\texttt{gcd}\ (\pi_1 x)\ (\pi_2 x)\ y$; i.e.,

$$\texttt{hasgcd}\ M \ \equiv\ \Sigma y{:}\mathbf{N}.\texttt{gcd}\ (\pi_1 M)\ (\pi_2 M)\ y$$

for an arbitrary term M of type $\mathbf{N} \times \mathbf{N}$.

Let M denote the following proof of $\texttt{gcd}\ 4\ 6\ 2$.

$$\texttt{Lemma}_2\ 4\ 6\ 2\ \texttt{True}\ (\texttt{Lemma}_2\ 2\ 4\ 2\ \texttt{True}\ (\texttt{Lemma}_1\ 0\ 2\ \texttt{True}))$$

Then $\langle 2, M\rangle$ is a proof of $\texttt{hasgcd}\ \langle 4,6\rangle$. (Suffixes of pairs are omitted here.) Let f be an unknown of type $\Pi x{:}(\mathbf{N} \times \mathbf{N}).\texttt{hasgcd}\ x$. The problem of generalizing M is then formulated by the equation

$$f\langle 4,6\rangle \ =\ \langle 2, M\rangle.$$

In order to use the induction operator $\mathbf{R}^+$ for solving the above equation, I substitute the following term for f.

$$\lambda x{:}(\mathbf{N} \times \mathbf{N}).\mathbf{R}^+(sx)xp_1p_2dab$$

The types of the unknowns are declared as follows.

$$\begin{array}{rcl}
s & \in & \mathbf{N} \times \mathbf{N} \to \mathbf{N} \\
p_1 & \in & \Pi x{:}(\mathbf{N} \times \mathbf{N}).|f_1 x| \\
p_2 & \in & \Pi x{:}(\mathbf{N} \times \mathbf{N}).|f_2 x| \\
d & \in & (\mathbf{N} \times \mathbf{N}) \to (\mathbf{N} \times \mathbf{N}) \\
a & \in & \Pi x{:}(\mathbf{N} \times \mathbf{N}).|f_1 x| \to (\texttt{hasgcd}\ (dx)) \to (\texttt{hasgcd}\ x) \\
b & \in & \Pi x{:}(\mathbf{N} \times \mathbf{N}).|f_2 x| \to (\texttt{hasgcd}\ x)
\end{array}$$

f_1 and f_2 are also unknowns whose type is $\mathbf{N} \times \mathbf{N} \to \texttt{Bool}$. This means that the predicates P_1 and P_2 in the induction schema are also inferred.

For solving the equation, one must obtain the following value for d.

$$\lambda x{:}(\mathbf{N} \times \mathbf{N}).\langle(\texttt{mod}\ (\pi_2 x)\ (\pi_1 x)), (\pi_1 x)\rangle$$

Notice that this term contains the function $\texttt{mod}$. Here is a question.

How can the unification procedure find the function mod?

Since the function mod explicitly appears in the declaration of the constants, it seems that the procedure can easily find the function mod. However, it encounters equations such as the following one.

$$d\langle 4,6\rangle \;=\; \langle 2,4\rangle$$

In order to solve this equation, the procedure must appropriately rewrite $\langle 2,4\rangle$ to $\langle(\texttt{mod}\ 6\ 4),4\rangle$ before unification, or synthesize the function mod by itself. This is not an easy problem.

One solution of this problem is to use the type structure of the example proof M. During the type check of M with the typing rules of **LF**, occurrences of terms in M are related with one another. For example, the occurrence of 2 in $\langle 2,4\rangle$ is related with an occurrence of mod 6 4, which is reduced to 2 during the type check. Using this information, the above equation can be rewritten as follows.

$$d\langle 4,6\rangle \;=\; \langle(\texttt{mod}\ 6\ 4),4\rangle$$

This makes it possible to obtain the value of d by simple projection and imitation with mod as a constant. (In this problem, it is also necessary to relate the occurrences of M in the definition of hasgcd M.) The same technique can also be used in an extension of **LF** with a term rewriting system as a built-in equality [7].

The following values of the unknowns are finally obtained.

$$\begin{aligned}
f_1 &= \lambda x{:}(\mathbf{N}\times\mathbf{N}).\texttt{isnonzero}\ (\pi_1 x)\\
f_2 &= \lambda x{:}(\mathbf{N}\times\mathbf{N}).\texttt{iszero}\ (\pi_1 x)\\
d &= \lambda x{:}(\mathbf{N}\times\mathbf{N}).\langle(\texttt{mod}\ (\pi_2 x)\ (\pi_1 x)),(\pi_1 x)\rangle\\
a &= \lambda x{:}(\mathbf{N}\times\mathbf{N}).\lambda X{:}(\texttt{isnonzero}\ (\pi_1 x)).\lambda Y{:}(\texttt{hasgcd}\ (dx)).\\
&\qquad \texttt{Lemma}_2\ (\pi_1 x)\ (\pi_2 x)\ (\texttt{mod}\ (\pi_2 x)\ (\pi_1 x))\ X\ Y\\
b &= \lambda x{:}(\mathbf{N}\times\mathbf{N}).\lambda X{:}(\texttt{iszero}\ (\pi_1 x)).\texttt{Lemma}_1\ (\pi_1 x)\ (\pi_2 x)\ X
\end{aligned}$$

The values of the generators are as follows.

$$\begin{aligned}
s\langle 4,6\rangle &= 2\\
p_1\langle 4,6\rangle &= \texttt{True}\\
p_1\langle 2,4\rangle &= \texttt{True}\\
p_2\langle 0,2\rangle &= \texttt{True}
\end{aligned}$$

4 Remaining Issues and Future Directions

I first note that information on termination is usually not present in examples or in a proof of an example. For instance, the function d in the induction schema $\mathbf{R}^+$ can be obtained by unification, but it must independently proved that $P_2[d^i x]$ eventually becomes true.

In this paper, it has been argued that higher-order unification is a useful and powerful tool for instantiating a given recursion or induction schema by examples. For this purpose, it is vital to develop an efficient implementation of higher-order unification. An experimental implementation is reported in [7].

The selection of an appropriate schema can also be considered as an operation of higher-order unification, i.e., e-projection. However, the use of e-projection should be carefully guided by examples and heuristic rules in order to avoid combinatorial explosion. In this sense, the central issue of programming-by-example and proving-by-example is still to be solved.

However, having a unified framework is very important theoretically as well as practically, because new insights on the framework can be applied on both programming-by-example and proving-by-example.

Therefore, one research direction in the future is to make the framework more powerful. This corresponds to using stronger calculi than that of the paper. I list some of the possibilities below.

- adding parameters to inductive definitions
- introducing a term rewriting system as a built-in equality
- using impredicative calculi

It is also important to study other frameworks for representing proofs than typed λ-calculi because they are not always the best one. For example, equational proofs are not easily represented and manipulated in them.

Acknowledgements

I deeply thank Prof. Takayasu Ito for giving me the opportunity to present my work at TACS. I also thank Prof. Hayao Nakahara for reading the manuscript of the paper.

References

[1] Angluin, D., Smith, C. H.: Inductive inference: Theory and methods, *Computing Surveys,* Vol.15, No.3 (1983), pp.237-269.

[2] Barendregt, H.: Introduction to generalized type systems, *Theoretical Computer Science — Proceedings of the Third Italian Conference,* World Scientific, 1989, pp.1-37.

[3] Dybjer, P.: An inversion principle for Martin-Löf's type theory, *Proceedings of the Workshop on Programming Logic,* PMG-R54, Univeristy of Göteborg and Chalmers University of Technology, 1989, pp.177-188.

[4] Elliott, C. M.: Higher-order unification with dependent function types, *Rewriting Techniques and Applications* (Dershowitz, N. ed.), LNCS355 (1989), pp.121-136.

[5] Elliott, C. M.: Some extensions and applications of higher-order unification, Ph.D Thesis, School of Computer Science, Carnegie Mellon University, 1990.

[6] Ellman, T.: Explanation-based learning: A survey of programs and perspectives, *ACM Computing Surveys,* Vol.21, No.2 (1989), pp.163-221.

[7] Hagiya, M.: Programming by example and proving by example using higher-order unification, *10th International Conference on Automated Deduction,* LNAI449 (1990), pp.588-602.

[8] Hagiya, M.: Synthesis of rewrite programs by higher-order and semantic unification, *Proceedings of the First International Workshop on Algorithmic Learning Theory* (1990), pp.396-410. *Also in New Generation Computing,* Vol.8, No.4 (1991), pp.403-420.

[9] Hagiya, M.: On reduction and projection in type theory with inductive definitions, *in preparation.*

[10] Harper, R., Honsell, F., Plotkin, G.: A framework for defining logics, *Symposium on Logic in Computer Science,* 1987, pp.194-204.

[11] Huet, G. P.: A unification algorithm for typed λ-calculus, *Theoretical Computer Science,* Vol.1 (1975), pp.27-57.

[12] Huet, G., Lang, B.: Proving and applying program transformations expressed with second-order patterns, *Acta Informatica,* Vol.11 (1978), pp.31-55.

[13] Kodratoff, Y.: A class of functions synthesized from a finite number of examples and a LISP program scheme, *International Journal of Computer and Information Science,* Vol.8, Nol.7 (1979), pp.489-521.

[14] Ling, X.: Inventing theoretical terms in inductive learning of functions — search and constructive methods, *Methodologies for Intelligent Systems* (Ras, Z. W. ed.), Vol.4 (1989), pp.332-341.

[15] Shavlik, J. W., DeJong, G. F.: An explanation-based approach to generalizing number, *Proceedings of IJCAI 87,* 1987, pp.236-238.

[16] Snyder, W., Gallier, J.: Higher-order unification revisited: Complete sets of transformations, *Journal of Symbolic Computation,* Vol.8, Nos 1&2 (1989), pp.101-140.

[17] Summers, P.D.: A methodology for LISP program construction from examples, *Journal of ACM,* Vol.24, No.1 (1977), pp.161-175.

[18] Van Harmelen, F., Bundy, A.: Explanation-based generalization = partial evaluation, *Artificial Intelligence,* Vol.36 (1988), pp.401-412.

A. Typing Rules

It is assumed that the i-th production rule of inductive type α is of the form

$$\frac{A_{i1} \quad \cdots \quad A_{in_i} \quad B_{i1} \quad \cdots \quad B_{ir_i}}{\alpha} \, c_i,$$

where

$$B_{ij} \equiv C_{ik1} \to \cdots \to C_{ikq_{ik}} \to \alpha.$$

Let $\bar{M}$, $\bar{x}_i$, $\bar{y}_i$ and $\bar{z}_i$ be sequences of terms or variables as follows.

$$\begin{aligned} \bar{M} &\equiv M_1 \cdots M_{n_i+r_i} \\ \bar{x}_i &\equiv x_{i1} \cdots x_{in_i} \\ \bar{y}_i &\equiv y_{i1} \cdots y_{ir_i} \\ \bar{z}_i &\equiv z_{i1} \cdots z_{ir_i} \end{aligned}$$

$x{:}A \in \Gamma$ means that $x{:}A$ is a member of Γ. Typing rules are as follows.

$$\frac{x{:}A \in \Gamma}{\Gamma \vdash x \in A}$$

$$\frac{\Gamma, x{:}A \vdash M \in B}{\Gamma \vdash \lambda x{:}A.M \in A \to B}$$

$$\frac{\Gamma \vdash M \in A \to B \quad \Gamma \vdash N \in A}{\Gamma \vdash MN \in B}$$

$$\frac{(\forall j) \ \Gamma \vdash M_j \in A_{ij} \quad (\forall k) \ \Gamma \vdash M_{n_i+k} \in B_{ik}}{\Gamma \vdash c_i \bar{M} \in \alpha}$$

$$\frac{\Gamma \vdash M \in \alpha \quad (\forall i) \ \Gamma, \Delta_i \vdash N_i \in A}{\Gamma \vdash e(M; \ \cdots, \ c_i \bar{x}_i \bar{y}_i . \bar{z}_i . N_i, \ \cdots) \in A}$$

In the last rule,

$$\begin{aligned} \Delta_i &\equiv x_{i1}{:}A_{i1}, \cdots, x_{in_i}{:}A_{in_i}, y_{i1}{:}B_{i1}, \cdots, y_{ir_i}{:}B_{ir_i}, z_{i1}{:}D_{i1}, \cdots, z_{ir_i}{:}D_{ir_i} \\ D_{ik} &\equiv C_{ik1} \to \cdots \to C_{ikq_{ik}} \to A. \end{aligned}$$

B. Reduction Rules

A reduction rule for an elimination term is of the form

$$e(c_i \bar{M}; \ \cdots, \ c_i \bar{x}_i \bar{y}_i . \bar{z}_i . N_i, \ \cdots) \rhd N_i[M_j/x_{ij}, \ M_{n_i+k}/y_{ik}, \ L_{ik}/z_{ik}],$$

where in the right hand side, M_j is substituted for x_{ij} $(1 \le j \le n_i)$, M_{n_i+k} is substituted for y_{ik} $(1 \le k \le r_i)$ and L_{ik} is substituted for z_{ik} $(1 \le k \le r_i)$ in N_i. L_{ik} is defined as follows.

$$L_{ik} \equiv \lambda w_1{:}C_{ik1}. \cdots .\lambda w_{q_{ik}}{:}C_{ikq_{ik}}.e(M_{n_i+k} w_1 \cdots w_{q_{ik}}; \ \cdots, \ c_i \bar{x}_i . \bar{y}_i . \bar{z}_i . N_i, \ \cdots)$$

The branches of the elimination term in L_{ik} are the same as those of the original elimination term.

From LP to LP: Programming with Constraints

Jean-Louis Lassez
IBM T.J. Watson Research Center
P.O.Box 704
Yorktown Heights N.Y. 10598, U.S.A.
jll@watson.ibm.com

Abstract

Constraint methods for problem solving have a long history. Recently the problem of introducing constraints as primitive constructs in programming languages has been addressed. A main task that the designers and implementers of such languages face is to use and adapt the concepts and algorithms from the extensive studies on constraints done in areas such as Mathematical Programming, Symbolic Computation, Artificial Intelligence, Program Verification and Computational Geometry. Borrowing from these areas and synthesizing the various notions leads to an emerging conception of programming with constraints that we will describe here informally.

1 Introduction

Constraints are key elements in areas such as Operations Research, Constructive Solid Geometry, Robotics, CAD/CAM, Spreadsheets, Model-based Reasoning, Theorem Proving and Program Verification. Most of Mathematical Programming can be characterized as the problem of optimizing a function whose variables are subject to satisfy a set of arithmetic constraints. Other types of constraints are also considered: Hammer [24] [25] is at the origin of the field of pseudo Boolean programming where logical and numerical conditions are interwoven. This area is very actively pursued with the recent works of Jeroslow [36], Chandru and Hooker [11][12].

Much work has been done in AI on Constraint Satisfaction Problems based on the pionniering papers by Freuder, Macworth, Montanari and Pearl (see Davis [20] and Pearl [53] for references). The main thrust of that work is algorithmic and heuristic, trying to solve hard combinatorial problems. Languages have been designed specifically to solve constraints problems [7][59]. A somewhat orthogonal approach is now also a very active research area. Instead of designing languages to solve Constraint Satisfaction problems, constraints are used as primitive elements in the design of programming systems. Constraints handling techniques have been incorporated in a number of programming systems including CLP($\Re$), CHIP, CAL, CIL, Prolog III, BNR-Prolog, Mathematica and Trilogy.

The CLP scheme [33] provides a formal framework for reasoning with and about constraints in the rule based context of logic programming. Within this framework, one can generate a class of programming languages customized to deal with constraints over specific domains of computation. The key idea here is that the important semantic properties of Horn clauses do not depend on the Herbrand Universe or Unification. These semantic properties and their associated programming methodology hold for arithmetic constraints and solvability as well as in many other domains (strings, graphs, booleans,...) as they do for terms. Consequently even though one deals with different languages working in different domains, they all share fundamental semantic properties and form a well defined class of languages. The CLP scheme provides then a main example of the use of constraints as *the* primitive building blocks of a class of programming languages, since logic formulae can be themselves considered as constraints. The Logic Programming Paradigm has three main directions: Horn clause programming, Concurrent programming and Deductive Databases. The CLP scheme extended the first direction. In the same spirit constraints have been introduced in committed choice languages in Maher [49], and in the work of Saraswat [55], and in Database querying languages by Kanellakis, Kuper and Revesz [39]. The link between classical AI work on constraints, and Logic Programming has been described by van Hentenryck [61]. A general framework for constraint programming is proposed in [56] which integrates much of these approaches. The work on database query languages of [39] is also actively pursued and provides an important link with traditional methods of symbolic computation as well as constraints work in computational geometry. Cox, McAloon and Tretkoff [15] provide a analysis of the complexity of various CLP languages, obtained by varying the the logic (propositional, relational, functional), and the constraints (integer, rational, complex). Such work will lead to a strong link with the field of pseudo Boolean programming that we mentioned earlier.

Darlington and Guo [16] design constraint based functional languages, and it should not be long before we see constraint based object oriented languages. In fact as we will hint later, it might be a very natural approach.

Not surprisingly there are and will be many different paradigms reflecting the integration of constraints and languages. The main differences come from the aims of the language: general purpose programming language, database or knowledge based query language, or a tool for problem solving. In that last case the domain of application, operations research, graphics etc..., will heavily affect the design of the language. Will we then have a collection of adhoc theories and languages? In mathematical programming the focus is on optimization, in artificial intelligence the focus is on constraint satisfaction and constraint propagation, in program verification the focus is on solvability. These foci should be reflected in the design of the associated languages, but constraint programming should also have its own focus and theory. We will describe here one approach to this problem derived from our follow up of the CLP paradigm. Depending on how much constraints are needed one uses an LP language, or a *c*LP language, or a *Clp* language (and sometimes we even use C). But non-logical constraints (in particular numeric constraints) are, in the present stage of CLP, treated as second class citizens. Work is in progress to introduce meta level programming and other techniques in CLP($\Re$) to manipulate more naturally constraints as input and output [26][50].

Nevertheless what is needed is a treatment of specific domains of constraints in a manner as systematic as logic constraints were treated. This is the problem that we will address here. Only after will we consider the integration of the various modules. In the next section we will briefly recall the main points that make logic formulae (or logic constraints) suitable in principle for language design. In a third section we will argue that a similar situation exists for other domains of constraints such as arithmetic constraints and Boolean constraints, and stress the analogy as an important research direction (still at the level of principles). In a fourth section we see that at the design and implementation level the problems are far more difficult to solve than for logic formulae. To try to circumvent these problems one must make heavy use of results and algorithms from symbolic computation, operations research, computational geometry etc... What is needed here is efficient algorithms for carefully selected sets of constraints. As in the case of logic formulae we have to sacrifice generality to achieve acceptable efficiency. Examples from the domain of linear constraints will be provided. In a last section we will see the analogies across many domains of constraints from symbolic computation, geometry, algebra etc and give the motivations which led us to propose a calculus of constraints [48]. This calculus is a first step towards providing a general theory for the emerging paradigm we described.

2 From Logic Programming ...

One will find in Chang and Lee's book [13] a review of the early works of Black, Darlington, Slagle, Green and Raphael, Waldinger and Lee, on the use of theorem proving for the design of Deductive Question Answering Systems. A more systematic approach and a restriction to Horn clauses led to Logic Programming and its associated languages and databases. The fundamental ideas and results that make logic formulae suitable for such systems are:

A logic formula is viewed as an implicit and concise representation of its set of logical consequence. That is viewed as a database or a program possessing knowledge.

A Query $Q(x, y)$ is answered by a set of substitutions (or constraint in the case of CLP) which establish a relationship between the variables, satisfied if and only if $Q(x, y)$ is a logical consequence of the formula. In other words the query-answer system allows the extraction of all knowledge implicitly stored in the formula.

A SINGLE algorithm, Resolution, is sufficient to answer all queries.

The semantics of the system are easily described through model theory which accommodates the declarative aspects, while proof theory describes the operational aspects. The results on soundness and completeness guarantee the correctness of the system.

In the case of CLP which takes constraints as input as well as output the language used to describe input and output may be lifted to the same level as the programming language itself.

All these points are important, and will be addressed in the next section, but the key one in terms of programming paradigm is the use of resolution. Often one sees definitions of a declarative programming language which create a confusion with specification languages. (What is to be computed as opposed to How it is to be computed). A specification language does not need to be executable, or could be executable through a package of thousands of subroutines. What makes Logic Based languages declarative is resolution. Its universal power, since it can handle all computable functions, relieves (*in principle*, we will address this later) the user from much programming.

The last point also needs some emphasis. The language of Logic is very expressive. But the output of a standard logic programming language is restricted to substitutions. So we can specify very complex objects but we can get only a very restrictive and primitive output, which is most frustrating. The introduction of constraints helps alleviate this problem, as illustrated in [34].

3 ... to Lazy Programming

Now we are to argue that the properties of logic formulae just described have counterparts for other domains, in particular for those most important from a computation point of view. Certainly a candidate is real arithmetic. The reader is referred to Van Den Vries [60] for a high level exposition of Tarski's elimination theory for real closed fields.

Tarski proved the following great theorem:

Theorem 1 (Tarski) *To any formula* $\phi(X_1, X_2, \ldots, X_m)$ *in the vocabulary* $\{0, 1, +, ., =, \leq\}$ *one can effectively associate two objects: (i) a quantifier free formula* $\theta(X_1, \ldots, X_m)$ *in the same vocabulary, and (ii) a proof of the equivalence* ϕ–θ *that uses only the axioms for real closed fields.*

What it means is that we can view an arithmetic formula (multivariate polynomials, inequalities, and, or, not, disjunction, conjunction, existential and universal quantifiers) as representing the set of all its logical consequences, that is the set of all arithmetic formulae that it entails. And that in order to obtain one of these consequences, a *single* algorithm, *quantifier elimination* is sufficient, in analogy with logic formulae and resolution.

From a semantic point of view we have the same advantage as in the case of Logic since we are dealing with the very old and well understood language of Mathematics. Let us give examples of quantifier elimination. A very simple and familiar example is the equation of degree two:

$$\exists x \; ax^2 + bx + c = 0$$

We all know from high school that an equivalent formula is:

$$b^2 - 4ac \; > \; 0$$

This formula may be obtained by eliminating the existential quantifier (or equivalently eliminating the variable x) from the equation. All such consequences of arithmetic formulae can indeed be obtained by eliminating quantifiers (or variables).

A typical problem in Geometry is to find the convex hull of a given set of points. A point of coordinates $(x_1, \ldots, x_n)$ is in the convex hull of a set of m points iff there exists λ_j's such that the system

$$\{x_1 = \Sigma\alpha_1^j\lambda_j, \; \ldots, \; x_n = \Sigma\alpha_n^j\lambda_j, \; \Sigma\lambda_j = 1, \; \lambda_j \geq 0, \; j = 1, \ldots, \; m\}$$

is satisfied, where $\{(\alpha_1^j, \; \ldots, \; \alpha_n^j)\}$ are the coordinates of the points. The representation of the convex hull is an equivalent set of relations solely between the x_i's. It can be obtained by eliminating all λ_j's in the system. For example, to compute the convex hull of the set of points

$$\{(1,0,0), \; (0,1,0), \; (0,0,1)\}$$

we write

$$\{x_1 = \lambda_1, \; x_2 = \lambda_2, \; x_3 = \lambda_3, \; \lambda_1 + \lambda_2 + \lambda_3 = 1, \; \lambda_i \geq 0\}.$$

By eliminating the λ_i's we obtain $\{x_1 + x_2 + x_3 = 1, \; x_1 \geq 0, \; x_2 \geq 0, \; x_3 \geq 0\}$ which is the convex hull of the given points. An interesting byproduct is that we have a trivial proof of the classic theorem that the convex hull of a finite set of points is a polyhedral set, since Gauss-Jordan reduction and Fourier elimination do not introduce non-linearities or disjunctions. More complex examples and references will be given later.

Elimination theory was a very active area at the turn of the century, modern work on algebraic geometry was more directed towards abstraction and declarative aspects. However with the recent applications to Robotics and CAD/CAM [10] elimination theory is making a strong comeback in algebraic geometry under the influence of Abhyankar (see Kapur and Mundy's forthcoming volume[41]). What remains to be shown is that one can develop a rich querying system along the lines of the one for logic formulae. It is a major research problem. In order not to brake the flow of the high level discussion in this section, we have given in a later section an example of how this can be achieved in a particular case.

Another domain of interest is Boolean algebra. We will not elaborate on it here, just through a simple example show that it is another area where fundamental results allow for a possible systematic treatment of a querying system along lines similar to those of logic or arithmetic formulae. We refer to the book "Boolean Reasoning" [8] for further information. Our remarks on Boolean algebra come from that book. C.I Lewis in 1918 stated that "For purpose of application of the algebra to ordinary reasoning, elimination is a process more important than solution, since most processes of reasoning take place through the elimination of middle terms". Let us see what role elimination plays in Boolean algebra on a simple example: Consider an AND gate to have inputs x_1 and x_2 and output z_1. Let us connect the output of the AND gate to the input of an OR gate whose second input is labelled x_3 and whose output is labelled z_2. The system of equations: $\{z_1 = x_1.x_2,\ z_2 = x_3 + z_1\}$ defines the circuit by reflecting its structure. But if we care only about the functionality of the circuit, not its structure, we want a relationship solely between input and output variables. Boole showed us that we can achieve this simply by eliminating the other variables from the system thereby obtaining: $z_2 = x_3 + x_1.x_2$. Of course one could give far more involved examples, but our aim here was just to show that we also have for that domain an "universal" query answering algorithm.

So we see that paradigmatic aspects of reasoning or programming with logic formulae also apply to other important domains and mathematical objects. Let us review the three main points, for a given domain:

A set of constraints is viewed as an implicit representation of the set of all constraints that it entails.

There is a query system such that an answer to a query $Q(x, y)$ is a relationship that is satisfied if and only if the query is entailed by the system.

And most importantly:

There exists a SINGLE algorithm to answer all queries (an oracle).

As mentioned in the case of Resolution, it is these oracles who can answer any query about an important area that lead to really high level languages. In other words what is described here is the opposite situation to conventional programming where the primitive elements are small objects and high level is achieved bottom up by creating macros and a large collection of subroutines. Here the approach is top down where we try to have as primitive elements of the language objects that are as powerful as possible, and the number of basic algorithms is kept to a minimum. The effect is striking, a logic based language can be described rigorously and succinctly in a few words: the syntax is Horn clauses, the interpreter is SLD resolution. For standardization purposes one would need more details, but nevertheless these few words provide an accurate description. To achieve a similar description capturing the essence of ADA would require substantially more text! Since the use of these oracles is to avoid programming unless it is absolutely necessary, it seems appropriate to call "*Lazy Programming*" this approach to programming with constraints. So in Lazy Programming one queries a constraint based formulation of the problem at hand, and oracles (Resolution, various forms of quantifier elimination, etc) perform the computation.

Before we address in the next section the "real" problems where we will see how hard it is to be lazy, let us mention research directions that are important in our context.

One is to develop query systems for numeric and Boolean constraints. For reasons that will be made clearer in the next section, specialized cases should be considered. The one we present later shows that if symbolic computation is very appropriate at the specification level, in order to achieve efficiency we have to consider and synthesize results and algorithms from linear programming and computational geometry as well.

Another direction which could be explored is the relationship between the oracle algorithms, as an ad hoc collection is not what is warranted. The analogy between the intended querying systems should be reflected in the algorithms on which they are based. Clearly all elimination algorithms are conceptually at least very closely related. By looking again at Resolution, we see also a notion of elimination: at each step we eliminate the occurrence of a predicate. Two powerful algorithms which are quite relevant to constraints programming are Knuth-Bendix and Buchberger's algorithm for constructing Grobner bases. Their relationship has been studied and a synthesis established [37][38]. In [9] Buchberger studies the relationships between the two aforementioned algorithms and Resolution. Buchberger in that paper proposes to establish certain basic *algorithm types* as a natural analogue to the concept of *datatype*. Naturally the oracles we discussed would form one of these types.

A problem that we do not address here is how to integrate the various modules corresponding to different domains of constraints. The CLP scheme is certainly a candidate, giving to logic formulae a predominant role. An object oriented framework could be also be considered which could provide more flexibility.

4 Computers do not run (only) on Principles

When they do they have a tendency to blow up. The advent of Resolution in the mid sixties raised (wild) hopes that automatic reasoning systems would be immediately available. The enormous difficulties met by the first attempts at implementation led a major part of the community to reject Resolution with the same fervor as it praised it initially. We now know that in order to obtain really practical logic based systems a number of substantial compromises had to be made. A major one was to restrict the domain to Horn clauses. Further major work was also essential at the design and implementation level. For other domains of constraints we are at present in a situation similar to the situation of Resolution in the late sixties. The hopes have been raised of a revolution in applications such as Robotics, Graphics, Constructive Solid Geometry, etc But the attempts at creating really practical systems have met with enormous difficulties, far more severe than in the case of Logic formulae. In the next section we will illustrate some of the problems and describe initial attempts at circumventing them. We refer the reader to the book by Hoffman [29], papers by D. Arnon, B. Buchberger, Kapur and Mundy in [40] for applications of symbolic computation methods. Also the paper by M. Coste in [14] provides a high level introduction to quantifier elimination.

We now describe the main problems. Their severity and attempts at circumventing them in the linear case will be described in the next section.

SIZE of Output and Intermediate Swell If the main problem with resolution was speed, with quantifier elimination we have a far worse problem: the size of the output can be doubly exponential [18]. So it seems that there is really no point in going further since even if by magic we were able to obtain the output, we would be so overwhelmed than it would be useless. However one should realize that much of the complexity of the output may be due to the method of elimination. Indeed there is no canonical form for arithmetic constraints, equivalent expressions may have widely differing sizes. The elimination methods will not necessarily provide the shortest one, as there is no clear notion of simplification to guide the methods. The recent work of Renegar (see [41][54]) gives a thorough comparison of the various methods as well as very significant new bounds. Now even in the case where the output size is reasonable, we may still have intermediate computation of doubly exponential size. The two problems are of course linked as the output of a variable elimination problem may well represent an intermediate computation in a further elimination process.

Finite or Infinite Precision Another major problem discussed in [19] is infinite precision arithmetic. Consider the polynomial: P(x)= (x+1)(x+2)......(x+20) now let us change one coefficient of P(x) by adding a tiny perturbation, so tiny that it seems negligible: Q(x)= P(x)+ $2^{-23}x^{19}$. If P(x) has clearly twenty obvious real roots, Q(x) has only ten real roots and the imaginary part of the other roots is comparatively very big. Therefore we can see that round off errors can create instabilities unacceptable in a solver. One can of course resort to infinite precision arithmetic. But then the problem comes that first computations are considerably slowed down and worse the size of the representation of coefficients can grow arbitrarily, aborting the computation.

5 Reasoning with Linear constraints

Let us now illustrate these problems in the very simple case of conjunctions of linear constraints. Even though it is a "trivial" case from a quantifier elimination point of view (no non-linearity, no OR , no implication, no NOT, no universal quantification), it still is of great importance from a practical point of view (we will see that it includes linear programming as a particular instance). Also it will make the problems more concrete and suggest more easily than in the general case means of circumventing them. It will illustrate how basic results from linear programming and computational geometry can be used in order to achieve efficiency.

5.1 A Querying System for linear constraints

The reader is referred to [43] for a more formal introduction, to [30][27] for applications of this system. Given a set S of constraints as a conjunction of linear equalities, inequalities and negative constraints (disjunctions of inequations), we consider the following queries:

1. Is S solvable?
2. If S is not solvable, what are the causes of unsolvability?
3. Does S contain any redundancy or implicit equalities?
4. Is S equivalent to another given set S'?
5. Does S imply $x = 2$?
6. Does there exist α such that S implies $x = \alpha$?
7. Does there exist $\alpha, \beta, \ldots, \gamma$ such that S implies $\alpha x + \beta y \ldots = \gamma$.
8. Does there exist $\alpha, \beta, \ldots, \gamma$ such that S implies $\alpha x + \beta y \ldots \leq \gamma$ and $\alpha \leq 2\beta$?

The first query is a typical problem of Linear Programming as it corresponds to the first phase of the simplex. The second query is characteristic of constraints manipulating system where the constraints in store can be modified to restore solvability using feedback information provided by the solver. Query 3 deals with the simplification of the constraints representation. Redundancy is a major factor of complexity in constraints processing. The removal of redundancy and of implicit equalities are key steps in building a suitable canonical representation for the constraints [44][45][47]. Query 4 addresses the problem of constraint representation. It is taken care of by the canonical representation we just referred to. Queries 5 and 6 are classic Constraint Satisfaction Problems (CSP) which look for variables with grounded value. Query 7 is a generalization of CSP to linear relations: variables are bound to satisfy given linear relations. Finally, the last query generalizes the above with an inequality relation.

These various problems can be expressed within a general framework whose foundation is the concept of *parametric query.*

Definition 1 *A parametric query Q is of the form*

$$\exists \alpha, \beta, \gamma, \ldots, \forall x, y, \ldots : S \Rightarrow \alpha x + \beta y + \ldots \leq \gamma \wedge R(\alpha, \beta, \ldots, \gamma)?$$

where S is the set of constraints in store and R is a set of linear relations on the parameters $\alpha, \beta, \ldots, \gamma$.

A parametric query asks under what conditions on $\alpha, \beta, \ldots, \gamma$, the constraint in Q is implied by the constraints in store. Specific queries can be formulated in this framework by varying the parameters. For instance,

- *Is x bound to a specific value a?*
  $\exists \alpha, \beta, \ldots, \gamma, \forall x, y, \ldots, S \Rightarrow \alpha x + \beta y + \ldots = \gamma$ with $\alpha = 1, \beta = 0, \delta = 0, \ldots, \gamma = a$.
- *Is x ground?*
  Same as above but with γ unconstrained.

- *Does S imply $2x + 3y \leq 0$?*
  All parameters set to 0 except $\alpha = 2$ and $\beta = 3$.

- *What are the constraints implied by the projection of S on the $\{x,y\}$-plane?*
  All parameters except α, β, and γ are set to 0 and there is no relation R.

The test for solvability and the classic optimization problem can also be expressed in this way:

- *Is S solvable?*
  All parameters except γ are set to 0 and there is no relation R. By Fourier's theorem [22] S will be solvable iff the answer does not allow γ to be negative.

- *What is the maximum of $x + y$?*
  With the objective function $f = x + y$ we set $\alpha = 1$ and $\beta = 1$. All other parameters are set to 0 except γ. The answer will give a lower bound for γ which corresponds to the maximum of f. That is $min(\gamma) = max(f)$ which is essentially the duality theorem of Linear Programming.

Parametric queries are analogous to Logic Programming queries which ask if there exists an assignment to the variables in the query so that the query becomes a logical consequence of the program clauses and generalize CSP's which are restricted to constraints of the type $x = a$. Whatever the query is, its answer is obtained by elimination (be it Gaussian or Fourier or other form). The previous elimination examples could have been trivially framed in the context of parametric query. Let us show now a more elaborate use of the queries:

5.2 Example

We wish to characterize the set of affine functions f mapping a given polyhedral set S into a given polyhedral set Q. This problem came about from reading a book about fractals [4] where such functions have to be constructed in order to generate compact functional representation of images. Even though we are still a long way to provide a partially automated process, the construction we provide is of interest in itself and could still be relevant in the long run for similar problems. Namely, if $S = \{Ax \leq b\}$ and $Q = \{A'X \leq b'\}$ are the polyhedral sets, we want to characterize

$$f(x_1, \ldots, x_n) = \begin{cases} X_1 = \alpha_1^1 x_1 + \ldots + \alpha_1^n x_n + \beta_1 \\ \vdots \\ X_m = \alpha_m^1 x_1 + \ldots + \alpha_m^n x_n + \beta_m \end{cases}$$

such that $f(S) \subseteq Q$. Let D be the matrix of α_i^j's and $E = A'D$. Replacing all X_i's in Q by the corresponding $\alpha_i^1 x_1 + \ldots + \alpha_i^n x_n + \beta_i$, we obtain $Q' = \{Ex \leq b' - A'\beta\}$. Each constraint in Q' is treated as a parametric query on S. The conjunction of all answers defines a polyhedron. The coordinates of the points in the polyhedron provide the coefficients and constants of the functions. For instance, if

$$S = \{x + y \leq 1, -x \leq 0, \ -y \leq 0\}$$

and

$$Q = \{-X - Y \leq 1, \ X \leq 0, \ Y \leq 0\}.$$

Replacing X by $a_1x + b_1y + c_1$ and Y by $a_2x + b_2y + c_2$, we have

$$Q' = \{-(a_1 + a_2)x - (b_1 + b_2)y \leq 1 + c_1 + c_2, \ a_1x + b_1y \leq -c_1, \ a_2x + b_2y \leq -c_2\}.$$

Each constraint in Q' is treated as a parametric query and the answers are:

$$\{c_1 + c_2 \geq -1, \ a_1 + a_2 + c_1 + c_2 \geq -1, \ b_1 + b_2 + c_1 + c_2 \geq -1\},$$

$$\{c_1 \leq 0, \ a_1 + c_1 \leq 0, \ b_1 + c_1 \leq 0\}$$

and

$$\{c_2 \leq 0, \ a_2 + c_2 \leq 0, \ b_2 + c_2 \leq 0\}$$

respectively. The intersection of the polyhedra represented by these three answers forms a polyhedron with 27 extreme points. Some of these points correspond to a function which gives $f(S) = Q$. Functions constructed with the other points give images strictly included in Q. In the above example, only two functions constructed with these points map S exactly to Q. They are

$$f(x, y) = \begin{cases} X = -x \\ Y = -y \end{cases}$$

and

$$f(x, y) = \begin{cases} X = -y \\ Y = -x \end{cases}$$

The intended application was to provide a heuristic help to find a particular map of S. One could first generate the images of the extreme points. Any map we wish will be a linear combination of the extreme points. By visual inspection one could see which extreme points posses characteristics of the target map. Moving in the convex hull of these points is easy and one could rapidly converge towards the required image, at which stage the point obtained would give us the intended map. The practical issue is that the number of extreme points generated even in simple cases is unmanageable. To restrict the space of functions one would need to introduce non linearities and the problem then requires far more sophisticated algorithms.

5.3 Elimination

Parametric queries are more complex than simple conjunctions of constraints as they involve universal quantifiers, non linearity and implication. However by using a result linked to duality in linear programming, we can reduce the problem to a case of conjunction of linear constraints.

Theorem 2 (The Subsumption Theorem) *A constraint C is implied by a set of constraints S iff C is a quasi-linear combination of constraints in S.*

A *quasi-linear* combination of constraints is a positive linear combination with the addition of a positive constant on the righ-hand side. For instance, let S be the set

$$\{2x + 3y - z \leq 1,\ x - y + 2z \leq 2,\ x - y + z \leq 0\}$$

and Q be the query

$$\exists \alpha, \beta, \forall x, y, S \Rightarrow \alpha x + \beta y \leq 1?$$

The following relations express that the constraint in Q is a quasi-linear combination of the constraints in S.

$$\begin{array}{l} 2\lambda_1 + \lambda_2 + \lambda_3 = \alpha \\ 3\lambda_1 - \lambda_2 - \lambda_3 = \beta \\ -\lambda_1 + 2\lambda_2 + \lambda_3 = 0 \\ \lambda_1 + 2\lambda_2 + q = 1 \\ \lambda_1 \geq 0, \lambda_2 \geq 0, \lambda_3 \geq 0, q \geq 0 \end{array}$$

where the λ_i's are the multipliers of the constraints in S. It is from this simpler formulation that variables will be eliminated.

Consider the problem of variable elimination for a conjunction of linear constraints. The basic algorithm is Fourier's[22], (see also [31]) The severity of the problem is illustrated by the table below:

Number of variables eliminated	Number of constraints generated	Actual number of constraints needed
0	32	18
1	226	40
2	12,744	50
3	39,730,028	19
4	390,417,582,083,242	2

The middle column tells us the size of the outputs if Fourier's method was to be used to eliminate between 1 to 4 variables from an initial set of 32 constraints. Whereas, the right most column gives the minimum size of equivalent outputs. Fourier's elimination is in fact doubly exponential. We see that a main reason for this is that it generates an enormous amount of redundant information. So one could alleviate the problems of size of output or size of intermediate computation by either removing redundancy or better preventing the generation of redundant information. However, assuming it is done, we have an exponential improvement, but we are still left with exponential size for intermediate computation and potential exponential size for output. The way to attack this problem is to look for output bound algorithms (an important area of study in computational geometry), that will guarantee that we get a solution when its size is small, bypassing the problem of intermediate swell. Also in the case where the size of the output is unmanageable, there is no point in computing it. However, we may sacrifice completeness and search for an approximation of reasonable size. That brings us back to avoiding intermediate swell.

5.4 Intermediate Swell

A method for eliminating variables, called the extreme points method, was derived from the formalism of parametric queries. This method is interesting as it shows that variable elimination can be viewed as a straightforward generalization of a linear program in its specification and as a generalization of the simplex in its execution.

Let $S = Ax \leq b$ and let V be the set of variables to be eliminated, the associated generalized linear program in then defined as:

Definition 2 *Generalized Linear Program (GLP)*

$$extr(\Phi(\Delta))$$

$$\Phi = \begin{cases} \sum \lambda_i a_{i_1} = \alpha_1 \\ \vdots \\ \sum \lambda_i a_{i_k} = \alpha_k \\ \sum \lambda_i b_i = \beta \end{cases}$$

$$\Delta = \begin{cases} \sum \lambda_i a_{i_{k+1}} = 0 \\ \vdots \\ \sum \lambda_i a_{i_m} = 0 \\ \sum \lambda_i = 1 \\ \lambda_i \geq 0 \end{cases}$$

where *extr* denotes the set of extreme points. Δ represents the conditions to be satisfied by a combination of constraints of S that eliminates the required variables. The normalization of the λ's ensures that Δ is a polytope.

Theorem 3 *$extr(\Phi(\Delta))$, solutions of GLP, determine a finite set of constraints which defines the projection of S.*

This means that the coordinates of the extreme points of $\Phi(\Delta)$ are the coefficients of a set of constraints that define the projection. The objective function in the usual linear program can be viewed as a mapping from R^n to R, the image of the polyhedron defined by the constraints being an interval in R. The optimization consists in finding a maximum or a minimum, that is one of the extreme points of the interval. In a GLP, the objective function represents a mapping from R^n to R^m and instead of looking for one extreme point, we look for the set of all extreme points. At the operational level, we can execute this GLP by generalizing the simplex method. The extreme points of $\Phi(\Delta)$ are images of extreme points of Δ. So we compute the set of extreme points of Δ, map them by Φ and eliminate the images which are not extreme points. It is important to note that although the extreme points method is better that Fourier in general because it eliminates the costly intermediate steps, there are still two main problems: the computation of the extreme points of Δ can be extremely costly even when the size of the projection is small and also the method produces a highly redundant output. See [32] for a comparison between this method and Fourier's.

5.5 Using Geometry

We refer to [42] for a more detailed description of the geometric approach to quantifier elimination. Much of the shortcomings of the algebraic methods come from the fact that they spend all their time eliminating variables (no pun intended) which is an operation whose complexity is linked to the size of the input. Now it is well known that quantifier elimination can be viewed as an operation of projection. Exploiting this remark in a systematic manner leads to more output bound algorithms which guarantee both an output when its size is reasonable and an approximation otherwise. The idea in the bounded case is trivial: by running linear programs we obtain constraints whose supporting hyperplanes bound both the polytope to be projected and its projection. The traces of these hyperplanes on the projection space provide an approximation containing the projection. At the same time the extreme points provided by the linear programs project on points of the projection. The convex hull of these points is a polytope that is included in the projection. Iterating this process will lead to the projection. Whether we have an output bound algorithm or not will however depend on the choice of points (more details in the reference). The difficulties are that we do not want to make any assumption on the input. The input can represent an arbitrary polyhedral set: bounded or not, full dimensional or not, redundant or not, empty or not. We want first to determine if the set is solvable, then if not full dimensional, it is simplified by standard linear programming techniques into a set of equations that defines its affine hull and a set of inequalities which defines a full-dimensional polyhedral set in a smaller space. A straightforward variable elimination in the set of equations gives the affine hull of the projection. This will be part of the final output. This simplification based on geometrical considerations allows us to eliminate as many variables as possible by using only linear programming and gaussian elimination before getting into the costly part of elimination.

Now we consider two cases depending on whether the polyhedral set defined by the input set of constraints is bounded or not.

In the bounded case, the algorithm works directly on the input constraints. The projection is computed by successive refinements of an initial approximation. The initial approximation is obtained by computing enough extreme points of the projection so that their convex hull is full-dimensional. The points are obtained by running linear programs on the initial set of constraints. Next, successive refinements consist in adding new extreme points and updating the convex hull: if a constraint in the convex hull does not belong to the projection then a new extreme point is determined and the convex hull is updated. The costly convex hull construction is done in the projection space thus the main complexity of the algorithm is linked to the size of the output. The process stops when either the projection has been found or the size of the approximation has reached a user-supplied bound.

In the unbounded case, the problem is reformulated using the generalized linear program representation which is bounded by definition. We compute now *by projection*, $\Phi(\Delta)$. The output will contain the convex hull of $\Phi(\Delta)$ but also the set of its extreme points, from which we can derive the constraints which define the projection we request. The advantage over the extreme points method is that we compute directly the extreme points of $\Phi(\Delta)$. We do not need to compute the extreme points of Δ, this computation being the source of enormous intermediate computation and high redundancy in the output.

5.6 Effect of Round Off Errors

Round off errors create problems, but none as drastic as those reported in the general case. We are using here standard linear programming techniques and the substantial literature, specialized algorithms, help alleviate the problem. Furthermore infinite precision arithmetic seems to work. Even though computation is far slower, we obtain results, and we run most examples in the two modes in order to study the effects of round off errors. We had indeed a surprising result, that we report now. Running an example in infinite precision arithmetic we obtained as output a set (conjunction) of 15 linear constraints, the same input treated with finite precision gave us a set S of over a hundred constraints. S did not contain any redundancy. Checking the steps of the computation did not lead us to see any instability. More surprisingly the two sets appeared equivalent when queried. What happened was an unsuspected effect of round off errors combined with redundancy. The output may be viewed as a polytope. In this type of computation a redundant constraint often has a supporting hyperplane containing an extreme point of the polytope. A round off error may translate the redundant constraint (as little as one may consider) towards the polytope, and change it by replacing the extreme point by a tiny facet. Now a polytope defined by n constraints may have 2^n extreme points. If each is replaced by a tiny little facet we obtain an approximation of the polytope which may be excellent from a geometric or topological or other point of view. However at the level of syntactic representation we have a disastrous situation the polytope is represented by n constraints its otherwise excellent approximation is represented by n+2^n constraints. This is a worse but analogous situation to the representation of numbers where 0.9999... may be an excellent but syntactically cumbersome approximation of 1.

5.7 Simplification

Another advantage of the linear case that we study is that we have (even with some negation allowed) a notion of canonical form [47]. So there is a clear notion of a "simplest" or most useful representation, as opposed to the general case. However it is not as good as for sets of equalities where a single algorithm gives both solvability and the canonical representation. Here we have to run separate algorithms for solvability, detection of implicit equalities, redundancy removal, variable elimination and other simplifications which lead to the requested canonical form. In theory this is not a problem as all these can be achieved by running Gaussian elimination and linear programs. In practice it can slow down computation considerably, reducing the benefits that later use of the canonical form will bring. (Should we simplify at the end or at each step when simplification is costly?). In order to alleviate this problem and make a systematic use of simplification it is important to try to integrate these algorithms as much as possible. The relationship established between linear programming and Fourier's elimination will help us achieve significant progress in that direction. It is a problem that we address now.

Here we consider the particular case of generalized linear program where all variables are eliminated. This case corresponds to Fourier algorithm test for solvability. But the generalized linear program can be executed by the Simplex and consequently is far more efficient. It also inherits nice properties from the standard dual Simplex such as good incremental behavior, no need to introduce slack variables and no restriction to have the problem variables positive. More importantly as a side effect of the solvability test we obtain much information about the geometric structure of the polyhedron associated to the constraints and about their algebraic properties. Such information is essential in a general system to reason about constraints. We do not provide here formal arguments to substantiate the claims summarized in the table below. It is sufficient to state that proof are easily derived from the basic properties of Fourier algorithm [22] and the standard results from Linear Programming.

Suppose Fourier algorithm is applied to $S = \{Ax \leq b\}$. The output Q is either ϕ or a finite set of inequalities of the form $0 \leq d$, where $d \in \Re$. If $Q = \phi$, S is solvable. Otherwise S is solvable iff all inequalities in Q are tautologies. S contains implicit equalities iff $0 \leq 0$ belongs to Q. An implicit equality is a constraint in S where $\leq$ can be replaced by $=$ without changing the semantics of S. Since all constraints in Q are of the form $0 \leq d$, it is sufficient to look at the minimum of the d's to determine the solvability of S and the existence of implicit equalities.

The generalized linear program D which corresponds to Fourier solvability algorithm is

$$\text{minimize } \varphi$$

$$\varphi = \sum_i \lambda_i b_i$$

$$\Delta = \begin{cases} \sum_i \lambda_i a_{ij} = 0 \\ \sum_i \lambda_i = 1 \\ \lambda_i \geq 0 \ \forall i \end{cases}$$

Notice that D is a variant of the dual Linear Program, hence is called the quasi-dual. The dual space here is the space of linear combinations rather than the usual economic or geometric interpretation. Now we consider each row in the table below.

Quasi-Dual D	Fourier algorithm	Properties of S
Unsolvable	$Q = \phi$	• *Strongly* solvable • Full dimensional • No implicit equalities • Unbounded and no projection has parallel facets • Inscribed spheres have unbounded radius
$min(\varphi(\lambda)) > 0$	$Q \neq \phi$ $0 \leq d \in Q \Rightarrow d \in \Re^+$	• Solvable • Full dimensional • No implicit equalities • Bounded or exists projection with parallel facets • Inscribed spheres have bounded radius
$min(\varphi(\lambda)) = 0$	$0 \leq 0 \in Q$ $0 \leq d \in Q \Rightarrow d \notin \Re^-$	• *Weakly* Solvable • Not full dimensional • Exists implicit equalities • An evident minimal subset of implicit equalities • Inscribed spheres have radius zero
$\exists\lambda : \varphi(\lambda) < 0$	$\exists d \in \Re^- : 0 \leq d \in Q$	• Unsolvable • An evident minimal infeasible subset

D unsolvable, that is Δ empty, corresponds to the case when Fourier algorithm gives $Q = \phi$. Hence, S is solvable and the associated polyhedron is full dimensional. Notice that because Q is empty no contradictions can ever be generated regardless of the values of the right hand side constants in the constraints of S. This is why we say that S is *strongly* solvable. It can be shown easily that the polyhedron is unbounded and no projection of S contains parallel facets. Therefore all inscribed spheres have unbounded radius.

If the minimal value of $\varphi(\lambda)$ is strictly positive Fourier algorithm generates a non-empty set of tautologies and therefore S is solvable. It is not strongly solvable as different values for b could lead to unsolvability. The associated polyhedron is full dimensional and it is either bounded or one of its projections contains parallel facets. Consequently, all inscribed spheres have a bounded radius.

In case where the minimal value of $\varphi(\lambda)$ is equal to zero, Fourier algorithm generates at least one $0 \leq 0$. This indicates that S is solvable and contains implicit equalities. Consequently S is not full dimensional and all inscribed spheres are reduced to points (radius zero). S is *weakly* solvable because an arbitrarily small change in b may give unsolvability. The corresponding extreme point for this minimal value gives us the first minimal set of implicit equalities in S. If we wish to identify all other implicit equalities, we add to the representation of Δ the constraint $\varphi(\lambda) = 0$ giving the new polytope

$$\Delta' : \{\varphi(\lambda) = 0,\ A^T\lambda = 0,\ \Sigma\lambda_i = 1,\ \lambda_i \geq 0\}.$$

From the extreme points of Δ' we derive the indices of the constraints in S that are implicit equalities.

In the course of minimization, if $\varphi(\lambda)$ becomes negative then we can stop the process immediately as this means that Fourier algorithm generates at least one contradiction. Thus, S is unsolvable. As in the previous case we obtain a first minimal infeasible subset. To identify all the minimal subsystems of S that cause the unsolvability, again we need to augment the representation of Δ by adding the constraint $\varphi(\lambda) \leq 0$. For simplicity's sake, we use the weak inequality instead of the strict one. The new polytope is

$$\Delta' : \{\varphi(\lambda) \leq 0,\ A^T\lambda = 0,\ \Sigma\lambda_i = 1,\ \lambda_i \geq 0\}.$$

Each vertex of Δ' that corresponds to a strictly negative value of $\varphi(\lambda)$ is associated with a minimal infeasible subsystem of S.

Beringer made two important observations [5]. The first one is that if the constraints in S are appropriately normalized then $min(\varphi(\lambda))$ (when positive) is in fact the maximal radius of the inscribed spheres. The other is a relation between the quasi-dual and Helly's theorem. Helly's theorem states that a set of $n \geq d+1$ convex sets in $\Re^d$ is unsolvable iff there exists a subset of $d+1$ convex sets which is unsolvable. When D is solvable, the quasi-dual Simplex follows Helly's theorem. Each basis corresponds to the selection of exactly $d+1$ constraints. $\varphi(\lambda)$ is a measure of solvability, by minimizing it we therefore search for a subset of $d+1$ constraints which is least likely to be solvable.

5.8 Summary

Much of the work on quantifier elimination has been done by mathematicians who have their own agenda. Much progress has been done on abstract complexity studies and in theorem proving. But in order to have significant applications outside of theorem proving, more efforts should be spent on defining meaningful subcases that might lead to practical algorithms. Also more effort should be spent systematically synthesizing the wealth of information we have on constraints from symbolic computation, mathematical programming, artificial intelligence, computational geometry etc One area that seems promising is linear constraints. As we have seen linear programming can be viewed as a very particular case of quantifier elimination. This lead to an interesting analysis of quantifier elimination as a generalized linear programming problem. In fact, the whole area of sensitivity analysis could be viewed as falling into the scope of quantifier elimination. By throwing in techniques from computational geometry one can substantially improve, in important cases, the practical efficiency of the algorithms. This synthesis also proved useful to find solvability algorithms and canonical representations with good applications related properties.

6 Crypto Intuitionism: Towards a Constraint Sequent Calculus

One of the main theoretical and practical issues in Logic is an efficient implementation of negation. One approach is to have a weaker form of negation, as in intuitonistic logic, another approach is to restrict the use of negation to simple subformulae. In [48], we introduce, in an abstract setting, the notion of *negatable constraints.* They represent the constraints which can be negated "for free" in a system that is without increasing the complexity of the associated solver. This corresponds to an intuitionistic behavior of disjunction (hence the dubious label of "crypto-intuitionism"). This property is closely linked to the existence of a canonical form which is particularly suitable for constraint propagation and querying. The proposed axiomatization is sufficiently general to account for a variety of examples that come up in affine geometry, group theory, symbolic computation, term algebras and elsewhere. It is also interesting to note that some of the axioms appear in a characterization of matroids. We will use our previous setting of linear constraints to introduce these notions and suggest how they may be systematically abstracted. A starting point for this study was a recurring phenomenon linked to the fundamental property of Horn clauses (see e.g. [23]) given in the following theorem:

Theorem 4 *Let P be a set of Horn clauses and $A_i = \exists x_1, \ldots, x_m\ B_i$ where B_i is a conjunction of atomic formulae.*
Then $P \Rightarrow A_1 \vee A_2 \vee \ldots \vee A_n$ iff $P \Rightarrow A_i$ for some i.

This property, as explained in the reference is at the basis of the good behavior of Horn clauses with respect to querying. We now see it appear in other contexts. Linear equality constraints define affine spaces. The well known geometric property

Proposition 1 *An affine space is contained in an union of affine spaces iff it is contained in one member of this union.*

is used in [39] to show the homomorphism theorem in database theory. Let us call this property the *strong compactness property.* It implies that equality constraints are negatable. Indeed consider a system of equality constraints and a conjunction of inequations (that is negated equalities). How do we test this system for solvability? A replacement of each inequation by a disjunction of strict inequalities would lead to a combinatorial explosion and transform the problem into a linear programming problem. However this is not needed since the strong compactness property implies that we can test the set of equality constraints independently with each inequation. The set is not solvable iff the hyperplane associated with one of the inequations contains the affine space defined by the equality constraints. The key factor behind the strong compactness property is the notion of dimension: one cannot cover an object of dimension d with a finite (even denumerable in that case) number of objects of dimension strictly smaller than d.

In [46] the problem of sets of equations and inequations in the Herbrand universe was addressed using the analogy with the situation of linear arithmetic equalities and inequations that we just described. All that was needed was to introduce the notion of dimension of the set of solutions to an equality in the Herbrand universe: the number of domain variables in an idempotent mgu (which is an invariant). To test for solvability does not lead to a combinatorial explosion, and the unification algorithm remains sufficient.

Theorem 5 (Strong Compactness) *Let E and $E_1, \ldots, E_n$ be equation sets and suppose the Herbrand universe is infinite.*

If $E \approx E_1 \vee \ldots \vee E_n$ then, for some E_j, $E \approx E_j$.

We can easily find similar examples of negatable constraints in domains that benefit from the notion of dimension. Let us give a simple example with a different flavor. Let the domain be a completely divisible group G. Let the constraints be with one argument: $H(x)$ is satisfied iff x belongs to subgroup H of G. All constraints are negatable. The strong compactness property is established by an application of the pigeon-hole principle. Other instances of this phenomenon will be found in [48] and an interesting one for classes of Boolean algebras in [51].

Let us now consider the problem of canonical form, in the case of (positive) linear constraints. A first use is for standardization of representation: two sets of constraints in canonical form should be equal iff they represent the same polyhedral set. This can be easily achieved if the polyhedral set is full dimensional: a triangle in a two dimensional space is uniquely described by a set of three constraints. If the set is not full dimensional there is an infinite number of non redundant equivalent sets of constraints defining the same polyhedral set. The solution adopted in [47] is quite natural: break the syntactic representation in two parts. One is the uniquely representable set of equalities defining the affine hull of the polyhedral set, the other is a unique set of inequalities as we are back to the full dimensional case. What is the link with the equalities as negatable constraints? Let us note first that the strong compactness property still holds:

Theorem 6 *If P is a polyhedral set and if the X_j are affine sets, then $P \subseteq \bigcup_j X_j$ implies $P \subseteq X_{j_0}$ for some fixed j_0.*

So the equality constraints are still negatable, we have no combinatorial explosion and solvability is still a linear programming problem despite the presence of inequations. But if the constraints are in canonical representation we are in a better situation as the solvability problem reduces to Gaussian elimination despite the presence of inequalities. What happens is that a polyhedral set behaves exactly in the same way as its affine hull in the presence of inequations: an hyperplane contains a polyhedral set iff it contains its affine hull.

The same results would be achieved with convex sets instead of polyhedral sets, or even taking dense subsets of affine spaces. An axiomatization of this phenomenon leads to three axioms which are part of the characterization of matroids, the missing axiom being the exchange property. From these one can extend the notion of canonical representation to sytems of constraints containing negative constraints. Important results follow. Essentially they imply that we can separate, in the canonical form, the different types of constraints in a semantically meaningful way.

In the case of linear constraints the canonical form method yields a completeness theorem in terms of the propagation of the equality, inequality and negative information contained in a set of generalized constraints.

Theorem 7 (Constraint Propagation Theorem) . *Let (E, I, N) be a set of consistent generalized constraints in canonical form with eliminable variables y and parameters x. Then we have*

(1) $(E, I, N) \models ay = bx$ iff $E \models ay = bx$ (2) $(E, I, N) \models ax \leq \beta$ iff $I \models ax \leq \beta$ (3) $(E, I, N) \models \overline{\{Cx = d\}}$ iff $N \models \overline{\{Cx = d\}}$ where $\overline{\{Cx = d\}}$ is a precise negative constraint.

In terms of implementation it means that we can use the solvers more efficiently. Equality relations between the variables appear automatically, and the system is overall simplified. In terms of querying the system, it means that if the query is about say negatable constraints then we need consult only the negatable part of the canonical representation.

Acknowledgements

I want to thank Tien Huynh, Joxan Jaffar, Catherine Lassez, Michael Maher, Kim Marriott and Ken McAloon, without whom .... Also this paper represents a summary of a series of lectures given at the Tata Institute, Bombay. The comments of the participants and of Pr. Shyamasundar is gratefully acknowledged.

References

[1] A. Aiba and K.Sakai, CAL: A Theoretical Background of Constraint Logic Programming and its Applications, *Journal of Symbolic Computation*, Vol 8 No 6 1989.

[2] D.S. Arnon, Geometric Reasoning with Logic and Algebra, in *Geometric Reasoning*, D. Kapur and J.L. Mundy eds., MIT Press 1989.

[3] D.S. Arnon, Towards a Deductive Database for Elementary Algebra and Geometry, *Proceedings of NACLP 90 Workshop on Deductive Databases.*

[4] M. Barnsley, Fractals Everywhere, Academic Press 1988.

[5] H. Béringer, private communication.

[6] W.W. Bledsoe, A New Method for Proving Certain Presburger Formulas, *Advance Papers 4th Int. Joint Conf. on Artif. Intell.*, Tbilissi, Georgia, USSR, Sept. 1975.

[7] A. Borning, The Programming Language Aspects of THINGLAB - A Constraint Oriented Simulation Laboratory, *ACM Transactions on Programming Languages and Systems*, 3 (1981) 252-387.

[8] F.M. Brown, Boolean Reasoning: The Logic of Boolean Equations, Kluwer Academic Pub. 1990.

[9] B. Buchberger, History and Basic Features of the Critical-Pair/Completion Procedure, in *Rewriting Techniques and Applications J-P. Jouannaud Ed.*, Academic Press 1987.

[10] J.F.Canny, The Complexity of Robot Motion Planning, MIT Press 1987.

[11] V. Chandru and J. Hooker, Logical Inference: A Mathematical Programming Perspective *AI in Manufacturing:Theory and Practise*, Edited by S.T. Kumara, R.L Kashyap, and A.L. Soyster, Wiley 1988

[12] V. Chandru and J. Hooker, Optimization Methods for Logical Inference, to appear.

[13] C-L Chang and R.C-T. Lee, Symbolic Logic and Mechanical Theorem Proving, Academic Press 1973.

[14] M. Coste, Geometry and Robotics, J.-D. Boissonat and J.-P. Laumond Eds, Springer Verlag Lecture Notes in Computer Science.

[15] J. Cox, K. McAloon and C. Tretkoff, Computational Complexity and Constraint Logic Programming Languages, *Annals of Mathematics and Artificial Intelligence*, to appear.

[16] J. Darlington and Y-K. Guo, Constraints Functional Programming, Technical Report, Department of Computing, Imperial College, to appear.

[17] J.H. Davenport, Robot Motion Planning, in *Geometric Reasoning*, J. Woowark ed., Oxford Science Publications.

[18] J.H. Davenport and J. Heintz, Real Quantifier Elimination is Doubly Exponential, in *Algorithms in Real Algebraic Geometry*, D.S. Arnon and B. Buchberger ed., Academic Press 1988.

[19] J-H. Davenport,Y. Siret and E. Tournier, Computer Algebra, Systems and Algorithms for Algebraic Computation, Academic Press 1988.

[20] E. Davis, Constraint Propagation with Interval Labels, *Journal of Artificial Intelligence*, 1987.

[21] R.J. Duffin, On Fourier's Analysis of Linear Inequality Systems, *Mathematical Programming Study 1*, pp. 71-95, 1974.

[22] J.B.J. Fourier, reported in: Analyse des travaux de l'Académie Royale des Sciences, pendant l'année 1824, Partie Mathématique, *Histoire de l'Académie Royale des Sciences de l'Institut de France 7* (1827) xlvii-lv. (Partial English translation in: D.A. Kohler, Translation of a Report by Fourier on his work on Linear Inequalities, *Opsearch* 10(1973) 38-42.)

[23] J. Gallier and S.Raatz, Hornlog: A Graph-based Interpreter for General Horn Clauses, *Journal of Logic Programming*, Vol 4, No 2 June 87.

[24] P. Hammer and I. Rosenberg, Applications of Pseudo Boolean Programming to the Theory of Graphs, *Z. Wahrscheinlichkeitsheorie und Verw. Gebiete 3*, 1964.

[25] P. Hammer and S. Rudeanu, Boolean Methods in Operations Research, Springer Verlag 1968.

[26] N. Heintze, S. Mychaylov, P. Stuckey and R. Yap, On Meta programming in CLP(R), *Proceedings NACLP 1989* MIT Press.

[27] R. Helm, T. Huynh, C. Lassez and K. Marriott, A Linear Constraint Technology for User Interfaces, to appear.

[28] R. Helm, K. Marriott and M. Odersky, Constraint Based Query Optimization for Spatial Databases, *Proceedings of ACM Conference on Principles of Database Systems*, Denver 1991.

[29] C. Hoffman, Geometric and Solid Modelling, Morgan Kauffman Pub. 1989.

[30] T. Huynh, L. Joskowicz, C. Lassez and J-L. Lassez, Reasoning About Linear Constraints Using Parametric Queries in *Foundations of Software Technology and Theoretical Computer Science*, Lecture Notes in Computer Sciences, Springer-Verlag vol. 472 December 1990.

[31] T. Huynh, C. Lassez and J-L. Lassez, Fourier Algorithm Revisited, *2nd International Conference on Algebraic and Logic Programming*, Springer-Verlag Lecture Notes in Computer Sciences, 1990.

[32] T. Huynh and J-L. Lassez, Practical Issues on the Projection of Polyhedral Sets, IBM Research Report, T.J. Watson Research Center, 1990.

[33] J. Jaffar and J-L. Lassez, Constraint Logic Programming, *Proceedings of POPL 1987*, Munich.

[34] J. Jaffar and J-L. Lassez, From Unification to Constraints, *Logic Programming Conference,* Tokyo, Springer Verlag Lecture Notes in Computer Science, June 1987.

[35] J. Jaffar and S. Michaylov, Methodology and Implementation of a CLP System, *Proceedings of the 1987 Logic Programming Conference*, Melbourne, MIT Press.

[36] R. G. Jeroslow, Logic Based Decision Support, *Annals of Discrete Mathematics*, North Holland 1989.

[37] A. Kandri-Rody and D. Kapur, On relationships between Buchberger's Grobner basis algorithm and the Knuth Bendix Completion Procedure, *General Electric Tech report N0 83CRD286*, Schenectady New York 1983.

[38] A. Kandri-Rodi, D. Kapur and F. Winkler Knuth-bendix Procedure and Buchberger Algorithm a Synthesis, *Proceedings International Symposium on Symbolic and Algebraic Computation 1989.*

[39] P. Kanellakis, G. Kuper and P. Revesz, Constraint Query Languages, *Proceedings of the ACM Conference on Principles of Database Systems*, Nashville 90.

[40] D. Kapur and J.L. Mundy, Geometric Reasoning, MIT Press 1989.

[41] D.Kapur and J.L. Mundy, Symposium on Symbolic and Numeric Computation, *Saratoga Springs 1990, Proceedings forthcoming*, Academic Press.

[42] C. Lassez and J-L. Lassez, Quantifier Elimination for Conjunctions of Linear Constraints via a Convex Hull Algorithm, IBM research Report, T.J. Watson Research Center, 1991.

[43] J-L. Lassez, Querying Constraints, *Proceedings of the ACM conference on Principles of Database Systems*, Nashville 1990.

[44] J-L. Lassez, T. Huynh and K. McAloon, Simplification and Elimination of Redundant Arithmetic Constraints, *Proceedings of NACLP 89*, MIT Press.

[45] J-L. Lassez and M.J. Maher, On Fourier's Algorithm for Linear Arithmetic Constraints, IBM Research Report, T.J. Watson Research Center, 1988, Journal of Automated Reasoning, to appear.

[46] J-L. Lassez, M.J. Maher and K. Marriott, Unification Revisited, *Foundations of Logic Programming and Deductive Databases*, J. Minker ed., Morgan-Kaufmann 1988.

[47] J-L. Lassez and K. McAloon, A Canonical Form for Generalized Linear Constraints, IBM Research Report RC 15004, IBM T.J. Watson Research Center, *Journal of Symbolic Computation*, to appear.

[48] J-L Lassez and K. McAloon, A Constraint Sequent Calculus, *Proceedings of LICS 90*, Philadelphia.

[49] M. Maher, A Logic Semantics for a class of Committed Choice Languages, *Proceedings of ICLP4*, MIT Press 1987.

[50] M. Maher and P. Stuckey, Expanding Query power in Constraint Logic Programming Languages, *Proceedings of NACLP 1989*, MIT Press.

[51] K. Marriott and M. Odersky, Systems of Negative Boolean Constraints, forthcoming.

[52] K. Mukai, Situations in Constraint, US-JAPAN AI Symposium, 1987, Tokyo.

[53] J. Pearl, Constraints and Heuristics, *AI Journal*, 1988.

[54] J. Renegar, On the Computational Complexity and Geometry of the First Order Theory of the Reals, Part I, II and III, Technical Reports, School of Operations Research and Industrial Engineering, Cornell 1989.

[55] V. Saraswat, Concurrent Constraint Logic Programming, MIT Press, to appear.

[56] V. Saraswat, F. Rossi and P. van Hentenryck, Towards a General Framework for Constraint Programming, forthcoming.

[57] J.T. Schwartz and M. Sharir, A Survey of Motion Planning and Related Geometric Reasoning, in *Geometric Reasoning*, D. Kapur and J.L. Mundy ed., MIT Press 1989.

[58] R.E. Shostak, On the SUP-INF method for proving Presburger formulas, *JACM*, 24 (1977) 529-543.

[59] G. Steele and G. Sussman, CONSTRAINTS - a Constraint Based Programming Language, *AI Journal*, 1982.

[60] L. Van Den Vries, Alfred Tarski's Elimination Theory for Closed Fields, *The Journal of Symbolic Logic, vol.53 n.1*, March 1988.

[61] P. van Hentenryck, Constraint Satisfaction in Logic Programming, The MIT Press 1989.

Polynomial Recursion Analysis in Pascal Like Programs

Dieter Armbruster
Institut für Informatik
Universität Stuttgart
D–7000 Stuttgart 1
Germany
Email: armbr@azu.informatik.uni-stuttgart.de

Abstract

Besides being of theoretical interest the knowledge about a procedure's calling behavior is valuable for an optimizing compiler. It is well known, however, that such properties like recursivity or reachability of procedures are unfortunately *undecidable* for programs in *ALGOL–like* languages and are still worse than *P–Space Complete* in the *ISO–Pascal* case.
We extend this language hierarchy (with respect to parameter restrictions) at the lower end to *Wirth's Pascal* and show that there the recursivity problem for procedures is decidable within *polynomial time*. In order to establish this (rather unexpected) result we

1. reduce recursivity of a procedure to a reachability problem – with both properties being defined on an infinite tree representation of the program;
2. show the equivalence between reachability in such an *infinite tree* on the one hand and reachability in the *finite graph* representation on the other hand;
3. solve then the reachability problem in this graph in $O(ns)$ of a program with n procedures as vertices and s call statements as edges.

1 Introduction

The development of new computer architectures with reduced but fast instruction sets (RISC [PA85]) requires the use of knowledge about the run time behaviour of procedures (subsuming functions) during compilation of programs in block structered languages like Pascal – thereby causing the renaissance of some classical compiler optimization problems. While for the present comfortable (but slow) microprogrammed machine instructions (e.g. a subroutine call) it does not seem to be promising to distinguish between recursive and non–recursive procedures, this situation changes for reduced, uncomfortable (but faster) instruction sets. Compilers for the latter can no longer afford to generally assume the worst case with respect to the calling behavior of procedures which means that every procedure is taken for being recursive. Thus, if the memory access for static data is faster than for dynamic data on a stack, the compiler can exploit this fact for non–recursive procedures by allocating memory for their local data in the static area. A further partitioning of "recursivity" into "strong" and "weak" recursivity yields another chance of optimization: When a weak recursive procedure is called there is no need to create an activation record (or frame) for it since it can use part of the record of the strong recursive procedure which is statically surrounding the weak recursive procedure and which is located further down in the rubtime stack. (For this partitioning see the final remarks in section 7.) In the following, however, we will concentrate on the theoretical aspects rather than on implementational ones.

Unfortunately the problem of determining whether or not a procedure is *actually* recursive or *actually* reachable (i.e. at run time) cannot be decided – even for programs without any I/O (this stems from the ability of such programs to simulate any Turing machine). Therefore we have to be content with approximating the *actual* properties; we call this approximations *tree recursivity* and *tree reachability*, since they are defined on the *execution tree* of a *program scheme* [WI82, LA73] rather than on the runtime stack (in the literature these approximations are also called *formal recursivity* and *formal reachability*).

We will informally define these notions in section 2, whereas section 3 deals with the graph representation of such a program scheme and presents an algorithm to compute reachabilty in this graph. Section 4 then shows the equivalence between reachabilty in the graph on one hand and in the tree on the other hand. As the last step in the reasoning chain we transform in section 5 tree recursivity into tree reachability and state the main result (tree recursivity $\Longleftrightarrow$ graph reachability) in section 6. Remarks on *strong/weak recursivity* (section 7) and finally the references (section 8) conclude the paper.

2 Informal Definitions

2.1 Program Scheme and its Execution Tree

A **program scheme** is a program where all data, labels, and their related statements are removed (with the intention to get a better decidability) leaving only (possibly nested) **procedure declarations** with **parameters of type procedure** and **statement parts** (= **body** minus local procedure declarations) with zero or more **call statements**. Thus, the statement part of procedure Q in fig. 1 consists of the two statements "$x(y)$" and "$Q(P, R)$", whereas the body (and consequently the statement part as well) of P is empty. (We denote the actuals by capitals and the formals by lower case letters.) If procedure P is declared locally in procedure Q (Q is **static predecessor** of P) then every call to Q generates a modified copy of the declaration of P by replacing those global formals in the body of P which are in Q's parameter list by the actual parameters (= arguments) of this call to Q. This is the well known copy rule semantics of blockstructered programs.

With this program scheme we associate an **execution tree** which simulates the execution of the scheme in a nondeterministic way: Starting with the main program *PROG* which represents the root of the tree we create a successor node for each call in the statement part of *PROG*, thereby labelling the node with the (call) statement itself. Inductively: Having reached a node labelled $U(\ldots V \ldots)$, we create children for this node – one child for each call in the statement part of procedure U. The label of such a successor node is formed by replacing all formals in the call statement by those names that appear on the corresponding parameter positions in the static predecessor nodes – according to the semantics of, say, Pascal. Note that all names in the labels are *non*formal. This construction yields a (possibly infinite) execution tree $E(PROG)$ of our program scheme *PROG*.

```
PROG:
{ procedure Q(x:proc(proc()), y:proc())
    { procedure P(z:proc()) {...}
      procedure R() {...}
      x(y)
      Q(P,R)
    }
  procedure A(w:proc()) { w() }
  procedure B() {...}

  Q(A,B)
}
```

```
1:        PROG
            |
2:       Q(A,B)
          /   \
3:    A(B)    Q(P,R)
       /       /   \
4:   B( )    P(R)  Q(P,R)
                    /   \
5:                ...   ...
```

Figure 1: A program scheme and its execution tree

Now, a procedure P in *PROG* is **tree recursive** resp. **tree reachable** iff there is a branch in $E(PROG)$ which begins at *PROG* and along which P is called at least twice resp. once. Fig.1 should help clarifying the notions (the first formal of Q is a procedure with one formal, its second a procedure without any formals).

It should be clear by now that *non tree recursivity* and *non tree reachability* imply the corresponding *actual* properties – but not vice versa, since for example the *actual* reachability (i.e. the actual execution) of a *tree* reachable procedure might depend on the value of some data.

By resorting to this tree approximation – what do we gain with respect to decidability? The answer depends on the important notion of *mode depth*:

2.2 On the Influence of the Mode Depth

In a program scheme the **mode depth MD** of a formal or nonformal name x without any arguments resp. parameters when being used in a call statement resp. in a declaration is defined to be 1. Then, inductively, the mode depth of a name y which is used as $y(\ldots x_j \ldots)$ is

$$MD(y) = max(MD(x_j)) + 1,$$

and the mode depth of a program $PROG$ is

$$MD(PROG) = max(MD(P_i)),$$

with P_i being the procedure names of $PROG$. For example, in fig.1, $MD(w) = 1$, hence $MD(A) = 2$; $MD(B) = 1$, hence $MD(Q) = MD(PROG) = 3$.
For **finite mode (= FM) programs** (e.g. ISO–Pascal [ISO81]), $MD(P_i)$ is finite, whereas for **FM2–programs** (e.g. Wirth's Pascal), $MD(P_i) \leq 2$. Note that therefore in FM–programs all formal parameters can be specified completely, as it is done in ISO–Pascal. Thus, a call like $P(P)$ which is legal in an **infinite mode** allowing language (e.g. ALGOL60) would be syntactically illegal in a finite mode language because its formal parameter cannot be specified completely (without resorting to recursive types).

2.3 The Environment of Our Problem

Now we can give the answer of the above question concerning the gain in decidability: For an *infinite mode* language both, recursivity and reachability in the tree was shown to be still *undecidable* [LA73], whereas for *finite modes* the problems are decidable [AR85] – although with complexity as bad as *complete in deterministic exponential time* [ME85]. However, we obtain our rather unexpected *polynomial* result by a restriction to $MD \leq 2$, i.e. to Wirth's Pascal. There, a formal procedure call can no more have any arguments (remember, the only parameters we deal with are of type *procedure*) whereas a nonformal call can have both – formal and nonformal arguments – as in the FM case.

On our way to this result we need another underlying structure for the calling behaviour: namely a *graph* – with the procedures and formal names as vertices and the call statements as edges.

3 Graph Representation of Program Schemes and Graph Reachability

3.1 Graph Representation

Informally, the graph here is defined as follows:
Initially it consists only of vertices – one for each procedure name and one for each formal parameter occuring in the program scheme. The labels of the vertices are the names of the procedures resp. the formal parameters itself. Each call statement in a scheme of a FM2 program has one of the following forms (note that $z(\ldots y \ldots)$ is excluded):

$$A(\ldots D \ldots), \qquad A(\ldots y \ldots), \qquad z(\,).$$

Starting with the vertice of the main program $PROG$ we add an edge $PROG \rightarrow A$ for each call $A(\ldots)$ in $PROG$'s statement part, and an edge $x \rightarrow D$ for each argument D on the position of the formal parameter x anywhere in $PROG$'s statement part (note that we encounter here only the first of the above three forms).
We repeat this step for each call in the statement part of each procedure which is reachable in the graph from node $PROG$ until no more edge can be added, thereby treating the other two forms analogously (see also section 4). A similar approach – though without guaranteeing reachability – can be found in [WA76].

Note that in general both, the source and the destination of an edge may be a node labelled with a formal name; we can interpret $A \rightarrow \psi$ as "the nonformal A calls the (non)formal ψ" and $x \rightarrow \psi$ as "the formal parameter x is replaced by the (non)formal argument ψ". Figure 2 is an example of this construction.

```
PROG:
{ procedure A( )  { }
  procedure Q(x:proc())  { x( ) }
  procedure P( )  { Q(A) }
  Q(P)
}
```

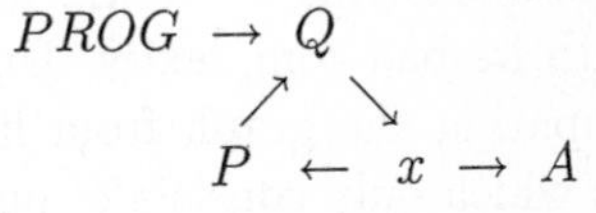

Figure 2: A program scheme and its graph representation

3.2 The Graph Construction

The following algorithm describes more precisely how to construct the reachability graph of a program scheme:

Input: FM2 program scheme with $\mathcal{P}$, the set of its procedure names, and $\mathcal{F}$, the set of its formal parameters, and s statements. Let $A \in \mathcal{P}$, $\psi \in \mathcal{P} \cup \mathcal{F}$, and x, $y \in \mathcal{F}$.

Output: $\mathcal{R} \subseteq \mathcal{P}$, the set of all procedures which are graph reachable from the main program *PROG*.

Method:

```
1   Initialize R = {PROG};
2   For all unmarked P ∈ R do
3       Mark P;
4       For all call statements c in the statement part of P do
5           If c = A(...ψ...) with ψ on the position of x
                add edges  P → A  and  x → ψ;
6           If c = y( )
                add edge  P → y,   y ∈ F;
7       Reconstruct R on the updated graph
        (using depth or breadth first searching).
```

Notes on the complexity:
Let us assume a limit on the length of parameterlists; then the inner loop (4–5–6) is executed at most once for each statement yielding $O(s)$ which is also the complexity of line 7. Together with the $O(n)$ of the outer loop (2—7), we end up with $\mathbf{O(sn)}$ of the whole algorithm.

Since this graph can be constructed in *polynomial* time it would be nice if we could use it as the underlying structure for our recursion analysis – rather than the execution tree with its bad complexity. Unfortunately, things are not that easy, as can be seen by comparing the graph from fig.2 with the corresponding tree for the above FM2 scheme which only consists of one finite branch:

$$1: \ PROG \ —— \ 2: \ Q(P) \ —— \ 3: \ P(\,) \ —— \ 4: \ Q(A) \ —— \ 5: \ A(\,)$$

According to the graph we find P to be recursive whereas the tree reveals its (actual) nonrecursivity. That is, graph analysis yields a less accurate but much cheaper *approximation of recursivity.* However, the last example shows no difference as far as *reachability* is concerned – and this is no coincidence as we will see.

4 Graph Reachability versus Tree Reachability

Let's look back at the FM3 program in fig.1 and conceive its graph (the algorithm of the graph construction for $MD \geq 3$ needs more passes over the scheme – but is of no interest here):

$$\begin{array}{ccccccccccccc} & & & & & & & & z & & & & \\ & & & & & & & & \downarrow & & & & \\ PROG & \longrightarrow & Q & \longrightarrow & x & \longrightarrow & A & \longrightarrow & w & \longrightarrow & y & \longrightarrow & B \\ & & \downarrow & & & & & & \downarrow & & & & \\ & & P & & & & & & R & & & & \end{array}$$

Comparing this graph with the corresponding execution tree in fig.1 we realize that for FM3 programs, graph and tree reachability do *not* coincide anymore, since R is not tree reachable. Although the second argument B in the call $Q(A, B)$ is tree reachable this is not true for the call $Q(P, R)$. This possible "constipation" of programs with $MD \geq 3$ is the reason for the intractability of reachability and recursivity problems. Therefore we exclude it for **permeable** programs:

Definition 1 *In the execution tree of a* **permeable program** *the i-th argument a_i of a procedure call $Q(\ldots a_i \ldots)$ is used (i.e. either called or passed on as an argument) iff the i-th argument b_i of any other call $Q(\ldots b_i \ldots)$ is used.*

This — at first glance — exotic and arbitrarily defined property is inherent to all FM2 programs, as can be proven by means of a very technical lemma (see [AR85]). It asserts in the execution tree of a FM2–program that if we reach P after n nodes below a call to Q in node α_q at tree level q ($\alpha_q = Q(\ldots)$) and if P's static link passes via α_q (note that Q then is a static predecessor of P), then we have an analogous situation for any other call $\alpha_r = Q(\ldots)$ elsewhere in the tree, i.e., we must reach another P n nodes below α_r and this P's static link passes via α_r.

This Lemma is used in the proof of theorem 1 and the next lemma:

Lemma 1 *Each program PROG with $MD(PROG) \leq 2$, i.e. each FM2 program, is permeable.*

With this notion of permeability we can prove our first main result:

Theorem 1 *Let P be a procedure in a FM2 program.*
P is graph reachable $\iff$ P is tree reachable.

Proof (sketch):
Let $\mathcal{P}$ be the set of the program's procedure names and $\mathcal{F}$ the set of its formal parameters. We will show: The path

$$(PROG = P_0, P_1,\ f_{1_1}, f_{1_2}, \ldots, f_{1_i}, \ldots,\ P_2, \ldots, P_i,\ f_{i_1}, \ldots, f_{i_j}, \ldots,\ P_n = P),$$

$f_{i_j} \in \mathcal{F}$, $0 \leq j \leq f = \mid \mathcal{F} \mid$, $0 \leq i \leq n = \mid \mathcal{P} \mid$ is in the graph iff the branch $(PROG, P_1, \ldots, P)$ is in the tree. This is proven by an induction on P_i and a subinduction on f_{i_j}, thereby analyzing the effects of the graph creating statements on the construction of the tree. The permeability of the program plays a key role in the proof.

We are now equipped with an $O(sn)$ tool for determining the (tree = graph) reachability of a procedure. But we asked for more – for tree recursivity. If we possessed a way to (polynomially) reduce tree recursivity to tree reachability we had solved the problem.

5 Reducing Tree Recursivity to Tree Reachability

We reduce the problem "is P tree recursive?" to "is P' (tree) reachable?". The idea is simple:
After having encountered a call to a copy of procedure P in a branch during a (nondeterministic) search through the execution tree, we have to change some "state" in order to memorize this event. Any further hit of P can then be recognized as *recursion*. To implement this change of state we duplicate each declaration of a `procedure Q(...x...)` in the program to get the pair

`procedure Q1(...x1..., ...x2...)` and `procedure Q2(...x1..., ...x2...)`

on the same nesting level as Q. The call ids in the statement parts of $Q1$ and $Q2$ receive the suffix 1 and 2 resp., *except* for the statement part of $P1$ where the call ids have suffix 2. The argument lists get also duplicated – analogously to the formal parameter lists. Note that the mode depths are not changed by this transformation. Now, let's follow a branch BR and its transformed $BR1$ simultaneously, starting at $PROG$ resp. $PROG1$: On our way to reach the first P resp. $P1$, all ids in $BR1$ have suffix 1. It is directly after $P1$ that the suffix switches to 2 and remains 2 for all successors of $P1$. So, iff there is a second call to P in BR we must reach $P2$ in $BR1$. The role of the duplicated parameter lists becomes clear now: they make the ...2–procedures statically available when needed. We demonstrate this transformation T_P in fig.3 (omitting the type specifications of the parameters).

Note: Within ...2–procedures we do not need any ...1–names since they can never be used. Therefore we simplified the transformation in fig.3 which now yields in the worst case (all procedures nested within each other) only $O(n^2)$ procedures in $PROG1$ – as opposed to $O(2^n)$ without omitting this useless procedures. Moreover, if we impose an (arbitrarily) limit on the nesting depth we even end up with $O(n)$ new procedures.
Since the transformation itself is essentially a parsing mechanism with output (it can be implemented by means of solely synthesized attributes) it can certainly be done in linear time with respect to the program length.

We are now ready to make a theorem out of it (note that it applies to general FM–programs and therefore "tree reachable" is *not* equivalent to "reachable"):

Theorem 2 *Let P be a procedure in a FM program $PROG$.*
P is tree recursive $\iff$ $P2$ is tree reachable in $PROG1 = T_P(PROG)$.

The proof is a formalization of the above transformation mechanism: the branches BR and $BR1$ are constructed inductively on the different cases that may arise: a successor may be called by a nonformal, local formal, or global formal statement.

This brings us to our final result.

6 Main Result

Combinig the last theorems we get for FM2 programs the main

Theorem 3 *Let P be a procedure in a FM2 program $PROG$.*
P is tree recursive $\iff$ $P2 \in \mathcal{R}(PROG1)$, with $PROG1 = T_P(PROG)$.

In words: In order to determine whether or not a procedure P in a FM2–program is tree recursive we first transform the program scheme $PROG$ to get $PROG1$. Then we construct its graph representation – thereby computing all reachable procedures in $PROG1$. If and only if $P2$ – the transformed of P – is among them, then P is tree recursive in $PROG$.

7 Strong and weak recursivity

The presented transformation mechanism is general enough to solve similar problems. In [AR88], for example, it is used to establish a polynomial method which determines whether or not a procedure P has the *most recent* property (in fact, there the transformation is applied twice – first to P's static predecessor Q and then to $Q2$, the transformed of Q).

But there is still another interesting property which can be determined polynomially by this method – the *weak/strong recursivity.* Our definition of recursivity does not distinguish between different copies of a local procedure P which get created by each call (according to the copy rule) of P's static predecessor. If we do distinguish, then recursivity is partitioned into two disjoint subsets – namely into weak and strong recursivity. Remember that (plain) recursivity of procedure P (as defined in sect. 2.1) required name "P" to appear at least twice on some branch in the execution tree. Now, if P is to be strongly recursive then these two appeareances of P must denote the very same copy of P; if P is to be weakly recursive then no two names "P" on some branch may refer to the same copy of P, i.e., every appearance of "P" on a branch denotes a different copy of P. More formal: If we distinguish between different copies of P by appending a superscript $s \geq 0$ to P, then s can be interpreted as a static pointer to the call of that copy of Q that generated this copy P^s of P.

For example:

```
PROG:                                        1: PROG^0
  { proc Q(..)                                   |
      { proc P(..)      { Q(..) }            2: Q^1(..)
        P(..)                                    |
      }                                      3: P^2(..)
    Q(..)                                        |
  }                                          4: Q^1(..)
                                                 |
                                             5: P^4(..)
                                                 |
                                                ...
```

Each call to Q creates a new copy of P. Both, P and Q are recursive, but Q is strongly (any call to Q is to the one and only copy Q^1 which was created by the call of $PROG^0$), whereas P is weakly (any call to P is dynamically preceded by a call to its static predecessor Q^1 which creates new copies $P^2, P^4, \ldots$ each time Q^1 is called). Therefore, there are no two "P^i" on any branch in $PROG$'s execution tree.

In terms of implementation weak recursivity of P means that its local datas don't need an activation record of their own – they can be allocated together (i.e. at the same time and place) with Q's activation record. In a forthcoming paper I will show how our mechanism reveals also strong recursivity and – together with (plain) recursivity – consequently weak recursivity.

8 References

[AR88] D. Armbruster: *A Polynomial Determination of the Most–Recent Property.* Theoretical Computer Science 56, 3–15, 1988.

[AR85] D. Armbruster: *Entscheidbarkeit und Bestimmung der Rekursivität von Prozeduren.* Dissertation, University of Stuttgart, 1985.

[ISO81] ISO/TC79/SC5N: *Specification for Computer Language Pascal.* Third draft proposal, 1981–11–04.

[LA73] H. Langmaack: *On Correct Procedure Parameter Transmission in Higher Programming Languages.* Acta Informatica 2, 110—142, 1973.

[ME85] A. R. Meyer: *Complexity of Program Flow Analysis for Strictness ...*, private comminication, August 1985.

[PA85] D. A. Patterson: *Reduced Instruction Set Computers.* Comm. of the ACM 28, 1, 8—21, 1985.

[WA76] K. Walter: *Recursion Analysis for Compiler Optimization.* Comm. of the ACM 19, 9, 514—516, Sept. 1976.

[WI82] K. Winklmann: *On the Complexity of Some Problems Concerning the Use of Procedures I.* Acta Informatica 18, 299—318, 1982.

```
PROG:
  { procedure A(x)  { A(..) }


    procedure Q(z)
      { procedure P(y)
          { P(z) }




        Q(P)
        z()










      }

    Q(A)
  }
```

```
PROG1:
  { procedure A1(x1,x2)  { A1(..,..) }
    procedure A2(x2)     { A2(..) }

    procedure Q1(z1,z2)
      { procedure P1(y1,y2)
          { P2(z2) }          <-- suffix change!
        procedure P2(y2)
          { P2(z2) }

        Q1(P1,P2)
        z1()
      }

    procedure Q2(z2)
      { procedure P2(y2)
          { P2(z2) }

        Q2(P2)
        z2()
      }

    Q1(A1,A2)
  }
```

Figure 3: $PROG1 \;=\; T_P(PROG)$

Complexity of Proving Program Correctness

Hardi Hungar
Dept. of Computer Science
University of Oldenburg
D-2900 Oldenburg, GERMANY
hardi.hungar@arbi.informatik.uni-oldenburg.de

Abstract

The spectrum of a formula is the set of finite data structures in which it is valid. It is known that for some program logics the classes of spectra form complete subclasses of well known complexity classes. This means that for those logics we know how hard it is to *decide* the set of finite models. We extend those results by determining complexity classes corresponding to partial correctness assertions about programs from sublanguages of Clarke's language **L4**.

We proceed to show that syntax-directed proof systems are adequate tools for *proving* partial correctness assertions: It is not more difficult to construct a proof for a valid assertion than to decide its validity. This holds if the programs are simple while-programs or if they belong to some sublanguage of **ALGOL** like **L4**, for which relatively complete proof systems are rather sophisticated.

1 Introduction

1.1 Setup

We study partial correctness in the usual framework: programming languages are parametrized by a *signature* which introduces names and types of the operations on the data domain. An *interpretation* of these symbols provides the domain. It fixes the semantics of programs and formulas. A natural question to ask is: What is the computational complexity of a set like

$$\{ \langle I, \{p\}\,\pi\,\{q\}\rangle \mid \pi \in \Pi,\ I \models \{p\}\,\pi\,\{q\} \},$$

where Π is a programming language, p and q stand for first-order formulas and I ranges over the set of interpretations?

But it is rather pointless to put exactly this question because the set above is not decidable for any reasonable programming language: We know that halting of while programs is undecidable if they are interpreted in $\mathcal{N}$, the (infinite) domain of natural numbers. And also whether a first-order formula is true in $\mathcal{N}$ or not can not always be computed. But both problems are contained in the set via assertions $\{true\}\ \pi\ \{false\}$ resp. $\{true\}\ \mathbf{skip}\ \{p\}$.

Therefore, we demand I to be finite. For many programming languages the resulting set is decidable. This is true in particular for those programming languages which have a relatively complete (in the sense of Cook [3]) Hoare-style proof system.

Our main purpose is to compare the (inherent) complexity of program correctness with the complexity of *proof constructing machines* which do not only decide the validity of assertions but also construct a derivation (in a Hoare-style proof system) for every valid assertion. To this end we have to establish the complexity of decision procedures at first and afterwards that of proving machines.

Our considerations will be somewhat restricted, though. The complexity will be measured in the size of the interpretation only. We will not take into account the length of the partial correctness assertions in the second component.[1]

1.2 Results

The most important notions of this paper are *spectrum* and *spectral complexity.*

Assuming a natural encoding of finite interpretations, every partial correctness assertion defines a formal language: the set of codes of those interpretations where it is valid. This language is called the *spectrum* of the assertion. The *spectrum class* of a programming language is the set of spectra of assertions about programs from that language.

Spectrum classes can often be related to complexity classes which are defined by time or space bounds on accepting Turing machines. We say that the spectrum class of a programming language is *complete* for a complexity class iff it is a subclass (i.e. every spectrum is decidable within the given bounds) and there is a simple (easy to compute) function making a spectrum of a partial correctness assertion out of every problem of the complexity class. Thus, if a spectrum class is complete for a complexity class, we know how hard it is to decide the spectra: They are exactly as hard to decide as the problems of the complexity class. We will use the term *spectral complexity of a programming language* in this case.

The spectral complexities of some programming languages are already known. We will discuss those results later. For some programming languages, namely **L4**-programs with bounded type depth, we have to determine the spectral complexities. This is done by showing that each of those sublanguages of **L4** is equivalent to a functional language with recursion of appropriate higher type. (The spectral complexities of those functional languages are known.) This establishes a hierarchy of programming

[1] For some programming languages (like **RFCT**, which is one of the languages considered here) deciding machines are of unbounded complexity in the second component

languages of increasing spectral complexity, all of them having a relatively complete proof system.

Knowing the spectral complexities is the basis for studying whether it is more difficult to construct derivations in Hoare-style proof systems for valid assertions than just to decide the validity of the assertions. We find out that both tasks are of the same degree of difficulty: Whatever syntax directed proof-system we considered, we always were able to give efficient proof constructing procedures. This substantiates the vague feeling that syntax directed proof-systems are natural and adequate.

1.3 Related work

The spectral complexities of (program) logics have been studied before. There are papers of Fagin [4] and Immerman [10] addressing such questions. More relevant to us are results from the work of Kfoury, Tiuryn and Urzyczyn [14, 19] and also of Harel and Peleg [8]. We had to adapt the definitions which were used there in order to answer the questions stated above. Therefore, our definitions (e.g. the notion of a spectrum) are not exactly the same. But the main results hold in our context as well. Thus we know the spectral complexities of deterministic and nondeterministic while-programs, of programs with simple recursion and of some languages with higher order recursion as well. In addition to [14] papers of Goerdt [7] and Juszczyk [13] help us to derive the spectral complexities of the sublanguages of **L4**. But in none of the papers cited above the complexity of proof construction has been studied.

There is yet another approach to the complexity of program correctness. In [11, 12] Jones and Muchnik fixed the interpretation (a finite domain of characters) and added **read** and **accept** commands to the programming languages. Programs could then be considered as automatas accepting formal languages. They asked for the complexity of procedures deciding e.g. whether the language accepted by a program is empty, measured in the size of the program. This does not collide with our work. Roughly spoken, Jones and Muchnik fixed the interpretation and computed complexities depending on the size of the program whereas the program is fixed and complexities are measured in the size of the interpretation as long as we are concerned with spectral complexities. Qualitatively, the results are comparable: The computational complexity increases if more advanced constructs are allowed. The complexity of syntax directed proving, however, is not addressed by Jones and Muchnik.

2 Preliminaries

2.1 Signatures, Interpretations and Formulas

Signatures are sets of symbols for functions and relations (with positive arities) and for constants. We assume that they contain at least the constant symbol ω, one function symbol and the binary relation symbol $\simeq$. If there is just one function symbol, which in addition is unary, we need at least one relation symbol besides $\simeq$. These restrictions either are necessary for syntax-directed proof systems or they save us from considering exceptional cases in definitions and results (cf. [8, 19]).

An *interpretation* of a signature consists of a *domain*, which is simply a set, and elements and appropriate (total) functions and relations for the symbols. $\simeq$ always gets equality on the domain as its meaning. If I is an interpretation, we will often refer to the domain of I by simply writing I.

If I and J are interpretations of the same signature, then a function from I to J is called an *isomorphism* if it is bijective and respects constants and values of functions and relations. A subset D of I^n is *closed with respect to isomorphism* if for any isomorphism $\phi : I \to I$ and any $\vec{d} \in I^n$ it holds: $\vec{d} \in D \Leftrightarrow \phi(\vec{d}) \in D$.

Terms, *boolean expressions* and *first-order formulas* are defined as usual. If I is an interpretation, then $Th(I)$ denotes the set of first-order formulas which are true in I, the *theory* of I.

Very important for proving partial correctness assertions in finite interpretations is the following expressibility lemma.

Lemma 1 (Expressibility Lemma) *If I is a finite interpretation and D is closed w.r.t. isomorphism then D is definable by a first-order formula.*

Proof

Let $diag_I(\vec{y})$ be a formula with $|I|$ free variables defining names (which are unique up to isomorphism) for the elements of I. Then

$$\exists \vec{y}.(diag_I(\vec{y}) \wedge \bigvee_{\vec{d} \in D} \vec{x} \simeq \vec{y}_{\vec{d}})$$

defines D. □

2.2 Programming Languages

We study essentially three different programming languages. They all are sublanguages of an idealized **ALGOL**:

(N)WP (non)deterministic while-programs

RFCT programs with regular formal call trees [17]

L4 programs with finitely typed procedures which do not use nonlocal variables [1]

The syntax of (idealized) **ALGOL** is as follows. *Statements*, *blocks* and *environments* are generated by the following production system.

S ::= $x := t$ | S;S | **if** b **then** S **else** S **fi** | S **or** S | **while** b **do** S **od** |
error | B | $g(\vec{x} : \vec{g})$
B ::= **begin var** x; S **end** | **begin** E S **end**
E ::= ε | **proc** $f(\vec{x} : \vec{h})$; B ; E ,

where x is a variable, t is a term, b is a boolean expression, f and g are procedure identifiers and $\vec{x}$ resp. $\vec{g}$ and $\vec{h}$ are vectors of variables resp. procedure identifiers.

The notions of free and bound identifiers are as usual. Programs of **ALGOL** are those statements without free procedure identifiers. Their *semantics*, a binary relation on the set of states, is provided by the static-scope copy rule (parameter passing by call-by-name), see e.g. [16]. The symbol **or** is interpreted as nondeterministic choice.

Viewed as a binary relation on the valuations of its free variables the semantics of every program is closed w.r.t. isomorphism. By Lemma 1, it is expressible by a first-order formula in every finite interpretation. Hence every finite interpretation is *expressive.*

Let **WP** be the set of **ALGOL**-programs without blocks, procedures and **or**, **NWP**-programs may contain **or**.

RFCT is defined as in [18]. It consists of all programs where the computation tree which is generated by the copy rule meets a certain regularity property. We will not spell out the (long) definition. What we need is the axiomatization of **RFCT** from [17] (see also [18]) and the fact that any program in **RFCT** is equivalent to a program without procedures as parameters [17].

To define **L4**, we need the notion of a *finite type.* Finite types are generated by

$$\tau \ ::= \ (n : \underbrace{\tau \ldots \tau}_{k}), \quad n, k \in \mathcal{N}$$

The *depth* $|\tau|$ of τ is 0 for $\tau = (0 : \varepsilon)$, 1 for $(n : \varepsilon)$ with $n \geq 1$, and k+1 for $(n : \tau_1 \ldots \tau_n)$, where k is the maximum of $\{|\tau_1|, \ldots, |\tau_k|\}$.

Let every procedure identifier be equipped (implicitly) with a type. An **ALGOL**-program has *finite types* if all occurrences of procedure identifiers are in accordance with their types. For example: If $g(x\,y : h)$ is a procedure call and the type of h is $(3 : \varepsilon)$, then the type of g has to be $(2 : (3 : \varepsilon))$.

L4 is the set of **ALGOL**-programs with finite types where no procedure refers to non-local variables, i.e. every variable occurring within the body of a procedure declaration is either a formal parameter of the procedure or declared within its body. For $k \in \mathcal{N}$ let $\mathbf{L4}^k$ be the subset of **L4** where all occurring types are of depths less or equal to k.

As intermediary language we also need $\mathbf{RVL4}^k$, the set of **ALGOL**-programs with finite types of depth less or equal to k, where global variables may be *read* by procedures, and where parameter passing is by value/result. (That is, nonlocal variables

Let us first explain some components of this declaration. *stack* is a procedure of type depth 2, *back*, *up* and *next* are of type depth 1. *next* may be declared elsewhere (e.g. on top level). It is a procedure which enumerates one by one all elements of the interpretation which can be generated from the initial contents of the free variables of the program (which are kept in $\vec{z}$), compare e.g. [19]. The enumeration starts with ω. Note that the value of x as any value occurring during execution of the program can be generated from the input. $g(\vec{y} : \vec{g})$ is the critical call. E_{mod} differs from E in that references to x (which we assume to look like $\tilde{x} := x$) are replaced by $\tilde{x} := \omega;\ back(\vec{z}\,\tilde{x}\,:)$.

The critical call in S is replaced by

$$\textbf{begin var } enum;\ enum := \omega;\ stack(\vec{z}\,\vec{y}\ enum\ x : skip) \textbf{ end}$$

skip is a procedure which stops without changing its parameters (like *next*, it may be declared once on top level in the program).

This is what happens during the execution of the transformed program instead of execution of the critical call: At first, *stack* calls itself recursively until *enum* and x are equal. Thereby a chain of different bindings of the procedure parameter *back* is created. The first one is *skip*, the other ones are different incarnations of *up*. Every element of the chain is a global formal parameter of its successor. The last element is global to those procedures occurring within the critical call which were declared in E in theoriginal program and which now are declared in E_{mod}(i.e. to those procedures which might refer to x nonlocally). The length of the chain is the number of times *next* has to be called to reach the value of x. Whenever the value of x is needed, the last element of the chain is called. Then one by one all the elements of the chain are invoked, recomputing the value of x in their parameter *counter*.

We need one procedure like *stack* for each critical call. The types of the procedures in E are not changed during the translation. (Except for the fact that the values of the input are made accessible throughout the program by adding the variable vector $\vec{z}$ to the parameter list of every procedure. But this does not change type depths since there are no procedures of type depth zero.) But we add procedures of depths one (*up*, *next* and *skip*) and two (*stack*). Thus our transformation does not work for programs of type depth one. But in those programs it is easy to denest procedure declarations. This also eliminates nonlocal references.

Note however that our transformation depends on the fact that all the values a variable might take can be generated systematically from the input. This would be difficult if ground functions were partial. □

Thus we have a lower bound on the spectral complexity of $\mathbf{L4}^k$. That the spectrum of $\mathbf{L4}^k$ indeed is contained in $DTIME(\exp^k(O(\log|I|)))$ follows by combining results from [7] and [15]. This proves the following theorem.

Theorem 3 *For $k \geq 1$, the spectral complexity of* $\mathbf{L4}^k$ *is* $DTIME(\exp^k(O(\log|I|)))$.

We also can construct proofs within these bounds.

Theorem 4 *For every* $\{p\}\,\pi\,\{q\}$ *with* $\pi \in \mathbf{L4}^k$, $k \geq 1$, *there is a proof constructor which works in* $DTIME(\exp^k(O(\log|I|)))$.

Proof

L4has been axiomatized by German, Clarke and Halpern in [5]. The proof system is even more complicated than the one for **RFCT**. One has to reason about statements with free procedure identifiers. This reflects the following fact: The semantics of a statement S within a program π is a binary relation on the set of states which depends on the bindings of the formal procedure identifiers global to it. And there might be an unbounded number of semantically different bindings of those procedure identifiers. (With **RFCT**-programs the situation is different. There is no need to deal with free procedures because it suffices to consider a finite number of different procedure environments for each statement.) Therefore we need a new notion of 'mgca'. If S is a statement with global formal procedures $\vec{h}$, global declared procedures $\vec{g}$ and free variables $\vec{x}$, the mgca used in the completeness proof of [5] takes the form

$$mgca_S(\vec{h}, \vec{v}_{\vec{h}}) \;=\; codes(\vec{v}_{\vec{h}}, \vec{h}) \wedge mgca_{\vec{g}}(\vec{v}_{\vec{h}}, \vec{g}) \rightarrow \{\vec{x} \simeq \vec{x}'\}\,\mathrm{S}\,\{post(\vec{v}_{\vec{h}}, \vec{x}, \vec{x}')\}$$

$\vec{v}_{\vec{h}}$ are variables of a new sort: Just like ordinary variables, their values are elements of the domain of the interpretation. But their range is not limited to one partial correctness assertion. They are used to code the semantics of procedures and transport those semantics into the postcondition within the third subformula, just like $\vec{x}'$ transports values from the precondition (input values) to the postcondition. (In the proof system, procedure identifiers may occur within statements but not within pre- or postconditions). The first subformula expresses '$\vec{v}_{\vec{h}}$ *codes* $\vec{h}$'. The second one captures the semantics of $\vec{g}$, the third one the semantics of S, provided that $\vec{h}$ are bound to procedures whose semantics are coded by $\vec{v}_{\vec{h}}$. Both the second and the third subformula express the semantics of the procedures resp. statement uniform in terms of $\vec{v}_{\vec{h}}$.

The second subformula is a conjunction of formulas which play a role similar to the assumptions in Olderog's proof system: They have to be verified for the bodies of the procedures and have to be eliminated by applications of an appropriate version of the recursion rule.

What we have to do is a little bit more than in the case of Olderog's proof system: We do not only have to compute the semantics of all the statements within the program, we also need a coding (which is not a built-in feature of the axiom system). Some care is needed in choosing the coding. We can use an adaptation of a binary representation of monotone higher order functions, cf. [7]. The length of the code of a procedure of type depth k is $\exp^k(O(\log|I|))$.

To get the semantics of the statements S we proceed in roughly the same way as in the proof of Theorem 2: We do a fixpoint approximation. An argument which is analogous to the one used there about the lengths of chains gives the desired bound on the computational complexity. The computed semantics are translated into mgcas. Having determined the mgcas, the rest is simple. □

An interesting point about the proof construction is the following. The distinction between formal and declared procedures in mgcas is not necessary. Defined as above a mgca is not even a most general assertion about S, since it does not depend on S alone, but also on its environment of procedure declarations (It is only most general within the context of the given program). Treating declared procedures like formal ones - like it is done in a compositional semantics - is possible in the proof system from [5]. Mgcas would become really 'most general assertions' and the proofs would be conceptually simpler from a theoretical point of view. But it would also increase the 'type depth' of every S which is in the scope of a procedure declaration at least by one (The highest type depth of declared procedures within a program is one plus the highest type depth of formal procedures) Thus would increase the complexity of proof construction exponentially.

4 Conclusions

We have examined the most important examples of proof systems for partial correctness assertions about sequential programs. In each case it turned out that proof construction in finite interpretations is of the same degree of complexity as the problem itself. This means: One can ask for a proof instead of being content with the simple answer 'yes' or 'no'.

What are conceivable directions of future work? There are at least two:

- looking at other systems, e.g. for concurrent programs. Another interesting candidate is Goerdt's proof system for a functional language with higher order recursion [6]
- trying to determine the complexity in the size of $\Phi_\Sigma(I)$ *and* $\{p\}\,\pi\,\{q\}$.

Acknowledgement

I sincerely thank Michał Grabowski for many discussions.

References

[1] Clarke, E. M. *Programming languages for which it is impossible to obtain good Hoare axiom systems,* JACM **26** (1979) 129–147.

[2] Clarke, E. M. *The characterization problem for Hoare logic,* Rep. CMU-CS-84-109, Carnegie-Mellon Univ. (1984).

[3] Cook, S. A. *Soundness and completeness of an axiom system for program verification,* SIAM J. Comp. **7** (1978) 70–90.

[4] Fagin, R. *Generalized first-order spectra and polynomial-time recognizable sets,* SIAM-AMS Proc. **7** (1974) 43–73.

[5] German, S. M., Clarke, E. M. and Halpern, J. Y. *Reasoning about procedures as parameters in the language L4,* Inf. and Comp. **83** (1989) 265–359. (Earlier version: 1st LiCS (1986) 11–25)

[6] Goerdt, A. *A Hoare calculus defined by recursion on higher types,* in: Proc. Logics of Programs 1985, LNCS 193, 106–117.

[7] Goerdt, A. *Characterizing complexity classes by general recursive definitions in higher types,* in: E. Börger and H. Kleine-Büning, CSL '88, Proceedings, LNCS 385 (1988).

[8] Harel, D. and Peleg, D. *On static logics, dynamic logics, and complexity classes,* Inf. and Contr. **60** (1984) 86–102.

[9] Hartmanis, J., Immerman, N. and Mahany, S. *One-way log-tape reductions,* 19th FoCS (1978) 65–72.

[10] Immerman, N. *Languages which capture complexity classes,* 15th SToC (1983) 347–354.

[11] Jones, N. D. and Muchnik, S. S. *Even simple programs are hard to analyze,* JACM **24** (1977) 338–350.

[12] Jones, N. D. and Muchnik, S. S. *The complexity of finite memory programs with recursion,* JACM **25** (1978) 312–321.

[13] Juszczyk, M. *On equivalence between language L4 and recursive definitions of higher types,* not published (submitted for MFCS'89) Warsaw (1989).

[14] Kfoury, A. J., Tiuryn, J. and Urzyczyn, P. *The hierarchy of finitely typed functions,* 2nd LiCS (1987) 225–235.

[15] Kfoury, A. J. and Urzyczyn, P. *Finitely typed functional programs. Part II: Comparisons to imperative languages,* Res. Rep. Boston Univ. (1988).

[16] Langmaack, H. *On correct procedure parameter transmission in higher programming languages,* Acta Inf. **2** (1973) 110–142.

[17] Olderog, E.-R. *Charakterisierung Hoarescher Systeme für ALGOL-ähnliche Programmiersprachen,* Dissertation, Univ. Kiel (1981).

[18] Olderog, E.-R. *A characterization of Hoare's logic for programs with PASCAL-like procedures,* 15th SToC (1983) 320–329.

[19] Tiuryn, J. and Urzyczyn, P. *Some relationships between logics of programs and complexity theory,* TCS **60** (1988) 83–108. (Earlier version: 24th FoCS (1983) 180–184)

Some Normalization Properties of Martin-Löf's Type Theory, and Applications

David A. Basin*

Department of Artifici... ...elligence

University of Ed...

Edinburgh EH1 1...

basin@aipna...

Douglas ...

Department of C...

Cornell ...

Ithaca, NY...

howe@cs.co...

Abstract

For certain kinds of applications of type theories, the faithfulness of formalization in the theory depends on intensional, or structural, properties of objects constructed in the theory. For type theories such as LF, such properties can be established via an analysis of normal forms and types. In type theories such as Nuprl or Martin-Löf's polymorphic type theory, which are much more expressive than LF, the underlying programming language is essentially untyped, and terms proved to be in types do not necessarily have normal forms. Nevertheless, it is possible to show that for Martin-Löf's type theory, and a large class of extensions of it, a sufficient kind of normalization property does in fact hold in certain well-behaved subtheories. Applications of our results include the use of the type theory as a logical framework in the manner of LF, and an extension of the *proofs-as-programs* paradigm to the synthesis of verified computer hardware. For the latter application we point out some advantages to be gained by working in a more expressive type theory.

*Supported by NATO under a grant awarded in 1990.

†Supported in part by ONR contract N00014-88-K-0409.

1 Introduction

For certain kinds of applications of type theories, the faithfulness of formalization in the theory depends on intensional, or structural, properties of objects constructed in the theory. One example of this is the use of a typed lambda calculus, such as LF [10], as a "general logic". One can embed a natural deduction logic in the calculus by introducing typed constants for each rule and for each term and formula constructor of the logic. The constants are typed in such a way that for each sentence P of the logic there is a type T whose members correspond to proofs of the sentence. The encoding is faithful when the existence of a member of T implies the provability of P. To prove faithfulness, one analyzes the normal forms of members of T and observes that their construction from the constants is isomorphic to a proof. See [10] for a discussion of the advantages of the LF approach to encoding logics.

Another example is a widely used method for formalizing the combinational logic of digital circuits [4]. Here one represents a circuit as a relation over the booleans, so that a circuit with n ports (inputs and outputs) is represented as an n-ary relation which is true exactly when the ports have values consistent with the logic of the circuit. The relations are built from operators which express the logic of transistors, gates, registers, etc. If *bool* is the type of booleans, then a circuit with 2 ports could be represented as a function of type $bool \times bool \rightarrow bool$. If we can form subtypes in our type theory, then we might write

$$\{ R : bool \times bool \rightarrow bool \mid Spec(R) \}$$

to represent the collection of all circuits satisfying some specification. A term t in this type is a function computing boolean values as specified. However, we need to know more than this if we want our representation to be faithful. In particular, we need to know that t is built from the operators for transistors, etc., in such a way that it can be viewed as a circuit. Here again we would like to analyze normal forms.

In this paper we show how the kinds of encodings just discussed can be done directly and faithfully in Martin-Löf's polymorphic type theory, and also in a class of "computational" extensions of it.

Martin-Löf's polymorphic type theory, which we will henceforth refer to as TT, was designed as a formal basis for constructive mathematics. It contains a functional programming language and a highly expressive type system. Some of its descendents have been used in a number of interactive proof development systems (for example, Nuprl [6], Veritas [8], Isabelle [16] and a system based on [15] currently under development). Nuprl, in particular, has been extensively used to formalize mathematics and programming. Our results should apply, with minor modifications, to the type theory of Nuprl, but this has not been checked.

The difficulty in establishing the required normalization properties in TT is that TT gains its expressiveness and flexibility partly at the cost of some of the traditional properties of type systems. In particular, the underlying programming language of

TT is untyped, and terms that belong to types cannot, in general, be normalized in the usual λ-calculus sense (although they are guaranteed to evaluate to weak head-normal form). For example, if $\perp$ is any diverging term of the untyped λ-calculus and T is an empty type, then

$$\lambda x.\ \perp\ \in T \rightarrow T.$$

Thus the techniques for proving faithfulness in LF are not directly applicable to TT.

Our main result is that a sufficient kind of normalization property does in fact hold for TT. From this property, we can derive several useful results about the faithfulness of encodings in TT. Before describing these results, we consider an example.

Suppose we have proven the sequent

$$T{:}U_1,\ z{:}T,\ s{:}T \rightarrow T,\ r{:}Ax \vdash t \in T$$

in TT, where r does not occur free in t and where Ax is the encoding in TT, via the *propositions-as-types* correspondence, of some logical statement involving T, z and s. This sequent says that under the hypotheses that T, z and s have the given types and satisfy Ax, t has type T (U_1 can be thought of as the collection of all "small" types).

Since T is a hypothetical type, and the only operations given for constructing members of T are z and s, we expect that t should be equivalent to a program of the form $s(s(\ldots(z)\ldots))$. There is little hope of proving such a property by a metatheoretic analysis of TT's inference system. The rules of this type theory are too numerous and complex.

Instead, we take a semantic approach, using the semantics developed by Allen [1]. In this semantics, the meaning of a type is a set of closed terms (together with an equivalence relation over the set). A term belongs in a type if and only if it evaluates to a value of the right form. For example, the members of N are all terms that evaluate to a numeral.

To obtain a normal form for t in the above example, we might proceed as follows. Since the sequent is provable, it is true. Its truth implies that for any particular type T, and for any values $z \in T$ and $s \in T \rightarrow T$ such that Ax is satisfied, the term t must evaluate to a value of a form appropriate for T. If such T, z, and s exist, then there is a sequence of computation steps taking this instance of t to a value. Now consider applying the same sequence to t, a term which may have free occurrences of the *variables* T, z and s. We get a sequence of "symbolic computation" steps that must also terminate, although it might be shorter than the original sequence. Since the computation system is lazy, the result of this new sequence may only be partly normalized, so we may need to repeat the whole process with some of the subterms.

However, we have the following difficulty. Suppose, for example, that Ax asserts both that that T is isomorphic to the type of natural numbers and that s solves the halting problem for Turing machines. Since all members of function types in the semantics are computable, no such s can exist. Hence there are no terms T, z, s, r of TT for which the hypotheses are true. Thus the sequent is vacuously true for any

t whatsoever, in particular for $t = \perp$. Nevertheless, it would clearly be useful to use the type theory to reason about such apparently inconsistent contexts, and still be guaranteed a normalization property.

This difficulty can in fact be ruled out because TT is *open-ended* in the sense that its theorems are true in any semantics constructed from a collection of new base types and a computation language that extends that of TT. For the example above, we could use an extension of TT that includes an "oracle" deciding the halting problem.

More generally, we want to show that if

$$x_1 : A_1,\ \ldots,\ x_n : A_n,\ r : Ax \vdash t \in T$$

is provable in TT, where $T, A_1, \ldots, A_n$ are from a well-behaved subtheory of TT and t is an arbitrary term in which r does not occur free, and if there is some extension of TT in which we can satisfy the hypotheses, then we can effectively find a term t in the subtheory which is in normal form and which is equal to t (as a member of T). The subtheory we deal with in this paper is based on the LF type theory. It is suitably well-behaved and is expressive enough for the examples we have in mind. We also fix a particular "maximal" extension in which to satisfy the hypotheses. This extension is a full classical model of TT in which all function types have representatives of all functions with appropriate domain and range.

The core of the paper is a pair of fairly general technical lemmas. We use these lemmas to obtain several particular theorems which can be applied to the practical examples outlined above. Suppose

$$\Gamma,\ r : Ax \vdash t \in T$$

is provable in TT, where

$$\Gamma = x_1 : A_1,\ \ldots,\ x_n : A_n$$

is the translation into TT of an LF context, T is an LF type in this context, t is any term of TT in which r is not free, and Ax represents a formula of higher-order logic in which the types of quantified variables are the LF types well-formed in Γ. We show that either of the following conditions is sufficient to find an LF term t' in normal form such that $\Gamma \vdash t' \in T$ in LF and

$$\Gamma,\ r : Ax \vdash t = t' \in T$$

is true in TT:

1. Ax is the trivial proposition *true*.

2. All the types well-formed in Γ are simple types (built from $\rightarrow$ and base types), and the hypotheses can be satisfied (in a certain way) in the classical extension.

These conditions cover many cases of practical interest, including the use of TT as a logical framework (where Ax is *true*) and the use of TT as a foundation for reasoning about combinational logic (where Ax expresses the logic properties of the circuit constructors). It should be possible to obtain more general results along these lines within the same technical framework.

The classical model is a reasonable place to look for objects to satisfy hypotheses with. However, it also plays a crucial technical role. The functions and values that are introduced in the classical extension have a simple structure. The proofs of the technical lemmas rely heavily on this simple structure, and we do not know how to eliminate this reliance.

In the open-ended spirit of TT, we prove the above results not just for TT *per se*, but for any extension of it which has the same type constructors but a larger computation language. We assume that any such language is presented with a certain kind of structural operational semantics. The proofs of the technical lemmas involve a detailed analysis of these presentations. The technical work of this paper builds on the work in [13], which introduces the operational semantics formalism and constructs the classical extension of TT.

There are some advantages to being able to use a highly expressive type theory for the practical applications mentioned above. For example, within stronger type theories, the type theory itself can serve as a meta-language for developing derived inference rules and tactics[11]; this is not possible within the weaker LF type theory. Another benefit to using a rich type theory is that one can reason about parameterized terms where the parameters come from arbitrary (not necessarily LF) types. For example, in the domain of hardware verification and synthesis, it is best to verify large regular circuits such as adders and multipliers by verifying parameterized versions (e.g., an n-bit adder) and later instantiating the parameters to produce a term representing a specific circuit. We provide an example of this kind of development at the end of this paper.

Some closely related work is presented in [5]. The main result there is that LF-like encodings in Nuprl are faithful in the case where the encoded logic has a complete semantics that can be introduced into the Nuprl semantics. The notion of faithfulness used there is weaker, since it only guarantees that provability in the object logic is equivalent to provability in the encoding, and does not guarantee any structural correspondence between proofs and terms of the type theory. Furthermore, the only proof given is for encodings of first-order logic.

The remainder of the paper is organized as follows. In the next section we supply some of the necessary background, summarize the relevant sections of [12, 13] and briefly describe the semantic approach of [1]. We then state and sketch the proofs of the results referred to above. In the last section we describe some applications.

2 Background

2.1 Structured Computation Systems

Language

A *lazy computation language* L is a triple (O, K, α) where O and K are sets of *operators* with $K \subset O$ and

$$\alpha \in O \to \{\, (k_1, \ldots, k_n) \mid n, k_i \geq 0 \,\}.$$

We call the members of K *canonical* operators. For $\tau \in O$, $\alpha(\tau)$ is the *arity* of τ and specifies the number and binding structure of the operator's arguments.

Fix a countably infinite set of variables. We inductively define the *second-order terms of arity n*. A variable is a second-order term of arity 0. If τ is an operator with arity $(k_1, \ldots, k_n)$, if $b_1, \ldots, b_n$ are second-order terms of arity $k_1, \ldots, k_n$ respectively, and if $\overline{x}$ is a list of m variables, then then $\overline{x}.\tau(b_1, \ldots, b_n)$ is a second-order term of arity m. The b_i in this term are the *operands* of the operator τ. We add binding structure by specifying that in a second-order term $x_1, \ldots, x_m. t$, each x_i binds in t. A *term* is a second-order term of arity 0.

We identify second-order terms that are α-equal (the same up to renaming of bound variables). We write $t[a_1, \ldots, a_n/x_1, \ldots, x_n]$ for the result of simultaneous substituting in t the terms $a_1, \ldots, a_n$ for $x_1, \ldots, x_n$, respectively. We will simplify this to $t[a_1, \ldots, a_n]$ when the variable list can be inferred from the context.

A term $\tau(\overline{t})$ is *canonical* if τ is a canonical operator, and *noncanonical* otherwise. The closed terms will be the programs of our computation systems. The closed canonical terms will be exactly the results of evaluating programs; thus a term will be considered to be fully evaluated exactly if its outermost operator is canonical.

Inference rules for evaluation, described below, are specified using an extension of the set of terms. For each $i \geq 1$ we fix an infinite set of variables which we will call the *second-order variables of arity i*. The ordinary variables from above are the second-order variables of arity 0. A *term schema* is built in the same way as a term, except that we also include expressions of the form $P[\overline{t}]$ where P is a second-order variable of arity i ($i \geq 0$) and $\overline{t}$ is a list of i terms. We identify $P[]$ and P. Because of the use we will make of second-order variables, we will usually capitalize the free second-order variables of a term schema and refer to them as *metavariables* (note that variables of arity $i > 0$ are always free).

A second-order substitution is a partial map σ from second-order variables to second-order terms of corresponding arity. The definition of the application of σ to terms is similar to the definition for ordinary substitution, except that $\sigma(P[a_1, \ldots, a_n]) = t[\sigma(a_1), \ldots, \sigma(a_n)/x_1, \ldots, x_n]$ if $\sigma(P)$ is $x_1, \ldots, x_n. t$. A *simple term schema* has the form $\tau(\overline{x}_1. P_1[\overline{x}_1]; \ldots; \overline{x}_n. P_n[\overline{x}_n])$ where the P_i are distinct metavariables. It is (non-) canonical if τ is (non-) canonical.

Evaluation Rules

Let L be a lazy computation language. An *evaluation rule* for L is a rule whose premises and conclusion are of the form $a \Downarrow b$, where a and b are term schemas or metavariables of arity 0. The set of premises of a rule may be infinite but must be well-ordered (that is, ordered by some total well-founded relation). In addition, in order to guarantee certain properties of evaluation, we impose the following syntactic conditions on a rule. Let I be the set that well-orders the premises, and for $i \in I$, let $a_i \Downarrow b_i$ be the ith premise. Let $a \Downarrow b$ be the conclusion of the rule. We require the following: (1) a is a noncanonical simple term schema; (2) for all $i \in I$, b_i is a metavariable or a canonical simple term schema, and has no metavariables in common with a or with b_j for $j \neq i$; (3) for each $i \in I$ and metavariable P of a_i, P occurs in a or in b_j for some $j <_I i$; (4) b is a metavariable, and for some i, b is b_i and does not occur in any other premise. The metavariable b is called the *output variable*, and the ith premise in the last condition is called the *output premise.*

The last restriction is only a convenience: rules allowing a more general form for b can be modified to meet this restriction by adding a few premises. For example, a rule with no output premise and with conclusion $a \Downarrow v$, for some canonical v, can be taken as shorthand for a rule with output premise $v \Downarrow P$ and conclusion $a \Downarrow P$.

An *instance* of a rule is the result of applying to its premises and conclusion a second-order substitution whose domain is the set of metavariables occurring in the rule. An instance is closed if each formula is closed (i.e. both terms are closed).

Let R be a set of evaluation rules over a lazy computation language L. We inductively define, for terms a and b, *derivations (in R) of $a \Downarrow b$*. If a is canonical then $a \Downarrow a$ is a derivation of itself. If a is noncanonical then a derivation of $a \Downarrow b$ consists of a rule instance with conclusion $a \Downarrow b$ and premises $\{ a_i \Downarrow b_i \,|\, i \in I \}$, together with derivations of $a_i \Downarrow b_i$ for each $i \in I$. A derivation is *closed* if every rule instance in it is closed. When we write $a \Downarrow b$ we will mean that the formula $a \Downarrow b$ has closed derivation.

A *structured computation system* S consists of a lazy computation language L and a set R of evaluation rules over L. The relation $\cdot \Downarrow \cdot$ specified by R is the *evaluation relation* of S. The evaluation relation has the property that if $a \Downarrow b$ then b is canonical, and if a is canonical then $a \Downarrow b$ if and only if $b = a$. A closed term b is a *value* of a if $a \Downarrow b$. A closed formula $a \Downarrow b$ is *determinate* if it is true and if for all closed terms v, $a \Downarrow v$ implies $v = b$. S is *deterministic* if every true closed formula over S is determinate. S is *strongly deterministic* if it is deterministic and if for every closed instance r of a rule of S, if the conclusion of r is $a \Downarrow b$ and its premises are $\{ a_i \Downarrow b_i \mid i \in I \}$, and if there is a $j \in I$ such that a_j has no value and $a_i \Downarrow b_i$ is determinate for $i < j$, then a has no value.

For example, the lazy untyped λ-calculus can be cast as a structured computation system. Take $O = \{ \lambda, ap \}$ and $K = \{ \lambda \}$. Define α by $\alpha(\lambda) = (1)$ and $\alpha(ap) = (0,0)$. Write $\lambda x.\, b$ for $\lambda(x.b)$, and $a(b)$ for $ap(a, b)$. The single evaluation rule is

$$\frac{F \Downarrow \lambda x.\, B[x] \quad B[A] \Downarrow C}{F(A) \Downarrow C.}$$

Languages with eager evaluation can also be cast as lazy computation systems. For example, we can specify the call-by-value λ-calculus by changing the above rule to

$$\frac{F \Downarrow \lambda x.\, B[x] \quad A \Downarrow V \quad B[V] \Downarrow C}{F(A) \Downarrow C.}$$

Non-lazy data constructors can be dealt with by introducing a non-canonical operator for each constructor. For example, for a pairing operator $\langle \cdot, \cdot \rangle$, introduce a non-canonical operator *pair* with the following rule.

$$\frac{A \Downarrow V \quad A' \Downarrow V'}{pair\,(A; A') \Downarrow \langle V, V' \rangle}$$

If S and S' are structured computation systems, then S' *extends* S if the language of S' extends that of S, and if for every rule r of S', if the operator in the conclusion of r is in the language of S then r is in S (so S' does not extend the semantics of any of the operators of S).

Some of the results below state that certain terms can be found *effectively*. For this to be true, it is required that the structured computation system be effectively presented.

A Computational Preorder

Let S be a structured computation system. The preorder $\leq$ is defined as the largest binary relation over the closed terms of S such that $a \leq a'$ if and only if: $a \Downarrow \theta(\overline{x}_1.\, t_1; \ldots; \overline{x}_n.\, t_n)$, for θ canonical, implies there are terms $t'_1, \ldots, t'_n$ such that $a' \Downarrow \theta(\overline{x}_1.\, t'_1; \ldots; \overline{x}_n.\, t'_n)$ and such that for each i, $1 \leq i \leq n$ and every sequence of closed terms $\overline{a}$ of the appropriate length, $t[\overline{a}/\overline{x}] \leq t'[\overline{a}/\overline{x}]$. Define $a \leq b$, for a and b open terms, if $\sigma(a) \leq \sigma(b)$ for every substitution σ such that $\sigma(a)$ and $\sigma(b)$ are closed. Finally, define $a \sim b$ if $a \leq b$ and $b \leq a$.

Following are some examples related to the computation system of TT. $\langle 2+2, 3\rangle \sim \langle 4, 3\rangle$. $\lambda x.\, x+2 \sim \lambda x.\, 2+x$. $y \not\sim \lambda x.\, y(x)$. $(\lambda x.\, b)(a) \sim b[a/x]$. Finally, for the pure untyped λ-calculus, the following are equivalent for closed terms a and a': (1) $a \sim a'$; (2) for all $n \geq 0$ and closed $b_1, \ldots, b_n$, $ab_1 \ldots b_n$ has a value if and only if $a'b_1 \ldots b_n$ does; (3) for every context (*i.e.* term with a hole) $C[\cdot]$, $C[a]$ has a value if and only if $C[a']$ does.

In [13] we prove the following.

Theorem 1 *The preorder $\leq$ of S is a congruence:*

$$\tau(\overline{x}_1.t_1; \ldots; \overline{x}_n.t_n) \leq \tau(\overline{x}_1.t'_1; \ldots; \overline{x}_n.t'_n)$$

whenever $t_i \leq t'_i$ for each i. If follows that if $a \leq a'$ and $b \leq b'$ then $b[a/x] \leq b'[a'/x]$.

A trivial consequence is that these properties also hold of $\sim$.

2.2 Type Theory

Let S_{TT} be the computation system of TT [14]. It is trivial to cast S_{TT} as a structured computation system.

The inductive construction in [1] gives a semantics of TT as a *type system*, which is a partial function ϕ mapping closed terms to partial equivalence relations[1] over closed terms. If $\phi(T)$ is defined we say T is a type in ϕ. For T a type in ϕ, we write $t \in_\phi T$ when $(t,t) \in \phi(T)$, and $t = t' \in_\phi T$ when $(t,t') \in \phi(T)$. The terms t such that $t \in_\phi T$ are the *members* of T. Two types are *equal* if they are assigned the same partial equivalence relation.

A slightly more complicated construction gives a semantics for Nuprl [6]. The main difference is that Nuprl has an intensional, or structural, type equality.

Theorem 2 *The rules of TT and Nuprl are "computationally open-ended", in the sense that for any deterministic S which extends S_{TT}, the construction in [1] yields a type system ϕ_S in which the rules of TT are true.*

We will refer to such an S as a *model* of TT, and will write $t \in_S T$ in place of $t \in_{\phi_S} T$, and similarly for $t = t' \in_S T$.

The rules of TT deal with judgements under hypotheses. The inference system can be given a sequent formulation. In this paper we will only need to mention sequents of the form

$$x_1 : A_1, \ldots, x_n : A_n \vdash C$$

where C is of the form $t \in T$ or $t = t' \in T$. We will use TT as a subscript, as in

$$x_1 : A_1, \ldots, x_n : A_n \vdash_{TT} C,$$

when the sequent is provable in TT. The semantics of the type theory can be extended to a semantics of sequents, although this is somewhat complicated. We will use S as a subscript when a sequent is true in the semantics generated from S.

There are a number of type constructors in TT. As examples, we consider Π types and universes. The term $\Pi\, x \in A\,.\, B$ is a type exactly if A is a type and for every $a \in A$, $B[a/x]$ is a type (we will ignore equality—for example, in this case we should also require that the type family B respect the equality of A). Its members are the terms t where $t \Downarrow \lambda x.\, b$ for some b such that $b[a/x] \in B[a/x]$ for every $a \in A$. Any term T such that $T \Downarrow \Pi\, x {\in} A\,.\, B$ is a type which is equal as a type to $\Pi\, x {\in} A\,.\, B$. For each i there is a type U_i whose members are types and which is closed under all the type constructors except U_j for $j \geq i$.

We will need the following result from [12].

Theorem 3 *Let S be a model of TT and let T be a type in S. If $T \leq_S T'$ then T' is a type which is equal to T. If $t \in_S T$ and $t \leq_S t'$ then $t = t' \in_S T$.*

---

[1] A *partial equivalence relation* is a symmetric, transitive relation.

TT is also open-ended with respect to universe inhabitation. This property is rather difficult to characterize (see [2]), but a weak form is sufficient here. In particular, we can incorporate an arbitrary collection of *base types* meeting the following restrictions. Let S be a model of TT, and let ϕ_S be the type system generated from S. Define a *constant* to be a canonical term with no subterms (that is, it is a canonical operator of arity ()). Let X be a set of constants which are not in the domain of ϕ_S, and let ϕ' be a type system over S whose domain is X and such that for every $c \in X$, if $t = t' \in_{\phi'} c$ then there exists a constant c' such that $t \Downarrow c'$ and $t' \Downarrow c'$. Then ϕ' can be extended to a type system for TT in which all the new base types are members of U_1.

Although the results below apply to an arbitrary S, they refer to provability only in TT. These results are actually more general, since the only property of provability used is that it implies truth in all extensions of S. Thus we could extend TT with new rules as long as they are true in all extensions of S.

2.3 Classical Models of Type Theory

Let S be a deterministic model of TT. In [13] we show how to extend S to a "classical" model S_c obtained by injecting enough oracles into S to ensure "full inhabitation" of function types in the following sense. Let A and B be types in S_c and let $a \mapsto b_a$ be any *function*, in the usual mathematical sense, mapping members of A to members of B, such that for all members a and a' of A, if $a = a' \in_{S_c} A$ then $b_a = b_{a'} \in_{S_c} B$. Then there is a *term* $f \in_{S_c} A \to B$ such that for every $a \in_{S_c} A$, $f(a) = b_a \in_{S_c} B$. The obvious generalization of this property to Π types holds as well. It follows that the propositions-as-types expression of the law of the excluded middle is sound in S_c (although we will not need this fact). In order to guarantee that S_c is deterministic we actually need to assume slightly more about S then that it is itself deterministic. See [13] for details on this complication (which does not appear to rule out any interesting computation systems).

In this section we present only the parts of the construction of S_c that are required for the subsequent development. We start by choosing a large chunk V of the cumulative hierarchy of set theory. V can be thought of as simply a very large set with $\emptyset$ as the only "primitive" element. To be more precise, define V_α, for each ordinal α, by transfinite induction:

$$V_\alpha = P(\bigcup_{\beta<\alpha} V_\beta).$$

where $P(S)$ is the power set of S. Set $V = V_\alpha$ for some suitably large limit ordinal.

The language of S_c is obtained from that of S by adding, for each n-ary function f ($n \geq 0$) which as a set is a member of V, a noncanonical operator o_f, called an *oracle*, whose arity is $(0, \ldots, 0)$. For use in the normalization results below, we also add, for each $v \in V$, a canonical operator κ_v, called an *atom*, of arity (). We can define an encoding i of the set of terms of S_c in V, using the standard set-theoretic encodings of pairing, integers etc.

In order to guarantee that S_c be deterministic, we define evaluation rules for an operator o_f only when f satisfies a certain "minimality" property, the details of which are of no concern here. The main property of evaluation we will need is the following.

Lemma 1 *Let $f \in V$ be a minimal function and let $t_1, \ldots, t_n$ be closed terms.*

$$o_f(t_1; \ldots; t_n) \Downarrow c$$

if and only if there exists $(i(u_1), \ldots, i(u_n))$ in the domain of f such that

$$f(i(u_1), \ldots, i(u_n)) = c$$

and for each i, $u_i \leq t_i$.

Henceforth we will identify a term with its code in V.

We will need a large collection of base types in order to provide instantiations of LF contexts. Let $\mathcal{A}$ be a large set of atoms (say the set of all κ_v for $v \in V_\alpha$, where α is an inaccessible cardinal number[2]). We introduce base types, as described in the previous section, one for every partial equivalence relation over $\mathcal{A}$. Pick arbitrary atoms to name these base types. Henceforth, we will assume that the type system corresponding to S_c includes these base types.

3 A Normalization Lemma

In this section we prove a normalization property for open terms t that have a value in the classical semantics when closed terms from a certain class are substituted for free variables. We will call the members of this class of substitutable terms "LF-like" since they correspond to the functions which can inhabit types or kinds in a set theoretic semantics of LF.

The normalization lemma is rather technical. Its significance is mainly as a tool for proving the results of the next section. It is proved with an involved (and somewhat nasty) syntactic argument.

Let V, S and S_c be as in the previous section, except that we additionally require that S be strongly deterministic. We first define a suitably well-behaved class of terms of S_c. We inductively define sets $\mathcal{F}_n$, $n \geq 0$. $\mathcal{F}_0 = \{\kappa_v \mid v \in V\}$. $\lambda x.\, o_f(x) \in \mathcal{F}_{n+1}$ if $f \neq \emptyset$ and there exists $k \geq 0$ such that $u \in \mathcal{F}_k$ and $v \in \mathcal{F}_n$ whenever $(u, v) \in f$. We call the members of $\mathcal{F}$ the *LF-like terms*, and the members of $\mathcal{F}_n$ the *LF-like terms of arity n*. We will often treat a function $f \in V$ as an LF-like term by identifying it with $\lambda x.\, o_f(x)$. Also, we will sometimes consider κ_v to be an LF-like function of arity 0. An LF-like term of arity n can be thought of as a curried function taking n arguments, which must be LF-like terms, and returning an atom.

[2] This is absurdly large for our purposes, but the construction of S_c already uses an infinite sequence of inaccessible cardinals.

We now define a notion of *domain* for the LF-like terms (and functions). For $t \in \mathcal{F}$,

$$D_t = \begin{cases} () & \text{if } t \text{ has arity } 0 \\ \{ (u_1, \ldots, u_n) \mid u_1 \in \mathit{dom}(f) \ \& \ (u_2, \ldots, u_n) \in D_{f(u)} \} & \text{if } t = \lambda x.\, o_f(x) \end{cases}$$

Next, we define the application of an LF-like term to a member of its domain.

$$\begin{aligned} \mathit{val}(\kappa_v, ()) &= \kappa_v \\ \mathit{val}(\lambda x.\, o_f(x), (u_1, \ldots, u_n)) &= \mathit{val}(f(u_1), (u_2, \ldots, u_n)) \end{aligned}$$

The following holds: for $t \in \mathcal{F}_n$, $ta_1 \ldots a_n \Downarrow c$ if and only if there exists $(u_1, \ldots, u_n) \in D_t$ such that $\mathit{val}(t, \overline{u}) = c$ and for each i, $u_i \leq a_i$.

For technical reasons, we also need a notion of "full η-expansion" of an LF-like term, analogous to the $\beta\eta$-long normal form of the typed λ-calculus. Instead of using types to determine what this expansion is, we us the arity information contained in members of $\mathcal{F}$. First, for t a term and $u \in \mathcal{F}_n$, define

$$\eta(t, u) = \begin{cases} t & \text{if } n = 0 \\ \lambda x_1 \ldots x_n.\, ta_1 \ldots a_n & \text{if } n > 0 \end{cases}$$

where, in the second case, none of the variables in $\overline{x}$ are free in t, and $a_i = \eta(x_i, v_i)$ for some arbitrary $\overline{v} \in D_u$. Now define, for $u \in \mathcal{F}_n$,

$$u^\eta = \begin{cases} u & \text{if } n = 0 \\ \lambda x_1 \ldots x_n.\, o_f(a_1)a_2 \ldots a_n & \text{if } u = \lambda x.\, o_f(x) \end{cases}$$

where, in the second case, the a_i are as before.

We will use LF-like terms to give meaning to the free variables of a term proven well-typed in some LF context. An *oracle assignment* is a mapping ξ from a finite set of variables to the set of LF-like functions of V. For the same technical reasons as were referred to above, we need to restrict the form of terms to which we can apply ξ. Let t be a term such that for every free variable z of t, $z \in \mathit{dom}(\xi)$ and every free occurrence of z in t heads a subterm of the form $za_1 \ldots a_n$ where n is the arity of $\xi(z)$ and where for some $\overline{u} \in D_{\xi(z)}$, each a_i is of the form $\eta(b_i, u_i)$. The term $\xi(t)$ is obtained from t by successively replacing subterms $za_1 \ldots a_n$, where n is the arity of $\xi(z)$, by $o_{\xi(z)}(a_1)a_2 \ldots a_n$ if $n > 0$, and by $\xi(z)$ otherwise.

Finally, a term is in *λ-normal form* if it contains no operators other than λ and application, and if it contains no redexes.

Lemma 2 *Let ξ be an oracle assignment and let t be a term of S such that $\xi(t)$ is defined and $\xi(t) \Downarrow \kappa_v$ in S_c for some $v \in V$. Then we can effectively find $t' \in S$ in λ-normal form such that $t \leq_S t'$.*

The proof of this lemma involves a rather complicated analysis of derivations in S_c and in S. Space limitations preclude including the proof here. However, the basic idea is fairly simple. $\xi(t)$ evaluates to an atom. Consider transforming this evaluation into a "pseudo-evaluation" where all terms of the form $o_f(a_1)a_2 \ldots a_n$ are replaced by $za_1 \ldots a_n$ where $\xi(z) = f$. A subevaluation which originally reduced a term $o_f(a_1)a_2 \ldots a_n$ to an atom is replaced by a single step which simply reduces $za_1 \ldots a_n$ to itself. The result of the pseudo-evaluation is a term of the form $za_1 \ldots a_n$. We inductively can find normal forms for $a_1, \ldots, a_n$.

We can compute t' from t given just the arity information of an oracle assignment. We augment S with "pseudo-axioms" $za_1 \ldots a_n \Downarrow za_1 \ldots a_n$ for each z free in t, where n is the arity of z given by the oracle assignment, and then find a derivation e of $t \Downarrow a$ for some a. a must have the form $za_1 \ldots a_n$, and inductively repeating the procedure on the a_i gives $\overline{a'}$ such that $a_i \leq a_i'$. Hence $t \leq z\overline{a'}$. The proof of Lemma 2 guarantees that such an e exists. Strong determinism of S guarantees that any e will suffice.

With a moderate amount of extra work we can prove not only $t \leq_S t'$, but in fact $t \leq_{S'} t'$ for any S' extending S that in which evaluation is deterministic.

4 Normalization in an LF-like Subtheory of TT

Let S and S_c be as in the previous section. We assume familiarity with LF. We write $\Gamma \vdash_{LF} t \in T$ for the LF judgement that t has type T in the context Γ[3]. For t an LF term, type or kind, obtain *the erasure of* t, $\epsilon(t)$, by erasing the types of bound variables in λ-abstractions and by replacing *Type* by U_1. Extend ϵ to contexts in the obvious way. It is straightforward to show that ϵ gives an interpretation of LF in TT. In particular, if $\Gamma \vdash_{LF} T \in \mathit{Type}$ then $\epsilon(\Gamma) \vdash_{TT} \epsilon(T) \in U_1$, and if $\Gamma \vdash_{LF} t \in T$ then $\epsilon(\Gamma) \vdash_{TT} \epsilon(t) \in \epsilon(T)$. Furthermore, $=_{\beta\eta}$ in LF implies provable equality of erasures in TT. When no confusion is likely to result, we will identify an LF object with its erasure.

We first prove a lemma which gives conditions under which the conclusion of Lemma 2 can be strengthened to include the property that the λ-normal form is in fact the erasure of some well-typed LF term. The main condition is the existence of a certain class of models of an LF context. After the lemma we give several consequences of practical import.

An LF type or kind has the form

$$\Pi\, x_1 \in A_1 . \ldots \Pi\, x_n \in A_n . B$$

where B is either *Type* or atomic: of the form $P\overline{a}$ for some variable P. The *arity* of this type is n.

Let $\Gamma = [x_1 : A_1, \ldots, x_n : A_n]$ be an LF context. A *model* M of Γ is a sequence $a_1, \ldots, a_n$ of LF-like terms of S_c satisfying the following. (1) The arity of a_i is the arity of A_i.

[3]here, contexts include LF signatures

(2) $A_i[a_1, \ldots, a_{i-1}/x_1, \ldots, x_{i-1}]$ is a type in S_c and $a_i \in_{S_c} A_i[a_1, \ldots, a_{i-1}]$. (3) If A_i has arity $m \geq 0$, then, writing

$$A_i[a_1, \ldots, a_{i-1}] = \Pi\, y_1 \in B_1 \,.\, \ldots \Pi\, y_m \in B_m \,.\, C,$$

if $a_i b_1 \ldots b_m$ has a value in S_c then the value is an atom and for all j,

$$b_j \in B_j[b_1, \ldots, b_{j-1}].$$

The last condition says that the objects we put in function types only return values on arguments of the right type. This is needed in the next lemma when we prove that certain normal forms can be well-typed in LF. In S_c, every function type is fully-inhabited, in the sense of Section 2.3, by functions which have values only on the domain of the type.

Write $M \models \Gamma$ if M is a model of Γ, and write $M(t)$ for $t[\overline{a}/\overline{x}]$. If the free variables of t and T are bound by Γ, then define $M \models t \in T$ if $M(t) \in_{S_c} M(T)$.

The proof of the following is a straightforward induction on the size of t.

Lemma 3 *Let t be a term in λ-normal form. Let Γ be an LF context and let T be a term such that $\Gamma \vdash_{LF} T \in Type$. Let $\mathcal{M}$ be a non-empty set of models of Γ. Suppose that for all $M \in \mathcal{M}$, $M \models t \in T$, and if T', T'' are LF types in Γ with different $\beta\eta$-long normal forms, then there exists $M \in \mathcal{M}$ such that $M(T')$ and $M(T'')$, as types in S_c, have no LF-like members in common. Then we can effectively find a term t' such that $\Gamma \vdash_{LF} t' \in T$ and $t = \epsilon(t')$.*

The required type information for t' can be computed in a single top-down pass over t since we are given the type for t.

The following theorem directly justifies the use of TT as a logical framework in the sense of LF.

Theorem 4 *Suppose that $\Gamma \vdash_{LF} T \in Type$ and that t is a term of S such that $\Gamma \vdash_{TT} t \in T$. Then we can effectively find a t' in λ-normal form such that $\Gamma \vdash_{LF} t' \in T$ and $\Gamma \vdash_S t = t' \in T$.*

Proof (sketch). Without loss of generality we may assume that T is atomic, and t has the form required for $\xi(t)$ to be defined for some oracle assignment ξ derived from a model of Γ in the obvious way. Since T is atomic, in any model M of Γ, $M(T)$ is a base type κ_u so $M(t) \Downarrow \kappa_v$ for some $v \in u$. By Lemma 2 and Theorem 3, there is a t' in λ-normal form such that $\Gamma \vdash_{TT} t = t' \in T$. It is straightforward to show that the class $\mathcal{M}$ of all models of Γ satisfies the conditions of Lemma 3, so we are done. □

For the statement of the next theorem, define the *simple types* over $c_1, \ldots, c_n$ to be all terms constructed from $c_1, \ldots, c_n$ and $\rightarrow$. Also, define the *base types* of a context Γ to be the variables x such that $x : A$ appears in Γ.

Theorem 5 *Let* $\Gamma = [x_1 : A_1, \ldots, x_n : A_n]$ *be an LF context where each* A_i *is either Type or is a simple type over* $x_1, \ldots, x_{i-1}$. *Let* Ax *be a type of* TT *(under the hypotheses* Γ*) representing, via propositions-as-types, a formula of higher-order logic with equality where: (1) the types of quantified variables are simple types over the base types of* Γ *and the (non-atom) base types of* TT *(for example, the type of integers); (2) the function symbols come from* Γ*; (3) the terms mentioned in* Ax *are well-typed in the sense of the simply-typed* λ*-calculus. Let* T *be a term such that* $\Gamma \vdash_{LF} T \in Type$*, and let* t *be a term of* S *in which* r *does not occur free. Suppose that*

$$\Gamma,\ r\!:\!Ax \vdash_{TT} t \in T$$

and that Γ *has a model* M *such that for some term* r *of* S_c, $M \models r \in Ax$. *Then we can effectively find a* t' *in* λ*-normal form such that* $\Gamma \vdash_{LF} t' \in T$ *and* $\Gamma, r\!:\!Ax \vdash_S t = t' \in T$.

Proof (sketch). Because of the restriction on Γ, all the LF types well-formed under Γ are simple types (composed of $\rightarrow$ and variables x such that $x \in Type$ is in Γ). Hence we can modify M, by making copies of intersecting base types if necessary, so that $\{M\}$ satisfies the conditions of Lemma 3. Then $M \models t \in T$, so we can proceed as in Theorem 4. □

We can easily extend TT to include Nuprl's subset type. The type $\{\, x \in A \mid B \,\}$ has as members all terms $a \in A$ such that $B[a/x]$ has a member. The proof rules for this type are given in [6]. Define the *squash* of a type A, denoted $\downarrow(A)$, to be $\{\, x \in Unit \mid A \,\}$ where *Unit* is a fixed type with a single member. Note that $\downarrow(A)$ has as its unique member the member of *Unit* if A is non-empty, otherwise it is empty. The rules of Nuprl guarantee that a squashed proposition may not be used during computationally significant parts of proofs. Hence, the effect of replacing Ax with $\downarrow(Ax)$ is to remove explicit variable occurrence restrictions in Theorem 5. We can now prove the following.

Theorem 6 *Suppose* $\Gamma,\ r\!:\downarrow(Ax) \vdash_{TT} t \in T$ *and that all the conditions of Theorem 5 hold except the restriction on occurrences of* r *in* t. *Then we can effectively find* t' *in* λ*-normal form such that* $\Gamma,\ r\!:\downarrow(Ax) \vdash_S t = t' \in T$.

5 Applications

In this section we describe an extension of the *proofs-as-programs* paradigm to the synthesis of programs with specific intensional properties. Theorem 6 provides a theoretical basis for using the proofs-as-programs paradigm to construct proof-objects that have desired structural and behavioral properties. In this section we illustrate this with an example: a context for developing and reasoning about representations of CMOS transistor-level circuits.

Terms representing CMOS circuits (which we henceforth call "circuit terms") are defined relative to a context which provides the appropriate constructors and axioms. Primitive circuit terms are either *power*, *ground*, or are one of two kinds of transistors

(n-type and p-type). Circuit terms are composed using an operator *Join*, and wires are introduced between similarly named ports by an operator *Wire*. The constructors, along with related types, are declared in the context Γ_{CMOS}, listed below.

$$T{:}U_1,\ B{:}U_1,\ \mathit{Ntran}{:}B \to B \to B \to T,\ \mathit{Ptran}{:}B \to B \to B \to T,$$
$$\mathit{Pwr}{:}B,\ \mathit{Gnd}{:}B,\ \mathit{tt}{:}T,\ \mathit{ff}{:}T,\ \mathit{Join}{:}T \to T \to T,\ \mathit{Wire}{:}(B \to T) \to T,$$

T can be thought of as the type of circuits and B as the type of ports.

Circuits terms are built in extensions to Γ_{CMOS} that contain additional declarations of port names. For example, a term t such that

$$\Gamma_{CMOS}, p_1{:}B, ..., p_n{:}B \vdash_{TT} t \in T$$

is intended to represent a circuit whose ports are named by the variables p_i. As an example, within the context Γ_{CMOS} extended by $i{:}T$ and $o{:}T$ the term

$$\mathit{Join}(\mathit{Ptran}(i, \mathit{Pwr}, o), \mathit{Ntran}(i, o, \mathit{Gnd})) \tag{1}$$

is of type T and represents a CMOS inverter.

While the context Γ_{CMOS} is sufficient for specifying and reasoning about the structure of circuits, it is inadequate for reasoning about their logical properties. We rectify this by augmenting Γ_{CMOS} with axioms for the types and constructors.

We axiomatize a simple *switch model semantics*[4], where each circuit with ports $a_1, \ldots, a_n$ is represented by a relation $R(a_1, ..., a_n)$ which is true precisely when the a_i have values that are consistent with the logic of the circuit. Under this interpretation, we may think of circuits as constraints. Composing circuits combines constraints: if R_1 and R_2 are circuits, then their join $\mathit{Join}(R_1(a_1, ..., a_n), R_2(a_1, .., a_n))$ represents a circuit which is true when the a_i satisfy both relations. Hence *Join* corresponds to conjunction. Given a function from B into T, e.g.,

$$\lambda w.\, R(a_1, ..., a_{i-1}, w, a_{i+1}, ..., a_n),$$

Wire internalizes the port w and the resulting relation should be true when there is some value for w that makes the relation true. Hence, the *Wire* operator corresponds to existential quantification over T. Transistors are axiomatized as relations that respect their switching values. For example, when the signal at the gate of an n-type transistor is high (equal to *Pwr*) than the source and the drain are connected and hence have the same value.

Our axioms for this interpretation are as follows. Here $tr(b)$ is defined as the *type* $b = \mathit{Pwr} \in B$, which encodes the proposition that b and *Pwr* are equal members of B. We will use the same notation for the analogous operation for T.

$$\begin{aligned}
&\forall b{:}B.\, (b = \mathit{Pwr} \in B \vee b = \mathit{Gnd} \in B) \wedge \neg(\mathit{Pwr} = \mathit{Gnd} \in B)\\
&\forall b{:}T.\, (b = \mathit{tt} \in T \vee b = \mathit{ff} \in T) \wedge \neg(\mathit{tt} = \mathit{ff} \in T)\\
&\forall g, s, d{:}B.\, tr(ntran(g, s, d)) \Leftrightarrow (tr(g) \Rightarrow (tr(s) \Leftrightarrow tr(d)))\\
&\forall g, s, d{:}B.\, tr(ptran(g, s, d)) \Leftrightarrow (\neg tr(g) \Rightarrow (tr(s) \Leftrightarrow tr(d)))\\
&\forall x, y{:}T.\, tr(\mathit{Join}(x, y)) \Leftrightarrow tr(x) \wedge tr(y)\\
&\forall f{:}B \to T.\, tr(\mathit{Wire}(f)) \Leftrightarrow \exists b{:}B.\, tr(f(b))
\end{aligned}$$

We extend Γ_{CMOS} by adding the squashed conjunction of these axioms.

Within the scope of Γ_{CMOS} we may both verify that circuits terms have specific logical properties and synthesize circuit terms from specifications of their properties. To verify that an explicitly given circuit t with ports $p_1, \ldots, p_n$ satisfies a specification *Spec*, we prove

$$\Gamma_{CMOS}, p_1\!:\!B, ..., p_n\!:\!B \vdash t \in \{\, t\!:\!T \mid tr(t) \Leftrightarrow \mathit{Spec} \,\}$$

More interestingly, a circuit satisfying *Spec* could be *synthesized* from a proof in TT. This takes advantage of the fact that it is possible to implement TT in a way that suppresses explicit members of types. A user, or theorem proving program, deals with sequents of the form $\Gamma \vdash A$. From a complete proof of such a sequent, a term t can be synthesized, or *extracted*, such that $\Gamma \vdash t \in A$ is provable in TT. Thus a circuit t could be synthesized from a proof of

$$\Gamma_{CMOS}, p_1\!:\!B, ..., p_n\!:\!B \vdash \{\, t\!:\!T \mid tr(t) \Leftrightarrow \mathit{Spec} \,\}$$

Since the provability of this implies that $t \in T$ is provable in the same context, Theorem 6 gives us a t' satisfying the specification which also directly represents a circuit. Hence, our work can be seen as providing a basis for generalizing the proofs-as-programs paradigm to synthesizing proven correct circuit terms from proofs of their specifications.

As a verification example, the reader may check that the inverter circuit (1 above) is satisfied if and only if the ports i and o are assigned different values in T. That is, the following is provable in TT.

$$\Gamma_{CMOS}, i\!:\!T, o\!:\!T \vdash \mathit{inv} \in \{\, t\!:\!T \mid tr(t) \Leftrightarrow (tr(i) \Leftrightarrow \neg tr(o)) \,\}.$$

Alternatively, the circuit term may be synthesized. Any proof of

$$\Gamma_{CMOS}, i\!:\!T, o\!:\!T \vdash \{\, t\!:\!T \mid tr(t) \Leftrightarrow (tr(i) \Leftrightarrow \neg tr(o)) \,\}$$

constructs a circuit term that logically implements an inverter.

One advantage of working within a rich type theory like TT as opposed to the weaker LF is that we may parameterize circuit terms by arbitrary types in TT. For such parameterized terms, when the parameter types are not LF types, our normalization result no longer applies. However, for any type-correct instantiation of the parameters, the resulting term will be a member of T and Theorem 6 will again apply. This result is satisfactory as in practice those working in hardware verification generally wish ultimately to build correct "concrete" circuits (e.g., 16-bit adders) as opposed to circuit schemas (e.g., n-bit adders) themselves.

As an example of this, we indicate how we might specify an adder schema that operates on variable width numbers. Such a schema will operate on sequences of ports of the same length. Let $\{1\,..\,n\}$ denote the type $\{\, m\!:\!N \mid 1 \leq m \leq n \,\}$. The type of port-value sequences (or *bit-vectors*) of length n is $\mathit{Bvec}(n) = \{1\,..\,n\} \rightarrow B$. To specify the adder we need auxiliary functions to interpret port values as bits and sequences of port values as unsigned numbers. To accomplish the former we require a function of type[4]

$$Val = \{\, f : B \to \{0\,..\,1\} \mid f(Pwr) = 1 \in int \wedge f(Gnd) = 0 \in int \,\}.$$

To accomplish the latter, we may define by recursion on n a function *nval* such that for any $val \in Val$, $n \in N$, and $v \in Bvec(n)$

$$nval(val, n, v) = val(v_1) + 2 * val(v_2) + \ \dots\ + 2^{n-1} * val(v_n).$$

With these in hand, the specification of parameterized n-bit adders is

$$\Gamma_{CMOS} \vdash \Pi\, n \in N\,.\, \Pi\, a, b, c \in Bvec(n)\,.\, \Pi\, cin, cout \in B\,.\, \{\, t : T \mid tr(t) \Leftrightarrow AddSpec \,\}$$

where *AddSpec* is the proposition

$$\begin{aligned} \forall val: Val.\, nval(val, n, a) + nval(val, n, b) + val(cin) \\ = nval(val, n, c) + 2^n * val(cout) \quad \in N. \end{aligned}$$

Suppose we have constructed a term t meeting the above specification. Theorem 6 does not directly apply since the type of t involves non-LF types. However, the theorem does apply to any application of t to specific arguments. Suppose $m > 0$. Let us extend Γ_{CMOS} with $3 * m + 2$ port names $a_1, ..., a_m$, $b_1, ..., b_m$, $c_1, ..., c_m$, cin and $cout$; these represent the ports of the two input numbers, the output number, the carry-in bit and the carry-out bit respectively. Call the resulting context Γ_{add}. Now we can write functions a, b, c of type $Bvec(m)$ such that $a(1) = a_1$, $a(2) = a_2$ etc. Since the term $t(m)(a)(b)(c)(cin)(cout)$ is in the type T under the assumptions of Γ_{add}, we can now apply the theorem as before and conclude that the term is equivalent to a circuit.

Providing a formal proof of the above specification would take us outside the scope of this paper; the reader may find details of proofs conducted in Nuprl for similar specifications in [3]. Such specifications are proved by induction and different proofs will construct terms representing different kinds of parameterized adders (e.g., ripple-carry, carry look ahead, etc.).

As with software development, the simultaneous synthesis and verification of hardware can simplify the design process. This methodology can put to particularly good advantage when circuit terms can be constructed and reasoned about in parts. [9] and [7] give examples of this kind of development methodology applied to the top down synthesis of proven correct combinational logic and sequential circuits. [3] provides examples of using type theory to synthesize recursive circuit schemas from their schematic specification (such as the n-bit adder just specified). Our results here give a method of rigorously demonstrating that this kind of development is correct within TT.

---

[4]Because the context axioms are squashed they may not be used computationally; hence one may not directly define a function that computes over members of T.

References

[1] S. F. Allen. A non-type theoretic definition of Martin-Löf's types. In *Proceedings of the Second Annual Symposium on Logic in Computer Science*, pages 215–221. IEEE, 1987.

[2] S. F. Allen. *A Non-Type-Theoretic Semantics for Type-Theoretic Language.* PhD thesis, Cornell University, 1987.

[3] D. A. Basin. Extracting circuits from constructive proofs. In *IFIP-IEEE International Workshop on Formal Methods in VLSI Design*, Miami, USA, January 1991.

[4] A. Camilleri, M. Gordon, and T. Melham. Hardware verification using higher-order logic. In D. Borrione, editor, *From HDL Descriptions to Guaranteed Correct Circuit Designs*, pages 43–67. Elsevier Science Publishers B. V. (North-Holland), 1987.

[5] R. Constable and D. Howe. Nuprl as a [illegible]reddi, editor, *Logic in Computer Science*, pages 77–90. Ac[illegible]

[6] R. L. Constable, et al. *Implementing M*[illegible]*prl Proof Development System.* Prentice-Hall, Englewoo[illegible]6.

[7] M. P. Fourman. Formal methods for m[illegible]*rence on Modeling the Innovation: Communications, Aut*[illegible]*n Systems*, Rome, Italy, 1990.

[8] F. Hanna, N. Daeche, and M. Longley[illegible]fication language based on type theory. In *Hardware Specification, Verification and Synthesis: Mathematical Aspects*, Ithaca, New York, 1989. Springer-Verlag.

[9] F. K. Hanna, M. Longley, and N. Daeche. Formal synthesis of digital systems. In *IMEC-IFIP International Workshop on: Applied Formal Methods For Correct VLSI Design*, volume 2, pages 532–548, Leuven, Belgium, 1989.

[10] R. Harper, F. Honsell, and G. Plotkin. A framework for defining logics. In *The Second Annual Symposium on Logic in Computer Science.* IEEE, 1987.

[11] D. Howe. Computational metatheory in Nuprl. *Proc. of 9th International Conference on Automated Deduction*, pages 238–257, 1988.

[12] D. Howe. Equality in lazy computation systems. *Proc. Fourth Annual Symposium on Logic in Computer Science, IEEE*, pages 198–203, June 1989.

[13] D. Howe. On computational open-endedness in Martin-Löf's type theory. To appear in *Proc. Sixth Annual Symposium on Logic in Computer Science, IEEE.*

[14] P. Martin-Löf. Constructive mathematics and computer programming. In *Sixth International Congress for Logic, Methodology, and Philosophy of Science*, pages 153–175, Amsterdam, 1982. North Holland.

[15] B. Nördstrom, K. Petersson, and J. M. Smith. *Programming in Martin-Löf's Type Theory*, volume 7 of *International Series of Monographs on Computer Science.* Oxford Science Publications, 1990.

[16] L. C. Paulson. Natural deduction proof as higher-order resolution. *Journal of Logic Programming*, (3):237–258, 1985.

Parametricity of Extensionally Collapsed Term Models of Polymorphism and Their Categorical Properties

Ryu Hasegawa
Research Institute for Mathematical Sciences
Kyoto University
Kyoto 606, Japan
ryu@kurims.kurims.kyoto-u.ac.jp

Abstract

In the preceding paper, the author proved that parametric natural models have many categorical data types: finite products, finite coproducts, initial and terminal fixed points. In this paper, we show the second order minimum model is parametric, and thus enjoys the property. In addition to that, we give representation of internal right and left Kan extensions. We also show that extensionally collapsed models of closed types/terms collection are partially parametric, and that they have a part of the categorical data types above.

1 Introduction

When we speak of *term models* of lambda calculi, there are two possibilities: one is the collection of all terms including open terms, and the other the collection of closed terms. The former is used to prove completeness for simply typed lambda calculus [8] and for second order lambda calculus [5]. In contrast, it is even misleading to call the collection of closed terms a model. It does not satisfy extensionality in case of second order lambda calculus [16] (even in case of system **T** [2]). It is, however, still worth while considering the collection of closed terms (of closed types), in particular, for second order lambda calculus.

One reason is that it is natural for second order lambda calculus to have empty types. It is showed in [16] that the completeness by the collection of all terms is applied only for the axioms and inference rules including the rule called *nonempty*, which is not sound for models having empty types. On the other hand, although the collection of closed terms is not a model, it gives an interpretation such that some types may be interpreted as an empty set.

Another reason we are concerned with in this paper is that the collection of closed terms is a *parametric* interpretation [22, 13]. Second order lambda calculus is often called *polymorphic* lambda calculus. It is because a universal type $\forall X.\sigma$ behaves as a type of polymorphic data. A *polymorphic data* is a family of terms $\{M_X \mid X \text{ ranges over types}\}$. A term M of type $\forall X.\sigma$ is regarded to be a polymorphic data whose X-indexed member is extracted by applying X to the term M.

If M is a closed term of type $\forall X.\sigma$, its normal form is $M = \Lambda X.N[X]$. It means that the members of M as a polymorphic data have uniform definitions $N[X]$ with parameter X. Strachey called polymorphism with uniform definitions *parametric* polymorphism in contrast to *ad hoc* polymorphism. Polymorphism of second order lambda calculus is parametric in nature.

Reynolds invented to use binary relations to reflect parametricity in semantics [20]. In the preceding paper [13], the author adopt the same idea in the framework of BMM models, and obtained a result that if an interpretation is a parametric natural model (see the following sections) then it has many canonical categorical data types, as finite products, finite coproducts, cartesian closedness, initial and terminal fixed points of some endofunctors. In fact, the universal conditions these categorical constructions should satisfy just corresponds to parametricity.

The result is, however, valid only for parametric *models*. Although the collection of closed terms is parametric, it is not a model. Breazu-Tannen and Coquand developped *polymorphic extensional collapse* which can be used to obtain models from closed types/terms interpretation. Then we face a problem whether the extensionally collapsed models are parametric. We show that all syntactically definable universal types are parametric. Then the models have a part of categorical data types mentioned above.

Another model treated in this paper is the second order minimum model by Moggi and Statman [18]. It is obtained from a special theory, called the maximum consistent theory, which satisfies the ω rule. We show the second order minimum model is fully parametric and the categorical data types above all exist in the model. Furthermore we give representation of internal right and left Kan extensions, including left and right adjoints as a special case.

2 Syntax of polymorphism

Suppose given a set $\mathcal{K}$ of *type constants*. A *type judgement* has the form $\Gamma \vdash \sigma$ where Γ is a finite sequence of mutually distinct type variables. There are four inference rules for generating type judgements.

(Ty proj) $\qquad \Gamma \vdash X \qquad (X \text{ appears in } \Gamma)$

(Ty const) $\qquad \Gamma \vdash A \qquad (A \text{ in } \mathcal{K})$

(Ty $\Rightarrow$) $$\frac{\Gamma \vdash \sigma \qquad \Gamma \vdash \tau}{\Gamma \vdash \sigma \Rightarrow \tau}$$

(Ty $\forall$) $$\frac{\Gamma, X \vdash \sigma}{\Gamma \vdash \forall X.\sigma}$$

As usual, we do not distinguish types which differ only in bound type variables.

Suppose given a set $\mathcal{C}$ of *individual constants*, to each of which a *closed* type is assigned. We denote the type by Type(c) for $c \in \mathcal{C}$. A *term judgement* is written $\Gamma\,;\,\Theta \vdash M : \sigma$ where Θ is a type assignment for individual variables of the form $x_1 : \sigma_1, \ldots, x_n : \sigma_n$. It is assumed here that $\Gamma \vdash \sigma_i$ $(i = 1, \ldots, n)$ and $\Gamma \vdash \sigma$ hold. Term judgement has six inference rules.

(te proj) $$\Gamma; \Theta \vdash x : \sigma \qquad (x : \sigma \in \Theta)$$

(te const) $$\Gamma; \Theta \vdash c : \mathrm{Type}(c) \qquad (c \in \mathcal{C})$$

where Γ is arbitrary, since Type(c) is assumed to be closed.

(te $\Rightarrow$I) $$\frac{\Gamma; \Theta, x : \sigma \vdash M : \tau}{\Gamma; \Theta \vdash \lambda x^{\sigma}.M : \sigma \Rightarrow \tau}$$

(te $\Rightarrow$E) $$\frac{\Gamma; \Theta \vdash M : \sigma \Rightarrow \tau \qquad \Gamma; \Theta \vdash N : \sigma}{\Gamma; \Theta \vdash MN : \tau}$$

(te $\forall$I) $$\frac{\Gamma, X; \Theta \vdash M : \tau}{\Gamma; \Theta \vdash \Lambda X.M : \forall X.\tau}$$

where X does not appear as free type variables in Θ.

(te $\forall$E) $$\frac{\Gamma; \Theta \vdash M : \forall X.\tau}{\Gamma; \Theta \vdash M\{\sigma\} : \tau[X{:=}\sigma]}$$

where σ is such that $\Gamma \vdash \sigma$ holds.

Four conversion rules (β), (η), (Type β) and (Type η) are defined as usual. We call $\Sigma = (\mathcal{K}, \mathcal{C})$ a *signature*. Let $\lambda^{\forall}(\Sigma)$ denote the second order lambda calculus generated by the inference rules above with the four conversion rules.

3 Parametric semantics

Polymorphism of second order lambda calculus is parametric polymorphism. $\forall X.\sigma$ is regarded to be a type of polymorphic data and the closed terms of the type have uniform definitions with parameter X. Then a problem is how to reflect uniformity (= parametricity) in semantics. Reynolds proposed in [20] an idea to use binary relations. In usual semantics [5], a variable type is interpreted as a function from the type domain (a set of sets) to itself. In Reynolds idea, a variable type has another interpretation as an endofunction on the set of binary relations between members of the type domain. Let F be such an interpretation of a variable type, and $\{a_X \in F(X) \mid X$ ranges over the type domain$\}$ a polymophic data. Reynolds asserted that a *parametric* polymorphic data should be subject to the condition $(a_A, a_B) \in F(r)$ for all r a subset of $A \times B$ (i.e., a binary relation from A to B). He introduced binary relations in trying to construct the full set-theoretic model [20] (but failed [21]). In the author's preceding paper, Reynolds parametricity is translated into BMM models [4, 5] to yield *relational models*. Adjoining binary relations makes difference. For example, Girard's coherence space model [9, 10] is not a BMM model (due to Moggi, see [6]), while it is a relational model [13]. We discuss below briefly the framework of relational model. A similar approach is developped by Wadler [22]. It also closely relates to the parametric HEO model by Bainbridge, Freyd, Scedrov and Scott [1, 13].

We are concerned with binary relations, for which identity relations are important but composition not. So we define an *r-frame* as the one obtained from category by removing the part involved in composition.

Definition 3.1 An *r-frame* is a pair of classes $(\mathcal{U}, \mathcal{R})$ with three maps $d_0, d_1 : \mathcal{R} \rightrightarrows \mathcal{U}$ (the domain and codomain maps) and $id : \mathcal{U} \to \mathcal{R}$ (identity map). $\mathcal{U}$ is the class of *objects*, and $\mathcal{R}$ is the class of *(binary) relations.*

R-frames are denoted by bold capital letters, as $\mathbf{T} = (\mathcal{U}, \mathcal{R})$. The notation $\mathrm{Obj}(\mathbf{T})$ and $\mathrm{Rel}(\mathbf{T})$ are used to indicate $\mathcal{U}$ and $\mathcal{R}$ respectively. For $A, B \in \mathcal{U}$, a binary relation r from A to B (i.e., $d_0(r) = A$, $d_1(r) = B$) is denoted as $r : A \twoheadrightarrow B$.

Definition 3.2 An *r-frame morphism* $F : \mathbf{T} \to \mathbf{T}'$ is a pair of functions $F : \mathrm{Obj}(\mathbf{T}) \to \mathrm{Obj}(\mathbf{T}')$ and $F : \mathrm{Rel}(\mathbf{T}) \to \mathrm{Rel}(\mathbf{T}')$ (both denoted by F) such that if $r : A \twoheadrightarrow B$ then $F(r) : F(A) \twoheadrightarrow F(B)$ (in other words, F preserves d_0 and d_1).

Note that it is not required for F to preserve id. An n-ary r-frame morphism is similarly defined. The case of $n = 0$ is worth being mentioned. Such an r-frame morphism is $F : \mathbf{1} \to \mathbf{T}$ where $\mathbf{1}$ is the r-frame consisting of one object 1 and one relation $id_1 : 1 \twoheadrightarrow 1$. Namely F is a pair of $A \in \mathrm{Obj}(\mathbf{T})$ and a relation $r : A \twoheadrightarrow A$ in $\mathrm{Rel}(\mathbf{T})$.

Definition 3.3 A *relation of r-frame morphisms* $q : F \twoheadrightarrow G$ for $F, G : \mathbf{T} \rightrightarrows \mathbf{T}'$ is a function $q : \mathrm{Rel}(\mathbf{T}) \to \mathrm{Rel}(\mathbf{T}')$ such that if $r : A \twoheadrightarrow B$ then $q(r) : F(A) \twoheadrightarrow G(B)$.

Note that the definition of q depends only on the object function part of F and G. An *identity relation of r-frame morphisms* $id_F : F \twoheadrightarrow F$ is defined by $id_F = F$.

Now we turn to defining relational model.

A type domain is an r-frame $\mathbf{T} = (\mathcal{U}, \mathcal{R})$. For each $n \leq 0$, $[\mathbf{T}^n \to \mathbf{T}]$ is an r-frame such that $\mathrm{Obj}\,[\mathbf{T}^n \to \mathbf{T}]$ is a class of r-frame morphisms $F : \mathbf{T}^n \to \mathbf{T}$ ($\mathbf{T}^0 = \mathbf{1}$) and $\mathrm{Rel}\,[\mathbf{T}^n \to \mathbf{T}]$ is a class of relations of r-frame morphisms $q : F \twoheadrightarrow G$ where

$F, G \in \mathrm{Obj}\,[\mathbf{T}^n \to \mathbf{T}]$. In order to interpret implication and universal types, we should be given two r-frame morphisms

$$\Rightarrow : \mathbf{T}^2 \to \mathbf{T}$$
$$\forall : [\mathbf{T} \to \mathbf{T}] \to \mathbf{T}\,,$$

and one function $I : \mathcal{K} \to \mathcal{U}$ (but for simplicity, we write just A for $I(A)$) to interpret constant types. From the $\forall$ above, we obtain $\tilde{\forall} : [\mathbf{T} \to \mathbf{T}] \to [\mathbf{T}^0 \to \mathbf{T}]$ as $\tilde{\forall} F = (\forall F, \forall id_F : \forall F \rightarrow\!\!\!\!\!\rightarrow \forall F)$ for $F \in \mathrm{Obj}\,[\mathbf{T} \to \mathbf{T}]$, and $\tilde{\forall} q = \forall q$ for $q \in \mathrm{Rel}\,[\mathbf{T} \to \mathbf{T}]$.

A type judgement is interpreted as an object of $[\mathbf{T} \to \mathbf{T}]$ ($n = |\Gamma|$).

(Ty proj) $[\![\Gamma \vdash X_i]\!]$ is the i-th projection.

(Ty const) $[\![\Gamma \vdash A]\!]$ is a constant r-frame morphism returning A for objects and id_A for relations

(Ty $\Rightarrow$) $[\![\Gamma \vdash \sigma \Rightarrow \tau]\!] = \Rightarrow \circ ([\![\Gamma \vdash \sigma]\!], [\![\Gamma \vdash \tau]\!])$.

(Ty $\forall$) $[\![\Gamma \vdash \forall X.\sigma]\!] = \tilde{\forall}[\![\Gamma, X \vdash \sigma]\!]$.

For all types to be interpreted well, it is necessary that $[\mathbf{T}^n \to \mathbf{T}]$ ($n \leq 0$) is closed under projections, weakenings (i.e., adjunction of dummy variables), $\Rightarrow$, $\forall$, and composition. For the detail, see [13].

To each $A \in \mathcal{U}$, a set (possibly empty) D_A is associated, and to each $r : A \rightarrow\!\!\!\!\!\rightarrow B$ is associated a subset $D_r \subseteq D_A \times D_B$. For the present purpose, however, it suffices to regard A and D_A, r and D_r to be identical. Accordingly each $F \in \mathrm{Obj}\,[\mathbf{T}^n \to \mathbf{T}]$ and $q \in \mathrm{Rel}\,[\mathbf{T}^n \to \mathbf{T}]$ have natural meanings as functions sending sets (of the form D_A) to sets and set-theoretic binary relations (of the form D_r) to set-theoretical binary relations.

The following term interpretation is the same as the counterpart of BMM interpretation [5, 4]. We associate *expansion functions*

$$\Phi^{\Rightarrow}_{A,B} : A \Rightarrow B \to (A \to B) \quad \text{to each } A, B \in \mathcal{U}$$
$$\Phi^{\forall}_{F} : \forall F \to \Pi(X \in \mathcal{U})F(X) \quad \text{to each } F \in \mathrm{Obj}\,[\mathbf{T} \to \mathbf{T}]$$

where $(A \to B)$ is the set of functions from A to B and $\Pi(X \in \mathcal{U})F(X)$ is the collection of $\mathcal{U}$-indexed families such that the component of index X belongs to $F(X)$. We also assume a function I which assigns to each $c \in \mathcal{C}$ an element of $[\![\vdash \mathrm{Type}(c)]\!]$. For simplicity, $I(c)$ is written c in most cases.

A term judgement $\Gamma\,;\,\Theta \vdash M : \sigma$ is interpreted as a member of $\Pi(\underline{X} \in \mathcal{U}^{|\Gamma|})([\![\Gamma \vdash \mathrm{Type}\,\Theta]\!](\underline{X}) \to [\![\Gamma \vdash \sigma]\!](\underline{X}))$ (we use underline to denote a sequence). $[\![\Gamma \vdash \sigma]\!]$ is recursively defined but $[\![\Gamma\,;\,\Theta \vdash M : \sigma]\!]$ is not. Instead the latter should be subject to a condition. See for the detail [4, p.93][13] (a little different with that in [5]).

Definition 3.4 A *second order relational interpretation* of $\lambda^{\forall}(\Sigma)$ (or *interpretation* in short) is a tuple

$$\xi = (\mathbf{T}, [\mathbf{T}^n \to \mathbf{T}](n \leq 0), \Rightarrow, \forall, D, \Phi^{\Rightarrow}, \Phi^{\forall}, I, [\![\,]\!]) .$$

In an interpretation, all types and terms are given meanings by $[\![\,]\!]$. However $[\![\,]\!]$ does not always respect conversions. Namely even if $M \rhd N$, it does not necessarily hold that $[\![\Gamma\,;\,\Theta \vdash M : \sigma]\!] = [\![\Gamma\,;\,\Theta \vdash N : \sigma]\!]$. It is easy to overcome this defect.

Definition 3.5 A *second order relational model* of $\lambda^{\forall}(\Sigma)$ (or in short *model*) is an interpretation in which all components of $\Phi^{\Rightarrow}$ and of $\Phi^{\forall}$ are one-to-one.

In a model, $[\![\,]\!]$ is uniquely determined by the other data, and it respects conversions. But the interpretation is still important notion since the collection of closed types and terms is an interpretation but not a model.

An ordinary BMM interpretation is a special case of relational interpretation. We have only to ignore the binary relation part. Formally let $\mathcal{R}$ consist of only identity relations id_A for $A \in \mathcal{U}$, and all $F \in \mathrm{Obj}\,[\mathbf{T}^n \to \mathbf{T}]$, $q \in \mathrm{Rel}\,[\mathbf{T}^n \to \mathbf{T}]$ send identity relations to identity relations.

If $\Rightarrow: \mathbf{T}^2 \to \mathbf{T}$ and $\forall : [\mathbf{T} \to \mathbf{T}] \to \mathbf{T}$ have canonical meanings as follows (logical, in other terms, an analogue of second order logical relation [17]), then we say ξ is a natural interpretation.

Definition 3.6 (i) $\Phi^{\Rightarrow}$ is *natural* if, for $r : A \twoheadrightarrow A'$ and $s : B \twoheadrightarrow B'$, the relation $r \Rightarrow s$ is defined as $r \Rightarrow s : f \mapsto f'$ iff $s : \Phi^{\Rightarrow}_{A,B}(f)(a) \mapsto \Phi^{\Rightarrow}_{A',B'}(f')(a')$ for any $r : a \mapsto a'$. (N.B. we write $r : a \mapsto a'$ for $(a, b) \in r$.)

(ii) $\Phi^{\forall}$ is *natural* if, for $q : F \twoheadrightarrow F'$ in $\mathrm{Rel}\,[\mathbf{T} \to \mathbf{T}]$, the relation $\forall q : \forall F \twoheadrightarrow \forall F'$ is defined as $\forall q : a \mapsto a'$ iff $q(r) : \Phi^{\forall}_{F}(a)(A) \mapsto \Phi^{\forall}_{F'}(a')(A')$ for any $r : A \twoheadrightarrow A'$.

(iii) An interpretation ξ is *natural* if both $\Phi^{\Rightarrow}$ and $\Phi^{\forall}$ are natural.

The next theorem by Reynolds is the principal theorem [20, 22, 13].

Theorem 3.7 (Abstraction Theorem) *Let ξ be a natural interpretation and suppose that for every $c \in C$ there holds $[\![\vdash \mathrm{Type}(c)]\!] : c \mapsto c$. Then, for any $\Gamma\,;\,\Theta \vdash M : \sigma$ and n relations $\underline{r} : \underline{A} \twoheadrightarrow \underline{B}$ ($n = |\Gamma|$), if $[\![\Gamma \vdash \mathrm{Type}\,\Theta]\!](\underline{r}) : \underline{a} \mapsto \underline{a'}$ then there holds*

$$[\![\Gamma \vdash \sigma]\!](\underline{r}) : b \mapsto b'$$

where $b = [\![\Gamma\,;\,\Theta \vdash M : \sigma]\!](\underline{A})(\underline{a})$ and $b' = [\![\Gamma\,;\,\Theta \vdash M : \sigma]\!](\underline{A'})(\underline{a'})$.

Finally we define semantical parametricity.

Definition 3.8 (i) $a \in \forall F$ is *parametric* if, for any $r : A \multimap B$, there holds

$$F(r) : \Phi_F^{\forall}(a)(A) \mapsto \Phi_F^{\forall}(a)(B)\,.$$

(Using $[\![\,]\!]$, we can write it $F(r) : [\![a\{A\}]\!] \mapsto [\![a\{B\}]\!]$.)

(ii) $\forall F$ is *parametric* if all $a \in \forall F$ is pararmetric.

(iii) An interpretation ξ is parametric if all $\forall F$ is parametric.

In a natural model ξ such that all $F \in \mathrm{Obj}\,[\mathbf{T} \to \mathbf{T}]$ preserves identities, we can characterize parametricity by the assetion that ξ is parametric iff $\forall : [\mathbf{T} \to \mathbf{T}] \to \mathbf{T}$ preserves identities (i.e., $\forall id_F = id_{\forall F}$). The following theorem [20] that is valid only for parametric natural models is used below.

Theorem 3.9 (Identity Extension Lemma) *Let ξ be a parametric natural model. Then every syntactically defined r-frame morphism $[\![\Gamma \vdash \sigma]\!]$ preserves identity relations.*

4 Polymorphic extensional collapse of pretheories

As is well-known, the collection of closed types/terms of second order lambda calculus is a BMM interpretation but not a BMM model [4]. Polymorphic extensional collapse by Breazu-Tannen and Coquand [4] gives a method to obtain a BMM model from the closed types/terms collection. In this section, we show every syntactically defined universal type is parametric for extensionally collapsed models of the closed types/terms collection.

First we construct a BMM interpretation $\xi_{\Sigma,E}$ from a pretheory E of closed terms of $\lambda^{\forall}(\Sigma)$. Next we give an extensionally collapsed model $Coll(\xi, \mathcal{P})$ for a logical per collection $\mathcal{P}$ as in [4], but this time we adjoin binary relations to $Coll(\xi, \mathcal{P})$ so that it gives a natural relational model. Then it is proved that every syntactically defined universal type is parametric. The result is, in fact, an immediate consequence of Abstraction Theorem.

A *pretheory* E is an equivalence relation of closed terms of $\lambda^{\forall}(\Sigma)$ such that $M\,E\,N$ implies that M and N have the same closed type, and is subject to the condition

(1) E respects (β) and (Type-β) conversions

(2) E is congruent w.r.t. application and Type application.

(1) means that if M' is obtained from M by reducing some β (or Type-β) redex in M then $M\,E\,M'$, and (2) means that if $M\,E\,M'$ of type $\sigma \Rightarrow \tau$ and $N\,E\,N'$ of type σ then $(MN)\,E\,(M'N')$, and that if $M\,E\,M'$ of type $\forall X.\sigma$ then $(M\{\tau\})\,E\,(M'\{\tau\})$ for any closed type τ. Of course α-conversion is dealt implicitly. Let $[M]$ denote the equivalence class of M modulo E.

This definition is different with that in [18] in respect that our pretheory does not necessarily respect η and Type-η conversions.

A *theory* is a pretheory E such that there is a model ξ and $M\,E\,N$ is defined by $[\![M]\!] = [\![N]\!]$.

We have a straightforward construction of a BMM interpretation $\xi_{\Sigma,E}$ by collecting all the closed types and closed terms and dividing them by E. It is formalized as follows.

- $\mathcal{U}$ is the set of closed types (modulo the names of bound type variables). For each $\sigma \in \mathcal{U}$, D_σ is the set of $[M]$ where M is such that $;\vdash M : \sigma$.
- Obj $[\mathbf{T}^n \to \mathbf{T}]$ (i.e., $\mathcal{U}^n \to \mathcal{U}$) is the set of type judgements $\Gamma \vdash \sigma$ ($|\Gamma| = n$) modulo the names of bound and/or free type variables. For $\sigma_1, \ldots, \sigma_n \in \mathcal{U}^n$, $(\Gamma \vdash \tau)(\underline{\sigma})$ is defined to be $\tau[\Gamma := \underline{\sigma}]$.
- $\Rightarrow(\sigma, \tau) = \sigma \Rightarrow \tau$, and $\forall(X \vdash \sigma) = \forall X.\sigma$.
- $\Phi^{\Rightarrow}_{\sigma,\tau}([M])$ is a function sending $[N]$ to $[MN]$. $\Phi^{\forall}_{X\vdash\sigma}([M])$ is a function sending τ to $[M\{\tau\}]$.
- $[\![\Gamma\,;\Theta \vdash M : \sigma]\!](\underline{\tau})(\underline{[N]})$ is defined to be $[M[\Gamma := \underline{\tau}][\Theta := \underline{N}]]$.

Well-definedness of $\Phi^{\Rightarrow}$ (and $\Phi^{\forall}$) follows from the assumption that E is congruent w.r.t. application (Type application).

Lemma 4.1 $[\![\Gamma\,;\Theta \vdash M : \sigma]\!]$ *is well-defined.*

(*Proof*) We must check that if $\underline{N}\,E\,\underline{N'}$ then

$$[\![\Gamma\,;\Theta \vdash M : \sigma]\!](\underline{\tau})(\underline{N}) = [\![\Gamma\,;\Theta \vdash M : \sigma]\!](\underline{\tau})(\underline{N'})\,.$$

Since E is reflexive, $(\Lambda\underline{X}\lambda\underline{x}^\sigma M)\,E\,(\Lambda\underline{X}\lambda\underline{x}^\sigma M)$. where $\Gamma = \underline{X}$ and $\Theta = \underline{x : \sigma}$. Then use (Type) application and (Type-) β conversions to show

$$(M[\Gamma := \underline{\tau}][\Theta := \underline{N}])\,E\,(M[\Gamma := \underline{\tau}][\Theta := \underline{N'}])\,. \qquad \square$$

We must also check that $[\![\Gamma \vdash \sigma]\!]$ and $[\![\Gamma\,;\Theta \vdash M : \sigma]\!]$ fulfill their required conditions. We omit the detail.

Theorem 4.2 $\xi_{\Sigma,E}$ *is a BMM interpretation.*

Remark 4.3 If E satisfies the ω rule

- if $(MN)\,E\,(M'N')$ for all $N\,E\,N'$ then $M\,E\,M'$, and
- if $(M\{\tau\})\,E\,(M\{\tau'\})$ for all τ then $M\,E\,M'$,

then $\xi_{\Sigma,E}$ is a model (i.e., all components of $\Phi^{\Rightarrow}$ and $\Phi^{\forall}$ are all one-to-one).

Next we construct a relational model $Coll(\xi, \mathcal{P})$ from any BMM interpretation ξ and logical per collection $\mathcal{P}$. We use the notation $(\text{-})^o$ to distinguish the constructions of the 'o'riginal interpretation from those of a model $Coll(\xi, \mathcal{P})$ to be defined. For example, $\mathcal{U}^o$, $\Rightarrow^o$, etc.

Definition 4.4 ([4]) Suppose given a signature Σ and a BMM interpretation ξ. A *logical per collection* $\mathcal{P}$ is a pair $(\mathcal{P}^U, \mathcal{P}^K)$ where

- $\mathcal{P}^U$ is a $\mathcal{U}$-indexed family $\{\mathcal{P}_A \mid A \in \mathcal{U}^o\}$ where $\mathcal{P}_A$ is a set of pers on D^o_A such that
  - if $R \in \mathcal{P}_A$ and $S \in \mathcal{P}_B$ then $R \Rightarrow^p S \in \mathcal{P}_{A \Rightarrow^o B}$ where $R \Rightarrow^p S$ is a per defined as $f\,(R \Rightarrow^p S)\,f'$ iff $\Phi^{\Rightarrow^o}_{A,B}(f)(a)\; S\; \Phi^{\Rightarrow^o}_{A',B'}(f')(a')$ for any $a\,R\,a'$.
  - suppose Q is a function sending $R \in \mathcal{P}_A$ to $Q(R) \in \mathcal{P}_{FA}$ where F is an object of $[\mathbf{T} \to \mathbf{T}]^o$. Then $\forall^p Q \in \mathcal{P}_{\forall^o F}$ where $\forall^p Q$ is a per defined as $f\,(\forall^p Q)\,f'$ iff $\Phi^{\forall^o}_F(f)(A)\;(Q(R))\;\Phi^{\forall^o}_F(f')(A)$ for any $R \in \mathcal{P}_A$.
- $\mathcal{P}^K$ is a function assigning a per in $\mathcal{P}_A$ to each $A \in \mathcal{K}$.

Note there exists at least one logical per collecion, namely the collection of all pers with arbitrary $\mathcal{P}^K$.

Our construction of an extensionally collapsed model $Coll(\xi, \mathcal{P})$ follows [4], but with adjoined binary relations. Note that in the construction below binary relations have no effect in the object part (i.e., the part involved in BMM models). Now we begin with the definition of $Coll(\xi, \mathcal{P})$.

- $\langle A, R\rangle$ belongs to $\mathcal{U}$ iff $A \in \mathcal{U}^o$ and $R \in \mathcal{P}_A$. $D_{\langle A,R\rangle}$ is the subquotient set A/R. For $a \in Dom(R)$ (i.e., $a\,R\,a$), let $[a]_R$ denote an equivalence class of a.
- $r : \langle A, R\rangle \twoheadrightarrow \langle B, S\rangle$ belongs to $\mathcal{R}$ iff it is a subset of $A/R \times B/S$.
- $\langle F, Q\rangle$ is an object of $[\mathbf{T}^n \to \mathbf{T}]$ iff $F \in \mathrm{Obj}\,[\mathbf{T}^n \to \mathbf{T}]^o$ and Q is a pair of functions (Q_p, Q_r) where Q_p sends $R_i \in \mathcal{P}_{A_i}$ $(i = 1, \ldots, n)$ to $Q_p(\underline{R}) \in \mathcal{P}_{F(\underline{A})}$, and Q_r sends $r_i : \langle A_i, R_i\rangle \twoheadrightarrow \langle B_i, S_i\rangle$ $(i = 1, \ldots, n)$ to $Q_r(\underline{r}) : \langle F(\underline{A}), Q_p(\underline{R})\rangle \twoheadrightarrow \langle F(\underline{B}), Q_p(\underline{S})\rangle$. The behaviour of $\langle F, Q\rangle$ is determined by

$$\langle F, Q\rangle(\underline{\langle A, R\rangle}) \stackrel{def}{=} \langle F(\underline{A}), Q_p(\underline{R})\rangle$$
$$\langle F, Q\rangle(\underline{r}) \stackrel{def}{=} Q_r(\underline{r})\,.$$

- $p : \langle F, Q\rangle \twoheadrightarrow \langle F', Q'\rangle$ belongs to $\mathrm{Rel}\,[\mathbf{T}^n \to \mathbf{T}]$ iff p sends $r_i : \langle A_i, R_i\rangle \twoheadrightarrow \langle A'_i, R'_i\rangle$ $(i = 1, \ldots n)$ to $p(\underline{r}) : \langle F(\underline{A}), Q_p(\underline{R})\rangle \twoheadrightarrow \langle F'(\underline{A'}), Q'_p(\underline{R'})\rangle$ (note that p is not involved in Q_r and Q'_r).

- $\Rightarrow: \mathbf{T}^2 \to \mathbf{T}$ is determined by; for objects, $\langle A, R\rangle \Rightarrow \langle B, S\rangle \stackrel{def}{=} \langle A \Rightarrow^o B, R \Rightarrow^p S\rangle$; for relations $r : \langle A, R\rangle \rightarrowtriangle \langle A', R'\rangle$ and $s : \langle B, S\rangle \rightarrowtriangle \langle B', S'\rangle$, the relation $r \Rightarrow s$ is defined as $r \Rightarrow s : [f]_{R \Rightarrow^p S} \mapsto [f']_{R' \Rightarrow^p S'}$ iff $s : [\Phi^{\Rightarrow^o}_{A,B}(f)(a)]_S \mapsto [\Phi^{\Rightarrow^o}_{A',B'}(f')(a')]_{S'}$ for any $r : [a]_R \mapsto [a']_{R'}$. It is well-defined by the definition of $\Rightarrow^p$.

- $\forall : [\mathbf{T} \to \mathbf{T}] \to \mathbf{T}$ is determined by; for an object, $\forall\langle F, Q\rangle \stackrel{def}{=} \langle \forall^o F, \forall^p Q_p\rangle$; and for a relation $p : \langle F, Q\rangle \rightarrowtriangle \langle F', Q'\rangle$, the relation $\forall p$ is defined as $\forall p : [f]_{\forall^p Q_p} \mapsto [f']_{\forall^p Q'_p}$ iff $p(r) : [\Phi^{\forall^o}_F(f)(A)]_{Q_p(R)} \mapsto [\Phi^{\forall^o}_{F'}(f')(A')]_{Q'_p(R')}$ for any $r : \langle A, R\rangle \rightarrowtriangle \langle A', R'\rangle$. Well-definedness follows from the definition of $\forall^p(\text{-})$.

- $\Phi^{\Rightarrow}_{\langle A,R\rangle\langle B,S\rangle}([f]_{R\Rightarrow^p S})$ is a function sending $[a]_R$ to $[\Phi^{\Rightarrow^o}_{A,B}(f)(a)]_S$.

- $\Phi^{\forall}_{\langle F,Q\rangle}([f]_{\forall^p(Q_p)})$ is a function sending $\langle A, R\rangle$ to $[\Phi^{\forall^o}_F(f)(A)]_{Q_p(R)}$.

- $I(A) \stackrel{def}{=} \langle A, \mathcal{P}^K(A)\rangle$ and $I(c) = [c]_R$ where R is the per part of $[\![\vdash \text{Type}\,\Theta]\!]$. Remark that $I(c)$ makes sense only in case there holds $c\,R\,c$. In this case we say c is *self-related* in $\mathcal{P}$.

- $[\![\Gamma\,;\,\Theta \vdash M : \sigma]\!](\underline{\langle A, R\rangle})(\underline{[a]}_{[\![\Gamma\vdash\text{Type}(a)]\!](\underline{R})})$ is defined to be $[[\![\Gamma\,;\,\Theta \vdash M : \sigma]\!]^o(\underline{A})(\underline{a})\,]_{[\![\Gamma\vdash\sigma]\!](\underline{R})}$ where $[\![\Gamma \vdash \sigma]\!](\underline{R})$ is the per part of $[\![\Gamma \vdash \sigma]\!](\underline{\langle A, R\rangle})$.

Lemma 4.5 *(i) $\Phi^{\Rightarrow}_{\langle A,R\rangle\langle B,S\rangle}$ and $\Phi^{\forall}_{\langle F,Q\rangle}$ are all one-to-one.*

(ii) $\Phi^{\Rightarrow}$ and $\Phi^{\forall}$ are natural.

(*Proof*) Immediate from definitions. □

Well-definedness of $[\![\Gamma\,;\,\Theta \vdash M : \sigma]\!]$ (in case all individual constant is self-related in $\mathcal{P}$) is proved as in [4], or by Abstraction Theorem remarking that $\Rightarrow^p$ and $\forall^p$ is defined so that $\Phi^{\Rightarrow}$ and $\Phi^{\forall}$ are natural w.r.t. pers in $\mathcal{P}$.

What remains to check is the conditions for $[\![\Gamma \vdash \sigma]\!]$ and $[\![\Gamma\,;\,\Theta \vdash M : \sigma]\!]$. They are satisfied, in fact, inheriting the conditions $[\![\Gamma \vdash \sigma]\!]^o$ and $[\![\Gamma\,;\,\Theta \vdash M : \sigma]\!]^o$ fulfill.

Theorem 4.6 *If all individual constant is self-related in $\mathcal{P}$, then $Coll(\xi, \mathcal{P})$ is a natural model.*

Now let us focus on polymorphic extensional collapse of closed types/terms interpretation $Coll(\xi_{\Sigma,E}, \mathcal{P})$. We say $c \in C$ is *self-related in $\mathcal{R}$* iff $[\![\vdash \text{Type}(c)]\!] : c \mapsto c$.

Theorem 4.7 *Consider $Coll(\xi_{\Sigma,E}, \mathcal{P})$ and suppose all individual constant is self-related in $\mathcal{R}$. All syntactically defined universal type $[\![\vdash \forall X.\sigma]\!]$ is parametric.*

(*Proof*) Since $Coll(\xi_{\Sigma,E}, \mathcal{P})$ is a natural model, Abstraction Theorem asserts that, for any $\vdash M : \forall X.\sigma$, there holds $[\![\vdash \forall X.\sigma]\!] : [\![M]\!] \mapsto [\![M]\!]$, that is, $[\![M]\!]$ is parametric. But any member of $[\![\vdash \forall X.\sigma]\!]$ have the form $[\![M]\!]$ for some closed term $M : \forall X.\sigma$. Therefore $[\![\vdash \forall X.\sigma]\!]$ is parametric. □

There are many syntactically undefinable universal types $\forall\langle F, Q\rangle$. A question is whether all $\forall\langle F, Q\rangle$ is parametric or there is any counterexample.

Remark 4.8 If the signature Σ is empty, the theorem can be extended a little. For example, $[\![\forall X(((\langle A, R\rangle \Rightarrow \langle B, S\rangle \Rightarrow X) \Rightarrow X)]\!]$ is parametric for any $\langle A, R\rangle$ and $\langle B, S\rangle$. Every element of the type has the form $\Lambda X \lambda y^{\langle A,R\rangle \Rightarrow \langle B,S\rangle \Rightarrow X} y[M]_R[N]_S$. Hence $[M]_R$ and $[N]_S$ can be treated as individual constants of constant types $\langle A, R\rangle$ and $\langle B, S\rangle$. Similar arguments show that $[\![\forall X(((\langle A, R\rangle \Rightarrow X) \Rightarrow ((\langle B, S\rangle \Rightarrow X) \Rightarrow X)]\!]$ is parametric.

5 Second order minimum model

Moggi and Statman discovered a construction of maximum consistent theory [18]. We denote it by E_m. The theory is interesting because of its satisfying the ω rule. Hence the corresponding BMM interpretation ξ_{ϕ,E_m} (ϕ is the empty signature) turns into a BMM model. Indeed ξ_{ϕ,E_m} is easily lifted into a parametric natural model. In this section we assume the signature is always empty

A pretheory is *consistent* iff it is *not* the case that $\texttt{true}\, E\, \texttt{false}$ where $\texttt{true} = \Lambda X \lambda x^X \lambda y^X x$ and $\texttt{false} = \Lambda X \lambda x^X \lambda y^X y$ of type $\texttt{Bool} = \forall X(X \Rightarrow X \Rightarrow X)$. All pretheory but one is consistent. Indeed if $\texttt{true}\, E\, \texttt{false}$ then any two closed terms of the same type are equivalent modulo E.

The set of all consistent pretheories has the structure of a lattice w.r.t. inclusion [18]. There is a maximal element of the lattice, called the *maximum consistent theory*. It is characterized as follows.

Definition 5.1 E_m is a pretheory defined as $M\, E_m\, N$ (M, N of type σ) iff, for all closed term K of type $\sigma \Rightarrow \texttt{Bool}$, there holds $KM =_{\beta\eta} KN$.

It is easily checked that E_m is actually a pretheory. And if we note that $\texttt{true}$ and $\texttt{false}$ are the only $\beta\eta$-normal closed terms of type $\texttt{Bool}$, and at the same time the only β-normal closed terms, then the following proposition is easily proved.

Proposition 5.2 *E_m is maximal in the lattice of consistent pretheories.*

We can infer, from the following proposition [18], that E_m is a theory.

Proposition 5.3 *E_m satisfies the ω rule:*
(i) for $M, M' : \sigma \Rightarrow \tau$, if $MN\, E_m\, M'N$ for all $N : \sigma$ then $M\, E_m\, M'$.
(ii) for $M, M' : \forall X.\sigma$, if $M\{\tau\}\, E_m\, M'\{\tau\}$ for all τ, then $M\, E_m\, M'$.

(*Proof*) Let E' be the theory of $Coll(\xi_{\phi,E_m}, All)$ where All is the collection of all pers. By the construction of polymorphic extensional collapse, $E_m \subseteq E'$. Since E_m is maximal, $E_m = E'$. Then (i) follows by replacing E_m by E'. As for (ii), if $M\{\tau\}\, E_m\, M'\{\tau\}$ for all τ, then $M\, E'\, M'$ by the construction of $Coll(\xi_{\phi,E_m}, All)$. (A direct proof is also possible.) □

By the ω rule, ξ_{ϕ,E_m} is a BMM model, called the *second order minimum model*. A quesion is whether there are any other consistent theories satisfying the ω rule. For those theories, if any, the following argument is valid.

Here we adjoin binary relations to ξ_{ϕ,E_m} so that it is to be a relational model. The additional structure is given as follows.

- $r : \sigma \multimap \tau$ iff $r \subseteq D_\sigma \times D_\tau$. $\mathcal{R}$ is the collection of such r's.
- $p : (\Gamma \vdash \tau) \multimap (\Gamma \vdash \tau')$ belongs to Rel $[\mathbf{T}^n \to \mathbf{T}]$ iff p sends $\underline{r} : \underline{\sigma} \multimap \underline{\sigma}'$ to $p(r) : \tau[\Gamma := \underline{\sigma}] \multimap \tau'[\Gamma := \underline{\sigma}']$.
- For $r : \sigma \multimap \sigma'$ and $s : \tau \multimap \tau'$, the relation $r \Rightarrow s$ is defined as $r \Rightarrow s : [M] \mapsto [M']$ ($M : \sigma \Rightarrow \tau$, $M' : \sigma' \Rightarrow \tau'$) iff $s : [MN] \mapsto [M'N']$ for any $r : [N] \mapsto [N']$.
- For $p : (X \vdash \sigma) \multimap (X \vdash \sigma')$, the relation $\forall p$ is defined as $\forall p : [M] \mapsto [M']$ ($M : \forall X.\sigma$, $M' : \forall X.\sigma'$) iff $p(r) : [M\{\tau\}] \mapsto [M'\{\tau'\}]$ for any $r : \tau \multimap \tau'$.

Since all $F \in$ Obj $[\mathbf{T}^n \to \mathbf{T}]$ is syntactically definable, the behaviour of F for relation arguments is completely determined by $r \Rightarrow s$ and $\forall p$. Note that $r \Rightarrow s$ and $\forall p$ are defined so that $\Phi^{\Rightarrow}$ and $\Phi^{\forall}$ are natural. Then the next theorem is immediate.

Theorem 5.4 ξ_{ϕ,E_m} *(with the additional structure above) is a parametric natural model.*

(*Proof*) For parametricity, all universal type is syntactically defined and its elements are all interpretations of some closed terms of the type. Then parametricity follows from Abstraction Theorem. □

6 Categorical properties

An interesting feature of parametric model is about categorical data types. Prawitz showed [19] that in intuitionistic second order logic implication and universal quantification represent other logical connectives, as

$$\begin{aligned} \bot &= \forall X.X \\ A \wedge B &= \forall X((A \Rightarrow B \Rightarrow X) \Rightarrow X) \\ A \vee B &= \forall X((A \Rightarrow X) \Rightarrow (B \Rightarrow X) \Rightarrow X) \\ \exists X.F(X) &= \forall Y(\forall X(F(X) \Rightarrow Y) \Rightarrow Y). \end{aligned}$$

It is showed in [13] that if a model ξ has enough binary relations and is a parametric natural model then in the categorya $\mathbf{C}_\xi$ generated by ξ (see below) the representations of Prawitz have natural meanings. For example, $\bot$ is an initial object, $A \wedge B$ is a product of A and B, and $A \vee B$ is a coproduct of A and B.

Definition 6.1 Let ξ be a model. A category $\mathbf{C}_\xi$ is defined as $\mathrm{Obj}(\mathbf{C}_\xi) = \mathcal{U}$, $\mathbf{C}_\xi = A \Rightarrow B$, $1_A = [\![\lambda x^A x]\!]$ and $g \circ f = [\![\lambda x^A g(fx) : A \Rightarrow C]\!]$ $(f : A \to B$ and $g : B \to C)$.

To each arrow $f \in A \Rightarrow B$, we associate a binary relation $|f| : A \rightharpoondown B$, a *graph* of f, defined as $|f| : a \mapsto b$ iff $b = \Phi^{\Rightarrow}_{A,B}(f)(a)$. A model ξ *has enough relations* iff all graphs $|f|$ belong to $\mathcal{R}$. The following theorem is a general property of a natural model which has enough relations.

Theorem 6.2 *Suppose ξ is a natural model which has enough binary relations. Then, in the category $\mathbf{C}_\xi$,*

(i) if $\bot = \forall X.X$ is parametric, $\bot$ is an initial object.

(ii) if $\top = \forall X(X \Rightarrow X)$ is parametric, then $\top$ is a terminal object.

(iii) if $A+B = \forall X((A \Rightarrow X) \Rightarrow (B \Rightarrow X) \Rightarrow X)$ is parametric, then $A+B$ is a coproduct of A and B.

(iv) if $A \times B = \forall X((A \Rightarrow B \Rightarrow X) \Rightarrow X)$ is parametric, then $A \times B$ is a product of A and B. Moreover if $A \times B$ is parametric for all A then adjunction $(\text{-}) \times B \dashv B \Rightarrow (\text{-})$ holds.

(N.B. we write, for example, simply $\forall X.X$ for $[\![\forall X.X]\!]$.)

Since ξ_{ϕ,E_m} has enough relations (in fact, it has all binary relations) and parametric (Theorem 5.4), the above theorem is applied for ξ_{ϕ,E_m}. As for $Coll(\xi_{\Sigma,E}, \mathcal{P})$, if the signature Σ is empty, by the remark following Theorem 4.7, the above theorem is applied, too. In these cases, however, the theorem is proved also by directly analyzing the closed terms of the types.

See [13] for the proof of the theorem. In an appropriate setting, even the converse is proved. For example, if $\forall X.X$ is an initial object then it is parametric w.r.t. the collection of all graphs. The essence of the proof of the theorem is to use parametricity for graphs in place of commutativity of diagrams.

Other syntactically definable data types are initial and terminal fixed points of *universally strong* endofunctors.

Definition 6.3 $F \in \mathrm{Obj}\,[\mathbf{T} \to \mathbf{T}]$ is a *universally strong functor* iff both

(i) there is a *universal strength* $\overline{F} \in \forall X \forall Y((X \Rightarrow Y) \Rightarrow (FX \Rightarrow FY))$ so that $\overline{F}$ induces a functor $\mathbf{C}_\xi \to \mathbf{C}_\xi$, and

(ii) for $f \in A \Rightarrow B$, there holds $F(|f|) = |\overline{F}(f)|$ where $\overline{F}(f)$ means $[\![\overline{F}\{A\}\{B\}(f)]\!]$.

For an endofunctor $F : \mathbf{C} \to \mathbf{C}$, an initial object of a comma category $(F \downarrow Id)$ is called, if any, an *initial fixed point* of F, and a terminal object of $(Id \downarrow F)$ a *terminal fixed point* of F. Initial fixed points are used to encode algebraic types and terminal fixed points to encode some lazy stream types [3, 11, 23].

The following theorem is a general property of parametric natural models [13].

Theorem 6.4 *Suppose ξ is a natural model which has enough relations, and $F : \mathbf{C}_\xi \to \mathbf{C}_\xi$ is a universally strong functor. Then*

(i) if $\mu F = \forall X((FX \Rightarrow X) \Rightarrow X)$ is parametric, then μF is an initial fixed point of F.

(ii) if $\nu F = \exists X((X \Rightarrow FX) \times X)$ and $\forall X(((X \Rightarrow FX) \times X) \Rightarrow \nu F)$ are parametric, then νF is a terminal fixed point of F.

To apply the theorem to the minimum model and extensionally collapsed model, we should know what objects of $[\mathbf{T} \to \mathbf{T}]$ are universally strong functors.

For $\Gamma \vdash \sigma$ and $X \in \Gamma$, we say X is $+$ $(-, 0)$ variant if X occurs at most positively (at most negatively, possibly both positively and negatively) in σ. Moreover we say, for example, $X, Y, Z \vdash \forall W((Y \Rightarrow X) \Rightarrow Z) \Rightarrow Y$ is $+0-$ variant where X, Y, Z are $+$, 0, $-$ variant respectively.

$X \vdash \sigma$ of $+$ variant is a candidate of a universally strong functor. In fact, is has a universal strength, constructed by induction on σ. But do not look over the second condition of Definition 6.3. For that, we need the next lemma and parametricity.

Lemma 6.5 *Let ξ be a natural model, $f \in A \Rightarrow A'$, and $r : B \rightarrowtriangle B'$.*

(i) for $F = [\![X, Y \vdash \sigma]\!]$ where $X, Y \vdash \sigma$ is $+0$ variant,

$$F(id_A, r); |\overline{F}(f, 1_{B'})| \subseteq F(|f|, r) \subseteq |\overline{F}(f, 1_B)|; F(id_{A'}, r)\,.$$

(ii) for $F = [\![X, Y \vdash \sigma]\!]$ where $X, Y \vdash \sigma$ is -0 variant,

$$|\overline{F}(f, 1_B)|^{op}; F(id_{A'}, r) \subseteq F(|f|, r) \subseteq F(id_A, r); |\overline{F}(f, 1_{B'})|^{op}\,.$$

(N.B. $r^{op} : a \mapsto b$ iff $r : b \mapsto a$. And $r; s : a \mapsto c$ iff there is b such that $r : a \mapsto b$ and $s : b \mapsto c$.)

Proposition 6.6 *If ξ is a parametric natural model, every $[\![X \vdash \sigma]\!]$ of $+$ variant is a universally strong functor.*

(*Proof*) Use the lemma above together with Identity Extension Lemma. □

Since the minimum model ξ_{ϕ,E_m} is a parametric natural model, for all $X \vdash \sigma$ of $+$ variant, $\forall X((\sigma \Rightarrow X) \Rightarrow X)$ and $\exists X((X \Rightarrow \sigma) \times X)$ are initial and terminal fixed points of $(X \vdash \sigma)$.

For $Coll(\xi_{\phi,E}, \mathcal{P})$, the situation is more subtle, because the model is only partially parametric (we shall assume the signature is empty ϕ). We must investigate Identity Extension Lemma for partially parametric models. A sufficient condition for $[\![\Gamma \vdash \sigma]\!]$ of $+$ variant to give a universally strong functor is that X is not captured in the scope of universal quanitifier. This covers, for example, the 'power set of power sets' functor $F = [\![X \vdash (X \Rightarrow \texttt{Bool}) \Rightarrow \texttt{Bool}]\!]$. Functors for defining algebraic types are also parametric. For example, the natural numbers object is an initial fixed point of $F = [\![X \vdash \top + X]\!]$ which is universally strong by the remark following Theorem 4.7.

Example 6.7 For $\xi = \xi_{\phi,E_m}$ and $= Coll(\xi_{\phi,E}, \mathcal{P})$, the following data types are initial (terminal) fixed points in the category $\mathbf{C}_\xi$.

(i) the type of ordinals [11]:

$$\mu X(\top + (\texttt{Nat} \Rightarrow X))$$

where Nat is $\mu X(\top + X)$ the type of natural numbers.

(ii) the type of infinite lists of A [23]:

$$\nu X(A \times X).$$

Second order types also provide representation of internal right and left Kan extensions. It seems to be new, as far as the author knows, but is a straightforward analogue of the representation by ends [15]. What follows is applicable for the minimum model ξ_{ϕ,E_m}, but not clear for $Coll(\xi_{\phi,E}, \mathcal{P})$, since the represetations include parameters.

Definition 6.8 Let ξ be a parametric natural model. $\mathbf{Us}(\mathbf{C}_\xi)$ is a category defined as; $\mathrm{Obj}(\mathbf{Us}(\mathbf{C}_\xi))$ is the collection of all universally strong functors; $\mathbf{Us}(\mathbf{C}_\xi)(F, G)$ is defined to be $\forall X(FX \Rightarrow GX)$ together with

$$1_F = [\![\Lambda X \lambda x^{FX} x]\!]$$
$$f' \circ f = [\![\Lambda X \lambda x^{FX} f'\{X\}(f\{X\}x)]\!]$$

for $f : F \to F'$ and $f' : F' \to F''$.

$\mathbf{Us}(\mathbf{C}_\xi)$ is a $\mathbf{C}_\xi$-enriched category, It is also a subcategory of the functor category $\mathbf{C}_\xi^{\mathbf{C}_\xi}$, since all $f \in \mathbf{Us}(\mathbf{C}_\xi)(F, G)$ is a natural transformation by the following lemma.

Lemma 6.9 *Let F and G be universally strong functors. If $\forall X(FX \Rightarrow GX)$ is parametric, then every $f \in \forall X(FX \Rightarrow GX)$ is a natural transformation.*

Recall the definition of right Kan extension. Let $\mathbf{C}$, $\mathbf{D}$ and $\mathbf{S}$ be categories, and $K : \mathbf{C} \to \mathbf{D}$ and $T : \mathbf{C} \to \mathbf{S}$. A right Kan extension of T along K is a functor $\mathrm{Ran}_K T : \mathbf{D} \to \mathbf{S}$, such that adjunction at T

$$\mathbf{S}^{\mathbf{C}}((\text{-}) \circ K, T) \cong \mathbf{S}^{\mathbf{D}}((\text{-}), \mathrm{Ran}_K T)$$

holds where $\mathbf{S}^{\mathbf{C}}$ and $\mathbf{S}^{\mathbf{D}}$ are the functor categories. We say a universally strong functor $\mathrm{Ran}_K T : \mathbf{C}_\xi \to \mathbf{C}_\xi$ is an *internal right Kan extension* of T along K (K and T are both universally strong endofunctors on $\mathbf{C}_\xi$) if

$$\mathbf{Us}(\mathbf{C}_\xi)((\text{-}) \circ K, T) \cong \mathbf{Us}(\mathbf{C}_\xi)((\text{-}), \mathrm{Ran}_K T)$$

is a natural equivalence in (-) where the equivalence is an isomorphism in $\mathbf{C}_\xi$ (recall $\mathbf{Us}(\mathbf{C}_\xi)$ is a $\mathbf{C}_\xi$-enriched category). An internal left Kan extension $\mathrm{Lan}_K T$ is defined dually.

Theorem 6.10 *In $\mathbf{C}_\xi$ for ξ a parametric natural model (thus in particular for $\xi = \xi_{\phi,E_m}$),*

(i) $\mathrm{Ran}_K T = \forall X(((\text{-}) \Rightarrow KX) \Rightarrow TX)$ *gives an internal right Kan extension of T along K.*

(ii) $\mathrm{Lan}_K T = \exists X((KX \Rightarrow (\text{-})) \times TX)$ *gives an internal left Kan extension of T along K.*

Corollary 6.11 *Let ξ be a parametric natural model and $K : \mathbf{C}_\xi \to \mathbf{C}_\xi$ a universally strong functor.*

(i) If K preserves $\mathrm{Ran}_K 1_{\mathbf{C}_\xi}$, then K has an internal left adjoint $\forall X(((\text{-}) \Rightarrow KX) \Rightarrow X)$.

(ii) If K preserves $\mathrm{Lan}_K 1_{\mathbf{C}_\xi}$, then K has an internal right adjoint $\exists X((KX \Rightarrow (\text{-})) \times X)$.

$A \times B = \forall X((A \Rightarrow B \Rightarrow X) \Rightarrow X)$ is a special case of (i) by $K = B \Rightarrow (\text{-})$. There is no other case, however, as pointed out in [7], namely,

Corollary 6.12 *Let ξ be a parametric natural model.*

(i) Any universally strong functor K preserving $\mathrm{Ran}_K 1_{\mathbf{C}_\xi}$ is representable as

$$K \cong (\forall X((\top \Rightarrow KX) \Rightarrow X)) \Rightarrow (\text{-})\,.$$

(ii) Any universally strong functor K perserving $\mathrm{Lan}_K 1_{\mathbf{C}_\xi}$ is corepresentable as

$$K \cong (\exists X((KX \Rightarrow \top) \times X)) \times (\text{-})\,.$$

I conjecture that if we consider a full subcategory of $Coll(\xi_{\Sigma,E}, \mathcal{P})$ consisting of all syntactically defined objects, then all the theorems above are applied. But the detail has not yet been checked.

Remark 6.13 Huwig and Poigné showed [14] that some kinds of looping combinators cannot coexist with cartesian closedness. For example, if $\mathbf{2} = \mathbf{1} + \mathbf{1}$ exists in a non-degenerating cartesian closed category, no arrow $Y : (\mathbf{2} \Rightarrow \mathbf{2}) \to \mathbf{2}$ can be a looping combinator (i.e., an arrow such that for any $f : \mathbf{2} \to \mathbf{2}$, there holds $Y \circ \lceil f \rceil = f \circ Y \circ \lceil f \rceil : \mathbf{1} \to \mathbf{2}$). Hence in $\mathbf{C}_\xi$ where $\xi = \xi_{\phi,E_m}$ or $Coll(\xi_{\phi,E}, \mathcal{P})$, there is no looping combinator of $\mathbf{2}$. More generally we can show that, in any natural interpretation with full binary relations, if $Y \in (\texttt{Bool} \Rightarrow \texttt{Bool}) \Rightarrow \texttt{Bool}$ is a looping combinator and $[\![\vdash (\texttt{Bool} \Rightarrow \texttt{Bool}) \Rightarrow \texttt{Bool}]\!] : Y \mapsto Y$ then $[\![\texttt{true}]\!] = [\![\texttt{false}]\!]$ is derived.

Acknowledgements

I would like to thank Susumu Hayashi for recommending me to submit the study to TACS meeting, and the referees for helpful advice, especially an indication about degeneration by looping combinators.

References

[1] E. S. Bainbridge, P. J. Freyd, A. Scedrov and P. J. Scott, Functorial Polymorphism, Theoret. Comput. Sci. 70 (1990) 35–64; Corrigendum, 71 (1990) 431.

[2] H. P. Barendregt, The lambda calculus, Its syntax and semantics, (North-Holland, Amsterdam, 1984) Revised edition.

[3] C. Böhm and A. Berrarducci, Automatic synthesis of typed Λ-programs on term algebras, Theoret. Comput. Sci. 39 (1985) 135–154.

[4] V. Breazu-Tannen and T. Coquand, Extensional models for polymorphism, Theoret. Comput. Sci. 59 (1988) 85–114.

[5] K. B. Bruce, A. R. Meyer and J. C. Mitchell, The semantics of second-order lambda calculus, Inform. Comput. 85 (1990) 76–134.

[6] T. Coquand, C. Gunter and G. Winskell, Domain theoretic models of polymorphism, Inform. and Comput. 81 (1989) 123–167.

[7] P. Freyd, Structural polymorphism, privately circulated, University of Pennsylvania (1989).

[8] H. Friedman, Equality between functionals, in:Logic Colloquium '73, Boston, Lecture Notes in Mathematics 453 (Springer, Berlin, 1975) 22–37.

[9] J.-Y. Girard, The system F of variable types, fifteen years later, Theoret. Comput. Sci. 45 (1986) 159–192.

[10] J.-Y. Girard, P. Taylor and Y. Lafont, Proofs and types, (Cambridge University Press, Cambridge, 1989).

[11] T. Hagino, A typed lambda calculus with categorical type constructors, in: D. H. Pitt, A. Poingé, D. E. Rydeheard, eds., Category Theory and Computer Science, Lecture Notes in Comput. Sci. 283 (Springer, Berlin, 1987) 12–39.

[12] R. Hasegawa, Parametric polymorphism and internal representaions of recursive type definitions, Master Thesis, RIMS, Kyoto University (1989).

[13] R. Hasegawa, Categorical datatypes in parametric polymorphism, in: Fourth Asian Logic Conference, 1990, Tokyo, submitted to Ann. Pure Appl. Logic.

[14] H. Huwig and A. Poigné, A note on inconsistencies caused by fixpoint in a cartesian closed category, Theoret. Comp. Sci. 73 (1990) 101–112.

[15] S. MacLane, Categories for the working mathematician, (Springer, Berlin, 1971).

[16] A. R. Meyer, J. C. Mitchell, E. Moggi, R. Statman, Empty types in polymorphic lambda calculus (preliminary report), in:Fourteenth Annual Symp. on Principles of Programming Languages, Munich, West Germany, 1987 (ACM, 1987) 253–262.

[17] J. C. Mitchell and A. Meyer, Second-order logical relations (extended abstract), in:R. Parikh ed., Proceedings of the Conference on Logics of Programs, Brooklyn, 1985, Lecture Notes in Comp. Sci. 193 (Springer, Berlin, 1985) 225–236.

[18] E. Moggi, The maximum consistent theory of the second order $\beta\eta$ lambda calculus, privately circulated, 1986.

[19] D. Prawitz, Natural Deduction, (Almqvist & Wiksell, Stockholm, 1965).

[20] J. C. Reynolds, Types, abstraction, and parametric polymorphism, in:R. E. A. Mason, ed., Information Processing 83 (North-Holland, Amsterdam, 1983) 513–523.

[21] J. C. Reynolds, Polymorphism is not set theoretic, in:G. Kahn, D.B. MacQueen, G. Plotkin, eds., Semantics of Data Types, Lecture Notes in Comput. Sci. 173 (Springer, Berlin, 1984) 145–156.

[22] P. Wadler, Theorems for free!, in:Fourth International Conf. Functional Programming Languages and Computer Architecture, London (ACM, 1989).

[23] G. C. Wraith, A note on categorical datatypes, in:D. H. Pitt, D. E. Rydeheard, P. Dybjer, A. M. Pitts, A. Poigné, eds., Category Theory and Computer Science, Lecture Notes in Comput. Sci. 389 (Springer, Berlin, 1989) 118–127.

Programs with Cont … Linear Logic

Shi…
Research Institute for Mathemat… Sciences
Kyoto University, Kyoto 606, JAPAN
sin@kurims.kyoto-u.ac.jp

Abstract

A programming language with continuations is studied in the framework of Girard's linear logic[1] . The execution of a program with continuations is in general *non-deterministic*: the result of computation depends on the evaluation strategy, e.g. call-by-value evaluation, call-by-name evaluation, $\cdots$, etc. In this paper, we first introduce $\lambda_c^{\rightarrow}$, a programming language with continuations, and then define the translation from $\lambda_c^{\rightarrow}$ to linear logic, which eliminates the non-determinism of $\lambda_c^{\rightarrow}$. The relation between computation of $\lambda_c^{\rightarrow}$ and normalization of linear logic is also shown.

1 Introduction

1.1 Continuations

The notion of *continuation* was born in order to give semantics of jump-statements in the Scott-Strachey's denotational semantics [9]. The word continuation means *the rest of computation* informally.

The programming language Scheme, which is one of many Lisp's dialects, is a result of applying this notion. In Scheme, we can treat continuations very flexibly like values, e.g. integer, symbols, lists, etc. The primitive function *call-with-current-continuation*, often abbreviated to *call/cc*, supports this facility in Scheme. The following program is an example of those using *call/cc*:

[1]We obey Girard's notation [3] except that we use the symbol $\wp$ as the multiplicative disjunction: "*par*".

```
(call/cc
        (lambda(exit)
                (for-each
                        (lambda (x) (if (negative?  x) (exit x)))
                        '(54 0 37 -3 245 19))
                #t))
```

$\overset{\text{The result}}{\rightarrow}$ -3 (This example is cited from the *revised*[3] *report* [8].)

A. Filinski presented a new view of continuations. He studied the *duality* between values and continuations in the framework of category theory [2]. This duality allows us to identify

a function from values of type A to values of type B

with

a function from continuations of type B to continuation of type A.

Although programming languages with continuations are very expressive, they have a unpleasant feature: their computation is *not confluent* unlike usual λ-calculus. In other words, results of computation depend on the evaluation strategy, e.g. call-by-value evaluation, call-by-name evaluation, etc. The following is a typical example:

(call/cc (lambda (exit)
((lambda(x) 1) (exit 2))))

↙ (call-by-name) (call-by-value) ↘

1 2

1.2 Linear logic and traditional logics

Traditional classical logic has a weak point that proof normalization is *non-deterministic* [4]:

Example 1 [Non-determinism of classical logic]

$$\dfrac{\dfrac{\overset{\vdots\,\pi}{\vdash B}}{\vdash B, C}\,\text{R-}\mathcal{W} \qquad \dfrac{\overset{\vdots\,\pi'}{\vdash B}}{C \vdash B}\,\text{L-}\mathcal{W}}{\dfrac{\vdash B, B}{\vdash B}\,\text{R-}\mathcal{C}}\,\mathit{CUT}$$

$$\swarrow \qquad\qquad\qquad\qquad \searrow$$

$$\dfrac{\dfrac{\overset{\vdots\,\pi}{\vdash B}}{\vdash B, B}\,\text{R-}\mathcal{W}}{\vdash B}\,\text{R-}\mathcal{C} \qquad\qquad\qquad\qquad \dfrac{\dfrac{\overset{\vdots\,\pi'}{\vdash B}}{\vdash B, B}\,\text{R-}\mathcal{W}}{\vdash B}\,\text{R-}\mathcal{C}$$

■

In [4], it is pointed out that the non-determinism of classical logic is caused by the *unrestricted* use of weakening-rules and contraction-rules to both sides of sequents. Intuitionistic logic avoids this problem by restricting the application of right weakening-rules and right contraction-rules. (In intuitioistic logic, we cannot write a proof corresponding to the above example.)

Girard's (classical) linear logic solves this non-determinism by the *careful* use of these structural rules. The "deterministic" proof normalization is one of the advantages of linear logic. The following is proofs in classical linear logic, corresponding to the above.

Example 2 [The corresponding proofs in linear logic]

$$\dfrac{\dfrac{\dfrac{\overset{\vdots\,\pi}{\vdash ?!B}}{\vdash ?!B, ?!C}\,?\text{W} \qquad \dfrac{\dfrac{\overset{\vdots\,\pi'}{\vdash ?!B}}{\vdash ?!B, ?C^{\perp}}\,?\text{W}}{\vdash ?!B, !?C^{\perp}}\,!}{\vdash ?!B, ?!B}\,\text{CUT}}{\vdash ?!B}\,?\text{C} \qquad\qquad \dfrac{\dfrac{\dfrac{\dfrac{\overset{\vdots\,\pi}{\vdash ?!B}}{\vdash ?!B, ?C^{\perp}}\,?\text{W}}{\vdash ?!B, !?C^{\perp}}\,! \qquad \dfrac{\overset{\vdots\,\pi'}{\vdash ?!B}}{\vdash ?!B, ?!C}\,?\text{W}}{\vdash ?!B, ?!B}\,\text{CUT}}{\vdash ?!B}\,?\text{C}$$

$$\downarrow \qquad\qquad\qquad\qquad \downarrow$$

$$\dfrac{\dfrac{\overset{\vdots\,\pi}{?!B}}{\vdash ?!B, ?!B}\,?\text{W}}{\vdash ?!B}\,?\text{C} \qquad\qquad\qquad\qquad \dfrac{\dfrac{\overset{\vdots\,\pi'}{?!B}}{\vdash ?!B, ?!B}\,?\text{W}}{\vdash ?!B}\,?\text{C}$$

■

We find that some information about determinism is added to the proof by this translation.

1.3 Classical logic and programming language with continuations

The formulae-as-types correspondence, also referred to as the Curry-Howard isomorphism, had been restricted to intuitionistic logic until T. G. Griffin, C. Murthy and R. L. Constable extended this to the correspondence between classical logic and a programming language with continuations [5] [7]. For example, call/cc corresponds to the classical proof:

$$\dfrac{\dfrac{\dfrac{[k:\neg A] \qquad \dfrac{\dfrac{\dfrac{[x:A] \quad [k:\neg A]}{\bot}\to\mathcal{E}}{A\to B}\to\mathcal{I}(x) \qquad [f:(A\to B)\to A]}{A}\to\mathcal{E}}{\bot}\to\mathcal{E}}{\dfrac{\neg\neg A}{A}\neg\neg\mathcal{E}}\to\mathcal{I}(k)}{((A\to B)\to A)\to A}\to\mathcal{I}(f)$$

(The conclusion $((A \to B) \to A) \to A$ is famous as *Pierce's law* which cannot be proved in intuitionistic logic.)

They also showed the correspondence between the *continuation-passing style transformation* (abbreviated to CPS-transformation) and $\neg\neg$-transformation which embeds classical logic into intuitionistic logic:

$$\begin{array}{ccc} \lambda^{\to}_{\mathcal{C},\mathcal{A}} & \overset{\text{CPS}}{\longrightarrow} & \lambda^{\to}_{\mathcal{A}} \\ \| & & \| \\ \text{classical logic} & \overset{\neg\neg}{\longrightarrow} & \text{intuitionistic logic} \end{array}$$

where $\lambda^{\to}_{\mathcal{C},\mathcal{A}}$ is the simple typed lambda calculus with the continuation primitives $\mathcal{C}$ and $\mathcal{A}$ [1] and $\lambda^{\to}_{\mathcal{A}}$ the simple typed lambda calculus with $\mathcal{A}$. $\mathcal{C}$ and $\mathcal{A}$ correspond to $\neg\neg$-elimination rule and $\bot$-elimination rule, respectively. And further, Murthy and Constable studied the connection between these transformations and evaluation strategies.

1.4 Motivation of this paper

We can eliminate the non-determinism from the traditional classical logic by the following ways:

Intuitionistic logic We inhibit right weakening rule and right contraction rule.

Linear logic We treat weakening rule and contraction rule more carefully.

While Griffin, Murthy and Constable studied $\neg\neg$-transformation (=CPS-transformation) as an embedding of classical logic into intuitionistic logic, we study another embedding: the translation from classical logic to (classical) linear logic.

2 The programming language $\lambda_c^{\rightarrow}$

At first, we define the programming language $\lambda_c^{\rightarrow}$, which is an extension of the simply typed λ-calculus by addition of the continuation primitive *call/cc*.

2.1 The syntax of $\lambda_c^{\rightarrow}$

Types of $\lambda_c^{\rightarrow}$ are defined in the same way as in the simply typed λ-calculus.

Definition 3 [Types of $\lambda_c^{\rightarrow}$] *Types* of $\lambda_c^{\rightarrow}$ are defined inductively as follows:

$$A ::= \alpha \mid A \rightarrow B$$

where $\alpha, \beta, \cdots$ are metavariables over *atomic types*, and $A, B, \cdots$ over types. ∎

Definition 4 [Terms of $\lambda_c^{\rightarrow}$] A *term* of $\lambda_c^{\rightarrow}$ is defined inductively as follows:

$$M ::= x \mid \lambda x{:}A.M \mid (MN) \mid call/cc_{A,B} \mid abort_{A,B}\{M\}$$

where $x, y, \cdots$ are metavariables over *variables* and $M, N, \cdots$ over types.

$\lambda x{:}A.M$, (MN), $call/cc_{A,B}$, $abort_{A,B}\{M\}$ are called a *λ-abstraction*, a *function application*, a *constant call/cc*, and an *abort-term* respectively.

In particular, terms except abort-terms $abort_{A,B}\{M\}$ are called *program terms*.

∎

2.2 Typing of $\lambda_c^{\rightarrow}$

The typing of the programming language $\lambda_c^{\rightarrow}$ is given in this section. The typing of terms which includes abort-terms is very complicated because of its global nature.

Definition 5 [Type environments] A *type environment* is a set of ordered-pairs consisting of a variable and a type such that variable-parts of these pairs are different from each other (i.e., $x \neq y$ for every $[x : A], [y : B]$ in the set).

For Example, $\{[x : \alpha], [y : \beta], [f : \alpha \rightarrow \beta]\}$ is a type environment, however $\{[x : \alpha], [x : \beta], [f : \alpha \rightarrow \beta]\}$ is *not* a type environment, where $\Gamma, \Delta, \cdots$ are metavariables over type environments. ∎

Definition 6 $[\Gamma \vdash M : A]$ The relation $\Gamma \vdash M : A$ is defined by the following *type inference rules*. A tree, which has $\Gamma \vdash M : A$ as the root and type inference rules as nodes and leaves, is called *type derivation tree*. The type inference rules of $\lambda_c^{\rightarrow}$ are as follows:

1. $$\frac{}{\{[x:A]\} \vdash x:A}\ Var$$

2. $$\frac{}{\vdash call/cc_{A,B} : ((A \to B) \to A) \to A}\ Con_{call/cc}$$

3. $$\frac{\Gamma \vdash M : B}{\Gamma \setminus \{[x:A]\} \vdash \lambda x{:}A.M : A \to B}\ Lam$$

4. $$\frac{\Gamma_1 \vdash M : A \to B \quad \Gamma_2 \vdash N : A}{\Gamma_1 \cup \Gamma_2 \vdash (M\,N) : B}\ App$$
   where $x \neq y$ for every $[x:A] \in \Gamma_1$ and $[y:B] \in \Gamma_2$.

5. $$\frac{\Gamma \vdash M : A}{\Gamma \vdash abort_{A,B}\{M\} : B}\ Special_{abort}$$

■

Definition 7 [Abort-typing-condition] Suppose that A is a type, Γ a type environment, and M a term such that $\Gamma \vdash M : A$. M satisfies the *abort-typing-condition* $\overset{\text{iff}}{\Leftrightarrow}$ For every abort-term $abort_{A,B}\{N\}$ occuring in M, its body N is a term such that $\Gamma' \vdash N : A$ for some type environment Γ'. ■

Definition 8 [Typing of $\lambda_c^{\to}$] M is a term of type A in type environment Γ $\overset{\text{iff}}{\Leftrightarrow}$ $\Gamma \vdash M : A$ and M satisfies the abort-typing-condition. ■

Proposition 9 [Basic properties]

1. If $\Gamma \vdash M : A$, then Γ is *truly* a type environment, that is, $x \neq y$ for every $[x:A], [y:B] \in \Gamma$.

2. If $\Gamma \vdash M : A$, then the set of variables occuring in Γ equals to the set of free variables in M.

■

The type inference rules in this paper is different with the usual rules. For example, the application rule is usually given as follows:

$$\frac{\Gamma \vdash M : A \to B \quad \Gamma \vdash N : A}{\Gamma \vdash (MN) : A}\ App$$

([6]:page 19)

The difference is the treatment of type environments. The reason why we economize the size of a type environment is that we like to simplify the definition of the translation from terms to proofs, T.

2.3 The computation rule of $\lambda_c^{\rightarrow}$

In this section, we define a *call-by-value* computation of $\lambda_c^{\rightarrow}$ in the style of Felleisen [1].

Definition 10 [Values] A *value* V of $\lambda_c^{\rightarrow}$ is defined inductively as

$$V ::= x \mid \lambda x{:}A.M \mid call/cc_{A,B}$$

where x denotes a variable, A a type, and M a term. ∎

Definition 11 [Evaluation contexts] An *evaluation context* $E[]$ is defined inductively as

$$E[\,] ::= [\,] \mid (E[\,]\ N) \mid (V\ \ E[\,])$$

where [] represents a "hole".

If $E[\,]$ is an evaluation context, then $E[M]$ denotes the term which results from the substitution of M for the hole of $E[\,]$. ∎

Definition 12 [Computation of $\lambda_c^{\rightarrow}$] The computation $\rightarrow_{comp}$is defined by: $\rightarrow_{comp} = \rightarrow_{\beta_v} \cup \rightarrow_{call/cc} \cup \rightarrow_{abort}$. Each relation is defined as follow:

$$\begin{array}{l} E[(\lambda x{:}A.M)V] \rightarrow_{\beta_v} E[M[x := V]], \\ E[(call/cc_{A,B}V)] \rightarrow_{call/cc} E[V(\lambda x{:}A.abort_{A,B}\{E[x]\})], \\ E[(abort_{A,B}\{M\})] \rightarrow_{abort} M. \end{array}$$

∎

Proposition 13 [Preservation of the abort-typing-condition] If M is a term of type A and N a term such that $M \rightarrow_{comp} N$, then N is also a term of type A. In other word, the abort-typing-condition is preserved during computation. ∎

3 Translation from $\lambda_c^{\rightarrow}$ to linear logic

We introduce the translation from $\lambda_c^{\rightarrow}$ to linear logic in this section. We define the translation from types of $\lambda_c^{\rightarrow}$ to propositions of linear logic, translation τ, and then the translation from terms to proofs, translation T, which maps a term of type A to a proof-net with conclusion $\tau(A)$.

3.1 Translation τ

To start with, we summarize traditional translations from λ-calculi to linear logic.

Linear λ-calculus is a simply typed λ-calculus introduced by Y. Lafont. The main feature of this calculus is the restriction of λ-abstraction: we can λ-abstract only a variable which occurs once and only once. For example, a term $\lambda f.\lambda x.(fx)$ is correct, however, $\lambda g.(gx)x$ is not. Types of the calculus are translated to propositions of linear logic by the following translation τ_{LLC}:

Definition 14 [The translation τ_{LLC}] The translation τ_{LLC} from types of linear λ-calculus to propositions of linear logic is defined as follows:

$$\begin{aligned} \tau_{LLC}(\alpha) &= \alpha \text{ (where } \alpha \text{ is an atomic type)} \\ \tau_{LLC}(A \to B) &= \tau_{LLC}(A) \multimap \tau_{LLC}(B) \end{aligned}$$

∎

A propostion $A \multimap B$ is regarded as the type of functions which receive a value of type A, use it *once and only once*, and return a value of type B.

This proposition is also regarded as the type of functions which receive a value of type $B^{\perp}$, use it *once and only once*, and return a value of type $A^{\perp}$ because

$$A \multimap B = B^{\perp} \multimap A^{\perp}.$$

From the viewpoint of Filinski's value-continuation duality, the proposition $A \multimap B$ is regarded as a type of functions which receive a *continuation* of type B , uses it once and only once, and return a *continuation* of type A.

Therefore we can say informally as follows:

a value of type $A^{\perp}$ = a continuation of type A

Next, let us examine the translation from the polymorphic λ-calculus F to linear logic ([3]:page 82).

Definition 15 [The translation $\tau_{\text{System F}}$] The translation $\tau_{\text{System F}}$ from types of System F to propositions of linear logic is defined as follows:

$$\begin{aligned} \tau_{\text{System F}}(\alpha) &= \alpha \text{ (where } \alpha \text{ is a proposition variable)} \\ \tau_{\text{System F}}(A \to B) &= !\tau_{\text{System F}}(A) \multimap \tau_{\text{System F}}(B) \\ \tau_{\text{System F}}(\forall\alpha.A) &= \Lambda\alpha.\tau_{\text{System F}}(A) \end{aligned}$$

∎

$!A \multimap B$ is a type of functions which receive a value of type A, use it *more than zero-times*, and return a value of type B. The modality ! represents the ability of duplication and deletion.

From the viewpoint of continuation, this proposition is also considered as a type of functions which receive a *continuation* of type B, use it *once and only once*, and return a *continuation* of type $!A$, because

$$!A \multimap B = B^{\perp} \multimap (!A)^{\perp}$$

We find that a received continuation cannot be deleted or duplicated in contrast to values.

For deletion and duplication of continuations, we try to add the modality ! to the underlined part of $\underline{B^{\perp}} \multimap (!A)^{\perp}$, and obtain

$$!B^{\perp} \multimap (!A)^{\perp} \quad = \quad !A \multimap ?B \ .$$

Unfortunately, the function of type $!A \multimap ?B$ cannot be applied to the value of type $?A$ in linear logic. For this reason, we use $!A \multimap !B$ instead of $!A \multimap B$ and add ! to the underlined part of $\underline{!A} \multimap !B$ as before, finally obtaining

$$!A \multimap ?!B \ \ (=!((!B)^{\perp}) \multimap (!A)^{\perp}).$$

In contrast to the former case, a function of type $!A \multimap ?!B$ can be applied to a value of type $?!A$ in linear logic.

The formal definition is as follows:

Definition 16 [Translation τ] The translation τ of $\lambda_c^{\rightarrow}$ types to linear logic propositions is defined as follow:

$$\begin{array}{rcl} \tau(\alpha) & = & \alpha \\ \tau(A \rightarrow B) & = & ?\tau(A)^{\perp} \wp ?!\tau(B) \\ & (= & !\tau(A) \multimap ?!\tau(B)) \end{array}$$

∎

Notation 17 [$\tau(\Gamma)$]

Suppose that Γ is type environment $\{[x_1 : A_1], \cdots, [x_n : A_n]\}$. Then $\tau(\Gamma)$ denotes the following sequence:

$$\tau(A_1), \cdots, \tau(A_n).$$

∎

3.2 Translation T

The translation T from typed terms of $\lambda_c^{\rightarrow}$ to proof-nets [3] of linear logic is defined in this section.

For simplicity and readablity of the definition, we give the translation from type derivation trees to proof-nets because type derivation trees have additional information about free variables.

$$\begin{array}{ccccc} \text{Typed term} & \longrightarrow & \text{Type derivation tree} & \overset{\text{translation } T}{\longrightarrow} & \text{Proof-net} \\ \Gamma \vdash M : A & & \begin{array}{c} :\Pi \\ \Gamma \vdash M : A \end{array} & & \begin{array}{ccc} \multicolumn{3}{c}{\cdots\cdots\cdots\cdots} \\ \vdots & T(\Pi) & \vdots \\ ?\tau(\Gamma)^{\perp} & & ?!\tau(A) \end{array} \end{array}$$

Definition 18 [Translation T] The translation T from type derivation trees to proof-nets of linear logic is defined inductively in the following. This translation maps a type derivation tree with the root $\Gamma \vdash M : A$ to the proof-net with conclusion $\tau(\Gamma)^{\perp}, ?!\tau(A)$.

1. If a type derivation tree Π is

$$\frac{}{\{[x : A]\} \vdash x : A}\,Var,$$

then the proof-net $T(\Pi)$ is as follows:

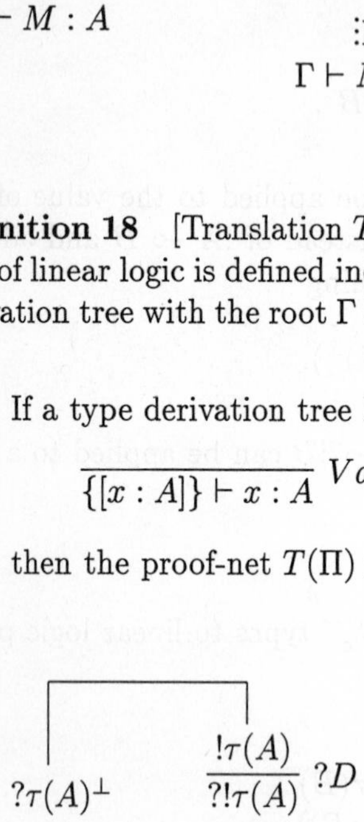

2. If a type derivation tree Π is

$$\frac{}{\vdash call/cc_{A,B} : ((A \rightarrow B) \rightarrow A) \rightarrow A}\,Con_{call/cc},$$

then the proof-net $T(\Pi)$is as follows:

$$\frac{!\tau(A)}{?!\tau(A)}\ ?D$$

$?\tau(A)^\perp$

weakening-box

$$\frac{?\tau(A)^\perp \quad ?!\tau(B)}{?\tau(A)^\perp \wp ?!\tau(B)}\ \wp$$

$?!\tau(A)$

!-box

$$\frac{!(?\tau(A)^\perp \wp ?!\tau(B)) \quad !?\tau(A)}{\dfrac{!(?\tau(A)^\perp \wp ?!\tau(B))\otimes !?\tau(A)}{?(!(?\tau(A)^\perp \wp ?!\tau(B))\otimes !?\tau(A))}\ ?D}\ \otimes \qquad \frac{?!\tau(A) \quad ?!\tau(A)}{?!\tau(A)}\ ?C$$

$$\frac{?(!(?\tau(A)^\perp \wp ?!\tau(B))\otimes !?\tau(A)) \quad ?!\tau(A)}{?(!(?\tau(A)^\perp \wp ?!\tau(B))\otimes !?\tau(A))\ \wp ?!\tau(A)}\ \text{!-box}$$

$$\frac{!(?(!(?\tau(A)^\perp \wp ?!\tau(B))\otimes !?\tau(A))\ \wp ?!\tau(A))}{?!(?(!(?\tau(A)^\perp \wp ?!\tau(B))\otimes !?\tau(A))\ \wp ?!\tau(A))}\ ?D$$

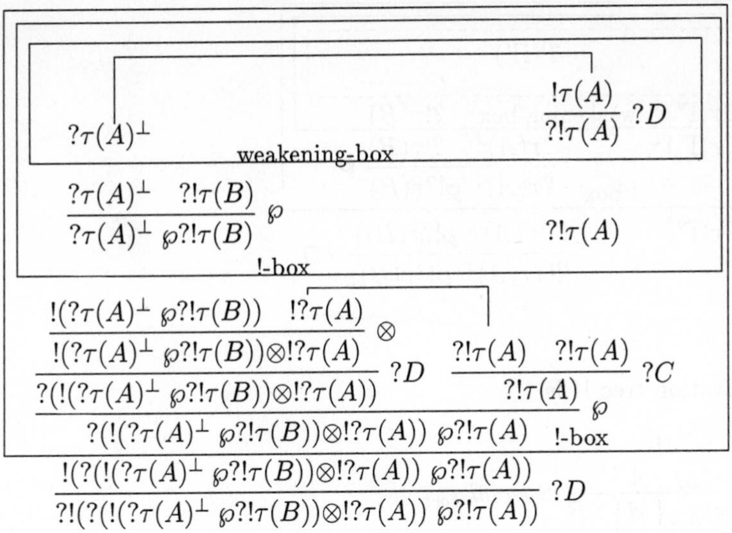

$$
\begin{aligned}
?!(\tau(((A \to B) \to A) \to A)) \ &=\ ?!(?\tau((A \to B) \to A)^\perp \wp ?!\tau(A)) \\
&=\ ?!(?(!\tau(A \to B)\otimes !?\tau(A)^\perp)\ \wp ?!\tau(A)) \\
&=\ ?!(?(!(?\tau(A) \wp ?!\tau(B))\otimes !?\tau(A)^\perp)\ \wp ?!\tau(A))
\end{aligned}
$$

3. If a type derivation tree Π is

$$
\begin{array}{c}
\vdots\ \Pi' \\
\frac{\Gamma \vdash M : B}{\Gamma' \vdash \lambda x{:}A.M : A \to B}\ \textit{Lam}
\end{array}
$$

where $\Gamma' = \Gamma \setminus [x : A]$,

(a) and if $[x : A] \in \Gamma$, then the proof-net $T(\Pi)$ is as follows:

$$T(\Pi')$$

$?\tau(\Gamma')^\perp$

$$\frac{?\tau(A)^\perp \quad ?!\tau(B)}{?\tau(A)^\perp \wp !?\tau(B)}\ \wp$$

!-box

$$?\tau(\Gamma')^\perp \qquad \frac{!(?\tau(A)^\perp \wp !?\tau(B))}{?!(?\tau(A)^\perp \wp !?\tau(B))}\ ?D$$

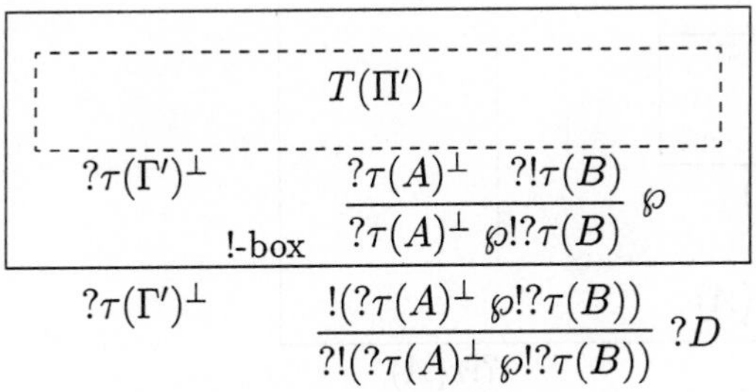

$$(?!\tau(A \to B) \equiv ?!(?\tau(A)^\perp \wp ?!\tau(B)))$$

(b) else (i.e. $[x : A] \notin \Gamma$) the proof-net $T(\Pi)$ is as follows:

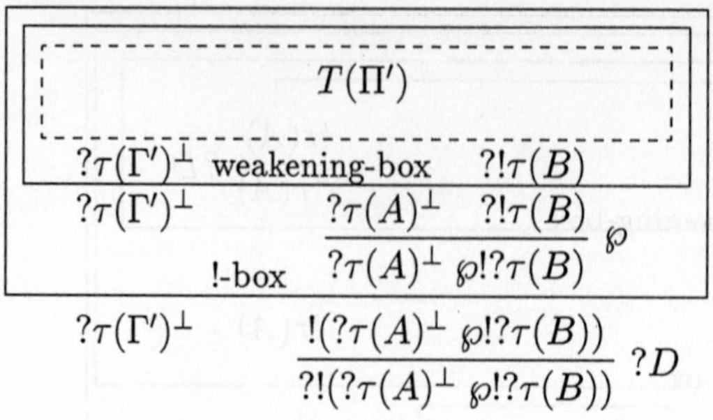

4. If a type derivation tree Π is

$$\dfrac{\begin{array}{c}\vdots\ \Pi' \\ \Gamma \vdash M : A\end{array}}{\Gamma \vdash abort_{A,B}\{M\} : B}\ Special_{abort}$$

then the proof net $T(\Pi)$ is as follows:

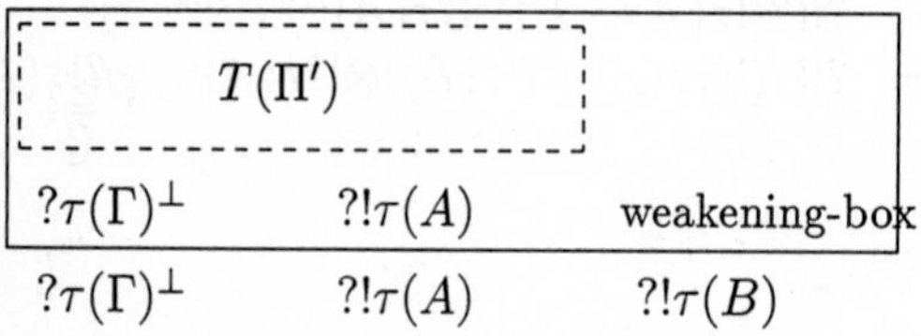

The treatment of the proposition $?!\tau(A)$ in the conclusions of the above proof-net is very special. We leave this proposition until the whole term is translated. Then, we let this out of boxes through their auxiliary doors:

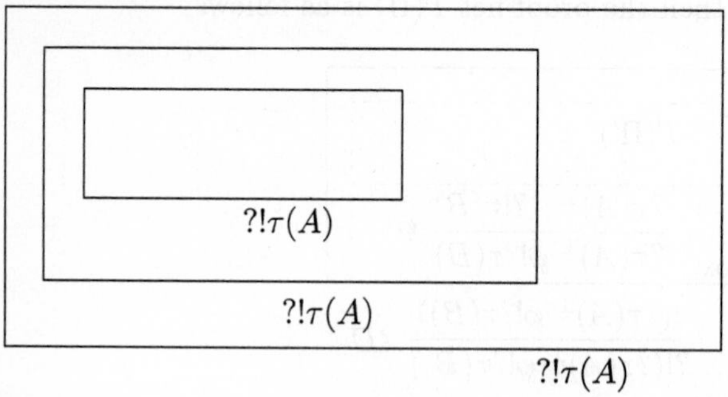

At last, we link this with the same proposition in the conclusion of the whole term:

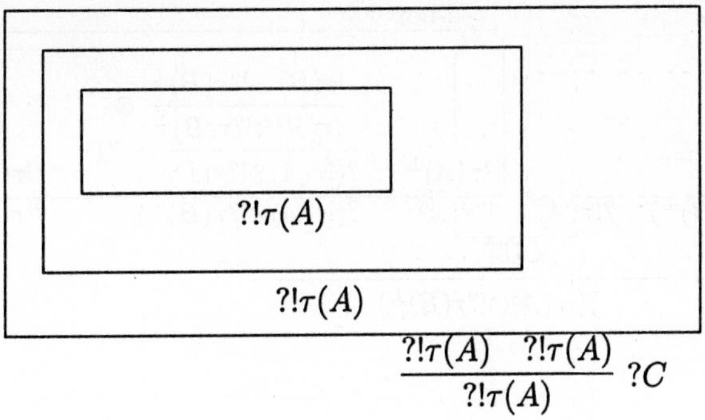

5. If a type derivation tree Π is

$$\dfrac{\dfrac{}{\vdash call/cc_{A,B} : ((A \to B) \to A) \to A}\, Con_{call/cc} \qquad \begin{array}{c}\vdots\,\Pi' \\ \Gamma \vdash N : (A \to B) \to A\end{array}}{\Gamma \vdash (call/cc_{A,B} N) : A}\, App$$

then the proof-net $T(\Pi)$ is as follows:

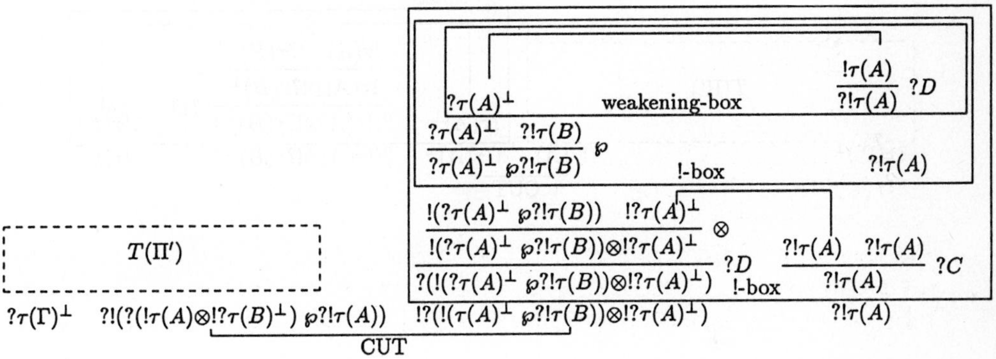

$$\left(\begin{array}{rcl} !?\tau((A \to B) \to A)^{\perp} & \equiv & !?(?\tau(A \to B)^{\perp}\, \wp ?!\tau(A))^{\perp} \\ & \equiv & !?(!\tau(A \to B) \otimes !?\tau(A)^{\perp}) \\ & \equiv & !?(!(?\tau(A)^{\perp}\, \wp ?!\tau(B)) \otimes !?\tau(A)^{\perp}) \end{array}\right)$$

6. If a type derivation tree Π is

$$\dfrac{\dfrac{}{\{[f : A \to B]\} \vdash f : A \to B}\, Var \qquad \begin{array}{c}\vdots\,\Pi' \\ \Gamma \vdash N : A\end{array}}{\Gamma \cup \{[f : A \to B]\} \vdash (fN) : B}\, App$$

(a) and if $[f : A \to B] \in \Gamma$, then the proof-net $T(\Pi)$ is as follows:

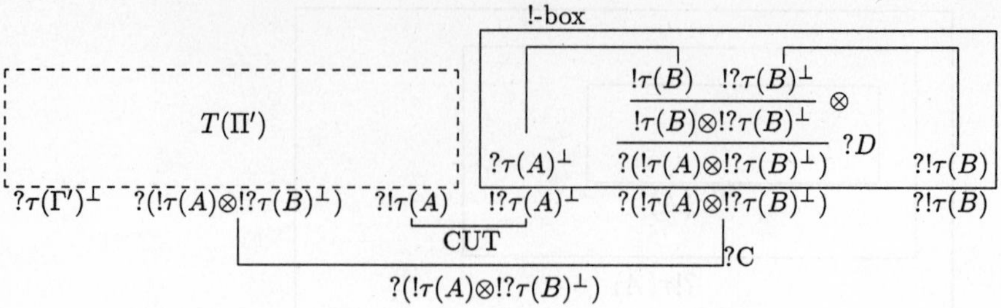

$$\left(\begin{array}{lcl} ?\tau(A \to B)^\perp & \equiv & ?(?\tau(A)^\perp \wp ?!\tau(B))^\perp \\ & \equiv & ?(!\tau(A)\otimes!?\tau(B)^\perp) \end{array} \right)$$

(b) else (i.e. $[f : A \to B] \notin \Gamma$), then the proof-net $T(\Pi)$ is as follows:

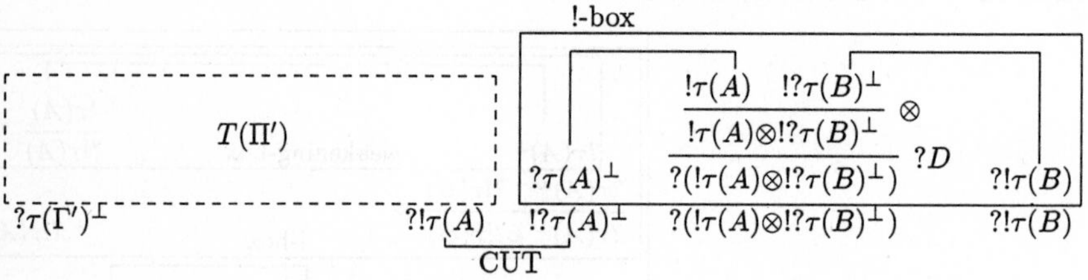

7. If a type derivation tree Π is

$$\dfrac{\dfrac{\dfrac{\vdots\,\Pi_1}{\Gamma_1 \vdash M : B}}{\Gamma_1' \vdash \lambda x{:}A.M : A \to B}\,Lam \qquad \dfrac{\vdots\,\Pi_2}{\Gamma_2 \vdash N : B}}{\Gamma_1' \cup \Gamma_2 \vdash ((\lambda x{:}A.M)N) : B}\,App$$

where $\Gamma_1 \equiv \Gamma \setminus \{[x : A]\}$,

(a) and if $[x : A] \in \Gamma_1$, then the proof-net $T(\Pi)$ is as follows:

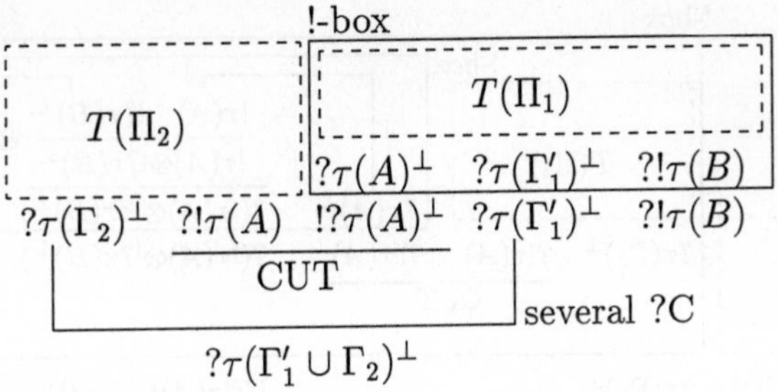

Notation 19 ["several $?C$"] "several $?C$" denotes that the same variable-type pairs in Γ_1' and Γ_2 are linked respectively by $?C$-link(contraction link). ∎

(b) Else (i.e. $[x : A] \notin \Gamma_1$) the proof-net $T(\Pi)$ is as follows:

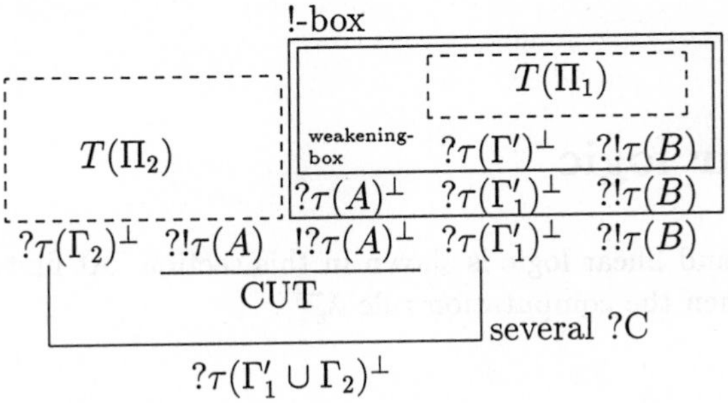

8. If a type derivation tree Π is

$$\frac{\begin{array}{c}\vdots\,\Pi_1\\ \Gamma_1 \vdash M : A \to B\end{array} \quad \begin{array}{c}\vdots\,\Pi_2\\ \Gamma_2 \vdash N : A\end{array}}{\Gamma_1 \cup \Gamma_2 \vdash (MN) : B}\ App$$

where the last type inference rule of Π_1 is *not* Var,Lam,or $Con_{call/cc}$, then the proof-net $T(\Pi)$ is as follows:

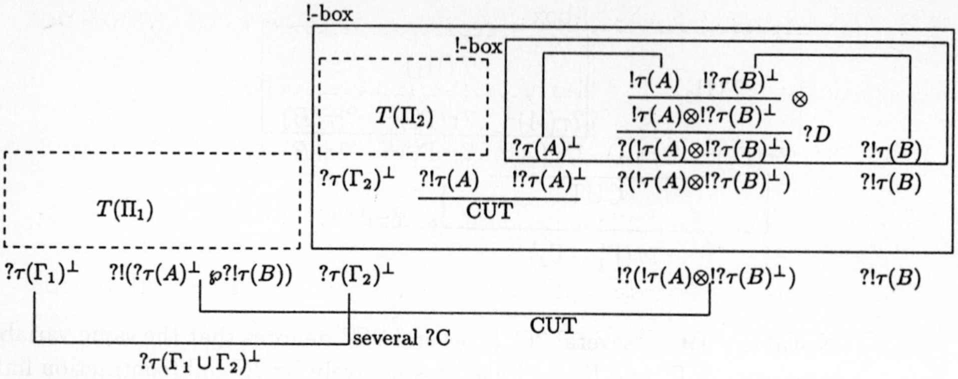

4 $\lambda_c^{\rightarrow}$ and linear logic

The relation between $\lambda_c^{\rightarrow}$ and linear logic is shown in this section. At first, we study evaluation contexts, and then the computation rule $\lambda_c^{\rightarrow}$.

4.1 Evaluation contexts in proof-nets

Suppose that

$$M = E[(M'V)]$$

where $E[]$ is an evaluation context and M' a λ-abstraction: $(\lambda x : A.M')$ or a constant: $call/cc_{A,B}$. (That is, M is a term which is a left hand of $\rightarrow_{\beta_v}$or $\rightarrow_{call/cc}$.)

By the definition of the translation T, $T(M)$ is the following proof-net:

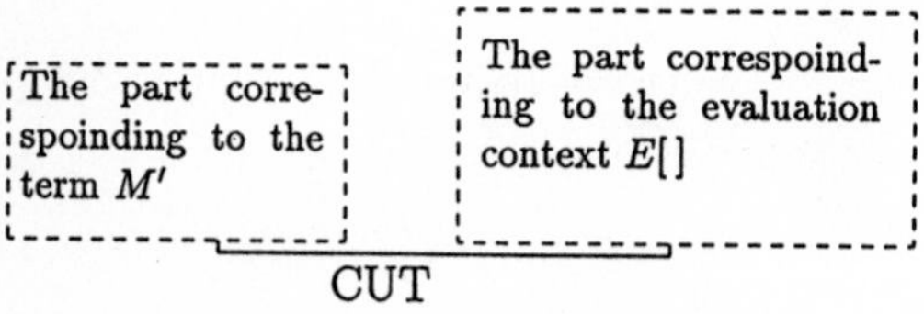

The part corresponding to $E[]$ is a *ghost box*[2]. And the underlined part of $E[\underline{((\lambda x{:}A.M')V)}]$, $E[\underline{(call/cc_{A,B}V)}]$ is outmost in the proof-net $T(M)$.

[2] [3]:page 65

4.2 Computation of $\lambda_c^{\rightarrow}$ and normalization of proof-net

We extend the normalization step of proof-net in [3].

Definition 20 [$\rightarrow_{\text{proof net}}$] $\rightarrow_{\text{proof net}}$is defined as

$$\rightarrow_{\text{proof net}} = \rightarrow_{\text{SC}} \cup \rightarrow_{\text{CC}} \cup \rightarrow_{\text{AC}},$$

where $\rightarrow_{\text{SC}}$is the *symmetric contraction*[3], $\rightarrow_{\text{CC}}$is the *commutative contraction*[4], and $\rightarrow_{\text{AC}}$ is the *additional contraction:*

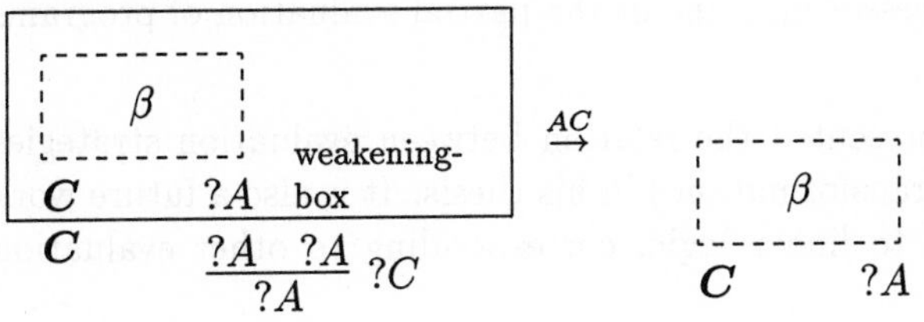

■

The addition of the new rule $\rightarrow_{\text{AC}}$ to the usual normalization $\rightarrow_{\text{SC}} \cup \rightarrow_{\text{CC}}$ is not bad because $\rightarrow_{\text{AC}}$ keeps the denotation of a proof-net in the coherent semantics and decreases the size[5] of a proof-net, so this extension does not affect the invariance of denotation during the normalization and the strong normalisability of proof-nets.

Theorem 21 [Main result] If M, N are terms such that

$$M \rightarrow_{comp} N,$$

then

$$T(M) \rightarrow^*_{\text{proof net}} T(N),$$

where $\rightarrow^*_{\text{proof net}}$ is the reflexive and transitive closure of $\rightarrow_{\text{proof net}}$. ■

The proof of this theorem is straightforward but very tedious. The important point is that evaluation contexts are mapped to ghost boxes.

5 Conclusions and future works

This paper has shown that

[3] [3]:page 62

[4] [3]:page 65

[5] [3]:page 70

- the definition of the syntax of the programming language with continuations $\lambda_c^{\rightarrow}$,
- the definition of the computation rule of $\lambda_c^{\rightarrow}$ and the translation of $\lambda_c^{\rightarrow}$ to linear logic, and
- the relation between the computation of $\lambda_c^{\rightarrow}$ and the normalization of proof net.

The computation rule of $\lambda_c^{\rightarrow}$ given in this paper is very sequentialized in comparison with the normalization of proof-nets. The computation of $\lambda_c^{\rightarrow}$ can be remade more "parallel". The parallelization based on linear logic may be another approach to the program execution on a multi-processor machine or the partial evaluation of programs with continuations.

C. Murthy and R. L. Constable presented the relation between evaluation strategies and $\neg\neg$-transformation (= CPS-transformation) in his thesis. It is also a future work to discover translations from $\lambda_c^{\rightarrow}$ to linear logic, corresponding to other evaluation strategies.

6 Acknowledgements

I am deeply indebted to Masami Hagiya for his many helps for preparing this paper. I would like to thank Susumu Hayashi for his comments on the draft of this paper.

References

[1] M. Felleisen, D. Friedman, E. Kohlbecker, and B. Duba. A syntactic theory of sequential control. *Theoretical Computer Science*, 52:205–237, 1987.

[2] A. Filinski. Declarative continuations and categorical duality. Master's thesis, University of Copenhagen, Aug 1989. DIKU Raport Nr. 89/11, ISSN 0107-8283.

[3] J.-Y. Girard. Linear logic. *Theoretical Computer Science*, 50:1–102, 1987.

[4] J.-Y. Girard, P. Taylor, and Y. Lafont. *Proofs and Types*, volume 7 of *Cambridge Tracts in Computer Science.* Cambridge University Press, 1989.

[5] T. G. Griffin. A formulae-as-types notion of control. In *Conference Record of the Seventeenth Annual ACM Symposium on Principles of Programming Languages*, 1990.

[6] G. Huet. A uniform approach to type theory. *Rapports de Recherche*, 795, Feb. 1988.

[7] C. Murth and R. L. Constable. Finding computational content in classical proofs, July 1990.

[8] J. Rees and W. Clinger. Revised^3 repord on the algorithmic language scheme. *SIGPLAN Notices*, 21(12):37–79, 1986.

[9] J. E. Stoy. *Denotational Semantics: The Scott-Strachey Approach to Programming Language Theory.* MIT Press, 1977.

π-Calculus Semantics of Object-Oriented Programming Languages

David Walker
Department of Computer Science
University of Technology, Sydney
NSW 2007, Australia

Abstract

The π-calculus provides a foundation for the study of computational systems with evolving communication structure. A system is viewed as a collection of agents which may share named communication links. Agents interact by passing to one another along shared links the names of other links. Semantics for a pair of parallel object-oriented programming languages are presented by translation into the π-calculus. The semantics are compared briefly with existing semantics of related languages.

1 Introduction

The π-calculus provides a foundation for the study of concurrent systems with evolving communication structure. The paper [7] contains an introduction to the calculus through a sequence of examples, while in [8] its elementary theory is developed in detail. In addition to the examples in [7], evidence of the expressive power of the calculus is provided by [6], in which encodings of λ-calculus in the π-calculus are studied; by [9], where a communications protocol used in a mobile telephone network is modelled; and by [11] which contains a translation of CCS with value-passing into the π-calculus. In the present paper we develop this theme further, providing semantics for a pair of parallel object-oriented programming languages by translating them into the π-calculus. The translations build on earlier work on the π-calculus and the translation of a parallel imperative language into CCS from [5]. They illustrate how the calculus may be used to provide succinct, natural and illuminating representations of systems described in an object-oriented style.

The first language considered is a mild enrichment of the language P of [4]; the second is closely related to the parallel object-oriented language POOL [1]. The languages differ essentially from one another only in the mechanisms they provide for interaction between objects: in the first language, interaction occurs via communication of data in the style of the programming language CSP; in the second, a rendezvous mechanism is employed. The encodings of these mechanisms in the π-calculus are very close to natural operational intuitions. Several variations of the translations have been examined; we believe it is not easy to find translations notably simpler than those presented.

The semantics offered here should be compared with alternative semantics of related languages, for example the semantics for POOL presented in [2, 3, 10]. This point is discussed further in the final section of the present paper. Here we note only that the domain equations adopted in [3] for giving a denotational semantics for POOL using metric spaces provide important insight into the language's semantic structure. The translations into the π-calculus do not in themselves yield comparable insight. Rather, they provide a striking operational account taking as primitive only the passing of named links between computational entities. Certainly a more abstract treatment than that offered here is required. We hope that with the development of model theory for the π-calculus, the translations, and modifications of them, will yield illuminating and relatively simple semantics for a range of object-oriented languages, and in particular will provide a clear view of the central concept: the object.

The following section contains a brief introduction to the π-calculus [7, 8]. This is followed by descriptions of the languages and their translations into the π-calculus. The paper ends with some discussion.

2 The π-calculus

This section contains a very brief introduction to the π-calculus [7, 8]. The π-calculus is a process calculus in which systems with evolving communication structure may be naturally expressed. A computational system is viewed as a collection of independent *agents*, each of which may share some communication links with other agents. Each link has a *name*. An interaction between two agents P and Q sharing a link named x consists in a handshake communication in which the name y of another link[1] is passed from P to Q along (the link named) x. A distinctive feature of the calculus is that it provides a simple treatment of the communication of *private* names. As illustrated in the examples cited in the introduction and in the translations below, this provides considerable power and convenience in modelling computational systems whose communication structures evolve dynamically.

We use x, y, z to range over an infinite set of *names*, and A to range over *agent identifiers*, each of which has a nonnegative arity. The *agents* of the π-calculus, ranged over by P, Q, R are as follows:

$$P \ ::= \ \Sigma_{i \in I} P_i \ \mid \ \alpha . P \ \mid \ P|Q \ \mid \ (y)P \ \mid \ [x{=}y]P \ \mid \ A(\tilde{y})$$

[1] or possibly the name x itself

where I is a *finite* set, α ranges over $\overline{x}y, x(y), \tau$, and $\tilde{y} = y_1 \dots y_n$ with n the arity of A. In $x(y).P$ and $(y)P$, the occurrence of y in parentheses is a binding occurrence whose scope is P. We write $fn(P)$ for the set of names occurring free in P.

The intended interpretation of agents is as follows:

- A *summation* $\Sigma_{i \in I} P_i$ behaves as one or other of the P_i. We write $\mathbf{0}$ for the empty summation. We often write α as an abbreviation for $\alpha.\mathbf{0}$.

- The *prefix* $\overline{x}y.P$ sends the name y along the name x and then behaves as P; $x(y).P$ receives a name z along x and then behaves as $P\{z/y\}$, i.e. as P with z substituted for all free occurrences of y (substitution may force change of bound names in P); $\tau.P$ performs the *silent action* τ and then behaves as P.

- A *composition* $P \mid Q$ behaves as P and Q acting independently in parallel but with the possibility of communication using shared names; such a communication results in a silent action.

- A *restriction* $(y)P$ behaves as P except that y is private to P: no agent may interact with a (component agent of) P along y; however, component agents of P may interact with one another along y.

- A *match* $[x{=}y]P$ behaves as P if $x = y$ and as $\mathbf{0}$ otherwise.

- Finally, an agent identifier A has an associated defining equation $A(\tilde{x}) \stackrel{\text{def}}{=} P$ with the x_i distinct and $fn(P) \subseteq \tilde{x}$; $A(\tilde{y})$ behaves as $P\{\tilde{y}/\tilde{x}\}$.

The behaviour of agents is given via a family of labelled transition relations $\xrightarrow{\alpha}$ between agents where α ranges over $\overline{x}y, x(y), \tau, \overline{x}(y)$. The intended interpretation of $P \xrightarrow{\alpha} Q$ is that P may perform the action α and thereby evolve into Q. The first three kinds of action correspond to the prefixes above; the fourth represents the passing along x of a private name y. Such an action typically arises from an agent of the form $(y)\overline{x}y.P$. For the transition rules defining the transition relations we refer to [8]. Using the transitional semantics, behavioural equivalences between agents may be defined and a rich algebraic theory developed. See [7, 8] for more details.

The translations make use of *constant* names. We refer to [7] for a discussion of their rôle in the calculus. We recall from [7] a particularly useful form of recursively- defined agent: the replicator. The agent $\alpha * P$ is defined by

$$\alpha * P \stackrel{\text{def}}{=} \alpha.(P \mid \alpha * P)$$

Finally we recall also that

$$x : [y_1 \Rightarrow P_1,\ y_2 \Rightarrow P_2, \dots]$$

is an abbreviation for

$$x(z).([z{=}y_1]P_1 + [z{=}y_2]P_2 + \dots)$$

3 The Languages

A program of either of the languages we consider describes the computational behaviour of a system of entities called *objects*. In the first language $\mathcal{L}_1$, which is a mild enrichment of the language P of [4], an object consists of a sequential statement together with a family of variables local to the object. Variables may contain data values such as integers or references to objects. The second language $\mathcal{L}_2$ is closely related to the parallel object-oriented language POOL [1]. In addition to the features of an $\mathcal{L}_1$-object, an $\mathcal{L}_2$-object possesses a number of procedures or *methods*.

The languages differ essentially from one another only in the mechanisms they provide for interaction between objects. In $\mathcal{L}_1$, objects interact via a synchronous communication mechanism in which a data value is sent from one object to another and assigned to a variable of the receiving object. In order for such an interaction to be possible, one of the sending object's variables must contain a reference to the receiving object. There are two modes of reception of a data value. In the first, one of the receiving object's variables must contain a reference to the sending object, while in the second the receiving object may accept a value (of the appropriate type) from any object. Interaction between objects in $\mathcal{L}_2$ occurs via a rendezvous mechanism in which a method is invoked in one object on receipt of a message from a second object. The sending object's activity is suspended until the method invocation is completed and a value returned to it by the receiving object.

Objects may be created during a computation. Moreover the communication structure among objects may evolve through the communication of references to objects. Each object is an instance of some *class*, and a program consists of a sequence of class declarations and a (conventional) indication of which of these classes furnishes the *root object* which alone exists at the initiation of a computation. We now describe the languages in detail, beginning with $\mathcal{L}_1$.

The language $\mathcal{L}_1$

We begin with a set of program variables ranged over by X, Y, Z. The class of $\mathcal{L}_1$-expressions ranged over by E is given as follows:

$$
\begin{array}{rcll}
E & ::= & X & \\
 & \mid & k & (k = 0, 1, 2, \ldots) \\
 & \mid & b & (b = \text{true, false}) \\
 & \mid & \textbf{nil} & \\
 & \mid & \textbf{self} & \\
 & \mid & E_1 + E_2 & \\
 & \mid & E_1 = E_2 & \\
 & \mid & \neg E & \\
 & \mid & E_1 \wedge E_2 &
\end{array}
$$

Each well-formed expression is of one of the types *nat*, *bool* and *ref*; the type of a variable is given via a declaration. **nil** and **self** are of type *ref*; **nil** signifies a reference to no object while, loosely speaking, **self** signifies the object in which it occurs. This simple language of expressions is adequate for illustrating the principal points of interest in the encoding. Richer languages may be accommodated by extending the techniques described below; see also [7] and [11].

We assume further a set of class names ranged over by C. The class of $\mathcal{L}_1$-statements ranged over by S is given as follows:

$$
\begin{array}{rcll}
S & ::= & \mathbf{skip} & \\
 & | & X := E & \\
 & | & X := \mathbf{new}_C & (C \text{ a class name}) \\
 & | & X!E & \\
 & | & X?Y & \\
 & | & ?Y & \\
 & | & S_1; S_2 & \\
 & | & \mathbf{if}\ E\ \mathbf{then}\ S_1\ \mathbf{else}\ S_2 & \\
 & | & \mathbf{while}\ E\ \mathbf{do}\ S &
\end{array}
$$

Statements of the forms $X := \mathbf{new}_C$, $X!E$ and $X?Y$ are well-formed only if X is of type *ref*. The effect of $X := \mathbf{new}_C$ is to create a new object of class C and to assign to X a reference to it. In $X!E$ the value of the expression E is sent to the object to which X contains a reference (if it exists), while in $X?Y$ a value is received from the object to which X contains a reference (if it exists) and assigned to Y. In $?Y$ a value is received from some object and assigned to Y. In any communication arising from $X!E$ and $Y?Z$ or from $X!E$ and $?Z$, the types of E and Z must agree. The remaining constructs have their usual meanings. $X := E$ is well-formed only if X and E share a common type; **if** E **then** S_1 **else** S_2 and **while** E **do** S are well-formed only if E is of type *bool*.

The class of $\mathcal{L}_1$-declarations is given as follows with t ranging over types. First there are sequences of variable declarations:

$$Vdec \ ::= \ \mathbf{var}\ X_1 : t_1, \ldots, X_n : t_n$$

with the X_i distinct from one another. Next there are class declarations:

$$Cdec \ ::= \ \mathbf{class}\ C\ \mathbf{is}\ Vdec\ \mathbf{in}\ S$$

with every variable occurring in S being declared in *Vdec*. And finally there are program declarations:

$$Pdec \ ::= \ \mathbf{program}\ P\ \mathbf{is}\ Cdec_1, \ldots, Cdec_n$$

where if $Cdec_i \equiv \mathbf{class}\ C_i\ \mathbf{is}\ Vdec_i\ \mathbf{in}\ S_i$, then: the C_i are distinct from one another; and if $X := \mathbf{new}_{C'}$ occurs in one of the S_i then C' is one of the C_j. By convention, C_1 is the class of the single root object which alone exists at the initiation of a computation.

On creation, an object augments the computation by executing the statement appearing in the declaration of the class of which it is an instance with its own family of local variables determined by the variable declaration part of the class declaration.

The language $\mathcal{L}_2$

$\mathcal{L}_2$ shares many features with $\mathcal{L}_1$. To describe its expressions we assume a set of method names ranged over by M. The class of $\mathcal{L}_2$-expressions is obtained by augmenting the definition of the class of $\mathcal{L}_1$-expressions with one extra clause:

$$\begin{array}{rcl} E & ::= & \ldots \\ & | & E_1!M(E_2) \end{array}$$

An expression of the form $E_1!M(E_2)$ is well-formed only if E_1 is of type *ref*. If the value of E_1 is a reference to an object, the value of the expression is the value returned by that object after an invocation of the method M with parameter E_2. Such an invocation may occur if the object referred to executes an **answer** statement as described below.

The class of $\mathcal{L}_2$-statements is obtained by deleting from the definition of the class of $\mathcal{L}_1$-statements the clauses for $X!E$, $X?Y$ and $?Y$, and adding instead one new clause:

$$\begin{array}{rcl} S & ::= & \ldots \\ & | & \textbf{answer}(M_1, \ldots, M_k) \end{array}$$

A statement $\textbf{answer}(M_1, \ldots, M_k)$ requires that for some i with $1 \leq i \leq k$, the statement comprising the body of the declaration of M_i (see below) be executed with a parameter supplied by an object seeking to evaluate an expression $E_1!M_i(E_2)$ with E_1 a reference to the object containing the **answer** statement. On termination of the method invocation a value is returned to the sending object, this being the value of the expression $E_1!M_i(E_2)$. Note that under this interpretation an $\textbf{answer}(M_1, \ldots, M_k)$ statement requires that an appropriate method be invoked. An alternative in which if no invocation requests are outstanding the **answer** statement may successfully terminate is also possible. With a little more work this too may be encoded in the π-calculus.

The class of $\mathcal{L}_2$-declarations contains in addition to sequences of variable declarations, sequences of method declarations of the form:

$$Mdec \; ::= \; \textbf{method } M_1(X_1, Y_1) \textbf{ is } S_1, \ldots, M_n(X_n, Y_n) \textbf{ is } S_n$$

with the M_i distinct from one another. In a method declaration **method** $M(X,Y)$ **is** S, X is the formal parameter supplied by an invoking expression $E_1!M(E_2)$, and Y a variable in which will be stored the value to be returned as the value of that expression on completion of the execution of the body S. We consider only one-parameter methods, the extension of the translation to the many-parameter case being quite straightforward.

The clause for $\mathcal{L}_2$-class declarations is:

$$Cdec \;::=\; \textbf{class}\ C\ \textbf{is}\ Vdec,\ Mdec\ \textbf{in}\ S$$

with every variable and every method name occurring in S being declared in *Vdec* and *Mdec*.

Finally, the clause for $\mathcal{L}_2$-program declarations is:

$$Pdec \;::=\; \textbf{program}\ P\ \textbf{is}\ Cdec_1, \ldots, Cdec_n$$

with caveats and interpretation similar those in the case of $\mathcal{L}_1$.

4 The Translations

Each entity of each syntactic category is represented as an agent[2], the representations of complex entities being constructed from those of their constituents. There are delicate relationships between certain parts of the translations, and for this reason some details may not be entirely clear when read in isolation. We begin with the translation of $\mathcal{L}_1$.

The translation of $\mathcal{L}_1$

To give a feel for the overall structure of the translation we begin with declarations. First we consider variables of non-reference types. We assume that for each variable X there are constant names r_X and w_X. As discussed in [7], the introduction of constant names may be avoided. However rather than introducing a further level of encoding we admit them here.

With t being either *nat* or *bool* we define:

$$[\![\textbf{var}\ X : t]\!] \stackrel{\text{def}}{=} Loc_X$$

where

$$\begin{aligned} Loc_X &\stackrel{\text{def}}{=} w_X(y).\, Reg_X(y) \\ Reg_X(y) &\stackrel{\text{def}}{=} \overline{r_X}y.\, Reg_X(y) + w_X(z).\, Reg_X(z) \end{aligned}$$

Loc_X represents a memory location at which the name of a link to an agent representing a value may be stored. Such a name may be written via the link w_X, while the name currently stored may be read via the link r_X. Assignment to X will be represented

[2] more accurately, as a mapping from names to agents

by the storing of the name of a link to the agent encoding the new data value. Note that on its declaration no link name is stored; an attempt to read from the variable will fail.

The translation of the declaration of a variable of type *ref* is slightly different. However it is convenient to use the same agent constants relying on context to resolve any ambiguity. We use two further constant names: `NIL` and `REF`. We define:

$$[\![\mathbf{var}\ X : \mathit{ref}]\!] \stackrel{\text{def}}{=} \mathit{Loc}_X$$

where

$$\begin{aligned} \mathit{Loc}_X &\stackrel{\text{def}}{=} \overline{r_X}\,\mathtt{NIL}.\,\mathit{Loc}_X + w_X : [\mathtt{NIL} \Rightarrow \mathit{Loc}_X,\ \mathtt{REF} \Rightarrow w_X(y).\,\mathit{Reg}_X(y)] \\ \mathit{Reg}_X(y) &\stackrel{\text{def}}{=} \overline{r_X}\,\mathtt{REF}.\,\overline{r_X}y.\,\mathit{Reg}_X(y) + w_X : [\mathtt{NIL} \Rightarrow \mathit{Loc}_X,\ \mathtt{REF} \Rightarrow w_X(z).\,\mathit{Reg}_X(z)] \end{aligned}$$

`REF` and `NIL` signify, respectively, that X does or does not contain a reference to an object; note the use of the match construct in the definitions. Otherwise the behaviour is similar to the case of X of non-reference type. Note that on its declaration X is deemed to contain no reference to an object.

A sequence of variable declarations is represented as the composition of the agents representing the individual declarations:

$$[\![\mathbf{var}\ X_1 : t_1, \ldots, X_n : t_n]\!] \stackrel{\text{def}}{=} [\![\mathbf{var}\ X_1 : t_1]\!] \mid \cdots \mid [\![\mathbf{var}\ X_n : t_n]\!]$$

Next we consider class declarations. We assume for each class name C a constant name c of the π-calculus. The translation is:

$$[\![\mathbf{class}\ C\ \mathbf{is}\ \mathit{Vdec}\ \mathbf{in}\ S]\!](c) \stackrel{\text{def}}{=} \overline{c}(w) * [\![\mathit{Vdec}\ \mathbf{in}\ S]\!](w)$$

where

$$[\![\mathit{Vdec}\ \mathbf{in}\ S]\!](w) \stackrel{\text{def}}{=} (N)([\![\mathit{Vdec}]\!] \mid [\![S]\!](w))$$

with $N = \{r_X, w_X \mid X \text{ occurs in } \mathit{Vdec}\}$. Recall from [7] that $\alpha * P$ is a *replicator*.

As explained below, each statement S is represented as an agent $[\![S]\!](w)$ with w playing the rôle of a reference to the object of which S is a part. The agent representing the class declaration may provide at c an indefinite number of private instances of the agent $[\![\mathit{Vdec}\ \mathbf{in}\ S]\!]$ which represents an object with statement agent $[\![S]\!]$ composed with agents representing the local variables. Note the rôle of the restriction operator in localizing the scope of the variables. Note also the means by which the agent representing the class declaration produces a new instance of the class accessible only to the recipient of the private name w. As explained below, the recipient will be an agent representing the expression $\mathbf{new}_C$.

Finally if $\mathit{Pdec} \equiv \mathbf{program}\ P\ \mathbf{is}\ \mathit{Cdec}_1, \ldots, \mathit{Cdec}_n$ is a program declaration, its translation is as follows:

$$[\![\mathit{Pdec}]\!](w) \stackrel{\text{def}}{=} (c_1, \ldots, c_m)([\![\mathit{Cdec}_1]\!](c_1) \mid \cdots \mid [\![\mathit{Cdec}_n]\!](c_n) \mid c_1(w).\,\mathbf{0})$$

Note how the initiation of the computation with the single root object of class C_1 is represented using the trigger $c_1(w).\mathbf{0}$.

Next we consider the translation of expressions of non-reference type. Each such expression E is represented as an agent $[\![E]\!](v)$ with v the name of a link through which the agent may communicate its value. Such agents have a transient existence: they may yield their value only once. However as explained below, more permanent forms are also used in the translation. We assume four more constant names: ZERO, ONE, TRUE and FALSE. We have:

$$\begin{aligned}
[\![k]\!](v) &\stackrel{\text{def}}{=} (\overline{v}\,\texttt{ONE}.\,)^k\,\overline{v}\,\texttt{ZERO}\\
[\![\mathit{true}]\!](v) &\stackrel{\text{def}}{=} \overline{v}\,\texttt{TRUE}\\
[\![\mathit{false}]\!](v) &\stackrel{\text{def}}{=} \overline{v}\,\texttt{FALSE}\\
[\![E_1+E_2]\!](v) &\stackrel{\text{def}}{=} (v_1,v_2)([\![E_1]\!](v_1) \mid [\![E_2]\!](v_2) \mid [\![+]\!](v_1,v_2,v))\\
[\![E_1=E_2]\!](v) &\stackrel{\text{def}}{=} (v_1,v_2)([\![E_1]\!](v_1) \mid [\![E_2]\!](v_2) \mid [\![=]\!](v_1,v_2,v))\\
[\![\neg E]\!](v) &\stackrel{\text{def}}{=} (v_1)([\![E_1]\!](v_1) \mid [\![\neg]\!](v_1,v))\\
[\![E_1\wedge E_2]\!](v) &\stackrel{\text{def}}{=} (v_1,v_2)([\![E_1]\!](v_1) \mid [\![E_2]\!](v_2) \mid [\![\wedge]\!](v_1,v_2,v))
\end{aligned}$$

where

$$\begin{aligned}
[\![+]\!](v_1,v_2,v) &\stackrel{\text{def}}{=} v_1:[\texttt{ZERO}\Rightarrow [\![+]\!]'(v_2,v),\ \texttt{ONE}\Rightarrow \overline{v}\,\texttt{ONE}.\,[\![+]\!](v_1,v_2,v)]\\
[\![+]\!]'(v_2,v) &\stackrel{\text{def}}{=} v_2:[\texttt{ZERO}\Rightarrow \overline{v}\,\texttt{ZERO},\ \texttt{ONE}\Rightarrow \overline{v}\,\texttt{ONE}.\,[\![+]\!]'(v_2,v)]\\
[\![=]\!](v_1,v_2,v) &\stackrel{\text{def}}{=} v_1:[\texttt{ZERO}\Rightarrow v_2:[\texttt{ZERO}\Rightarrow \overline{v}\,\texttt{TRUE},\ \texttt{ONE}\Rightarrow \overline{v}\,\texttt{FALSE}],\\
&\qquad\ \ \texttt{ONE}\Rightarrow v_2:[\texttt{ZERO}\Rightarrow \overline{v}\,\texttt{FALSE},\ \texttt{ONE}\Rightarrow [\![=]\!](v_1,v_2,v)]]\\
[\![\neg]\!](v_1,v) &\stackrel{\text{def}}{=} v_1:[\texttt{FALSE}\Rightarrow \overline{v}\,\texttt{TRUE},\ \texttt{TRUE}\Rightarrow \overline{v}\,\texttt{FALSE}]\\
[\![\wedge]\!](v_1,v_2,v) &\stackrel{\text{def}}{=} v_1:[\texttt{FALSE}\Rightarrow \overline{v}\,\texttt{FALSE},\ \texttt{TRUE}\Rightarrow v_2(y).\,\overline{v}y]
\end{aligned}$$

Note that in these definitions we abbreviate $\alpha.\mathbf{0}$ to α.

For X of non-reference type we have:

$$[\![X]\!](v) \stackrel{\text{def}}{=} r_X(y).\,y(u).\,\mathit{Copy}(u,v)$$

where

$$\mathit{Copy}(u,v) \stackrel{\text{def}}{=} u(z).\,\overline{v}z.\,\mathit{Copy}(u,v)$$

Some explanation of this representation is required. However, it is much more readily appreciated in conjunction with the translation of the assignment statement $X := E$, so we proceed to this first. Three preparatory steps are required.

The first involves the introduction of a further constant name *done* and the following definition:

$$\mathit{Done} \stackrel{\text{def}}{=} \overline{\mathit{done}}\,\mathit{done}.\,\mathbf{0}$$

The rôle of *Done* is to provide a signal of successful termination of a statement. This will be elaborated below.

The second step is the introduction of a derived operator *before* as follows:

$$P \textit{ before } Q \stackrel{\text{def}}{=} (done)(P \mid done(z).\, Q) \quad \text{where } z \notin fn(Q)$$

Finally the third step involves the introduction of a family of agents representing the evaluation of expressions (of all types). We set:

$$\begin{aligned} Eval(v_1, v) \stackrel{\text{def}}{=} v_1 : [\ & \texttt{ZERO} \Rightarrow Nateval_0(v), \\ & \texttt{ONE} \Rightarrow Nateval_1(v_1, v), \\ & \texttt{FALSE} \Rightarrow Booleval_F(v), \\ & \texttt{TRUE} \Rightarrow Booleval_T(v), \\ & \texttt{NIL} \Rightarrow Refeval_N(v), \\ & \texttt{REF} \Rightarrow Refeval_R(v_1, v)] \end{aligned}$$

where

$$\begin{aligned} Nateval_0(v) &\stackrel{\text{def}}{=} Done \mid \overline{v}(w) * [\![0]\!](w) \\ Nateval_k(v_1, v) &\stackrel{\text{def}}{=} v_1 : [\texttt{ZERO} \Rightarrow Done \mid \overline{v}(w) * [\![k]\!](w), \\ &\qquad\quad \texttt{ONE} \Rightarrow Nateval_{k+1}(v_1, v)] \qquad \text{if } k \geq 1 \\ Booleval_F(v) &\stackrel{\text{def}}{=} Done \mid \overline{v}(w) * [\![false]\!](w) \\ Booleval_T(v) &\stackrel{\text{def}}{=} Done \mid \overline{v}(w) * [\![true]\!](w) \\ Refeval_N(v) &\stackrel{\text{def}}{=} Done \mid \overline{v}(w) * Nil(w) \\ Refeval_R(v_1, v) &\stackrel{\text{def}}{=} v_1(u).\, (Done \mid \overline{v}(w) * Ref(w, u)) \end{aligned}$$

where

$$\begin{aligned} Nil(w) &\stackrel{\text{def}}{=} \overline{w}\,\texttt{NIL} \\ Ref(w, u) &\stackrel{\text{def}}{=} \overline{w}\,\texttt{REF}.\, \overline{w}u \end{aligned}$$

Note in passing that the encoding of data values may be extended easily to arbitrary sets of values built recursively from a finite set of constructors.

Then for X and E of common non-reference type we have:

$$[\![X := E]\!](w) \stackrel{\text{def}}{=} (v)((v_1)([\![E]\!](v_1) \mid Eval(v_1, v)) \textit{ before } \overline{w_X}v.\, Done)$$

Thus the assignment is represented by the evaluation of E followed by the passing to Reg_X of a private link to the replicator representing the value of E and a signal (to the agent representing the subsequent command) of successful termination. Note from the definition of *Eval* that an indefinite number of private instances of the agent representing the value of E may be obtained via the link stored in Reg_X.

The definition of $[\![X]\!]$ may now be clearer. The evaluation of an expression X (of non-reference type) is represented by the reception from Reg_X of the name of a private link to the replicator representing the current value of X, followed by the reception from the replicator of the name of a private link to an agent capable of yielding the value, followed in turn by the transmission of the value piecemeal. To gain some feel for the representation the reader may care to examine the encoding of a fragment such as:

$$\textbf{var}\ X : \mathit{nat},\ Y : \mathit{nat}\ \textbf{in}\ X := 3;\ Y := X + X$$

The translation of the sending statement is similar. We have:

$$\begin{aligned} [\![X!E]\!](w) \overset{\text{def}}{=}\ & r_X(u).\,[u = \mathtt{REF}]\, r_X(x). \\ & (v)((v_1)([\![E]\!](v_1) \mid \mathit{Eval}(v_1, v))\ \mathit{before}\ \overline{x}v.\,\mathit{Done}) \end{aligned}$$

First the name x of the link to the agent representing the receiving object is read from Reg_X. Then E is evaluated and the private link to the replicated version of its value passed along x.

The receiving statements are represented as follows:

$$[\![X?Y]\!](w) \overset{\text{def}}{=} r_X(u).\,[u = \mathtt{REF}] r_X(x).\,x(y).\,\overline{w_Y}y.\,\mathit{Done}$$

in which the name x of the link to the sending object is read from Reg_X, the name y of the private link to the replicated version of the incoming data value is received along x, and this name is sent to Reg_Y. Secondly:

$$[\![?Y]\!](w) \overset{\text{def}}{=} w(y).\,\overline{w_Y}y.\,\mathit{Done}$$

Here one point of the parameter w in the representation of statements is seen. The reception of a value from an unspecified object is represented by the reception of a name along the link named w. The other rôle of this parameter is in the translation of the expression **self** as described below.

The translation of expressions of type *ref* is as follows:

$$\begin{aligned} [\![\textbf{nil}]\!](w, v) &\overset{\text{def}}{=} \overline{v}\,\mathtt{NIL} \\ [\![\textbf{self}]\!](w, v) &\overset{\text{def}}{=} \overline{v}\,\mathtt{REF}.\,\overline{v}w \\ [\![X]\!](w, v) &\overset{\text{def}}{=} \mathit{Copy}(r_X, v) \end{aligned}$$

Note the presence of two parameters in these definitions. The first of these will be the parameter in the translation $[\![S]\!](w)$ of the statement in which the expression in question occurs. Also, compare the representation $[\![X]\!]$ with the corresponding definition for X of non-reference type. In this case no passing of private links to copies of agents representing data values is required.

The translations of the assignment, sending and receiving statements for reference types are as follows:

$$\begin{aligned} [\![X := E]\!](w) \overset{\text{def}}{=} (v)([\![E]\!](w, v) \mid v : [\ & \mathtt{NIL} \Rightarrow \overline{w_X}\,\mathtt{NIL}.\,\mathit{Done}, \\ & \mathtt{REF} \Rightarrow \overline{w_X}\,\mathtt{REF}.\,v(u).\,\overline{w_X}u.\,\mathit{Done}]) \end{aligned}$$

$$[\![X!E]\!](w) \stackrel{\text{def}}{=} (v)([\![E]\!](w,v) \mid r_X(u).\,[u = \texttt{REF}]\, r_X(x).\,(y)\overline{x}y.\; v : [\texttt{NIL} \Rightarrow \overline{y}\,\texttt{NIL}.\,\mathit{Done},\ \texttt{REF} \Rightarrow \overline{y}\,\texttt{REF}.\,v(u).\,\overline{y}u.\,\mathit{Done}])$$

$$[\![X?Y]\!](w) \stackrel{\text{def}}{=} r_X(u).\,[u = \texttt{REF}]\, r_X(x).\,x(y).\; y : [\texttt{NIL} \Rightarrow \overline{w_Y}\,\texttt{NIL}.\,\mathit{Done},\ \texttt{REF} \Rightarrow \overline{w_Y}\,\texttt{REF}.\,y(u).\,\overline{w_Y}u.\,\mathit{Done}]$$

$$[\![?Y]\!](w) \stackrel{\text{def}}{=} w(y).\,y : [\ \texttt{NIL} \Rightarrow \overline{w_Y}\,\texttt{NIL}.\,\mathit{Done},\ \texttt{REF} \Rightarrow \overline{w_Y}\,\texttt{REF}.\,y(u).\,\overline{w_Y}u.\,\mathit{Done}]$$

Compare these clauses with the corresponding representations in the case of non-reference types. A value of type *ref* is communicated via a *molecular action* (see [7]). A more uniform treatment of the encoding of expressions is possible. We adopt the present approach in order to illustrate the possibilities and also because the alternative does not appear to be simpler.

The final assignment involves the creation of a new object:

$$[\![X := \mathbf{new}_C]\!](w) \stackrel{\text{def}}{=} c(z).\,\overline{w_X}\,\texttt{REF}.\,\overline{w_X}z.\,\mathit{Done}$$

Referring back to the translation of class declarations, this assignment is represented by the reception from the agent representing the declaration of C of a private link z to an agent representing a new object of class C followed by the sending of this link to Reg_X.

It remains only to deal with the standard statement constructs. We have:

$$\begin{aligned}
[\![\mathbf{skip}]\!](w) &\stackrel{\text{def}}{=} \mathit{Done}\\
[\![S_1; S_2]\!](w) &\stackrel{\text{def}}{=} [\![S_1]\!](w)\ \mathit{before}\ [\![S_2]\!](w)\\
[\![\mathbf{if}\ E\ \mathbf{then}\ S_1\ \mathbf{else}\ S_2]\!](w) &\stackrel{\text{def}}{=} (v)([\![E]\!](v) \mid v : [\texttt{TRUE} \Rightarrow [\![S_1]\!](w),\ \texttt{FALSE} \Rightarrow [\![S_2]\!](w)])\\
[\![\mathbf{while}\ E\ \mathbf{do}\ S]\!](w) &\stackrel{\text{def}}{=} W(w)
\end{aligned}$$

where

$$W(w) \stackrel{\text{def}}{=} (v)([\![E]\!](v) \mid v : [\texttt{TRUE} \Rightarrow ([\![S]\!](w)\ \mathit{before}\ W(w)),\ \texttt{FALSE} \Rightarrow \mathit{Done}])$$

These clauses are fairly self-explanatory (see [5]). This completes the translation of $\mathcal{L}_1$.

The translation of $\mathcal{L}_2$

The $\mathcal{L}_2$-translations of those constructs common to the two languages are identical to their $\mathcal{L}_1$-translations. The translations of the other constructs, method declarations,

answer statements, and method invocation expressions, are intimately related to one another.

Suppose **method** $M(X,Y)$ **is** S is a single method declaration taking a parameter of non-reference type and returning a value of non-reference type. Then the translations are as follows where for each method name M we assume a constant name m of the π-calculus:

$$[\![\mathbf{method}\ M(X,Y)\ \mathbf{is}\ S]\!](m) \stackrel{\mathrm{def}}{=} \overline{m}(z) * M(z)$$

where

$$M(z) \stackrel{\mathrm{def}}{=} (N)(Loc_X \mid Loc_Y \mid z(w).\, z(x).\, \overline{w_X}x.\, ([\![S]\!](w)\ \mathit{before}\ r_Y(v').\, \overline{z}v'))$$

with $N = \{r_X, w_X, r_Y, w_Y\}$;

$$[\![\mathbf{answer}(M_1,\ldots,M_k)]\!](w) \stackrel{\mathrm{def}}{=} w(u).\, u : [m_i \Rightarrow u(v).\, m_i(z).\, \overline{z}w.\, \overline{z}v.\, z(v').\, \overline{u}v'.\, \mathit{Done}]_{i=1}^{k}$$

and

$$\begin{aligned}[\![E_1!M(E_2)]\!](v) \stackrel{\mathrm{def}}{=} (v_3)\ \ & ((v_1)([\![E_1]\!](v_1) \mid v_1(u).\, [u = \mathrm{REF}]\, v_1(w).\, \mathit{Done}) \\ & \mathit{before}\ ((v_2)([\![E_2]\!](v_2) \mid \mathit{Eval}(v_2, v_3)) \\ & \quad \mathit{before}\ (u)\overline{w}u.\, \overline{u}m.\, \overline{u}v_3.\, u(v').\, v'(v'').\, \mathit{Copy}(v'', v)))\end{aligned}$$

The agent representing $E_1!M(E_2)$ first obtains the name of the link w to the agent representing the object to which E_1 refers (if it exists), and then the parameter E_2 is evaluated. Its activity is then suspended until the agent representing the object referred to is able to receive a communication along this link, indicating the execution of an **answer** statement. Then a private link u is communicated from the expression agent to the **answer** statement agent, and along this link there follows the name m representing the method M. If the method requested is among those offered, modelled using the match construct, the private link v_3 to the replicated version of the value of E_2 is sent along u, and then the **answer** agent requests from the agent representing the appropriate method declaration a private copy of the agent representing the method body (with private local variable agents). To this agent it communicates the parameter w indicating in which object it occurs – this is necessary as the body may contain **answer** statements or occurrences of the expression **self** – followed by the private link to the replicated value of the parameter. The method body agent stores this link in its local Reg_X, the agent $[\![S]\!]$ becomes active, and on completion the name stored in the local Reg_Y is returned to the **answer** agent. This agent in turn returns this name to the $E_1!M(E_2)$ expression agent, along the private link u previously established between them, and then indicates successful termination. Finally a link to a private copy of the value is obtained and the value is copied piecemeal via the *Copy* agent.

It is straightforward to modify the translation to handle the case when either the parameter or the value of the invoking expression is of type *ref*. Similarly, the representation of many-parameter methods is not difficult. As mentioned earlier, the interpretation of the **answer** statement adopted here is such that it may successfully terminate only after a method has been invoked. A representation of an alternative in which this is not the case is possible but is not given here.

If several objects are suspended awaiting an opportunity to invoke a method in a given object then according to the translation given here, when an **answer** statement is executed, only one will have this opportunity. Moreover if the method requested by the selected object is not among those offered in the **answer** statement, the agent representing the **answer** statement will be unable to proceed. An alternative in which incoming messages are stored in queues, with method invocations occurring in an order determined in some way by the queues' contents, may also be represented with a little more work.

It remains only to complete the translation of $\mathcal{L}_2$-declarations. The translation of a sequence $Mdec_1, \ldots, Mdec_n$ of method declarations with M_i the method name appearing in $Mdec_i$ is:

$$[\![Mdec_1, \ldots, Mdec_n]\!](m_1, \ldots, m_n) \stackrel{\text{def}}{=} [\![Mdec_1]\!](m_1) \mid \cdots \mid [\![Mdec_n]\!](m_n)$$

The translation of an $\mathcal{L}_2$-class declaration is:

$$[\![\mathbf{class}\ C\ \mathbf{is}\ Vdec,\ Mdec\ \mathbf{in}\ S]\!](c) \stackrel{\text{def}}{=} \overline{c}(w) * [\![Vdec,\ Mdec\ \mathbf{in}\ S]\!](w)$$

where

$$[\![Vdec,\ Mdec\ \mathbf{in}\ S]\!](w) \stackrel{\text{def}}{=} (N)([\![Vdec]\!] \mid [\![Mdec]\!] \mid [\![S]\!](w))$$

with

$$N = \{r_X, w_X \mid X \text{ occurs in } Vdec\} \cup \{m \mid M \text{ occurs in } Mdec\}$$

Finally the translation of a program declaration is as for $\mathcal{L}_1$ with the above definitions. This completes the translation of $\mathcal{L}_2$.

5 Discussion

The principal aim of this paper has been to illustrate the expressive power of the π-calculus. That the behaviour of any system expressible in a language such as POOL may be viewed entirely as a 'name game' in which the sole purpose of communication is to exchange names which may be used in further communications is not, perhaps, in itself surprising. That, however, a calculus as simple, elegant and tractable as the π-calculus provides such a treatment is noteworthy.

The semantics provided by the translations should be compared with existing semantics such as those for POOL in [2, 3, 10]. In [2] an operational semantics for POOL based on a transition system is presented. A configuration has four components: a set of (labelled) statements to be executed by the existing objects; a state recording the current values of the 'instance variables' and of the 'local variables' of the existing objects; a type function recording the class of each of the existing objects; and a unit recording the definitions of the classes. Transitions between configurations are given by a set of axioms and rules. It is likely that a relationship may be established between this operational semantics and the π-calculus semantics, but at the time of writing this has not been completed. The relationship with the semantics of [10] also deserves to be investigated in detail.

As mentioned in the introduction the domain equations adopted in [3] for giving a denotational semantics for POOL provide insight into the language's semantic structure, insight which is lacking from the translation into the π-calculus as it stands. However the π-calculus seems to provide a suitable forum in which to examine in undiluted form many issues pertinent to object-oriented languages. Recent work of Milner on sorts and types in the π-calculus allows the translations to be recast so as to capture more structure. It is hoped that further development of type and model theories of the π-calculus will allow the operational account provided by the translations to be supplemented by more abstract semantic descriptions.

Acknowledgments

I am grateful to Robin Milner, John Potter and the referees for comments on this paper.

References

[1] P. America, *Issues in the design of a parallel object-oriented language*, Formal Aspects of Computing, vol.1 no.4 pp.366–411 (1989).

[2] P. America, J. de Bakker, J. Kok and J. Rutten, *Operational semantics of a parallel object-oriented language*, in 13th POPL, 194–208 (1986).

[3] P. America, J. de Bakker, J. Kok and J. Rutten, *Denotational semantics of a parallel object-oriented language*, Information and Computation, vol.83 no.2 (1989).

[4] P. America and F. de Boer, *A Proof System for Process Creation*, Philips Research Laboratories Report RWR-116-DO-90506-DO (1990).

[5] R. Milner, *Communication and Concurrency*, Prentice-Hall (1989).

[6] R. Milner, *Functions as Processes*, Research Report 1154, INRIA (1990).

[7] R. Milner, J. Parrow and D. Walker, *A Calculus of Mobile Processes, Part I*, University of Edinburgh report ECS-LFCS-89-85, to appear in J. Information and Computation.

[8] R. Milner, J. Parrow and D. Walker, *A Calculus of Mobile Processes, Part II*, Univeristy of Edinburgh report ECS-LFCS-89-86, to appear in J. Information and Computation.

[9] F. Orava and J. Parrow, *Algebraic description of mobile networks: An example*, to appear in Proc. 10th IFIP Symposium on Protocol Specification, Testing and Verification, North-Holland (1990).

[10] F. Vaandrager, *Process algebra semantics for POOL*, Technical Report CS-R8629, CWI Amsterdam (1986).

[11] D. Walker, *Some results on the π-calculus*, in *Concurrency: Theory, Language, and Architecture*, A. Yonezawa and T. Ito (eds.), Springer LNCS 491, 21–35 (1991).

Wrapper Semantics of an Object-Oriented Programming Language with State

Andreas V. Hense
LS Programmiersprachen u. Übersetzerbau
FB 14, Informatik
Universität des Saarlandes
6600 Saarbrücken 11, Fed. Rep. of Germany
hense@cs.uni-sb.de

Abstract

The semantics of class inheritance has first been given in operational form (method-lookup-semantics). While this semantics is well suited for implementing object-oriented programming languages, it may conceal the true nature of inheritance. The development of denotational semantics for object-oriented languages has culminated in object creation as fixed point operation. Cook gave a semantics on this basis, using so called *wrappers*. This semantics abstracts from the internal state of objects (*instance variables*).

In this paper we show how wrapper semantics can be extended to an object-oriented programming language *with state* while keeping the structure of the original definitions. For this purpose we define a direct denotational semantics of a small example language. The insertion of state into class definitions can be done before or after the related fixed point operation. The choice of the alternative considerably influences the semantic domains and clauses.

1 Introduction

Object-oriented programming is subject of intensive research and at the same time spreading into industrial contexts. The semantics of object-oriented programming has been described operationally for a long time. We feel that classes and inheritance – two key points in object-oriented programming – are so complicated that they deserve a thorough treatment. Although the operational method-lookup-semantics seems to be intuitive at first glance, the essence of inheritance – namely the difference between inheriting from a class and using a class [20] – may be concealed behind operational details.

Our work is based on the following notion of object-oriented programming [19]: an object-oriented programming language must support the concepts of *objects*, *object classes*, and *class inheritance*. An object has a set of operations and a state. Objects communicate with each other by sending messages. The result of a message sent to an object (the *receiver*) is not completely determined by the actual parameters, but depends on the state of the receiver. Object classes can serve as templates for creating objects. They specify operations and may also contain their implementation. Class inheritance is a mechanism for the composition of specifications and implementations. There is late binding for operations modified in subclasses.

What has been the development of semantics relevant to this article? The first semantics of SMALLTALK [6], which often serves as an archetype of object-oriented programming languages, was described op[illegible]. We owe the first denotational semantics of SMALLTALK to Wolczko [illegible]mantics still has some operational elements: inheritance is des[illegible]. A denotational SMALLTALK-semantics in continuation s[illegible] Both semantics are long because they describe a "real" la[illegible]nted more readable semantics because he focused on cent[illegible]ed programming; he used fixed points for modeling *self*. [illegible]ics of inheritance without state using so called *wrappe*[illegible] good intuition of class inheritance. It remains to be sho[illegible]antics also works for a language with state.

Why is state important for object-oriented [illegible] The object-oriented programming style implies that objects in the real wor[illegible] modeled by objects in the programming language. Real objects change, yet maintain their identity. Therefore we need the assignment operator [1]. With the introduction of the assignment operator we lose referential transparency but we gain expressive power [5].

We show that wrapper semantics and internal state are orthogonal notions in a certain sense: we give the denotational semantics of a full object-oriented language while keeping the structure of wrapper semantics.[1] For this purpose we define the object-oriented programming language O'SMALL. The name O'SMALL gives a hint at the purpose and the origin of the language. Gordon [7] described an imperative language called SMALL by giving it a denotational semantics. O'SMALL is an object-oriented extension of SMALL. The reason for describing an extension of a well known language concept instead of describing the prototype SMALLTALK is "inheritance at another level": we only show the differences between object-oriented and imperative languages; the description of the latter is well known [15,7]. Our goal has been to minimize complicated constructions and to preserve the intuitiveness of the wrapper mechanism.

[1]first appeared in [8]

Section 2 starts with an introductory example written in O'SMALL. O'SMALL is a full object-oriented programming language *with state.* In section 3, we give the central definitions of inheritance *without* state: objects have no instance variables and there are no assignments. The example language in this section is 'functional O'SMALL'. Functional O'SMALL has no imperative features (assignments) but it has parameterized classes. To see the differences between O'SMALL and functional O'SMALL, compare figures 2 and 4. Functional O'SMALL is not defined formally. Section 4 contains the semantics of O'SMALL (with state). The formal concepts without state of section 3 are now transferred into a world with state. The semantics of O'SMALL does not use continuations (*direct semantics*).

To prevent confusion, the state in the sections of this paper is shown as a flag that can be turned on and off:

section	2	3	4
state	ON	OFF	ON

2 An introductory example

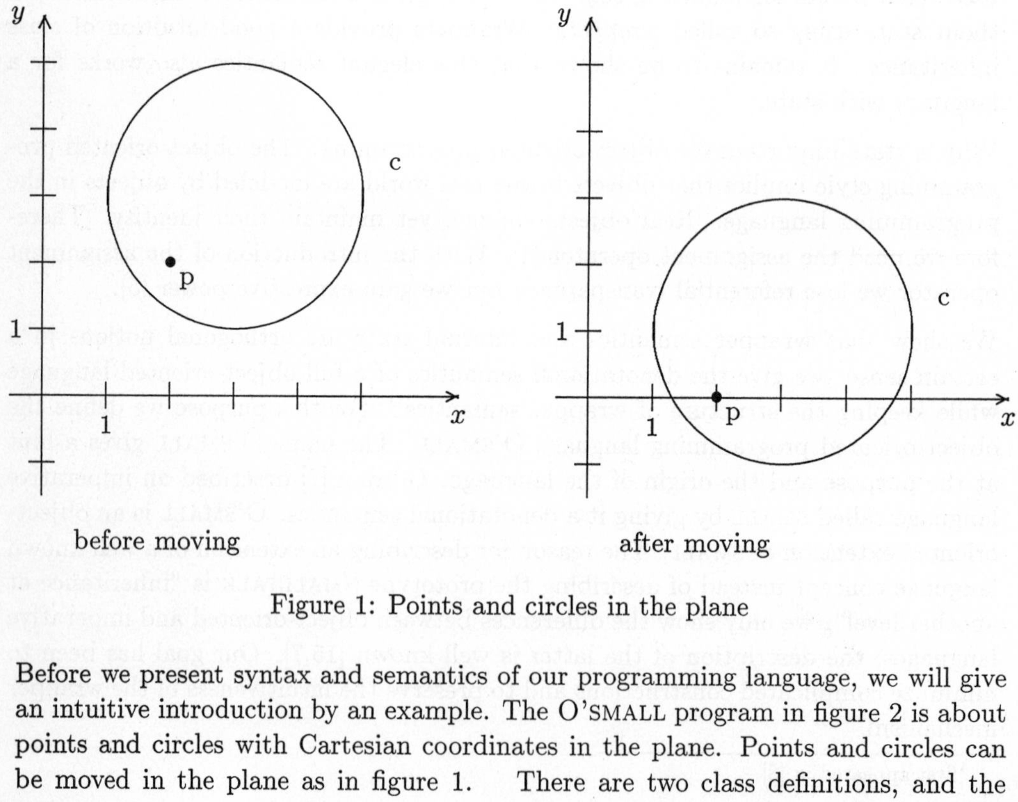

Figure 1: Points and circles in the plane

Before we present syntax and semantics of our programming language, we will give an intuitive introduction by an example. The O'SMALL program in figure 2 is about points and circles with Cartesian coordinates in the plane. Points and circles can be moved in the plane as in figure 1. There are two class definitions, and the

```
class Point inheritsFrom Base
def var xComp := 0; var yComp := 0
in meth x() xComp
   meth y() yComp
   meth move(X,Y) xComp := X+self.x; yComp := Y+self.y
   meth distFromOrg()  sqrt( sqr(self.x)  +  sqr(self.y) )
   meth closerToOrg(point) self.distFromOrg < point.distFromOrg
ni

class Circle inheritsFrom Point
def var radius := 0
in meth r() radius
   meth setR(r) radius := r
   meth distFromOrg() max(0, super.distFromOrg - self.r)
ni

def var p := new Point;
    var c := new Circle
in p.move(2,2); c.move(3,3); c.setR(2);
   output p.closerToOrg(c); {results in FALSE}
   p.move(0,-2);            c.move(0,-2);
   output p.closerToOrg(c)  {results still in FALSE}
ni
```

Figure 2: Example program in O'SMALL

inheritance tree is as in figure 3. The class `Base` is a class "without contents" (see section 4.5); `Base` is always at the root of the inheritance tree.

Objects of class `Point` have two instance variables representing the Cartesian coordinates of the point. A point object created with `new` is in the origin because its instance variables are initialized to zero. There are two methods for inspecting the instance variables. Instance variables are not directly visible from outside. The method `move` changes the position of the receiver. In object-oriented terminology, the O'SMALL expression `p.m(a)` stands for the sending of `m` with argument `a` to the receiver `p`. There is a method for the distance from the origin and a method that returns TRUE if the receiver is closer to the origin than the argument. Booleans, numbers, and some standard functions on them are primitive.

The class `Circle`, which inherits instance variables and methods from `Point`, has an additional instance variable for the radius, methods for reading and changing the radius, and it redefines `distFromOrg`. For the redefinition of `distFromOrg`, the `distFromOrg`-definition of the superclass is referred to by `super.distFromOrg`.

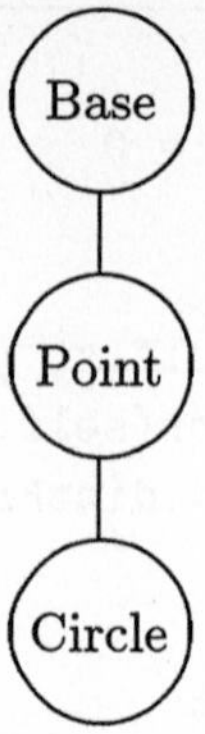

Figure 3: Inheritance graph

The output of the program in figure 2 results in: FALSE FALSE. This is what we intended. We are now able to compare points and circles with respect to their closeness to the origin, and always get consistent behavior.

3 Semantics of inheritance

The contents of this section are adapted from [4]. Note that this semantics abstracts from state. So it is not a description of the O'SMALL which was introduced informally in figure 2. The semantics of O'SMALL will be the topic of section 4. In this section 'functional O'SMALL' will be used in examples.

3.1 Fixed point semantics

Self-reference and applications of functions to themselves pose mathematical problems. Yet, recursive procedures or functions are common in programming, and we will also need them in the remainder of this article. Scott [13] provided a basis for mathematical structures (cpo's[2]) that are suited for the description of recursive programs. For an overview refer to [2,9]. Let us give an informal example of a recursive definition in an O'SMALL like notation.[3]

```
method fac(n)    if n=0 then 1 else n * fac(n-1)
```

This definition is recursive or self-referential. In SMALLTALK and O'SMALL, self-reference is standardized syntactically with the pseudo-variable `self`. Before we continue and apply the fixed point technique to classes, we need some definitions and notions:

[2]complete partial order [2]

[3]the concrete syntax of O'SMALL has no equality symbol for method definitions

Definition 3.1 A *record* is a finite mapping from a set of labels to a set of values. A record is denoted by $\begin{bmatrix} x_1 & \mapsto & v_1 \\ & \vdots & \\ x_n & \mapsto & v_n \end{bmatrix}$ with labels x_i and values v_i. All labels that are not in the list are mapped to $\perp$. The empty record, where all labels are mapped to $\perp$, is denoted by $[]$.

We list some correspondence between object-oriented terminology and the current framework: *Objects* are records. *Message sending* is record selection (denoted by a dot), *message selectors* are labels, and *methods* are values of records. The values may refer recursively to the whole record; there is no direct simultaneous recursion between components. Note that in this section objects have no state.

Instead of just applying a function to an argument, object-oriented languages send a message to an object – for the pseudo variable `self` the object itself. For the above example, we thus obtain the O'SMALL program fragment:

```
method fact(n)    if n=0 then 1 else n * self.fact(n-1)
```

This is a method definition that may appear in a class. To access this method, we have to send a message with selector `fact` to an object of this class. But because the definition is self-referential, one does still not know what it denotes. With fixed point analysis we can construct denotations of self-referential definitions, and in cpo's, unique solutions are guaranteed to exist. We transform the above definition into non-recursive form by explicitly abstracting the self-reference. A λ-calculus-like meta language is used for semantic considerations.

$$Fact = \lambda s.[fact \mapsto \lambda n. \text{ if } n = 0 \text{ then } 1 \text{ else } n * s.fact(n-1)]$$

Fact maps records to records. Its definition is not recursive. The abstracted variable s plays the role of `self`. The fixed point theorem [16] guarantees the existence of a least fixed point for all continuous functions mapping elements of a cpo to elements of the same cpo.[4] All functions considered here are continuous. Let F be such a function. Then we write $\text{FIX}(F)$ for the least fixed point of F. If $f = \text{FIX}(F)$ then $F(f) \doteq f$. This holds because f is a fixed point. The function *fac*, we intended to define in the first place, is now the fact-component of *Fact*'s fixed point:

$$fac = \text{FIX}(Fact).fact$$

3.2 Classes and fixed points

A *class* is a function whose fixed point is an object. *Fact* is an example of a class with only one method. Let us look at another example of a class. Figure 4 shows a program in functional O'SMALL whose semantics will be discussed now. We focus on the first class-definition.

[4] original theorem for complete lattices

```
class Point(a,b) inheritsFrom Base
   meth x() a
   meth y() b
   meth distFromOrg()  sqrt( sqr(self.x)  +  sqr(self.y) )
   meth closerToOrg(point) self.distFromOrg < point.distFromOrg

class Circle(a,b,c) inheritsFrom Point(a,b)
   meth r() c
   meth distFromOrg() max(0, super.distFromOrg - self.r)

def var p := new Point(2,2)
    var c := new Circle(3,3,2)
in
    .
    .
    .
ni
```

Figure 4: Program in functional O'SMALL

$$Point = \lambda a.\lambda b.\lambda s. \begin{bmatrix} x & \mapsto & a \\ y & \mapsto & b \\ distFromOrg & \mapsto & \sqrt{(s.x)^2 + (s.y)^2} \\ closerToOrg & \mapsto & \lambda p.\ s.distFromOrg < p.distFromOrg \end{bmatrix}$$

Point is the class of points in the plane[5]. An object p of class *Point* is created by:

$$p = \text{FIX}(Point\ 2\ 2) = \begin{bmatrix} x & \mapsto & 2 \\ y & \mapsto & 2 \\ distFromOrg & \mapsto & \sqrt{8} \\ closerToOrg & \mapsto & \lambda p.\ \sqrt{8} < p.distFromOrg \end{bmatrix}$$

3.3 Inheritance and wrappers

On the semantic level, classes are functions of the form $\lambda s.B$ where s is the standardized variable representing self-reference. *Inheritance* is the construction of a new class (the *subclass*) using an existing class (the *superclass*). The formal parameters for self-reference of the superclass and of the subclass "are the same" (this will become clearer after definition 3.5).

[5]to be precise: (Point a_1 a_2) is a class

The additional definitions or modifications in the subclass are modeled by *wrappers*. A wrapper is a function taking two objects as input and returning a new object. The first input object is the parameter for self-reference, like the parameter of self reference of classes. The second input object is the parameter for "super-reference". Wrappers have this special form here, because the language we describe has the pseudo-variables `self` and `super`. If in a hypothetical language, there were further pseudo-variables, wrappers would have more parameters.

The inheritance function of definition 3.5 combines a wrapper and a class such that a new class results. For the definition of the inheritance function, we need further definitions:

Definition 3.2 Let $dom(m) = \{x \mid m(x) \neq \perp\}$. The *left-preferential combination of records* is defined by:

$$(m \oplus n)(x) = \begin{cases} m(x) & \text{if } x \in dom(m) \\ n(x) & \text{if } x \in dom(n) - dom(m) \\ \perp & \text{otherwise} \end{cases}$$

Definition 3.3 Let $*$ be a binary operator on records. The *self-distributing version* of $*$ is denoted by $\boxed{*}$ and is defined by: $C_1 \boxed{*} C_2 = \lambda s.C_1(s) * C_2(s)$

C_1 and C_2 are classes in the above definition.

Definition 3.4 $\triangleright$ combines a function w that maps records to records and a record c such that a new record results: $w \triangleright c = (w\ c) \oplus c$

Definition 3.5 The *inheritance function* $\boxed{\triangleright}$ applies a wrapper W to a class C and returns a class: $W \boxed{\triangleright} C$

Consequently the domain of wrappers is: Wrapper = Object → Object → Object

Let us now take a look at the second class definition of figure 4. Circles are defined as a subclass of the already defined points. The wrapper *CIRCLE* [6] contains the differences between points and circles. The variable p is used like the pseudo-variable super in SMALLTALK or O'SMALL.

$$CIRCLE = \lambda a.\lambda b.\lambda c.\lambda s.\lambda p. \begin{bmatrix} r & \mapsto & c \\ distFromOrg & \mapsto & max(0, p.distFromOrg - s.r) \end{bmatrix}$$

The *Circle*-class is created by:

$$Circle = \lambda a.\lambda b.\lambda c.(CIRCLE\ a\ b\ c) \boxed{\triangleright} (Point\ a\ b)$$

[6] to be precise: (*CIRCLE* a_1 a_2 a_3) is a wrapper)

An object c of class *Circle* is created by:

$$c = \text{FIX}(\mathit{Circle}\ 3\ 3\ 2) = \begin{bmatrix} x & \mapsto & 3 \\ y & \mapsto & 3 \\ r & \mapsto & 2 \\ \mathit{distFromOrg} & \mapsto & \sqrt{18} - 2 \\ \mathit{closerToOrg} & \mapsto & \lambda p.\ \sqrt{18} - 2 < p.\mathit{distFromOrg} \end{bmatrix}$$

Wrappers are central to the semantics of inheritance. In every class declaration, a superclass is named. If nothing is inherited, *Base* is named as superclass. *Base* is the class whose objects are empty records. The semantics of a class definition is a wrapper being wrapped around the superclass, and this results in a new class. As pointed out above, we can get objects by applying the fixed point operator to a class. If in this context classes have no additional parameters, the objects of a class are all equal, because in this section they have no state. In the context of section 4.5, where objects do have state, they can become different as their state changes. The above definitions are also used in [3] for the definition of method systems.

Method systems are a model of object-oriented programming languages. Method systems describe inheritance only. They do *not* describe state, i.e. there are no assignments, no instance variables etc. In [3] a *denotational semantics* for method systems based on wrapper application is given. This denotational semantics is proved to be equivalent to a *method lookup semantics*, the operational semantics of inheritance in SMALLTALK.

4 An object-oriented language with state

In this section we show how to extend the semantics of inheritance without state of section 3 to a semantics of an object-oriented programming language, i.e. we add the state we abstracted from in section 3. The semantics consists of the abstract syntax (section 4.4) and the mapping from the syntactic domains to the semantic domains defined by the semantic clauses (section 4.5). The semantic clauses use auxiliary functions (section A) intended to enhance readability. The semantic functions defined in the following, are all continuous, because they are built by standard constructions (function composition) from continuous functions. Therefore, their smallest fixed points exist in cpo's. However, domain theory has not been the focus of our attention.

4.1 Designing O'SMALL

We designed the programming language O'SMALL for the semantics description of object-oriented programming languages. It is based on SMALL [7], an imperative programming language for semantics description. We chose SMALL and Gordon's notation for direct semantics because it is standard. For the formulation of examples, O'SMALL is provided with a concrete syntax. The description of the concrete syntax is not included in this paper.

Some properties of O'SMALL are listed now: A class definition consists of a clause where the instance variables are declared, and a method clause. Instance variables are not visible outside the object. Method definitions are restricted to the method clause of class definitions. Therefore, methods can only be called via message sending. Instance variables are encapsulated: they are only accessible to methods defined in the class, but not to methods defined in a subclass. Encapsulated instance variables have been postulated in [14,21].

There is *call by reference* for parameters of methods. After an assignment `x:=y`, `x` denotes the same object as `y`. There is thus a correspondence between call by reference and reference semantics of object assignment.

4.2 Extending the semantic domains

In the description of the imperative programming language SMALL, there are three semantic domains for values. For the description of O'SMALL, these domains have to be extended. There are *Storable values* that can be put into locations in the store. *Denotable values* can be bound to an identifier in an environment. *Expressible values* can be the result of expressions. Storable values are so called R-values and files. Files serve for input and output. R-values are the results of evaluating the right hand sides of assignments. We extend R-values by objects. Denotable values are locations in the store, R-values, procedures and functions. We extend the denotable values by classes. In this language expressible values are the same as denotable values.

4.3 The new semantic domains

The newly introduced semantic domains are *Object*, *Class*, and *Wrapper*. Objects, classes, and wrappers were introduced in section 3. Their domains were:

$$\begin{aligned} \text{Object} &= \text{Record} \\ \text{Class} &= \text{Object} \to \text{Object} \\ \text{Wrapper} &= \text{Object} \to \text{Object} \to \text{Object} \end{aligned}$$

These domains have to be modified to include state. *Object* remains unchanged, except that the record values are different now because the state is hidden inside them. The domain of wrappers is completely determined by the domain of classes, because wrappers take fixed points of classes and return classes.

To understand the semantic *domain of classes*, we take a closer look at class declaration and object creation. When a class is declared, the current environment is enriched by the class name. The class name is bound to the result of a wrapper application. In this wrapper application, the wrapper for the current class is applied to the superclass. The store remains unchanged, because the instance variables are not allocated at class-declaration time. An object is created by application of the fixed point operator to the class.

The problem with the introduction of state is as follows. The method environment is recursive, and a fixed point operation has to be applied. The allocation of instance variables must not be recursive – otherwise repeated allocation in the store may be the result. There are two possible choices for the domain of classes. One choice consists of feeding the current store before applying the fixed point operation. This results in

$$\text{Store} \rightarrow [(\text{Object} \rightarrow \text{Object}) \times \text{Store}]$$

as the domain of classes. The store has to appear in the domain and in the codomain, because the instance variables of objects must be allocated. (Object $\rightarrow$ Object) appears in the codomain because the fixed point operation has to be applied. The domain looks simple, but the semantic clauses for object creation and class definition become cluttered. We decided to keep the clutter in these clauses to a minimum, and therefore opt for the second choice: the store is fed after the fixed point operation. For the fixed point operator to be applied to it, the domain of the class must be

$$\alpha \rightarrow \alpha$$

where α is any domain (the domain of classes was *Object* $\rightarrow$ *Object* in section 3). A function is needed for the allocation of all instance variables of the new object. They include the instance variables declared in superclasses. This function has to "know" the current store and has to return it with the instance variables inside it; the store must thus appear in the domain and the codomain of the function. In addition, this function has to return an object. Therefore, the result of the application of the fixed point operator to the class is:

$$\text{Store} \rightarrow [\text{Object} \times \text{Store}]$$

Although we have not been aware of monads when developing this semantics, this type happens to be the type of *state transformers* [18].[7] The type of state transformers is

$$\text{ST}_\alpha = \text{Store} \rightarrow [\alpha \times \text{Store}]$$

Thus, the above type is $\text{ST}_{\text{Object}}$. We will be using this concise form of writing throughout the rest of this paper. $\text{ST}_{\text{Object}}$ is the α we have been looking for: classes are functions on state transformers, and their type is:

$$\text{ST}_{\text{Object}} \rightarrow \text{ST}_{\text{Object}}$$

[7] the terms 'type' and 'domain' are used synonymously here

4.4 Syntax of O'SMALL

Our way of describing semantics goes back to [15,7]. Meta variables ranging over domains are listed on the right hand side.

4.4.1 Syntactic domains

There are primitive syntactic domains

Ide	the domain of identifiers	I
Bas	the domain of basic constants	B
BinOp	the domain of binary operators	O

and compound syntactic domains:

Pro	the domain of programs	P
Exp	the domain of expressions	E
CExp	the domain of compound expressions	C
Var	the domain of variable declarations	V
Cla	the domain of class declarations	K
Meth	the domain of method declarations	M

Method declarations are distinguished from variable and class declarations because methods are declared in classes only. In lieu of commands [7], we have compound expressions. Their syntactic appearance is similar to commands but compound expressions return a value, whence the name.

4.4.2 Syntactic clauses

P ::= K C

K ::= class I_1 inheritsFrom I_2 def V in M | K_1 K_2 | ϵ

C ::= E | I := E | output E | if E then C_1 else C_2 |
while E do C | def V in C | C_1;C_2

E ::= B | true | false | read | I | E.I(E_1,...,E_n) | new E | E_1 O E_2

V ::= var I := E | V_1 V_2 | ϵ

M ::= meth I(I_1,...,I_n) C | M_1 M_2 | ϵ

Class, variable, and method declarations may be empty.

4.5 Semantics of O'SMALL

4.5.1 Semantic domains

Primitive semantic domains:

Unit	the one-point-domain	u
Bool	the domain of booleans	b
Loc	the domain of locations	l
Bv	the domain of basic values	

Unit is the domain needed for the result of compound expressions that do not return a useful value (`while`-expression). The element of *Unit* is denoted by *unit.* Locations are addresses of cells in the store. Compound semantic domains are defined by the following domain equations:

ST_α	$= \mathrm{Store} \rightarrow [\alpha \times \mathrm{Store}]$	state transformers	x
$\mathrm{Record}_{\alpha,\beta}$	$= \alpha \rightarrow [\beta + \{\bot\}]$	records	
Env	$= \mathrm{Record}_{Ide,Dv}$	environments	r
Object	$= \mathrm{Record}_{Ide,Dv}$	objects	o
Dv	$= \mathrm{Loc} + \mathrm{Rv} + \mathrm{Method}_n + \mathrm{Class}$	denotable values	d
Sv	$= \mathrm{File} + \mathrm{Rv}$	storable values	v
Rv	$= \mathrm{Unit} + \mathrm{Bool} + \mathrm{Bv} + \mathrm{Object}$	R-values	e
File	$= \mathrm{Rv}^*$	files	i
Ans	$= \mathrm{File} \times \{\mathrm{error}, \mathrm{stop}\}$	program answers	a
Store	$= \mathrm{Record}_{Loc,Sv}$	stores	s
Method_n	$= \mathrm{Dv}^n \rightarrow \mathrm{ST}_{\mathrm{Dv}}$	method values	m
Class	$= \mathrm{ST}_{\mathrm{Object}} \rightarrow \mathrm{ST}_{\mathrm{Object}}$	class values	c
Wrapper	$= \mathrm{ST}_{\mathrm{Object}} \rightarrow \mathrm{Class}$	wrapper values	w

Domains Method_n are needed for each $n \in \mathbb{N}_0$. The type of state transformers appears with various parameter types in the remainder of this paper.

4.5.2 Semantic clauses

The following semantic functions are primitive:

$\mathsf{B} \;:\; \text{Bas} \rightarrow \text{Bv}$

$\mathsf{O} \;:\; \text{BinOp} \rightarrow \text{Rv} \rightarrow \text{Rv} \rightarrow \text{ST}_{\text{Dv}}$

B takes syntactic basic constants and returns semantic basic values. O takes a syntactic binary operator (e.g. +), two R-values, and a store; it returns the result of the binary operation and leaves the store unchanged. The remaining semantic functions will be defined by clauses and have the following types:

$\mathsf{P} \;:\; \text{Pro} \rightarrow \text{File} \rightarrow \text{Ans}$

$\mathsf{R}, \mathsf{E} \;:\; \text{Exp} \rightarrow \text{Env} \rightarrow \text{ST}_{\text{Dv}}$

$\mathsf{C} \;:\; \text{CExp} \rightarrow \text{Env} \rightarrow \text{ST}_{\text{Dv}}$

$\mathsf{V} \;:\; \text{Var} \rightarrow \text{Env} \rightarrow \text{ST}_{\text{Env}}$

$\mathsf{K} \;:\; \text{Cla} \rightarrow \text{Env} \rightarrow \text{ST}_{\text{Env}}$

$\mathsf{M} \;:\; \text{Meth} \rightarrow \text{Env} \rightarrow \text{Env}$

Differing from [7], we use record notation for environments and stores. Alternatives are denoted in braces. *err*, *inp* and *out* are locations and not identifiers in the following clause. Note that the dot of λ-abstractions is the operator with the least precedence. An abstracted variable is bound until the end of the clause. This is only in a few cases indicated by extra parentheses. For the definition of auxiliary functions in the following clauses, refer to section A.

$\mathsf{P}[\![\text{K C}]\!] \; \text{i} = \text{extractans} \; \text{s}_{final}$

where

$$\text{extractans} = \lambda\text{s}.(\text{s out}, \begin{Bmatrix} \text{error, if (s err)} \\ \text{stop , otherwise} \end{Bmatrix})$$

$$(\text{r}_{class}, \_) = \mathsf{K}[\![\text{K}]\!] \; \text{r}_{initial} \; \text{s}_{initial}$$

$$(\_, \text{s}_{final}) = \mathsf{C}[\![\text{C}]\!] \; \text{r}_{class} \; \text{s}_{initial}$$

$$\text{r}_{initial} = \left[\text{Base} \mapsto \lambda\text{o}.\lambda\text{s}.\text{result} \; [] \right]$$

$$\text{s}_{initial} = \begin{bmatrix} \text{err} & \mapsto & \text{false} \\ \text{inp} & \mapsto & \text{i} \\ \text{out} & \mapsto & \epsilon \end{bmatrix}$$

An answer from a program is gained by running it with an input. The store is initialized with the error flag set to *false*, the input, and an empty output. The initial environment contains the "empty" class *Base*. The initial environment is enriched by the declared classes. Then the compound expression is evaluated. Objects of the base class are records where every label is mapped to $\perp$. In addition to the output, an error flag shows if the program has come to a normal end (*stop*) or if it stopped with an error (*error*).

$$\mathsf{R}[\![\mathrm{E}]\!]\ \mathrm{r} \ = \mathsf{E}[\![\mathrm{E}]\!]\ \mathrm{r} \star \mathrm{deref} \star \mathrm{Rv?}$$

The semantic function R produces R-values.

$$\mathsf{E}[\![\mathrm{B}]\!]\ \mathrm{r} = \mathrm{result}(\mathsf{B}[\![\mathrm{B}]\!])$$

$$\mathsf{E}[\![\mathrm{true}]\!]\ \mathrm{r} = \mathrm{result\ true}$$

$$\mathsf{E}[\![\mathrm{false}]\!]\ \mathrm{r} = \mathrm{result\ false}$$

$$\mathsf{E}[\![\mathrm{read}]\!]\ \mathrm{r} = \mathrm{cont\ inp} \star \lambda \mathrm{i}.\lambda \mathrm{s}. \left\{ \begin{array}{ll} \mathrm{seterr\ s} & \mathrm{, if\ i} = \epsilon \\ (\mathrm{hd\ i}, [\mathrm{inp} \mapsto \mathrm{tl\ i}] \oplus \mathrm{s}), & \mathrm{otherwise} \end{array} \right\}$$

$$\mathsf{E}[\![\mathrm{I}]\!]\ \mathrm{r} = \mathrm{result\ (r\ I)} \star \mathrm{Dv?}$$

$$\mathsf{E}[\![\mathrm{E.I(E_1,\ldots,E_n)}]\!]\ \mathrm{r} = \mathsf{R}[\![\mathrm{E}]\!]\ \mathrm{r} \star \mathrm{Object?} \star \lambda \mathrm{o.(result(o\ I)}\star\mathrm{Method?}\star$$
$$\lambda \mathrm{m}.\mathsf{R}[\![\mathrm{E_1}]\!]\ \mathrm{r}\star\lambda \mathrm{d_1}.\ \ldots \mathsf{R}[\![\mathrm{E}_n]\!]\ \mathrm{r}\star\lambda \mathrm{d}_n.\mathrm{m(d_1,\ldots,d}_n))$$

The last clause is for message sending, which is record field selection. The first expression is evaluated as an R-value. The result of this evaluation must be an object. The resulting record *o* is applied to the message selector *I*. This should result in a method that is then applied to the parameters.

$$\mathsf{E}[\![\mathrm{new\ E}]\!]\ \mathrm{r} \ = \mathsf{E}[\![\mathrm{E}]\!]\ \mathrm{r} \star \mathrm{Class?} \star \lambda \mathrm{c}.\lambda \mathrm{s}.(\mathrm{F{\scriptsize IX}\ c})\mathrm{s}$$

The evaluation of *E* yields a class. The fixed point operator FIX is applied to this class. The state transformer resulting from the application of FIX, is applied to the current store *s*.

$$\mathsf{E}\ [\![\mathrm{E_1\ O\ E_2}]\!]\ \mathrm{r} = \mathsf{R}[\![\mathrm{E_1}]\!]\ \mathrm{r} \star \lambda \mathrm{e_1}.\mathsf{R}[\![\mathrm{E_2}]\!]\ \mathrm{r} \star \lambda \mathrm{e_2}.\mathsf{O}[\![\mathrm{O}]\!]\ (\mathrm{e_1, e_2})$$

$$\mathsf{C}[\![\mathrm{E}]\!]\ \mathrm{r} = \mathsf{E}[\![\mathrm{E}]\!]\ \mathrm{r}$$

$$\mathsf{C}[\![\mathrm{I := E}]\!]\ \mathrm{r} = \mathsf{E}[\![\mathrm{I}]\!]\ \mathrm{r} \star \mathrm{Loc?} \star \lambda \mathrm{l}.\ \mathsf{R}[\![\mathrm{E}]\!]\ \mathrm{r} \star (\mathrm{update\ l})$$

$$\mathsf{C}[\![\mathrm{output\ E}]\!]\ \mathrm{r} = \mathsf{R}[\![\mathrm{E}]\!]\ \mathrm{r} \star \lambda \mathrm{e}.\lambda \mathrm{s}.(\mathrm{unit}, [\mathrm{out} \mapsto \mathrm{append(s\ out,e)}] \oplus \mathrm{s})$$

$$\mathsf{C}[\![\mathrm{if\ E\ then\ C_1\ else\ C_2}]\!]\ \mathrm{r} = \mathsf{R}[\![\mathrm{E}]\!]\ \mathrm{r} \star \mathrm{Bool?} \star \mathrm{cond}(\mathsf{C}[\![\mathrm{C_1}]\!]\ \mathrm{r}, \mathsf{C}[\![\mathrm{C_2}]\!]\ \mathrm{r})$$

$$\mathsf{C}[\![\mathrm{while\ E\ do\ C}]\!]\ \mathrm{r} = \mathsf{R}[\![\mathrm{E}]\!]\ \mathrm{r} \star \mathrm{Bool?} \star$$
$$\mathrm{cond}(\mathsf{C}[\![\mathrm{C}]\!]\ \mathrm{r} \star \lambda \mathrm{e}.\mathsf{C}[\![\mathrm{while\ E\ do\ C}]\!]\ \mathrm{r}, \mathrm{result\ unit})$$

$$\mathsf{C}[\![\mathrm{def\ V\ in\ C\ end}]\!]\ \mathrm{r} = \mathsf{V}[\![\mathrm{V}]\!]\ \mathrm{r} \star \lambda \mathrm{r'}.\mathsf{C}[\![\mathrm{C}]\!]\ (\mathrm{r'}\oplus\mathrm{r})$$

$$\mathsf{C}[\![\mathrm{C_1; C_2}]\!]\ \mathrm{r} = \mathsf{C}[\![\mathrm{C_1}]\!]\ \mathrm{r} \star \lambda \mathrm{e}.\mathsf{C}[\![\mathrm{C_2}]\!]\ \mathrm{r}$$

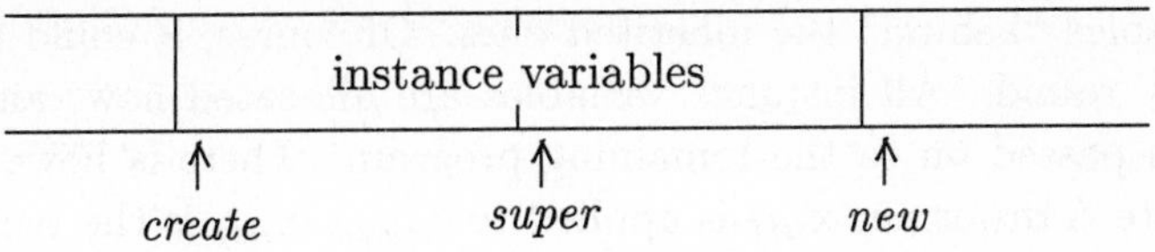

Figure 5: The store during object creation

The result of assignment, output-term, and while-loop is *unit*. In a sequence of expressions, the transmitted value is discarded. This practice has been adopted from ML [11].

$$\mathsf{K}[\![\text{class } I_1 \text{ inheritsFrom } I_2 \text{ def } V \text{ in } M]\!]\ r$$
$$= E[\![I_2]\!]\ r \ \star\ \text{Class?}\ \star\ \lambda c.\text{result}[I_1 \mapsto w\ \boxed{\triangleright}\ c]$$

where

$$w = \lambda x_{self}.\lambda x_{super}.\lambda s_{create}.\ (\mathsf{M}[\![M]\!]\ (\begin{bmatrix} \text{self} & \mapsto & r_{self} \\ \text{super} & \mapsto & r_{super} \end{bmatrix} \oplus r_{local} \oplus r)\ ,\ s_{new})$$

where

$$(r_{super}, s_{super}) = x_{super}\ s_{create}$$
$$(r_{local}, s_{new}) = \mathsf{V}[\![V]\!]\ r\ s_{super}$$
$$(r_{self}, \_) = x_{self}\ s_{create}$$

Classes have type $ST_{\text{Object}} \rightarrow ST_{\text{Object}}$ and wrappers $ST_{\text{Object}} \rightarrow ST_{\text{Object}} \rightarrow ST_{\text{Object}}$.[8] The result of the evaluation of a class declaration is the binding of a class to the class name. The store remains unchanged when a class is declared. The wrapper w takes a state transformer for `self`, a state transformer for `super`, and a store as parameters. The store parameter is fed at object creation time, x_{self} at fixed point operation time, and x_{super} at wrapper application time. The wrapper evaluates the method definitions in an environment being determined at declaration time – except that the locations for the instance variables have to be determined at object creation time. The local environment is only visible in the class itself and not in any subclass. Thus, we have encapsulated instance variables.

Let us consider what happens at object creation time during the evaluation of the inner where-clause above. Figure 5 shows the store with arrows pointing at the first free cell of the store with the respective index. x_{super} is applied to the store at object creation time. This results in the method environment of the superclass; but also the part of the instance variables defined in the superclass are allocated, and the first free cell of the store is indicated by *super* in the figure. The new instance variables for the current class are declared in *V*. *V* has to be evaluated in s_{super} to put the new

[8] for detailed inspection of this clause, refer also to section A

instance variables "behind" the inherited ones. Of course, it could have been done the other way round. All instance variables are allocated now, and the resulting store (s_{new}) is passed on to the remaining program. There is however a third line where the state transformer x_{self} is applied to s_{create}. x_{self} is the recursive part and r_{self} is the resulting recursive environment. x_{self} has to be applied to s_{create} because its instance variables are the ones that have just been allocated. The careful reader may have noticed that the store resulting from the last state transformation is not needed. This is indicated by an underscore. The reason for this is, that the instance variables of the current class have been allocated already. The method environment is recursive, the instance variable environment is not.

$$\mathsf{K}[\![\mathrm{K}_1\ \mathrm{K}_2]\!]\ \mathrm{r} = \mathsf{K}[\![\mathrm{K}_1]\!]\ \mathrm{r}\ \star\ \lambda \mathrm{r'}.\ \mathrm{r'}\oplus(\mathsf{K}[\![\mathrm{K}_2]\!]\ (\mathrm{r'}\oplus\mathrm{r}))$$

$$\mathsf{K}[\![\epsilon]\!]\ \mathrm{r} = \mathrm{result}\ [\,]$$

$$\begin{array}{lcl}
\mathsf{V}[\![\mathrm{var\ I} := \mathrm{E}]\!]\ \mathrm{r} & = & \mathsf{R}[\![\mathrm{E}]\!]\ \mathrm{r}\ \star\ \lambda \mathrm{d}.\ \mathrm{new}\star\lambda \mathrm{l}.\lambda \mathrm{s}.\ ([\mathrm{I}\mapsto \mathrm{l}],\ [\mathrm{l}\mapsto \mathrm{d}]\oplus \mathrm{s}) \\
\mathsf{V}[\![\mathrm{V}_1\ \mathrm{V}_2]\!]\ \mathrm{r} & = & \mathsf{V}[\![\mathrm{V}_1]\!]\ \mathrm{r}\ \star\ \lambda \mathrm{r'}.\ \mathrm{r'}\oplus(\mathsf{V}[\![\mathrm{V}_2]\!]\ (\mathrm{r'}\oplus\mathrm{r})) \\
\mathsf{V}[\![\epsilon]\!]\ \mathrm{r} & = & \mathrm{result}\ [\,] \\
\mathsf{M}[\![\mathrm{meth\ I}(\mathrm{I}_1,\ldots,\mathrm{I}_n)\ \mathrm{C}]\!]\ \mathrm{r} & = & \left[\ \mathrm{I}\ \mapsto\ \ \lambda \mathrm{d}_1.\ \ldots.\lambda \mathrm{d}_n.\ \mathsf{C}[\![\mathrm{C}]\!]\left(\begin{bmatrix} \mathrm{I}_1 & \mapsto & \mathrm{d}_1 \\ & \vdots & \\ \mathrm{I}_n & \mapsto & \mathrm{d}_n \end{bmatrix} \oplus \mathrm{r}\right)\ \right] \\
\mathsf{M}[\![\mathrm{M}_1\ \mathrm{M}_2]\!]\ \mathrm{r} & = & (\mathsf{M}[\![\mathrm{M}_2]\!]\ \mathrm{r})\ \oplus\ (\mathsf{M}[\![\mathrm{M}_1]\!]\ \mathrm{r}) \\
\mathsf{M}[\![\epsilon]\!]\ \mathrm{r} & = & [\,]
\end{array}$$

Method definitions are not recursive. Recursion and the calling of other methods is possible by sending messages to `self`.

4.6 The current class

In SMALLTALK it is possible to create a new instance of a class `A` inside class `A`, i.e. inside methods defined in class `A`, by the expression `self class new`. Let `self class new` occur in the definition of the method `m` defined in class `A`. Let `B` be a subclass of `A` where `m` is inherited without being redefined. Then the expression `self class new`, sent to an object of class `B`, will return an object of class `B`. Cook [4] needs an additional level of inheritance to describe the possibilities of a SMALLTALK-expression like `self class new`, where the class constructor (i.e. the class name) is referred to "in a relative way".

For the "relative" reference to the class constructor inside the class, we extend O'SMALL by the pseudo variable `current`. `current` denotes the class of the receiver of a message. Thus, `current new` in O'SMALL has the same effect as `self class`

new in SMALLTALK. Note that in O'SMALL **new** is no message; it has to be defined in the semantics. An additional level of inheritance could be easily introduced into the semantics. But on the contrary of what might be expected, an additional level of inheritance is superfluous in O'SMALL. It is enough to bind *current* to $\lambda x.x_{self}$. Here, the abstracted variable x is just needed to get the right type of a class. x_{self} is the state transformer of the class, and can be used to allocate new instance variables. The class definition clause is thus changed to:

$$\mathsf{K}[\![\mathrm{I}_1 \text{ inheritsFrom } \mathrm{I}_2 \text{ def V in M}]\!]\ \mathrm{r}$$
$$= \mathsf{E}[\![\mathrm{I}_2]\!]\ \mathrm{r}\ \star\ \mathrm{Class?}\ \star\ \lambda \mathrm{c.result}[\mathrm{I}_1 \mapsto \mathrm{w} \boxed{\triangleright} \mathrm{c}]$$

where

$$\mathrm{w} = \lambda \mathrm{x}_{self}.\lambda \mathrm{x}_{super}.\lambda \mathrm{s}_{create}.\ (\mathsf{M}[\![\mathrm{M}]\!]\ (\begin{bmatrix} \mathrm{self} & \mapsto & \mathrm{r}_{self} \\ \mathrm{current} & \mapsto & \lambda \mathrm{x.x}_{self} \\ \mathrm{super} & \mapsto & \mathrm{r}_{super} \end{bmatrix} \oplus \mathrm{r}_{local} \oplus \mathrm{r})\ ,\ \mathrm{s}_{new})$$

where

$$(\mathrm{r}_{super}, \mathrm{s}_{super}) = \mathrm{x}_{super}\ \mathrm{s}_{create}$$
$$(\mathrm{r}_{local}, \mathrm{s}_{new}) = \mathsf{V}[\![\mathrm{V}]\!]\ \mathrm{r}\ \mathrm{s}_{super}$$
$$(\mathrm{r}_{self}, \_) = \mathrm{x}_{self}\ \mathrm{s}_{create}$$

5 Conclusion

We have started with a semantics of inheritance as presented in [3]. This semantics does not include state, and the question if it is applicable to an object-oriented programming language with state remained open in [4]. With our denotational semantics for O'SMALL, we hope to have answered this question in the affirmative. For the description of objects with state, the domains of classes and wrappers had to be adjusted accordingly. The introduction of state was possible without making the central semantic clauses of class declaration and object creation complicated, at least at the surface; the complications are limited to the local definitions of the class-declaration clause. The creation of objects of the current class is possible without an extra level of inheritance. There exists an executable version of this semantics in Miranda [17].

One direction of future research with our semantics, is the discussion of different known concepts of object-oriented programming languages (multiple inheritance, classes as objects, etc.). Another direction is the development of an efficient and provably correct implementation.

Acknowledgements

Thanks to Reinhold Heckmann, Fritz Müller, and Reinhard Wilhelm for many valuable contributions and discussions, to Andreas Gündel for constructively criticising O'SMALL, and to Carl Gunter and Mario Wolczko for commenting on earlier drafts.

References

[1] H. Abelson, G. J. Sussman, and J. Sussman. *Structure and Interpretation of Computer Programs.* MIT Press, 1985.

[2] H. P. Barendregt. *The Lambda Calculus – Its Syntax and Semantics.* Volume 103 of *Studies in Logic and The Foundations of Mathematics*, Noth-Holland, revised 1984 edition, 1981.

[3] W. Cook and J. Palsberg. A denotational semantics of inheritance and its correctness. In *Object-Oriented Programming Systems, Languages and Applications*, pages 433–444, ACM, Oct. 1989.

[4] W. R. Cook. *A Denotational Semantics of Inheritance.* Technical Report CS-89-33, Brown University, Dept. of Computer Science, Providence, Rhode Island 02912, May 1989.

[5] M. Felleisen. On the expressive power of programming languages. *Lecture Notes in Computer Science*, 432:134–151, 1990. European Symposium on Programming.

[6] A. Goldberg and D. Robson. *Smalltalk-80: the Language.* Addison-Wesley, 1989.

[7] M. Gordon. *The Denotational Description of Programming Languages: An Introduction.* Springer-Verlag, New York/Heidelberg/Berlin, 1979.

[8] A. Hense. *The Denotational Semantics of an Object Oriented Programming Language.* Technical Report A 01/90, Universität des Saarlandes, Fachbereich 14, Jan. 1990.

[9] J. Hindley and J. Seldin. *Introduction to Combinators and λ-Calculus.* Volume 1 of *London Mathematical Society Student Texts*, Cambridge University Press, 1986.

[10] S. Kamin. Inheritance in Smalltalk-80. In *Symposium on Principles of Programming Languages*, pages 80–87, ACM, Jan. 1988.

[11] R. Milner. A proposal for standard ML. In *Symposium on Lisp and Functional Programming*, pages 184–197, ACM, Austin Texas, 1984.

[12] U. S. Reddy. Objects as closures: abstract semantics of object-oriented languages. In *Symposium on Lisp and Functional Programming*, pages 289–297, ACM, 1988.

[13] D. Scott. Data types as lattices. *SIAM J. Comput.*, 5:522–587, 1976.

[14] A. Snyder. Encapsulation and inheritance in object-oriented programming languages. In *Object-Oriented Programming Systems, Languages and Applications*, pages 38–45, ACM, Sep. 1986.

[15] J. E. Stoy. *Denotational Semantics: The Scott-Strachey Approach to Programming Language Theory.* MIT press, 1977.

[16] A. Tarski. A lattice-theoretical fixed point theorem and its applications. *Pacific Journal of Mathematics*, 5:285–309, 1955.

[17] D. Turner. Miranda: a non-strict functional language with polymorphic types. *Lecture Notes in Computer Science*, 201:1–16, 1985. Functional Programming Languages and Computer Architecture.

[18] P. Wadler. Comprehending monads. In *Symposium on Lisp and Functional Programming*, pages 61–78, ACM, 1990.

[19] P. Wegner. The object-oriented classification paradigm. In B. Shriver and P. Wegner, editors, *Research Directions in Object Oriented Programming*, pages 479–560, MIT Press, 1987.

[20] P. Wegner and S. Zdonik. Inheritance as an incremental modification mechanism or what like is and isn't like. *Lecture Notes in Computer Science*, 322:55–77, Aug. 1988. European Conference on Object-Oriented Programming.

[21] M. Wolczko. Encapsulation, delegation and inheritance in object-oriented languages. 1990. (submitted for publication).

[22] M. Wolczko. Semantics of Smalltalk-80. *Lecture Notes in Computer Science*, 276:108–120, 1987. European Conference on Object-Oriented Programming.

A Auxiliary functions

We need a generic function $\star$ for the composition of commands and declarations. This function stops the execution of the program when an error occurs. Let there be two functions f and g with the following types:

$$f : \left\langle \begin{array}{c} \mathit{Store} \\ D_1 \to \mathit{Store} \end{array} \right\rangle \to [D_2 \times \mathit{Store}], \quad g : D_2 \to \mathit{Store} \to [D_3 \times \mathit{Store}]$$

The lines inside the angular delimiters represent alternatives. The alternatives in the following text are not free but depend on the choices of the alternatives above: if in the above delimiters one chooses the upper alternative, one must choose the upper alternative below (and vice versa). The composition of f and g has type

$$f \star g : \left\langle \begin{array}{c} Store \\ D_1 \rightarrow Store \end{array} \right\rangle \rightarrow [D_3 \times Store]$$

and is defined by

$$f \star g = \left\langle \begin{array}{c} \lambda s_1 \\ \lambda d_1.\lambda s_1 \end{array} \right\rangle . \left\{ \begin{array}{l} (\bot, s_2),\text{ if } s_2\ err \\ g\ d_2\ s_2,\text{ otherwise} \end{array} \right. \quad \text{where} \quad (d_2, s_2) = \left\langle \begin{array}{c} f s_1 \\ f d_1 s_1 \end{array} \right\rangle$$

$\star$ is left associative. The definition of $\triangleright$ in section 3 is based on the left-preferential combination of records (denoted by $\oplus$). This symbol is also overloaded in the semantic equations: if the arguments of $\oplus$ are of the domain *Fixed* then $\oplus$ stands for:

$$x_1 \oplus x_2 \ = \ \lambda s.(r_1 \oplus_{lpr} r_2, s') \ where \ (r_1, s') = x_1 s, \ (r_2, \_) = x_2 s$$

where $\oplus_{lpr}$ stands for the operation on records that is defined in definition 3.2. This is the only change of the inheritance function (definition 3.5). Here are further auxiliary functions. Let D be any semantic domain:

cond : [D × D] → Bool → D .... Alternative

$\text{cond}(d_1, d_2) = \lambda\text{b}. \left\{ \begin{array}{l} d_1,\text{ if b} \\ d_2,\text{ otherwise} \end{array} \right.$

cnt : Loc → $\text{ST}_{[\text{Sv} + \{\bot\}]}$ .... Contents of a location

cnt = λl.λs.(s l, s)

cont : Dv → ST_{Sv} .... Contents of a location with domain checking

cont = Loc? $\star$ cnt $\star$ Sv?

D? : D' → $\text{ST}_{\text{D'}}$, with D ⊆ D' .... Domain checking

$\text{D?} = \lambda\text{d}. \left\{ \begin{array}{l} \text{result d, if (isD d)} \\ \text{seterr , otherwise} \end{array} \right.$

deref : Dv → ST_{Dv} .... Dereferencing

$\text{deref} = \lambda\text{d}. \left\{ \begin{array}{l} \text{cont d , if (isLoc d)} \\ \text{result d, otherwise} \end{array} \right.$

new : ST_{Loc} .... Getting a new location in the store

new s = (l,s) or = ($\bot$, [err ↦ true] $\oplus$ s)

If new s = (l,s) then s l = $\bot$ is guaranteed.

result : D → ST_{D} .... Side effect free evaluation

result d = λs.(d, s)

seterr : ST_{D} .... Setting the error flag

seterr = λs.($\bot$, [err ↦ true] $\oplus$ s)

update : Loc → Dv → ST_{Dv} .... Updating of a location

update l = Sv? $\star$ λd.λs.(unit, [l ↦ d] $\oplus$ s)

Sharing Actions and Attributes in Modal Action Logic

Mark Ryan, José Fiadeiro and Tom Maibaum
Department of Computing, Imperial College, London SW7 2BZ, Great Britain
mdr@doc.ic.ac.uk

Abstract

Distributed systems may be specified in Structured Modal Action Logic by decomposing them into *agents* which interact by sharing *attributes* (memory) as well as *actions*.

In the formalism we describe, specification texts denote theories, and theories denote the set of semantic structures which satisfy them. The semantic structures are Kripke models, as is usual for modal logic. The "possible worlds" in a Kripke model are the states of the agent, and there is a separate relation on the set of states for each action term.

Agents potentially share actions as well as attributes in a way controlled by locality annotations in the specification texts. These become locality axioms in the logical theories the texts denote. These locality axioms provide a refined way of circumscribing the effects of actions.

Safety and liveness conditions are expressed (implicitly) by deontic axioms, which impose obligations and deny permissions on actions. We show that "deontic defaults" exist so that the specifier need not explicitly grant permissions or avoid obligations in situations where normative behaviour is not an issue.

1 Introduction

The idea of using Modal Action Logic for specifying distributed systems is well-established [3, 4, 5]. Additionally the frame problem can be overcome by specifying *structure* on specifications—the system is split into *agents* (or objects, or components) which interact by sharing actions. This is the approach taken by Fiadeiro & Maibaum [1], and fits well with object-oriented specification: an object has a private memory and public procedures for its manipulation.

But often, as we discuss below, it is more natural to share *attributes* between agents than to share *actions*. In this paper we give a logical semantics to a pseudo-language in which both attribute and action sharing are allowed. The logic is called Structured Modal Action Logic (Structured MAL).

The agent is the unit of structure. An agent is any component of the system being described which has an independent existence; it may be passive or active. Agents are composable. A collection of agents can be viewed as a single agent in a precise way to be described later. The single agent incorporates the behaviours of the individual agents. As already stated, agents can interact by sharing attributes or by sharing actions. An *attribute* is part of the state of the system—a predicate or function which varies not only with its arguments but also with the state of the agent to which it belongs. In general agents should be as self-contained as possible; the actions of an agent should only update attributes of that agent, and vice versa. But clearly some interaction between agents is necessary. The interaction is precisely controlled by means of *locality axioms*. For each agent, the specifier must declare which of the actions and attributes are local and which are sharable with other agents. A sharable action is one which can update the attributes of a superagent (one which incorporates it) — these attributes may come from other agents which the superagent incorporates. Similarly, a sharable attribute is one which can be updated by the action of a superagent.

Throughout this paper we will make use of the **lift-system** example. The atomic agents which might make up the specification include:

- **button**, with the action 'press' and the attribute 'lit' (buttons have lights on them)
- **door**, with the actions 'open' and 'close' and the attribute 'posn' (their position).
- **person**, with, among others, the action 'press-button'.

Of course there are other agents, but we will concentrate on these three for the purpose of motivating the two types of interaction which Structured MAL adopts. These agents make up the lift specification:

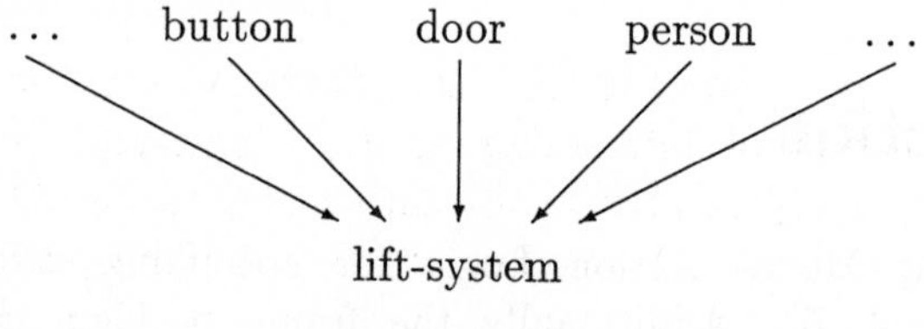

When the person selects a button and presses it, this is really an in action which both the person and the button participate. True, the person initiates the action; the button participates in it in a purely passive way. But since the button moves in and out, and could do so independently of the person if incorporated in a specification in a different way, the natural choice is to specify this interaction by joint participation of actions, that is, action sharing. We do this by having a press action in both the agents **person** and **button** say person.press and door.press, and then including the axiom person.press = door.press in the **lift-system**.

Now consider what happens when the lift arrives at a floor and the door opens. The light of the appropriate button is extinguished. We could specify that both the door and the button jointly participate in an action which opens the door and extinguishes the light. But it makes more sense to say that the door's opening extinguishes the light — the button has nothing to do with it. The action 'open' of the agent **door** directly updates the attribute 'lit' of **button**. This is attribute sharing.

Both these examples are fairly marginal. One could make a case for specifying the first one as an example of attribute sharing and the second one as an example of action sharing. The specifier is free to do this if he or she wishes. In Structured MAL, both types of sharing can be used freely.

Each agent specification has a collection of actions and attributes — the collection is known as its *signature*. In addition, the specification language also says which actions and attributes are *local* and which are *sharable*. If an action is declared as local to an agent, an axiom is generated which states that the action can only update the attributes of that agent. Similarly, a local attribute comes with an axiom which says that it can only be changed by an action belonging to the agent in which it is defined. These *locality axioms* are examined in Section 5.

Locality axioms are not an explicit part of the specification in the way that other axioms are. They are part of the theory presentations which the specifications denote. What we have is a three tiered system which looks like this:

specification texts	(a text in the specification language)
↓	
specifications	(theory presentations connected together by morphisms)
↓	
agents	(models of the theories)

A specification text is a text in the specification language. It specifies the behaviour of a collection of interacting agents. This text denotes a family of theory presentations, one presentation for each agent specified, connected together by *morphisms*. A model of a theory presentation is an agent which satisfies the specification.

The best way to think of this is to bear in mind that the level of primary interest is the middle level. That level consists of theories connected by morphisms. The level above, the specification language level, says how this is to work by using high level constructs like inheritance, clientship and parameterisation. At the middle level there may be more agent specifications (theories) than in the specification text, because many of them will be by-products of the high-level constructs used. At the bottom level, models of the theories correspond to agents which meet the specifications.

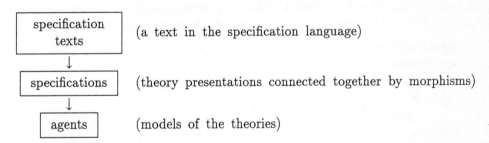

The term *morphism* comes from category theory. Indeed, theory presentations and their morphisms form a category in which, following general categorical principles [2], colimits explain how to build a complex system from a diagram that expresses how its components are interconnected. See [1] for the application of this principle to the specification of object-oriented systems. As far as we are concerned here, a morphism is simply a map with certain properties between theory presentations with which we can specify agent interaction. A precise definition comes later. The agent diagram above is an example of a morphism diagram.

2 Agents and morphisms

Agents are the units of structure. Each agent is an encapsulation of behaviour — it consists of a state (the values of its attributes) which is changed as it performs actions. An action or an attribute may be entirely local to an agent, or it may be shared with other agents. If an action is local to an agent **X**, it can only change the values of the attributes of **X**. Of course it need not change them all, but it cannot affect any others. If an attribute is local to **X**, it can only be changed by the actions of **X**. We will call these two types of locality *action locality* and *attribute locality*, respectively.

The lift example starts with the 'atomic' agents **button** and **door**. Buttons have lights and illuminate when pressed. They are extinguished by actions which are external to them (the opening of the door). So **button** looks like this:

> **agent** button
> **attributes**
> s lit : bool;
> **actions**
> ℓ press;
> **axioms**
> [press]lit;
> **end**

This is the text which the specifier writes in the specification language. The ℓ and s annotations mean local and sharable, respectively. The signature of the theory presentation which this denotes consists of the attribute lit and the action press. The theory presentation has two axioms; one comes from the specification text, and says simply that lit is true after press has taken place[1]. The other is the locality axiom for the local action press, and says that press can only affect the attributes of the agent **button**. How this is done will be revealed in section 5. The attribute 'lit' is sharable, because it will have to be updated by actions taking place in other agents (namely, the opening of the door).

[1]In fact, the light only comes on if the lift is at a floor *other than* the one being requested. An elegant way of handling this fact by means of *defaults* is described in [6].

The attribute lit has values of sort boolean. Atomic formulas are equalities of values in a sort, often of the form 'attribute = value'. If the sort concerned is boolean, we glibly let attribute values stand as formulas in the obvious way. Thus '[press]lit' is an abbreviation for '[press](lit = true)'.

Doors also have one attribute, their position, and two actions, open and close.

agent door
attributes
  ℓ posn : (op, cl);
actions
  s open;
  ℓ close;
axioms
  [open](posn = op)
  [close](posn = cl)
end

The attribute 'posn' has the enumerated sort (op, cl). Everything is local except the action open, which has to be sharable to be able to extinguish the lights.

Inside each lift there is a panel of lift buttons. For an n-floor system, the agent **lift-buttons** is made of n copies of **button**. At the specification language level, its specification looks like this:

agent lift-buttons
includes button **via** 1;
includes button **via** 2;
⋮
includes button **via** n;
end

The clause '**includes** button **via** 1' means that at the theory presentation level there is a morphism, named 1, from **button** to **lift-buttons**. The morphism maps the action symbol press in **button** to the action symbol 1.press in **lift-buttons**. The clause '**includes** subagent **via** morphism-name' implicitly declares all signature symbols and axioms of subagent in the agent being specified, but renaming the signature symbols by prefixing them by the morphism name. At the theory presentation level, the theory which **lift-buttons** denotes has n sharable attributes 1.lit, 2.lit, ..., n.lit and n local actions 1.press, ..., n.press, one 'lit' attribute and one 'press' action for each button.

We need to describe one more agent before we can describe a **lift**: it is the 'agent' **lift-position**.

agent lift-position
attributes
  ℓ floor : 1..n
actions
  ℓ up;
  ℓ down;
axioms
  $(\text{floor} = f) \wedge (f < n) \rightarrow [\text{up}](\text{floor} = f + 1)$
  $(\text{floor} = f) \wedge (f > 1) \rightarrow [\text{down}](\text{floor} = f - 1)$
  $\text{per(up)} \rightarrow \text{floor} < n$
  $\text{per(down)} \rightarrow \text{floor} > 1$
end

The axioms containing the formulas per(up) and per(down) are deontic axioms; they express the fact that the lift is only *permitted* to move up or down when the floor variable is within the right bounds. There are also deontic axioms which express *obligations.* These deontic axioms are described in section 3.

The reader may be surprised that **lift-position** deserves the status of an agent, but there is an advantage of having it as a separate agent rather than just including its attributes and actions in the specification of **lift**, which is that the local actions up and down are then constrained to being able to update the value of floor only. Remember that an action local to an agent gets a locality axiom in the theory presentation which says that it can only affect the attributes of that agent. The smaller the agent, the more powerful the locality axiom. Indeed, a principle of this approach, the "structuring principle", is that all structuring should be done by judicious choice of agents, and hence of locality constraints. The specifier need never get involved in including explicit locality axioms in specifications; they should all be implied by making actions and attributes local or sharable.

The lift itself consists of the agents **lift-buttons**, **door** and **lift-position**:

agent lift
includes door **via** door;
includes lift-buttons
  localising 1.lit,...,n.lit ;
includes lift-position;
axioms
  $(\text{floor} = 1) \rightarrow [\text{open}]\neg 1.\text{lit};$
  $\vdots$
  $(\text{floor} = n) \rightarrow [\text{open}]\neg n.\text{lit};$
  $\text{per(up)} \vee \text{per(down)} \rightarrow \text{door.posn=cl};$
end

The **localising** clause makes the attributes i.lit local in the agent lift. (Without this clause, they would retain the sharable status with which they were defined in the agent **button**.) This has the effect of adding a locality axiom in **lift**, in the way described later.

The theory presentation denoted by this specification text has all the signature elements and the axioms of its constituents. Since no renaming of the actions and attributes is necessary, the morphisms are labelled 'id' (for identity). **lift** also has an additional axiom, which we have referred to previously: $(\text{floor} = f) \rightarrow [\text{open}]\neg f.\text{lit}$. It says that when the door opens, the light corresponding to the floor at which the door has opened switches off. Here is the morphism diagram at the theory presentation level:

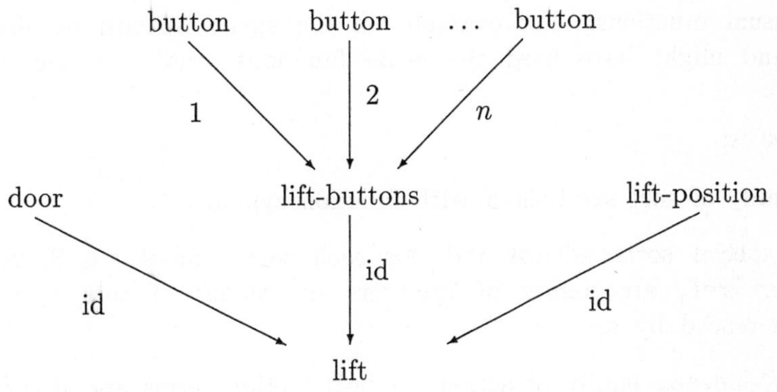

3 Language and logic

In this section we describe the language and the logic used in the theory presentations, which are denoted by agent descriptions in the specification language.

We have mentioned that we have two types of locality, action locality and attribute locality. To be able to give the locality axioms that go with these two kinds, our language must be sufficiently rich to compare actions and to compare attributes. Comparing actions does not represent a problem because they will just be terms of the sort **action**. But by comparing attributes we mean comparing the actual attributes, not their values. Therefore we must distinguish between references and values — a distinction well known in programming languages. When we write $A = B$ we mean that attributes A and B have the same value. But $\&A = \&B$ means A and B are actually the same attribute — they refer to the same "cell". & is the reference or 'address-of' operator. To de-reference attribute names we use the $*$ operator. Thus $*\&A$ is the value of $\&A$, otherwise written A.

As we said, the specifier does not have to use these operators; they will only be needed for locality axioms, which, by the structuring principle mentioned above, the specifier will never have to provide explicitly. The locality axioms will be implicit in the specification texts. Nevertheless, the locality axioms are explicit in the theory presentations which the specifications denote, so we need to have the logical language to describe them.

3.1 Signatures

We said that a signature is the extralogical language in the theory presentation, *i.e.* the attribute and action symbols. It also consists of the sort symbols used and the usual functions. For example, in the agent **button** we used the sort boolean, and might have used the usual functions 'and', 'or' *etc.* which come with it.

A signature is:

- A family of sort symbols S with function symbols
- The special sorts **action** and, for each sort symbol $s \in S$, $\mathbf{ref}_s$. Terms of sort $\mathbf{ref}_s$ are names of (pointers to) values of sort s, and will be de-referenced by $*$.
- An S^*-indexed family of action symbols (action terms are of sort **action**)
- An $S^* \times S$-indexed family of attribute symbols (attribute terms formed from the attribute symbol $A : s_1 \times \ldots \times s_n \times s$ are of sort s).

Notice that actions and attributes can be parameterised by terms of sorts of the signature. (In the lift example, there happened not to be any parameterised actions or attributes.)

At the theory presentation level we do not distinguish between local and sharable actions and attributes. At this level that information is carried by the locality axioms. The annotations l and s appear at the specification language level, and the 'specification compiler' generates the locality axioms from them.

3.2 Language of theory presentations

This section describes the language of the theory presentations. As we have said, the language used by the specifier to write axioms is only a subset of this: the specifier does not need to make explicit use of the operators & and *, in view of what we have called the structuring principle.

We will describe the language for a signature with sorts S. In addition to the symbols of the signature, we have for each sort s in S enumerably many variables x, y,... of the sort s and α,... of the sort $\mathbf{ref}_s$, and enumerably many variables $x, y \ldots :$ **action**.

- Terms are formed using
  - variables of the sorts
  - function symbols of the sorts S with appropriately sorted term parameters; constant symbols of the sorts are simply zero-arity function symbols.
  - attribute symbols, again with appropriately sorted term parameters. Zero-arity attribute symbols vary only with the state of the agent.

    The values of functions are invariant across states, whereas attributes change from state to state.
  - action symbols, again with zero or more appropriately sorted term parameters.
  - for each attribute term $\mathbf{A} : s$, there is a term $\&\mathbf{A} : \mathbf{ref}_s$ (its "reference"). Notice that $\mathbf{A}$ is an attribute term, not an attribute symbol; in other words its parameters are instantiated by appropriately sorted terms. This means that an attribute symbol has a different reference for each set of (semantically distinct) actual parameters.
  - for each term $\alpha : \mathbf{ref}_s$ there is a term $*\alpha : s$ (its "contents").
- atomic formulas are equalities of terms ($t_1 = t_2$), and deontic formulas (per($\mathbf{a}$) and obl($\mathbf{a}$) for action terms $\mathbf{a}$). As we have said, if t is a term of sort boolean, we will sometimes abbreviate the atomic formula $t =$ true by t.
- formulas are made from smaller formulas with the usual connectives and the modal-action operators; if ϕ and ψ are formulas and $\mathbf{a}$ is an action term, then $\phi \wedge \psi$, $\phi \vee \psi$, $\phi \rightarrow \psi$, $\neg\phi$, and $[\mathbf{a}]\phi$ are formulas.

3.3 Interpretation

Having described the language in which agents are described at a logical level, it is now time to see what models there are of such descriptions. Remember that an agent description is a pair consisting of a signature and a theory presentation (a finite set of axioms). Such a pair comes from an agent described by a specification text. At the logical level, all agent descriptions are simply ⟨signature,presentation⟩ pairs.

The semantic structures are Kripke models, as usual for modal logic. See [3] for details of Kripke frames for multi-modal logics. In the semantics that follows, for each agent there is a Kripke frame. Agent composition corresponds to taking the product of Kripke frames, modulo shared actions and attributes. The "possible worlds" in a frame are the states of the agent, and there is a separate relation on the set of states for each action term. The states interpret non-modal formulas locally (*i.e.* without reference to other states) by evaluating the terms in the sets which interpret the sorts, for atomic propositions, and by the usual truth-table definitions for the non-modal connectives.

An interpretation structure for a signature with sorts S consists of:

- for each sort s in S, a non-empty domain of individuals D_s; and for each function symbol $f : s_1 \times \ldots s_n \to s$, a function $[\![f]\!] : D_{s_1} \times \ldots \times D_{s_n} \to D_s$
- a set of states W, and a designated initial state $w_0 \in W$
- a set $\text{ACT} \subseteq W \rightarrow W$, which will be used to interpret action terms (terms of sort **action**).
- for each sort s, a set $\text{REF}_s \subseteq W \rightarrow D_s$. These will be used to interpret reference terms (terms of sort $\mathbf{ref}_s$).
- for each action symbol $a : s_1 \times \ldots \times s_n \to \mathbf{action}$, a function $[\![a]\!] : D_{s_1} \times \ldots \times D_{s_n} \to \text{ACT}$, as before
- for each attribute symbol $A : s_1 \times \ldots \times s_n \to s$, a function $[\![A]\!] : D_{s_1} \times \ldots \times D_{s_n} \to \text{REF}_s$
- a pair of sets P and O. Both are subsets of $\text{ACT} \times W$. They are used to interpret the deontic formulas.

An interpretation structure is therefore a set of states and a means of interpreting action terms as functions between states and a way of evaluating state-dependent formulas within states.

To interpret the quantifiers we start by assigning each variable of the language to an individual of the appropriate sort. This is an awkward technicality, and the reader may like to ignore all references to assignments in the passage below the following definition.

An assignment $\mathcal{A}$ is a map from variables to individuals in the carrier set of the variable's sort.

- $x : s$ is assigned to $\mathcal{A}(x) \in D_s$
- $\alpha : \mathbf{ref}_s$ is assigned to $\mathcal{A}(\alpha) \in \text{REF}_s$
- $x : \mathbf{action}$ is assigned to $\mathcal{A}(x) \in \text{ACT}$

We now show how to evaluate formulas in states, relative to an assignment $\mathcal{A}$. First we have to evaluate terms, as follows.

1. Variables: if x is a variable of sort s then its interpretation in the state w, written $[\![x]\!]_w^{\mathcal{A}}$, is $\mathcal{A}(x)$ in D_s. Similarly, if $\alpha : \mathbf{ref}_s$ then $[\![\alpha]\!]_w^{\mathcal{A}} = \mathcal{A}(\alpha)$ and if $x : \mathbf{action}$ then $[\![x]\!]_w^{\mathcal{A}} = \mathcal{A}(x)$.

2. Attributes: if $A(t_1,\ldots,t_n)$ is an attribute term of sort s, then its interpretation in state w, written $[\![A(t_1,\ldots,t_n)]\!]^{\mathcal{A}}_w$, is $[\![A]\!]([\![t_1]\!]^{\mathcal{A}}_w,\ldots,[\![t_n]\!]^{\mathcal{A}}_w)(w)$. That is to say, to interpret $A(t_1,\ldots,t_n) : s$ in w, apply $[\![A]\!]$ to the interpretations of $t_1,\ldots,t_n$ in w, yielding a function from $W \to D_s$. This function is the reference (address) of the attribute concerned, which is then applied to w to yield the required result.

3. Actions: if $a(t_1,\ldots,t_n)$: **action** then $[\![a(t_1,\ldots,t_n)]\!]^{\mathcal{A}}_w = [\![a]\!]([\![t_1]\!]^{\mathcal{A}}_w,\ldots,[\![t_n]\!]^{\mathcal{A}}_w) \in$ ACT

4. References: $[\![\&A(t_1,\ldots,t_n)]\!]^{\mathcal{A}}_w = [\![A]\!]([\![t_1]\!]^{\mathcal{A}}_w,\ldots,[\![t_n]\!]^{\mathcal{A}}_w)$

5. Values: $[\![*\alpha]\!]^{\mathcal{A}}_w = [\![\alpha]\!]^{\mathcal{A}}_w(w)$. The interpretation of reference terms is covered by case 4 and this case. There are no constants or functions of sort $\mathbf{ref}_s$ — the only terms of sort $\mathbf{ref}_s$ are terms like $\&A(t_1,\ldots,t_n)$ and variables.

Formulas are true or false in a state. We will write $[\![\phi]\!]^{\mathcal{A}}$ for the set of states in which ϕ is true. First we deal with the atomic formulas, which are equalities between terms and permissions and obligations of actions.

- The atomic formula $t_1 = t_2$ is true in a state w if t_1 and t_2 have the same interpretations in w. Formally, $w \in [\![t_1 = t_2]\!]^{\mathcal{A}}$ iff $[\![t_1]\!]^{\mathcal{A}}_w = [\![t_2]\!]^{\mathcal{A}}_w$.
- The atomic formula per(**a**) is true in w if $\langle [\![\mathbf{a}]\!]^{\mathcal{A}}_w, w\rangle$ is in P. That is to say, P is just a set specifying what actions are permitted in what states.
- Similarly, $w \in$ obl(**a**) if $\langle [\![\mathbf{a}]\!]^{\mathcal{A}}_w, w\rangle$ is in O. O is a set specifying what actions are obliged in what states.

In the discussion above, **a** is an action term (a term of type **action**), that is, an action symbol (some a) together with term parameters. Notice that permission or obligation to perform an action **a** depends on its parameters (so an agent may have permission to perform the action with some parameters and not with others).

Now for the interpretation of the connectives.

- $w \in [\![\phi \wedge \psi]\!]^{\mathcal{A}}$ iff $w \in [\![\phi]\!]^{\mathcal{A}}$ and $w \in [\![\psi]\!]^{\mathcal{A}}$.
- $w \in [\![\phi \vee \psi]\!]^{\mathcal{A}}$ iff $w \in [\![\phi]\!]^{\mathcal{A}}$ or $w \in [\![\psi]\!]^{\mathcal{A}}$.
- $w \in [\![\phi \rightarrow \psi]\!]^{\mathcal{A}}$ iff $w \notin [\![\phi]\!]^{\mathcal{A}}$ or $w \in [\![\psi]\!]^{\mathcal{A}}$.
- $w \in [\![\neg\phi]\!]^{\mathcal{A}}$ iff $w \notin [\![\phi]\!]^{\mathcal{A}}$.
- $w \in [\![[\mathbf{a}]\phi]\!]^{\mathcal{A}}$ iff $[\![\mathbf{a}]\!]^{\mathcal{A}}_w(w) \in [\![\phi]\!]^{\mathcal{A}}$. That is to say, to evaluate whether $[\mathbf{a}]\phi$ is true in w, first evaluate the action **a** in w. The result is a function in ACT. Then apply this function to w, yielding another state $[\![\mathbf{a}]\!]^{\mathcal{A}}_w(w)$. The answer is then given by whether ϕ is true in this new state.

- $w \in [\![\forall x.\, \phi]\!]^{\mathcal{A}}$ if $w \in [\![\phi]\!]^{\mathcal{A}'}$ for all assignments $\mathcal{A}'$ which differ from $\mathcal{A}$ at most by the assignment of x.
- $w \in [\![\exists x.\, \phi]\!]^{\mathcal{A}}$ if $w \in [\![\phi]\!]^{\mathcal{A}'}$ for at least one assignment $\mathcal{A}'$ which differs from $\mathcal{A}$ at most by the assignment of x.

The treatment of quantifiers we have given in the last two clauses above is standard. Recall that for all formulas ϕ, $[\![\phi]\!]^{\mathcal{A}}$ is evaluated relative to an assignment $\mathcal{A}$. We will sometimes ignore this complication and just write $[\![\phi]\!]$, which we justify by the following: If ϕ has no free variables then $[\![\phi]\!]^{\mathcal{A}}$ is independent of the assignment $\mathcal{A}$.

3.4 Logic

We are now in a position to give the consequence relation which defines our logic. Let Γ be the theory presentation corresponding to an agent specification **X**. To compute the consequences of the specification, we first look at the agents which satisfy it. These are models of Γ. Formally, an interpretation structure $[\![\cdot]\!]$ together with an assignment $\mathcal{A}$ is a model of a sentence ϕ if for every state w of the interpretation structure, $w \in [\![\phi]\!]^{\mathcal{A}}$. A model of a *set* of sentences Γ is a ⟨structure,assignment⟩ pair which is a model of each of the sentences of Γ.

A model of Γ thus corresponds to an agent which satisfies the specification **X**. It has a collection of states and undergoes actions which transform it from state to state. But this does not fully reflect the information contained in Γ, because only some actions are permitted in a state, and others may be obliged. We need to look at sequences of actions, *life-cycles*, to reflect this.

Given a model $[\![\cdot]\!]$, a life-cycle is a sequence of state-transitions $\langle e_1, e_2, \ldots \rangle$ where each e_i is in ACT. This is any sequence of actions that the agent can go through. Such a sequence is *normative* if it respects the deontic part of the specification, *i.e.* if each action which takes place is permitted, and if every obligation incurred is discharged. For permissions, this just means that for each n the pair $\langle e_n, w_n \rangle$ must be in P, where w_n is the state arrived at just before the transition e_n, that is, $w_n = e_{n-1}(e_{n-2}(\ldots e_1(w_0)\ldots))$.

One could treat obligations in MAL the other way around: whenever $\langle e, w_n \rangle$ is in O and w_n is $e_{n-1}(e_{n-2}(\ldots e_1(w_0)\ldots))$ for some n, then e must be e_n. However, in Structured MAL it was decided that obligations should be weaker than the 'immediate' obligations mentioned above. Instead of requiring immediate fulfillment, they require eventual fulfillment. That is, when an agent incurs an obligation it must carry out the action at some point in the future, not necessarily immediately. This is characterised in terms of life-cycles as follows: $\langle e_1, e_2, \ldots \rangle$ is normative with respect to obligations if for all e_i in the cycle, if $w_i = e_i(e_{i-1}(\ldots e_1(w_0)\ldots))$ and $\langle e, w_i \rangle \in O$ for some e, then $e = e_j$ for some $j > i$.

Now to define consequences of the specification of **X**. A is a consequence of **X** if it is true in all states that an agent satisfying **X** could get into. Let $[\![\cdot]\!]$ be a model of the theory presentation Γ denoted by **X**. Let $\langle e_1, e_2, \ldots\rangle$ be a normative life-cycle of $[\![\cdot]\!]$. A is a consequence if it is true in all states $e_i(e_{i-1}(\ldots e_1(w_0)\ldots))$.

A life cycle in which an agent incurs an obligation to perform the action **a**, and though it never does perform **a** it performs another action which, in the particular state in which it is performed, is equivalent to **a** in the sense of achieving the same transformation of that state, is not normative. One might think that because our definition of normativity looks only at denotations and not at terms, this would count as normative, but brief reflection should be enough to convince the reader that this is in general not so.

3.5 Deontic axioms

Since reasoning from a specification Γ involves consideration only of normative life-cycles (ones in which actions performed are permitted and obligations incurred are discharged), permissions default to 'on' and obligations to 'off'. This means that the specifier never has to assert permissions – the logic only takes into consideration models in which actions which occur are permitted. Similarly, the specifier never needs to deny obligations. The effect of this is that permissions should be *denied* in a specification, and obligations should be *asserted*. Typically, deontic axioms will look like

$$\text{per(a)} \rightarrow \textit{condition}$$
$$\textit{condition} \rightarrow \text{obl(a)}$$

More precisely: there should be positive occurrences of obligations and negative occurrences of permissions in deontic axioms.

We say 'should', but the specifier is not barred from writing per(a) $\leftarrow$ condition or per(a) $\leftrightarrow$ condition. There are however disadvantages in doing so. The problem is that agents which inherit the agent for which we are writing deontic axioms may need to put more constraints on permissions (*i.e.* deny permission in further circumstances) and constraining permission to match a single condition will contradict this. There are examples of this in section 6. If permissions are written in the recommended way, they are easy to 'add-up'. Adding up per(a) $\rightarrow$ cond_1, per(a) $\rightarrow$ cond_2, and per(a) $\rightarrow$ cond_3 yields per(a) $\rightarrow$ $\text{cond}_1 \wedge \text{cond}_2 \wedge \text{cond}_3$. It should be obvious that the same remarks apply to obligations, except that further axioms *add* obligations instead of removing permissions. Axioms add up similarly: $\text{cond}_1 \rightarrow \text{obl(a)}$ and $\text{cond}_2 \rightarrow \text{obl(a)}$ make $\text{cond}_1 \vee \text{cond}_2 \rightarrow \text{obl(a)}$.

The reader may object that having only negative occurrences of permissions makes it impossible to prove permissions. As this stands this is true, but it *must* be true given the way permissions are defined. We cannot assert permissions because we can not know that they are not going to be denied in agents which inherit the agent in question. But once we have completed the specification we can logically 'close' the deontic axiom, asserting per(a) $\leftrightarrow$ $cond_1 \wedge cond_2 \wedge cond_3 \ldots$ Then permissions can be proved.

Again, the same remarks apply to obligations with the obvious changes: here we should say: having only positive occurrences of obligations makes it impossible to *use* them in proofs, until we logically close the conjunction of the axioms in the way described.

4 Structure

In Sections 1 and 2 we motivated the idea that agents can be composed in a variety of ways. In this section we will look at this in more detail. The primitive relation between agents is that of *morphism*. If there is a morphism from **X** to **Y**, **X** is identical in behaviour with some sub-agent of **Y**. The morphism is a map between signatures which shows us how to rename the signature elements to demonstrate the sub-agent relation.

A morphism is a map between agent specifications **X** and **Y** taking

- each sort in **X** to a sort in **Y** (the special sorts **action** and $\mathbf{ref}_s$ are preserved)
- each action symbol in **X** to an action symbol in **Y**
- each attribute symbol in **X** to an attribute symbol in **Y**

such that the translation under the mapping of each theorem of **X** is a theorem of **Y**.

Of course the map must respect the sorts of the action and attribute symbols in the language. A symbol in **X** is mapped on to a symbol in **Y** whose sort is the sort which is mapped on to by the sort of **X**.

The following diagrams show examples of morphisms in the lift specification. **floor** is constructed as an aggregation of two **buttons** (see page 4), an 'up' button and a 'down' button. Each **button** is mapped to **floor**, with morphisms called 'up' and 'down'. As already indicated, we use the dot notation in naming the attributes and actions of **floor**. For example, the attribute 'lit' is mapped by the morphism 'up' to the attribute 'up.lit'. The next morphism is an example of refinement. We have decided that there should be only one light on each floor, which will represent the state of both buttons. When the user presses either of the buttons, the light illuminates and the user is not able to see which of the buttons was pressed. The morphism collapses the distinction between 'up.lit' and 'down.lit'. First we show how the agents are defined, and then the morphisms.

```
agent floor
includes button via up;
includes button via down;
end
```

```
agent floor′
attributes
    s lit : bool;
includes floor via id where
    up.lit is lit
    down.lit is lit;
end
```

This example also shows the flexibility of the specification language. Given that we have specified **button** as on page 4, these specifications are really just abbreviations for the following more verbose ones:

```
agent floor
attributes
    s  up.lit : bool;
    s  down.lit : bool;
actions
    ℓ  up.press;
    ℓ  down.press;
axioms
    [up.press]up.lit;
    [down.press]down.lit;
end
```

```
agent floor′
attributes
    s  lit : bool;
actions
    ℓ  up.press;
    ℓ  down.press;
axioms
    [up.press]lit;
    [down.press]lit;
end
```

At the theory presentation level, the connections are as follows.

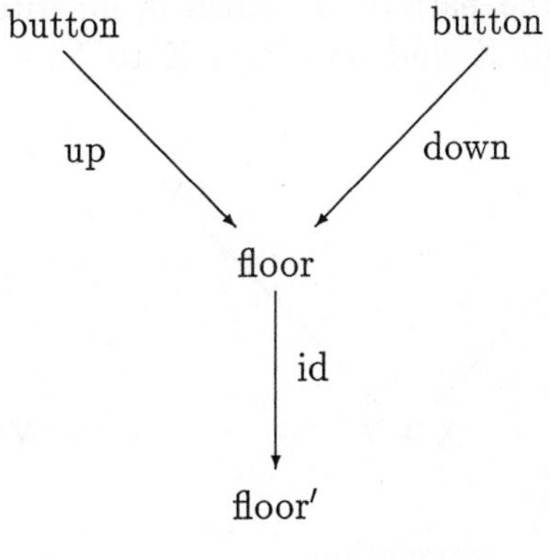

4.1 Inheritance and clientship

Agents can exist in a variety of relationships one to another. Two important relationships used in object-oriented design are *inheritance* and *clientship*. If **Y** inherits **X**, all the actions and attributes of **X** are also attributes of **Y**, but **Y** may have more besides. For example, consider the abstract agents **vehicle** and **car**. **Car** inherits all the actions and attributes of **vehicle**, but has more of its own besides. Now consider the agent **engine**. We might be tempted to say that **vehicle** inherits all its actions and attributes. This will certainly be true for actions like *start* or attributes like *running*. But we may want to say that some attributes or actions, like the attribute *flooded*, are attributes or actions which apply to the engine alone. It does not make sense to say that the vehicle is flooded — or at least, it is not the same as saying that the engine is flooded. **Vehicle** inherits only some of the actions and attributes of **engine**. This is clientship.

These object-oriented relationships, and many others, are captured by the sub-agent relation. **X** is a sub-agent of **Y** if there is a *morphism* from the specification of **X** to that of **Y**. Roughly speaking, this means that all the actions and attributes of **X** are (under appropriate renaming) actions and attributes of **Y**. We will now describe how three object-oriented constructs are captured by morphisms.

- Inheritance is captured by a single morphism. If **Y** inherits **X** then there is a morphism from the specification of **X** to that of **Y**.
- Aggregation is captured by two morphisms. If **X + Y** is the aggregation of **X** and **Y**, then there are morphisms from **X** to **X + Y** and from **Y** to **X + Y**. The aggregation may involve identifying some actions and attributes between **X** and **Y**, in which case we can form an abstraction **Z** of **X + Y**.
- Clientship is also captured by two morphisms. If **X** is a client of **Y**, that is to say it inherits selectively from **Y**, then we construct morphisms as follows. Let **Z** be the part of **Y** which is inherited by **X**. Then we have a morphism from **Z** to **X** and one from **Z** to **Y**.

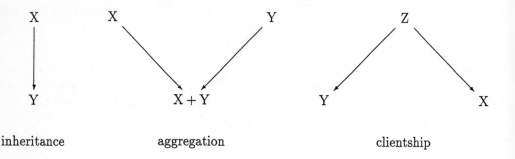

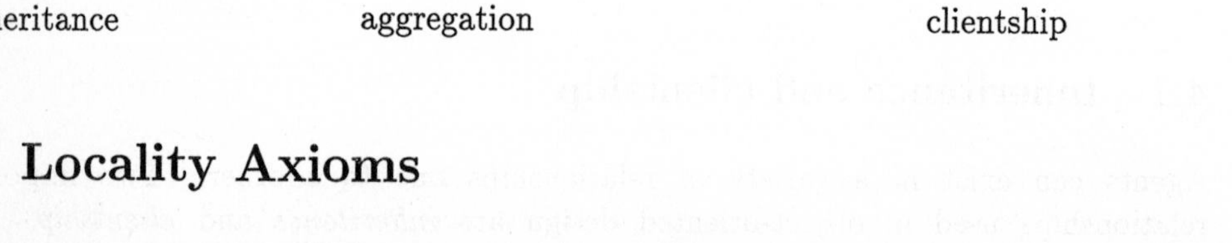

inheritance aggregation clientship

5 Locality Axioms

We said in the introduction that the key benefit of structure was the ability to impose a notion of *locality* by which we can control the effects of actions. Without locality the structuring we have introduced would be wasted — all reasoning would have to take place in the biggest agent. But the 'biggest agent' that **button** is a part of is the **lift-system**, or perhaps the whole building or even the street that we are specifying. We would like to conclude properties of **button** or **door** without reference to these big systems.

Examples

Here are examples where attributes and actions should be local to the agents in which they are defined:

1. Only the actions in the agent **door** (*i.e.* 'open' and 'close') can affect the attribute 'posn'. This is locality for *attributes*:

   Only the actions of X can affect the attributes of X

2. The actions in agent **button** (*i.e.* 'press') can only affect the attribute 'lit'. This is locality for *actions*:

   The actions of X can *only* affect the attributes of X

Non-examples

There are instances where locality fails, showing why some actions and attributes *must* be sharable to allow the interaction between agents we want. For example, the axiom $(\text{floor} = 1) \rightarrow [\text{open}]\neg 1.\text{lit}$ in the agent **lift**, which says the light at the current floor is extinguished by the door opening, violates both types of locality. The action 'open' has to affect the attribute 'lit' which is declared outside the agent in which 'open' is declared; and the attribute 'lit' is changed by an action (open) declared outside the agent in which it is declared.

We need to have locality for some actions and attributes and not for others. In the specification language we have a mechanism for stating which action and attribute symbols are local and which are not. At the theory presentation level, this means that some attributes and some actions have a locality axiom. But as we are about to see, within an agent community there are degrees of sharability.

Locality axioms

Remember that the specifications of agents indicate whether the actions and attributes are local or sharable. For example, the attribute 'lit' is sharable in **button**, because as we have remarked it will be updated by the action 'open' in **door**. But the action 'press' in **button** is local. And 'lit' (or '*i*.lit' as it is then known) in **lift** is local, because it will not be updated by any actions introduced in ever-bigger agents. Similarly, 'open' in **door** is sharable (it has to update i.lit), and it remains sharable in **lift** because it will have more work to do in **lift-system**. (It will have to extinguish the floor lights.)

Local attribute or action symbols have a locality axiom in the theory presentation denoted by the agent specification.

For example, 'posn' is a local attribute. The locality axiom is

$$\forall a : \textbf{action}, \forall v : (\text{op,cl}) \;\; (a = \text{open} \vee a = \text{close} \vee (\text{posn} = v \rightarrow [a](\text{posn} = v))).$$

It means that no action other than 'open' and 'close' can affect the value of 'posn'; for either an action is 'open' or 'close', or the value of posn is unchanged by the action.

'Press' is a local action symbol in **button**: its locality axiom is

$$\forall \alpha : \textbf{ref}_{\text{bool}}(\alpha = \&\text{lit} \vee ((*\alpha = v) \rightarrow [\text{press}](*\alpha = v))$$

which means: no attribute other than the attribute 'lit' can be affected by the action 'press'.

General form

We will now show the general form of locality axioms. Unfortunately they look rather ugly in this form, but the purpose of this section is to show that for any action or attribute symbol in an agent we can construct a locality axiom.

Suppose A is an attribute symbol local to an agent with action symbols $a_1, \ldots, a_n$. The locality axiom should say that every action which occurs is either an instance of one of these actions or leaves A unchanged.

$$\forall \mathbf{a} : \textbf{action} \bigvee_{i=1}^{n} (\exists \underline{x_i}.\;\; (\mathbf{a} = a_i(\underline{x_i}))) \;\; \vee \;\; \forall \underline{y}, v.\;\; (A(\underline{y}) = v) \rightarrow [\mathbf{a}](A(\underline{y}) = v))$$

The axiom says: either **a** is one of the actions of the agent with appropriate parameters, or it leaves the value of the attribute (with any parameters) unchanged. We have used $\underline{x_i}$ to mean a vector of variables. The number and sort of these variables is determined by the sort of the action symbol for each value of i. Similarly, $\underline{y}$ is a vector of variables whose sorts match the parameters of A.

Action locality: Now suppose the action symbol a is local to an agent with the following attribute symbols:

$$A_1^{s_1}, A_2^{s_1}, \ldots, A_{n_{s_1}}^{s_1}, A_1^{s_2}, A_2^{s_2}, \ldots, A_{n_{s_2}}^{s_2}, \ldots$$

For each sort s, we suppose that there are n_s attribute symbols with values of the sort s. Then for each sort s and each reference term α of sort $\textbf{ref}_s$, *either* α is the reference of one of the parameterised attribute symbols with values of sort s, *or* **a** (with any parameters) leaves the value of α unchanged.

The schematic form of the locality axiom is thus:

$$\bigwedge_{s\in S}(\forall\alpha:\mathbf{ref}_s\bigvee_{i=1}^{n_s}\exists\underline{x_i}.\,\alpha=\&A_i^s(\underline{x_i}))\;\vee\;\forall\underline{y},v:s.\,((*\alpha=v)\rightarrow[a(\underline{y})](*\alpha=v))$$

These axioms are complicated, but it is worth repeating that the specifier does not have to write them down or ever use the operators $*$ and &. Locality axioms are generated by the specification 'compiler' on the basis of the locality declarations the specifier makes.

To understand their effect, the crucial point about locality axioms is that (like all axioms) they are inherited by agents via morphisms. But the scope of the quantifiers $\forall\alpha:\mathbf{ref}$ and $\forall a:\mathbf{action}$ increases as we move to bigger and bigger agents. Notice that the natural requirement that morphisms cannot map *local* symbols to *sharable* ones is enforced by the fact that the locality axioms are inherited under morphisms.

6 Auto-teller examples

The following example, of an autoteller system in a bank, shows some of the ideas in this paper in action. An autoteller (cash-dispenser) allows bank customers to withdraw money from their accounts by inserting a plastic card and typing a personal identification number at the keypad. The machine compares the identification number with the number magnetically coded on the card. It asks the customer the amount of cash required (by putting an appropriate message on its VDU screen) and, after checking one of the bank's databases, dispenses the cash. It records the transaction on an internal recorder, and prints the transaction on a chit which it gives to the customer. It has an internal hopper in which it can retain the card if the customer consistently types the wrong identification number.

From the English-language specification we identify the following components:

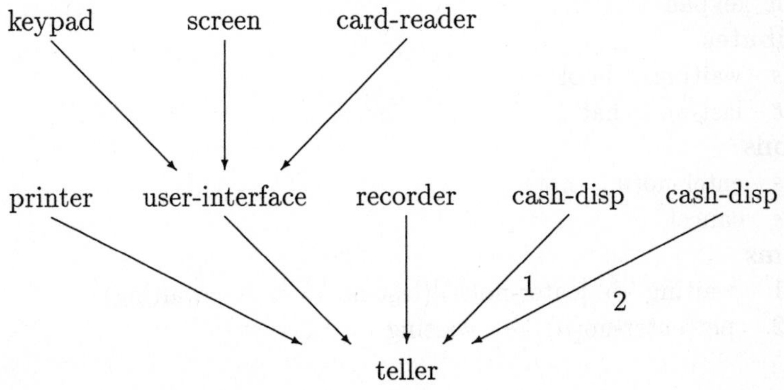

The user-interface is made up from the keypad, the screen, and the card-reader. In turn the teller is made up from the printer, the user-interface, the recorder and (say) two cash-dispensers containing notes of different denominations. A teller-system consists of (say) m tellers and n databases.

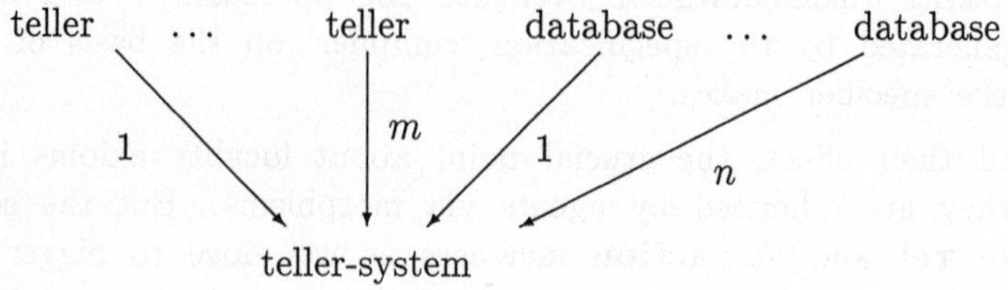

But here we will deal with just the following fragment of these diagrams:

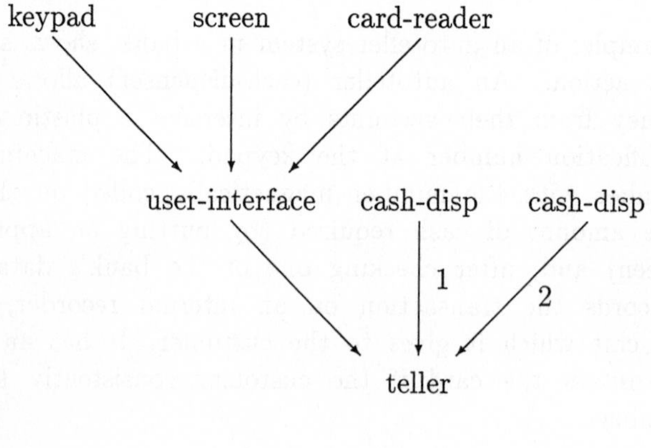

We are now in a position to axiomatise the agents.

agent keypad
attributes
  s waiting : bool
  ℓ last-no : nat
actions
  s enter-no(n : nat)
  s cancel
axioms
  1. waiting $\rightarrow$ [enter-no(n)](last-no $= n \wedge \neg$waiting)
  2. per(enter-no(n)) $\rightarrow$ waiting
end

A keypad has two attributes which define its state, waiting and last-no. Waiting specifies whether the agent is in a state of accepting a numerical input on its keypad. Last-no contains the last number typed. The agent keypad also has two actions, enter-no(n) (the user enters the number n), and cancel (the user elects to abort the transaction – we imagine that the cancel button is part of the keypad). Notice that the keypad does not, and should not, distinguish between the various types of numbers entered (identification numbers, amounts etc).

The keypad's first axiom states that last-no is updated by the action enter-no(n) if the agent is in the waiting state, and also that it then ceases to be in the waiting state. What happens if the agent is not in the waiting state is not defined, although the second axiom states that an occurrence of the action enter-no(n) would then be non-normative.

The keypad has a complex interface with the other components, as can be seen by the fact that both actions and one attribute are shared. The attribute waiting is shared because it will be updated by actions in the user-interface. Similarly, enter-no(n) and cancel are sharable because they have to update attributes there too.

Now for the card-reader:

> **agent** card-reader
> **attributes**
> ℓ has-card : bool
> ℓ card : (r, u)
> ℓ card-no : nat
> **actions**
> s accept-r(n : nat)
> ℓ accept-u
> ℓ return
> ℓ keep
> **axioms**
> 1. has-card $\rightarrow$ obl(return) $\vee$ obl(keep);
> 2. [accept-r(n)](card-no $=$ n $\wedge$ has-card $\wedge$ card $=$ r);
> 3. [accept-u](has-card $\wedge$ card $=$ u);
> 4. [return]$\neg$has-card;
> 5. [keep]$\neg$has-card;
> 6. per(return) $\vee$ per(keep) $\rightarrow$ has-card ;
> 7. per(accept-r(n)) $\vee$ per(accept-u) $\rightarrow$ $\neg$has-card;
>
> **end**

The card-reader has three local attributes which respectively indicate: whether there is a card inside it; whether the card inside (if any) is readable or unreadable; and the personal identification number coded on the magnetic strip of the card. Notice that (r, u) is an enumerated sort. The card-reader can accept a readable card with number n (accept-r(n)), or accept an unreadable card (perhaps one which is damaged or wrongly inserted) (accept-u). It can then return or keep the card. Of these actions, only accept-r(n) need be sharable; it has to update attributes of the user-interface.

The axioms say the following:

1. If the reader has a card, it has an obligation to keep the card or to return it. That is, a life-cycle is non-normative if it has a state in which has-card is true but which is not eventually followed by a return action or a keep action.

2 and 3. After accepting a readable card, the appropriate attributes are updated.

4 and 5. After keeping (transferring to internal hopper) or returning a card there is no longer a card.

6. The agent may keep or return a card only if it has one...

7. ...and accept one only if it does not have one.

The last of the agents which make up the user-interface is the screen. It has just one sharable attribute, the message which it displays. Clearly it has to be sharable; if it was local, it would never get updated as there are no actions in that agent.

agent screen
attributes
    s message : string
end

Now we are in a position to tie these components together in the user-interface.

agent user-interface
attributes
    ℓ entering-id;
    ℓ entering-amt;
actions
    ℓ request-amt;
includes keypad
includes card-reader
includes screen
axioms
    1. $\neg$(entering-id $\wedge$ entering-amt);
    2. entering-id $\rightarrow$ (message='Enter id' $\wedge$ $\exists n$ obl(enter-no(n)) $\vee$ obl(cancel));
    3. entering-amt $\rightarrow$ (message='Enter amount' $\wedge$ $\exists n$ obl(enter-no(n)) $\vee$ obl(cancel
    4. [accept-r(n)](entering-id $\wedge$ waiting);
    5. last-no=card-no $\wedge$ entering-id $\wedge$ $\neg$waiting $\rightarrow$ obl(request-amt);
    6. [request-amt](entering-amt $\wedge$ waiting);
    7. [cancel]obl(return)
end

The user-interface includes all the actions and attributes and axioms of its constituents. It also has the attributes entering-id and entering-amt and the action request-amt, all of which are local. The purpose of these is to guide it through the sequence of events to do with verifying the card and dispensing the cash. The axioms mean:

1. The machine is never at once processing the identifier and the amount.

2. While expecting the customer identifier, the screen displays the appropriate message and a number must be entered on the keypad.

   The clause $\exists n$ obl(enter-no(n)) means that there is an obligation to enter *a* number, but not any specific number. In other words, the user fulfills this obligation by typing an arbitrary number. The reader may consider how one could specify an obligation to enter some specific number.

3. Similarly when expecting an amount.

4. After accepting a readable card the machine enters the expecting-identifier state and activates the keypad

5 and 6. If the machine is processing the identifier and the customer has typed a number which was found to be correct, the machine enters the processing-amount state.

7. If the cancel button is pressed the machine must return the card.

The cash dispenser dispenses cash if it has enough left:

> **agent** cash-disp
> **attributes**
> ℓ qty-left : nat;
> **actions**
> ℓ dispense(q : nat);
> **axioms**
> $x =$ qty-left $\land\ x > q \rightarrow$ [dispense(q)](qty-left $= x - q$);
> per(disp(q)) $\rightarrow q >$ qty-left
> **end**

The auto-teller itself is left with the rather boring task of deciding how much of each denomination is to be dispensed. Note that the dispensers are obliged to dispense if (and permitted only if) the right conditions are met. Recall the form of deontic axioms described in section 3.5.

agent teller
includes user-interface
includes cash-disp **via** 1
includes cash-disp **via** 2
axioms

entering-amt $\wedge$ $\neg$waiting $\wedge$
n_1 = last-no div denom$_1$ $\wedge$ n_2 = (last-no mod denom$_1$) div denom$_2$ $\rightarrow$
obl(1.dispense(n_1)) $\wedge$ obl(2.dispense(n_2));

per(1.dispense(n_1)) $\vee$ per(2.dispense(n_2)) $\rightarrow$
entering-amt $\wedge$ $\neg$waiting $\wedge$
n_1 = last-no div denom$_1$ $\wedge$ n_2 = (last-no mod denom$_1$) div denom$_2$;

end

One perhaps counter-intuitive feature of the logic which this example brings out is the relative weakness of the locality axioms compared with the frame rule. For example, we cannot deduce from the axioms of the card-reader that the return action does not affect the card-no attribute. That is because they are in the same agent and there is no locality axiom to that effect. The important points here are that (i) it does not matter – we do not need the assumption that return does not affect card-no; and (ii), that an implementation which chose to reset card-no after returning the card to some null value would be a perfectly good implementation, even a likely one.

The structuring principle says that whenever we need to make such constraints we must do so by structuring the agents in a way which gives rise to the right locality axioms.

Acknowledgments

This work is one of the results of the SERC FOREST Project at Imperial College, London. Mark Ryan is funded by that project. José Fiadeiro is on leave from Departamento de Matematica, Instituto Superior Tecnico, Lisboa, Portugal, as a grantee of the Commission of the European Communities.

References

[1] J. Fiadeiro and T. Maibaum. Describing, structuring and implementing objects. In *Proc. REX Workshop on Foundations of Object-Oriented Languages.* Springer-Verlag, in print.

[2] J. Goguen. A categorial manifesto. Technical Report PRG-72, Programming Research Group, University of Oxford, March 1989.

[3] R. Goldblatt. *Logics of Time and Computation.* CSLI Lecture Notes, 1987.

[4] S. Khosla and T. S. E. Maibaum. The perscription and description of state based systems. In B. Banieqbal, H. Barringer, and A. Pnueli, editors, *Temporal Logic in Specification.* 1989. Lecture Notes in Computer Science 398.

[5] T. S. E. Maibaum. A logic for the formal requirements specification of real-time embedded systems. Technical report, Imperial College, London, 1987. Deliverable R3 for FOREST (Alvey).

[6] Mark Ryan. Defaults and revision in structured theories. In *Logic in Computer Science (LICS)*, July 1991.

First Order Data Types and First Order Logic

Ralf Treinen*
FB14 – Dept. of Computer Science
Universität des Saarlandes
W6600 Saarbrücken, Germany
treinen@cs.uni-sb.de

Abstract

This paper concerns the relation between parameterized first order data types and first order logic. Augmenting first order logic by data type definitions yields in general a strictly stronger logic than first order logic. Some modeltheoretic properties of the new logic are investigated. While the new logic always fulfills the downward Skolem-Löwenheim property, compactness is fulfilled if and only if for the given data type definition the new logic has the same expressive power than first order logic. This last property is shown to be undecidable.

1 Introduction

The use of modules for data abstraction is now a well-established principle in software design, see for instance [2]. From the programmers point of view a module is a piece of encapsulated software that propagates only a well-defined subset of its data structures and operations to its environment, we call this the *export* part of the module. Outside the module these data structures and operations are accessible only via their names, the implementation remains hidden from the users of the module. The module may use data structures and operations defined elsewhere in the program, this leads to the important concept of parameterization: The *parameter* part of module specifies the sorts and operations that have to be supplied to the module. In the following we will always consider modules as parameterized modules, even if the the parameter part is not stated explicitly in the syntax. This interpretation of modules reflects in the semantics: The semantics of a module now has to be defined as a function that maps the denotations of the parameter part to the denotations of the export part.

*Present Address: DFKI, Stuhlsatzenhausweg 3, W 6600 Saarbrücken, Germany.
email: treinen@dfki.uni-sb.de

Among the modularization concepts known from programming languages we here only mention the clusters of CLU ([18]), the packages of Ada[1] ([1]), the modules of MODULA-2([31]) and the structures of ML ([22]). Generic data types as in ML or Miranda[2] ([28]) provide another parameterization concept by abstracting basic sorts from data type definitions. Furthermore parameterization comes naturally with specification languages, no matter whether they are operational, axiomatic (algebraic) or algorithmic ([9]). A non-exhaustive list of specification languages using parameterization is Alphard ([25]), CLEAR ([4]), ACT ONE ([8]) and OBSCURE ([15], [16]). All these languages differ substantially in the methods used for implementing, resp. specifying, data structures and operations. In this paper we take an abstract approach and present an idealized language for expressing modules. The language follows the Algorithmic Specification language of [19] and can be seen as a programming language as well as a specification language. We only consider modules defining data structures and operations, higher order functions are not included in our language. We have a purely functional point of view, that is modules construct new "exported" *algebras* from given "parameter" algebras.

We do not distinguish between the import- and the parameter part of a module as it has been done in [8]: In our sense the import part comprises all the sorts and operations that may be used by a module but are not defined in it. In [8] this is called the import part, while the parameter part in [8] designates some sorts and operations that are common to the import and the export part. We choose the name "parameter" in order to emphasize that the semantics of a module depends exactly on the meaning of these sort and operation symbols.

In our idealized language functions are defined by general recursive programs as in functional programming languages, but without syntactic sugar as for instance the let-construct or pattern matching. Data structures are defined by constructor functions, this kind of data definition is known from languages like ML, Miranda or Algorithmic Specifications. The Algorithmic Specification method furthermore introduces subset and quotient operations on algebras, but as shown in [19] these are not relevant for the logic and we are allowed to drop them here. Although restricted in expressive power we claim that our idealized language provides a representation of interesting subsets of the languages above (also the imperative ones in the case of absence of global variables, such that the functional perspective is retained).

This idealized language can be seen as a generalization of program schemes (see for instance [11]). In fact, when we restrict the module language by excluding the definition of new sorts we meet exactly the situation of recursive program schemes, where for some module a parameter algebra corresponds to an interpretation of a program scheme. While in the theory of program schemes one is interested in deriving properties of schemes that hold for all interpretations from some fixed class, we are here interested in another question.

Our interest in modules is motivated by their use in the top-down design of software.

[1] Ada is a registered trademark of the United States Departement of Defense.

[2] Miranda is a registered trademark of Research Software Ltd.

Given some properties of the export algebra of a module, we would like to know the exact requirements to the parameter algebra that ensure that the properties are satisfied. This leads to the central notion of a weakest parameter condition: For a given module m, a formula v over the parameter signature of m is called a *weakest parameter condition* of a formula w over the export signature of m if for each parameter algebra P: P fulfills v iff the semantics of m, applied to P, fulfills w.

In order to investigate the existence of weakest parameter conditions we incorporate the semantics of modules into a new logic that extends first order logic. In this new logic the models are parameter algebras and the formulas are first order formulas over the export signature of some given module. We always refer to some fixed module, that is the modules themselves do not occur in the formulas of our new logic. In the terminology of [14], our logic is an endogenous logic about modules, not an exogenous one.

The Logic of Effective Definitions (EDL) of [26] considers completely unstructered schemes that are a generalization of recursive program schemes. Model theoretic and proof theoretic properties of EDL are discussed in [26]. A downward Skolem-Löwenheim result for EDL is given there, making use of the corresponding property of infinitary logic. Our downward Skolem-Löwenheim result bases just on properties of first order logic. In contrast to EDL our logic incorporates data structures defined by constructors. Furthermore we concentrate on the relation between first order logic and the new logic as described above.

This paper is organized as follows: In the next section we first shortly review the notions we use in the rest of the paper. In Section 3 we define syntax and semantics of our module language and show some basic properties of the semantics. Section 4 defines the central notions with regard to the logic. The fundamental model-theoretic properties of our new logic are investigated in Section 5. Section 6 addresses decidability questions. Some of the proofs are omitted in this paper. For more complete proofs and definitions the reader is referred to [27].

2 Preliminaries

For complete definitions of the basic notions on signatures and algebras we refer the reader to [8]. If Σ is a signature containing the sort symbol s and function symbol f and A a Σ-algebra, then s^A denotes the carrier set of sort s in A and f^A the function that is the denotation of f in A. If Σ_1 is a subsignature of Σ_2 and A a Σ_2-algebra then $A\mid_{\Sigma_1}$ denotes the restriction of A to Σ_1.

A *variable family* for a signature $\Sigma = (S, F)$ is a family $X = (X_s)_{s\in S}$ of sets of variable symbols that are pairwise disjoint and disjoint to F. For a variable family $X = (X_s)_{s\in S}$ and (S, F)-algebra A $\Gamma_{X,A}$ or shortly Γ_A denotes the set of A-assignments. If X is a variable family for the signature $\Sigma = (S, F)$, $T_\Sigma(X)$ is the set of terms built with F and X. The set of ground terms $T_\Sigma(\emptyset)$ is also written as T_Σ. For $t \in T_\Sigma(X)$ the sort of t *sort*$(t) \in S$ and the set of free variables of t *free*$(t) \subseteq X$ are defined as usual, $T_{\Sigma,s}(X)$ denotes the subset of terms with sort s. A Σ-algebra A induces an interpretation function for terms: $A: T_\Sigma(X) \to (\Gamma_{X,A} \to A)$

We assume from the reader basic knowledge on first order logic (see for instance [10], [5]). We only consider first order logic with equality as the only predicate symbol, therefore we can consider algebras as models in the sense of first order logic. We write $A, \alpha \models w$ if the formula w is satisfied by the model A and the assignment $\alpha \in \Gamma_A$, if w is a sentence we write $A \models w$ in this case. This generalizes to sets W of sentences by $A \models W$ if $A \models w$ for all $w \in W$. For a class $\mathcal{C}$ of algebras we write $\mathcal{C} \models w$ if $A \models w$ for each $A \in \mathcal{C}$.

We use a somewhat sloppy notation for extensions of algebras adopted from [5]. If A is a (S, F)-algebra, $(S \cup \{c\}, F)$ an extension of (S, F) by one constant symbol c of sort s and $a \in s^A$, then we denote by (A, a) the $(S \cup \{c\}, F)$-algebra that coincides with A on (S, F) and assignes a to c.

$\Join$ is the equivalence junctor. For a sentence w and terms t_1, t_2 of the same sort where t_1 does not have a bound variable occurrence in w, $w(t_1/t_2)$ denotes the sentence obtained by substituting every occurrence of t_1 in w by t_2. It is understood that bound variables are renamed such that no free variable of t_2 is captured by a quantifier of w.

A Σ-algebra A is an *elementary submodel* of a Σ-algebra B if $A \subseteq B$ and for all Σ-formulas w and all A-assignments $\alpha \in \Gamma_A \subseteq \Gamma_B$: $A, \alpha \models w$ iff $B, \alpha \models w$. This is a stronger notion than being a submodel, especially elementary submodels have the same first order theory ([5]).

We use some basic notions from the theory of the semantics of programs, see for instance [20].

3 Modules

3.1 Syntax

In the following we are always interested in standard signatures:

Definition 1 *A signature (S, F) is called a* standard signature *([19]) if: S contains the sort bool and F contains the function symbols $true :\to bool$, $false :\to bool$ and for each $s \in S$ $\bot_s :\to s$, $\texttt{ifthenelse}_s : bool, s, s \to s$ and $=_s: s, s \to bool$.*

Definition 2 *A* module *is a tuple*

$$(PS_m, PF_m, NS_m, K_m, NF_m, EF_m, PR_m)$$

where PS_m, PF_m, NS_m, K_m and NF_m are pairwise disjoint sets and

- *(PS_m, PF_m) is a standard signature, called Σ_{Pm}. PS_m contains the* parameter sorts *of m.*

$$
\begin{array}{lll}
\textbf{PAR} & \textbf{SORTS}\ elem & \\
 & \textbf{OPNS}\ +\!: elem, elem \rightarrow elem & \\
\textbf{BODY} & \textbf{SORTS}\ list & \\
 & \textbf{CONS} & atom\colon elem \rightarrow list \\
 & & cons\colon elem, list \rightarrow list \\
 & \textbf{FCTS} & app\colon list, list \rightarrow list \\
 & & sum\colon list \rightarrow elem \\
 & & isin\colon elem, list \rightarrow bool \\
 & \textbf{PROG} & app(l_1, l_2) \Leftarrow \texttt{if is}_{atom}?(l_1)\ \texttt{then}\ cons(\texttt{select}^1_{atom}(l_1), l_2) \\
 & & \qquad\qquad \texttt{else} \\
 & & \qquad\qquad cons(\texttt{select}^1_{cons}(l_1), app(\texttt{select}^2_{cons}(l_1), l_2)) \\
 & & sum(l) \quad \Leftarrow \texttt{if is}_{atom}?(l)\ \texttt{then select}^1_{atom}(l) \\
 & & \qquad\qquad \texttt{else select}^1_{cons}(l) + sum(\texttt{select}^2_{cons}(l)) \\
 & & isin(e, l) \ \Leftarrow \texttt{if is}_{atom}?(l)\ \texttt{then select}^1_{atom}(l) = e \\
 & & \qquad\qquad \texttt{else if select}^1_{cons}(l) = e\ \texttt{then}\ true \\
 & & \qquad\qquad\qquad \texttt{else}\ isin(e, \texttt{select}^2_{cons}(l))
\end{array}
$$

Figure 1: An example of a module definition.

- *$(PS_m \cup NS_m, PF_m \cup K_m \cup NF_m)$ is a signature and the range of all function symbols in K_m is an element of NS_m. Extending this signature by the following set of function symbols:*

$$
\begin{array}{ll}
 & \{\texttt{ifthenelse}_s\colon bool, s, s \rightarrow s \mid s \in NS_m\} \\
\cup & \{=_s\colon s, s \rightarrow bool \mid s \in NS_m\} \\
\cup & \{\texttt{is}_c?\colon s \rightarrow bool \mid s \in NS_m\} \\
\cup & \{\texttt{select}^j_c\colon s \rightarrow s_j \mid c \in K_m\,,\ c\colon s_1, \ldots, s_j, \ldots, s_n \rightarrow s\} \\
\cup & \{\bot_s\colon \rightarrow s \mid s \in NS_m\}
\end{array}
$$

  we obtain a standard signature $\Sigma_{Am} = (AS_m, AF_m)$.

- *PR_m is a recursive program of the form $(f_i(x_{i,1}, \ldots, x_{i,l_i}) \Leftarrow t_i)_{i=1,\ldots,n}$ where $NF_m = \{f_1, \ldots, f_n\}$, for all i the $x_{i,j}$ are pairwise distinct and of appropriate sort and $t_i \in T_{\Sigma_{Am}}(\{x_{i,1}, \ldots, x_{i,l_i}\})$ of appropriate sort.*

- *EF_m is a subset of AF_m such that $\Sigma_{Em} := (AS_m, EF_m)$ is a standard signature.*

The pair $(\Sigma_{Pm}, \Sigma_{Em})$ constitutes the signature of the module m.

We do not consider hiding of sorts here since this is not relevant from the logical point of view. Figure 1 contains an example of a module written in a more user friendly syntax. We will be somewhat sloppy in syntax and will not mention the standard parts of the signatures, drop the sort indices if known from the context and allow mixfix syntax if convenient. Furthermore we will not mention EF_m if identical to AF_m.

In order to formulate Theorem 2 we will need the notion of an extension of a module by a set of constants.

Definition 3 *Let m be a module and C a set of constant symbols disjoint from all components of m. Then the* extension of m by C *is the module*

$$(PS_m, PF_m \cup C, NS_m, K_m, NF_m, EF_m, PR_m)$$

3.2 Semantics

The semantics of modules as defined in this section again resembles [19]. In contrast to [19] where the semantics is defined denotationally we here take an approach that is adopted from the algebraic semantics method ([12]). The advantage of the algebraic semantics is that it makes the distinction between the recursion structure given by the program and the interpretation of the base functions explicit. Furthermore we will make use of the iterations of a term later in the logic.

An algebra over a standard signature will be called standard if it assignes the intended meanings to the standard parts of the signature.

Definition 4 *Let $\Sigma = (S, F)$ be a standard signature. A Σ-algebra A is called a* standard algebra ([19]) *if*

- $bool^A = \{\underline{\text{true}}, \underline{\text{false}}, \bot_{bool}\}$ *and* $true^A = \underline{\text{true}}$, $false^A = \underline{\text{false}}$, $\bot_{bool}^A = \bot_{bool}$
- *for all* $s \in S$ $\texttt{ifthenelse}_s^A$ *is the sequential* $if - then - else$ *function ([20]).*
- *For each function symbol $f \in F$ the denotation f^A is continuous with respect to the following ordering $\sqsubseteq_s$:*

$$x_1 \sqsubseteq_s x_2 \quad \text{iff} \quad x_1 = x_2 \ \text{or} \ x_1 = \bot_s^A$$

Alg_Σ denotes the class of all standard algebras with signature Σ.

Note that, since a standard signature contains a constant symbol $\bot_s$ of each sort s, a standard algebra always contains a distinguished carrier $\bot_s^A$ of each sort s.

Now we define an intermediate algebra A^* that extends the parameter algebra A by the newly defined sorts and operations except the recursive functions. This intermediate algebra will then be used in order to define the semantics of the recursive functions and to obtain the complete semantics of the module.

Definition 5 *Let m be a module with signature (Σ_P, Σ_E) and $A \in Alg_{\Sigma_P}$. We define an algebra A^* with signature $(AS_m, AF_m \setminus NF_m)$ as follows:*

- $A^* |_{\Sigma_P} := A$
- *In order to define the carrier sets of the new sorts let C_A denote the following set of formal constants:*

$$C_A := \{c_a \colon \rightarrow s \mid s \in PS_m, a \in s^A, a \neq \bot_s^A\}$$

and $s^A := T_{\Sigma \cup C_A, s} \cup \{\bot_s\}$ for all $s \in NS_m$.

- $\bot_s^A := \bot_s$ *for all $s \in NS_m$*
- *For all $s \in NS_m$* $\texttt{ifthenelse}_s$ *and $=_s$ obtain their meaning according to the definition of standard algebra*
- *For all $k \colon s_1, \ldots, s_n \rightarrow s \in K_m$:*

$$k^{A^*}(x_1, \ldots, x_n) := \begin{cases} k(x_1, \ldots, x_n) & \textit{if } x_i \neq \bot_{s_i}^A \textit{ for all } i \\ \bot_s^A & \textit{otherwise} \end{cases}$$

- *For all $c \colon s_1, \ldots, s_n \rightarrow s \in K_m$:*

$$\texttt{is}_c?^{A^*}(x) := \begin{cases} \underline{\text{true}} & \textit{if } x = c(x_1, \ldots, x_n) \textit{ for some } x_i \\ \bot_{bool} & \textit{if } x = \bot_s^A \\ \underline{\text{false}} & \textit{otherwise} \end{cases}$$

- *For all $c \colon s_1, \ldots, s_n \rightarrow s \in K_m$:*

$$\texttt{select}_c^{j\,A^*}(x) := \begin{cases} x_j & \textit{if } x = c(x_1, \ldots, x_j, \ldots, x_n) \\ & \quad \textit{for some } x_i \neq \bot_{s_i}^A, i = 1 \ldots n \\ \bot_{s_j}^A & \textit{otherwise} \end{cases}$$

Lemma 1 *A^* is a standard algebra.*

Definition 6 *Let m be a module with signature (Σ_P, Σ_E) and $t \in T_{\Sigma_{E_m}}(X)$. Then for each $n \in \mathbb{N}$, $t\langle n \rangle$ is the term obtained by n-fold application of the full substitution computation rule on t and then replacing each occurrence of recursive function symbols by $\bot$.*

In the terminology of [12], Definition 3.22, this is the n-th element t^n of the Kleene sequence of t.

The reader is referred to [12] for a formal definition.

Definition 7 *Let m be a module with signature (Σ_P, Σ_E). Then $\mathcal{M}(m)$ is a function*

$$\mathcal{M}(m)\colon Alg_{\Sigma_P} \to Alg_{\Sigma_E}$$

where for all $A \in Alg_{\Sigma_P}$:

- $\mathcal{M}(m)(A) \mid_{(AS_m, EF_m \setminus NF_m)} := A^* \mid_{(AS_m, EF_m \setminus NF_m)}$
- *for all $f : s_1, \ldots, s_n \to s \in NF_m \cap EF_m$, $a_i \in s_i^{A^*}$:*

$$f^{\mathcal{M}(m)(A)}(a_1, \ldots, a_n) := \bigsqcup_{i \geq 0} A^*(f(x_1, \ldots, x_n)\langle i \rangle)(\alpha[x_i \leftarrow a_i])$$

  for an arbitrary assignment $\alpha \in \Gamma_{A^*}$.

The choice of the assignment α is arbitrary since $x_1, \ldots x_n$ are the only free variables in the terms under consideration. The existence of the least upper bound of this set of values is a simple consequence of the fact that all cpo's are flat.

Lemma 2 *$\mathcal{M}(m)(A)$ is a standard algebra.*

Lemma 3 *Let m be a module with signature (Σ_P, Σ_E), $A \in Alg_{\Sigma_P}$, $B = \mathcal{M}(m)(A)$, $f\colon s_1, \ldots, s_n \to s \in EF \cap NF_m$ and $a_i \in s^B$. Let $\alpha \in \Gamma_B$ with $\alpha(x_i) = a_i$ for all $i = 1, \ldots, n$. Then*

- *either $f^B(a_1, \ldots, a_n) = \bot_s^B$ and $B(f(x_1, \ldots, x_n)\langle j \rangle)(\alpha) = \bot_s^B$ for all $j \in \mathbb{N}$*
- *or $f^B(a_1, \ldots, a_n) = c \neq \bot_s^B$ and there is a j_0 such that for all $j \geq j_0$: $B(f(x_1, \ldots, x_n)\langle j \rangle)(\alpha) = c$*

3.3 Basic Properties of the Semantics

Our semantics obeys the *persistency* condition. Intuitively this means that the sorts and operations of the parameter algebra are not modified by the semantics of a module.

Lemma 4 *Let m be a module with signature (Σ_P, Σ_E) and $A \in Alg_{\Sigma_P}$. Then*

$$\mathcal{M}(m)(A) \mid_{\Sigma_P \cap \Sigma_E} = A \mid_{\Sigma_P \cap \Sigma_E}$$

We now show two lemmas that we will need for the proof of Theorem 1, the straightforward proofs are omitted here.

Lemma 5 *Let m be a module with signature (Σ_P, Σ_E), $A, B \in Alg_{\Sigma_P}$ and $A \subseteq B$. Then $\mathcal{M}(m)(A) \subseteq \mathcal{M}(m)(B)$*

Lemma 6 *Let m be a module with signature (Σ_P, Σ_E), $\Sigma_P \subseteq \Sigma_E$, $A \in Alg_{\Sigma_P}$ and $B' \in Alg_{\Sigma_E}$ with $B' \subseteq \mathcal{M}(m)(A)$.
Then $B' = \mathcal{M}(m)(B' \mid_{\Sigma_P})$.*

4 Logic

4.1 Basic Definitions and Properties

Definition 8 *For a standard signature $\Sigma = (S, F)$ let WFF_Σ be the set of first order sentences over the language $\langle S, F, \{=_s \mid s \in S\}\rangle$ where each $=_s$ is a binary predicate symbol.*

If m is a module with signature (Σ_P, Σ_E) we denote WFF_{Σ_P} by $PWFF_m$ and WFF_{Σ_E} by WFF_m.

Let us emphasize that we only consider sentences, that is first order formulas without free variables. Besides the usual conventions on the syntax of first order logic we use the following abbreviations:

$$
\begin{array}{rcl}
(t_1 \sqsubseteq t_2) & \text{stands for} & (t_1 = \bot \lor t_1 = t_2) \\
\forall x \in s \,.\, w & \text{stands for} & \forall x : s \,.\, x = \bot_s \lor w \\
\exists x \in s \,.\, w & \text{stands for} & \exists x : s \,.\, x \neq \bot_s \land w
\end{array}
$$

We now come to the central definition of this paper. For a sentence $w \in WFF_\Sigma$ and (not necessarily standard) algebra A we write as usual $A \models w$ if A is a model of w, see again [10] for complete definitions. The point is that we can now use the semantics of a module with signature (Σ_P, Σ_E) in order to express properties of standard Σ_P-algebras by Σ_E-sentences.

Definition 9 *Let m be a module with signature (Σ_P, Σ_E), $A \in Alg_{\Sigma_P}$ and $w \in WFF_m$. We define*

$$A]\!\models_m w \quad \Leftrightarrow \quad \mathcal{M}(m)(A) \models w$$

For $W \subseteq WFF_m$ we write $A]\!\models_m W$ if $A]\!\models_m w$ for all $w \in W$. $]\!\models_m w$ means $A]\!\models_m w$ for all $A \in Alg_{\Sigma_P}$. Furthermore $Th_m(A) := \{w \in WFF_m \mid A]\!\models_m w\}$

For example let m be the module of Figure 1 and Nat the extension of the algebra of natural numbers to a standard algebra. Then

$$Nat]\!\models_m \forall l_1, l_2 : list \,.\, sum(app(l_1, l_2)) = sum(l_1) + sum(l_2)$$

As an immediate consequence of the persistency of the semantics (Lemma 4) we get

Lemma 7 *Let m be a module with signature (Σ_P, Σ_E), $w \in WFF_{\Sigma_P \cap \Sigma_E}$. Then for alle algebras $A \in Alg_{\Sigma_P}$:*

$$A \models w \quad \textit{iff} \quad A]\!\models_m w$$

This means that our new logic is at least as expressive as first order logic. Later we will see that, depending on the module under consideration, there is in general indeed a gain in expressiveness.

4.2 Classes of Parameter Algebras

We are not always interested in parameter algebras from the whole class Alg_{Σ_P}. Instead it is often natural to restrict the parameter algebras to some subclass of Alg_{Σ_P}. The choice of this subclass should depend only on the input signature. We put some reasonable constraints on the possible classes of parameter algebras that we will need in the following.

We call a class of algebras *compact* if the compactness theorem of first order logic holds in this class of models.

Definition 10 *A class C of Σ-algebras is called* compact *if for each set $W \subseteq WFF_\Sigma$ of formulas the following holds:*

If each finite subset of W has a model in C then W has a model in C

The choice of a particular class of parameter algebras is formally expressed by the concept of a *domain operator*:

Definition 11 *A domain operator $\Im$ maps each standard signature Σ to a subclass $\Im_\Sigma$ of Alg_Σ such that the following holds:*

1. *$\Im_\Sigma$ is compact.*
2. *$\Im_\Sigma$ is closed under elementary submodels.*
3. *For any sort symbol s in Σ and constant symbol c not in Σ:*

$$\Im_{\Sigma\cup\{c:s\}} = \{(A, a) \mid A \in \Im_\Sigma \text{ and } a \in s^A\}$$

The next lemma shows that a wide class of mappings satisfies the constraints of Definition 11:

Lemma 8 *Let ι be a mapping that maps each standard signature $\Sigma = (S, F)$ to some set of formulas $\iota(\Sigma) \subseteq WFF_\Sigma$ where only constants from $\{true, false\} \cup \{\bot_s \mid s \in S\}$ are allowed. Then the operator mapping each signature Σ to the class of standard algebras that are models of $\iota(\Sigma)$ is a domain operator.*

Proof: First observe that for given standard signature Σ the class of Σ-standard algebras can de described by some set of first order axioms. Therefore the compactness property and the closure under elementary submodels are easy consequences of the pertaining theorems of first order logic: The compactness theorem (Theorem 1.3.22 in [5]), respectively the sharpened Skolem-Löwenheim Theorem (Theorem 3.1.6 in [5]). The proof of the third constraint is trivial. □

As a consequence the following operators are indeed domain operators:

1. The operator $\Im^{f}$ mapping each signature to the full class of standard algebras.
2. The operator $\Im^{strict}$ mapping each signature to the class of standard algebras where all functions except $if - then - else$ are strict.
3. The operator mapping each signature to the class of standard algebras where all functions are sequential ([29]).

We therefore claim that the constraints in Definition 11 are reasonable. Note that we did not require closure of the domain operator under the semantics of modules, although this would be an acceptable constraint in view of vertical composition of modules. To be precise, we do *not* require that $\mathcal{M}(m)(A) \in \Im_{\Sigma_E}$ for $A \in \Im_{\Sigma_P}$.

4.3 Parameter Conditions

The notion of a parameter condition links first order logic to our new logic.

Definition 12 *Let m be a module with signature (Σ_P, Σ_E), $\Im$ a class operator and $w \in WFF_m$. A sentence $v \in PWFF_m$ is a $\Im, m$-*parameter condition *of w if for all $A \in \Im_{\Sigma_P}$:*

$$A \models v \quad \Rightarrow \quad A]\models_m w$$

*A sentence $v \in PWFF_m$ is a $\Im, m$-*weakest parameter condition *of w if for all $A \in \Im_{\Sigma_P}$:*

$$A \models v \quad \Leftrightarrow \quad A]\models_m w$$

The following lemma is immediate by the definition:

Lemma 9 *Weakest parameter conditions are unique up to equivalence, that is: let m be a module with signature (Σ_P, Σ_E), $\Im$ a domain operator and $w \in WFF_m$. Then for all weakest parameter conditions $v_1, v_2 \in PWFF_m$: $\Im_{\Sigma_P} \models v_1 \leftrightarrow v_2$*

We illustrate the important notion of a weakest parameter condition with some examples.

1. Let m be the module of Figure 1. The formula

$$\forall l_1, l_2 \in list \,.\, sum(app(l_1, l_2)) = sum(l_1) + sum(l_2)$$

has the $\Im^{strict}$, m-weakest parameter condition:

$$\forall x_1, x_2, x_3 \in elem \,.\, x_1 + (x_2 + x_3) = (x_1 + x_2) + x_3$$

2. Let m be again the module of Figure 1. The class of standard algebras that fulfill the formula

$$w := \exists l \in list\,.\,\forall x \in elem\,.\,isin(x, l) = true$$

is exactly the class of finite Σ_{Pm}-algebras with nonempty carrier set. Since the class of finite algebras cannot be described by means of first order logic ([5]) w does not have a $\Im^f, m$-weakest parameter condition.

These last examples show that our new logic is more expressive than first order logic. In the next section we will discuss the model theoretic properties of the new logic that reflect this gain in expressiveness.

The following lemma gives a special case in which a $\Im, m$-weakest parameter condition always exists:

Lemma 10 *Let m be a module with $NF_m = \emptyset$ and $\Im$ a domain operator. Then for each $w \in WFF_m$ there exists a $\Im, m$-weakest parameter condition. Furthermore for each formula w the weakest parameter condition is computable.*

Proof: The proof follows from procedures for solving equational problems in term algebras ([6], [23]). See [3] for details how to apply these results to the semantics of modules. □

5 Properties of the New Logic

We now consider two basic model-theoretic properties of our new logic. Lindström ([17]) has shown that first order logic is the only logic fulfilling countable compactness and the Skolem-Löwenheim property (see also [24], [5]). Besides the fact that he considers logical systems with the whole class of algebras as domain (instead of standard algebras in our case) his theorem applies in our case only to an endogenous variant of our logic where all possible modules are considered. Here we are interested in obtaining theorems about the logical properties of distinguished modules.

5.1 Downward Skolem-Löwenheim

Theorem 1 *Let m be a module with signature (Σ_P, Σ_E), $\Im$ a domain operator and $A \in \Im_{\Sigma_P}$.*

Then for each family $Z = (Z_s)_{s \in PS}$ of sets with cardinality at most $\aleph_0$ and $Z_s \subseteq s^A$ there is a $B \in \Im_{\Sigma_P}$ of cardinality $\aleph_0$ that contains Z such that $\mathcal{M}(m)(B)$ is an elementary submodel of $\mathcal{M}(m)(A)$.

Proof: Without loss of generality let Z contain $\aleph_0$ many elements. Furthermore we may assume $\Sigma_P \subseteq \Sigma_E$ since elementary submodels are invariant under restriction of the signature.

By the sharpened downward Skolem Löwenheim Theorem of first order logic (Theorem 3.1.6 of [5]) there is an elementary submodel B' of $\mathcal{M}(m)(A)$ with cardinality $\aleph_0$ containing Z.
Let $B := B' |_{\Sigma_P}$. B contains Z and therefore has cardinality $\aleph_0$. By Theorem 6: $B' = \mathcal{M}(m)(B)$. Since B' is an elementary submodel of $\mathcal{M}(m)(A)$, B is also an elementary submodel of A. By the closure of $\Im_{\Sigma_P}$ under elementary submodels $B \in \Im_{\Sigma_P}$. □

Corollary 1 *Let m be a module with signature (Σ_P, Σ_E) and $A \in \Im_{\Sigma_P}$ of infinite cardinality. Then there is a $B \in \Im_{\Sigma_P}$ of cardinality $\aleph_0$ with $Th_m(A) = Th_m(B)$.*

Proof: Let B be the model according to Theorem 1. By the properties of elementary submodels $\mathcal{M}(m)(A)$ and $\mathcal{M}(m)(B)$ have the same first order theory and so $Th_m(A) = Th_m(B)$. □

5.2 Compactness

From first order logic it is known that the most applications of the compactness theorem require the introduction of new constant symbols in some intermediate step. These new constants in some sense allow to express an existential quantification over an infinite conjunction of formulas. Therefore the compactness theorem can be used in order to show that a theory has a model containing an element satisfying some infinite set of formulas (see for instance Proposition 2.2.7 in [5]). In order to argue about compactness properties of our logic we therefore have to consider extensions of given modules, since including them into the parameter part is the only way to incorporate new constant symbols.

Definition 13 *Let m be a module with signature (Σ_P, Σ_E) and $\Im$ a domain operator. We say that $]\models_m$ is* $\Im$-compact *if for each $W \subseteq WFF_m$ the following holds:*

> *If for each finite $F \subseteq W$ there is a $A \in \Im_{\Sigma_P}$ with $A]\models_m F$, then there exists $B \in \Im_{\Sigma_P}$ with $B]\models_m W$*

Theorem 2 *Let m be a module and $\Im$ a domain operator. Then the following statements are equivalent:*

1. *For each extension m' of m, $]\models_{m'}$ is $\Im$-compact.*
2. *For each extension m' of m and $w \in WFF_{m'}$ w has a $\Im, m'$-weakest parameter condition*

Proof:

$(1) \Longleftarrow (2)$

This is an easy consequence of the definition of a weakest parameter condition and of the compactness property of the domain operator $\Im$.

$(1) \Longrightarrow (2)$

Assume that for each extension m' of m $]\models_{m'}$ is compact. We define the set W as the set of all formulas that belong to some arbitrary extension of m. Strictly speaking this is a set only if we fix some set of possible constant symbols, but we do not bother about set theoretic peculiarities here.

$$W := \bigcup_{m' \text{ extends } m} WFF_{m'}$$

For each $w \in W$ define

- $\phi_1(w)$ is the number of occurrences of existential quantifiers in w ranging over some new sort
- $\phi_2(w)$ is the number of occurrences of existential quantifiers in w ranging over some parameter sort plus the number of occurrences of $\neg$, $\wedge$ in w.

With the help of these notions we define a relation $\sqsubseteq$ on W by

$$w_1 \sqsubseteq w_2 :\Longleftrightarrow (\phi_1(w_1), \phi_2(w_1)) \leq_{\text{lex}} (\phi_1(w_2), \phi_2(w_2))$$

where $\leq_{\text{lex}}$ is the lexicographic extension of the ordering $\leq$ on natural numbers. From the properties of lexicographic orderings it is obvious that $\sqsubseteq$ is a well founded quasi ordering ([7]).

Now let $w \in W$ be a minimal formula with respect to $\sqsubseteq$ such that there exists an extension m' of m with $w \in WFF_{m'}$ and w does not have a weakest $\Im, m'$-parameter condition. Σ' denotes the parameter signature of m'. First we show that w must be an atomic formula. Note that for a given formula $v \in W$ we can restrict our attention to the minimal extension m^* of m such that $v \in WFF_{m^*}$. The addition of further constants does not affect the existence of a weakest parameter condition. We say that $v \in W$ has a weakest parameter condition (without mentioning the module) if it has a $\Im, m^*$-weakest parameter condition where m^* is the extension of m by the constants occurring in v.

1. Suppose $w = \exists x : s \,.\, v$ where s is a parameter sort. Let c be a new constant symbol not occurring in m' or w. By the minimality condition $v(x/c)$ has a weakest parameter condition r. We obtain a contradiction by showing that $\exists y : s \,.\, r(c/y)$ is a weakest parameter condition of w where y does not occur freely in r.

   Let m'' denote the extension of m' by $\{c \colon s\}$ and $A \in \Im_{\Sigma'}$.

$$
\begin{array}{lll}
 & A \models \exists y : s\,.\,r(c/y) & \\
\Leftrightarrow & (A, a) \models r & \text{for some extension } (A, a) \text{ of } A \\
\Leftrightarrow & (A, a)]\!\models_{m''} v(x/c) & \text{since } r \text{ is a } \Im, m'' \text{ weakest parameter condition of } v(x/c) \\
\Leftrightarrow & (A, a)]\!\models_{m''} \exists x : s\,.\,v & \text{since } c \text{ does not occur in } m'' \text{ or } w \\
\Leftrightarrow & A]\!\models_{m'} \exists x : s\,.\,v & \text{since } c \text{ does not occur in } m' \text{ or } w
\end{array}
$$

2. Suppose $w = \exists x : s\,.\,v(x)$ where s is a new sort. Define

$$C_s := T_{K,s}(X_{par}) \cup \{\bot_s\}$$

where X_{par} is the family of variables of parameter sort. From the definition of the semantics it is immediate that for each $A \in \Im_{\Sigma'}$ and $a \in s^{\mathcal{M}(m')(A)}$ there is a $t \in C_s$ and an assignment $\alpha \in \Gamma_A$ with

$$\mathcal{M}(m')(A)(t)(\alpha) = a \tag{1}$$

For each finite set $F \subseteq C_s$, the formula

$$\bigvee_{t \in F} \exists free(t)\,.\,v(x/t)$$

has by minimality of w a $\Im, m'$-weakest parameter condition r_F which is itself a $\Im, m'$-parameter condition of w. Since w by assumption does not have a weakest parameter condition, for each finite $F \subseteq C_s$ there is a $A \in \Im_{\Sigma'}$ with

$$A]\!\models_{m'} \{\exists x : s\,.\,v\} \cup \{\forall free(t)\,.\,\neg v(x/t) \mid t \in F\}$$

Since $]\!\models_{m'}$ is compact there is an $A \in \Im_{\Sigma'}$ with

$$A]\!\models_{m'} \{\exists x : s\,.\,v\} \cup \{\forall free(t)\,.\,\neg v(x/t) \mid t \in C_s\}$$

This contradicts (1).

3. Suppose $w = \neg v$. By minimality of w v has a weakest parameter condition r. Then $\neg r$ must be a weakest parameter condition of w.

4. Suppose $w = v_1 \vee v_2$. By minimality of w v_1 and v_2 have weakest parameter conditions r_1 and r_2, respectively. Then $r_1 \vee r_2$ must be a weakest parameter condition of w.

We now know that w must be of the form $t_1 = t_2$. This formula is equivalent to

$$\underbrace{(t_1 = t_2 \wedge t_1 \neq \bot)}_{v_1} \vee \neg(\underbrace{t_1 \neq \bot}_{v2} \vee \underbrace{t_2 \neq \bot}_{v_3})$$

As in the cases (3),(4) above it follows that at least one of v_1, v_2, v_3 does not have a weakest parameter condition. Without loss of generality we assume that v_1 does not have a weakest parameter condition.

By Lemma 10 we know that for each natural number n there is a $\Im, m'$-weakest parameter condition r_n of $t_1\langle n\rangle = t_2\langle n\rangle \wedge t_1\langle n\rangle \neq \bot$. Observe that $]\models_{m'} \neg r_n \supset \neg r_m$ for $n > m$. Since r_n is a parameter condition for v_1 and since v_1 by assumption does not have a weakest parameter condition, for each finite set F of natural numbers there is a $A \in \Im_{\Sigma'}$ with

$$A]\models_{m'} \{v_1\} \cup \{\neg r_n \mid n \in F\}$$

By the compactness property of $]\models_{m'}$ there is a $A \in \Im_{\Sigma'}$ with

$$A]\models_{m'} \{t_1 = t_2 \wedge t_1 \neq \bot\} \cup \{t_1\langle n\rangle \neq t_2\langle n\rangle \vee t_1\langle n\rangle = \bot \mid n > 0\}$$

According to the properties of monotonic functions there are two possibilities:

- For all n: $\mathcal{M}(m')(A)(t_1\langle n\rangle = \bot$. This contradicts $\mathcal{M}(m')(A)(t_1) \neq \bot$ by Lemma 3.
- There is a n_0 such that $\mathcal{M}(m')(A)(t_1\langle n_0\rangle) \neq \bot$. Then for all $n > n_0$ $\mathcal{M}(m')(A)(t_1\langle n\rangle) \neq \bot$ and therefore $\mathcal{M}(m')(t_1\langle n\rangle) \neq \mathcal{M}(m')(t_2\langle n\rangle)$. This contradicts $\mathcal{M}(m')(A)(t_1) = \mathcal{M}(m')(A)(t_2)$ by Lemma 3.

□

6 Decidability Questions

We now show that the existence of weakest parameter conditions is in general undecidable, even if the module does not introduce new sorts.

In order to show undecidability of the existence of weakest parameter conditions we have to take care that the domain operator under consideration is rich enough. If the domain operator is too trivial a weakest parameter condition always exists. Take for example any domain operator that maps each standard signature to some class containing one single algebra. Here a weakest parameter condition always exists, it is either `TRUE` or `FALSE`. Therefore we require the domain operator to be non-trivial. In order to define non-triviality we use some notions from [30]:

Definition 14 *A domain operator $\Im$ is called* non-trivial *if for each hierarchical type $T = (\Sigma, E, P)$ where P is the specification BOOL, E is a finite set of Σ-equations and T is hierarchy-persistent the extension of the initial model of T to a standard algebra is contained in $\Im_\Sigma$.*

The extension of A to a standard algebra *is obtained by extending the signature to a standard signature, assigning $\bot$,* `ifthenelse` *and $=$ their standard meaning and extending all functions of A strictly.*

We use a result about two-head automata that turned out to be useful for undecidability results in the field of program schemes. For a definition of two-head automata the reader is referred to [11] from which we borrow the notations and to [21]. Here we consider only automata over a fixed input alphabet $\{0, 1\}$. We use the following result

PAR **SORTS** *tapeposition*
value
OPNS $start\colon \to tapeposition$
$next\colon tapeposition \to tapeposition$
$contents0\colon tapeposition \to bool$
$a\colon \to value$
$f\colon value \to value$
$test\colon value \to bool$
BODY **FCTS** $H\colon \to bool$
$F_q\colon tapeposition, tapeposition, value \to bool$
for all states q of the automaton
PROG $H \Leftarrow F_{q_0}(start, start, a)$
$F_q(p_1, p_2, x) \Leftarrow$ `if` $contents0(p_1)$
`then` $F_{\delta(q,0)}(next(p_1), p_2, x)$
`else` $F_{\delta(q,1)}(next(p_1), p_2, x)$
for all states $q \in K_1$
$F_q(p_1, p_2, x) \Leftarrow$ `if` $contents0(p_2)$
`then` $F_{\delta(q,0)}(p_1, next(p_2), x)$
`else` $F_{\delta(q,1)}(p_1, next(p_2), x)$
for all states $q \in K_2$
$F_r(p_1, p_2, x) \Leftarrow F_r(p_1, p_2, x)$
$F_a(p_1, p_2, x) \Leftarrow$ `if` $test(x)$
`then` *true*
`else` $F_{q_0}(start, start, f(x))$
EXPORT $H\colon \to bool$

Figure 2: A module simulating a two-head automaton used for Theorem 3

Lemma 11 ([21]) *It is not semidecidable whether for a THA A the language accepted by A, $\mathcal{L}_A$ for short, is empty.*

The module of Figure 2 simulates a THA in the following sense. To a given Σ_P algebra B we associate the input tape $tape_B$ that is defined by

$$tape_B(i) := \begin{cases} 0 & \text{if } B(contents0(next^i(start))) = true \\ 1 & \text{if } B(contents0(next^i(start))) = false \end{cases}$$

Obviously each possible input tape is a $tape_B$ for some Σ_P algebra B.

Lemma 12 *Let A be a two-head automaton and m be the pertaining module according* *to Figure 2. For each $B \in Alg_{\Sigma_P}$ and $\alpha \in \Gamma_B$:*

$$\begin{aligned} tape_B \in \mathcal{L}_A &\Rightarrow \mathcal{M}(m)(B)(F_{q_0}(start, start, x))(\alpha) = \\ &\quad \mathcal{M}(m)(B)(\texttt{if}\ test(x)\ \texttt{then}\ true\ \texttt{else}\ F_{q_0}(start, start, f(x)))(\alpha) \\ tape_B \notin \mathcal{L}_A &\Rightarrow \mathcal{M}(m)(B)(F_{q_0}(start, start, x))(\alpha) = \bot \end{aligned}$$

Proof: This follows easily from the definitions. □

Lemma 13 *Let m be the module associated to the THA A according to Figure 2 and $\Im$ a non trivial domain operator.*

1. *If $\mathcal{L}_A = \emptyset$ then $]\models_m H = \bot$*
2. *If $\mathcal{L}_A \neq \emptyset$ then the formula $(H \neq \bot)$ does not have a $\Im, m$-weakest parameter condition.*

Proof: (1) follows immediately from Lemma 12. For part (2), let $t \in \mathcal{L}_A$ and n be the last position of t visited by any of the heads of A when feeded with input t. Suppose v is a $\Im, m$ weakest import condition of $(H \neq \bot)$.

We can describe the relevant part of t (that is the initial part of t up to position n) by a finite set of equations:

$$e_t := \bigwedge_{i=0\ldots n} \begin{cases} contents0(next^i(start)) = true & \text{if } t(i) = 0 \\ contents0(next^i(start)) = false & \text{if } t(i) = 1 \end{cases}$$

From Lemma 12 we conclude that for each $B \in Alg_{\Sigma_P}$ with $B \models e_t$:

$$B\,]\models_m H \neq \bot \Leftrightarrow B \models test(f^i(a)) = true \text{ for some } i \tag{2}$$

On the other hand each set of the form

$$\{v, e_t\} \cup \{test(f^i(a)) = false \mid i \leq n_0\}$$

has by non-triviality of $\Im$ a model in $\Im_{\Sigma_P}$, namely the extension of the initial model of $(BOOL, \Sigma_P, E)$ to a standard algebra where

$$\begin{aligned} E &= \{e_t\} \\ &\cup \{test(f^i(a)) = false \mid i \leq n_0\} \\ &\cup \{test(f^{n_0+1}(x)) = true\} \end{aligned}$$

By compactness of $\Im$ there is an algebra in $\Im_{\Sigma_P}$ satisfying

$$\{v, e_t\} \cup \{test(f^i(a)) = false \mid i \in \mathbb{N}\}$$

This contradicts (2). □

As a consequence we can in each formula, if $\mathcal{L}_A = \emptyset$, replace H bei $\bot_{bool}$ thus obtaining a $\Im, m$-weakest parameter condition. Therefore we get the first undecidability result of this section:

Theorem 3 *For a non-trivial domain operator $\Im$ the following sets are not semidecidable:*

- *the set of modules m such that all formulas $w \in WFF_m$ have a $\Im, m$-weakest parameter condition*

- *the set of pairs (w, m) where m is a module, $w \in WFF_m$ and w has a $\Im, m$-weakest parameter condition*

With a similar proof we can also show that the sets of Theorem 3 are not semidecidable. Here we state only the theorem:

Theorem 4 *For a non-trivial domain operator $\Im$ the following sets are not semidecidable:*

- *the set of modules m such that some formula $w \in WFF_m$ does not have a $\Im, m$ weakest parameter condition*
- *the set of pairs (w, m) where m is a module and $w \in WFF_m$ and w does not have a $\Im, m$ weakest parameter condition*

Acknowledgements

I wish to thank Thomas Lehmann, Joachim Philippi and Jacques Loeckx for comments and discussions.

References

[1] American National Standards Institute. *The Programming Language Ada Reference Manual.* LNCS vol. 155. Springer, 1983.

[2] J. Bishop. *Data Abstraction in Programming Languages.* Addison–Wesley, 1986.

[3] P. Buhmann. Disunifikation in modularen Termalgebren. Master's thesis, Universität des Saarlandes, 1991. In preparation.

[4] R. M. Burstall and J. A. Goguen. Semantics of CLEAR, a specification language. In D. Björner, editor, *Abstract Softare Specifications*, pages 292–332. Springer LNCS, vol. 86, 1980.

[5] C. C. Chang and H. J. Keisler. *Model Theory.* Studies in Logic and the Foundations of Mathematics, vol. 73. North-Holland Publishing Company, third edition, 1990.

[6] H. Comon and P. Lescanne. Equational problems and disunification. *Journal of Symbolic Computation*, 7(3,4):371–425, 1989.

[7] N. Dershowitz. Termination of rewriting. *Journal of Symbolic Computation*, 3:69–116, 1987.

[8] H. Ehrig and B. Mahr. *Fundamentals of Algebraic Specification, vol. 1.* EATCS-Monographs on Theoretical Computer Science. Springer-Verlag, 1985.

[9] H. Ehrig and B. Mahr. *Fundamentals of Algebraic Specification, vol. 2.* EATCS-Monographs on Theoretical Computer Science. Springer-Verlag, 1990.

[10] H. B. Enderton. *Mathematical Introduction to Logic.* Academic Press, 1972.

[11] S. A. Greibach. *Theory of Program Structures: Schemes, Semantics, Verification.* Lecture Notes in Computer Science, Vol. 35. Springer Verlag, 1975.

[12] I. Guessarian. *Algebraic Semantics.* Lecture Notes in Computer Science, Vol. 99. Springer Verlag, 1979.

[13] R. Harper, D. MacQueen, and R. Milner. Standard ML. Technical Report ECS-LFCS-86-2, Edinburgh University, 1986.

[14] D. Kozen and J. Tiuryn. Logics of programs. In J. van Leeuwen, editor, *Handbook of Theoretical Computer Science, volume B*, chapter 14, pages 789–840. Elsevier Science Publishers, 1990.

[15] T. Lehmann and J. Loeckx. The specification language of OBSCURE. In D. Sannella and A. Tarlecki, editors, *5th Workshop on Specification of Abstract Data Types*, pages 131–153. Springer LNCS, vol. 332, 1987.

[16] T. Lehmann and J. Loeckx. OBSCURE, a specification language for abstract data types. Technical Report A 19-90, Universität des Saarlandes, 1990. Submitted for publication.

[17] P. Lindström. On extension of elementary logic. *Theoria*, 35:1–11, 1969.

[18] B. Liskov and J. Guttag. *Abstraction and Specification in Program Development.* MIT press, 1986.

[19] J. Loeckx. Algorithmic specifications: A constructive specification method for abstract data types. *ACM Trans. Prog. Lang. Syst.*, 9(4), 1987.

[20] J. Loeckx and K. Sieber. *The Foundations of Program Verification.* Wiley/Teubner, 2nd edition, 1987.

[21] D. C. Luckham, D. M. R. Park, and M. S. Paterson. On formalized computer programs. *J. Comput. Syst. Sci.*, 4:220–249, 1970.

[22] D. MacQueeen. Modules for standard ML. In [13], 1986.

[23] M. J. Maher. Complete axiomatisations of the algebra of finite, rational and infinite trees. In *Third Anual Symposium on Logic in Computer Science*, pages 348–357, Edinburgh, Scotland, july 1988. IEEE.

[24] J. D. Monk. *Mathematical Logic.* Graduate Texts in Mathematics, vol. 37. Springer, 1976.

[25] M. Shaw, editor. *Alphard: Form and Content.* Springer, 1981.

[26] J. Tiuryn. A survey of the logic of effective definitions. In E. Engeler, editor, *Proceedings of the Workshop on Logics of Programs*, pages 198–245. Springer LNCS, vol. 125, 1981.

[27] R. Treinen. First order data types and first order logic. Interner Bericht A 01/91, Universität des Saarlandes, Jan. 1991.

[28] D. A. Turner. Miranda: A non-strict functional language with polymorphic types. In J.-P. Jouannaud, editor, *IFIP International Conference on Functional Programming Languages and Computer Architecture*, pages 1–16. Springer LNCS, vol. 201, 1985.

[29] J. Vuillemin. Correct and optimal implementations of recursion in a simple programming language. *J. Comput. Syst. Sci.*, 9:332–354, 1974.

[30] M. Wirsing, P. Pepper, H. Partsch, W. Dosch, and M. Broy. On hierarchies of abstract data types. *Acta Informatica*, 20:1–33, 1983.

[31] N. Wirth. *Programming in MODULA-2.* Springer, third edition, 1985.

Efficient Program Synthesis: Semantics, Logic, Complexity

Max I. Kanovich
Tver' State University, Tver' 170000, USSR

Abstract

The problem of program synthesis is considered.

(1) A computational semantics is introduced for relational knowledge bases. Our semantics naturally arises from practical experience of databases and knowledge bases.

(2) It is stated that the corresponding logic coincides exactly with the intuitionistic one.

(3) Our methods of proof of the general theorems turn out to be very useful for designing new efficient algorithms.
In particular, one can construct a program synthesizer that runs in linear space.
As a corollary, we can explain why there exist programs that solve PSPACE-complete problems "in a reasonable time" despite of their theoretical exponential uniform lower bound.

1 Introduction

The problem of program synthesis in relational knowledge bases is related with the membership problems in relational detabases and is formulated in the following way.

A knowledge base KB is given. (A system of laws and constraints Deps is the core of KB). Tasks of the form "for the knowledge base KB, find Z from X"are proposed.

One would like

(1) to analyze the task: determine whether the "functional dependency" $(X \to Z)$ follows from the laws of KB;

(2) to synthesize a solution of the task: using the laws of KB, to compose an algorithm (a program) which, from a give input list X, computes an output list Z.

General theorems of complexity theory show that the problem of analyzing such a "computational" task and synthesizeing a program for its solution is unsolvable. Even when we restrict the class of knowledge bases, we are confronted with all the theoretical troubles concerning NP- and PSPACE-completeness. On the other hand, there is much experience in constructing programs for practical computational tasks. One of the stimuli for the work was the desire to understand this phenomenon: that a certain system can work successfully and efficiently in practice while its complexity is proved to have exponential uniform lower bound.

We investigate knowledge bases that contain

(1) entities of both simple and functional types (functionals of higher types are permitted),

(2) functional, operator, and variant dependencies.

We define semantics and logic of tasks in these knowledge bases, and , on the basis of a specialized calculus, construct algorithms that can solve a PSPACE-complete problem in small (linear) space and in quasipolynomial time.

To illustrate the problem we use an example that involeves many of the questions one must answer in developing a useful theory of knowledge bases and computational tasks.

Suppose we have an office with two clerks and we want to consider simple entities (attributes) such as

"person" (let its domain be the set {Sidorov, Johnson}) ,
"year", "salary", "pension", "amount", "total (for a year)",
"(expericence) level",

and the functional entity "pay_ roll" of the type (person $\rightarrow$ amount):
An implementation of the functional entity pay_roll is a program (a finite function) mapping the persons to be paid into the amounts due to each.

We can postulate the following dependencies for the problem:

$D1$: (year , level $\rightarrow$ salary)
('given a year and a level, salary can be calculated'),

$D2$: (salary $\rightarrow$ amount)
('amount can be calculated from salary'),

$D3$: (pension $\rightarrow$ amount)
('amount can be calculated from pension'),

$D4$: (year , person $\rightarrow$ level OR pension)
('given a year and a person, eigher level or pension is defined'),

$D5$: (pay_roll $\rightarrow$ total)
('for a given implementation of pay_roll, total can be calculated:
total = pay_roll(Sidorov) + pay_roll(Johnson) ').

We may propose a four-state table to represent a database T':

year	person	level	salary	pension	amount	pay_roll	total
1990	Sidorov	low	10	undef	10	p'	30
1990	Johnson	high	40	undef	40	p''	45
1991	Sidorov	undef	undef	5	5	p''	45
1991	Johnson	high	40	undef	40	p''	45

where is p' and p'' are programs such that

$$p'(\text{Sidorov}) = 10; \quad p''(\text{Sidorov}) = 5$$
$$p'(\text{Johnson}) = 20; \quad p''(\text{Johnson}) = 40.$$

Let us recall that p' and p'' are possible implementations (values) of the entity pay_roll. The instance T' seems to show that the following task:

"For a give year, determine the value of total",

is unsolvable because

(1) all the dependencies are satisfied on the instance T',

(2) the implementations of the functional entity pay_roll are in accordance with the values of person and amount, but

(3) the functional dependency D' : (year $\rightarrow$ total) is not satisfied on the instance T'.

On the other hand, we can construct a scheme-program to solve this task:
Let a value of year be given.
First, we create an implementation of pay_roll of the type (person $\rightarrow$ amount):

1. For a given person, according to the variant dependency $D4$, either level or pension is defined.
2. If level is defined then amount is computed with the help of the functional dependencies $D1$ and $D2$.
3. If pension is defined then amount is computed by the dependency $D3$.

Now, applying the dependency $D5$ to this implementation, total is calculated.

This contradiction can be explained. The point is that there is no **full** accordance between entities pay_roll, person and amount on T'. E.g. if we fix the value of year by setting: year=1990, we have a truncated database T'':

year	person	level	salary	pension	amount	pay_roll	total
1990	Sidorov	low	10	undef	10	p'	30
1990	Johnson	high	40	undef	40	p''	45

In this new database the dependency between person and amount becomes functional: there is a function p such that amount = p(person) on T", but both p' and p'' do not agree with this function p.

2 Relational Knowledge Bases

Let us first give a definition of relational knowledge bases.

A relational knowledge base is said to be a tuple

$$KB = (\text{Names, Functs, Doms, Deps})$$

where

(1) Names $= (A[1], A[2], \cdots, A[n] \cdots)$
is a recursively enumerable sequence of names of "entities" (or "attributes").

(2) The set Names is divided into two parts: some entities are declared as "functional entities"; Functs is a recursively enumerable set of names of all "functional entities" together with their finite types: the type of a functional entity F is an expression of the form $(X \rightarrow Y)$, where X and Y are lists of the names of entities from Names, the list X is called "the argument list".

(3) Doms is a recursively enumerable sequence of domains of entities from Names: the domain of entity V is denoted by $Dom(V)$.
(An "empty" entity B such that $Dom(B)$ is empty can be considered).
For a list X, $Dom(X)$ is the Cartesian product of domains of all entities from the list X.
The crucial point of the definition is that, for functional entities, we require that in order to specify some concrete value of a functional entity it is not sufficient to give its set-theoretical description; instead, it is necessary to present a program calculating this function. So the domain of a functional entity F of the type $(X \rightarrow Y)$ is defined to be the set of all programs mapping $Dom(X)$ into $Dom(Y)$.

(4) Deps is a recursively enumerable set of laws, constraints, dependencies etc. connected with our problem area.
It is convenient to consider knowledge bases on two levels: the "scheme (or structural)" level and the "object" level.
For the sake of brevity, we consider only the following kinds of constraints: functional, operator and variant dependencies:

(4.1) A "functional dependency" [3] is an expression
$$D : (X \rightarrow Y)$$
where X and Y are lists of names of entities from Names (D is name of the dependency). This expression should be perceived as the assertion:
"There is a function (a functional of higher type) from $Dom(X)$ into $Dom(Y)$".
It should be noted that names of functional entities may be contained in the lists X and Y.

(4.2) An "operator dependency" [5,8] is an expression
$$D : ((X' \rightarrow Y') \rightarrow Y),$$
where X', Y' and Y are lists of names of entities. This expression is treated as the functional dependency
$$D : (F \rightarrow Y)$$
where F is a functional entity of type $(X' \rightarrow Y')$.

(4.3) A "variant dependency" [9] is an expression
$D : (X \to Y' \ or \ Y'')$
where X, Y' and Y'' are lists of names of entities from Names.
The lists Y' and Y'' are called "alternative lists".
This expression should be perceived as the assertion:
"For some values of X, the values of Y' can be calculated, and, for the rest values of X, the values of Y'' can be defined".

3 Relational Database

As models for a knowledge base we consider relational databases [3].

First, define the notion of a "possible state". We assume that there is a symbol 'undef' that represents undefinedness.

A sequence $s = (a[1], a[2], \cdots, a[n] \cdots)$,
where for every n, $a[n]$ is from $Dom(A[n])$ or equals 'undef', is called the state of an object. Every $a[n]$ is denoted also by $A[n](s)$ and is treated as
"the value of the entity $A[n]$ in the state s".
For a list $X = B', B'', \cdots$, we denoted $X(s) = (B'(s), B''(s), \cdots)$, if some $B(s)$ is equal to "undef" we shall take $X(s)$ to be undefined.

By an instance of a database we call an arbitrary set of states.

Informally, we are interested in the instances that are consistent with all the laws from the relational knowledge base.

We say that a functional dependency $D : (X \to Y)$ is satisfied on an instance T if there exists a program g mapping $Dom(X)$ into $Dom(Y)$ such that, for every state s from T, if $X(s)$ is defined then $Y(s)$ is defined and $Y(s) = g(X(s))$

An operator dependency $D : ((X' \to Y') \to Y)$ is satisfied on an instance T if, for every list of entity names W, if the functional dependency $C : (W, X' \to Y')$ is satisfied on T then the functional depencency $H : (W \to Y)$ is satisfied on T.

This definition is based on the following "principle of conservation": When the values of entities are kept fixed, all the laws must be preserved. That is to say: for a list W, let g be a program computing Y' from the list W, X' on the whole database T. When we fix values for the entities from W, say $W = w$, we thus truncate the database. On the new database the dependency between X' and Y' becomes functional, namely, one can extract a program p from g such that $Y' = p(X')$ on the new database. According to the operator dependency D, Y can be computed from p and, finally, Y is computed from w.

It should be noted that this definition is also correlated with Kleene's s-m-n theorem [2].

A variant dependency $D : (X \to Y' \ or \ Y'')$ is said to be satisfied on an instance T if there exists a program q mapping $Dom(X)$ into the set {1,2}, a program g' mapping

$Dom(X)$ into $Dom(Y')$, and a program g'' mapping $Dom(X)$ into $Dom(Y'')$ such that, for every state s from T, if $X(s)$ is defined then

(i) if $q(X(s)) = 1$ then $Y'(s)$ is defined and $Y'(s) = g'(X(s))$,

(ii) if $q(X(s)) = 2$ then $Y''(s)$ is defined and $Y''(s) = g''(X(s))$.

We say that an instance T is in full accordance with a functional entity F of the type $(X' \to Y')$ if

(a) for every state s from T, if both $X'(s)$ and $F(s)$ are defined then $Y'(s)$ is defined and $Y'(s) = F(s)(X'(s))$ (let us recall that $F(s)$ is a program of the type $(X' \to Y')$),

(b) the operator dependency $D : ((X' \to Y') \to F)$ is satisfied on T.

An instance T is called consistent with a relational knowledge base KB if

(1) all the dependences from KB are satisfied on T,

(2) T is in full accordance with every functional entity F from KB.

4 Tasks. Solvable Tasks

We consider tasks of the following form.

Suppose that we wish to calculate values of all variables from a goal list Z for the case where values of all input variables from a list X are given using the dependencies from the relational knowledge base KB. In short we denote this "computational task" by

$$Task = (KB; X \Rightarrow Z).$$

Next, we give a precise definition (a natural semantics) of the concept "solvability of a computational task".

A computational task $(KB; X \Rightarrow Z)$ is said to be solvable if, for every instance T that is consistent with KB, the functional dependency $H : (X \to Z)$ is satisfied on T.

According to the definition, to justify unsolvability of a task $(KB; X \Rightarrow Z)$ means to find a refutation, e.g., an instance T such that T is in full accordance with all the laws from KB, but there is a state s from T that $X(s)$ is defined and $Z(s)$ is undefined.

Theorem 5.1 implies that all reasonable definitions are equivalent and demonstrates that our definition of solvable tasks is very robust and does not depend on the particular choice of a level of constructivity.

Theorem 4.1 *Consider a simpler case: knowledge bases are finite and contain no variant dependency, and, for every entity V, the set $Dom(V)$ is infinite. Then the set of all solvable tasks is PSPACE-complete.*

Proof. Follows from PSPACE-completeness of the intuitionistic propositional logic.

For a finite knowledge base KB, it should be noted that a task $Task$ can be represented by a propositional formula $fTask$ if one interprets "," as conjunction, "$\rightarrow$" as implication, "*or*" as disjunction, the entity with the empty domain as false. Theorems 6.1 and 6.3 imply that the task T is solvable if and only if the formula $fTask$ belongs to the intuitionistic propositional logic.

5 The General Theorem on Computational Tasks

Theorem 5.1 *Let KB be a finite knowledge base and, for each entity V, let $Dom(V)$ be either infinite or empty. Then a task $(KB; X \Rightarrow Z)$ is solvable if and only if it can be solved by a (scheme) program.*

Proof. ¿From right to left it is evident. Theorems 6.3 and 6.2 yield the nontrivial implication that can be considered as a justification of the automatic program synthesis itself. The interest in such synthesis would be much less if one could produce a solvable computational task that could not be solved by a program (see below a remark on infinite knowledge bases).

In order to prove this theorem and theorems on complexity of knowledge bases a special Tasks Calculus is invented and the consistency and completeness theorems are stated for this calculus.

6 Tasks Calculus

For lists X and Y, we denote their concatenation by $X * Y$.

The empty list is denoted by 0.

By formulas we mean expressions of one of the following three forms

$$(X \rightarrow Y),$$
$$((X' \rightarrow Y') \rightarrow Y),$$
$$(X \rightarrow X' \text{ or } X''),$$

where X, X', X'', Y, Y' are lists of names from $Names$.

A relational knowledge base

$$KB = (Names, Functs, Doms, Deps)$$

is represented in the language by a set of formulas $A \times (KB)$:

(i) a functional or variant dependency $D : (X \rightarrow E)$ is represented in $A \times (KB)$ by the formula $(X \rightarrow E)$,

(ii) an oparator dependency $D : ((X' \rightarrow Y') \rightarrow Y)$ is represented in $A \times (KB)$ by the formula $((X' \rightarrow Y') \rightarrow Y)$,

(iii) a functional entity F of the type $(X \to Y)$ is represented in $A \times (KB)$ by two formulas: the formula $(F * X \to Y)$ and the formula $((X \to Y) \to F)$.

E.g. for the knowledge base KB from Introduction, $A \times (KB)$ is the set of following seven formulas:

(year , level → salary),
(salary → amount),
(pension → amount),
(year , person → level or pension),
(pay_roll → total),
(pay_roll , person → amount),
((person → amount) → pay_roll).

A task sequent is said to be an expression of the form

$G \Rightarrow Z$

where G is a multiset of formulas, Z is a list of names from $Names$. Informally, the sequent $G \Rightarrow Z$ represents the following task:

"For the given set of dependencies G, determine Z".

The following notational conventions are followed throughout this paper:

B	Arbitrary name from $Names$
$X, X', X'', Y, Y', Y'', W, W', W'', Z, Z'$	Arbitrary lists of names
G, G', G''	Arbitrary multisets of formulas
E	Arbitrary list of names or an expression: X' *or* X''

For a sequent $G \Rightarrow Z$, by $Out(G)$ we denote the set of all B such that a formula of the form $(0 \to W' * B * W'')$ is contained in G.

A sequent $G \Rightarrow Z$, is called an axiom if either

(a) Z is contained in $Out(G)$, or

(b) for some B such that $Dom(B)$ is empty, a formula of the form $(0 \to W' * B * W'')$ is contained in G.

Let us give the inference rules for the Tasks Calculus:

Composition:
$$\frac{G, (0 \to W' * B * W''), (Y' * Y'' \to E) \Rightarrow Z}{G, (0 \to W' * B * W''), (Y' * B * Y'' \to E) \Rightarrow Z}$$

Subprogram:
$$\frac{G, (0 \to X') \Rightarrow Y' \qquad G, (0 \to Y) \Rightarrow Z}{G, ((X' \to Y') \to Y) \Rightarrow Z}$$

Branching:
$$\frac{G, (0 \to X') \Rightarrow Z \qquad G, (0 \to X'') \Rightarrow Z}{G, (0 \to X' \text{ or } X'') \Rightarrow Z}$$

A derivation in this calculus is a finite sequence of task sequents such that each member of it is either an axiom sequent or the result of application of one of the inference rules to preceding sequents.

Theorem 6.1 *If a sequent*

$$A \times (KB), (0 \to X) \Rightarrow Z$$

is derivable in the Tasks Calculus, then the computational task $(KB; X \Rightarrow Z)$ *is solvable.*

Proof. Follows from that all rules of the Tasks Calculus are correct on tasks.

Each inference rule can be perceived as a formalization of a constructive step in a natural reasoning related with a process of solving tasks:

(Composition) If a knowledge base contains a dependency $D : (0 \to B)$ (that means B is computed) and a dependency $D' : (B \to Y)$ (that means Y is computed from B) then we can compute Y with the help of a composition and, therefore, the true law $D'' : (0 \to Y)$ can be add to the knowledge base.

(Subprogram) If, for a functional entity F of the type $(X' \to Y')$, we want to add the dependency $D : (0 \to F)$ ("a procedure F is implemented") to a set of laws G, then we must synthesize a subprogram for this F, namely, solve the 'subtask' $G, (0 \to X') \Rightarrow Y'$.

(Branching) If, for a variant dependency $D : (0 \to X' \textit{ or } X'')$ that means either X' or X'' is computed, we are able to solve both 'subtasks' $G, (0 \to X') \Rightarrow Z$ and $G, (0 \to X'') \Rightarrow Z$ then we can solve the main task.

Taking into account what has been said, a program can be extracted **directly** from a derivation in the Tasks Calculus.

Theorem 6.2 *According to an arbitrary derivation of a sequent* $A \times (KB), (0 \to X) \Rightarrow Z$*, one can easily assemble a scheme program for the computational task* $(KB; X \Rightarrow Z)$*.*

This minimal set of rules of tasks reasoning is turned out to cover all possible rules of tasks reasoning.

Theorem 6.3 *Let* KB *be a finite knowledge base and, for each entity* V*, let* $Dom(V)$ *be either infinite or empty. If a computational task* $(KB; X \Rightarrow Z)$ *is solvable then the sequent:* $A \times (KB), (0 \to X) \Rightarrow Z$ *is derivable in the Tasks Calculus.*

Proof. A database T that demonstrates the unsolvability of a computational task $Task$ can be easily transformed into a Kripke model K that refutes the corresponding propositional formula $fTask$.

But there is no straightforward inverse transformation because it should ensure the full accordance with all the functional entities, which is a very strong and tough condition. In particular, considering "self- and cross-referential" functional entities and variant dependencies, we need the recursion theorem and unbounded domains.

Assume that the sequent $A \times (KB), (0 \rightarrow X) \Rightarrow Z'$ is not derivable.

First, we construct a Kripke-like skeleton for a refutable database.

We say that a sequent S is reduced to a sequent S' if

(a) either S' can be transformed into S with the help of the composition rule, or

(b) for S of the form $G, ((X' \rightarrow Y') \rightarrow Y) \Rightarrow Z'$ and S' of the form $G, (0 \rightarrow Y) \Rightarrow Z'$, the sequent $G, (0 \rightarrow X') \Rightarrow Y'$ is derivable.

A sequent S' is said to be a reduction limit of a sequent S if

(a) S can be transformed into S' by means of a finite sequence of applications of reductions, and

(b) S' cannot be reduced to any sequent.

Note that if S if not derivable then its reduction limit is not derivable either.

Now we construct a tree of limit sequents as follows:

The root is claimed to be a reduction limit of the sequent

$$A \times (KB), (0 \rightarrow X) \Rightarrow Z.$$

For every vertex v of the form $G, ((X' \rightarrow Y') \rightarrow Y) \Rightarrow Z'$, we construct a son v' of it such that v' is a reduction limit of the sequent $G, (0 \rightarrow X') \Rightarrow Y'$.

For every vertex v of the form $G, (0 \rightarrow X' \textit{ or } X'') \Rightarrow Z'$, we

(i) select a sequent S from the following two sequents:
$G, (0 \rightarrow X') \Rightarrow Z'$ and $G, (0 \rightarrow X'') \Rightarrow Z'$,
such that S is not derivable, and

(ii) construct a son v' of v such that v' is a reduction limit of S.

It should be noted that this tree is forced to be finite and all its vertices are not derivable.

For a vertex v of the form $G \Rightarrow Z'$, the set $Out(G)$ will be also denoted by $Out(v)$. Since v is not an axiom, Z' is not contained in $Out(v)$.

We say that a vertex v is **good** if, for every formula $(Y \rightarrow X' \textit{ or } X'')$ from $A \times (KB)$, if Y is contained in $Out(v)$ then either X' or X'' is contained in $Out(v)$.

Lemma 6.1 *For every vertex v of the form $G \Rightarrow Z'$, there is a good descendant v' of the form $G' \Rightarrow Z'$.*

Lemma 6.2 *For each vertex v:*

(1) For every formula $(X' \to Y')$ from $A \times (KB)$, if X' is contained in $Out(v)$ then Y' is contained in $Out(v)$.

(2) For every formula $((X' \to Y') \to Y)$ from $A \times (KB)$, if, for all good descendants v' of v such that X' is contained in $Out(v')$, Y' is contained in $Out(v')$ then Y is contained in $Out(v)$.

(3) For every functional entity F of the type $(X' \to Y')$, the entity F is contained in $Out(v)$ if and only if, for all good descendants v' of v such that X' is contained in $Out(v')$, Y' is contained in $Out(v')$.

The set of all good vertices together with the 'evaluation' *Out* represents a refutable Kripke model.

Second, a refutable database is constructed.

Without loss of generality, we consider the case:

(1) for every simple entity V, $Dom(V)$ is either the set of all non-negative numbers or empty,

(2) for every functional entity V, $Dom(V)$ is the set of all Gödel numbers of all partial recursive functions,

(3) for every functional entity F of the type $(X' \to Y')$, the length of both X' and Y' is equal to 1,

(4) there is no operator dependency.

Lemma 6.3 *There exists a one-to-one increasing primitive recursive function t such that, for every partial recursive function h, one can realize a "fixed point" b such that, for every i and v, the integer $t(b,i,v)$ is the Gödel number of a program p that*

$$p(x) = h(b,i,v,x), \quad \text{for all } x.$$

Let us define an "evaluation function" *eval* as follows:
For the root v, we set:

$$\begin{aligned} eval(z,i,v) &= t(z,i,v), && \text{if } A[i] \text{ is contained in } Out(v),\\ eval(z,i,v) &= \text{'undef'}, && \text{otherwise.} \end{aligned}$$

All good vertices and the root are called basic vertices. By $base(v)$ we denote the nearest basic proper ancestor of v.
For every vertex v that is not the root, we set:

$$\begin{aligned} eval(z,i,v) &= eval(z,i,base(v)), && \text{if } A[i] \text{ is contained in } Out(base(v)),\\ eval(z,i,v) &= t(z,i,v), && \text{if } A[i] \text{ is not contained in } Out(base(v)),\\ & && \quad \text{and } A[i] \text{ is contained in } Out(v) \text{ and}\\ & && \quad \text{the vertex } v \text{ is good},\\ eval(z,i,v) &= \text{'undef'}, && \text{otherwise.} \end{aligned}$$

We can realize a recursive function h such that, for every z, i, v and x,

(1) $h(z,i,v,0) = h(z,i,v',0)$ implies $v = v'$,

(2) for every functional entity $A[i]$ of the type $(A[j] \to A[k])$, that $eval(z,i,v)$ is defined, and for every descendant v' of v, that $eval(z,j,v')$ is defined, there is a descendant v'' of v such that $eval(z,j,v'') = eval(z,j,v')$ and $h(z,i,v,eval(z,j,v')) = eval(z,k,v'')$.

Using Lemma 6.3, let us select a "fixed point" b for this function h.

Now, a state $s(v)$ is assigned to every vertex v as follows:

$$s(v) = (eval(b,1,v), eval(b,2,v), eval(b,3,v), \cdots, eval(b,i,v), \cdots).$$

Let T be the set of all such $s(v)$.

For a list W and a tuple w from $Dom(W)$, by $T/[W = w]$ we denote the set of all states s from T such that $W(s)$ is defined and $W(s) = w$.

Let $T[v]$ be the set of all states assigned to descendants of v.

Lemma 6.4 *For every W and w, there exists a basic vertex v such that $T/[W = w]$ is equal to $T[v]$.*

Proof. By induction on the length of W.

Lemma 6.5 *For every formula $(X' \to Y')$ from $A \times (KB)$, the functional dependency $D: (X' \to Y')$ is satisfied on T.*

Proof. For v' and v'', let $X'(s(v'))$ be defined and $X'(s(v'')) = X'(s(v'))$. By Lemma 6.4, there is a basic vertex v such that v is a common ancestor of v' and v'', and $X'(s(v)) = X'(s(v'))$. Since X' is contained in $Out(v)$, Lemma 6.2 implies that Y' is contained in $Out(v)$ and, therefore, $Y'(s(v')) = Y'(s(v)) = Y'(s(v''))$.

Lemma 6.6 *For every functional entity $A[i]$ of the type $(A[j] \to A[k])$, the instance T is in full accordance with $A[i]$.*

Proof. We prove the both lines of the definition.

(a) For a given state $s(v)$, in which $A[i]$ is defined, let v' be a basic ancestor of v such that $eval(b,i,v) = eval(b,i,v') = t(b,i,v')$. This $t(b,i,v')$ is a Gödel number of a program p such that, for all x, $p(x) = h(b,i,v',x)$. Thus, $A[i]$ has the value p on the whole instance $T[v']$. Taking into account the formula $(A[i], A[j] \to A[k])$ from $A \times (KB)$, Lemma 6.2 implies that $D: (A[j] \to A[k])$ is satisfied on $T[v']$.
If $A[j]$ is defined in $s(v)$, then
$$p(eval(b,j,v)) = h(b,i,v',eval(b,j,v)) = eval(b,k,v).$$
It yields the line (a) in the definition of full accordance.

(b) For a list W and a tuple w, let the functional dependency $D : (A[j] \to A[k])$ be satisfied on $T/[W = w]$. By Lemma 6.4, there is a basic vertex v such that this instance is equal to $T[v]$.
Assume that $A[i]$ is not contained in $Out(v)$. By Lemma 6.2, there is a good descendant v' of v such that $A[j]$ is contained in $Out(v')$ but $A[k]$ is not contained in $Out(v')$ and therefore $A[k]$ is undefined in the state $s(v')$, which is a contradiction.
Hence we may conclude that $A[i]$ is to be contained in $Out(v)$ and, for every state s from $T/[W = w]$, we have: $A[i](s) = A[i](s(v))$.
Thus validity of the dependency $D : (W, A[j] \to A[k])$ implies validity of the dependency $H : (W \to A[i])$.

Lemma 6.7 *For every good vertex v, the variant dependency $D : (Y \to X'$ or $X'')$ from KB is satisfied on the instance $T[v]$.*

Proof. For a given y from $Dom(Y)$, let us examine the instance $T[v]/[Y = y]$. By Lemma 6.4, let v' be a good descendant of v such that this instance is equal to $T[v']$. The list Y is contained in $Out(v')$. Hence either X' or X'' is contained in $Out(v')$. Therefore, either $H' : (0 \to X')$ or $H'' : (0 \to X'')$ is satisfied on $T[v']$.

Lemma 6.8 *For every good vertex v, the instance $T[v]$ is consistent with KB.*

Proof. Follows from Lemmas 6.5–6.7.

To complete the proof of the theorem, by Lemma 6.1 we find a good vertex v of the form $G', (0 \to X) \Rightarrow Z$. For this v,

(1) the instance $T[v]$ is consistent with KB,

(2) the input list X is defined in the state $s(v)$, but

(3) the goal list Z is undefined in the state $s(v)$.

Hence the task $(KB; X \Rightarrow Z)$ is unsolvable.

Corollary 6.1 *For a given finite G, let KB be the knowledge base such that $A \times (KB) = G$. Then a sequent $G \Rightarrow Z$ is derivable if and only if the task $(KB; 0 \Rightarrow Z)$ is solvable.*

Proof. Follows from Theorems 6.1 and 6.3.

Corollary 6.2

(1) For the composition rule, its conclusion is derivable if and only if its premise is derivable.

(2) For the subprogram rule, if its left premise is derivable then its conclusion is derivable if and only if its right premise is derivable.

(3) For the branching rule, its conclusion is derivable if and only if both its premises are derivable.

Proof. Follows from Corollary 6.1.

7 Complexity of an Algorithm of Analysis and Synthesis

Let us consider the following algorithm based on the Tasks Calculus.

Input. A computational task $Task = (KB; X \Rightarrow Z)$.

Output. A scheme program for $Task$ if $Task$ is solvable, or negative answer otherwise.

Method. A derivation of the sequent $A \times (KB), (0 \to X) \Rightarrow Z$ is being searched for.

If this search is successful then, with the help of Theorem 6.2, the derivation is transformed into the scheme program for $Task$.

Otherwise, the answer is: "$Task$ is unsolvable".

Theorem 7.1 *Let KB be finite and, for each entity V, let $Dom(V)$ be either infinite or empty. Then this algorithm runs correctly on all computational tasks.*

Follows from Theorems 6.1 and 6.3.

Theorem 7.2 *For a given computational task $Task = (KB; X \Rightarrow Z)$, one can*

(a) recognize whether $Task$ is solvable or not,

(b) construct a minimal scheme program for $Task$,

in deterministic **linear** *space*

$$O(L)$$

where L is the number of all occurrences of entity names in KB.

Proof. We can search for a derivation of the sequent $A \times (KB), (0 \to X) \Rightarrow Z$ with the help of a depth-first search.

Taking into account Corollary 6.2, for a given sequent $G \Rightarrow Z'$ that is assigned to a vertex of this search tree, the search stack needs to contain no more than

(1) a number of names of 'variant' and 'operator' formulas (without repetitions),

(2) the set $Out(G)$ (without repetitions).

Thus we get a linear bound on the stack size.

It should be noted that when we consider the tasks for which the degree of subtasks interaction (see below) is bounded, more complicated traversal of a tree may be required (cf. Theorems 7.3 and 7.5).

Taking into account the PSPACE-completeness, all known algorithms of analysis and synthesis are forced to perform an exponential search for "almost all" computational tasks. In spite of this, all examples of "bad" tasks are unnatural.

We introduce some level (rank) r to computational tasks, so that natural (realistic) tasks have a small level r.
Now let us explain what subtasks are and how they interact.

According to what has been said, in performing the task $(KB; X \Rightarrow Z)$ there may appear 'subtasks', e.g. in such cases as follows:

(a) For a functional entity F of the type $(X' \rightarrow Y')$, we must solve a subtask $(KB'; X' \Rightarrow Y')$, the input of it is the "argument list" X'.

(b) If we use a variant dependency $D : (X' \rightarrow Y' \ or \ Y'')$ for computing Z', we have to solve two subtasks $(KB'; Y' \Rightarrow Z')$ and $(KB''; Y'' \Rightarrow Z')$, the inputs of these subtasks are the "alternative lists" Y' and Y''.

In performing the main task, subtasks can interact, namely, we can solve a subtask provided that values of inputs of some other subtasks are given in addition. Embedding of subprograms is related to this phenomenon. The maximal number of subtasks with different inputs which can interact in the process of performing the main task at a moment is called the degree of subtasks interaction.

Let us give formal definitions.

By $In(KB, X, r)$ we denote the set of all lists W that is a concatenation of the following $r+1$ lists:
the input list X and r ("argument" and/or "alternative") lists from KB.

We say that an operator dependency $D : ((X' \rightarrow Y') \rightarrow Y)$ is satisfied down to depth r over X on an instance T if, for every W from $In(KB, X, r)$, if the functional dependency $C : (W * X' \rightarrow Y')$ is satisfied on T then the functional dependency $H : (W \rightarrow Y)$ is satisfied on T.

We say that an instance T is in accordance down to depth r over X with a functional entity F of the type $(X' \rightarrow Y')$ if

(a) for every state s from T, if both $X'(s)$ and $F(s)$ are defined then $Y'(s)$ is defined and $Y'(s) = F(s)(X'(s))$,

(b) the operator dependency $D : ((X' \rightarrow Y') \rightarrow F)$ is satisfied down to depth r over X on T.

We say that a variant dependency $D : (Y \to X' \; or \; X'')$ is satisfied down to depth r over X on an instance T if, for every W from $In(KB, X, r)$ such that the dependency $C : (W \to Y)$ is satisfied on T, if both dependencies of the form $C' : (W * X' \to Z')$ and $C'' : (W * X'' \to Z')$ are satisfied on T then the dependency $H : (W \to Z')$ is satisfied on T.

An instance T is called consistent with a relational knowledge base KB down to depth r over X if

(1) all the dependences from KB are satisfied on T down to depth r over X,

(2) T is in accordance down to depth r over X with every functional entity F from KB.

A computational task $(KB; X \Rightarrow Z)$ is said to be solvable with the degree of subtasks interaction r if, for every instance T that is consistent with KB down to depth r over X, the dependency $H : (X \to Z)$ is satisfied on T.

Theorem 7.3 [9] *For a given computational task* $Task = (KB; X \Rightarrow Z)$, *one can*

(a) recognize whether $Task$ *is solvable or not,*

(b) construct a program for $Task$,

in **quasipolynomial** *running time*

$$O(\; L * n * n * \exp(3(r+1) * \ln(m) - 3\ln((r+1)!)) \;)$$

where L is the number of all occurrences of entity names in KB,
n is the number of different entity names from KB,
m is the total number of different "argument lists" and "alternative lists" from KB,
r is the minimal degree of subtasks interaction with which $Task$ can be solved.

If the minimal degree of subtasks interaction with which a task can be solved is equal to 0, we say that this task is solvable with separable subtasks [8].

Theorem 7.4 [8] *We get a quadratic time synthesis algorithm for solving computational tasks with separable subtasks.*

Theorem 7.5 *We can solve computational tasks with separable subtasks in parallel near-linear time.*

Finally, let $Task[Embedding = r]$ be a set of all tasks for which there exist programs such that embedding of their subprograms and conditional statements is not greater than r.

For every r, this class is a proper subclass of the class of all tasks that are solvable with degree r of subtasks interaction.

On the other hand, Theorem 6.3 implies

Corollary 7.1 *For each entity V, let $Dom(V)$ be either infinite or empty. Then a task $(KB; X \Rightarrow Z)$ is solvable if and only if it is contained in the class $Task[Embedding = m]$, where m is the total number of different "argument lists" and "alternative lists" from KB.*

Theorem 7.6 *For a given computational task $Task = (KB; X \Rightarrow Z)$, we can*

(a) recognize whether $Task$ is solvable or not,

(b) construct a program for $Task$,

in **quasipolynomial** running time

$$O(L * n * exp(r \ln(m))$$

in **subquadratic** space

$$O(L + n * d)$$

where d is the number of different "alternative lists" in KB,
r is the minimal integer that
$Task$ is contained in the class $Task[Embedding = r]$.

Proof. By refining on Theorem 7.2.

Theorem 7.7 *For every r, the class $Task[Embedding = r]$ is running in parallel near-linear time.*

So, treating computational tasks on the basis of our calculus, an exponential execution time should be expected in the worst case, as is customary. But such cases arise for very unnatural tasks that need maximum cross-linking of all possible subprograms, even in the best programs. Our sysnthesizer runs in polynomial time on all natural tasks; the degree of the polynomial is determined by the minimal depth of interacting of subtasks that can be achieved in some solution for the main task.

8 Finite vs. Infinite Knowledge Bases

It should be pointed out that Theorem 5.1 is valid for all infinite knowledge bases containing no variant dependencies, as well as for many infinite knowledge bases having such dependencies.

Nevertheless, we can show an infinite knowledge base KB (containing only a single variant dependency) and a $Task(KB; X \Rightarrow Z)$ such that

(1) this $Task$ is solvable, but still

(2) there is no program for this $Task$.

9 Conclusion

In conclusion it should be pointed out that on the basis of similar "lossless" calculi one can get algorithms that run in polynoomial (and even linear or subquadratic) time also for

(1) the membership problem in the theory of relational databases with functional and multivalued dependencies,

(2) recoginzing the validity of Horn formulas in the one-placed predicate logic,

(3) flow analysis of "and-or" graphs,

(4) recognizing derivability of formulas of some kind in the classical and intuitionistic propositional and modal calculi, etc.

References

[1] A.Aho, J.Hopcroft and J.Ullman, The Design and Analysis of Computer Algorithms, (1976).

[2] H.Rogers, Theory of Recursive Functions and Effective Computability, (1967).

[3] J.D.Ullman, Principles of Database Systems, (1980).

[4] M.R.Garey and D.S.Johnson, Computers and Intractability, (1979).

[5] G.E.Mints and E.Kh.Tyugu, Propositional logic programming and the PRIZ system. J. Logic Programming, 9, N 2-3 (1990),179-193.

[6] I.O.Babaev, S.S.Lavrov et al., Third Conf. Application of the Methods of Mathematical Logic, Tallinn, (1983), 29-41. (Russian)

[7] A.Ja.Dikovskii, Third Conf. Application of the Methods of Mathematical Logic, Tallinn, (1983), 42-51. (Russian)

[8] A.Ja.Dikovskii and M.I.Kanovich, Computational models with separable subtasks. Proceedings of Academy of Sci. of USSR, Technical Cybernetics, 5 (1985), 36-60. (Russian)

[9] M.I.Kanovich, Quasipolynmial algorithms for recognizing the satisfiabiblity and derivability of propositional formulas. Soviet Mathematics Doklady, 34, N 2 (1987), 273-277.

[10] M.I.Kanovich, Efficient program synthesis in computational models. J. Logic Programming, 9, N 2-3 (1990), 159-177.

Principal Type-Schemes of BCI-Lambda-Terms

Sachio Hirokawa*
Dept. of Computer Science
College of General Education
Kyushu University
Fukuoka 810, JAPAN
hirokawa@ec.kyushu-u.ac.jp

Abstract

A BCI-λ-term is a λ-term in which each variable occurs exactly once. It represents a proof figure for implicational formula provable in linear logic. A principal type-scheme is a most general type to the term with respect to substitution. The notion of "relevance relation" is introduced for type-variables in a type. Intuitively an occurrence of a type-variable b is relevant to other occurrence of some type-variable c in a type α, when b is essentially concerned with the deduction of c in α. This relation defines a directed graph $G(\alpha)$ for type-variables in the type. We prove that a type α is a principal type-scheme of BCI-λ-term iff (a), (b) and (c) holds:

(a) Each variable occurring in α occurs exactly twice and the occurrences have opposite sign.

(b) $G(\alpha)$ is a tree and the right-most type variable in α is its root.

(c) For any subtype γ of α, each type variable in γ is relevant to the right-most type variable in γ.

A type-schemes of some BCI-λ-term is minimal iff it is not a non-trivial substitution instance of other type-scheme of BCI-λ-term. We prove that the set of BCI-minimal types coincides with the set of principal type-schemes of BCI-λ-terms in $\beta\eta$-normal form.

1 Introduction

A BCI-λ-term is a λ-term in which each variable occurs exactly once. By formulas-as-types correspondence [13], it represents a proof figure for implicational formula

*Supported by a Grant-in-Aid for Encouragement of Young Scientists No.02740115 of the Ministry of Education.

provable in linear logic by Girard [3]. Implicational fragment of linear logic is equivalent to BCI-logic, which is obtained from intuitionistic logic by removing contraction rules and weakening rules. In this logic, one can use an assumption exactly once. This restriction is described as a condition on $(\rightarrow I)$-rule for BCI-logic in natural deduction formulation and a condition on abstraction in formation of BCI-λ-terms.

A principal type-scheme of a λ-term is a most general type-scheme of the λ-term. If a λ-term has a type-scheme, then it has a most general type-scheme. This fact is known as principal type-scheme theorem [4]. It is a basis for type-inference systems for functional programming languages. Algorithms of type-inference have been studied well. But principal type-schemes and structures of principal type-assignment figures have not been examined enough. We shall look into the structures of principal type-assignment to BCI-λ-terms. By Hindley [6], any BCI-λ-term has a type-scheme. So the set of principal type-schemes of BCI-λ-terms is identical to that of BCI-λ-terms in β-normal form. Therefore we only have to examine the structure of principal type-assignment figures for BCI-λ-terms in β-normal form.

It is known that the principal type-assignment corresponds to the following condensed detachment rule (D-rule)

$$\frac{\alpha \rightarrow \beta \quad \gamma}{\beta\theta}$$

where θ is a most general unifier of α and γ. The set of provable formulas from a set of axioms via D-rule corresponds to the set of principal type-schemes of combinators which are constructed from basic combinators having the axioms as their types.

If we take $\{S, K, I\}$ as the axioms, then the corresponding λ-terms is identical to the set of all closed λ-terms. By converse principal type-scheme theorem [4, 2, 12], the set of principal type-schemes and the set of type-schemes are identical for SKI-λ-terms.

Given a set T of closed λ-terms, T is said to be D-complete when

$$ts(T) = pts(T)$$

where ts(T) is the set of type-schemes and pts(T) is the set of principal type-schemes of λ-terms in T respectively. (For more detail and precise treatment of D-rule, see [8].) It is quite recent that this holds for T=BCIW and BB'IW-λ-terms. (See [16, 18, 12].) However, this does not hold for BCI-λ-terms or for BCK-λ-terms [8]. (See Figure 1.)

In the first draft of [8] Hindley and Meredith raised a problem of characterization of $pts(BCI)$ and $pts(BCK)$. Meyer and Bunder proved the following result in [16].

$$pts(BCI) = ts(BCI) \cap F_2$$

Here F_2 is the set of types with the two-property in which every type variable occurs exactly twice.

The above equality characterizes the set of principal type-schemes among type-schemes BCI-λ-terms and not among arbitrary types. So the two-property is a necessary and sufficient condition for a type-scheme of a BCI-λ-term to be principal. In

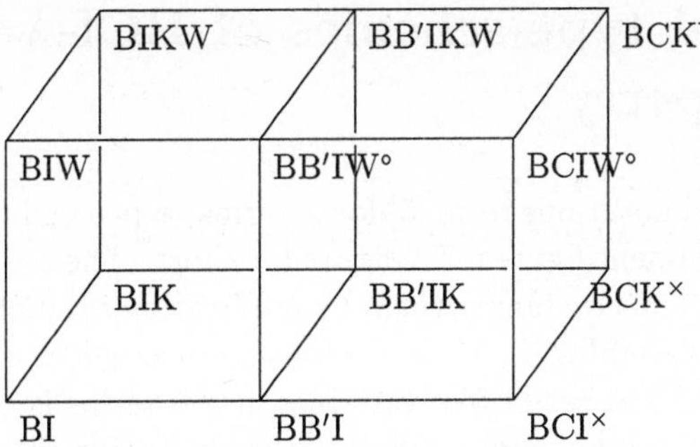

Figure 1: Lambda-terms and Logic

this paper, we give a necessary and sufficient condition for a type to be a principal type-scheme of some BCI-λ-term. The condition is written in terms of types and it does not need any notion of provability nor typability. To describe the condition, we introduce a notion of "relevance relation" between type variables in a type. Intuitively an occurrence of a type variable b is relevant to other occurrence of some type variable c in a type α, when b is essentially concerned to the deduction of c in α. This relation was found by an analysis of positive and negative occurrences of type variables in principal type-assignment figures for BCI-λ-terms in β-normal form. This relation defines a directed graph $G(\alpha)$ for type-variables in the type. We prove that a type α is a principal type-scheme of BCI-λ-term iff (a), (b) and (c) holds:

(a) Each variable occurring in α occurs exactly twice and the occurrences have opposite sign.

(b) $G(\alpha)$ is a tree and the right-most type variable in α is its root.

(c) For any subtype γ of α, each type variable in γ is relevant to the right-most type variable in γ.

A formula α is BCI-minimal iff it is provable in BCI-logic and it is not a non-trivial substitution instance of other BCI-provable formula. Every BCI-formula is a substitution instance of some BCI-minimal formula. The notion of minimality was introduced by Komori [15] with respect to the uniqueness of proof figure. The author conjectured in [10] that BCK-formula is minimal iff it is a principal type-scheme of some BCK-λ-term in $\beta\eta$-normal form. We solve this conjecture concerning to BCI-λ-terms by showing

$$BCI - minimal = pts(BCI - \beta\eta).$$

We conjecture more strong characterization that says α is BCI-minimal iff α satisfies (a), (b), (c) and (a*): if a subtype γ occurs twice in α, then γ is a type variable.
We shall discuss on this conjecture with respect to decision problem of BCI-formulas.

We use some lemmas without proof from [10, 11, 12].

2 Principal type-schemes of BCI-λ-terms and the two-property

We use the standard notations from [5] for λ-terms, types and type-assignment system. We call a type assignment figure a TA-figure for short. The set of types are constructed from type-variables and combining them by implication symbol '$\rightarrow$'. We use the letters $x, y, z, \cdots$ for term-variables, $L, M, N, \cdots$ for λ-terms, $a, b, c, \cdots$ for type-variables and $\alpha, \beta, \gamma, \cdots$ for types. The set of free variables in a λ-terms is denoted by $FV(M)$. We say that a type α is general than β iff β is a substitution instance of α. We consider only the λ-terms which do not contain any constant. Therefore the set of assumptions in a type-assignment figure for a λ-term M have the form $\{x_1 : \alpha_1, \cdots, x_n : \alpha_n\}$ where $x_1, \cdots, x_n$ are all of free variables in M. When a λ-term M is type-assigned to α with an assumption set $B = \{x_1 : \alpha_1, \cdots, x_n : \alpha_n\}$, we write $B|-M : \alpha$. When the pair (B, α) is a most general type-assignment for the term M with respect to substitution, (B, α) is said to be a principal pair of M and we denote it by $B||-M : \alpha$. When $B = \emptyset$, α is said to be a principal type-scheme of the term and we denote it by $||-M : \alpha$.

A λ-term is said to be a BCI-λ-term when each variable occurs exactly once.

Definition 1 (BCI-λ-terms) *The set of BCI-λ-terms is defined inductively as follows.*

(1) Every variable is a BCI-λ-term.

(2) If M is a BCI-λ-term and x is a free variable in M then $(\lambda x.M)$ is a BCI-λ-term.

(3) If M and N are BCI-λ-terms and $FV(M) \cap FV(N) = \emptyset$ then (MN) is a BCI-λ-term.

We denote by BCI,BCI-β, BCI-η and BCI-$\beta\eta$ the sets of closed BCI-λ-terms, the set of closed BCI-λ-terms in β-normal form, the set of closed BCI-λ-terms in η-normal form and the set of closed BCI-λ-terms in $\beta\eta$-normal form respectively.

Definition 2 *Given a set T of closed λ-terms, we denote by $ts(T)$ and $pts(T)$ the set of type-schemes of λ-terms in T and the set of principal type-schemes of λ-terms in T respectively.*

Remark 1 *It is known that every BCI-λ-term has a type and that every BCI-λ-term has a principal type-scheme. (See [6]). It is trivial that ts(BCI)=ts(BCI-β). The subject-reduction theorem and the subject-expansion theorem hold for BCI-λ-terms, i.e., for any closed BCI-λ-term M and N, when M is β-reducible to N, $|-M : \alpha$ iff $|-N : \alpha$. Therefore we have pts(BCI-β)=pts(BCI). (See [6].)*

Lemma 1 *(1) Let $xM_1 \cdots M_n$ be a BCI-λ-term in β-normal form, $B||{-}xM_1 \cdots M_n : \alpha$ and $B_i = \{y : \beta \in B \mid y \in FV(M_i)\}$. Then α is a type variable a, $x : \alpha_1 \to \cdots \to \alpha_n \to a \in B$ for some $\alpha_1, \cdots, \alpha_n$ and the following (a),(b) and (c) hold.*

(a) $B_i||{-}M_i : \alpha_i$.

(b) $var(B_i, \alpha_i) \cap var(B_j, \alpha_j)$ for $i \neq j$.

(c) $a \notin var(B_i, \alpha_i)$.

Here $var(B_i, \alpha_i)$ is the set of type variables in B_i and α_i.

(2) Let $\lambda x.M$ be a BCI-λ-term in β-normal form. If $B||{-}\lambda x.M : \alpha$ then $\alpha = \gamma \to \beta$ and $B \cup \{x : \gamma\}||{-}M : \beta$.

Proof. See [10]. ■

Definition 3 (two-property) *A type α has the two-property iff every type variable in α occurs exactly twice in α. We denote by F_2 the set of all types having the two-property. A pair (B, α) of assumption set $B = \{x_1 : \alpha_1, \cdots, x_n : \alpha_n\}$ and a type α has the two-property iff $\alpha_1 \to \cdots \to \alpha_n \to \alpha$ has the two-property.*

The following characterization theorem was proved in [16]. It states that a type-scheme of a closed BCI-λ-term is a principal type-scheme of some closed BCI-λ-term iff it has the two-property. Another proof is in [9]. We prove this theorem as a special case of the following Lemma 2. Our proof is written in the words of λ-calculus and type assignment to λ-terms.

Theorem 1

$$pts(BCI) = ts(BCI) \cap F_2.$$

Lemma 2 *Let (B, α) be a pair of an assumption set and a type for some BCI-λ-term. Then $B||{-}M : \alpha$ for some BCI-λ-term M iff (B, α) has the two-property.*

Proof of Lemma 2. ($\Rightarrow$) By induction on M.

Case 1. $M = x$. Then α is a type variable. Let $\alpha = a$. Then $B = \{x : a\}$. Therefore (B, a) has the two-property.

Case 2. $M = xM_1 \cdots M_n (n \geq 1)$. By Lemma 1, α is a type variable a and the TA-figure for $B||{-}xM_1 \cdots M_n : a$ has the following form.

$$\frac{x : \alpha_1 \to \cdots \to \alpha_n \to a \quad M_1 : \alpha_1 \quad \cdots \quad M_n : \alpha_n}{xM_1 \cdots M_n : a}$$

To prove the two-property of (B, a), assume that b is an arbitrary type variable in (B, a). Apply Lemma 1 for $xM_1 \cdots M_n$. Let $B_i = \{y : \beta \in B \mid y \in FV(M_i)\}$. Then (c),(d) and (e) of Lemma 1 hold.

Subcase 2.1 $b = a$. By (d) and (e), a occurs exactly twice in $x : \alpha_1 \to \cdots \to \alpha_n \to a$ and $xM_1 \cdots M_n : a$.

Subcase 2.2 $b \neq a$. Since b occurs in B, b occurs in some B_i. By (d), such B_i is unique. By induction hypothesis for $B_i||{-}M_i : \alpha_i$, b occurs exactly twice in (B_i, α_i). Therefore b occurs exactly twice in $B = B_1 \cup \cdots B_n \cup \{x : \alpha_1 \to \cdots \to \alpha_n \to a\}$. Thus b occurs exactly twice in (B, a).

Case 3 $M = \lambda x.N$. By Lemma 1, we have $\alpha = \gamma \to \beta$ and the TA-figure for $B||{-}\lambda x.N : \gamma \to \beta$ has the following form.

$$\frac{N : \beta}{\lambda x.N : \beta \to \gamma}$$

Then we have $B \cup \{x : \gamma\}||{-}N : \beta$. By induction hypothesis $(B \cup \{x : \gamma\}, \beta)$ has the two-property. Therefore $(B, \beta \to \gamma)$ has the two-property. This completes the proof for $(\Rightarrow)$. ∎

To prove $(\Leftarrow)$ we need some results from [12].

Definition 4 *Let V be a set of type variables and $\theta = [a_1 := \alpha_1\ , \cdots, a_n := \alpha_n]$ be a simultaneous substitution such that $a_i \in V$. When $n = 1$, θ is said to be a single substitution. A single substitution θ is*

trivial w.r.t. V	*iff*	$\theta = [a := b], b \notin V.$
arrow w.r.t. V	*iff*	$\theta = [a := b \to c], a \in V, b, c \notin V, b \neq c.$
contraction w.r.t. V	*iff*	$\theta = [a := b], a, b \in V, a \neq b.$

Lemma 3 (Decomposition of substitution) *Any substitution θ is decomposed into*

$$\theta = \sigma_1 \cdots \sigma_k \tau_1 \cdots \tau_l \rho_1 \cdots \rho_m,$$

where σ_i's are arrow substitutions, τ_i's are contraction substitutions and ρ_i's are trivial substitutions.

Proof. See [12]. ∎

Lemma 4 *If N is a BCI-λ-term in β-normal form, $B||{-}N : \alpha$ and θ is an arrow substitution with respect to (B, α), then there is a BCI-λ-term M in β-normal form which is η-reducible to N and $B\theta||{-}M : \alpha\theta$.*

Proof See [12]. ■

Proof of Lemma 2 (continued) ($\Leftarrow$) Since (B, α) is a pair of an assumption set and a type for some BCI-λ-term N, we have $B|\!-N : \alpha$. By the principal type-scheme theorem [4, 2, 11], we can construct an assumption set C, a type β and a substitution θ such that $C|\!|\!-N : \beta$ and we have $(B, \alpha) = (C, \beta)\theta$. By decomposition of θ, we have $\theta = \sigma_1 \cdots \sigma_k\ \tau_1 \cdots \tau_l\ \rho_1 \cdots \rho_m$, where σ_i's are arrow substitutions, τ_i's are contraction substitutions and ρ_i's are trivial substitutions. Since (B, α) has the two-property, this decomposition does not contain any contraction substitution. Thus we have $\theta = \sigma_1 \cdots \sigma_k\ \rho_1 \cdots \rho_m$. By Lemma 4, we can construct a λ-term M such that $B|\!|\!-M : \alpha$ and M is η-reducible to N. Since N is a BCI-λ-term, so is M. Thus (B, α) is a principal pair for a BCI-λ-term M. ■

As a corollary of Theorem 1, we prove that any logic is not D-complete if it is subset of BCI-logic. In other words, if T is a non-empty subset of closed BCI-λ-terms, then $pts(T) \overset{\subset}{\neq} ts(T)$. Remember that BCI is the set all closed BCI-λ-terms and that pts(T) is the set of principal type-schemes of λ-terms in T and that ts(T) is the set of type-schemes of λ-terms in T.

Theorem 2 *If $\emptyset \neq T \subseteq BCI$ then $pts(T) \overset{\subset}{\neq} ts(T)$.*

Proof. Le $\alpha \in ts(T)$ and a be a type variable in α and b be any type variable. Consider a substitution $\theta = [a := b \to b \to b]$. Then the type variable b occurs three times in $\alpha\theta$. Therefore $\alpha\theta \notin pts(BCI)$ by Theorem 1. Therefore $\alpha\theta \notin pts(T)$. ■

3 Relevance relation

Theorem 1 in the previous section does not imply that a type with the two-property is a principal type-scheme of some closed BCI-λ-term. The type $\alpha = ((a \to b) \to b) \to a$ has the two-property. But it is not a type of any BCI-λ-term. In fact, it is not provable even in classical logic. Moreover, even if a type is provable in LJ and has the two-property, it is not always a principal type-scheme of some BCI-λ-term. Consider $\gamma = a \to a \to b \to b$ which is a type of $\lambda xyz.z$. But γ is not a type-scheme of any BCI-λ-term in β-normal form. Therefore it is not a principal type-scheme of any BCI-λ-term. Thus we have pts(BCI) $\overset{\subset}{\neq} F_2$.

In [14] Jaskowski proved

$$LJ \cap F_{1,2} = ts(BCK) \cap F_{1,2}.$$

Here $F_{1,2}$ is the set types with one-two-property in which every type variable occurs at most twice. It would be tempting to hope that $LJ \cap F_2 = ts(BCI) \cap F_2$. But it is not the case. The above example $\gamma = a \to a \to b \to b$ belongs to $LJ \cap F_2$ but it does not belong to $ts(BCI) \cap F_2$.

Theorem 1 gives a characterization of principal type-schemes of BCI-λ-terms. However it still needs typability to BCI-λ-terms. By terms-as-proof correspondence, it means the provability in BCI-logic. In this section, we shall give a detailed analysis of principal type-assignment figures to BCI-λ-terms. A relation between each occurrences of type variables is clarified. As a result, we introduce the notion of "relevance relation" of type variables Intuitively, a type variable b is relevant to another type variable c when b is used to deduce c in a type-scheme. This notion is defined to type variables in arbitrary types. These types does not have to be a type-scheme of any λ-term. We show a necessary and sufficient condition for a type-scheme to be a principal type-scheme of some closed BCI-λ-term. The point is that lambda-terms are not necessary to describe this condition.

Definition 5 (core) *The core of a type-scheme α is the right-most type variable in α. We denote it by $core(\alpha)$.*

When it is clear from the context, we use the word 'core' to specify not only a type variable, but also its occurrence of the type variable.

The sign of a subtype in a type-scheme is defined as usual.

Definition 6 (positive/negative subtype) *α is positive in α. If an occurrence of γ is positive (negative) in β, then the occurrence of γ in $\alpha \to \beta$ is positive (negative) in $\alpha \to \beta$. If an occurrence of γ is positive (negative) in α, then the occurrence of γ in $\alpha \to \beta$ is negative (positive) in $\alpha \to \beta$.*

Definition 7 (essentially balancedness) *([1]) A type-scheme α is essentially balanced iff each variable occurring in α occurs exactly twice and the occurrences have opposite sign.*

Definition 8 (relevance relation) *Let b and c be type variables in a type-scheme α. We write $b \succ_\alpha c$ iff α contains an occurrence of subtype γ of the form $\gamma = \alpha_1 \to \cdots \to (\gamma_1 \cdots \to \gamma_k \to b) \to \cdots \to \alpha_n \to c$ such that the occurrence of c is negative in α. We define '$\succ_\alpha^*$' as the transitive and reflexive closure of '$\succ_\alpha$'. When $b \succ_\alpha^* c$, we say that b is relevant to c in α.*

Definition 9 (relevance graph G(α)) *Given a type-scheme α, we denote by $G(\alpha)$ the directed graph whose nodes are type variables in α and whose edges are ordered pairs (b, c) of type variables in α such that $b \succ_\alpha c$.*

Consider a BCI-λ-term $\lambda xyzu.z(x(\lambda v.yv))u$ and its principal type-scheme $\alpha = ((e \to a) \to b) \to (e \to a) \to (b \to c \to d) \to c \to d$. It has the following TA-figure.

The signs are written to each occurrence of type variables in the end-formula.

$$\cfrac{\cfrac{z : d \to a \to e \qquad \cfrac{x : (b \to c) \to d \qquad \cfrac{\cfrac{y : b \to c \quad v : b}{yv : c}}{\lambda v.yv : b \to c}}{x(\lambda v.yv) : d} \qquad u : a}{z(x(\lambda v.yv))u : e}}{\lambda xyzu.z(x(\lambda v.yv))u : ((b^- \to c^+) \to d^-) \to (b^+ \to c^-) \to (d^+ \to a^+ \to e^-) \to a^- \to e^+}$$

Its relevance graph is shown in Figure 2. It is similar to Böhm tree of M.

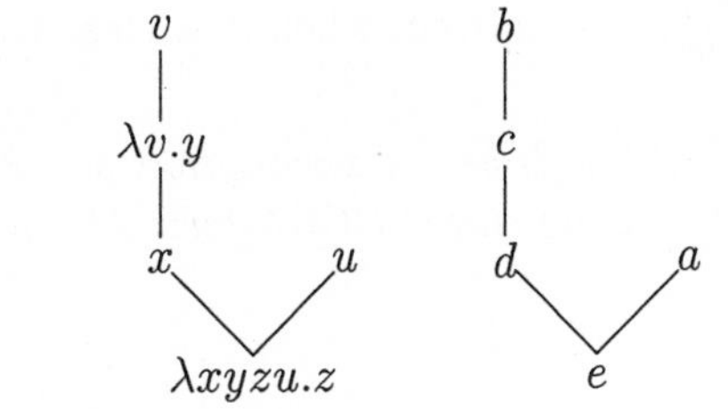

Figure 2: Böhm tree and relevance graph $G(\alpha)$

Theorem 3 *A type-scheme α is a principal type-scheme of some closed BCI-λ-term iff the following (a),(b) and (c) hold.*

(a) α is essentially balanced.

(b) $G(\alpha)$ is a tree with a root core(α), i.e., the following (i),(ii) and (iii) hold.

(i) core(α) is the root of $G(\alpha)$: $a \succ_\alpha^* core(\alpha)$ for all $a \in var(\alpha)$.

(ii) $G(\alpha)$ has no cycle: if $a \succ_\alpha^* b$ and $b \succ_\alpha^* a$, then $a = b$.

(iii) $G(\alpha)$ is not collapsed: if $c \succ_\alpha a$ and $c \succ_\alpha b$ for some c then $a = b$.

(c) For any subtype γ in α and for any type-variable a in γ, $a \succ_\alpha^* core(\gamma)$.

We can not remove the condition (c). A type-scheme $(((c^+ \to a^-) \to b^+) \to c^-) \to b^- \to a^+$ satisfies the conditions (a) and (b). But it is not provable in classical logic. Therefore is is not a type-scheme of any BCI-λ-term.

The proof of if-part shall be given later. Only-if-part is proved by induction on M, where we encounter an M which contains free variables. So we need to extend the notions of signs, essentially balancedness and relevance relation to pairs (B, α) of an assumption set B and a type-scheme α.

Definition 10 *Let $B = \{x_1 : \alpha_1, \cdots, x_n : \alpha_n\}$ be an assumption set and α be a type-scheme. Given an occurrence of subtype γ in α_i, the sign of the occurrence γ in (B, α) is the opposite of the sign of γ in α_i. If γ is an occurrence of subtype in α, the sign of the γ is identical to the sign of γ in α_i. (B, α) is essentially balanced iff $\alpha_1 \to \cdots \to \alpha_n \to \alpha$ is essentially balanced. Let $b, c \in var(B, \alpha)$. We write $b \succ_{(B,\alpha)} c$ iff $b \succ_\delta c$ where $\delta = \alpha_1 \to \cdots \to \alpha_n \to \alpha$. '$\succ^*_{(B,\alpha)}$' is the transitive and reflexive closure of '$\succ_{(B,\alpha)}$'. $G(B, \alpha)$ is the graph whose nodes are type variables in (B, α) and whose edges are ordered pairs (b, c) such that $b \succ_{(B,\alpha)} c$.*

Only-if-part of Theorem 3 is a special case of the following lemma. Sometimes, subscripts (B, α) for $\succ_{(B,\alpha)}$ and $\succ^*_{(B,\alpha)}$ are omitted, when it is clear from the context.

Lemma 5 *Let $B = \{x_1 : \alpha_1, \cdots, x_m : \alpha_m\}$ be an assumption set and α be a type-scheme. If (B, α) is a principal pair of some closed BCI-λ-term M, then the following (a), (b) and (c) hold.*

(a) (B, α) is essentially balanced.

(b) $G(B, \alpha)$ is a tree with the root $core(\alpha)$:

(i) $\forall b \in var(B, \alpha)\ b \succ^* core(\alpha)$.

(ii) $\forall b, c \in var(B, \alpha)\ b \succ^* c, c \succ^* b \Rightarrow b = c$.

(iii) $\forall b, c \in var(B, \alpha)\ (\exists c \in var(B, \alpha) d \succ b, d \succ b) \Rightarrow b = c$.

(c) For any subtype γ of α_i or of α, $\forall b \in var(\gamma)\ b \succ^* core(\gamma)$.

Proof. We prove the lemma by induction on M. We can assume that M is in β-normal form.

Case 1. $M = x$. Then $\alpha = a$ for some type variable a. So we have $B = \{x : a\}$. Thus (a),(b) and (c) hold.

Case 2. $M = xM_1 \cdots M_n (n \geq 1)$. Then by Lemma 1, $\alpha = a$ for some type variable a and a type assignment figure for $B||\!-M : a$ has the following form.

$$\frac{x : \gamma_1 \to \cdots \to \gamma_n \to a \quad M_1 : \gamma_1 \quad \cdots \quad M_i : \gamma_i \quad \cdots \quad M_n : \gamma_n}{xM_1 \cdots M_i \cdots M_n : a}$$

Let $B_i = \{x_j : \alpha_j \in B \mid x_j \in FV(M_j)\}$.

First we prove (a). By Lemma 1 we have $B_i||\!-M_i : \gamma_i$. By induction hypothesis for M_i, (B_i, γ_i) is essentially balanced. To prove that (B, a) is essentially balanced, let b an arbitrary type variable in (B, a). If $b = a$, then by Lemma 1, a does not occur in (B_i, γ_i). Therefore a is essentially balanced in (B, a). If $b \in var(B)$, then by Lemma 1, there is unique B_i such that $b \in var(B_i)$. By induction hypothesis for (B_i, γ_i), b is essentially balanced in (B_i, γ_i). Since b does not occur in other (B_j, γ_j), b is essentially balanced in (B, a).

Next we prove (b-i). Let $b \in var(B,a)$. If $b = a$, then we have $a \succ^* core(\alpha)$, since $\alpha = a$. If $b \neq a$, then there is unique B_i such that $b \in var(B_i)$. By induction hypothesis for (B_i, γ_i), we have $b \succ^*_{(B_i,\gamma_i)} core(\gamma_i)$. Since $x : \gamma_1 \to \cdots \to \gamma_n \to a \in B$ we have $core(\gamma_i) \succ^*_{(B_i,\gamma_i)} a$. Thus we have $b \succ^*_{(B_i,\gamma_i)} a$.

Next we prove (b-ii). Let $b, c \in var(B,a)$, $b \succ^*_{(B,a)} c$ and $c \succ^*_{(B,a)} b$.

If $b = a$, then $a \succ^*_{(B,a)} c$. Let $\delta = \alpha_1 \to \cdots (\gamma_1 \to \cdots \to \gamma_n \to a) \to \alpha_m \to a$. Note that that there is not any type d such that $a \succ_{(B,a)} d$. If $a \succ_{(B,a)} d$ for some d, then there is an occurrence of some subtype $\delta_1 \to \cdots \to (\xi_1 \to \cdots \to \xi_k \to a) \to \cdots \to \delta_p \to d$ of such that the occurrence of d is negative in δ. By Lemma 1, a does not occur in (B_i, γ_i). Therefore a occurs exactly twice in δ. Therefore $d = a$. However a=core(δ) is positive in δ. A contradiction. Thus there is not any type d such that $a \succ_{(B,a)} d$. Therefore if $a \succ^*_{(B,a)} c$, then $c = a$. We can prove (b-ii) similarly for the case $c = a$. Now assume that $b, c \neq a$. Since there is not any type d such that $a \succ_{(B,a)} d$, a does not appear in the relevance relation between $b \succ^*_{(B,a)} c$ nor in $c \succ^*_{(B,a)} b$. Since $var(B_i, \gamma_i) \cap var(B_j, \gamma_j) = \emptyset$, these relevance relations are derived from subtypes in some unique (B_i, γ_i). By induction hypothesis we have $b = c$.

Next we prove (b-iii). Let $b, c, d \in var(B,a)$, $d \succ_{(B,a)} b$ and $d \succ_{(B,a)} c$. Then $\delta = \alpha_1 \to \cdots \to (\gamma_1 \to \cdots \to \gamma_n \to a) \to \alpha_m \to a$ contains some occurrences of subtype $\xi = \xi_1 \to \cdots \to (\zeta_1 \to \cdots \to \zeta_k \to d) \to \cdots \to \xi_l \to b$ and $\nu = \nu_1 \to \cdots \to (\mu_1 \to \cdots \to \mu_k \to d) \to \cdots \to \nu_l \to c$ such that the core(ξ) and core(ν) is negative in δ. Therefore the occurrence of core($\zeta_1 \to \cdots \to \zeta_k \to d$) and core($\mu_1 \to \cdots \to \mu_k \to d$) are positive in δ. Since (B,a) is essentially balanced, the positive occurrence of d in δ is unique. Therefore $b = c$.

Next we prove (c). Assume that γ is a subtype of α_i or that γ is a subtype of α. If $core(\gamma) = a$, (c) is clear from (b-i). If $core(\gamma) \neq a$, then γ is a subtype of some α_i. If $core(\alpha_i) = a$ and $\alpha_i = \gamma \to \cdots \to \gamma_n \to a$, then γ is a subtype of some γ_j. By induction hypothesis for (B_j, γ_j), we have $b \succ^*_{(B_j,\gamma_j)} core(\gamma)$. Therefore $b \succ^*_{(B,\gamma)} core(\gamma)$. If $core(\alpha_i) \neq a$, then $x_i : \alpha_i \in B_j$ for some B_j. By induction hypothesis for (B_j, γ_j), we have $b \succ^*_{(B_j,\gamma_j)} core(\gamma)$. Therefore $b \succ^*_{(B,\gamma)} core(\gamma)$.

Case **3**. $M = \lambda x.N$. Then by Lemma 1, $\alpha = \beta \to \gamma$ and $B \cup \{x : \beta\} || - N : \gamma$. By induction hypothesis, $(B \cup \{x : \beta\}, \gamma)$ is essentially balanced. Therefore (B, α) is essentially balanced. Thus (a) holds. Since $G(B, \beta \to \gamma)$ is identical to $G((B \cup \{x : \beta\}, \gamma)$, (b) holds by induction hypothesis. (c)is Clear. ∎

Proof of if-part of Theorem 3. By induction on the number N of type variables in α.

Base step. $N = 2$. Then $\alpha = a \to a$ for some type variable a. This is a principal type-scheme of BCI-λ-term $\lambda x.x$.

Induction step. $N > 2$. Let $\alpha = \xi_1 \to \cdots \to \xi_m \to e$. First we claim that the core of some ξ_{i_0} is e, i.e., that $\xi_{i_0} = \zeta_1 \to \cdots \to \zeta_k \to e$. By condition (a), e is essentially balanced in α. Since the core of α is positive in α, the negative occurrence of e appears in some ξ_{i_0}. Consider the core of ξ_{i_0}. Then we have $e \succ^*_\alpha core(\xi_{i_0})$ by condition (c). On the other hand we have $core(\xi_{i_0}) \succ^*_\alpha e$ by condition (b-i). By (b-ii) we have $e = core(\xi_{i_0})$. This proves the first claim.

Let $e_j = core(\xi_j)(j = 1, \cdots, k)$. Since α is essentially balanced, each e_j is distinct to each other and $e_j \neq e$. We divide the set of type-schemes $S = \{\xi_1, \cdots, \xi_{i_0-1}, \xi_{i_0+1}, \cdots, \xi_n\}$ into k subsets $S_1, \cdots, S_k$ by $S_j = \{\xi_i \mid core(\xi_i) \succ^*_\alpha e_j\}(j = 1, \cdots, k)$. We enumerate each member of S_j as $S_j = \{\xi_{j,1}, \cdots, \xi_{j,l_j}\}$. We can see that this becomes a partition of $\xi_1, \cdots, \xi_{i_0-1}, \xi_{i_0+1}, \cdots, \xi_n$ as follows. By (b-i), for each $i = 1, \cdots, i_0 - 1, i_0 + 1, \cdots, n$, $core(\xi_i)$ is relevant to e in α. Since the negative occurrence of e in α is unique, this relation goes through some e_j. Therefore $core(\xi_i)$ is relevant to e_j in α for some j. By (b-iii), such e_j is unique for each ξ_i. Therefore $S_1, \cdots, S_k$ is a partition of S.

Now we put $\alpha_j = \xi_{j,1} \to \cdots \to \xi_{j,l_j} \to \zeta_j$ $(j = 1, \cdots, k)$ and show that α_j satisfies (a),(b) and (c).

(a) Let $a \in var(\alpha_j)$. Since α is essentially balanced, a is essentially balanced in α. If α occurs in other $\alpha_{j'} = \xi_{j',1} \to \cdots \to \xi_{j',l_{j'}} \to \zeta_{j'}$, then a is relevant to e_j and to $e_{j'}$ in α by the definition of $\alpha'_j s$. By (b-ii), it follows that $e_j = e_{j'}$. Therefore a occurs only in α_j. Thus a is essentially balanced in α_j.

Before we prove (b) and (c), we claim that if an occurrence of a subtype γ in α contains a type c such that $c \succ^*_\alpha e_j$, then the occurrence of γ is either in ζ_j or in some ξ_q such that $core(\xi_q) \succ^*_\alpha e_j$. Let γ be such an occurrence of subtype. Remember that $\alpha = \xi_1 \to \cdots \to (\zeta_1 \to \cdots \to \zeta_k \to e) \to \cdots \to \xi_n \to e$. If $core(\gamma) = e$ then we have $c \succ^*_\alpha e$ by (c). On the other hand we have $c \succ^*_\alpha e_j$. By (b-iii), it follows that $e = e_j$. A contradiction. Therefore $core(\gamma) \neq e$. Thus γ is either a subtype of ξ_q or a subtype of ζ_q. If γ is a subtype of ξ_q, then $c \succ^*_\alpha core(\xi_q)$ by (c). Since $core(\xi_q) \succ^*_\alpha e_{j'}$ for some j', it follows that $c \succ^*_\alpha e_{j'}$. Therefore $e_{j'} = e_j$. Thus $core(\xi_q) \succ^*_\alpha e_j$. If γ is a subtype of ζ_q, then $c \succ^*_\alpha core(\zeta_q) = e_q$. This proves the claim.

(b-i) is clear from the definition of α_j. From the above claim, the connection relation $\succ^*_\alpha$ for type variables in α_j is determined by occurrences of subtypes in α_j. Thus (b-ii) and (b-iii) hold for α_j. (c) is immediated from the above claim.

Therefore α_j satisfies (a),(b) and (c). By induction hypothesis for α_j, there is a closed BCI-λ-term $L_j = \lambda x_1 \cdots x_{j,l_j}.M_j$ such that $||\!-L_j : \alpha_j$. Since it is principal type assignment, a type assignment figure for $L_j : \alpha_j$ of the following form.

$$\frac{M_j : \zeta_j}{\lambda x_1 \cdots x_{j,l_j}.Lj : \xi_{j,1} \to \cdots \to \xi_{j,l_j} \to \zeta_j}$$

Now we put $M = \lambda x_1 \cdots x \cdots x_n.xM_1 \cdots M_k$. Then M is type-assigned to $\alpha = \xi_1 \to \cdots \to (\zeta_1 \to \cdots \to \zeta_k \to e) \to \cdots \to \xi_n \to e$ by the following type assignment figure.

$$\frac{\dfrac{x : \zeta_1 \to \cdots \to \zeta_k \to e \quad M_1 : \zeta_1 \quad \cdots \quad M_k : \zeta_k}{xM_1 \cdots M_k : e}}{\lambda x_1 \cdots x \cdots x_n.xM_1 \cdots M_k : \xi_1 \to \cdots \to (\zeta_1 \to \cdots \to \zeta_k \to e) \to \cdots \to \xi_n \to e}$$

Since $\alpha = \xi_1 \to \cdots \to (\zeta_1 \to \cdots \to \zeta_k \to e) \to \cdots \to \xi_n \to e$ is essentially balanced, α has the two-property. By Theorem 1, α is a principal type-scheme of M. ∎

4 BCI-minimal-types and BCI-λ-terms in $\beta\eta$-normal form

We say that α is more general than β when β is a substitution instance of α. This relation becomes a pre-order. BCI-minimal types are the set of minimal types in ts(BCI) with respect to this pre-order. The notion of minimality was introduced by Komori [15] concerning to the uniqueness of proof figure for BCK-logic. In [10], the author of the present paper conjectured that a type is BCK-minimal iff it is a principal-type-scheme of some closed BCK-λ-term in $\beta\eta$-normal form. In this section, we prove that the conjecture is true for BCI-λ-terms.

Definition 11 (BCI-minimal) *A type α in ts(BCI) is said to be $BCI - minimal$ iff α is not a non-trivial substitution instance of other type in ts(BCI). We denote the set of BCI-minimal-types by BCI-minimal.*

Theorem 4 *([10]) If two closed BCI-λ-terms in β-normal form have the same principal-type-scheme, then they are identical.*

Proof. See [10]. ∎

Remember that BCI and BCI-$\beta\eta$ denotes the set closed BCI-λ-terms and the set closed BCI-λ-terms in $\beta\eta$-normal form.

Theorem 5

$$pts(BCI - \beta\eta) \underset{\neq}{\subset} pts(BCI).$$

Proof. Consider a BCI-λ-term $\lambda xy.xy$ and its principal-type-scheme $(a \to b) \to a \to b$. Note that $\lambda xy.xy$ is not in η-normal form. Assume that $||\!- M : \alpha$ for some closed BCI-λ-term M in β-normal form. By Theorem 4 it follows that $M = \lambda xy.xy$. Therefore $\alpha \notin pts(BCI - \beta\eta)$. ∎

Theorem 6 (Characterization of BCI-minimal types)

$$pts(BCI - \beta\eta) = BCI - minimal.$$

In the proof of this theorem, we use a transformation of TA-figure. It is a rewriting along a "connected" occurrences of the same type in a TA-figure. A connection is a series of the occurrences of the same type in a TA-figure. Each occurrence of the type in the same connection has the same meaning through the deduction.

Definition 12 (connection [11]) *Let P be a TA-figure for $B|-M : \beta$. Two occurrences of the same type γ in P are said to be directly connected to each other iff one of (1),(2) and (3) holds:*

(1) Both γ appear at the same position in α in distinct occurrences of the same assumption $x : \alpha$.

$$\cdots x : \alpha \cdots x : \alpha \cdots$$

(2) (a) One γ appears at a position in α of the major premise $M : \alpha \to \beta$ of an $(\to E)$ rule and the other γ appears at the same position in α of the minor premise $N : \alpha$ of the $(\to E)$ rule, or

(b) one γ appears at a position in β of the major premise $M : \alpha \to \beta$ of an $(\to E)$ rule and the other γ appears at the same position in β of the consequence $MN : \beta$ of the $(\to E)$ rule.

$$\frac{M : \alpha \to \beta \quad N : \alpha}{MN : \beta}\ (\to E)$$

(3) (a) One γ appears at a position in α of the assumption $x : \alpha$ and the other γ appears at the same position in α of the consequence $\lambda x.M : \alpha \to \beta$, or

(b) one γ appears at a position in β of $M : \beta$ and the other γ appears at the same position in β of $\lambda x.M : \alpha \to \beta$.

$$\begin{array}{c}[x : \alpha] \\ \vdots \\ \dfrac{M : \beta}{\lambda x.M : \alpha \to \beta}\ (\to I)\end{array}$$

The connection relation is the reflexive transitive closure of the direct connection relation.

Proof of Theorem 6. First we prove pts(BCI-η) $\supseteq$ BCI-minimal.

Let α be a BCI-minimal type. Then there is a closed BCI-λ-term M in β-normal form such that $||-M : \alpha$. Let P be a TA-figure for $||-M : \alpha$. Assume that M is not in η-normal form. Then M contains some subterm $\lambda x.Nx$ such that $x \notin FV(N)$. Since M is in β-normal form, so is $\lambda x.Nx$. Therefore N has the form $N = yN_1 \cdots N_n$ and P has the following form.

$$
P_1 \left\{ \dfrac{y:\alpha_1\to\cdots\to\alpha_n\to\beta\to\gamma \quad N_1:\alpha_1 \quad \cdots \quad Nn:\alpha_n}{yN_1\cdots N_n:\beta\to\gamma} \right. \qquad
\left. \dfrac{\dfrac{yN_1\cdots N_n:\beta\to\gamma \qquad x:\beta}{yN_1\cdots N_n x:\gamma}}{\lambda x.yN_1\cdots N_n x:\beta\to\gamma} \right\} P_2
$$

$$
\begin{array}{c} \vdots \\ M:\alpha \end{array}
$$

Let P_1 be the sub-TA-figure with the end-formula $\lambda x.yN_1\cdots N_n:\beta\to\gamma$ and let P_2 be the sub-TA-figure with the end-formula $\lambda x.yN_1\cdots N_n x:\beta\to\gamma$. In P_1 replace $\beta\to\gamma$ by a new type variable c. Let P_1^* be the result of P_1. Note that in P the predicate $\beta\to\gamma$ of $\lambda x.yN_1\cdots N_n x:\beta\to\gamma$ does not connect to the predicate of any major premiss of $(\to I)$. This is proved by induction on $|\!-M:\alpha$. Below the type-assignment formula $\lambda x.yN_1\cdots N_n x:\beta\to\gamma$ in P, replace the connection of $\beta\to\gamma$ by c and replace the occurrence of the subterm $\lambda x.yN_1\cdots N_n x$ by $yN_1\cdots N_n$. After that rewriting, replace P_2 by P_1^*. Then we obtain a TA-figure for $|\!-M[\lambda x.yN_1\cdots N_n x/yN_1\cdots N_n]:\delta$ where $\alpha=\delta[c:=\beta\to\gamma]$. This contradicts the minimality of α. Therefore M is in η-normal form.

Next we prove pts(BCI-$\beta\eta$) $\subseteq$ BCI-minimal. Let $\alpha\in$ pts(BCI-$\beta\eta$). Then we have $||\!-M:\alpha$ for some closed BCI-λ-term M in $\beta\eta$-normal form. To prove the minimality of α, assume that $\alpha=\beta\theta_1$ for some $\beta\in$ pts(BCI-β) and some substitution θ_1. Since $\beta\in$ ts(BCI-β) there is a closed BCI-λ-term N in β-normal form such that $|\!-N:\beta$. By principal type-scheme theorem, we have $||\!-N:\gamma$ for some γ. Thus we have $\beta=\gamma\theta_2$ for some substitution θ_2. Therefore $\alpha=\gamma\theta_2\theta_1$. Since $\alpha\in$ pts(BCI-β), α has the two-property. Thus the decomposition of $\theta_1\theta_2$ does not contain any contraction substitution. Thus the decomposition consists only of arrow substitutions and trivial substitutions. By Lemma 4 there is a closed λ-term M^* in β-normal form such that $||\!-M^*:\alpha$ and M^* is η-reducible to N. Therefore M^* is a closed BCI-λ-term in β-normal form. Thus we have $||\!-M:\alpha$ and $||\!-M^*:\alpha$. By Theorem 4 we have $M=M^*$. Therefore N is in η-normal-form. So we have $M=N$. Thus $\theta_2\theta_1$ is trivial. Thus θ_1 is trivial. Therefore α is BCI-minimal. ∎

After the first draft of this paper, H.Ono and Y.Komori pointed out that the proof of Theorem 6 can be simpler if we use the following result by Babaev and Solove'ev [1] and Mints [17].

Theorem 7 *([1, 17]) If two λ-terms in $\beta\eta$-normal form has the same balanced type-scheme as their types, then they are identical.* ∎

Another proof of Theorem 6. First we prove $pts(BCI-\beta\eta)\supseteq BCI-minimal$. Note that $ts(T)=ts(T-\beta)=ts(T-\beta\eta)$ for any set T of closed λ-terms. In fact, if $|\!-M:\alpha$ for some $M\in T$, then M has $\beta\eta$-normal form $M*$ by strong normalization theorem. Thus $ts(T)\subseteq ts(T-\beta\eta)$. Therefore we have $ts(T)=ts(T-\beta)=ts(T-\beta\eta)$.

Now let $\alpha \in$ BCI-minimal. Then there is a closed BCI-λ-term M such that $|\!-M : \alpha$. We can take such M as $\beta\eta$-normal form. Since α is BCI-minimal, α is a principal type-scheme of M. Thus $pts(BCI - \beta\eta) \supseteq BCI - minimal$.

Next we prove $pts(BCI - \beta\eta) \subseteq BCI - minimal$. Let $\alpha \in pts(BCI - \beta\eta)$. Then we have $||\!-M : \alpha$ for some closed BCI-λ-term M in $\beta\eta$-normal form. To prove the minimality, assume that α is a substitution instance of other type β in $ts(BCI - \beta)$. Then there is a closed BCI-λ-term N in $\beta\eta$-normal form and a substitution θ such that $|\!-N : \beta$ and $\alpha = \beta\theta$. Then we have $|\!-N : \alpha$. By Theorem 3, α is balanced. By Theorem 7 it follows that $M = N$. Therefore β is trivial variant of α. Thus α is BCI-minimal. ∎

We conjecture the following characterization of BCI-minimal types which will be a strong form of Theorem 3.

Conjecture: A type -scheme α is a BCI-minimal iff the following (a), (a*), (b) and (c). hold.

(a) α is essentially balanced.

(a*) If a subtype γ occurs twice in α, then γ is a type variable.

(b) $G(\alpha)$ is a tree with a root core(α).

(c) For any subtype γ in α and for any type-variable a in γ, $a \succ_\alpha^* core(\gamma)$.

If a type is BCI-minimal then it is a principal type of some BCI-λ-term. So, the above conjecture says that the difference between minimality and principality is only (a*).

If the above conjecture is true, then we could construct a decision procedure for BCI-formulas. The procedure looks strange in the sense that it does not search the proof. We denote F_2^* the set of types which satisfy (a) and (a*). Given a type α, first enumerate all $\xi \in F_2^*$ such that α is a substitution instance of ξ. For each ξ, calculate the relevance graph $G(\xi)$. Check if ξ satisfies (b) and (c). If ξ satisfies (b) and (c), then ξ is a BCI-minimal type and α is BCI-provable. If no such ξ exists, then α is not BCI-provable.

Acknowledgements

The author would like to thank to J. R. Hindley for careful reading of the first draft of this paper and for many valuable information on literature. He also thanks to H. Ono and Y. Komori for their stimulating discussion.

References

[1] A.A. Babaev, S.V. Solov'ev. A coherence theorem for canonical morphism in cartesian closed categories. *Zapiski nauchnykh Seminarov Lenigradskogo Otdeleniya matematichskogo Instituta im. V.A. Steklova An SSSR* 88:3-29, 1979.

[2] C.-B. Ben-Yelles. *Type-assignment in the lambda-calculus.* PhD thesis, University College, Swansea, 1979.

[3] J.-Y. Girard. Linear logic. *Theoret. Comput. Sci.* 50:1-101, 1987.

[4] J.R. Hindley. The principal type-scheme of an object in combinatory logic. *Trans. Amer. Math. Soc.* 146:29-60 1969.

[5] J. R. Hindley and J. P Seldin. *Introduction to Combinators and Lambda-Calculus.* Cambridge Univ. Press, London, 1986.

[6] J. R. Hindley. BCK-combinators and linear lambda-terms have types. *Theoret. Comp. Sci.* 64:97-105, 1989.

[7] J. R. Hindley. The Meyer-Bunder theorem: Every inhabited type is a P.T.S. in BB'IW-combinatory logic. Manuscript 1989.

[8] J. R. Hindley and D. Meredith. Principal type-schemes and condensed detachment. *J. Symbolic Logic* 50:90-105, 1990.

[9] J. R. Hindley. BCK and BCI logics, condensed detachment and the 2-property, a summary. Report, Univ. of Wolongon, Aug 1990.

[10] S. Hirokawa. Principal types of BCK-lambda terms. submitted.

[11] S. Hirokawa. Principal type assignment to lambda terms. submitted.

[12] S. Hirokawa. Converse principal-type-scheme theorem in lambda-calculus. *Studia Logica* (to appear).

[13] W. A. Howard. The formulae-as-types notion of construction. In J. R. Hindley and J. P Seldin, editors, *To H.B. Curry, Essays on Combinatory Logic, Lambda Calculus and Formalism*, pages 479–490. Academic Press, 1980.

[14] S. Jaskowski. Über Tautologien, in welchen keine Variable merh Als zweimal vorkommt. *Zeitschrift für Math. Logik* 9:219-228, 1963.

[15] Y. Komori. BCK algebras and lambda calculus. In *Proceedings of 10th Symp. on Semigroups, Sakado 1986*, pages 5-11. Josai University, 1987.

[16] R. K. Meyer and M. W. Bunder. Condensed detachment and combinators. *J. Automated Reasoning* (to appear).

[17] G. E. Mints. A simple proof of the coherence theorem for cartesian closed categories. Manuscript 1982.

[18] G. E. Mints and T. Tammet. Condensed detachment is complete for relevant logic: proof using computer. *J. Automated Reasoning* (to appear).

Intersection and Union Types

Franco BARBANERA, Mariangiola DEZANI-CIANCAGLINI
Dipartimento di Informatica dell'Universita' di Torino
Corso Svizzera, 185 10149 Torino ITALY
barba, dezani@di. unito. it

Abstract

A type assignment with *union* and *intersection* types is introduced. Relevant syntactical and semantic properties of this system are proved.

Introduction.

One of the most interesting approaches for studying polymorphic type disciplines for functional programming is the predicate type theory for λ-calculus, in which types are assigned to untyped λ-terms by means of a system of inference rules.

Intersection types were introduced in [12] as a generalization of the predicate type discipline by Curry, mainly with the aim of describing the functional behaviour of all solvable λ-terms. In the intersection type discipline the usual "→"-based type language for λ-calculus was extended by adding a constant ω as a universal type and a new connective "∧" for the intersection of two types. With suitable axioms and rules to assign types to λ-terms, this gave a system in which:
(i) the set of types given to a λ-term does not change under β-conversion, and
(ii) the sets of solvable and normalizing λ-terms can be characterized very neatly by the types of their members.
Moreover this system was proved to be sound and complete [4] [15].

The aim of the present paper is foundational: to study the intersection type discipline enriched with a new type constructor "∨" allowing us to form *union* types. The typing rules for introduction and elimination of "∨" are essentially inspired by the "formulas-as-types" analogy, viewing ∨ as the logical connective "or". New clauses, which take into account the intuitive meaning of "∨" as union, are added to the pre-order relation on types of [4]. Moreover we add a clause which is not implied by set-theoretic arguments, but which is useful to preserve typing under reductions of λ-terms. The so obtained pre-order relation is used in a type assignment rule.

We prove that our type assignment system with intersection and union types still satisfies the properties (i) and (ii). These proofs are done by associating to each type a finite set of intersection types and to each deduction in the full system a set of deductions in the intersection type assignment system. Moreover we prove the Approximation Theorem, which says that the types of a λ-term are all and only the types of its approximants.

A natural way of defining the semantics of a predicate type theory is to interpret the underlying untyped language in a domain D and the types as subsets of D, in such a way that the interpretation of a λ-term is contained in the interpretation of every type which can be assigned to that λ-term. A classical way of giving the semantics of disjunction is to consider possible worlds where knowledge can expand, i.e. where there are different states of knowledge. Of course there are incompatible ways of extending the knowledge: a tree of possibilities will be a possible world, and a branch in such a tree will determine a possible history of knowledge in that possible world. These are the basic ideas leading to Beth-Kripke models for intuitionistic logic [6] [18]. We introduce a notion of type interpretation inspired by Beth models. Essentially we make sure that whenever a λ-term M has a union type $\sigma\vee\tau$ in a given state of knowledge w, then M will eventually have one of σ and τ in every state extending w. We shall prove the soundness and completeness of our type assignment system with respect to this notion of type interpretation. Moreover we consider two other notions of type interpretation : one inspired by the second order interpretation given in logic to the disjunction, and the other inspired by the translation into types without unions. Our type assignment system is proved to be sound and complete with respect to both these type interpretations.

As byproducts of these results we have also interesting properties for the type assignment systems obtained by weakening the pre-order relation on types (so, in particular, for the subsystem of [21] restricted to $\rightarrow$, $\wedge$ and $\vee$). In fact all these systems characterize the sets of solvable and normalizing λ-terms and are sound with respect to the four notions of type interpretations introduced in the present paper.

A consequence of the Approximation Theorem is that the class of typable λ-terms does not increase by adding the union type constructor to intersection types. Some results however indicate that we obtain more meaningful types. In particular, allowing also a limited polymorphism, "infinite unions" and "infinite intersections", we succeed in typing in a uniform way some interesting classes of λ-terms, like the λ-terms representing numbers known as Berarducci numerals [5] and, in general, the λ-terms of ∗-algebras (∗-algebras are λ-representations of free algebras [7]).

We discussed the present approach to the design of a type system with intersection and union types during the workshop "Computer Science Logic" (Kaiserlauten, 1989) and during the meeting of the ESPRIT BRA Working Group 3230 on "Common Foundation of Logic and Functional Programming" (Paris, 1991).

1. Type Assignment System: Definitions and Main Properties.

The set of types is built out of an infinite set of type variables and the type constant ω, by means of the function space ("$\rightarrow$"), union ("$\vee$") and intersection ("$\wedge$") type constructors.

1.1 <u>Definition</u> (*Types*).
The set T of *types* is inductively defined by
- $\phi_0, \phi_1, \ldots \in T$ type variables
- $\omega \in T$ type constant
- $\sigma, \tau \in T \Rightarrow (\sigma\rightarrow\tau), (\sigma\wedge\tau), (\sigma\vee\tau) \in T$.

Convention : we omit parentheses according to the precedence rule: "$\wedge$ and $\vee$ over $\rightarrow$".

We define a preorder $\leq$ on the so obtained types which is justified by the interpretation of ω as universal type, of $\rightarrow$ as function space constructor, of $\wedge$ as intersection and of $\vee$ as union between types. This preorder uses a predicate $P: \mathbf{T} \rightarrow \{\mathbf{tt}, \mathbf{ff}\}$ which is true for a type σ if $\vee$ occurs in σ only on the left of some arrows. This means that σ could be written without $\vee$ occurrences (modulo the equivalence relation induced by $\leq$). This will be clarified by the results of Section 2.

1.2 Definition (*Preorder on Types*).

(i) The predicate $P: \mathbf{T} \rightarrow \{\mathbf{tt}, \mathbf{ff}\}$ is defined by:

$P(\phi) = P(\omega) = \mathbf{tt}$ $\qquad P(\sigma \rightarrow \tau) = P(\tau)$

$P(\sigma \wedge \tau) = P(\sigma)$ and $P(\tau)$ $\qquad P(\sigma \vee \tau) = \mathbf{ff}$.

(ii) The relation $\leq$ on T is inductively defined as the reflexive and transitive closure of:

$$\begin{array}{ll}
\tau \leq \omega & \omega \leq \omega \rightarrow \omega \\
\tau \leq \tau \wedge \tau & \tau \vee \tau \leq \tau \\
\sigma \wedge \tau \leq \sigma, \ \sigma \wedge \tau \leq \tau & \sigma \leq \sigma \vee \tau, \ \tau \leq \sigma \vee \tau \\
\sigma \wedge (\tau \vee \rho) \leq (\sigma \wedge \tau) \vee (\sigma \wedge \rho) & (\sigma \rightarrow \rho) \wedge (\sigma \rightarrow \tau) \leq \sigma \rightarrow \rho \wedge \tau \\
(\sigma \rightarrow \rho) \wedge (\tau \rightarrow \rho) \leq \sigma \vee \tau \rightarrow \rho & \sigma \leq \sigma', \ \tau \leq \tau' \Rightarrow \sigma \wedge \tau \leq \sigma' \wedge \tau' \\
\sigma \leq \sigma', \ \tau \leq \tau' \Rightarrow \sigma \vee \tau \leq \sigma' \vee \tau' & \sigma' \leq \sigma, \ \tau \leq \tau' \Rightarrow \sigma \rightarrow \tau \leq \sigma' \rightarrow \tau' \\
P(\sigma) \Rightarrow \sigma \rightarrow \rho \vee \tau \leq (\sigma \rightarrow \rho) \vee (\sigma \rightarrow \tau) . &
\end{array}$$

$\sigma \sim \tau$ is short for $\sigma \leq \tau \leq \sigma$. Then, if the set of types is considered modulo $\sim$, $\leq$ becomes a partial order.

1.3 Remark. Clause $P(\sigma) \Rightarrow \sigma \rightarrow \rho \vee \tau \leq (\sigma \rightarrow \rho) \vee (\sigma \rightarrow \tau)$ is not necessary when types are interpreted as arbitrary sets. It holds when we interpret types as upward closed subsets of a Scott domain. In such a case the condition corresponding to P is "to contain a least element". For example in [1] types are interpreted as *compact-open* subsets and condition P becomes "to be a *consistent prime* ".
The main reason we introduce this clause is that we are looking for a type assignment system in which types are preserved under reduction of subjects (see Remark 1.6).

A *typing statement* is an expression of the form $M: \sigma$, where M is a λ-term and σ a type; M is called the *subject* of the typing statement.
A *basis*, the finite set of assumptions a typing statement depends on, is a set of *basic* typing statement of the form $x: \sigma$, where x is a variable and σ a type. In a basis no two typing statements have the same subject.
A *statement* is an expression of the form $B \vdash M: \sigma$, where B is a basis and $M: \sigma$ is a typing statement.
Given a basis B without occurrences of x, the basis $B \cup \{x: \sigma\}$ will be denoted by $B, x: \sigma$.

1.4 *Definition* (*Type Assignment System*).
The axioms and rules to derive typing statements are:

$$(Ax)\ \frac{}{B,x:\sigma \vdash x:\sigma} \qquad (\omega)\ \frac{}{B \vdash M:\omega}$$

$$(\to E)\ \frac{B \vdash M:\sigma\to\tau \quad B \vdash N:\sigma}{B \vdash MN:\tau} \qquad (\to I)\ \frac{B,x:\sigma \vdash M:\tau}{B \vdash \lambda x.M:\sigma\to\tau}$$

$$(\wedge)\ \frac{B \vdash M:\sigma \quad B \vdash M:\tau}{B\vdash M:\sigma\wedge\tau} \qquad (\vee)\ \frac{B,x:\sigma \vdash M:\rho \quad B,x:\tau \vdash M:\rho \quad B \vdash N:\sigma\vee\tau}{B\vdash M[N/x]:\rho}$$

$$(\leq)\ \frac{B \vdash M:\sigma \quad \sigma\leq\tau}{B \vdash M:\tau} \ .$$

Union types were first introduced in [21], where the properties of the formal system are not investigated, but only a brief discussion of their use in a possible system to argue about the types-as-ideals semantics is given.
The rules for $\wedge$ and $\vee$ given in [21] are

$$(\wedge I)\ \frac{B \vdash M:\sigma \quad B \vdash M:\tau}{B \vdash M:\sigma\wedge\tau} \qquad (\wedge E)\ \frac{B \vdash M:\sigma\wedge\tau}{B \vdash M:\sigma} \qquad \frac{B \vdash M:\sigma\wedge\tau}{B \vdash M:\tau}$$

$$(\vee I)\ \frac{B \vdash M:\sigma}{B \vdash M:\sigma\vee\tau} \quad \frac{B \vdash M:\tau}{B \vdash M:\sigma\vee\tau} \qquad (\vee E)\ \frac{B,x:\sigma \vdash M:\rho \quad B,x:\tau \vdash M:\rho \quad B \vdash N:\sigma\vee\tau}{B \vdash M[N/x]:\rho}$$

Rules ($\wedge$E) and ($\vee$I) are admissible in our system. In fact ($\wedge$E) and ($\vee$I) are particular cases of application of rule ($\leq$) (which is not a rule of [21]) since $\sigma\wedge\tau\leq\sigma, \sigma\wedge\tau\leq\tau, \sigma\leq\sigma\vee\tau$ and $\tau\leq\sigma\vee\tau$.

Note that the given inference rules modify the basis only by erasing premises. The following admissible rules modify the basis by replacing premises.

$$(\leq L)\ \frac{B,x:\sigma \vdash M:\tau \quad \rho\leq\sigma}{B,x:\rho \vdash M:\tau} \qquad (\vee L)\ \frac{B,x:\sigma \vdash M:\rho \quad B,x:\tau \vdash M:\rho}{B,x:\sigma\vee\tau \vdash M:\rho} \ .$$

Let us prove their admissibility.
For rule ($\leq$L), given a derivation, each occurrence of the axiom

$$(Ax)\ \frac{}{B,x:\sigma \vdash x:\sigma}$$

can be replaced by the following deduction

$$(Ax)\ \frac{}{B, x{:}\rho \vdash x{:}\rho} \qquad (\leq)\ \frac{B, x{:}\rho \vdash x{:}\rho \quad \rho \leq \sigma}{B, x{:}\rho \vdash x{:}\sigma}\ .$$

For rule ($\vee$L) note that if $B \vdash M{:}\tau$ is derivable and $B \subseteq B'$ then also $B' \vdash M{:}\tau$ is derivable. Moreover, typing statements and derivations are independent from the name of (free) term variables. This means in particular that the assumptions of ($\vee$L) imply $B, y{:}\sigma \vdash M[y/x]{:}\rho$ $\;B, y{:}\tau \vdash M[y/x]{:}\rho$ where y does not occur in B and M. So the following deduction shows the admissibility of rule ($\vee$L).

$$(\vee)\ \frac{B, x{:}\sigma\vee\tau, y{:}\sigma \vdash M[y/x]{:}\rho \quad B, x{:}\sigma\vee\tau, y{:}\tau \vdash M[y/x]{:}\rho \quad B, x{:}\sigma\vee\tau \vdash x{:}\sigma\vee\tau}{B,\ x{:}\sigma\vee\tau \vdash M{:}\rho}$$

In the following proofs we shall freely use these admissible rules.

1.5 Remarks.

(i) In the intersection type assignment system rule ($\leq$) can be replaced by rules ($\wedge$E) and

$$(\eta)\ \frac{B \vdash \lambda x.Mx{:}\sigma \quad x \notin FV(M)}{B \vdash M{:}\sigma}\ .$$

The same property does not hold here; in fact by using rules ($\wedge$E), (η) and ($\vee$I) we can derive all the clauses defining the relation $\leq$ but $\sigma\wedge(\tau\vee\rho) \leq (\sigma\wedge\tau)\vee(\sigma\wedge\rho)$ and $P(\sigma) \Rightarrow \sigma\to\rho\vee\tau \leq (\sigma\to\rho)\vee(\sigma\to\tau)$.

Nevertheless rule (η) is an admissible rule in the present type assignment; this is proved in Section 2.

(ii) In [15] a subset of intersection types (the *normal types*) is defined, showing that this restriction is trivial, in the sense that every deduction could be paralleled by a deduction containing only normal types. Analogously, in a first version of the present paper we introduced a subset of T proving the same property for the type assignment system of Definition 1.4.

(iii) Intersection does not correspond to conjunction in the standard formulas-as-types isomorphism, as already noted in [17]; a simple example is the type $\sigma\to\tau\to\sigma\wedge\tau$ (an axiom of Hilbert system) which cannot be deduced for any closed λ-term. Also union does not correspond to disjunction; an example is again given by an axiom of Hilbert system: $(\sigma\to\tau)\to(\rho\to\tau)\to\sigma\vee\rho\to\tau$. But union can be considered as symmetrical to intersection, since we can deduce $\vdash \lambda xy.xy{:}(\sigma\to\tau)\wedge(\rho\to\tau)\to\sigma\vee\rho\to\tau$.

An interesting property of the intersection type assignment is the invariance of types under β-conversion and η-reduction. We will prove in Section 2 that adding union types preserves this property; this proof is based on the results for the intersection type discipline using a suitable translation of types and deductions. The invariance of types under β-η-reduction is needed to assure that all reducts of a well typed λ-term have its types. The implications on the possible construction of a type inference system for functional programming languages based on the type discipline presented in this paper are straightforward.

The intersection type assignment is already not invariant under η-expansion of subjects (a trivial example is $\vdash \lambda x.x{:}\phi\to\phi$ and $\not\vdash \lambda xy.xy{:}\phi\to\phi$).

1.6 Remark . The type assignment system obtained by erasing the clause $P(\sigma) \Rightarrow \sigma\to\rho\vee\tau \leq (\sigma\to\rho)\vee(\sigma\to\tau)$ in the definition of $\leq$ is not invariant under β-η-reduction of subjects. The problem is that in rule ($\vee$) we lose the correspondence between subterms and subdeductions; many occurrences of the same subterm correspond in fact to a unique subdeduction. For example one can deduce the type $(\sigma\to\sigma\to\tau)\wedge(\rho\to\rho\to\tau)\to(\mu\to\sigma\vee\rho)\to\mu\to\tau$ both for $\lambda xyz.x(yz)(yz)$ and for $\lambda xyz.x((\lambda t.t)yz)((\lambda t.t)yz)$, but this type cannot be deduced for $\lambda xyz.x(yz)((\lambda t.t)yz)$ or $\lambda xyz.x((\lambda t.t)yz)(yz)$. Benjamin Pierce showed us this example. Then in this system types are not preserved either under β-reduction or under β-expansion. A similar example shows that types are not preserved under η-reduction.
Instead types are invariant under β-η-reductions and β-expansions which are done simultaneously on all the occurrences of the same subterm which correspond to the same subdeduction. To formally represent these reductions and prove this property requires a different machinery and will be done elsewhere [20].

In Section 2 we prove another important property, which is strictly connected with invariance of types under β-convertibility; if a type σ is deducible for a λ-term M (starting from a given basis) then σ is deducible for an approximant of M (starting from the same basis). Moreover we prove that the introduction of union types in the intersection type discipline preserves the characterization of solvable and normalizing λ-terms.

Usually, in type assignment systems λ-terms are interpreted as objects of the domain D of a λ-model and types as subsets of D, in such a way that the interpretation of a λ-term is contained in the interpretation of every type which can be assigned to that λ-term.

Let us recall (cfr. [22] and [3]) that a λ-model $\mathcal{M} = \langle D, \cdot , \varepsilon\rangle$ is a set D together with a binary operation $\cdot$ and elements $\mathbf{K}$, $\mathbf{S}$, $\varepsilon \in D$ such that:

$(K \cdot d) \cdot e = d$ $\qquad\qquad ((S \cdot d) \cdot e) \cdot f = (d \cdot f) \cdot (e \cdot f)$

$(\varepsilon \cdot d) \cdot e = d \cdot e$ $\qquad\qquad \forall e\ (d_1 \cdot e = d_2 \cdot e) \Rightarrow \varepsilon \cdot d_1 = \varepsilon \cdot d_2$

$\varepsilon \cdot \varepsilon = \varepsilon.$

Given a λ-model $\mathcal{M} = \langle D, \cdot, \varepsilon\rangle$ and a mapping (*environment*)
ζ: Term-Variables$\to$D, the meaning of a λ-term in M is inductively defined by:

$[\![x]\!]_\zeta = \zeta(x)$ $\qquad\qquad [\![MN]\!]_\zeta = [\![M]\!]_\zeta \cdot [\![N]\!]_\zeta$

$[\![\lambda x.M]\!]_\zeta = \varepsilon \cdot d$ where $d \cdot e = [\![M]\!]_{\zeta[e/x]}$ for all $e \in D$.

Types can be interpreted as subsets of D taking into account that ω represents the universal type, $\to$ represents the function space constructor, $\wedge$ and $\vee$ the intersection and union between types, respectively. Therefore given a λ-model $\mathcal{M} = \langle D, \cdot, \varepsilon\rangle$ a straightforward definition of type interpretation is a mapping $\mathfrak{v} : T\to 2^D$ such that :

(i) $\mathfrak{v}(\omega) = D$

(ii) $\mathfrak{v}(\sigma\to\tau) = \{\, d\in D \mid \forall e\in\mathfrak{v}(\sigma)\ d\cdot e\in\mathfrak{v}(\tau) \,\}$

(iii) $\mathfrak{v}(\sigma\wedge\tau) = \mathfrak{v}(\sigma)\cap\mathfrak{v}(\tau)$

(iv) $\mathfrak{v}(\sigma\vee\tau) = \mathfrak{v}(\sigma)\cup\mathfrak{v}(\tau)$

(v) $P(\sigma) \Rightarrow \mathfrak{v}(\sigma\to\rho\vee\tau) \subseteq \mathfrak{v}(\sigma\to\rho)\cup\mathfrak{v}(\sigma\to\tau)$.

The soundness of our type assignment system with respect to this notion of type interpretation can be easily proved by induction on deductions.

But since we want a completeness result without requiring any saturation condition, we introduce a notion of type interpretation which is strictly inspired by Beth forcing [6]. The authors thank Roger Hindley for an enlightening discussion on this point. Let us define first a suitable notion of possible worlds relative to a given λ-model.

1.7 <u>Definition</u> (*Possible Worlds*).
Given a λ-model $\mathcal{M}$ whose domain is D, a *possible world* $\mathcal{W}$ for $\mathcal{M}$ is a triple:

$$\mathcal{W} = \langle \mathcal{P}, \sqsubseteq, \{A_w\}_{w\in\mathcal{P}} \rangle$$

where:

- $\mathcal{P}$ is a nonempty set of elements, representing *states of knowledge*
- $(\mathcal{P}, \sqsubseteq)$ is a partial ordering which can be represented as a finitely branching tree
- for each $w \in \mathcal{P}$, A_w is a finite set of pairs $\langle d, \phi \rangle$ where $d \in D$ and ϕ is a type variable (*the atomic facts* known at state w)
- $w \sqsubseteq w'$ (w' *extends* w) $\Rightarrow$ $A_w \subseteq A_{w'}$.

As usual, a *bar* $\mathfrak{b}_w$ for a state w is any collection of states (extending w) such that any maximal branch going through w intersects (i.e. goes through one of the elements of) $\mathfrak{b}_w$.

The notion of world naturally suggests a notion of type interpretation.

1.8 <u>Definition</u> (*Beth Type Interpretation*).
Every possible world $\mathcal{W}$ for $\mathcal{M} = \langle D, \cdot, \varepsilon \rangle$ defines a mapping $\upsilon : T \to \mathcal{P} \to 2^D$ as follows :

(i) $\upsilon(\omega, w) = D$
(ii) $\upsilon(\phi, w) = \{d \in D \mid \exists\, \mathfrak{b}_w\ \forall w' \in \mathfrak{b}_w\ \langle d, \phi \rangle \in A_{w'}\}$
(iii) $\upsilon(\sigma \to \tau, w) = \{ d \in D \mid \forall w' \sqsupseteq w\ \forall e \in \upsilon(\sigma, w')\ d \cdot e \in \upsilon(\tau, w') \}$
(iii) $\upsilon(\sigma \wedge \tau, w) = \upsilon(\sigma, w) \cap \upsilon(\tau, w)$
(iv) $\upsilon(\sigma \vee \tau, w) = \{ d \in D \mid \exists\, \mathfrak{b}_w\ \forall w' \in \mathfrak{b}_w\ d \in \upsilon(\sigma, w') \cup \upsilon(\tau, w') \}$.

We say that υ is a *Beth type interpretation* iff :
(v) $P(\sigma) \Rightarrow \upsilon(\sigma \to \rho \vee \tau, w) \subseteq \upsilon((\sigma \to \rho) \vee (\sigma \to \tau), w)$ for all $w \in \mathcal{P}$.

In what follows we will consider only possible worlds which induce Beth type interpretations.

1.9 <u>Remark</u>. In [21] types are interpreted as *ideals*, i.e. nonempty subsets of a Scott domain closed under approximations and limits of increasing chains. This assures that the interpretation of second order types is never empty. Note that the usual inference rules are not complete if the interpretation of some type in each model is the empty set.
Alternative inference rules which allow empty interpretations of types are presented in [23]. The traditional inference system turns out to be complete for *Kripke λ-models* which may have empty types [24]. Both these papers deal with typed λ-calculus. The main difference between the present approach and the Kripke λ-models of [24] is that while we use the standard notion of λ-model of untyped λ-calculus changing only the definition of type interpretation, Mitchell and Moggi build possible worlds in which each knowledge state supplies a meaning for typed λ-terms.

The notion of semantic satisfability for our system is defined as usual.

1.10 *Definition* (*Satisfability*).
Let $\mathcal{W}$, ζ be as above and υ be a type interpretation.
(i) $\mathcal{W}, \zeta, w \models M{:}\sigma$ iff $[\![M]\!]_\zeta \in \upsilon(\sigma, w)$.
(ii) $\mathcal{W}, \zeta, w \models B$ iff $\forall x{:}\sigma \in B$ $\mathcal{W}, \zeta, w \models x{:}\sigma$.
(iii) $B \models M{:}\sigma$ iff $\forall\, \mathcal{W}, \zeta, w$: $[\mathcal{W}, \zeta, w \models B \Rightarrow \mathcal{W}, \zeta, w \models M{:}\sigma]$.

We will prove that the set inclusion among type interpretations respects the preorder relation $\leq$ between types. This will imply the semantic soundness of the given type inference system.
Moreover we will prove semantic completeness building a suitable possible world for the term model of λ-calculus (this will be done in Section 3).

We will show that our type assigment system is also sound and complete choosing an interpretation of the type constructor $\vee$ inspired by rule ($\vee$) and by the definition of disjunction in minimal second order logic [27] (this idea was suggested to us by Stefano Berardi). In this case we can define directly the type interpretation avoiding the introduction of possible worlds.

1.11 *Definition* (*Second Order Type Interpretation*).
If D is the domain of a λ-model, a mapping $\upsilon_s : T \to 2^D$ is a *second order type interpretation* iff:
(i) $\upsilon_s(\omega) = D$
(ii) $\upsilon_s(\sigma\to\tau) = \{\, d\in D \mid \forall e\in\upsilon_s(\sigma)\ d\cdot e\in\upsilon_s(\tau) \,\}$
(iii) $\upsilon_s(\sigma\wedge\tau) = \upsilon_s(\sigma)\cap\upsilon_s(\tau)$
(iv) $\upsilon_s(\sigma\vee\tau) = \{\, d\in D \mid \forall\rho\ \forall e\in\upsilon_s((\sigma\to\rho)\wedge(\tau\to\rho))\ \ e\cdot d\in\upsilon_s(\rho) \,\}$
(v) $\sigma\leq\tau \Rightarrow \upsilon_s(\sigma) \subseteq \upsilon_s(\tau)$.

1.12 Remarks.
(i) Note that the interpretation of $\wedge$ by an analogous operator suggested by the definition of disjunction in minimal second order logic, i.e.
$\upsilon_s(\sigma\wedge\tau) = \{d\in D \mid \forall\rho\ \forall e\in\upsilon_s(\sigma\to\tau\to\rho)\ e\cdot d\in\upsilon_s(\rho)\}$, looks meaningless. As remarked by Benjamin Pierce (Private Communication) a possible second order type interpretation of $\wedge$ is instead :
$\upsilon_s(\sigma\wedge\tau) = \{\, d\in D \mid \forall\rho\ \forall e\in\upsilon_s((\sigma\to\rho)\vee(\tau\to\rho))\ \ e\cdot d\in\upsilon_s(\rho) \,\}$.
(ii) It is always true that $\upsilon_s(\sigma)\cup\upsilon_s(\tau)\subseteq\upsilon_s(\sigma\vee\tau)$, since $d\in\upsilon_s(\sigma)\cup\upsilon_s(\tau)$ and $e\in\upsilon_s((\sigma\to\rho)\wedge(\tau\to\rho))$ imply $e\cdot d\in\upsilon_s(\rho)$.
(iii)(by Mario Coppo). When types are interpreted as *ideals* it is easy to check that $\upsilon_s(\sigma\vee\tau)\subseteq\upsilon_s(\sigma)\cup\upsilon_s(\tau)$. This can be proved by contradiction. If $\upsilon_s(\sigma\vee\tau)\not\subseteq\upsilon_s(\sigma)\cup\upsilon_s(\tau)$ then there exists a *finite* element d_0 such that $d_0\in\upsilon_s(\sigma\vee\tau)$ and $d_0\notin\upsilon_s(\sigma)\cup\upsilon_s(\tau)$. Let e_0 be a finite element such that $e_0\notin\upsilon_s(\rho)$ for a type ρ (a possible choice is $e_0=d_0$ and $\rho\equiv\sigma$ or $\rho\equiv\tau$) and let f_0 be the *step function* :

$$f_0(d) = \begin{cases} e_0 & \text{if } d_0 \sqsubseteq d \\ \bot & \text{otherwise} \end{cases}$$

$f_0\in\upsilon_s((\sigma\to\rho)\wedge(\tau\to\rho))$ since $\forall d\in\upsilon_s(\sigma)\cup\upsilon_s(\tau)\ f_0(d)=\bot$.
On the other hand $f_0(d_0) = e_0\notin\upsilon_s(\rho)$, contradiction.

1.13 *Definition* (*Second Order Semantic Satisfability*).
Let $\mathcal{M}$, ζ be as above and υ_s be a second order type interpretation.
(i) $\mathcal{M}, \zeta, \upsilon_s \models_s M{:}\sigma$ iff $[\![M]\!]_\zeta\in\upsilon_s(\sigma)$.

(ii) $\mathcal{M}, \zeta, \upsilon_s \models_S B$ iff $\forall x{:}\sigma \in B \;\; \mathcal{M}, \zeta, \upsilon_s \models_S x{:}\sigma$.
(iii) $B \models_S M{:}\sigma$ iff $\forall\, \mathcal{M}, \zeta, \upsilon_s$: $[\mathcal{M}, \zeta, \upsilon_s \models_S B \Rightarrow \mathcal{M}, \zeta, \upsilon_s \models_S M{:}\sigma]$.

In Section 3 we shall introduce another notion of type interpretation, directly suggested by the translation in intersection types, and we will prove also the soundness and completeness with respect to this notion.

2. Conversion and Approximation Theorems.

We prove the conversion and the approximation theorems by defining suitable translations from T to finite subsets of types without union ($T_\wedge$) and from deductions in $\vdash$ to sets of deductions in the intersection type assignment system ($\vdash^\wedge$).

2.1 Definition (*Intersection Type Assignment System*).
(i) $T_\wedge$ is the set of types built out of type variables and the constant ω using only the type constructors $\rightarrow$ and $\wedge$.
(ii) $\leq^\wedge$ is the relation defined by restricting all clauses in 1.2 to types in $T_\wedge$.
(iii) The system $\vdash^\wedge$ is the system $\vdash$ where only types in $T_\wedge$ are used.

$T_\wedge$ and $\vdash^\wedge$ are therefore the set of types and the type assignment system of [4]. Obviously in $\vdash^\wedge$ rule ($\vee$) is not allowed and in rule ($\leq$) the relation $\leq$ is replaced by $\leq^\wedge$.

2.2 Theorem (*Main Property of* $\vdash^\wedge$) [4].
Let $B \vdash^\wedge M{:}\sigma$ and $M =_\beta N$ or $M \rightarrow_\eta N$. Then $B \vdash^\wedge N{:}\sigma$.

Convention : $C(n,m)$ denotes the finite set of functions $\chi{:}\{1,..,n\}\rightarrow\{1,..,m\}$.

2.3 Lemma (*The mapping* $\mathfrak{m}$).
(i) Let $\sigma \sim \sigma_1\vee..\vee\sigma_n$ and $\tau \sim \tau_1\vee..\vee\tau_m$.
Then $\sigma\rightarrow\tau \sim \bigvee_{\chi\in C(n,m)}\bigwedge_{1\leq i\leq n}(\sigma_i\rightarrow\tau_{\chi(i)})$.
(ii) Let $\sigma\in T$. Then there exists a finite set $\mathfrak{m}(\sigma) = \{\sigma_1,..,\sigma_n\}$ of types in $T_\wedge$ such that $\sigma \sim \sigma_1\vee..\vee\sigma_n$.
Proof.
(i) Easy from 1.2.
(ii) We build the set $\mathfrak{m}(\sigma)$ by induction on σ.
- $\sigma \equiv \omega, \phi$. $\mathfrak{m}(\sigma) = \{\sigma\}$.
For the induction step, let (by the induction hypothesis) $\mathfrak{m}(\rho) = \{\rho_1,..,\rho_p\}$ with $\rho \sim \rho_1\vee..\vee\rho_p$ and $\mathfrak{m}(\tau) = \{\tau_1,..,\tau_m\}$ with $\tau \sim \tau_1\vee..\vee\tau_m$.
$\sigma \equiv \rho\rightarrow\tau$.
We can use (i) obtaining $\mathfrak{m}(\sigma) = \{\bigwedge_{1\leq i\leq p}(\rho_i\rightarrow\tau_{\chi(i)}) \mid \chi\in C(p,m)\}$ since $\rho\rightarrow\tau \sim \bigvee_{\chi\in C(p,m)}\bigwedge_{1\leq i\leq n}(\rho_i\rightarrow\tau_{\chi(i)})$.
- $\sigma \equiv \rho\wedge\tau$.
It is easy to check that $(\rho_1\vee..\vee\rho_p)\wedge(\tau_1\vee..\vee\tau_m) \sim \bigvee_{1\leq i\leq p, 1\leq j\leq m}(\rho_i\wedge\tau_j)$. We put then $\mathfrak{m}(\tau\wedge\rho) = \{\rho_i\wedge\tau_j \mid 1\leq i\leq p, 1\leq j\leq m\}$.
- $\sigma \equiv \rho\vee\tau$.
In this case $\mathfrak{m}(\rho\vee\tau) = \mathfrak{m}(\rho)\cup\mathfrak{m}(\tau)$. ◻

For example if $\sigma \equiv \phi_0 \vee \phi_1 \to \phi_2 \vee \phi_3$ then $m(\sigma) = \{\phi_0 \to \phi_2 \wedge \phi_1 \to \phi_2,\ \phi_0 \to \phi_2 \wedge \phi_1 \to \phi_3,$ $\phi_0 \to \phi_3 \wedge \phi_1 \to \phi_2,\ \phi_0 \to \phi_3 \wedge \phi_1 \to \phi_3\}$.
Obviously $\sigma' \in m(\sigma)$ implies $\sigma' \leq \sigma$.
In the following lemma we prove that m agrees with $\leq$.

2.4 <u>Lemma</u> (*Main Property of* m).
$\sigma \leq \tau$ implies $\forall \sigma' \in m(\sigma)\ \exists \tau' \in m(\tau)$ such that $\sigma' \leq^{\wedge} \tau'$.
<u>Proof</u>.
(i) By induction on the derivation of $\sigma \leq \tau$. We give only the most interesting cases.
Let $m(\sigma) = \{\sigma_1, .., \sigma_n\}$, $m(\tau) = \{\tau_1, .., \tau_m\}$, $m(\rho) = \{\rho_1, .., \rho_p\}$.
$(\sigma \to \rho) \wedge (\sigma \to \tau) \leq \sigma \to \rho \wedge \tau$.
It is easy to check that
$m((\sigma \to \rho) \wedge (\sigma \to \tau)) = \{\wedge_{1 \leq i \leq n} (\sigma_i \to \rho_{\chi(i)}) \wedge (\sigma_i \to \tau_{\chi'(i)}) \mid \chi \in C(n,m),\ \chi' \in C(n,p)\}$
and
$m(\sigma \to \rho \wedge \tau) = \{\wedge_{1 \leq i \leq n} (\sigma_i \to \rho_{\chi(i)} \wedge \tau_{\chi'(i)}) \mid \chi \in C(n,m), \chi' \in C(n,p)\}$, from which the thesis follows.
$\sigma \to \rho \vee \tau \leq (\sigma \to \rho) \vee (\sigma \to \tau)$ with $P(\sigma) = \mathbf{tt}$.
It is easy to check that
$m(\sigma \to \rho \vee \tau) = \{\wedge_{1 \leq i \leq n} (\sigma_i \to \mu_{\chi(i)}) \mid \{\mu_1, .. \mu_{p+m}\} = m(\rho) \cup m(\tau),\ \chi \in C(n, p+m)\}$
and
$m((\sigma \to \rho) \vee (\sigma \to \tau)) = \{\wedge_{1 \leq i \leq n} (\sigma_i \to \rho_{\chi(i)}) \mid \chi \in C(n,p)\} \cup \{\wedge_{1 \leq i \leq n} (\sigma_i \to \tau_{\chi(i)}) \mid \chi \in C(n,m)\}$,
from which the thesis follows.
$\mu \leq \sigma,\ \tau \leq \upsilon \Rightarrow \sigma \to \tau \leq \mu \to \upsilon$. Let $m(\mu) = \{\mu_1, .., \mu_q\}$ and $m(\upsilon) = \{\upsilon_1, .., \upsilon_r\}$.
$m(\sigma \to \tau) = \{\wedge_{1 \leq i \leq n} (\sigma_i \to \tau_{\chi(i)}) \mid \chi \in C(n,m)\}$. We have $\wedge_{1 \leq i \leq n} (\sigma_i \to \tau_i) \in m(\sigma \to \tau)$.
Then $\wedge_{1 \leq i \leq n} (\sigma_i \to \tau_i) \leq^{\wedge} \sigma_i \to \tau_i$ for all i $(1 \leq i \leq n)$. By the induction hypothesis we have that for all i $(1 \leq i \leq n)$ there exists g(i) such that $\tau_i \leq^{\wedge} \upsilon_{g(i)}$.
Hence for all i $(1 \leq i \leq n)$ $\sigma_i \to \tau_i \leq \sigma_i \to \upsilon_{g(i)}$ (1).
By the induction hypothesis we have also that for all h $(1 \leq h \leq q)$ there exists f(h) such that $\mu_h \leq^{\wedge} \sigma_{f(h)}$.
Then for all h $(1 \leq h \leq q)$ $\sigma_{f(h)} \to \upsilon_{g(f(h))} \leq^{\wedge} \mu_h \to \upsilon_{g(f(h))}$ and then from (1) we get $\wedge_{1 \leq i \leq n} (\sigma_i \to \tau_i) \leq^{\wedge} \wedge_{1 \leq h \leq q} (\mu_h \to \upsilon_{g(f(h))})$ with $\wedge_{1 \leq h \leq q} (\mu_h \to \upsilon_{g(f(h))}) \in m(\mu \to \upsilon)$. □

To each basis B with types in $\mathbf{T}$, m naturally associates a (finite) set of bases $\mathfrak{B}(B)$ with types in $\mathbf{T}_{\wedge}$; for each statement of B of the shape $x{:}\sigma$ each basis B' of $\mathfrak{B}(B)$ contains a statement $x{:}\sigma'$ for a unique choice of $\sigma' \in m(\sigma)$.

2.5 <u>Definition</u> (*Set of Bases* $\mathfrak{B}(B)$).
$\mathfrak{B}(B) = \{B' \mid FV(B) = FV(B')$ and $[x{:}\sigma \in B \Rightarrow \exists! \sigma' \in m(\sigma)\ x{:}\sigma' \in B']\}$.

For example if $B = \{x{:}\phi_0 \vee \phi_1,\ y{:}\phi_2 \vee \phi_3\}$ then $\mathfrak{B}(B) = \{B_1, B_2, B_3, B_4\}$ where $B_1 = \{x{:}\phi_0, y{:}\phi_2\}$, $B_2 = \{x{:}\phi_0, y{:}\phi_3\}$, $B_3 = \{x{:}\phi_1, y{:}\phi_2\}$ and $B_4 = \{x{:}\phi_1, y{:}\phi_3\}$.

By rule $(\leq L)$ $B \vdash M{:}\sigma \Rightarrow \forall B' \in \mathfrak{B}(B)\ B' \vdash M{:}\sigma$, but $\mathfrak{B}(B)$ enjoys more interesting properties.

2.6 <u>Theorem</u> (*Main Property of* $\mathfrak{B}(B)$).
$B \vdash M{:}\sigma \Leftrightarrow \forall B' \in \mathfrak{B}(B)\ \exists \sigma' \in m(\sigma)\ B' \vdash^{\wedge} M{:}\sigma'$.

Proof.

$\Leftarrow$) By definition of $\mathbf{m}(\sigma)$ we have $\sigma'\leq\sigma$ and then by $(\leq)$ we get $\forall B'\in\mathbf{B}(B)$ $B'\vdash M:\sigma$.

By construction if $B = \{x_j: \tau_j \mid 1\leq j\leq n\}$ then $\mathbf{B}(B) = \{\{x_j: \tau_j'\} \mid \tau_j'\in\mathbf{m}(\tau_j)\}$.

Let $\mathbf{m}(\tau_1) = \{\mu_1,\ldots,\mu_m\}$; by construction there is B" such that all the $B_i = B'', x_1:\mu_i$ $(1\leq i\leq m)$ are elements of $\mathbf{B}(B)$ (in general there are many such B").

It is clearly sufficient to prove that $B_i \vdash M:\sigma$ for $1\leq i\leq m$ implies $B'', x_1:\tau_1 \vdash M:\sigma$. This can be obtained by applying rule $(\vee L)$ m times to get $B'', x_1: \mu_1\vee..\vee\mu_m \vdash M:\sigma$ and lastly rule $(\leq L)$, since by definition $\tau_1\sim \mu_1\vee..\vee\mu_m$.

$\Rightarrow$) By induction on a proof of $B\vdash M:\sigma$.

For rule (ω) it is trivial.

$$(Ax)\quad \frac{}{B,x:\sigma \vdash x:\sigma}\ .$$

Let $B'\in\mathbf{B}(B,x:\sigma)$. Then it has to be $B'= B'',x:\sigma'$ with $\sigma'\in\mathbf{m}(\sigma)$. We then get by (Ax) $B'',x:\sigma' \vdash^{\wedge} x:\sigma'$.

$$(\rightarrow I)\quad \frac{B,x:\rho \vdash N:\tau}{B \vdash \lambda x.N: \rho\rightarrow\tau}\ .$$

By the induction hypothesis $\forall B'\in\mathbf{B}(B)\ \forall\rho'\in\mathbf{m}(\rho)\ \exists\tau'_{\rho'}\in\mathbf{m}(\tau)\ B',x:\rho' \vdash^{\wedge} N:\tau'_{\rho'}$ ($\tau'_{\rho'}$ depends on ρ' and B').

Using $(\rightarrow I)$ we get $\forall B'\in\mathbf{B}(B)\ \forall\rho'\in\mathbf{m}(\rho)\ B'\vdash^{\wedge}\lambda x.N:\rho'\rightarrow\tau'_{\rho'}$ and then using $(\wedge)$ $\forall B'\in\mathbf{B}(B)\ B'\vdash^{\wedge} \lambda x.N: \wedge_{\rho'\in\mathbf{m}(\rho)}(\rho'\rightarrow\tau'_{\rho'})$.

It is easy to check that $\wedge_{\rho'\in\mathbf{m}(\rho)}(\rho'\rightarrow\tau'_{\rho'})\in\mathbf{m}(\rho\rightarrow\tau)$.

$$(\rightarrow E)\quad \frac{B \vdash M:\rho\rightarrow\sigma \qquad B \vdash N:\rho}{B \vdash MN:\sigma}\ .$$

By the induction hypothesis we have $\forall B'\in\mathbf{B}(B)\ \exists\rho_{B'}\in\mathbf{m}(\rho)\ B'\vdash^{\wedge} N:\rho_{B'}$ (1) and $\forall B'\in\mathbf{B}(B)\ \exists\mu_{B'}\in\mathbf{m}(\rho\rightarrow\sigma)\ B'\vdash^{\wedge} M:\mu_{B'}$ (2).

It is easy to check that if $\mathbf{m}(\rho) = \{\rho_1,..,\rho_m\}$ and $\mathbf{m}(\sigma) = \{\sigma_1,..,\sigma_n\}$ then $\mu_{B'} \equiv \wedge_{1\leq i\leq m}(\rho_i\rightarrow\sigma_{\chi(i)})$ for some $\chi\in C(m,n)$. Then from (2), by $(\wedge E)$, we get $\forall B'\in\mathbf{B}(B)\ B'\vdash^{\wedge} M: \rho_{B'}\rightarrow\sigma'$ for some $\sigma'\in\mathbf{m}(\sigma)$ (3).

Hence by $(\rightarrow E)$ from (3) and (1) we get $\forall B'\in\mathbf{B}(B)\ \exists\sigma'\in\mathbf{m}(\sigma)\ B'\vdash^{\wedge} MN:\sigma'$.

$$(\wedge)\quad \frac{B \vdash M:\tau \qquad B \vdash M:\rho}{B \vdash M:\tau\wedge\rho}\ .$$

By the induction hypothesis $\forall B'\in\mathbf{B}(B)\ \exists\tau'\in\mathbf{m}(\tau)\ B' \vdash^{\wedge} M:\tau'$ and $\forall B'\in\mathbf{B}(B)\ \exists\rho'\in\mathbf{m}(\rho)\ B' \vdash^{\wedge} M:\rho'$. Therefore $B' \vdash M:\tau'\wedge\rho'$ using $(\wedge)$. By definition $\tau'\wedge\rho'\in\mathbf{m}(\tau\wedge\rho)$.

$$(\vee)\quad \frac{B,x:\tau \vdash M:\sigma \qquad B,x:\rho \vdash M:\sigma \qquad B \vdash N:\tau\vee\rho}{B \vdash M[N/x]:\sigma}\ .$$

By the induction hypothesis $\forall B'\in\mathbf{B}(B)\ \forall\tau'\in\mathbf{m}(\tau)\ \exists\sigma'\in\mathbf{m}(\sigma)\ B',x:\tau' \vdash^{\wedge} M:\sigma'$ and $\forall B'\in\mathbf{B}(B)\ \forall\rho'\in\mathbf{m}(\rho)\ \exists\sigma''\in\mathbf{m}(\sigma)\ B',x:\rho' \vdash^{\wedge} M:\sigma''$. Again by the induction hypothesis $\forall B'\in\mathbf{B}(B)\ \exists\mu\in\mathbf{m}(\tau\vee\rho)\ B' \vdash^{\wedge} N:\mu$. By definition $\mu\in\mathbf{m}(\tau)\cup\mathbf{m}(\rho)$. Let us assume that $\mu\in\mathbf{m}(\tau)$; in this case we obtain a proof of $B' \vdash^{\wedge} M[N/x]:\sigma'$ simply by replacing each axiom of the shape $B'',x:\mu \vdash^{\wedge} x:\mu$ by a proof of $B'' \vdash^{\wedge} N:\mu$ in a proof of $B',x:\mu \vdash^{\wedge} M:\sigma'$ (notice that by construction $B' \subseteq B''$). The case $\mu \in m(\rho)$ can be treated in the same way.

$$(\leq)\ \frac{B \vdash M:\sigma \quad \sigma \leq \tau}{B \vdash M:\tau}.$$

By the induction hypothesis $\forall B' \in \mathfrak{B}(B)\ \exists \sigma' \in m(\sigma)\ B' \vdash^{\wedge} M:\sigma'$. By Lemma 2.4 $\exists \tau' \in m(\tau)\ \sigma' \leq^{\wedge} \tau'$ and therefore $B' \vdash^{\wedge} M:\sigma'$ by rule $(\leq^{\wedge})$. □

The meaning of Theorem 2.6 is that to each deduction in $\vdash$ we can associate (in a unique way) a set of deductions in $\vdash^{\wedge}$ for the same λ-term. The main technical points of this theorem are the elimination of rule $(\vee)$ and the replacement of rule $(\leq^{\wedge})$ for rule $(\leq)$. This allows us to extend easily to union types the most important syntactic properties of the intersection type discipline, i.e. the invariance of types under β-conversion (and η-reduction) of subjects and the Approximation Theorem.

2.7 _Theorem_ (*β-conversion and η-reduction Theorem*).
Let $B \vdash M:\sigma$ and $M =_{\beta} N$ or $M \rightarrow_{\eta} N$. Then $B \vdash N:\sigma$.
Proof.

$B \vdash M:\sigma$	$\Rightarrow$	$\forall B' \in \mathfrak{B}(B)\ \exists \sigma' \in m(\sigma)\ B' \vdash^{\wedge} M:\sigma'$	by Theorem 2.6
	$\Rightarrow$	$\forall B' \in \mathfrak{B}(B)\ \exists \sigma' \in m(\sigma)\ B' \vdash^{\wedge} N:\sigma'$	by Theorem 2.2
	$\Rightarrow$	$B \vdash M:\sigma$ by Theorem 2.6.	□

Note that $\sigma \not\sim \omega$ implies $\sigma' \not\sim \omega$ for all $\sigma' \in m(\sigma)$ and if ω does not occur in σ then ω does not occur in all $\sigma' \in m(\sigma)$. Therefore by Theorem 2.6 ($\Rightarrow$) the following characterization of solvable and normalizing terms, stated in [4] for the intersection type discipline, is still valid.

2.8 _Theorem_ (*Characterization of Solvable and Normalizing λ-terms*).
(i) $\exists B,\ \tau \not\sim \omega$ such that $B \vdash M:\tau \iff M$ is solvable.
(ii) $\exists B,\ \tau$ without occurrences of ω such that $B \vdash M:\tau \iff M$ has normal form.

2.9 _Remark_.
Let $\vdash^{-}$ denote derivability in a type assignment system obtained by weakening $\leq$, i.e. by dropping some clauses in Definition 1.2(ii). In particular we can obtain the system of [21] (restricted to $\rightarrow, \wedge$ and $\vee$) by leaving only the clauses corresponding to $(\wedge E)$ and $(\vee I)$. Clearly it holds:
$[B \vdash^{-} M:\sigma \Rightarrow B \vdash M:\sigma]$ and $[B' \vdash^{\wedge} M:\sigma' \Rightarrow B' \vdash^{-} M:\sigma']$ (if σ' and all types in B' belong to $T_{\wedge}$). Therefore Theorem 2.8 extends immediately to all systems $\vdash^{-}$.

We introduce the usual notions of λ-Ω-calculus and approximants [31] [3].

2.10 _Definition_ (*λ-Ω-calculus*).
The set of λ-Ω-terms is obtained by adding the constant Ω to the formation rules of λ-terms. To the usual reductions rules we add the following two:

$$\Omega M \rightarrow \Omega \qquad\qquad \lambda x.\Omega \rightarrow \Omega.$$

A λ-Ω-term A is in β-Ω-normal form iff it cannot be reduced using β and Ω reduction rules.

2.11 *Definition* (*Approximants*).
Let M, A be λ-Ω-terms, A in β-Ω-normal form.
A is an *approximant* of M ($A \sqsubseteq M$) iff $\exists M' =_\beta M$ such that A matches M' except at occurrences of Ω in M.

All the type assignment definitions above and the ones given in the following can be extended to λ-Ω-terms without modifications.

2.12 *Theorem* (*Approximation Theorem for* $\vdash^\wedge$) [30].
$B \vdash^\wedge M:\sigma \iff \exists A \sqsubseteq M$ such that $B \vdash^\wedge A:\sigma$.

2.13 *Theorem* (*Approximation Theorem*).
$B \vdash M:\sigma \iff \exists A \sqsubseteq M$ such that $B \vdash A:\sigma$.
Proof.
$B \vdash M:\sigma \iff \forall B' \in \mathcal{B}(B)\ \exists \sigma' \in m(\sigma)\ B' \vdash^\wedge M:\sigma'$ by Theorem 2.6
$\iff \forall B' \in \mathcal{B}(B)\ \exists \sigma' \in m(\sigma)\ \exists A_{B',\sigma'} \sqsubseteq M\ \ B' \vdash^\wedge A_{B',\sigma'}:\sigma'$ by Th.2.12
$\iff \exists A \sqsubseteq M\ \forall B' \in \mathcal{B}(B)\ \exists \sigma' \in m(\sigma)\ B' \vdash^\wedge A:\sigma'$
(for $\Rightarrow$ choose $A = \bigsqcup_{B',\sigma'} A_{B',\sigma'}$ and use Theorem 2.12 ($\Leftarrow$))
$\iff \exists A \sqsubseteq M$ such that $B \vdash A:\sigma$ by Theorem 2.6. □

3. Soudness and Completeness.

As already said in Section 1, we consider three type interpretations :
- the type interpretation suggested by the translation of Section 2
- the second order type interpretations
- the Beth type interpretation.

The soundness proof is in all cases quite straightforward; for this proof it is essential that each type interpretation respects the preorder relation $\leq$.
We will consider these interpretations in increasing order of difficulty of proofs.

Type interpretations based on intersection types.

3.1 *Definition* (*Type Interpretations Based on Intersection Types*).
If D is the domain of a λ-model, a mapping $\upsilon_\wedge$: $T_\wedge \to 2^D$ is a *pre-type interpretation* iff :

(i) $\upsilon_\wedge(\omega) = D$
(ii) $\upsilon_\wedge(\sigma \to \tau) = \{ d \in D \mid \forall e \in \upsilon_\wedge(\sigma)\ \ d \cdot e \in \upsilon_\wedge(\tau) \}$
(iii) $\upsilon_\wedge(\sigma \wedge \tau) = \upsilon_\wedge(\sigma) \cap \upsilon_\wedge(\tau)$.

Each pre-type interpretation $\upsilon_\wedge$ induces a mapping $\upsilon_\vee$: $T \to 2^D$ (*type interpretation based on intersection types*) defined by:

$$\upsilon_\vee(\sigma) = \cup_{\sigma' \in m(\sigma)} \upsilon_\wedge(\sigma').$$

Obviously each pre-type interpretation is a type interpretation for $T_\wedge$.
Let the induced notion of semantic satisfability $\models^\vee$ be defined as usual (it is sufficient to rephrase Definition 1.13).
Let $\models^\wedge$ denotes semantic satisfability for the intersection types. The soundness and completeness of this system (i.e. that $B \models^\wedge M:\sigma \iff B \vdash^\wedge M:\sigma$) has been proved using different models [4] [15].

$\upsilon^+((\sigma\to\rho)\wedge(\tau\to\rho)) = \upsilon^+(\sigma\vee\tau\to\rho)$ since $(\sigma\to\rho)\wedge(\tau\to\rho) \sim \sigma\vee\tau\to\rho$.

$$\begin{aligned}\upsilon^+(\sigma\vee\tau) &= \{[M] \mid B^+ \vdash M:\sigma\vee\tau\}\\ &\subseteq \{[M] \mid \forall\rho\ \forall N\ [\ B^+ \vdash N:\sigma\vee\tau\to\rho \Rightarrow B^+ \vdash NM:\rho\ ]\}\\ &= \{[M] \mid \forall\rho\ \forall[N]\in\upsilon^+(\sigma\vee\tau\to\rho)\ [NM]\in\upsilon^+(\rho)\}.\end{aligned}$$

$$\begin{aligned}\{[M] \mid \forall\rho\ \forall[N]\in\upsilon^+(\sigma\vee\tau\to\rho)\ [NM]\in\upsilon^+(\rho)\}\\ &= \{[M] \mid \forall\rho\ \forall N\ (\ B^+ \vdash N:\sigma\vee\tau\to\rho \Rightarrow B^+ \vdash NM:\rho)\}\\ &\subseteq \{[M] \mid B^+ \vdash (\lambda x.x)M:\sigma\vee\tau)\} \text{ by choosing } \rho \equiv \sigma\vee\tau \text{ and } N \equiv \lambda x.x\\ &\subseteq \{[M] \mid B^+ \vdash M:\sigma\vee\tau\ \} \text{ by Theorem 2.7}\\ &= \upsilon^+(\sigma\vee\tau).\end{aligned}$$

□

3.7 _Theorem_ (*Completeness*).

$B \models_s M:\sigma \quad \Rightarrow \quad B \vdash M:\sigma$.

Proof.

$\mathcal{MT}$, υ^+, ζ_o satisfy B by definition, in fact $x:\sigma\in B$ implies $[x]\in\upsilon^+(\sigma)$. Then

$$\begin{aligned}B \models_s M:\sigma &\Rightarrow [\ \forall\, \mathcal{M},\ \upsilon_s,\ \zeta \models B \ \Rightarrow\ [\![M]\!]_\zeta\in\upsilon_s(\sigma)\ ] \text{ by definition}\\ &\Rightarrow [\![M]\!]_{\zeta_o}\in\upsilon^+(\sigma) \text{ since } \mathcal{MT},\ \upsilon^+,\ \zeta_o \models B\\ &\Rightarrow [M]\in\upsilon^+(\sigma) \text{ by 3.5(i)}\\ &\Rightarrow B^+ \vdash M:\sigma \quad \text{by 3.5(ii)}\\ &\Rightarrow B \vdash M:\sigma\ .\end{aligned}$$

□

Beth Type Interpretations.

3.8 _Lemma_ (*Properties of Beth Type Interpretations*).

(i) Let $v\sqsubseteq w$. Then $\upsilon(\sigma,v) \subseteq \upsilon(\sigma,w)$.

(ii) Let b_w be a bar for w. Then $\forall w'\in b_w\ [d\in\upsilon(\sigma,w') \Rightarrow d\in\upsilon(\sigma,w)]$.

(iii) $\sigma \leq \tau \Rightarrow \forall\, \mathcal{W},\ w:\ \ \upsilon(\sigma,w) \subseteq \upsilon(\tau,w)$.

Proof.

(i) By induction on σ.

- $\sigma \equiv \phi$.

Let $d\in\upsilon(\phi,v)$, then by definition $\exists b_v\ \forall v'\in b_v\ \langle d,\phi\rangle\in A_{v'}$. If there is $v'\in b_v$ such that $v'\sqsubseteq w$ then $\langle d,\phi\rangle\in A_w$ by definition. Otherwise let b_w be the set of all states in b_v which are greater than w; by definition b_w is a bar for w. We have then that $\forall w'\in b_w\ \langle d,\phi\rangle\in A_{w'}$ and then by definition $d\in\upsilon(\phi,w)$.

- $\sigma \equiv \rho\to\tau$.

$$\begin{aligned}\upsilon(\sigma,v) &= \{\ d\in D \mid \forall v'\sqsupseteq v\ \forall e\in\upsilon(\sigma,v')\ d\cdot e\in\upsilon(\tau,v')\ \}\\ &\subseteq \{\ d\in D \mid \forall w'\sqsupseteq w\ \forall e\in\upsilon(\sigma,w')\ d\cdot e\in\upsilon(\tau,w')\ \} \quad \text{since } w\sqsupseteq v\\ &= \upsilon(\tau,w).\end{aligned}$$

- $\sigma\equiv\rho\wedge\tau$.

Straightforward by the induction hypothesis.

- $\sigma \equiv \rho\vee\tau$.

Let $d\in\upsilon(\rho\vee\tau,v)$, then by definition $\exists b_v\ \forall v'\in b_v\ d\in\upsilon(\rho,v')$ or $d\in\upsilon(\tau,v')$. If there is $v'\in b_v$ such that $v'\sqsubseteq w$ then $d\in\upsilon(\rho,w)$ or $d\in\upsilon(\tau,w)$ by the induction hypothesis. Otherwise let b_w be the set of all states in b_v which are greater than w; by definition b_w is a bar for w. We have then that $\forall w'\in b_w\ d\in\upsilon(\rho,w')$ or $d\in\upsilon(\tau,w')$ and then by definition $d\in\upsilon(\rho\vee\tau,w)$.

(ii) By induction on σ.

- $\sigma \equiv \phi$.

We have $\forall w'\in b_w\ \ d\in\upsilon(\phi,w')$ and then by definition of υ we get

$\forall w'\in\mathfrak{b}_w\ \exists\mathfrak{b}_{w'}\ \forall v\in\mathfrak{b}_{w'}\ \langle d,\phi\rangle\in A_V$. Let us take $\mathfrak{b}'_w=\bigcup_{w'\in\mathfrak{b}_w}\mathfrak{b}_{w'}$. $\mathfrak{b}'_w$ is a bar for w and moreover $\forall v\in\mathfrak{b}'_w\ \langle d,\phi\rangle\in A_V$. Then by definition $d\in\mathfrak{v}(\phi,w)$.

- $\sigma\equiv\rho\to\tau$.

By hypothesis $\exists\mathfrak{b}_w\ \forall w'\in\mathfrak{b}_w\ d\in\mathfrak{v}(\rho\to\tau,w')$.
By definition this implies $\forall w'\in\mathfrak{b}_w\ \forall v'\sqsupseteq w'\ [e\in\mathfrak{v}(\rho,v')\Rightarrow d\cdot e\in\mathfrak{v}(\tau,v')]$.
We want to show that $d\in\mathfrak{v}(\rho\to\tau,v')$, i.e. $\forall v\sqsupseteq v'\ [e\in\mathfrak{v}(\rho,v)\Rightarrow d\cdot e\in\mathfrak{v}(\tau,v)]$.
Given any $v\sqsupseteq w$ if there is $w'\in\mathfrak{b}_w$ such that $w'\sqsubseteq v$ then $d\in\mathfrak{v}(\rho\to\tau,v)$ by (i). Otherwise let $\mathfrak{b}_v$ be the set of all states in $\mathfrak{b}_w$ which are greater than v; by definition $\mathfrak{b}_v$ is a bar for v. If $e\in\mathfrak{v}(\rho,v)$ then $e\in\mathfrak{v}(\rho,v'')$ for all $v''\in\mathfrak{b}_v$ by (i) and then $d\cdot e\in\mathfrak{v}(\tau,v'')$ by hypothesis (since $v''\sqsupseteq v''\in\mathfrak{b}_v$). Thus $\forall v''\in\mathfrak{b}_v\ d\cdot e\in\mathfrak{v}(\tau,v'')$ and then $d\cdot e\in\mathfrak{v}(\tau,v)$ by the induction hypothesis.

- $\sigma\equiv\rho\wedge\tau$.

$$\begin{aligned}\forall w'\in\mathfrak{b}_w\ d\in\mathfrak{v}(\rho\wedge\tau,w') &\Rightarrow \forall w'\in\mathfrak{b}_w\ d\in\mathfrak{v}(\rho,w') \text{ and } d\in\mathfrak{v}(\tau,w') \text{ by definition}\\ &\Rightarrow d\in\mathfrak{v}(\rho,w) \text{ and } d\in\mathfrak{v}(\tau,w) \text{ by the ind. hyp.}\\ &\Rightarrow d\in\mathfrak{v}(\rho\wedge\tau,w) \text{ by definition.}\end{aligned}$$

- $\sigma\equiv\rho\vee\tau$.

$\forall w'\in\mathfrak{b}_w\ d\in\mathfrak{v}(\rho\vee\tau,w')\Rightarrow\forall w'\in\mathfrak{b}_w\ \exists\mathfrak{b}_{w'}\ \forall w''\in\mathfrak{b}_{w'}\ d\in\mathfrak{v}(\rho,w'')$ or $d\in\mathfrak{v}(\tau,w'')$ by definition. We have that $\bigcup_{w'\in\mathfrak{b}_w}\mathfrak{b}_{w'}$ is still a bar for w and $\forall w''\in\bigcup_{w'\in\mathfrak{b}_w}\mathfrak{b}_{w'}\ d\in\mathfrak{v}(\rho,w'')$ or $d\in\mathfrak{v}(\tau,w'')$ i.e., by definition, $d\in\mathfrak{v}(\rho\vee\tau,w)$.
(iii) By induction on $\leq$ using 1.8 (v). □

3.9 *Theorem* (*Semantic Soundness*).
(i) Let $B,x{:}\tau\models M{:}\sigma$ and $B\models N{:}\tau$. Then $B\models M[N/x]:\sigma$.
(ii) $B\vdash M{:}\sigma\ \Rightarrow\ B\models M{:}\sigma$.

Proof.

(i) Let choose any $\mathcal{W},\zeta,w$ such that $\mathcal{W},\zeta,w\models B$. Let $d=[\![N]\!]_\zeta$ and $\zeta'=\zeta[d/x]$. By hypothesis $d\in\mathfrak{v}(\tau,w)$ and then $\mathcal{W},\zeta',w\models B,x{:}\tau$. Therefore by hypothesis we get $[\![M]\!]_{\zeta'}\in\mathfrak{v}(\sigma,w)$. Now we have finished, since $[\![M]\!]_{\zeta'}=[\![M]\!]_{\zeta[d/x]}=[\![M[N/x]]\!]_\zeta$.
(ii) By induction on deductions.
When the last applied rule is ($\leq$) the soundness follows from 3.8 (iii).
The most interesting case is when the last applied rule is :

$$(\vee)\quad\frac{B,x{:}\sigma\vdash M{:}\rho\qquad B,x{:}\tau\vdash M{:}\rho\qquad B\vdash N{:}\sigma\vee\tau}{B\vdash M[N/x]{:}\rho}.$$

By the induction hypothesis we have that

$$\begin{aligned}\mathcal{W},\zeta,w\models B \text{ and } [\![x]\!]_\zeta\in\mathfrak{v}(\sigma,w) &\Rightarrow [\![M]\!]_\zeta\in\mathfrak{v}(\rho,w),\\ \mathcal{W},\zeta,w\models B \text{ and } [\![x]\!]_\zeta\in\mathfrak{v}(\tau,w) &\Rightarrow [\![M]\!]_\zeta\in\mathfrak{v}(\rho,w) \text{ and}\\ \mathcal{W},\zeta,w\models B &\Rightarrow [\![N]\!]_\zeta\in\mathfrak{v}(\sigma\vee\tau,w)\\ &\Rightarrow \exists\mathfrak{b}_w\forall w'\in\mathfrak{b}_w\ [\![N]\!]_\zeta\in\mathfrak{v}(\sigma,w') \text{ or } [\![N]\!]_\zeta\in\mathfrak{v}(\tau,w').\end{aligned}$$

Let $w'\in\mathfrak{b}_w$ and $[\![N]\!]_\zeta\in\mathfrak{v}(\sigma,w')$. By (i) $[\![M[N/x]]\!]_\zeta\in\mathfrak{v}(\rho,w')$.
Analogously if $[\![N]\!]_\zeta\in\mathfrak{v}(\tau,w')$.
Therefore we conclude $\mathcal{W},\zeta,w\models B\Rightarrow\exists\mathfrak{b}_w\forall w'\in\mathfrak{b}_w\ [\![M[N/x]]\!]_\zeta\in\mathfrak{v}(\rho,w')$ which implies $\mathcal{W},\zeta,w\models B\Rightarrow[\![M[N/x]]\!]_\zeta\in\mathfrak{v}(\rho,w)$ by 3.8(ii). □

To prove the completeness we build a suitable world for the term model relative to a given basis B_0. First we need some technical definitions.
To each basis B we have associated a (finite) set of bases $\mathbf{B}(B)$ as in 2.5.
Let $\{\sigma_n\}_{n\in\omega}$ be an enumeration of all types of $\mathbf{T}$.

The states of knowledge of our world will represent sets of statements of our type assigment system.
First we build a finitely branching tree $\mathcal{T}$ (whose nodes are labelled with bases) starting from a given basis B_0. In $\mathcal{T}$ the basis associated to a father is always less powerful (from the point of view of the deducible statements) than the bases associated to each of its sons: more precisely if B is the label of a node whose son is labelled B' then $B \vdash M{:}\sigma$ implies $B' \vdash M{:}\sigma$ (in general the viceversa does not hold).
To each node of $\mathcal{T}$ with label B we associate a state of knowledge w_B which represents the set of typing statements deducible from B. The knowledge states inherit the order relation from that between the corresponding bases.
For each state of knowledge w_B the set of atomic facts is the subset of pairs of w_B whose second elements are type variables.

3.10 Definition (*Term World for the Term Model*).
(i) The tree $\mathcal{T}$ generated by a basis B_0 is inductively defined by:
- the root is labelled by B_0
- if B is the label of a node at (even) level 2n, then it has two sons: B and $B, z{:}\sigma_n$
- if B is the label of a node at odd level then their sons are all the bases belonging to $\mathfrak{B}(B)$.
(ii) $w_B = \{<[M],\sigma> \mid B \vdash M{:}\sigma\}$.
(iii) The partial order ($\mathcal{PT}, \sqsubseteq$) is defined by:
$\mathcal{PT} = \{ w_B \mid B \text{ labels a node of } \mathcal{T}\}$
$w_B \sqsubseteq w_{B'}$ iff B is (the label of) an ancestor of (the node labelled) B'.
(iv) $A_{wB} = \{<[M],\phi> \mid <[M],\phi> \in w_B$ and ϕ is a type variable$\}$.
(v) The term world $\mathcal{WT}$ is the possible world defined by:

$$\mathcal{WT} = <\mathcal{PT}, \sqsubseteq, \{A_{wB}\}_{wB\in\mathcal{PT}}>.$$

3.11 Lemma (*Properties of* $\mathcal{WT}$).
(i) $B \vdash M{:}\sigma\vee\tau \Rightarrow \exists \mathfrak{b}_{wB}\ \forall w_{B'}\in\mathfrak{b}_{wB}\ \ B' \vdash M{:}\sigma$ or $B' \vdash M{:}\tau$.
(ii) $w_B \sqsubseteq w_{B'} \Rightarrow B \subseteq B'$.
(iii) $\upsilon_T(\sigma, w_B) = \{[M] \mid B \vdash M{:}\sigma\}$ is the Beth type interpretation defined by $\mathcal{WT}$.
Proof.
(i) Let us take as $\mathfrak{b}_{wB}$ the set $\{w_{B'} \mid B'\in\mathfrak{B}(B)\}$. By Theorem 2.6 we have that
$\forall B'\in\mathfrak{B}(B)\ \exists\rho\in m(\sigma)\cup m(\tau)\ B' \vdash^{\wedge} M{:}\rho$ and hence by ($\leq$) we get
$\forall B'\in\mathfrak{B}(B)\ B' \vdash M{:}\sigma$ or $B' \vdash M{:}\tau$.
(ii) Immediate from the construction.
(iii) The clause (v) of definition 1.8 is satisfied by rule ($\leq$).
We prove that $\upsilon_T(\sigma, w_B) = \{[M] \mid B\vdash M{:}\sigma\}$ satisfies the other clauses of 1.8 by induction on σ.
For ω it follows from rule (ω).
For ϕ it is true since, by definition, $\{w_B\}$ is a bar for w_B.

$$\begin{aligned}\upsilon_T(\sigma\to\tau, w_B) &= \{[M] \mid B\vdash M{:}\sigma\to\tau\}\\ &\subseteq \{[M] \mid \forall w_{B'}\sqsupseteq w_B\ \forall N\,[\,B' \vdash N{:}\sigma \Rightarrow B' \vdash MN{:}\tau\,]\}\\ &= \{[M] \mid \forall w_{B'}\sqsupseteq w_B\ \forall\,[N]\in\upsilon_T(\sigma, w_{B'})\ \ [MN]\in\upsilon_T(\tau, w_{B'})\}.\end{aligned}$$

To prove the inverse inclusion let us assume $\forall w_{B'}\sqsupseteq w_B$:
$\forall N\,[\,B'\vdash N{:}\sigma \Rightarrow B' \vdash MN{:}\tau\,]$.
Let $\mathfrak{B}(B) = \{B_i \mid i\in I\}$ and $B_i' = B_i, z{:}\sigma$ where z does not occur in M. It is easy to verify that $w_{Bi'}\sqsupseteq w_B$ for all $i\in I$, therefore:
$\forall N\,[\,B_i' \vdash N{:}\sigma \Rightarrow B_i' \vdash MN{:}\tau] \quad\Rightarrow\quad B_i' \vdash^{\wedge} Mz{:}\tau$

$$\Rightarrow\ B_i \vdash^{\wedge} \lambda z.Mz:\sigma\to\tau \text{ by } (\to I)$$
$$\Rightarrow\ B_i \vdash^{\wedge} M:\sigma\to\tau \text{ by Theorem 2.2 .}$$

Therefore from $\forall i\in I\ B_i \vdash^{\wedge} M:\sigma\to\tau$ we have $B \vdash M:\sigma\to\tau$ by 2.6.

$$\begin{aligned}
\upsilon_T(\sigma\wedge\tau, w_B) &= \{[M] \mid B \vdash M:\sigma\wedge\tau\}\\
&= \{[M] \mid B \vdash M:\sigma\}\cap\{[M] \mid B \vdash M:\tau\}\\
&= \upsilon_T(\sigma, w_B)\cap\upsilon_T(\tau, w_B).\\
\upsilon_T(\sigma\vee\tau, w_B) &= \{[M] \mid B \vdash M:\sigma\vee\tau\}\\
&= \{[M] \mid \exists \mathfrak{b}_{wB}\ \forall w_{B'}\in\mathfrak{b}_{wB}\ [\ B' \vdash M:\sigma \text{ or } B' \vdash M:\tau\ ]\} \text{ by (i)}\\
&= \{[M] \mid \exists \mathfrak{b}_{wB}\ \forall w_{B'}\in\mathfrak{b}_{wB}\ [M]\in\upsilon_T(\sigma, w_{B'})\cup\upsilon_T(\tau, w_{B'})\}. \quad \Box
\end{aligned}$$

3.12 Theorem (*Completeness*).
$B \models M:\sigma \quad\Rightarrow\quad B \vdash M:\sigma$.

Proof.
We build $\mathcal{T}$ starting from $B_0 = B$. Let ζ_o be as in 3.5(i) .
$\mathcal{WT}$, ζ_o, w_B satisfy B by definition, in fact $x:\sigma\in B$ implies $[x]\in\upsilon_T(\sigma, w_B)$. Then

$$\begin{aligned}
B \models M:\sigma &\Rightarrow [\ \forall \mathcal{W},\zeta,w \models B \Rightarrow [\![M]\!]_\zeta\in\upsilon_T(\sigma, w_B)\ ] \text{ by definition}\\
&\Rightarrow [\![M]\!]_{\zeta_o}\in\upsilon_T(\sigma, w_B) \text{ since } \mathcal{WT},\ \zeta_o,\ w_B \models B\\
&\Rightarrow [M]\in\upsilon_T(\sigma, w_B) \text{ by definition of } \zeta_o\\
&\Rightarrow B \vdash M:\sigma \quad \text{by definition of } \upsilon_T . \quad \Box
\end{aligned}$$

3.13 Remark. The soundness results of Section 1 and the three soundness results of Section 3 still hold for all the systems $\vdash^-$ as defined in Remark 2.9. Obviously these systems are sound also if we take out the conditions corresponding to the removed clauses of $\leq$ from the definitions of type interpretations.

4. Applications to Typing Data Structures.

An open problem for intersection types is that of characterizing the class of functions and data structures which can be represented by means of λ-terms which can be typed. In a sense all partial recursive functions are representable, since all λ-terms can be typed. This is proved in [12] and is formally stated in [19].This answer is but satisfactory, since for example we do not have a representation of natural numbers and of the successor and predecessor functions which can be typed respectively by $\upsilon, \upsilon\to\upsilon$ and $\upsilon\to\upsilon$ for a suitable type υ.

More formally, let us consider, following [19], a free algebra $\mathcal{A}$ and a mapping $\mathfrak{r}:\mathcal{A}\to\Lambda$ (where Λ is the set of all λ-terms). We say that a λ-term M *represents* a function f *non-uniformly* with respect to a type assigment system $\mathbf{S}$ iff, for all $\mathfrak{a}_1,\ldots,\mathfrak{a}_k\in\mathcal{A}$, $M\mathfrak{r}(\mathfrak{a}_1)\ldots\mathfrak{r}(\mathfrak{a}_k)$ can be typed in $\mathbf{S}$ and $M\mathfrak{r}(\mathfrak{a}_1)\ldots\mathfrak{r}(\mathfrak{a}_k) =_{\beta\eta} \mathfrak{r}(f(\mathfrak{a}_1,\ldots,\mathfrak{a}_k))$. We say that M represents f *strictly* if moreover there is a type τ such that, for all $\mathfrak{a}\in\mathcal{A}$, $\mathfrak{r}(\mathfrak{a})$ has type τ in $\mathbf{S}$ and M has type $\underbrace{\tau\to\ldots\to}_{k}\tau\to\tau$.

In the intersection type discipline, while, as said before, all partial recursive functions are non-uniformly representable, the class of strictly representable functions, although non exactly characterized, seems to be very poor. Leivant in [19] conjectures that the functions strictly representable in the intersection type discipline are already strictly representable in Curry's type discipline. This motivates the introduction of infinite type intersections in [19]; the main result is that all primitive recursive functions are strictly representable in the so obtained type discipline. The price which must be paid is that of having infinite derivations.

Our proposal is to allow infinite unions and intersections of types, but to limit their introduction at the last but one step of derivations. In this way the derivations are infinite in quite a trivial way. Moreover we allow second order types of level three, i.e. we introduce an operator $\forall$ of universal quantification, but we do not permit more than three nested occurrences of it. We do not have an exact characterization of the functions which can be strictly represented in the so obtained type discipline, but we shall show how functions defined by primitive recursion over Berarducci numerals (defined in [5]) and in general over $*$-algebras (defined in [7]) can be strictly typed. The typing of Berarducci numerals is interesting since it has been proved that they cannot be typed in second order type discipline [14].
The good properties of $*$-algebras are illustrated in [7].

Let us firstly introduce types with infinite unions and intersections. We strongly limit the use of infinity; we have only a rule which introduces infinite intersections (there is no corresponding elimination rule) and we require its application to be followed only by applications of rule ($\leq$). Our choice is motivated by the fact that this extension alone allows the desired typing.

4.1 *Definition* (*Infinite Types*).
(i) The set T_∞ of *infinite types* is defined by

- $\sigma\in T \Rightarrow \sigma, \forall\phi.\sigma\in T_1$ - $\sigma,\tau\in T_1 \Rightarrow \sigma\to\tau, \sigma\wedge\tau, \sigma\vee\tau\in T_1$
- $\sigma\in T_1 \Rightarrow \sigma, \forall\phi.\sigma\in T_2$ - $\sigma\in T_2 \Rightarrow \sigma\in T_\infty$
- $\sigma_i\in T_2\ (i\in I) \Rightarrow \mathbb{A}_{i\in I}\,\sigma_i, \mathbb{V}_{i\in I}\,\sigma_i\in T_\infty$ - $\sigma,\ \tau\in T_\infty \Rightarrow \forall\phi.\sigma, \sigma\to\tau\in T_\infty$.

(ii) The relation $\leq$ is extended to infinite types by adding the clauses:

$\sigma_k \leq \mathbb{V}_{i\in I}\,\sigma_i$ for each $k\in I$
$\mathbb{V}_{i\in I}\,\sigma_i \leq \sigma$ if $\sigma_i\equiv\sigma$ for each $i\in I$
$\mathbb{A}_{i\in I}(\sigma_i\to\tau_i) \leq \mathbb{V}_{i\in I}\,\sigma_i \to \mathbb{V}_{i\in I}\,\tau_i$.

(iii) The type assignment system is extended to infinite types by adding the rules to introduce and to eliminate $\forall$ and the infinitary rule ($\mathbb{A}\infty$):

$$(\forall I)\ \frac{B\vdash M{:}\sigma \quad \phi\notin FV(B)}{B\vdash M{:}\forall\phi.\sigma} \qquad (\forall E)\ \frac{B\vdash M{:}\forall\phi.\sigma}{B\vdash M{:}\sigma[\tau/\phi]} \qquad (\mathbb{A}\infty)\ \frac{B\vdash M{:}\sigma_i \quad \forall i\in I}{B\vdash M{:}\mathbb{A}_{i\in I}\,\sigma_i}$$

with the condition that an application of rule ($\mathbb{A}\infty$) can only be followed by applications of rule ($\leq$).

Berarducci numerals.

Berarducci numerals have the nice feature that both the iteration and primitive recursion operator have simple representations as λ-terms. They are defined by

<u>zero</u> $\equiv \lambda xy.y$ <u>successor</u> $\equiv \lambda xy.yxy$
<u>predecessor</u> $\equiv \lambda x.x(\lambda yz.y)$ <u>discriminator</u> $\equiv \lambda x.x(\lambda uvw.$<u>false</u>)<u>true</u>

where as usual <u>false</u> $\equiv \lambda xy.y$ and <u>true</u> $\equiv \lambda xy.x$.
The <u>iterator</u> which is a solution of the system of equations:

<u>iterator</u> <u>zero</u> f a = a   <u>iterator</u> (<u>successor</u> n) f a = f (<u>iterator</u> n f a)

is <u>iterator</u> $\equiv \lambda xy.x(\lambda uvw.y(uvw))$.

The recursor which is a solution of the system of equations:

recursor zero f a = a recursor (successor n) f a = f n (recursor n f a)

is recursor ≡ λxyz. z(λuvw.xu(uvw))y.

If we define iteratively:

$\pi_0 \equiv \forall\phi\psi.\phi\to\psi\to\psi$ $\pi_{n+1} \equiv \forall\phi\psi.((\pi_n\to\phi\to\psi)\wedge\phi)\to\psi$

and the type of numerals as $\mathbf{N} \equiv \mathbb{V}_{0\leq n\leq\infty}\,\pi_n$ it is easy to verify that zero, successor, predecessor and discriminator have the expected types. More precisely we can derive:

$\vdash$ zero : π_0 which implies $\vdash$ zero : $\mathbf{N}$

$\vdash$ successor : $\pi_n\to\pi_{n+1}$ for $0\leq n\leq\infty$

which imply $\vdash$ successor : $\mathbf{N}\to\mathbf{N}$

$\vdash$ predecessor : $\pi_0\to\pi_0$ and $\vdash$ predecessor : $\pi_{n+1}\to\pi_n$ for $0\leq n\leq\infty$

which imply $\vdash$ predecessor : $\mathbf{N}\to\mathbf{N}$

$\vdash$ discriminator : $\pi_0\to\forall\phi\psi.\phi\to\psi\to\phi$ and

$\vdash$ discriminator : $\pi_{n+1}\to\forall\phi\psi.\phi\to\psi\to\psi$ for $0\leq n\leq\infty$

which imply $\vdash$ discriminator : $\mathbf{N}\to$ **bool**

where **bool** $= (\forall\phi\psi.\phi\to\psi\to\phi)\vee(\forall\phi\psi.\phi\to\psi\to\psi)$, since $\vdash$ true : $\forall\phi\psi.\phi\to\psi\to\phi$ and $\vdash$ false : $\forall\phi\psi.\phi\to\psi\to\psi$.

Moreover, with some work, we can derive $\vdash$ iterator : $\forall\phi.\mathbf{N}\to(\phi\to\phi)\to\phi\to\phi$ and $\vdash$ recursor : $\forall\phi.\mathbf{N}\to(\mathbf{N}\to\phi\to\phi)\to\phi\to\phi$.

*-algebras.

Let $\mathcal{A}$ be a free algebra, generated by the constructors $\mathbf{c}_1,\dots,\mathbf{c}_m$, of arities $r_1,\dots,r_m$ respectively. Let us firstly represent the elements of $\mathcal{A}$ by pure applicative terms: each constructor $\mathbf{c}$ of arity r is represented by an identifier c and if $\mathbf{c}(\mathbf{a}_1,..,\mathbf{a}_r)$ is an element of $\mathcal{A}$ let us represent it by $ca_1..a_rc_1...c_m$ where a_i is the representation of the element $\mathbf{a}_i$. We obtain a canonical λ-representation of $\mathbf{a}$ simply by closing a, i.e. we define $\mathbf{r}(\mathbf{a})=\lambda c_1...c_m.a$. The so obtained set of λ-terms is called the *-algebra which represents the free algebra $\mathcal{A}$ in [7].

The features of *-algebras with respect to Church algebras (as defined in [8]) are illustrated in [7]; we recall only that the representations of the recursor R is a simple normal form in *-algebras. The *-algebra which represents the natural numbers is a trivial variant of Berarducci numerals.

From the typing point of view, all iteratively defined functions are strictly representable using Church algebras and second order type discipline [8]. The negative result of [14] indicates that this is no more true for *-algebras.

We show instead that all primitive recursive functions are strictly representable using *-algebras and infinite unions and intersections of types.

To write the type τ of the canonical representations of the elements of $\mathcal{A}$ in the case of *-algebras we can assume without loss of generality that the constructor c_1 has arity 0. Then if we define iteratively:

$\alpha_0 \equiv \forall\phi_1...\phi_m\psi.(\phi_1\wedge(\phi_1\to...\to\phi_m\to\psi))\to\phi_2\to...\to\phi_m\to\psi$

$\alpha_{j+1} \equiv \forall\phi_1...\phi_m\psi.\phi_1\to...\to\phi_{i-1}\to(\phi_i\wedge\gamma_j)\to\phi_{i+1}\to...\to\phi_m\to\psi$

where $\gamma_j \equiv \alpha_{i1}\to...\to\alpha_{iri}\to\phi_1\to...\to\phi_m\to\psi$ and j corresponds (using a suitable coding) to the integer list i, $i_1,\dots,i_{ri}$, we have $\tau \equiv \mathbb{V}_{0\leq n\leq\infty}\,\alpha_n$.

The representation of the recursor is: $R = \lambda h_1...h_m.\langle H_1h_1,\dots,H_mh_m\rangle$ where

$H_i = \lambda he_1...e_{ri}c_1...c_m.h(e_1c_1...c_m)...(e_{ri}c_1...c_m)e_1...e_{ri}$.

If we define $\beta_i \equiv \underbrace{\tau \rightarrow \ldots \rightarrow \tau}_{2r_i} \rightarrow \tau$ it is quite cumbersome but straightforward to check that we can deduce for R the following type : $\beta_1 \rightarrow \ldots \rightarrow \beta_m \rightarrow \tau \rightarrow \tau$.

5. Related Works and Directions for Further Research

Union Types

Intersection types have been used by Reynolds in [28] and [29] to get expressive power for his programming language FORSYTHE. The main difference from our approach is that FORSYTHE is a typed calculus; moreover FORSYTHE includes records, lists etc. But if we restrict ourselves to the pure λ-terms we have the natural correspondence between the type assigment system of [4] and the typed calculus of [28]: this is proved in [2] . Currently Pierce [25] [26] is investigating an extension of the type system of FORSYTHE in which union types are present. Pierce is of course in a typed environment, but the rules of typed λ-terms formation dealing with union types, developed independently, resemble very much the ones used in our system. He gives very interesting motivations and examples of the use of union types in actual programming. The following is an example of Pierce showing that some real expressive power is gained when union types are allowed.
The type for the IF operator is such that the term $\mathbf{n}$ = IF b THEN 1 ELSE -1
has the following type: $\mathbf{n}$: Neg-num ∨ Pos-num.
If we now try to tell if $\mathbf{n}$ is zero, using the function
Is-Zero : (Neg-num→False) ∧ (Zero→True) ∧ (Pos-num→False)
we get (Is-Zero $\mathbf{n}$) : False.
Without using union types the best information we could get about (Is-Zero $\mathbf{n}$) is that it is just a boolean value.
Therefore we can conclude with Pierce that union types allow a restricted form of abstract interpretation to be performed during typechecking.
A PER model validating the typing and equality rules is given in [25].
[26] adds second order polymorphic types and shows that in the so obtained system many common data types can be encoded without any type or term constants.
In [26] other current researches involving union types are described (including "recursively" the present one).

Infinite Types

As stated above, a type assignment system $J^{\infty}\lambda$ with infinite intersections of types was independently introduced and investigated by Leivant in [19]. The main differences with our system are that $J^{\infty}\lambda$ has an elimination rule for infinite types and rules for infinite types can be used everywhere in a derivation.
In the present paper restrictions are made since we are only interested in particular problems of uniform typing. The aims of Leivant are wider. He wishes to investigate infinite intersections as a master formalism in which several typings, such as stratified quantificational polymorphism, can be interpreted and related. His discipline naturally stratifies into subdisciplines, allowing type formation only up to certain levels. Leivant characterizes the class of functions definable in these subdisciplines. Moreover, a strong normalization theorem is proved for $J^{\infty}\lambda$.

Directions for Further Research

It would be no doubt worth investigating our restriction on infinite intersection from the point of view of Leivant, i.e. focusing on the class of functions definable. Infinite union types are also worth investigating in contexts where no restriction or weaker restrictions are given.

In the intersection type language we can build λ-models (filter models) in which the interpretation of a λ-term coincides with the set of all types that can be assigned to it [4]. Filter models turn out to be a very rich class containing in particular each inverse-limit space, and have been widely used to study properties of D_∞-λ-models [11].

It is not clear how to derive filter models in the case of intersection and union types without introducing saturation conditions. Take for example the basis $B=\{x:\mu, y:\mu\}$, where $\mu \equiv (\sigma\wedge(\sigma\to\tau))\vee(\rho\wedge(\rho\to\tau))$. Obviously $B \vdash xx:\tau$ but $B \nvdash xy:\tau$. Since the sets of types which can be derived for x and y coincide, one would have, for a suitable filter d and all enviroments ζ which satisfy B, that $[\![x]\!]_\zeta = [\![y]\!]_\zeta = d$. But this leads to a contradiction when we interpret xx and xy, since both $\tau \in d \cdot d$ and $\tau \notin d \cdot d$ should hold!

Union types could also be used to type a λ-calculus enriched with a join and a parallel operator, a language for parallel functions introduced in [9] and [10]. Boudol considers the intersection type discipline without type variables. The advantages of introducing union and type variables would be:

- the possibility of defining a semantics in which the interpretation of a λ-term increases by reduction
- a more expressive typing.

This is essentially the subject of [20].

Acknowledgements.

We are very grateful to Stefano Berardi, Mario Coppo, Roger Hindley, Furio Honsell, Robert Meyer, Benjamin Pierce and Simona Ronchi della Rocca for helpful discussions about the subject of this paper. Particular thanks to Andrea Manchèe.

REFERENCES.

[1] Abramsky S., Domain Theory in Logical Form, *Annals of Pure and Applied Logics* 51 (1991), 1-77.

[2] Altenkirch T., Ein Konstruktiver Ansatz zur Konjunktiven Typisierung des λ-kalkuls, Diplomarbeit, TU Berlin, (1983).

[3] Barendregt H.P., The Lambda Calculus : its Syntax and Semantics, *Studies in Logic and the Foundations of Math. 103* , North-Holland, (1984).

[4] Barendregt H.P., Coppo M., Dezani-Ciancaglini M., A Filter Lambda Model and the Completeness of Type Assignment, *J. Symbolic Logic* 48 (1983), 931-940.

[5] Berarducci A., Programmazione Funzionale e Rappresentabilità in alcuni sistemi di Logica Combinatoria, Tesi di Laurea, Università di Roma,(1983).

[6] Beth E.W., *The Foundation of Mathematics* , North Holland, (1959) (2nd ed. 1965).

[7] Böhm C., Functional Programming and Combinatory Algebras, MFCS 88, *LNCS* 324 (1985), 14-26.
[8] Böhm C., Berarducci A., Automatic Synthesis of Typed λ-programs on Term Algebras, *Theor. Comp. Sci.* 39 (1985), 135-154.
[9] Boudol G., A Lambda-Calculus for Parallel Functions, Rapport de Recherche INRIA 1231, (1990).
[10] Boudol G., A Lambda-Calculus for (Strict) Parallel Functions, Internal Report, INRIA Sophia-Antipolis, (1991).
[11] Coppo M., Dezani-Ciancaglini M., Honsell F., Longo G., Extended Type Structures and Filter Lambda Models, *Logic Colloquium* 82, North-Holland, (1984), 241–262.
[12] Coppo M., Dezani-Ciancaglini M., Venneri B., Functional Characters of Solvable Terms, *Zeit. Math. Logik* 27 (1981), 45-58.
[13] Curry H., Feys R., *Combinatory Logic*, North-Holland, (1958).
[14] Giannini P., Some Negative Results on Berarducci Numerals, Internal Report, Universita' di Torino, (1988).
[15] Hindley R., The Simple Semantic for Coppo-Dezani-Sallé Types, ISP 82, *LNCS* 137 (1982), 212-226.
[16] Hindley R., The Completeness Theorem for Typing Lambda Terms, *Theor. Comp. Sci.* 22 (1983), 1-17.
[17] Hindley R. Coppo-Dezani Types do not Correspond to Propositional Logic, *Theor. Comp. Sci.* 28 (1984), 235-236.
[18] Kripke S., A Completeness Theorem in Modal Logic, *Journal of Symbolic Logic* 24 (1959), 1-14.
[19] Leivant D., Discrete Polymorphism, *Proc. VI ACM Conference on LISP and Functional Programming*, (1990), 288-297.
[20] de'Liguoro U., Non-Deterministic Lambda-Calculus: Models and Types, Thesis Proposal, Università di Roma, (1991).
[21] MacQueen D., Plotkin G., Sethi R., An Ideal Model for Recursive Polymorphic Types, *Information and Control* 71 (1986), 95-130.
[22] Meyer A., What is a Model of the Lambda Calculus?, *Information and Control* 52 (1982), 87-122.
[23] Meyer A., Mitchell J.C., Moggi E., Statman R., Empty Types in Polymorphic Lambda Calculus, *Proc. 14th ACM Symposium on Principles of Programming Languages*, (1985), 253-262.
[24] Mitchell J., Moggi E., Kripke-style Models for Typed Lambda Calculus, *Annals of Pure and Applied Logics* 51 (1991), 99-124.
[25] Pierce B., Preliminary Investigation of a Calculus with Intersection and Union Types, Internal Report, Carnegie Mellon University, (1990).
[26] Pierce B., Programming with Intersection Types, Union Types and Polymorphism, Technical Report, CMU-CS-91-106, Carnegie Mellon University, (1991).
[27] Prawitz D., *Natural Deduction*, Almqvist & Wiksell, Stockolm, (1965).
[28] Reynolds J.C., Preliminary Design of the Programming Language FORSYTHE, Report CMU-CS-88-159, Carnegie Mellon University, (1988).
[29] Reynolds J.C., Syntactic Control of Interference Part 2, ICALP 89, *LNCS* 372 (1989), 704-722.
[30] Ronchi della Rocca S., Characterization Theorems for a Filter Lambda Model, *Information and Control* 54 (1982), 201-216.
[31] Wadsworth C., The Relation between Computational and Denotational Properties for D_∞-models of the Lambda Calculus, *S.I.A.M. J. on Computing* 5 (1976), 488-521.

The Coherence of Languages with Intersection Types

John C. Reynolds*
School of Computer Science
Carnegie Mellon University
Pittsburgh, PA 15213-3890, USA
john.reynolds@cs.cmu.edu

Abstract

When a programming language has a sufficiently rich type structure, there can be more than one proof of the same typing judgement; potentially this can lead to semantic ambiguity since the semantics of a typed language is a function of such proofs. When no such ambiguity arises, we say that the language is *coherent*. In this paper we prove the coherence of a class of lambda-calculus-based languages that use the intersection type discipline, including both a purely functional programming language and the Algol-like programming language Forsythe.

1 Introduction

As the type structure of programming languages has become richer, the problem of avoiding semantic ambiguity has become more difficult. In [5], this problem was resolved for first-order languages with implicit conversions (i.e. subtypes) and generic operators. In the present paper, we consider the more general case of higher-order languages with implicit conversions and intersection types [2]. For such languages, we will find that the usual kind of semantic equations give meaning, not to phrases of the language itself, but rather to proofs of typing judgements about such phrases. Thus to insure against semantic ambiguity, we must prove that distinct proofs of the same typing judgement possess the same meaning. Following [1] (which treats a closely

*This research was sponsored in part by National Science Foundation Grant CCR-8922109 and in part by the Avionics Lab, Wright Research and Development Center, Aeronautical Systems Division (AFSC), U.S. Air Force, Wright-Patterson AFB, OH 45433-6543 under Contract F33615-90-C-1465, Arpa Order No. 7597. The views and conclusions contained in this document are those of the author and should not be interpreted as representing the official policies, either expressed or implied, of the U.S. Government.

related problem for a language with implicit conversions and polymorphism), we call this property *coherence.*

The kind of language for which we will prove coherence is a lambda calculus extended to include object manipulation, fixed points, and conditionals. More precisely, our results hold for a class of such languages obtained by varying such entities as primitive types, constants, and semantic categories, subject to appropriate constraints.

Two particular cases of importance are a purely functional language (albeit without recursively defined types), and a syntactically desugared version of the Algol-like language Forsythe [7]. Certain aspects of the general treatment, notably the inclusion of operations for object construction, field selection, merging, and conditional branching, are specifically motivated by the desire to encompass Forsythe.

Our results depend upon some basic properties of intersection types (also called conjunctive types) that are proved in [6] and summarized in the following section.

2 Types and Their Semantics

We consider the set of types defined by the abstract grammar

$$\theta ::= \rho \mid \theta \to \theta \mid \iota{:}\,\theta \mid \mathbf{ns} \mid \theta \,\&\, \theta$$

where the metavariable ι ranges over identifiers, and the metavariable ρ ranges over primitive types. Here $\to$ is the usual operator for constructing types of procedures (or, in an applicative language, functions), & is the binary intersection operator, and **ns** (called ω in [2]) denotes the intersection of zero types. The construction $\iota{:}\,\theta$ is meant to denote a type that is isomorphic to θ, but (in an intuitive sense) disjoint from θ. (In programming terminology, one can regard $\iota{:}\,\theta$ as the type of objects or records with a single field named ι ranging over the type θ.)

We write $\theta \leq \theta'$ to indicate that θ is a subtype of θ'. The subtype relation $\leq$ is the least preorder on the set of types such that

$$\theta \leq \mathbf{ns} \qquad \theta_1 \,\&\, \theta_2 \leq \theta_1 \qquad \theta_1 \,\&\, \theta_2 \leq \theta_2$$

$$\text{If } \theta \leq \theta_1 \text{ and } \theta \leq \theta_2 \text{ then } \theta \leq \theta_1 \,\&\, \theta_2 \,.$$

$$\text{If } \rho \leq_{\text{prim}} \rho' \text{ then } \rho \leq \rho' \,. \qquad \text{If } \theta \leq \theta' \text{ then } \iota{:}\,\theta \leq \iota{:}\,\theta' \,.$$

$$\text{If } \theta_1' \leq \theta_1 \text{ and } \theta_2 \leq \theta_2' \text{ then } \theta_1 \to \theta_2 \leq \theta_1' \to \theta_2' \,.$$

$$\iota{:}\,\theta_1 \,\&\, \iota{:}\,\theta_2 \leq \iota{:}\,(\theta_1 \,\&\, \theta_2)$$

$$(\theta \to \theta_1) \,\&\, (\theta \to \theta_2) \leq \theta \to (\theta_1 \,\&\, \theta_2)$$

$$\mathbf{ns} \leq \iota{:}\,\mathbf{ns} \qquad \mathbf{ns} \leq \theta \to \mathbf{ns}$$

where $\leq_{\text{prim}}$ is a given subtype preorder for primitive types. We write $\theta \simeq \theta'$ when θ and θ' are equivalent, i.e. when $\theta \leq \theta'$ and $\theta' \leq \theta$.

The first four of the above relationships establish that **ns** is a greatest type and that $\theta_1 \,\&\, \theta_2$ is a greatest lower bound of θ_1 and θ_2. Note that we say "a" rather than "the"; since we have a preorder rather than a partial order, greatest types and greatest lower bounds are unique only to within equivalence.

The specific choice of the primitive types and their subtype relation is not relevant to the coherence property. However, we will impose two requirements: First, the preordered set of primitive types must be pairwise bounded complete, i.e. every pair of primitive types with an upper bound must have a least upper bound. Second (so that we can introduce conditionals), there must be a particular primitive type **bool**.

Under the first of these assumptions, it is shown in [6] that

Proposition 1 *If $\theta_1 \,\&\, \theta_2 \leq \theta'$ then there are θ_1' and θ_2' such that $\theta_1 \leq \theta_1'$, $\theta_2 \leq \theta_2'$, and $\theta' \simeq \theta_1' \,\&\, \theta_2'$.*

Proposition 2 *Every pair of types has a least upper bound. In particular, there is a function $\sqcup$ mapping pairs of types into types such that $\theta_1 \sqcup \theta_2$ is a least upper bound of θ_1 and θ_2, and*

$$\theta \sqcup \mathbf{ns} \simeq \mathbf{ns}$$

$$\theta_1 \sqcup (\theta_2 \,\&\, \theta_3) \simeq (\theta_1 \sqcup \theta_2) \,\&\, (\theta_1 \sqcup \theta_3)$$

$$\rho \sqcup \iota{:}\, \theta \simeq \mathbf{ns}$$

$$\rho \sqcup (\theta_1 \rightarrow \theta_2) \simeq \mathbf{ns}$$

$$\iota{:}\, \theta_1 \sqcup (\theta_2 \rightarrow \theta_3) \simeq \mathbf{ns}$$

$$\rho_1 \sqcup \rho_2 \simeq \rho_1 \sqcup_{\mathrm{prim}} \rho_2 \text{ when } \rho_1 \sqcup_{\mathrm{prim}} \rho_2 \text{ exists}$$

$$\rho_1 \sqcup \rho_2 \simeq \mathbf{ns} \text{ when } \rho_1 \sqcup_{\mathrm{prim}} \rho_2 \text{ does not exist}$$

$$\iota{:}\, \theta_1 \sqcup \iota{:}\, \theta_2 \simeq \iota{:}\, (\theta_1 \sqcup \theta_2)$$

$$\iota_1{:}\, \theta_1 \sqcup \iota_2{:}\, \theta_2 \simeq \mathbf{ns} \text{ when } \iota_1 \neq \iota_2$$

$$(\theta_1 \rightarrow \theta_1') \sqcup (\theta_2 \rightarrow \theta_2') \simeq (\theta_1 \,\&\, \theta_2) \rightarrow (\theta_1' \sqcup \theta_2') \,.$$

(As with greatest lower bounds, least upper bounds are unique only to within an equivalence. Note, by the way, that the function $\sqcup$, unlike &, is not a type constructor.)

In proving coherence, we will assume that the semantics of our language is based upon a category $\mathcal{K}$ with the following properties:

1. The category $\mathcal{K}$ is Cartesian closed.

2. There is a subcategory $\mathcal{S}$ of $\mathcal{K}$ such that every finite diagram in $\mathcal{S}$ has a limit in $\mathcal{S}$ that is also a limit in $\mathcal{K}$. (In particular, we assume that $\mathcal{S}$ and $\mathcal{K}$ have the same distinguished product.)

3. There is a functor $\underset{\mathcal{S}}{\Longrightarrow}$ from $\mathcal{S}^{\text{op}} \times \mathcal{S}$ to $\mathcal{S}$ that is a restriction of the exponentiation functor $\underset{\mathcal{K}}{\Longrightarrow}$ from $\mathcal{K}^{\text{op}} \times \mathcal{K}$ to $\mathcal{K}$. (This does not imply that $\mathcal{S}$ is Cartesian closed, since it need not contain application and abstraction morphisms.) For each object k of $\mathcal{S}$, the functor $k \underset{\mathcal{S}}{\Longrightarrow} -$ preserves limits in $\mathcal{S}$.

4. There is a functor $[\![-]\!]_{\text{prim}}$ from the preordered set of primitive types (viewed as a category) to $\mathcal{S}$ that assigns meanings to the primitive types ρ and implicit conversions to the morphisms $\rho \leq_{\text{prim}} \rho'$ of the primitive subtype relation.

For a purely functional language, for example, $\mathcal{K}$ is the category CPO whose objects are complete partial orders with least elements and whose morphisms are continuous functions, and $\mathcal{S}$ is the subcategory whose morphisms are strict. For Forsythe, on the other hand, both $\mathcal{K}$ and $\mathcal{S}$ are subcategories of the functor category CPO^{Σ} used by F. Oles to describe the semantics of Algol-like languages [3, 4]. Specifically, $\mathcal{K}$ is the full subcategory whose objects are functors that map morphisms into strict functions, $\mathcal{S}$ is the further subcategory whose morphisms are natural transformations that map objects into strict functions, and Σ is an appropriate category of "store shapes".

In [6], it is shown from the above general properties of $\mathcal{K}$ that one can define a semantic functor $[\![-]\!]$ characterized as follows:

Proposition 3 *There is a "semantic" functor $[\![-]\!]$ from the preordered set of types (viewed as a category) to $\mathcal{S}$ that satisfies*

1. *$[\![-]\!]$ is an extension of $[\![-]\!]_{\text{prim}}$.*

2. *$[\![\theta_1 \to \theta_2]\!] = [\![\theta_1]\!] \underset{\mathcal{S}}{\Longrightarrow} [\![\theta_2]\!]$ and $[\![\theta_1 \to \theta_2 \leq \theta_1' \to \theta_2']\!] = [\![\theta_1' \leq \theta_1]\!] \underset{\mathcal{S}}{\Longrightarrow} [\![\theta_2 \leq \theta_2']\!]$.*

3. *$[\![\iota\colon \theta]\!] = [\![\theta]\!]$ and $[\![\iota\colon \theta \leq \iota\colon \theta']\!] = [\![\theta \leq \theta']\!]$.*

4. *$[\![\mathbf{ns}]\!]$ is a terminal object.*

5. *$[\![\theta_1 \,\&\, \theta_2]\!]$, along with the implicit conversions $[\![\theta_1 \,\&\, \theta_2 \leq \theta_1]\!]$ and $[\![\theta_1 \,\&\, \theta_2 \leq \theta_2]\!]$, is a pullback of $[\![\theta_1]\!]$, $[\![\theta_2]\!]$, and $[\![\theta_1 \sqcup \theta_2]\!]$:*

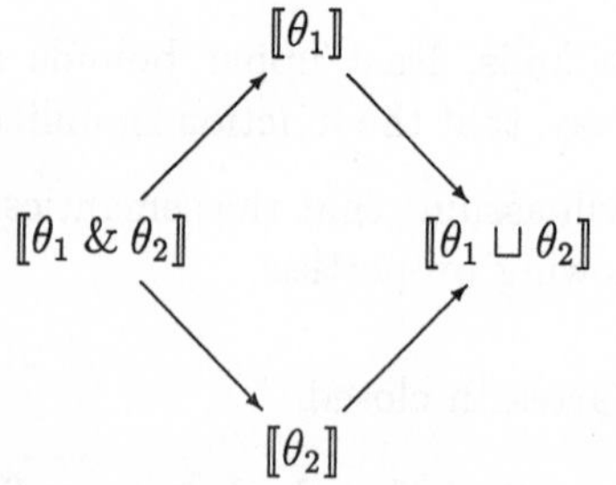

(As illustrated by this diagram, we adopt the convention that an unlabeled arrow from $[\![\theta]\!]$ to $[\![\theta']\!]$ denotes the implicit conversion $[\![\theta \leq \theta']\!]$. Later, we will also use this convention for products of implicit conversions.)

Actually, the functor constructed in [6] only gives isomorphisms, such as $[\![\theta_1 \to \theta_2]\!] \simeq [\![\theta_1]\!] \underset{\mathcal{S}}{\Rightarrow} [\![\theta_2]\!]$ and $[\![\iota\colon \theta]\!] \simeq [\![\theta]\!]$. Without any loss of generality, however, we can make the present exposition far more concise by assuming that these isomorphisms are equalities.

Notice that, because of the last part of the above proposition, the semantics of types is not compositional in the conventional sense, since the meaning $[\![\theta_1 \,\&\, \theta_2]\!]$ of $\theta_1 \,\&\, \theta_2$ depends, not only upon the meanings of θ_1 and θ_2, but also upon the meaning of $\theta_1 \sqcup \theta_2$ and the implicit conversions among these meanings.

A *type assignment* π is a mapping from a finite set of identifiers into types; the appropriate preordering is that $\pi \leq \pi'$ whenever $\operatorname{dom} \pi' \subseteq \operatorname{dom} \pi$ and, for all $\iota \in \operatorname{dom} \pi'$, $\pi\iota \leq \pi'\iota$. We write $[\![-]\!]^*$ for the functor from the preordered set of type assignments (viewed as a category) to $\mathcal{S}$, such that

$$[\![\pi]\!]^* \overset{\text{def}}{=} \prod_{\iota \in \operatorname{dom} \pi}^{\mathcal{S}} [\![\pi\iota]\!] \,,$$

and $[\![\pi \leq \pi']\!]^*$ is the unique morphism making the diagram

$$\begin{array}{ccc}
\prod\limits_{\iota \in \operatorname{dom} \pi}^{\mathcal{S}} [\![\pi\iota]\!] & \xrightarrow{\ \mathsf{p}\ } & [\![\pi\iota]\!] \\
{\scriptstyle [\![\pi \leq \pi']\!]^*}\big\downarrow & & \big\downarrow \\
\prod\limits_{\iota \in \operatorname{dom} \pi'}^{\mathcal{S}} [\![\pi'\iota]\!] & \xrightarrow{\ \mathsf{p}'\ } & [\![\pi'\iota]\!]
\end{array}$$

(where p and p' denote projection morphisms) commute in $\mathcal{S}$ for every $\iota \in \operatorname{dom} \pi'$.

3 Phrases and their Semantics

We write $\pi \vdash p : \theta$ for the judgement that a phrase p has type θ under the type assignment π, and $\mathcal{P}_{\pi\theta}$ for the set of phrases p for which $\pi \vdash p : \theta$ is a valid typing judgement. The valid typing judgements of our language are those that are provable from a certain set of inference rules. At the outset, it is important to note that some of these rules, such as the rule for subtypes:

$$\frac{\pi \vdash p : \theta_1}{\pi \vdash p : \theta} \quad \text{when } \theta_1 \leq \theta$$

are not syntax-directed, since they allow one to infer a judgement about a phrase from a previous judgement about the *same* phrase.

The semantics of phrases (or more precisely of typing judgements, since a phrase satisfying several judgements will have several meanings) is given by a family of semantic functions

$$\mu_{\pi\theta} \in \mathcal{P}_{\pi\theta} \to ([\![\pi]\!]^* \underset{\mathcal{K}}{\to} [\![\theta]\!]) \,.$$

Conventionally, one would expect to define these functions by a collection of semantic equations, one for each "reason" that a phrase belongs to one of the $\mathcal{P}_{\pi\theta}$, i.e. for each inference rule. But as soon as one tries to write a semantic equation for a non-syntax-directed rule, such as the intuitively obvious rule

$$\mu_{\pi\theta}[p] = \mu_{\pi\theta_1}[p] \,;\, [\![\theta_1 \leq \theta]\!] \qquad \text{when } \pi \vdash p : \theta_1 \text{ and } \theta_1 \leq \theta$$

for subtypes, it becomes clear that something is awry: Since conventional semantic equations are cases of a definition by induction on the size of phrases, they should not define the meaning of a phrase in terms of another meaning of the same phrase. (Note, by the way, that we use a semicolon to denote composition in diagrammatic order.)

In fact, instead of defining the meaning of phrases, the semantic equations for our language define the meaning of proofs that such phrases satisfy typing judgements. They actually define a function μ (distinguished from $\mu_{\pi\theta}$ by the absence of subscripts) that maps each proof P of a judgement $\pi \vdash p : \theta$ into a morphism in $[\![\pi]\!]^* \xrightarrow[\mathcal{K}]{} [\![\theta]\!]$. The definition is by induction on the size of the proof, with a case analysis on the rule used at the main step of the proof.

For each inference rule

$$\frac{J_1 \quad J_2 \quad \ldots \quad J_n}{J}$$

the corresponding semantic equation gives the meaning of the proofs that use the rule at their main step, as a function of the meanings of the subproofs of the judgements that are premisses of the rule. In stating the semantic equation, we will write P for the proof of J whose meaning is being defined and P_i for the subproof of the premiss J_i. For example, the semantic equation for the subtype rule is

$$\mu[P] = \mu[P_1] \,;\, [\![\theta_1 \leq \theta]\!] \,.$$

The property of coherence bridges the gap between the function μ that is actually defined by the semantic equations and the functions $\mu_{\pi\theta}$ that give meanings to typing judgements independently of their proofs. We say that μ is *coherent* iff $\mu[P_1] = \mu[P_2]$ whenever P_1 and P_2 both prove the same typing judgement. This is exactly the property needed to make the obvious definition

$$\mu_{\pi\theta}[p] \stackrel{\text{def}}{=} \mu[P] \text{ for any } P \text{ proving } \pi \vdash p : \theta$$

unambiguous.

4 Inference Rules and Semantic Equations

In this section we give the inference rules and semantic equations for the class of languages for which we will prove coherence. The first three of these rules are the only ones that are not syntax-directed.

- Subtypes

$$\frac{\pi \vdash p : \theta_1}{\pi \vdash p : \theta} \quad \text{when } \theta_1 \leq \theta \qquad \mu[P] = \mu[P_1] \,;\, [\![\theta_1 \leq \theta]\!] \,.$$

- Nonsense

$$\frac{}{\pi \vdash p : \mathbf{ns}} \qquad \mu[P] = u_\pi \,,$$

where u_π is the unique morphism from $[\![\pi]\!]^*$ to the terminal element $[\![\mathbf{ns}]\!]$.

- Intersections

$$\frac{\pi \vdash p : \theta_1 \qquad \pi \vdash p : \theta_2}{\pi \vdash p : \theta_1 \,\&\, \theta_2} \qquad \mu[P] = \beta \,,$$

where β is the unique mediating morphism into the pullback:

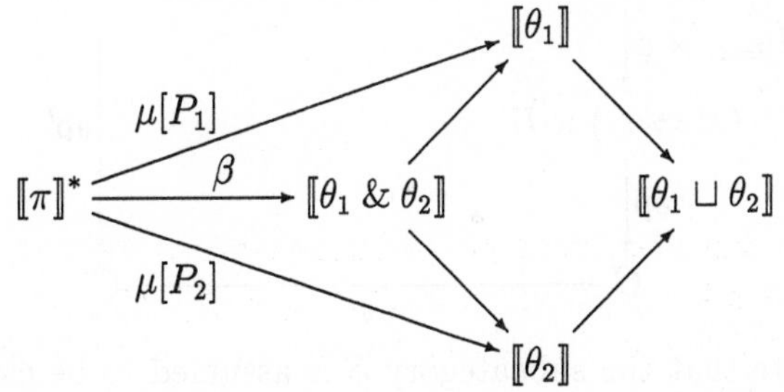

This semantic equation only makes sense if the perimeter of the above diagram commutes. In the next section, as part of the proof of coherence, we will establish that this condition is always met.

- Identifiers

$$\frac{}{\pi \vdash \iota : \pi(\iota)} \quad \text{when } \iota \in \operatorname{dom} \pi \qquad \mu[P] = \mathsf{p} \,,$$

where p is the projection morphism from $[\![\pi]\!]^* = \prod^{S}_{\iota \in \operatorname{dom} \pi} [\![\pi\iota]\!]$ to $[\![\pi\iota]\!]$.

- Constants

$$\frac{}{\pi \vdash c : \theta_c} \qquad \mu[P] = u_\pi \,;\, \mu_c \,.$$

Here θ_c is the type of the constant c, μ_c is its meaning, which must be a morphism from the terminal element $[\![\mathbf{ns}]\!]$ to $[\![\theta_c]\!]$, and u_π is the unique morphism from $[\![\pi]\!]^*$ to the terminal element.

We will not specify any particular constants. It should be noted, however, that when θ_c is an intersection of procedural types, e.g. $(\theta_1 \to \theta_1') \,\&\, (\theta_2 \to \theta_2')$, the requirement that μ_c must be a morphism from $[\![\mathbf{ns}]\!]$ to $[\![\theta_c]\!]$ is a nontrivial constraint that has the same effect as the naturality constraints on generic operators in [5].

The semantics of the next two rules relies upon the Cartesian closed nature of $\mathcal{K}$. For all objects B and C there is an *exponentiation* object $B \Rightarrow C$ and an *application* morphism $\mathsf{ap} \in (B \Rightarrow C) \times B \to C$ such that, for all objects A and morphisms $\rho \in A \times B \to C$, there is exactly one *abstraction* morphism $\mathsf{ab}\,\rho \in A \to (B \Rightarrow C)$ making

$$\begin{array}{ccc} A \times B & \xrightarrow{\mathsf{ab}\,\rho \times I_B} & (B \Rightarrow C) \times B \\ & \searrow^{\rho} & \downarrow \mathsf{ap} \\ & & C \end{array}$$

commute in $\mathcal{K}$. Moreover, the exponentiation operator $\Rightarrow$ extends to a functor from $\mathcal{K}^{\mathrm{op}} \times \mathcal{K}$ to $\mathcal{K}$ with the following action on morphisms: if $\phi \in B' \to B$ and $\psi \in C \to C'$ then $\phi \Rightarrow \psi$ is the unique morphism in $(B \Rightarrow C) \to (B' \Rightarrow C')$ making

$$\begin{array}{ccc} (B \Rightarrow C) \times B' & \xrightarrow{(\phi \Rightarrow \psi) \times I_{B'}} & (B' \Rightarrow C') \times B' \\ I_{B \Rightarrow C} \times \phi \downarrow & & \\ (B \Rightarrow C) \times B & & \downarrow \mathsf{ap}' \\ \mathsf{ap} \downarrow & & \\ C & \xrightarrow[\psi]{} & C' \end{array}$$

commute in $\mathcal{K}$. Note that the subcategory $\mathcal{S}$ is assumed to be closed under products and exponentiations of both objects and morphisms.

- Applications

$$\frac{\pi \vdash p_1 : \theta_1 \to \theta \qquad \pi \vdash p_2 : \theta_1}{\pi \vdash p_1\, p_2 : \theta} \qquad\qquad \mu[P] = \langle \mu[P_1], \mu[P_2] \rangle \,;\, \mathsf{ap}\,,$$

where $\langle \mu[P_1], \mu[P_2] \rangle$ is the mediating morphism from the object $[\![\pi]\!]^*$ to the product $([\![\theta_1]\!] \underset{\mathcal{K}}{\Rightarrow} [\![\theta]\!]) \times [\![\theta_1]\!]$, and ap is the application morphism from this product to $[\![\theta]\!]$.

- Abstractions

$$\frac{[\,\pi \mid \iota{:}\, \theta_1\,] \vdash p_1 : \theta_2}{\pi \vdash \lambda\iota.\ p_1 : \theta_1 \to \theta_2} \qquad\qquad \mu[P] = \mathsf{ab}(\P \,;\, \mu[P_1])\,.$$

Here $[\,\pi \mid \iota{:}\, \theta_1\,]$ denotes the type assignment with domain $\mathrm{dom}\,\pi \cup \{\iota\}$ that maps ι into θ_1 and all other ι' in its domain into $\pi\iota'$, while $\P$ denotes the unique morphism making

$$\begin{array}{ccc} [\![\pi]\!]^* \times [\![\theta_1]\!] & & \\ \P \downarrow & \searrow & \\ [\![\,[\,\pi \mid \iota{:}\,\theta_1\,]\,]\!]^* & \longrightarrow & [\![\theta_1]\!] \end{array} \qquad \text{and} \qquad \begin{array}{ccc} [\![\pi]\!]^* \times [\![\theta_1]\!] & \longrightarrow & [\![\pi]\!]^* \\ \P \downarrow & & \downarrow \\ [\![\,[\,\pi \mid \iota{:}\,\theta_1\,]\,]\!]^* & \longrightarrow & [\![\pi\iota']\!] \end{array}$$

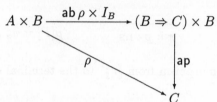

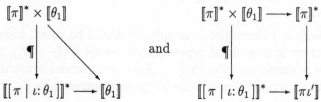

commute, the latter for all $\iota' \in \operatorname{dom} \pi - \{\iota\}$. (The unlabeled arrows in these diagrams denote the evident projection morphisms.)

Notice that abstractions do not contain type information, so that our inference rules describe an implicitly typed language. Of course, in practice one must use an explicitly typed language, since there is no type-inference decision procedure for intersection types [2]. But explicit type information is not needed to establish coherence; indeed the property of coherence is stronger when formulated for the implicitly typed case, since it implies that changing explicit type information cannot change semantics.

The next two cases deal with operations for constructing objects and extracting their fields (which are central to the object-oriented capabilities of Forsythe). Intuitively, $\iota \equiv p$ constructs an object with a single field whose name is ι and whose value is p, while $p.\iota$ extracts the value of the field named ι from the object p. In the actual semantics, however, $[\![\iota\colon\theta]\!] = [\![\theta]\!]$, i.e. single-field objects are identical to their field values, so that the semantic equations are trivial.

- Object Construction

$$\frac{\pi \vdash p_1 : \theta_1}{\pi \vdash (\iota \equiv p_1) : (\iota\colon\theta_1)} \qquad \mu[P] = \mu[P_1]\,.$$

- Field Selection

$$\frac{\pi \vdash p_1 : (\iota\colon\theta)}{\pi \vdash p_1.\iota : \theta} \qquad \mu[P] = \mu[P_1]\,.$$

The next four rules describe the Forsythe "merging" operation. The essential idea is that a phrase p_1, p_2 should take on the meanings of both p_1 and p_2. However, to avoid ambiguity, the phrase p_2 is required to be either a lambda expression or an object constructor, whose meaning "overwrites" the corresponding type of meaning of p_1. (The object-constructor case provides a limited kind of object concatenation that is much simpler than, for example, the approach of [8].)

- Merging

$$\frac{\pi \vdash \lambda\iota.\, p_2 : \theta_1 \to \theta_2}{\pi \vdash (p_1, \lambda\iota.\, p_2) : \theta_1 \to \theta_2} \qquad \mu[P] = \mu[P_1]$$

$$\frac{\pi \vdash p_1 : \theta}{\pi \vdash (p_1, \lambda\iota.\, p_2) : \theta} \quad \text{when } \theta \text{ is a primitive type or has the form } \iota\colon\theta_1 \qquad \mu[P] = \mu[P_1]$$

$$\frac{\pi \vdash \iota \equiv p_2 : (\iota\colon\theta_1)}{\pi \vdash (p_1, \iota \equiv p_2) : (\iota\colon\theta_1)} \qquad \mu[P] = \mu[P_1]$$

$$\frac{\pi \vdash p_1 : \theta}{\pi \vdash (p_1, \iota \equiv p_2) : \theta} \quad \text{when } \theta \text{ is a primitive type or has the form } \theta_1 \to \theta_2 \text{ or } \iota'\colon\theta_1 \text{ where } \iota' \neq \iota \qquad \mu[P] = \mu[P_1]\,.$$

Finally, we give rules for fixed-point and conditional constructions. In these cases we cannot give an explicit semantics without specifying a particular semantic category; for example, the semantics are different for Forsythe than for a purely functional langauge. So we state the semantic equations in terms of unspecified entities Y_k and cd_θ for which we can give sufficient conditions to ensure coherence.

- Fixed Points

$$\frac{\pi \vdash p_1 : \theta \to \theta}{\pi \vdash \mathbf{rec}\, p_1 : \theta} \qquad \mu[P] = \mu[P_1]\,;\mathsf{Y}_{[\![\theta]\!]}\,.$$

Here $\mathsf{Y}_k \in (k \Rightarrow k) \to k$ is an object-indexed family of morphisms in $\mathcal{K}$ that satisfies the following condition: If p, ρ, ρ' is a pullback in $\mathcal{S}$ of

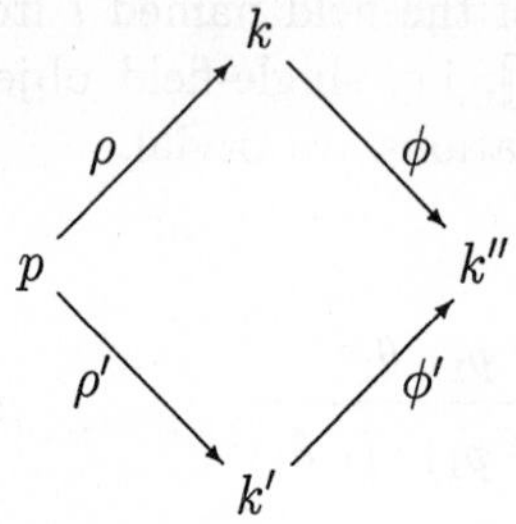

and if the diagram

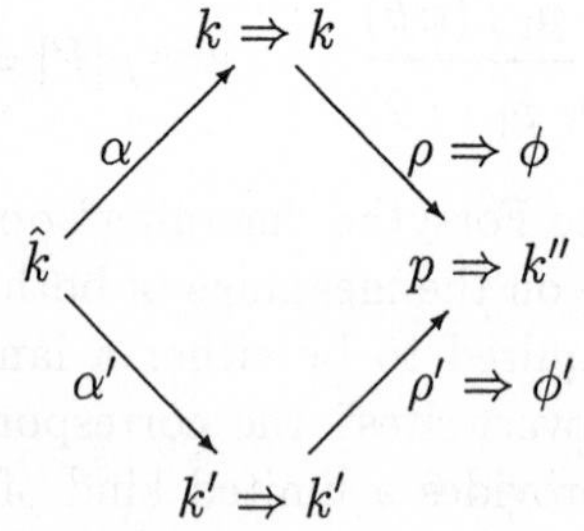

commutes in $\mathcal{K}$ then

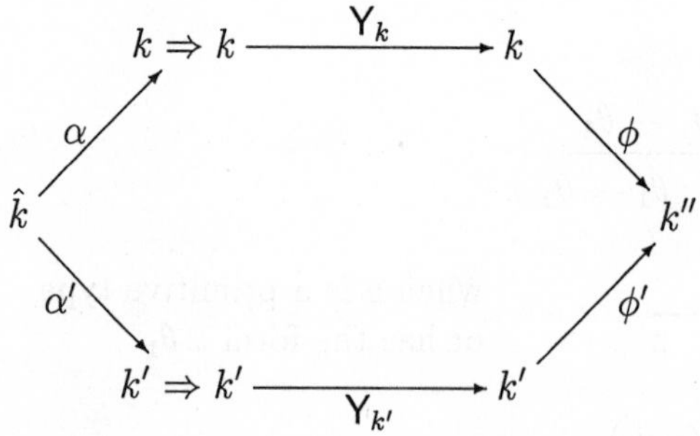

commutes in $\mathcal{K}$.

- Conditionals

$$\frac{\pi \vdash p_1 : \mathbf{bool} \qquad \pi \vdash p_2 : \theta \qquad \pi \vdash p_3 : \theta}{\pi \vdash \mathbf{if}\, p_1\, \mathbf{then}\, p_2\, \mathbf{else}\, p_3 : \theta} \qquad \mu[P] = \langle \mu[P_1], \mu[P_2], \mu[P_3]\rangle;\mathsf{cd}_\theta,$$

where $\langle \mu[P_1], \mu[P_2], \mu[P_3] \rangle$ is the mediating morphism from $[\![\pi]\!]^*$ to $[\![\mathbf{bool}]\!] \times [\![\theta]\!] \times [\![\theta]\!]$. Here cd_θ is a type-indexed family of morphisms in $\mathcal{K}$ that is required to be a natural transformation from the functor $[\![\mathbf{bool}]\!] \times [\![-]\!] \times [\![-]\!]$ to the functor $[\![-]\!]$ (regarded as functors from the preordered set of types to $\mathcal{K}$). (See Appendix.)

The reader who is familiar with [7] will notice that we have omitted a number of inference rules for various constructions in Forsythe. However, in an implicitly typed version of this language these constructions can all be defined as syntactic sugar, i.e. as abbreviations for phrases in the more basic language described above (with the inclusion of extra constants, such as *add*, that do not actually occur in Forsythe).

5 A Proof of Coherence

We will now prove that the inference rules and semantic equations in the previous section define a semantic function μ that is coherent. In fact, we will prove a stronger property of μ:

Proposition 4 *Suppose P proves $\pi \vdash p : \theta$, P' proves $\pi' \vdash p : \theta'$, $\pi'' \leq \pi$, $\pi'' \leq \pi'$, $\theta \leq \theta''$, and $\theta' \leq \theta''$. Then*

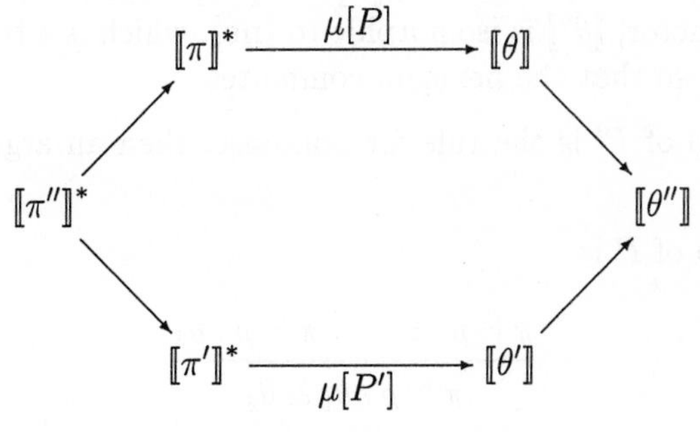

commutes in $\mathcal{K}$.

The special case where $\pi = \pi' = \pi''$ and $\theta = \theta' = \theta''$ gives the coherence property. (Also, the special case where $\pi = \pi' = \pi''$ and $\theta'' = \theta \sqcup \theta'$ will be needed to show that the function μ is well-defined in the case of intersections.)

Proof: The proof is by induction on the sum of the sizes of the proofs P and P'.

(1a) If the main step of P is

$$\frac{\pi \vdash p : \theta_1}{\pi \vdash p : \theta} \quad \text{when } \theta_1 \leq \theta$$

then $\mu[P] = \mu[P_1] ; [\![\theta_1 \leq \theta]\!]$. In the diagram

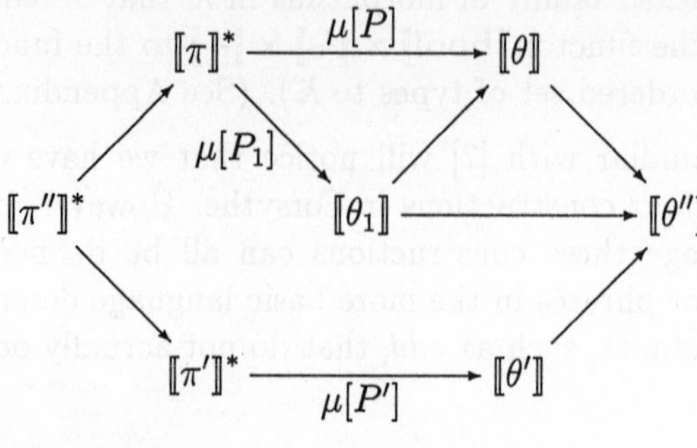

the inner hexagon commutes by the induction hypothesis, the leftmost triangle by the semantic equation, and the rightmost triangle since $[\![-]\!]$ is a functor. Thus the outer hexagon commutes.

(1b) If the main step of P' is the rule for subtypes, then an argument symmetric to that of (1a) applies.

(2a) If the main step of P is

$$\frac{}{\pi \vdash p : \mathbf{ns}}$$

then $\mu[P]$ is the unique morphism from $[\![\pi]\!]^*$ to $[\![\mathbf{ns}]\!]$. Then θ is **ns**, so that $\theta'' \simeq \mathbf{ns}$, and since $[\![-]\!]$ is a functor, $[\![\theta'']\!]$ is isomorphic to $[\![\mathbf{ns}]\!]$, which is a terminal object. Thus $[\![\theta'']\!]$ is also terminal, so that the hexagon commutes.

(2b) If the main step of P' is the rule for nonsense, then an argument symmetric to that of (2a) applies.

(3a) If the main step of P is

$$\frac{\pi \vdash p : \theta_1 \qquad \pi \vdash p : \theta_2}{\pi \vdash p : \theta_1 \,\&\, \theta_2}$$

then $\mu[P]$ is the unique mediating morphism into the pullback:

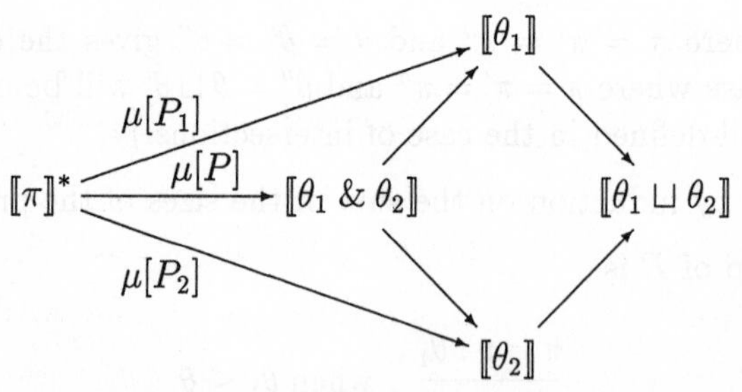

This semantic equation only makes sense if the perimeter of the diagram commutes, but this condition is insured by the induction hypothesis, applied to P_1 and P_2.

Since $\theta = \theta_1 \& \theta_2 \leq \theta''$, Proposition 1 shows that there are θ_1'' and θ_2'' such that $\theta_1 \leq \theta_1''$, $\theta_2 \leq \theta_2''$, and $\theta'' \simeq \theta_1'' \& \theta_2''$. Thus everything in

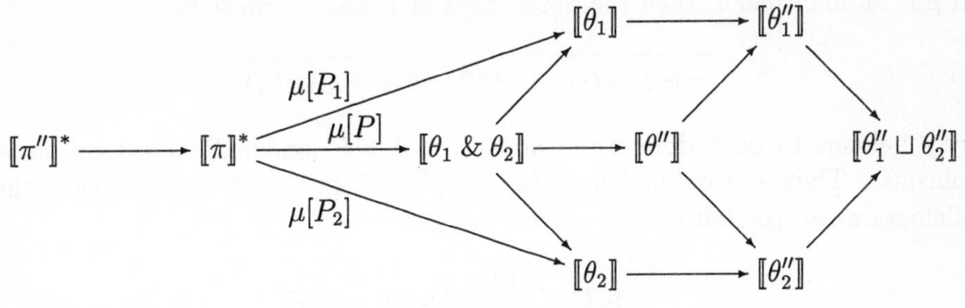

commutes, and $[\![\theta'']\!]$ is a pullback of $[\![\theta_1'']\!]$, $[\![\theta_2'']\!]$, and $[\![\theta_1'' \sqcup \theta_2'']\!]$.

It follows that the outside paths in

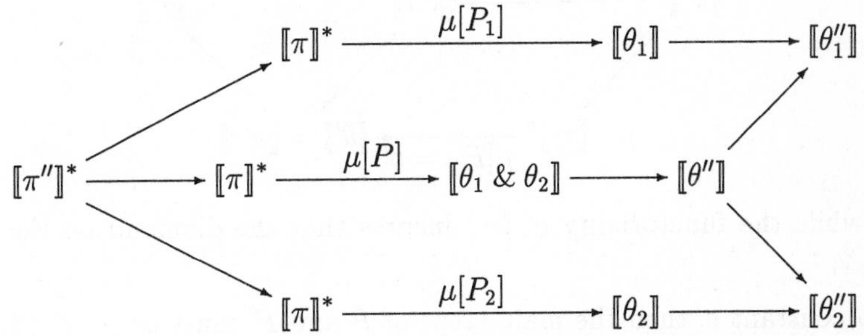

are a cone for this pullback and, since the inner polygons commute, the middle path is a mediating morphism. But, by two applications of the induction hypothesis, to P_1 and P' and to P_2 and P' respectively, the inner polygons in

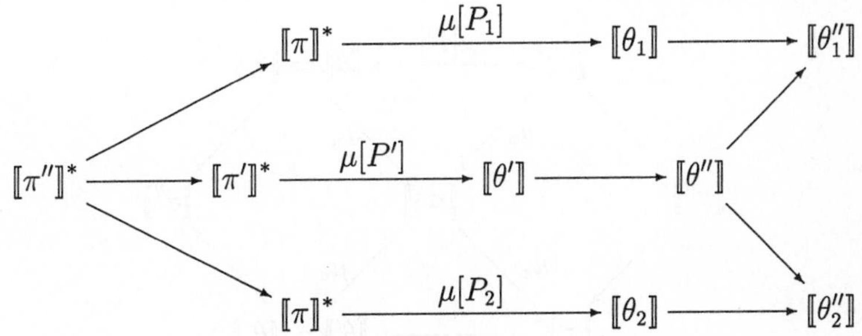

also commute, so that the middle path here is also a mediating morphism. Then the equality of the mediating morphisms gives the desired result.

(3b) If the main step of P' is the rule for intersections, then an argument symmetric to that of (3a) applies.

At this stage, we have considered all of the cases where the main step of P or P' is a non-syntax-directed rule. In the remaining cases, since both P and P' prove judgements about the same phrase p, their main steps must be syntax-directed rules for the same syntactic construction. Except in the case of the merging constructions, there is exactly one rule, which must be used as the main step of both proofs, for each construction.

(4) If p is an identifier ι, then the main steps of P and P' must be

$$\frac{}{\pi \vdash \iota : \pi(\iota)} \qquad \text{and} \qquad \frac{}{\pi' \vdash \iota : \pi'(\iota)}$$

where ι belongs to both $\operatorname{dom} \pi$ and $\operatorname{dom} \pi'$, and $\mu[P]$ and $\mu[P']$ must be projection morphisms. Then the definition of $[\![\pi'' \leq \pi]\!]^*$ and $[\![\pi'' \leq \pi']\!]^*$ insures that the two parallelograms on the left of

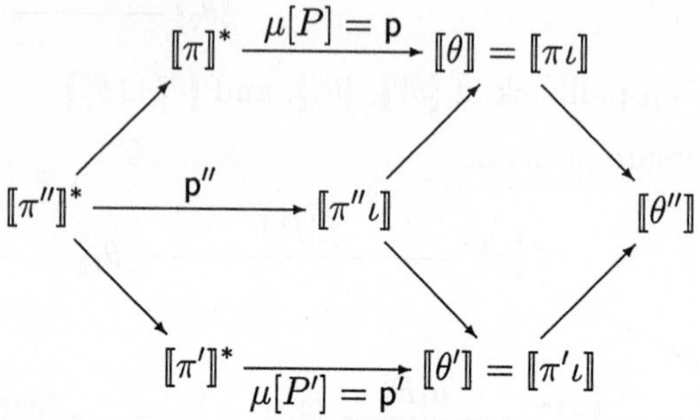

commute, while the functoriality of $[\![-]\!]$ insures that the diamond on the right commutes.

(5) If p is a constant c, then the main steps of P and P' must be

$$\frac{}{\pi \vdash c : \theta_c} \qquad \text{and} \qquad \frac{}{\pi' \vdash c : \theta_c}$$

with $\mu[P] = u_\pi \,;\, \mu_c$ and $\mu[P'] = u'_\pi \,;\, \mu_c$. Then the triangles in

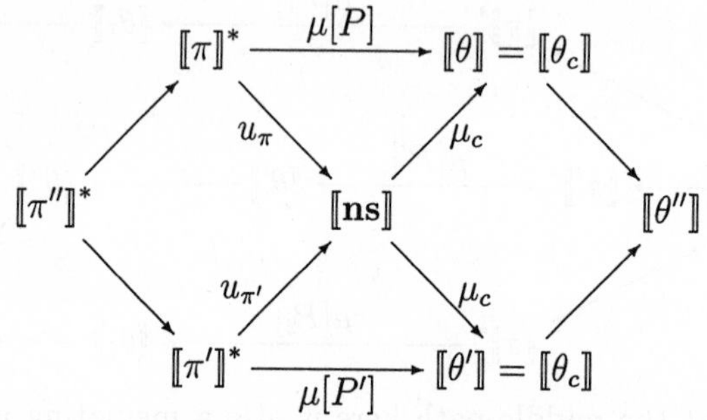

commute, the left diamond commutes since $[\![\mathbf{ns}]\!]$ is terminal, and the right diamond commutes trivially.

(6) If p is an application $p_1\, p_2$, then the main steps of P and P' must be

$$\frac{\pi \vdash p_1 : \theta_1 \to \theta \qquad \pi \vdash p_2 : \theta_1}{\pi \vdash p_1\, p_2 : \theta} \qquad \text{and} \qquad \frac{\pi' \vdash p_1 : \theta'_1 \to \theta' \qquad \pi' \vdash p_2 : \theta'_1}{\pi' \vdash p_1\, p_2 : \theta'}$$

with $\mu[P] = \langle \mu[P_1], \mu[P_2] \rangle \;;\, \mathsf{ap}$ and $\mu[P'] = \langle \mu[P'_1], \mu[P'_2] \rangle \;;\, \mathsf{ap}'$. Since both $\theta_1 \to \theta$ and $\theta'_1 \to \theta'$ are subtypes of $(\theta_1 \,\&\, \theta'_1) \to \theta''$, the application of the induction hypothesis to P_1 and P'_1 shows that

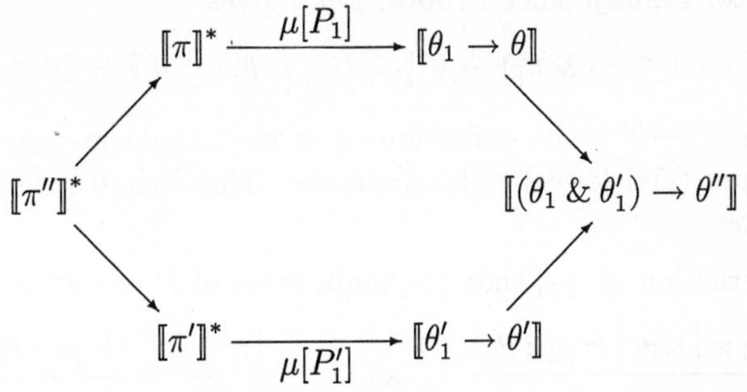

(1)

commutes. On the other hand, since θ_1 and θ'_1 are both subtypes of $\theta_1 \sqcup \theta'_1$, the application of the induction hypothesis to P_2 and P'_2 shows that the perimeter of

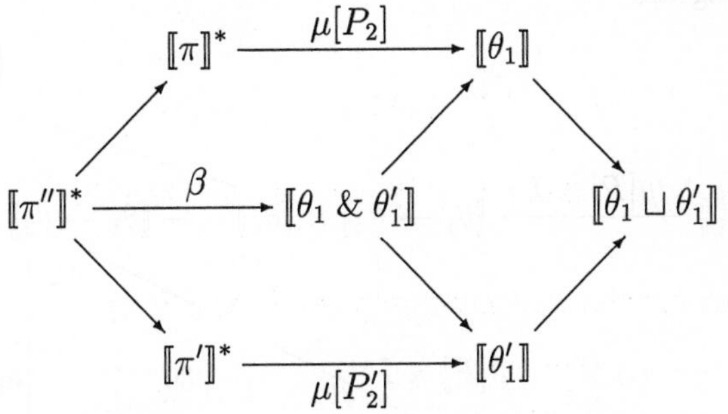

(2)

commutes, so that the definition of intersection as a pullback establishes that there is a unique morphism β making the two parallelograms commute. Now consider the diagram

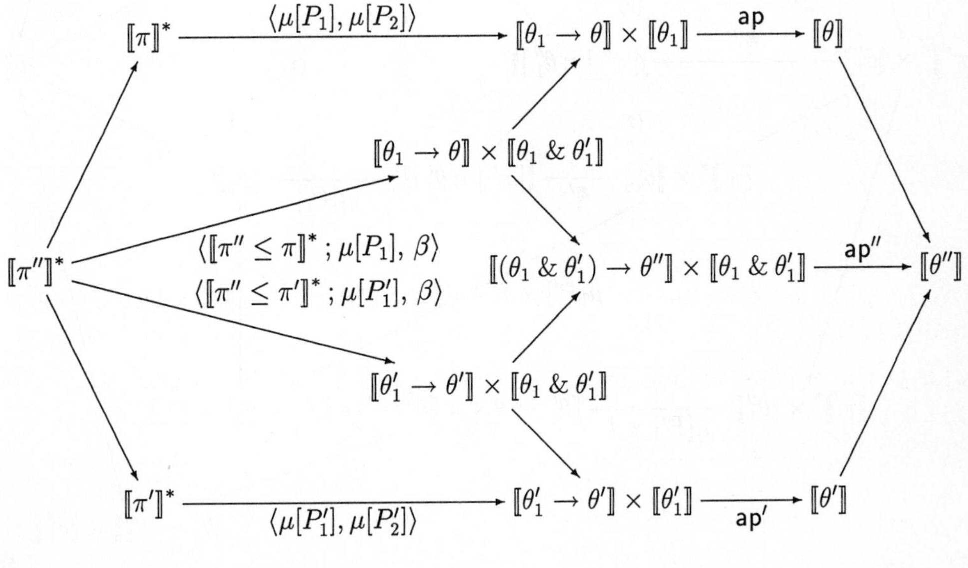

From the commutativity of Diagram 1 and elementary properties of products, the central quadrilateral commutes. From the commutativity of the parallelograms in Diagram 2 and elementary properties of products, the quadrilaterals at the upper and lower left commute. Finally, since Proposition 3 gives

$$[\![\theta_1 \to \theta \leq (\theta_1 \,\&\, \theta_1') \to \theta'']\!] = [\![(\theta_1 \,\&\, \theta_1') \leq \theta_1]\!] \Rightarrow [\![\theta \leq \theta'']\!]$$

(and similarly for $\theta_1' \to \theta'$), the definition of $\Rightarrow$ on morphisms implies that the pentagons at the upper (and lower) right commute. The desired result follows from the semantic equations.

(7) If p is an abstraction $\lambda\iota.\, p_1$, then the main steps of P and P' must be

$$\frac{[\,\pi \mid \iota{:}\,\theta_1\,] \vdash p_1 : \theta_2}{\pi \vdash \lambda\iota.\, p_1 : \theta_1 \to \theta_2} \quad \text{and} \quad \frac{[\,\pi' \mid \iota{:}\,\theta_1'\,] \vdash p_1 : \theta_2'}{\pi' \vdash \lambda\iota.\, p_1 : \theta_1' \to \theta_2'}$$

with $\mu[P] = \mathsf{ab}(\P\,; \mu[P_1])$ and $\mu[P'] = \mathsf{ab}(\P'\,; \mu[P_1'])$. Let $\theta_1'' = \theta_1 \,\&\, \theta_1'$ and $\theta_2'' = \theta_2 \sqcup \theta_2'$, and consider the diagram

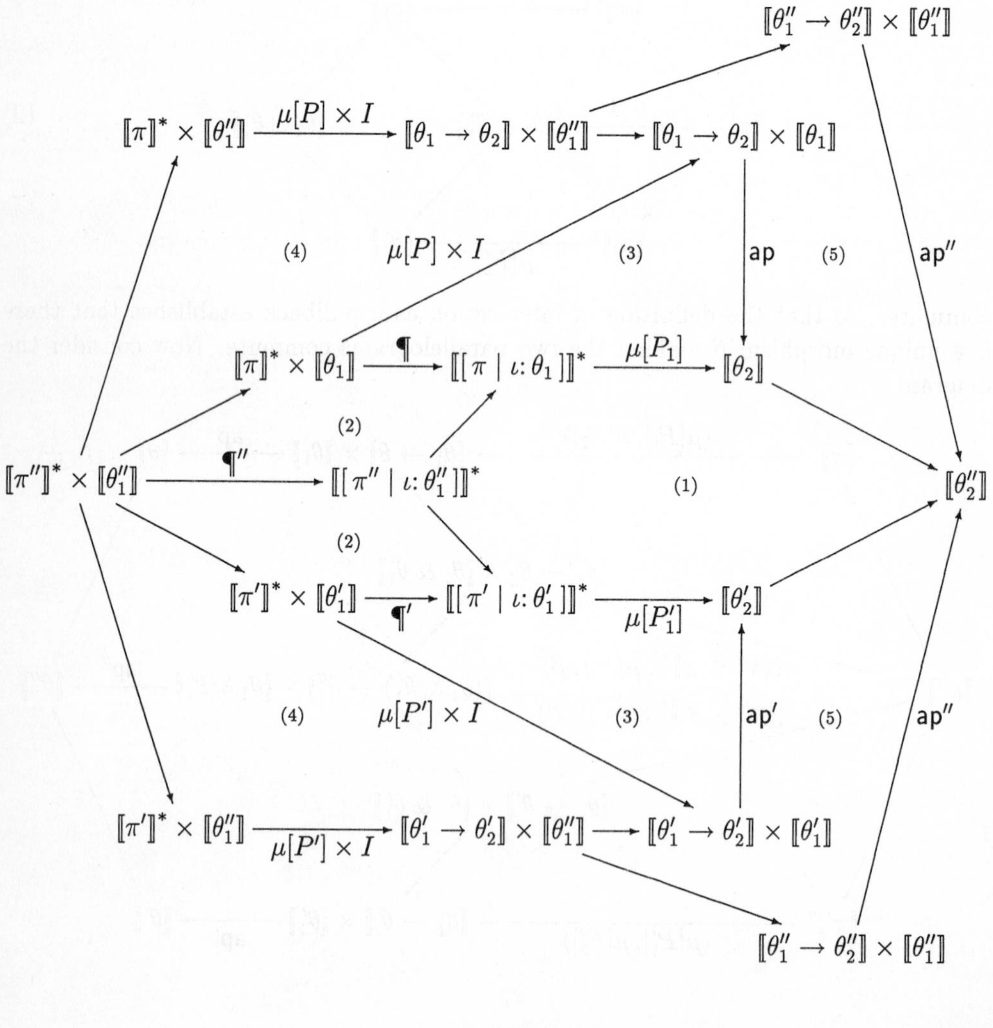

The commutativity of (1) is established by the induction hypothesis, that of (2) by the definition of ¶ and properties of products, that of (3) by the semantic equation and the property of Cartesian closure, that of (4) by properties of products, and that of (5) by Proposition 3 and the definition of $\Rightarrow$ on morphisms.

From the commutativity of the perimeter, using properties of products again, we get

$$\left((\llbracket \pi'' \leq \pi \rrbracket^* \,;\, \mu[P] \,;\, \llbracket \theta_1 \to \theta_2 \leq \theta_1'' \to \theta_2'' \rrbracket) \times I_{\llbracket \theta_1'' \rrbracket}\right) ; \mathsf{ap}'' =$$

$$\left((\llbracket \pi'' \leq \pi' \rrbracket^* \,;\, \mu[P'] \,;\, \llbracket \theta_1' \to \theta_2' \leq \theta_1'' \to \theta_2'' \rrbracket) \times I_{\llbracket \theta_1'' \rrbracket}\right) ; \mathsf{ap}'' .$$

Then the uniqueness of abstraction morphisms establishes the commutativity of the inner hexagon in

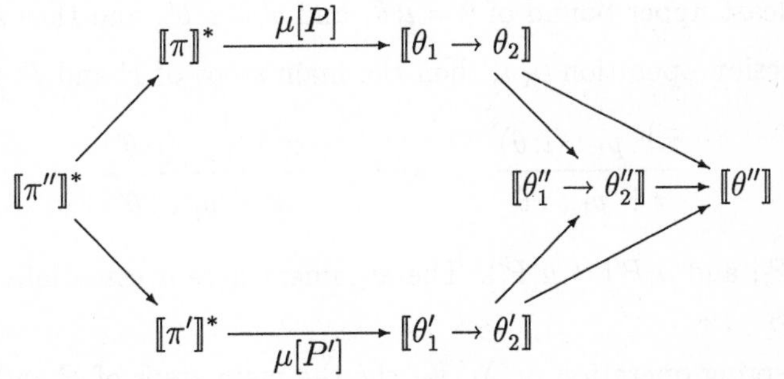

The rest of the diagram is justified by the fact that $\theta_1'' \to \theta_2'' = (\theta_1 \mathbin{\&} \theta_1') \to (\theta_2 \sqcup \theta_2')$ is a least upper bound of $\theta = \theta_1 \to \theta_2$ and $\theta' = \theta_1' \to \theta_2'$, and thus a subtype of θ''.

(8) If p is an object constructor $\iota \equiv p_1$, then the main steps of P and P' must be

$$\frac{\pi \vdash p_1 : \theta_1}{\pi \vdash (\iota \equiv p_1) : (\iota \colon \theta_1)} \quad \text{and} \quad \frac{\pi' \vdash p_1 : \theta_1'}{\pi' \vdash (\iota \equiv p_1) : (\iota \colon \theta_1')}$$

with $\mu[P] = \mu[P_1]$ and $\mu[P'] = \mu[P_1']$. The induction hypothesis gives the commutativity of

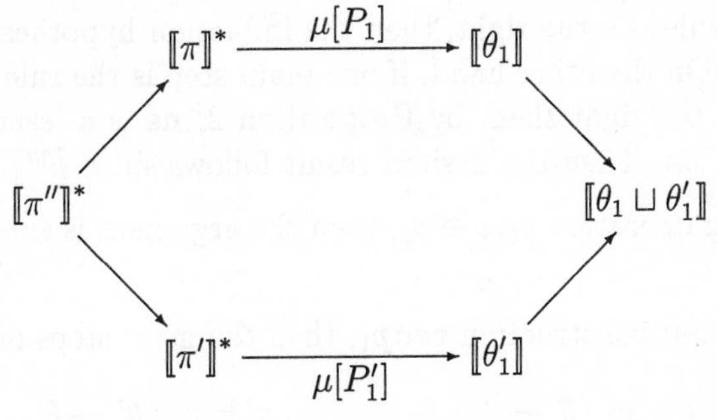

so that, by the semantic equation and Proposition 3,

$$\begin{array}{ccccc} & [\![\pi]\!]^* & \xrightarrow{\mu[P]} & [\![\iota:\theta_1]\!] & \\ \nearrow & & & & \searrow \\ [\![\pi'']\!]^* & & & & [\![\iota:(\theta_1 \sqcup \theta'_1)]\!] \\ \searrow & & & & \nearrow \\ & [\![\pi']\!]^* & \xrightarrow[\mu[P']]{} & [\![\iota:\theta'_1]\!] & \end{array}$$

commutes. Then, as in the previous case, the desired result follows from the fact that $\iota\colon(\theta_1 \sqcup \theta'_1)$ is a least upper bound of $\theta = \iota\colon\theta_1$ and $\theta' = \iota\colon\theta'_1$, and thus a subtype of θ''.

(9) If p is a selection operation $p_1.\iota$, then the main steps of P and P' must be

$$\frac{\pi \vdash p_1 : (\iota\colon\theta)}{\pi \vdash p_1.\iota : \theta} \qquad \text{and} \qquad \frac{\pi' \vdash p_1 : (\iota\colon\theta')}{\pi' \vdash p_1.\iota : \theta'}$$

with $\mu[P] = \mu[P_1]$ and $\mu[P'] = \mu[P'_1]$. The argument here is essentially the same as in the previous case.

(10) If p is a merging operation $p_1, \lambda\iota.\, p_2$, the the main steps of P and P' must be

$$\frac{\pi \vdash \lambda\iota.\, p_2 : \theta_1 \to \theta_2}{\pi \vdash (p_1, \lambda\iota.\, p_2) : \theta_1 \to \theta_2} \qquad \text{or} \qquad \frac{\pi \vdash p_1 : \theta}{\pi \vdash (p_1, \lambda\iota.\, p_2) : \theta} \qquad \begin{array}{l}\text{when } \theta \text{ is a primitive} \\ \text{type or has the form } \iota\colon\theta_1\end{array}$$

and

$$\frac{\pi' \vdash \lambda\iota.\, p_2 : \theta'_1 \to \theta'_2}{\pi' \vdash (p_1, \lambda\iota.\, p_2) : \theta'_1 \to \theta'_2} \qquad \text{or} \qquad \frac{\pi' \vdash p_1 : \theta'}{\pi' \vdash (p_1, \lambda\iota.\, p_2) : \theta'} \qquad \begin{array}{l}\text{when } \theta' \text{ is a primitive} \\ \text{type or has the form } \iota\colon\theta'_1\end{array}$$

with $\mu[P] = \mu[P_1]$ and $\mu[P'] = \mu[P'_1]$. If the main steps of P and P' are both rules on the left or both rules on the right, then the induction hypothesis gives the desired result immediately. On the other hand, if one main step is the rule on the left and the other is the rule on the right then, by Proposition 2, **ns** is a least upper bound of θ and θ', so that $\theta'' \simeq \mathbf{ns}$. Then the desired result follows since $[\![\theta'']\!]$ is terminal.

(11) If p is a merging operation $p_1, \iota \equiv p_2$, then the argument is similar to the previous case.

(12) If p is a fixed-point construction $\mathbf{rec}\, p_1$, then the main steps of P and P' must be

$$\frac{\pi \vdash p_1 : \theta \to \theta}{\pi \vdash \mathbf{rec}\, p_1 : \theta} \qquad \text{and} \qquad \frac{\pi' \vdash p_1 : \theta' \to \theta'}{\pi' \vdash \mathbf{rec}\, p_1 : \theta'}$$

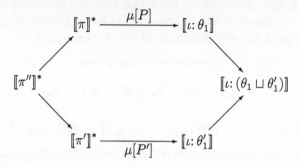

with $\mu[P] = \mu[P_1] ; \mathsf{Y}_{[\![\theta]\!]}$ and $\mu[P'] = \mu[P_1'] ; \mathsf{Y}_{[\![\theta']\!]}$. Since $[\![\theta \mathbin{\&} \theta']\!]$ is a pullback of $[\![\theta]\!]$, $[\![\theta']\!]$, and $[\![\theta \sqcup \theta']\!]$, and since by the induction hypothesis

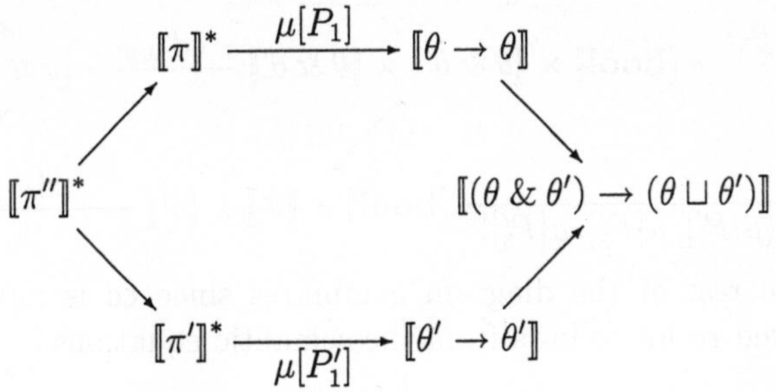

commutes, the condition satisfied by the Y_k implies the commutativity of

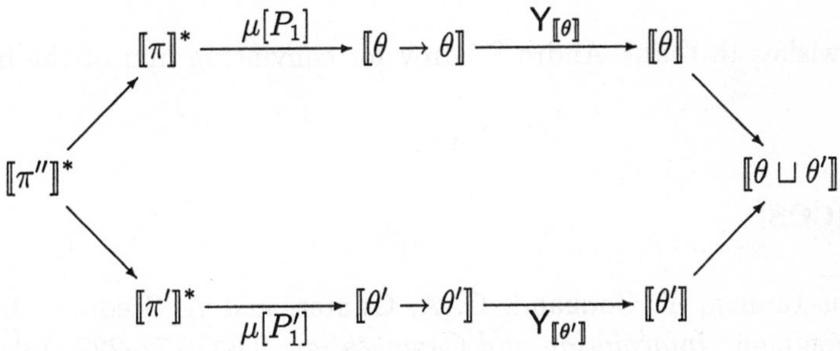

Then the desired result follows from the semantic equations and $\theta \sqcup \theta' \leq \theta''$.

(13) If p is a conditional construction **if** p_1 **then** p_2 **else** p_3, then the main steps of P and P' must be

$$\frac{\pi \vdash p_1 : \mathbf{bool} \qquad \pi \vdash p_2 : \theta \qquad \pi \vdash p_3 : \theta}{\pi \vdash \mathbf{if}\, p_1 \,\mathbf{then}\, p_2 \,\mathbf{else}\, p_3 : \theta} \qquad \frac{\pi' \vdash p_1 : \mathbf{bool} \qquad \pi' \vdash p_2 : \theta' \qquad \pi' \vdash p_3 : \theta'}{\pi' \vdash \mathbf{if}\, p_1 \,\mathbf{then}\, p_2 \,\mathbf{else}\, p_3 : \theta'}$$

with $\mu[P] = \langle \mu[P_1], \mu[P_2], \mu[P_3] \rangle ; \mathsf{cd}_\theta$ and $\mu[P'] = \langle \mu[P_1'], \mu[P_2'], \mu[P_3'] \rangle ; \mathsf{cd}_{\theta'}$. By the induction hypothesis for each of the three premisses, the perimeters of

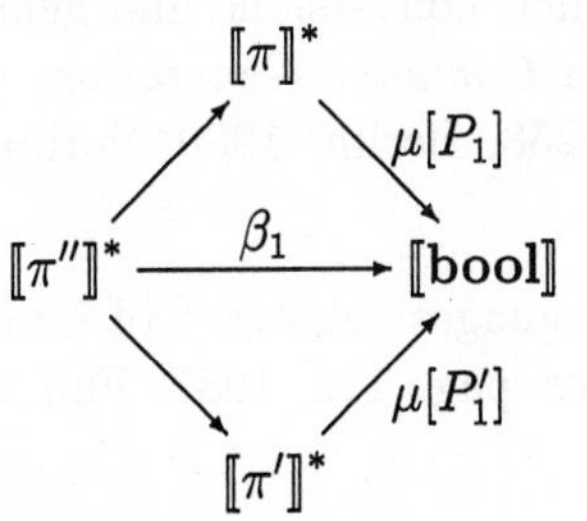

and

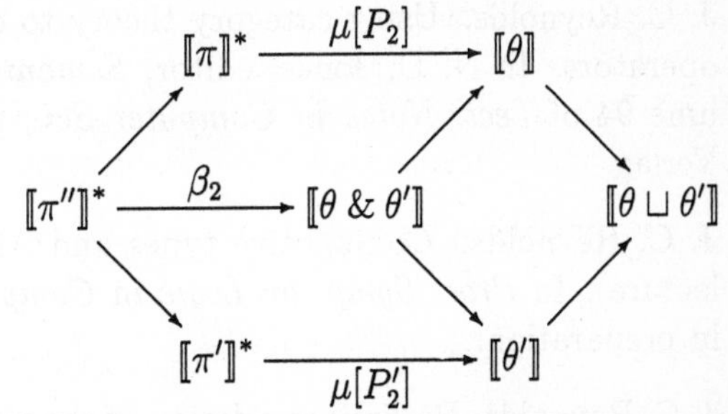

and a similar diagram for P_3 and P_3' must commute. Thus, trivially in the first case and by the definition of $\theta \& \theta'$ as a pullback in the remaining cases, there are morphisms β_1, β_2, and β_3 that make the interior triangles and parallelograms commute. Then the lefthand parallelograms in

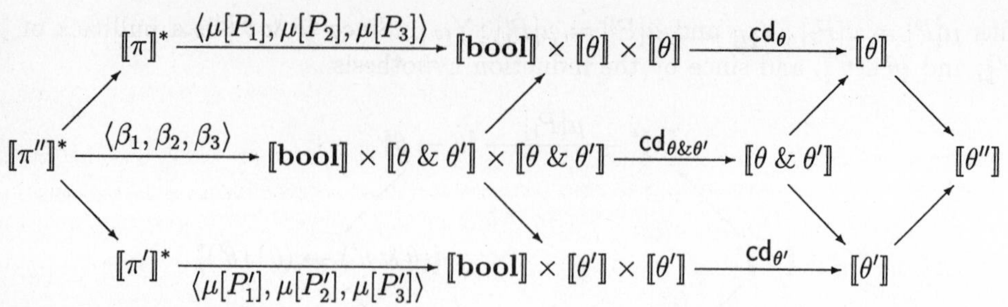

commute, and the rest of the diagram commutes since cd is natural and $[\![-]\!]$ is a functor. The desired result follows from the semantic equations. *(End of Proof)*

Acknowledgement

The author wishes to thank Andre Scedrov for convincing him of the importance of coherence.

References

[1] V. Breazu-Tannen, T. Coquand, C. A. Gunter, and A. Scedrov. Inheritance as implicit coercion. *Information and Computation*, 93(1):172–222, July 1991.

[2] M. Coppo, M. Dezani-Ciancaglini, and B. Venneri. Functional characters of solvable terms. *Z. Math. Logik Grundlagen Math.*, 27:45–58, 1981.

[3] F. J. Oles. *A Category-Theoretic Approach to the Semantics of Programming Languages.* Ph. D. dissertation, Syracuse University, August 1982.

[4] F. J. Oles. Type algebras, functor categories, and block structure. In M. Nivat and J. C. Reynolds, editors, *Algebraic Methods in Semantics*, pages 543–573. Cambridge Univ. Press, Cambridge, England, 1985.

[5] J. C. Reynolds. Using category theory to design implicit conversions and generic operators. In N. D. Jones, editor, *Semantics-Directed Compiler Generation*, volume 94 of *Lect. Notes in Computer Sci.*, pages 211–258, Berlin, 1980. Springer-Verlag.

[6] J. C. Reynolds. Conjunctive types and Algol-like languages (abstract of invited lecture). In *Proc. Symp. on Logic in Computer Science*, page 119, 1987. Full text in preparation.

[7] J. C. Reynolds. Preliminary design of the programming language Forsythe. Report CMU-CS-88-159, Carnegie Mellon University, June 21, 1988.

[8] M. Wand. Type inference for record concatenation and multiple inheritance. In *Proc. Fourth Annual Symp. on Logic in Computer Science*, pages 92–97, 1989.

A Conditionals in Forsythe

To complete the definition of Forsythe and show that it is coherent, we would have to specify the categories $\mathcal{K}$ and $\mathcal{S}$, the morphism families Y_k and cd_θ, and the meaning of various constants, and demonstrate that these entities satisfy the assumptions stated in this paper. For the most part, such a development is beyond the scope of our presentation. In this appendix, however, we consider one aspect that is closely related to the rest of the paper and does not involve the details of functor-category semantics.

In Forsythe, the conditional construction is first defined for primitive types and then defined by induction for all types. Here we show that if the initial definition for primitives is a natural transformation then the inductively defined extension is a natural transformation.

Let B be the functor from the preordered set of types to $\mathcal{K}$ such that $B(-) = [\![\mathbf{bool}]\!] \times (-) \times (-)$, and assume that cd is a natural transformation from $B[\![J(-)]\!]$ to $[\![J(-)]\!]$, where J is the injection from primitive types to types. Then we extend $\mathsf{cd}_\theta \in B[\![\theta]\!] \rightarrow [\![\theta]\!]$ to all types θ as follows:

- $\mathsf{cd}_{\theta_1 \rightarrow \theta_2} = \mathsf{ab}\Big(\Psi_{[\![\theta_1 \rightarrow \theta_2]\!],[\![\theta_1]\!]}\,;\, B(\mathsf{ap})\,;\, \mathsf{cd}_{\theta_2}\Big)$,

where $\Psi_{k,k'}$ is the evident morphism from the product $([\![\mathbf{bool}]\!] \times k \times k) \times k'$ to the product $[\![\mathbf{bool}]\!] \times (k \times k') \times (k \times k')$ that "duplicates its second argument".

- $\mathsf{cd}_{\iota:\theta} = \mathsf{cd}_\theta$.
- $\mathsf{cd}_{\mathbf{ns}}$ is the unique morphism from $B[\![\mathbf{ns}]\!]$ to $[\![\mathbf{ns}]\!]$.
- $\mathsf{cd}_{\theta_1 \& \theta_2}$ is the unique morphism into the pullback:

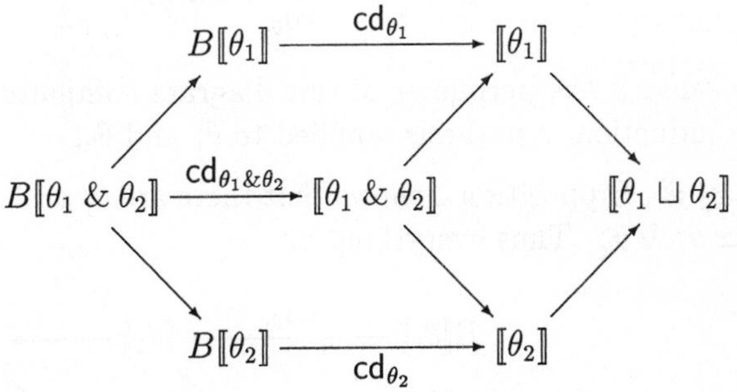

The final case of the definition only makes sense if the perimeter of the diagram commutes, but the following proposition will establish that this condition is always met.

Proposition 5 *Suppose $\hat{\theta}$ is a lower bound, and θ'' is an upper bound, of θ and θ'. Then*

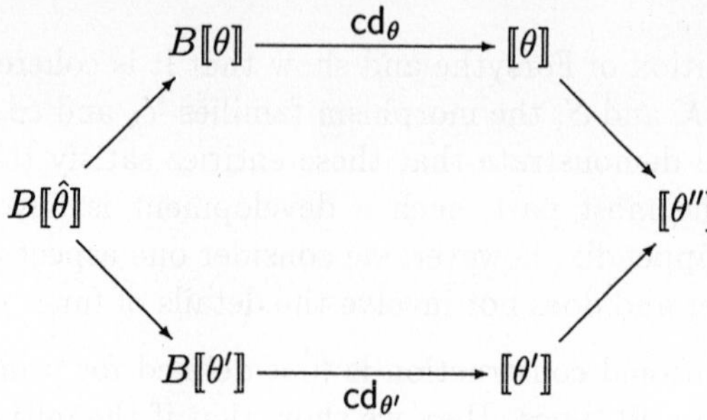

commutes in $\mathcal{K}$.

Notice that this proposition, in the special case where $\hat{\theta} = \theta \leq \theta' = \theta''$, implies the naturality of cd.

Proof: The proof is by induction on the sum of the sizes of the types θ and θ'.

(1a) If $\theta = \mathbf{ns}$ then $\theta'' \simeq \mathbf{ns}$, so that $[\![\theta'']\!]$ is terminal, and the hexagon commutes.

(1b) If $\theta' = \mathbf{ns}$ then an argument symmetric to (1a) applies.

(2a) If $\theta = \theta_1 \mathbin{\&} \theta_2$ then cd_θ is the unique mediating morphism into the pullback:

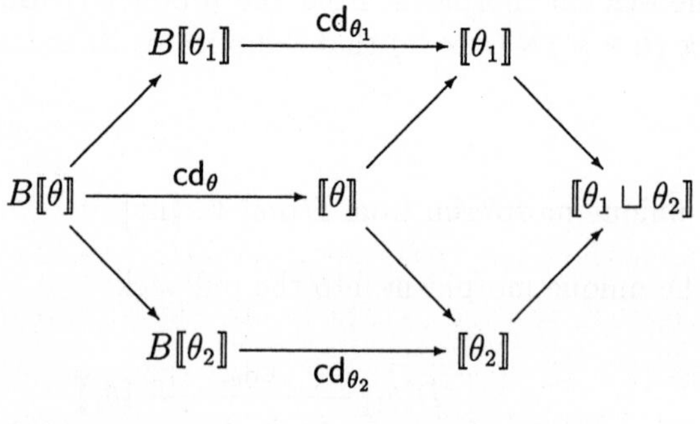

This only makes sense if the perimeter of this diagram commutes, but this condition is insured by the induction hypothesis, applied to θ_1 and θ_2.

Since $\theta = \theta_1 \mathbin{\&} \theta_2 \leq \theta''$, Proposition 1 shows that there are θ_1'' and θ_2'' such that $\theta_1 \leq \theta_1''$, $\theta_2 \leq \theta_2''$, and $\theta'' \simeq \theta_1'' \mathbin{\&} \theta_2''$. Thus everything in

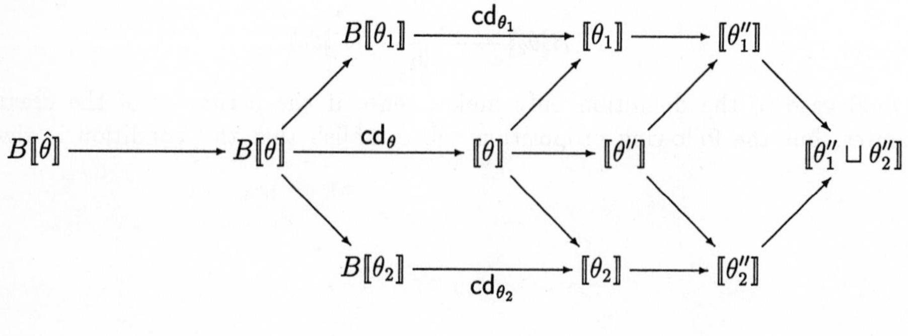

commutes, and $[\![\theta'']\!]$ is a pullback of $[\![\theta_1'']\!]$, $[\![\theta_2'']\!]$, and $[\![\theta_1'' \sqcup \theta_2'']\!]$.

It follows that the outside paths in

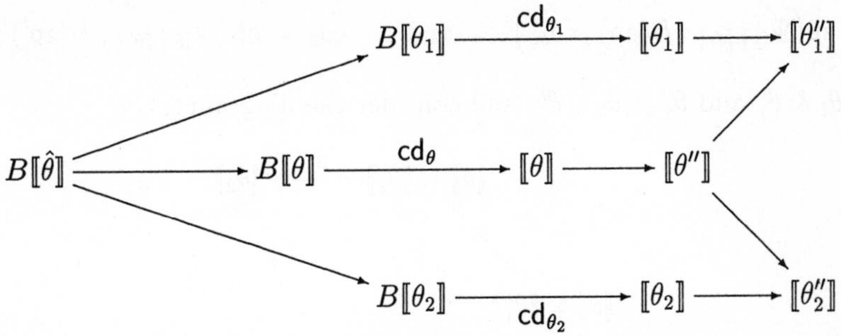

are a cone for this pullback and, since the inner polygons commute, the middle path is a mediating morphism. But, by two applications of the induction hypothesis, to θ_1 and θ' and to θ_2 and θ' respectively, the inner polygons in

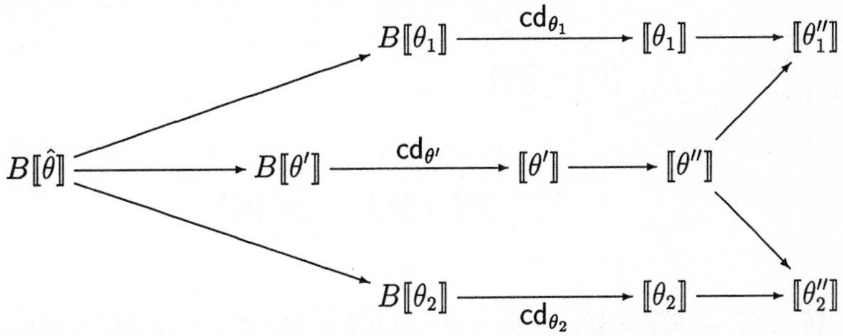

also commute, so that the middle path here is also a mediating morphism. Then the equality of the mediating morphisms gives the desired result.

(2b) If $\theta' = \theta_1 \;\&\; \theta_2$ then an argument symmetric to (2a) applies.

(3) In the remaining cases, Proposition 2 shows that **ns** is a least upper bound of θ and θ' unless θ and θ' are both primitive types and have a primitive least upper bound, or both procedural types, or both object types with the same field name. But when **ns** is a least upper bound, $[\![\theta'']\!]$ must be terminal.

(4) If $\theta = \rho$ and $\theta' = \rho'$ are primitive types with a least upper bound, then the naturality of cd for primitive types gives the commutativity of

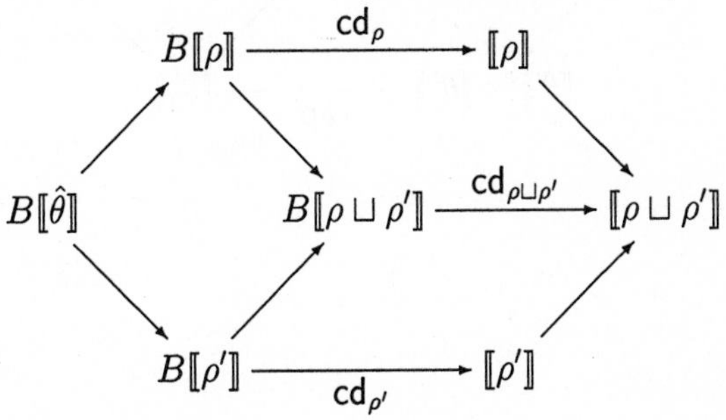

and the desired result follows since $\rho \sqcup \rho' = \theta \sqcup \theta' \le \theta''$.

(5) If $\theta = \theta_1 \to \theta_2$ and $\theta' = \theta'_1 \to \theta'_2$ then

$$\mathsf{cd}_\theta = \mathsf{ab}\Big(\Psi_{[\![\theta]\!],[\![\theta_1]\!]} \,;\, B(\mathsf{ap}) \,;\, \mathsf{cd}_{\theta_2}\Big) \qquad \text{and} \qquad \mathsf{cd}_{\theta'} = \mathsf{ab}\Big(\Psi_{[\![\theta']\!],[\![\theta'_1]\!]} \,;\, B(\mathsf{ap}') \,;\, \mathsf{cd}_{\theta'_2}\Big)\,.$$

Let $\theta''_1 = \theta_1 \mathbin{\&} \theta'_1$ and $\theta''_2 = \theta_2 \sqcup \theta'_2$, and consider the diagram

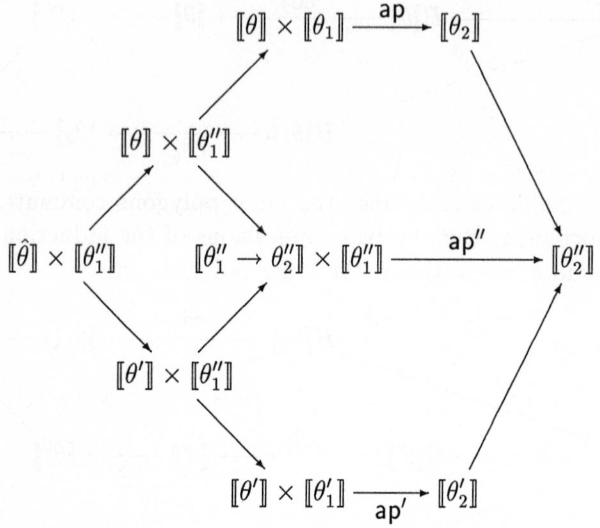

Since

$$[\![\theta \le \theta''_1 \to \theta''_2]\!] = [\![\theta_1 \to \theta_2 \le \theta''_1 \to \theta''_2]\!] = [\![\theta''_1 \le \theta_1]\!] \Rightarrow [\![\theta_2 \le \theta''_2]\!]\,,$$

(and similarly for θ'), the definition of $\Rightarrow$ on morphisms implies that the upper (and lower) pentagons commute. Thus the perimeter commutes, and by the definition of $\theta_2 \mathbin{\&} \theta'_2$ as a pullback, there is a unique mediating morphism β that makes the two parallelograms in

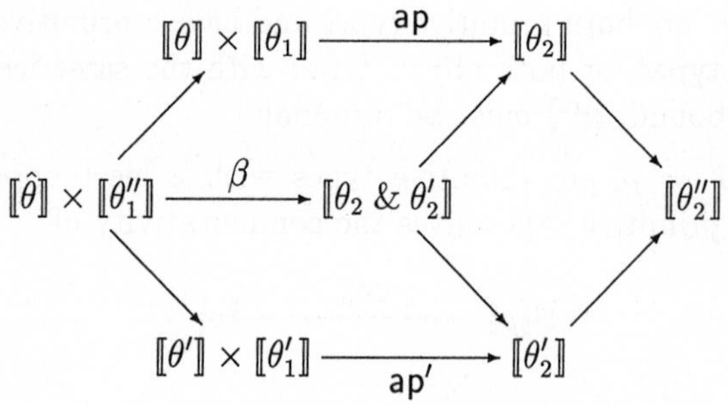

commute. Now consider the diagram

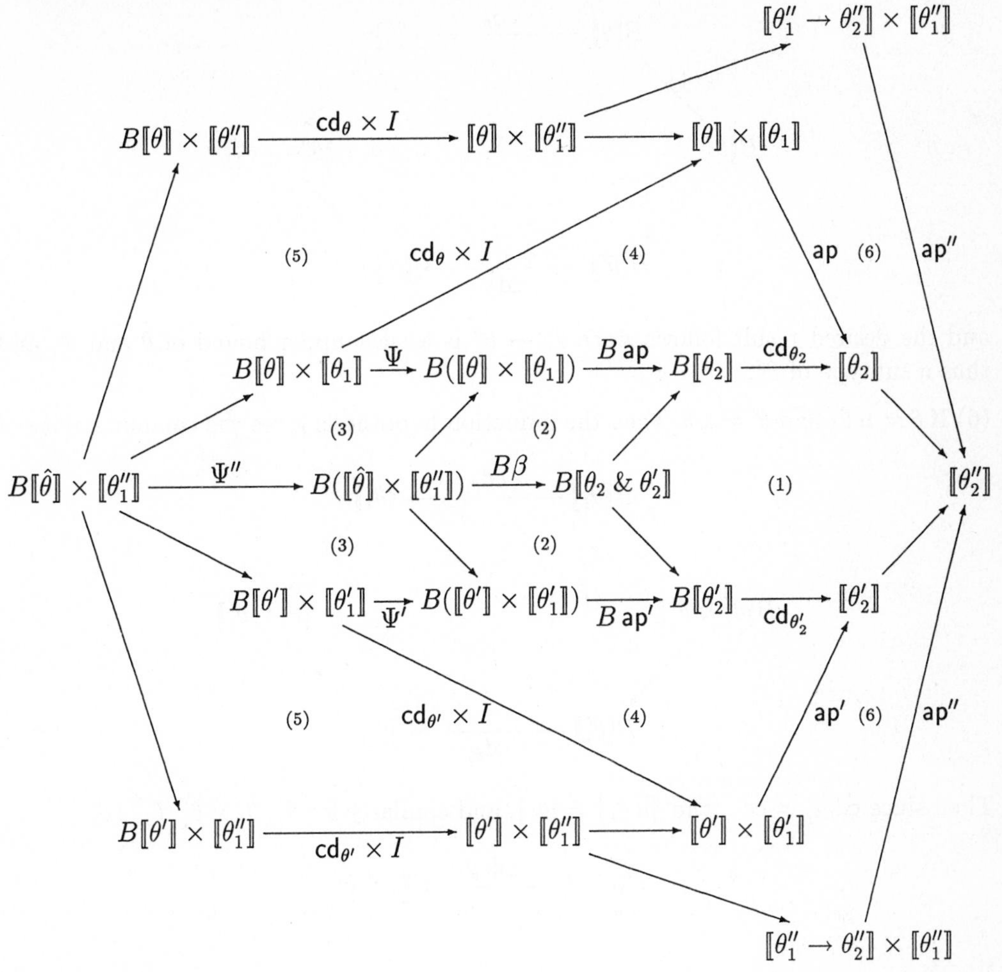

The commutativity of (1) is established by the induction hypothesis, that of (2) by applying B to the previous diagram, that of (3) by properties of products that insure that Ψ is natural, that of (4) by the definition of cd_θ and the property of Cartesian closure, that of (5) by properties of products, and that of (6) by Proposition 3 and the definition of $\Rightarrow$ on morphisms.

From the commutivity of the perimeter, using properties of products again, we get

$$\Big((B[\![\hat{\theta} \leq \theta]\!] \,;\, \mathsf{cd}_\theta \,;\, [\![\theta \leq \theta_1'' \rightarrow \theta_2'']\!]) \times I_{[\![\theta_1'']\!]}\Big) \,;\, \mathsf{ap}'' =$$

$$\Big((B[\![\hat{\theta} \leq \theta']\!] \,;\, \mathsf{cd}_{\theta'} \,;\, [\![\theta' \leq \theta_1'' \rightarrow \theta_2'']\!]) \times I_{[\![\theta_1'']\!]}\Big) \,;\, \mathsf{ap}'' \,.$$

Then the uniqueness of abstraction morphisms establishes the commutativity of

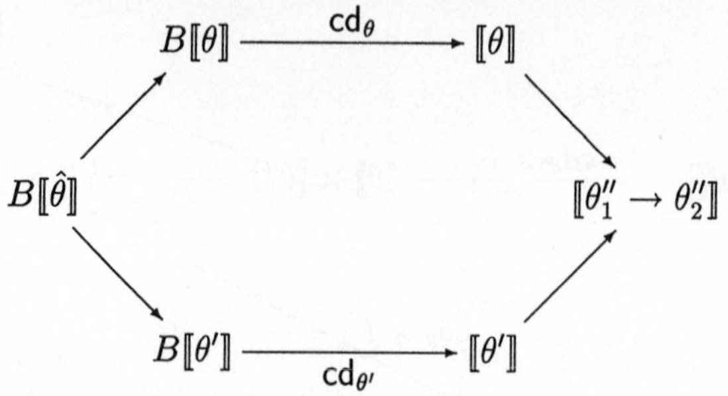

and the desired result follows since $\theta''_1 \rightarrow \theta''_2$ is a least upper bound of θ and θ', and thus a subtype of θ''.

(6) If $\theta = \iota\colon \theta_1$ and $\theta' = \iota\colon \theta'_1$ then the induction hypothesis gives the commutativity of

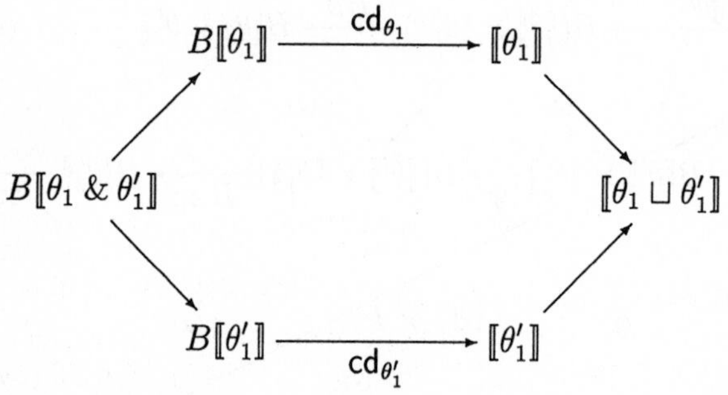

Then since $\mathsf{cd}_{\iota:\theta_1} = \mathsf{cd}_{\theta_1}$ and $[\![\iota\colon \theta_1]\!] = [\![\theta_1]\!]$, and similarly for θ'_1, $\theta_1 \,\&\, \theta'_1$, $\theta_1 \sqcup \theta'_1$,

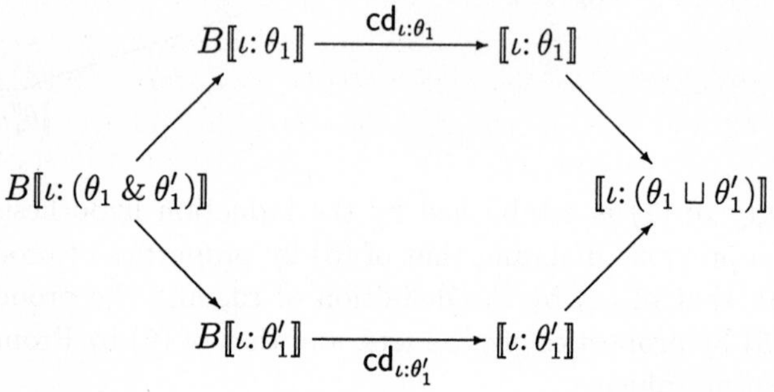

commutes. The desired result follows since $\hat{\theta} \leq \iota\colon \theta_1 \& \iota\colon \theta'_1 \leq \iota\colon (\theta_1 \& \theta'_1)$ and $\iota\colon (\theta_1 \sqcup \theta'_1) \simeq \iota\colon \theta_1 \sqcup \iota\colon \theta'_1 \leq \theta''$.

(End of Proof)

Singleton, Union and Intersection Types for Program Extraction

Susumu Hayashi *
Department of Applied Mathematics and Informatics
Ryukoku University
Seta, Ohtsu, Shiga, Japan
hayashi@whale.ryukoku.ac.jp

In memory of my mother, Yoshie Hayashi

Abstract

Two type theories, ATT and ATTT, are introduced. ATT is an impredicative type theory closely related to the polymorphic type theory of implicit typing of MacQueen et al. [MPS86]. ATTT is another version of ATT that extends the Girard-Reynolds second order lambda calculus. ATT has notions of intersection, union and singleton types. ATTT has a notion of refinement types as in the type system for ML by Freeman and Pfenning [FP91], plus intersection and union of refinement types and singleton refinement types. We will show how singleton, union and intersection types serve for development of programs without unnecessary codes via a variant of the Curry-Howard isomorphism. More exactly, they give a way to write types as specifications of programs without unnecessary codes which is inevitable in the usual Curry-Howard isomorphism.

1 Introduction

We introduce two constructive type theories: ATT (A Type Theory) and ATTT (ATT more Typed). ATT is an impredicative type theory closely related to the polymorphic type theory of implicit typing in [MPS86]. It is designed to develop programs without unnecessary codes via the Curry-Howard isomorphism. Constructive type theories are known as a basis for program development via constructive logic. But, when they were applied to the practice of formal program development of programs, they proved inadequate in practice. One defect of type theories is that developed programs *must*

*Partly supported by Grant No. 02249209 of the Japanese Ministry of Education.

often include unnecessary codes for computation (see [HN88, Hay90]). This comes from the identification of proofs and programs. Our main aim here is to remedy this defect by introducing singleton, union and intersection types. Union and intersection types hide entities from the scene and singleton type exposes them. By these, we can exclude purely logical parts of proofs from extracted programs.

We will introduce another type theory ATTT (A triple tee) as well. ATTT is a system based on the idea of "refinement" of types. ATTT is a conservative extension of the Girard-Reynolds second order lambda calculus, which we will refer as $\lambda 2$. Thus it can be used to develop typed programs in $\lambda 2$. Program extraction in ATTT is related to

The aim of this paper is to introduce ATT and ATTT and establish their fundamental mathematical properties. Applications of ATT and ATTT for the practice of program extraction will appear elsewhere.

2 A type theory ATT

Before giving a formal syntax of ATT, we will give an intuitive explanation of the syntax and the intended semantics. ATT has objects, types and kinds. These three syntactic categories are roughly defined by the following grammar:

$$\begin{array}{rcl} K & ::= & \mathit{Type}. \\ A & ::= & x \mid c \mid A \rightarrow A \mid A \wedge A \mid A \vee A \mid \\ & & \bigwedge x \in K.A \mid \bigvee x \in K.A \mid \\ & & \bigwedge x \in A.A \mid \bigvee x \in A.A \mid \\ & & \{M\}_A. \\ M & ::= & x \mid c \mid \lambda x.M \mid MM. \end{array}$$

We will use another constant, *Kind*, which does not appear in this grammar. In the grammar above, M, A and K denote objects, types and kinds, respectively. As it is a second order system, ATT has only one kind *Type*. So the kind level is inessential for ATT, but we include it for coherence with GTS-style presentations of type theories [Bar90], which will be used in this paper. (Although we follow GTS-presentation as far as possible, our notations and terminologies may sometimes diverge from the ones of GTS.)

The intended semantics of ATT assumes a fixed domain D of untyped partial λ-calculus. Objects are elements of the domain. Normally, types in programming languages are interpreted as sets with common structure. Types of ATT, however, are interpreted as *arbitrary* subsets of D. In particular, the empty set is a type, as ATT is designed to achieve a kind of Curry-Howard isomorphism. The kind *Type* is the set of all subsets of D. The constant *Kind* is the singleton set of *Type*.

Now we give a rigorous formulation of ATT. Although ATT is a second order system, we have to formulate it as higher order systems like CoC [CH88], since the formation of singleton types is depends on the typing of objects. A singleton type $\{A\}_B$ is well formed only when B is a type of A.

Firstly, we define *preterms* (called pseudo terms in [Bar90]). Preterms are defined by the following grammar:

$$\begin{aligned} T \ ::= \ & x \mid c \mid \lambda x.T \mid TT \mid \\ & T \to T \mid T \wedge T \mid T \vee T \mid \\ & \bigwedge x \in T.T \mid \bigvee x \in T.T \mid \\ & \{T\}_T. \end{aligned}$$

Here, c and x stand for constants and variables, respectively. For program development, we have to extend this grammar by adding some basic types such as the type of natural numbers. To this end, we keep the definition of constants open. But we assume that at least *Type* and *Kind* are constants. These two constants are called *sorts*. In the following, s stands for a sort.

The symbols $\lambda, \bigwedge, \bigvee$ are "quantifiers," so that occurrences of the variables x in T_1 of $\lambda x.T_1, \bigwedge x \in T_0.T_1, \bigvee x \in T_0.T_1$ are bound by these quantifiers. The notion of bound occurrences and free occurrences are defined as usual. The set of free variables of a preterm T will be written $FV(T)$. The operation of α-conversion is defined as usual and we will identify two α-convertible preterms. Substitution of preterms is defined as usual. When a preterm B is substituted for a variable x in a preterm A, we denote the resulting preterm by $A[x:=B]$.

The reduction and conversion of preterms are defined as usual by β-reduction. When B is obtained form from A by successive β-reductions, we will write $A \twoheadrightarrow_\beta B$. When A and B are convertible, we will write $A =_\beta B$.

A *Judgment* of ATT is of the form $A \in B$, where A and B are preterms. A *Context* is a sequence of judgements of the form $x \in A$, where x is a variable. We will denote a context by Γ. A *Sequent* (hypothetical judgement) of ATT is the form $\Gamma \vdash J$, where J is a judgment. Let Γ be $x_1 \in A_1, \ldots, x_n \in A_n$. Then $\Gamma[x:=B]$ is $x_1 \in A_1[x:=B], \ldots, x_n \in A_n[x:=B]$. Similarly, if J is the judgment $A \in B$, then $J[x:=C]$ is $A[x:=C] \in B[x:=C]$.

A *legal sequent* of ATT is a sequent derivable by the following axiom and inference rules:

Axiom

$$\langle\,\rangle \vdash \mathit{Type} \in \mathit{Kind}$$

Start rule

$$\frac{\Gamma \vdash A \in s}{\Gamma, x \in A \vdash x \in A}$$

where x is Γ-fresh, i.e., x is not declared in Γ.

Weakening rule

$$\frac{\Gamma \vdash A \in B \quad \Gamma \vdash C \in s}{\Gamma, x \in C \vdash A \in B}$$

where x is Γ-fresh.

Conversion rule

$$\frac{\Gamma \vdash A \in B \quad \Gamma \vdash B' \in s \quad B =_\beta B'}{\Gamma \vdash A \in B'}$$

Subject reduction

$$\frac{\Gamma \vdash A \in B \quad A \twoheadrightarrow_\beta A'}{\Gamma \vdash A' \in B}$$

Rules for function space

$\rightarrow$-formation

$$\frac{\Gamma \vdash A \in \mathit{Type} \quad \Gamma \vdash B \in \mathit{Type}}{\Gamma \vdash (A \rightarrow B) \in \mathit{Type}}$$

$\rightarrow$-introduction

$$\frac{\Gamma \vdash A \in \mathit{Type} \quad \Gamma \vdash B \in \mathit{Type} \quad \Gamma, x \in A \vdash C \in B}{\Gamma \vdash (\lambda x.C) \in (A \rightarrow B)}$$

$\rightarrow$-elimination

$$\frac{\Gamma \vdash F \in (A \rightarrow B) \quad \Gamma \vdash C \in A}{\Gamma \vdash (FC) \in B}$$

Rules for union

$\vee$-formation

$$\frac{\Gamma \vdash A \in \mathit{Type} \quad \Gamma \vdash B \in \mathit{Type}}{\Gamma \vdash A \vee B \in \mathit{Type}}$$

$\vee$-introduction

$$\frac{\Gamma \vdash A \in \mathit{Type} \quad \Gamma \vdash B \in \mathit{Type} \quad \Gamma \vdash C \in A}{\Gamma \vdash C \in A \vee B}$$

$$\frac{\Gamma \vdash A \in \mathit{Type} \quad \Gamma \vdash B \in \mathit{Type} \quad \Gamma \vdash C \in B}{\Gamma \vdash C \in A \vee B}$$

$\vee$-elimination

$$\frac{\Gamma \vdash C \in A \vee B \quad \Gamma, x \in A \vdash D \in E \quad \Gamma, x \in B \vdash D \in E}{\Gamma \vdash D[x := C] \in E[x := C]}$$

where E is not a sort.

$\bigvee$-formation

$$\frac{\Gamma \vdash A \in s \quad \Gamma, x \in A \vdash B \in \mathit{Type}}{\Gamma \vdash (\bigvee x \in A.B) \in \mathit{Type}}$$

$\bigvee$-introduction

$$\frac{\Gamma \vdash A \in s \quad \Gamma, x \in A \vdash B \in \mathit{Type} \quad \Gamma \vdash D \in A \quad \Gamma \vdash C \in B[x := D]}{\Gamma \vdash C \in (\bigvee x \in A.B)}$$

$\bigvee$-elimination

$$\frac{\Gamma \vdash C \in (\bigvee x \in A.B) \quad \Gamma, x \in A, y \in B \vdash D \in E}{\Gamma \vdash D[y := C] \in E[y := C]}$$

where x is not in $FV(D) \cup FV(E)$ and E is not a sort.

Rules for intersection

$\wedge$-formation

$$\frac{\Gamma \vdash A \in \mathit{Type} \quad \Gamma \vdash B \in \mathit{Type}}{\Gamma \vdash A \wedge B \in \mathit{Type}}$$

$\wedge$-introduction

$$\frac{\Gamma \vdash A \in \mathit{Type} \quad \Gamma \vdash B \in \mathit{Type} \quad \Gamma \vdash C \in A \quad \Gamma \vdash C \in B}{\Gamma \vdash C \in A \wedge B}$$

$\wedge$-elimination

$$\frac{\Gamma \vdash C \in A \wedge B}{\Gamma \vdash C \in A} \qquad \frac{\Gamma \vdash C \in A \wedge B}{\Gamma \vdash C \in B}$$

$\bigwedge$-formation

$$\frac{\Gamma \vdash A \in s \quad \Gamma, x \in A \vdash B \in \mathit{Type}}{\Gamma \vdash (\bigwedge x \in A.B) \in \mathit{Type}}$$

$\bigwedge$-introduction

$$\frac{\Gamma \vdash A \in s \quad \Gamma, x \in A \vdash B \in \mathit{Type} \quad \Gamma, x \in A \vdash C \in B}{\Gamma \vdash C \in (\bigwedge x \in A.B)}$$

where x is not in $FV(C)$.

$\bigwedge$-elimination

$$\frac{\Gamma \vdash C \in (\bigwedge x \in A.B) \quad \Gamma \vdash D \in A}{\Gamma \vdash C \in B[x := D]}$$

Rules for singleton

singleton-formation

$$\frac{\Gamma \vdash B \in \mathit{Type} \quad \Gamma \vdash A \in B}{\Gamma \vdash \{A\}_B \in \mathit{Type}}$$

singleton-introduction

$$\frac{\Gamma \vdash B \in \mathit{Type} \quad \Gamma \vdash A \in B}{\Gamma \vdash A \in \{A\}_B}$$

singleton-elimination

$$\frac{\Gamma \vdash P_1 \in \{A\}_C \wedge \{B\}_C \quad \Gamma \vdash P_2 \in D[x := A] \quad \Gamma, x \in C \vdash D \in Type}{\Gamma \vdash P_2 \in D[x := B]}$$

$$\frac{\Gamma \vdash A \in \{B\}_C}{\Gamma \vdash A \in C}$$

Here we will give some comments on the formalism. ATT has the rule of subject reduction as a basic rule. The rule is an admissible rule for many type theories like CoC. Readers may think that the rule is unnecessary. But we have not succeeded to prove the rule for ATT without the rule. Furthermore, Pierce and Freeman have observed an example which would be an counterexample for the rule in a type system closely related to ATT. We conjecture that subject reduction fails for ATT without subject reduction as a basic rule. In this paper, we do not use the rule of subject reduction at all. Hence we can survive without the rule. But it would be useful for optimization and transformation of programs. So we added it as a basic rule. But the rule is optional. All results in this paper remain true for the system without the rule of subject reduction except the definition of subtyping judgment in section 2.5.

The first elimination rule for singleton may look rather strange. We do not know if this is the *only* right formulation of singleton-elimination. But this is the best formulation we know at the time this paper is written. Later, we will define a propositional equality by means of singleton and intersection types. Then this rule will turn into the equality rule used by Turner in his type theory NTT [Tur89]. Furthermore, we have been able to derive almost all properties which we need. One which we cannot derive is the same rule but substituting B for x in P_2 of the conclusion. But this would not be a correct rule from type theoretic point of view. At least, in the presence of the stronger rule as a basic inference rule, the transformation from ATT to ibMPS presented later does not work.

2.1 Basic notions and lemmas

We will define some basic notions and prove some basic lemmas which are necessary to understand the structure of ATT.

Definition 1 If a sequent is derivable by the inference rules above, then it is called a *legal sequent*. If $\Gamma \vdash A \in B$ is a legal sequent, then Γ is called *legal context*, $A \in B$ is *legal judgment*, and A and B are *(legal) terms*. To emphasize the context Γ, we will often say "a preterm A is a term *under the context* Γ." □

Church-Rosser property of preterms can be proved by standard methods, e.g., the one in [Mar72].

Lemma 1 *If two preterms are β-convertible, then they can be reduced to a common preterm.*

The following two lemmas are proved by induction on derivations.

Lemma 2 *If $x_1 \in A_1, \ldots, x_n \in A_n \vdash J$ is a legal sequent, then (i) if $i \neq j$, then $x_i \neq x_j$, (ii) the free variables of the term A_i are a subset of $\{x_1, \ldots, x_{i-1}\}$, and (iii) the free variables of the judgment J are a subset of $\{x_1, \ldots, x_n\}$.*

Lemma 3 *Assume that $x_1 \in A_1, \ldots, x_n \in A_n \vdash B \in C$ is a legal sequent. Then B is not the sort Kind. Furthermore, for each i, A_i is not the sort Kind and one of the followings holds:*

1. *A_i is the sort Type and $x_1 \in A_1, \ldots, x_{i-1} \in A_{i-1} \vdash A_i \in Kind$ is derivable.*
2. *$x_1 \in A_1, \ldots, x_{i-1} \in A_{i-1} \vdash A_i \in Type$ is derivable.*

The following lemma ensures that substitution is legal. It is proved by induction on derivations using lemma 2.

Lemma 4 (substitution) *If $\Gamma_1, x \in A, \Gamma_2 \vdash J$ and $\Gamma_1 \vdash C \in A$ are legal sequents, then so is $\Gamma_1, \Gamma_2[x := C] \vdash J[x := C]$.*

The following lemma ensures that a generalized rule of weakening holds. It is proved by induction on derivations using lemma 3.

Lemma 5 (generalized weakening) *When a context Γ is obtained from another context Γ' by dropping some judgments in Γ', then we say that Γ' contains Γ. If $\Gamma \vdash J$ is a legal sequent and Γ' is a legal context which contains Γ, then $\Gamma' \vdash J$ is a legal sequent.*

The first part of the following lemma is a special case of lemma 4 above and the second part is easily proved by induction on derivations. The second part was called "context replacement" by Luo [Luo90].

Lemma 6 (replacement) *(i) If $\Gamma \vdash A \in B$ and $\Gamma, x \in B \vdash x \in B'$ are derivable, then $\Gamma \vdash A \in B'$ is derivable. (ii) If $\Gamma, x \in A, \Gamma' \vdash J$ and $\Gamma, x \in A' \vdash x \in A$ are derivable, then $\Gamma, x \in A', \Gamma' \vdash J$ is derivable.*

2.2 Classification of terms

Every term of ATT (except the sort *Kind*) is classified into one of object, type and kind. As ATT is a second order system, this classification can be done by purely syntactical observation. Firstly, we define object, type and kind by their shapes. Then we prove that this classification is sound, e.g., if a term A is a type, then $A \in \mathit{Type}$ is derivable. Assume a preterm A is legal under context Γ. By lemma 2, all free variables of A are declared in Γ. Let x be a free variable of A. If it is declared by $x \in \mathit{Type}$, then we call it a *type variable* of Γ. Otherwise, we call it an *object variable* of Γ. So all free variables of *any* legal term under Γ are classified into type variables and object variables. We extend this classification to legal terms.

Definition 2 (classification under a variable classification) Assume that $FV(A)$ is a union of two disjoint sets *Obj* and *Typ*. The variables of *Obj* are called object variables, and the variables of *Typ* are called type variables. Then objects, types and kinds under the classification of free variables $\langle \mathit{Obj}, \mathit{Typ} \rangle$ are defined as follows:

objects

1. An object variable is an object.
2. If A and B are objects, then so is (AB).
3. If A is an object under the classification $\langle \mathit{Obj} \cup \{x\}, \mathit{Typ} \rangle$, then $\lambda x.A$ is an object under the classification $\langle \mathit{Obj}, \mathit{Typ} \rangle$.

types

1. A type variable is a type.
2. If A and B are types, then so are $A \to B$, $A \vee B$ and $A \wedge B$.
3. If A is an object and B is a type, then $\{A\}_B$ is a type.
4. If A is a type and B is a type under the classification $\langle \mathit{Obj} \cup \{x\}, \mathit{Typ} \rangle$, then $\bigwedge x \in A.B$ and $\bigvee x \in A.B$ are types under the classification $\langle \mathit{Obj}, \mathit{Typ} \rangle$.
5. If A is a type under the classification $\langle \mathit{Obj}, \mathit{Typ} \cup \{x\} \rangle$, then $\bigwedge x \in \mathit{Type}.A$ and $\bigvee x \in \mathit{Type}.A$ are types under the classification $\langle \mathit{Obj}, \mathit{Typ} \rangle$.

kinds The constant *Type* is a kind. □

Now we classify legal terms under a context using the classification above.

Definition 3 (classification under a context) Assume a preterm A is legal under context Γ. Let *Obj* be the set of object variables of Γ, and let *Typ* be the set of type variables of Γ. If A is an object under the classification $\langle \mathit{Obj}, \mathit{Typ} \rangle$, then A is an *object under* Γ. *Types* and *kinds under* Γ are defined in the same way. □

The following lemma shows that classification corresponds to our intutive notions of terms, types and kinds.

Lemma 7 *1. If $x_1 \in A_1, \ldots, x_n \in A_n$ is a legal context, then either A_i is a type under the context $x_1 \in A_1, \ldots, x_{i-1} \in A_{i-1}$ or A_i is a kind, i.e., $A_i \equiv \mathit{Type}$.*

2. If $\Gamma \vdash A \in B$ is a legal sequent, then exactly one of the following holds:

(a) A is an object and B is a type under Γ.

(b) A is a type and B is a kind, i.e. $B \equiv \mathit{Type}$.

(c) A is a kind, i.e. $A \equiv \mathit{Type}$, and B is the sort Kind.

Proof. By induction on derivations. Note that the uniqueness of the classification is trivial, as the sets of objects, types, kinds, and the sort *Kind* are syntactically disjoint. □

The sort *Type* is an element of *Kind* by the axiom. It is coherent with the classification above. We shall check that a type as defined above is an element of the sort *Type*, as *Type* is intended to be the collection of types. Namely, we shall prove the following lemma.

Lemma 8 *If $\Gamma \vdash A \in B$ is derivable and B is a type, then $\Gamma \vdash B \in \mathit{Type}$ is derivable.*

This lemma can be proved by induction on derivations using the following type inversion lemma and lemma 4.

Lemma 9 *1. Let* op *be one of $\rightarrow$, $\vee$, $\wedge$. If $\Gamma \vdash (A \ \mathsf{op}\ B) \in \mathit{Type}$ is derivable, then so are $\Gamma \vdash A \in \mathit{Type}$ and $\Gamma \vdash B \in \mathit{Type}$.*

2. Let OP *be one of $\bigvee$, $\bigwedge$. If $\Gamma \vdash (\mathsf{OP}\, x \in A.B) \in \mathit{Type}$ is derivable, then so are $\Gamma \vdash A \in \mathit{Type}$ and $\Gamma, x \in A \vdash B \in \mathit{Type}$.*

3. If $\Gamma \vdash \{A\}_B \in \mathit{Type}$ is derivable, then so are $\Gamma \vdash B \in \mathit{Type}$ and $\Gamma \vdash A \in B$.

Proof. Each case is proved by induction on derivations. For the rules other than formation, introduction and elimination, it is trivial. Note that we need the Church-Rosser property for the case of the conversion rule to prove that B' is *Type*, if B is *Type*. For the case of subject reduction, we use the conversion rule and lemma 6. A sequent $\Gamma \vdash A \in \mathit{Type}$ does not match the conclusions of any introduction rules. If $\Gamma \vdash A \in B$ is a conclusion of an elimination rule, then B is a type. For elimination of union and intersection, this is a trivial implication of lemma 7 since the side condition of these rules excludes the case where B is *Type*. The cases for the other elimination rules are also proved by the same lemma. Let's check only $\bigwedge$-elimination. By lemma 7, B is a type, since $\bigwedge x \in A.B$ is a type. Similarly, D is a type or an object. Hence, $B[x := D]$ is not *Type* or *Kind*. Hence, it must be a type by the same lemma. Other cases are similar and easily proved. So the only rules left are the formation rules. Let's consider the case of singleton-formation. Assume that $\Gamma \vdash \{A\}_B \in \mathit{Type}$ is a conclusion of a formation rule, then the rule must be singleton-formation. Then $\Gamma \vdash B \in \mathit{Type}$ and $\Gamma \vdash A \in B$ are the premises of the rule. Hence, they are derivable. The other cases are the same. □

Note that if a term is proved to be an element of *Type*, then it is one of the forms of the lemma above or a type variable. Hence, by lemma 9, any element of *Type* is formed by successive applications of the formation rules.

2.3 Semantics of ATT

A semantics of ATT can be given on any reasonable concrete model of partial untyped lambda calculus. Unfortunately, we cannot find any good reference for this kind of models of partial untyped lambda calculus. (A good reference for the typed case is [Mog88].) One possible approach is to start with models of ordinary (total) untyped lambda calculus. But this construction will invalidate an important proposition that if a term is typable then it denotes a meaningful value. So we will give a semantics using a particular domain theoretic model of partial untyped lambda calculus by Plotkin [Plo85].

Plotkin reconstructed D_∞ in the category of cpo's and continuous partial functions. In his sense, a cpo may or may not have bottom element. His D_∞ is a non-empty cpo with two total continuous functions i and j

$$\mathsf{D}_\infty \underset{j}{\overset{i}{\rightleftarrows}} [\mathsf{D}_\infty \rightharpoonup \mathsf{D}_\infty] \qquad \text{satisfying } i \circ j = i$$

Note that $[\mathsf{D}_\infty \rightharpoonup \mathsf{D}_\infty]$ is the set of partial continuous functions from D_∞ to D_∞. (For Plotkin's D_∞, $j \circ i = id$ also holds. But this is not necessary, as η-conversion is not considered in ATT.) Now we can interpret lambda terms as in the usual D_∞.

1. If x is a variable, then $[\![x]\!]_\rho = \rho(x)$.
2. $[\![(AB)]\!]_\rho = (i([\![A]\!]_\rho))([\![B]\!]_\rho)$.
3. $[\![\lambda x.A]\!]_\rho = j(\mathsf{fun}\, v \in \mathsf{D}_\infty.[\![A]\!]_{\rho[x:=v]})$.

The notation $\rho[x := v]$ denotes the function that maps the variable x to v and any variable y except x to $\rho(y)$. The notation $\mathsf{fun}\, x \in A.B$ stands for the lambda notation at the metalevel. Note that $[\![(AB)]\!]_\rho$ can be undefined, as $i([\![A]\!]_\rho)$ is a partial function. So an interpretation of a term may be undefined. Using Plotkin's semantics, a semantics of ATT is given as follows.

Definition 4 (interpretation) Let TYPE be the set of subsets of D_∞ and KIND be the singleton $\{\mathsf{TYPE}\}$. Let $\langle \mathit{Obj}, \mathit{Typ} \rangle$ be a partition of the variables into object variables and type variables. A function ρ from the set of variables to $\mathsf{D}_\infty \cup \mathsf{TYPE} \cup \mathsf{KIND}$ is called an *assignment*, if $\rho(x)$ is in D_∞ for an object variable x and $\rho(x)$ is in TYPE for a type variable x. For simplicity, we assume that the only constants of ATT are *Type* and *Kind*. Let M be an object, a type, or a kind under $\langle Obj, Typ \rangle$. We define interpretation $[\![M]\!]_\rho$ of M. (This interpretation may be undefined. Later, we will see the interpretation of any legal term is defined.)

objects An object is a lambda term. The interpretation of an object M is given by the interpretation of lambda term $[\![M]\!]_\rho$ given above.

types
1. If x is a type variable, then set $[\![x]\!]_\rho = \rho(x)$.
2. $[\![A \to B]\!]_\rho = \{f \in \mathsf{D}_\infty | \forall x \in [\![A]\!]_\rho.((i(f))(x) \in [\![B]\!]_\rho)\}$.
3. $[\![A \vee B]\!]_\rho = [\![A]\!]_\rho \cup [\![B]\!]_\rho$.
4. $[\![A \wedge B]\!]_\rho = [\![A]\!]_\rho \cap [\![B]\!]_\rho$.
5. $[\![\{A\}_B]\!]_\rho = \{x \in \mathsf{D}_\infty | x = [\![A]\!]_\rho \text{ and } [\![A]\!]_\rho \in [\![B]\!]_\rho\}$.
6. $[\![\bigwedge x \in A.B]\!]_\rho = \bigcap_{v \in [\![A]\!]_\rho}([\![B]\!]_{\rho[x:=v]})$.
7. $[\![\bigvee x \in A.B]\!]_\rho = \bigcup_{v \in [\![A]\!]_\rho}([\![B]\!]_{\rho[x:=v]})$.

sorts $[\![Type]\!]_\rho = \mathsf{TYPE}$ and $[\![Kind]\!]_\rho = \mathsf{KIND}$. □

The soundness theorem is proved by induction on derivations.

Theorem 1 (soundness) *Assume that $\Gamma \vdash A \in B$ is derivable. Let ρ be an environment with respect to the partition of variables induced by the context Γ. Then $[\![A]\!]_\rho$ and $[\![B]\!]_\rho$ are defined and $[\![A]\!]_\rho$ is an element of $[\![B]\!]_\rho$. Hence the interpretation of any legal term is defined.*

Although we gave a semantics in the category of sets, it would be possible to give a semantics in other categories with some conditions. Rosolini [Ros86] and others have introduced notions of partial categories which is intended for categories of partial maps. Following D. Scott's semantics of lambda calculus in cartesian closed categories, we would be able to give a semantics of partial lambda calculus in partial cartesian closed categories. Then the partial CCC would be embeddable into a topos. In the topos, we would be able to give semantics of ATT, as we can define singleton, union and intersection by the constructive logic of the topos. This would be straightforward but is yet to be worked out.

Pierce [Pie90] has given a PER-semantics for a type system closely related to ATT. Pierce did not consider singleton type, but it would be interpreted by

$$x\ [\![\{A\}_B]\!]_\rho\ y = x\ [\![B]\!]_\rho\ y \text{ and } x\ [\![B]\!]_\rho\ [\![A]\!]_\rho.$$

This semantics works for ATT as well. Then the rule of extensionality of functions can be added to the system as in Martin-Löf's type theory of [Mar72]. But Pierce has pointed out an anomaly of this semantics: As the union of PER's is not in general a PER, we have to collapse it by taking the transitive closure to interpret union types. This causes some expected equalities between types to fail. See [Pie90] for details.

2.4 Eliminating the non-computational part

In this section, we will show that the non-computational part of the proof is eliminable by a simple translation. This translation translates derivations in ATT into another type theory, ibMPS, which is a variant of the type theory of MacQueen et al. [MPS86]. As a corollary of the soundness of the translation, we obtain a strong normalization theorem for ATT.

The system ibMPS (inhabitable basic MacQueen, Plotkin and Sethi system) is roughly defined as follows:

$$\begin{aligned} \text{ibMPS} \;=\; & \text{ATT} - \text{singleton types} \\ & \quad - \text{first order big union and intersection types} \\ & \quad - \text{conversion rule} \end{aligned}$$

The first order big union and intersection types mean types of the form $\bigwedge x \in A.B$ or $\bigvee x \in A.B$, where A is a type.

As we dropped the singleton types, types of ibMPS can be defined independently from the definition of legal terms as in the usual second order type theories. It is more natural to reformulate ibMPS in this way, but we do not do so here to avoid repetitions and to save space. We only list changes of ibMPS from ATT. Note that some rules for intersections and unions are changed. These changes come from the other changes.

Definition 5 (ibMPS) The system ibMPS is defined by changing ATT as follows:

1. Drop $\{T\}_T$ from the syntax of the preterms, and drop all the rules for singleton types.

2. Change all the rules for $\bigwedge$ and $\bigvee$, and $\vee$-elimination rule as follows:

$$\frac{\Gamma, x \in \mathit{Type} \vdash B \in \mathit{Type}}{\Gamma \vdash (\bigwedge x \in \mathit{Type}.B) \in \mathit{Type}} \qquad \frac{\Gamma, x \in \mathit{Type} \vdash B \in \mathit{Type}}{\Gamma \vdash (\bigvee x \in \mathit{Type}.B) \in \mathit{Type}}$$

$$\frac{\Gamma, x \in \mathit{Type} \vdash B \in \mathit{Type} \quad \Gamma, x \in \mathit{Type} \vdash C \in B}{\Gamma \vdash C \in (\bigwedge x \in \mathit{Type}.B)}$$

$$\frac{\Gamma \vdash C \in (\bigwedge x \in \mathit{Type}.B) \quad \Gamma \vdash D \in \mathit{Type}}{\Gamma \vdash C \in B[x := D]}$$

$$\frac{\Gamma, x \in \mathit{Type} \vdash B \in \mathit{Type} \quad \Gamma \vdash D \in \mathit{Type} \quad \Gamma \vdash C \in B[x := D]}{\Gamma \vdash C \in (\bigvee x \in \mathit{Type}.B)}$$

$$\frac{\Gamma \vdash C \in (\bigvee x \in \mathit{Type}.B) \quad \Gamma, x \in \mathit{Type}, y \in B \vdash D \in E}{\Gamma \vdash D[y := C] \in E}$$

$$\frac{\Gamma \vdash C \in A \vee B \quad \Gamma, x \in A \vdash D \in E \quad \Gamma, x \in B \vdash D \in E}{\Gamma \vdash D[x := C] \in E}$$

   In the last two rules, E is not *Type* or *Kind*.

3. Drop the conversion rule. □

It is easy to prove the following lemma by induction of derivations.

Lemma 10 (inhabitation rule) *The following is an admissible rule of* ibMPS.

$$\frac{\Gamma, x \in A, \Gamma' \vdash B \in C}{\Gamma, \Gamma' \vdash B \in C},$$

where x is not a free variable of B, and A is not Type.

The inhabitation rules maintains that all types are inhabited (cf. [Mit90]). Note that ATT is regarded as having an empty type; otherwise singleton-elimination is not sound. Existence of an empty type is a characteristic of type systems based on the Curry-Howard isomorphism. On the other hand, in many systems purely for types in programming languages, types can be assumed to be inhabited. In this sense, we are translating a type theory for the Curry-Howard isomorphism (verification system) into a type theory for a programming language (computation system).

Definition 6 (translation from ATT to ibMPS) We define a translation $M \mapsto M^*$ from preterms of ATT to preterms of ibMPS as follows:

1. $c^* = c$.
2. $x^* = x$.
3. $(\lambda x.A)^* = (\lambda x.A^*)$.
4. $(AB)^* = (A^*B^*)$.
5. $(A \mathsf{\ op\ } B)^* = (A^* \mathsf{\ op\ } B^*)$, where op is one of $\rightarrow$, $\wedge$, $\vee$.
6. $(\mathsf{OP}\, x \in \mathit{Type}.B)^* = \mathsf{OP}\, x \in \mathit{Type}.B^*$, where OP is one of $\bigwedge$, $\bigvee$.
7. $(\mathsf{OP}\, x \in A.B)^* = B^*$, where A is not *Type* and OP is one of $\bigwedge$, $\bigvee$.
8. $(\{A\}_B)^* = B^*$. □

The translation is naturally expanded to translations of judgments, contexts and sequents. Then the translation preserves derivability.

Theorem 2 *If* $\Gamma \vdash J$ *is derivable in* ATT, *then so is* $\Gamma^* \vdash J^*$ *in* ibMPS.

Proof. By induction of derivations. Let us check only the cases of $\bigwedge$-introduction and singleton-elimination, as the other cases are proved similarly.

Let us consider the case of $\bigwedge$-introduction. Assume that the last rule of the derivation is as follows:

$$\frac{\Gamma \vdash A \in s \quad \Gamma, x \in A \vdash B \in \mathit{Type} \quad \Gamma, x \in A \vdash C \in B}{\Gamma \vdash C \in (\bigwedge x \in A.B)}$$

If A is not *Type*, then the translation of the conclusion is $\Gamma^* \vdash C^* \in B^*$. By the induction hypothesis, the translation of the last premise, $\Gamma^*, x \in A^* \vdash C^* \in B^*$, is derivable. By the inhabitation rule, $\Gamma^* \vdash C^* \in B^*$ is derivable. If A is *Type*, then the translation of the rule is the $\bigwedge$-introduction rule of ibMPS.

Now consider the case of singleton-elimination. Assume that the last rule of the derivation is as follows:

$$\frac{\Gamma \vdash P_1 \in \{A\}_C \wedge \{B\}_C \quad \Gamma \vdash P_2 \in D[x := A] \quad \Gamma, x \in C \vdash D \in \mathit{Type}}{\Gamma \vdash P_2 \in D[x := B]}$$

Since $\{A\}_C$ is a legal term, C is a type and so x is an object variable. Since the translation eliminates all subterms which are objects, we see $(D[x := A])^* \equiv (D[x := B])^* \equiv D^*$. Hence the translation of the conclusion of the rule is the same as the translation of the second premise and so it is derivable form the induction hypothesis. □

The terms of ibMPS are strongly normalizable. A proof for a related system can be found in [Lei86] and it is applicable to ibMPS. So we do not give a proof here.

Theorem 3 *Every term of* ibMPS *is strongly normalizable.*

We can prove strong normalization property of ATT from this theorem.

Corollary 1 *Every term of* ATT *is strongly normalizable.*

Proof. Let M be a term of ATT. Then M^* is strongly normalizing by the previous theorem and theorem 2. If M is an object, then M^* is identical to M. So M is strongly normalizing. If M is a type, then its subterms, which are objects, are legal terms of ATT by lemma 9. Since reduction can happen only in such subterms, M is strongly normalizing. □

The following is also obvious:

Corollary 2 ATT *is a conservative extension of* ibMPS.

2.5 Some definable types and judgments

In this section, we will define some derived notions including dependent products and sums at the level of types.

(1) **Dependent product.** ATT does not have a dependent product Π unlike Martin-Löf type theories. Such a dependent product of types is definable by means of intersection types and function spaces. Assume that A and B are types. Then we define

$$\Pi x \in A.B \stackrel{\text{def}}{=} \bigwedge x \in A.(\{x\}_A \rightarrow B)$$

The formation and elimination rules for Π are easily derivable.

We will derive the introduction rule. Assume that the following three sequents are derived:

$$(1) \quad \Gamma \vdash A \in \mathit{Type}, \quad (2) \quad \Gamma, x \in A \vdash B \in \mathit{Type}, \quad (3) \quad \Gamma, x \in A \vdash C \in B.$$

Let y and z be a fresh variables. By renaming the variable x of (3) to z and applying generalized weakening, we can derive

$$\Gamma, x \in A, y \in \{x\}_A, z \in A \vdash C[x := z] \in B[x := z].$$

Since $y \in A$ is derivable under $\Gamma, x \in A, y \in \{x\}_A$, we can derive

$$\Gamma, x \in A, y \in \{x\}_A \vdash C[x := y] \in B[x := y]$$

by substitution. On the other hand, we can derive $y \in \{y\}_A \wedge \{x\}_A$ under the same context. Then we can derive the Π-introduction rule roughly as follows:

$$\dfrac{\dfrac{\dfrac{\Gamma, x \in A, y \in \{x\}_A \vdash y \in \{y\}_A \wedge \{x\}_A \quad \Gamma, x \in A, y \in \{x\}_A \vdash C[x := y] \in B[x := y]}{\Gamma, x \in A, y \in \{x\}_A \vdash C[x := y] \in B[x := y][y := x]}}{\Gamma, x \in A \vdash \lambda y.(C[x := y]) \in (\{x\}_A \rightarrow B)}}{\Gamma \vdash \lambda x.C \in \bigwedge x \in A.(\{x\}_A \rightarrow B)}$$

In the second inference, we omitted the first two premises of $\rightarrow$-introduction, which are easily derived. Note that we identify the two α-convertible terms $\lambda y.C[x := y]$ and $\lambda x.C$ in the last step of the inference.

(2) **Cartesian product.** Using $\bigwedge$ at the level of types, we can define the cartesian product of two types by the standard method for polymorphic lambda calculi.

$$A \times B \stackrel{\text{def}}{=} \bigwedge X \in \mathit{Type}.((A \rightarrow B \rightarrow X) \rightarrow X)$$

Note that the arrows $\rightarrow$ above are basic constructors of ATT. Pairing $\langle A, B\rangle$ and projections, $\mathit{fst}(A)$, $\mathit{snd}(A)$, are defined in the standard way.

(3) **Dependent sum.** The dependent sum of types is definable by means of union types and cartesian products. Assume that A and B are types. Then we define

$$\Sigma x \in A.B \stackrel{\text{def}}{=} \bigvee x \in A.(\{x\}_A \times B)$$

Note that this dependent sum is a *strong* sum [Coq86], as the first component of a member a of $\Sigma x \in A.B$ is obtained by $fst(a)$. Note that a preterm $\Sigma x \in Type.B$ can be defined as above, but cannot be a type, as such a strong sum implies a contradiction [Coq86]. To derive $(\Sigma x \in Type.B) \in Type$, $\{x\}_{Type} \in Type$ has to be derived. But, to derive it by the rule of singleton-formation, $Type \in Type$ is required but it is not derivable. Note that the standard definition of dependent sum of types is also possible in ATT:

$$\Sigma x \in A.B \stackrel{\text{def}}{=} \bigwedge y \in Type.((\Pi x \in A.(B \to y)) \to y)$$

Since ATT has a strong sum, this sum turns out to be a strong sum. (This was pointed out by Luo.)

(3) **Subset Type.** A subset type is definable as follows:

$$\{x \in A|B\} \stackrel{\text{def}}{=} \bigvee x \in A. \bigvee y \in B.\{x\}_A$$

Note that subset type is a kind of dependent sum $\mathsf{SUM}\, x \in A.B$ which exposes information from A and hides information from B. The strong sum defined above exposes information from both A and B. The union type $\bigvee x \in A.B$ hides information from A and exposes information from B.

(4) **Propositional equality.** Martin-Löf type has a basic type $Eq(A, M, N)$ called propositional equality. In higher order type theories like CoC, Leibnitz equality can be defined as a type (proposition). But it cannot be in second order theories. Having singleton types, an equality type can be defined in ATT as follows:

$$Eq(A, M, N) \stackrel{\text{def}}{=} \{M\}_A \wedge \{N\}_A$$

It is inhabited iff M and N are the same object of the type A. This equality is an equivalence relation, i.e., the following rules hold:

$$\frac{M \in A \quad A \in Type}{M \in Eq(A, M, M)} \quad \frac{C \in Eq(A, N, M)}{C \in Eq(A, M, N)} \quad \frac{C_1 \in Eq(A, M, N) \quad C_2 \in Eq(A, N, P)}{C_2 \in Eq(A, M, P)}$$

The rule of singleton-elimination serves as the equality rule. Note that our propositional equality is closer to Leibnitz equality than to Martin-Löf's, as it is not an extensional equality.

(5) **Equality judgment.** Martin-Löf type theory has an equality judgment $M = N \in A$. A similar judgment can be defined by

$$M = N \in A \stackrel{\text{def}}{=} M \in \{N\}_A$$

Note that the following rules hold:

$$\frac{C \in Eq(A, M, N)}{M = N \in A} \qquad \frac{M = N \in A}{M \in Eq(A, M, N)} \qquad \frac{M = N \in A}{N \in Eq(A, M, N)}$$

The following proposition ensures that our definition of equality is reasonable.

Proposition 1 (equality reflection) *Assume that* $M \in A$ *and* $N \in A$ *are derivable under the empty context. Then* $M = N \in A$ *is derivable under the empty context iff* M *and* N *are* β*-convertible.*

Proof. The "if" direction is trivial. Let us prove the "only if" direction. Let NT be the set of normalizable terms of untyped lambda calculus. β-convertibility is an equivalence relation on it. Let D be the set of β-conversion equivalence classes of NT. Then D is a model of partial untyped lambda calculus. Note that the interpretation is identical, i.e., $[\![M]\!]_\rho$ is the term obtained from M by the substitution induced by the assignment ρ. Interpreting *Type* as the powerset of D, an interpretation of ATT is obtained. Note that $[\![\{A\}_B]\!]_\rho$ is the singleton of $[\![A]\!]_\rho$. Soundness is easily checked by induction on derivations. If $M = N \in A$, i.e., $M \in \{N\}_A$, is derivable under the empty context, then the equivalence classes of M and N must be identical by soundness and the interpretation of singleton. Hence M and N are β-convertible.

The proof of soundness theorem resembles Scedrov's proof of normalization for $\lambda 2$ in [Sce89]. But there is a subtlety. Our interpretation of types must allow the empty set to make the singleton-elimination sound. In Scedrov's proof, the interpretation of a type must be a non-empty set of equivalence classes. This is necessary to verify the soundness of $\rightarrow$-introduction. His proof goes as follows. When $\Gamma, x \in A \vdash C \in B$ is derived, $[\![C]\!]_\rho \in [\![B]\!]_\rho$ and so C is normalizable, if ρ is an assignment satisfying the context $\Gamma, x \in A$. Because $[\![A]\!]_\rho$ is always non-empty, we see that $\lambda x.C$ is normalizable, if there is an assignment satisfying the context Γ. Thus, the non-emptiness of types is used to assure that $\lambda x.C$ is normalizable. But this is not necessary in our case, as we have already proved all legal terms in ATT are strongly normalizable. So we can allow the empty set. □

Equality reflection was first proved by Luo for Leibnitz equality in his system ECC [Luo90] by a syntactical analysis of normalized terms. It seems difficult to prove it for ATT by syntactical analysis. The possibility and importance of equality reflection for ATT was pointed out by Luo.

(6) **Subtype judgment.** ATT has a notion of subtypes. For example, $A \wedge B$ is a subtype of A and B, as any term which belongs to $A \wedge B$ belongs to A and B as well. The subtype judgment $A \leq B$, i.e., A is a subtype of B, can be defined by

$$A \leq B \stackrel{\text{def}}{=} \lambda x.x \in (A \rightarrow B).$$

If $\Gamma \vdash A \leq B$ is derivable, then $\Gamma, x \in A \vdash x \in B$ is derivable. (Note that subject reduction is necessary to show this.) The reverse is trivial, if A and B are types under Γ.

Many other important notions can be defined in ATT, e.g., a variant of the conditional formulas of PX. But we do not include them here. They will appear elsewhere together with some interpretations of logic into ATT (variants of the Curry-Howard isomorphism).

2.6 Application to program extraction

In this section, we sketch how program extraction is achieved in ATT. (The details will appear elsewhere.)

By the types and judgments defined in the previous section, we can write specifications of programs as types of ATT just as in Nuprl and CoC. (In practice, these are not enough. We have to add some additional types such as recursive types and recursion operators for them. But this is another matter.) A typical specification with a subset type is $\Pi x \in A.\{y \in B|C\}$ (see [NPS90]). By this type, we mean the set of functions f from $A \rightarrow B$ such that $C[y := f(x)]$ is inhabited. Unfolding the definition of Π and the subset type, we have the following type:

$$\bigwedge x \in A.(\{x\}_A \rightarrow \bigvee y \in B. \bigvee z \in C.\{y\}_B).$$

The translation of this type into ibMPS is $A \rightarrow B$. Hence a function f of this type has the type $A \rightarrow B$ in ibMPS and so also in ATT. Furthermore, the condition on f is fulfilled.

Subset types are used to hide unnecessary information in specifications. If one does not need to have the information from C of $\Pi x \in A. \Sigma y \in B.C$, then one replaces the Σ with a subset type. But this hides all of the information from C. In ATT, finer hiding of information is possible. Suppose that we need the information y_2 but not y_1 in $\Pi x \in A. \Sigma y_1 \in B_1. \Sigma y_2 \in B_2.C$. If the Σ for y_1 is changed to a subset type, then it hides y_2 as well. When the Σ is replaced by $\bigvee$, then the specification become what we expect. Note that we cannot always exchange y_1 and y_2, as y_1 may appear in B_2. The type former $\bigvee$ works just like the $\check{\exists}$-existential quantifier in [TH90]. This observation was the start point of the development of ATT.

3 ATTT: ATT more Typed

ATT is a type system based on untyped lambda calculus. Although untyped lambda calculus serves well as a semantics of type systems, there are some more natural semantics, e.g., coherence semantics. In this section, we introduce another type theory called ATTT based on Girard-Reynolds' $\lambda 2$. As the coherence space gives a semantics of $\lambda 2$, it also gives a semantics of ATTT.

The basic idea of ATTT is to keep types just as in $\lambda 2$ and introduce the notion of refinement (or refinement type) of types for specifications of programs. A refinement of a type T is a subset of T. In some semantics, e.g., in coherence semantics, a type is always inhabited. A refinement is an arbitrary subset of a type, so it can be empty.

The refinement approach of ATTT is closely related to the notion of a modified realizability interpretation. Modified realizability determines a set of realizers and their functionality. Let's consider the modified realizability of the formula $\forall x \in A.\exists y \in B.(f(x) =_C g(y))$. A term a is a realizer of the formula iff a is a term of type $A \rightarrow B$ and $\forall x \in A.(f(x) = g(a(x)))$ holds. In ATTT, the formula is interpreted by the following *refinement* of the type $A \rightarrow B$:

$$\bigwedge x \in A.(\{x\}_A \rightarrow \bigvee y \in B.\bigvee p \in Eq(C, f(x), g(y)).\{y\}_B).$$

The type $A \rightarrow B$ gives the functionality of the realizers of the formula and the refinement above gives the set of realizers of the formula. This will become clearer when we give a translation of ATTT into $\lambda 2$ below.

The idea of refinement types was first introduced by Freeman and Pfenning [FP91] in the context of ML. Our notion of refinement was influenced by their work, although the aim and presentation are different. Freeman and Pfenning write $A : B :: C$ iff A is an element of the refinement type B and B is a refinement of C. We will not introduce new judgment $A : B :: C$ but will introduce a new kind *refine*(A) for each type A. This denotes the set of the refinements of A. Hence, the equivalent of $A : B :: C$ is the pair of judgments $A \in B$ and $B \in$ *refine*(C).

3.1 Formulation of ATTT

The preterms of ATTT are defined by the following grammar:

$$\begin{array}{rcl} T & ::= & x \mid c \mid \lambda x \in T.T \mid TT \mid \mathit{refine}(T) \mid \\ & & T \rightarrow T \mid T \wedge T \mid T \vee T \mid \\ & & \Pi x \in T.T \mid \bigwedge x \in T.T \mid \bigvee x \in T.T \mid \\ & & \{T\}_T. \end{array}$$

Note that *refine* is not a constant but is a syntactical operator. *Sorts* of ATTT are *Kind, Type, RKind* and preterms of the form of *refine*(A). In the following, s stands for a sort. Among the sorts, *RKind* and *refine*(A) are called *refinement sorts* and *refine*(A) is called a *refinement kind.* We will give inference rules of ATTT below:

The axiom, start rule, weakening rule, conversion rule, and rule of subject reduction are the same as in ATT, so we do not reproduce them here. Besides these general rules, ATTT has two rules for refinement.

refine-formation

$$\frac{\Gamma \vdash M \in \mathit{Type}}{\Gamma \vdash \mathit{refine}(M) \in \mathit{RKind}}$$

refine-subtyping

$$\frac{\Gamma \vdash C \in A \quad \Gamma \vdash A \in \mathit{refine}(B)}{\Gamma \vdash C \in B}$$

Rules for dependent product

Π-formation

$$\frac{\Gamma, x \in \mathit{Type} \vdash A \in \mathit{Type}}{\Gamma \vdash (\Pi\, x \in \mathit{Type}.A) \in \mathit{Type}} \qquad \frac{\Gamma, x \in \mathit{Type} \vdash R \in \mathit{refine}(A)}{\Gamma \vdash (\Pi\, x \in \mathit{Type}.R) \in \mathit{refine}(\Pi\, x \in \mathit{Type}.A)}$$

Π-introduction

$$\frac{\Gamma, x \in \mathit{Type} \vdash A \in \mathit{Type} \quad \Gamma, x \in \mathit{Type} \vdash B \in A}{\Gamma \vdash (\lambda x \in \mathit{Type}.B) \in (\Pi\, x \in \mathit{Type}.A)}$$

$$\frac{\Gamma, x \in \mathit{Type} \vdash R \in \mathit{refine}(A) \quad \Gamma, x \in \mathit{Type} \vdash B \in R}{\Gamma \vdash (\lambda x \in \mathit{Type}.B) \in (\Pi\, x \in \mathit{Type}.R)}$$

Π-elimination

$$\frac{\Gamma \vdash F \in (\Pi\, x \in \mathit{Type}.A) \quad \Gamma \vdash B \in \mathit{Type}}{\Gamma \vdash (FB) \in A[x := B]}$$

Rules for function space

→-formation

$$\frac{\Gamma \vdash A \in \mathit{Type} \quad \Gamma \vdash B \in \mathit{Type}}{\Gamma \vdash A \to B \in \mathit{Type}} \qquad \frac{\Gamma \vdash C \in \mathit{refine}(A) \quad \Gamma \vdash D \in \mathit{refine}(B)}{\Gamma \vdash C \to D \in \mathit{refine}(A \to B)}$$

→-introduction

$$\frac{\Gamma \vdash A \in \mathit{Type} \quad \Gamma \vdash B \in \mathit{Type} \quad \Gamma, x \in A \vdash C \in B}{\Gamma \vdash (\lambda x \in A.C) \in A \to B}$$

$$\frac{\Gamma \vdash C \in \mathit{refine}(A) \quad \Gamma \vdash D \in \mathit{refine}(B) \quad \Gamma, x \in C \vdash E \in D}{\Gamma \vdash (\lambda x \in A.E) \in C \to D}$$

→-elimination

$$\frac{\Gamma \vdash F \in A \to B \quad \Gamma \vdash C \in A}{\Gamma \vdash (FC) \in B}$$

Rules for union

∨-formation

$$\frac{\Gamma \vdash A \in \mathit{refine}(C) \quad \Gamma \vdash B \in \mathit{refine}(C)}{\Gamma \vdash A \vee B \in \mathit{refine}(C)}$$

∨-introduction

$$\frac{\Gamma \vdash A \in \mathit{refine}(C) \quad \Gamma \vdash B \in \mathit{refine}(C) \quad \Gamma \vdash D \in A}{\Gamma \vdash D \in A \vee B}$$

$$\frac{\Gamma \vdash A \in \mathit{refine}(C) \quad \Gamma \vdash B \in \mathit{refine}(C) \quad \Gamma \vdash D \in B}{\Gamma \vdash D \in A \vee B}$$

∨-elimination

$$\frac{\Gamma \vdash C \in A \vee B \quad \Gamma, x \in A \vdash D \in E \quad \Gamma, x \in B \vdash D \in E}{\Gamma \vdash D[x := C] \in E[x := C]}$$

where E is not a sort.

⋁-formation

$$\frac{\Gamma \vdash A \in s \quad \Gamma, x \in A \vdash B \in \mathit{refine}(C)}{\Gamma \vdash (\bigvee x \in A.B) \in \mathit{refine}(C)}$$

where s is not *Kind*.

⋁-introduction

$$\frac{\Gamma \vdash A \in s \quad \Gamma, x \in A \vdash B \in \mathit{refine}(C) \quad \Gamma \vdash D \in A \quad \Gamma \vdash E \in B[x := D]}{\Gamma \vdash E \in (\bigvee x \in A.B)}$$

where s is not *Kind*,

⋁-elimination

$$\frac{\Gamma \vdash C \in (\bigvee x \in A.B) \quad \Gamma, x \in A, y \in B \vdash D \in E}{\Gamma \vdash D[y := C] \in E[y := C]}$$

where x is not in $FV(D) \cup FV(E)$ and E is not a sort.

Rules for intersection

∧-formation

$$\frac{\Gamma \vdash A \in \mathit{refine}(C) \quad \Gamma \vdash B \in \mathit{refine}(C)}{\Gamma \vdash A \wedge B \in \mathit{refine}(C)}$$

∧-introduction

$$\frac{\Gamma \vdash A \in \mathit{refine}(C) \quad \Gamma \vdash B \in \mathit{refine}(C) \quad \Gamma \vdash D \in A \quad \Gamma \vdash D \in B}{\Gamma \vdash D \in A \wedge B}$$

∧-elimination

$$\frac{\Gamma \vdash C \in A \wedge B}{\Gamma \vdash C \in A} \qquad \frac{\Gamma \vdash C \in A \wedge B}{\Gamma \vdash C \in B}$$

$\bigwedge$-formation

$$\frac{\Gamma \vdash A \in s \quad \Gamma, x \in A \vdash B \in \mathit{refine}(C)}{\Gamma \vdash (\bigwedge x \in A.B) \in \mathit{refine}(C)}$$

where s is not *Kind.*

$\bigwedge$-introduction

$$\frac{\Gamma \vdash A \in s \quad \Gamma, x \in A \vdash B \in \mathit{refine}(C) \quad \Gamma, x \in A \vdash D \in B}{\Gamma \vdash D \in (\bigwedge x \in A.B)}$$

where x is not in $FV(D)$ and s is not *Kind.*

$\bigwedge$-elimination

$$\frac{\Gamma \vdash C \in (\bigwedge x \in A.B) \quad \Gamma \vdash D \in A}{\Gamma \vdash C \in B[x := D]}$$

Rules for singleton

singleton-formation

$$\frac{\Gamma \vdash B \in \mathit{Type} \quad \Gamma \vdash A \in B}{\Gamma \vdash \{A\}_B \in \mathit{refine}(B)}$$

singleton-introduction

$$\frac{\Gamma \vdash B \in \mathit{Type} \quad \Gamma \vdash A \in B}{\Gamma \vdash A \in \{A\}_B}$$

singleton-elimination

$$\frac{\Gamma \vdash P_1 \in \{A\}_C \wedge \{B\}_C \quad \Gamma \vdash P_2 \in D[x := A] \quad \Gamma, x \in C \vdash D \in s}{\Gamma \vdash P_2 \in D[x := B]}$$

where s is the kind *Type* or a refinement kind.

Note that the second elimination rule of ATT is not present in ATTT, because it is derivable in ATTT. If $\{A\}_B$ is a legal term, then $\{A\}_B \in \mathit{refine}(B)$ is derivable. *refine*-subtyping implies $C \in B$, if $C \in \{A\}_B$.

Legal sequents and terms, etc. are defined as in ATT. Basic lemmas, e.g., the Church-Rosser property, substitution etc., hold for ATTT as well. Lemma 3 must be changed as follows:

Lemma 11 *Assume that* $x_1 \in A_1, \ldots, x_n \in A_n \vdash B \in C$ *is a legal sequent. Then* B *is neither Kind nor RKind. Furthermore, for each* i, A_i *is neither Kind nor RKind, and one of the followings holds:*

1. A_i *is the kind Type and* $x_1 \in A_1, \ldots, x_{i-1} \in A_{i-1} \vdash A_i \in \mathit{Kind}$ *is derivable.*
2. A_i *has the form* $\mathit{refine}(D)$ *and* $x_1 \in A_1, \ldots, x_{i-1} \in A_{i-1} \vdash A_i \in \mathit{RKind}$ *is derivable.*
3. $x_1 \in A_1, \ldots, x_{i-1} \in A_{i-1} \vdash A_i \in \mathit{Type}$ *is derivable.*
4. $x_1 \in A_1, \ldots, x_{i-1} \in A_{i-1} \vdash A_i \in \mathit{refine}(D)$ *is derivable for some* D.

3.2 Classification of terms of ATTT

We classify the terms of ATTT as in the classification in ATT. It is more complicated than in the case of ATT, as we have now introduced the notion of refinement.

Definition 7 (classification under variable classification) Assume that $FV(A)$ is a union of three disjoint sets *Obj*, *Typ* and *Ref*. The variables of *Obj* are called object variables, the variables of *Ref* are called refinement variables, and the variables of *Typ* are called type variables. Then objects, types, refinements, kinds and refinement kinds (r-kinds for short) under the classification of free variables $\langle Obj, Typ, Ref\rangle$ are defined as follows:

objects 1. An object variable is an object.

2. If A and B are objects, then so is (AB).
3. If A is an object under the classification $\langle Obj \cup \{x\}, Typ, Ref\rangle$ and B is a type, then $\lambda x \in B.A$ is an object under the classification $\langle Obj, Typ, Ref\rangle$.

types 1. A type variable is a type.

2. If A and B are types, then so is $A \to B$.
3. If A is a type and B is a type under the classification $\langle Obj, Typ \cup \{x\}, Ref\rangle$, then $\Pi x \in Type.A$ is a type under the classification $\langle Obj, Typ, Ref\rangle$.

refinements 1. A refinement variable is a refinement.

2. If A is an object and B is a type, then $\{A\}_B$ is a refinement.
3. If A and B are refinements, then so are $A \to B$, $A \vee B$ and $A \wedge B$.
4. If A is a refinement under the classification $\langle Obj, Typ \cup \{x\}, Ref\rangle$, then $\Pi x \in Type.A$ is a refinement under the classification $\langle Obj, Typ, Ref\rangle$.
5. If A is a type or a refinement, and B is a refinement under the classification $\langle Obj \cup \{x\}, Typ, Ref\rangle$, then $\bigwedge x \in A.B$ and $\bigvee x \in A.B$ are refinements under the classification $\langle Obj, Typ, Ref\rangle$.
6. If A is an r-kind and B is a refinement under the classification $\langle Obj, Typ, Ref \cup \{x\}\rangle$, then $\bigwedge x \in A.B$ and $\bigvee x \in A.B$ are refinements under the classification $\langle Obj, Typ, Ref\rangle$.

kind The constant *Type* is a kind.

r-kind If A is a type, then *refine*(A) is an r-kind. □

As in the case of ATT, any legal term of ATTT is uniquely classified into one of the classifications above, or one of *Kind* and *RKind*. ATTT-versions of the basic lemmas for ATT also hold. It should be clear how to formulate and prove them and so we will not include them here.

3.3 Translation of ATTT into $\lambda 2$

Now we give a translation of ATTT into a GTS-formulation of $\lambda 2$. The GTS-formulation of $\lambda 2$ is given by dropping $\mathit{refine}(T)$, $T \vee T$, $T \wedge T$, $\bigvee x \in T.T$, $\bigwedge x \in T.T$ and $\{T\}_T$ from the grammar of preterms. The conversion rule, rule of subject reduction and all of the rules for these are also dropped, e.g., the second inference rule of Π-formationis dropped. (Note that the rule of subject reduction is an admissible rule of $\lambda 2$.) The system was called $\lambda 2$ in [Bar90]. We will call the system $\lambda 2$, as $\lambda 2$ is essentially the same as $\lambda 2$.

Definition 8 (translation of preterms of ATTT into $\lambda 2$) We define a *nondeterministic* translation from ATTT to $\lambda 2$. That is, we define a binary relation $M \rightsquigarrow M'$ between preterms M of ATTT and preterms M' of $\lambda 2$, as follows:

1. $\mathit{RKind} \rightsquigarrow \mathit{Kind}$ and $c \rightsquigarrow c$ for the other constant c.
2. $\mathit{refine}(A) \rightsquigarrow \mathit{Type}$.
3. $x \rightsquigarrow x$.
4. If $A \rightsquigarrow A'$ and $B \rightsquigarrow B'$, then $(\lambda x \in A.B) \rightsquigarrow (\lambda x \in A'.B')$.
5. If $A \rightsquigarrow A'$ and $B \rightsquigarrow B'$, then $(AB) \rightsquigarrow (A'B')$.
6. If $A \rightsquigarrow A'$ and $B \rightsquigarrow B'$, then $(\Pi x \in A.B) \rightsquigarrow (\Pi x \in A'.B')$ and $(A \rightarrow B) \rightsquigarrow (A' \rightarrow B')$
7. If $A \rightsquigarrow A'$ and $B \rightsquigarrow B'$, then $A \ \mathsf{op}\ B \rightsquigarrow A'$ and $A \ \mathsf{op}\ B \rightsquigarrow B'$, where op is one of $\wedge$, $\vee$.
8. If $A \rightsquigarrow A'$ and $B \rightsquigarrow B'$, then $(\mathsf{OP}\, x \in \mathit{refine}(A).B) \rightsquigarrow B'[x := A']$, where OP is one of $\bigwedge$, $\bigvee$.
9. If $B \rightsquigarrow B'$ and A is not an r-kind, then $(\mathsf{OP}\, x \in A.B) \rightsquigarrow B'$, where OP is one of $\bigwedge$, $\bigvee$.
10. If $B \rightsquigarrow B'$, then $\{A\}_B \rightsquigarrow B'$.

If $M \rightsquigarrow M'$ holds, then we call M' a *translation of* M. □

The translation of judgments is naturally defined. If $A \rightsquigarrow A'$ and $B \rightsquigarrow B'$, then $A \in B \rightsquigarrow A' \in B'$. The translation of contexts and sequents is not straightforward, however.

Definition 9 (translation of contexts and sequents) Let Γ be $x_1 \in A_1, \ldots, x_n \in A_n$ and $A_i \leadsto A_i'$ for $i = 1, \ldots, n$. Set

$$\Gamma = \Gamma_0, x_{p_1} \in \mathit{refine}(T_{p_1}), \Gamma_1, \ldots, x_{p_m} \in \mathit{refine}(T_{p_m}), \Gamma_m$$

such that any judgment in Γ_j $(j = 1, \ldots, m)$ is not of the form $x \in \mathit{refine}(T)$. That is, $x_{p_1} \in A_{p_1}, \ldots, x_{p_m} \in A_{p_m}$ is the enumeration of all of the judgments in Γ whose A_i is an r-kind and $\mathit{refine}(T_{p_j}) = A_{p_j}$.

Let Γ_j' be the context obtained from Γ_j by replacing each judgment $x_i \in A_i$ by $x_i \in A_i'$. For $j = 1, \ldots, m$, let σ_j be the substitution $[x_{p_1} := T_{p_1}] \cdots [x_{p_j} := T_{p_j}]$. In particular, we will denote σ_m by $[\Gamma]$. Set

$$\Gamma' = \Gamma_0', \Gamma_1'\sigma_1, \ldots, \Gamma_m'\sigma_m.$$

Then we call Γ' a *translation of the context* Γ and write $\Gamma \leadsto \Gamma'$.

Next, we define the translation of a sequent. Let S be $\Gamma \vdash B \in C$. Assume that $\Gamma \leadsto \Gamma'$, $B \leadsto B'$ and $C \leadsto C'$. Set

$$S' = \Gamma' \vdash B'[\Gamma] \in C'[\Gamma].$$

Then we call S' a *translation of the sequent* S and write $S \leadsto S'$. □

For example, $x \in \mathit{Type}, z \in x \vdash x \in \mathit{Type}$ is a translation of the legal sequent

$$x \in \mathit{Type}, y \in \mathit{refine}(x), z \in y \vdash (y \wedge \{z\}_x) \in \mathit{refine}(x).$$

The soundness of the translation is stated as follows:

Theorem 4 *If S is a legal sequent of* ATTT *and $S \leadsto S'$, then S' is a legal sequent of $\lambda 2$.*

Note that if M is an object or a type, then it is a preterm of $\lambda 2$, and any translation of M is identical to M. By this observation, the following is obvious:

Corollary 3 ATTT *is a conservative extension of $\lambda 2$.*

An inversion principle similar to the type inversion principle for ATT (lemma 9) holds for ATTT. Hence, we can prove the strong normalization property as in the case of ATT.

Corollary 4 *Every term of* ATTT *is strongly normalizable.*

Note that strong normalization property of legal objects and types is obvious by the conservativity result.

Theorem 4 is a corollary of the following proposition which can be proved by simultaneous induction on derivations. The proof is straightforward, but lengthy. So we do not include it.

Proposition 2 *1. If S is a legal sequent of* ATTT *and $S \leadsto S'$, then S' is a legal sequent of $\lambda 2$.*

2. If S is a legal sequent of ATTT *and $S \leadsto S'$ and $S \leadsto S''$, then S' and S'' are identical.*

3. If $\Gamma \vdash A \in \mathit{refine}(B)$ is a legal sequent of ATTT *and*

$$(\Gamma \vdash A \in \mathit{refine}(B)) \leadsto (\Gamma \vdash A' \in C),$$

then A' is identical to B.

As a corollary of this proposition, we can prove the following:

Corollary 5 *If $\Gamma \vdash A \in \mathit{refine}(B)$ and $\Gamma \vdash A \in \mathit{refine}(B')$ are legal sequents of ATTT, then B and B' are identical.*

We will call the unique type B of $A \in \mathit{refine}(B)$ *the type of A* written $\mathit{type}(A)$. Note that $\mathit{type}(A)$ depends on the context under which A is legal. For simplicity, we omit context in the notation.

3.4 Semantics of ATTT

The semantics of ATTT is fairly simple. We start with the so called BMM-semantics of $\lambda 2$ (see [BMM90] for BMM-semantics). The BMM-semantics is a set theoretical semantics, that is, each type of $\lambda 2$ is interpreted as a set. Let $[\![A]\!]_\rho$ be the interpretation of type A under assignment ρ. Then we interpret refinement kinds by

$$[\![\mathit{refine}(A)]\!]_\rho = \mathit{Pow}([\![A]\!]_\rho).$$

Pow(X) is the powerset of X. Hence, refinements of a type are subsets of the interpretation of the type. Singleton, intersection and union refinements are interpreted in the usual sense of set theory. Then it is straightforward to check the semantics is sound. A more intrinsic semantics could be given in appropriate categories, such as the topos of Pitts [Pit87]. Furthermore, we conjecture that there is a PL-category-like second-order categorical framework for ATTT.

As remarked in section 2.3, the PER-semantics for ATT has some anomalies. But this is not so in ATTT, because we can state the extensionality rule only for types and not for refinements.

Extensionality

$$\frac{\Gamma \vdash A \in \mathit{Type} \quad \Gamma \vdash B \in \mathit{Type} \qquad \Gamma, f \in (A \to B), g \in (A \to B), x = y \in A \vdash f(x) = g(y) \in B}{\Gamma, f \in (A \to B), g \in (A \to B) \vdash f = g \in (A \to B)}$$

Note that we can define the equality judgment only for types and not for refinements, since $a = b \in A$ is $a \in \{b\}_A$ and so A must be a type. Hence, two functions from refinement $R_1 \to R_2$ must be compared in the type $\mathit{type}(R_1) \to \mathit{type}(R_2)$.

4 Related works

Many authors have studied union and intersection types from disparate motivations, e.g., [FP91, MPS86, BDC91, Pie90, Pie91, Rey88]. A more complete list of the literature on the subject and a fine survey of them can be found in [Pie91]. But we here list only related work devoted to the same aim as ours: program extraction.

No literature has considered the suite of types, Singleton, Union and Intersection Types, SUIT in short, for program extraction. One exception is the work by Parigot and Krivine. They considered first order and second order intersections for a similar purpose to program extraction [Par88, Par89, KP90]. Parigot uses a type closely related to singleton types in [Par89]. But they do not consider union types, because they use functions explicitly rather than existential quantifiers.

Although none of types of SUIT is used explicitly, Paulin's modified realizability interpretation for CoC [PM89] and Burstall's deliverable [BM91] seem closely related to our work. Actually, these two were our constant sources of ideas. As we pointed out, ATTT is an axiomatization of modified realizability. The translation from ATTT to $\lambda 2$ seems to be a counterpart of Paulin's extraction operator $\mathcal{E}$ in [PM89]. There would be a formal relationship between Paulin's realization method and a higher order version of ATTT.

Burstall's deliverable is closely related to modified realizability and so to Paulin's work. His motivation was to separate proofs and programs in program development via CoC or ECC. This is closed to our motivation of separating logic and computation. In ATTT, refinements serve as the device of logic and types serve as the device of computation. Unlike the deliverable approach, the logical part, i.e., inference on refinement, is not kept at all in the terms developed. Deliverables keep programs and proofs separately as terms of CoC. In our case, the program part of a deliverable is the term A of the derived judgment $A \in B$ and the proof is kept in the derivation of the judgment. The exact relationships to Paulin and Burstall's work remains to be studied.

5 Future work

Decidability of typechecking with SUIT seems hopeless. Typing with SUIT is just difficult as verification. Typechecking in the deliverable approach is reduced to typechecking of CoC and so is automatic. This is because of the presence of a term recording a history of proofs separately from programs. We think that this approach separates proofs and programs too much. There seems no apparent association of subparts of the proof-term and program-term of a deliverable. It would be difficult to see that a subterm of a program-term was verified by a part of the proof-term, and in what way. We are working to add annotations recording history of derivations to terms of our type theories. Such annotations keep all the logical information of inference rules, but they should not be respected by the system. That is, these annotations should work like the documentation part in Knuth's WEB language. With these annotations, typechecking in ATT and ATTT would become decidable.

The application of SUIT to program extraction was briefly mentioned. We have already had some applications of SUIT for the aim, which will appear elsewhere. But SUIT in practice of program extraction has not been well studied. In particular, we have not considered SUIT in backward reasoning. Bob Harper has pointed out that an anomaly of subset type with backward reasoning encountered in Nuprl project would appear in our setting and might cause a problem. We are trying to understand and remedy this anomaly by the history annotations mentioned above.

We have designed higher order versions of ATT and ATTT. Their metatheories are yet to be studied. We believe that there is a general method for adding SUIT to a type theory at least in the way of ATTT without interfering with any features of the original type theory. Such a method might give a general way to add logic to type theory.

The right semantics of ATT and ATTT is yet to investigate as noted in the paper. Furthermore, semantics of SUIT fully consistent with extensionality is yet to study. We conjecture that there is no such semantics.

Subject reduction in the presence of union and intersection types has not been studied well. In the deliverable approach, equivalence of programs can be verified in CoC using equalities attached to data types. But, this cannot be done in our approach, as the only way to transform of programs into another is β-reduction of subject reduction. This is one of the most serious problems yet to be solved with SUIT approach.

Acknowledgments

I thank Zhaohui Luo, Christine Paulin, Benjamin Pierce and Yukihide Takayama for fruitful discussions and helpful comments on the paper.

References

[Bar90] H. Barendregt. Introduction to generalized type systems. Technical Report no.90-8, University of Nijmegen, May 1990.

[BDC91] F. Barbanera and M. Dezani-Ciancaglini. Intersection and union types. In *Theoretical Aspect of Computer Science, Sendai*, 1991. To appear.

[BM91] R. Burstall and J. McKinna. Deliverable: an approach to program development in the calculus of constructions. An earlier version is in the preliminary proceeding of the Logical Frameworks BRA meeting at Sophia Antipolis 1990, April 1991.

[BMM90] K.B. Bruce, A.R. Meyer, and J. C. Mitchell. The semantics of second-order lambda calculus. *Information and Computation*, 85:76–134, 1990.

[CH88] Th. Coquand and G. Huet. Calculus of constructions. *Information and Computation*, 76:95–120, 1988.

[Coq86] Th. Coquand. An analysis of Girard's paradox. In *Proceedings of First Annual Symposium on Logic in Computer Science*, 1986.

[FP91] T. Freeman and F. Pfenning. Refinement types for ML. In *ACM SIGPLAN'91 Conference on Programming Language Design and Implementation, Toronto, Ontario.* ACM Press, June 1991.

[Hay90] S. Hayashi. Constructive mathematics and computer-aided reasoning systems. In P.P. Petkov, editor, *MATHEMATICAL LOGIC*, pages 43–52. Plenum Press, New York, 1990.

[HN88] S. Hayashi and H. Nakano. *PX: A Computational Logic.* The MIT Press, Cambridge, Mass., 1988.

[KP90] J.-L. Krivine and M. Parigot. Programmimg with proofs. *Journal of Information Processing and Cybernetics EIK*, 26:149–167, 1990.

[Lei86] D. Leivant. Typing and convergence in the lambda calculus. *Theoretical Computer Science*, 44:51–68, 1986.

[Luo90] Z. Luo. *An Extended Calculus of Constructions.* PhD thesis, Department of Computer Science, University of Edinburgh, July 1990.

[Mar72] P. Martin-Löf. A theory of types. Unpublished manuscript, 1972.

[Mit90] J. C. Mitchell. Type systems for programming languages. In J. van Leeuwen, editor, *Handbook of Theoretical Computer Science, Volume B*, pages 365–458. North-Holland, 1990.

[Mog88] E. Moggi. *The Partial Lambda-Calculus.* PhD thesis, Department of Computer Science, University of Edinburgh, 1988.

[MPS86] D. MacQueen, G. Plotkin, and R. Sethi. An ideal model for recursive polymorphic types. *Information and Control*, 71:95–130, 1986.

[NPS90] B. Nordström, K. Petersson, and J.M. Smith. *Programming in Martin-Löf's type theory, an introduction.* Clarendon Press, Oxford, 1990.

[Par88] M. Parigot. Programming with proofs: a second order type theory. In *ESOP '88 (Lecture Notes in Computer Science No. 300).* Springer-Verlag, 1988.

[Par89] M. Parigot. Recursive programming with proofs. In *Proceedings of Symposium Mathematiques et Informatique, Luminy, France*, October 1989. To appear in Theoretical Computer Science.

[Pie90] B.C. Pierce. Preliminary investigation of a calculus with intersection and union types. Unpublished manuscript, June 1990.

[Pie91] B.C. Pierce. Programming with intersection types, union types, and polymorphism. Technical Report CMU-CS-91-106, School of Computer Science, Carnegie Mellon University, Feburary 1991.

[Pit87] A.M. Pitts. Polymorphism is set theoretic constructively. In D.H. Pitt et al., editors, *Category theory and computer science (Lecture Notes in Comuter Science No. 283)*, pages 12–39, Berlin, 1987. Springer-Verlag.

[Plo85] G. Plotkin. Lectures given at ASL Stanford meeting. Unpublished lecture notes, July 1985.

[PM89] C. Paulin-Mohring. Extracting F_ω's programs from proofs in the calculus of construction. In *Proceedings of 16th Annual ACM Symposium on Principles of Programming Languages*, 1989.

[Rey88] J.C. Reynolds. Preliminary design of the programming language Forsythe. Technical Report CMU-CS-88-159, School of Computer Science, Carnegie Mellon University, June 1988.

[Ros86] G. Rosolini. *Continuity and effectiveness in topoi.* PhD thesis, Department of Computer Science, Carnegie-Mellon University, 1986.

[Sce89] A. Scedrov. Normalization revisited. In J. W. Gray and A. Scedrov, editors, *Categories in Computer Science and Logic, (Contemporary Mathematics Vol. 92)*, pages 357–369. American Mathematical Society, Providence, Rhode Island, 1989.

[TH90] Y. Takayama and S Hayashi. Extended projection method and realizability interpretation. Submitted to Information and Computation, 1990.

[Tur89] D. Turner. A new formulation of constructive type theory. In P. Dybjer et al., editors, *Proceedings of the Workshop on Programming Logic*, pages 258–294, 1989. Report 54, Programming Methodology Group, Department of Computer Science, Chalmers University of Technology and University of Göteborg.

Subtyping + Extensionality: Confluence of $\beta\eta$top reduction in $\mathbf{F}_{\leq}$

Pierre-Louis Curien[1], Giorgio Ghelli[2]

Abstract: We contribute to the syntactic study of $\mathbf{F}_{\leq}$, a variant of second order λ-calculus $\mathbf{F}$ which appears as a paradigmatic kernel language for polymorphism and subtyping. The type system of $\mathbf{F}_{\leq}$ has a maximum type Top and bounded quantification. We endow this language with the familiar β-rules (for terms and types), to which we add extensionality rules: the η-rules (for terms and types), and a rule (top) which equates all terms of type Top. These rules are suggested by the axiomatization of cartesian closed categories. We show that this theory $\beta\eta\mathrm{top}_{\leq}$ is decidable, by exhibiting an effectively weakly normalizing and confluent rewriting system for it. Our proof of confluence relies on the confluence of a corresponding system on $\mathbf{F}_1$ (the extension of $\mathbf{F}$ with a terminal type), and follows a general pattern that we investigate for itself in a separate paper.

After giving some background on the language $\mathbf{F}_{\leq}$ (section 1), we make observations on the confluence problem of $\beta\eta$ in various typed λ-calculi (section 2). We discuss some difficulties arising from the multiplicity of typing proofs in $\mathbf{F}_{\leq}$ (section 3), which lead us to study the corresponding problem in an explicit calculus $\mathbf{cF}_{\leq}$, whose terms codify typing proofs in $\mathbf{F}_{\leq}$ (section 4). We add the (top) rule which equates all terms of type Top (section 5). In the rest of the paper (sections 6 through 10) we state our confluence results (theorem 1 in section 9, and theorem 2 in section 10), and we offer a technical survey of the constructions which lead us to them. We conclude in section 11.

1 $\mathbf{F}_{\leq}$ *background*

$\mathbf{F}_{\leq}$ is a basic language expressing *structural subtyping* and *polymorphism*. It allows for an encoding of most familiar structures with subtyping such as records and variants, and is a kernel for the language Quest developed by Luca Cardelli [Ca]. It is essentially the language Fun of [CaWe] (unlike $\mathbf{F}_{\leq}$, Fun has recursive types and values, and has records, variants and existential types as primitives). $\mathbf{F}_{\leq}$ was introduced in [CG1] (see also [BrLo] and [CaLo]). We briefly recall the syntax of $\mathbf{F}_{\leq}$, and hint at a few encodings. The reader will find more material in [CaLo,GheTh,CaMaMiSce].

[1] LIENS (CNRS), 45 rue d'Ulm, 75230 Paris Cedex 05, France. This work was carried on with the partial support of E.E.C., Esprit Basic Research Action 3003 CLICS .
[2] Dipartimento di Informatica, Università di Pisa, Corso Italia 40, I-56100, Pisa, Italy, ghelli@dipisa.di.unipi.it.
This work was carried on with the partial support of E.E.C., Esprit Basic Research Action 3070 FIDE and of Italian C.N.R., P.F.I. "Sistemi informatici e calcolo parallelo".

The types and expressions of $\mathbf{F}_{\leq}$ are defined as follows:

$$A ::= t \mid Top \mid A{\rightarrow}A \mid \forall t{\leq}A.\, A$$
$$a ::= x \mid top \mid \lambda x{:}A.\, a \mid a(a) \mid \Lambda t{\leq}A.\, a \mid a\{A\}$$

In the second order abstraction $\Lambda t{\leq}A.a$, the bound A restricts the types which can be accepted as parameters to be subtypes of A. The type Top is a supertype of all types, so that unbounded second order lambda abstraction can be recovered as $\Lambda t{\leq}Top.a$. The term top is the (unique) term of type Top . The typing rules are given in appendix A.

Here are a few examples of subtypings. In $\mathbf{F}_{\leq}$ the known encoding of the type of booleans in second order λ-calculus, $TF \equiv \forall t.t{\rightarrow}t{\rightarrow}t$, has four subtypes:

- $TF \equiv \forall t{\leq}Top.\, t{\rightarrow}t{\rightarrow}t$ (the booleans)
- $F \equiv \forall t{\leq}Top.\, Top{\rightarrow}t{\rightarrow}t$ (just false)
- $T \equiv \forall t{\leq}Top.\, t{\rightarrow}Top{\rightarrow}t$ (just true)
- $\bot \equiv \forall t{\leq}Top.\, Top{\rightarrow}Top{\rightarrow}t$ (an empty type)

One can prove the following inclusions: $\bot{\leq}T$, $\bot{\leq}F$, $T{\leq}TF$ and $F{\leq}TF$. Moreover, there is no term of type $\bot$, and only one β normal form $true_T = \Lambda t{\leq}Top.\lambda x{:}t.\lambda y{:}Top.\, x$ of type T. In TF we find the following normal forms: $true_T$ again, and

$true_{TF} = \Lambda t{\leq}Top.\, \lambda x{:}t.\, \lambda y{:}t.\, x$

(and similarly $false_F$ and $false_{TF}$). We shall see in section 3 that $true_F$ and $true_{TF}$, $false_F$ and $false_{TF}$ are provably βη equal. So the subtypes of TF correspond exactly to the subsets of {true,false}.

We now briefly hint at the encoding of records. The essence of record subtyping is the possibility of obtaining subtypes by adding fields. This is captured by Cardelli's n-ary tuples [CaLo], which satisfy the following subtyping rule:

$$A_i{\leq}A'_i \Rightarrow A_1{\otimes}\ldots{\otimes}A_n{\otimes}B \leq A'_1{\otimes}\ldots{\otimes}A'_n\,.$$

A tuple can be encoded in $\mathbf{F}_{\leq}$ as the right associative product of its component types and of Top. For example $A_1{\otimes}\ldots{\otimes}A_n{\otimes}B$ and $A'_1{\otimes}\ldots{\otimes}A'_n$ are encoded respectively as

$(A_1{\times}\ldots{\times}(A_n{\times}(B{\times}Top))\ldots)$ and $(A'_1{\times}\ldots{\times}(A'_n{\times}(Top))\ldots)$,

and the inequality follows from $A_i{\leq}A'_i$ and $B{\times}Top{\leq}Top$. This encoding of tuples can be easily extended to records [CaLo].

In a previous paper [CG1], we initiated a study of the syntactic theory of $\mathbf{F}_{\leq}$. We addressed a *coherence* problem: in presence of subtyping, there may be several proofs establishing that a given expression has a given type. Similarly there may be several proofs of a subtyping judgement $A{\leq}B$. In [CG1] we have exhibited a complete equational axiomatization of the following equivalence relation between typing proofs: two proofs are equivalent when they prove the same typing or subtyping judgement (see proposition 3 of this paper). To prove the coherence[3] of a proposed interpretation, it is thus enough to check that the axioms of [CG1] are satisfied.

We also proved, as fallouts of this coherence study: a) the property that a typable expression always has a *minimum* type (once the types (bounds) of the free (type) variables are fixed), and b) the *completeness* of a natural *type-checking* algorithm. The key tool was the definition of a (weakly) normalizing rewriting system on typing proofs. It was convenient to introduce a language $\mathbf{cF}_{\leq}$ whose terms are the typing proofs of $\mathbf{F}_{\leq}$. This language, which we called explicit, will be also extensively used in this paper.

2 *Confluence of* $\beta\eta$ *reduction on typed* λ*-calculi*

The main purpose of this paper is to investigate the *confluence* (and the decidability) of a theory in $\mathbf{F}_{\leq}$ involving both β rules and extensionality rules. It is known that $\beta\eta$-confluence holds in the (simply) typed λ-calculus, but not on the raw (i.e. possibly not typable) terms of this calculus. Consider the following critical pair[4] (where x is not free in b):

(*) $\lambda x{:}A.(\lambda y{:}B.b)x \;\rightarrow_\eta\; \lambda y{:}B.b, \qquad \lambda x{:}A.(\lambda y{:}B.b)x \;\rightarrow_\beta\; \lambda x{:}A.b[y\leftarrow x] =_\alpha \lambda y{:}A.b.$

If we do not take typing rules into account, the two reducts cannot be compared. But when the redex $\lambda x{:}A.(\lambda y{:}B.b)x$ is well typed (in the simply typed or second-order λ-calculus), then A and B coincide, so that the critical pair is solved. The situation is less simple in the higher-order λ-calculus, where A and B may be interconvertible. But in the higher-order λ-calculus the type conversion system is separate from the term conversion system: thus we can get, by a separate argument, that A,B both converge to say C, and both $\lambda x{:}A.b$ and $\lambda y{:}B.b$ converge to $\lambda y{:}C.b$. The situation is much more complex with dependent types, since then the solution of the critical pair (*) circularly calls for the decision of the equality of A and B, which may contain terms. A way to go around this circularity had been found by D. Van Daalen [Daal] (see also [Salv,CG2]).

In presence of subtyping, the expression $\lambda x{:}A.(\lambda y{:}B.b)x$ is well typed, and has type $A\rightarrow C$, as soon as $A\leq B$ is provable and b has type C. One may uncautiously try to solve the critical pair (*) by adding the following equation, and by orienting it:

$\lambda y{:}B.b = \lambda y{:}A.b \quad (A\leq B).$

We argue that this equation should be oriented from left to right. In typed systems, one always looks for some kind of subject reduction property, namely, roughly speaking, if the left hand side of an equation is typed, then the right hand side should also be typed. Consider the left hand side.

---

[3] *Coherence* amounts to the property that the interpretation of a term t is independent of a particular typing proof of t (a semantic interpretation function is defined by induction on typing proofs, not on terms, so a priori different typing proofs of a same judgement could be interpreted differently).

[4] Recall that in the terminology of rewriting theory, a critical pair is formed by the superposition of the left hand sides of two rules.

Suppose that $\lambda y{:}B.b$ is well typed. Then in any typing proof of $\lambda y{:}B.b$ we must show, at some stage, that b is well typed under the assumption y:B. A fortiori, when $A \leq B$, b is well typed under the assumption y:A, thus also $\lambda y{:}A.b$ is well typed. This argument does not work the other way around. Take for instance $A \equiv A_1 \rightarrow A_2$ and $B \equiv Top$. If the rule were oriented from right to left then $\lambda y{:}A_1 \rightarrow A_2.yx$ would reduce to $\lambda y{:}Top.yx$, which cannot be well typed. So we tentatively add to the $\beta\eta$ reduction system the following rule:

(1) $\lambda y{:}B.b \rightarrow \lambda y{:}A.b \quad (A \leq B)$.

But, even with this orientation, the rule fails to satisfy subject reduction, as shown in the next section.

3 Typed reduction

Let us be more specific about what we mean by subject reduction in $F_{\leq}$. We say that a rule satisfies *subject reduction* in $F_{\leq}$ if, for any typable redex R, and *any* type of R, the reduct R' can be typed with the *same* type; informally the rule decreases minimum types.

This property is satisfied by β and η (first and second order), but it does not hold for rule (1). Take $b \equiv y$. Then the minimum types of $\lambda y{:}B.y$ and $\lambda y{:}A.y$ are $B \rightarrow B$ and $A \rightarrow A$, respectively, and $A \rightarrow A$ is not a subtype of $B \rightarrow B$ if A and B are different. So it is not always correct to identify a (1) redex by only matching the subexpression to be replaced: the resulting term will not be necessarily well typed. Specifically, suppose that the (1) reduction takes place in the context $\lambda z{:}(B \rightarrow B) \rightarrow C.\ z[\ ]$. Then, of the two expressions $\lambda z{:}(B \rightarrow B) \rightarrow C.\ z(\lambda y{:}B.y)$ and $\lambda z{:}(B \rightarrow B) \rightarrow C.\ z(\lambda x{:}A.x)$, only the first one can be typed.

What is then a correct application of (1)? The point is that we not only have to match a subexpression against the left hand side of (1), but also to match types in some sense. In the specific example we considered, given a context C[ ], the replacement of, say $C[\lambda y{:}B.y]$ by $C[\lambda x{:}A.x]$, is safe if some typing proof of $C[\lambda y{:}B.y]$ assigns a supertype of $A \rightarrow A$ to the redex $\lambda y{:}B.y$. In general, we shall allow the replacement of $\lambda y{:}B.b$ by $\lambda x{:}A.b$ only if some typing proof of $C[\lambda y{:}B.b]$ assigns type $A \rightarrow C$, for some C, to the redex $\lambda y{:}B.b$ [5] (remember that $A \rightarrow C$ is one the types of $\lambda x{:}A.(\lambda y{:}B.b)x$).

A way to formalize this restriction is to specify the valid typings and the valid rewriting rules *at the same time*. One introduces judgements $\Gamma \vdash a \rightarrow b{:}A$; our rule is now expressed (correctly) as follows:

$$(\lambda t) \qquad \frac{\Gamma \vdash \lambda x{:}B.b{:}\ A \rightarrow C \qquad (A \neq B)}{\Gamma \vdash \lambda x{:}B.b \rightarrow \lambda x{:}A.b{:}\ A \rightarrow C}$$

(it can be proved that the premise entails $A \leq B$). For example, λt implies that $true_T{:}TF$ rewrites to $true_{TF}{:}TF$ (cf. section 1).

[5] Notice that $A \rightarrow C$ is not the minimum type of $\lambda y{:}B.b$.

Replacement of subexpressions is controlled by *typed congruence rules*, which duplicate the typing rules. So, for example:

$$(\rightarrow\text{Elim})\quad \frac{\Gamma \vdash a \rightarrow a' : A \rightarrow B \quad \Gamma \vdash b : A}{\Gamma \vdash ab \rightarrow a'b : B}$$

$$(\text{Subsump})\quad \frac{\Gamma \vdash a \rightarrow a' : A \quad \Gamma \vdash A \leq B}{\Gamma \vdash a \rightarrow a' : B}$$

It can be shown that, in the present case, this axiomatization accepts only replacements which result in well-typed terms (formally, if $\Gamma \vdash a \rightarrow a' : A$ is provable, then so are $\Gamma \vdash a : A$ and $\Gamma \vdash a' : A$). Generalizing, the above axiomatization relies on inference rules of the following shapes:

$$(\text{Axiom})\quad \frac{\Gamma \vdash a : A}{\Gamma \vdash a \rightarrow a' : A}$$

$$(\text{Typed Congruence})\quad \frac{\Gamma \vdash a \rightarrow a' : A \quad \ldots}{\Delta \vdash C[a] \rightarrow C[a'] : B}$$

λt and $\rightarrow$Elim are examples of (Axiom) and (Typed Congruence), respectively.

This style of axiomatization, while logically clear, does not fit nicely with known techniques to prove decidability via confluence (Knuth-Bendix completion in particular): reduction and typing are too tightly related. In the simply typed λ-calculus, reduction and typing are usually separated. One specifies β as a rewrite rule on raw terms, with untyped congruence rules:

$$(\text{Untyped Congruence})\quad \frac{a \rightarrow a'}{C[a] \rightarrow C[a']}$$

Then the typed theory can be defined by:

$$\frac{\Gamma \vdash a : A \quad a \rightarrow a'}{\Gamma \vdash a \rightarrow a' : A}$$

Untyped presentations are more handy than typed ones. One may wonder which kinds of typed presentations can be transformed into an equivalent untyped one. Call a typed presentation *type independent* when for any instance $\Delta \vdash b : B$ of the premise $\Gamma \vdash a : A$ of an axiom

$$\frac{\Gamma \vdash a{:}A}{\Gamma \vdash a \rightarrow a'{:}A}$$

and for any type B' s.t. $\Delta \vdash$ b:B' is provable, then B' matches A (this is achieved in particular if A is a type metavariable not occurring freely in Γ, a). We say furthermore that a typed presentation satisfies *typed* subject reduction when a':A follows from a:A for each axiom. We believe that each untyped presentation satisfying subject reduction (as defined in the first paragraph of this section) is equivalent to a typed presentation which is type independent and satisfies typed subject reduction, and vice-versa. Notice that the rule λt above is not type independent.

In a system like simply typed λ-calculus, and more widely in systems where types of expressions are uniquely determined from the environment, type independence holds for free, and typed subject reduction amounts to subject reduction.

Summarizing, we have on one side calculi with uniquely determined types for which untyped presentations can be given, and on the other side systems like $\beta+\eta+\lambda t$ where a typed presentation is needed. But a theory corresponding closely to $\beta+\eta+\lambda t$ can be expressed in the explicit calculus **cF**$_{\leq}$ which has uniquely determined types. We shall first establish a confluence result relative to this theory in **cF**$_{\leq}$, and then transfer it to **F**$_{\leq}$.

4 *Expressing λt in the explicit calculus cF$_{\leq}$*

The language **cF**$_{\leq}$ keeps a complete record of the typing proofs in **F**$_{\leq}$. The key departure between **F**$_{\leq}$ and **cF**$_{\leq}$ is in the subsumption rule: in **F**$_{\leq}$, when a:A and A≤B, then a:B. In **cF**$_{\leq}$ there is a language of subtyping proofs (or coercions): if a:A, and c:A≤B (i.e. c is a proof of A≤B), then we write c<a>:B; the reader will find the complete language **cF**$_{\leq}$ in appendix B. For example, Id:A≤A, and if c:A≤B, d:A'≤B', then c→d: B→A' ≤ A→B'. In **cF**$_{\leq}$, typable expressions have unique types, allowing for a separation of reduction and typing. Let us revisit the critical pair (*) with this new apparatus:

(**) λx:A.(λy:B.b)(c<x>) $\rightarrow_{\text{“}\eta\text{”}}$ (c→Id)<λy:B.b> [6]
λx:A.(λy:B.b)(c<x>) $\rightarrow_{\beta}$ λx:A.b[y←c<x>]$=_{\alpha}\lambda$y:A.[y←c<y>].

The coercions in (**) come from proofs that A→C is a type of λx:A.(λy:B.b)x and λy:B.b . The coercions c and c→Id prove A≤B and B→C≤A→C, respectively.

The equational consequence of (**) which is now considered is:

(2) (c→Id)<λy:B.b> → λy:A.[y←c<y>].

The substitution occurring in the right hand indicates an orientation from left to right, confirming

[6]Notice that this is not η proper. The general form of the η rule in **cF**$_{\leq}$, called cη, is λy:A.d<a(c<y>)> → (c→d)<a>.

the choice made in section 2. Informally, rule (2) adapts the input type of a function to its *context type*, i.e. the type that the function has as a subexpression in its context.

5 Where Top comes in

Actually rule (2) takes only care of the case where the context type is an arrow type. If the context type is Top, then the following new critical pair arises (Top_A (Top for short) is the proof of A≤Top and c•d proves A≤C if d proves A≤B and c proves B≤C; see appendix B):

$$\mathrm{Top}\langle(c\to \mathrm{Id})\langle\lambda y{:}B.a\rangle\rangle \to (\mathrm{Top}\bullet(c\to \mathrm{Id}))\langle\lambda y{:}B.a\rangle \to \mathrm{Top}\langle\lambda y{:}B.a\rangle^{7}$$
$$\mathrm{Top}\langle(c\to \mathrm{Id})\langle\lambda y{:}B.a\rangle\rangle \to \mathrm{Top}\langle\lambda y{:}A.a[y\leftarrow c\langle y\rangle]\rangle.$$

This suggests to include the rule

$$\mathrm{Top}\langle a\rangle \to \mathrm{top}$$

in the theory. Informally, "observed from Top, all terms are equal", and categorically, "Top is terminal". Actually this rule as such does *not* force terminality: The variable x (with x:Top in the environment) and the term top are not equated. We reinforce the rule to

(top) $a{:}\,\mathrm{Top} \Rightarrow a \to \mathrm{top}$.

Notice that (top), unlike λt, is not an equational consequence of the other rules, it really changes the equational theory considered.

Expressed in $\mathbf{F}_{\leq}$, the rule (top) becomes:

$$\text{(top)}\quad \frac{\Gamma \vdash a{:}\,\mathrm{Top}}{\Gamma \vdash a\to \mathrm{top}{:}\,\mathrm{Top}}$$

(notice that in the terminology introduced in section 3, this axiom is not type independent in $\mathbf{F}_{\leq}$).

Thus critical pair considerations have lead us to consider both extensionality rules η and (top), rather than η in isolation. In [GheTh] it is proved that all the terms of type Top are observationally equivalent, in the sense that the result of the β evaluation of an expression of basic type is not affected by the replacement of any subexpression of type Top by any other expression of type Top.

Summarizing, we consider the equational theory $\beta\eta\mathrm{top}_{\leq}$ in $\mathbf{F}_{\leq}$ consisting of first and second order β and η, and (top). As suggested by the discussions in sections 3 and 4, we shall first work with a "corresponding" theory $c\beta\eta\mathrm{top}_{\leq}$ on $c\mathbf{F}_{\leq}$ which consists of first and second order β and cη

---

[7] $(\mathrm{Top}\bullet(c\to \mathrm{Id})) \to \mathrm{Top}$ is one of the coherence rules of [CG1] (notice that $\mathrm{Top}\bullet(c\to \mathrm{Id})$) and Top are two different proofs of the same subtyping B→C≤Top.

(cf. footnote 6), (top), and a set of equations (groups I and II + Id + Comp, see appendix B) which are introduced for coherence (cf. section 1, see [CG1] and Proposition 3 below).

6 Our proof plan

We are now ready to describe our proof plan:

1) We exhibit a rewriting system cR in $\mathbf{cF}_{\leq}$ which is equivalent to $c\beta\eta top_{\leq}$ as an equational theory, and show that it is confluent and weakly normalizing (with an effective normalizing strategy). The proof of confluence relies on a translation to a confluent system on $\mathbf{F_1}$ (the extension of F with a terminal type) and use a general technique discussed in section 8.

2) We transfer confluence and effective weak normalization of cR in $\mathbf{cF}_{\leq}$ to the corresponding system R in $\mathbf{F}_{\leq}$ (for confluence we use again the general technique of section 8). Decidability of $\beta\eta top_{\leq}$ in $\mathbf{F}_{\leq}$ follows immediately, because $\beta\eta top_{\leq}$ is the equational theory of R.

We devote the rest of the paper to survey the realization of this plan. We first continue the game of critical pairs (section 7). Then, we introduce the general method (section 8), and sketch how we use it to carry out part 1 (section 9) and part 2 (section 10) of the proof plan.

7 Knuth-Bendix continued

Our proofs of confluence for both cR and R do *not* rely on local confluence (see section 8). However, playing the game of completions is a useful guide in designing cR and R, since the systems are to be locally confluent anyway. We focus on the interactions between (top) and η.

Intuitively, if all the terms in Top are equivalent, then also all the terms in, say, A→Top are equivalent. This can be seen directly from critical pairs (we work on $\mathbf{cF}_{\leq}$, but similar "critical pairs" arise also in $\mathbf{F}_{\leq}$). Suppose a:A→Top;

$$\lambda y{:}A.ay \rightarrow_{top} \lambda y{:}A.top, \qquad \lambda y{:}A.ay \rightarrow_{\eta} a$$

So we add the following stronger version of (top):

(gentop) $\Gamma \vdash a{:}\ T,\ T \in \text{IsoTop and } a \neq top(T) \quad \Rightarrow \quad a \rightarrow top(T)$

where IsoTop is the set of all the types like A→... →Top, ∀t≤A...Top, possibly mixing first order and second order quantifications. top(T) is the term λx:A...top or Λt≤A...top of type T (see appendix A for a formal definition).

There is another critical pair involving top and η, arising intuitively from the fact that top(T) is equivalent to any variable of type T. If $c:A\leq T$ and $T\in$ IsTop , then:

$$\lambda y{:}A.d\langle a(c\langle y\rangle)\rangle \rightarrow_{top} \lambda y{:}A.d\langle a(top(T))\rangle, \quad \lambda y{:}A.d\langle a(c\langle y\rangle)\rangle \rightarrow_{c\eta} (c\rightarrow d)\langle a\rangle .$$

Thus we have to add the following variant of η in $\mathbf{cF}_{\leq}$:

$$(c\eta_{top}) \qquad \lambda y{:}A.d\langle a(top(T))\rangle \rightarrow (c\rightarrow d)\langle a\rangle .$$

where c is a proof of $A\leq T$; since in [CG1] we defined a notion of normal form coercion, we can choose c to be the normal form proof of $A\leq T$.

We shall stop here our investigation of critical pairs. One has to take into account the coherence axioms, which lead to other critical pairs of less interest. The complete listing of cR is given in appendix B.

8 *A general technique to prove confluence of weakly normalizing systems*

Now we present the general technique which we use to prove our confluence results.

Proposition 1: Let $(A,\rightarrow)$ and $(B,\rightarrow')$ be two abstract reduction systems (i.e. sets equipped with a binary relation) and G be a set mapping from A to B. Suppose that the following properties hold:

(C1) $(B,\rightarrow')$ is confluent,
(C2) $(A,\rightarrow)$ is weakly normalizing,
(C3) If $a\rightarrow a'$ in A, then $G(a)='G(a')$ in B (equivalently: if $a=a'$, then $G(a)='G(a')$),
(C4) G translates $\rightarrow$ normal forms into $\rightarrow'$ normal forms,
(C5) G is injective on $\rightarrow$ normal forms.

where = (=') is the reflexive, symmetric and transitive closure of $\rightarrow$ ($\rightarrow'$). Then $(A,\rightarrow)$ is confluent.

Proof: Easy (see [CG2]). □

We refer to [CG2] for a discussion and some examples of applications of the method. We shall apply this method twice, to get successively the confluence of cR and the confluence of the corresponding system R on $\mathbf{F}_{\leq}$.

Notation: We shall use hereafter "≡" for syntactic equality, to distinguish it from provable equality "=".

9 *Confluence of* cR

We apply proposition 1 with $(A,\to)=(cF_{\leq},cR)$ and $(B,\to')=(F_1,R_1)$ where F_1 is second order λ-calculus, extended with a terminal type[8], and R_1 is a confluent completion of βηtop on F_1. Here is the syntax of F_1 :

$$A ::= t \mid Top \mid A\to A \mid \forall t.\, A$$
$$a ::= x \mid top \mid \lambda x{:}A.\, a \mid a(a) \mid \Lambda t.\, a \mid a\{A\}$$

The theory βη top on F_1 consists of the same rules as $\beta\eta top_{\leq}$ on $F_{\leq}$. The presence of (top) introduces critical pairs in the corresponding rewriting theory (which are similar to those discussed in 7); completion leads us to a locally confluent rewriting system R_1 whose underlying equational theory is the theory βηtop. The confluence of R_1 is proved in [CDC]. The typing rules of F_1, the theory βηtop and the system R_1 are given in appendix C.

The mapping G is a translation * from $cF_{\leq}$ to F_1 which encodes subtyping proofs by suitable terms of F_1. It is a variant of the translation proposed in [BCGS], which was used to produce models for subtyping out of models of (polymorphic) λ-calculus. The full definition of * is given in appendix D. We discuss here some important cases of the definition. The idea is to associate with every proof of a subtyping judgement A≤B an F_1 term a of type B* which has at most one occurence of a distinguished free variable (written []) of type A*. We shall write a[b] instead of a[[]←b] [9]. The translation preserves typings in the sense that if a:A, then a*:A*. Here are some cases in the definition of the translation:

- the axiom Id_A proving A≤A is translated into the single variable []:A*
- an assumption t_A proving t≤A, where t is a type variable, is translated into $t^{\#}$[] (i.e. $t^{\#}$ applied to []): $t^{\#}$ is a new variable of type t→A*, which we choose to denote by $t^{\#}$ to keep track of the name t.
- if e≡c→d is a proof of A'→B ≤ A→B', built from proofs c, d of A≤A', B≤B', then the translation of e is λz:A*.d*[[]c*[z]], where [] has type A'*→B*.
- c<b> is translated to c*[b*]: coercion application is modeled by substitution.

<u>Theorem 1</u>: $(cF_{\leq},cR)$ is effectively weakly normalizing and confluent.

Proof: (C1) (confluence of R_1) is proved in [CDC]. The proofs of (C2) (weak normalization of cR), (C3) and (C4) (preservation of equality and normal forms) are carried out in [CG3] (we actually prove effective weak normalization). Property (C5) (injectivity on normal forms[10]) is the most interesting. We briefly sketch the argument, and refer to [CG3] for details. We

[8] We keep calling it Top for simplicity, although no subtyping is present in F_1.
[9] Thus, e.g. λx.[x] is λy.x; this conflicts with the standard use of [ ] to denote holes in contexts where captures are allowed: if C[ ]=λx.[] is viewed as a context, then C[x] is λx.x.
[10] Notice that * is not injective outside the set of normal forms: think of (Id→Id)<x> and λz:A.xz which are both translated to λz:A.xz.

exhibit a left inverse to the restriction of * to normal forms. The basic idea is to take profit of the difference between η and and its counterpart $c\eta$ in $\mathbf{cF}_{\leq}$. Taking a normal form a in $\mathbf{cF}_{\leq}$, we know from (C4) that a* is a normal form in $\mathbf{F}_1$. But considered as a term in $\mathbf{cF}_{\leq}$[11], a* is not a normal form. The repeated use of (variants of) $c\eta$ on a* has the quite "magic" effect of reconstructing the coercions that * had interpreted. We hope that the following example will give the flavour of what is going on.

Suppose that we start with the cR normal form $a\equiv(t\to Id)\langle x\rangle$, where $x{:}A\to B$ and $t\leq A$ are assumed in the environment; and $t\to Id$ proves $A\to B\leq t\to B$. The translation a* is $\lambda z{:}t.x(t^{\#}z)$, which is an R_1 normal form in $\mathbf{F}_1$. When embedding this expression back to $\mathbf{cF}_{\leq}$, we turn the special variable $t^{\#}$ back to a coercion, and get $\lambda z{:}t.x(t\langle z\rangle)$, which is *not* a cR normal form. We apply (a degenerate form of) $c\eta$ and obtain back $(t\to Id)\langle x\rangle$. The general argument is by induction on the size of normal forms. □

10 Confluence of R.

It remains to transfer the confluence of cR back to a corresponding system R in $\mathbf{F}_{\leq}$. The system R is defined by taking as axioms the (typed) coercion erasures of the axioms of cR[12], and closing them under typed congruence rules (cf. section 3). The precise definition of R is given in appendix A. The following proposition states the relation between the two systems formally.

Proposition 2: For any a,a',Γ, $\Gamma\vdash a\to a'{:}A$ holds in $(\mathbf{F}_{\leq},R)$ iff both

i) there exist b,b' whose coercion erasures are a,a', such that $\Gamma\vdash b{:}A$ and $b\to b'$ in $(\mathbf{cF}_{\leq},cR)$.

ii) the coercion erasures a and a' of b and b' are different (this is trivial in the only if direction)

Proof: By tedious induction on derivations. □

Notation: If b:A is a $\mathbf{cF}_{\leq}$ term whose coercion erasure is a, we shall also say that b is a *coercion fattening* of a:A. Thus a coercion fattening codifies a typing proof.

To prove confluence of R, we use again proposition 1, taking $(A,\to)=(\mathbf{F}_{\leq},R)$ and $(B,\to')=(\mathbf{cF}_{\leq},cR)$. The translation takes a term b of $\mathbf{F}_{\leq}$ (actually a judgement) to one of its coercion fattenings b' in $\mathbf{cF}_{\leq}$. More specifically, we impose b' to be a normal form w.r.t. to the rewriting system cR1 consisting of I+II+III-$c\lambda t$-$c\Lambda t$+$c\lambda t1$+$c\Lambda t1$ (see appendix B) where $c\lambda t1$, $c\Lambda t1$ are the rules:

[11] Indeed, roughly speaking, $\mathbf{F}_1$ can be considered as a sublanguage of $\mathbf{cF}_{\leq}$ where no use is made of the subtyping facility.

[12] The coercion erasure of a $\mathbf{cF}_{\leq}$ term a is the term b of $\mathbf{F}_{\leq}$ such that a codifies a typing proof of b.

(cλt1) $\quad$ (c→d)<λx:A.a> → (c→Id)<λx:A.d<a>> $\quad$ d≠Id .

(cΛt1) $\quad$ (∀t≤c.d)<Λt≤A.a>→ (∀t≤c.Id)<Λt≤A.(d<a>)> $\quad$ d≠Id

cR1, roughly, is composed of those of the rules in cR which preserve the coercion erasure. It is, as an equational theory, equivalent to the system considered in [CG1]. We can thus rephrase the coherence result of [CG1] as:

Proposition 3: If Γ⊢b:A and Γ⊢b':A are provable in $cF_{\leq}$, and if b and b' have the same coercion erasure, then b and b' are interconvertible in cR1. The equational theory induced by cR1 is included in cR.

Proof: Easy. For the record, the theory considered in [CG1] is I+II+III' where III'=III-cλt-cΛt+λ+Λ and

(λ) $\quad$ λx:A. c<b> → (Id_A→c) <λx:A. b >

(Λ) $\quad$ Λt≤A. c<b> → (∀t≤Id_A. c) <Λt≤A. b> . □

Before proceeding further, let us give some hints about our choice of translation. We take a term into a coercion fattening of it, because we then get injectivity for free, since fattening has erasure as left inverse. We take a fattening in cR1 normal form because we want to map R normal forms into cR normal forms; we use the system cR1 because we have to stay within the set of coercion fattenings of the translated term.

The proof of confluence relies on the following three lemmas:

Lemma 1: cR1 is effectively weakly normalizing.

Proof: By a slight adaptation of the proof of weak normalization of I+II+III given in [CG1]. □

Lemma 2: If b→b' in ($cF_{\leq}$,cR) and b is in cR1 normal form, then the coercion erasures of b and b' are different.

Proof: Suppose that b is in cR1 normal form. All the rules in cR-I-II-III change the coercion erasure, and the only possible cλt redexes must have the form (c→ Id)<λx:A.a>, where c:A'<A (otherwise there would be an (Id→) redex); this special case of cλt also changes the coercion erasure. □

Lemma 3: The coercion erasure of a cR normal form is an R normal form.

Proof: See [CG3]. □

Theorem 2: ($F_{\leq}$,R) is effectively weakly normalizing and confluent.

Proof: (C1) (confluence of cR) holds by theorem 1. (C3) (preservation of interconvertibility) is shown by transitivity. If a$\to$a', then by proposition 2 (only if part) there is a coercion fattening b of a s.t. b$\to$b' in cR, for some coercion fattening b' of a'. Since G(a) is by definition a coercion fattening of a, then, by proposition 3, b and G(a) (respectively b' and G(a')) are provably equal in cR. As for (C4) (preservation of normal forms), notice first that by definition G maps an $F_{\leq}$ normal form a to a cR1 normal form b. Suppose that b is not a cR normal form; then b reduces in cR to b' and, by lemma 2 and proposition 2 (if part), a would reduce, in R, to the coercion erasure of b', which is not possible since a is in R normal form. (C5) (injectivity on normal forms) is obvious since G has coercion erasure as left inverse. As for (C2) (weak normalization of R) let b be an $F_{\leq}$ term, and take the coercion erasure of a cR normalizing sequence from G(b). G(b) is weakly normalizing by theorem 1, and the coercion erasure of the cR sequence is an R sequence, intermixed with reflexive steps, by proposition 2. This sequence ends with a normal form by lemma 3. □

Corollary 1: The theories $\beta\eta top_{\leq}$ and $c\beta\eta top_{\leq}$ are decidable.

Proof: By theorems 1 and 2, noticing that the theories of R, cR are $\beta\eta top_{\leq}$, $c\beta\eta top_{\leq}$. □

11 Conclusion and acknowledgements

We have explored a confluent theory of subtyping involving β rules and extensionality rules. The solution we found confirms us in the belief that explicit calculi of coercions are useful intermediate languages to study the syntactic properties of subtyping. On the way, we have singled out a general technique to establish the confluence of weakly normalizing systems. Our study also prompted us to revisit the decidability problem for theories of (polymorphic) λ-calculi with the explicit presence of a terminal type.

First steps to the work presented here were taken in [GheTh], where confluence was studied for the theory βη on a simpler system Fbq which has no Top type, and has unbounded quantification as well as bounded quantification. Without this preliminary experience, we feel that we would not have had the courage to go into the constructions presented here. It was also proved in [GheTh] that the theory $\beta\eta top_{\leq}$ on $F_{\leq}$ is equivalent to the theory $c\beta\eta top_{\leq}$ on $cF_{\leq}$, a result that we do not use here.

We might try to extend the present work by including additional rules in the theory. In particular, we did not consider the following so-called "hexagon" or "parametricity" rule, which is introduced in [CaMaMiSce] :

$$\frac{\Gamma \vdash b=b' : \forall t{\le}A.B \quad \Gamma \vdash A' \le A'' \le A}{\Gamma \vdash b\{A'\}=b'\{A''\} : B[t^{+} \leftarrow A', t^{-} \leftarrow A'']}$$

where $^{+}$ and $^{-}$ stand respectively for the positive and negative occurrence of the type variable t. This rule, in conjunction with $\beta\eta$ $top_{\le}$, appears essential to prove some (weak forms of) isomorphisms between types in $F_{\le}$, for instance between $\exists$t.t (encoded as $\forall$u.($\forall$t.t$\rightarrow$u)$\rightarrow$u) and Top.

The present work was started during an active period of e-mail exchange between the authors and L. Cardelli, G. Longo, S. Martini, and A. Scedrov, whom we want to thank alll: these fruitful discussions provided an essential stimulus for the present work.

References

[BCGS] V. Breazu-Tannen, T. Coquand, C. Gunter, A. Scedrov, Inheritance and Explicit Coercion, to appear in Information and Computation, preliminary version in Proc. Logic in Computer Science 89.

[BrLo] K. Bruce, G. Longo, A Modest Model of Records, Inheritance and Bounded Quantification, Information and Computation 87, 1/2, pp.196-240 (1990).

[CaMaMiSce] L. Cardelli, S. Martini, J. Mitchell, A. Scedrov, An Extension of System F with Subtyping, in these Proceedings.

[CaWe] L. Cardelli, P. Wegner, On Understanding Types, Data Abstraction and Polymorphism, ACM Computing Surveys 17 (4) (1985).

[Ca] L. Cardelli, Typeful Programming, DEC SRC Research Report 45 (1989).

[CaLo] L. Cardelli, G. Longo, A Semantic Basis for Quest, DEC SRC Research Report 55, short version in Proc. Conf. on Lisp and Functional Programming 1990, Nice (1990).

[CDC] P.-L. Curien, Roberto Di Cosmo, Confluence in the typed λ-calculus extended with Surjective Pairing and a Terminal Type, Proc. ICALP 91, to appear in LNCS.

[CG1] P.-L. Curien, G. Ghelli, Coherence of Subsumption, Mathematical Structures in Computer Science, to appear; short version in Proc. CAAP 90, LNCS 431.

[CG2] P.-L. Curien, G. Ghelli, On Confluence of Weakly Normalizing Systems, Proc. RTA 91, to appear in LNCS.

[CG3] P.-L. Curien, G. Ghelli, Subtyping + Extensionality: Confluence of $\beta\eta$top reduction in $F_{\le}$, long version, Technical Report, University of Pisa and LIENS, to appear (1991).

[Daal] D. van Daalen, The Language Theory of Automath, PhD Thesis, Technical University of Eindhoven, 1980.

[GheTh] G. Ghelli, Proof-theoretic Studies about a Minimal Type System Integrating Inclusion and Parametric Polymorphism, PhD Thesis, TD-6/90, Univ. of Pisa, 1990.

[Kri] J.-L. Krivine, λ-calcul, Types et Modèles, Masson (1990).

[Salv] A. Salvesen, The Church-Rosser Theorem for LF with $\beta\eta$-reduction, draft (1989).

Appendix A: the System $F_{\leq}$.

Syntax $A ::= t \mid Top \mid A \rightarrow A \mid \forall t \leq A.\ A$

$a ::= x \mid top \mid \lambda x{:}A.\ a \mid a(a) \mid \Lambda t \leq A.\ a \mid a\{A\}$

Notation: A<B stands for A≤B and A≠B

Environments (sequences whose individual components have the form x:A or t)

(Øenv) () env

(≤env) $\dfrac{\Gamma \text{ env} \quad \Gamma \vdash A \text{ type} \quad t \notin \Gamma^{13}}{\Gamma, t \leq A \quad \text{env}}$ (: env) $\dfrac{\Gamma \text{ env} \quad \Gamma \vdash A \text{ type} \quad x \notin \Gamma}{\Gamma, x{:}A \quad \text{env}}$

Types

(VarForm) $\dfrac{\Gamma, t \leq A, \Gamma' \text{ env}}{\Gamma, t \leq A, \Gamma' \vdash t \quad \text{type}}$ (TopForm) $\dfrac{\Gamma \text{ env}}{\Gamma \vdash Top \quad \text{type}}$

(→ Form) $\dfrac{\Gamma \vdash A \text{ type} \quad \Gamma \vdash B \text{ type}}{\Gamma \vdash A \rightarrow B \quad \text{type}}$ (∀ Form) $\dfrac{\Gamma, t \leq A \vdash B \text{ type}}{\Gamma \vdash \forall t \leq A.\ B \quad \text{type}}$

Subtypes

(Var≤) $\dfrac{\Gamma, t \leq A, \Gamma' \text{ env}}{\Gamma, t \leq A, \Gamma' \vdash t \leq A}$ (Top≤) $\dfrac{\Gamma \vdash A \text{ type}}{\Gamma \vdash A \leq Top}$

(→≤) $\dfrac{\Gamma \vdash A \leq A' \quad \Gamma \vdash B \leq B'}{\Gamma \vdash A' \rightarrow B \leq A \rightarrow B'}$ (∀≤) $\dfrac{\Gamma \vdash A \leq A' \quad \Gamma, t \leq A \vdash B \leq B'}{\Gamma \vdash \forall t \leq A'.B \leq \forall t \leq A.B'}$

(Id≤) $\dfrac{\Gamma \vdash A \text{ type}}{\Gamma \vdash A \leq A}$ (Trans≤) $\dfrac{\Gamma \vdash A \leq B \quad \Gamma \vdash B \leq C}{\Gamma \vdash A \leq C}$

Expressions /typed congruence rules for reduction:

(Var:) $\dfrac{\Gamma, x{:}A, \Gamma' \text{ env}}{\Gamma, x{:}A, \Gamma' \vdash x{:}\ A}$ (Top) $\dfrac{\Gamma \text{ env}}{\Gamma \vdash top{:}\ Top}$

(→ Intro) $\dfrac{\Gamma, x{:}\ A \vdash b\ (\rightarrow b'){:}\ B}{\Gamma \vdash \lambda x{:}A.b\ (\rightarrow \lambda x{:}A.b'){:}\ A \rightarrow B}$ (→ Elim) $\dfrac{\Gamma \vdash f\ (\rightarrow f'){:}\ A \rightarrow B \quad \Gamma \vdash a{:}\ A^{14}}{\Gamma \vdash f(a)\ (\rightarrow f'(a)){:}\ B}$

(∀ Intro) $\dfrac{\Gamma, t \leq A \vdash b\ (\rightarrow b'){:}\ B}{\Gamma \vdash \Lambda t \leq A.b\ (\rightarrow \Lambda t \leq A.b'\ ){:}\ \forall t \leq A.B}$ (∀ Elim) $\dfrac{\Gamma \vdash f\ (\rightarrow f'){:}\ \forall t \leq A.\ B \quad \Gamma \vdash A' \leq A}{\Gamma \vdash f\{A'\}\ (\rightarrow f'\{A'\}){:}\ B[t \leftarrow A']}$

(Subsump) $\dfrac{\Gamma \vdash a\ (\rightarrow a'){:}\ A \quad \Gamma \vdash A \leq B}{\Gamma \vdash a\ (\rightarrow a'){:}\ B}$

---

[13] A variable t (x)∈Γ if it is present in a left hand side of an element t ≤ A (x : A) of the environment.

[14] And symmetrically in the argument a

Axioms of βηtop equivalence:

(β) $\dfrac{\Gamma \vdash (\lambda x{:}A.a)b{:}\ U}{\Gamma \vdash (\lambda x{:}A.a)b \to a[x \leftarrow b] : U}$ (η) $\dfrac{\Gamma \vdash \lambda x{:}A.ax{:}\ U \quad x \text{ not free in } a}{\Gamma \vdash \lambda x{:}A.ax \to a : U}$

(β2) $\dfrac{\Gamma \vdash (\Lambda t{\le}A.a)\{A'\}{:}\ U}{\Gamma \vdash (\Lambda t{\le}A.a)\{A'\} \to a[t \leftarrow A'] : U}$ (η2) $\dfrac{\Gamma \vdash \lambda t{\le}A.a\{t\}{:}U \quad t \text{ not free in } a}{\Gamma \vdash \lambda t{\le}A.a\{t\} \to a : U}$

(top) $\dfrac{\Gamma \vdash a{:}\ Top}{\Gamma \vdash a{=}top : Top}$

Rewriting system R: β+η+β2+η2+

(λt)	$\Gamma \vdash$	$\lambda x{:}A.b$	$\to$	$\lambda x{:}A'.b : A' \to U$	$A'<A$
(Λt)	$\Gamma \vdash$	$\Lambda t{\le}A.b$	$\to$	$\Lambda t{\le}A'.b : \forall t{\le}A'.U$	$A'<A$
(gentop)	$\Gamma \vdash$	a	$\to$	$top(T)\ \ {:}Top(T)$	$T \in IsoTop,\ a \ne top(T)$
(η_{top})	$\Gamma \vdash$	$\lambda x{:}A.a(top(T))$	$\to$	$a\ \ {:}U$	$x \notin FV(a), A \le T, T \in IsoTop$

Notation: IsoTop is the minimum subset of the set of all types in $\mathbf{F}_{\le}$ such that:

$Top \in IsoTop; \qquad T \in IsoTop \ \Rightarrow\ A \to T \in IsoTop,\ \ \forall t{\le}A.T \in IsoTop$

The canonical element of a type $T \in$ IsoTop, denoted top(T), is defined as:

$top(Top) = top; \qquad top(A \to T) = \lambda x{:}A.top(T); \qquad top(\forall t{\le}A.T) = \Lambda t{\le}A.top(T)$

Appendix B: The system $\mathbf{cF}_{\le}$

Syntax:
$A ::= t \mid Top \mid A \to A \mid \forall t{\le}A.\ A$
$a ::= x \mid \lambda x{:}A.\ a \mid a(a) \mid \Lambda t{\le}A.\ a \mid a\{A,c\} \mid c\langle a\rangle$
$c ::= t_A \mid Top_A \mid c \to c \mid \forall t{\le}c.\ c \mid Id_A \mid c \bullet c$

Typing rules: (we list only those distinct from the corresponding ones in $\mathbf{F}_{\le}$)

Subtypes

(Var≤) $\dfrac{\Gamma, t{\le}A, \Gamma' \ env}{\Gamma, t{\le}A, \Gamma' \vdash t_A{:}\ t{\le}A}$ (Top≤) $\dfrac{\Gamma \vdash A\ type}{\Gamma \vdash top_A{:}\ A{\le}Top}$

(→≤) $\dfrac{\Gamma \vdash c{:}\ A{\le}A' \quad \Gamma \vdash d{:}\ B{\le}B'}{\Gamma \vdash c{\to}d{:}\ A'{\to}B \le A{\to}B'}$ (∀≤) $\dfrac{\Gamma \vdash c{:}A{\le}A' \quad \Gamma, t{\le}A \vdash d{:}\ B{\le}B'}{\Gamma \vdash \forall t{\le}c.d{:} \forall t{\le}A'.B \le \forall t{\le}A.B'}$

(Id≤) $\dfrac{\Gamma \vdash A\ type}{\Gamma \vdash Id_A{:}\ A{\le}A}$ (Trans≤) $\dfrac{\Gamma \vdash c{:}\ A{\le}B \quad \Gamma \vdash d{:}\ B{\le}C}{\Gamma \vdash d{\bullet}c{:}\ A{\le}C}$

Terms

(Coerce) $\dfrac{\Gamma \vdash a: A \qquad \Gamma \vdash c: A \le B}{\Gamma \vdash c<a>: B}$ (∀ Elim) $\dfrac{\Gamma \vdash f:\forall t \le A.B \quad \Gamma \vdash c:A' \le A}{\Gamma \vdash f\{A',c\}: B[t \leftarrow A']}$

Theory:

I *Coercions:*

(Ass)	$(c \bullet d) \bullet e$	=	$c \bullet (d \bullet e)$
(IdL)	$Id_B \bullet c$	=	c
(IdR)	$c \bullet Id_A$	=	c
(Id→)	$Id_A \to Id_B$	=	$Id_{A \to B}$
(Id∀)	$\forall t \le Id_A.\ Id_B$	=	$Id_{\forall t \le A.B}$
(Top)	$Top_B \bullet c$	=	Top_A
(VarTop)	t_{Top}	=	Top_t
(TopId)	Top_{Top}	=	Id_{Top}

II *Coercions:*

(→')	$(c \to d) \bullet (c' \to d')$	=	$(c' \bullet c) \to (d \bullet d')$
(→")	$(c \to d) \bullet ((c' \to d') \bullet e)$	=	$((c' \bullet c) \to (d \bullet d')) \bullet e$
(∀')	$\forall t \le c.\ d \bullet \forall t \le c'.d'$	=	$\forall t \le c' \bullet c.\ d \bullet (d'[t_B \leftarrow c \bullet t_A])$
(∀")	$\forall t \le c.\ d \bullet (\forall t \le c'.d' \bullet e)$	=	$(\forall t \le c' \bullet c.\ d \bullet (d'[t_B \leftarrow c \bullet t_A])) \bullet e$

Expressions:

(Id)	$Id<a>$	=	a	
(Comp)	$c<d<a>>$	=	$(c \bullet d) <a>$	
(β)	$(\lambda x:A.b)(a)$	=	$b[x \leftarrow a]$	
(cη)	$\lambda x:A.c<b(d<x>)>$	=	$(d \to c)<b>$	$x \notin FV(b)$
(β2)	$(\Lambda t \le A.b)\{A',c\}$	=	$b[t \leftarrow A'][t_A \leftarrow c]$	
(cη2)	$\Lambda t \le A.d<b\{t,c \bullet \ldots \bullet e \bullet t_A\}>$	=	$(\forall t \le c \bullet \ldots \bullet e.d)<b>$	$t \notin FV(b,c)$
(top)	a	=	top	$\Gamma \vdash a: Top$

Rewriting system cR: The equations of the theory (from left to right) - top +

(App')	$((c \to d)<a>)(b)$	→	$d<a(c<b>)>$	
(App")	$((c \to d) \bullet e<a>)(b)$	→	$d<(e<a>)(c<b>)>$	
(App2')	$((\forall t \le c.d)<f>)\{A,e\}$	→	$d[t_B \leftarrow e][t \leftarrow A]<f\{A,c \bullet e\}>$	$e:A \le B$
(App2")	$((\forall t \le c.d) \bullet c'<f>)\{A,e\}$	→	$d[t_B \leftarrow e][t \leftarrow A]<(c'<f>)\{A,c \bullet e\}>$	
(cλt)	$(c \to d)<\lambda x:A.a>$	→	$\lambda x:A'.d<a[x \leftarrow c<x>]>$	$c:A' \le A$
(cΛt)	$(\forall t \le c.d)<\Lambda t \le A.a>$	→	$\Lambda t \le A'.(d<a[t_A \leftarrow c \bullet t_{A'}]>)$	$c:A' \le A$

$(c\eta_1)$	$\lambda x{:}A.b(d<x>)$	$\rightarrow$	$(d\rightarrow Id)<b>$	$x\notin FV(b)$
$(c\eta_2)$	$\lambda x{:}A.c<b(x)>$	$\rightarrow$	$(Id\rightarrow c)<b>$	$x\notin FV(b)$
$(c\eta_3)$	$\lambda x{:}A.b(x)$	$\rightarrow$	b	$x\notin FV(b)$
$(c\eta 2_1)$	$\Lambda t\leq A.d<b\{t,t_A\}>$	$\rightarrow$	$(\forall t\leq Id_A.d)<b>$	$t\notin FV(b)$
$(c\eta 2_2)$	$\Lambda t\leq A.b\{t,c\bullet\ldots\bullet e\bullet t_A\}$	$\rightarrow$	$(\forall t\leq c\bullet\ldots\bullet e.Id)<b>$	$t\notin FV(b,c)$
$(c\eta 2_3)$	$\Lambda t\leq A.b\{t,t_A\}$	$\rightarrow$	b	$t\notin FV(b)$
$(c\eta 2_4)$	$\Lambda t\leq A.d<b\{t,Top_t\}>$	$\rightarrow$	$(\forall t\leq Top_A.d)<b>$	$t\notin FV(b)$
$(c\eta 2_5)$	$\Lambda t\leq A.b\{t,Top_t\}$	$\rightarrow$	$(\forall t\leq Top_A.Id)<b>$	$t\notin FV(b)$

(gentop)	a	$\rightarrow$	$top(T)$	$\Gamma\vdash a{:}T\in IsoTop,\ a\neq top(T)$
$(c\eta_{top})$	$\lambda x{:}A.c<b(top(T))>$	$\rightarrow$	$(d\rightarrow c)<b>$	$d=NF(A\leq T), T\in IsoTop,\ x\notin FV(b)$
$(c\eta_{top'})$	$\lambda x{:}A.b(top(T))$	$\rightarrow$	$(d\rightarrow Id)<b>$	$d=NF(A\leq T), T\in IsoTop,\ x\notin FV(b)$

where $NF(A\leq T)$ is a normal form proof of $A\leq T$, as defined in [CG1].

Notation:

$III=Id+Comp+App'+App''+App2'+App2''+c\lambda t+c\Lambda t$

$\eta = c\eta+c\eta_1+c\eta_2+c\eta_3+c\eta_{top}+c\eta_{top'}+c\eta 2+c\eta 2_1+c\eta 2_2+c\eta 2_3+c\eta 2_4+c\eta 2_5+Comp$

$c\eta = \eta+TopId$

$R1=I+II+III-c\lambda t-c\Lambda t+c\lambda t1+c\Lambda t1$ ($c\lambda t1+c\Lambda t1$ are listed below)

$(c\lambda t1)$	$(c\rightarrow d)<\lambda x{:}A.a>$	$\rightarrow$	$(c\rightarrow Id)<\lambda x{:}A.d<a>>$	$d\neq Id$
$(c\Lambda t1)$	$(\forall t\leq c.d)<\Lambda t\leq A.a>$	$\rightarrow$	$(\forall t\leq c.Id)<\Lambda t\leq A'.(d<a>)>$	$d\neq Id$

Appendix C: The system F_1

Syntax: $A ::= t \mid Top \mid A\rightarrow A \mid \forall t.\ A$

$a ::= x \mid top \mid \lambda x{:}A.\ a \mid a(a) \mid \Lambda t.\ a \mid a\{A\}$

Typing rules: (we list only those distinct from the corresponding ones in $F_{\leq}$)

Environments (sequences whose individual components have the form x:A or t)

(tenv) $$\frac{\Gamma\ env \quad t\notin\Gamma}{\Gamma,\ t\quad env}$$

Types

(VarForm) $$\frac{\Gamma, t, \Gamma'\ \ env}{\Gamma, t, \Gamma'\vdash t\ \ type}$$

(∀ Form) $$\frac{\Gamma, t\vdash B\ \ type}{\Gamma\vdash \forall t.B\ \ type}$$

Expressions

(∀ Intro) $$\frac{\Gamma, t\vdash b{:}\ B}{\Gamma\vdash \Lambda t.b : \forall t.B}$$

(∀ Elim) $$\frac{\Gamma\vdash f{:}\forall t.B \quad \Gamma\vdash A\ type}{\Gamma\vdash f\{A\}{:}\ B[t\leftarrow A]}$$

<u>Equational theory</u>:

(β)	$(\lambda x{:}A.a)b$	$=$	$a[x\leftarrow b]$	
(η)	$\lambda x{:}A.ax$	$=$	a	x not free in a
(top)	a	$=$	$top : Top$	$\Gamma\vdash a{:}T$ and $a\neq top$
$(\beta 2)$	$(\Lambda t.a)\{A'\}$	$=$	$a[t\leftarrow A']$	
$(\eta 2)$	$\Lambda t.a\{t\}$	$=$	a	t not free in a

<u>Rewriting Theory:</u> The above rules - (top) +

(gentop)	a	$\rightarrow$	$top(T)$	$\Gamma\vdash a{:}T\in IsoTop$ and $a\neq top(T)$
(η_{top})	$\lambda x{:}T.a(top(T))$	$\rightarrow$	a	$T\in IsoTop$, x not free in a

where IsoTop and top(T) are as in appendix B, dropping bounds "$\leq A$" where appropriate.

Appendix D: The translation * from $cF_{\leq}$ to F_1

<u>Coercions</u>:

$t_A{}^* = top(A^*)$	$A\in IsoTop$
$Id_A{}^* = top(A^*)$	$A\in IsoTop$
$t_A{}^* = t^{\#}[]$	$A\notin IsoTop$ and $[]: t$
$Id_A{}^* = []$	$A\notin IsoTop$ and $[]: A$
$Top_A{}^* = top$	
$(c_{A'A}\rightarrow d_{B'B})^* = \lambda z{:}A'^*.d^*[[](c^*[z])]$	z fresh and $[]{:}A\rightarrow B'$
$(c\circ d)^* = c^*[d^*]$	if $[]{:}A$ in d^*, then $[]{:}A$
$(\forall t\leq c_{A'A}.d_{B'B})^* = \Lambda t.\lambda t^{\#}{:}t\rightarrow A'^*.d^*[[]\{t\}(clos_t(c^*[t^{\#}[]]))]$	bound variables in c^* are renamed to avoid capturing t $[]{:}\forall t.(t\rightarrow A)\rightarrow B'$

<u>Terms</u>:

$x^*=x$	
$(ab)^*=a^*b^*$	
$(\lambda x{:}A.a)^*=\lambda x{:}A^*.a^*$	unless $\exists B\notin IsoTop, t_B.\ a=t_B\langle x\rangle$
$(\lambda x{:}A.a)^*=t^{\#}$	if $\exists B\notin IsoTop, t_B.\ a=t_B\langle x\rangle$
$(a\{A,c\})^*=a^*\{A^*\}(clos_{A^*}(c^*))$	
$(\Lambda t\leq A.a)^*=\Lambda t.\lambda t^{\#}{:}t\rightarrow A^*.a^*$	
$(c\langle a\rangle)^*=c^*[a^*]$	
$top^*= top$	
$clos_A(a) = d$ if $a=d[]$, $\lambda x{:}A.a[x]$ otherwise	a is the translation of a coercion

<u>Types:</u> $t^*=t$; $Top^*= Top$; $(A\rightarrow B)^*= A^*\rightarrow B^*$; $(\forall t\leq A.B)^*=\forall t.(t\rightarrow A^*).B^*$

An extension of system *F* with subtyping

Luca Cardelli [1] *Simone Martini* [2] *John C. Mitchell* [3] *Andre Scedrov* [4]

Abstract

System F is a well-known typed λ-calculus with polymorphic types, which provides a basis for polymorphic programming languages. We study an extension of F, called $F_{<:}$, that combines parametric polymorphism with subtyping.

The main focus of the paper is the equational theory of $F_{<:}$, which is related to PER models and the notion of parametricity. We study some categorical properties of the theory when restricted to closed terms, including interesting categorical isomorphisms. We also investigate proof-theoretical properties, such as the conservativity of typing judgments with respect to F.

We demonstrate by a set of examples how a range of constructs may be encoded in $F_{<:}$. These include record operations and subtyping hierarchies that are related to features of object-oriented languages.

1. Introduction

System F [16] [21] is a well-known typed λ-calculus with polymorphic types, which provides a basis for polymorphic programming languages. We study an extension of F that combines parametric polymorphism [24] with subtyping. We call this language $F_{<:}$, where $<:$ is our symbol for the subtype relation. $F_{<:}$ is closely related to the language $F_{\leq}$ identified by Curien, and used by Curien and Ghelli primarily as a test case for certain mathematical techniques [15] [10]. $F_{\leq}$ is, in turn, a fragment of the language *Fun* of [9]. In spite of $F_{<:}$'s apparent minimality, it has become apparent that a range of constructs may be encoded in it (or in $F_{\leq}$); these include many of the record operations and subtyping features of [5], [8], and related work, which are connected to operations used in object-oriented programming. We illustrate some of the power of $F_{<:}$ in Section 3; see also [6].

In addition to the connections with object-oriented programming, we have found that the study of $F_{<:}$ raises semantic questions of independent interest. A major concern in this paper is an equational theory for $F_{<:}$ terms. The equational axioms for most systems of typed λ-calculi arise

[1] *Digital Equipment Corporation, Systems Research Center, 130 Lytton Ave, Palo Alto CA 94301.*
[2] *Dipartimento di Informatica, Università di Pisa, Corso Italia 40, I-56125 Pisa, Italy. This author is partially supported by the CNR-Stanford collaboration grant 89.00002.26.*
[3] *Computer Science Department, Stanford University, Stanford CA 94305.*
[4] *Department of Mathematics, University of Pennsylvania, 209 South 33rd Street, Philadelphia, PA 19104-6395. This author is partially supported by the ONR Contract N00014-88-K-0635 and by NSF Grant CCR-87-05596.*

Simone Martini and Andre Scedrov would like to thank John C. Mitchell, the Computer Science Department, and the Center for the Study of Language and Information at Stanford University for their hospitality during those authors' extended stay in 1989-1990, when much of this research was done.

Luca Cardelli and Simone Martini would like to thank Pierre-Louis Curien, Giorgio Ghelli, and Giuseppe Longo for many stimulating discussions related to this work. In particular, Curien helped in the early proof of $Top \sim \exists(X)X$.

naturally as a consequence of characterizing type connectives by adjoint situations (for example). In addition, it is often the case that provable equality may be captured by a reduction system obtained by orienting the equational axioms in a straightforward way. However, both of these properties appear to fail for $F_{<:}$. A simple example illustrates some of the basic issues.

A straightforward polymorphic type is $\forall(A)A \to A \to A$, which is commonly referred to as *Bool* since in system *F* and related systems there are two definable elements of this type. These elements are written as the following normal forms:

$$true \triangleq \lambda(A)\, \lambda(x{:}A)\, \lambda(y{:}A)\, x$$
$$false \triangleq \lambda(A)\, \lambda(x{:}A)\, \lambda(y{:}A)\, y$$

In $F_{<:}$, however, there are two additional normal forms of type *Bool*. These arise because we have a maximal type *Top*, which has all other types as subtypes. The main idea behind the additional terms is that we can change the type of any argument not used in the body of a term to *Top*, and still have a term of the same type (by antimonotonicity of the left operand of $\to$ with respect to <:). This gives us the following two normal forms of type *Bool*.

$$true' \triangleq \lambda(A)\, \lambda(x{:}A)\, \lambda(y{:}Top)\, x$$
$$false' \triangleq \lambda(A)\, \lambda(x{:}Top)\, \lambda(y{:}A)\, y$$

However, *true* and *true'* are completely equivalent terms when considered at type *Bool*. Specifically, for any type *A*, the terms *true(A)* and *true'(A)* define extensionally equal functions of type $A \to A \to A$. Put proof-theoretically, if we take any term *a* containing *true* with the property that when reducing *a* to normal form we apply each occurrence of *true* to two arguments, then we may replace any or all occurrences of *true* by *true'* and obtain a provably equal term. For this reason, it seems natural to consider *true* = *true'*, and similarly *false* = *false'*, even though these terms have different normal forms. When we add these two equations to our theory, we restore the pleasing property that *Bool* contains precisely two equivalence classes of normal forms.

While our initial examination of the equational theory of $F_{<:}$ was motivated by a vague intuition about observable properties of normal forms, our primary guide is the PER semantics of polymorphic λ-calculus with subtyping [4] [7] [15] [23]. One relevant characteristic of PER models is the *parametric* behavior of polymorphic functions. Specifically, since polymorphic functions operate independently of their type parameter, they may be considered equivalent at all their type instances. In $F_{<:}$ we can state a consequence of this notion of parametricity, namely that whenever the two type instances have a common supertype, the terms will be equal when considered as elements of that supertype (see the rule *(Eq appl2)* in section 2.2). Hence the syntax of $F_{<:}$ can state, at least to some extent, the semantic notion of parametricity investigated in [22], [14], and [1]. A general principle we have followed is to adopt axioms that express parametricity properties satisfied by PER models, but not to try to explicitly capture the exact theory of PER models [18]. This leads us to a new angle on parametricity which may prove useful in further study, and also gives us a set of axioms that are sufficient to prove *true* = *true'*, and other expected equations, without appearing contrived to fit these particular examples.

While $F_{<:}$ differs from each of the λ-calculi mentioned above, several properties of $F_{<:}$ transfer easily from related work. For syntactic properties we have strong normalization [15]; canonical type derivations, coherence, minimum typing [10]; and confluence of the β-η-*TopCollapse* equational theory [11]. The PER semantics follows easily from the work in [4], [7], [15], and [23]. While an alternative semantics could perhaps be developed in the style of [3] and [14], we do not explore that possibility here.

The main results of this paper are an equational theory for $F_{<:}$, some proof-theoretic properties developed in section 2 including conservativity of $F_{<:}$ typing over F, a set of examples in section 3 demonstrating the expressiveness of $F_{<:}$ (some reported earlier in [7] and in [15] with attribution), and some categorical properties in section 4 of the theory when restricted to closed terms.

2. System $F_{<:}$

$F_{<:}$ is obtained by extending F [16] [21] with a notion of subtyping (<:). This extension allows us to remain within a pure calculus. That is, we introduce neither the basic types, nor the structured types, normally associated with subtyping in programming languages. Instead, we show that these programming types can be obtained via encodings within the pure calculus. In particular, we can encode record types with their subtyping relations [5].

2.1 Syntax

Subtyping is reflected in the syntax of types by a new type constant *Top* (the supertype of all types), and by a subtype bound on second-order quantifiers: $\forall(X<:A)A'$ (*bounded quantifiers* [9]). Ordinary second-order quantifiers are recovered by setting the quantifier bound to *Top*; we use $\forall(X)A$ for $\forall(X<:Top)A$. The syntax of values is extended by a constant *top* of type *Top*, and by a subtype bound on polymorphic functions: $\lambda(X<:A)a$; we use $\lambda(X)a$ for $\lambda(X<:Top)a$.

Syntax

$A,B ::=$	Types
X	type variables
Top	the supertype of all types
$A \rightarrow B$	function spaces
$\forall(X<:A)B$	bounded quantifications
$a,b ::=$	Values
x	value variables
top	the canonical value of type *Top*
$\lambda(x{:}A)b$	functions
$b(a)$	applications
$\lambda(X<:A)b$	bounded type functions
$b(A)$	type applications

The $\rightarrow$ operator associates to the right. The scoping of λ and $\forall$ extends to the right as far as possible. Types and terms can be parenthesized.

A subtyping judgment is added to F's judgments. Moreover, the equality judgment on values is made relative to a type; this is important since values in $F_{<:}$ can have many types, and two values may or may not be equivalent depending on the type that those values are considered as possessing.

Judgments

$\vdash E\ env$	E is a well-formed environment
$E \vdash A\ type$	A is a type
$E \vdash A <: B$	A is a subtype of B
$E \vdash a : A$	a has type A
$E \vdash a \leftrightarrow b : A$	a and b are equal members of type A

We use *dom(E)* for the set of variables defined by an environment E. As usual, we identify terms up to renaming of bound variables; that is, using $B\{X{\leftarrow}C\}$ for the substitution of C for X in B:

$$\forall(X<:A)B \;\equiv\; \forall(Y<:A)\,B\{X{\leftarrow}Y\}$$

$$\lambda(X<:A)b \;\equiv\; \lambda(Y<:A)\,b\{X{\leftarrow}Y\} \qquad \lambda(x:A)b \;\equiv\; \lambda(y:A)\,b\{x{\leftarrow}y\}$$

These identifications can be made directly on the syntax; that is, without knowing whether the terms involved are the product of formal derivations in the system. By adopting these identifications, we avoid the need of a type equivalence judgment for quantifier renaming.

Moreover, in formal derivations we restrict ourselves to terms where all bound variables are distinct, to environments where variables are defined at most once, and to judgments where all bound and environment-defined variables are distinct. A more formal approach would use de Bruijn indices for free and bound variables [12].

2.2 Rules

The inference rules of $F_{<:}$ are listed below; the only essential difference between these and the ones of $F_{\leq}$ [15] [10], is in the more general *(Eq appl2)*. We now comment on the most interesting aspects of the rules; see also the discussion about *(Eq appl2)* in section 2.4.

The subtyping judgment, $E \vdash A <: B$, is, for any E, a reflexive and transitive relation on types with a *subsumption* property: that is, a member of a type is also a member of any supertype of that type. Every type is a subtype of *Top*. The function space operator $\rightarrow$ is antimonotonic in its first argument and monotonic in its second. A bounded quantifier is antimonotonic in its bound and monotonic in its body under an assumption about the free variable.

The rules for the typing judgment, $E \vdash a : A$, are the same as the corresponding rules in F, except for the extension to bounded quantifiers. However, additional typing power is hidden in the subsumption rule, which allows a function to take an argument of a subtype of its input type.

Most of the equivalence rules, $E \vdash a \leftrightarrow b : A$, are unremarkable. They provide symmetry, transitivity, congruence on the syntax, and β and η equivalences. Two rules, however, stand out. The first, *(Eq collapse)* (also called the *Top-collapse* rule), states that any two terms are equivalent when "seen" at type *Top*; since no operations are available on members of *Top*, all values are indistinguishable at that type. The second, *(Eq appl2)*, is the congruence rule for polymorphic type application, giving general conditions under which two expressions $b'(A')$ and $b''(A'')$ are equivalent at a type C. This rule has many intriguing consequences, which will be amply explored in the sequel. (We occasionally write $E \vdash A,B<:C$ for $E \vdash A<:C \wedge E \vdash B<:C$, and so on.)

Environments

(Env ∅)

$$\frac{}{\vdash \emptyset\ env}$$

(Env x)

$$\frac{E \vdash A\ type \quad x \notin dom(E)}{\vdash E,x{:}A\ env}$$

(Env X)

$$\frac{E \vdash A\ type \quad X \notin dom(E)}{\vdash E,X<:A\ env}$$

Types

(Type X)

$$\frac{\vdash E,X<:A,E'\ env}{E,X<:A,E' \vdash X\ type}$$

(Type Top)

$$\frac{\vdash E\ env}{E \vdash Top\ type}$$

(Type →)

$$\frac{E \vdash A\ type \quad E \vdash B\ type}{E \vdash A{\rightarrow}B\ type}$$

(Type ∀)

$$\frac{E,X<:A \vdash B\ type}{E \vdash \forall(X<:A)B\ type}$$

Subtypes

(Sub refl)
$$\frac{E \vdash A\ type}{E \vdash A <: A}$$

(Sub trans)
$$\frac{E \vdash A <: B \quad E \vdash B <: C}{E \vdash A <: C}$$

(Sub X)
$$\frac{\vdash E, X <: A, E'\ env}{E, X <: A, E' \vdash X <: A}$$

(Sub Top)
$$\frac{E \vdash A\ type}{E \vdash A <: Top}$$

(Sub →)
$$\frac{E \vdash A' <: A \quad E \vdash B <: B'}{E \vdash A \rightarrow B <: A' \rightarrow B'}$$

(Sub ∀)
$$\frac{E \vdash A' <: A \quad E, X <: A' \vdash B <: B'}{E \vdash \forall(X <: A)B <: \forall(X <: A')B'}$$

Values

(Subsumption)
$$\frac{E \vdash a : A \quad E \vdash A <: B}{E \vdash a : B}$$

(Val x)
$$\frac{\vdash E, x : A, E'\ env}{E, x : A, E' \vdash x : A}$$

(Val top)
$$\frac{\vdash E\ env}{E \vdash top : Top}$$

(Val fun)
$$\frac{E, x : A \vdash b : B}{E \vdash \lambda(x : A)b : A \rightarrow B}$$

(Val appl)
$$\frac{E \vdash b : A \rightarrow B \quad E \vdash a : A}{E \vdash b(a) : B}$$

(Val fun2)
$$\frac{E, X <: A \vdash b : B}{E \vdash \lambda(X <: A)b : \forall(X <: A)B}$$

(Val appl2)
$$\frac{E \vdash b : \forall(X <: A)B \quad E \vdash A' <: A}{E \vdash b(A') : B\{X \leftarrow A'\}}$$

Equivalence

(Eq symm)
$$\frac{E \vdash a \leftrightarrow b : A}{E \vdash b \leftrightarrow a : A}$$

(Eq trans)
$$\frac{E \vdash a \leftrightarrow b : A \quad E \vdash b \leftrightarrow c : A}{E \vdash a \leftrightarrow c : A}$$

(Eq x)
$$\frac{E \vdash x : A}{E \vdash x \leftrightarrow x : A}$$

(Eq collapse)
$$\frac{E \vdash a : Top \quad E \vdash b : Top}{E \vdash a \leftrightarrow b : Top}$$

(Eq fun)
$$\frac{E, x : A \vdash b \leftrightarrow b' : B}{E \vdash \lambda(x : A)b \leftrightarrow \lambda(x : A)b' : A \rightarrow B}$$

(Eq appl)
$$\frac{E \vdash b \leftrightarrow b' : A \rightarrow B \quad E \vdash a \leftrightarrow a' : A}{E \vdash b(a) \leftrightarrow b'(a') : B}$$

(Eq fun2)
$$\frac{E, X <: A \vdash b \leftrightarrow b' : B}{E \vdash \lambda(X <: A)b \leftrightarrow \lambda(X <: A)b' : \forall(X <: A)B}$$

(Eq appl2)
$$\frac{E \vdash b' \leftrightarrow b'' : \forall(X <: A)B \quad E \vdash A', A'' <: A \quad E \vdash B\{X \leftarrow A'\}, B\{X \leftarrow A''\} <: C}{E \vdash b'(A') \leftrightarrow b''(A'') : C}$$

(Eq eta)
$$\frac{E \vdash b \leftrightarrow b' : A \rightarrow B \quad y \notin dom(E)}{E \vdash \lambda(y : A)b(y) \leftrightarrow b' : A \rightarrow B}$$

(Eq eta2)
$$\frac{E \vdash b \leftrightarrow b' : \forall(X <: A)B \quad Y \notin dom(E)}{E \vdash \lambda(Y <: A)b(Y) \leftrightarrow b' : \forall(X <: A)B}$$

(Eq beta)
$$\frac{E, x : A \vdash b \leftrightarrow b' : B \quad E \vdash a \leftrightarrow a' : A}{E \vdash (\lambda(x : A)b)(a) \leftrightarrow b'\{x \leftarrow a'\} : B}$$

(Eq beta2)
$$\frac{E, X <: A \vdash b \leftrightarrow b' : B \quad E \vdash A' <: A}{E \vdash (\lambda(X <: A)b)(A') \leftrightarrow b'\{X \leftarrow A'\} : B\{X \leftarrow A'\}}$$

2.3 Basic properties

We now state some basic lemmas about $F_{<:}$ derivations. Most of these are proven by (simultaneous) induction on the size of the derivations; the proofs are long, but straightforward if carried out in the order indicated. We conclude the section with an application of these lemmas, showing that typing is preserved under β-η-reductions.

Notation

Let ϑ stand for either $C\ \mathit{type}$, $C{<:}C'$, $c{:}C$, or $c{\leftrightarrow}c'{:}C$.

Lemma (Implied judgments)

(ϑ/env) $\quad \vdash E,F\ \mathit{env} \;\Rightarrow\; \vdash E\ \mathit{env}$ $\quad$ and $\quad E,F \vdash \vartheta \;\Rightarrow\; \vdash E\ \mathit{env}$

$(env/type)$ $\quad \vdash E,X{<:}D,E'\ \mathit{env} \;\Rightarrow\; E \vdash D\ \mathit{type}$ $\quad$ and $\quad \vdash E,x{:}D,E'\ \mathit{env} \;\Rightarrow\; E \vdash D\ \mathit{type}$

Lemma (Bound change)

$\vdash E,X{<:}D',E'\ \mathit{env},\ E \vdash D\ \mathit{type} \;\Rightarrow\; \vdash E,X{<:}D,E'\ \mathit{env}$

$E,X{<:}D',E' \vdash C\ \mathit{type},\ E \vdash D\ \mathit{type} \;\Rightarrow\; E,X{<:}D,E' \vdash C\ \mathit{type}$

Lemma (Weakening)

Let β stand for either $X{<:}D$ or $x{:}D$. Assume $\vdash E,\beta\ \mathit{env}$, and $X,x \notin dom(E')$. Then,

$\vdash E,E'\ \mathit{env} \Rightarrow \vdash E,\beta,E'\ \mathit{env}$ $\quad$ and $\quad E,E' \vdash \vartheta \Rightarrow E,\beta,E' \vdash \vartheta$

Assume $\vdash E,F\ \mathit{env}$ and $dom(F) \cap dom(E') = \emptyset$. Then,

$\vdash E,E'\ \mathit{env} \Rightarrow \vdash E,F,E'\ \mathit{env}$ $\quad$ and $\quad E,E' \vdash \vartheta \Rightarrow E,F,E' \vdash \vartheta$

Lemma (Implied judgments, continued)

$(sub/type)$ $\quad E \vdash C{<:}C' \;\Rightarrow\; E \vdash C\ \mathit{type},\ E \vdash C'\ \mathit{type}$

Lemma (Bound weakening)

Let $\langle\beta,\beta'\rangle$ stand for either $\langle X{<:}D, X{<:}D'\rangle$ or $\langle x{:}D, x{:}D'\rangle$. Assume $E \vdash D'{<:}D$. Then,

$\vdash E,\beta,E'\ \mathit{env} \Rightarrow \vdash E,\beta',E'\ \mathit{env}$ $\quad$ and $\quad E,\beta,E' \vdash \vartheta \Rightarrow E,\beta',E' \vdash \vartheta$

Lemma (Type substitution)

Assume $E \vdash D'{<:}D$. Then,

$\vdash E,X{<:}D,E'\ \mathit{env} \Rightarrow \vdash E,E'\{X{\leftarrow}D'\}\ \mathit{env}$ $\quad$ and $\quad E,X{<:}D,E' \vdash \vartheta \Rightarrow E,E'\{X{\leftarrow}D'\} \vdash \vartheta\{X{\leftarrow}D'\}$

Lemma (Value substitution)

Assume either $E \vdash d{:}D$, or d is any term and $x \notin FV(\vartheta)$; then

$\vdash E,x{:}D,E'\ \mathit{env} \Rightarrow \vdash E,E'\ \mathit{env}$ $\quad$ and $\quad E,x{:}D,E' \vdash \vartheta \Rightarrow E,E' \vdash \vartheta\{x{\leftarrow}d\}$

Lemma (Implied judgments, continued)

$(val/type)$ $\quad E \vdash c : C \Rightarrow E \vdash C\ \mathit{type},$

(eq/val) $\quad E \vdash c{\leftrightarrow}c' : C \Rightarrow E \vdash c : C,\ E \vdash c' : C,$

Lemma (Eq subsumption)

$E \vdash c{\leftrightarrow}c' : C,\ E \vdash C{<:}D \;\Rightarrow\; E \vdash c{\leftrightarrow}c' : D$

Lemma (Implied judgments, continued)

(val/eq) $\quad E \vdash c : C \;\Rightarrow\; E \vdash c{\leftrightarrow}c : C$

Lemma (Congruence)

$E \vdash d{\leftrightarrow}d' : D \wedge E,x{:}D,E' \vdash c{:}C \;\Rightarrow\; E,E' \vdash c\{x{\leftarrow}d\}{\leftrightarrow}c\{x{\leftarrow}d'\} : C$

Lemma (Renaming)

Assume $Y \notin dom(E,X{<:}D,E')$. Then,

$\vdash E,X{<:}D,E'\ \mathit{env} \Rightarrow \vdash E,Y{<:}D,E'\{X{\leftarrow}Y\}\ \mathit{env}$ and $E,X{<:}D,E' \vdash \vartheta \Rightarrow E,Y{<:}D,E'\{X{\leftarrow}Y\} \vdash \vartheta\{X{\leftarrow}Y\}$

Assume $y \notin dom(E,x{:}D,E')$. Then,

$\vdash E,x{:}D,E'\ \mathit{env} \Rightarrow \vdash E,y{:}D,E'\ \mathit{env}$ $\quad$ and $\quad E,x{:}D,E' \vdash \vartheta \Rightarrow E,y{:}D,E' \vdash \vartheta\{x{\leftarrow}y\}$

Lemma (Exchange)

Let β stand for either $X{<:}D$ or $x{:}D$. Let β' stand for either $X'{<:}D'$ or $x'{:}D'$. Assume $\vdash E,\beta'\ \mathit{env}$.

$\vdash E,\beta,\beta',E'\ \mathit{env} \Rightarrow \vdash E,\beta',\beta,E'\ \mathit{env}$ $\quad$ and $\quad E,\beta,\beta',E' \vdash \vartheta \Rightarrow E,\beta',\beta,E' \vdash \vartheta$

Lemma (Substitution exchange)

Let β stand for either $x':D'$ or $X'<:D'$. Then,

$\vdash E,X<:D,\beta,E'\ env \Rightarrow\ \vdash E,\beta\{X\leftarrow D\},X<:D,E'\ env$

$E,X<:D,\beta,E' \vdash C\ type \Rightarrow E,\beta\{X\leftarrow D\},X<:D,E' \vdash C\ type$

The following two lemmas draw conclusions about the shape of terms and derivations, from the fact that certain subtyping and typing judgments have been derived.

Lemma (Subtyping decomposition)

- If $E \vdash A<:X$, then $A\equiv Y_1$ for some type variable Y_1 and either $Y_1\equiv X$, or for some $n\geq 1$, $Y_1<:Y_2\in E .. Y_n<:X\in E$
- If $E,X<:B,E' \vdash X<:A$, then either $A\equiv X$ or $E,X<:B,E' \vdash B<:A$.
- If $E \vdash Top<:A$, then $A\equiv Top$.
- If $E \vdash B'\rightarrow B''<:A$, then either $A\equiv Top$ or $A\equiv A'\rightarrow A''$, $E \vdash A'<:B'$ and $E \vdash B''<:A''$
- If $E \vdash A<:B'\rightarrow B''$, then either $A\equiv A'\rightarrow A''$ for some A',A'', with $E \vdash B'<:A'$ and $E \vdash A''<:B''$, or $A\equiv X_1$ and for some $A',A'',n\geq 1$: $X_1<:X_2 \in E .. X_n<:A'\rightarrow A'' \in E$ with $E \vdash B'<:A'$ and $E \vdash A''<:B''$
- If $E \vdash \forall(X<:B')B''<:A$, then either $A\equiv Top$ or $A\equiv\forall(X<:A')A''$, $E \vdash A'<:B'$ and $E,X<:A' \vdash B''<:A''$
- If $E \vdash A<:\forall(X<:B')B''$, then either $A\equiv\forall(X<:A')A''$ for some A',A'', with $E \vdash B'<:A'$ and $E,X<:B' \vdash A''<:B''$, or $A\equiv X_1$ and for some $A',A'',n\geq 1$: $X_1<:X_2 \in E .. X_n<:\forall(X<:A')A'' \in E$ with $E \vdash B'<:A'$ and $E,X<:B' \vdash A''<:B''$

Lemma (Typing decomposition)

- If $E,x:D,E' \vdash x:C$, then $E \vdash D<:C$
- If $E \vdash top:A$, then $A\equiv Top$
- If $E \vdash \lambda(x:B')b : A$, then either $A\equiv Top$, or for some A',A'',B'', $A\equiv A'\rightarrow A''$ with $E\vdash A'<:B'$, $E \vdash B''<:A''$, and $E,x:B' \vdash b : B''$.
- If $E \vdash b(c) : B''$ then for some B', $E\vdash b : B'\rightarrow B''$ and $E \vdash c : B'$
- If $E \vdash \lambda(X<:B')b : A$, then either $A\equiv Top$, or for some A',A'',B'', $A\equiv\forall(X<:A')A''$ with $E \vdash A'<:B'$, $E,X<:A' \vdash B''<:A''$, and $E,X<:B'\vdash b : B''$.
- If $E \vdash b(C) : D$ then for some B',B'',X, $E\vdash C<:B'$, $E \vdash B''\{X\leftarrow C\} <: D$, and $E \vdash b : \forall(X<:B')B''$.

We conclude with a proposition about the preservation of typing under β and η reduction. The second-order η case is by far the hardest, and it requires the following lemma about the elimination of unused free variables (FV).

Lemma (Non-occurring type variable)

If $X\notin FV(c,E')$ and $E,X<:D,E'\vdash c : C$ then for some C_0 with $X\notin FV(C_0)$

$E,X<:D,E' \vdash c : C_0$ and $E,X<:D,E' \vdash C_0<:C$

Proposition (Preservation of typing under β-η-reductions)

(β1) $E \vdash (\lambda(x:B)b)(c) : A \Rightarrow E \vdash b\{x\leftarrow c\} : A$ **(η1)** $E \vdash \lambda(x:B)c(x) : A,\ x\notin FV(c) \Rightarrow E \vdash c : A$

(β2) $E \vdash (\lambda(X<:B)b)(C) : A \Rightarrow E \vdash b\{X\leftarrow C\} : A$ **(η2)** $E \vdash \lambda(X<:B)c(X) : A,\ X\notin FV(c) \Rightarrow E \vdash c : A$

Note that this proposition is non-trivial; for example, the (β1) case does not follow simply from the *(Eq beta)* rule and the eq/val lemma. Moreover, the derivation of $E \vdash b\{x\leftarrow c\} : A$ will have in general quite a different shape than the derivation of $E \vdash (\lambda(x:B)b)(c) : A$.

2.4 Derived rules

Most of the lemmas in the previous section can be written down as derived inference rules. Here we discuss some derived rules of special significance.

First, the eq-subsumption lemma in the previous section gives us a very interesting rule that lifts subsumption to the equality judgment; we remark that this is proven via the *(Eq beta)* rule.

(Eq subsumption)

$$\frac{E \vdash a \leftrightarrow a' : A \quad E \vdash A <: B}{E \vdash a \leftrightarrow a' : B}$$

Note that, in general, it is not true that $E \vdash a \leftrightarrow a' : B$ and $E \vdash A <: B$ imply $E \vdash a \leftrightarrow a' : A$.

The following two lemmas concern the equivalence of functions modulo domain restriction; the first one will find a useful application in section 3.1.

Lemma (Domain restriction)

If $f: A \rightarrow B$, then f is equivalent to its restriction $f|_{A'}$ to a smaller domain $A'<:A$, when they are both seen at type $A' \rightarrow B$. That is:

(Eq fun')

$$\frac{E \vdash A'<:A \quad E \vdash B<:B' \quad E,x:A \vdash b \leftrightarrow b' : B}{E \vdash \lambda(x:A)b \leftrightarrow \lambda(x:A')b' : A' \rightarrow B'}$$

Lemma (Bound restriction)

If $f: \forall(X<:A)B$, then f is equivalent to its restriction $f|_{A'}$ to a smaller bound $A'<:A$, when they are both seen at type $\forall(X<:A')B$. That is:

(Eq fun2')

$$\frac{E \vdash A'<:A \quad E,X<:A' \vdash B<:B' \quad E,X<:A \vdash b \leftrightarrow b' : B}{E \vdash \lambda(X<:A)b \leftrightarrow \lambda(X<:A')b' : \forall(X<:A')B'}$$

We now turn to the *(Eq appl2)* rule. This rule asserts that if a polymorphic function $b : \forall(X<:A)B$ is instantiated at two types $A'<:A$ and $A''<:A$, then both instantiations evaluate to the same value with respect to any result type that is an upper bound of $B\{X \leftarrow A'\}$ and $B\{X \leftarrow A''\}$.

(Eq appl2)

$$\frac{E \vdash b' \leftrightarrow b'' : \forall(X<:A)B \quad E \vdash A'<:A \quad E \vdash A''<:A \qquad E \vdash B\{X \leftarrow A'\}<:C \quad E \vdash B\{X \leftarrow A''\}<:C}{E \vdash b'(A') \leftrightarrow b''(A'') : C}$$

Note that this rule asserts that the result of $b(A)$ is independent of A, in the proper result type.

A simpler derived rule (used in $F_{\leq}$ [10]) is obtained by setting $A'=A''$:

(Eq appl2 A'=A")

$$\frac{E \vdash b' \leftrightarrow b'' : \forall(X<:A)B \quad E \vdash A'<:A}{E \vdash b'(A') \leftrightarrow b''(A') : B\{X \leftarrow A'\}}$$

However, the *(Eq appl2)* rule is most useful when $A' \neq A''$ and we can find an interesting upper bound to $B\{X \leftarrow A'\}$ and $B\{X \leftarrow A''\}$. This motivates the following derived rule, which is often used in practice.

Denote by $B\{X^- \leftarrow C, X^+ \leftarrow D\}$ the substitution of C for the negative occurrences of X in B, and of D for the positive ones. Take $A'<:A''$ ($<: A$), then we have (see [15, Sec. 14.3] for a proof):

$$B\{X\leftarrow A'\} \equiv B\{X^-\leftarrow A',X^+\leftarrow A'\} <: B\{X^-\leftarrow A',X^+\leftarrow A''\}$$
$$B\{X\leftarrow A''\} \equiv B\{X^-\leftarrow A'',X^+\leftarrow A''\} <: B\{X^-\leftarrow A',X^+\leftarrow A''\}$$

Hence, for $A'<:A''<:A$ we have a (non trivial) common supertype for $B\{X\leftarrow A'\}$ and $B\{X\leftarrow A''\}$. This fact then justifies the rule:

(Eq appl2-+)

$$\frac{E\vdash b'\leftrightarrow b'' : \forall(X<:A)B \quad E\vdash A'<:A''<:A}{E\vdash b'(A')\leftrightarrow b''(A'') : B\{X^-\leftarrow A',X^+\leftarrow A''\}}$$

This rule is in fact a special case of *dinaturality* of type application [3], where the dinaturality is required only with respect to coercions $A'<:A''$, for all A',A'' subtypes of A. We have the diagram:

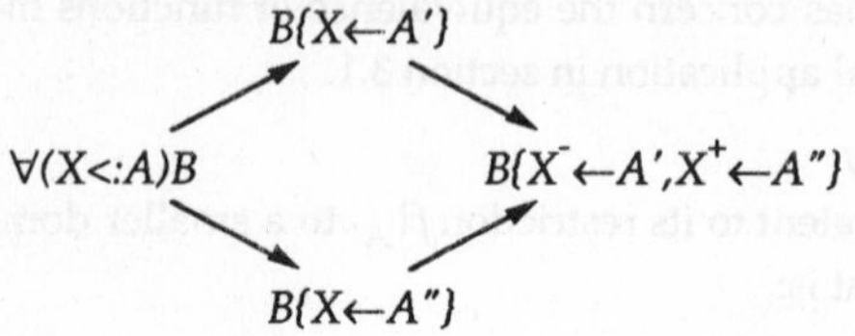

The two arrows on the left are the A' and A'' instances of generic type application $x(X)$, where x is a variable of type $\forall(X<:A)B$, and B might have the type variable X free. The two arrows on the right are coercions induced by $A'<:A''$. Here $\forall(X<:A)B$ is constant in X, so the coercion $A'<:A''$ has no effect on this type. Hence the diagram above is just a brief version of:

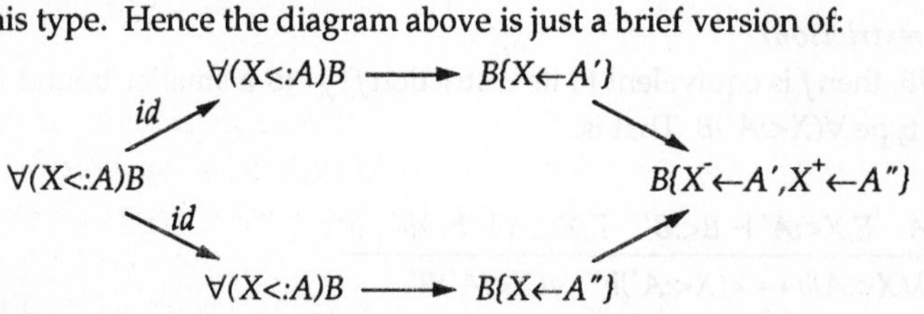

where now the two horizontal arrows are the A' and A'' instances of $x(X)$. In the terminology of [3, p.42], the family given by $\{x(X)\mid X<:A\}$ is dinatural in the coercions.

We conclude this section with an application of *(Eq appl2)*, which is used insections 3.3 and 4.

Proposition (Eq-substitution)

Assume $E,X<:A,x{:}\ S\vdash b{:}B$ and X positive in S and B.
If $E\vdash A_1,A_2 <: A$, $E\vdash s_1{:}S\{X\leftarrow A_1\}$, $E\vdash s_2{:}S\{X\leftarrow A_2\}$, $E\vdash s_1\leftrightarrow s_2{:}S\{X\leftarrow A\}$
then $E\vdash b\{X\leftarrow A_1,x\leftarrow s_1\}\leftrightarrow b\{X\leftarrow A_2,x\leftarrow s_2\}{:}\ B\{X\leftarrow A\}$

Proof Let $M \triangleq \lambda(X<:A)\lambda(x{:}S)b$, then $E\vdash M : \forall(X<:A)S\to B$. Now prove:

(1) $E\vdash M(A_1)(s_1) \leftrightarrow M(A)(s_1) : B\{X\leftarrow A\}$ by *(Eq appl2)* and *(Eq appl)*, since X is positive in S and B
(2) $E\vdash M(A_2)(s_2) \leftrightarrow M(A)(s_2) : B\{X\leftarrow A\}$ similarly to (1)
(3) $E\vdash M(A)(s_1) \leftrightarrow M(A)(s_2) : B\{X\leftarrow A\}$ by *(Eq appl2)* and *(Eq appl)*, since $E\vdash s_1\leftrightarrow s_2{:}S\{X\leftarrow A\}$.

Conclude by *(Eq trans)*, *(Beta2)*, and *(Beta)*.

□

The proposition can be easily generalized to the case where there are several variables $x_1{:}\ S_1, \ldots, x_n{:}\ S_n$ (X positive in all of them) and terms $E\vdash s_1{:}S\{X\leftarrow A_1\},\ldots, E\vdash s_n{:}S\{X\leftarrow A_n\}$, with $E\vdash A_1,\ldots,A_n <: A$ and $E\vdash s_1\leftrightarrow\ldots\leftrightarrow s_n{:}S\{X\leftarrow A\}$.

2.5 PER semantics

For the PER semantics, the reader can consult [4], [7], [15], and [23]. The interpretation of $F_{<:}$ in PER is explained in those papers, except that the *(Eq appl2)* must be shown sound. The soundness for this rule is relatively straightforward, and omitted.

2.6 Conservativity of typing

Besides the presence of subtypes, the main new feature of $F_{<:}$ with respect to F lays in its equational theory, which extends the standard β-η equality in two directions, adding a terminal type *Top* and introducing the rule *(Eq appl2)*.

First of all, the equational theory (↔) of $F_{<:}$ is not conservative over F, the reason being the rule *(Eq appl2)*. Consider, for example:

Proposition

$E \vdash B\ type,\ \ E \vdash c : \forall(X)X{\to}B,\ \ E \vdash a : A \ \Rightarrow\ E \vdash c(Top)(top) \leftrightarrow c(A)(a) : B$

Proof

$E \vdash c(Top)(top) \leftrightarrow c(Top)(a) : B$	val/eq lemma *(Eq appl2) (Eq collapse) (Eq appl)*
$E \vdash c(Top)(a) \leftrightarrow c(A)(a) : B$	val/eq lemma *(Eq appl2) (Eq appl)*
$E \vdash c(Top)(top) \leftrightarrow c(A)(a) : B$	*(Eq trans)*

□

By applying this fact twice via *(Eq trans)* we can show:

$$y : \forall(X)X{\to}Bool \vdash y(Bool)(true) \leftrightarrow y(Bool)(false) : Bool$$

which is an F-judgment equating two different β-η-normal forms. It is well- known that no such judgment is derivable in F. A further application of *(Eq fun)* produces two closed terms with the same property.

As for the *typing* theory, however, $F_{<:}$'s rules are designed in such a way as to maintain and carefully generalize those of F. Writing $\vdash_F$ for derivations in F, and $\vdash_{<:}$ for derivations in $F_{<:}$, we can prove the following result.

Theorem

If $E \vdash_{<:} a : A$, where E, a, and A are in the language of F, then $E \vdash_F a : A$.

The proof of this statement (inspired by some results in [15]) requires a detour on *normal form proofs* in $F_{<:}$, a subject studied in [10] for a slightly different system, but sharing with $F_{<:}$ the same typing judgments. The reason for the detour is that trivial proofs by induction on the derivation of $E \vdash_{<:} a : A$ do not work, since $F_{<:}$ has "cut rules" (e.g. *(Subsumption)* or *(Val appl)*) that may introduce non-F types.

2.6.1 Normal and minimal proofs in $F_{<:}$

Subtype proofs

A *normal form proof* of $E \vdash_{<:} A{<:}B$ is a proof using either a single application of *(Sub Refl)* if $A{\equiv}B$, or it is a proof using only the rules *(Sub Top)*, *(Sub→)*, *(Sub ∀)*, or one of the following two rules:

(Sub X-Iter)

$$\frac{\vdash_{<:} E,X<:A,E'\ env \qquad k\geq 1}{E,X<:A,E' \vdash_{<:} X <: E^k(X)}$$

(Sub X-Trans)

$$\frac{\vdash_{<:} E,X<:A,E'\ env \qquad E,X<:A,E' \vdash_{<:} E^*(X)<:B}{E,X<:A,E' \vdash_{<:} X <: B}$$

where $E^1(X) = E(X)$, and $E^{k+1}(X) = E(X)$ if $E(X)$ is not a variable, or $E^{k+1}(X) = E^k(E(X))$ otherwise. Moreover, let k be the least k for which $E^k(X)$ is not a variable; then define $E^*(X) = E^k(X)$.

Type proofs

Normal form proofs and minimal normal form proofs of $E \vdash_{<:} a : A$ are simultaneously defined as follows.

A *normal form proof* of $E \vdash_{<:} a : A$ is either a minimal normal form proof or has the following shape:

$$\frac{E \vdash_{<:} a : A' \qquad E \vdash_{<:} A' <: A}{E \vdash_{<:} a : A}$$

where $A' \not\equiv A$, $E \vdash_{<:} a : A'$ is given by a minimal normal form proof, and $E \vdash_{<:} A' <: A$ is given by a normal form proof.

A *minimal normal form proof* of $E \vdash_{<:} a : A$ is a proof using only the rules: *(Val x)*; *(Val top)*; *(Val fun)* with the restriction that the premise is given by a minimal normal form proof; *(Val fun2)* with the restriction that the premise is given by a minimal normal form proof; or one of the following two rules *(Val appl-min)* and *(Val appl2-min)*.

(Val appl-min)

$$\frac{E \vdash_{<:} b : A \rightarrow B \qquad E \vdash_{<:} a : A}{E \vdash_{<:} b(a) : B}$$

where $E \vdash_{<:} a : A$ is given by a normal form proof and $E \vdash_{<:} b : A \rightarrow B$ is given by either a minimal normal form proof or by a proof of the shape:

$$\frac{E \vdash_{<:} b : X \qquad E \vdash_{<:} X <: E^*(X)}{E \vdash_{<:} b : E^*(X)}$$

where $E \vdash_{<:} b : X$ is given by a minimal normal form proof, X is a variable, $E^*(X) \equiv A \rightarrow B$, and $E \vdash_{<:} X <: E^*(X)$ is given by a single application of *(Sub X-Iter)*.

(Val appl2-min)

$$\frac{E \vdash_{<:} b : \forall(X<:A)B \qquad E \vdash_{<:} A' <: A}{E \vdash_{<:} b(A') : B\{X \leftarrow A'\}}$$

where $E \vdash_{<:} A' <: A$ is given by a normal proof and $E \vdash_{<:} b : \forall(X<:A)B$ is given by either a minimal normal form proof or by a proof of the shape:

$$\frac{E \vdash_{<:} b : X \qquad E \vdash_{<:} X <: E^*(X)}{E \vdash_{<:} b : E^*(X)}$$

where $E \vdash_{<:} b : X$ is given by a minimal normal form proof, X is a variable, $E^*(X) \equiv \forall(X<:A)B$, and $E \vdash_{<:} X <: E^*(X)$ is given by a single application of *(Sub X-Iter)*.

Proposition [10]

For any provable judgment $E \vdash_{<:} a : A$, there exists a (unique) normal form proof.

2.6.2 $F_{<:}$ typing is conservative over *F* typing

It is not difficult to see *F* as a subsystem of $F_{<:}$. As for the language, just define a translation function β so that:

$$\beta(\forall X.A) \equiv \forall(X{<:}Top)\,\beta(A) \qquad \beta(\Lambda X.M) \equiv \lambda(X{<:}Top)\,\beta(M)$$

and which is the identity on all the other constructs. A well formed environments *E* in *F* consist of a collection $E1 \equiv X_1,\ldots,X_h$ of type variables and a list $E2 \equiv x_1{:}\ S_1,\ \ldots,\ x_h{:}\ S_h$ of type assumptions, where at most the type variables in *E1* can appear free. Then:

$$\beta(E) \equiv X_1{<:}Top,\ \ldots,\ X_h{<:}Top,\ x_1{:}\beta(S_1),\ \ldots,\ x_h{:}\beta(S_h).$$

By this, it is almost obvious that to any *F*-derivation $E \vdash_F a{:}A$ corresponds an $F_{<:}$-derivation $\beta(E) \vdash \beta(a){:}\beta(A)$ that never uses (Subsumption) (and thus subtyping rules) or *Top* rules and where (Eq appl2) is always applied in its special case when $A' \equiv A''$ and $C \equiv B\{X \leftarrow A'\}$. In the following, we will argue directly in the language of $F_{<:}$ (thus dispensing from β).

Lemma

Let *E* be an *F*-environment, and let *A* and *B* be *F*-types.

$E \vdash_{<:} A{<:}B$ iff $A \equiv B$.

Lemma

Let *E* be an *F*-environment, *a* be an *F*-term, and let $E \vdash_{<:} a : A$ be a minimal normal form proof. Then *A* is an *F*-type and $E \vdash_F a : A$.

Proof By induction on the minimal normal form proof $E \vdash_{<:} a : A$. □

Theorem (Conservativity of typing over F)

Let *E* be an *F*-environment, *a* be an *F*-term and *A* be an *F*-type.

$E \vdash_{<:} a : A \ \Rightarrow\ E \vdash_F a : A$

Proof Consider a normal form proof of $E \vdash_{<:} a : A$. Note that it is necessarily a minimal normal form proof. Then the thesis reduces to that of the lemmas. □

3. Expressiveness

Since $F_{<:}$ is an extension of *F*, one can already carry out all the standard encodings of algebraic data types that are possible in *F* [2]. However, it is not clear that anything of further interest can be obtained from the subtyping rules of $F_{<:}$, which only involve an apparently useless type *Top* and the simple rules for → and ∀. In this section we begin to show that we can in fact construct rich subtyping relations on familiar data structures.

3.1 Booleans

In the sequel we concentrate on inclusion of structured types, but for this to make sense we need to show that there are some non-trivial inclusions already at the level of basic types. We investigate here the type of booleans, which also illustrates some consequences of the $F_{<:}$ rules.

Starting from the encoding of Church's booleans in *F*, we can define three subtypes of *Bool* as follows (cf. [13]):

$$Bool \triangleq \forall(A)\,A\to A\to A \qquad True \triangleq \forall(A)\,A\to Top\to A$$
$$None \triangleq \forall(A)\,Top\to Top\to A \qquad False \triangleq \forall(A)\,Top\to A\to A$$

where:

$None <: True,\ None <: False,\ True <: Bool,\ False <: Bool$

Looking at all the closed normal forms (that is, the *elements*) of these types, we have:

$$true_{Bool} : Bool \triangleq \lambda(A)\,\lambda(x{:}A)\,\lambda(y{:}A)\,x \qquad true_{True} : True \triangleq \lambda(A)\,\lambda(x{:}A)\,\lambda(y{:}Top)\,x$$
$$false_{Bool} : Bool \triangleq \lambda(A)\,\lambda(x{:}A)\,\lambda(y{:}A)\,y \qquad false_{False} : False \triangleq \lambda(A)\,\lambda(x{:}Top)\,\lambda(y{:}A)\,y$$

We obtain four elements of type *Bool*; in addition to the usual two, $true_{Bool}$ and $false_{Bool}$, the extra $true_{True}$ and $false_{False}$ have type *Bool* by subsumption. However, we can show that $true_{Bool}$ and $true_{True}$ are provably equivalent at type *Bool*, by using the domain restriction lemma (*Eq fun'*) from section 2.4.

$$\frac{\dfrac{\dfrac{\dfrac{E,A{<:}Top,x{:}A,y{:}Top \vdash x \leftrightarrow x : A \qquad E \vdash A{<:}Top}{E,A{<:}Top,x{:}A \vdash \lambda(y{:}Top)\,x \leftrightarrow \lambda(y{:}A)\,x : A{\to}A}\ (Eq\ fun')}{E,A{<:}Top \vdash \lambda(x{:}A)\,\lambda(y{:}Top)\,x \leftrightarrow \lambda(x{:}A)\,\lambda(y{:}A)\,x : A{\to}A{\to}A}}{E \vdash \lambda(A)\,\lambda(x{:}A)\,\lambda(y{:}Top)\,x \leftrightarrow \lambda(A)\,\lambda(x{:}A)\,\lambda(y{:}A)\,x : \forall(A)\,A{\to}A{\to}A}}{E \vdash true_{True} \leftrightarrow true_{Bool} : Bool}$$

Similarly, we can show that $E \vdash false_{False} \leftrightarrow false_{Bool} : Bool$. Hence, there really are only two different values in *Bool*, one value each in *True* and *False*, and none in *None*.

3.2. Simple records

We restrict ourselves to the encoding of *simple records* (the ones with a fixed number of components [7]); *extensible records* are treated in [6].

Cartesian products are encoded, as usual, as $A{\times}B \triangleq \forall(C)(A{\to}B{\to}C){\to}C$; note that by this definitions $\times$ is monotonic in both its arguments.

A *tuple type* is an iterated cartesian product; we consider only the ones ending with *Top*:

$$Tuple(A_1,..,A_n,Top) \triangleq A_1{\times}(..{\times}(A_n{\times}Top)..) \qquad n\geq 0$$

These types have the property that a tuple type with more components is a subtype of a corresponding tuple type with fewer components. For example:

$$Tuple(A, B, Top) \equiv A{\times}B{\times}Top <: A{\times}Top \equiv Tuple(A, Top)$$
because $A{<:}A$, $B{\times}Top{<:}Top$, and $\times$ is monotonic.

Tuple values are similarly encoded by iterated pairing, ending with *top*. The basic operations on tuple values are: $a\llcorner i$, dropping the first i components of tuple a; and $a.i$, selecting the i-th component of a. These are defined by iterating the product projections.

Let L be a countable set of *labels*, enumerated by a bijection $\iota\in L{\to}Nat$. We indicate by l^i, with a superscript, the i-th label in this enumeration. Often we need to refer to a list of n distinct labels out of this enumeration; we then use subscripts, as in $l_1..l_n$. So we may have, for example, $l_1,l_2,l_3 = l^5,l^1,l^{17}$. More precisely, $l_1..l_n$ stands for $l^{\sigma(1)},..,l^{\sigma(n)}$ for some injective $\sigma\in 1..n{\to}Nat$.

A record type has the form $Rcd(l_1{:}A_1,..,l_n{:}A_n,C)$; in this presentation C will always be *Top*. Once the enumeration of labels is fixed, a record type is encoded as a tuple type where the record components are allocated to tuple slots as determined by the index of their labels; the component of label l^i into the i-th tuple slot. The remaining slots are filled with *Top* "padding". For example:

$$Rcd(l^2{:}C, l^0{:}A, Top) \triangleq Tuple(A, Top, C, Top)$$

Since record type components are canonically sorted under the encoding, two record types that differ only in the order of their components will be equal under the encoding. Hence we can consider record components as unordered.

From the encoding, we derive the familiar rule for simple records [5]:

$$\frac{E \vdash A_1 <: B_1 \;..\; E \vdash A_n <: B_n \quad E \vdash A_{n+1}\, type \;..\; E \vdash A_m\, type}{E \vdash Rcd(l_1{:}A_1,..,l_n{:}A_n,..,l_m{:}A_m,Top) <: Rcd(l_1{:}B_1,..,l_n{:}B_n,Top)}$$

This holds because any additional field $l_k{:}A_k$ $(n<k\leq m)$ on the left is absorbed either by the *Top* padding on the right, if $\iota(l_k)<max(\iota(l_1)..\iota(l_n))$, or by the final *Top*, otherwise.

Record values are similarly encoded; for example: $rcd(l^2{=}c,\ l^0{=}a,\ top) \triangleq tuple(a,\ top,\ c,\ top)$. Record selection is reduced to tuple selection by setting $r.l_i \triangleq r.\iota(l_i)$.

From these encodings we obtain all the usual typing rules for records. Moreover, the derived equational theory exhibits a form of observational equivalence:

$$\frac{\begin{array}{c} E \vdash a_1{\leftrightarrow}b_1 : A_1 \;..\; E \vdash a_n{\leftrightarrow}b_n : A_n \\ E \vdash a_{n+1} : B_{n+1} \;..\; E \vdash a_p : B_p \quad E \vdash b_{n+1} : C_{n+1} \;..\; E \vdash b_q : C_q \end{array}}{E \vdash rcd(l_1{=}a_1,..,l_n{=}a_n,..,l_p{=}a_p,top) \leftrightarrow rcd(l_1{=}b_1,..,l_n{=}b_n,..,l_q{=}b_q,top) : Rcd(l_1{:}A_1,..,l_n{:}A_n,Top)}$$

That is, two records are equivalent if they coincide on the components that are observable at a given type. This holds ultimately because any two values are equivalent at type *Top*.

3.3. Lists

Following [2] we can define the algebra of parametric lists. *List[A]* stands for the homogeneous lists of type *A*.

$$List[A] \triangleq \forall(L)\, L{\to}(A{\to}L{\to}L){\to}L$$

We have:

$$A <: B \;\Rightarrow\; List[A] <: List[B]$$

$nil: \forall(A)\ List[A] \triangleq$
$\quad \lambda(A)\,\lambda(L)\,\lambda(n{:}L)\,\lambda(c{:}A{\to}L{\to}L)\ n$

$cons: \forall(A)\ A{\to}List[A]{\to}List[A] \triangleq$
$\quad \lambda(A)\,\lambda(hd{:}A)\,\lambda(tl{:}List[A])$
$\quad\quad \lambda(L)\,\lambda(n{:}L)\,\lambda(c{:}A{\to}L{\to}L)$
$\quad\quad\quad c(hd)(tl(L)(n)(c))$

$length: \forall(A)\ List[A]{\to}Nat \triangleq$
$\quad \lambda(A)\,\lambda(l{:}List[A])$
$\quad\quad l(Nat)(zero)(\lambda(a{:}A)\lambda(n{:}Nat)succ(n))$

As an application of *(Eq appl2)* we can now show some interesting facts. Namely, any two empty lists are equal in *List[Top]*, and have the same length in *Nat*. Similarly for two singleton lists, and so on. In the proof, we will use the Eq-substitution proposition of Section 2.4.

Take *b:B* and *c:C*, then:

$\vdash nil(B) \leftrightarrow nil(C) : List[Top]$ (Eq appl2)

$\vdash length(Top)(nil(B)) \leftrightarrow length(Top)(nil(C)) : Nat$ (Eq appl2, Eq appl)

$\vdash cons(B)(b)(nil(B)) \leftrightarrow cons(C)(c)(nil(C)) : List[Top]$ by Eq-substitution, starting from $X{<:}Top,\ x{:}X, l{:}List[X] \vdash cons(X)(x)(l) : List[X]$

$\vdash length(B)(cons(B)(b)(nil(B))) \leftrightarrow length(C)(cons(C)(c)(nil(C))) : Nat$
by Eq-substitution, starting from $X{<:}Top,\ l{:}List[X] \vdash length\,(X)(l) : Nat$

Note that we have proven an interesting property of the behavior of *length* uniquely from its type; any function $f: \forall(A)\ List[A] \to Nat$ has such a property. This fact is related to the theorems proved by Wadler in [25] using only the types of terms. A difference is that our proof is carried out within $F_{<:}$, whereas Wadler uses parametricity properties beyond the proof system of F.

4. The category of closed terms

It is well known that the usual second-order encodings for products and coproducts, while logically sound, do not define, under β-η-equality, true categorical constructions. One can easily prove the existence of a term making a certain diagram commute, but its uniqueness does not follow from the standard equational rules.

As an example of the expressive power of *(Eq appl2)*, we show that those encodings are really categorical constructions when the underlining equational theory is the one of $F_{<:}$. In the same vein, motivated by the semantic isomorphisms obtained in [3] and [14] as consequences of parametricity, we investigate some provable isomorphisms in a suitable setting. The framework for our discussion is a category whose objects are the sets of closed terms of a closed type.

4.1 Definitions and basic properties

Recall first (see [LS 86] or [MS 89]) that given a typed λ-calculus language and a λ-theory **T**, a category $Cl(\mathbf{T})$ is determined by taking as objects of $Cl(\mathbf{T})$ the (closed) types of **T**. As for morphisms, choose first one variable for each type and define the morphisms from A to B to be equivalence classes of typing judgments $x{:}A \vdash t{:}B$, where x is the chosen variable of type A, and the equivalence relation is given by the equality judgments $x{:}A \vdash t \leftrightarrow t'{:}B$ of **T**. We will write $[x{:}A \vdash t{:}B]$ for the morphism given by the judgment $x{:}A \vdash t{:}B$. Identity is given by $[x{:}A \vdash x{:}A]$ and composition is defined by substitution:

$$[y{:}B \vdash s{:}C] \circ [x{:}A \vdash t{:}B] = [x{:}A \vdash s\{y \leftarrow t\}{:}C]$$

The category $Cl(F_{<:})$, obtained by applying this construction to $F_{<:}$, has a terminal object, given by Top. For any object A, the canonical morphism from A to Top is $[x{:}A \vdash top{:}Top]$; uniqueness is guaranteed by *(Eq collapse)*.

Now, given an arbitrary (small) category **C** with a terminal object 1, consider the canonical functor $\ulcorner\_\urcorner : \mathbf{C} \to \mathbf{Sets}$ given by:

For any object A:
$\ulcorner A \urcorner = \mathbf{C}(1,A)$ (the set of all morphisms $1 \to A$)
For any morphism $f \in \mathbf{C}(A,B)$:
$\ulcorner f \urcorner$ is the mapping from $\ulcorner A \urcorner$ to $\ulcorner B \urcorner$ given by composing with f
(that is $\ulcorner f \urcorner(p) = f \circ p$ for $p \in \mathbf{C}(1,A)$)

Note that $\ulcorner\_\urcorner$ is not faithful if **C** is not well-pointed. Given $f,g \in \mathbf{C}(A,B)$, in fact, $\ulcorner f \urcorner$ and $\ulcorner g \urcorner$ are set-theoretical mappings and, therefore, in order to have $\ulcorner f \urcorner = \ulcorner g \urcorner$ it is sufficient that $f \circ p = g \circ p$ for any $p \in \mathbf{C}(1,A)$. The values of the functor $\ulcorner\_\urcorner : \mathbf{C} \to \mathbf{Sets}$ over all the objects and morphisms of **C** give a subcategory of **Sets** that can be denoted with $\ulcorner \mathbf{C} \urcorner$.

The category we are interested in is $\ulcorner Cl(F_{<:}) \urcorner$. We will prove, as consequences of *(Eq appl2)*, that it has finite products and coproducts. For this, however, it is convenient to introduce the category <u>CL</u>, equivalent to $\ulcorner Cl(F_{<:}) \urcorner$, for which we can give a more explicit description.

Remark

$\vdash A\ type$	reads "A is a closed type"
$\vdash a{:}A$	reads "a is a closed term of closed type A"

Definition (cl-equality)

We say $\vdash f \leftrightarrow^{cl} f' : A \to B$ iff
for all a, $\vdash f,f':A\to B, \vdash a{:}A \Rightarrow \vdash f(a) \leftrightarrow f'(a) : B$

The *objects* of $\ulcorner Cl(F_{<:})\urcorner$ are, for any $\vdash A\ type$, the sets of morphisms $[z{:}Top \vdash t{:}A]$. By *(Eq collapse)* and congruence, $[z{:}Top \vdash t{:}A] = [z{:}Top \vdash t\{z\leftarrow top\}{:}A]$. The term $t\{z\leftarrow top\}$ is closed and $z{:}Top \vdash t\{z\leftarrow top\}{:}A$ iff $\vdash t\{z\leftarrow top\}{:}A$. Any object of $\ulcorner Cl(F_{<:})\urcorner$ is therefore isomorphic to the the set of equivalence classes $[\vdash a{:}A]$ of closed terms of a closed type; the equivalence relation is given by the equality judgments $\vdash a\leftrightarrow a'{:}A$ (write $\vdash A\ type$ for such a set). These sets are the objects of the category <u>CL</u>.

The *morphisms* of $\ulcorner Cl(F_{<:})\urcorner$ are, for any morphism $f=[x{:}A \vdash t{:}B]$ of $Cl(F_{<:})$, mappings from $\ulcorner A\urcorner$ to $\ulcorner B\urcorner$ given by, for any $[z{:}Top \vdash a{:}A]$, $\ulcorner f\urcorner([z{:}Top \vdash a{:}A]) = [z{:}Top \vdash t\{x\leftarrow a\}{:}B]$. By β- and η-conversion one obtains a category equivalent to $\ulcorner Cl(F_{<:})\urcorner$ by stipulating that a morphism of <u>CL</u> from $\vdash A\ type$ to $\vdash B\ type$ is an equivalence class of derivable term judgments:

$$\vdash f{:}A\to B$$

where the morphism equivalence is

$$(\vdash f{:}A\to B) = (\vdash f'{:}A\to B) \quad \text{iff} \quad \vdash f \leftrightarrow^{cl} f'{:}A\to B.$$

The *identity* and the *composition* judgment judgments are, for any $\vdash h{:}A\to B$ and $\vdash g{:}B\to C$:

$$id_A \triangleq \vdash \lambda(x{:}A)x : A\to A \qquad\qquad g\circ h \triangleq \vdash \lambda(x{:}A)g(h(x)) : A\to C$$

(We also ambiguously use $g\circ h \triangleq \lambda(x{:}A)g(h(x))$.)

We remark that morphism equivalence is *not* provable equality. For two morphisms $\vdash f{:}A\to B$ and $\vdash f'{:}A\to B$ to be equal it is sufficient that f and f' agree on the *closed* terms of type A. Similarly, the following two definitions correspond to isomorphism and uniqueness (for morphisms) in <u>CL</u>.

Definition (cl-isomorphism)

We say $\vdash A \sim^{cl} B$ iff there exist $\vdash f{:}A\to B, \vdash g{:}B\to A$ such that

$\vdash g\circ f \leftrightarrow^{cl} id_A : A\to A \qquad\qquad \vdash f\circ g \leftrightarrow^{cl} id_B : B\to B$

Definition (cl-uniqueness)

We say $\vdash f{:}A\to B$ is the cl-unique f satisfying $P(f)$ iff
for any other $\vdash f'{:}A\to B$ satisfying $P(f')$ we have $\vdash f \leftrightarrow^{cl} f' : A\to B$.

In order to prove that <u>CL</u> has finite products and coproducts, we need some more lemmas in $F_{<:}$, and especially the crucial consequence of *(Eq appl2)* expressed in the eq-var-substitution lemma, below.

Lemma (Type monotonicity)

Let $E,X{<:}B \vdash C <: D <: B$ and $E,X{<:}B,E' \vdash S\ type$. Then

(i) X positive in $S \quad\Rightarrow\quad E,X{<:}B,E' \vdash S\{X\leftarrow C\} <: S\{X\leftarrow D\}$

(ii) X negative in $S \quad\Rightarrow\quad E,X{<:}B,E' \vdash S\{X\leftarrow D\} <: S\{X\leftarrow C\}$

Definition (Pointed on X)

Given a type variable X, a type S is *pointed on* X iff X is positive in S and
$S \equiv \forall(Y_1{<:}B_1)\ldots\forall(Y_k{<:}B_k)T_1\to(\ldots\to(T_h\to X)\ldots)$ for $k\geq 0, h\geq 0$.

Lemma (Generalized collapse)

Let $E,X{<:}Top \vdash S\ type$, with S pointed on X.

$E \vdash D\ type$ and $E \vdash s : S\{X{\leftarrow}D\} \quad \Rightarrow \quad E,X{<:}Top,x{:}S \vdash x{\leftrightarrow}s : S\{X{\leftarrow}Top\}$

By generalised collapse and the eq-substitution proposition (Sect. 2.4) we obtain the following lemma, which expresses a parametricity property: A (possibly open) term a of a closed type A is provably equal to any term obtained by substituting specific types and terms for its free variables.

Lemma (Eq-var-substitution)

Assume, for i=1..n, $E',X{<:}Top \vdash S_i\ type$ and S_i pointed on X. Let $E \equiv E',X{<:}Top,x_1{:}\ S_1,\ldots, x_n{:}S_n$.

If $\vdash A\ type$, $E \vdash a{:}A$, $E' \vdash D\ type$ and $E' \vdash t_i{:}\ S_i\{X{\leftarrow}D\}$ for i=1..n,

then $E \vdash a \leftrightarrow a\{X{\leftarrow}D, x_1{\leftarrow}t_1, \ldots, x_n{\leftarrow}t_n\} : A$.

4.2 <u>CL</u> finite products and coproducts; well-pointedness

4.2.1 Terminal objects

Proposition

For any object $\vdash C\ type$, there is a unique morphism $\vdash 1_C : C{\rightarrow}Top$.

4.2.2 Binary products

Definition

$A \times B \triangleq \forall(C)\,(A{\rightarrow}B{\rightarrow}C){\rightarrow}C$

Proposition

For any pair of objects $\vdash A\ type$, $\vdash B\ type$, the object $\vdash A{\times}B$ type is their categorical product.

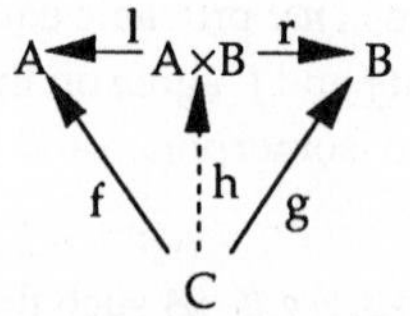

That is, there exist $\vdash l{:}A{\times}B{\rightarrow}A$, $\vdash r{:}A{\times}B{\rightarrow}B$ such that for any $\vdash C\ type$, and for any $\vdash f{:}C{\rightarrow}A$, $\vdash g{:}C{\rightarrow}B$, there exists a unique (i.e. cl-unique) $\vdash h{:}C{\rightarrow}A{\times}B$ such that $\vdash l{\circ}h \leftrightarrow^{cl} f : C{\rightarrow}A$ and $\vdash r{\circ}h \leftrightarrow^{cl} g : C{\rightarrow}B$.

Corollary $\vdash A \sim^{cl} A',\ \vdash B \sim^{cl} B' \quad \Rightarrow \quad \vdash A{\times}B \sim^{cl} A'{\times}B'$

4.2.3 Initial objects

Definition

$Bot \triangleq \forall(X)X$

Proposition

For any object $\vdash C\ type$, there is a unique morphism $\vdash 0_C : Bot{\rightarrow}C$.

Remark

$Bool{\rightarrow}Bot$ is also an initial object since there are no terms of type $Bool{\rightarrow}Bot$. The unique map is the equivalence class of $\lambda(x{:}\ Bool{\rightarrow}Bot)\ x(true)(C)$, which includes $\lambda(x{:}\ Bool{\rightarrow}Bot)\ x(false)(C)$. More generally, any empty type V for which there exists a term $\vdash f{:}V{\rightarrow}Bot$ is initial. The canonical morphism is the equivalence class of $\lambda(x{:}V)\ f(x)(C)$, which is cl-unique since there are no closed terms $\vdash c{:}V$.

4.2.4 Binary coproducts

Definition

$A + B \triangleq \forall(C)\ (A{\rightarrow}C){\rightarrow}(B{\rightarrow}C){\rightarrow}C$

Proposition

For any pair of objects $\vdash A\ type$, $\vdash B\ type$, the object $\vdash A{+}B\ type$ is their categorical coproduct.

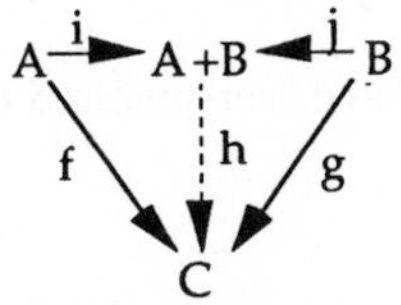

That is, there exist $\vdash i{:}A{\rightarrow}A{+}B$, $\vdash j{:}B{\rightarrow}A{+}B$ such that for any $\vdash C\ type$, and for any $\vdash f{:}A{\rightarrow}C$, $\vdash g{:}B{\rightarrow}C$, there exists a unique (i.e. cl-unique) $\vdash h{:}A{+}B{\rightarrow}C$ such that $\vdash h{\circ}i \leftrightarrow^{cl} f : A{\rightarrow}C$ and $\vdash h{\circ}j \leftrightarrow^{cl} g : B{\rightarrow}C$.

Proof Define: $i \triangleq \lambda(x{:}A)\lambda(C)\lambda(f{:}A{\rightarrow}C)\lambda(g{:}B{\rightarrow}C)f(x)$ then $\vdash i : A \rightarrow A{+}B$

$j \triangleq \lambda(y{:}B)\lambda(C)\lambda(f{:}A{\rightarrow}C)\lambda(g{:}B{\rightarrow}C)g(y)$ then $\vdash j : B \rightarrow A{+}B$

$case \triangleq \lambda(C)\lambda(f{:}A{\rightarrow}C)\lambda(g{:}B{\rightarrow}C)\lambda(c{:}A{+}B)c(C)(f)(g)$

then $\vdash case : \forall(C)\ (A{\rightarrow}C){\rightarrow}(B{\rightarrow}C){\rightarrow}(A{+}B){\rightarrow}C$

We will only show that, for any $\vdash c{:}A{+}B$, $\vdash C\ type$, $\vdash D\ type$, $\vdash f{:}A{\rightarrow}C$, $\vdash g{:}B{\rightarrow}C$ and $\vdash k{:}C{\rightarrow}D$,

$\vdash case(D)(k{\circ}f)(k{\circ}g)(c) \leftrightarrow (k{\circ}case(C)(f)(g))(c) : D.$

The normal form of c must have one of the shapes:

$c \equiv \lambda(C')\lambda(f'{:}H)\lambda(g'{:}G)f'(a)$

for some $C'{<:}Top \vdash A{\rightarrow}C <: H$, $C'{<:}Top \vdash B{\rightarrow}C' {<:} G$, and $C'{<:}Top, f'{:}H, g'{:}G \vdash a{:}A$

$c \equiv \lambda(C')\lambda(f'{:}H)\lambda(g'{:}G)g'(b)$

for some $C'{<:}Top \vdash A{\rightarrow}C <: H$, $C'{<:}Top \vdash B{\rightarrow}C' {<:} G$, and $C'{<:}Top, f'{:}H, g'{:}G \vdash b{:}B$

By bound weakening lemma,

$C'{<:}Top, f'{:}A{\rightarrow}C', g'{:}B{\rightarrow}C' \vdash a{:}A$ and $C'{<:}Top, f'{:}A{\rightarrow}C', g'{:}B{\rightarrow}C' \vdash b{:}B.$

By (Eq fun'), either $\vdash c \leftrightarrow \lambda(C')\lambda(f'{:}A{\rightarrow}C')\lambda(g'{:}B{\rightarrow}C')f'(a) : A{+}B$

or $\vdash c \leftrightarrow \lambda(C')\lambda(f'{:}A{\rightarrow}C')\lambda(g'{:}B{\rightarrow}C')g'(b) : A{+}B$

In the first case we have:

$\vdash case(D)(k{\circ}f)(k{\circ}g)(c) \leftrightarrow c(D)(k{\circ}f)(k{\circ}g) \leftrightarrow k(f(a\{C'{\leftarrow}D, f'{\leftarrow}k{\circ}f, g'{\leftarrow}k{\circ}g\})) : D$

$\vdash (k{\circ}case(C)(f)(g))(c) \leftrightarrow k(f(a\{C'{\leftarrow}C, f'{\leftarrow}f, g'{\leftarrow}g\})) : D$

From eq-var-substitution lemma:

$C'{<:}Top, f'{:}A{\rightarrow}C', g'{:}B{\rightarrow}C' \vdash a \leftrightarrow a\{C'{\leftarrow}D, f'{\leftarrow}k{\circ}f, g'{\leftarrow}k{\circ}g\} : A$

$C'{<:}Top, f'{:}A{\rightarrow}C', g'{:}B{\rightarrow}C' \vdash a \leftrightarrow a\{C'{\leftarrow}C, f'{\leftarrow}f, g'{\leftarrow}g\} : A$

Conclude by transitivity and (Eq appl).

The second case is similar.

□

Corollary $\vdash A \sim^{cl} A', \ \vdash B \sim^{cl} B' \ \Rightarrow \ \vdash A+B \sim^{cl} A'+B'$

4.2.5 Well-pointedness

Recall that a category **C** with a terminal object *1* is well-pointed iff for any pair of objects *A* and *B* and any $f,g \in \mathbf{C}(A,B)$ we have:

$f=g$ iff for any $h \in \mathbf{C}(1,A), f \circ h = g \circ h$.

Proposition

CL is well-pointed. That is, for any $\vdash A\ type$, $\vdash B\ type$, and any $\vdash f,g : A \to B$, we have:

$\vdash f \leftrightarrow^{cl} g : A \to B \quad \Leftrightarrow \quad$ for any $\vdash h : Top \to A, \ \vdash f \circ h \leftrightarrow^{cl} g \circ h : Top \to B$

4.3 CL Isomorphisms

For the following isomorphisms we have been inspired by [3] and [14].

4.3.1 Double negation

We prove that, for any $\vdash A\ type$ we have $A \sim \forall(C)(A \to C) \to C$. This is an isomorphism holding in the models studied in [3], but having no known proof in *F* (see the remark below).

Proposition

$\vdash A\ type \ \Rightarrow \ \vdash A \sim^{cl} \forall(C)(A \to C) \to C$

Proof

Define: $f \triangleq \lambda(x{:}\forall(C)(A \to C) \to C)\ x(A)(id(A))$ $\quad g \triangleq \lambda(y{:}A)\ \lambda(C)\ \lambda(z{:}A \to C)\ z(y)$

Then: $\vdash f{:}\ (\forall(C)(A \to C) \to C) \to A$ and $\vdash g{:}\ A \to (\forall(C)(A \to C) \to C)$.

Take *a* such that $\vdash a{:}A$. Then, by β-conversion:

$\vdash f(g(a)) \leftrightarrow a : A$

Take closed *b* such that $\vdash b : \forall(C)(A \to C) \to C$. Then *b* has a normal form of the shape

$b = \lambda(C)\ \lambda(z{:}D)\ z(a1)$

for some $C{<:}Top \vdash A \to C {<:} D$ and $C{<:}Top, z{:}D \vdash a1{:}A$. By bound weakening lemma,

$C{<:}Top, z{:}A \to C \vdash a1{:}A$

and hence

$\vdash b \leftrightarrow \lambda(C)\ \lambda(z{:}A \to C)\ z(a1)$.

Then

$\vdash g(f(b)) \leftrightarrow \lambda(C)\ \lambda(z{:}A \to C)\ z(a1\{C \leftarrow A, z \leftarrow id(A)\}) : \forall(C)(A \to C) \to C$

By eq-var-substitution lemma,

$C{<:}Top, z{:}A \to C \vdash a1 \leftrightarrow a1\{C \leftarrow A, z \leftarrow id(A)\} : A$

Hence,

$C{<:}Top, z{:}A \to C \vdash z(a1) \leftrightarrow z(a1\{C \leftarrow A, z \leftarrow id(A)\}) : C$

That is:

$\vdash \lambda(C)\ \lambda(z{:}A \to C)\ z(a1) \leftrightarrow \lambda(C)\ \lambda(z{:}A \to C)\ z(a1\{C \leftarrow A, z \leftarrow id(A)\}) : \forall(C)(A \to C) \to C$

Combining the two equations above:

$\vdash g(f(b)) \leftrightarrow \lambda(C)\ \lambda(z{:}A \to C)\ z(a1) \leftrightarrow b : \forall(C)(A \to C) \to C$

□

Remark

Christine Paulin-Mohring has shown that, even for A closed, $A \sim \forall(C)(A\to C)\to C$ is not provable in F via the isomorphism we have used in the proof above. (It is not known whether some other isomorphism would work.) To see this, let T be $\forall(R)R\to R$; the term:

$$\lambda(P)\ \lambda(x{:}(T\to T)\to P)$$
$$x\ (\lambda(y{:}T)\ y\ (P\to T)\ (\lambda(u{:}P)y)\ (x(\lambda(v{:}T)v)))$$
$$:\forall(P)((T\to T)\to P)\to P$$

is not convertible to any term of the form $\lambda(P)\ \lambda(x{:}(T\to T)\to P)\ x(c)$ where $c{:}T\to T$ is a closed term. Roberto di Cosmo has shown that A is not isomorphic, in the usual sense, to $\forall(C)(A\to C)\to C$ in F.

4.3.2 Other isomorphisms

Existentials

Define $\exists(X{<:}A)B \triangleq \forall(V)(\forall(X{<:}A)B\to V)\to V$ and $\exists(X)B \triangleq \exists(X{<:}Top)B$. Then:

$\exists(X{<:}A)X \sim A$ (corollary: $\exists(X)X \sim Top$)

Domain restriction

$C \sim \forall(X)\ X\to C$

$A\to C \sim \forall(X{<:}A)\ X\to C$

Categorical

$(A\times B)\times C \sim A\times(B\times C)$ $\quad (A+B)+C \sim A+(B+C)$

$A\times Top \sim Top\times A \sim A$ $\quad A+Bot \sim Bot+A \sim A$

Various

$Top\to A \sim A$	(simple top collapse)
$A\to Top \sim Top$	(simple top collapse)
$Top \sim \forall(C)\ C\to C$	(analyzing the normal forms)
$Bot\to A \sim Top$	(analyzing the normal forms)
$A\to Bot \sim Bot$ for A nonempty	(vacuous $f\circ g \leftrightarrow^{cl} id$ conditions: both types are empty)
$\forall(X)\ (A\to X) \sim A\to\forall(X)\ X$	(β-η suffices)

References

[1] S.Abramsky, J.C.Mitchell, A.Scedrov, P.Wadler: ***Relators***, to appear.

[2] C.Böhm, A.Berarducci: ***Automatic synthesis of typed λ-programs on term algebras***, Theoretical Computer Science, 39, pp. 135-154, 1985.

[3] E.S.Bainbridge, P.J.Freyd, A.Scedrov, P.J.Scott: ***Functorial polymorphism***, Theoretical Computer Science, vol.70, no.1, pp 35-64, 1990.

[4] K.B.Bruce, G.Longo: ***A modest model of records, inheritance and bounded quantification***, Information and Computation, 87(1/2):196-240, 1990.

[5] L.Cardelli: ***A semantics of multiple inheritance***, in Information and Computation 76, pp 138-164, 1988.

[6] L.Cardelli: ***Extensible records in a pure calculus of subtyping***, to appear.

[7] L.Cardelli, G.Longo: ***A semantic basis for Quest***, Proceedings of the 6th ACM LISP and Functional Programming Conference, ACM Press, 1990.

[8] L.Cardelli, J.C.Mitchell: ***Operations on records***, Proc. of the Fifth Conference on Mathematical Foundations of Programming Language Semantics, New Orleans, 1989. To appear in Mathematical Structures in Computer Science, 1991.

[9] L.Cardelli, P.Wegner: ***On understanding types, data abstraction and polymorphism***, Computing Surveys, Vol 17 n. 4, pp 471-522, December 1985.

[10] P.-L.Curien, G.Ghelli: ***Coherence of subsumption***, Mathematical Structures in Computer Science, to appear.

[11] P.-L.Curien, G.Ghelli: ***Subtyping + extensionality: confluence of $\beta\eta$-reductions in $F_{\leq}$***, to appear.

[12] N.G.de Bruijn: ***Lambda-calculus notation with nameless dummies***, in Indag. Math. 34(5), pp. 381-392, 1972.

[13] J.Fairbairn: ***Some types with inclusion properties in $\forall$, $\rightarrow$, μ***, Technical report No 171, University of Cambridge, Computer Laboratory.

[14] P.J.Freyd: ***Structural polymorphism***, to appear in TCS.

[15] G.Ghelli: ***Proof theoretic studies about a mininal type system integrating inclusion and parametric polymorphism***, Ph.D. Thesis TD-6/90, Università di Pisa, Dipartimento di Informatica, 1990.

[16] J-Y.Girard: ***Une extension de l'interprétation de Gödel à l'analyse, et son application à l'élimination des coupures dans l'analyse et la théorie des types***, Proceedings of the second Scandinavian logic symposium, J.E.Fenstad Ed. pp. 63-92, North-Holland, 1971.

[17] J.Lambek, P.J.Scott: ***Introduction to higher order categorical logic***, Cambridge University Press, 1986.

[18] J.C.Mitchell: ***A type inference approach to reduction properties and semantics of polymorphic expressions***, Logical Foundations of Functional Programming, ed. G. Huet, Addison-Wesley, 1990.

[19] J.C.Mitchell, P.J.Scott: ***Typed λ-models and cartesian closed categories***, in Categories in Computer Science and Logic, J.W.Gray and A.Scedrov Eds. Contemporary Math. vol. 92, Amer. Math. Soc., pp 301-316, 1989.

[20] A.M.Pitts: ***Polymorphism is set-theoretic, constructively***, in Category Theory and Computer Science, Proceedings Edinburgh 1987, D.H.Pitt, A.Poigne, and D.E.Rydeheard Eds. Springer Lecture Notes in Computer Science, vol. 283, pp 12-39, 1987.

[21] J.C.Reynolds: ***Towards a theory of type structure***, in Colloquium sur la programmation pp. 408-423, Springer-Verlag Lecture Notes in Computer Science, n.19, 1974.

[22] J.C.Reynolds: ***Types, abstraction, and parametric polymorphism***, in Information Processing '83, pp 513-523, R.E.A.Mason ed., North Holland, Amsterdam, 1983.

[23] A.Scedrov: ***A guide to polymorphic types***, in Logic and Computer Science, pp 387-420, P.Odifreddi ed., Academic Press, 1990.

[24] C.Strachey: ***Fundamental concepts in programming languages***, lecture notes for the International Summer School in Computer Programming, Copenhagen, August 1967.

[25] P.Wadler: ***Theorems for free!***, Proc. of the Fourth International Conference on Fuctional Programming and Computer Architecture, ACM Press, 1989.

Will Logicians be Replaced by Machines?

Dana S. Scott
Hilmann University Professor
of Computer Science, Philosophy
and Mathematical Logic
Carnegie Mellon University
Pittsburgh, Pennsylvania, USA

Abstract

Many workers have been and will be soon displaced by machines, and we have to ask whether it is only a matter of time before teachers are as well. The lecture will review the march of technology and how developments are apt to affect teaching and research in many subjects. To be able to understand the emerging situation, we also have to reflect on the nature of studies in the Foundations of Mathematics.

Author Index

Lecture Notes in Computer Science

For information about Vols. 1–441
please contact your bookseller or Springer-Verlag

Vol. 442: M. Main, A. Melton, M. Mislove, D. Schmidt (Eds.), Mathematical Foundations of Programming Semantics. Proceedings, 1989. VI, 439 pages. 1990.

Vol. 443: M.S. Paterson (Ed.), Automata, Languages and Programming. Proceedings, 1990. IX, 781 pages. 1990.

Vol. 444: S. Ramani, R. Chandrasekar, K.S.R. Anjaneyulu (Eds.), Knowledge Based Computer Systems. Proceedings, 1989. X, 546 pages. 1990. (Subseries LNAI).

Vol. 445: A.J.M. van Gasteren, On the Shape of Mathematical Arguments. VIII, 181 pages. 1990.

Vol. 446: L. Plümer, Termination Proofs for Logic Programs. VIII ,142 pages. 1990. (Subseries LNAI).

Vol. 447: J.R. Gilbert, R. Karlsson (Eds.), SWAT ´90. 2nd Scandinavian Workshop on Algorithm Theory. Proceedings, 1990. VI, 417 pages. 1990.

Vol. 448: B. Simons, A. Spector (Eds.), Fault Tolerant Distributed Computing. VI, 298 pages. 1990.

Vol. 449: M.E. Stickel (Ed.), 10th International Conference on Automated Deduction. Proceedings, 1990. XVI, 688 pages. 1990. (Subseries LNAI).

Vol. 450: T. Asano, T. Ibaraki, H. Imai, T. Nishizeki (Eds.), Algorithms. Proceedings, 1990. VIII, 479 pages. 1990.

Vol. 451: V. Marík, O. Stepánková, Z. Zdráhal (Eds.), Artificial Intelligence in Higher Education. Proceedings, 1989. IX, 247 pages. 1990. (Subseries LNAI).

Vol. 452: B. Rovan (Ed.), Mathematical Foundations of Computer Science 1990. Proceedings, 1990. VIII, 544 pages. 1990.

Vol. 453: J. Seberry, J. Pieprzyk (Eds.), Advances in Cryptology – AUSCRYPT '90 Proceedings, 1990. IX. 462 pages. 1990.

Vol. 454: V. Diekert, Combinatorics on Traces. XII, 165 pages. 1990.

Vol. 455: C.A. Floudas, P.M. Pardalos, A Collection of Test Problems for Constrained Global Optimization Algorithms. XIV, 180 pages. 1990.

Vol. 456: P. Deransart, J. Maluszyn´ski (Eds.), Programming Language Implementation and Logic Programming. Proceedings, 1990. VIII, 401 pages. 1990.

Vol. 457: H. Burkhart (Ed.), CONPAR '90 – VAPP IV. Proceedings, 1990. XIV, 900 pages. 1990.

Vol. 458: J.C.M. Baeten, J.W. Klop (Eds.), CONCUR '90. Proceedings, 1990. VII, 537 pages. 1990.

Vol. 459: R. Studer (Ed.), Natural Language and Logic. Proceedings, 1989. VII, 252 pages. 1990. (Subseries LNAI).

Vol. 460: J. Uhl, H.A. Schmid, A Systematic Catalogue of Reusable Abstract Data Types. XII, 344 pages. 1990.

Vol. 461: P. Deransart, M. Jourdan (Eds.), Attribute Grammars and their Applications. Proceedings, 1990. VIII, 358 pages. 1990.

Vol. 462: G. Gottlob, W. Nejdl (Eds.), Expert Systems in Engineering. Proceedings, 1990. IX, 260 pages. 1990. (Subseries LNAI).

Vol. 463: H. Kirchner, W. Wechler (Eds.), Algebraic and Logic Programming. Proceedings, 1990. VII, 386 pages. 1990.

Vol. 464: J. Dassow, J. Kelemen (Eds.), Aspects and Prospects of Theoretical Computer Science. Proceedings, 1990. VI, 298 pages. 1990.

Vol. 465: A. Fuhrmann, M. Morreau (Eds.), The Logic of Theory Change. Proceedings, 1989. X, 334 pages. 1991. (Subseries LNAI).

Vol. 466: A. Blaser (Ed.), Database Systems of the 90s. Proceedings, 1990. VIII, 334 pages. 1990.

Vol. 467: F. Long (Ed.), Software Engineering Environments. Proceedings, 1969. VI, 313 pages. 1990.

Vol. 468: S.G. Akl, F. Fiala, W.W. Koczkodaj (Eds.), Advances in Computing and Information – ICCI ´90. Proceedings, 1990. VII, 529 pages. 1990.

Vol. 469: I. Guessarian (Ed.), Semantics of Systeme of Concurrent Processes. Proceedings, 1990. V, 456 pages. 1990.

Vol. 470: S. Abiteboul, P.C. Kanellakis (Eds.), ICDT ´90. Proceedings, 1990. VII, 528 pages. 1990.

Vol. 471: B.C. Ooi, Efficient Query Processing in Geographic Information Systems. VIII, 208 pages. 1990.

Vol. 472: K.V. Nori, C.E. Veni Madhavan (Eds.), Foundations of Software Technology and Theoretical Computer Science. Proceedings, 1990. X, 420 pages. 1990.

Vol. 473: I.B. Damgård (Ed.), Advances in Cryptology – EUROCRYPT ´90. Proceedings, 1990. VIII, 500 pages. 1991.

Vol. 474: D. Karagiannis (Ed.), Information Syetems and Artificial Intelligence: Integration Aspects. Proceedings, 1990. X, 293 pages. 1991. (Subseries LNAI).

Vol. 475: P. Schroeder-Heister (Ed.), Extensions of Logic Programming. Proceedings, 1989. VIII, 364 pages. 1991. (Subseries LNAI).

Vol. 476: M. Filgueiras, L. Damas, N. Moreira, A.P. Tomás (Eds.), Natural Language Processing. Proceedings, 1990. VII, 253 pages. 1991. (Subseries LNAI).

Vol. 477: D. Hammer (Ed.), Compiler Compilers. Proceedings, 1990. VI, 227 pages. 1991.

Vol. 478: J. van Eijck (Ed.), Logics in AI. Proceedings, 1990. IX, 562 pages. 1991. (Subseries in LNAI).

Vol. 480: C. Choffrut, M. Jantzen (Eds.), STACS 91. Proceedings, 1991. X, 549 pages. 1991.

Vol. 481: E. Lang, K.-U. Carstensen, G. Simmons, Modelling Spatial Knowledge on a Linguistic Basis. IX, 138 pages. 1991. (Subseries LNAI).

Vol. 482: Y. Kodratoff (Ed.), Machine Learning – EWSL-91. Proceedings, 1991. XI, 537 pages. 1991. (Subseries LNAI).

Vol. 483: G. Rozenberg (Ed.), Advances In Petri Nets 1990. VI, 515 pages. 1991.

Vol. 484: R. H. Möhring (Ed.), Graph-Theoretic Concepts In Computer Science. Proceedings, 1990. IX, 360 pages. 1991.

Vol. 485: K. Furukawa, H. Tanaka, T. Fullsaki (Eds.), Logic Programming '89. Proceedings, 1989. IX, 183 pages. 1991. (Subseries LNAI).

Vol. 486: J. van Leeuwen, N. Santoro (Eds.), Distributed Algorithms. Proceedings, 1990. VI, 433 pages. 1991.

Vol. 487: A. Bode (Ed.), Distributed Memory Computing. Proceedings, 1991. XI, 506 pages. 1991.

Vol. 488: R. V. Book (Ed.), Rewriting Techniques and Applications. Proceedings, 1991. VII, 458 pages. 1991.

Vol. 489: J. W. de Bakker, W. P. de Roever, G. Rozenberg (Eds.), Foundations of Object-Oriented Languages. Proceedings, 1990. VIII, 442 pages. 1991.

Vol. 490: J. A. Bergstra, L. M. G. Feljs (Eds.), Algebraic Methods 11: Theory, Tools and Applicatlons. VI, 434 pages. 1991.

Vol. 491: A. Yonezawa, T. Ito (Eds.), Concurrency: Theory, Language, and Architecture. Proceedings, 1989. VIII, 339 pages. 1991.

Vol. 492: D. Sriram, R. Logcher, S. Fukuda (Eds.), Computer-Aided Cooperative Product Development. Proceedings, 1989 VII, 630 pages. 1991.

Vol. 493: S. Abramsky, T. S. E. Maibaum (Eds.), TAPSOFT '91. Volume 1. Proceedings, 1991. VIII, 455 pages. 1991.

Vol. 494: S. Abramsky, T. S. E. Maibaum (Eds.), TAPSOFT '91. Volume 2. Proceedings, 1991. VIII, 482 pages. 1991.

Vol. 495: 9. Thalheim, J. Demetrovics, H.-D. Gerhardt (Eds.), MFDBS '91. Proceedings, 1991. VI, 395 pages. 1991.

Vol. 496: H.-P. Schwefel, R. Männer (Eds.), Parallel Problem Solving from Nature. Proceedings, 1991. XI, 485 pages. 1991.

Vol. 497: F. Dehne, F. Fiala. W.W. Koczkodaj (Eds.), Advances in Computing and Intormation - ICCI '91 Proceedings, 1991. VIII, 745 pages. 1991.

Vol. 498: R. Andersen, J. A. Bubenko jr., A. Sølvberg (Eds.), Advanced Information Systems Engineering. Proceedings, 1991. VI, 579 pages. 1991.

Vol. 499: D. Christodoulakis (Ed.), Ada: The Choice for '92. Proceedings, 1991. VI, 411 pages. 1991.

Vol. 500: M. Held, On the Computational Geometry of Pocket Machining. XII, 179 pages. 1991.

Vol. 501: M. Bidoit, H.-J. Kreowski, P. Lescanne, F. Orejas, D. Sannella (Eds.), Algebraic System Specification and Development. VIII, 98 pages. 1991.

Vol. 502: J. Bārzdiņš, D. Bjørner (Eds.), Baltic Computer Science. X, 619 pages. 1991.

Vol. 503: P. America (Ed.), Parallel Database Systems. Proceedings, 1990. VIII, 433 pages. 1991.

Vol. 504: J. W. Schmidt, A. A. Stogny (Eds.), Next Generation Information System Technology. Proceedings, 1990. IX, 450 pages. 1991.

Vol. 505: E. H. L. Aarts, J. van Leeuwen, M. Rem (Eds.), PARLE '91. Parallel Architectures and Languages Europe, Volume I. Proceedings, 1991. XV, 423 pages. 1991.

Vol. 506: E. H. L. Aarts, J. van Leeuwen, M. Rem (Eds.), PARLE '91. Parallel Architectures and Languages Europe, Volume II. Proceedings, 1991. XV, 489 pages. 1991.

Vol. 507: N. A. Sherwani, E. de Doncker, J. A. Kapenga (Eds.), Computing in the 90's. Proceedings, 1989. XIII, 441 pages. 1991.

Vol. 508: S. Sakata (Ed.), Applied Algebra, Algebraic Algorithms and Error-Correcting Codes. Proceedings, 1990. IX, 390 pages. 1991.

Vol. 509: A. Endres, H. Weber (Eds.), Software Development Environments and CASE Technology. Proceedings, 1991. VIII, 286 pages. 1991.

Vol. 510: J. Leach Albert, B. Monien, M. Rodríguez (Eds.), Automata, Languages and Programming. Proceedings, 1991. XII, 763 pages. 1991.

Vol. 511: A. C. F. Colchester, D.J. Hawkes (Eds.), Information Processing in Medical Imaging. Proceedings, 1991. XI, 512 pages. 1991.

Vol. 512: P. America (Ed.), ECOOP '91. European Conference on Object-Oriented Programming. Proceedings, 1991. X, 396 pages. 1991.

Vol. 513: N. M. Mattos, An Approach to Knowledge Base Management. IX, 247 pages. 1991. (Subseries LNAI).

Vol. 514: G. Cohen, P. Charpin (Eds.), EUROCODE '90. Proceedings, 1990. XI, 392 pages. 1991.

Vol. 515: J. P. Martins, M. Reinfrank (Eds.), Truth Maintenance Systems. Proceedings, 1990. VII, 177 pages. 1991. (Subseries LNAI).

Vol. 516: S. Kaplan, M. Okada (Eds.), Conditional and Typed Rewriting Systems. Proceedings, 1990. IX, 461 pages. 1991.

Vol. 517: K. Nökel, Temporally Distributed Symptoms in Technical Diagnosis. IX, 164 pages. 1991. (Subseries LNAI).

Vol. 518: J. G. Williams, Instantiation Theory. VIII, 133 pages. 1991. (Subseries LNAI).

Vol. 519: F. Dehne, J.-R. Sack, N. Santoro (Eds.), Algorithms and Data Structures. Proceedings, 1991. X, 496 pages. 1991.

Vol. 520: A. Tarlecki (Ed.), Mathematical Foundations of Computer Science 1991. Proceedings, 1991. XI, 435 pages. 1991.

Vol. 521: B. Bouchon-Meunier, R. R. Yager, L. A. Zadek (Eds.), Uncertainty in Knowledge-Bases. Proceedings, 1990. X, 609 pages. 1991.

Vol. 522: J. Hertzberg (Ed.), European Workshop on Planning. Proceedings, 1991. VII, 121 pages. 1991. (Subseries LNAI).

Vol. 523: J. Hughes (Ed.), Functional Programming Languages and Computer Architecture. Proceedings, 1991. VIII, 666 pages. 1991.

Vol. 524: G. Rozenberg (Ed.), Advances in Petri Nets 1991. VIII, 572 pages. 1991.

Vol. 525: O. Günther, H.-J. Schek (Eds.), Large Spatial Databases. Proceedings, 1991. XI, 471 pages. 1991.

Vol. 526: T. Ito, A. R. Meyer (Eds.), Theoretical Aspects of Computer Software. Proceedings, 1991. X, 772 pages. 1991.